INTERACTIVE CASEBOOK SERIES^{SM}

CONTRACTS

A Contemporary Approach

THIRD EDITION

Christina L. Kunz
PROFESSOR EMERITA
MITCHELL HAMLINE SCHOOL OF LAW

Carol L. Chomsky
PROFESSOR OF LAW
UNIVERSITY OF MINNESOTA LAW SCHOOL

Jennifer S. Martin
PROFESSOR OF LAW
ST. THOMAS UNIVERSITY SCHOOL OF LAW (FLORIDA)

Elizabeth R. Schiltz
HERRICK PROFESSOR OF LAW
UNIVERSITY OF ST. THOMAS SCHOOL OF LAW (MINNESOTA)

WEST
ACADEMIC
PUBLISHING

Interactive Casebook Series is a servicemark registered in the U.S. Patent and Trademark Office.

© 2010 Thomson Reuters
© 2013 LEG, Inc. d/b/a West Academic Publishing
© 2018 LEG, Inc. d/b/a West Academic
    444 Cedar Street, Suite 700
    St. Paul, MN 55101
    1-877-888-1330

West, West Academic Publishing, and West Academic are trademarks of West Publishing Corporation, used under license.

Printed in the United States of America

ISBN: 978-1-68328-815-2

In memory of Halbert Kunz, the first lawyer I knew—C.L.K.

For Steve—C.L.C.

To Tom, Emma, Leeland, and Marshall—J.S.M.

In memory of Bernice A. Kaczynski, my best teacher—E.R.S.

Acknowledgements and Illustration Credits

First and foremost, we thank our husbands, our families, and our friends, who lived through and worked around our writing schedules and were fellow travelers on our book odyssey. We are grateful for their good spirits, their patience, and their support.

We are grateful to Louis Higgins and to West Academic Publishing for giving us the opportunity to join in pioneering this new teaching format in textbooks. The features of the Interactive Casebook Series—the chance to incorporate case histories, diagrams, questions, and commentary at just the right place in the text—have challenged us to think through each set of cases and explanations and to make our teaching strategies accessible for both instructors and students. We have found that the format and content enlivens the reading experience for students and leads them to learn more actively. And the process of writing in this format has reshaped our concept of a casebook and has sparked new ideas about how to teach more effectively.

We thank our fellow teachers who offered comments on the book to help us improve the text. We thank our friend and colleague, Professor Stephen Sepinuck from Gonzaga University School of Law, who gave us valuable suggestions for improving the book, as well as his own charts and diagrams. We are also grateful to Professor Deborah Gerhardt at University of North Carolina School of Law for her suggestions.

Our students played invaluable roles in the development and editing of this book, making suggestions about our manuscript editions and providing feedback to make the final product better. We thank them for their insights and suggestions.

We want to retrospectively thank two research assistants who worked on the second edition, Matti Adam and Lucie O'Neill, from William Mitchell College of Law (now Mitchell Hamline School of Law). We hope they will forgive us for inadvertently leaving them out of the Acknowledgements for the second edition. We continue to value their contributions.

The logistics of creating a book of this type are challenging, and we thank Jon Harkness, Greg Olson, and Whitney Esson for their dedication to producing the polished final product you have in your hands.

Finally a toast to this wonderful team of four co-authors, our weekly video calls, and the richness and ease of our collaboration.

C.L.K., C.L.C., J.S.M., & E.R.S.
March 2018

Case opinions appear with the permission of Thomson Reuters. Below are the attributions and credits for the photographs and images, by page number:

23	The two photographs accompanying Lucy v. Zehmer appear with the generous permission of Professor Franklin Snyder at Texas A&M University School of Law. The restaurant receipt appears in the record of the case.
30	Photograph of the barque appears at http://en.wikipedia.org/wiki/Barque (public domain).
50	Photograph of Justice Benjamin Cardozo is in the Library of Congress (public domain).
57	Photograph of John Cheever appears at http://en.wikipedia.org/wiki/John_Cheever (Library of Congress, public domain).
79–80	Advertisements from the Great Minneapolis Surplus Store appear courtesy of the Minnesota Historical Society.
90	Carbolic Smoke Ball advertisement is in the public domain and appears at http://en.wikipedia.org/wiki/Carlill_v_Carbolic_Smoke_Ball_Co.
135	Photograph of the "Consent To Be Photographed" sandwich board appears courtesy of the photographer, Christina L. Kunz.
196	Photograph of E. Allan Farnsworth appears courtesy of Columbia Law School.
239	Photograph of Samuel Williston appears courtesy of Historical & Special Collections, Harvard Law School Library http://law.harvard.edu/library/special/index.html (original dimensions 19.5 x 24.3 cm; unknown photographer).
240	Photograph of Arthur Corbin is in the public domain.
319	Portrait of Lord Mansfield is in the public domain in the New York Public Library's Digital Collections.
342	Photograph of Judge Spottswood W. Robinson, III is in the public domain, https://commons.wikimedia.org/wiki/File:Spottswood_William_Robinson.jpg.

448   Photograph of Walker-Thomas Furniture Store sign is in the public domain on www.flickr.com.

449   Photograph of the Walker-Thomas Furniture Store windows appears with the permission of Professor Franklin Snyder at Texas A&M University School of Law.

527   Photograph of Elizabeth Arden appears at http://en.wikipedia.org/wiki/Elizabeth_Arden (public domain).

542   Photograph of Judge Henry Friendly is in the Bettmann Archive and appears courtesy of Corbis Images.

572   Photograph of Justice Roger Traynor at http://www.courts.ca.gov/documents/2007_Supreme_Court_Booklet_withinserts.pdf (page 52) (public domain).

628   Photograph of Judge Richard Posner appears courtesy of Judge Posner's office at the Seventh Circuit Court of Appeals.

750   Pictures of the music hall appear at http://en.wikipedia.org/wiki/Royal_Surrey_Gardens (public domain).

756   Map is from the 2004 CIA Factbook (public domain).

757   Photograph of the canal appears at http://en.wikipedia.org/wiki/Suez_Canal (public domain).

763   Photograph of King Edward VII is in the public domain and appears on numerous websites.

767   Photograph of the flat in *Krell v. Henry* appears courtesy of the photographer, Jessica Zaiken.

824   Picture of the steam engine appears at http://www.constructionlawtoday.com/2009/06/consequential-damages-in-construction-contracts-and-architects-agreements-part-3-why-treat-consequential-and-direct-damages-differently/ (public domain).

824   Photograph of the mill in Hadley is courtesy of Michael Thorpe, Gloucester City Council, which granted permission for its use in all educational or nonprofit contexts; it formerly appeared at http://lawprofessors.typepad.com/contractsprof_blog/2005/06/hadleys_mill.html (last viewed in spring 2013).

825   Photograph of Vanessa Redgrave was taken by Elena Torre from Viareggio, Italia, and appears courtesy of a Creative Commons Attribution—Share Alike 2.0 Generic License; it appears at http://commons.wikimedia.org/wiki/File:Vanessa_Redgrave_by_Elena_Torre.jpg.

829   Photograph of the Houston Astrodome (1965) appears at https://commons.wikimedia.org/wiki/File:Astrodome_1965.jpeg (public domain).

837   Photograph of Shirley MacLaine appears at https://en.wikipedia.org/wiki/Shirley_MacLaine#/media/ (public domain).

863   Photograph of Justice Shirley Abrahamson appears with the permission of the Director of State Courts, Wisconsin Supreme Court.

913   Photograph of railway wagon appears courtesy of the photographer, Christina L. Kunz.

Summary of Contents

ACKNOWLEDGEMENTS AND ILLUSTRATION CREDITS v

TABLE OF CASES xxv

TABLE OF RESTATEMENT AND UCC PROVISIONS xxxvii

CHAPTER 1. *Introduction* 1

§ 1. Overview 1

§ 2. Sources of Contract Law and Authority 5

    § 2.1. Judicial Opinions 5

    § 2.2. Restatements of the Law 6

    § 2.3. Statutory Law 8

    § 2.4. International Commercial Law and the CISG 9

§ 3. Features of This Book 10

CHAPTER 2. *Promise and Assent* 15

§ 1. Introduction 15

§ 2. Is Meaning Judged Objectively or Subjectively? 17

§ 3. Promise as Expression of Commitment 31

§ 4. Lack of Commitment: Illusory Promises 33

§ 5. Promises with Indefinite or Incomplete Terms 38

CHAPTER 3. *Assent Through Offer and Acceptance* 65

§ 1. Introduction 67

§ 2. Sequential Assent by Offer and Acceptance Under the Common Law ... 67

    § 2.1. Defining "Offer" 69

        § 2.1.1. Advertisements and Rewards as Offers 75

        § 2.1.2. Offers in the Commercial Bidding Process 98

    § 2.2. How Long Does an Offer Last? 101

        § 2.2.1. Lapse 101

        § 2.2.2. Death or Incapacity of the Offeror or Offeree 105

§ 2.3. Defining Acceptance 106

§ 2.3.1. Distinguishing Between Acceptance and Counter-Offer ...107

§ 2.3.2. The Mirror Image Rule 112

§ 2.3.3. Permitted Method and Manner of Acceptance
(Including Acceptance by Promise or by Performance)...........116

§ 2.3.4. Acceptance by Conduct 126

§ 2.3.5. Acceptance by Inaction 129

§ 2.3.6. What Terms Are Accepted? 136

§ 2.4. Rejection by the Offeree 150

§ 2.5. Revocation by the Offeror 152

§ 2.5.1. Limitations on the Power to Revoke: Unilateral
Contracts 156

§ 2.5.2. Limitations on the Power to Revoke: Option Contracts
and Firm Offers 157

§ 2.6. Time of Effectiveness of Contract Formation
Communications..159

§ 2.6.1. The Mailbox Rule for Acceptances 159

§ 2.6.2. Time of Acceptance by Conduct 164

§ 3. Sequential Offer and Acceptance Under UCC Article 2 166

§ 3.1. General Rules of Offer and Acceptance.............................169

§ 3.2. Rejection of the Mirror Image Rule: UCC § 2–207 169

§ 3.2.1. Defining Acceptance Under § 2–207 171

§ 3.2.1.1. Acceptance by Expression of Commitment:
§ 2–207(1) 171

§ 3.2.1.2. Acceptance by Conduct: § 2–207(3) 176

§ 3.3. Terms of a Contract Formed Under § 2–207 177

§ 3.3.1. Terms of a Contract Formed Under § 2–207(1):
Understanding § 2–207(2)..178

§ 3.3.2. Terms of a Contract Formed Under § 2–207(3) 179

§ 3.4. Integrating Your Understanding of § 2–207 181

CHAPTER 4. *Consideration* 195

§ 1. Introduction 196

§ 2. Defining Consideration..197

§ 2.1. Articulating Consideration as a Benefit-Detriment Test 198

§ 2.2. Articulating Consideration as a Bargained-for Exchange 205

§ 3. Common Disputes Involving Consideration.............................223

§ 3.1. Conditional Gifts 224

§ 3.2. Illusory Promises 230

§ 3.3. Settlement Agreements Based on Worthless (Invalid) Claims 233

§ 3.4. Contract Modification and the Pre-Existing Duty Rule 241

§ 3.5. Discharge of Duty and the Pre-Existing Duty Rule 251

§ 4. Stretching the Limits of Consideration Doctrine 261

CHAPTER 5. *Alternatives to Consideration* 271

§ 1. Introduction 272

§ 2. Promissory Estoppel...274

§ 3. Promise for Benefit Already Received ("Promissory Restitution") 312

§ 4. Liability for Restitution 329

CHAPTER 6. *Defenses to Contract Enforcement* 353

§ 1. Introduction 354

§ 2. Defenses Based on Lack of Capacity to Contract.......................356

§ 2.1. Infancy 357

§ 2.2. Mental Illness or Defect..368

§ 2.3. Intoxication 384

§ 3. Defenses Related to Defects in Mutual Assent............................386

§ 3.1. Mistake...387

§ 3.1.1. Mutual Mistake...389

§ 3.1.2. Unilateral Mistake 399

§ 3.2. Misrepresentation...404

§ 3.3. Duress and Undue Influence..415

§ 3.3.1. Duress..415

§ 3.3.2. Undue Influence..431

§ 3.4. Unconscionability 440

§ 3.4.1. Codifications of the Unconscionability Defense.............450

§ 3.4.2. Substantive and Procedural Unconscionability.................452

§ 3.4.3. Unconscionability Issues in Arbitration Agreements.........459

§ 4. Violation of Public Policy 471

CHAPTER 7. *Statute of Frauds*...489

§ 1. Introduction 490

§ 2. Manner and Effect of Invoking the Statute of Frauds 493

§ 3. Is the Contract Within the Statute of Frauds?.............................493

§ 3.1. Is the Contract Within a Category of Contracts Covered by the Statute of Frauds? 494

§ 3.2. Does the Agreement Fall Within an Exception to the Writing Requirement?...500

§ 3.2.1. Exceptions for Contracts for the Sale of Goods...............500

§ 3.2.2. Part Performance Exception................................501

§ 3.2.3. Equitable and Promissory Estoppel 503

§ 4. Is There a Writing That Satisfies the Statute of Frauds? 507

§ 4.1. What Kind of Writing Is Required?..............................507

§ 4.2. Writing or Writings? 521

§ 4.3. The Statute of Frauds in Electronic Commerce....................530

CHAPTER 8. *Content and Meaning of the Contract* 537

§ 1. Introduction 539

§ 2. Interpreting Express Contract Terms.................................541

§ 2.1. The Types of Evidence Relevant to Interpretation.................541

§ 2.1.1. A Case Study in Interpretation.............................541

§ 2.1.2. The Special Role of "Course of Performance," "Course
of Dealing," and "Trade Usage".................................549

§ 2.2. Canons of Construction 552

§ 2.3. Subjective Intent vs. Objective Meaning.........................560

§ 2.4. Is Interpretation a Question of Fact or Law?...................561

§ 3. Using Extrinsic Evidence to Understand a Contract..................564

§ 3.1. Determining Ambiguity...565

§ 3.2. The Parol Evidence Rule 579

§ 3.2.1. Applying the Parol Evidence Rule: Two Sets of
Questions...581

§ 3.2.2. The Nature of the Written Contract.......................581

§ 3.2.3. The Nature of the Evidence Introduced 601

§ 3.3. Reviewing § 3: Using Extrinsic Evidence to Understand a
Contract 610

§ 4. Implied Contract Terms and Provisions...............................611

§ 4.1. Terms Implied from the Circumstances...........................613

§ 4.2. Duty of Good Faith..625

§ 4.2.1. The General Duty of Good Faith in Performance or
Enforcement 627

§ 4.2.2. Duty of Good Faith in Requirements and Output
Contracts..639

§ 4.2.3. Duty of Good Faith in Exercising Termination Rights 642

§ 5. Express Conditions 645

§ 5.1. General Introduction to Conditions..............................645

§ 5.2. Types of Conditions 647

§ 5.2.1. Conditions to Contract Formation Versus Contract
Performance..647

§ 5.2.2. Conditions Precedent, Conditions Subsequent, and Concurrent Conditions 648

§ 5.2.3. Express Conditions and Implied Conditions.....................649

§ 5.3. Identifying and Enforcing Express Conditions 650

§ 5.4. Waiver and Excuse of Conditions...666

§ 5.4.1. Waiver of Conditions...666

§ 5.4.2. Excuse of Condition to Avoid Forfeiture.....................668

CHAPTER 9. *Performance, Breach, and Excuse* 683

§ 1. Introduction 684

§ 2. Implied Conditions and Order of Performance 685

§ 3. Performance and Breach Under the Common Law...........................690

§ 3.1. Implied Conditions and the Doctrine of Substantial Performance...690

§ 3.2. Substantial Performance or Material Breach?..............................701

§ 3.3. Partial or Total Breach? 706

§ 4. Repudiation 724

§ 4.1. Defining Repudiation (Renunciation) 725

§ 4.2. Anticipatory Repudiation...728

§ 4.3. Reasonable Insecurity About Future Performance 733

§ 5. Performance and Breach Under UCC Article 2.................................745

§ 6. Excuse from Performance: Impossibility, Impracticability, and Frustration of Purpose 748

§ 6.1. Impossibility 748

§ 6.2. Impossibility Broadens into Impracticability 754

§ 6.3. Frustration of Purpose...762

§ 6.4. When *Do* Courts Grant Excuse? 776

CHAPTER 10. *Remedies* 781

§ 1. Overview...782

§ 2. Remedies at Law (Damages) 786

§ 2.1. Expectation Damages...790

§ 2.1.1. Categories of Expectation Damages 790

§ 2.1.2. Thinking Sensibly About Expectation Damages 792

§ 2.1.3. Measuring Typical Direct Damages.............................795

§ 2.1.4. Special Problems in Measuring Direct Damages 800

§ 2.1.4.1. Damages Resulting from Anticipatory Repudiation...800

§ 2.1.4.2. Owner's Cost to Complete Versus Diminution in Value 802

§ 2.1.4.3. Damages for "Lost Profits" and "Lost Volume" 815
§ 2.1.5. Indirect Expectation Damages 818
§ 2.1.5.1. Incidental Damages 819
§ 2.1.5.2. Consequential Damages....................................820
§ 2.1.6. Mitigation of Damages (Avoidable Damages) 833
§ 2.2. Reliance Damages..847
§ 2.3. Restitution Damages 851
§ 2.3.1. Damages for the Party Who Materially Breaches 854
§ 2.3.2. Damages for the Party Who Is Prevented from
Performing 860
§ 2.4. Agreed and Liquidated Damages 862
§ 2.5. Punitive Damages..875
§ 3. Equitable Remedies: The "Extraordinary Remedies"...................881
§ 3.1. Specific Performance..882
§ 3.2. Prohibitory Injunction...894
§ 3.3. Specific Restitution..905
§ 4. Putting the Concepts Together 906

CHAPTER 11. *Third-Party Rights and Duties* 909
§ 1. Introduction 909
§ 2. Assignment of Rights and Delegation of Duties........................910
§ 2.1. Common Law Approach..912
§ 2.2. UCC and Restatement Provisions 920
§ 2.3. Beyond the Basics..923
§ 3. Third-Party Beneficiaries 925
§ 3.1. Common Categories of Third-Party Beneficiaries 927
§ 3.2. Beyond the Basics..933

INDEX..937

Table of Contents

ACKNOWLEDGEMENTS AND ILLUSTRATION CREDITS v

TABLE OF CASES xxv

TABLE OF RESTATEMENT AND UCC PROVISIONS xxxvii

CHAPTER 1. *Introduction* 1
§ 1. Overview 1
§ 2. Sources of Contract Law and Authority 5
    § 2.1. Judicial Opinions 5
    § 2.2. Restatements of the Law 6
    § 2.3. Statutory Law 8
    § 2.4. International Commercial Law and the CISG 9
§ 3. Features of This Book 10

CHAPTER 2. *Promise and Assent* 15
§ 1. Introduction 15
§ 2. Is Meaning Judged Objectively or Subjectively? 17
    Embry v. Hargadine, McKittrick Dry Goods Co. 18
    Lucy v. Zehmer 22
§ 3. Promise as Expression of Commitment 31
    PROBLEMS: WAS A PROMISE MADE? (2-1 TO 2-8) 32
§ 4. Lack of Commitment: Illusory Promises 33
    PROBLEMS: ILLUSORY PROMISES (2-9, 2-10) 36
§ 5. Promises with Indefinite or Incomplete Terms 38
    Quake Construction v. American Airlines 39
    Sun Printing & Publishing Ass'n v. Remington Paper & Power Co. .. 50
    Academy Chicago Publishers v. Cheever 57

CHAPTER 3. *Assent Through Offer and Acceptance* 65
§ 1. Introduction 67
§ 2. Sequential Assent by Offer and Acceptance Under the Common Law ... 67

§ 2.1. Defining "Offer" 69

§ 2.1.1. Advertisements and Rewards as Offers 75

Lefkowitz v. Great Minneapolis Surplus Store, Inc. 76

Leonard v. PepsiCo 82

PROBLEM: ADVERTISEMENTS AND REWARDS (3-1) 97

§ 2.1.2. Offers in the Commercial Bidding Process..........................98

PROBLEMS: WAS AN OFFER MADE? (3-2 TO 3-4) 99

§ 2.2. How Long Does an Offer Last?...101

§ 2.2.1. Lapse 101

§ 2.2.2. Death or Incapacity of the Offeror or Offeree....................105

PROBLEM: DEATH OF THE OFFEROR (3-5) 105

§ 2.3. Defining Acceptance 106

§ 2.3.1. Distinguishing Between Acceptance and Counter-Offer ...107

Ardente v. Horan..108

PROBLEMS: ACCEPTANCE OR COUNTER-OFFER? (3-6 TO 3-8)..............111

§ 2.3.2. The Mirror Image Rule...112

PROBLEMS: MIRROR-IMAGE RULE (3-9, 3-10)...........................114

§ 2.3.3. Permitted Method and Manner of Acceptance
(Including Acceptance by Promise or by Performance)............116

PROBLEMS: PREPARATIONS FOR OR THE BEGINNING OF PERFORMANCE
(3-11 TO 3-13) 119

PROBLEM: OFFER AND ACCEPTANCE (3-14)...............................123

§ 2.3.4. Acceptance by Conduct 126

§ 2.3.5. Acceptance by Inaction 129

PROBLEMS: ASSENT THROUGH CONDUCT OR INACTION (3-15 TO
3-17) 134

§ 2.3.6. What Terms Are Accepted? 136

Reading Critically: *Meyer v. Uber* and Notice of Terms to the
Offeree 137

§ 2.4. Rejection by the Offeree 150

§ 2.5. Revocation by the Offeror 152

PROBLEMS: REJECTION AND REVOCATION (3-18 TO 3-20) 155

§ 2.5.1. Limitations on the Power to Revoke: Unilateral
Contracts 156

§ 2.5.2. Limitations on the Power to Revoke: Option Contracts
and Firm Offers..157

PROBLEMS: IRREVOCABLE OFFERS (3-21 TO 3-23) 158

§ 2.6. Time of Effectiveness of Contract Formation
Communications..159

§ 2.6.1. The Mailbox Rule for Acceptances..159

    UETA § 15. Time . . . of Sending and Receipt............................161

§ 2.6.2. Time of Acceptance by Conduct...164

PROBLEMS: TIME OF EFFECTIVENESS OF ACCEPTANCE (3-24, 3-25) 165

§ 3. Sequential Offer and Acceptance Under UCC Article 2 166

§ 3.1. General Rules of Offer and Acceptance.....................................169

§ 3.2. Rejection of the Mirror Image Rule: UCC § 2–207......................169

    § 3.2.1. Defining Acceptance Under § 2–207.................................171

        § 3.2.1.1. Acceptance by Expression of Commitment:

            § 2–207(1)...171

        § 3.2.1.2. Acceptance by Conduct: § 2–207(3).......................176

§ 3.3. Terms of a Contract Formed Under § 2–207...............................177

    § 3.3.1. Terms of a Contract Formed Under § 2–207(1):

        Understanding § 2–207(2)..178

    § 3.3.2. Terms of a Contract Formed Under § 2–207(3) 179

§ 3.4. Integrating Your Understanding of § 2–207 181

    Egan Machinery Co. v. Mobil Chemical Co. 184

PROBLEMS: CONTRACTS AND THEIR TERMS UNDER UCC § 2–207 (3-26 TO

    3-30) 189

CHAPTER 4. *Consideration* 195

§ 1. Introduction 196

§ 2. Defining Consideration..197

§ 2.1. Articulating Consideration as a Benefit-Detriment Test 198

§ 2.2. Articulating Consideration as a Bargained-for Exchange 205

    United States v. Meadors 206

PROBLEMS: IS THERE CONSIDERATION? (4-1 TO 4-8)....................................221

§ 3. Common Disputes Involving Consideration 223

§ 3.1. Conditional Gifts...224

PROBLEM: CONDITIONAL GIFTS (4-9)..229

§ 3.2. Illusory Promises...230

PROBLEM: ILLUSORY PROMISES (4-10) 232

§ 3.3. Settlement Agreements Based on Worthless (Invalid) Claims.....233

    Dyer v. National By-Products, Inc....234

PROBLEM: SETTLEMENT AGREEMENTS AND CONSIDERATION (4-11)............240

§ 3.4. Contract Modification and the Pre-Existing Duty Rule................241

    Angel v. Murray 242

PROBLEMS: CONTRACT MODIFICATION AND CONSIDERATION (4-12 TO

    4-14)..250

§ 3.5. Discharge of Duty and the Pre-Existing Duty Rule 251

       Problems: Contract Discharge and Consideration (4-15 to 4-17)...260

§ 4. Stretching the Limits of Consideration Doctrine 261

      Lawrence v. Ingham County Health Dept. Family Planning/Pre-Natal Clinic 262

Chapter 5. *Alternatives to Consideration* 271

§ 1. Introduction 272

§ 2. Promissory Estoppel...274

      Restatement § 90. Promise Reasonably Inducing Definite and Substantial Action..277

      Restatement (Second) § 90. Promise Reasonably Inducing Action or Forbearance 278

      Conrad v. Fields 280

      Hayes v. Plantations Steel Co. 287

      Maryland Nat'l Bank v. United Jewish Appeal Fed'n of Greater Wash. 292

      Pavel Enterprises v. A.S. Johnson Co....305

§ 3. Promise for Benefit Already Received ("Promissory Restitution")..........312

      Mills v. Wyman 313

      Drake v. Bell..318

      Webb v. McGowin 322

§ 4. Liability for Restitution...329

      Nursing Care Services, Inc. v. Dobos..332

      Mitchell v. Moore 335

      Bloomgarden v. Coyer...342

      Problems: Promissory Estoppel, Promissory Restitution, and Restitution (5-1 to 5-9) 347

Chapter 6. *Defenses to Contract Enforcement* 353

§ 1. Introduction 354

§ 2. Defenses Based on Lack of Capacity to Contract...................................356

      § 2.1. Infancy 357

          Webster Street Partnership, Ltd. v. Sheridan 359

      § 2.2. Mental Illness or Defect...368

          Fingerhut v. Kralyn Enterprises, Inc. 369

      § 2.3. Intoxication 384

      Problems: The Incapacity Defenses (6-1, 6-2).......................................385

§ 3. Defenses Related to Defects in Mutual Assent.......................................386

      § 3.1. Mistake..387

PROBLEMS: DISTINGUISHING MISTAKE OF FACT, LAW, OPINION, AND
    PREDICTION (6-3 TO 6-7) 388
    § 3.1.1. Mutual Mistake...389
        Lenawee County Board of Health v. Messerly....................392
    § 3.1.2. Unilateral Mistake...399
    PROBLEMS: THE MISTAKE DEFENSE (6-8 TO 6-10) 402
  § 3.2. Misrepresentation...404
    PROBLEMS: THE MISREPRESENTATION DEFENSE (6-11 TO 6-14).................414
  § 3.3. Duress and Undue Influence...415
    § 3.3.1. Duress..415
        EverBank v. Marini...418
        PROBLEMS: THE DURESS DEFENSE (6-15 TO 6-17)...........................430
    § 3.3.2. Undue Influence..431
        G.A.S. v. S.I.S....433
  § 3.4. Unconscionability 440
    Williams v. Walker-Thomas Furniture Co. 442
    § 3.4.1. Codifications of the Unconscionability Defense...............450
    § 3.4.2. Substantive and Procedural Unconscionability.................452
    § 3.4.3. Unconscionability Issues in Arbitration Agreements.........459
        Disappearing Claims and the Erosion of Substantive Law 460
        Italian Colors and Freedom of Contract Under the Federal
        Arbitration Act...464
    PROBLEM: THE UNCONSCIONABILITY DEFENSE (6-18) 468
§ 4. Violation of Public Policy 471
  Tunkl v. Regents of the University of California 474
PROBLEMS: CONTRACT DEFENSES (6-19 TO 6-21)......................................486

CHAPTER 7. *Statute of Frauds*...489
§ 1. Introduction 490
§ 2. Manner and Effect of Invoking the Statute of Frauds 493
PROBLEM: BURDEN OF PROOF IN THE STATUTE OF FRAUDS (7-1) 493
§ 3. Is the Contract Within the Statute of Frauds?.............................493
  § 3.1. Is the Contract Within a Category of Contracts Covered by the
    Statute of Frauds? 494
    PROBLEMS: THE ONE-YEAR PROVISION (7-2 TO 7-7)...........................497
  § 3.2. Does the Agreement Fall Within an Exception to the Writing
    Requirement?...500
    § 3.2.1. Exceptions for Contracts for the Sale of Goods.................500
    § 3.2.2. Part Performance Exception 501

§ 3.2.3. Equitable and Promissory Estoppel 503

§ 4. Is There a Writing That Satisfies the Statute of Frauds? 507

     § 4.1. What Kind of Writing Is Required? 507

         Howard Construction Co. v. Jeff-Cole Quarries, Inc. 511

         PROBLEMS: WHAT KIND OF WRITING IS REQUIRED? (7-8 TO 7-12)...........520

     § 4.2. Writing or Writings? 521

         Crabtree v. Elizabeth Arden Sales Corp. 525

     § 4.3. The Statute of Frauds in Electronic Commerce............................530

PROBLEMS: APPLYING THE STATUTE OF FRAUDS (7-13 TO 7-16) 532

CHAPTER 8. *Content and Meaning of the Contract* 537

§ 1. Introduction 539

§ 2. Interpreting Express Contract Terms..541

     § 2.1. The Types of Evidence Relevant to Interpretation 541

         § 2.1.1. A Case Study in Interpretation...541

             Frigaliment Importing Co. v. B.N.S. International Sales Corp.........542

         § 2.1.2. The Special Role of "Course of Performance," "Course
             of Dealing," and "Trade Usage" 549

     § 2.2. Canons of Construction 552

         PROBLEMS: CANONS OF CONSTRUCTION (8-1, 8-2) 552

     PROBLEMS: INTERPRETING EXPRESS TERMS (8-3 TO 8-5) 558

     § 2.3. Subjective Intent vs. Objective Meaning.......................................560

     § 2.4. Is Interpretation a Question of Fact or Law?.................................561

§ 3. Using Extrinsic Evidence to Understand a Contract 564

     § 3.1. Determining Ambiguity...565

         C. & A. Construction Co. v. Benning Construction Co. 566

         Pacific Gas & Electric Co. v. G.W. Thomas Drayage & Rigging Co. 572

     § 3.2. The Parol Evidence Rule 579

         § 3.2.1. Applying the Parol Evidence Rule: Two Sets of
             Questions 581

         § 3.2.2. The Nature of the Written Contract.....................................581

             UAW-GM Human Resource Center v. KSL Recreation Corp. 584

             PROBLEM: MERGER OR INTEGRATION CLAUSES (8-6)............................599

         § 3.2.3. The Nature of the Evidence Introduced 601

         PROBLEMS: PAROL EVIDENCE RULE (8-7 TO 8-16).....................................607

     § 3.3. Reviewing § 3: Using Extrinsic Evidence to Understand a
     Contract 610

§ 4. Implied Contract Terms and Provisions..611

     § 4.1. Terms Implied from the Circumstances..613

Fisher v. Congregation B'nai Yitzhok...613

First National Bank of Lawrence v. Methodist Home for the Aged 617

Wood v. Lucy, Lady Duff-Gordon 623

§ 4.2. Duty of Good Faith...625

    § 4.2.1. The General Duty of Good Faith in Performance or
Enforcement 627

        Market Street Associates Limited Partnership v. Frey 627

    § 4.2.2. Duty of Good Faith in Requirements and Output
Contracts..639

    § 4.2.3. Duty of Good Faith in Exercising Termination Rights 642

§ 5. Express Conditions 645

§ 5.1. General Introduction to Conditions..................................645

§ 5.2. Types of Conditions 647

    § 5.2.1. Conditions to Contract Formation Versus Contract
Performance..647

    § 5.2.2. Conditions Precedent, Conditions Subsequent, and
Concurrent Conditions...648

    § 5.2.3. Express Conditions and Implied Conditions.....................649

§ 5.3. Identifying and Enforcing Express Conditions............................650

    Morrison v. Bare...651

    Internatio-Rotterdam, Inc. v. River Brand Rice Mills, Inc. 656

    Peacock Construction Co. v. Modern Air Conditioning, Inc. 660

§ 5.4. Waiver and Excuse of Conditions....................................666

    § 5.4.1. Waiver of Conditions..666

    § 5.4.2. Excuse of Condition to Avoid Forfeiture............................668

        J.N.A. Realty Corp. v. Cross Bay Chelsea, Inc. 671

CHAPTER 9. *Performance, Breach, and Excuse*...............................683

§ 1. Introduction 684

§ 2. Implied Conditions and Order of Performance 685

    PROBLEMS: IMPLIED CONDITIONS (9-1, 9-2).....................................688

§ 3. Performance and Breach Under the Common Law.............................690

§ 3.1. Implied Conditions and the Doctrine of Substantial
Performance...690

    Jacob & Youngs v. Kent...692

    PROBLEM: IMPLIED VERSUS EXPRESS CONDITIONS (9-3)............................700

§ 3.2. Substantial Performance or Material Breach?............................701

    PROBLEMS: SUBSTANTIAL PERFORMANCE OR MATERIAL BREACH? (9-4,
9-5) 705

§ 3.3. Partial or Total Breach?..706

    Sackett v. Spindler...711

    Problems: Partial or Total Breach? (9-6, 9-7)............................717

§ 4. Repudiation 724

  § 4.1. Defining Repudiation (Renunciation) 725

  § 4.2. Anticipatory Repudiation..728

    Hochster v. De la Tour 729

  § 4.3. Reasonable Insecurity About Future Performance 533

    Problem: Right to Adequate Assurance (9-8) 736

    Hornell Brewing Co. v. Spry 737

§ 5. Performance and Breach Under UCC Article 2...745

  Problem: Performance Under UCC Article 2 (9-9) 747

§ 6. Excuse from Performance: Impossibility, Impracticability, and
Frustration of Purpose 748

  § 6.1. Impossibility 748

    Taylor v. Caldwell 749

  § 6.2. Impossibility Broadens into Impracticability 754

  § 6.3. Frustration of Purpose...762

    Krell v. Henry..762

    Adbar, L.C. v. New Beginnings C-Star 770

  § 6.4. When *Do* Courts Grant Excuse? 776

  Problems: Impossibility, Impracticability, and Frustration of Purpose
(9-10, 9-11)...779

Chapter 10. *Remedies* 781

§ 1. Overview..782

  Problem: Comparing Remedial Principles (10-1)...............................784

§ 2. Remedies at Law (Damages) 786

  Problems: Comparing Types of Damages (10-2, 10-3)........................787

  § 2.1. Expectation Damages..790

    § 2.1.1. Categories of Expectation Damages 790

    § 2.1.2. Thinking Sensibly About Expectation Damages 792

    Problems: Determining Expectation Damages (10-4 to 10-9) 793

    § 2.1.3. Measuring Typical Direct Damages................................795

    § 2.1.4. Special Problems in Measuring Direct Damages 800

      § 2.1.4.1. Damages Resulting from Anticipatory
Repudiation...800

      § 2.1.4.2. Owner's Cost to Complete Versus Diminution in
Value 802

Lyon v. Belosky Construction, Inc. 804

PROBLEM: DAMAGES FOR DEFECTIVE PERFORMANCE (10-10).......806

Peevyhouse v. Garland Coal & Mining Co. 808

§ 2.1.4.3. Damages for "Lost Profits" and "Lost Volume" 815

§ 2.1.5. Indirect Expectation Damages 818

§ 2.1.5.1. Incidental Damages 819

PROBLEM: INCIDENTAL DAMAGES (10-11) 819

§ 2.1.5.2. Consequential Damages..820

§ 2.1.6. Mitigation of Damages (Avoidable Damages) 833

Parker v. Twentieth Century-Fox Film Corp. 837

PROBLEM: MITIGATION OF DAMAGES (10-12) 846

§ 2.2. Reliance Damages...847

§ 2.3. Restitution Damages 851

§ 2.3.1. Damages for the Party Who Materially Breaches 854

Eker Brothers, Inc. v. Rehders..856

§ 2.3.2. Damages for the Party Who Is Prevented from Performing 860

PROBLEM: RESTITUTION DAMAGES (10-13)..............................862

§ 2.4. Agreed and Liquidated Damages 862

Wassenaar v. Panos..863

PROBLEMS: LIQUIDATED DAMAGES (10-14, 10-15) 871

§ 2.5. Punitive Damages...875

Romero v. Mervyn's..875

§ 3. Equitable Remedies: The "Extraordinary Remedies"...............................881

§ 3.1. Specific Performance..882

Ammerman v. City Stores Co. 884

Laclede Gas Co. v. Amoco Oil Co...888

PROBLEM: SPECIFIC PERFORMANCE (10-16) 894

§ 3.2. Prohibitory Injunction..894

American Broadcasting Companies v. Wolf..............................895

§ 3.3. Specific Restitution..905

§ 4. Putting the Concepts Together 906

CHAPTER 11. *Third-Party Rights and Duties*....................................909

§ 1. Introduction 909

§ 2. Assignment of Rights and Delegation of Duties.................................910

§ 2.1. Common Law Approach 912

PROBLEM: DIAGRAMMING ASSIGNMENT/DELEGATION TRANSACTIONS (11-1) 920

§ 2.2. UCC and Restatement Provisions 920

§ 2.3. Beyond the Basics..923

§ 3. Third-Party Beneficiaries 925

Problem: Diagramming Third-Party Beneficiary Transactions (11-2)........927

§ 3.1. Common Categories of Third-Party Beneficiaries 927

§ 3.2. Beyond the Basics..933

Problem: Third-Party Beneficiaries (11-3)......................................934

Index...937

Table of Cases

The principal cases are in bold type. The Example and Analysis cases are in italics type. Cases cited or discussed in the text are in roman type. Cases cited in principal cases and within other quoted materials are not included. References are to pages.

3637 Green Road Co. v. Specialized Component Sales, 69 N.E.3d 1083 (Ohio Ct. App. 2016), *498, 502*

Abbot of Westminster v. Clerke, 73 Eng. Rep. 59, 63 (K.B. 1536), 749

Academy Chicago Publishers v. Cheever, 144 Ill.2d 24, 161 Ill.Dec. 335, 578 N.E.2d 981 (Ill.1991), **57**

Adams v. Lindsell, 1817 WL 2056 (KB 1818), 160

Adbar, L.C. v. New Beginnings C-Star, 103 S.W.3d 799 (Mo.App. E.D.2003), **770**

Alabama Football, Inc. v. Wright, 452 F.Supp. 182 (N.D.Tex.1977), 777

Alliance Wall Corp. v. Ampat Midwest Corp., 17 Ohio App.3d 59, 477 N.E.2d 1206 (1984), *173*

Aluminum Co. of America v. Essex Group, Inc., 499 F.Supp. 53 (W.D.Pa.1980), 777

American Broadcasting Companies, Inc. v. Wolf, 52 N.Y.2d 394, 438 N.Y.S.2d 482, 420 N.E.2d 363 (N.Y.1981), **895**

American Express Co. v. Italian Colors Restaurant, 570 U.S. 228, 133 S.Ct. 2304, 186 L.Ed.2d 417 (2013), 459

American Home Mortg., Inc., In re, 379 B.R. 503 (Bkrtcy.D.Del.2008), 722

American Software, Inc. v. Ali, 54 Cal.Rptr.2d 477 (Cal.App. 1 Dist.1996), *455*

Ammerman v. City Stores Co., 394 F.2d 950, 129 U.S.App.D.C. 325 (D.C.Cir.1968), **884**

Angel v. Murray, 113 R.I. 482, 322 A.2d 630 (R.I.1974), **242**

Appeal of (see name of party)

Ardente v. Horan, 117 R.I. 254, 366 A.2d 162 (R.I.1976), **108**

Argall v. Cook, 43 Conn. 160 (1875), 257

AT&T Mobility LLC v. Concepcion, 563 U.S. 333, 131 S.Ct. 1740, 179 L.Ed.2d 742 (2011), 459

Augstein v. Leslie, 2012 WL 4928914 (S.D.N.Y. Oct. 17, 2012), *96*

Ayers v. Shaffer, 286 Va. 212, 748 S.E.2d 83 (2013), *431*

Baehr v. Penn-O-Tex Oil Corp., 258 Minn. 533, 104 N.W.2d 661 (Minn.1960), *215*
Bak-A-Lum Corp. of America v. Alcoa Bldg. Products, Inc., 69 N.J. 123, 351 A.2d 349 (N.J.1976), *642*
Barker's Estate, In re, 158 Misc. 803, 287 N.Y.S. 841 (Surrogate's Ct. 1936), *204*
Barrer v. Women's Nat. Bank, 761 F.2d 752, 245 U.S.App.D.C. 349 (D.C.Cir.1985), *409*
Birdsall v. Saucier, 1992 WL 37731 (Conn.Super.1992), *258*
Blanton v. Friedberg, 819 F.2d 489 (4th Cir.1987), *860*
Bloomgarden v. Coyer, 479 F.2d 201, 156 U.S.App.D.C. 109 (D.C.Cir.1973), **342**
BMW of North America, LLC v. MiniWorks, LLC, 166 F. Supp. 3d 976 (D. Ariz. 2010), *102*
Bonebrake v. Cox, 499 F.2d 951 (8th Cir.1974), 168
Bouton v. Byers, 50 Kan.App.2d 35, 321 P.3d 780 (2014), *789*
British Waggon Co v. Lea & Co., 1880 WL 14338 (QBD 1880), *913*
Britton v. Turner, 6 N.H. 481 (N.H.1834), *854*
Brooks Towers Corp. v. Honkin-Conkey Construction Co., 454 F.2d 1203 (10th Cir. 1972), *130*
Brown v. Kern, 21 Wash. 211, 57 P. 798 (Wash.1899), 242
Burger King Corp. v. Family Dining, Inc., 426 F. Supp. 485 (E.D. Pa. 1977), *668*
Burns v. McCormick, 233 N.Y. 230, 135 N.E. 273 (N.Y.1922), 501
Bush v. Protravel Intern., Inc., 192 Misc.2d 743, 746 N.Y.S.2d 790 (N.Y.City Civ. Ct.2002), 774

C. & A. Const. Co., Inc. v. Benning Const. Co., 256 Ark. 621, 509 S.W.2d 302 (Ark.1974), **566**
Care Display, Inc. v. Didde-Glaser, Inc., 225 Kan. 232, 589 P.2d 599 (Kan.1979), 168
Central Drug Store v. Adams, 184 Tenn. 541, 201 S.W.2d 682 (Tenn. 1947), *555*
Certa v. Wittman, 35 Md.App. 364, 370 A.2d 573 (Md.App.1977), 473
C. Itoh & Co. (America) Inc. v. Jordan Intern. Co., 552 F.2d 1228 (7th Cir.1977), *177, 180*
Clark, Appeal of, 57 Conn. 565, 19 A. 332 (Conn.1889), *199*
Cleveland, Estate of v. Gorden, 837 S.W.2d 68 (Tenn.Ct.App.1992), 347
Coca-Cola Co. v. Babyback's Intern., Inc., 841 N.E.2d 557 (Ind.2006), 502
Collins v. Thompson, 679 F.2d 168 (9th Cir. 1982), *150*
Columbia Nitrogen Corp. v. Royster Co., 451 F.2d 3 (4th Cir.1971), 551
Conagra v. Bartlett Partnership, 248 Neb. 933, 540 N.W. 2d 333 (1995), *753*
Conrad v. Fields, 2007 WL 2106302 (Minn.App.2007), **280**
Construction Aggregates Corp. v. Hewitt-Robins, Inc., 404 F.2d 505 (7th Cir.1968), 174

Corn Products Refining Co. v. Fasola, 109 A. 505 (N.J.Err. & App.1920), *733*

Cosden Oil & Chemical Co. v. Karl O. Helm Aktiengesellschaft, 736 F.2d 1064 (5th Cir.1984), 801

Couldery v. Bartrum, 19 Ch.D. 394, 399 (1880), 257

Crabtree v. Elizabeth Arden Sales Corporation, 305 N.Y. 48, 110 N.E.2d 551 (N.Y.1953), **525**

Crane Ice Cream Co. v. Terminal Freezing & Heating Co., 147 Md. 588, 128 A. 280 (Md.1925), *916*

C.R. Klewin, Inc. v. Flagship Properties, Inc., 220 Conn. 569, 600 A.2d 772 (Conn.1991), 496

Cumber v. Wane, 93 Eng. Rep. 613 (1718), 256

Dahl v. HEM Pharmaceuticals Corp., 7 F.3d 1399 (9th Cir. 1993), *122*

Dean v. Myers, 466 So.2d 952 (Ala.1985), 496

De Haviland v. Warner Bros. Pictures, 67 Cal.App.2d 225, 153 P.2d 983 (Cal.App. 2 Dist.1944), 844

Dorton v. Collins & Aikman Corp., 453 F.2d 1161 (6th Cir.1972), 174

Dougherty v. Salt, 227 N.Y. 200, 125 N.E. 94 (N.Y.1919), *203*

Douglas v. Pflueger Hawaii, Inc., 110 Hawai'i 520, 135 P.3d 129 (2006), *357*

Drake v. Bell, 55 N.Y.S. 945 (N.Y.Sup.1899), **318**

Drennan v. Star Paving, 333 P.2d 757, 51 Cal.2d 409 (1958), *301*

Dyer v. National By-Products, Inc., 380 N.W.2d 732 (Iowa 1986), **234**

Earle v. Angell, 157 Mass. 294, 32 N.E. 164 (Mass.1892), 105

Egan Machinery Co. v. Mobil Chemical Co., 660 F.Supp. 35 (D.Conn.1986), **184**

Eker Brothers, Inc. v. Rehders, 150 N.M. 542 (Ct. App. 2011), **856**

Embry v. Hargadine, McKittrick Dry Goods Co., 127 Mo.App. 383, 105 S.W. 777 (1907), **18**

Estate of (see name of party)

EverBank v. Marini, 200 Vt. 490, 134 A.3d 189, 2015 VT 131 (2015), **418**

Fairmount Glass Works v. Crunden-Martin Woodenware Co., 106 Ky. 659, 51 S.W. 196 (1899), *71*

Farley v. Cleaveland, 4 Cow. 432, 15 Am.Dec. 387 (N.Y. 1825), 928

Feld v. Henry S. Levy & Sons, Inc., 37 N.Y.2d 466, 373 N.Y.S.2d 102, 335 N.E.2d 320 (N.Y.1975), *640*

Fingerhut v. Kralyn Enterprises, Inc., 71 Misc.2d 846, 337 N.Y.S.2d 394 (N.Y.Sup.1971), **369**

Finnin v. Bob Lindsay, Inc., 366 Ill.App.3d 546, 304 Ill.Dec. 196, 852 N.E.2d 446 (Ill.App. 3 Dist.2006), 112

First Development Corp. of Kentucky v. Martin Marietta Corp., 959 F.2d 617 (6th Cir 1992), *153, 162*

First Nat. Bank of Lawrence v. Methodist Home for the Aged, 181 Kan. 100, 309 P.2d 389 (Kan.1957), **617**

Fisher v. Congregation B'Nai Yitzhok, 177 Pa.Super. 359, 110 A.2d 881 (Pa. Super.1955), **613**

Florida Power & Light Co. v. Westinghouse Elec. Corp., 826 F.2d 239 (4th Cir.1987), 777

Foakes v. Beer, L.R. 9 A.C. 605 (H.L. 1884), 257

Ford Motor Credit Co. v. McDaniel, 613 S.W.2d 513 (Tex.Civ.App.Corpus Christi 1981), 556

Foster & Kleiser v. Baltimore County, 57 Md.App. 531, 470 A.2d 1322 (1984), 72

Frigaliment Importing Co. v. B.N.S. Intern. Sales Corp., 190 F.Supp. 116 (S.D.N.Y.1960), **542**

Frostifresh Corp. v. Reynoso, 52 Misc.2d 26, 274 N.Y.S.2d 757 (N.Y.Dist.Ct.1966), *457*

Galloway v. Santander Consumer USA, Inc., 819 F.3d 79 (4th Cir. 2016), *122*

G.A.S. v. S.I.S., 407 A.2d 253 (Del.Fam.Ct.1978), **433**

Gill v. Johnstown Lumber Co., 151 Pa. 534, 25 A. 120 (Pa.1892), 723

Gonzalez v. Jurella, 2015 WL 9943596 (D. Conn. Sept. 22, 2015), *384*

Goodman v. Dicker, 169 F.2d 684, 83 U.S.App.D.C. 353 (D.C.Cir.1948), *850*

Groves v. John Wunder Co., 205 Minn. 163, 286 N.W. 235 (1939)

Hadley v. Baxendale, 1854 WL 7208 (Ex Ct 1854), *821*

Halbman v. Lemke, 99 Wis.2d 241, 298 N.W.2d 562 (Wis.1980), *366*

Hall v. Hall, 222 Cal.App.3d 578, 271 Cal.Rptr. 773 (Cal.App. 4 Dist.1990), 502

Hamer v. Sidway, 32 N.Y.St.Rep. 521, 11 N.Y.S. 182 (N.Y.Sup.Gen.Term 1890), *201*

Hanford v. Connecticut Fair Ass'n, 92 Conn. 621, 103 A. 838 (Conn.1918), 777

Harding v. Cargo of 4,698 Tons of New Rivers Steam Coal, 147 F. 971 (D.Me.1906), 554

Hayes v. Plantations Steel Co., 438 A.2d 1091 (R.I.1982), **287**

Herm Hughes & Sons, Inc. v. Quintek, 834 P.2d 582 (Utah Ct. App. 1992), *174*

Heuerman v. B & M Const., Inc., 358 Ill.App.3d 1157, 295 Ill.Dec. 549, 833 N.E.2d 382 (Ill.App. 5 Dist.2005), 168

Higgins v. Lauritzen, 209 Mich.App. 266, 530 N.W.2d 171 (Mich.App.1995), 168

Hills Materials Co. v. Rice, 982 F.2d 514 (Fed.Cir.1992), 554

Hochster v. De La Tour, 1853 WL 7479 (QB 1853), **729**

Holler v. Holler, 364 S.C. 256, 612 S.E.2d 469 (S.C.App.2005), *416*

Hollywood Fantasy Camp v. Gabor, 151 F.3d 203 (5th Cir. 1998), 116

Holter v. National Union Fire Ins. Co. of Pittsburgh, Pa., 1 Wash.App. 46, 459 P.2d 61 (Wash.App. Div. 2 1969), *555*

Home Elec. Co. v. Underdown Heating & Air Conditioning Co., 86 N.C. App. 540, 358 S.E.2d 539 (1987), 304

Hornell Brewing Co., Inc. v. Spry, 174 Misc.2d 451, 664 N.Y.S.2d 698 (N.Y.Sup.1997), **737**

Houston Dairy, Inc. v. John Hancock Mut. Life Ins. Co., 643 F.2d 1185 (5th Cir.1981), *102, 127*

Howard Const. Co. v. Jeff-Cole Quarries, Inc., 669 S.W.2d 221 (Mo.App. W.D.1983), **511**

Hume v. United States, 132 U.S. 406, 10 S.Ct. 134, 33 L.Ed. 393 (1889), 441

Hutton v. Monograms Plus, Inc., 78 Ohio App.3d 176, 604 N.E.2d 200 (Ohio App. 2 Dist.1992), 664

Hyde v. Dean of Windsor, 78 Eng. Rep. 798 (Q.B. 1597), 749

Idaho Power Co. v. Westinghouse Elec. Corp., 596 F.2d 924 (9th Cir.1979), *175*

In re (see name of party)

Internatio-Rotterdam, Inc. v. River Brand Rice Mills Inc., 259 F.2d 137 (2nd Cir.1958), **656**

Jacob & Youngs v. Kent, 230 N.Y. 239, 129 N.E. 889 (N.Y.1921), **692**, *802*

James Baird Co. v. Gimbel Bros., Inc., 64 F.2d 344 (2d Cir.1933), *301*

James B. Berry's Sons Co. of Illinois v. Monark Gasoline & Oil Co., 32 F.2d 74 (8th Cir.1929), *734*

Jay Dreher Corporation v. Delco Appliance Corporation, 93 F.2d 275 (2nd Cir.1937), *735*

J.N.A. Realty Corp. v. Cross Bay Chelsea, Inc., 42 N.Y.2d 392, 397 N.Y.S.2d 958, 366 N.E.2d 1313 (N.Y.1977), **671**

Johnson v. Calvert, 19 Cal.Rptr.2d 494, 851 P.2d 776 (Cal.1993), *482*

JRG Capital Investors I, LLC v. Doppelt, 2012 WL 2529256 (S.D.Tex.2012), *556*

Kannavos v. Annino, 356 Mass. 42, 247 N.E.2d 708 (Mass.1969), *412*

Kenford Co., Inc. v. Erie County, 108 A.D.2d 132, 489 N.Y.S.2d 939 (N.Y.A.D. 4 Dept.1985), *828*

K & G Const. Co. v. Harris, 223 Md. 305, 164 A.2d 451 (Md.1960), **717, 724**

Khiterer v. Bell, 6 Misc.3d 1015(A), 800 N.Y.S.2d 348 (N.Y.City Civ.Ct.2005), *702, 803*

Kingston v. Preston, 99 Eng. Rep. 437 (K.B.1773), *687*

Kirksey v. Kirksey, 8 Ala. 131 (Ala.1845), 274

Klapp v. United Ins. Group Agency, Inc., 468 Mich. 459, 663 N.W.2d 447 (Mich.2003), *562*

Koehring Co. v. Glowacki, 77 Wis.2d 497, 253 N.W.2d 64 (Wis.1977), 173

Krell v. Henry, 1903 WL 12966 (CA 1903), **762**

The Kronprinzessin Cecilie, 244 U.S. 12, 37 S.Ct. 490, 61 L.Ed. 960 (1917), 777

Laclede Gas Co. v. Amoco Oil Co., 522 F.2d 33 (8th Cir.1975), **888**

Lakeman v. Pollard, 43 Me. 463 (Me.1857), 777

Lake River Corp. v. Carborundum Co., 769 F.2d 1284 (7th Cir.1985), 873

Lawrence v. Fox, 20 N.Y. 268 (N.Y.1859), *927*

Lawrence v. Ingham County Health Dept. Family Planning/Pre-Natal Clinic, 160 Mich.App. 420, 408 N.W.2d 461 (Mich.App.1987), **262**

Lee v. Joseph E. Seagram & Sons, Inc., 552 F.2d 447 (2nd Cir.1977), *605*

Lefkowitz v. Great Minneapolis Surplus Store, Inc., 251 Minn. 188, 86 N.W.2d 689 (Minn.1957), **76**

Lenawee County Bd. of Health v. Messerly, 417 Mich. 17, 331 N.W.2d 203 (Mich.1982), **392**

Leonard v. Pepsico, Inc., 88 F.Supp.2d 116 (S.D.N.Y.1999), **82**

Lloyd v. Murphy, 25 Cal.2d 48, 153 P.2d 47 (Cal.1944), 778

Lockheed Electronics Co. v. Keronix, Inc., 114 Cal.App.3d 304, 170 Cal.Rptr. 591 (Cal.App. 2 Dist.1981), *175*

Lowy v. United Pac. Ins. Co., 67 Cal.2d 87, 60 Cal.Rptr. 225, 429 P.2d 577 (Cal.1967), 723

Lucy v. Zehmer, 196 Va. 493, 84 S.E.2d 516 (Va.1954), **22**

Lyon v. Belosky Const. Inc., 247 A.D.2d 730, 669 N.Y.S.2d 400 (N.Y.A.D. 3 Dept.1998), **804**

MacPherson v. Buick Motor Co., 217 N.Y. 382, 111 N.E. 1050 (N.Y.1916), 51

Market Street Associates Ltd. Partnership v. Frey, 941 F.2d 588 (7th Cir.1991), **627**

Maryland Nat. Bank v. United Jewish Appeal Federation of Greater Washington, Inc., 286 Md. 274, 407 A.2d 1130 (Md.1979), **292**

Mattei v. Hopper, 51 Cal.2d 119, 330 P.2d 625 (1958), 664

McCaull-Webster Elevator Co. v. Steele Bros., 43 S.D. 485, 180 N.W. 782 (1921), 775

McCloskey & Co. v. Minweld Steel Co., 220 F.2d 101 (3rd Cir.1955), *725*, *800*

McIntosh v. Murphy, 52 Haw. 29, 469 P.2d 177, 54 A.L.R.3d 707 (1970), *504*

Meadors, United States v., 753 F.2d 590 (7th Cir.1985), **206**

Mealey v. Kanealy, 226 Iowa 1266, 286 N.W. 500 (Iowa 1939), *554*

Meincke v. Northwest Bank & Trust Co., 745 N.W.2d 95 (Iowa App.2007), *217*

Menorah Chapels at Millburn v. Needle, 386 N.J.Super. 100, 899 A.2d 316 (N.J.Super.A.D.2006), 723

Meyer v. Kalanick, 200 F. Supp. 3d 408 (S.D.N.Y. 2016), *138*

Meyer v. Uber Technologies, Inc., 868 F.3d 66 (2d Cir. 2017), *138*

Middletown Concrete Products, Inc. v. Black Clawson Co., 802 F.Supp. 1135 (D.Del.1992), *597*

Mills v. Wyman, 20 Mass. 207 (Mass.1825), **313**

Mineral Park Land Co. v. Howard, 172 Cal. 289, 156 P. 458 (Cal.1916), 777

Mitchell v. Moore, 729 A.2d 1200 (Pa.Super.1999), **335**

Monahan v. Finlandia University, 69 F. Supp. 3d 681 (W.D. Mich. 2014), *163*

Moraine Products, Inc. v. Parke, Davis & Co., 43 Mich.App. 210, 203 N.W.2d 917 (Mich.App.1972), *554*

Morrison v. Bare, 2007 WL 4415307 (Ohio App. 9 Dist.2007), **651**

Mouton v. Kershaw, 59 Wis. 316, 18 N.W. 172 (1884), *70*

Muther-Ballenger v. Griffin Electronic Consultants, 100 N.C.App. 505, 897 S.E.2d 247 (1990), *604*

Myers v. Smith, 48 Barb. 614 (N.Y.Sup.Gen.Term 1867), 112

Nanakuli Paving and Rock Co. v. Shell Oil Co., Inc., 664 F.2d 772 (9th Cir.1981), *550*

Naylor Benzon & Co Ltd v. Krainische Industrie Gesellschaft, 1 K.B. 331 (1881), 472

Neibarger v. Universal Cooperatives, Inc., 439 Mich. 512, 486 N.W.2d 612 (Mich.1992), 168

Neri v. Retail Marine Corp., 30 N.Y.2d 393, 334 N.Y.S.2d 165, 285 N.E.2d 311 (N.Y.1972), *815*

Newport Associates Phase I Developers Ltd. v. Travelers Cas. And Sur. Co., 2013 WL 10090299 (N.J. Sup. Ct. 2015), *556*

Nichols v. Raynbred, 80 Eng. Rep. 238 (K.B. 1615), 686

Nigro v. Lee, 63 A.D.3d 1490, 882 N.Y.S.2d 346 (2009), *407*

Nirvana Int'l, Inc. v. ADT Security Services, Inc., 881 F. Supp. 2d 556 (S.D.N.Y. 2012), *130*

Nordyne, Inc. v. International Controls & Measurements Corp., 262 F.3d 843 (8th Cir.2001), *73*

Northern Corp. v. Chugach Elec. Ass'n, 518 P.2d 76 (Alaska 1974), 776

Northern Indiana Public Service Co. v. Carbon County Coal Co., 799 F.2d 265 (7th Cir.1986), *758*

Nursing Care Services, Inc. v. Dobos, 380 So.2d 516 (Fla.App. 4 Dist.1980), **332**

Orange & Rockland Utilities, Inc. v. Amerada Hess Corp., 59 A.D.2d 110, 397 N.Y.S.2d 814 (N.Y.A.D. 2 Dept.1977), *641*

Ortelere v. Teachers' Retirement Board of City of New York, 25 N.Y.2d 196, 303 N.Y.S.2d 362, 250 N.E.2d 460 (1969), 382

Owen v. Hendricks, 433 S.W.2d 164 (Tex.1968), *521*

Owen v. Tunison, 131 Me. 42, 158 A. 926 (1932), *71*

Owens v. M.E. Schepp Ltd. Partnership, 218 Ariz. 222, 182 P.3d 664 (Ariz.2008), 501

Pacific Gas & Elec. Co. v. G. W. Thomas Drayage & Rigging Co., 69 Cal.2d 33, 69 Cal.Rptr. 561, 442 P.2d 641 (Cal.1968), **572**

Palsgraf v. Long Island R. Co., 248 N.Y. 339, 162 N.E. 99 (N.Y.1928), 51

Paradine v. Jane, 82 Eng. Rep. 897 (K.B. 1647), 748

Parker v. Twentieth Century-Fox Film Corp., 89 Cal.Rptr. 737, 474 P.2d 689 (Cal.1970), **837**

Pass v. Shelby Aviation, Inc., 2000 WL 388775 (Tenn.Ct.App.2000), 168

Pauma Band of Luiseno Mission Indians of the Pauma & Yuima Reservation v. California, 813 F.3d 1155 (9th Cir. 2015), *853*

Pavel Enterprises, Inc. v. A.S. Johnson Co., Inc., 342 Md. 143, 674 A.2d 521 (Md.1996), 303, **305**

Peacock Const. Co., Inc. v. Modern Air Conditioning, Inc., 353 So.2d 840 (Fla.1977), **660**

Peevyhouse v. Garland Coal & Min. Co., 382 P.2d 109 (Okla.1962), **808**

Pennsy Supply, Inc. v. American Ash Recycling Corp. of Pennsylvania, 895 A.2d 595 (Pa.Super.2006), *227*

Pinnel's Case, 77 Eng. Rep. 237 (C.P. 1602), 256

Pittsburgh-Des Moines Steel Co. v. Brookhaven Manor Water Co., 532 F.2d 572 (7th Cir.1976), 724

Pittsley v. Houser, 125 Idaho 820, 875 P.2d 232 (Idaho App.1994), 168

Popkin v. Security Mut. Ins. Co. of New York, 48 A.D.2d 46, 367 N.Y.S.2d 492 (N.Y.A.D. 1 Dept.1975), *555*

Provencal v. Vermont Mut. Ins. Co., 132 N.H. 742, 571 A.2d 276 (1990), *103*

Quake Const., Inc. v. American Airlines, Inc., 141 Ill.2d 281, 152 Ill.Dec. 308, 565 N.E.2d 990 (Ill.1990), **39**

Quaker State Mushroom Co., Inc. v. Dominick's Finer Foods, Inc. of Illinois, 635 F. Supp. 1281 (N.D. Ill. 1986), *151*

Questar Builders, Inc. v. CB Flooring, LLC, 410 Md. 241, 978 A.2d 651 (Md.2009), *231, 643*

Raffles v. Wichelhaus, 1864 WL 5985 (Unknown Court 1864), 30

Redgrave v. Boston Symphony Orchestra, Inc., 855 F.2d 888 (1st Cir.1988), *825*

Register.com, Inc. v. Verio, Inc., 356 F.3d 393 (2d Cir. 2004), 147

Renovest Co. v. Hodges Development Corp., 135 N.H. 72, 600 A.2d 448 (N.H.1991), 649, 667

Rhode Island State Dept. of Transp. v. Providence and Worcester R. Co., 674 A.2d 1239 (R.I.1996), 115

Richardson v. Greensboro Warehouse & Storage Co., 223 N.C. 344, 26 S.E.2d 897 (N.C.1943), 113

Rich Products Corp. v. Kemutec, Inc., 66 F.Supp.2d 937 (E.D.Wis.1999), 175

Ricketts v. Scothorn, 57 Neb. 51, 77 N.W. 365 (Neb.1898), 276

Roberts Contracting Co., Inc. v. Valentine-Wooten Road Public Facility Bd., 2009 Ark. App. 437, 320 S.W.3d 1 (Ark.App.2009), *703, 862*

Rockingham County v. Luten Bridge Co., 35 F.2d 301 (4th Cir.1929), *833*

Rogers Communications Inc. v. Bell Aliant Regional Communications Income Fund, 2007 CarswellNat 7307(CRTC 2007), *557*

Romero v. Mervyn's, 109 N.M. 249, 784 P.2d 992 (N.M.1989), **875**

Roylex, Inc. v. Avco Community Developers, Inc., 559 S.W.2d 833 (Tex.Civ.App.Hous (14 Dist.) 1977), *555*

Rye v. Phillips, 203 Minn. 567, 282 N.W. 459 (Minn.1938), 241

Sackett v. Spindler, 248 Cal.App.2d 220, 56 Cal.Rptr. 435 (Cal.App. 1 Dist.1967), **711**, *799, 836*

San Carlos Irrigation & Drainage Dist. v. United States, 23 Cl. Ct. 276 (1991), 708

Schneberger v. Apache Corp., 890 P.2d 847 (Okla.1994), 815

Schnell v. Nell, 17 Ind. 29 (Ind.1861), *218*

Seaver v. Ransom, 224 N.Y. 233, 120 N.E. 639 (N.Y.1918), *929*

Security Stove & Mfg. Co. v. American Ry. Express Co., 227 Mo.App. 175, 51 S.W.2d 572 (Mo.App.1932), *848*

Sibree v. Tripp, 153 Eng. Rep. 745 (1846), 256

Sierra Diesel Injection Service, Inc. v. Burroughs Corp., Inc., 656 F.Supp. 426 (D.Nev.1987), *595*

Singer v. Adamson, 2003 WL 23641985 (Mass.Land Ct.2003), 532

Sitogum Holdings, Inc. v. Ropes, 352 N.J.Super. 555, 800 A.2d 915 (N.J.Super. Ch.2002), *453*

S.M.R. Enterprises, Inc. v. Southern Haircutters, Inc., 662 S.W.2d 944 (Tenn. Ct.App.1983), *556*

Soldau v. Organon Inc., 860 F.2d 355 (9th Cir. 1988), *162*

Southern Idaho Pipe & Steel Co. v. Cal-Cut Pipe & Supply, Inc., 98 Idaho 495, 567 P.2d 1246 (Idaho 1977), 173

Spector, United States v., 55 F.3d 22 (1st Cir. 1995), 120

Stanley v. A. Levy & J. Zentner Co., 60 Nev. 432, 112 P.2d 1047 (Nev.1941), 496

Stanley Gudyka Sales Co. v. Lacy Forest Products, 915 F.2d 273 (7th Cir. 1990), *709*

Stearns v. Emery-Waterhouse Co., 596 A.2d 72 (Me. 1991), *506*

Sterling v. Taylor, 55 Cal.Rptr.3d 116, 152 P.3d 420 (Cal.2007), *508*

Stroupes v. Finish Line, Inc., 2005 WL 5610231 (E.D. Tenn. March 16, 2005), *357*

Stump Home Specialties Mfg., Inc., United States v., 905 F.2d 1117 (7th Cir. 1979), 207

Sub-Zero Freezer Co., Inc. v. Cunard Line Ltd., 2002 WL 32357103 (W.D.Wis.2002), 774

Sullivan v. O'Connor, 363 Mass. 579, 296 N.E.2d 183 (Mass.1973), 269

Sun Printing & Publishing Ass'n v. Remington Paper & Power Co., 235 N.Y. 338, 139 N.E. 470 (1923), **50**

Taylor v. State Farm Mut. Auto. Ins. Co., 175 Ariz. 148, 854 P.2d 1134 (Ariz.1993), 579

Taylor v. Caldwell, 1863 WL 6052 (KB 1863), **749**, 750

Texaco, Inc. v. Pennzoil, Co., 729 S.W.2d 768 (Tex.App.Hous. (1 Dist.) 1987), 49

Textile Unlimited, Inc. v. A..BMH and Co., Inc., 240 F.3d 781 (9th Cir.2001), 175

The Score Board, Inc., In re, 238 B.R. 585 (D.N.J. 1999), 365

Toker v. Perl, 103 N.J.Super. 500, 247 A.2d 701 (N.J.Super.L.1968), *458*

Toker v. Westerman, 113 N.J.Super. 452, 274 A.2d 78 (N.J.Dist.Ct.1970), 441, *457*

Tomczak v. Koochiching County Highway Dept., 1999 WL 55501 (Minn.App.1999), *225*

Totem Marine Tug & Barge, Inc. v. Alyeska Pipeline Service Co., 584 P.2d 15 (Alaska 1978), *426*

Transatlantic Financing Corp. v. United States, 363 F.2d 312, 124 U.S.App.D.C. 183 (D.C.Cir.1966), *755*

Travis v. Tacoma Public School Dist., 120 Wash.App. 542, 85 P.3d 959 (Wash. App. Div. 2 2004), 113

Trident Center v. Connecticut General Life Insurance Co., 847 F.2d 564 (9th Cir. 1988), 578

True North Composites, LLC v. Trinity Industries, Inc., 2003 WL 21206154 (Fed. Cir.2003), 168

Tunkl v. Regents of University of Cal., 60 Cal.2d 92, 32 Cal.Rptr. 33, 383 P.2d 441 (Cal.1963), **474**

UAW-GM Human Resource Center v. KSL Recreation Corp., 228 Mich.App. 486, 579 N.W.2d 411 (Mich.App.1998), **584**

UMG Recordings, Inc. v. Augusto, 628 F.3d 1175 (9th Cir. 2011), *131*

United States v. _____ (see opposing party)

Unke v. Thorpe, 75 S.D. 65, 59 N.W.2d 419 (S.D.1953), *753*

U.S. Bancorp Equipment Finance, Inc. v. Ameriquest Holdings LLC, 55 UCC Rep. Serv. 2d 423 (D. Minn. 2004), 774

U.S. Industries, Inc. v. Semco Mfg., Inc., 562 F.2d 1061 (8th Cir.1977), 172

Viking Supply v. National Cart Co., 310 F.3d 1092 (8th Cir. 2002), *768*

Vitex Mfg. Corp. v. Caribtex Corp., 377 F.2d 795 (3rd Cir.1967), *817*

Wagner v. Rainier Mfg. Co., 230 Or. 531, 371 P.2d 74 (Or.1962), 112

Warren v. Skinner, 20 Conn. 559 (1850), 257

Wassenaar v. Panos, 111 Wis.2d 518, 331 N.W.2d 357 (Wis.1983), **863**

Webb v. McGowin, 27 Ala.App. 82, 168 So. 196 (Ala.App.1935), **322**

Webster Street Partnership, Ltd. v. Sheridan, 220 Neb. 9, 368 N.W.2d 439 (Neb.1985), **359**

Whitelaw v. Brady, 3 Ill.2d 583, 121 N.E.2d 785 (Ill.1954), 112

Wil-Fred's Inc. v. Metropolitan Sanitary Dist. of Greater Chicago, 57 Ill.App.3d 16, 14 Ill.Dec. 667, 372 N.E.2d 946 (Ill.App. 1 Dist.1978), *400*

Williams v. Lloyd W. Jones, 82 Eng. Rep. 95 (K.B. 1628), 749

Williams v. Walker-Thomas Furniture Co., 350 F.2d 445, 121 U.S.App.D.C. 315 (D.C.Cir.1965), **442**

Wood v. Boynton, 64 Wis. 265, 25 N.W. 42 (Wis.1885), *389*

Wood v. Lucy, Lady Duff-Gordon, 222 N.Y. 88, 118 N.E. 214 (N.Y.1917), **623**

Yaros v. Trustees of University of Pennsylvania, 742 A.2d 1118 (Pa. Super. 1999), *103*

Table of Restatement and UCC Provisions

Restatement (First) of Contracts

§ 90. Promise Reasonably Inducing Definite and Substantial Action...............277

§ 133. Definition of Donee Beneficiary, Creditor Beneficiary, Incidental
    Beneficiary..931

§ 135. Duties Created by a Gift Promise...931

§ 136. Duties Created by a Promise to Discharge a Duty 931

Restatement (Second) of Contracts

Chapter 1. Meaning of Terms

§ 1. Contract Defined..215

§ 2. Promise; Promisor; Promisee; Beneficiary 16, 34, 647

Chapter 2. Formation of Contracts—Parties and Capacity

§ 12. Capacity to Contract...356

§ 14. Infants..358

§ 15. Mental Illness or Defect 383

§ 16. Intoxicated Persons 384

Chapter 3. Formation of Contracts—Mutual Assent
Topic 2. Manifestation of Assent in General

§ 19. Conduct as Manifestation of Assent 126

Topic 3. Making of Offers

§ 24. Offer Defined...70

§ 26. Preliminary Negotiations 87

§ 30. Form of Acceptance Invited..116

§ 32. Invitation of Promise or Performance 119

§ 33. Certainty 60

Topic 4. Duration of the Offeree's Power of Acceptance

§ 38. Rejection 150, 151

§ 39. Counter-Offers 107, 150

§ 41. Lapse of Time 101, 103, 104

§ 42. Revocation by Communication from Offeror Received by Offeree 152

§ 43. Indirect Communication of Revocation 153, 154

§ 45. Option Contract Created by Part Performance or Tender 157, 300

§ 46. Revocation of General Offer 153

Topic 5. Acceptance of Offers

§ 50. Acceptance of Offer Defined 106

§ 62. Effect of Performance by Offeree Where Offer Invites Either Performance
    or Promise 119

§ 63. Time When Acceptance Takes Effect 160

§ 69. Acceptance by Silence or Exercise of Dominion 129, 132, 133

Chapter 4. Formation of Contracts—Consideration
Topic 1. The Requirement of Consideration

§ 71. Requirement of Exchange; Types of Exchange 215, 218, 233

§ 72. Exchange of Promise for Performance 218

§ 73. Performance of Legal Duty 218, 249

§ 74. Settlement of Claims 237

§ 79. Adequacy of Consideration; Mutuality of Obligation 215

Topic 2. Contracts without Consideration

§ 84. Promise to Perform a Duty in Spite of Non-occurrence of a
    Condition 667, 668

§ 86. Promise for Benefit Received 328

§ 87. Option Contract 302, 503

§ 89. Modification of Executory Contract 247, 249

§ 90. Promise Reasonably Inducing Action or Forbearance 277, 278, 298,
    302, 503, 788, 847

Chapter 5. The Statute of Frauds

§ 110. Classes Covered..494, 496

Topic 4. The Land Contract Provision

§ 129. Action in Reliance; Specific Performance...501

Topic 6. Satisfaction of the Statute by a Memorandum

§ 131. General Requisites of a Memorandum...507

§ 133. Memorandum Not Made as Such 507, 508

§ 134. Signature...508

§ 136. Time of Memorandum...508

§ 137. Loss or Destruction of a Memorandum..508

Topic 7. Consequences of Non-Compliance

§ 139. Enforcement by Virtue of Action in Reliance 503, 506

Chapter 6. Mistake

§ 151. Mistake Defined 387

§ 152. When Mistake of Both Parties Makes a Contract Voidable 398, 402

§ 153. When Mistake of One Party Makes a Contract Voidable 399, 402

§ 154. When a Party Bears the Risk of a Mistake 398, 402

§ 157. Effect of Fault of Party Seeking Relief 399, 402

Chapter 7. Misrepresentation, Duress and Undue Influence
Topic 1. Misrepresentation

§ 159. Misrepresentation Defined..410

§ 161. When Non-Disclosure is Equivalent to an Assertion....................410, 633

§ 162. When a Misrepresentation is Fraudulent or Material 410, 411

§ 167. When a Misrepresentation is an Inducing Cause 410

§ 168. Reliance on Assertions of Opinion..410

§ 169. When Reliance on a Assertion of Opinion is Not Justified 410

Topic 2. Duress and Undue Influence

§ 174. When Duress by Physical Compulsion Prevents Formation of a
Contract 420, 421, 422

§ 175. When Duress by Threat Makes a Contract Voidable....................421, 422

§ 176. When a Threat Is Improper 422, 423, 426, 429

§ 177. When Undue Influence Makes a Contract Voidable 431

Chapter 8. Unenforceability on Grounds of Public Policy
Topic 1. Unenforceability in General
§ 178. When a Term Is Unenforceable on Grounds of Public Policy 473

Chapter 9. The Scope of Contractual Obligations
Topic 1. The Meaning of Agreements
§ 201. Whose Meaning Prevails..561

Topic 2. Considerations of Fairness and the Public Interest
§ 205. Duty of Good Faith and Fair Dealing..625
§ 208. Unconscionable Contract or Term 451

Topic 3. Effect of Adoption of a Writing
§ 211. Standardized Agreements 446
§ 212. Interpretation of Integrated Agreements 561
§ 214. Evidence of Prior or Contemporaneous Agreements and
  Negotiations 602, 603
§ 216. Consistent Additional Terms..593

Topic 5. Conditions and Similar Events
§ 224. Condition Defined..645, 647, 648, 655
§ 229. Excuse of a Condition to Avoid Forfeiture 668
§ 230. Event that Terminates a Duty...648

Chapter 10. Performance and Non-Performance
Topic 1. Performances to be Exchanged Under an Exchange of Promises
§ 234. Order of Performances 690

Topic 2. Effect of Performance and Non-Performance
§ 237. Effect on Other Party's Duties of a Failure to Render Performance 701
§ 241. Circumstances Significant in Determining Whether a Failure Is
  Material 704, 708, 715
§ 242. Circumstances Significant in Determining When Remaining Duties
  Are Discharged 708

Topic 3. Effect of Prospective Non-Performance

§ 251. When a Failure to Give Assurance May Be Treated as a Repudiation...735, 736

Chapter 11. Impracticability of Performance and Frustration of Purpose

§ 261. Discharge by Supervening Impracticability 754, 755, 775

§ 262. Death or Incapacity of Person Necessary for Performance....................754

§ 263. Destruction, Deterioration or Failure to Come Into Existence of Thing Necessary for Performance 754

§ 264. Prevention by Government Regulation or Order..................................754

§ 265. Discharge by Supervening Frustration 768, 769, 775

§ 266. Existing Impracticability or Frustration 775

§ 269. Temporary Impracticability or Frustration..779

§ 270. Partial Impracticability 779

Chapter 12. Discharge by Assent or Alteration
Topic 1. The Requirement of Consideration

§ 273. Requirement of Consideration or a Substitute......................................256

Topic 2. Substituted Performance, Substituted Contract,
Accord and Account Stated

§ 278. Substituted Performance...251, 253

§ 279. Substituted Contract...252, 255

§ 280. Novation 253

§ 281. Accord and Satisfaction 253

Topic 3. Agreement of Rescission, Release and Contract Not to Sue

§ 283. Agreement of Rescission 252

Chapter 14. Contract Beneficiaries

§ 302. Intended And Incidental Beneficiaries 932

§ 304. Creation of Duty to Beneficiary...932

§ 315. Effect of A Promise of Incidental Benefit 932

Chapter 15. Assignment and Delegation
Topic 1. What Can Be Assigned or Delegated

§ 317. Assignment of a Right..921, 922

§ 318. Delegation of Performance of Duty..921, 922

§ 322. Contractual Prohibition of Assignment 921, 922

Chapter 16. Remedies
Topic 2. Enforcement by Award of Damages

§ 355. Punitive Damages 875, 879

§ 356. Liquidated Damages and Penalties..862, 867

Topic 4. Restitution

§ 374. Restitution in Favor of Party in Breach................................855, 857, 858

Restatement (Third) of Restitution & Unjust Enrichment

§ 1. Restitution and Unjust Enrichment 330

§ 2. Limiting Principles 330, 346

§ 20. Protection of Another's Life or Health 341

§ 21. Protection of Another's Property 341

§ 22. Performance of Another's Duty 341

§ 28. Unmarried Cohabitants 341

Uniform Commercial Code

Article 1. General Provisions
Part 1. General Provisions

§ 1–103. Construction of [Uniform Commercial Code] to Promote Its Purposes
and Policies; Applicability of Supplemental Principles of Law........167, 770

Part 2. General Definitions and Principles of Interpretation

§ 1–201. General Definitions

(b)(37) "Signed"..510

(b)(43) "Writing" 510

§ 1–205. Reasonable Time; Seasonableness 172

Part 3. Territorial Applicability and General Rules

§ 1–303. Course of Performance, Course of Dealing, and Usage of Trade 550

§ 1–304. Obligation of Good Faith...625

Article 2. Sales
Part 1. Short Title, General Construction and Subject Matter

§ 2–102. Scope; Certain Security and Other Transactions Excluded from this Article..167, 229

§ 2–105. Definitions: Transferability; "Goods"; 'Future" Goods; "Lot"; "Commercial Unit" 167

§ 2–106. Definitions: "Contract"; "Agreement"; "Contract for Sale"; "Sale"; "Present Sale"; "Conforming" to Contract; "Termination"; "Cancellation"..167

Part 2. Form, Formation and Readjustment of Contract

§ 2–201. Formal Requirements; Statute of Frauds.........494, 500, 510, 513, 514, 516, 517, 518

§ 2–202. Final Written Expression; Parol or Extrinsic Evidence 582

§ 2–204. Formation in General 169, 184, 192

§ 2–205. Firm Offers..158, 167, 300

§ 2–206. Offer and Acceptance in Formation of Contract......164, 167, 169, 184, 192

§ 2–207. Additional Terms in Acceptance. 114, 169–193, 516, 540, 741

§ 2–209. Modification, Rescission and Waiver...............................247, 249, 250

§ 2–210. Delegation of Performance; Assignment of Rights 920, 921, 922

Part 3. General Obligation and Construction of Contract

§ 2–302. Unconscionable Contract or Clause.................................445, 451, 453

§ 2–305. Open Price Term 612

§ 2–306. Output, Requirements and Exclusive Dealings 639, 641, 919

§ 2–307. Delivery in Single Lot or Several Lots......................................446, 612

§ 2–308. Absence of Specified Place of Delivery..612

§ 2–309. Absence of Specific Time Provisions; Notice of Termination 612

§ 2–313. Express Warranties by Affirmation, Promise, Description, Sample ...407

§ 2–314. Implied Warranty: Merchantability; Usage of Trade 612

§ 2–315. Implied Warranty: Fitness for Particular Purpose.............................612

Part 5. Performance

§ 2–503. Manner of Seller's Tender of Delivery...745

§ 2–508. Cure by Seller of Improper Tender or Delivery; Replacement...746, 747

Part 6. Breach, Repudiation and Excuse

§ 2–601. Buyer's Rights on Improper Delivery 745, 747

§ 2–602. Manner and Effect of Rightful Rejection 746, 747

§ 2–603. Merchant Buyer's Duties as to Rightfully Rejected Goods 746

§ 2–604. Buyer's Options as to Salvage of Rightfully Rejected Goods 746

§ 2–606. What Constitutes Acceptance of Goods 746, 747

§ 2–607. Effect of Acceptance; Notice of Breach; Burden of Establishing Breach After Acceptance; Notice of Claim or Litigation to Person Answerable Over 747

§ 2–608. Revocation of Acceptance in Whole or in Part 746, 747

§ 2–609. Right to Adequate Assurance 735, 736, 741, 742, 743, 744, 920

§ 2–610. Anticipatory Repudiation 732

§ 2–611. Retraction of Anticipatory Repudiation 732

§ 2–612. "Installment Contract"; Breach 745

§ 2–615. Excuse by Failure of Presupposed Conditions. 754, 755, 770, 890

§ 2–616. Procedure on Notice Claiming Excuse. 890

Part 7. Remedies

§ 2–704. Seller's Right to Identify Goods to the Contract Notwithstanding Breach or to Salvage Unfinished Goods 835

§ 2–706. Seller's Resale Including Contract for Resale 795, 796

§ 2–708. Seller's Damages for Non-acceptance or Repudiation 796, 816, 818

§ 2–710. Seller's Incidental Damages. 795, 796, 819

§ 2–712. "Cover"; Buyer's Procurement of Substitute Goods 797

§ 2–713. Buyer's Damages for Non-delivery or Repudiation 797, 800

§ 2–715. Buyer's Incidental and Consequential Damages 715, 797, 819, 820, 833

§ 2–716. Buyer's Right to Specific Performance or Replevin 882, 892

§ 2–718. Liquidation or Limitation of Damages 862

CONTRACTS

A Contemporary Approach

THIRD EDITION

CHAPTER 1

Introduction

Table of Contents

§ 1. Overview...1

§ 2. **Sources of Contract Law and Authority**...5

    § 2.1. Judicial Opinions...5

    § 2.2. Restatements of the Law...6

    § 2.3. Statutory Law...8

    § 2.4. International Commercial Law and the CISG.......................9

§ 3. **Features of This Book**..10

§ 1. Overview

You no doubt have a general notion, and probably mental images, of contracts and contract formation. A buyer and a seller of a product rise from a table and shake hands after hours of negotiation; a home buyer and seller sign a series of documents to "close" a home sale; a car owner leaves her car with the dealer to have maintenance work done on the vehicle; an executive purchases a suit at a department store and leaves the suit for alterations; a tenant and a landlord agree to the terms of a lease; a child and a parent agree that excellent grades in school will result in an increase in allowance. Indeed, you have likely entered into many similar agreements in your own life. What makes all of these "contracts"—or are they all contracts?

In common language, "contract" may refer to a document representing an agreement (though as we will see, a contract does not have to be in writing), to an agreement-in-fact between or among people (whether or not that agreement is legally enforceable), to a legally binding obligation arising from an agreement-in-fact, or (going a bit farther afield!) to an arrangement with a paid assassin or the agreement between bridge partners regarding how many tricks they will take in a hand. We will most often use "contract" to mean "a promise or a set of promises for the breach of which the law gives a remedy"*—that is, a legally binding obligation arising from a promise. This book focuses on determining under what circumstances the law will recognize the existence of and enforce such an obligation, and on the consequences—the remedies available—once a contract is recognized to exist.

Contract law governs promises, agreements, and exchanges and is one of the basic building blocks of law in the United States. Many of the transactions you encounter in your own daily life are grounded in contract, and the principles of contract law pervade many other areas, including commercial, consumer, family, property, and corporate law. Do an online search for news related to the word "contract" and you will no doubt find a broad range of public and private transactions that involve creating or interpreting or enforcing a wide variety of contracts.

This book considers the following sequence of issues related to contract creation and enforcement:

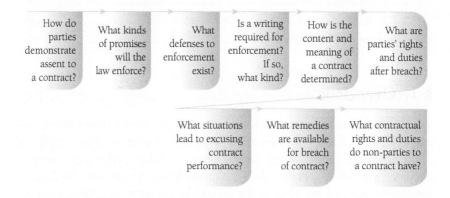

The issues identified in the diagram matter for purposes of contract drafting and planning, as well as for litigating contract claims. In the litigation context, some of the issues relate to elements a plaintiff must establish to enforce a promise; others are defenses that may be raised by the party resisting enforcement of the promise. Seen through that litigation lens, the issues addressed in the contracts course may be portrayed this way:

---

* Restatement (Second) of Contracts § 1. See page 6 for a description of the Restatement and its authority as a source of doctrinal rules.

Plaintiff's arguments to enforce a promise:	Defendant's arguments to defeat a contract claim:
A contract was created (Chs. 2, 3 & 4) or the facts show there is another rationale for enforcing a promise (Ch. 5).	One or more defenses bar contract enforcement (Ch. 6).
If someone other than plaintiff formed the contract with defendant, plaintiff is entitled to enforce it (Ch. 11).	The contract should have been represented in a signed writing and was not (Ch. 7).
The terms of the contract (Ch. 8) have been breached by the other party (Ch. 9), causing injury to plaintiff.	Circumstances justify excusing a breach (Ch. 9).
Plaintiff's injury should be compensated or alleviated by damages or some other relief (Ch. 10).	Some damages should not be recoverable because plaintiff failed to mitigate (Ch. 10).

One of the challenges of studying contract law is that determining the rights and liabilities of parties to an alleged contract often requires a sequential analysis of the entire contract relationship between them. As reflected in the charts above, one cannot determine whether a remedy exists for an alleged breach without considering whether the parties manifested assent, whether any defenses might be plausibly claimed to exist, whether any writing required for enforcement exists, what terms the parties agreed to, whether and how seriously one or both parties breached, and what remedies might be available and appropriate. As a result, although you will learn the concepts that govern the analysis of each step as you progress through the course, only at the end will you be able to fully respond to the question: "Do the circumstances presented create enforceable contractual obligations, and who will be responsible for what?" Each building block is important, but none can stand on its own. Consequently, you will have to live with a degree of uncertainty and incompleteness until the whole picture emerges later in the course.

In the midst of this uncertainty and incompleteness, however, you will find certain consistencies in analysis that mark contract doctrine, no matter which issues are being considered. Courts, commentators, lawyers, and contracting parties will return, again and again, to underlying principles and assumptions that are the foundations of contract law, or of United States law in general. You should seek out, take note of, and critique those principles and how they operate to support (or challenge) outcomes of disputes. Examples of those principles include

- Freedom of contract: Parties should decide for themselves what responsibilities to undertake, with only the smallest of restrictions, and should not ask the court to choose for them;

- Predictability and security: Parties operate more effectively when they can comfortably predict and order their lives according to the legal implications of their actions;

- Commercial reasonableness: Rules should reflect the way parties actually conduct business;

- Fairness: Parties should be protected from being misled, unreasonably pressured, or otherwise led into contracts that do not represent their true choices or that shock the conscience.

If several principles are implicated, they may be in harmony with one another or conflict. Sometimes the meaning and implications of the principles themselves will be contested (e.g., What contract rule will produce the most predictability? How much can and should contract law seek to deliver justice or protect against unfairness and how much should parties be relied upon to protect themselves?).

Lawrence Friedman has noted, "Contract law is abstraction—what is left in the law relating to agreements when all particularities of person and subject-matter are removed."* Indeed, contract law often purports to provide a one-size-fits-all rule, even though the same rule may not fit comfortably with respect to the wide variety of parties (e.g., consumers, small businesses, large corporations), transaction types (e.g., small purchase, large commercial transaction), party relationships (e.g., one-time transaction, repeat players), and economic landscape (e.g., free market, lightly or heavily regulated). Sometimes, however, the general rule is stated in broad terms, allowing it to be applied differently when the particular circumstances of the type identified above justify different treatment.

Keeping in mind the abstract rules and their impact on the particular will help you both understand and critique the rules you will be studying. Seek out and pay attention to broader principles and inquire whether the general rules adequately address the particular. As you consider each case or rule, ask yourself:

- Why was this outcome reached or rule adopted?

- What assumptions about human behavior lie behind that result?

- What values are reflected in the choice made?

- Whose interests are being protected, whether purposefully or not, and how well?

---

* Lawrence Friedman, *Contract Law in America* 20 (1965).

- What impact will the rule likely have on subsequent contract formation and performance?

- Is there a rule you think would be better than the one adopted? Why would it be better?

These questions will help you to learn the rules of contract law better, while also expanding your understanding of the purposes and effect of legal rules in general.

§ 2. Sources of Contract Law and Authority

Where does the "law" of contracts come from? A variety of sources are cited by judges and commentators and used in this textbook. What follows is a brief introduction to those sources, their scope and authority. Understanding the nature of these sources now will help you make better sense of the reading and analyze it more effectively. Later, an understanding of the sources of contract law will help you in law practice when you research contract problems posed by your clients, whether in litigation or transactional contexts.

§ 2.1. Judicial Opinions

Contract law in the United States is, in its origins, foundations, and implementation, a creature of the common law. That means the legal rules are primarily derived from and stated in judicial opinions (though, as we will discuss below, statutory law plays an increasingly large role).

Contract law is also predominantly a matter of state, not federal, law. This means that state judges determine the common law contract rules for that jurisdiction. Judges generally rely on prior decisions by other judges—case precedents—in reaching their decisions, and they favor precedent from their own jurisdiction over precedent from other states and from federal courts. Precedent from a court's own jurisdiction is "mandatory precedent," while precedents from other jurisdictions are only "persuasive precedent," not binding.

This reliance on precedent results in a degree of uniformity among the states, with outcomes derived from common principles, but there is also a significant amount of variation in the rules adopted by the various jurisdictions. One of the most difficult parts of studying contract law is dealing with these variations. Judges from different jurisdictions may state a rule in different ways and might apply the same rule inconsistently. As you read the cases and commentary in this book, keep

FYI

Common law countries, such as the United States, Canada, Australia, the United Kingdom, India, and Pakistan, draw on the British common law tradition. Many other countries, including most of Europe, Asia, Central and South America, and large portions of Africa, draw instead upon a civil law tradition descended from Roman law. In civil law jurisdictions, the primary law is statutory rather than judicial, and legislation is compiled into comprehensive codes that provide the rules for judicial decision-making. In such jurisdictions, judges decide cases primarily by interpreting and applying statutory provisions rather than by developing rules or being bound by case law arising from similar circumstances. Although located within a common law country, Louisiana and Puerto Rico retain civil law systems derived from their French and Spanish histories. The borderlines between common law and civil law adjudication have become more blurred as common law countries adopt more comprehensive statutes and civil law jurisdictions accumulate judicial opinions clarifying and applying the statutory law.

in mind that you are studying the way particular judges articulate the contract rules in question, which will resemble but may not be identical to the way the rule is articulated by another judge or in another jurisdiction. When the rule varies among jurisdictions, there may (or may not) be a version that is followed by a clear majority or minority of jurisdictions. The existence of such variations makes it important to step back from the narrow rule at issue and consider the policies and principles that underlie the specific contract rule articulated by the courts. Indeed, you may find that the variations you see in outcomes and opinions are explicitly or implicitly driven by differences in how the courts balance competing policies. Dealing with the challenge of inconsistent rules statements and outcomes in the cases discussed in the course materials will help prepare you for the challenge of dealing with the same challenges that arise often in law practice!

§ 2.2. Restatements of the Law

In 1923, in part because of the uncertainties created by a system of common law rules based in so many jurisdictions, a group of prominent American judges, lawyers, and professors established the American Law Institute (ALI) for the purpose of bringing clarity and consistency to the common law. Over the years since its creation as a private nonprofit organization, the ALI has—among a variety of law reform projects—produced a series of subject-specific "Restatements" that seek to state the principles and rules of the common law as reflected in judicial opinions and,

Go Online

For more information on the ALI, go to www.ali.org.

sometimes, statutory enactments. Drafts of proposed provisions are prepared by a Reporter, an expert in the field appointed by the ALI Council. The Reporter works in consultation with knowledgeable advisors drawn from the ALI membership. After approval by the ALI Council, a draft is submitted to the full ALI membership for approval. The process of preparing a comprehensive Restatement and earning approval of the membership usually takes years and multiple redrafts.

Because the Restatements are the products of the ALI and its members, they are persuasive commentary about the law, but they are not themselves law, unless and until a court adopts a particular provision in an opinion or a legislature enacts a particular provision into statutory law. When a particular rule is not uniform among jurisdictions, the drafters of the Restatement must choose which version of the rule to propose for inclusion. Moreover, some Restatement provisions are promulgated to encourage courts to adopt what the drafters view to be more coherent or appropriate rules not yet widely embraced by courts, rather than simply to restate a rule that currently exists. For all these reasons, you cannot assume that the Restatement is "the law," though it is often a good guide to the rules in use by the courts, and some or all provisions may be used as the "law of the course" by your instructor. Note that courts adopt Restatement provisions on a rule-by-rule basis; a jurisdiction does not adopt an entire Restatement at once.

As one of its first projects, the ALI produced the Restatement of Contracts, officially adopted by the ALI in 1932. It adopted the Restatement (Second) of Contracts in 1979. Although the second Restatement more accurately reflects the law in many jurisdictions today, some courts continue to use provisions from the earlier version. Sometimes it is instructive to consider both versions to see how the law, or perception of the law, has changed over time. Currently, the ALI is In the process of drafting and critiquing a Restatement of the Law for Consumer Contracts. See www.ali.org/projects for information on the current status of that effort.

The Restatements are comprised of "black letter" statements of law, "Comments" that explain more about the provisions, "Illustrations" (often drawn from case law), and "Notes" written by the reporter(s). If your instructor has selected for your use a supplement containing Restatement provisions, you might scan the table of contents and some of those provisions to get a better sense of what the Restatement looks like and what it covers. You can find the entire table of contents and all the provisions of the first and second Restatements in online legal research resources as well. When this book refers you to relevant Restatement provisions at appropriate places in the text, you should read the provision, at least scan and sometimes read closely the Comments and Illustrations, and look at how that provision fits into adjacent provisions and indeed the whole Restatement.

§ 2.3. Statutory Law

Although this book focuses primarily on common law, some areas of contract law are instead governed by statutory provisions. Statutory law always supersedes common law rules on the same subject matter because legislative enactments have greater authority than judicial common law decisions.

What's That?

Since its founding as a private nonprofit organization in 1892, NCCUSL/ULC has worked to consider when uniformity among state laws would be desirable and practical and to draft, adopt, and advocate for uniform codes to address those areas of law. Each state names a group of commissioners to represent its voice in the adoption process. Internal drafting committees often spend years drafting proposed laws, with the help of outside observers and advisors. When a proposed uniform law is presented at the ULC annual meeting, each state has one vote, and a majority of states attending (and no less than 20) must approve a proposal before it is officially adopted as a Uniform or Model Act. There are presently more than 100 uniform and model acts promulgated by NCCUSL, ranging widely in subject matter. For more information, see www.uniformlaws.org.

The statute most referenced in these materials is the Uniform Commercial Code (the UCC). The UCC purports to be what its name suggests—a uniform statute for all commercial matters, encompassing the activities of consumers as well as merchants and other commercial entities. The UCC was jointly promulgated by the American Law Institute (already mentioned for its role with respect to the Restatements) and the National Conference of Commissioners on Uniform State Laws (NCCUSL), now known as the Uniform Law Commission (ULC). Like other uniform laws, the UCC is a proposal to the states and does not become law in a state until adopted by the state's legislature. The UCC is divided into "Articles," each addressing a different aspect of commercial transactions. This text will introduce you to selected portions of Article 1, which contains general provisions and definitions, and Article 2, which establishes rules of law for contracts for the sale of goods. Other Articles govern leases of goods (2A); bank transactions (3, 4 and 4A); letters of credit (5); documents of title (7); investment securities (8); and secured transactions (9). Some UCC provisions covered in this textbook supplement the common law, but other provisions differ from (and supersede) the common law, providing a comparative focus on how the rules governing different kinds of contracts differ, and whether they should.

The UCC has been adopted in whole or in part in all 50 states, as well as in the District of Columbia, Puerto Rico, and the U.S. Virgin Islands. States are free to adopt variations on uniform laws when enacting them, and many have done so with respect to particular provisions of the UCC. References in this book are to the uniform version.

When the ALI and the ULC make changes in a uniform law, the version in effect in some states may differ from the new uniform version for an often considerable period of time, as the states consider whether to make the proposed changes. Article 1 was revised in 2001 and that version has been adopted by all states and territories except Puerto Rico as of October 2017. This book focuses on provisions drawn from revised Article 1, though court opinions may refer to the unrevised version.

Not every attempt at revision of a uniform law is successful. In 2003, ALI and ULC adopted major changes to Articles 2 and 2A of the UCC, but the revisions were not received favorably by state legislatures, and the ALI and ULC withdrew them in 2011. References to Article 2 in this book are to the unamended (and still official) version.

In addition to state statutes, federal statutes govern a few aspects of specific types of contractual transactions. As federal law, they supersede competing provisions of state law and are included in this book when relevant to the discussion.

§ 2.4. International Commercial Law and the CISG

Increasingly, commercial transactions are being undertaken in a global context, so understanding the international law related to those transactions is critical in law practice. A review of international commercial law is beyond the scope of these materials, but you should be aware of the existence and importance of those sources and their impact on contract law.

The Convention on Contracts for the International Sale of Goods (CISG) is a United Nations treaty enacted by the United States and 86 other nations. It applies if the parties to a contract have their places of business in different countries, each of which has ratified the CISG, making the treaty relevant in many transactions between parties from more than one country.[*] When it applies, the CISG (as a part of

> **Go Online!**
>
> The list of countries ratifying the CISG is available through the website of the United Nations Commission on International Trade Law at www. uncitral.org/uncitral/en/uncitral_texts/ sale_goods/1980CISG_status.html. Pace University hosts an extensive website on the CISG at www.cisg.law.pace.edu.

---

[*] It also applies to these situations: (1) One party's place of business is in a country that has ratified the CISG and that country's law (including the CISG) is determined to be the governing law of the contract; (2) the parties' agreement chooses the CISG as governing law even though neither party is from a country that has ratified the CISG (but the mandatory rules of the applicable domestic law supersede any conflicting CISG rules); or (3) a tribunal decides to apply all of part of the CISG because it is an appropriate rule under the applicable law.

U.S. law through ratification) takes precedence over state law, including enacted UCC provisions. The CISG operates as a package of default rules, so the parties' agreement may exclude the application of the CISG or may vary its provisions.

The Principles of International Commercial Contracts was adopted by the International Institute for the Unification of Private Law (UNIDROIT) (pronounced "oo' ne dwah"). UNIDROIT is an independent intergovernmental organization whose purpose is to modernize and harmonize private law, in particular, commercial law, among the member countries, including the United States. Like the Restatement, the UNIDROIT principles represent an effort to state guiding rules of law for contracts. The principles are not binding law unless the parties to a contract agree that they should be. The Principles play only a secondary role, but may be useful as a source of guidance in international transactions where the CISG does not control.

The CISG and the UNIDROIT Principles were drafted with both common law and civil law rules in mind, in order to effectively serve an international constituency. The drafters created hybrid rules when possible and, if not, sought a balance between favoring common law rules and civil law rules.

§ 3. Features of This Book

As you begin your law school studies, you will quickly see that learning law is about much more than just learning a set of legal rules. It is also about acquiring a set of skills associated with learning and practicing law. That skill set includes the ability (1) to read judicial opinions (written in what may seem like a foreign language at first), (2) to figure out what law is "made" by the case, and (3) to understand how "black letter" statements of the law (such as Restatement provisions or rules derived from cases) would be applied to other fact situations. It also includes the ability (4) to think critically about the law as you learn it, (5) to understand the connections between law and public policy, and (6) to be creative in problem-solving by using legal concepts and doctrines. In effect, you need to learn how to learn the law using traditional legal material, and how to use the law you learn, because you will spend much of your professional life learning and applying law on your own, based on the foundation begun in law school.

To facilitate this kind of learning, this book includes both verbatim court opinions and summarized cases set out as "Examples and Analysis." In addition, it offers guidance on how to approach and analyze the material as you read to help you get the most out of your reading. This guidance appears in several kinds of text boxes associated with the reading:

Reading Critically

Offers questions to help frame your thinking as you read the material that follows the box so that you can be better prepared to discuss the specifics, as well as to think and talk about the policy implications.

Food for Thought

Stretches your analysis after you have read associated material, often by raising additional questions or suggesting a broader context to consider.

Think About It!

Presents questions urging you to think about particular important issues raised, directly or indirectly, by the text, often providing additional information or commentary.

Take Note!

Calls your attention to a particular aspect of a case or other material.

These are not "crutches" that tell you what to take away from the reading; rather, they are attempts to make the pedagogy more transparent by asking directed questions that will help you structure your thinking as you read and prepare for class. By considering the questions and comments in the text boxes, you will be better prepared to discuss the material in class, no matter what paths of analysis your teacher follows. And by paying attention to the questions themselves, you will learn something about how to structure your reading and analysis in all of your classes. Class discussion will, of course, push your understanding even further than your reading could, so the "reading the law critically" questions and other text-box guidance are a starting point, not an end-point.

This textbook also provides helpful supplemental information in text boxes appearing at the point in the text where you will need that information. They are of the following types:

What's That?

Explains the meaning of terms that appear in the main text.

Who's That?

Provides biographical information about a person mentioned in the text.

It's Latin to Me!

The law is fond of Latin terms and phrases; when you encounter these in the text for the first time, this box will explain their meaning.

Behind the Scenes

Provides further background about material in the text, often by adding additional facts not included in the associated judicial opinion or by describing the aftermath of the case.

Make the Connection

Notes connections between concepts or discussions in the main text and (1) earlier or later material in this textbook or (2) other courses or law school subject matter.

Business Lingo

Explains special business terms that arise in commercial transactions.

FYI

Supplies additional information to augment the text.

Practice Pointers

Offers advice relevant to legal practice inspired by the actions (or inactions) of legal counsel in the cases or prompted by a particular contract clause.

See It

Points you to or presents visual information that is relevant to the material in the text.

For More Information

Points you to additional resources to consult for more information on a subject.

Go Online

Directs you to relevant online resources that are worth consulting in relation to a matter being discussed.

Ethical Issues

Highlights relevant realworld situations that raise ethical concerns for attorneys.

Test Your Knowledge

These boxes, located at the end of each chapter, contain hyperlinks to online assessment questions that will help you test your understanding of the material in each chapter.

In electronic form, this textbook also provides live online links to cited sources. You need not follow every such link (indeed, you would be spending far too much time on this course if you did so!), but the links are there when you need or want additional information.

Some final notes on form: In the trial court opinions and appellate decisions appearing in the book, courts may refer to parties as appellant and appellee, plaintiff and defendant, petitioner and respondent, or some combination of such terms. To help you make sense of the facts of each case, this book identifies in the captions the role that each party played in the trial court (plaintiff or defendant) and in the appeal (petitioner or appellant, respondent or appellee, depending on the terminology in that jurisdiction), even though the published case may not do so.

Most cases have been edited to omit less relevant material. Text omissions are noted with ellipses (. . .) but citations are usually omitted without such notation. Typographical errors have in some instances been corrected without specifying the original text. Some cases (especially older ones) have been "styled" (e.g., by adding paragraph breaks and indentations) to make the opinions more readable. Explanatory text added to cases appears within square brackets. The courts' footnotes retain their original numbers. Authors' footnotes are marked with asterisks.

Finally, one of the goals of this textbook is to cultivate your critical reading of documents that create, or purport to create, contracts. This textbook introduces you to common kinds of contract clauses and their customary variations. This orientation toward "transactional skills" helps to counter-balance the emphasis on litigation that flows from the use of litigated cases as the basic source material for this and other courses. In law practice, the volume of transactional practice equals—if not exceeds—the volume of litigation practice on contract-related issues, so it is important for the first-year contracts course to emphasize both.

Chapter 2

Promise and Assent

How do parties demonstrate assent to a contract?

What kinds of promises will the law enforce?

What defenses to enforcement exist?

Is a writing required for enforcement? If so, what kind?

How is the content and meaning of a contract determined?

What are parties' rights and duties after breach?

What situations lead to excusing contract performance?

What remedies are available for breach of contract?

What contractual rights and duties do non-parties to a contract have?

Table of Contents

§ 1. Introduction 15

§ 2. Is Meaning Judged Objectively or Subjectively? 17

    Embry v. Hargadine, McKittrick Dry Goods Co. 18

    Lucy v. Zehmer 22

§ 3. Promise as Expression of Commitment 31

    PROBLEMS: WAS A PROMISE MADE? (2-1 TO 2-8) 32

§ 4. Lack of Commitment: Illusory Promises 33

    PROBLEMS: ILLUSORY PROMISES (2-9, 2-10) 36

§ 5. Promises with Indefinite or Incomplete Terms 38

    Quake Construction v. American Airlines 39

    Sun Printing & Publishing Ass'n v. Remington Paper & Power Co. 50

    Academy Chicago Publishers v. Cheever 57

§ 1. Introduction

Contracts are grounded in promises. Indeed, the Restatement (Second) of Contracts § 1 defines a contract as "a promise or a set of promises for which the law gives a remedy." But just what constitutes a promise? It is more than just a statement of present intention to do something in the future or a mere opinion about what may or may not happen. As we will see, in the materials that follow:

- A promise is a statement of *commitment* to the person on the receiving end of the promise—the promisee—that the promisor will do (or, sometimes, refrain from doing) some specified act.

- The statement must have sufficient *content and certainty* to justify the promisee in understanding that a commitment has been made and may be relied upon.

- The promise must be *communicated* to the promisee.

The Restatement (Second) of Contracts § 2(1) defines a promise as a "manifestation of intention to act or refrain from acting in a specified way, so made as to justify a promisee in understanding that a commitment has been made." That definition encompasses those same requirements—that there be a communication of commitment with sufficient certainty to justify reliance. The manifestation of commitment is at the core of contract, because it means the parties themselves create obligations to each other.

The promisor may communicate ("manifest") commitment by words (spoken or written), by conduct (e.g., the nod of a head, or a handshake, or other act that shows commitment is intended), or by a combination of words and conduct. Even if it appears at first that only words are involved, we will see that spoken or written words can be understood fully only in a context that includes conduct, as well as tone of voice and other surrounding circumstances.

Before we can determine whether a statement constitutes a promise—especially whether it communicates intent to commit—we must first consider a preliminary question: by what standard should the meaning of the communication be evaluated? In particular, should a party's communications be judged by a subjective standard (what the person was thinking at the time) or an objective standard (what a reasonable person would think that the communication meant)? This same choice between objective and subjective standards arises whenever the meaning of communications between contracting parties is at issue, so we will encounter the question repeatedly in our consideration of contract transactions.

§ 2. Is Meaning Judged Objectively or Subjectively?

Because contract law is grounded in the notion of enforcing parties' voluntarily created rights and obligations, it involves a search for the intent of the parties. That intent must be found in the communications between the parties to an alleged contract, including the words used in the agreement. But sometimes there are multiple meanings—what a party was thinking at the time of the communication (her subjective meaning), what the other party understood (his subjective meaning), and what a reasonable person would have understood (an objective meaning). As you will see in the two cases that follow, the objective meaning is most important in analyzing whether a contractual promise exists, with subjective meaning playing a subsidiary role. The cases and the "Reading Critically" questions preceding them will help you understand why that is the chosen standard and how the standard operates.

Reading Critically: *Embry* and *Lucy*

In both *Embry* and *Lucy*, one party claims a contractual commitment—a promise—was made; the other party says that did not happen. Some of the argument is about what was, in fact, said. But most of the dispute is about the meaning of the words that were admittedly spoken.

1. How does each court state the rule used to determine the meaning of the parties' communications? Why is that the standard chosen?

2. What meaning does the court attribute to the communications? Do you agree with the court's conclusion? Why or why not?

3. Who is the "reasonable person" whose objective view determines the outcome? Is it an objective observer apart from the parties without any knowledge of the particular circumstances (the proverbial "fly on the wall")? Or is it an objective person placed in the shoes of the sender or the recipient of a communication, with the knowledge that person had at the time of the communication?

4. Each party tries to prove a meaning favorable to his own claim. Did each party subjectively understand the meaning that same way at the time of the transaction? Would it matter if he did not?

5. The court in each case decides which party's stated understanding of the communications is the objectively reasonable meaning. What do you think would happen if the court thought that the two understandings were equally plausible?

6. What evidence is relevant to show the objective meaning of a communication? The subjective meaning? Is the subjective test harder or easier to satisfy? What are the advantages and disadvantages of the subjective and objective tests?

Embry v. Hargadine, McKittrick Dry Goods Co.

CHARLES R. EMBRY, Plaintiff-Appellant

v.

HARGARDINE, McKITTRICK DRY GOODS CO., Defendant-Appellee

Missouri Court of Appeals
105 S.W. 777 (Mo. Ct. App. 1907)

GOODE, J.

. . . . The appellant was an employee of the respondent company under a written contract to expire December 15, 1903, at a salary of $2,000 per annum. His duties were to attend to the sample department of respondent, of which he was given complete charge. It was his business to select samples for the traveling salesmen of the company, which is a wholesale dry goods concern, to use in selling goods to retail merchants. Appellant contends that on December 23, 1903, he was re-engaged by respondent, through its president, Thos. H. McKittrick, for another year at the same compensation and for the same duties stipulated in his previous written contract. On March 1, 1904, he was discharged, having been notified in February that, on account of the necessity of retrenching expenses, his services and that of some other employees would no longer be required. The respondent company contends that its president never re-employed appellant after the termination of his written contract, and hence that it had a right to discharge him when it chose.

The point with which we are concerned requires an epitome of the testimony of appellant and the counter testimony of McKittrick, the president of the company, in reference to the alleged re-employment. Appellant testified: That several times prior to the termination of his written contract on December 15, 1903, he had endeavored to get an understanding with McKittrick for another year, but had been put off from time to time. That on December 23d, eight days after the expiration of said contract, he called on McKittrick, in the latter's office, and said to him that as appellant's written employment had lapsed eight days before, and as there were only a few days between then and the 1st of January in which to seek employment with other firms, if respondent wished to retain his services longer he must have a contract for another year, or he would quit respondent's service then and there. That he had been put off twice before and wanted an understanding or contract at once so that he could go ahead without worry. That McKittrick asked him how he was getting along in his department, and appellant said he was very busy, as they were in the height of the season getting men out—had about 110 salesmen on the line and others in preparation. That McKittrick then said: "Go ahead, you're all right. Get your men out, and don't let that worry you." That appellant took McKittrick at his word and worked until February 15th without any question in his mind. It was on February 15th that he was notified his services would be discontinued on March 1st.

McKittrick denied this conversation as related by appellant, and said that, when accosted by the latter on December 23d, he (McKittrick) was working on his books in order to get out a report for a stockholders' meeting, and, when appellant said if he did not get a contract he would leave, that he (McKittrick) said: "Mr. Embry, I am just getting ready for the stockholders' meeting to-morrow. I have no time to take it up now. I have told you before I would not take it up until I had these matters out of the way. You will have to see me at a later time. I said: 'Go back upstairs and get your men out on the road.' I may have asked him one or two other questions relative to the department, I don't remember. The whole conversation did not take more than a minute."

Embry also swore that, when he was notified he would be discharged, he complained to McKittrick about it, as being a violation of their contract, and McKittrick said it was due to the action of the board of directors, and not to any personal action of his, and that others would suffer by what the board had done as well as Embry.

Appellant requested an instruction to the jury setting out, in substance, the conversation between him and McKittrick according to his version, and declaring that those facts, if found to be true, constituted a contract between the parties that defendant would pay plaintiff the sum of $2,000 for another year, provided the jury believed from the evidence that plaintiff commenced said work believing he was to have $2,000 for the year's work. This instruction was refused, but the court gave another embodying in substance appellant's version of the conversation, and declaring it made a contract "if you (the jury) find both parties thereby intended and did contract with each other for plaintiff's employment for one year from and including December 23, 1903, at a salary of $2,000 per annum." . . . .

. . . [I]t remains to determine whether or not this part of the instruction was a correct statement of the law in regard to what was necessary to constitute a contract between the parties; that is to say, whether the formation of a contract by what, according to Embry, was said, depended on the intention of both Embry and McKittrick. Or, to put the question more precisely: Did what was said constitute a contract of re-employment on the previous terms irrespective of the intention or purpose of McKittrick?

Judicial opinion and elementary treatises abound in statements of the rule that to constitute a contract there must be a meeting of the minds of the parties, and both must agree to the same thing in the same sense. Generally speaking, this may be true; but it is not literally or universally true. That is to say, the inner intention of parties to a conversation subsequently alleged to create a contract cannot either make a contract of what transpired, or prevent one from arising, if the words used were sufficient to constitute a contract. In so far as their intention is an influential element, it is only such intention as the words or acts of the parties indicate; not one secretly cherished which is inconsistent with those words or acts.

The rule is thus stated by a text-writer, and many decisions are cited in support of his text: "The primary object of construction in contract law is to discover the intention of the parties. This intention in express contracts is, in the first instance, embodied in the words which the parties have used and is to be deduced therefrom. This rule applies to oral contracts, as well as to contracts in writing, and is the rule recognized by courts of equity." 2 Paige, Contracts, § 1104. So it is said in another work: "Now this measure of the contents of the promise will be found to coincide in the usual dealings of men of good faith and ordinary competence, both with the actual intention of the promisor and with the actual expectation of the promisee. But this is not a constant or a necessary coincidence. In exceptional cases a promisor may be bound to perform something which he did not intend to promise, or a promisee may not be entitled to require that performance which he understood to be promised to him." Walds-Pollock, Contracts (3d Ed.) 309.

In Brewington v. Mesker, 51 Mo. App. 348, 356, it is said that the meeting of minds, which is essential to the formation of a contract, is not determined by the secret intention of the parties, but by their expressed intention, which may be wholly at variance with the former. In Machine Co. v. Criswell, 58 Mo. App. 471, . . . [the court noted that the intention of the parties] "must always be determined by the conduct, acts, and express declarations of the parties, and not by the secret intention existing in the mind or minds of the contracting parties. If the validity of such a contract depended upon secret intentions of the parties, then no oral contract of sale could be relied on with safety." Machine Co. v. Criswell, 58 Mo., loc. cit. 473. In Smith v. Hughes, L. R. 6 Q. B. 597, 607, it was said: "If, whatever a man's real intention may be, he so conducts himself that a reasonable man would believe that he was assenting to the terms proposed by the other party, and that other party upon that belief enters into the contract with him, the man thus conducting himself would be equally bound as if he had intended to agree to the other party's terms." . . . . In view of those authorities, we hold that, though McKittrick may not have intended to employ Embry by what transpired between them according to the latter's testimony, yet if what McKittrick said would have been taken by a reasonable man to be an employment, and Embry so understood it, it constituted a valid contract of employment for the ensuing year.

The next question is whether or not the language used was of that character, namely, was such that Embry, as a reasonable man, might consider he was re-employed for the ensuing year on the previous terms, and act accordingly. We do not say that in every instance it would be for the court to pronounce on this question, because, peradventure, instances might arise in which there would be such an ambiguity in the language relied on to show an assent by the obligor to the proposal of the obligee that it would be for the jury to say whether a reasonable mind would take it to signify acceptance of the proposal. Belt v. Goode, 31 Mo. 128; . . . .

With these rules of law in mind, let us recur to the conversation of December 23d between Embry and McKittrick as related by the former. Embry was demanding a renewal of his contract, saying he had been put off from time to time, and that he had only a few days before the end of the year in which to seek employment from other houses, and that he would quit then and there unless he was reemployed. McKittrick inquired how he was getting along with the department, and Embry said they, i.e., the employees of the department, were very busy getting out salesmen. Whereupon McKittrick said: "Go ahead, you are all right. Get your men out, and do not let that worry you." We think no reasonable man would construe that answer to Embry's demand that he be employed for another year, otherwise than as an assent to the demand, and that Embry had the right to rely on it as an assent. The natural inference is, though we do not find it testified to, that Embry was at work getting samples ready for the salesmen to use during the ensuing season. Now, when he was complaining of the worry and mental distress he was under because of his uncertainty about the future, and his urgent need, either of an immediate contract with respondent, or a refusal by it to make one, leaving him free to seek employment elsewhere, McKittrick must have answered as he did for the purpose of assuring appellant that any apprehension was needless, as appellant's services would be retained by the respondent. The answer was unambiguous, and we rule that if the conversation was according to appellant's version, and he understood he was employed, it constituted in law a valid contract of re-employment, and the court erred in making the formation of a contract depend on a finding that both parties intended to make one. It was only necessary that Embry, as a reasonable man, had a right to and did so understand.

. . . .

The judgment is reversed, and the cause remanded. All concur.

Lucy v. Zehmer

W. O. LUCY and J. C. LUCY, Complainants-Appellants

v.

A. H. ZEHMER and IDA S. ZEHMER, Defendants-Appellees

Supreme Court of Appeals of Virginia
84 S.E.2d 516 (Va. Ct. App. 1954)

BUCHANAN, J., delivered the opinion of the court.

This suit was instituted by W. O. Lucy and J. C. Lucy, complainants, against A. H. Zehmer and Ida S. Zehmer, his wife, defendants, to have specific performance of a contract by which it was alleged the Zehmers had sold to W. O. Lucy a tract of land owned by A. H. Zehmer in Dinwiddie county containing 471.6 acres, more or less, known as the Ferguson farm, for $50,000. J. C. Lucy, the other complainant, is a brother of W. O. Lucy, to whom W. O. Lucy transferred a half interest in his alleged purchase.

What's That?

The plaintiffs in this suit asked for "specific performance" of the purchase contract, seeking an order compelling the defendants to do what was promised—deliver a deed for the property. For a variety of reasons (see the note on the history of equity in Chapter 5, page 285), money damages are the preferred remedy for a breach of contract. Sometimes, though, damages are inadequate to remedy a breach, especially where a piece of real estate or some other unique item is the subject of the dispute. In those instances, a court will consider whether to award the disputed item itself ("specific performance") rather than damages for the value of that item. Chapter 10, page 882, covers the policies supporting and limiting the remedy of specific performance.

The instrument sought to be enforced was written by A. H. Zehmer on December 20, 1952, in these words: "We hereby agree to sell to W. O. Lucy the Ferguson Farm complete for $50,000.00, title satisfactory to buyer," and signed by the defendants, A. H. Zehmer and Ida S. Zehmer.

The answer of A. H. Zehmer admitted that at the time mentioned W. O. Lucy offered him $50,000 cash for the farm, but that he, Zehmer, considered that the offer was made in jest; that so thinking, and both he and Lucy having had several drinks, he wrote out "the memorandum" quoted above and induced his wife to sign it; that he did not deliver the memorandum to Lucy, but that Lucy picked it up, read it, put it in his pocket, attempted to offer Zehmer $5 to bind the bargain, which Zehmer refused to accept, and realizing for the first time that Lucy was serious, Zehmer assured him that he had no intention of selling the farm and that the whole matter was a joke. Lucy left the premises insisting that he had purchased the farm.

Depositions were taken and the decree appealed from was entered holding that the complainants had failed to establish their right to specific performance, and dismissing their bill. The assignment of error is to this action of the court.

W. O. Lucy, a lumberman and farmer, thus testified in substance: He had known Zehmer for fifteen or twenty years and had been familiar with the Ferguson farm for ten years. Seven or eight years ago he had offered Zehmer $20,000 for the farm which Zehmer had accepted, but the agreement was verbal and Zehmer backed out. On the night of December 20, 1952, around eight o'clock, he took an employee to McKenney, where Zehmer lived and operated a restaurant, filling station and motor court. While there he decided to see Zehmer and again try to buy the Ferguson farm. He entered the restaurant and talked to Mrs. Zehmer until Zehmer came in. He asked Zehmer if he had sold the Ferguson farm. Zehmer replied that he had not. Lucy said, "I bet you wouldn't take $50,000.00 for that place." Zehmer replied, "Yes, I would too; you wouldn't give fifty." Lucy said he would and told Zehmer to write up an agreement to that effect. Zehmer took a restaurant check and wrote on the back of it, "I do hereby agree to sell to W. O. Lucy the Ferguson Farm for $50,000 complete." Lucy told him he had better change it to "We" because

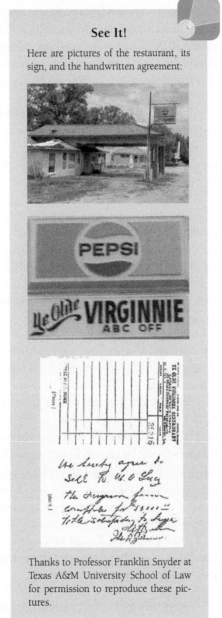

See It!

Here are pictures of the restaurant, its sign, and the handwritten agreement:

Thanks to Professor Franklin Snyder at Texas A&M University School of Law for permission to reproduce these pictures.

Mrs. Zehmer would have to sign it too. Zehmer then tore up what he had written, wrote the agreement quoted above and asked Mrs. Zehmer, who was at the other end of the counter ten or twelve feet away, to sign it. Mrs. Zehmer said she would for $50,000 and signed it. Zehmer brought it back and gave it to Lucy, who offered him $5 which Zehmer refused, saying, "You don't need to give me any money, you got the agreement there signed by both of us."

The discussion leading to the signing of the agreement, said Lucy, lasted thirty or forty minutes, during which Zehmer seemed to doubt that Lucy could raise $50,000. Lucy suggested the provision for having the title examined and Zehmer made the suggestion that he would sell it "complete, everything there," and stated that all he had on the farm was three heifers.

Lucy took a partly filled bottle of whiskey into the restaurant with him for the purpose of giving Zehmer a drink if he wanted it. Zehmer did, and he and Lucy had one or two drinks together. Lucy said that while he felt the drinks he took he was not intoxicated, and from the way Zehmer handled the transaction he did not think he was either.

December 20 was on Saturday. Next day Lucy telephoned to J. C. Lucy and arranged with the latter to take a half interest in the purchase and pay half of the consideration. On Monday he engaged an attorney to examine the title. The attorney reported favorably on December 31 and on January 2 Lucy wrote Zehmer stating that the title was satisfactory, that he was ready to pay the purchase price in cash and asking when Zehmer would be ready to close the deal. Zehmer replied by letter, mailed on January 13, asserting that he had never agreed or intended to sell.

Mr. and Mrs. Zehmer were called by the complainants as adverse witnesses. Zehmer testified in substance as follows:

He bought this farm more than ten years ago for $11,000. He had had twenty-five offers, more or less, to buy it, including several from Lucy, who had never offered any specific sum of money. He had given them all the same answer, that he was not interested in selling it. On this Saturday night before Christmas it looked like everybody and his brother came by there to have a drink. He took a good many drinks during the afternoon and had a pint of his own. When he entered the restaurant around eight-thirty Lucy was there and he could see that he was "pretty high." He said to Lucy, "Boy, you got some good liquor, drinking, ain't you?" Lucy then offered him a drink. "I was already high as a Georgia pine, and didn't have any more better sense than to pour another great big slug out and gulp it down, and he took one too."

After they had talked a while Lucy asked whether he still had the Ferguson farm. He replied that he had not sold it and Lucy said, "I bet you wouldn't take

$50,000.00 for it." Zehmer asked him if he would give $50,000 and Lucy said yes. Zehmer replied, "You haven't got $50,000 in cash." Lucy said he did and Zehmer replied that he did not believe it. They argued "pro and con for a long time," mainly about "whether he had $50,000 in cash that he could put up right then and buy that farm."

Finally, said Zehmer, Lucy told him if he didn't believe he had $50,000, "you sign that piece of paper here and say you will take $50,000.00 for the farm. " He, Zehmer, "just grabbed the back off of a guest check there" and wrote on the back of it. At that point in his testimony Zehmer asked to see what he had written to "see if I recognize my own handwriting." He examined the paper and exclaimed, "Great balls of fire, I got 'Firgerson' for Ferguson. I have got satisfactory spelled wrong. I don't recognize that writing if I would see it, wouldn't know it was mine."

After Zehmer had, as he described it, "scribbled this thing off," Lucy said, "Get your wife to sign it." Zehmer walked over to where she was and she at first refused to sign but did so after he told her that he "was just needling him [Lucy], and didn't mean a thing in the world, that I was not selling the farm." Zehmer then "took it back over there . . . and I was still looking at the dern thing. I had the drink right there by my hand, and I reached over to get a drink, and he said, 'Let me see it.' He reached and picked it up, and when I looked back again he had it in his pocket and he dropped a five dollar bill over there, and he said, 'Here is five dollars payment on it.' . . . I said, 'Hell no, that is beer and liquor talking. I am not going to sell you the farm. I have told you that too many times before.' "

Mrs. Zehmer testified that when Lucy came into the restaurant he looked as if he had had a drink. When Zehmer came in he took a drink out of a bottle that Lucy handed him. She went back to help the waitress who was getting things ready for next day. Lucy and Zehmer were talking but she did not pay too much attention to what they were saying. She heard Lucy ask Zehmer if he had sold the Ferguson farm, and Zehmer replied that he had not and did not want to sell it. Lucy said, "I bet you wouldn't take $50,000 cash for that farm," and Zehmer replied, "You haven't got $50,000 cash." Lucy said, "I can get it." Zehmer said he might form a company and get it, "but you haven't got $50,000.00 cash to pay me tonight." Lucy asked him if he would put it in writing that he would sell him this farm. Zehmer then wrote on the back of a pad, "I agree to sell the Ferguson Place to W. O. Lucy for $50,000.00 cash." Lucy said, "All right, get your wife to sign it." Zehmer came back to where she was standing and said, "You want to put your name to this?" She said "No," but he said in an undertone, "It is nothing but a joke," and she signed it.

She said that only one paper was written and it said: "I hereby agree to sell," but the "I" had been changed to "We". However, she said she read what she signed and was then asked, "When you read 'We hereby agree to sell to W. O. Lucy,' what did you interpret that to mean, that particular phrase?" She said she thought that was a cash sale that night; but she also said that when she read that part about "title satisfactory to buyer" she understood that if the title was good Lucy would pay $50,000 but if the title was bad he would have a right to reject it, and that that was her understanding at the time she signed her name.

On examination by her own counsel she said that her husband laid this piece of paper down after it was signed; that Lucy said to let him see it, took it, folded it and put it in his wallet, then said to Zehmer, "Let me give you $5.00," but Zehmer said, "No, this is liquor talking. I don't want to sell the farm, I have told you that I want my son to have it. This is all a joke." Lucy then said at least twice, "Zehmer, you have sold your farm," wheeled around and started for the door. He paused at the door and said, "I will bring you $50,000.00 tomorrow. . . . No, tomorrow is Sunday. I will bring it to you Monday." She said you could tell definitely that he was drinking and she said to her husband, "You should have taken him home," but he said, "Well, I am just about as bad off as he is."

The waitress referred to by Mrs. Zehmer testified that when Lucy first came in "he was mouthy." When Zehmer came in they were laughing and joking and she thought they took a drink or two. She was sweeping and cleaning up for next day. She said she heard Lucy tell Zehmer, "I will give you so much for the farm," and Zehmer said, "You haven't got that much." Lucy answered, "Oh, yes, I will give you that much." Then "they jotted down something on paper . . . and Mr. Lucy reached over and took it, said let me see it." He looked at it, put it in his pocket and in about a minute he left. She was asked whether she saw Lucy offer Zehmer any money and replied, "He had five dollars laying up there, they didn't take it." She said Zehmer told Lucy he didn't want his money "because he didn't have enough money to pay for his property, and wasn't going to sell his farm." Both of them appeared to be drinking right much, she said.

She repeated on cross-examination that she was busy and paying no attention to what was going on. She was some distance away and did not see either of them sign the paper. She was asked whether she saw Zehmer put the agreement down on the table in front of Lucy, and her answer was this: "Time he got through writing whatever it was on the paper, Mr. Lucy reached over and said, 'Let's see it.' He took it and put it in his pocket," before showing it to Mrs. Zehmer. Her version was that Lucy kept raising his offer until it got to $50,000.

The defendants insist that the evidence was ample to support their contention that the writing sought to be enforced was prepared as a bluff or dare to force Lucy to admit that he did not have $50,000; that the whole matter was a joke;

that the writing was not delivered to Lucy and no binding contract was ever made between the parties.

It is an unusual, if not bizarre, defense. When made to the writing admittedly prepared by one of the defendants and signed by both, clear evidence is required to sustain it.

In his testimony Zehmer claimed that he "was high as a Georgia pine," and that the transaction "was just a bunch of two doggoned drunks bluffing to see who could talk the biggest and say the most." That claim is inconsistent with his attempt to testify in great detail as to what was said and what was done. It is contradicted by other evidence as to the condition of both parties, and rendered of no weight by the testimony of his wife that when Lucy left the restaurant she suggested that Zehmer drive him home. The record is convincing that Zehmer was not intoxicated to the extent of being unable to comprehend the nature and consequences of the instrument he executed,

Make the Connection

Note the standard the court uses in ruling that Zehmer was not too intoxicated to assent to the contract. You will see this standard reappear in the material on mental incapacity to enter contracts in Chapter 6, page 368.

and hence that instrument is not to be invalidated on that ground. 17 C.J.S., Contracts, § 133 b., p. 483; *Taliaferro v. Emery,* 124 Va. 674, 98 S.E. 627. It was in fact conceded by defendants' counsel in oral argument that under the evidence Zehmer was not too drunk to make a valid contract.

The evidence is convincing also that Zehmer wrote two agreements, the first one beginning "I hereby agree to sell." Zehmer first said he could not remember about that, then that "I don't think I wrote but one out. " Mrs. Zehmer said that what he wrote was "I hereby agree," but that the "I" was changed to "We" after that night. The agreement that was written and signed is in the record and indicates no such change. Neither are the mistakes in spelling that Zehmer sought to point out readily apparent.

The appearance of the contract, the fact that it was under discussion for forty minutes or more before it was signed; Lucy's objection to the first draft because it was written in the singular, and he wanted Mrs. Zehmer to sign it also; the rewriting to meet that objection and the signing by Mrs. Zehmer; the discussion of what was to be included in the sale, the provision for the examination of the title, the completeness of the instrument that was executed, the taking possession of it by Lucy with no request or suggestion by either of the defendants that he give it back, are facts which furnish persuasive evidence that the execution of the contract was a serious business transaction rather than a casual, jesting matter as defendants now contend.

On Sunday, the day after the instrument was signed on Saturday night, there was a social gathering in a home in the town of McKenney at which there were general comments that the sale had been made. Mrs. Zehmer testified that on that occasion as she passed by a group of people, including Lucy, who were talking about the transaction, $50,000 was mentioned, whereupon she stepped up and said, "Well, with the high-price whiskey you were drinking last night you should have paid more. That was cheap." Lucy testified that at that time Zehmer told him that he did not want to "stick" him or hold him to the agreement because he, Lucy, was too tight and didn't know what he was doing, to which Lucy replied that he was not too tight; that he had been stuck before and was going through with it. Zehmer's version was that he said to Lucy: "I am not trying to claim it wasn't a deal on account of the fact the price was too low. If I had wanted to sell $50,000.00 would be a good price, in fact I think you would get stuck at $50,000.00." A disinterested witness testified that what Zehmer said to Lucy was that "he was going to let him up off the deal, because he thought he was too tight, didn't know what he was doing. Lucy said something to the effect that 'I have been stuck before and I will go through with it.'"

Think About It!

What matters for contract formation is the manifested intent of the parties when they reached agreement. Why would it be relevant to consider the testimony about what was said at Sunday's gathering, the day after the agreement was allegedly entered?

If it be assumed, contrary to what we think the evidence shows, that Zehmer was jesting about selling his farm to Lucy and that the transaction was intended by him to be a joke, nevertheless the evidence shows that Lucy did not so understand it but considered it to be a serious business transaction and the contract to be binding on the Zehmers as well as on himself. The very next day he arranged with his brother to put up half the money and take a half interest in the land. The day after that he employed an attorney to examine the title. The next night, Tuesday, he was back at Zehmer's place and there Zehmer told him for the first time, Lucy said, that he wasn't going to sell and he told Zehmer, "You know you sold that place fair and square." After receiving the report from his attorney that the title was good he wrote to Zehmer that he was ready to close the deal.

Not only did Lucy actually believe, but the evidence shows he was warranted in believing, that the contract represented a serious business transaction and a good faith sale and purchase of the farm.

In the field of contracts, as generally elsewhere, "We must look to the outward expression of a person as manifesting his intention rather than to his secret and unexpressed intention. 'The law imputes to a person an intention corresponding to the reasonable meaning of his words and acts.' " *First Nat. Bank v. Roanoke Oil Co.,* 169 Va. 99, 114, 192 S.E. 764, 770.

At no time prior to the execution of the contract had Zehmer indicated to Lucy by word or act that he was not in earnest about selling the farm. They had argued about it and discussed its terms, as Zehmer admitted, for a long time. Lucy testified that if there was any jesting it was about paying $50,000 that night. The contract and the evidence show that he was not expected to pay the money that night. Zehmer said that after the writing was signed he laid it down on the counter in front of Lucy. Lucy said Zehmer handed it to him. In any event there had been what appeared to be a good faith offer and a good faith acceptance, followed by the execution and apparent delivery of a written contract. Both said that Lucy put the writing in his pocket and then offered Zehmer $5 to seal the bargain. Not until then, even under the defendants' evidence, was anything said or done to indicate that the matter was a joke. Both of the Zehmers testified that when Zehmer asked his wife to sign he whispered that it was a joke so Lucy wouldn't hear and that it was not intended that he should hear.

The mental assent of the parties is not requisite for the formation of a contract. If the words or other acts of one of the parties have but one reasonable meaning, his undisclosed intention is immaterial except when an unreasonable meaning which he attaches to his manifestations is known to the other party. Restatement of the Law of Contracts, Vol. I, § 71, p. 74.

". . . The law, therefore, judges of an agreement between two persons exclusively from those expressions of their intentions which are communicated between them. . . ." Clark on Contracts, 4 ed., § 3, p. 4.

An agreement or mutual assent is of course essential to a valid contract but the law imputes to a person an intention corresponding to the reasonable meaning of his words and acts. If his words and acts, judged by a reasonable standard, manifest an intention to agree, it is immaterial what may be the real but unexpressed state of his mind. 17 C.J.S., Contracts, § 32, p. 361 . . . .

So a person cannot set up that he was merely jesting when his conduct and words would warrant a reasonable person in believing that he intended a real agreement, 17 C.J.S., Contracts, § 47, p. 390 . . . .

Whether the writing signed by the defendants and now sought to be enforced by the complainants was the result of a serious offer by Lucy and a serious acceptance by the defendants, or was a serious offer by Lucy and an acceptance in secret jest by the defendants, in either event it constituted a binding contract of sale between the parties.

. . . .

Reversed and remanded.

Food for Thought: Two Ships Named "Peerless" and the Absence of Objective Meaning

In both *Embry* and *Lucy,* the court was called upon to determine whether the plaintiff's understanding was objectively reasonable. Sometimes—especially when determining the meaning of a contract term—the court may be called upon to decide whether plaintiff's understanding or defendant's understanding (or some other meaning not proposed by either party) is the objectively reasonable one. But what happens if there is no clear objective meaning—if the court finds no basis for choosing one understanding over another? Sometimes a court can fill in an appropriate term, as it may do if the parties commit to a contract while omitting some terms (see § 5 below). But what happens if the disputed term is a crucial term, central to the claim that they have agreed at all? Is a contract formed?

Consider the old but well-known case of *Raffles v. Wichelhaus,* 159 Eng. Rep. 375 (Exch. 1864), in which the parties agreed in writing that the seller would send a load of cotton from Bombay to the buyers in Liverpool by way of a sailing ship, the Peerless—a "barque." (The photo shows the kind of barque that was the most common type of deep-water carrier in the mid-1800s. For more information, see http:// en.wikipedia.org/wiki/Barque.)

Because sailing speed and route depended on wind speed and direction, the parties did not specify a shipping date or an arrival date, in keeping with the usual practices of that era. There were, in fact, two ships named "Peerless" sailing from Bombay. The buyers said they had meant the ship that left Bombay in October; the sellers delivered cotton from the ship that left in December. Dif-

ferent arrival dates could affect the price the cotton would fetch upon resale in the English market; indeed, the cotton market was particularly volatile in the latter half of 1862 because of an imminent cotton famine. When the cotton arrived on the December "Peerless," the buyers refused to take delivery; the buyers would have suffered a loss in reselling the cotton (although it appears they would have lost more if the cotton had indeed arrived on the October ship, which they claim to have intended, so they may have been acting somewhat opportunistically). The seller sued for breach; the buyers defended by claiming that they meant (and therefore contracted for) the cotton on the October "Peerless." The seller demurred to this defense, essentially saying, "So what? My claim is good even if we each meant different ships. The contract was for cotton from a ship named Peerless, and that's what I delivered."

If the parties have differing subjective intent, even on a key term (such as the timing and therefore identity and value of the goods being purchased), that would not defeat contract formation as long as the subjective meaning of one of the parties was "the" reasonable (objective) meaning. However, if the court has no basis for choosing, as was possibly the case in *Raffles*, that could be seen as defeating contract formation, because neither party can show an "objective meeting of the minds."

In fact, the court made only a procedural ruling against the seller's demurrer, holding that the buyers' defense—that the cotton was delivered from a different ship, and therefore at a different time, than the buyer contracted for—*could* make a difference in whether the agreement was enforceable. The court never stated a substantive rule or hinted as to the likely outcome at trial. *See* A.W. Brian Simpson, *Contracts for Cotton to Arrive: The Case of the Two Ships Peerless*, 11 Cardozo L. Rev. 287 (1989). Some judges and commentators mistakenly state that the *Raffles* court held that no contract existed because there was no "meeting of the minds," based on the parties' actual (subjective) differing intent. That would have been a satisfying result, but *Raffles* itself cannot be used as precedent for that conclusion.

§ 3. Promise as Expression of Commitment

Both in popular and legal understanding, a promise is a speaker's expression of commitment to a course of action ("I promise I'll take you to dinner tonight"; "I promise that if you maintain a B-average GPA, I'll pay for a week-long trip to

Europe for you this summer"; "I promise that I'll buy your used car for $5000, if you will sell it to me"). A promisor need not use the word "promise." Indeed, no particular form of words is required to create a promise. What is required is a manifestation of commitment made by the speaker in a manner that justifies the recipient of the communication in concluding that a promise—a commitment—has been made.

As we know from studying *Embry* and *Lucy*, whether a communication expresses commitment will be judged by an objective standard, a factual inquiry taking into account the accompanying context and circumstances. We start with a series of problems, to highlight the kinds of factors involved in deciding whether a speaker has expressed commitment.

Problems: Was a Promise Made?

In each of the situations below, do you think a promise has been made? Why or why not? If you think no promise was made, what change in the language or circumstances would be enough to turn it into a promise?

2-1.   A wrote to B: "Dear Sir: We are authorized to sell Michigan fine salt, in full car-load lots of 80 to 95 barrels, delivered at your city, at $90 per barrel, to be shipped per your specified railroad company. Shall be pleased to receive your order."

2-2.   A wrote to B: "Will you sell me your [specified] property for $20,000?" B wrote back: "Because of improvements, it would not be possible for me to sell it unless I was to receive $30,000."

2-3.   A wrote to B, "I am writing several people, including yourself, who have previously expressed an interest in this property. Our price is $25,500. I will be interested in hearing from you further if you have any interest in this property."

2-4.   An advertisement placed in a weekly circular by Best Electronics:

    a.   "Sale on all tablets. Save up to $200!"

    b.   "20% off regular prices on all cameras. Sale ends Saturday!"

    c.   "Day after Thanksgiving sale! Door busters: first 10 customers get additional savings of 20%"

2-5. A wrote to B: "In response to your inquiry, we submit the attached quote for the repair work necessary on your car." The attachment described in detail the work to be performed and specified price for labor and materials.

2-6. Same as 2-5, except the price on the attachment was identified as "Cost Estimate."

2-7. Employer HealthCare, Inc. sends to Employee an Arbitration Policy that includes the following statement: "HealthCare, Inc. reserves the right to alter, amend, modify, or revoke this Arbitration Policy at its sole and absolute discretion at any time with or without notice."

2-8. Prospective purchaser of condominium sends to owner the following:

OFFER TO PURCHASE

I am pleased to submit the following terms and conditions under which I would like to enter into a purchase and sale agreement with the Seller for the above referenced property:

Purchase Price: $550,000

Inspection Period: Buyer shall have five (5) days to inspect and evaluate all aspects of the property ("Inspection Period") and inform Seller if the inspection results are unsatisfactory.

Closing: It is the intent of the parties to close no later than eight (8) days after the expiration of the Inspection Period.

Contingencies: Any obligation on the part of Buyer to purchase the Property would be contingent upon the Buyer acquiring a New First Mortgage acceptable to Buyer in its sole discretion.

Obligation: Either party to this agreement may (1) propose different terms from those summarized herein, (2) enter into negotiations with other parties and/or (3) unilaterally terminate all negotiations with the other party hereto.

---

§ 4. Lack of Commitment: Illusory Promises

As you saw in the Problems in the previous section, statements can sometimes appear to be expressing commitment ("I promise to do x") but at the same time contain words that deny a commitment is being made ("unless I later decide not to do x"). Such a statement is sometimes referred to as an "illusory promise":

something that appears to be a promise, but does not actually bind or obligate the promisor to anything. An illusory promise is composed of "words in a promissory form that promise nothing." Corbin on Contracts § 5.28 (2003). No promise exists if the promisor "retains an unlimited right to decide later the nature or extent of his performance. The unlimited choice in effect destroys the promise and makes it merely illusory." 1 Samuel Williston, Contracts, § 4:24 (4th Ed. 1990). The Restatement explains that "[w]ords of promise which by their terms make performance entirely optional with the 'promisor' whatever may happen, or whatever course of conduct in other respects he may pursue, do not constitute a promise." Restatement (Second) § 2 cmt. e.

As with all communications, a statement claimed to be illusory must be evaluated in context. Just as a statement of commitment may in fact be illusory, a statement that appears to be illusory may in context be a commitment, albeit to less than may first appear. A statement reserving the right to back out of a purchase agreement if an inspection shows the property to be "unsatisfactory" may be understood as making no commitment at all (because the inspection will always result in a list of at least minor deficiencies and the buyer can thus claim the property is no longer satisfactory) or as making a commitment (because the buyer is expressing commitment to the sale but wants to be protected from as-yet-unknown substantial problems with the property, and the parties would not go to the effort of signing a several-page document called a "Sales Agreement" if they considered the promises in it to be worthless). Determining whether a promise is illusory thus often requires considering the statement in the context in which the alleged promise was made in order to decide whether the reasonable recipient of the communication would understand it as promising something "real."

Take Note:
Termination vs. Cancellation

Because the right to terminate a contract is granted by a contract clause, it is not the same as the right to "cancel" a contract. The law grants an aggrieved party the right to cancel the contract after a total breach by the other party (see Chapter 9, page 706), and that right exists without any contract clause granting the right to cancel. The outcome after termination or cancellation is largely the same (that is, the contract's performance phase is ended, and one or both parties may have liability for past breaches and unpaid-for goods or services, continuing warranty obligations, etc.).

Although some courts and parties may use these terms (termination and cancellation) interchangeably, it is important to identify clearly which right is being invoked, whatever wording is used, in order to understand whether what is at issue is enforcement of a contract clause or breach of the contract.

The question whether an illusory promise has been made may arise when a contract-termination clause is included in an otherwise-valid agreement. A termination clause gives one or both parties the right to put an end to future performance obligations under the contract. Termination clauses come in two varieties:

- A termination-for-cause clause gives one or both parties the right to end performance obligations for any reason(s) specified in the clause. The specified reasons may or may not constitute breaches of the contract, just as they may or may not be events that lead the other party to be insecure about the likelihood of continued performance. For example, loan agreements may give the creditor the right to "call the loan" (accelerate payment and put an end to the extension of credit) upon events that make the creditor concerned that the debtor is becoming less credit-worthy, even though none of those events are a breach of the agreement.

- A termination-at-will or termination-for-convenience clause gives one or both parties the right to end the performance obligations for any reason (or for no reason). These clauses may be contained in contracts of indefinite or long duration, such as long-term service or employment contracts, or in distributorship arrangements between a manufacturer and distributor of goods. Such clauses also appear in contracts of set duration when one or both parties want the discretionary right to end the contract early without having to specify a reason.

Termination-at-will clauses are risky because they might lead a court to conclude that either or both of the parties' contract promises are illusory. If a party makes a promise to perform, but has the right to terminate the contract for any reason at any time, including the moment just after contract formation, then the so-called promise is not really a promise because that party has not really made a commitment to do something or refrain from doing something in the future. However, if the agreement otherwise illustrates an intent to enter a contractual relationship, courts will sometimes look for any limitation on the "at-will" aspect of the agreement, no matter how slim, to find that the promise is not illusory. As a result, termination-at-will clauses are sometimes drafted so that, e.g.,

- they cannot be exercised until a brief period of time has passed,

- the terminating party must give some advance notice before termination is effective, or

- the right to terminate exists only on the monthly or yearly anniversary of the agreement.

Each of these drafting practices ensures that the terminating party is bound to its promises for at least a short period of time, so the promises are not illusory.

Even if the termination clause has none of these limitations, a court may determine that the promises have sufficient substance to prevent them from being illusory, perhaps by finding an implied obligation to exercise the termination clause

Make the Connection

We will consider how courts may find an implied contract term and the meaning of an obligation to perform in good faith in Chapter 8.

in good faith. However, because of the risk that the promises will be found illusory, it is best to draft termination-at-will clauses using at least one of the above drafting practices.

Note that termination-for-cause clauses do not create a danger that a party's promise might be illusory, because the right to terminate arises only upon the event specified in the clause. The party with the right to terminate is bound to perform the contract unless and until the specified event occurs.

Problems: Illusory Promises

2-9. On March 10, Melissa Harvey was hired by National Golf Corporation (NGC) to work in the pro shop at the Bliss Hills Golf Course, a club managed by NGC, and was told she should report for work on March 22. On March 19, NGC gave Harvey a number of documents to review, including the NGC Worker Handbook. Page 20 of the handbook discussed arbitration and states:

> I agree that any claim of unlawful harassment or discrimination or claims of wrongful discharge, arising out of my employment with NGC, including public policy claims, contract claims and claims involving any applicable Federal, State, or Local statute, ordinance or regulation relating to the termination of my employment, employment discrimination, harassment or retaliation, will be resolved exclusively by final and binding arbitration and not by court action. I acknowledge that I am knowingly and voluntarily waiving my right to pursue such claims in court and instead will pursue them through arbitration. This arbitration shall be the exclusive means of resolving any dispute(s) listed in this agreement and no other action will be brought in any court or administrative forum.

Page 23 of the handbook included the following acknowledgment form, which Harvey signed:

> Acknowledgment

> My signature below indicates that I have read this NGC Worker Agreement and handbook and promise and agree to

abide by its terms and conditions. I further understand that the Company reserves the right to amend, supplement, rescind or revise any policy, practice, or benefit described in this handbook—other than employment at-will provisions—as it deems appropriate.

I acknowledge that my employment is at-will, which means that either the Company or I have the absolute right to end the employment relationship at any time with or without notice or reason. I further acknowledge that I have read and agree to be bound by the arbitration policy set forth on page 20 of this handbook.

Harvey gave the signed acknowledgment form to NGC when she started work. Are the promises of either Harvey or NGC illusory? If so, what changes would you suggest in the documents to make them not illusory?

2-10. FireFighting Company and the U.S. Forest Service signed a document entitled "Pacific Northwest Engine Tender Agreement" that listed fire equipment the Company would make available if called upon by the Forestry Service during the two years during which the Agreement would be in effect. The Agreement contained the following clauses:

(a) This Agreement does not preclude the Government from using an agency or other resources;

(b) This Agreement does not guarantee there will be a need for equipment offered nor does it guarantee orders will be placed against the awarded agreements;

(c) Because the equipment needs of the government and availability of contractor's equipment during an emergency cannot be determined in advance, it is mutually agreed that, upon request of the government, the contractor shall furnish the equipment offered herein to the extent the contractor is willing and able at the time of order.

Are the promises of either FireFighting Company or the U.S. Forest Service illusory? If so, what changes would you suggest in the documents to make them not illusory?

§ 5. Promises with Indefinite or Incomplete Terms

As we have seen, to be a promise, a statement must manifest commitment to a future course of action. What happens if the statement expresses commitment, but the details of that commitment are indefinite or incomplete? Commercial agreements often involve business constraints, time limitations, and incomplete knowledge, so even multi-page signed contract documents may be incomplete in one or more ways. The cases in this section explore the degree of uncertainty that the courts will tolerate. Courts are reluctant to enforce an indefinite or incomplete agreement because of concerns that the parties did not mean to make a "real" promise or that the parties' agreement is so incomplete or indefinite that the court will be unable to determine how to enforce it. Litigated cases in this area tend to focus on one or more of the following issues:

Make the Connection

If a contract is formed despite the existence of uncertainties, the contested or missing terms of the contract will need to be ascertained by the rules governing interpretation of the contract. See Chapter 8.

- *Uncertain commitment:* The parties' preliminary agreement, such as a "letter of intent" or a "memorandum of understanding," may reflect the parties' commitment to an agreement that they will further define later. But sometimes the preliminary agreement shows that one or both parties intend only to set up a pre-contractual framework for further negotiations, perhaps to enhance the chances of obtaining financing or to discourage competitors. How can a court distinguish between these two intents?

- *Vague terms:* The parties want to do business, but they have a difficult time bridging the gap between their views on one or more terms. Sometimes the parties try to solve that problem by drafting a clause that is intentionally vague. In other situations, the vagueness is unintentional, the result of inattention or sloppy drafting. How much vagueness will a court tolerate before it determines that the vagueness signals the parties have not truly reached agreement or concludes the court has no reliable way to resolve the vagueness and therefore cannot enforce the agreement?

- *Missing terms:* The parties might omit some terms because they could not come to agreement on them, or because the parties did not foresee an issue arising, or simply because of the parties' haste. Or the parties may specify that omitted terms can be supplied by one of the parties or may be filled in by later agreement of the parties. When is a contract not formed for lack of assent to the core of the transaction? How much can or should the court fill in? Which terms must the parties agree to for a court to find the promise(s) enforceable?

These issues illustrate the sometimes indistinct boundary between commitment and lack of commitment, and between enforceability and non-enforceability. As the cases demonstrate, the standard for making the required judgment is difficult to articulate with precision, and courts disagree on the standard and its application.

Reading Critically: *Quake Construction*, *Sun Printing*, & *Academy Chicago Publishers*

1. Which of the issues raised in the introductory note to this section (uncertain commitment, vague terms, and missing terms) does each case involve?

2. On what basis does each judge (speaking for the court, or in concurring or dissenting opinions, or in decisions appealed in the reported case) decide the parties did, or did not, enter into a binding agreement?

3. If the judge found, or would have found, no binding agreement existed, was it because the court thought the parties did not commit or because, despite the parties' commitment, the court could not (or would not) enforce the agreement? Do you agree with the outcome of the case? Why or why not?

4. Does the court lean toward or against enforcing incomplete agreements, as a matter of policy? What facts serve to persuade the court to enforce the agreement?

Quake Construction v. American Airlines

QUAKE CONSTRUCTION, INC., Plaintiff-Appellee

v.

AMERICAN AIRLINES, INC., and JONES BROS. CONSTRUCTION CORP., Defendants-Appellants

Supreme Court of Illinois
565 N.E.2d 990 (Ill. 1990)

Justice Calvo delivered the opinion of the court:

Plaintiff, Quake Construction, Inc. (Quake), filed a . . . complaint against defendants, American Airlines, Inc. (American), and Jones Brothers Construction

Corporation (Jones). In count I, plaintiff sought damages for breach of contract. . . . Upon defendants' motion, the circuit court of Cook County dismissed the complaint with prejudice . . . . On appeal, the Appellate Court reversed the dismissal . . . and remanded the cause to the circuit court. . . . We granted defendants' petition for leave to appeal . . . .

Quake alleged in its complaint the following facts. In February 1985, American hired Jones to prepare bid specifications, accept bids, and award contracts for construction of the expansion of American's facilities at O'Hare International Airport. Quake received an invitation to bid on the employee facilities and automotive maintenance shop project (hereinafter referred to as the project), and in April 1985 submitted its bid to Jones. Jones orally notified Quake that Quake had been awarded the contract for the project. Jones then asked Quake to provide the license numbers of the subcontractors Quake intended to use on the project. Quake notified Jones that the subcontractors would not allow Quake to use their license numbers until Quake submitted a signed subcontract agreement to them. Jones informed Quake that Quake would shortly receive a written contract for the project prepared by Jones. To induce Quake to enter into agreements with its subcontractors and to induce the subcontractors to provide Quake and Jones with their license numbers, Jones sent Quake the following letter of intent dated April 18, 1985:

> "We have elected to award the contract for the subject project to your firm as we discussed on April 15, 1985. A contract agreement outlining the detailed terms and conditions is being prepared and will be available for your signature shortly.
>
> Your scope of work as the general contractor includes the complete installation of expanded lunchroom, restroom and locker facilities for American Airlines employees as well as an expansion of American Airlines existing Automotive Maintenance Shop. The project is located on the lower level of 'K' Concourse. A sixty (60) calendar day period shall be allowed for the construction of the locker room, lunchroom and restroom area beginning the week of April 22, 1985. The entire project shall be complete by August 15, 1985.
>
> Subject to negotiated modifications for exterior hollow metal doors and interior ceramic floor tile material as discussed, this notice of award authorizes the work set forth in the following documents at a lump sum price of $1,060,568.00.

> **See It!**
>
> The "K" Concourse is in Terminal 3 at O'Hare. For a map, see www.ohare.com/PDF/PassengerInformation/D32011terminal3.pdf.

a)   Jones Brothers Invitation to Bid dated March 19, 1985.

b)   Specifications as listed in the Invitation to Bid.

c)   Drawings as listed in the Invitation to Bid.

d)   Bid Addendum # 1 dated March 29, 1985.

Quake Construction Inc. shall provide evidence of liability insurance in the amount of $5,000,000 umbrella coverage and 100% performance and payment bond to Jones Brothers Construction Corporation before commencement of the work. The contract shall include MBE, WBE and EEO goals as established by your bid proposal. Accomplishment of the City of Chicago's residency goals as cited in the Invitation to Bid is also required. As agreed, certificates of commitment from those MBE firms designated on your proposal modification submitted April 13, 1985, shall be provided to Jones Brothers Construction Corporation.

Jones Brothers Construction Corporation reserves the right to cancel this letter of intent if the parties cannot agree on a fully executed subcontract agreement."

Jones and Quake thereafter discussed and orally agreed to certain changes in the written form contract. Handwritten delineations were made to the form contract by Jones and Quake to reflect these changes. Jones advised Quake it would prepare and send the written contract to Quake for Quake's signature. No such formal written contract, however, was entered into by the parties.

At a preconstruction meeting on April 25, 1985, Jones told Quake, Quake's subcontractors, and governmental officials present that Quake was the general contractor for the project. On that same date, immediately after the meeting, American informed Quake that Quake's involvement with the project was terminated. Jones confirmed Quake's termination by a letter dated April 25, 1985. The damages Quake allegedly suffered included the money it spent in procuring the contract and preparing to perform under the contract, and its loss of anticipated profit from the contract.

Make the Connection

As noted in the preceding section of this chapter, "cancellation" is the word usually used to identify a party's legal right to stop performing a contract because of the other party's total breach (see p. 34 and the Chapter 9 discussion of cancellation and total breach). Even though the agreement here reserves to Jones Brothers the right to "cancel" the letter of intent, the effect of the clause is to create a right to "terminate" the agreement upon occurrence of an event (the failure to execute a written contract). You should use these words precisely in order to identify clearly which right is being invoked (ending performance because of breach or because the contract grants the right to end it), even (or especially) if a court uses the words more loosely.

The main issue is whether the letter of intent from Jones to Quake is an enforceable contract such that a cause of action may be brought by Quake. This court has previously set forth the principles of law concerning the enforceability of letters of intent:

Behind the Scenes

This is admittedly an odd termination, occurring so soon after Quake's bid was selected and immediately after Jones confirmed Quake as the contractor. Research turned up no explanation for this termination, but Chicago newspapers discussed the pressures to include minority and local contractors, bribery convictions of an alderman and a board member on the Chicago Transit Authority, and pressure to optimize the project budget and accompanying bonding.* How might such facts help explain the timing of the termination?

"The fact that parties contemplate that a formal agreement will eventually be executed does not necessarily render prior agreements mere negotiations, where it is clear that the ultimate contract will be substantially based upon the same terms as the previous document. . . . If the parties . . . intended that the . . . document be contractually binding, that intention would not be defeated by the mere recitation in the writing that a more formal agreement was yet to be drawn. However, parties may specifically provide that negotiations are not binding until a formal agreement is in fact executed. . . . If the parties construe the execution of a formal agreement as a condition precedent, then no contract arises unless and until that formal agreement is executed."

Chicago Investment Corp. v. Dolins (1985), 107 Ill.2d 120, 126–27, 89 Ill. Dec. 869, 481 N.E.2d 712. . . . Thus, although letters of intent may be enforceable, such letters are not necessarily enforceable unless the parties intend them to be contractually binding. . . .

. . . . If the language of an alleged contract is ambiguous regarding the parties' intent, the interpretation of the language is a question of fact which a circuit court cannot properly determine on a motion to dismiss. . . .

What's That?

A "condition precedent" is an event that must occur in order for a contract to be formed or in order for a performance duty to arise within a contract. Conditions precedent to contract formation are rarer than conditions precedent to contract performance, but the former nonetheless arise in situations such as the case quoted here. Chapters 8 and 9 cover express and implied conditions, respectively.

---

*   Dean Baquet & Douglas Frantz, *Politically Linked Georgia Firm Key to O'Hare Contracts,* Feb. 24, 1985, at 1; Editorial, *Getting It Right at O'Hare,* Chi. Trib., April 18, 1986, at 18; John Gorman, *Ex-Ald. Humes Admits Taking Series of Bribes,* Chi. Trib., May 2, 1989, at 3; Joel Kaplan & James Strong, *Medley's Conviction Casts Cloud over O'Hare Pact,* Chi. Trib., Aug. 31, 1989, at 22.

In determining whether the parties intended to reduce their agreement to writing, the following factors may be considered: whether the type of agreement involved is one usually put into writing, whether the agreement contains many or few details, whether the agreement involves a large or small amount of money, whether the agreement requires a formal writing for the full expression of the covenants, and whether the negotiations indicated that a formal written document was contemplated at the completion of the negotiations. (*Ceres,* 114 Ill.2d at 144, 102 Ill.Dec. 379, 500 N.E.2d 1 . . . .) Other factors which may be considered are: "where in the negotiating process that process is abandoned, the reasons it is abandoned, the extent of the assurances previously given by the party which now disclaims any contract, and the other party's reliance upon the anticipated completed transaction." *A/S Apothekernes Laboratorium for Specialpraeparater v. I.M.C. Chemical Group, Inc.* (N.D.Ill.1988), 678 F.Supp. 193, 196, aff'd (7th Cir.1989), 873 F.2d 155.

    . . . .

The circuit court in the case at bar dismissed Quake's complaint, relying principally on the following sentence in the letter: "Jones Brothers Construction Corporation reserves the right to cancel this letter of intent if the parties cannot agree on a fully executed subcontract agreement" (hereinafter referred to as the cancellation clause). The parties agreed during oral arguments that the subcontract agreement referred to in the cancellation clause concerned an agreement between Jones and Quake. Jones was the general contractor for the entire expansion project. Jones hired Quake as a subcontractor to handle only the work on the employee facilities and automotive shop. Quake, in turn, hired subcontractors to perform this work. The circuit court determined, based on the cancellation clause, that the parties agreed not to be bound until they entered into a formal written contract. Consequently, the circuit court held that the letter was not an enforceable contract and accordingly dismissed the complaint.

The appellate court, however, found the letter ambiguous. . . .

    . . . .

We agree with the appellate court majority's analysis and its conclusion that the letter was ambiguous. Consequently, we affirm the decision of the appellate court. The letter of intent included detailed terms of the parties' agreement. The letter stated that Jones awarded the contract for the project to Quake. The letter stated further "this notice of award authorizes the work." Moreover, the letter indicated the work was to commence approximately 4 to 11 days after the letter was written. This short period of time reveals the parties' intent to be bound by the letter so the work could begin on schedule. We also agree with the appellate court that the cancellation clause exhibited the parties' intent to be bound by the letter because no need would exist to provide for the cancellation of the letter unless the letter had some binding effect. The cancellation clause also implied the parties' intention to be bound by the letter at least until they entered into the formal contract. We agree with the appellate court that all of these factors evinced the parties' intent to be bound by the letter.

On the other hand, the letter referred several times to the execution of a formal contract by the parties, thus indicating the parties' intent not to be bound by the letter. The cancellation clause could be interpreted to mean that the parties did not intend to be bound until they entered into a formal agreement. Therefore, the appellate court correctly concluded that the letter was ambiguous regarding the parties' intent to be bound by it.

Defendants contend the letter of intent did not contain all of the terms necessary for the formation of a construction contract. Defendants assert construction contracts typically include terms regarding payment, damages and termination. Defendants argue the detail in the contract is usually extensive if the value and complexity of the construction project are great. Defendants also note the letter stated the contract would include the detailed terms and conditions of the parties' agreement. The letter indicated *the contract* would include the MBE, WBE and EEO (Minority Business Enterprise, Women's Business Enterprise, and Equal Employment Opportunity, respectively) goals established by Quake's bid proposal. Defendants point out the letter stated certain terms of the agreement still had to be negotiated. Without the formal contract, defendants assert, the parties could not have continued toward the completion of the project because the letter excluded many terms of the agreement which would have been included in the contract. Defendants thus argue the absence in the letter of all the terms of the agreement reveals the parties' intent not to be bound by the letter.

The appellate court stated the number and extent of the terms in the letter can indicate the parties' intent to be bound by the letter. The final contract only need be *substantially based* on the terms in the letter as long as the parties intended the letter to be binding. (*Chicago,* 107 Ill.2d at 126–27, 89 Ill.Dec. 869, 481 N.E.2d 712.) Many of the details regarding the project were included in the letter. The letter adopted by reference the contents of certain documents which included even further details concerning the project. We agree Jones accepted the MBE, WBE and EEO goals established by Quake. The letter merely indicated that those goals would be reiterated in the contract. We acknowledge that the absence of certain terms in the letter indicates the parties' intent not to be bound by the letter. This only confirms our holding that the letter is ambiguous as to the parties' intent.

. . . .

Defendants contend even if the letter contained all of the essential terms of a contract, the cancellation clause negated any inference that the parties intended to be bound by the letter. The clause, according to defendants, clearly established the parties' intent not to be so bound. Defendants argue the letter only sets forth the provisions which would be included in the contract if one is ever executed. Defendants point out both the circuit court and the appellate court dissent found the cancellation clause unambiguously declared the parties' intent not to be bound until the parties entered into a formal contract.

We do not find defendants' argument persuasive. The appellate court stated that, in addition to the detailed terms of the parties' agreement, the letter also contained a sentence in which Jones said it awarded the contract for the project to Quake. Moreover, the letter stated "this notice of award *authorizes* the work." (Emphasis added.) Furthermore, the appellate court pointed out, the letter was dated April 18, while at the same time the letter indicated that Quake was to begin work the week of April 22 and complete the work by August 15. We agree with the appellate court's conclusion that a "reasonable inference from these facts is that the parties intended that work on the Project would begin prior to execution of a formal contract and would be governed by the terms of the 'Letter of Intent.'" (181 Ill.App.3d at 914, 130 Ill.Dec. 534, 537 N.E.2d 863.) All of these factors indicate the negotiations were more than merely preliminary and the parties intended the letter to be binding. The factors muddle whatever otherwise "clear" intent may be derived from the cancellation clause.

Defendants acknowledge the letter was dated April 18 and it stated the work would commence the week of April 22. Defendants point out that the letter also indicated Jones would submit a formal contract to Quake "shortly." Defendants argue a contract could conceivably have been written and signed within that period of time. Defendants conclude the appellate court's assumption regarding the date of the letter and the commencement of the work was invalid. While defendants' interpretation of these facts is plausible, we believe it only lends credence to our conclusion the letter is ambiguous concerning the parties' intent. Thus, the trier of fact should decide which interpretation is valid.

. . . .

Defendants further contend that the cancellation clause is not ambiguous. Defendants assert parties may agree, in a letter of intent, to the course of, and discontinuance of, their negotiations. Defendants argue the letter of intent in the case at bar merely reflects the parties' agreement regarding the course of their negotiations.

We, like the appellate court, find the cancellation clause itself ambiguous as to the parties' intent. We do not agree with defendants' assertion that the cancellation clause so clearly indicates the parties' intent not to be bound by the letter that the clause negates other evidence in the letter of the parties' intent to be bound. The clause can be construed as a condition precedent to the formation of a contract. The clause, however, also states that Jones can "cancel" the letter. As the appellate court noted, if the parties did not intend to be bound by the letter, they had no need to provide for its cancellation. We also agree with the appellate court that the cancellation clause "implies that the parties could be bound by the 'Letter of Intent' in the absence of a fully executed subcontract agreement." (181 Ill.App.3d at 914, 130 Ill.Dec. 534, 537 N.E.2d 863.) Thus, the ambiguity within the cancellation clause itself enhances the other ambiguities in the letter.

. . . .

Defendants allege that the appellate court's decision puts the continued viability of letters of intent at risk. Defendants contend if we uphold the appellate court's decision finding the cancellation clause ambiguous, negotiating parties will have difficulty finding limiting language which a court would unquestionably consider unambiguous. We disagree. Courts have found letters of intent unambiguous in several cases referred to in this opinion. (See *Interway*, 85 Ill.App.3d 1094, 41 Ill.Dec. 117, 407 N.E.2d 615 . . . .) Furthermore, contract cases each turn on their own particular set of facts. . . . Thus, the existence or absence of particular language or words will not ensure that a letter of intent is unambiguous. Our decision here follows the settled law in Illinois concerning letters of intent: The intent of the parties is controlling.

Neither we nor the appellate court have decided whether in fact a contract exists, that is, whether the parties intended to be bound by the letter. We merely hold that the parties' intent, based on the letter alone, is ambiguous. Therefore, upon remand, the circuit court must allow the parties to present other evidence of their intent. The trier of fact should then determine, based on the evidence and the letter, whether the parties intended to be bound by the letter.

. . . .

For the foregoing reasons, we affirm the decision of the appellate court.

Affirmed.

JUSTICE STAMOS, specially concurring:

Because dismissal is unwarranted unless clearly no set of facts can be proved under the pleadings that will entitle a plaintiff to recover, I agree with the majority that the circuit court should not have dismissed [count I of] Quake's complaint. . . .

Instead of weighing as heavily for as against a construction contract, in my judgment the cancellation clause powerfully militates against any finding of such contract. . . .

The cancellation clause refers expressly to cancelling the *letter*, not to cancelling the construction contract that the letter anticipates. A construction contract certainly would bind the parties to that contract's terms, but upon acceptance by Quake the letter here would much more plausibly be viewed as, at most, only binding the parties to efforts at achieving a construction contract on the terms outlined. See, *e.g.*, *Evans, Inc. v. Tiffany & Co.* (N.D.Ill.1976), 416 F.Supp. 224 (obligation to negotiate derived from unclear letter of intent); see also *Precontractual Liability*, 87 Colum.L.Rev. at 250–69 (discussing letters of intent classified as "agreements with open terms" and "agreements to negotiate"); Knapp, *Enforcing the Contract to Bargain*, 44 N.Y.U.L.Rev. 673 (1969) (discussing need for recognizing good-faith bargaining duty as intermediate stage between ultimate contract and none); *cf.* Shell, *Substituting Ethical Standards for Common Law Rules in Commercial Cases: An Emerging Statutory Trend*, 82 Nw. U. L. Rev. 1198, 1199 & n.7 (1988) (noting case law on duty of good-faith negotiation pursuant to letters of intent).

. . . .

Hence, the letter itself, as distinguished from the anticipated construction contract, may be regarded as a contract in its own right: a contract to engage in negotiations. If so, it was this contract, not the anticipated construction contract, that might be cancelled by Jones pursuant to the cancellation clause. Indeed, the notion of cancelling a construction contract not yet entered into lacks meaning.

. . . .

. . . Yet, one might ask in reply: If the letter required only an effort to achieve a construction contract, and if failure of the effort would necessarily prevent any such contract from arising to bind the parties, how could the issue of cancelling a mere letter ever take on enough significance to explain inclusion of the cancellation clause? . . .

. . . .

. . . [S]everal hypotheses suggest themselves for explaining the present letter of intent's cancellation clause:

Because the letter can be regarded as creating an obligation on Jones to attempt to achieve a construction contract, existence of the clause might be explained as a device by which Jones could put an end to its obligation to negotiate.

The fact that this letter, like many others, was intended to induce action by third parties furnishes another possible explanation for including the cancellation clause: It would give Jones a way to put an end to any further inducement based on Jones' once-expressed intention.

A third possible explanation lies in the possibility that, as a result of the parties' subsequent conduct (such as commencement of construction work by Quake), an uncancelled letter of intent might become a link in a chain leading to a finding of contract.

Still another possible explanation lies in the fact that, commercially if not legally, letters of intent have a certain weight as trustworthy indicators of business decisions; accordingly, an issuer might wish to cancel a letter once a decision had changed, in order not to mislead those who might otherwise rely on it.

Any or all of these possibilities would adequately explain the clause, without any need whatever to conclude that the clause betokens an intent to be bound to a construction contract thought to be embodied in the letter. See also *Precontractual Liability*, 87 Colum.L.Rev. at 257–58 (discussing other possible rationales for clause).

If letters of intent are to be used, their drafters would be well advised to avoid ambiguity on the point of whether the issuers are bound. As ever, obscurantist language can produce desired practical effects in the short term, but can well lead eventually to litigation and undesired contractual obligations. Extreme examples exist. (See, *e.g.*, Note, *The $10.53 Billion Question—When Are the Parties Bound?: Pennzoil and the Use of Agreements in Principle in Mergers and Acquisitions*, 40 Vand.L.Rev. 1367 (1987).) Some counsel and clients may opt for ambiguity on grounds of expediency and may account for the probability of resultant litigation costs in the clients' overall business decisionmaking, but many others could benefit from more precision. In turn, counsel for recipients of such letters should remain alert to the likelihood that the instruments lack contractual force.

. . . .

The *Pennzoil* Case

In the final paragraph of the opinion, Justice Stamos cites an "extreme example" of "undesired contractual obligations" from the contested agreement between Texaco, Inc. and Pennzoil Co., litigated in *Texaco, Inc. v. Pennzoil Co.*, 729 S.W.2d 768 (Tex. Ct. App. 1987), *cert. denied*, 485 U.S. 994 (1988). The multi-billion dollar verdict in *Pennzoil* turned on a question of fact: whether Pennzoil's "agreement in principle" to merge with Getty Oil was a contract, despite the absence of an executed final writing. After the "agreement in principle" was made, Texaco tried to acquire Getty Oil for a higher price, and Pennzoil sued Texaco for tortious interference with Pennzoil's contract rights. (Of course, there could be no tortious interference with contract rights if no contract had been formed between Pennzoil and Getty.) Texaco paid Pennzoil $7.3 billion in compensatory damages and $1 billion in punitive damages—the largest civil judgment in history to that date. Much has been written on the dispute and the resulting rounds of litigation. For a small taste of the commentary, *see* T. Petzinger, *Oil & Honor: The Texaco-Pennzoil Wars* (1987); Stephen M. Bundy, *Commentary on "Understanding Pennzoil v. Texaco": Rational Bargaining and Agency Problems*, 75 Va. L. Rev. 335 (1989); David A. Lax, *Commentary on 'Understanding Pennzoil v. Texaco': Market Expectations of Bargaining Inefficiency and Potential Roles for External Parties in Disputes between Publicly Traded Companies*, 75 Va. L. Rev. 367 (1989); Robert H. Mnookin, *Rational Bargaining and Market Efficiency: Understanding Pennzoil v. Texaco*, 75 Va. L. Rev. 295 (1989).

Sun Printing & Publishing Ass'n v. Remington Paper & Power Co.

SUN PRINTING & PUBLISHING ASS'N, Plaintiff-Appellee

v.

REMINGTON PAPER & POWER CO., Defendant-Appellant

Court of Appeals of New York
139 N.E. 470 (N.Y. 1923)

CARDOZO, J.

Who's That?

Judge—later U.S. Supreme Court Justice—Benjamin Cardozo was one of the leading jurists in American history. Cardozo was born in 1870 in New York City, descended on his mother's side from a prominent Jewish family whose members emigrated to the American colonies before the Revolutionary War. His father, a judge on the New York Supreme Court (the general trial court), resigned and returned to private practice soon after Cardozo's birth in the midst of a judicial corruption scandal surrounding the Erie Railway takeover. Cardozo entered Columbia University as an undergraduate at age 15 and four years later enrolled in Columbia Law School. Some have suggested his choice of profession was in part to restore the reputation of his family after his father's resignation from the bench. After the Columbia law school faculty voted to add a third year to the standard two years of law school study, Cardozo and a number of other students chose instead to leave without their degrees (which were not required to take the bar or to practice law), and at the age of 21 he began his professional career. After 23 years as a trial and appellate lawyer, Cardozo was narrowly elected to the New York Supreme Court, taking office on January 1, 1914. Less than a month later, he was appointed to the New York Court of Appeals, at age 43 perhaps the youngest judge to serve on that court. He was later elected to a full term and then, in 1926, to be Chief Judge. He resigned in 1932 to accept appointment to the United States Supreme Court, where he served until his death in 1938.

Cardozo is probably best known for the major opinions he wrote during his 18 years on the New York Court of Appeals, including three contracts cases discussed in this book (*Dougherty v. Salt*, page 203, *Wood v. Lucy, Lady Duff-Gordon*, page 623, and *Jacob & Youngs v. Kent*, page 692) and the prominent torts cases of *Macpherson v. Buick Motor Co.*, 111 N.E. 1050 (1916) (ruling that manufacturers could be held liable for injuries to consumers) and *Palsgraf v. Long Island Rail Road Co.*, 162 N.E. 99 (1929) (developing the concept of proximate cause). He gave a series of lectures at Yale University, later published as *The Nature of the Judicial Process*, http://xroads.virginia.edu/~HYPER/CARDOZO/CarNat.html, a book that is still used widely by judges and scholars. Cardozo was a founding vice-president of the American Law Institute and wrote several books about the development of the law and about judicial decision-making.

An insight into Cardozo's jurisprudential philosophy may be gleaned from his comment that "justice is not to be taken by storm. She is to be wooed by slow advances." See Andrew Kaufman, *Cardozo and the Art of Biography* 20 Cardozo L. Rev. 1245 (1999); Andrew Kaufman, *Benjamin Cardozo on the Supreme Court*, 20 Cardozo L. Rev. 1259 (1999); Lawrence Cunningham, *Cardozo and Posner: A Study in Contracts*, 36 Wm. & Mary L. Rev. 1379 (1995).

Plaintiff agreed to buy and defendant to sell 1,000 tons of paper per month during the months of September, 1919, to December, 1920, inclusive, 16,000 tons in all. Sizes and quality were adequately described. Payment was to be made on the 20th of each month for all paper shipped the previous month. The price for shipments in September, 1919, was to be $3.73 3/4 per 100 pounds, and for shipments in October, November, and December, 1919, $4 per 100 pounds. 'For the balance of the period of this agreement the price of the paper and length of terms for which such price shall apply shall be agreed upon by and between the parties hereto fifteen days prior to the expiration of each period for which the price and length of term thereof have been previously agreed upon, said price in no event to be higher than the contract price for news print charged by the Canadian Export Paper Company to the large consumers, the seller to receive the benefit of any differentials in freight rates.'

Between September, 1919, and December of that year, inclusive, shipments were made and paid for as required by the contract. The time then arrived when there was to be an agreement upon a new price and upon the term of its duration. The defendant in advance of that time gave notice that the contract was imperfect, and disclaimed for the future an obligation to deliver. Upon this the plaintiff took the ground that the price was to be ascertained by resort to an established standard. It made demand that during each month of 1920 the defendant deliver 1,000 tons of paper at the contract price for news print charged by the Canadian Export Paper Company to the large consumers, the defendant to receive the benefit of any differentials in freight rates. The demand was renewed month by month till the expiration of the year. This action has been brought to recover the ensuing damage.

Seller and buyer left two subjects to be settled in the middle of December and at unstated intervals thereafter. One was the price to be paid. The other was the length of time during which such price was to govern. Agreement as to the one was insufficient without agreement as to the other. If price and nothing more had been left open for adjustment, there might be force in the contention that the buyer would be viewed, in the light of later provisions, as the holder of an option. Cohen & Sons v. Lurie Woolen Co., 232 N. Y. 112, 133 N. E. 370. This would mean that, in default of an agreement for a lower price, the plaintiff would have the privilege of calling for delivery in accordance with a price established as a maximum. The price to be agreed upon might be less, but could not be more, than 'the contract price for news print charged by the Canadian Export Paper Company to the large consumers.' The difficulty is, however, that ascertainment of this price does not dispense with the necessity for agreement in respect of the term during which the price is to apply. Agreement upon a maximum payable this month or to-day is not the same as an agreement that it shall continue to be payable next month or to-morrow. Seller and buyer understood that the price to be fixed in December for a term to be agreed upon would not be more than the price then charged by the Canadian Export Paper Company to the large consumers. They did not understand that, if during the term so established the price charged by the Canadian Export Paper Company was changed, the price payable to the seller would fluctuate accordingly. This was conceded by plaintiff's counsel on the argument before us. The seller was to receive no more during the running of the prescribed term, though the Canadian Maximum was raised. The buyer was to pay no less during that term, though the maximum was lowered. In the brief, the standard was to be applied at the beginning of the successive terms, but once applied was to be maintained until the term should have expired. While the term was unknown, the contract was inchoate.

The argument is made that there was no need of an agreement as to time unless the price to be paid was lower than the maximum. We find no evidence of this intention in the language of the contract. The result would then be that the defendant would never know where it stood. The plaintiff was under no duty to accept the Canadian standard. It does not assert that it was. What it asserts is that the contract amounted to the concession of an option. Without an agreement as to time, however, there would be not one option, but a dozen. The Canadian price to-day might be less than the Canadian price to-morrow. Election by the buyer to proceed with performance at the price prevailing in one month would not bind it to proceed at the price prevailing in another. Successive options to be exercised every month would thus be read into the contract. Nothing in the wording discloses the intention of the seller to place itself to that extent at the mercy of the buyer. Even if, however, we were to interpolate the restriction that the option, if exercised at all, must be exercised only once, and for the entire quantity permitted, the difficulty would not be ended. Market prices in 1920 happened to rise. The importance of the time element becomes apparent when we ask ourselves what the seller's position would be if they had happened to fall. Without an agreement as to time, the maximum would be lowered from one shipment to another with every reduction of the standard. With such an agreement, on the other hand, there would be stability and certainty. The parties attempted to guard against the contingency of failing to come together as to price. They did not guard against the contingency of failing to come together as to time. Very likely they thought the latter contingency so remote that it could safely be disregarded. In any event, whether through design or through inadvertence, they left the gap unfilled. The result was nothing more than 'an agreement to agree.' St. Regis Paper Co. v. Hubbs & Hastings Paper Co., 235 N. Y. 30, 36, 138 N. E. 495. Defendant 'exercised its legal right' when it insisted that there was need of something more. St. Regis Paper Co. v. Hubbs & Hastings Paper Co., supra; 1 Williston Contracts, § 45. The right is not affected by our appraisal of the motive. Mayer v. McCreery, 119 N. Y. 434, 440, 23 N. E. 1045.

We are told that the defendant was under a duty, in default of an agreement, to accept a term that would be reasonable in view of the nature of the transaction and the practice of the business. To hold it to such a standard is to make the contract over. The defendant reserved the privilege of doing its business in its own way, and did not undertake to conform to the practice and beliefs of others. United Press v. New York Press Co., 164 N. Y. 406, 413, 58 N. E. 527, 53 L. R. A. 288. We are told again that there was a duty, in default of other agreement, to act as if the successive terms were to expire every month. The contract says they are to expire at such intervals as the agreement may prescribe. There is need, it is true, of no high degree of ingenuity to show how the parties, with little change of language, could have framed a form of contract to which obligation would attach. The difficulty is that they framed another. We are not at liberty to revise while professing to construe.

. . . .

. . . . The action is not based upon a refusal to treat with the defendant and attempt to arrive at an agreement. Whether any such theory of liability would be tenable we need not now inquire. Even if the plaintiff might have stood upon the defendant's denial of obligation as amounting to such a refusal, it did not elect to do so. Instead, it gave its own construction to the contract, fixed for itself the length of the successive terms, and thereby coupled its demand with a condition which there was no duty to accept. Rubber Trading Co. v. Manhattan Rubber Mfg. Co., 221 N. Y. 120, 116 N. E. 789; 3 Williston, Contracts, § 1334. We find no allegation of readiness, and offer to proceed on any other basis. . . .

The order of the Appellate Division should be reversed, and that of the Special Term affirmed, with costs in the Appellate Division and in this court, and the question certified answered in the negative.

CRANE, J. (dissenting).

I cannot take the view of this contract that has been adopted by the majority. The parties to this transaction beyond question thought they were making a contract for the purchase and sale of 16,000 tons rolls news print. The contract was upon a form used by the defendant in its business, and we must suppose that it was intended to be what it states to be, and not a trick or device to defraud merchants. It begins by saying that, in consideration of the mutual covenants and agreements herein set forth the Remington Paper & Power Company, Incorporated, of Watertown, state of New York, hereinafter called the seller, agrees to sell and hereby does sell and the Sun Printing & Publishing Association of New York City, state of New York, hereinafter called the purchaser, agrees to buy and pay for and hereby does buy the following paper, 16,000 tons rolls news print. The sizes are then given. Shipment is to be at the rate of 1,000 tons per month to December, 1920, inclusive. There are details under the headings consignee, specifications, price and delivery, terms, miscellaneous, cores, claims, contingencies, cancellations.

Under the head of miscellaneous comes the following:

'The price agreed upon between the parties hereto, for all papers shipped during the month of September, 1919, shall be $3.73 3/4 per hundred pounds gross weight of rolls on board cars at mills.

'The price agreed upon between the parties hereto for all shipments made during the months of October, November and December, 1919, shall be $4.00 per hundred pounds gross weight of rolls on board cars at mills.

'For the balance of the period of this agreement the price of the paper and length of terms for which such price shall apply shall be agreed upon by and between the parties hereto fifteen days prior to the expiration of each period for which the price and length of term thereof has been previously agreed upon, said price in no event to be higher than the contract price for news print charged by the Canadian Export Paper Company to the large consumers, the seller to receive the benefit of any differentials in freight rates.

'It is understood and agreed by the parties hereto that the tonnage specified herein is for use in the printing and publication of the various editions of the Daily and Sunday New York Sun, and any variation from this will be considered a breach of contract.'

After the deliveries for September, October, November, and December, 1919, the defendant refused to fix any price for the deliveries during the subsequent months, and refused to deliver any more paper. It has taken the position that this document was no contract; that it meant nothing; that it was formally executed for the purpose of permitting the defendant to furnish paper or not, as it pleased.

Surely these parties must have had in mind that some binding agreement was made for the sale and delivery of 16,000 tons rolls of paper, and that the instrument contained all the elements necessary to make a binding contract. It is a strain upon reason to imagine the paper house, the Remington Paper & Power Company, Incorporated, and the Sun Printing & Publishing Association, formally executing a contract drawn up upon the defendant's prepared form which was useless and amounted to nothing. We must, at least, start the examination of this agreement by believing that these intelligent parties intended to make a binding contract. If this be so, the court should spell out a binding contract, if it be possible. I not only think it possible, but think the paper itself clearly states a contract recognized under all the rules at law. It is said that the one essential element of price is lacking; that the provision above quoted is an agreement to agree to a price, and that the defendant had the privilege of agreeing or not, as it pleased; that, if it failed to agree to a price, there was no standard by which to measure the amount the plaintiff would have to pay. The contract does state, however, just this very thing. Fifteen days before the 1st of January, 1920, the parties were to agree upon the price of the paper to be delivered thereafter, and the length of the period for which such price should apply. However, the price to be fixed was not 'to be higher than the contract price for news print charged by the Canadian Export Paper Company to large consumers.' Here, surely, was something definite. The 15th day of December arrived. The defendant refused to deliver. At that time there was a price for news print charged by the Canadian Export Paper Company. If the plaintiff offered to pay this price, which was the highest price the defendant could demand, the defendant was bound to deliver. This seems to be very clear.

But, while all agree that the price on the 15th day of December could be fixed, the further objection is made that the period during which that price should continue was not agreed upon. There are many answers to this.

We have reason to believe that the parties supposed they were making a binding contract; that they had fixed the terms by which one was required to take and the other to deliver; that the Canadian Export Paper Company price was to be the highest that could be charged in any event. These things being so, the court should be very reluctant to permit a defendant to avoid its contract. Wakeman v. Wheeler & Wilson Mfg. Co., 101 N. Y. 205, 4 N. E. 264, 54 Am. Rep. 676.

On the 15th of the fourth month, the time when the price was to be fixed for subsequent deliveries, there was a price charged by the Canadian Export Paper Company to large consumers. As the defendant failed to agree upon a price, made no attempt to agree upon a price, and deliberately broke its contract, it could readily be held to deliver the rest of the paper, 1,000 rolls a month, at this Canadian price. There is nothing in the complaint which indicates that this is a fluctuating price, or that the price of paper as it was on December 15th was not the same for the remaining 12 months. Or we can deal with this contract month by month. The deliveries were to be made 1,000 tons per month. On December 15th 1,000 tons could have been demanded. The price charged by the Canadian Export Paper Company on the 15th of each month on and after December 15, 1919, would be the price for the 1,000-ton delivery for that month. Or, again, the word as used in the miscellaneous provision quoted is not 'price,' but 'contract price'—'in no event to be higher than the contract price.' Contract implies a term or period, and, if the evidence should show that the Canadian contract price was for a certain period of weeks or months, then this period could be applied to the contract in question. Failing any other alternative, the law should do here what it has done in so many other cases—apply the rule of reason and compel parties to contract in the light of fair dealing. It could hold this defendant to deliver its paper as it agreed to do, and take for a price the Canadian Export Paper Company contract price for a period which is reasonable under all the circumstances and conditions as applied in the paper trade.

To let this defendant escape from its formal obligations when any one of these rulings as applied to this contract would [have] given a practical and just result is to give the sanction of law to a deliberate breach. Wood v. Lucy, Lady Duff-Gordon, 222 N. Y. 88, 118 N. E. 214; Moran v. Standard Oil Co., 211 N. Y. 187, 105 N. E. 217; United States Rubber Co. v. Silverstein, 229 N. Y. 168, 128 N. E. 123.

For these reasons I am for the affirmance of the courts below.

HISCOCK, C. J., and POUND, MCLAUGHLIN, and ANDREWS, JJ., concur with CARDOZO, J.

CRANE, J., reads dissenting opinion with which HOGAN, J., concurs.

Academy Chicago Publishers v. Cheever

ACADEMY CHICAGO PUBLISHERS, Plaintiff-Appellant

v.

MARY W. CHEEVER, Defendant-Appellee

Supreme Court of Illinois

578 N.E.2d 981 (Ill. 1991)

JUSTICE HEIPLE delivered the opinion of the court:

This is a suit for declaratory judgment. It arose out of an agreement between the widow of the widely published author, John Cheever, and Academy Chicago Publishers. Contact between the parties began in 1987 when the publisher approached Mrs. Cheever about the possibility of publishing a collection of Mr. Cheever's short stories which, though previously published, had never been collected into a single anthology. In August of that year, a publishing agreement was signed which provided, in pertinent part:

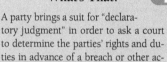

What's That?

A party brings a suit for "declaratory judgment" in order to ask a court to determine the parties' rights and duties in advance of a breach or other action resulting in possible liability.

"Agreement made this 15th day of August 1987, between Academy Chicago Publishers or any affiliated entity or imprint (hereinafter referred to as the Publisher) and Mary W. Cheever and Franklin H. Dennis of the USA (hereinafter referred to as Author).

Whereas the parties are desirous of publishing and having published a certain work or works, tentatively titled *The Uncollected Stories of John Cheever* (hereinafter referred to as the Work):

. . . .

2. The Author will deliver to the Publisher on a mutually agreeable date one copy of the manu-

Who's That?

John Cheever (1912–1982) is recognized as one of the most important fiction writers of the twentieth century. He was awarded the Pulitzer Prize for Fiction, the National Book Critics Circle Award, and the National Medal for Literature. For more information about his works and his role in American literature, see www.todayinliterature.com/biography/john.cheever.asp.

script of the Work as finally arranged by the editor and satisfactory to the Publisher in form and content.

. . . .

5. Within a reasonable time and a mutually agreeable date after delivery of the final revised manuscript, the Publisher will publish the Work at its own expense, in such style and manner and at such price as it deems best, and will keep the Work in print as long as it deems it expedient; but it will not be responsible for delays caused by circumstances beyond its control."

Academy and its editor, Franklin Dennis, assumed the task of locating and procuring the uncollected stories and delivering them to Mrs. Cheever. Mrs. Cheever and Mr. Dennis received partial advances for manuscript preparation. By the end of 1987, Academy had located and delivered more than 60 uncollected stories to Mrs. Cheever. Shortly thereafter, Mrs. Cheever informed Academy in writing that she objected to the publication of the book and attempted to return her advance.

Academy filed suit in the circuit court of Cook County in February 1988, seeking a declaratory judgment: (1) granting Academy the exclusive right to publish the tentatively titled, "The Uncollected Stories of John Cheever"; (2) designating Franklin Dennis as the book's editor; and (3) obligating Mrs. Cheever to deliver the manuscript from which the work was to be published.

The trial court entered an order declaring, *inter alia*: (1) that the publishing agreement executed by the parties was valid and enforceable; (2) that Mrs. Cheever was entitled to select the short stories to be included in the manuscript for publication; (3) that Mrs. Cheever would comply with her obligations of good faith and fair dealing if she delivered a manuscript including at least 10 to 15 stories totaling at least 140 pages; (4) Academy controlled the design and format of the work to be published, but control must be exercised in cooperation with Mrs. Cheever.

Academy appealed the trial court's order, challenging particularly the declaration regarding the minimum story and page numbers for Mrs. Cheever's compliance with the publishing agreement, and the declaration that Academy must consult with defendant on all matters of publication of the manuscript.

The appellate court affirmed the decision of the trial court with respect to the validity and enforceability of the publishing agreement and the minimum story and page number requirements for Mrs. Cheever's compliance with same. The appellate court reversed the trial court's declaration regarding control of publication, stating that the trial court erred in considering extrinsic evidence to interpret the agreement regarding control of the publication, given the explicit language of the agreement granting exclusive control to Academy. (200 Ill.App.3d 677, 146 Ill.Dec. 386, 558 N.E.2d 349.)

The parties raise several issues on appeal; this matter, however, is one of contract and we confine our discussion to the issue of the validity and enforceability of the publishing agreement.

Make the Connection

Chapter 8, page 564, includes coverage of when extrinsic evidence is admissible to interpret explicit language of a written agreement.

While the trial court and the appellate court agreed that the publishing agreement constitutes a valid and enforceable contract, we cannot concur. The principles of contract state that in order for a valid contract to be formed, an "offer must be so definite as to its material terms or require such definite terms in the acceptance that the promises and performances to be rendered by each party are reasonably certain." (1 Williston, Contracts §§ 38 through 48 (3d ed. 1957); 1 Corbin, Contracts §§ 95 through 100 (1963).) Although the parties may have had and manifested the intent to make a contract, if the content of their agreement is unduly uncertain and indefinite no contract is formed. 1 Williston § 37; 1 Corbin § 95.

The pertinent language of this agreement lacks the definite and certain essential terms required for the formation of an enforceable contract. (*Midland Hotel Corp. v. Reuben H. Donnelley Corp.* (1987), 118 Ill.2d 306, 113 Ill.Dec. 252, 515 N.E.2d 61.) A contract "is sufficiently definite and certain to be enforceable if the court is enabled from the terms and provisions thereof, under proper rules of construction and applicable principles of equity, to ascertain what the parties have agreed to do. (*Morey v. Hoffman* (1957), 12 Ill.2d 125, 145 N.E.2d 644.) The provisions of the subject publishing agreement do not provide the court with a means of determining the intent of the parties.

Trial testimony reveals that a major source of controversy between the parties is the length and content of the proposed book. The agreement sheds no light on the minimum or maximum number of stories or pages necessary for publication of the collection, nor is there any implicit language from which we can glean the intentions of the parties with respect to this essential contract term. The publishing agreement is similarly silent with respect to who will decide which stories will be included in the collection. Other omis-

Think About It!

Why do you think the parties structured the agreement as they did? What advantages did the flexible terms provide? How might parties retain this flexibility while also having a valid contract? How much can be left to the sole discretion of one party?

sions, ambiguities, unresolved essential terms and illusory terms are: No date certain for delivery of the manuscript. No definition of the criteria which would render the manuscript satisfactory to the publisher either as to form or content. No date certain as to when publication will occur. No certainty as to style or manner in which the book will be published nor is there any indication as to the price at which such book will be sold, or the length of time publication shall continue, all of which terms are left to the sole discretion of the publisher.

A contract may be enforced even though some contract terms may be missing or left to be agreed upon, but if the essential terms are so uncertain that there is no basis for deciding whether the agreement has been kept or broken, there is no contract. (*Champaign National Bank v. Landers Seed Co.* (1988), 165 Ill.App.3d 1090, 116 Ill. Dec. 742, 519 N.E.2d 957; Restatement (Second) of Contracts § 33 (1981).) Without setting forth adequate terms for compliance, the publishing agreement provides no basis for determining when breach has occurred, and, therefore, is not a valid and enforceable contract.

An enforceable contract must include a meeting of the minds or mutual assent as to the terms of the contract. (*Midland Hotel*, 118 Ill.2d at 313, 113 Ill. Dec. 252, 515 N.E.2d 61.) It is not compelling that the parties share a subjective understanding as to the terms of the contract; the parties' conduct may indicate an agreement to the terms of same. (*Steinberg v. Chicago Medical School* (1977), 69 Ill.2d 320, 13 Ill. Dec. 699, 371 N.E.2d 634.) In the instant case, however, no mutual assent has been illustrated. The parties did not and do not share a common understanding of the essential terms of the publishing agreement.

Think About It!

Might the *Quake Construction* lawsuit (page 39) on remand suffer the same fate as the *Academy Chicago Publishers* lawsuit?

In rendering its judgment, the trial court supplied minimum terms for Mrs. Cheever's compliance, including story and page numbers. It is not uncommon for a court to supply a missing material term, as the reasonable conclusion often is that the parties intended that the term be supplied by implication. However, where the subject matter of the contract has not been decided upon and there is no standard available for reasonable implication, courts ordinarily refuse to supply the missing term. (1 Williston § 42; 1 Corbin § 100.) No suitable standard was available for the trial court to apply. It is our opinion that the trial court incorrectly supplied minimum compliance terms to the publishing agreement, as the agreement did not constitute a valid and enforceable contract to begin with. As noted above, the publishing agreement contains major unresolved uncertainties. It is not the role of the court to rewrite the contract and spell out essential elements not included therein.

In light of our decision that there was no valid and enforceable contract between the parties, we need not address other issues raised on appeal. For the foregoing reasons, the decisions of the trial and appellate courts in this declaratory judgment action are reversed.

Reversed.

JUSTICES CLARK and FREEMAN took no part in the consideration or decision of this opinion.

Behind the Scenes

The Cheever litigation took four years and raged across four courtrooms and twelve state and federal courts in New York and Illinois. As described by the lawyers who represented Mrs. Cheever: "The fight was unusually fierce, even by today's litigation standards. Academy referred to the Cheever family as 'venal people' and 'a traveling freak show,' while Academy's own executives were likened in the news media to grave robbers and rapists. After Academy's loss of its last appeal, what remained was a nationwide injunction issued by the federal court in New York, barring Academy from publishing an anthology of 68 previously uncollected Cheever stories, which Academy had hoped would be a blockbuster book, but which *The Washington Post* characterized as 'a literary scavenger job.' "* The case's biggest irony was that the Cheever family won a complete victory, but conceded in 1988 that it would have to compile a book similar to the one that Academy Chicago Publishers originally envisioned in order to recover the family's legal costs.**

Jordan and Anita Miller, the principals in Academy Chicago Publishers, maintained throughout the litigation and afterwards that their agreement with Mary Cheever reflected the level of specificity and flexibility needed and generally recognized as reasonable in the publishing world, and that their small publishing house was being bullied by those with more resources. See Anita Miller, *Uncollecting Cheever: The Family of John Cheever vs. Academy Chicago Publishers* (1998). Richard Dooling, in his review of Miller's book in the New York Times, said the circumstances

---

* The quotation came from the lawyers' website, and was available at the time of the publication of this book's second edition. The law firm has apparently disbanded and the website is no longer there.
** See David Streitfeld, *Cheevers, Publisher End Fight*, Wash. Post, Jan. 25, 1992, at C5. For more information, see John Blades, *Cheever's Chaff: Chicago Academy Stymied in Fight with Family to Print All His Uncollected Tales*, Chi. Trib., Feb. 27, 1989, § 5, at 2; James Warren, *Contract Dispute: Publishers Tell Judge He Doesn't Get It, But Authors Say He Does*, Chi. Trib., Sept. 1, 1991, § 5, at 2.

seemed "more like the tale of a small publisher that carelessly drafted an important contract (without consulting a lawyer) and the family of a renowned author who foolishly signed it (without consulting a lawyer). Then both parties called in lawyers and fought for four years to best each other in a species of combat that differs from violence only insofar as there is usually no bloodshed in litigation. Perhaps both sides now appreciate Voltaire's observation: "I was never ruined but twice, once when I lost a lawsuit and once when I won one." Richard Dooling, "*The 5:48 is Cancelled*," at www.nytimes.com/books/98/12/27/reviews/981227.27doolint.html.

Academy Chicago Publishers survived the ordeal and continued to publish new titles, including John Cheever, *Fall River and Other Uncollected Stories*, published in 2009 when the stories reverted to the public domain. In 2013, the publisher was acquired by Chicago Review Press, Inc., and continues to exist as that publisher's imprint Academy Chicago. See http://www.chicagoreviewpress.com/academy-chicago-pages-526.php.

Think About It:
The Impact of Jurisprudential Philosophy

On what philosophical and policy grounds do the courts in *Quake, Sun Printing*, and *Academy Chicago Publishers* differ? Consider their views on the realities of the contract formation process and the role of law in responding to them. Which courts make it easier to form a contract, and which ones make it more difficult to form a contract? How do these approaches affect future contracting parties? Which approach do you think is more appropriate?

Consider, too, the evidence that each court takes into account. In each case, does the court limit the extrinsic evidence to be considered for guidance on the meaning of the agreement or look beyond the document to the broader context? In Chapter 8, we look further at the differences between the plain-meaning and context-based approaches to interpretation.

Food for Thought:
Indefinite or Incomplete Agreements

Toward the end of *Academy Chicago Publishers*, the court said, "A contract may be enforced even though some contract terms may be missing or left to be agreed upon, but if the essential terms are so uncertain that there is no basis for deciding whether the agreement has been kept or broken, there is no contract."

Why do parties continue to write indefinite and incomplete agreements, in the face of a doctrine that may invalidate them? One commentator has theorized that deliberately incomplete agreements that rely on self-enforcement (between the parties, without the court system) are more efficient than legally enforceable agreements. In a data pool of cases in which courts refused to enforce agreements because of indefiniteness, the intentionally incomplete agreements were generally "simple in form, clear in commitment, and structured to create opportunities for parties to reciprocate in ways that expand the contractual surplus." Other agreements, notably "agreements to agree," were often structured to allow one or both parties to watch the other party in action, thereby "providing an opportunity . . . to observe the other's character over time" and to screen out business partners who were not reciprocally fair. Even without a valid contract, this opportunity was valuable. Robert E. Scott, *A Theory of Self-Enforcing Indefinite Agreements*, 103 Colum L. Rev. 1641, 1643 (2003). Thus, even with a marginally valid or even invalid agreement, the parties might be satisfied with the end result of their negotiations. Legal validity is not always the goal. But one or both parties may end up ambushed and disadvantaged by the invalidity.

What competing policies underlie the varying attitudes displayed by the courts dealing with incomplete agreements? What is the right balance to be struck? Do you think the cases in this section show success in doing that?

Test Your Knowledge

To assess your understanding of the material in this chapter, <u>click here</u> to take a quiz.

CHAPTER 3

Assent Through Offer and Acceptance

How do parties demonstrate assent to a contract?

What kinds of promises will the law enforce?

What defenses to enforcement exist?

Is a writing required for enforcement? If so, what kind?

How is the content and meaning of a contract determined?

What are parties' rights and duties after breach?

What situations lead to excusing contract performance?

What remedies are available for breach of contract?

What contractual rights and duties do non-parties to a contract have?

Table of Contents

§ 1. Introduction 67
§ 2. Sequential Assent by Offer and Acceptance Under the Common Law 67
    § 2.1. Defining "Offer" 69
        § 2.1.1. Advertisements and Rewards as Offers 75
            Lefkowitz v. Great Minneapolis Surplus Store, Inc. 76
            Leonard v. PepsiCo 82
            PROBLEM: ADVERTISEMENTS AND REWARDS (3-1) 97
        § 2.1.2. Offers in the Commercial Bidding Process 98
            PROBLEMS: WAS AN OFFER MADE? (3-2 TO 3-4) 99
    § 2.2. How Long Does an Offer Last? 101
        § 2.2.1. Lapse 101
        § 2.2.2. Death or Incapacity of the Offeror or Offeree 105
            PROBLEM: DEATH OF THE OFFEROR (3-5) 105
    § 2.3. Defining Acceptance 106
        § 2.3.1. Distinguishing Between Acceptance and Counter-Offer ...107
            Ardente v. Horan 108

PROBLEMS: ACCEPTANCE OR COUNTER-OFFER? (3-6 TO 3-8)............111

§ 2.3.2. The Mirror Image Rule..112

PROBLEMS: MIRROR-IMAGE RULE (3-9, 3-10) 114

§ 2.3.3. Permitted Method and Manner of Acceptance
(Including Acceptance by Promise or by Performance)............116

PROBLEMS: PREPARATIONS FOR OR THE BEGINNING OF PERFORMANCE
(3-11 TO 3-13) 119

PROBLEM: OFFER AND ACCEPTANCE (3-14)................................123

§ 2.3.4. Acceptance by Conduct..126

§ 2.3.5. Acceptance by Inaction..129

PROBLEMS: ASSENT THROUGH CONDUCT OR INACTION (3-15 TO
3-17)..134

§ 2.3.6. What Terms Are Accepted? 136

§ 2.4. Rejection by the Offeree..150

§ 2.5. Revocation by the Offeror..152

PROBLEMS: REJECTION AND REVOCATION (3-18 TO 3-20)....................155

§ 2.5.1. Limitations on the Power to Revoke: Unilateral
Contracts...156

§ 2.5.2. Limitations on the Power to Revoke: Option Contracts
and Firm Offers..157

PROBLEMS: IRREVOCABLE OFFERS (3-21 TO 3-23)............................158

§ 2.6. Time of Effectiveness of Contract Formation
Communications...159

§ 2.6.1. The Mailbox Rule for Acceptances..................................159

UETA § 15. Time . . . of Sending and Receipt..........................161

§ 2.6.2. Time of Acceptance by Conduct....................................164

PROBLEMS: TIME OF EFFECTIVENESS OF ACCEPTANCE (3-24, 3-25)............165

§ 3. **Sequential Offer and Acceptance Under UCC Article 2** 166

§ 3.1. General Rules of Offer and Acceptance.................................169

§ 3.2. Rejection of the Mirror Image Rule: UCC § 2–207.....................169

§ 3.2.1. Defining Acceptance Under § 2–207................................171

§ 3.2.1.1. Acceptance by Expression of Commitment:
§ 2–207(1)...171

§ 3.2.1.2. Acceptance by Conduct: § 2–207(3)........................176

§ 3.3. Terms of a Contract Formed Under § 2–207............................177

§ 3.3.1. Terms of a Contract Formed Under § 2–207(1):
Understanding § 2–207(2)..178

§ 3.3.2. Terms of a Contract Formed Under § 2–207(3) 179

§ 3.4. Integrating Your Understanding of § 2–207 181

Egan Machinery Co. v. Mobil Chemical Co. 184

PROBLEMS: CONTRACTS AND THEIR TERMS UNDER UCC § 2–207 (3-26 TO
3-30) 189

§ 1. Introduction

In Chapter 2, we considered what characteristics make a statement a "promise." In this chapter, we look at how one or more promises are combined to establish the parties' mutual assent, to form a contract. Because contract law attempts to enforce obligations that parties have imposed on themselves, rather than enforcing community norms as in tort law, determining whether the parties have assented is the crucial first element in establishing contractual liability. Moreover, because contract liability is based on voluntary assumption of responsibility, contract law focuses on finding and implementing the intention of the parties, as well as that intention can be discerned.

> **Make the Connection**
>
> By its nature, assent must be voluntary and not based on mistaken or misrepresented information. This chapter focuses on the mechanics of manifesting assent, assuming no underlying concern with the nature of the agreement process. Chapter 6 examines "the dark side of mutual assent"—defenses to contract formation based on allegations that fraud, duress, undue influence, mistake, or misrepresentation undercuts the existence of true assent.

Manifestation of mutual assent may occur simultaneously, with the parties together agreeing to a single statement of terms, perhaps by signing the same document. That is the most straightforward method of communicating mutual assent, and finding the existence of that kind of mutual assent is mostly a matter of establishing that the stated terms include expressions of commitment, not illusory promises or too much uncertainty for enforcement.

Many agreements occur not through such simultaneous expressions of assent to agreed terms, however, but through a sequence of communications between the parties. Determining whether such a sequence of communications has resulted in contract formation requires mastering the terminology and analysis used by the courts to evaluate assent, and it is to that task we now turn. Different rules apply if the alleged contract is governed by the common law or by the Uniform Commercial Code (UCC), though the UCC draws on common law concepts as well. The following sections address these questions, both in the common law and under the UCC.

§ 2. Sequential Assent by Offer and Acceptance Under the Common Law

When evaluating whether parties have reached agreement through a series of back-and-forth communications, courts look for a pattern of communications constituting an "offer" by one party and an "acceptance" by the other. In essence, an "offer" is a commitment by one party to an exchange of future performances and an "acceptance" is a commitment by the other party to that same exchange. The existence of offer and acceptance may be simple to establish (e.g., Max says to Emily, "Will you mow my lawn next Friday? If so, I will promise to pay you $50" and Emily says to Max, "Yes, I will do that, for the promised $50"). This promise-for-a-promise is a manifestation of mutual assent. The sequence of offer and acceptance is reflected in the center column of the chart below.

But finding offer and acceptance may not be so simple. First, as reflected in the chart below, the web of communications between the parties may involve other "moves" that may prevent (or complicate) mutual assent.

- As shown in the left-hand column: Before an offer is accepted, it may terminate, through lapse, revocation, or (less frequently) death or incapacity of the offeror.

- As shown in the right-hand column: The offeree may respond to the offer with a rejection, which also results in termination of the offer and therefore no agreement. Or the offeree may respond with a "counter-offer" of its own, which typically constitutes a rejection of the original offer, but also restarts the quest for an acceptance.

The Offer and Acceptance Process

Second, there are challenging questions that may arise at each step of the agreement process.

- What form and content of communication is necessary to create an offer? What happens if the initial communication is an advertisement or a promise of a reward? Does that constitute an offer? Is a "price quote" an offer? What about catalogues?

- When does an offer lapse, especially if no time limit is specified?

- What form and content of communication is necessary to create an acceptance? Can the acceptance differ in any respect from the offer?

- What happens if communications "cross in the mail" (e.g., the offeror sends a revocation of the offer at the same time that the recipient of the offer sends an acceptance)?

- How do the rules of offer and acceptance apply to modern bidding processes, often governed by statutory requirements superimposed on the common law rules?

§ 2.1. Defining "Offer"

The first step in finding mutual assent by offer and acceptance is to determine whether either party has made an offer. In this section, we consider how offer has been defined, as well as factual examples that show the courts' judgments about which communications do and do not result in offers.

An offer, like a promise, is an expression of willingness to undertake an obligation or refrain from acting. There must be manifestation of commitment, as well as sufficient certainty to provide the basis for a court to enforce the promise. The promisor must be committing now, not withholding assent until later.

While a promise may be one-sided, an offer is two-sided: it is a promise that the offeror makes conditional (explicitly or implicitly) on the offeree doing something, or promising to do something, in return. It is a commitment to a proposed exchange ("I *promise* to do this if you *promise* to do that" or "I *promise* to do this if you *do* that"). The Restatement (Second) contains a typical definition: "An offer is the manifestation of willingness to enter into a bargain, so made as to justify another person in

> ### Take Note:
> ### Offers and Conditions
>
> An offer may specify a condition that must be satisfied in order for the offer to be valid—that is, the offeror is not committing until the condition arises. For example, the owner of a racehorse might promise to sell the horse to the offeree-buyer if the horse wins a specified race. If the horse does not win, the condition is not satisfied (and can never be satisfied), so the promise is not an operative offer (that is, it cannot be accepted). Alternatively, an offer might specify that it is valid only as long as a particular condition exists; when the condition ceases to exist, so does the offer. For instance, a person who wishes to buy a particular piece of real estate might promise to buy the property as long as 30-year fixed mortgage interest rates remain below 4%. If interest rates reach 4%, then the buyer's offer expires, because the condition ceased to exist.

understanding that his assent to that bargain is invited and will conclude it" (§ 24); a bargain is "an agreement to exchange promises or to exchange a promise for a performance or to exchange performances" (§ 3).

As with respect to promises, the content and context of an offer are relevant to determining its meaning—whether it constitutes an offer. As noted by one court: "Language suggesting a legal offer, such as 'I offer' or 'I promise' can be contrasted with language suggesting more preliminary negotiations, such as 'I quote' or 'are you interested.' Differing phrases are evidence of differing intent, but no one phrase is necessarily controlling. . . . In addition to the language used by the parties, it is also appropriate to consider the circumstances surrounding the making of the offer, including the context of any prior communications or course of dealing between the parties; whether the communication was private or made to the general public; whether the communication comes in reply to a specific request for an offer; and whether the communication contains detailed terms."[*]

Like all contract communications, a purported offer is judged by its objective meaning—whether a reasonable person in the position of the offeree would understand the communication to be an offer, which makes a commitment and allows the recipient to form a contract by saying "yes." In marginal cases, courts are often reluctant to rule that an offer was made, because the result might be significant liability that the purported offeror did not mean to undertake.

> **Example A:** *Mouton v. Kershaw*, 18 N.W. 172 (Wis. 1884).
>
> A wrote to B: "Dear Sir: We are authorized to offer Michigan fine salt, in full car-load lots of 80 to 95 barrels, delivered at your city, at $90 per barrel, to be shipped per your specified railroad company. Shall be pleased to receive your order." Did A make an offer to sell salt?

Analysis: You might recognize this as similar to Problem 2-1. The court held that, despite the existence of the word "offer" in the statement, and the specificity as to price and shipment method, it was not an offer, because no quantity was specified and there was no way to fill in a quantity if the parties did not agree to that themselves. If B said, "I accept," how much salt would the parties have agreed to buy and sell? The prospective buyer argued that the "offer" was for "such reasonable amount of salt as he might order, and as the appellants might reasonably expect him to order," but the court was not persuaded. As for evidence of commitment, saying "we are authorized to offer" might be considered one step short of saying "we are offering."

---

[*] *Honeywell Intern. Inc. v. Nikon Corp.*, 672 F. Supp. 2d 638, 642 (D. Del. 2009).

Example B: *Owen v. Tunison*, 158 A. 926 (Maine 1932).

A wrote to B: "Will you sell me your [specified] property for $20,000?" B wrote back: "Because of improvements, it would not be possible for me to sell it unless I was to receive $30,000." Did either A or B make an offer?

Analysis: You might recognize this as Problem 2-2. The court held that A initially made an inquiry, not an offer. "Will you sell" to me at a specified price is different than "I ask you to sell" to me at that price. B made an invitation to an offer ("If you're willing to sell to me, let me know"), but not an offer. The court relied on an analogous cases in which "I want [a certain price]" was not an offer. Likewise, the court held that B's statement was also not an offer, relying on a case that reached the same conclusion from a statement that an owner "would not consider less than half." The subjunctive tense ("I would" rather than "I will") and the negative terminology ("I won't sell unless I receive at least $30,000" rather than "I will sell for $30,000") contribute to the conclusion that no commitment is shown. Of course, if the context were different, the conclusion about the reasonable meaning of the statements might be different as well. If A had previously offered $18,000, then $19,000, then said he'd be willing to go "a little higher" and then asked "will you sell it to me for $20,000," the statement might be an offer.

Example C: *Fairmount Glass Works v. Crunden-Martin Woodenware Co.*, 51 S.W. 196 (Ky. 1899).

Buyer wrote to Seller on 4/20: "Please advise us the lowest price you can give us on our order for ten car loads of Mason green jars, complete, with caps, packed one dozen in a case, either delivered here, or f.o.b. cars your place, as you prefer. State terms and cash discount."

Seller replied on 4/23: "We quote you Mason fruit jars, complete, in one-dozen boxes, delivered in East St. Louis, Ill.: Pints $4.50, quarts $5.00, half gallons $6.50, per gross, for immediate acceptance, and shipment not later than May 15, 1895; sixty days' acceptance, cash in ten days. Please note that we make all quotations and contracts subject to the contingencies of agencies or transportation, delays or accidents beyond our control."

On 4/24, Buyer replied by telegram: "Your letter twenty-third received. Enter order ten carloads as per your quotation. Specifications mailed."

On 4/24, Seller replied by telegram: "Impossible to book your order. Output all sold."

Buyer sued Seller for breach of contract. The case turned on whether Fairmount's communication of 4/23 was an offer that was accepted by telegram on 4/24.

Analysis: The court held that Buyer's letter of 4/20 was an inquiry for the price and terms on which Seller would sell the goods. The court cited "a number of authorities holding that a quotation of prices is not an offer to sell . . . . There are a number of cases holding that the transaction is not completed until the order [made in response to the quotation] is accepted. But each case must turn largely upon the language there used. In this case we think there was more than a quotation of prices, although appellant's letter uses the word 'quote' in stating the prices given. The true meaning of the correspondence must be determined by reading it as a whole." Buyer's letter asked not for a general quotation of prices but for the price at which Seller would sell a specific quantity of jars. Seller's reply was therefore an offer to sell, reinforced by the statement "for immediate acceptance." Although the quantities of each size jar were not yet specified, Seller's offer allowed Buyer to name the quantity of each size jar and to fix the delivery date, as long as it was "not later than May 15."

Example D: *Foster & Kleiser v. Baltimore County*, 470 A.2d 1322 (Md. Ct. Spec. App. 1984).

In early February, Baltimore County submitted to County Mutual Acceptance Corporation (CMAC) a document that expressed Baltimore's interest in purchasing land owned by CMAC for the price of $183,000. The document contained a clause saying, "In the event that this Agreement is not approved by the Baltimore County Council, this Agreement shall become null and void . . . ." CMAC signed the document on February 6 and returned it to the County. The County Council approved the purchase on April 20. Foster & Kleiser had maintained billboards on the land being purchased by the County, but that lease was terminated by CMAC with 60 days notice on February 11. Foster & Kleiser sued Baltimore County for lease payments it claimed the County owed starting on February 6. The County defended by claiming it did not own the property until April 20, which was after the lease had terminated. The answer to that question depended on whether the document submitted by Baltimore County to CMAC was an offer or only part of preliminary negotiations, inviting CMAC to make an offer.

Analysis: The court concluded that Baltimore County did not make an offer because the quoted clause reserved to the County the right to decide later whether it wanted to commit. As a result, CMAC did not have the power to enter a binding obligation by accepting. Although written by Baltimore County, the document became an offer *by CMAC* when CMAC signed and sent the document back to the County. That offer was accepted when the City Council approved the agreement. The result might have been different if the offer came from someone other than the governmental body whose approval was necessary; the document might then be considered a binding commitment to enter a bargain, granting the recipient the power to accept, with performance conditional on approval from the relevant governmental body. It is the fact that the purported offeror retained authority to decide whether to commit that prevented the document in each case from being an offer.

Example E: *Nordyne, Inc. v. International Controls & Measurements Corp.*, 262 F.3d 843 (8th Cir. 2001).

Nordyne manufactures heating, ventilation, and air conditioning equipment. International Controls & Measurements Corp. (ICM) manufactures electronic defrost control boards for use in such equipment. For 10 years before the particular dispute arose, Nordyne had been purchasing control boards from ICM. In 1997, ICM began marketing a new version of the control panel Nordyne had been purchasing. The following sequence of communications occurred between the parties:

- 5/13: ICM sent Nordyne a quotation for the new version of the control panel.

- 7/29: After Nordyne told ICM one of the new features was not necessary to its operation, ICM sent Nordyne a new quotation for the modified unit, for Nordyne's estimated annual usage of 40,000 units at $9.87 per unit. The quotation said it was valid until 12/31/97. Printed at the bottom of the quotation was the following: "CONDITIONS ON REVERSE SIDE ARE PART OF THIS QUOTATION." The conditions on the back included a statement that "All orders are subject to acceptance by the Seller at its home office in Cicero, New York."

- 9/12: After Nordyne asked to see samples, ICM sent five samples with a letter from the ICM home office stating: "Full blown manufacturing of this device is awaiting your sign off of these check samples as approved for production. Please review the samples and 'sign off' this document and send it back by return fax so that we may fulfill your production requirements in a timely manner."

- 9/15: Nordyne signed the production approval.

- 9/17: Nordyne issued a purchase order for 20,000 units at the quoted price, and under the shipping, payment, and packaging terms set forth in the quotation on 7/29. The purchase order form stated "Please enter our order for the above, subject to terms and conditions printed on reverse side . . . . Please acknowledge by signing and returning the attached acknowledgment form giving date of shipment." On the reverse side of the purchase order appeared Terms and Conditions, including: "Buyer shall not be bound by this order until Buyer receives the acknowledgment copy of this order executed by Seller."

- 9/22: ICM signed the acknowledgment.

ICM made its first shipment on 9/30. Between that date and mid-August of the following year, ICM shipped Nordyne's entire order of 46,151 units at the rate of approximately one shipment per week.

For purposes of a breach of contract suit brought by Nordyne, the court had to determine which communication constituted an offer so it could then determine when the contract was created by acceptance. ICM argued that the offer was made on 7/29 when ICM sent Nordyne a quotation and was accepted when Nordyne signed the production approval on 9/15. Nordyne argued that the 7/29 quotation was not an offer "because (1) it was not for immediate acceptance, but was subject to ICM's approval at its home office, and to ICM's providing acceptable samples, and (2) it did not specify quantity and did not include a delivery schedule." Nordyne argued the offer was made on 9/17 in its purchase order, which was accepted when ICM signed the acknowledgment and returned it.

Analysis: The court agreed with ICM. "The general rule is that a price quotation, such as one appearing in a catalogue or on a flyer, is not an offer, but is rather a suggestion to induce offers by others. However, a price quotation, 'if detailed enough, can amount to an offer creating the power of acceptance; to do so it must reasonably appear from the price quote that assent to the quote is all that is needed to ripen the offer into a contract.' Factors relevant in determining whether a price quotation is an offer include the extent of prior inquiry, the completeness of the terms of the suggested bargain, and the number of persons to whom the price quotation is communicated." The court concluded that the quotation included sufficient terms to constitute an offer. Although the communication on 7/29 said home office approval was necessary, that approval was given on 9/12 in a communication that the court understood to be asking for Nordyne's acceptance of its offer, which Nordyne did on 9/15.

§ 2.1.1. Advertisements and Rewards as Offers

Whether advertisements—communications to the public—constitute legally effective offers (whether an offeree can create a contract by saying "yes" to accept) has posed challenging questions for applying contract doctrines developed with one-on-one bargaining in mind. The traditional view of advertisements was that they are generally not offers, based on one or more of the following rationales:

- An advertisement is best understood not as a promise to sell but as a general promotion or a statement of present intent or an invitation for customers to come in and begin a bargaining process.

- An advertisement usually does not specify any quantity and so could be for any quantity for each customer.

- An advertisement usually does not limit the number of possible contracting partners and so cannot reasonably be understood as a commitment to any specific recipients.

- Advertisements often omit essential terms or leave them uncertain.

- Advertisements are sometimes "too good to be true" or otherwise too promotional to be reasonably considered a commitment.

Public promises of rewards have some of the same characteristics as advertisements but present slightly different issues when determining whether they constitute offers. The two cases in this section wrestle with when an offer can arise from an advertisement or a public promise of a reward.

Reading Critically: *Lefkowitz*

1. The court considers two advertisements in this case. Was each one an offer? If not, why not? If so, what did each ad require for acceptance?

2. What rule defining offers can you extract from this case?

3. What role did the objective test play in this case?

4. Why wasn't the "house rule" effective? What could the store have done to make it effective?

5. In light of the result and analysis in *Lefkowitz*, look at some newspaper or internet advertisements. Which ones might be considered offers? Which would not?

Lefkowitz v. Great Minneapolis Surplus Store, Inc.

MORRIS LEFKOWITZ, Plaintiff-Respondent

v.

GREAT MINNEAPOLIS SURPLUS STORE, INC., Defendant-Appellant

Supreme Court of Minnesota
86 N.W.2d 689 (Minn. 1957)

MURPHY, JUSTICE.

This is an appeal from an order of the Municipal Court of Minneapolis denying the motion of the defendant for amended findings of fact, or, in the alternative, for a new trial. The order for judgment awarded the plaintiff the sum of $138.50 as damages for breach of contract.

This case grows out of the alleged refusal of the defendant to sell to the plaintiff a certain fur piece which it had offered for sale in a newspaper advertisement. It appears from the record that on April 6, 1956, the defendant published the following advertisement in a Minneapolis newspaper:

"Saturday 9 A.M. Sharp 3 Brand New Fur Coats Worth to $100.00
First Come First Served $1 Each"

On April 13, the defendant again published an advertisement in the same newspaper as follows:

"Saturday 9 A.M. 2 Brand New Pastel Mink 3-Skin Scarfs Selling for $89.50
Out they go Saturday. Each . . . $1.00
1 Black Lapin Stole [. . .] Beautiful, worth $139.50 . . . $1.00
First Come First Served"

The record supports the findings of the court that on each of the Saturdays following the publication of the above-described ads the plaintiff was the first to present himself at the appropriate counter in the defendant's store and on each occasion demanded the coat and the stole so advertised and indicated his readiness to pay the sale price of $1. On both occasions, the defendant refused to sell the merchandise to the plaintiff, stating on the first occasion that by a "house rule" the offer was intended for women only and sales would not be made to men, and on the second visit that plaintiff knew defendant's house rules.

The trial court properly disallowed plaintiff's claim for the value of the fur coats since the value of these articles was speculative and uncertain. The only evidence of value was the advertisement itself to the effect that the coats were "Worth to $100.00," how much less being speculative especially in view of the price for which they were offered for sale. With reference to the offer of the defendant on April 13, 1956, to sell the "1 Black Lapin Stole . . . worth $139.50 . . ." the trial court held that the value of this article was established and granted judgment in favor of the plaintiff for that amount less the $1 quoted purchase price.

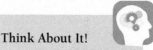

Think About It!

As reflected in the court's disallowance of the plaintiff's first claim, damages will not be awarded if the amount is speculative or cannot be proven with reasonable certainty. See Chapter 10. Could the plaintiff have proven certain-enough damages in Leftowitz?

The defendant contends that a newspaper advertisement offering items of merchandise for sale at a named price is a "unilateral offer" which may be withdrawn without notice. He relies upon authorities which hold that, where an advertiser publishes in a newspaper that he has a certain quantity or quality of goods which he wants to dispose of at certain prices and on certain terms, such advertisements are not offers which become contracts as soon as any person to whose notice they may come signifies his acceptance by notifying the other that he will take a certain quantity of them. Such advertisements have been construed as an invitation for an offer of sale on the terms stated, which offer, when received, may be accepted or rejected and which therefore does not become a contract of sale until accepted by the seller; and until a contract has been so made, the seller may modify or revoke such prices or terms. Montgomery Ward & Co. v. Johnson, 209 Mass. 89, 95 N.E. 290; . . . Craft v. Elder & Johnson Co., 38 N.E.2d 416, 34 . . . .

. . . . On the facts before us we are concerned with whether the advertisement constituted an offer, and, if so, whether the plaintiff's conduct constituted an acceptance.

There are numerous authorities which hold that a particular advertisement in a newspaper or circular letter relating to a sale of articles may be construed by the court as constituting an offer, acceptance of which would complete a contract. J. E. Pinkham Lumber Co. v. C. W. Griffin & Co., 212 Ala. 341, 102 So. 689 . . . .

The test of whether a binding obligation may originate in advertisements addressed to the general public is 'whether the facts show that some performance was promised in positive terms in return for something requested.' 1 Williston, Contracts (Rev. ed.) § 27.

See It

The following advertisements, courtesy of the Minnesota Historical Society, were the subject of the *Lefkowitz* case. In the first advertisement, the three fur coats appear under "Saturday." In the second advertisement, the two mink scarves and the black lapin stole appear in the middle circle, under "Dollar." Elsewhere in both ads, "6 Cocker Spaniel puppies" are free "to the first boys or girls accompanied by their parents."

The authorities above cited emphasize that, where the offer is clear, definite, and explicit, and leaves nothing open for negotiation, it constitutes an offer, acceptance of which will complete the contract. The most recent case on the subject is Johnson v. Capital City Ford Co., La. App., 85 So.2d 75, in which the court pointed out that a newspaper advertisement relating to the purchase and sale of automobiles may constitute an offer, acceptance of which will consummate a contract and create an obligation in the offeror to perform according to the terms of the published offer.

Whether in any individual instance a newspaper advertisement is an offer rather than an invitation to make an offer depends on the legal intention of the parties and the surrounding circumstances. Annotation, 157 A.L.R. 744, 751 . . . . We are of the view on the facts before us that the offer by the defendant of the sale of the Lapin fur was clear, definite, and explicit, and left nothing open for negotiation. The plaintiff[,] having successful[ly] managed to be the first one to appear at the seller's place of business to be served, as requested by the advertisement, and having offered the stated purchase price of the article, . . . was entitled to performance on the part of the defendant. We think the trial court was correct in holding that there was in the conduct of the parties a sufficient mutuality of obligation to constitute a contract of sale.

Think About It!

What do you think the court means when it refers to the "legal intention" of the parties? What evidence would be relevant to prove that intention?

This case and others state that an offer must be "clear, definite, and explicit, and [leave] nothing open for negotiation." That does not mean the offeror would refuse to negotiate, just that absolutely essential terms are stated and need not be negotiated before a contract can be agreed to. Recall, too, that a court can fill in some missing terms if it first concludes there is sufficient certainty to create a contract.

The defendant contends that the offer was modified by a 'house rule' to the effect that only women were qualified to receive the bargains advertised. The advertisement contained no such restriction. This objection may be disposed of briefly by stating that, while an advertiser has the right at any time before acceptance to modify his offer, he does not have the right, after acceptance, to impose new or arbitrary conditions not contained in the published offer. Payne v. Lautz Bros. & Co., City Ct., 166 N.Y.S. 844, 848 . . . .

Affirmed.

Make the Connection

Notice that the buyer accepted the offer here by engaging in the conduct specified in the offer. An offer to be accepted by performance is called an "offer for a unilateral contract." If instead the offer had called for acceptance by a return promise, then it would be an "offer for a bilateral contract." The bilateral aspect of the contract is the offeror's expectation that the offer will be accepted by a reciprocal promise rather than by a reciprocal performance. This distinction is covered more thoroughly later in this chapter (page 117).

Reading Critically: *Leonard*

1. The court discusses both advertisement and reward cases. How does the law treat these two categories of communications differently and similarly, in defining what is an offer?

2. What additional rules defining offers does this case add to your understanding?

3. What role does the objective test play in this case?

Leonard v. PepsiCo

JOHN D.R. LEONARD, Plaintiff

v.

PEPSICO, INC., Defendant

Southern District of New York
88 F. Supp. 2d 116 (S.D.N.Y. 1999),
aff'd on same grounds, 210 F.3d 88 (2d Cir. 2000)

KIMBA M. WOOD, DISTRICT JUDGE.

Plaintiff brought this action seeking, among other things, specific performance of an alleged offer of a Harrier Jet, featured in a television advertisement for defendant's "Pepsi Stuff" promotion. Defendant has moved for summary judgment pursuant to Federal Rule of Civil Procedure 56. For the reasons stated below, defendant's motion is granted.

I. Background

This case arises out of a promotional campaign conducted by defendant, the producer and distributor of the soft drinks Pepsi and Diet Pepsi. The promotion, entitled "Pepsi Stuff," encouraged consumers to collect "Pepsi Points" from specially marked packages of Pepsi or Diet Pepsi and redeem these points for merchandise featuring the Pepsi logo. Before introducing the promotion nationally, defendant conducted a test of the promotion in the Pacific Northwest from October 1995 to March 1996. A Pepsi Stuff catalog was distributed to consumers in the test market, including Washington State. Plaintiff is a resident of Seattle, Washington. While living in Seattle, plaintiff saw the Pepsi Stuff commercial that he contends constituted an offer of a Harrier Jet.

A. The Alleged Offer

Because whether the television commercial constituted an offer is the central question in this case, the Court will describe the commercial in detail. The commercial opens upon an idyllic, suburban morning, where the chirping of birds in sun-dappled trees welcomes a paperboy on his morning route. As the newspaper hits the stoop of a conventional two-story house, the tattoo of a military drum introduces the subtitle, "MONDAY 7:58 AM." The stirring strains of a martial air mark the appearance of a well-coiffed teenager preparing to leave for school, dressed in a shirt emblazoned with the Pepsi logo, a red-white-and-blue ball. While the teenager confidently preens, the military drumroll again sounds as the subtitle "T-SHIRT 75 PEPSI POINTS" scrolls across the screen. Bursting from his room, the teenager strides down the hallway wearing a leather jacket. The drumroll sounds again, as the subtitle "LEATHER JACKET 1450 PEPSI POINTS" appears. The teenager opens the door of his house and, unfazed by the glare of the early morning sunshine, puts on a pair of sunglasses. The drumroll then accompanies the subtitle "SHADES 175 PEPSI POINTS." A voiceover then intones, "Introducing the new Pepsi Stuff catalog," as the camera focuses on the cover of the catalog.[2]

Go Online!

You can view the original commercial and a modified version on YouTube.

The scene then shifts to three young boys sitting in front of a high school building. The boy in the middle is intent on his Pepsi Stuff Catalog, while the boys on either side are each drinking Pepsi. The three boys gaze in awe at an object rushing overhead, as the military march builds to a crescendo. The Harrier Jet is not yet visible, but the observer senses the presence of a mighty plane as the extreme winds generated by its flight create a paper maelstrom in a classroom devoted to an otherwise dull physics lesson. Finally, the Harrier Jet swings into view and lands by the side of the school building, next to a bicycle rack. Several students run for cover, and the velocity of the wind strips one hapless faculty member down to his underwear. While the faculty member is being deprived of his dignity, the voiceover announces: "Now the more Pepsi you drink, the more great stuff you're gonna get."

The teenager opens the cockpit of the fighter and can be seen, helmetless, holding a Pepsi. "[L]ooking very pleased with himself," (Pl. Mem. at 3,) the teenager exclaims, "Sure beats the bus," and chortles. The military drumroll sounds a final time, as the following words appear: "HARRIER FIGHTER 7,000,000 PEPSI POINTS." A few seconds later, the following appears in more stylized script: "Drink

---

2   At this point, the following message appears at the bottom of the screen: "Offer not available in all areas. See details on specially marked packages."

Pepsi—Get Stuff." With that message, the music and the commercial end with a triumphant flourish.

Inspired by this commercial, plaintiff set out to obtain a Harrier Jet. Plaintiff explains that he is "typical of the 'Pepsi Generation'" . . . he is young, has an adventurous spirit, and the notion of obtaining a Harrier Jet appealed to him enormously." Plaintiff consulted the Pepsi Stuff Catalog. The Catalog features youths dressed in Pepsi Stuff regalia or enjoying Pepsi Stuff accessories, such as "Blue Shades" ("As if you need another reason to look forward to sunny days."), "Pepsi Tees" ("Live in 'em. Laugh in 'em. Get in 'em."), "Bag of Balls" ("Three balls. One bag. No rules."), and "Pepsi Phone Card" ("Call your mom!"). The Catalog specifies the number of Pepsi Points required to obtain promotional merchandise. The Catalog includes an Order Form which lists, on one side, fifty-three items of Pepsi Stuff merchandise redeemable for Pepsi Points. Conspicuously absent from the Order Form is any entry or description of a Harrier Jet. The amount of Pepsi Points required to obtain the listed merchandise ranges from 15 (for a "Jacket Tattoo" ("Sew 'em on your jacket, not your arm.")) to 3300 (for a "Fila Mountain Bike" ("Rugged. All-terrain. Exclusively for Pepsi.")). It should be noted that plaintiff objects to the implication that because an item was not shown in the Catalog, it was unavailable.

The rear foldout pages of the Catalog contain directions for redeeming Pepsi Points for merchandise. These directions note that merchandise may be ordered "only" with the original Order Form. The Catalog notes that in the event that a consumer lacks enough Pepsi Points to obtain a desired item, additional Pepsi Points may be purchased for ten cents each; however, at least fifteen original Pepsi Points must accompany each order.

Although plaintiff initially set out to collect 7,000,000 Pepsi Points by consuming Pepsi products, it soon became clear to him that he "would not be able to buy (let alone drink) enough Pepsi to collect the necessary Pepsi Points fast enough." Reevaluating his strategy, plaintiff "focused for the first time on the packaging materials in the Pepsi Stuff promotion," and realized that buying Pepsi Points would be a more promising option. Through acquaintances, plaintiff ultimately raised about $700,000.

B. Plaintiff's Efforts to Redeem the Alleged Offer

On or about March 27, 1996, plaintiff submitted an Order Form, fifteen original Pepsi Points, and a check for $700,008.50. Plaintiff appears to have been represented by counsel at the time he mailed his check; the check is drawn on an account of plaintiff's first set of attorneys. At the bottom of the Order Form, plaintiff wrote in "1 Harrier Jet" in the "Item" column and "7,000,000" in the

"Total Points" column. In a letter accompanying his submission, plaintiff stated that the check was to purchase additional Pepsi Points "expressly for obtaining a new Harrier jet as advertised in your Pepsi Stuff commercial."

On or about May 7, 1996, defendant's fulfillment house rejected plaintiff's submission and returned the check, explaining that:

> The item that you have requested is not part of the Pepsi Stuff collection. It is not included in the catalogue or on the order form, and only catalogue merchandise can be redeemed under this program.

> The Harrier jet in the Pepsi commercial is fanciful and is simply included to create a humorous and entertaining ad. We apologize for any misunderstanding or confusion that you may have experienced and are enclosing some free product coupons for your use.

Plaintiff's previous counsel responded on or about May 14, 1996, as follows:

> Your letter of May 7, 1996 is totally unacceptable. We have reviewed the video tape of the Pepsi Stuff commercial . . . and it clearly offers the new Harrier jet for 7,000,000 Pepsi Points. Our client followed your rules explicitly . . . .

> This is a formal demand that you honor your commitment and make immediate arrangements to transfer the new Harrier jet to our client. If we do not receive transfer instructions within ten (10) business days of the date of this letter you will leave us no choice but to file an appropriate action against Pepsi . . . .

This letter was apparently sent onward to the advertising company responsible for the actual commercial, BBDO New York ("BBDO"). In a letter dated May 30, 1996, BBDO Vice President Raymond E. McGovern, Jr., explained to plaintiff that:

> I find it hard to believe that you are of the opinion that the Pepsi Stuff commercial ("Commercial") really offers a new Harrier Jet. The use of the Jet was clearly a joke that was meant to make the Commercial more humorous and entertaining. In my opinion, no reasonable person would agree with your analysis of the Commercial.

On or about June 17, 1996, plaintiff mailed a similar demand letter to defendant.

Litigation of this case initially involved two lawsuits, the first a declaratory judgment action brought by PepsiCo in this district . . . , and the second an action brought by Leonard in Florida state court . . . . PepsiCo brought suit in this Court . . . seeking a declaratory judgment stating that it had no obligation to furnish plaintiff with a Harrier Jet. . . . . In response . . ., Leonard brought suit in Florida state court . . . , although this case had nothing to do with Florida. That suit was removed to the Southern District of Florida. . . [and then] transferred to this Court . . . .

. . . . PepsiCo moved for summary judgment pursuant to Federal Rule of Civil Procedure 56. The present motion . . . follows three years of jurisdictional and procedural wrangling.

II. Discussion

A. The Legal Framework

1. Standard for Summary Judgment

On a motion for summary judgment, a court "cannot try issues of fact; it can only determine whether there are issues to be tried." Donahue v. Windsor Locks Bd. of Fire Comm'rs, 834 F.2d 54, 58 (2d Cir.1987) . . . . The party seeking summary judgment "bears the initial responsibility of informing the district court of the basis for its motion," which includes identifying the materials in the record that "it believes demonstrate the absence of a genuine issue of material fact." Celotex Corp., 477 U.S. at 323, 106 S.Ct. 2548.

. . . . Although a court considering a motion for summary judgment must view all evidence in the light most favorable to the non-moving party, and must draw all reasonable inferences in that party's favor, see Consarc Corp. v. Marine Midland Bank, N.A., 996 F.2d 568, 572 (2d Cir.1993), the nonmoving party "must do more than simply show that there is some metaphysical doubt as to the material facts." Matsushita Elec. Indus. Co. v. Zenith Radio Corp., 475 U.S. 574, 586 (1986). If, based on the submissions to the court, no rational fact-finder could find in the non-movant's favor, there is no genuine issue of material fact, and summary judgment is appropriate. See Anderson, 477 U.S. at 250.

. . . . "Summary judgment is proper when the 'words and actions that allegedly formed a contract [are] so clear themselves that reasonable people could not differ over their meaning.' " Krumme v. Westpoint Stevens, Inc., 143 F.3d 71, 83 (2d Cir.1998) . . . ; see also Wards Co. v. Stamford Ridgeway Assocs., 761 F.2d 117, 120 (2d Cir.1985) (summary judgment is appropriate in contract case where interpretation urged by non-moving party is not "fairly reasonable"). . . .

2. Choice of Law

. . . . Because this action was transferred from Florida, the choice of law rules of Florida, the transferor state, apply. See Ferens v. John Deere Co., 494 U.S. 516,

523–33, 110 S.Ct. 1274, 108 L.Ed.2d 443 (1990). Under Florida law, the choice of law in a contract case is determined by the place "where the last act necessary to complete the contract is done." Jemco, Inc. v. United Parcel Serv., Inc., 400 So.2d 499, 500–01 (Fla.Dist.Ct.App.1981) . . . .

The parties disagree as to whether the contract could have been completed by plaintiff's filling out the Order Form to request a Harrier Jet, or by defendant's acceptance of the Order Form. If the commercial constituted an offer, then the last act necessary to complete the contract would be plaintiff's acceptance, in the state of Washington. If the commercial constituted a solicitation to receive offers, then the last act necessary to complete the contract would be defendant's acceptance of plaintiff's Order Form, in the state of New York. The choice of law question cannot, therefore, be resolved until after the Court determines whether the commercial was an offer or not. The Court agrees with both parties that resolution of this issue requires consideration of principles of contract law that are not limited to the law of any one state. Most of the cases cited by the parties are not from New York courts. As plaintiff suggests, the questions presented by this case implicate questions of contract law "deeply ingrained in the common law of England and the States of the Union."

B. Defendant's Advertisement Was Not an Offer

1. Advertisements as Offers

The general rule is that an advertisement does not constitute an offer. The Restatement (Second) of Contracts explains that:

> Advertisements of goods by display, sign, handbill, newspaper, radio or television are not ordinarily intended or understood as offers to sell. The same is true of catalogues, price lists and circulars, even though the terms of suggested bargains may be stated in some detail. It is of course possible to make an offer by an advertisement directed to the general public (see § 29), but there must ordinarily be some language of commitment or some invitation to take action without further communication.

Restatement (Second) of Contracts § 26 cmt. b (1979). Similarly, a leading treatise notes that:

> It is quite possible to make a definite and operative offer to buy or sell goods by advertisement, in a newspaper, by a handbill, a catalog or circular or on a placard in a store window. It is not customary to do this, however; and the presumption is the other way. . . . Such advertisements are understood to be mere requests to consider and examine and negotiate; and no one can reasonably regard them as

otherwise unless the circumstances are exceptional and the words used are very plain and clear.

1 Arthur Linton Corbin & Joseph M. Perillo, Corbin on Contracts § 2.4, at 116–17 (rev. ed.1993) . . . . New York courts adhere to this general principle. See Lovett v. Frederick Loeser & Co., 124 Misc. 81, 207 N.Y.S. 753, 755 (N.Y.Mun.Ct.1924) (noting that an "advertisement is nothing but an invitation to enter into negotiations, and is not an offer which may be turned into a contract by a person who signifies his intention to purchase some of the articles mentioned in the advertisement") . . . .

An advertisement is not transformed into an enforceable offer merely by a potential offeree's expression of willingness to accept the offer through, among other means, completion of an order form. . . . . See . . . Alligood v. Procter & Gamble, 72 Ohio App.3d 309, 594 N.E.2d 668 (1991) (finding that no offer was made in promotional campaign for baby diapers, in which consumers were to redeem teddy bear proof-of-purchase symbols for catalog merchandise); Chang v. First Colonial Savings Bank, 242 Va. 388, 410 S.E.2d 928 (1991) (newspaper advertisement for bank settled the terms of the offer once bank accepted plaintiffs' deposit, notwithstanding bank's subsequent effort to amend the terms of the offer). Under these principles, plaintiff's letter of March 27, 1996, with the Order Form and the appropriate number of Pepsi Points, constituted the offer. There would be no enforceable contract until defendant accepted the Order Form and cashed the check.

The exception to the rule that advertisements do not create any power of acceptance in potential offerees is where the advertisement is "clear, definite, and explicit, and leaves nothing open for negotiation"; in that circumstance, "it constitutes an offer, acceptance of which will complete the contract." Lefkowitz v. Great Minneapolis Surplus Store, 251 Minn. 188, 86 N.W.2d 689, 691 (1957). . . .

The present case is distinguishable from Lefkowitz. First, the commercial cannot be regarded in itself as sufficiently definite, because it specifically reserved the details of the offer to a separate writing, the Catalog.[6] The commercial itself made no mention of the steps a potential offeree would be required to take to accept the alleged offer of a Harrier Jet. The advertisement in Lefkowitz, in contrast, "identified the person who could accept." Corbin, supra, § 2.4, at 119. See generally United States v. Braunstein, 75 F.Supp. 137, 139 (S.D.N.Y.1947) ("Greater precision of expression may be required, and less help from the court given, when the parties are merely at the threshold of a contract."); Farnsworth, supra, at 239 ("The fact that a proposal is very detailed suggests that

---

[6]   It also communicated additional words of reservation: "Offer not available in all areas. See details on specially marked packages."

it is an offer, while omission of many terms suggests that it is not."). Second, even if the Catalog had included a Harrier Jet among the items that could be obtained by redemption of Pepsi Points, the advertisement of a Harrier Jet by both television commercial and catalog would still not constitute an offer. . . . the absence of any words of limitation such as "first come, first served," renders the alleged offer sufficiently indefinite that no contract could be formed. . . . "A customer would not usually have reason to believe that the shopkeeper intended exposure to the risk of a multitude of acceptances resulting in a number of contracts exceeding the shopkeeper's inventory." Farnsworth, supra, at 242. There was no such danger in Lefkowitz, owing to the limitation "first come, first served."

The Court finds, in sum, that the Harrier Jet commercial was merely an advertisement. The Court now turns to the line of cases upon which plaintiff rests much of his argument.

2. Rewards as Offers

In opposing the present motion, plaintiff largely relies on a different species of unilateral offer, involving public offers of a reward for performance of a specified act. Because these cases generally involve public declarations regarding the efficacy or trustworthiness of specific products, one court has aptly characterized these authorities as "prove me wrong" cases. See Rosenthal v. Al Packer Ford, 36 Md.App. 349, 374 A.2d 377, 380 (1977). The most venerable of these precedents is the case of Carlill v. Carbolic Smoke Ball Co., [1893] 1 Q.B. 256 [, 1892 WL 9612] (Court of Appeal, 1892), a quote from which heads plaintiff's memorandum of law: "[I]f a person chooses to make extravagant promises . . . he probably does so because it pays him to make them, and, if he has made them, the extravagance of the promises is no reason in law why he should not be bound by them." Carbolic Smoke Ball, 1 Q.B. at 268 (Bowen, L.J.).

Long a staple of law school curricula, Carbolic Smoke Ball owes its fame not merely to "the comic and slightly mysterious object involved," A.W. Brian Simpson. Quackery and Contract Law: Carlill v. Carbolic Smoke Ball Company (1893), in Leading Cases in the Common Law 259, 281 (1995), but also to its role in developing the law of unilateral offers. The case arose during the London influenza epidemic of the 1890s. Among other advertisements of the time, for Clarke's World Famous Blood Mixture, Towle's Pennyroyal and Steel Pills for Females, Sequah's Prairie Flower, and Epp's Glycerine Jube-Jubes . . . appeared solicitations for the Carbolic Smoke Ball. The specific advertisement that Mrs. Carlill saw, and relied upon, read as follows:

> 100£ reward will be paid by the Carbolic Smoke Ball Company to any person who contracts the increasing epidemic influenza, colds, or any diseases caused by taking cold, after having used the ball three times

daily for two weeks according to the printed directions supplied with each ball. 1000£ is deposited with the Alliance Bank, Regent Street, [showing] our sincerity in the matter.

During the last epidemic of influenza many thousand carbolic smoke balls were sold as preventives against this disease, and in no ascertained case was the disease contracted by those using the carbolic smoke ball.

Carbolic Smoke Ball, 1 Q.B. at 256–57. "On the faith of this advertisement,". . . Mrs. Carlill purchased the smoke ball and used it as directed, but contracted influenza nevertheless.[8] The lower court held that she was entitled to recover the promised reward.

Affirming the lower court's decision, Lord Justice Lindley began by noting that the advertisement was an express promise to pay £100 in the event that a consumer of the Carbolic Smoke Ball was stricken with influenza. . . . The advertisement was construed as offering a reward because it sought to induce performance, unlike an invitation to negotiate, which seeks a reciprocal promise. . . . "[A]dvertisements offering rewards . . . are offers to anybody who performs the conditions named in the advertisement, and anybody who does perform the condition accepts the offer.". . .[9] Because Mrs. Carlill had complied with the terms of the offer, yet contracted influenza, she was entitled to £100.

Like Carbolic Smoke Ball, the decisions relied upon by plaintiff involve offers of reward. In Barnes v. Treece, 15 Wash.App. 437, 549 P.2d 1152 (1976), for example, the vice-president of a punchboard distributor, in the course of hearings before the Washington State Gambling Commission, asserted that, " 'I'll put a hundred thousand dollars to anyone to find a crooked board. If they find it, I'll pay it.' " Id. at 1154. Plaintiff, a former bartender, heard of the offer and located

---

[8]   Although the Court of Appeals's opinion is silent as to exactly what a carbolic smoke ball was, the historical record reveals it to have been a compressible hollow ball, about the size of an apple or orange, with a small opening covered by some porous material such as silk or gauze. The ball was partially filled with carbolic acid in powder form. When the ball was squeezed, the powder would be forced through the opening as a small cloud of smoke. . . . At the time, carbolic acid was considered fatal if consumed in more than small amounts. . . .

[9]   Carbolic Smoke Ball includes a classic formulation of this principle: "If I advertise to the world that my dog is lost, and that anybody who brings the dog to a particular place will be paid some money, are all the police or other persons whose business it is to find lost dogs to be expected to sit down and write a note saying that they have accepted my proposal?" Carbolic Smoke Ball, 1 Q.B. at 270 (Bowen, L.J.).

two crooked punchboards. Defendant, after reiterating that the offer was serious, providing plaintiff with a receipt for the punchboard on company stationery, and assuring plaintiff that the reward was being held in escrow, nevertheless repudiated the offer. . . . The court ruled that the offer was valid and that plaintiff was entitled to his reward. . . . The plaintiff in this case also cites cases involving prizes for skill (or luck) in the game of golf. See Las Vegas Hacienda v. Gibson, 77 Nev. 25, 359 P.2d 85 (1961) (awarding $5,000 to plaintiff, who successfully shot a hole-in-one); see also Grove v. Charbonneau Buick-Pontiac, Inc., 240 N.W.2d 853 (N.D.1976) (awarding automobile to plaintiff, who successfully shot a hole-in-one).

Other "reward" cases underscore the distinction between typical advertisements, in which the alleged offer is merely an invitation to negotiate for purchase of commercial goods, and promises of reward, in which the alleged offer is intended to induce a potential offeree to perform a specific action, often for noncommercial reasons. In Newman v. Schiff, 778 F.2d 460 (8th Cir.1985), for example, the Fifth Circuit held that a tax protestor's assertion that, "If anybody calls this show . . . and cites any section of the code that says an individual is required to file a tax return, I'll pay them $100,000," would have been an enforceable offer had the plaintiff called the television show to claim the reward while the tax protestor was appearing. . . . The court noted that, like Carbolic Smoke Ball, the case

Make the Connection

In §§ 2.4 & 2.5, this chapter discusses occurrences that terminate an offeree's power to accept an offer. One such occurrence is the lapse of the offer after a stated or reasonable time. In the cited case of *Newman v. Schiff*, the court seems to have concluded that an offer made during a TV show lapsed at the end of the show.

"concerns a special type of offer: an offer for a reward.". . . James v. Turilli, 473 S.W.2d 757 (Mo.Ct.App.1971), arose from a boast by defendant that the "notorious Missouri desperado" Jesse James had not been killed in 1882, as portrayed in song and legend, but had lived under the alias "J. Frank Dalton" at the "Jesse James Museum" operated by none other than defendant. Defendant offered $10,000 "to anyone who could prove me wrong.". . . The widow of the outlaw's son demonstrated, at trial, that the outlaw had in fact been killed in 1882. On appeal, the court held that defendant should be liable to pay the amount offered. . . .

In the present case, the Harrier Jet commercial did not direct that anyone who appeared at Pepsi headquarters with 7,000,000 Pepsi Points on the Fourth of July would receive a Harrier Jet. Instead, the commercial urged consumers to accumulate Pepsi Points and to refer to the Catalog to determine how they could redeem their Pepsi Points. The commercial sought a reciprocal promise, expressed through acceptance of, and compliance with, the terms of the Order Form. As noted previously, the Catalog contains no mention of the Harrier Jet. Plaintiff states that he "noted that the Harrier Jet was not among the items described in the catalog, but this did not affect [his] understanding of the offer." It should have.[10]

. . . . Because the alleged offer in this case was, at most, an advertisement to receive offers rather than an offer of reward, plaintiff cannot show that there was an offer made in the circumstances of this case.

C. An Objective, Reasonable Person Would Not Have Considered the Commercial an Offer

Plaintiff's understanding of the commercial as an offer must also be rejected because the Court finds that no objective person could reasonably have concluded that the commercial actually offered consumers a Harrier Jet.

1. Objective Reasonable Person Standard

In evaluating the commercial, the Court must not consider defendant's subjective intent in making the commercial, or plaintiff's subjective view of what the commercial offered, but what an objective, reasonable person would have understood the commercial to convey. See . . . Mesaros, 845 F.2d at 1581 ("A basic rule of contracts holds that whether an offer has been made depends on the objective reasonableness of the alleged offeree's belief that the advertisement or solicitation was intended as an offer.") . . . .

> If it is clear that an offer was not serious, then no offer has been made:

> What kind of act creates a power of acceptance and is therefore an offer? It must be an expression of will or intention. It must be an act that leads the offeree reasonably to conclude that a power to create a contract is conferred. This applies to the content of the power as well as to the fact of its existence. It is on this ground that we must exclude invitations to deal or acts of mere preliminary negotiation, and acts evidently done in jest or without intent to create legal relations.

Corbin on Contracts, § 1.11 at 30 . . . . An obvious joke, of course, would not give rise to a contract. . . . On the other hand, if there is no indication that the offer is "evidently in jest," and that an objective, reasonable person would find that the offer was serious, then there may be a valid offer. See . . . Lucy v. Zehmer, 196 Va. 493, 84 S.E.2d 516, 518, 520 (1954) (ordering specific performance of a

---

[10] In his affidavit, plaintiff places great emphasis on a press release written by defendant, which characterizes the Harrier Jet as "the ultimate Pepsi Stuff award." Plaintiff simply ignores the remainder of the release, which makes no mention of the Harrier Jet even as it sets forth in detail the number of points needed to redeem other merchandise.

contract to purchase a farm despite defendant's protestation that the transaction was done in jest as " 'just a bunch of two doggoned drunks bluffing' ").

. . . .

3. Whether the Commercial Was "Evidently Done In Jest"

Plaintiff's insistence that the commercial appears to be a serious offer requires the Court to explain why the commercial is funny. Explaining why a joke is funny is a daunting task; as the essayist E.B. White has remarked, "Humor can be dissected, as a frog can, but the thing dies in the process . . . ."[11] The commercial is the embodiment of what defendant appropriately characterizes as "zany humor."

First, the commercial suggests, as commercials often do, that use of the advertised product will transform what, for most youth, can be a fairly routine and ordinary experience. The military tattoo and stirring martial music, as well as the use of subtitles in a Courier font that scroll terse messages across the screen, such as "MONDAY 7:58 AM," evoke military and espionage thrillers. The implication of the commercial is that Pepsi Stuff merchandise will inject drama and moment into hitherto unexceptional lives.

What's That?

"Puffing" or "puffery" is a statement that the recipient has reason to know is intended to promote a product and is not intended to accurately state a fact or reliably state a promise. In the context in the cited case, the issue is whether the manufacturer's statement was indeed a warranty about the car's quality or was instead "puffery" and therefore not actionable by the eventual buyer.

The commercial in this case thus makes the exaggerated claims similar to those of many television advertisements: that by consuming the featured clothing, car, beer, or potato chips, one will become attractive, stylish, desirable, and admired by all. A reasonable viewer would understand such advertisements as mere puffery, not as statements of fact, see, e.g., Hubbard v. General Motors Corp., 95 Civ. 4362(AGS), 1996 WL 274018, at *6 (S.D.N.Y. May 22, 1996) (advertisement describing automobile as "Like a Rock," was mere puffery, not a warranty of quality) . . . and refrain from interpreting the promises of the commercial as being literally true.

Second, the callow youth featured in the commercial is a highly improbable pilot, one who could barely be trusted with the keys to his parents' car, much less the prize aircraft of the United States Marine Corps. Rather than checking the fuel gauges on his aircraft, the teenager spends his precious preflight minutes preening. The youth's concern for his coiffure appears to extend to his flying without a helmet. Finally, the teenager's comment that flying a Harrier Jet to school

---

[11] Quoted in Gerald R. Ford, *Humor and the Presidency* 23 (1987).

"sure beats the bus" evinces an improbably insouciant attitude toward the relative difficulty and danger of piloting a fighter plane in a residential area, as opposed to taking public transportation.

Third, the notion of traveling to school in a Harrier Jet is an exaggerated adolescent fantasy. In this commercial, the fantasy is underscored by how the teenager's schoolmates gape in admiration, ignoring their physics lesson. The force of the wind generated by the Harrier Jet blows off one teacher's clothes, literally defrocking an authority figure. As if to emphasize the fantastic quality of having a Harrier Jet arrive at school, the Jet lands next to a plebeian bike rack. This fantasy is, of course, extremely unrealistic. No school would provide landing space for a student's fighter jet, or condone the disruption the jet's use would cause.

FYI

According to www. snopes.com, in September 1997 the Pentagon declared that Harrier Jets cannot be sold in flyable condition, so the plaintiff could not have bought a flyable plane.

Fourth, the primary mission of a Harrier Jet, according to the United States Marine Corps, is to "attack and destroy surface targets under day and night visual conditions." United States Marine Corps, Factfile: AV-8B Harrier II (last modified Dec. 5, 1995) https://fas.org/man/dod-101/sys/ac/av-8.htm. Manufactured by McDonnell Douglas, the Harrier Jet played a significant role in the air offensive of Operation Desert Storm in 1991. . . . The jet is designed to carry a considerable armament load, including Sidewinder and Maverick missiles. See id. As one news report has noted, "Fully loaded, the Harrier can float like a butterfly and sting like a bee—albeit a roaring 14-ton butterfly and a bee with 9,200 pounds of bombs and missiles." Jerry Allegood, Marines Rely on Harrier Jet, Despite Critics, News & Observer (Raleigh), Nov. 4, 1990, at C1. In light of the Harrier Jet's well-documented function in attacking and destroying surface and air targets, armed reconnaissance and air interdiction, and offensive and defensive anti-aircraft warfare, depiction of such a jet as a way to get to school in the morning is clearly not serious even if, as plaintiff contends, the jet is capable of being acquired "in a form that eliminates [its] potential for military use."

Fifth, the number of Pepsi Points the commercial mentions as required to "purchase" the jet is 7,000,000. To amass that number of points, one would have to drink 7,000,000 Pepsis (or roughly 190 Pepsis a day for the next hundred years—an unlikely possibility), or one would have to purchase approximately $700,000 worth of Pepsi Points. The cost of a Harrier Jet is roughly $23 million dollars, a fact of which plaintiff was aware when he set out to gather the amount he believed necessary to accept the alleged offer. Even if an objective, reasonable person were not aware of this fact, he would conclude that purchasing a fighter plane for $700,000 is a deal too good to be true.[13]

Plaintiff argues that a reasonable, objective person would have understood the commercial to make a serious offer of a Harrier Jet because there was "absolutely no distinction in the manner" in which the items in the commercial were presented. Plaintiff also relies upon a press release highlighting the promotional campaign, issued by defendant, in which "[n]o mention is made by [defendant] of humor, or anything of the sort." These arguments suggest merely that the humor of the promotional campaign was tongue in cheek. Humor is not limited to what Justice Cardozo called "[t]he rough and boisterous joke . . . [that] evokes its own guffaws." Murphy v. Steeplechase Amusement Co., 250 N.Y. 479, 483, 166 N.E. 173, 174 (1929). In light of the obvious absurdity of the commercial, the Court rejects plaintiff's argument that the commercial was not clearly in jest. . . .

III. Conclusion

In sum, there are three reasons why plaintiff's demand cannot prevail as a matter of law. First, the commercial was merely an advertisement, not a[n] . . . offer. Second, the tongue-in-cheek attitude of the commercial would not cause a reasonable person to conclude that a soft drink company would be giving away fighter planes as part of a promotion. [Third reason pertaining to statute of frauds is omitted.]

For the reasons stated above, the Court grants defendant's motion for summary judgment. . . .

Think About It: Reconsidering the Presumption About Advertisements

In *Leonard v. Pepsico*, Judge Wood begins her reasoning with a paragraph of weighty authorities saying that "[t]he general rule is that an advertisement does not constitute an offer." She then quotes a Restatement comment that says advertisements are not "ordinarily" intended as offers to sell and that there "ordinarily" must be language of commitment to make an advertisement an offer.

---

[13] In contrast, the advertisers of the Carbolic Smoke Ball emphasized their earnestness, stating in the advertisement that "£1,000 is deposited with the Alliance Bank, [showing] our sincerity in the matter.". . .

Professor Jay Feinman argues that the "general rule" that an advertisement does not constitute an offer is inaccurate—that plenty of cases, including *Lefkowitz*, hold that a particular advertisement is an offer. Like all alleged offers, he says, advertisements should be judged on the circumstances—the certainty of the terms, the level of commitment, the means by which the accepting persons are selected from the members of the public receiving the advertisement, etc. Professor Feinman posits that advertisements-are-not-offers statements should be replaced by either (1) a presumption in favor of advertisements being offers or (2) no statement either way so that advertisements are examined in the same light as other alleged offers without any leaning one way or the other. Jay Feinman, *Is an Advertisement an Offer? Why It Is, and Why It Matters*, 58 Hastings L.J. 61 (2006).

According to Professor Melvin Eisenberg:

> *Lefkowitz* is open to several interpretations. It might be said that the advertisement was special because it involved foreseeable reliance—but so, really, does any other advertisement whose primary purpose is to induce customer response. Alternatively, it might be said that the advertisement in *Lefkowitz* was distinguishable from other advertisements on the ground that it stated the quantity available and the first-come-first-served method of allocating the quantity. However, it is implied in every advertisement that (only) a reasonable quantity is available and that the quantity will be allocated first come first served.

Melvin Aron Eisenberg, *Expression Rules in Contract Law and Problems of Offer and Acceptance,* 82 Cal. L. Rev. 1127, 1171 (1994).

Considering *Lefkowitz*, *Leonard*, and the commentaries by Eisenberg and Feinman, how do you think advertisements should be treated in determining whether an offer exists?

Look again at any advertisements you reviewed in response to Question 5 on page 76. Is your analysis of whether those advertisements are offers the same in light of *Leonard* and these commentaries?

Example F: *Augstein v. Leslie,* 2012 WL 4928914 (S.D.N.Y. Oct. 17, 2012).

In 2010, in Cologne, Germany, someone stole Rapper Ryan Leslie's backpack, containing his laptop, an external hard drive, jewelry, and cash.

Leslie posted a YouTube video saying he would pay $20,000 for return of the laptop, which contained unreleased music, rare concert footage, and Leslie's personal information. "I love coming to Germany and partying with you guys and sharing my music with you guys," Leslie said in the video. "So I am asking for your help, my laptop was stolen and I am offering $20,000 for the return. $20,000 is nothing compared to how valuable this laptop is to me." See the video at https://www.youtube.com/watch?v=YvVPjZ-wvkE. In a later Twitter post, Leslie reportedly raised the reward "for my intellectual property" to $1 million. About a month later, an auto-repair mechanic turned in the computer, saying he found it tucked in a garbage bag while walking his dog in a German forest. According to Leslie, the data on the laptop was corrupted, so Leslie would not pay the reward. The finder sued and filed a motion for summary judgment, seeking a ruling that the video was an enforceable offer for a reward, not an unenforceable advertisement, as claimed by Leslie.

Analysis: The court ruled that the statement was an enforceable reward, citing both *Leonard v. Pepsico* and *Carlill v. Carbolic Smoke Ball*. "Leslie . . . relies on the fact that the offer was conveyed over YouTube (a website where many advertisements and promotional videos are shared, along with any number of other types of video) to undermine the legitimacy of the offer. I do not find this reasoning persuasive. The forum for conveying the offer is not determinative, but rather, the question is whether a reasonable person would have understood that Leslie made an offer of a reward. I conclude that they would."

The jury later awarded $1.2 million to the plaintiff, the amount of the reward plus interest.

Problem: Advertisements and Rewards

3-1. On 8/23/17, the night before the Powerball lottery results were announced, a man posted (and then deleted) the following Tweet:

Hundreds of people retweeted the posting. If the poster had won the Powerball (he didn't), would his promise have been enforceable?

──────────

§ 2.1.2. Offers in the Commercial Bidding Process

Commercial bidding for contracts, either business-to-business or business-to-government, are governed by the general rules of offer and acceptance, supplemented by a regulatory or statutory framework when government contracts are involved. You will see cases involving commercial bidding in numerous places in this textbook. To apply the general rules about assent to those communications, you need a working understanding of how the bidding process works, as well as knowledge about the types of communications used in the bidding process.

Typical communications in a bidding process may involve one or more of the following types of documents:

- A **Request for Information (RFI)** is a screening and information-gathering device. A buyer either publishes the RFI or sends it to a limited number of preselected providers of the goods and services sought. The request states the general goals of the project and invites providers to describe their capabilities and skills as related to these goals. The providers' responses to the RFI allow the buyer to compare providers and to send information about "next steps" to them. An RFI is unlikely to be an offer because it is mainly a request for providers to submit general information about their suitability for the project. There is no discussion of terms such as price, dates, etc. that would suggest an expression of an offer.

- A **Request for Proposal (RFP)** is sent to providers who match the buyer's needs and who may have been identified from responses to an RFI. The RFP usually presents a specific set of requirements and goals (more specific than those in an RFI) and allows each candidate to suggest a solution based on its own creativity, skills, and resources. Again, there is no expression of an intent to enter into a binding contract, so it is unlikely to be an offer.

- A **Request for Quotations (RFQ)** states a non-negotiable desired service or product, the parameters and requirements of the product, and the rules for submitting qualified bids. It may be used after an RFI and RFP, or it may be a stand-alone document asking for bids on a project not previously discussed in an RFI or RFP. The RFQ may be published, or it may be sent to multiple recipients who may be interested in submitting a bid. The issuer of the RFQ is not yet committing to the project, much less to agreeing to work with any particular vendor who responds. An RFQ is likely to be an invitation to make offers, and the resulting bids are likely to be offers.

- A **Request for Bid (RFB)** is used as part of the highly regulated bidding process for government contracts, especially public works contracts. In competitive procurement, the government body or other project owner defines the project and then issues an RFB, which states a non-negotiable desired service or product, the parameters and requirements of the product, and the rules for submitting qualified bids. Suppliers/providers are invited to submit bids, and departures from stated specifications generally disqualify the bid. An RFB, like an RFQ, is likely to be considered an invitation to offers rather than an offer, and the resulting bids are likely to be offers. The law may restrict the government issuer's right to choose among the bids (e.g., it might have to accept the lowest bid that fulfills the project requirements).

FYI: Bidding Documents

Here are some links to websites discussing RFI, RFQ, and RFP:

www.techsoup.org/learningcenter/tech-plan/page5507.cfm

http://it.toolbox.com/blogs/original-thinking/outstanding-rfp-and-rfi-whats-the-difference-24312

Although there is a high degree of consistency of usage of these terms within the business community, government entities sometimes use them interchangeably, incorrectly, or in meaningless combinations (e.g., "Request for Bid Proposal"). Court decisions often do not take notice of the differences in the terms and sometimes do not focus enough on the function and content of the documents. When analyzing a client's situation or case law, it is thus essential to consider the language used, the parties' reasonable expectations, and the surrounding circumstances, in order to fully understand whether an offer has occurred in the bidding process.

Problems: Was an Offer Made?

Analyze each of the fact situations below to determine whether any of the parties made an offer. Be precise about which language and circumstances support finding an offer or no offer.

3-2. The following set of communications was exchanged between Owner and Customer:

- Owner placed an ad in the newspaper asking payment in cash for 40 acres of land, "vicinity: Greenwood, Colorado."

- Customer sent letter expressing interest, asking for more details.

- Owner sent Customer a flyer describing the property, giving the location, and stating the price.

- Customer replied by letter stating he was not sure he found the property, asking for its legal description, and suggesting a certain bank as escrow agent.

- Owner wrote back stating that "it sounds like you found the correct lot," that Customer's bank is acceptable as an escrow agent, and that Customer "must decide fast if you are really interested in purchasing the land because I expect to have a buyer in the next week or so." Two days later, Owner sold the land to a third party.

- Not knowing that Owner already sold the property, Customer replied to Owner's letter, saying that he was accepting Owner's offer to sell the property and was proceeding to deposit the purchase price immediately with the escrow agent.

When Customer discovered that Owner sold the land to a third party, he brought an action against Owner for breach of contract. Did Owner make an offer to sell the property? If so, in which communication? Did Customer make an offer to buy the property? If so, in which communication? Why are the other communications not offers?

3-3. United States Mint sent advertising materials to selected persons, including previous buyers of coins and coin collectors, describing commemorative coins to be issued and sold pursuant to orders received with payment. The materials gave the price of the coins, promised a discount to persons placing an order before a certain date, said that delivery would take place 6 to 8 weeks after the issuance date of the coins, reserved to the U.S. Mint the "right to limit quantities shipped, subject to availability," and encouraged potential purchasers to forward early payment because the "Mint may discontinue accepting orders should bullion prices increase significantly." Above the customer's signature line was the following language: "VERY IMPORTANT—PLEASE READ: Please accept my order for the coins I have indicated. I understand that all sales are final and not subject to refund. Verification of my order will be made by the U.S.

Mint. . . . If my order is received by [date], I will be entitled to purchase the coins at the . . . discount price shown. I have read, understand and agree to the above." Demand exceeded the Mint's expectations for $5 gold coins, and the supplies were exhausted quickly. Within a few months of the deadline, the $5 coins had doubled in value. The buyers in the dispute at issue placed several orders for the coins by the specified date, paying for some with checks and others by credit card. They received the coins paid for with checks, but did not receive any of the coins paid for by credit card. Investigation revealed that the third party vendor handling the credit card transactions had mistakenly rejected the buyers' otherwise valid credit card. The buyers sued the U.S. government for damages for breach of contract. Were the Mint's advertising materials an offer or a mere invitation to offers?

3-4. J. Cheney Mason, a prominent criminal defense lawyer, represented a defendant who had been accused of murdering several people in Orlando in 1997. In support of his alibi—that he was in Atlanta at the time of the killings—the defendant introduced into evidence an Atlanta hotel surveillance camera tape showing that he was in that hotel a few hours after the murder took place in Orlando. A few months after the defendant was convicted, Mason appeared on the TV show "Dateline," where he asserted that it would be impossible for anyone to have travelled from Orlando to the Atlanta hotel in the time allotted. In particular, he said that the trip from the Atlanta airport to the hotel could not be done in the required time—28 minutes. Mason went on to say, "I challenge anybody to show me, I'll pay them a million dollars if they can do it." The Dateline reporter asked for clarification about the time allotted, and Mason responded, "Twenty-eight minutes. Can't happen. Didn't happen." A law student in Texas accomplished just that, made a video of the trip, and demanded $1,000,000 from the defense attorney, who claimed that the so-called offer was a joke and therefore could not be accepted to form a contract. See www.courthousenews.com/2009/06/19/MAsonDateline.pdf (complaint). Should the law student receive the reward?

---

§ 2.2. How Long Does an Offer Last?

§ 2.2.1. Lapse

As reflected in Restatement (Second) § 41, an offer lapses at the time specified in the offer or, if no time is specified, at the end of a reasonable time. What is a "reasonable time" depends on all the circumstances of the transaction, including the way in which the offer is communicated and the nature of the performance expected.

> **Example G:** *Houston Dairy, Inc. v. John Hancock Mutual Life Ins. Co.*, 643 F.2d 1185 (5th Cir. 1981).
>
> John Hancock mailed a commitment letter to Houston Dairy on December 30, 1977, in which it agreed to lend Houston Dairy $800,000 at 9¼%, provided that within 7 days Houston Dairy returned the commitment letter with a written acceptance and enclose either a letter of credit or a cashier's check in the amount of $16,000 both as a "good faith deposit" and as a measure of damages should Houston Dairy default on repaying. Houston Dairy executed and returned the letter 18 days later. There were further discussions between agents of the parties about the method for completing final paperwork to close on the loan, but no other communications between the parties. On January 30, Houston Dairy was able to obtain a loan at 9% interest and requested a refund of its deposit of $16,000, claiming it had never accepted John Hancock's offer.

Analysis: John Hancock's offer lapsed after 7 days, as specified in the offer. Houston Dairy's return of the signed "commitment letter" constituted a new offer, and none of the subsequent communications between the parties resulted in an acceptance.

> **Example H:** *BMW of North America, LLC v. MiniWorks, LLC*, 166 F. Supp. 3d 976 (D. Ariz. 2010).
>
> BMW claimed MiniWorks was infringing on its trademark. BMW sent MiniWorks a proposed settlement, offering to refrain from filing a civil infringement suit if MiniWorks agreed in writing to cease and desist unauthorized uses of the mark. The letter said, "[I]t is our client's hope that this matter can be amicably resolved and that it will have your cooperation in discontinuing use of BMW's trademarks. Specifically, BMW requests that you [take certain actions to cease use of the mark and] countersign and return the acknowledgement on page 4 of this letter by June 21." The letter concluded: "We look forward to your response by June 21." MiniWorks signed and returned the letter on July 3.
>
> BMW claimed that MiniWorks continued to infringe on the mark and filed suit to enforce the settlement agreement. MiniWorks claimed that

it had not accepted the settlement offer, because it returned the signed document nearly two weeks after the stated deadline.

Analysis: The court ruled that the offer by BMW had not lapsed at the time the letter was returned because the language in the offer suggested rather than demanded a return by June 21. The later return was within a reasonable time and, therefore, could operate as an acceptance. The court also noted that if the return of the document on July 3 was too late, it would operate as an offer, and subsequent action by BMW indicated its assent. Under either analysis, there was a contract.

Example I: *Provencal v. Vermont Mut. Ins. Co.*, 571 A.2 276 (N.H. 1990).

Provencal was allegedly injured in a fall on 8/26/81, on property insured by Vermont Mutual. On 1/21/85, Vermont Mutual sent a settlement offer to Provencal in the amount of $6235. There was no stated expiration date for the offer. Provencal sent an acceptance to Vermont Mutual on 8/28/88. She later filed suit to enforce the settlement. Vermont Mutual claimed the offer had lapsed before acceptance.

Analysis: The court agreed that the offer had lapsed. "In determining what constitutes a reasonable time, 'all the circumstances existing when the offer and attempted acceptance [were] made' must be considered [citing the Restatement (Second) of Contracts § 41(2)]. Whether a delay in acceptance is reasonable depends on the situation of the parties and the subject matter of the contract." The statute of limitations for any claim by Provencal had expired 6 years after the fall, on 8/26/87. The insurer "chose to make a certain financial offer in light of the surrounding circumstances at the time, including the potential cost and the probable outcome of any litigation. Because the claim was obviously disputed, it is unlikely that an offer would have been extended absent the plaintiff's ability to seek a remedy in the courts. Clearly the situation of the parties changed substantially when the possibility of suit was eliminated. It is unreasonable to conclude, given the changed circumstances of the parties and the subject matter of the contract, that the offer remained open after the statute of limitations had run."

Example J: *Yaros v. Trustees of University of Pennsylvania*, 742 A.2d 1118 (Pa. Super. 1999).

Yaros brought a negligence action against the University after she fell at one of its ice-skating rinks. On the first day of the trial, the University offered Yaros a settlement offer of $750,000. Yaros's attorney responded that Yaros would accept $1.5 million in settlement up until the time she testified, after which she would not settle for any amount. The trial continued. Three days later, after the conclusion of testimony, the University offered Yaros $750,000 in settlement during a ten-minute recess prior to closing arguments. At the close of the conversation, the University's attorney said, "You've got to get back to me," and looked at the clock and placed his palms sideward. He did not communicate any express time limitations regarding the offer. Yaros's attorney stated he would talk to his client now, and he left the courtroom to do so. The University's attorney also left the courtroom, to go to the restroom. When Yaros's attorney returned to the courtroom, without Yaros, who was in the women's restroom, he asked the trial court for two minutes to speak to his client before closing arguments, to which the court agreed. Upon Yaros's return, her attorney did not confer with her, and closing arguments commenced immediately. During the University's closing, Yaros authorized her attorney to accept the settlement offer. After the University ended its closing, Yaros's attorney gave his rebuttal. At a sidebar conference following closings, Yaros's attorney stated that Yaros accepted the University's settlement offer. The University's attorney replied, "I don't know if it's still there, judge."

The next day, prior to jury deliberations, Yaros orally moved to enforce the settlement. Given the dispute over the continued existence of the settlement offer, the judge denied the motion to enforce pending evidentiary hearings on the matter and the jury's verdict. The jury came back with a defense verdict. Yaros filed a motion to enforce settlement.

The University claimed the offer lapsed prior to being accepted. It relied on the so-called "conversation rule": "Where parties bargain face to face or over the telephone, the time for acceptance does not ordinarily extend beyond the end of the conversation unless a contrary intention is indicated. A contrary intention may be indicated by express words or by the circumstances." Restatement (Second) § 41, comment d. The University insisted that because of the face-to-face nature of the negotiations, the offer terminated at the end of the conversation between counsel, or at the very latest at the beginning of closing arguments. The University also argued that when the University's attorney gestured by putting his palms sideward, this figuratively illustrated that the time that Yaros had to respond to the offer was limited and short.

Analysis: The court confirmed the application of the "conversation rule," but found that the circumstances (the need for Yaros's attorney to speak with her) and the actions of the attorney for the University (saying "get back to me" and making hand movements while looking at the clock) meant the offer was not to be understood as ending at the end of the conversation. It rejected the University's claim that "you've got to get back to me" could only be interpreted as "you've got to get back to me with an answer as soon as possible—which is, when we both come back into the courtroom: you from your discussion with your client and I from the Men's Room, so we can conclude this negotiation in the next few minutes before closings." The court also rejected the University's "strained interpretation" of its attorney's hand gesture, noting that the lawyer had used a similar gesture in an entirely different context. At best, the time during which the offer would exist was ambiguous, further reinforced by the University's statement to the judge "I don't know if [the settlement offer is] still there." Ultimately, the court found the settlement offer was accepted by Yaros before it lapsed.

§ 2.2.2. Death or Incapacity of the Offeror or Offeree

An offeree's power of acceptance is terminated upon the death or incapacity of either the offeror or the offeree. Note that this is a rule about termination of an *offer*, not termination of a *contract*. If a contract is formed, death or incapacity excuses performance of that contract only if the disability or death affects an individual necessary for performance. (*See* Chapter 9, page 754.) In some instances, a critical question therefore will be whether an offer was accepted (and the contract therefore formed) before the death or incapacity that would otherwise terminate the power of acceptance.

Problem: Death of the Offeror

3-5.   Consider the following facts suggested by the case of *Earle v. Angell*, 32 N.E. 164 (Mass. 1892):

> An elderly woman promises her nephew $500 if he will attend her funeral. Her nephew promises that he will come if he is notified in time. He does attend her funeral, and submits a claim to the estate for $500.

> If the aunt died before the contract was created, the offer terminated upon her death. If the contract was created before she died, however, then the contract survived her death, and the estate must pay. Does the estate have to pay the nephew?

---

§ 2.3. Defining Acceptance

After an offer has been made, the offeree gains the "power of acceptance," which means the offeree can create a contract by assenting to the offer. But that is not the only possible response to an offer. As reflected on the flowchart at the beginning of this chapter (page 68), the offeree might instead make a counter-offer, reject the offer, or remain silent and let the offer lapse. We have already discussed lapse (page 101). This section examines acceptances and counter-offers. We will address rejection later in this chapter, in § 2.4.

Like an offer, an acceptance must manifest the assenting party's commitment to be bound to the terms, and it must be communicated to the other party in an appropriate manner. See Restatement (Second) § 50. If the offeree clearly communicates to the offeror her assent to the terms offered, and does so in a timely fashion using the method and manner requested in the offer, that will constitute acceptance and a contract will be formed. Many questions may arise about whether that standard has been met, however:

- When is a purported acceptance a counter-offer, not an acceptance?

- Must the would-be acceptance be a "mirror image" of the offer?

> **Make the Connection**
>
> In Chapter 2, you learned that mutual assent occurs when the parties manifest definite commitment to reasonably certain terms (at least as to the essential terms). Recall *Quake Construction*, *Sun Printing*, and *Academy Chicago Publishers*. The same is true when assent is manifested consecutively in an offer and an acceptance. Both the offeror and the offeree must manifest a definite commitment to reasonably certain terms.

- Does the acceptance have to be communicated using a particular method of communication? Is a verbal response sufficient? What about a letter, email, or text?

- Does the acceptance have to be communicated in a particular manner (by making a promise or, instead, by starting to perform) or may the offeree choose? If acceptance is by performance, must the offeree notify the offeror of acceptance?

- When is an acceptance effective—when it is sent or when it is received?

- When can acceptance be by conduct or even by inaction (remaining silent)?

Those questions are addressed in the rest of this section.

§ 2.3.1. Distinguishing Between Acceptance and Counter-Offer

A response is a counter-offer if it demonstrates dissatisfaction with the offered terms and proposes alternative terms instead. Because an acceptance must express commitment to the offered contract, a counter-offer is not an acceptance. A counter-offer is also usually understood as terminating the original offer, unless the parties specify otherwise. "The termination of the power of acceptance by a counter-offer merely carries out the usual understanding of bargainers that one proposal is dropped when another is taken under consideration; if alternative proposals are to be under consideration at the same time, warning is expected." Restatement (Second) § 39, comment a. With the original offer terminated, the question then will be whether the counter-offer is accepted by the original offeror (or whether it is rejected or allowed to lapse, or yet another counter-offer is made).

What happens if an offeree neither unequivocally accepts ("I agree to your terms") or unequivocally makes a counter-offer ("I want these terms instead") but instead communicates assent but with some expression of dissatisfaction with the proposed terms? Some "grumbling" is allowed without undercutting the expression of assent, but if the "grumble" goes too far, then the offeree has not accepted and may have rejected and made a counter-offer.

> **Example K:** Restatement (Second) of Contracts § 39, Illustrations 1 and 2
>
> 1. A offers B to sell him a parcel of land for $5,000, stating that the offer will remain open for thirty days. B replies, "I will pay $4,800 for the parcel," and on A's declining that, B writes, within the thirty day period, "I accept your offer to sell for $5,000."
>
> 2. A makes the same offer to B as that stated in Illustration 1, and B replies, "Won't you take less?" A answers, "No."

Analysis: In Illustration 1, there is no contract unless A's reply to the counter-offer manifested an intention to renew his original offer. B's reply is a counter-offer and therefore terminates A's original offer, though A may renew the offer (e.g., "I won't take that amount, but I'm still ready to sell at $5,000").

In Illustration 2, B's response is an inquiry, not a counter-offer, and A's original offer stands. An acceptance thereafter by B within the thirty-day period is effective.

Reading Critically: *Ardente*

1. Trace the sequence of communications between the sellers and the prospective buyer. The court's ruling is in response to the defendant's motion for summary judgment, so the court views the facts most favorably for the plaintiff, but there is an alternative way to understand the legal implications of the communications. Which communication does the court think is an offer? Is there an earlier communication that might have been found to be an offer if the case had gone to trial? How would you support each result?

2. Why does the court conclude that the response to the offer is not an acceptance? What distinguishes a "conditional acceptance" from an acceptance with a request or suggestion? Why is a "conditional acceptance" not an operative acceptance?

Ardente v. Horan

ERNEST P. ARDENTE, Plaintiff-Appellant

v.

WILLIAM A. HORAN and KATHERINE L. HORAN, Defendants-Respondents

Supreme Court of Rhode Island
366 A.2d 162 (R.I. 1976) (unpublished opinion)

DORIS, JUSTICE.

Ernest P. Ardente, the plaintiff, brought this civil action in Superior Court to specifically enforce an agreement between himself and William A. and Katherine L. Horan, the defendants, to sell certain real property. The defendants filed an answer together with a motion for summary judgment pursuant to Super.R.Civ.P. 56. Following the submission of affidavits by both the plaintiff and the defendants and a hearing on the motion, judgment was entered by a Superior Court justice for the defendants. The plaintiff now appeals.

In August 1975, certain residential property in the city of Newport was offered for sale by defendants. The plaintiff made a bid of $250,000 for the property which was communicated to defendants by their attorney. After defendants' attorney advised plaintiff that the bid was acceptable to defendants, he prepared a purchase and sale agreement at the direction of defendants and forwarded it to plaintiff's attorney for plaintiff's signature. After investigating certain title conditions, plaintiff executed the agreement. Thereafter plaintiff's attorney returned the document to defendants along with a check in the amount of $20,000 and a letter dated September 8, 1975, which read in relevant part as follows:

> In this case as in others we have seen, a party to a transaction—the "principal"—may be bound to a contract entered into by an "agent" acting on behalf of the principal if the situation follows the rules governing agency law. The agent is not personally liable on the contract. An employee of a corporation may be acting on behalf of the corporation (which is a legal person). Here, both buyer and sellers are represented by their attorneys, who are their "agents."

> "My clients are concerned that the following items remain with the real estate: a) dining room set and tapestry wall covering in dining room; b) fireplace fixtures throughout; c) the sun parlor furniture. I would appreciate your confirming that these items are a part of the transaction, as they would be difficult to replace."

The defendants refused to agree to sell the enumerated items and did not sign the purchase and sale agreement. They directed their attorney to return the agreement and the deposit check to plaintiff and subsequently refused to sell the property to plaintiff. This action for specific performance followed.

In Superior Court, defendants moved for summary judgment on the ground that the facts were not in dispute and no contract had been formed as a matter of law. The trial justice ruled that the letter quoted above constituted a conditional acceptance of defendants' offer to sell the property and consequently must be construed as a counteroffer. Since defendants never accepted the counteroffer, it followed that no contract was formed, and summary judgment was granted.

. . . .

The plaintiff's . . . contention is that the trial justice incorrectly applied the principles of contract law in deciding that the facts did not disclose a valid acceptance of defendants' offer. . . . [W]e cannot agree.

The trial justice proceeded on the theory that the delivery of the purchase and sale agreement to plaintiff constituted an offer by defendants to sell the property. Because we must view the evidence in the light most favorable to the party against whom summary judgment was entered, in this case plaintiff, we assume as the trial justice did that the delivery of the agreement was in fact an offer.[3]

The question we must answer next is whether there was an acceptance of that offer. The general rule is that where, as here, there is an offer to form a bilateral contract, the offeree must communicate his acceptance to the offeror before any contractual obligation can come into being. A mere mental intent to accept the offer, no matter how carefully formed, is not sufficient. The acceptance must be transmitted to the offeror in some overt manner. Bullock v. Harwick, 158 Fla. 834, 30 So.2d 539 (1947). . . . A review of the record shows that the only expression of acceptance which was communicated to defendants was the delivery of the executed purchase and sale agreement accompanied by the letter of September 8. Therefore it is solely on the basis of the language used in these two documents that we must determine whether there was a valid acceptance. Whatever plaintiff's unexpressed intention may have been in sending the documents is irrelevant. We must be concerned only with the language actually used, not the language plaintiff thought he was using or intended to use.

Make the Connection

As we learned in *Lucy v. Zehmer*, the objective test is applied from the vantage point of a reasonable person in the position of the party receiving a communication—here, the offeror.

There is no doubt that the execution and delivery of the purchase and sale agreement by plaintiff, without more, would have operated as an acceptance. The terms of the accompanying letter, however, apparently conditioned the acceptance upon the inclusion of various items of personalty. In assessing the effect of the terms of that letter we must keep in mind certain generally accepted rules. To be effective, an acceptance must be definite and unequivocal. "An offeror is entitled to know in clear terms whether the offeree accepts his proposal. It is not enough that the words of a reply justify a probable inference of assent." 1 Restatement Contracts § 58, comment a (1932). The acceptance may not impose additional conditions on the offer, nor may it add limitations. "An acceptance which is equivocal or upon condition or with a limitation is a counteroffer and requires acceptance by the original offeror before a contractual relationship can exist." John Hancock Mut. Life Ins. Co. v. Dietlin, 97 R.I. 515, 518, 199 A.2d 311, 313 (1964). . . .

---

[3] The conclusion that the delivery of the agreement was an offer is not unassailable in view of the fact that defendants did not sign the agreement before sending it to plaintiff, and the fact that plaintiff told defendants' attorney after the agreement was received that he would have to investigate certain conditions of title before signing the agreement. If it was not an offer, plaintiff's execution of the agreement could itself be no more than an offer, which defend-ants never accepted.

However, an acceptance may be valid despite conditional language if the acceptance is clearly independent of the condition. Many cases have so held. Williston states the rule as follows:

> Frequently an offeree, while making a positive acceptance of the offer, also makes a request or suggestion that some addition or modification be made. So long as it is clear that the meaning of the acceptance is positively and unequivocally to accept the offer whether such request is granted or not, a contract is formed.

1 Williston, Contracts § 79 at 261–62 (3d ed. 1957). Corbin is in agreement with the above view. 1 Corbin, supra, § 84 at 363–65. Thus our task is to decide whether plaintiff's letter is more reasonably interpreted as a qualified acceptance or as an absolute acceptance together with a mere inquiry concerning a collateral matter.

In making our decision we recognize that, as one text states, "The question whether a communication by an offeree is a conditional acceptance or counter-offer is not always easy to answer. It must be determined by the same common-sense process of interpretation that must be applied in so many other cases." 1 Corbin, supra § 82 at 353. In our opinion the language used in plaintiff's letter of September 8 is not consistent with an absolute acceptance accompanied by a request for a gratuitous benefit. We interpret the letter to impose a condition on plaintiff's acceptance of defendants' offer. The letter does not unequivocally state that even without the enumerated items plaintiff is willing to complete the contract. In fact, the letter seeks "confirmation" that the listed items "are a part of the transaction". Thus, far from being an independent, collateral request, the sale of the items in question is explicitly referred to as a part of the real estate transaction. . . .

Accordingly, we hold that since the plaintiff's letter of acceptance dated September 8 was conditional, it operated as a rejection of the defendants' offer and no contractual obligation was created. . . .

Problems: Acceptance or Counter-Offer?

3-6. A businessperson offers to buy her partner's share of their business. Her partner writes back that she "accepts" and "proposes" that they "set December 15 as the closing date for the purchase."

3-7. Eight contractors make bids (offers) to build a school. The school district opens the bids, selects the winning bid, and sends a letter to that contractor "accepting your bid," stating additional terms that were not in the RFB or the bid, and saying that the final written agreement containing the bid terms and these new terms "is ready for your signature."

3-8.   A professor receives his annual reappointment letter from the university and signs it "under protest that the salary does not reflect guarantees under present and past personnel policies."

———————

§ 2.3.2. The Mirror Image Rule

Under the common law, an acceptance must be a "mirror image" of the offer, matching the terms of the offer. A typical articulation of the rule says that "acceptance [of an offer] must be 'positive, unconditional, unequivocal and unambiguous, and must not change, add to, or qualify the terms of the offer.' "[*] The mirror-image rule supports the offeror's traditional role as the "master of the offer": The offeror has made an offer proposing a contract on the offeror's terms, not on the offeree's terms.

The mirror-image rule was originally applied strictly, so that any variance from the offer was enough to prevent the purported acceptance from being effective. Consider the following ruling from an 1867 case: A brewer sent a letter to a malt grower 100 miles away, inquiring about buying malt for the summer brewing season. The grower replied by letter: "The malt I have for sale is at Weedsport. I will sell you ten thousand bushels of the malt . . . at $1.54 . . . per bushel, *delivered* on the boat at Weedsport." The brewer wrote back, "I will take your malt, ten thousand bushels, *deliverable* on boat at Weedsport, at 154 cents . . . ." The court considered the brewer's response to be "a manifest variance from the terms of the offer" and therefore a counter-offer. "The words ['deliverable' and 'delivered'] do not mean the same thing; they require, or may require, something to be done quite different as one or the other should be exacted," the court stated.[**]

Some jurisdictions continue to apply the rule strictly. In Illinois, for example, "the acceptance must conform exactly to the offer. . . . [A]ny changes to an offer, even minor changes, constitute a counteroffer rather than an acceptance."[***] Strictly applied, the mirror image rule prevents contract formation based on a small difference between the offer and purported acceptance, even when the parties reasonably thought they had formed a contract. As a result, a majority of jurisdictions now apply the mirror image rule more leniently, allowing minor differences between offer and acceptance.

———————

[*]   *Wagner v. Rainier Mfg. Co.*, 371 P.2d 74, 77 (Or. 1962).
[**]   *See Myers v. Smith*, 48 Barb. 614 (N.Y. Sup. Ct. 1867).
[***]   *Finnin v. Bob Lindsay, Inc.*, 852 N.E.2d 446, 448–49 (Ill. Ct. App. 2006) (quoting *Whitelaw v. Brady*, 121 N.E.2d 785 (Ill. 1954)).

For example, a teacher resigned from his position, specifying his last day of work as June 20 and his resignation effective August 31. The school district accepted the teacher's resignation, effective June 20. The teacher then attempted to rescind the resignation, claiming that, because of the difference in effective dates, there had been no acceptance of his offer to resign. The court held that the district had accepted the teacher's offer to resign, finding that the difference in effective date was an immaterial variation because it did not affect the teacher's work or pay.[*]

In another case, a seller offered to sell real estate to two buyers, who attempted to accept the offer with various additions and conditions. Seller protested that the changes prevented buyers' purported acceptance from being effective. When the buyers sued for damages for breach of contract, seller demurred. The court sided with the seller, reasoning that buyers attempted to add a "material and important" condition that title be acceptable to buyers' attorney. The court recognized that "immaterial differences in the phrasing of the offer and acceptance" should not defeat contract formation. It said that a court should "try to give to each writing a reasonable interpretation under which substantial justice may be reached according to the intent of the parties. But . . . there must be substantial agreement between offer and acceptance in all material particulars in order that such mutuality may appear. There must be no lack of identity between offer and acceptance, . . . and the parties must appear to have assented to the same thing in the same sense . . . ."[**]

These articulations are all grounded in the same inquiry: determining when the purported acceptance has deviated enough from the offer that the offeree should not be understood to have exercised his or her power of acceptance and instead to have made a counter-offer. (Note again the application of the objective test.) The offeree's response to the offer can be understood as being somewhere on the progression below, from acceptance to counter-offer, depending upon the facts and the court's rigor in applying the mirror-image rule:

---

[*]   *See Travis v. Tacoma Pub. Sch. Dist.*, 85 P.3d 959 (Wash. Ct. App. 2004).

[**]   *Richardson v. Greensboro Warehouse & Storage Co.*, 26 S.E.2d 897, 898 (N.C. 1943).

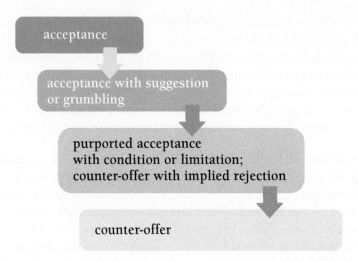

UCC § 2–207 expressly rejects the mirror image rule and substitutes a complex rule for determining when acceptance occurs if the offeree expresses commitment but specifies different terms. We will cover that rule later in this chapter.

Problems: Mirror-Image Rule

3-9. Providence & Worcester Railroad Co. (P&W) owned property in Providence, Rhode Island, that had on it railroad tracks not currently in use. P&W entered a contract to sell the land to Promet Corp. That sale was explicitly made subject to first submitting to the State of Rhode Island a 30-day option for the state to buy the property, as required by a statute regarding railroad property.

On December 12, 1985, P&W sent a copy of the P&W-Promet sales agreement to Joseph Arruda, assistant director for planning for the State Department of Transportation, along with the following letter:

Take Note!

As is usual in real estate sales, the purchase agreement is the contract, and the "closing" is the moment of performance, when the seller transfers the property and the buyer pays for the property.

Dear Mr. Arruda:

You are hereby notified, pursuant to Section 39–6.1–9 of the Rhode Island General Laws, that this company proposes to sell a certain parcel of land situated at East Providence, Rhode Island for $100,000 with a closing to be held on January 17, 1986.

> Pursuant to statute, the State of Rhode Island has a period of thirty (30) days from the date of this notification within which to accept this offer to sell under the same terms and conditions as outlined in the enclosed Real Estate Sales Agreement.
>
> If the State's rights are not exercised within such period, we shall deem ourselves free to sell the property to Promet Corp. in accordance with the terms of the enclosed Real Estate Sales Agreement.

On January 7, 1986, Herbert DeSimone, director of transportation for the state, delivered to P&W's agent the following letter:

> Pursuant to Rhode Island General Law, Section 39–6.1–9, I am writing to you on behalf of the State of Rhode Island to exercise its right to accept the offer to purchase 6.9 acres of land.
>
> Of course, you understand that certain wording in the Real Estate Sales Agreement [referring to the agreement between P&W and Promet] relating to 'buyer' and obligations concerning the removal of track would be inappropriate to the purpose of the State's purchase.
>
> Please contact Mr. Joseph F. Arruda of this department to arrange for a meeting to revise the existing offer to conform the State's acceptance.

The wording change noted in DeSimone's letter referred to (1) changing the name of the buyer in the agreement from "Promet" to "the State of Rhode Island" and (2) removing clauses in the P&W-Promet agreement requiring P&W to remove the unused railroad tracks before conveyance.

Did the State accept P&W's offer? *See State of Rhode Island Department of Transportation v. Providence and Worcester Railroad Co.*, 674 A.2d 1239 (R.I. 1996).

3-10. Fantasy Vacation Corp. (FVC) is in the business of selling fantasy vacation packages to buyers who will pay $7500 for a week of movie-making, including appearances with a "genuine" movie star. FVC sends Susan Starlet, the designated "star," a proposed 14-paragraph contract, specifying the dates and location of her appearance for an FVC vacation package, her duty to be "on call" from after breakfast until dinner each day, her acting roles and scenes, her release of publicity and filming rights, her duty to provide media appearances "as appropriate" during the specified days, FVC's duty to provide scripts and a director, FVC's duty to pay Starlet a $10,000 fee and up to $1000 for her expenses, and FVC's duty to provide Starlet with two first-class round-trip air tickets, hair and makeup services, wardrobe for the filming, hotel expenses, and a hotel suite with "two bathrooms if available." FVC's cover letter asks Starlet to sign the agreement as soon as possible and return it to FVC.

She signs the agreement and returns it, after making the following hand-written changes on the document: she inserts the word "one" in the sentence about media interviews, she adds "two bedrooms" to the hotel suite description, and she adds the words "to be supplied by Neiman Marcus department store" to the paragraph on wardrobe. Has she accepted FVC's offer? (If you think these facts are unrealistic, look at *Hollywood Fantasy Camp v. Gabor*, 151 F.3d 203 (5th Cir. 1998), but do your own analysis first and note that the facts here are slightly different and the court's conclusion is arguable).

---

§ 2.3.3. Permitted Method and Manner of Acceptance (Including Acceptance by Promise or by Performance)

The offeree's attempted acceptance will occur in a particular *manner* (by communication of a promise or by the beginning of performance) and, if by communicating a promise, by using a particular *method* (e.g., verbally, by letter, by telegram, by email). Sometimes "manner" and "method" are conflated into a discussion of the nature of the acceptance, but it is worth thinking about them separately to ensure clarity of analysis. Both aspects of acceptance are discussed in this section.

Because the offeror is master of the offer, the offer may specify the exclusive method and manner of acceptance. Most often, however, an offeror does not exercise this power. If the offer is silent as to the method or manner of acceptance, or if it includes only a preference or suggestion (not a demand), then the offeree is free to accept in any reasonable manner or method that is not precluded by the offer. See Restatement (Second) § 30(2).

For example, an offeror may communicate an offer in a writing, but say nothing about the *method* (the medium) of acceptance. The offeree

Take Note!

If a response to an offer is not an acceptance because not made using the proper method, it is likely a counter-offer on the proposed terms because the offeree has indicated her commitment to those terms, though communicating that in an unacceptable way. In the examples in the text, the offeree's telephone call or mail response would be a counter-offer on those terms, which the original offeror may now accept if he chooses, and his reaction to the phone call or letter may communicate that assent.

may send back a written acceptance or telephone a response. On the other hand, the offeror may say "in order to accept this offer, you must sign this contract document and return it to me." If the offeree telephones the offeror and says "I accept," there is no contract, because the method of acceptance did not conform to the offer's specification of the sole method of acceptance. Sometimes the method of delivery of the offer and other circumstances will implicitly communicate a restriction on the method to be used in responding. For example, if an offer is made by email and there is reason to think a speedy response is important (e.g., the market is volatile), responding via a letter sent through the U.S. mails might not be considered a reasonable method of communication, so a return letter would not be an acceptance.

Likewise, if an offeror does not specify the *manner* of acceptance—whether acceptance should be by communicating a promise or by performing—either manner of acceptance is appropriate. *No matter how acceptance is signified, however, what the offeror typically wants from the offeree at the moment of acceptance is a promise to perform.* Each party seeks the commitment of the other to a future performance in order to "seal the deal" rather than looking for immediate performance to signal agreement. Of course, both parties ultimately want performance of what is promised, but it is the exchange of promises that creates the contract. A contract formed by such a mutual exchange of promises is often called a **"bilateral contract,"** because both parties have made promises. The offer to enter such a contract is an "offer for a bilateral contract" because it seeks the commitment of the other party through a promise that constitutes acceptance. The offeree's promise may be made explicitly in words or implicitly by conduct (perhaps by the beginning of the requested performance). Regardless of the method of promising, the acceptance is the offeree's commitment to the performance that is sought by the offeror.

Sometimes, however, an offeror may specify that the manner of acceptance must be by actually performing the specified acts, not by promising. If acceptance is to be made only by performance, then no contract is formed (and neither the offeror nor the offeree is bound) until the offeree completes the performance. Such arrangements are called **"unilateral contracts"** because only *one* party makes a promise. The offer to enter such a contract is called an "offer for a unilateral contract." Note that in a unilateral contract, *both* parties eventually *perform*. It is unilateral because only one party *promises* to perform; the other party assents by performing, but does not promise in advance to do so. Once a contract is formed, whether it is unilateral or bilateral becomes irrelevant.

Offers for rewards are a prime example of offers for unilateral contracts. In the *Carbolic Smoke Ball* case (see *Leonard v. PepsiCo*, page 90), the company did not want purchasers of the product to promise to use it and catch influenza. Rather, the company promised that if a purchaser actually bought the smoke ball, used it as directed, and then caught the flu, the company would pay. Likewise, when someone offers a reward for return of a lost or stolen item, she is not asking anyone to promise to return the item. Rather, she is promising that if someone actually returns the item, she will pay the promised amount. Another common example is a business that offers a bonus to employees who remain with the business until a particular date but does not ask them to promise to remain; the business will pay if they do stay, but the employees are free to leave at any time.

Think About It!

Consider the newspaper advertisement in *Lefkowitz*, (page 76), in which the store specified that to buy the furs at the bargain price the offeree had to be the first person in line at the store by 9 a.m. on the next Saturday morning. Was that an offer for a unilateral or bilateral contract?

Why does it matter whether a contract is bilateral or unilateral? For both kinds of contracts, the critical issue is determining when the contract was formed. If an offeror makes an offer for a bilateral contract, then, at the moment the promises are exchanged, the contract is created and both parties are bound. If an offeror makes an offer for a unilateral contract, however, the offeree cannot create a contract by promising because the offeror did not ask for and will not accept a promise as the manner of acceptance. If the offer is not accepted until performance is complete, then the offeror is not bound until that moment and would therefore be free to withdraw the offer.

Make the Connection

In Chapter 5, we will discuss the concept of promissory estoppel, which might offer a path to recovery for someone who relies on a promise that does not ripen into a contract, perhaps offering relief for the employees who stay in their jobs after a promise of a later bonus. As you will see, however, a promise is enforceable under promissory estoppel only if reliance is reasonable, and it may not be considered reasonable for the promisee to rely on an offer for a unilateral contract, at least if the offeree knew or should have known that the promise can legally be withdrawn at any time during the promisee's performance.

That result is problematical, however. If employees are promised a bonus if they stay in their jobs until a particular date and in reliance on the promise they do remain, despite other opportunities, it is troubling if the employer can announce just before that date that the offer is withdrawn. Yet the definition of a unilateral contract leads to that result.

Courts and commentators have fashioned two rules that limit the effect of this dilemma. One—a limitation on revocation of an offer for a unilateral contract—we will discuss below, in the section addressing revocations (see page 152). The other is a rule that makes the existence of unilateral contracts less likely by interpreting an offer that is ambiguous as to manner of acceptance as being an offer for a bilateral (rather than unilateral) contract. That is, most offerors are understood as seeking a return promise as acceptance, unless the offer makes it very clear that a unilateral contract is desired. Clarity may come from explicit language in the offer ("I do not want your promise; only performance will do") or it may come from the circumstances (an offer for a reward); but because clarity is required as to the manner of acceptance, the circumstances must be unusual so that only a unilateral contract makes sense. Thus, if an offer is silent, vague, or ambiguous with respect to whether performance alone is permitted as a manner of acceptance, the offer will be understood as proposing a bilateral contract. The offeree may, of course, accept by means of an express return promise. But the offeree may, alternatively, accept through conduct that may reasonably be understood as signaling agreement, *and the beginning of performance is understood to be such a signal.* Once the offeree begins performance, both parties are bound. See Restatement (Second) of Contracts §§ 32 and 62.

The beginning of performance is thus an important moment in deciding whether an offer for a bilateral contract has been accepted. (It is also an important moment in applying the rule limiting revocation of an offer for a unilateral contract; see below at page 156.) In both circumstances, the courts have distinguished between mere preparation for performance and the beginning of performance. Sometimes the line between preparation and performance is hard to draw, as illustrated in the Problems below.

Problems: Preparations for or the Beginning of Performance

3-11. An organization offers an award for the best essay on a particular topic, and a potential essayist begins reading about the subject matter. Has the essayist begun performing or merely made preparations to perform?

3-12. A homeowner offers a painter $1000 to paint her house, and the painter purchases paint for the job. Has the painter begun performing or merely made preparations to perform?

3-13. A property owner offers to sell a piece of property. The offeree spends time and money contacting others to join him in the purchase as well as flying across the country to visit the property. Has the offeree begun performing or merely made preparations to perform?

The terms "unilateral" and "bilateral" contract are now used in only some jurisdictions (and are not used in the Restatement (Second)), but the conceptual issue—whether acceptance is to be by promise or performance—continues to matter. However, the rules described here and below have decreased the number of cases in which the distinction is significant, because most offers are construed to be for bilateral contracts and because, as we will see in a later section, a true offer for a unilateral contract often cannot be revoked once performance has begun.

Example L: *United States v. Spector*, 55 F.3d 22 (1st Cir. 1995).

Spector and two others (Murray and Mintz) were under investigation by the government for criminal violations of several statutes and had been informed that the government intended to file charges. As the expiration date for the statute of limitations approached, the three targets of the investigation sought a delay from the government to permit them to investigate the circumstances further and have an opportunity to persuade the government to change its position in certain respects. The three sent to the government a proposed agreement to extend the statute of limitations to 3/5/93, specifying that it would become effective "upon execution of all parties," and all parties did sign.

As the extended statute of limitations date approached, the three targets sought an additional delay. Their lawyer prepared a document that specified that the government would not bring charges before 4/9/93 and the individuals would agree to extend the statute of limitations until 4/16/93. The document specified that it would become effective "upon execution by Murray, Spector, and Mintz, and their respective counsel and the United States by its counsel." The document was signed by the individuals and their counsel but was never signed by government counsel.

The grand jury returned an indictment on 4/16/93. Spector moved to dismiss two counts of the indictment because the statute of limitations had expired as to those counts. If the extension agreement was not effective, the statute of limitations would have expired on 3/5/93, and Spector would be entitled to dismissal.

Analysis: The court dismissed the two counts of the indictment because the government never accepted the agreement. The document explicitly required the signature of government counsel and went so far as to specify with particularity that the acceptance of one of the individuals would be by fax, indicating a deliberate choice about the method and manner of acceptance. The government conceded that it had failed to sign the second extension because of "a minor, albeit presently embarrassing, clerical error," but argued that it had accepted through its performance of not bringing an indictment before 4/9/93. The court concluded that performance could not constitute acceptance in this instance. "The defendant was entitled not merely to forbearance from indictment, which he received, but to have the government's binding *promise* to forbear from indicting him, which he did not receive. That promise provided reassurance and certainty that he would not be indicted prior to the time period set forth in the agreement. . . . [W]here the government reaches an agreement with a potential criminal defendant, and where both parties expressly establish, in writing, the terms of their bargain and map out the conditions under which it will be effective, we think the parties are best held to the plain terms of that agreement, absent some good reason to depart. . . . '[T]he most meticulous standards of both promise and performance must be met by prosecutors engaging in plea bargaining.') The latter is particularly true where, as here, the government subsequently seeks specific performance of the defendant's agreement to waive a defense."

> **Example M:** *United States v. Papaleo*, 853 F.2d 16 (1st Cir. 1988).
>
> The government offered the following plea agreement: "[I]n exchange for defendant's . . . plea of guilty as to count one of the indictment, the Government at the time of sentencing will move for the dismissal of counts two and three." The defendant and the Government both signed the plea agreement. After the scheduled sentencing hearing was delayed, the government withdrew the plea. The defendant sought to enforce the plea agreement, claiming that he had accepted the government's offer of a bilateral contract.

Analysis: The court held that the offer was for a unilateral contract that could be accepted only by the defendant entering a guilty plea. The court noted that the plea agreement did not contain any explicit promise by the defendant. Indeed, under principles of criminal law, a court cannot force a defendant to plead guilty because of a promise in a plea agreement. "Absent more explicit promissory language, we will not read the ambiguous language of the 'agreement' as containing bilateral promises such as to bind the government to a contract unenforceable against the other party."

Example N: *Dahl v. HEM Pharmaceuticals Corp.*, 7 F.3d 1399 (9th Cir. 1993).

Dahl and 17 others afflicted with chronic fatigue syndrome participated in a one-year double-blind clinical trial of a new drug, Ampligen, manufactured by HEM. Some patients would receive doses of the drug; others would receive a placebo. Each patient signed a consent form that included a statement that if, at the end of the one-year study, statistical analysis showed efficacy of the drug compared to a placebo, the participant would receive one year of Ampligen without cost. Patients could withdraw from the study at any time, but if they remained in the study they were required to accept the risks of treatment, forgo other drugs, not become pregnant, and submit to uncomfortable testing.

The clinical trial showed the required efficacy. HEM filed an "investigational new drug application" to make the drug available by prescription to patients not in clinical trials. That application was denied, but the federal Food and Drug Administration approved holding an "open" clinical trial. HEM refused to provide a year's supply of Ampligen to Dahl and the other patients from the first clinical trial, which would be permitted by the FDA decision. Dahl and the other patients sued. HEM claimed that because the patients were free to withdraw at any time, HEM was not bound to provide the drug.

Analysis: The court enforced the promise to supply Ampligen to the patients. "Somehow the category of unilateral contracts appears to have escaped HEM's notice. The deal was, 'if you submit to our experiment, we will give you a year's supply of Ampligen at no charge.' . . . [T]he petitioners performed by submitting to the double-blind tests. They incurred the detriment of being tested upon for HEM's studies in exchange for the promise of a year's treatment of Ampligen. Upon completion of the double-blind tests, there was a binding contract."

Example O: *Galloway v. Santander Consumer USA, Inc.*, 819 F.3d 79 (4th Cir. 2016).

Jacqueline Galloway purchased a car and financed the purchase through an agreement with CitiFinancial Auto, Ltd., with monthly payments of $487.46. When she experienced difficulty making her payments, she sought a reduced payment schedule. CitiFinancial sent her an amended financing agreement that would reduce her payments to $365.57 and requested that she sign and return it "for further review, approval and consideration." Galloway returned the signed document. CitiFinancial did not sign the document, but sent Galloway a new schedule showing monthly payments of $366.43, 86 cents more than the amount reflected in the amended financing agreement. Galloway made payments in the amount reflected on the schedule ($366.43) for several years. Later, the financing agreement was assigned (transferred) to Santander Consumer USA, Inc. When Galloway fell behind on payments, Santander foreclosed on the car (reclaiming it to satisfy the unpaid amounts on the loan). At issue in the case was whether Galloway and CitiFinancial had agreed to the terms in the amended financing agreement, which included a provision requiring arbitration of disputes.

Analysis: The trial court concluded that when Galloway returned the amended financing agreement with her signature, she made an offer. CitiFinancial did not sign the agreement, but CitiFinancial either (1) accepted the offer by performance when it reduced her payments (even though the reduction was 86 cents less than proposed in the offer) or (2) made a counter-offer reducing the payments to $366.43 and Galloway accepted by performance when she made the reduced payment. The trial judge therefore enforced the arbitration provision in the amended financing agreement and dismissed Galloway's lawsuit. The dissenting judge would have reversed the dismissal, finding there to be a genuine issue of material fact as to whether the parties agreed to the written financing agreement that contained the arbitration clause.

Problem: Offer and Acceptance

3-14.   Robert Hinshaw was hired as the General Manager of Fisher Hydraulics in 2009 pursuant to a long-term contract. Less than a year later, Fisher was purchased by an investment company, Ligon Industries. The leadership of Ligon (Leon Nolen and John McMahon) became unhappy with the performance of Fisher Hydraulics and informed Hinshaw several times in 2015 and 2016 that they would accept his resignation. In January 2017, Hinshaw's attorney sent Nolen a letter (the "First Letter") that included the following:

> Dear Mr. Nolen:
>
> I am writing for the purpose of negotiating terms by which Mr. Hinshaw could resign from his position as General Manager.
>
> It has become obvious to Mr. Hinshaw that you no longer wish him to be employed by Ligon Industries. The expectations that

have been placed upon Mr. Hinshaw and his facility's performance now lead him to the conclusion that you are setting him up for failure.

Under the terms of his employment contract dated August 4, 2009, which was assumed by your company upon its purchase of Fisher Hydraulics, Mr. Hinshaw is entitled to severance payments if he is terminated other than for cause. "Cause" is defined to mean only "fraud, theft, being grossly insubordinate, and misappropriation of company assets." At no time has Mr. Hinshaw been accused of any such conduct, and I am sure you would agree that his performance has been outstanding. In fact, on numerous occasions, you and other members of management have held Fisher Hydraulics up as the example to be followed by the other facilities in the Ligon group.

Mr. Hinshaw's contract does not contain a non-compete agreement nor a confidentiality agreement. Under the circumstances, he would be more than willing to sign such an agreement under the proper terms. Specifically, we would propose that in return for the signing of a confidentiality agreement and a non-compete agreement, Mr. Hinshaw be awarded forty-eight (48) months of severance, based on the average compensation (both base salary and bonus) which he has received over the last three years. During the 48 month period he would also be willing to serve as a consultant. We would also expect that the annual bonus due Mr. Hinshaw for 2016 will be paid immediately and any unused vacation will be paid upon his effective resignation. Finally, we would ask that Mr. Hinshaw's medical insurance be paid by the company during the forty-eight (48) month period.

Please understand that Mr. Hinshaw would like nothing more than to retain his position as General Manager until such time as he would retire. However, at the age of fifty-nine, it would be very difficult for him to obtain new employment. Consequently, it would be in everyone's interest to negotiate a reasonable severance arrangement that would allow Mr. Hinshaw to exit gracefully from the company.

Please have your attorney contact me with your position in regard to this proposal.

The letter was received on Friday, January 12. McMahon and Nolen talked about the letter, which they characterized as making unreasonable demands and accusing them of unethical behavior, and they agreed they needed to "make a change." Nolen called Hinshaw and told him "that we accepted his resignation and that I wanted him to clean out his desk and to leave." Hinshaw left the Fisher facility that day and took home some personal items. Later on Friday, Hinshaw's counsel sent a second letter to McMahon and Nolen, stating that "Mr. Hinshaw has not resigned and has not tendered his resignation. He has simply made a proposal for his potential resignation. If you continue to insist that he leave the plant, we will consider that a termination without cause under this contract." Ligon's attorney also sent a letter to Hinshaw's attorney saying "Ligon currently does not desire a non-compete nor a confidentiality agreement."

The next day, Saturday, Nolen told three company employees that Hinshaw had resigned. On Sunday, McMahon sent a letter to Hinshaw's counsel that said the letter Hinshaw had sent, "in addition to being insubordinate, suggests that he no longer has the best interest of Fisher at heart and that a healthy and professional relationship between Ligon and Mr. Hinshaw no longer exists. Therefore, we advised Mr. Hinshaw to vacate his office as of Friday afternoon." Because he had not done so, the letter went on, arrangements would be made to allow Hinshaw to remove his personal belongings from his office.

On Monday, Hinshaw appeared at the company offices, but left when he was told Nolen did not want him there. That same day, his lawyer sent a letter to McMahon saying: "Given that the company has now removed him from the operation, we can only assume that the terms of our proposal have been accepted. I am sure that you will recognize this as acceptance by performance or conduct."

When Hinshaw did not receive the compensation and other terms he thought he was entitled to under the First Letter, he sued Ligon Industries to enforce the agreement he claimed existed. The company moved for summary judgment, claiming no contract existed on the terms in the First Letter.

In order to rule on the motion, the court must decide the following issues:

1) Did the First Letter constitute an offer? In particular, did it manifest Hinshaw's commitment to enter a contract? Was it sufficiently definite and certain to be an offer?

2) Assuming the First Letter constituted an offer, was it accepted by Ligon through the actions of Nolen and McMahon? How?

3) If the First Letter was not accepted, was a contract created by any other communications or conduct of the parties?

How would you advise the court to rule on the summary judgment motion? If summary judgment is not granted, how would you argue to a jury that there was, or was not, a contract based on the First Letter and the other communications and actions of the parties?

———

§ 2.3.4. Acceptance by Conduct

If invited or reasonable under the circumstances, a party's assent to an offer may be manifested by conduct (including but not limited to the beginning of performance) rather than by express words. But conduct is inherently ambiguous as a source of meaning, so judging whether particular conduct actually represents assent presents challenges and requires reflection on the context of the conduct. For example, you say to your friend, "If you will take care of my apartment while I'm on vacation in Prague, I promise to bring you a T-shirt from one of the underground jazz clubs there." You produce your apartment key, and your friend silently takes it from your hand. Has he promised to care for your apartment while you are away, accepting your offer? What if he simply nodded his head in response, or shook your hand and wished you a good trip? Does it matter if the key was given immediately after your statement or a week later? If he did assent by one or more of these actions, to what terms has he assented?

Restatement (Second) of Contracts § 19 says that conduct will be understood as assent when the party engaging in the conduct "intends to engage in the conduct" and "knows or has reason to know the other party may infer from his conduct that he assents." Note the application of the objective standard for understanding communications: it is the reasonable meaning of the conduct that matters, not the actor's intent, as long as the conduct itself is intentional.

> **Example P:** *Leibowitz v. Cornell University*, 584 F.3d 487 (2d Cir. 2009).
>
> Margaret Leibowitz taught at Cornell beginning in 1984 as a senior extension associate. Under school personnel policies, senior extension associates were appointed to five-year terms, renewable on the basis of department recommendations. After her teaching contract was not renewed in 2002, Margaret Leibowitz sued the school, claiming age and gender discrimination as well as state breach of contract claims. Cornell defended in part by relying on the terms included in the letters of reappointment sent to Leibowitz each time she was rehired. Leibowitz argued that the letters did not constitute express contracts because they do not bear her signature.

Analysis: The court concluded that Leibowitz had manifested assent to the contract and its terms when she performed teaching services after receiving the appointment letters. See also *Galloway*, Example O. Both *Leibowitz* and *Galloway* involved performance, or part performance, of contract obligations that arguably communicated assent to offered terms.

> **Example Q:** *Houston Dairy, Inc. v. John Hancock Mutual Life Ins. Co.*, 643 F.2d 1185 (5th Cir. 1981).
>
> As described in Example G, John Hancock mailed a commitment letter to Houston Dairy in which it agreed to lend Houston Dairy $800,000 if within 7 days Houston Dairy returned the commitment letter with a written acceptance and a cashier's check for $16,000. Houston Dairy executed and returned the letter 18 days later with a check. That was too late to be an acceptance, but could be considered an offer by Houston Dairy for a loan on the terms specified in the original commitment letter. John Hancock deposited the cashier's check and asked its lawyer to contact Houston Dairy's attorney to discuss closing on the loan. When Houston Dairy obtained a loan at a lower interest rate, John Hancock argued that it had accepted Houston Dairy's offer of a loan through its actions.

Analysis: The court concluded that the action of cashing the check did not constitute acceptance, because when a cashier's check is deposited, there is no notice to the entity providing the funds to the bank, and John Hancock sent no notice of its own. Moreover, as indicated in other cases involving similar facts, the action of cashing a check is ambiguous conduct that might or might not indicate acceptance depending on other circumstances. The conversation between the attorneys for the two parties also did not indicate acceptance because the request was to determine how the closing should be done, not to actually arrange the closing.

> **Example R:** *International Business Machines v. Johnson*, 629 F. Supp. 2d 321 (S.D.N.Y. 2009).
>
> David Johnson worked for International Business Machines (IBM) for more than 27 years. He received a salary and, along with other executives, an annual "equity grant" (stock in the company, or an option to purchase such stock). In 2005, IBM began to require senior executives to sign a noncompetition agreement in order to continue to be eligible to receive annual equity grants. The company sent the executives copies of the agreement, asking them to return a signed copy of the agreement within a few months.

Johnson objected to the noncompetition agreement. He initially delayed sending the agreement back. After two months, he received an email asking him again to return it, warning him that his 2005 equity grant would not take effect without a signed agreement, and setting a deadline of June 1. Johnson purposely signed the agreement on the line for IBM to sign, intending *not* to show agreement but to buy time to decide what to do. In the fall of 2005, IBM returned the improperly-signed agreement to Johnson, requesting that he sign in the appropriate space. The company later sent him a new blank agreement and requested he sign it but he refused to do so. In 2005 and 2006, Johnson received his equity grant after clicking on an "electronic equity acceptance form" that contained the following language:

> IBM's grant to you of stock options . . . are not effective until, and are conditioned upon (1) your accepting the terms and conditions of the award agreements . . . under which these equity awards are granted, including those provisions relating to the cancellation and rescission of awards **and** (2) your agreeing to the terms and conditions of the Noncompetition Agreement, which you have received under a separate cover. . . . .

> . . . . By pressing the ACCEPT button, you also agree that the grant of these awards by IBM is subject to the condition that, and your acceptance of such awards is not effective until, you agree to the terms and conditions of the Noncompetition Agreement by signing and returning the agreement as directed.

In 2007 and 2008, equity grants were paid to senior executives without the language conditioning them on the noncompetition agreement. Johnson never signed a noncompetition agreement as requested. In 2008, Johnson accepted a position with Dell, Inc. IBM filed suit, claiming breach of the purported noncompetition agreement and seeking a preliminary injunction to enforce its terms. Johnson defended by claiming he had never agreed to the noncompetition agreement.

Analysis: The court denied the preliminary injunction. The court concluded that Johnson's action in signing the agreement on the wrong line was ambiguous and that under contract interpretation principles, he ran the risk that the ambiguity would be construed against him, which could have resulted in a determination that he had assented to the contract. But IBM's subsequent actions suggested that the company did not interpret Johnson's actions as demonstrating assent. "In short, IBM faces a daunting, if not insurmountable, task in convincing a finder-of-fact that it treated Mr. Johnson's ambiguous conduct as an acceptance of its offer to enter into a non-competition agreement. Consequently, the Court cannot find, based on the limited record before it, that IBM has established a likelihood of success on the merits of its breach of contract claim." What actions by IBM suggested it did not consider he had accepted the offer? What actions might IBM suggest it believed he had accepted?

§ 2.3.5. Acceptance by Inaction

When we consider whether conduct shows assent, we at least know that the individual voluntarily undertook the particular action, though it may be challenging to determine if the action is meant to, or is reasonably understood to, manifest assent. Can *inaction*—the failure to speak in response to an offer—ever be understood as showing agreement? What if you left a voice-mail for your friend, offering a Prague T-shirt in return for apartment care and saying, "If I don't hear back from you by tomorrow, I'll assume you agree and will leave my key in your mailbox when I leave town." Can the friend's inaction or silence constitute acceptance?

Because contract formation is based on finding that both parties assented to the contract, we usually demand affirmative communication of assent through speech or conduct. But silence or inaction can constitute assent in a few limited circumstances described and illustrated in Restatement § 69 and the examples that follow.

Reading Critically: Acceptance by Silence or Dominion in the Restatement (Second)

Read Restatement (Second) § 69.

1. What three sets of circumstances are identified as allowing silence or inaction to be treated as acceptance?

2. Why is it reasonable to find assent under those circumstances when the offeree has not spoken or acted?

3. Are the examples that follow in accord with the Restatement provisions and examples? Do you agree with the outcomes?

Example S: *Nirvana Int'l, Inc. v. ADT Security Services, Inc.*, 881 F. Supp. 2d 556 (S.D.N.Y. 2012).

The owner of Nirvana International, a jewelry store, asked ADT Security Services to install a burglar alarm in the store. ADT provided a 6-page contract that contained a provision limiting ADT's liability for system failure to 10% of the price paid. The owner met with the ADT representative to review the contract terms. He initialed or signed pages 1 to 3 of the contract as required, but in the meeting said he had to think more about the provisions on pages 4 to 6, including the liability limitation. He later decided he did not want to approve the limitation, but did not communicate that to ADT. ADT installed the burglar alarm, even though the owner had not signed or initialed the remaining pages of the contract, and Nirvana paid the monthly monitoring fee. In a burglary during which the alarm did not send an alert to the police, Nirvana lost $2.4 million of merchandise. ADT refused to pay more than the amount specified in the contract. Nirvana sued, claiming damage from an allegedly faulty alarm system. ADT relied on the contractual limitation; Nirvana claimed it had not agreed to that term.

Analysis: The court concluded that Nirvana had implicitly agreed to the terms proposed by ADT when it accepted the benefits of the contract ("such as they were") by allowing installation of the alarm, knowing the conditions ADT required for installation. As in many cases involving allegations of silence as acceptance, there were also some actions that might be considered acceptance by conduct (paying the monthly monitoring fee), but the court pointed to the silent acceptance of benefits as crucial to the holding.

Example T: *Brooks Towers Corp. v. Honkin-Conkey Construction Co.*, 454 F.2d 1203 (10th Cir. 1972).

The parties entered an office building construction contract that included an initial contract price of $7.2 million, a designated completion date, and penalties for late performance. The parties implemented a specific procedure for Change Orders from the original plans and specifications: The owner's architect would issue a "Bulletin" detailing a change directed to the contractor, requesting a "Quotation" from the contractor. The court concluded that this was, in legal effect, a call for a bid. The contractor would then issue a "Quotation" setting forth a change in contract price, if any, together with a specific request for additional days to complete the contract as a result of the changes. The contractor requested extensions of some 300 days involving about 80 formal "Quotations." These "Quotations" were submitted directly to the architect and owner, who would jointly agree on each Quotation. Each Quotation form contained a portion for approval or disapproval of both contract price increases and completion date changes. In each instance, the architect completed the portion of the form dealing with the change in contract price. In a few instances, the architect expressly allowed or disallowed extensions of time. In the great majority of the Quotations, the architect did not make any entries relating to extensions. He testified that by not acting, he indicated his disapproval, or, perhaps more accurately, that the extensions were matters to be determined by the Owner and the Contractor. The Contractor relied upon the lack of express disapproval as a grant of the requests for extensions. After the architect returned the "Quotation" forms to the contractor, an amendment or "Change Order" reflecting the deletions, alterations or additions was prepared by the contractor and thereafter executed by the contractor and owner. The "Change Orders" did not refer to extensions of time.

After completion of the construction work, the owner filed suit, claiming damages for delay in completion. The contractor counterclaimed for amounts due under the contract and alleged the delays were approved when the architect returned the Quotations with approval of the described work and no statement about the extension of time requested.

Analysis: The court concluded that the "Quotations" were offers on the part of the contractor to undertake the requested changes, subject to specific price changes and additional days to complete the work. It also concluded that the silence of the architect with respect to extensions of time constituted an acceptance of the offer made by the contractor, in view of the dealings of the parties. "When the relations between the parties justify the offeror's expectation of a reply or where a duty exists to communicate either an acceptance or rejection, silence will be regarded as an acceptance."

Example U: *UMG Recordings, Inc. v. Augusto,* 628 F.3d 1175 (9th Cir. 2011).

As part of its marketing efforts for merchandise, UMG sent unsolicited CDs to music critics and radio DJs. Some of the CDs had on them the brief statement "Promotional Use Only—Not for Sale." Most of them bore a longer statement similar to the following:

This CD is the property of the record company and is licensed to the intended recipient for personal use only. Acceptance of this CD shall constitute an agreement to comply with the terms of the license. Resale or transfer of possession is not allowed and may be punishable under federal and state laws.

Augusto was not a music critic or DJ but managed to acquire a large number of the promotional CDs many of which he sold through online auctions at eBay.com. Augusto regularly advertised the CDs as "rare . . . industry editions" and referred to them as "Promo CDs." UMG filed suit against Augusto, claiming breach of copyright. Augusto claimed he was free to market the CDs because the original transfer of the CDs was a sale, not a license under the terms UMG specified on the CDs.

Analysis: The court reasoned as follows:

The sparest promotional statement, "Promotional Use Only—Not for Sale," does not even purport to create a license. But even the more detailed statement is flawed in the manner in which it purports to secure agreement from the recipient. . .

It is one thing to say, as the statement does, that "acceptance" of the CD constitutes an agreement to a license and its restrictions, but it is quite another to maintain that "acceptance" may be assumed when the recipient makes no response at all. This record reflects no responses. Even when the evidence is viewed in the light most favorable to UMG, it does not show that any recipients agreed to enter into a license agreement with UMG when they received the CDs.

In a footnote, the court went on to say:

Although our result does not depend on the point, there is even doubt that a license contract could arise from the absence of response of the recipients. The general rule of contract law is that the "mere receipt of an unsolicited offer does not impair the offeree's freedom of action or inaction or impose on him any duty to speak." Restatement (Second) of Contracts § 69 cmts. a, c. "Nothing in contract law [can] force the parties into a contractual arrangement when they do not intend to be bound." Raymond T. Nimmer & Jeff Dodd, Modern Licensing Law § 3:17 (2010).

The commentary on section 69 of the Restatement offers a pertinent illustration: "A sends B a [book] with a letter, saying, 'If you wish to buy this book send me $6.50 within one week after receipt hereof, otherwise notify me and I will forward postage for return.' B examines the book and *without replying* carefully lays it on a shelf to await A's messenger. There is no contract." Restatement (Second) of Contracts § 69 cmt. e, illus. 8 (emphasis added). The Restatement does provide an exception to the rule that silence and inaction do not constitute assent when, "because of prior dealings or otherwise, it is reasonable that the offeree should notify the offeror if he does not intend to accept." *Id.* § 69(1)(c). The record as it stands does not suggest that UMG could avail itself of this provision.

FYI

Unsolicited Merchandise and Buying Clubs

More than likely, you have received in the mail some goods you did not order (mailing labels, greeting cards, DVDs), accompanied by a request for payment or contribution. Under Restatement (Second) § 69, is a contract formed if the recipient of such a mailing keeps and uses the goods? Gives them away? Discards them? Puts them on a shelf and forgets about them?

Because of the uncertainty about the answers to such questions and as a result of abuses by marketers attempting to foist unwanted merchandise on consumers, state and federal regulators have sought to police some of the abuses. According to the Postal Reorganization Act of 1970, 39 U.S.C. § 3009, a person who receives "unordered merchandise" *by way of the U.S. Postal Service* usually may treat it as a gift:

(a)   Except for (1) free samples clearly and conspicuously marked as such, and (2) merchandise mailed by a charitable organization soliciting contributions, the mailing of unordered merchandise or of communications prohibited by subsection (c) of this section constitutes an unfair method of competition and an unfair trade practice in violation of section 45(a)(1) of title 15.

(b)   Any merchandise mailed in violation of subsection (a) of this section, or within the exceptions contained therein, may be treated as a gift by the recipient, who shall have the right to retain, use, discard, or dispose of it in any manner he sees fit without any obligation whatsoever to the sender. All such merchandise shall have attached to it a clear and conspicuous statement informing the recipient that he may treat the merchandise as a gift to him and has the right to retain, use, discard, or dispose of it in any manner he sees fit without any obligation whatsoever to the sender.

(c)   No mailer of any merchandise mailed in violation of subsection (a) of this section, or within the exceptions contained therein, shall mail to any recipient of such merchandise a bill for such merchandise or any dunning communications.

(d)   For the purposes of this section, "unordered merchandise" means merchandise mailed without the prior expressed request or consent of the recipient.

The Federal Trade Commission (FTC) explains the rule on its website, as well as providing information about abuses associated with "free trials" and "buying plans" in which the consumer signs up for a club and then "shops" until she cancels her membership in the club. See Federal Trade Commission, Consumer Information, Unordered Merchandise, www.consumer.ftc.gov/articles/0181-unordered-merchandise. Particularly problematic are "clubs" that charge monthly membership fees until the customer affirmatively cancels. "Customers " sometimes find themselves enrolled when they thought they had agreed only to pay a small shipping charge for a free trial and discovered the enrollment months later by noticing a charge on their debit or credit card statements, easily missed because of the small size. See www.consumer.ftc.gov/articles/0101-free-trial-offers.

State statutes also address abuses resulting from the mailing of unsolicited goods, sometimes giving the recipient a defense against any action for the price or return of the goods. *See, e.g.*, Wisc. Stat. § 241.28 (2017) (unsolicited goods are gifts); *see also* state statutes listed in Joseph M. Perillo, *Calamari and Perillo on Contracts* § 2.19, at 77 n.13 (6th ed. 2009).

Problems: Assent Through Conduct or Inaction

3-15.   Chris is walking along a wide public walkway on a city waterfront when she sees the signboard in the picture.

In all caps, it reads as follows:

Consent to be Photographed

In consideration for your admittance, and entering the premises and by your presence in this area, you consent to be photographed, filmed, interviewed and/or otherwise recorded. Your entry constitutes your consent to such photography, filming and/or recording and to any use, in any and all media, throughout the universe in perpetuity, or your appearance, voice, image and name for any purpose whatsoever in connection with the television production noted above.

You understand that the photography, filming and/or recording will be done in reliance on this consent given by you by entering this Area.

If you do not agree, please do not enter this area.

Chris doesn't want to make a three-block detour off and back onto the waterfront walkway so she continues walking past the signboard and sees the film crew.

Two months later, in Caesar's Palace in Las Vegas, she sees a similar signboard as she enters the pool area inside the hotel, where a film crew is working. She's wondering whether she assented to both sets of terms.

3-16. On the door of a restaurant is a sign that says that anyone entering the restaurant agrees to arbitrate any disputes concerning the restaurant. *See* the actual sign at www.motherjones.com/mojo/2008/01/eat-burger-waive-right-sue. Is it effective?

What if a patron walked into the restaurant wearing a T-shirt that read, "I do not assent to arbitration"? Professor Ian Ayres of Yale proposed to sell a "liabiliT shirt" saying, "Any disclaimer of liability notwithstanding, management, by serving me, accepts legal responsibility for any losses to my person or property that would result from my use of this establishment.©" Will either T-shirt have its intended effect for the wearer? *See* www.whynot.net/merchandise/history.php.

3-17.   As reported by the ContractsProf Blog, the *New York Times* on June 22, 2011, reported that passengers of livery car services have been pulled out of the cars and searched by police, based on "the Taxi/Livery Robbery Inspection Program," which permits drivers to join the program to allow police to "inspect their car at any time in order to ensure the driver's safety." Drivers indicate their participation in the program by affixing a decal to their rear and side windows. When passengers asked why they were being instructed to step out of the back seat of their livery car or cab and be searched, the police informed them that they had consented to be searched when they got into a car displaying decals indicating that the driver was part of the Inspection Program. http://lawprofessors.typepad. com/contractsprof_blog/2011/06/new-york-city-police-on-consent.html. Did the passengers assent to the search by getting into the livery cars? (Ignore the constitutional issues under the Fourth Amendment on search and seizure.)

---

§ 2.3.6. What Terms Are Accepted?

An acceptance, by definition, is agreement to the offered terms. Even the more lenient applications of the mirror image rule allow only grumbling about the terms or an inquiry about varying the terms offered; it does not undercut the notion that an acceptance is, by definition, assent to the deal that was offered. Indeed, under traditional contract doctrine, an offeree has assented to the terms of what is offered even if the offeree has not read or otherwise reviewed the terms in the offer. That rule has sometimes been described as a "duty to read" the

Make the Connection

Even assuming that the offeree has assented to every term in the offer, defenses such as mistake, fraud, misrepresentation, and unconscionability may be available to deny liability for some terms or their consequences. We will consider those defenses in Chapter 6. Terms may also be interpreted in ways that protect the offeree from unexpected consequences, and the doctrine of *contra preferendum*—construe against the drafter—may be used to limit the effect of the so-called duty to read, as we will also see in Chapter 8.

agreement, but as Professor Charles Knapp has noted, that is a misnomer: "The duty to read, although regarded as a part of contract law, is not a 'duty' imposed *by* contract, but rather a statement about how parties should behave during the contract-making process."[*] He suggests that, especially in view of modern contracting realities, we should stop calling it a duty:

> This is not only technically incorrect, but it also encourages judges (and others as well) to moralize or be condescending to persons who do not read everything they sign. Nobody does that, and in fact nobody is expected to. In standardized form contracting, it is not only *not* encouraged, it is essentially *discouraged*. Contract recitations that say, "I have read all of this contract" are patently false, and are known to be false—to the party who presents a written contract for signature as well as to the party who signs it. All those words really convey to the signer is this: "Although we know you haven't read much or any of this contract, and probably wouldn't understand its importance if you had, we expect to hold you to it."[**]

This result is consistent with the objective test, because it matches the likely conclusion of the reasonable person watching the process of contract formation and possibly the assumptions of the offeree herself.

The conclusion that all terms in the offer are accepted, whether read or not, also depends on the offeree at least having the opportunity to know what terms are being offered because they are communicated by the offeror in the document presented for signature. With many agreements now being concluded online, courts have repeatedly been presented with the question whether an online offer adequately communicates all or part of the offer's terms to the offeree and whether the offeror has sufficiently communicated to the offeree that particular conduct will manifest the offeree's assent. These questions often arise in lawsuits involving arbitration clauses and forum-selection clauses. The example below illustrates the challenges of applying traditional contract doctrines to these modern circumstances.

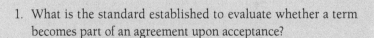

Reading Critically: *Meyer v. Uber* and
Notice of Terms to the Offeree

1. What is the standard established to evaluate whether a term becomes part of an agreement upon acceptance?

---

[*]   Charles Knapp, *Is There a Duty to Read?*, 66 Hastings L.J. 1083, 1085–86 (2015).

[**]   *Id.* at 1108–09.

2. Do you agree with the trial court or the appellate court in *Meyer v. Uber Technologies, Inc.*? Why?

3. Considering the examples described below and your own use of websites to purchase goods or services, what is your view of what constitutes meaningful communication of terms to, and assent by, an offeree?

4. What would you suggest sellers of goods or services do to ensure that offerees will be held to have agreed to the offered terms in these kinds of transactions? Do you think establishing additional rules for offer and acceptance in these kinds of cases would be a good idea? Why or why not? What rules would you advocate?

Example V: *Meyer v. Kalanick*, 200 F. Supp. 3d 408 (S.D.N.Y. 2016), *rev'd*, *Meyer v. Uber Technologies, Inc.*, 868 F.3d 66 (2d Cir. 2017).

In 2014, plaintiff Spencer Meyer downloaded onto his smartphone the Uber application software, which would permit him to use the Uber ride-hailing service. Meyer then registered for an Uber account with his smartphone, using the process depicted in the screenshots reproduced below. The first screen asked users to enter identifying information or use their Google Plus or Facebook accounts to provide such information. If they did so and clicked "Next," they were taken to a second screen with a "REGISTER" button, buttons to pay using PayPal or Google Wallet, and below those, in smaller print, the words "By creating an Uber account, you agree to the Terms of Service & Privacy Policy," with a hyperlink to those terms of service. If the user clicked the hyperlink, she would be taken to a screen that contains a button that accesses the terms and conditions then in effect. Those terms and conditions consisted of nine hard-copy pages of text. At the bottom of the seventh page was a paragraph titled *Dispute Resolution*, which said all disputes between "You and Company" would be settled by binding arbitration. In the middle of the paragraph, in bold, was the statement "You acknowledge and agree that you and Company are each waiving the right to a trial by jury or to participate as a plaintiff or class User in any purported class action or representative proceeding."

After using the service approximately ten times, Meyer brought suit against Uber's founder and (now former) chief executive officer, Travis Kalanick, on behalf of himself and others similarly situated, alleging that the Uber application allows third-party drivers to illegally fix prices. The federal district court joined Uber Technologies as a defendant. Uber and Kalanick moved to compel arbitration pursuant to the clause described above, which they claimed was part of the contract the parties had entered.

Analysis: The trial and appellate courts generally agreed on the law to be applied to determine whether the arbitration term was part of the contract the parties entered, but they disagreed about the application of the law to the facts. Both courts noted that electronic formation of contracts looks different than traditional formation of contracts, but the same fundamental principles of contract law apply. From the district court opinion:

> [W]hile the Internet may have reduced ever further a consumer's power to negotiate terms, "it has not fundamentally changed the principles of contract." Register.com, Inc. v. Verio, Inc., 356 F.3d 393, 403 (2d Cir.2004). One of these principles is that "[m]utual manifestation of assent . . . is the touchstone of contract." Specht v. Netscape Communications Corp., 306 F.3d 17, 29 (2002). Moreover, "[a]rbitration agreements are no exception to the requirement of manifestation of assent," and "[c]larity and conspicuousness of arbitration terms are important

in securing informed assent." *Id.* at 30. The Specht standard provides a way for courts to ascertain whether this fundamental principle of contract law has been vindicated, and it is this standard—whether plaintiff Meyer had "[r]easonably conspicuous notice of the existence of contract terms and unambiguous manifestation of assent to those terms"—that the Court will apply. *Id.* at 35.

From the appellate court opinion:

> To form a contract, there must be "[m]utual manifestation of assent, whether by written or spoken word or by conduct." California law is clear, however, that "an offeree, regardless of apparent manifestation of his consent, is not bound by inconspicuous contractual provisions of which he is unaware, contained in a document whose contractual nature is not obvious." "Thus, California contract law measures assent by an objective standard that takes into account both what the offeree said, wrote, or did and the transactional context in which the offeree verbalized or acted."
>
> Where there is no evidence that the offeree had actual notice of the terms of the agreement, the offeree will still be bound by the agreement if a reasonably prudent user would be on inquiry notice of the terms. Whether a reasonably prudent user would be on inquiry notice turns on the "[c]larity and conspicuousness of arbitration terms"; in the context of web-based contracts, . . . clarity and conspicuousness are a function of the design and content of the relevant interface.
>
> Thus, only if the undisputed facts establish that there is "[r]easonably conspicuous notice of the existence of contract terms and unambiguous manifestation of assent to those terms" will we find that a contract has been formed.

Both opinions referred to categories of online contracting that have often been referenced by courts—"clickwrap," where the user is presented with a choice to agree or not agree to terms by clicking a box (express assent by language) and "browsewrap," where the user is told that continuing to use a website constitutes assent (assent by conduct). Each website and contracting circumstance is different, however, so one cannot easily place a particular transaction into one or the other category. Nor do the categories define the outcome of the contract formation and contract terms questions. As the trial court noted, "electronic agreements fall along a spectrum in the degree to which they provide notice, and it is difficult to draw bright-line rules because each user interface differs from others in distinctive ways. Consequently, courts must embark on a 'fact-intensive inquiry' in order to make determinations about the existence of '[r]easonably conspicuous notice' in any given case." 200 F. Supp. at 420.

As already noted, though, courts may disagree about the application of the law to the facts. The trial court concluded that Meyer did not assent to the arbitration term:

> Here, . . . the notification was in a font that was barely legible on the smartphone device that a would-be Uber registrant could be expected to use.
>
> . . . .
>
> A review of numerous other cases finding that an electronic agreement was formed highlights the point that the Uber registration process in plaintiff Meyer's case involved a considerably more obscure presentation of the relevant contractual terms.[9] Further, by contrast to the

---

[9] See, e.g., Defillipis v. Dell Fin. Servs., 2016 WL 394003, at *3 (M.D. Pa. Jan. 29, 2016) ("an applicant had to affirmatively click a box agreeing: 'I have read and agree to the Privacy Policy and Terms & Conditions, which contain important account information.' "); Bassett v. Elec. Arts, Inc., 93 F.Supp.3d 95, 99 (E.D.N.Y.2015) ("Plaintiff would have been presented with four buttons, two of which are the links to the terms of service and privacy policy, one which reads 'I Do Not Accept,' and one which reads 'I Have Read And Accept Both Documents.' . . . If the registrant . . . does not click the button reading 'I . . . Accept,' the registration process stops and the online features cannot be activated."); Nicosia v. Amazon.com, Inc., 84 F. Supp. 3d 142, 150 (E.D.N.Y.2015) (the statement "By placing your order, you agree to Amazon.com's privacy notice and conditions of use" appears directly under "Review your order" and higher on the page than the button to click to "Place your order," so that "[t]o place his orders, Plaintiff had to navigate past this screen by clicking a square icon below and to the right of this disclaimer, which states: 'Place your order.' "); Whitt v. Prosper Funding, LLC, 2015 WL 4254062, at *1 (S.D.N.Y. July 14, 2015) ("An applicant could not complete a loan application without clicking the box indicating his or her acceptance of the Agreement."); Tompkins v. 23andMe, Inc., 2014 WL 2903752, at *3 (N.D. Cal. June 25, 2014) ("The account creation page requires customers to check a box next to the line, 'Yes, I have read and agree to the Terms of Service and Privacy Statement' . . . Similarly, during the registration process, . . . [c]ustomers must then click a large blue icon that reads 'I ACCEPT THE TERMS OF SERVICE' before finishing the registration process"); Swift v. Zynga Game Network, Inc., 805 F. Supp. 2d 904, 911 (N.D. Cal.2011) ("Plain-tiff admits that she was required to and did click on an 'Accept' button directly above a statement that clicking on the button served as assent to the YoVille terms of service along with a blue hyperlink directly to the terms of service."); Zaltz v. JDATE, 952 F.Supp.2d 439, 453–54 (E.D.N.Y.2013) ("defendant's reference to its Terms and Conditions of Service appear above the but-ton" that "a prospective user had to click in order to assent"); 5831 Partners LLC v. Shareasale.com, 2013 WL 5328324, at *7 & n. 4 (E.D.N.Y. Sept 23, 2013) ("defendant's reference to its Merchant Agreement appears adjacent to the activation button . . . in determining that the forum selection clause was reasonably communicated to plaintiff, [the Court] is solely relying on the second page of the sign up process (in which a prospective merchant must click to activate its account and is informed that 'By clicking and making a request to Activate, you agree to the terms and conditions in the Merchant Agreement.' "); Vernon v. Qwest Commc'ns Int'l, Inc., 925 F. Supp. 2d 1185, 1191 (D. Colo.2013) ("At each stage of the enrollment process the consumer was referred to the Subscriber Agreement and, in some instances, specifically to the existence of an arbitration clause."); Fteja, 841 F.Supp.2d 835 (the phrase "By clicking Sign Up, you are indicating that you have read and agree to the Terms of Policy" appeared directly below the button marked "Sign Up," and, this Court finds, the symmetry between the "Sign Up" phrases would help to catch the reader's

situation in Register.com, 356 F.3d 393 at 401–02, there is no evidence that plaintiff Meyer repeatedly visited Uber's registration screen.

Rather, Uber's interface here shares certain characteristics in common with instances in which courts have declined to hold that an electronic agreement was formed. Most obviously, Uber riders need not click on any box stating "I agree" in order to proceed to use the Uber app—a feature that courts have repeatedly made note of in declining to find that an electronic contract was formed. As the Seventh Circuit has stated, a court "cannot presume that a person who clicks on a box that appears on a computer screen has notice of all contents not only of that page but of other content that requires further action (scrolling, following a link, etc.)." Sgouros v. TransUnion Corp., 817 F.3d 1029, 1035 (7th Cir.2016).

Significantly for the purposes of determining whether plaintiff was on inquiry notice, the hyperlink here to the "Terms of Service & Privacy Policy" is by no means prominently displayed on Uber's registration screen. While the payment information and "Register" button are "very user-friendly and obvious," Berkson, 97 F.Supp.3d at 404, Uber's statement about "Terms of Service" appears far below and in much smaller font. As a result, "the design and content of" Uber's registration screen did not "make the 'terms of use' (*i.e.*, the contract details) readily and obviously available to the user." Id. at 402; *see also* Long, 200 Cal. Rptr.3d at 126 (recognizing "the practical reality that the checkout flow is laid out in such a manner that it tended to conceal the fact that placing an order was an express acceptance of [defendant's] rules and regulations.") (internal quotation marks and alterations omitted).

. . . .

Here, the Court finds that plaintiff Meyer did not have "[r]eason-ably conspicuous notice" of Uber's User Agreement, including its arbitration clause, or evince "unambiguous manifestation of assent to those terms." Id. Most importantly, the Uber registration screen, as explained supra, did not adequately call users' attention to the existence of Terms of Service, let alone to the fact that, by registering to use Uber, a user was agreeing to them. Like in Long, the "Terms of [Service]

---

eye); Guadagno v. E*Trade Bank, 592 F. Supp. 2d 1263, 1267, 1271 (C.D. Cal.2008) (users had to check a box acknowledging that they had reviewed the Account Agreement); Feldman v. Google, Inc., 513 F. Supp. 2d 229, 233, 237 (E.D. Pa.2007) (in order to activate their accounts, users had to click a box stating "Yes, I agree to the above terms and conditions" displayed in a scrollable text box); Major v. McCallister, 302 S.W.3d 227 (Mo. Ct. App. 2009) (the party seeking to enforce the contract "*did* put 'immediately visible notice of the existence of license terms'—i.e., 'By submitting you agree to the Terms of Use' and a blue hyperlink—right next to the button that Appellant pushed.").

hyperlink[ ]—[its] placement, color, size and other qualities relative to the [Uber app registration screen's] overall design—[is] simply too inconspicuous to meet [the Specht] standard." Long, 200 Cal.Rptr.3d at 125–26. When to this is coupled the fact that the key words "By creating an Uber account, you agree to" are even more inconspicuous, it is hard to escape the inference that the creators of Uber's registration screen hoped that the eye would be drawn seamlessly to the credit card information and register buttons instead of being distracted by the formalities in the language below. And this, the Court finds, is the reasonably foreseeable result.

Further still, the wording of Uber's hyperlink adds to the relative obscurity of Uber's User Agreement. The Court cannot simply assume that the reasonable (non-lawyer) smartphone user is aware of the likely contents of "Terms of Service," especially when that phrase is placed directly alongside "Privacy Policy." There is, after all, a "breadth of the range of technological savvy of online purchasers" (and smartphone users). Barnes & Noble, 763 F.3d at 1179; *see also* Long, 200 Cal.Rptr.3d at 127; Berkson, 97 F.Supp.3d at 400. The reasonable user might be forgiven for assuming that "Terms of Service" refers to a description of the types of services that Uber intends to provide, not to the user's waiver of his constitutional right to a jury trial or his right to pursue legal redress in court should Uber violate the law.[11] In other words, "the importance of the details of the contract" was "obscured or minimized by the physical manifestation of assent expected of a consumer seeking to purchase or subscribe to a service or product." Berkson, 97 F.Supp.3d at 402. There is a real risk here that Uber's registration screen "made joining [Uber] fast and simple and made it appear—falsely—that being a [user] imposed virtually no burdens on the consumer besides payment." Schnabel, 697 F.3d at 127–28.

Additionally, the hurdles for Uber users were not at an end even if they did click on the initial hyperlink. Such users were "taken to a screen that contains a button that accesses the 'Terms and Conditions' and 'Privacy Policy' then in effect." Once users reached the "Terms of

---

[11] It may be noted, a propos the expectations of the ordinary consumer, that according to a 2015 study carried out by the Consumer Financial Protection Bureau, "[o]ver three quarters of those who said they understood what arbitration is acknowledged they did not know whether their credit card agreement contained an arbitration clause. Of those who thought they did know, more than half were incorrect about whether their agreement actually contained an arbitration clause. Among consumers whose contract included an arbitration clause, fewer than 7 percent recognized that they could not sue their credit card issuer in court." See Consumer Financial Protection Bureau Study Finds That Arbitration Agreements Limit Relief for Consumers, Consumer Protection Financial Bureau, March 10, 2015, https://www.consumerfinance.gov/about-us/newsroom/cfpb-study-finds-that-arbitration-agreements-limit-relief-for-consumers/.

Service" (*i.e.*, the User Agreement), they had to scroll down several pages in order to come across the arbitration provision, located in a "dispute resolution" section. *See* Sgouros, 817 F.3d at 1033; Savetsky, 2015 WL 604767, at *4. While the "dispute resolution" heading in the User Agreement is bolded, as is the waiver (in the arbitration context) of the right to a jury trial or class proceeding, users would have had to reach this part of the agreement to discover the bolded text at all (unlike, for example, the prominent warning about the existence of an arbitration clause in Guadagno v. E*Trade Bank, 592 F.Supp.2d 1263, 1271 (C.D.Cal.2008)). Though "[a] party cannot avoid the terms of a contract on the ground that he or she failed to read it before signing," Specht, 306 F.3d at 30 (internal quotation marks omitted), the placement of the arbitration clause in Uber's User Agreement constituted, as a practical matter, a further barrier to reasonable notice.

At bottom, what is at stake is the "integrity and credibility" of "electronic bargaining." Specht, 306 F.3d at 35. When contractual terms as significant as the relinquishment of one's right to a jury trial or even of the right to sue in court are accessible only via a small and distant hyperlink titled "Terms of Service & Privacy Policy," with text about agreement thereto presented even more obscurely, there is a genuine risk that a fundamental principle of contract formation will be left in the dust: the requirement for "a manifestation of mutual assent." Schnabel, 697 F.3d at 119 (internal quotation marks omitted). One might be tempted to argue that the nature of electronic contracts is such that consumers do not read them, however conspicuous these contracts are, and that consumers have resigned themselves simply to clicking away their rights. But that would be too cynical and hasty a view, and certainly not the law. The purveyors of electronic form contracts are legally required to take steps to provide consumers with "reasonable notice" of contractual terms. *See* Specht, 306 F.3d at 20. User interfaces designed to encourage users to overlook contractual terms in the process of gaining access to a product or service are hardly a suitable way to fulfill this legal mandate.

In contrast, the appellate court concluded that Meyer *assented* to the arbitration term:

1. Reasonably conspicuous notice

In considering the question of reasonable conspicuousness, precedent and basic principles of contract law instruct that we consider the perspective of a reasonably prudent smartphone user. *See Schnabel* [v. *Trilegiant Corp.*, 697 F.3d 110, 118 (2d Cir. 2012)] at 124 ("[T]he touchstone of the analysis is whether reasonable people in the position of the parties would have known about the terms and the conduct that would be required to assent to them."). "[M]odern cell phones . . . are now such a pervasive and insistent part of daily life that the proverbial visitor from Mars might conclude they were an important feature of human anatomy." *Riley v. California*, ___ U.S. ___, 134 S.Ct. 2473, 2484, 189 L.Ed.2d 430 (2014). As of 2015, nearly two-thirds of American adults owned a smartphone, a figure that has almost doubled since 2011. *See* U.S. Smartphone Use in 2015, Pew Research Center, at 2 (Apr. 2015), http://assets.pewresearch.org/wp-content/uploads/sites/14/2015/ 03/ PI_Smartphones_0401151.pdf (last visited Aug. 17, 2017). Consumers use their smartphones for, among other things, following the news, shopping, social networking, online banking, researching health conditions, and taking classes. *Id.* at 5. In a 2015 study, approximately 89 percent of smartphone users surveyed reported using the internet on their smartphones over the course of the week-long study period. *Id.* at 33. A purchaser of a new smartphone has his or her choice of features, including operating systems, storage capacity, and screen size.

Smartphone users engage in these activities through mobile applications, or "apps," like the Uber App. To begin using an app, the consumers need to locate and download the app, often from an application store. Many apps then require potential users to sign up for an account to access the app's services. Accordingly, when considering the perspective of a reasonable smartphone user, we need not presume that the user has never before encountered an app or entered into a contract using a smartphone. Moreover, a reasonably prudent smartphone user knows that text that is highlighted in blue and underlined is hyperlinked to another webpage where additional information will be found.

Turning to the interface at issue in this case, we conclude that the design of the screen and language used render the notice provided reasonable as a matter of California law.[9] The Payment Screen is uncluttered, with only fields for the user to enter his or her credit card details, buttons to register for a user account or to connect the user's pre-existing PayPal account or Google Wallet to the Uber account, and the warning that "By creating an Uber account, you agree to the TERMS OF SERVICE & PRIVACY POLICY." The text, including the hyperlinks to the Terms and Conditions and Privacy Policy, appears directly below the buttons for registration. The entire screen is visible at once, and the user does not need to scroll beyond what is immediately visible to find notice of

---

[9] In evaluating the application interface, we use the actual-size screenshot of the last step in the registration process, as it would have appeared on Meyer's Samsung Galaxy S5.

the Terms of Service. Although the sentence is in a small font, the dark print contrasts with the bright white background, and the hyperlinks are in blue and underlined. This presentation differs sharply from the screen we considered in *Nicosia*, which contained, among other things, summaries of the user's purchase and delivery information, "between fifteen and twenty-five links," "text . . . in at least four font sizes and six colors," and several buttons and advertisements. *Nicosia* [*v. Amazon.com, Inc.*, 834 F.3d 220, 229 (2d Cir. 2016).] at 236–37. Furthermore, the notice of the terms and conditions in *Nicosia* was "not directly adjacent" to the button intended to manifest assent to the terms, unlike the text and button at issue here. *Id.* at 236.

In addition to being spatially coupled with the mechanism for manifesting assent—*i.e.*, the register button—the notice is temporally coupled. As we observed in *Schnabel*,

> inasmuch as consumers are regularly and frequently confronted with non-negotiable contract terms, particularly when entering into transactions using the Internet, the presentation of these terms at a place and time that the consumer will associate with the initial purchase or enrollment, or the use of, the goods or services from which the recipient benefits at least indicates to the consumer that he or she is taking such goods or employing such services subject to additional terms and conditions that may one day affect him or her.

Schnabel, 697 F.3d at 127. Here, notice of the Terms of Service is provided simultaneously to enrollment, thereby connecting the contractual terms to the services to which they apply. We think that a reasonably prudent smartphone user would understand that the terms were connected to the creation of a user account.

That the Terms of Service were available only by hyperlink does not preclude a determination of reasonable notice. *See Fteja* [*v. Facebook, Inc.*, 841 F.Supp.2d 829, 839 (S.D.N.Y. 2012)] ("[C]licking [a] hyperlinked phrase is the twenty-first century equivalent of turning over the cruise ticket. In both cases, the consumer is prompted to examine terms of sale that are located somewhere else."). Moreover, the language "[b]y creating an Uber account, you agree" is a clear prompt directing users to read the Terms and Conditions and signaling that their acceptance of the benefit of registration would be subject to contractual terms. As long as the hyperlinked text was itself reasonably conspicuous—and we conclude that it was—a reasonably prudent smartphone user would have constructive notice of the terms. While it may be the case that many users will not bother reading the additional terms, that is the choice the user makes; the user is still on inquiry notice.

Finally, we disagree with the district court's determination that the location of the arbitration clause within the Terms and Conditions was itself a "barrier to reasonable notice." *Meyer*, 200 F.Supp.3d at 421 (citing, *inter alia*, *Sgouros* [*v. TransUnion Corp.*, 817 F.3d 1029, 1033 (7th Cir. 2016)]). In *Sgouros*, the Seventh Circuit determined that the defendant's website actively misled users by "explicitly stating that a click on the button constituted assent for TransUnion to obtain access to the purchaser's personal information," without saying anything about "contractual terms," and without any indication that "the same click constituted acceptance of the Service Agreement." 817 F.3d at 1035–36. The website did not contain a hyperlink to the relevant agreement; instead, it had a scroll box that contained the entirety of the agreement, only the first three lines of which were visible without scrolling, and it had no prompt for the reader to scroll for additional terms. *See id.* at 1035–36 ("Where the terms are not displayed but must be brought up by using a hyperlink, courts outside of Illinois have looked for a clear prompt directing the user to read them. . . . No court has suggested that the presence of a scrollable window containing buried terms and conditions of purchase or use is, in itself, sufficient for the creation of a binding contract . . . ."). Here, there is nothing misleading. Although the contract terms are lengthy and must be reached by a hyperlink, the instructions are clear and reasonably conspicuous. Once a user clicks through to the Terms of Service, the section heading ("Dispute Resolution") and the sentence waiving the user's right to a jury trial on relevant claims are both bolded.

Accordingly, we conclude that the Uber App provided reasonably conspicuous notice of the Terms of Service as a matter of California law and turn to the question of whether Meyer unambiguously manifested his assent to those terms.

2. Manifestation of assent

Although Meyer's assent to arbitration was not express, we are convinced that it was unambiguous in light of the objectively reasonable notice of the terms, as discussed in detail above. See *Register.com* [*Register.com, Inc. v. Verio, Inc.*, 356 F.3d 393, 403 (2d Cir. 2004).] at 403 ("[R]egardless whether [a user] did or did not say, 'I agree' . . . [the user's] choice was either to accept the offer of contract, taking the information subject to the terms of the offer, or, if the terms were not acceptable, to decline to take the benefits."); *see also Schnabel*, 697

F.3d at 128 ("[A]cceptance need not be express, but where it is not, there must be evidence that the offeree knew or should have known of the terms and understood that acceptance of the benefit would be construed by the offeror as an agreement to be bound."). As we described above, there is ample evidence that a reasonable user would be on inquiry notice of the terms, and the spatial and temporal coupling of the terms with the registration button "indicate[d] to the consumer that he or she is . . . employing such services subject to additional terms and conditions that may one day affect him or her." *Schnabel*, 697 F.3d at 127. A reasonable user would know that by clicking the registration button, he was agreeing to the terms and conditions accessible via the hyperlink, whether he clicked on the hyperlink or not.

The fact that clicking the register button had two functions—creation of a user account and assent to the Terms of Service—does not render Meyer's assent ambiguous. The registration process allowed Meyer to review the Terms of Service prior to registration, unlike web platforms that provide notice of contract terms only after the user manifested his or her assent. Furthermore, the text on the Payment Screen not only included a hyperlink to the Terms of Service, but expressly warned the user that by creating an Uber account, the user was agreeing to be bound by the linked terms. Although the warning text used the term "creat[e]" instead of "register," as the button was marked, the physical proximity of the notice to the register button and the placement of the language in the registration flow make clear to the user that the linked terms pertain to the action the user is about to take.

The transactional context of the parties' dealings reinforces our conclusion. Meyer located and downloaded the Uber App, signed up for an account, and entered his credit card information with the intention of entering into a forward-looking relationship with Uber. The registration process clearly contemplated some sort of continuing relationship between the putative user and Uber, one that would require some terms and conditions, and the Payment Screen provided clear notice that there were terms that governed that relationship.

Accordingly, we conclude on the undisputed facts of this case that Meyer unambiguously manifested his assent to Uber's Terms of Service as a matter of California law.

————————————

As you see in the competing analyses in *Meyer*, in determining what constitutes reasonable notice of terms and adequate indication of assent, courts have to make judgments about what the reasonable user will notice and understand when offers are made. That is not an abstract question, though it is often treated that way. Increasingly there is data available to support judgments about what will likely be seen and understood. See, for example, the study undertaken by Jonathan Obar and Anne Oeldorf-Hirsch to assess user interactions with the consent materials of a fictitious social networking service, which revealed that the "quick-join clickwrap option," common to social networking services, hinders assent processes by making privacy and terms of service policies difficult to find and by discouraging engagement with privacy and reputation protections by suggesting that assent materials are unimportant. See Jonathan A. Obar & Anne Oeldorf-Hirsch, *Clickwrap Impact: Quick-Join Options and Ignoring Privacy and Terms of Service Policies of Social Networking Services*, in Proceedings of the 8th International Conference on Social Media & Society, available at SSRN: https://ssrn.com/abstract=3017277.

Food for Thought: Modifying Online Agreements

If you have a credit card or a bank account, you probably have received a written notice of changed contract terms, with a note saying that continued use of the card or account after a specified date will constitute assent to those new terms. This means of contract modification is sanctioned by regulations governing particular financial transactions. However, these regulations do not apply to companies' other attempts to modify agreements.

Sometimes vendors seek to change agreement terms by simply "posting" them on the company website or providing some other notice, rather than by obtaining affirmative assent from the other party. Some vendors include a contract provision saying "terms are subject to change at any time." In a small number of jurisdictions, courts have held that such a term causes the contract to be "illusory," because one party claims the right to change the terms and therefore is not committed to the supposed contract. In the majority of jurisdictions, though, the original contract is valid, and the issue becomes whether the later modification is effective.

A vendor who seeks to change its standard-form terms for hundreds, thousands, or even millions of customers may be able to do so easily if each user's visit to the website is a new contract (for instance, if each purchase from the vendor is a separate transaction) or if website subscribers assent to the proposed modification on their next online visit before the modification needs to take effect. However, if the customers have an ongoing relationship with the vendor, with new transactions occurring even if the customers do not visit the website, modifying the contract becomes a logistical nightmare if the vendor needs to obtain the assent of every customer (an "opt-in" system). As an alternative, some vendors have notified customers of an upcoming change in contract terms and have given them a specified number of days to expressly "opt out" of the modification or the contract, after which the remaining customers will be presumed to assent to the modified contract. In the bricks-and-mortar world, you will recall, silence is seldom valid assent. Should, or why should, the result be different in electronic settings? Considering your own online activity, have you encountered a change of terms of this sort? How did you handle the notice? Can you identify circumstances in which silence should, or should not, be considered to manifest assent?

§ 2.4. Rejection by the Offeree

An offeree's power of acceptance is terminated by the offeree's rejection of the offer, expressly or through conduct. Rejection also may occur by virtue of a counter-offer, which implicitly announces "I don't want your deal; I want the deal I now propose to you." A rejection usually is understood as terminating the offer because the offeror may reasonably understand it that way and therefore will not prepare to perform the promise nor act to revoke the offer. See Restatement (Second) § 38 comment a. However, a rejection does not terminate the offer (1) if the offeror indicates that the offer will stand despite rejection or (2) if the offeree indicates it will continue to consider the offer, despite initial rejection. See Restatement (Second) §§ 38, 39. As with other communications related to contract formation or interpretation, whether a statement is a rejection is a question of fact and is judged under the objective standard.

Example W: *Collins v. Thompson*, 679 F.2d 168 (9th Cir. 1982).

Prisoners at the Washington State Reformatory filed a class action alleging that conditions of confinement at the prison were unconstitutional. On January 19, 1981, the state submitted to the court a proposed consent decree, providing for reduction of the inmate population to the single cell capacity of 656 on a schedule calling for a first reduction to 865 on March 1. On February 6, the state discovered an error in the consent decree and submitted a revised proposal on February 13, calling for the first reduction in population to occur by April 1 rather than March 1. On February 26, the inmates moved for approval of the settlement with the March 1 date or, in the alternative, for notice to the class reflecting

the change to April 1. The state moved for court approval of the settlement with the April 1 date, while the prisoners moved for adoption of
the March 1 date. The court refused both requests, concluding that the
parties had not yet reached agreement as to the content of the decree.
Thereafter, on May 15, the inmates filed a Notice of Acceptance of Order
of Settlement, seeking adoption of the February 6 proposal, using the
April 1 date. The state opposed, arguing that the prisoners' actions in
strenuously pursuing the enforcement of the proposed consent decree
with the March 1 date constituted a rejection of the February 13 offer.

Analysis: The district court ruled that the inmates' "alternative motion on February 26, 1981 clearly indicated that the plaintiffs were not rejecting the entire
settlement and that they fully intended settlement even if the date were the April
1st date," relying on Restatement (Second) of Contracts § 38 that a "manifestation
of intention not to accept an offer is a rejection *unless the offeree manifests an intention
to take it under further advisement.*" The Court of Appeals affirmed, finding that
factual conclusion not clearly erroneous.

Example X: *Quaker State Mushroom Co., Inc. v. Dominick's Finer Foods, Inc.
of Illinois*, 635 F. Supp. 1281 (N.D. Ill. 1986).

Quaker State and Dominick's had a one-year contract for sale of mushrooms, which expired in March 1983. Eight months after expiration,
Dominick's submitted four orders for mushrooms—on 10/23, 11/9, and
two orders on 12/2—at the price that would have applied if the previous
contract still existed. After receiving the first order, Quaker State realized
it did not have inventory to fulfill the order. It mailed a notice of price
increase dated 11/10 that included the statement "All orders subject to
final confirmation of this office." There were no further communications
between the parties, but Quaker State shipped the mushrooms that had
been ordered and Dominick's accepted delivery. Quaker State demanded
payment at the increased price noted in its 11/10 communication. Dominick's instead paid the lower price listed in its orders. Quaker State filed
suit for the difference in price and moved for summary judgment. The
result depended on determining if the parties reached agreement and, if
so, at what point in the sequence of communications.

Analysis: The court ruled that Dominick's orders were offers, but they were
rejected by Quaker State's notice that it required a higher price than listed in the
orders. That notice was not a counter-offer, however, because the notice indicated

Ethical Issues

The court rejected Quaker State's motion for summary judgment because the "reasonable value" was an issue of fact that could not be determined without a hearing. The court went on to chastise the parties, noting that the dispute involved only approximately $19,000 (if Quaker State was entitled to the higher price it sought) and "should never have mushroomed into full-blown litigation. Had the parties simply split the difference initially, they probably would have been not much worse off than they are now, after having had to pay lawyers' fees and other costs to conduct discovery and brief summary judgment motions. A trial in this case would be an economic absurdity." The court therefore ordered the parties to meet before the next status hearing to discuss settlement or consider agreeing to prompt and final arbitration (and suggested in a footnote that a fair settlement might be for Dominick's to pay the lower price for its first two orders and the higher price for the last two).

that orders were subject to confirmation. There was therefore no offer in existence when the mushrooms were shipped by Quaker State or accepted by Dominick's.

Under UCC Article 2, just as under the common law, parties can create a contract through their conduct (e.g., shipping mushrooms and accepting the shipment), and parties may leave some terms—including price—undetermined, but a contract is created only if parties manifest the intention to enter a contract through their actions and despite the uncertainty. The court concluded that, because Quaker State and Dominick's had communicated their difference of opinion about the price to be charged for the mushrooms, the parties did not manifest intention to enter a contract at any point in the transaction.

Since no contract existed between the parties, Dominick's would be liable not for breach of contract but for the reasonable value of the mushrooms, under general principles of restitution (see Chapters 5 and 10).

§ 2.5. Revocation by the Offeror

A revocation is a communication that manifests the offeror's intention not to enter into the contract previously proposed by the offeror. It terminates the offeree's power of acceptance. See Restatement (Second) § 42. The offeror's intent is usually expressed through *direct* communication ("I revoke my offer"). Revocation may, instead, be manifested *indirectly* if: (i) the offeror takes action that shows that the offeror no longer intends to commit to the offered bargain; and (ii) the offeree learns of that action (e.g., Marian offers to sell a piece of property to Jorge but then enters a contract to sell the property to someone else and Jorge learns about the sale). Because direct communication is favored, indirect revocation typically requires the action taken by the offeror clearly show the offer no longer can exist (e.g., that Marian is discussing a sale with a third party will not be sufficient) and the information indirectly acquired by the offeree must be trustworthy (e.g., an unverified rumor that Marian has sold the property may not be sufficient). See Restatement (Second) § 43 (requiring "definite" action by the offeror "inconsistent with an intention to enter the proposed contract" and "reliable" information acquired by the offeree to that effect).

Typically a revocation must be communicated to the offeree, just as the offer was. However, if the offer was made publicly by general advertisement or flyer (e.g., notice of a reward), the revocation may be communicated by a similar method of dissemination. As long as no better method of communication is available, a general communication will effectively revoke the offer, even if a particular individual does not become aware of the revocation and acts on the original offer. See Restatement (Second) § 46.

As with other communications related to assent, factual questions may arise regarding the application of these rules, such as whether particular language is "manifestation of an intention" not to enter into the transaction (under § 42), whether "no better means of notification is reasonably available" (under § 46), whether action by the offeror is "definite action" that is "inconsistent" with an intention not to enter into the transaction (under § 43), and whether the offeree has acquired "reliable" information about the offeror's action (also under § 43).

> **Example Y:** *First Development Corp. of Kentucky v. Martin Marietta Corp.,* 959 F.2d 617 (6th Cir 1992).
>
> On August 16, Sam Pollitt, on behalf of First Development Corp. of Kentucky (FDCK), submitted an offer to purchase a piece of riverfront property from Martin Marietta Corp. (MM) for $300,000. MM allowed the offer to expire because it had too many contingencies that in essence would allow FDCK to have 7½ months to decide unilaterally whether or not it would go forward with the purchase. On September 7, after the expiration of FDCK's offer, MM made an offer to FDCK to sell the property for $550,000, with the offer to expire in 30 days. After the offer was sent, a third party—Harmony Landing—initiated purchase discussions with MM. Based on those discussions, MM sent a signed contract document to Harmony, which arrived on September 19. After a telephone conversation in which a few minor modifications were agreed to, Harmony signed the contract document on September 21 or 22 and immediately sent it back to MM. MM received the signed contract on September 22 or 23. The agreement between MM and Harmony provided that Harmony would pay a nonrefundable $10,000 for a 60-day option to purchase the property, which would allow it to seek certain building permits. If Harmony wished to continue to consider the purchase, it would pay a nonrefundable $40,000 for an additional 10-month option

to purchase the property. If Harmony eventually decided to move forward with the purchase, the $50,000 would be applied to the purchase price of $550,000.

Meanwhile, on September 21, the real estate agent for MM told Pollitt of Harmony's interest in the property, but the agent was not aware of the imminent signing of a contract. On September 21, Pollitt looked at the property again, decided to accept MM's offer, typed an acceptance of MM's offer, and placed it in his desk drawer. On the morning of September 22, Pollitt put the acceptance into the company's mail depository for stamping and mailing. At 2:30 pm that afternoon, Pollitt returned a phone call from the agent, who told Pollitt that MM had accepted an option contract for sale of the property. At the conclusion of the call, Pollitt told the agent he intended to accept MM's offer. Pollit then retrieved the typed acceptance from the company's mail depository, and at 4:15 pm Pollitt delivered it to the agent. MM returned the acceptance to Pollitt, and FDCK filed suit for a permanent injunction, seeking to prevent MM from selling the property to Harmony and ordering MM to deliver the property to FDCK under the offer MM sent on September 7. The result of the suit turned on whether MM revoked its offer before FDCK accepted it.

Analysis: The trial judge entered a permanent injunction and ordered MM to convey the land to FDCK. On appeal, the majority ruled that MM had revoked its offer before FDCK's acceptance because Pollitt knew before the acceptance was delivered that the land was no longer available and was off the market. A dissenting judge disagreed, because FDCK knew only that there was an option contract on sale of the land, and did not have definite knowledge of the terms of that option contract. This particular option contract might have made Harmony's option to buy effective only if FDCK did not accept MM's offer to sell it to FDCK, so the offeree had not "acquire[d] reliable information" that the offeror had "take[n] definite action inconsistent with an intention to enter into the proposed contract" (Restatement (Second) § 43. Do you agree with the majority or with the dissent?

Make the Connection

Under the so-called "mailbox rule," the outcome might have been different if Pollitt had already deposited the acceptance in the US mails, rather than simply placed it in the company mail collection for later stamping and mailing. See § 2.6.

Problems: Rejection and Revocation

3-18. A popular cabaret singer makes an offer to perform on June 10th for $3500 in a performance hall owned by the offeree in Seattle. While the offeree is exploring how much income he could make selling tickets and related merchandise for her performance, he hears from his booking agent that the cabaret singer has just scheduled a month-long tour in Australia for June. The offeree quickly mails an acceptance to the singer. Is there acceptance? Would there be acceptance if the offeree instead hears from a reliable source that the singer has scheduled concerts on June 8th in Miami and June 11th in New Orleans?

3-19. AMC issues an RFQ for a project. Supplier B responds with a bid (expiring in a month) that includes a very competitive price, but a slightly different timeline than in the RFQ, because Supplier B has competing obligations for part of the proposed timeline in the RFQ. A week later, AMC opens the eight bids received. AMC is intrigued with the expertise of Supplier B and the price of B's bid. The AMC bid supervisor immediately calls Supplier B and says, "I need to check your timeline with my project manager, because it may be problematic. If you can do the work a month after our RFQ timeline, but in 2/3 of the time specified in the RFQ, we can close the deal now." After investigating the job further for three days, Supplier B tells AMC that it cannot do the job so quickly. Then AMC tries to accept Supplier B's earlier bid, still within the one-month period specified in the offer. Supplier B argues that that bid is no longer available for consideration. Who's right? (Select two answers.)

    a. Supplier B is correct, because its initial bid has been impliedly rejected by AMC's counter-offer.

    b. Supplier B is correct, because its initial bid lapsed upon AMC's counter-offer.

    c. Supplier B is correct, because AMC revoked Supplier B's offer by AMC's counter-offer.

    d. AMC is correct, because B's bid was not rejected.

    e. AMC is correct, because Supplier B's initial bid had not yet lapsed.

3-20. Betta has a ski equipment store at a popular ski area. Her supplier sends her a catalog with the upcoming season's "hot sellers for cold days; shipment within ten days." She fills out the order sheet inside the catalog, ordering

12 boot-warmer appliances (which plug into a cigarette lighter outlet in a car and blow warm air into cold boots), and sends it to the supplier. Eight days later, Betta gets a handwritten postcard from the seller, saying that the boot-warmers are in stock and are available for a new 10% discount, if Betta orders at least 15. Betta reconsiders her order of 12 and phones in an order for 16 instead. Two days later, Betta receives a box in the mail with 12 boot-warmers. A day later, she receives a box with 16 boot-warmers. When was a contract formed and on what terms?

—————————

§ 2.5.1. Limitations on the Power to Revoke: Unilateral Contracts

Because an offer is merely a promise of what the offeror will do *if* the offeree accepts the offer, it is not binding on the offeror until acceptance. As a result, the offeror may revoke its offer at any time before acceptance, even if the offeror said it would keep the offer open for a specific period of time. The "promise" to keep the offer open defines when the offer will lapse but does not unilaterally bind the offeror. If the offeree wants the offered deal, the offeree need only accept it.

However, if the offer is for a unilateral contract (see page 117), the rule can operate unfairly, as illustrated by two well-known hypotheticals:

- *The Brooklyn Bridge Hypothetical*: A says to B, "If you walk across the Brooklyn Bridge, I will give you $500." B eagerly starts across the bridge and is within a few feet of the end when A yells, "I revoke!"

- *The Flagpole Hypothetical*: A says to B, "If you climb this flagpole, I will give you $500." B eagerly starts to climb the flagpole and is within a few feet of the top when A yells, "I revoke!"

Because these offers may be accepted only by performance, not by return promise, acceptance occurs only when the offeree has fully performed—when B gets all the way across the bridge or climbs to the top of the flagpole. Until that time, the offeree cannot prevent the offeror from revoking the offer, since acceptance by promise ("I promise to cross the bridge") is not possible (it's a unilateral contract!) and maybe not desirable (B doesn't want to be in breach if she can't get to the top of the flagpole).

The courts have fashioned two rules to limit the risks for the offeree in these circumstances. The first rule we saw on page 119: If an offer is ambiguous, vague, or silent regarding whether it is an offer for a bilateral or unilateral contract, then it will be understood as being an offer for a bilateral contract, seeking a return promise, and the beginning of performance will operate as an acceptance.

The second rule applies to the true unilateral contract situation, in which the offeree can accept only by performance. Once the offeree begins performance, an "option contract" is created by operation of law, giving the offeree the opportunity to complete the requested performance and thus accept the offer for a unilateral contract. If the offeree does not complete performance in accordance with the terms of the offer, the offeror is free to withdraw the offer. See Restatement (Second) § 45.

Think About It!

In response to offers for both bilateral and unilateral contracts, the beginning of performance (distinguished from mere preparation for performance) is significant. For offers for bilateral contracts, the beginning of performance constitutes acceptance of the offer. For offers for unilateral contracts, it means there is an option contract for the offeree to complete performance and accept. Given similar facts, would you expect courts to be more likely to find that the offeree began performance in a bilateral or in a unilateral contract situation?

In effect, this rule makes an offer for a unilateral contract temporarily irrevocable once the offeree begins performance. The offeree is not bound to continue or complete performing but has the opportunity to do so. If the offeree completes the performance, there is a binding contract, so the offeror has a duty to fulfill the promise in the offer. If the offeree does not complete performance, the offeror has no duty to perform.

§ 2.5.2. Limitations on the Power to Revoke: Option Contracts and Firm Offers

Offers may be at least temporarily irrevocable under the following additional circumstances:

The Parties Create an Option Contract: Any offer can be made irrevocable if the parties agree that the offeree will pay the offeror (or provide something else of value) to keep the offer open, usually for a specified period of time. This creates an "option contract" in favor of the offeree on the underlying deal. For example, if a seller offers to sell particular real estate to a prospective buyer, who wants time to explore financing or obtain building or zoning permits, the parties may mutually assent to an option contract, under which the buyer pays the seller for the seller's promise not to revoke the offer during the specified period. If no time is specified in the option contract terms, a court may determine that the option is available for a "reasonable time" (or, in proper circumstances, may decide the contract is too indeterminate to be enforceable). Whether the buyer eventually accepts the seller's offer to sell the real estate is in the discretion of the buyer, as the option-holder. In effect, the seller has entered into a "side-contract" with the potential buyer to keep its offer-to-sell open for the agreed-upon period of time.

In an option contract, because the offeror is bound by contract to keep the offer open as agreed, the offer is not governed by the usual rules on termination of the power of acceptance. In addition to being irrevocable, it cannot be terminated by rejection or counter-offer. Whether death or incapacity affects the option depends on the rules regarding excuses from contract performance (*see* Chapter 9) rather than on the rules for termination of the power of acceptance. Acceptance of the offer that is the subject of the option contract is effective when it reaches the offeror, unless the offer for the option contract specifies otherwise. (This is an exception to the "mailbox rule," which is covered below on page 159.)

The Offer Is a "Firm Offer" Under Article 2: If the transaction is governed by UCC Article 2 because its predominant purpose involves a contract for the sale of goods (see the discussion on page 166), UCC § 2–205 applies. Under this section, a signed offer by a merchant promising that the offer will be held open is enforceable for the amount of time expressed (or for a reasonable time, if no time is given), up to three months. If the offer is on a form supplied by the offeree, the offeror must "sign" (usually, initial) the assurance of irrevocability. The firm-offer rule in § 2–205 supplements the common-law rules on irrevocability, which remain applicable for sale-of-goods contracts.

Some states have similar statutes that apply to a broader group of transactions than does UCC § 2–205, specifying, for example, that a signed writing promising that an offer will be held open is enforceable.[*]

In Chapter 5, we will explore one additional rule of law that could affect the revocability of an offer. That concept—promissory estoppel—makes a promise enforceable when a promisee justifiably relies on the promise, even though no contract was formed. The question addressed in Chapter 5 is when that concept should be available to bind an offeror in circumstances when the offeree has the opportunity to create liability by accepting the offer.

Problems: Irrevocable Offers

If multiple rules could apply, give all possible results.

3-21. Company A sends an email to Company B inquiring about the price of 300 electrical engines, model 45JR2. On October 1, Company B replies by email, "Our price for 300 engines, model 45JR2, is $5200. We guarantee that price until October 14, during which time the 300 engines can be shipped within two days of ordering. We await your order. Samuel Seller, Sales Agent, Company B." Assume that the price quote is an offer. Five

---

[*] *See, e.g.*, N.Y. Gen. Oblig. L. § 5–1109 (McKinney 2001).

days later, Company B emails Company A an email withdrawing the offer. Two days later, Company A emails Company B a purchase order for the 300 engines for $5200. Company B refuses to acknowledge the order or ship the engines. Did the offer still exist when the offeree tried to accept?

3-22.   A makes an oral offer to B to settle a contract dispute, saying that it can be accepted only by B paying to A $752 in cash no later than July 1. On July 1, B goes to A's apartment in order to pay the money to A. B knocks on the door, A opens the door just a crack (with the chain still on the door) to see who it is, and B fans a stack of dollar bills in A's face. A then says, "But I revoke the offer." Did the offer still exist when the offeree tried to accept? Does the result change if A yells "I revoke" through the door before he opens it?

3-23.   In letters received by a prospective buyer and its broker, Seller offers, in writing, to sell real estate to the buyer and to pay a percentage of the sales price as a commission to Broker, if within six days Broker is successful in getting the buyer to accept the offer. On the fourth day, Seller mails Broker a writing revoking the offer. On the morning of the sixth day, Broker obtains the prospective buyer's acceptance of the offer. That afternoon, Broker receives Seller's revocation. Broker notifies Seller of Buyer's acceptance that evening by letter by messenger. Broker claims breach of the contract and sues Seller for the commission. Did the offer still exist when the Broker tried to accept?

---

§ 2.6. Time of Effectiveness of Contract Formation Communications

§ 2.6.1. The Mailbox Rule for Acceptances

Because a party's assent must be manifested to the other party, the default assumption in determining the existence of offer and acceptance is that a communication must be delivered to the other party to be effective. For example, because an offeree cannot act on an offer without knowing about it, a communication becomes effective as an offer only upon delivery to the offeree. The same is true of revocations: Because the offeree reasonably believes an offer may be accepted until notified otherwise, a revocation is effective only upon delivery to the offeree. And the same is true of rejections: Because the offeror reasonably believes that the offeree has the power of acceptance until notified otherwise, a rejection of an offer is effective only upon delivery to the offeror.

Applying the default assumption to all contract-formation communications causes no difficulty when the parties are in face-to-face conversation, because the communications are sent and received at the same time. If the parties are at a distance, however, the default rule that communications are effective only when received poses some challenges when applied to acceptances.

Acceptance marks agreement by both parties. At the moment the offeree dispatches her acceptance, there is a manifestation of agreement by both parties, but the offeror does not yet know that. If the acceptance is not effective until received by the offeror, however, the offeree remains at risk that the offer could be withdrawn before the acceptance and may hesitate to rely on the existence of a contract until she knows the offeror received it. But she will not know when the acceptance arrives without a responsive confirmation, producing continuing uncertainty as well as the necessity of an additional communication beyond an offer and an acceptance.

In England, this dilemma was addressed in 1818 by adoption of the "mailbox rule" in *Adams v. Lindsell*, 106 Eng. Rep. 250 (K.B. 1818), and courts in the United States soon followed suit. The mailbox rule—really an exception to the default rule requiring delivery of contract communications—says that an acceptance, if properly addressed and sent in a reasonable manner invited by the offer, is effective when it is "put out of the offeree's possession" (see Restatement (Second) § 63). As a result, a contract is formed when the offeree has manifested intent to enter the contract, before the offeror is aware, even if the acceptance never arrives.

The mailbox rule solves one set of problems but potentially creates others. First, the offeror is bound to a contract before receiving the acceptance, even if the offeror attempts to revoke between dispatch and receipt of the acceptance. (The offeror is bound even if the acceptance is never received, but this is a more unusual situation.) Second, having the acceptance be effective upon dispatch creates a dilemma if the offeree sends an acceptance (effective upon dispatch) and thereafter sends a faster-arriving rejection or counter-offer (effective when received), perhaps because the market shifts in a direction unfavorable to the offeree or just because the offeree changed his mind. Should first-in-time prevail (e.g., acceptance is effective because sent before the other communication arrived), even though the offeror receives conflicting information (e.g., both an acceptance and a counter-offer, or an acceptance and a rejection)?

Because the offeror is "master of the offer," some difficulties for the offeror (e.g., being bound before the acceptance arrives) can be addressed by having the offer explicitly require delivery of an acceptance, not just dispatch, to be effective, or require a speedy form of delivery (electronic acknowledgment, perhaps). Or the offeror can contact the offeree directly (perhaps by phone) to revoke, rather than rely on less speedy communications.

Other difficulties have been addressed by interpretations of or limitations on the mailbox rule to ensure that the offeree cannot use the rule to gain an unfair advantage. Thus an acceptance is not effective upon dispatch if the offeree also sends a rejection or counter-offer; the offeror is entitled to rely on whichever communication (rejection, counter-offer, or acceptance) arrives first. Such adjustments strike a balance by permitting offerees to assume the existence of a contract once they send an acceptance, while protecting the offeror from confusion and preventing the offeree from speculating on the market or otherwise "gaming" the rules.

Today, with immediate communications available by telephone, email, and fax, and many contracts entered through electronic means, concerns about when an acceptance becomes effective may arise less often, but it was a challenging issue when most communications were carried out by letters sent by post or messenger, and it remains an issue when mail or other methods of non-instantaneous communication are used. Even seemingly instantaneous forms of communication may raise questions about when those communications are to be considered "sent" and "received," since they still spend time in transit and may not be viewed by the intended recipient immediately upon arrival at a destination. In the 47 states adopting the Uniform Electronic Transactions Act (UETA), the following section helps to settle these kinds of questions by defining when an electronic record is sent or received:

UETA § 15. Time . . . of Sending and Receipt

(a) Unless otherwise agreed between the sender and the recipient, an electronic record is sent when it:

    (1) is addressed properly or otherwise directed properly to an information processing system that the recipient has designated or uses for the purpose of receiving electronic records or information of the type sent and from which the recipient is able to retrieve the electronic record;

    (2) is in a form capable of being processed by that system; and

    (3) enters an information processing system outside the control of the sender or of a person that sent the electronic record on behalf of the sender or enters a region of the information processing system designated or used by the recipient which is under the control of the recipient.

(b) Unless otherwise agreed between a sender and the recipient, an electronic record is received when:

    (1) it enters a processing system that the recipient has designated or uses for the purpose of receiving electronic records or information of the type sent and from which the recipient is able to retrieve the electronic record; and

    (2) it is in a form capable of being processed by that system.

. . . .

(e) An electronic record is received under subsection (b) even if no individual is aware of its receipt.

. . . .

Example Z: *First Development Corp. of Kentucky v. Martin Marietta Corp.*, 959 F.2d 617 (6th Cir. 1992).

Reread the facts in Example Y on page 153.

Analysis: If Pollitt had put his acceptance directly into the U.S. Postal Service mail, instead of placing it in the company's mail depository for stamping, he would have accepted the offer before it was withdrawn—and Martin Marietta would have ended up committed to two enforceable contracts involving sale of the land. How might Martin Marietta have changed the offer to prevent the mailbox rule from applying in this fashion?

Example AA: *Soldau v. Organon Inc.*, 860 F.2d 355 (9th Cir. 1988).

Organon Inc. discharged John Soldau from employment. Afterwards, Organon sent Soldau a letter, offering to pay him double the normal severance payment if he released all his claims against the company that might arise from his discharge. Soldau signed and dated the document and deposited it in the mail. When he returned home, he found that he had already received a check from Organon with the increased severance payment. Soldau returned to the post office and convinced a U.S. Postal Service employee to open the mail depository and return the envelope to him. He later sued Organon, claiming his discharge violated state and federal law, including the Age Discrimination in Employment Act. Organon moved to dismiss the lawsuit on the basis of the agreement that

Soldau had signed. Soldau claimed there was no agreement because he had not accepted the company's offer.

Analysis: The court held that, under the mailbox rule, Soldau had accepted Organon's offer when he placed the signed document in the mail, even though he later retrieved the envelope and it was not delivered to Organon.

> **Example BB:** *Monahan v. Finlandia University*, 69 F. Supp. 3d 681 (W.D. Mich. 2014), vacated in unpublished opinion, Case # 2:14–cv–00064– RHB (6th Cir. Sept. 1, 2015).
>
> Joseph Monahan was employed by Finlandia as Dean of the International School of Business and Executive Vice-President for External Relations in 2007–2008. On July 1, 2008, Finlandia wrote to Monahan that his administrative appointments were not being renewed, but it offered him employment as a tenured professor for 2008–2009. The appointment form said, "Please sign, date, and return this letter as evidence that you accept this appointment." The cover letter accompanying the appointment form said "Please return on or before July 15th. Should the signed letter not be received by this date, the position will not be held."
>
> Monahan signed the form on July 10 and properly addressed it to Finlandia. On July 14, Monahan mailed the form by express mail, second-day delivery. The letter arrived on July 16, but was misplaced in the Finlandia mailroom.
>
> On July 21, Finlandia sent Monahan a letter saying it had not received his reply and was not holding the position for him, as indicated in its earlier communication. Monahan sent Finlandia a copy of the receipt showing he had sent the form on July 14. Finlandia found that the form had been received on July 16. Because that was after the date specified in its offer, Finlandia continued to maintain that the offer of employment had not been effectively accepted.

Analysis: The trial court concluded that the letter of appointment did not specify a specific method or time frame for acceptance, but the cover letter specified the acceptance had to be received by July 15 to be effective. That changed the mailbox rule, so the acceptance was not effective when mailed. Finlandia therefore was free to consider the offer lapsed on July 15 or to withdraw the offer. But, the court concluded, Finlandia had not done so. The court thought that the letter Finlandia sent on July 21 indicated that it *had* continued to hold the offer open after July 15, until after the acceptance was received

The court of appeals disagreed. It vacated and remanded the case, concluding that no contract had been formed. The purported acceptance arrived too late, after the offer had lapsed. Finlandia could have revived its offer, or accepted Monahan's counter-offer, but it did neither.

§ 2.6.2. Time of Acceptance by Conduct

If an acceptance may be or must be made by performance or other conduct, is the acceptance effective when the conduct occurs or at some later time? Does the offeree have to take any additional steps after engaging in the conduct that will signify acceptance? The general rule is that the acceptance is valid at the time of the conduct, but if the conduct would not reliably come to the offeror's attention within a reasonable time, the offeree must take reasonable steps to notify the offeror of acceptance. No such notification is required if the offer waives it or if the offeror actually learns of the acceptance within a reasonable time, even if that was not likely at the time of the acceptance.

If the offeree fails to give the required notice, the offeror will be able to choose whether or not to recognize the existence of a contract, though the way in which the legal rules reach that result varies:

- In some jurisdictions, the acceptance is considered ineffective, so no contract is formed, but if the offeror eventually learns of the conduct signifying acceptance, the offeror may create a contract by treating the attempted acceptance as an offer and giving his own assent.

- In other jurisdictions, a contract is formed when the offeree performs the acts constituting acceptance, but the offeror may consider his contractual duties as "discharged" (nullified) because of the offeree's failure to notify the offeror of acceptance.

- UCC § 2–206(2) allows the offeror to choose whether to treat the offer as lapsed because notice of acceptance was not given.

If no contract is formed, restitutionary relief may be necessary to prevent the offeror from being unjustly enriched by any performance given by the offeree.

Consider the following example: Ben mails to a screen-printing shop a written purchase order for 50,000 specialty T-shirts for an upcoming marathon. Ben's order requests that, if the shop agrees to print the shirts, it start production immediately, to be sure the shirts will be ready in time for the event. The shop accepts Ben's offer when it starts to produce the T-shirts, but it still must give notice to Ben with reasonable promptness. If it fails to do so, the consequence depends on whether UCC Article 2 governs the contract. If the sale is considered to be predominantly a sale of goods (T-shirts) under Article 2, Ben could treat his offer as lapsed or could recognize the contract despite the absence of timely notice. If the contract was instead considered to be predominantly a service contract (for silk-screening), then either no contract would be formed or a contract would be formed but Ben could consider his duty under the contract to be discharged. Either way, Ben would be free to recognize a contract or give assent to the shop's offer (made by conduct and communication to Ben) by accepting the T-shirts or making a new promise to pay.

Problems: Time of Effectiveness of Acceptance

3-24. When is or should the following acceptances be effective?

     a. An acceptance sent via UPS or Federal Express

     b. An acceptance expressed by clicking "I agree" on a website

     c. An acceptance sent via text message

     d. An acceptance sent by letter, which never arrives

     e. An acceptance sent by letter, which never arrives, in response to an offer saying "I must hear from you within 10 days"

     f. An acceptance sent by email, which bounces back as "undeliverable"

     g. An acceptance sent by email from an email address widely known for sending spam, so it gets caught in the offeror's spam filter and never shows up in the offeror's email inbox

3-25. Shep owns a coffee shop in a quaint back alley of a commercial district. One morning, he arrives to find that his shop has been vandalized—smashed front plate-glass window, painted graffiti on the shop's sign, and missing coffee machines and bags of coffee beans. He posts a dozen copies of the following announcement in the neighborhood:

Help Stop Vandalism!

Shep's Coffee Shop was broken into and vandalized on the night of December 10. Shep will pay $300 to the first person providing him with information identifying the perpetrators. Contact Shep at 651-234-5678 with any information. Thanks!

Sherry works down the street from the coffee shop and sees one of the postings. She takes a picture of the graffiti on her cell phone and begins asking around to see if someone can identify the graffiti style or maker. She also begins to do some research on break-ins in the area. Will it be necessary for her to take reasonable steps to notify Shep of her acceptance, after she completes performance?

a. No, because no notice of acceptance is necessary for an offer that can be accepted only by performance.

b. No, because her acceptance will make notification unnecessary.

c. No, because the offeror is master of the offer, and Shep's offer did not state that notification would be required.

d. No, because Shep will find out about the acceptance within a reasonable time after acceptance.

e. Yes, notification will be necessary.

Would your answer be different if the reward had been for anyone providing information directly to the police?

---

§ 3. Sequential Offer and Acceptance Under UCC Article 2

We have noted the existence of UCC Article 2 (see Chapter 1) and looked at the contents of one of its provisions (see page 158 on § 2–205), without addressing to which contracts Article 2 would apply. This section introduces you to a broader range of Article 2 provisions—those that govern contract formation. We begin with a discussion of the scope of Article 2 as a whole, so that you will have the tools to determine whether Article 2 applies to a particular transaction and what impact that may have on the common-law rules that would otherwise apply to the contract.

Scope of UCC Article 2

"Transaction in Goods"/"Sale of Goods"

As noted in Chapter 1, the Uniform Commercial Code (UCC) is a uniform state statute that has been nearly universally adopted by U.S.

states and territories. UCC Article 2 is in effect in 49 states (all but Louisiana, which is a civil-law jurisdiction). As noted in § 1–103(b): "Unless displaced by the particular provisions of [the Uniform Commercial Code], the principles of law and equity, including the law merchant and the law relative to capacity to contract, principal and agent, estoppel, fraud, misrepresentation, duress, coercion, mistake, bankruptcy, and other validating or invalidating cause supplement its provisions." That means that, when the UCC applies to a transaction:

- Provisions that change the common law rule supersede the common law rule.

- If Article 2 is silent on a particular topic, then the common law rule applies.

- If Article 2 contains a new rule that does not conflict with the common law, it supplements the common-law rules, which remain applicable. The firm-offer rule in § 2–205 (see page 158) is an example of a supplementary Article 2 rule. It adds to, but does not interfere with, the common law rules on irrevocability of offers.

As you will see, Article 2 contains relatively few competing rules on contract formation, so in most instances a court determining whether a contract exists will rely on the common law rules of offer and acceptance. But one set of Article 2 provisions—§§ 2–206 and 2–207—significantly change the rules of contract formation applied when the offer and acceptance are not mirror images, so it will be important for you to be able to distinguish contracts inside and outside the scope of Article 2.

According to UCC § 2–102, Article 2 applies to "transactions in goods." Although a few Article 2 provisions apply to transactions other than sales, the language of almost all of the provisions limits coverage to contracts for "sales" of "goods:"

- A "sale" is defined in § 2–106 as the "passing of title from the seller to the buyer for a price". Sales are distinguished from transactions such as leases, gifts, and mortgages.

- "Goods" are defined in § 2–105 as "all things . . . which are moveable at the time of identification to the contract". Goods are distinguished from contract subjects such as services, real property, and intangibles (e.g., good will and data).

The most difficult questions about the scope of Article 2 are raised when a transaction involves both a sale of goods and some other kind of transaction. For example, does Article 2 govern a purchase of carpeting that involves not only a sale of goods but also installation of those goods (a service)? Does it govern the hiring of a mechanic to replace one's car brakes, which involves both providing labor (services) and selling parts (goods)? In such cases, courts apply the "predominant purpose" test; they look at the mixed contracts and ask "whether their predominant factor, their thrust, their purpose, reasonably stated, is the rendition of service, with goods incidentally involved (e.g., contract with artist for painting) or is a transaction of sale, with labor incidentally involved (e.g., installation of a water heater in a bathroom)," *Bonebrake v. Cox*, 499 F.2d 951, 960 (8th Cir. 1974). In determining the predominant purpose, courts consider a variety of factors, including the language of the contract (how does it talk about the parties' relationship and their performance responsibilities?), the primary reason the parties entered the contract, the relative costs of the goods and services, the nature of the provider's business (primarily a goods merchant or a service provider?), and any other circumstances relevant to determining the "predominant purpose" behind the contract. *See, e.g., Pass v. Shelby Aviation, Inc.*, 2000 WL 388775 (Tenn. Ct. App. Apr. 13, 2000).

Examples of cases finding predominantly a contract for sale of goods and, therefore, Article 2 coverage include *Pittsley v. Houser*, 875 P.2d 232 (Idaho Ct. App. 1994) (sale and installation of carpet); *Neibarger v. Universal Cooperatives, Inc.*, 486 N.W.2d 612 (Mich. 1992) (sale of milking system); and *True North Composites, LLC v. Trinity Industries, Inc.*, 65 Fed. App. 266 (Fed. Cir. 2003) (contract for custom design and manufacture of railcars). Examples of cases finding predominantly a sale of services and therefore no Article 2 coverage include *Pass v. Shelby Aviation, Inc.*, 2000 WL 388775 (Tenn. Ct. App.) (contract to repair and service airplane); *Higgins v. Lauritzen*, 530 N.W.2d 171 (Mich. Ct. App. 1995) (contract for installation of a water system); *Care Display, Inc. v. Didde-Glaser, Inc.*, 589 P.2d 599 (Kan. 1979) (contract for custom design and construction of themed booths for trade fair); and *Heuerman v. B&M Construction, Inc.*, 833 N.E.2d 382 (Ill. Ct. App. 2005) (contract with trucking company to deliver gravel).

§ 3.1. General Rules of Offer and Acceptance

The general rules for contract formation under Article 2 appear in § 2–204. Section 2–204(3) allows a contract to be formed, even though the content is indefinite, as long as the parties intended to make a contract and there is a reasonably certain basis for giving a remedy. This rule reflects but also loosens the common law rule discussed in Chapter 2 (see page 38). The rest of § 2–204 is equally flexible. Section 2–204(1) says a contract for sale of goods "may be made in any manner sufficient to show agreement, including conduct by both parties which recognizes the existence of a contract," and § 2–204(2) says an agreement may be found even though the moment of its making is undetermined. Article 2 does not explain how to show "agreement," so courts use common law principles of assent to define whether a contract for sale has been made.

Read § 2–206(1)(a), which addresses the general manner of acceptance and states a rule similar to the common law rule: Unless unambiguously indicated by language or circumstances, an offer to make a contract "shall be construed as inviting acceptance in any manner and by any medium reasonable in the circumstances." As in the common law, the offeror can mandate or the circumstances may require a particular manner or medium of acceptance, but if not, any reasonable manner or medium of acceptance is allowed. That includes acceptance by communication or acceptance by performance.

Read § 2–206(1)(b), which specifies a particular application of the rule in § 2–206(1)(a) that any reasonable manner of acceptance is generally permitted. Under § 2–206(1)(b), an offer to purchase goods for prompt shipment may be accepted either by a promise (e.g., a written confirmation sent to the buyer) or by performance (actually shipping the goods). Either way, what is created is a bilateral contract, on the terms specified in the offer—even if the goods that are shipped do not match the specifications in the offer. Note the additional rule in § 2–206(2): If acceptance is by performance (including by shipment), "an offeror who is not notified of acceptance within a reasonable time may treat the offer as having lapsed before acceptance."

We turn now to a UCC section that rejects the common-law mirror-image rule and creates a complicated set of rules on contract formation that supersede and significantly change the common law.

§ 3.2. Rejection of the Mirror Image Rule: UCC § 2–207

UCC § 2–207 expressly rejects the common law mirror image rule, which requires that an acceptance be a manifestation of assent to exactly the terms of the offer. Rejecting the mirror image rule has consequences both for deciding whether a contract has been entered (that is, whether the offeree will be understood to have manifested assent when the acceptance differs from the offer) and for identifying the terms that will be part of any resulting contract (because if the offer and acceptance do not have to match, determining what terms are part of the contract is much more complex).

The rejection of the mirror image rule is a bow to the realities of modern contracting behavior. As standard forms and boilerplate terms became more common because of the ubiquity of mass printing and reproduction technologies, business parties would often craft lengthy contract forms favorable to their own interests. When communicating with others to enter contracts, they would each use their own contract forms. The parties would directly negotiate critical aspects (the goods or services being exchanged, price, deadlines for performance) and then each would attach to the "offer" and "acceptance" a set of its own standard terms and conditions for the contract, typically diverging on some or even many points from the document received from the other party, in minor or major ways. Under traditional contract doctrine, any divergence at all between the forms would mean that a contract would not be created by the exchange of those documents. And yet the parties often thought they had entered a contract with each other, sometimes shipping and receiving goods or performing and receiving services and making payment. Often no one would read the other party's form—until a problem arose and the parties ended up in a dispute about the terms of the contract.

Under the common law, the result was surprising, to at least one and perhaps both of the parties. If the parties had not begun performance, there was no contract in existence at all. The parties may have agreed on the basics (what was being exchanged and the price) and even on many more details of the exchange, and each may have "signed off" on the deal, but the forms didn't agree, so there was no contract. If the parties had gone further, and actually performed under the contract, their conduct would create a contract, but on what terms? Party A sent a document committing to a set of terms (an offer), and Party B responded with its own differing document (not an acceptance, but a counter-offer). After Party B sent its counter-offer, additional documents might be exchanged between the parties, none of them creating a contract because each one contained terms that differed from the previous document. If the parties performed, the standard interpretation was that the last party to send a document had made "the final offer" and the other party's performance accepted the terms in that last document. This came to be known as the "last shot rule."

This last-shot rule ran contrary to the parties' expectation that a contract was created by their exchange of documents and that those documents, not the last-sent document, determined the contract terms. The unfairness (or at least imbalance) of the last-shot rule and the resulting asymmetry between business expectations and the legal result was at odds with the philosophy of the nascent Uniform Commercial Code and of customary concepts of commercial liability—that the law should follow good business practices and lead to legal results consistent with the beliefs of reasonable persons. Accordingly, the drafting committee working on UCC Article 2 abandoned the mirror image rule and formulated a replacement rule in § 2–207. The problem addressed in § 2–207 is often dubbed "the battle of the forms" because it primarily deals with transactions involving exchanges of form contracts, though the section's coverage is not expressly limited to such exchanges. The section allows contracts to be formed even with significant variations between offer and acceptance, so it also must identify what terms are in the contract created by communications with non-matching sets of terms.

This UCC provision has had mixed successes and failures, but it was a visionary attempt to reduce the anomalies resulting from applying the mirror image rule to situations involving standard forms. As you will see, § 2–207 is not a model of clarity, and it is challenging to both understand what it says and make sense of how to use it. You will need to read, and re-read, the provision, and annotate it with the additional guidance offered by this textbook and examples.

§ 3.2.1. Defining Acceptance Under § 2–207

Just as under the common law, acceptance under § 2–207 may be by communication or by conduct. These two paths to contract formation result in different determinations about which terms are part of the contract. We start with an analysis of the two paths to forming a contract, and then discuss what terms are part of the contract created under each path.

§ 3.2.1.1. Acceptance by Expression of Commitment: § 2–207(1)

Read UCC § 2–207(1). It applies when a contract is created by an offer and an acceptance that do not match each other precisely. It rejects the mirror-image rule by stating that a communication may be an acceptance "even though it states terms additional to or different from those offered . . . ." However, the communication operates as an acceptance only if it is a "definite and seasonable expression of acceptance" and it does not operate as an acceptance if "acceptance is expressly made conditional on assent to the additional or different terms." Each of these clauses requires further explanation.

First, what makes a statement a **"definite and seasonable expression of acceptance"**?

- "[D]efinite . . . expression of acceptance" means that the offeree's language must show a willingness to commit to the contract by accepting the offer. To determine whether a particular communication expresses commitment, look at the language used by the offeree, just as we looked at language to decide if a statement is a promise under the common law (see Chapter 2, page 17). For instance, if a buyer sends an order to a seller, and the seller responds with the statement "Your order will be shipped within 30 days," that constitutes a definite expression of acceptance of the order. If, instead, the seller says, "We have received your order and will give it our prompt and careful attention," the seller's response is not a "definite . . . expression of acceptance," but merely notification of receipt of the offer.

> **See It**
>
> The chart on page 183 illustrates the application of § 2–207 to answer the questions:
>
> - Has a contract been formed under § 2–207?
>
> - If so, what are the terms of the resulting contract?
>
> You may find it helpful to look at the chart periodically as you read through the textual explanations of the workings of § 2–207.

- "Seasonable" is defined in § 1–205(b) as "at or within the time agreed or, if no time is agreed, at or within a reasonable time." In context, that means the response to the offer should be made within the time specified by the offer or, if none is specified, within a reasonable time after the offer, judging reasonableness based on all of the circumstances.

Because § 2–207 allows the acceptance to differ from the offer, courts have found one more requirement to be implicit in "definite and seasonable expression of acceptance": the acceptance must not "diverge[ ] *significantly* as to a *dickered* term."[*] A "dickered term" is a term about which the parties have explicitly negotiated or that does not appear in standard-form language. If the acceptance diverges significantly as to a dickered term, the offeree is not really accepting the deal offered. Consequently, it is critical to consider whether the difference between the offer and the purported acceptance is in a standard or a dickered term and whether the difference is significant. Examples of typically dickered terms are the item number, color, delivery date, quantity, and price, because such terms are specific to the transaction and not part of the standard-form language. Warranties, payment terms (e.g., how to deliver payment), remedy provisions and the like are often in standard-form language but may become dickered terms if the parties discuss them explicitly and directly.

---

[*] *See, e.g., U.S. Industries, Inc. v. Semco Manufacturing, Inc.*, 562 F.2d 1061, 1067 (8th Cir. 1977).

Example CC: *Koehring Co. v. Glowacki*, 253 N.W.2d 64 (Wisc. 1977).

Seller sent a letter to multiple potential purchasers listing machinery for sale "as is, where is." The buyer offered to buy for $16,500 "FOB, our truck, your plant, loaded" (a term that would have required seller to move the machinery onto the truck, at a cost of $1200 to $2100). Seller sent a telegram saying the bid was "accepted" but reiterating the "as is, where is" term. The court held that seller's response was a counter-offer because there was an "absence of agreement between the parties as to whether the sales price included loading risks and costs," which constituted a considerable expense.

Example DD: *Southern Idaho Pipe & Steel Co. v. Cal-Cut Pipe & Supply, Inc.*, 567 P.2d 1246 (Idaho 1977), cert. denied, 434 U.S. 1056 (1978).

Seller sent buyer an offer to sell pipe. Buyer struck out seller's delivery date, inserted a date two months later, then signed and returned the form with a $20,000 check, which seller deposited. The court found an acceptance because the buyer's change did not "diverge[ ] so radically from the terms of the offer"; the seller "failed to establish the urgency" of the earlier date and appeared to acquiesce easily to the new date.

Example EE: *Alliance Wall Corp. v. Ampat Midwest Corp.*, 477 N.E.2d 1206 (Ohio Ct. App. 1984).

In an exchange of communications, the buyer and seller agreed on the number of aluminum panels to be purchased and the price but identified different shipping dates. Finding that the communications showed the shipping date was important to the parties, the court concluded that no contract was created by the exchanges of purchase orders and acknowledgments. (The goods were shipped and paid for, however, so a contract was formed by conduct under § 2–207(3). As discussed below, contract formation by conduct is subject to different rules for determining the contract's terms.)

> **Example FF:** *Herm Hughes & Sons, Inc. v. Quintek*, 834 P.2d 582 (Utah Ct. App. 1992).
>
> Seller's form offer required the buyer to pay invoices in full within 10 days to receive an 8% discount on the price. Buyer's form acceptance required buyer to pay only 90% of past bills in order to receive the 8% discount. The court held that this was a significant difference as to a dickered term, so no contract was created by the documents.

As noted above, § 2–207(1) also says that a response cannot be considered an acceptance if it is **"expressly made conditional on assent to additional or different terms."** This language has caused particular difficulty in interpretation, with courts divided on what it means.

All courts agree that, to satisfy this provision, the response must explicitly say that it will not be an acceptance unless the additional or different terms become part of the contract. This kind of *express condition* is typically flagged by phrases such as "provided that," "subject to," "conditional on," "but only if," or "except that the accepting party must also . . . ," each of which shows explicitly that the responding party does not mean to accept without its *own* terms being included.

Take Note!

If a response to an offer is *not* an acceptance because it is "expressly made conditional on assent to additional or different terms," then—if it expresses commitment to entering a contract, but only on different terms from the offer—the communication is a counter-offer under the common law rules that apply if there is not a superseding UCC rule. Whether that counter-offer ends up as the starting point for contract formation depends on further application of both common law principles and § 2–207.

A majority of courts require still more—that an offeree follow the statutory language precisely by also saying, expressly, that the acceptance is conditioned *on the offeror's "assent"* to the additional or different terms.[*] In the view of those courts, it is not enough to say "acceptance means my terms will prevail," or that "this acceptance is subject to my terms and conditions." The acceptance must explicitly state both the conditional relationship *and the requirement that the offeror assent to the additional or different terms.* For example, no acceptance occurs if the response to an offer to sell is a purchase order that says it is *"subject to [your] acceptance* of the

---

[*]   *See e.g. Dorton v. Collins & Aikman Corp.*, 453 F.2d 1161, 1168 (6th Cir. 1972) A minority of courts hold that a counter-offer results when a condition is attached to the new terms in the purported acceptance (for instance, "I accept, subject to the terms below."). The condition need not be attached to *the offeree's assent to* the new terms in the purported acceptance. *See, e.g., Construction Aggregates Corp. v. Hewitt-Robins, Inc.*, 404 F.2d 505 (7th Cir. 1968) (minority approach).

Additional Terms and Conditions on the reverse side" because the purchase order expressly specifies that the acceptance is "subject to" the offeree's "acceptance" of the additional terms.* Similarly, no acceptance occurs if the response says, "Seller's willingness to sell to you is *conditioned on your acceptance* of these terms of sale."** Each of these formulations says the acceptance requires the offeror's assent to the additional or different terms. That makes the offeree's communication not an acceptance, but a counter-offer.

In jurisdictions following this strict approach, if a form of words is used that appears to accept, subject to additional or different terms, but it does not satisfy this higher standard—that is, it does not "expressly [make the acceptance] conditional on assent to the additional or different term" as understood in that jurisdiction—the response *will* be considered to be an acceptance, even though it might otherwise seem that the offeror does not mean it that way.

> **Example GG:** *Idaho Power Co. v. Westinghouse Elec. Corp.*, 596 F.2d 924 (9th Cir. 1979).
>
> A buyer responded to a seller's offer with a purchase order that said: "Acceptance of this order shall be deemed to constitute an agreement upon the part of the seller to the conditions named hereon and supersedes all previous agreements."

Analysis: The court held that the purchase order was not expressly conditional on assent to the buyer's terms because "the language used does not clearly reveal that [Buyer] was 'unwilling to proceed with the transaction unless . . . assured of [Seller's] assent to additional or different terms.' "

> **Example HH:** *Lockheed Electronics Co. v. Keronix, Inc.*, 170 Cal. Rptr. 591 (Ct. App. 1981).
>
> An offer stated that "I agree to contract only if your acceptance contains all of my terms, and I hereby object to any additional terms." The acceptance included the offer's terms and added terms of its own.

Analysis: The acceptance was not expressly conditional on assent to those additional terms and so operated as an acceptance.

---

* *See Rich Products Corp. v. Kemutec, Inc.*, 66 F. Supp. 2d 937 (E.D. Wisc. 1999) (emphasis supplied).
** *See Textile Unlimited, Inc. v. A..BMH & Co.*, 240 F.3d 781, 788 (9th Cir. 2001) (emphasis supplied).

Taking all of these issues into account, we can paraphrase § 2–207(1) as follows: *A purported acceptance that does not diverge significantly from the offer (as to the dickered terms) is an acceptance (of an offer), even though it does not mirror the offer, unless it states (in the way required by the jurisdiction) that the offeree's assent to the offer is conditional on the offeror's assent to the new terms in the purported acceptance.* If the offeree responds with something that seems to make a commitment ("a definite and seasonable expression of acceptance") but it also says acceptance is expressly conditional on the offeror's assent to the additional or different terms (under the rule applicable in the jurisdiction), it is not an acceptance, but a counter-offer. We will see below the consequences of that understanding.

§ 3.2.1.2. Acceptance by Conduct: § 2–207(3)

If there is an exchange of documents between the parties that does not create a contract under § 2–207(1), that does not end the matter. **Read the first sentence of UCC § 2–207(3).** It says that "conduct by both parties which recognizes the existence of a contract is sufficient to establish a contract for sale although the writings of the parties do not otherwise establish a contract."

The reference to "the writings of the parties" indicates that § 2–207(3) does not apply unless and until the parties exchanged writings that failed to manifest the parties' assent. If writings have not been exchanged (e.g., an offer was sent but the offeree did not respond), a contract may still be created by conduct under the common law, but § 2–207(3) would not apply.

The reference to "conduct by both parties" means that action by only one party is not sufficient to create a contract under § 2–207(3). For example, if seller sends an offer, buyer sends a counter-offer, and seller ships the goods, there is conduct only by the seller, and no contract is created under § 2–207(3). A typical sequence of events that does create a contract under § 2–207(3) is (1) one party makes an offer; (2) the other party sends a response that expresses a definite and seasonable expression of acceptance, includes additional terms, and makes acceptance expressly conditional on the offeror's agreement to those additional terms, making it a counter-offer under § 2–207(1); (3) the seller ships the goods; and (4) the buyer accepts delivery of the goods. The parties exchanged writings that failed to create a contract, and then both parties acted as if they had formed a contract.

Example II: *C. Itoh & Co. (America) Inc. v. The Jordan International Co.,* 552 F.2d 1228 (7th Cir. 1977).

Itoh submitted a purchase order to Jordan for a quantity of steel coils. In response, Jordan sent an acknowledgment form that had, on its face, this statement:

> Seller's acceptance is, however, expressly conditional on Buyer's assent to the additional or different terms and conditions set forth below and printed on the reverse side. If these terms and conditions are not acceptable, Buyer should notify Seller at once.

One of the terms on the reverse side was a broad provision for arbitration of any claims arising under the contract. Itoh did not respond to the acknowledgment. Jordan delivered the steel coils to Itoh. Itoh paid for the coils and sold them to Riverview Steel Corporation. Riverview notified Itoh that the coils were defective and refused to pay for them. Itoh sued Jordan, which moved to dismiss the case on the basis of the arbitration clause. Jordan argued that the acknowledgment created a contract, and that the arbitration clause was included in that contract.

Analysis: The Court determined that the strict rule applied to the question whether the acknowledgment "expressly made [acceptance] conditional on assent to the additional or different terms" under § 2–207(1), but that under either the strict or more lenient rule, Jordan's acknowledgment was not an acceptance and therefore became a counter-offer. Either party could have walked away from the transaction at that point, but "neither Jordan nor Itoh elected to follow that course; instead, both parties proceeded to performance, Jordan by delivering and Itoh by paying for the steel coils." A contract was created by the conduct of the parties under § 2–207(3). We will consider the fate of the arbitration clause below.

§ 3.3. Terms of a Contract Formed Under § 2–207

If a contract is formed under § 2–207(1), the contract is created by the writings of the parties but the terms in the offer and acceptance do not match. Similarly, if a contract is created under § 2–207(3), it is created by conduct, after the terms in the offer and counter-offer did not match. So what terms are in those contracts? The two subsections below address this question.

§ 3.3.1. Terms of a Contract Formed Under § 2–207(1): Understanding § 2–207(2)

If a contract is created by an exchange of offer and acceptance under § 2–207(1), the decision as to which terms are in the resulting contract is controlled by § 2–207(2). Before we can explore the workings of § 2–207(2), however, we need to clarify one more bit of terminology. Recall that § 2–207(1) allows creation of a contract even though the acceptance contains terms "additional to" or "different from" those in the offer. "Additional terms" are terms on subjects not addressed in the offer (e.g., the acceptance has a provision on warranties for the goods, but the offer says nothing about warranties). "Different terms" are terms on a topic addressed differently in the offer and the acceptance (e.g., the offer contains a one-year warranty, but the acceptance disclaims all warranties).

Now **read UCC § 2–207(2) and Comments 4 and 5.** You will see that § 2–207(2) refers only to "additional" terms, so we will start with an outline of the rule(s) specified in § 2–207(2) about what happens to additional terms in the acceptance:

- An additional term in an offeree's acceptance is a proposal of a term to be added to the contract (essentially a request to modify the contract formed in § 2–207(1)). It becomes part of the contract if the other party (the original offeror) assents to the "proposal."

- If both parties are merchants, then the additional terms in the offeree's acceptance become part of the contract unless

  a) the offer expressly says, in effect, that an acceptance must be only on the terms in the offer and no other terms (a kind of "my way or the highway" clause); or

  b) the additional term(s) would materially alter the contract otherwise proposed in the offer (with some guidance on what counts as "material" in Comments 4 and 5); or

  c) the offeror has already notified the offeree that he or she objects to the additional term(s) in the acceptance or does so within a reasonable time after receiving the acceptance.

As a result of these rules, the contract created by two merchants by offer and acceptance under § 2–207(1) contains the terms in the offer plus offeree's additional terms that pass the tests of § 2–207(2). If one or both parties is not a merchant, the contract created under § 2–207(1) contains the terms in the offer plus any additional terms proposed by offeree that are affirmatively agreed-to by the offeror.

What happens to "different" terms in the acceptance? Section 2–207 does not say. Courts have adopted two different rules:

- The majority approach for contracts between merchants is a "knock-out rule"—the different terms cancel each other out, and the gaps are filled in by supplementary provisions under the UCC.

- The minority approach for contracts between merchants is the "first shot rule"—the offeror, as the "master of the offer," prevails, and the different term in the acceptance is dropped.

For exchanges not "between merchants," the courts have not fashioned an answer, perhaps because the situation rarely arises.

> ### Take Note: § 2–207 and Confirmations
>
> Section 2–207(1) says that a "written confirmation" sent "within a reasonable time," like a "definite and seasonable expression of acceptance," can "operate[ ] as an acceptance" even though it contains additional or different terms. Since by definition a "confirmation" is sent only after a contract is agreed to, a written confirmation cannot truly act as an acceptance, but the inclusion of confirmations in § 2–207(1) means that additional or different terms in a written confirmation will be treated just like additional or different terms in a response to an offer, except that they will be judged based on whether they are additional to or different from *the contract*, rather than from the offer. Note that terms on competing confirmation forms that are additional to what is in the contract but different from each other will cancel each other out under § 2–207(2)(c), because the differing terms in the two confirmations are deemed to object to each other.

§ 3.3.2. Terms of a Contract Formed Under § 2–207(3)

If a contract is created under § 2–207(3), by conduct of both parties after an exchange of communications that do not result in offer and acceptance, the terms of that contract are decided according to the second sentence of subsection (3). **Read § 2–207(3).**

Under § 2–207(3), the documents did not establish a contract, but the "terms on which the writings of the parties agree" become part of the contract. Other terms do not. This rule is known colloquially as the "knock-out rule," because the other terms in the parties' writings are "knocked out."* Any missing terms are filled in with "supplementary terms incorporated under any other provisions of this Act." As you will learn in Chapter 8, these supplementary terms include

- "Course of performance" (the parties' patterns of dealings in *this* contract)

- "Course of dealing" (the parties' patterns of dealings in their *past* contracts)

- "Usage of trade" (customs in the vocation, trade, geographic area, etc.)

- Default provisions (also known as "gap-fillers"; these rules in UCC Article 2 fill in missing terms not filled in by course of performance, course of dealing, or usage of trade, including, e.g., place for delivery, time for shipment, time for payment, and even price)

Example JJ: *C. Itoh & Co. (America) Inc. v. The Jordan International Co.,* 552 F.2d 1228 (7th Cir. 1977).

As described in Example II above, Itoh sent a purchase order and Jordan responded with an acknowledgment that was a counter-offer because it made acceptance expressly conditional on Itoh's assent to additional terms. Among the additional terms was an arbitration provision. When Itoh sued Jordan, Jordan moved to dismiss the case on the basis of the arbitration clause.

Analysis: The court denied Jordan's motion to dismiss, concluding that the arbitration provision did not become part of the contract created under § 2–207(3). The court said that "disputed additional terms (i.e., those terms on which the writings of the parties do not agree) which are necessarily excluded from a [§ 2–207(3)] contract by the language, 'terms on which the writings of the parties agree,' cannot be brought back into the contract under the guise of 'supplementary terms.' " The court went on to note that "contract formation under subsection (3) gives neither party the relevant terms of his document, but fills out the contract with the standardized provisions of Article Two."

Because nothing in the UCC (including course of dealing, course of performance, or usage of trade) supplied an arbitration provision, the court denied Jordan's motion to dismiss. The court went on to explain the policy behind the result:

───────────

* This is a different knock-out rule than the majority rule governing different terms, as discussed in the previous section.

We are convinced that this conclusion does not result in any unfair prejudice to a seller who elects to insert in his standard sales acknowledgement form the statement that acceptance is expressly conditional on buyer's assent to additional terms contained therein. Such a seller obtains a substantial benefit under Section 2–207(1) through the inclusion of an "expressly conditional" clause. If he decides after the exchange of forms that the particular transaction is not in his best interest, Subsection (1) permits him to walk away from the transaction without incurring any liability so long as the buyer has not in the interim expressly assented to the additional terms. Moreover, whether or not a seller will be disadvantaged under Subsection (3) as a consequence of inserting an "expressly conditional" clause in his standard form is within his control. If the seller in fact does not intend to close a particular deal unless the additional terms are assented to, he can protect himself by not delivering the goods until such assent is forthcoming. If the seller does intend to close a deal irrespective of whether or not the buyer assents to the additional terms, he can hardly complain when the contract formed under Subsection (3) as a result of the parties' conduct is held not to include those terms. Although a seller who employs such an "expressly conditional" clause in his acknowledgement form would undoubtedly appreciate the dual advantage of not being bound to a contract under Subsection (1) if he elects not to perform and of having his additional terms imposed on the buyer under Subsection (3) in the event that performance is in his best interest, we do not believe such a result is contemplated by Section 2–207. Rather, while a seller may take advantage of an "expressly conditional" clause under Subsection (1) when he elects not to perform, he must accept the potential risk under Subsection (3) of not getting his additional terms when he elects to proceed with performance without first obtaining buyer's assent to those terms. Since the seller injected ambiguity into the transaction by inserting the "expressly conditional" clause in his form, he, and not the buyer, should bear the consequence of that ambiguity under Subsection (3).

§ 3.4. Integrating Your Understanding of § 2–207

Applying § 2–207 is challenging because you must analyze multiple documents, apply multiple standards to those documents, and possibly reach multiple possible answers (e.g., a court may conclude that a document is or is

See It!

A humorous review of § 2–207 can be found in the YouTube video entitled "This Form Is Your Form," by "profblaw."

not an acceptance). But it *is* possible to create a methodical approach to analyzing § 2–207! To help you do that, consider the flowchart and the ordered bullet list of questions below, each of which detail the flow of analysis under § 2–207. You may find one of these overviews more helpful than the other. You may find it most helpful to craft your own!

To determine if a sequence of documents and conduct creates a contract and the terms of that contract, ask the following questions:

- Which document states an offer?

- Does the response contain a "definite and seasonable expression of acceptance"?

    o If it does not, was it a counter-offer, with further communications that might create a contract under § 2–207? (If so, continue analyzing the sequence of communications.) Or was there a contract created by the conduct of both parties?

    o If it does, was acceptance made expressly conditional on the offeror's assent to the additional or different terms?

        ▪ If made expressly conditional, were there further communications that might create a contract under § 2–207? (If so, continue analyzing the sequence of communications.) Or was there a contract created by the conduct of both parties?

        ▪ If not made expressly conditional, a contract was formed.

If a contract was created by the documents, rather than by conduct, there is another bullet list of questions to be answered to determine whether the additional or different terms become part of the contract:

- Is the term additional or is it different?

- If different, has the jurisdiction adopted the majority or minority rule? (Or what would the answer be under both the majority and minority rules.)

- If additional,

    o Are both parties merchants? If not, the term is a proposal, so look for affirmative assent by the offeror.

    o If parties are both merchants,

- Did the offer limit acceptance to the terms of the offer?

- Would the additional term materially alter the contract?

- Did the offer object to the additional term, before or after it was proposed?

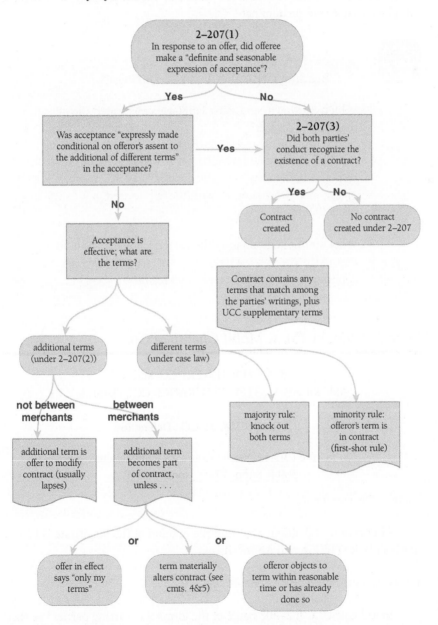

You can use the flowchart, the bullet list of questions, or your own depiction of § 2–207 to help you navigate the case and problems below. Remember that § 2–207 applies only to contracts predominantly for sale of goods, and only if the purported acceptance includes additional or different terms. In other contracts under Article 2, § 2–204 and § 2–206 apply, and the common law rules apply where the UCC is silent. Common law rules also govern contracts in which the sale of goods does not predominate.

Reading Critically: *Egan Machinery Co.*

1. Which document and what language constituted the offer in the contract for sale?

2. Which document and what language was sent by the offeree in response to the offer? Was the document an acceptance? Why or why not? Do you agree with the application of § 2–207 to reach that result?

3. What was the additional or different term at issue? Did it become part of the contract? Why or why not? Do you agree with the application of § 2–207 to reach that result?

Egan Machinery Co. v. Mobil Chemical Co.

EGAN MACHINERY CO. and
AMERICAN MUTUAL INSURANCE CO., Plaintiffs
v.
MOBIL CHEMICAL CO., Defendant

United States District Court, D. Connecticut
660 F. Supp. 35 (D. Conn. 1986)

EGINTON, DISTRICT JUDGE.

After review and absent objection the opinion of the Magistrate is hereby ADOPTED, RATIFIED, and AFFIRMED.

THOMAS P. SMITH, UNITED STATES MAGISTRATE.

In a classic UCC § 2–207 battle of the forms the warring parties use their boilerplate armies in an attempt to control the high ground by making their assent conditional on their right to set the conditions of the contract. In fashioning a peace between the combatants the court first looks to whether the exchanged forms created a contract. If a contract has been formed in this way, the court next determines which additional or different terms control by reference to § 2–207(2). *Daitom, Inc. v. Pennwalt Corporation*, 741 F.2d 1569 (10th Cir.1984). In deciding defendant's renewed motion for summary judgment, the court here considers the significance of two boilerplate contract clauses. The first is plaintiff's assertion that "this offer is accepted on the condition that our Standard Conditions of Sale, which are attached hereto and made a part hereof, are accepted by you." The second is defendant's clause stating: "Important—this order expressly limits acceptance to terms stated herein, and any additional or different terms proposed by seller are

What's That?

The *Egan Machinery Co.* case is a decision by a federal district court judge, ratifying a written opinion by a United States magistrate judge, a position created by statute. Federal magistrate judges have jurisdiction to hear nondispositive matters in civil cases before the federal district court and to hear preliminary criminal proceedings (e.g., arraignments). They also consider administrative appeals (e.g., Social Security Act determinations), issue Reports and Recommendations to the presiding federal district court judge, and conduct full trials if the parties waive their right to a hearing before a federal district court ("Article III") judge. The magistrate judges are selected by the chief judge of the district court for eight-year terms. As reflected here, a report and recommendation from a magistrate judge is presented to the federal district court to whom the case is assigned; it may be accepted by that judge as is or modified.

rejected unless expressly agreed to in writing." For the reasons set out below, the court concludes that a contract was created by the exchange of forms and that the additional term at issue here—an indemnity provision—did not become part of the contract. Accordingly, summary judgment should enter for the defendant.

The facts pertinent to the instant motion are easily recounted. In response to the defendant's Request for Bid on a two-sided eighty inch precoater, the plaintiff submitted two Quotations, one on April 5, 1973, and one on April 27, 1973. These Quotations describe in detail the components of the precoater, the precoater's operation, and those material[s] to be supplied by the plaintiff and the defendant. Aside from price, conditions of sale are not included in the Quotations.

On May 2, 1973, the defendant submitted a Requisition/Purchase order ("Order") for the precoater described in the plaintiff's quotations. The Requisition/Purchase Order contained the following language:

Please enter our order for the following, subject to conditions set forth in this order and on the reverse side hereof. Important—this order expressly limits acceptance to terms stated herein, and any additional or different terms proposed by the seller are rejected unless expressly agreed to in writing.

The conditions listed in the Order did not include an indemnification provision.

In response to the defendant's Order, the plaintiff submitted an Order Acknowledgment ("Acknowledgment") on May 8, 1973. This Acknowledgment provided that

> This order is accepted on the condition that our Standard Conditions of Sale, which are attached hereto and made a part hereof, are accepted by you, notwithstanding any modifying or additive conditions contained on your purchase order. Receipt of this acknowledgment by you without prompt written objection thereto shall constitute an acceptance of these terms and conditions.

Paragraph 12 of the plaintiff's Standard Conditions of Sale, the provision at issue here, provides that

> The purchaser shall use and shall require its employees to use all safety devices and guards and maintain the same in proper working order. Purchaser shall use and require its employees to use safe operating procedures in operating the equipment. If purchaser fails to observe the obligations contained in this paragraph, purchaser agrees to indemnify and save Egan harmless from any liability or obligation incurred by Egan to persons injured directly or indirectly in connection with the operation of the equipment. Purchaser further agrees to notify Egan promptly and in any event within 30 days, of any accident or malfunction involving Egan's equipment which results in personal injury or damage to property and to cooperate fully with Egan in investigating and determining the causes of such accident or malfunction. In the event the purchaser fails to give such notice to Egan, purchaser agrees to indemnify and save Egan harmless from any claims arising from such accident or malfunction.

Make the Connection

This is an indemnification clause that shifts the cost of third parties' losses resulting from poor training and supervision from the manufacturer to the purchaser. *Angel v. Murray*, Ch. 4, page 242 also involved an indemnification clause.

In October 1977 one of the defendant's employees was injured while operating the precoater purchased from the plaintiff. The employee filed suit against the plaintiff and its insurer, Amico. This action culminated in a stipulated judgment by which Amico, as the plaintiff's insurer, paid the Mobil employee $75,000. The instant action then followed the stipulated judgment.

The defendant filed its initial motion for summary judgment on June 20, 1984. On November 24, 1985, this court denied that motion without prejudice and alerted counsel to *Daitom, Inc. v. Pennwalt Corporation*, 741 F.2d 1569 (10th Cir. 1984), a case cited by neither party but which the court considered sound and persuasive on the issues raised by the defendant's motion. Heeding the court's suggestion, both parties on the pending renewed motion for summary judgment have looked to *Daitom* for a useful analytical framework and for substantive law. As a result, the issues to be resolved are narrow.

Before reaching those issues, however, a few points need be briefly mentioned. The first is that Connecticut's version of UCC § 2–207, Conn. Gen. Stat. § 42a–2–207, applies here. But because the Connecticut Supreme Court has not addressed the issues presented by the defendant's motion, this court, sitting in diversity, must make an estimate of what that court would do if faced with the same issues. *Brastex Corp. v. Allen International, Inc.*, 702 F.2d 326, 330 (2d Cir.1983). Next, it is well settled that to prevail on a motion for summary judgment the moving party must demonstrate the absence of any genuine issue of material fact and that it is entitled to judgment as a matter of law. *Heyman v. Commerce and Industry Ins. Co.*, 524 F.2d 1317, 1320 (2d Cir.1975). Summary judgment may be employed in disputes involving the interpretation of unambiguous contracts. *Wards Co., Inc. v. Stamford Ridgeway Associates*, 761 F.2d 117, 120 (2d Cir.1985).

The arguments of the parties can also be sketched briefly. In opposing the motion, the plaintiff argues that no contract was formed by the exchange of documents because its conditional acceptance clause meets the specificity requirement of § 2–207(1)'s exception provision. Continuing, the plaintiff argues that a contract was formed instead by the conduct of the parties and that according to the UCC's gap fillers of custom and usage it became a genuine issue of material fact as to whether the indemnity provision became a term of the contract, thus making summary judgment inappropriate.

In contrast, the defendant argues that a contract was formed by the exchange of documents because the plaintiff failed to explicitly declare its unwillingness to proceed with the contract unless its conditions, including the indemnity provision, were accepted. Moreover, the defendant contends the indemnity provision did not become part of the contract because it was an additional term that the defendant rejected by not expressly assenting to it.

Turning first to the claimed conditional acceptance language of the plaintiff's Order Acknowledgment,[26] it is clear, following the lead of *Daitom*, and predicting that the Connecticut Supreme Court would do the same, that the clause is not sufficiently explicit to declare the plaintiff's intention to abort the contract unless it were sure of the defendant's assent to additional or different terms because the clause does not come out and state just that. *Daitom, supra*, 741 F.2d at 1577. Courts have required that clauses such as the one here be strictly construed. *Reaction Molding Technologies v. General Electric Co.*, 588 F.Supp. 1280, 1288 (E.D.Pa.1984). The conditional acceptance clause will convert an acceptance into a counter-offer only where the offeree clearly reveals its unwillingness to proceed with the transaction unless it is assured of the offeror's assent to additional or different terms. *Dorton v. Collins & Aikman Corp.*, 453 F.2d 1161, 1168 (6th Cir.1972). This the plaintiff's clause did not do.

The plaintiff's clause here falls short of creating a conditional acceptance partly because it fails to declare in clear terms the plaintiff's unwillingness to go forward unless its additional [or] different terms are assented to by the defendant. Instead, the clause speaks in generalities, using limiting rather than conditional language. *Reaction Molding, supra*, 588 F.Supp. at 1258, presuming the defendant's acceptance of its Standard Conditions at Sale unless the defendant responded with prompt written objection. This is not enough. The focus of § 2–207(1) is on explicit, not implicit, statements of intent. See *Dorton, supra*, 453 F.2d at 1168.

Moreover, the single case upon which the plaintiff relies is distinguishable. In *Uniroyal, Inc. v. Chambers Gasket and Manufacturing*, 177 Ind.App. 508, 380 N.E.2d 571 (1978), the seller's disputed clause used the word "conditional" and required the buyer to notify the seller in writing within seven days if it does not accept the conditions of sale. Such specific references are lacking in the clause at issue here.

The plaintiff's failure to explicitly declare its unwillingness to proceed with the contract unless its conditions were accepted compels the conclusion that a contract was formed by the exchanged forms on the consistent terms but leaves unresolved the issue of whether the indemnity provision became a term of the contract. In resolving this issue it should be noted first that the indemnity provision must be considered an additional term not only because there is no conflicting term but because the plaintiff has so acknowledged it. With this established, the question narrows, under the *Daitom* analysis, to whether the defendant's offer, under § 2–207(2), expressly limits acceptance to the terms of the offer. This it

---

[26] The defendant's Requisition/Purchase order became the offer in this exchange of documents partly because it was the first exchanged form with conditions, *Reaction Molding Technologies v. General Electric Co.*, 585 F.Supp. 1097, 1106–07 (E.D. Pa. 1984) (citing J. White & R. Summers, Uniform Commercial Code at 27), and partly because the plaintiff's Order/Acknowledgment form characterizes itself as an acceptance with the phrase "this order is accepted."

clearly did with the statement, "important—this order expressly limits acceptance to terms stated herein, and any additional or different terms proposed by the seller are rejected unless expressly agreed to in writing." Nearly identical language was found equal to the task of limitation in *Lockheed Electronics Co., Inc. v. Keronix, Inc.*, 114 Cal App.3d 304, 170 Cal.Rptr. 591, 30 U.C.C.Rep. 827 (1981), and, similarly, it is sufficient for the defendant's purposes here. As a result, the indemnity provision proposed by the plaintiff did not become part of the contract.

As the indemnity provision at issue here did not become a term of the contract, the defendant's motion should be granted.

The parties are entitled to seek timely review.

Problems: Contracts and Their Terms Under UCC § 2–207

3-26. Which one of the following (if included in an offer) most likely "expressly limits acceptance to the terms of the offer" under § 2–207(2)(a)?

    a. "The terms of this offer are subject to the assent of the offeree."

    b. "This offer's terms can be accepted only by a written assent delivered to Offeror."

    c. "Only these terms, and no others, will be included in the contract."

3-27. Gerry runs an office furniture store that sells bookcases, file cabinets, desks, shelving, office chairs, and other office furniture. Vera looks at the store's online catalog, sees four items that she needs for her business, and mails Gerry a purchase order (P.O.) for those items. On Vera's P.O. is the following preprinted term: "The terms of this purchase order supersede seller's catalog terms. If a contract is formed, only the terms of this purchase order prevail. All goods will be of sufficient quality to remain serviceable for 1 year after sale." Vera's form does not have any term about remedies.

Gerry receives the purchase order and sends back an acknowledgment form, promising shipment at the end of the week, but he does not read Vera's term quoted above. The pre-printed terms in Gerry's acknowledgment form state: "Seller expressly disclaims all warranties on the quality of the goods sold. Buyer's remedies for any breach are limited to a refund of the amount paid for items sold." (In UCC Article 2, the default remedy for breach is *not* limited to a refund of the purchase price.)

    a. Do the parties have a contract? If so, how was it created (under which part of § 2–207)?

    b. Assuming a contract was created, is the refund limitation on Gerry's form part of the contract?

    c. Assuming a contract was created, is there a warranty that the goods will remain serviceable for a year?

3-28. Same facts as above, except that when Gerry receives the P.O., he sends back an acknowledgment form that says, "This acknowledgment supersedes all previous documents. Any contract formed with any buyer can be created only on the terms in this acknowledgment. Acceptance of any purchase order is conditional on the following terms: Seller expressly disclaims all warranties on the quality of the goods sold. Buyer's remedies for any breach are limited to a refund of the amount paid for items sold." Gerry delivers the four items. Vera accepts delivery and pays for them.

    a. Do the parties have a contract? If so, how was it created (under which part of § 2–207)?

    b. Assuming a contract was created, is the refund limitation on Gerry's form part of the contract?

    c. Assuming a contract was created, does the contract contain a warranty that the goods will remain serviceable for a year?

3-29. Buyer was hired to build dikes to be used in the process of extracting minerals from the Dead Sea. Buyer entered into negotiations with Seller for a conveyor system needed to move sand, gravel and rock to the construction site. The parties discussed and reached agreement on many of the terms that would be included in the agreement, but the discussions made clear that a contract would not exist until there was assent by both parties to a written agreement. The Seller's local office sent a letter to its headquarters in New York that concluded:

> This contract has been negotiated on the basis of our May 25 cost/plus letter. Copies of this cost/plus letter and other pertinent correspondence have been sent to our Legal Department for approval. It is not certain at this time whether Buyer will write their own version of the purchase order or whether they will accept our cost/plus letter. We have informed Buyer that its order will not be accepted until one of our corporate officers approves of all conditions and agreements.

Buyer thereafter issued a purchase order, incorporating the dickered terms on which the parties had agreed, along with its standard terms and conditions. The purchase order was sent to Seller's headquarters, which returned an executed copy of the purchase order along with a letter that said, "This acceptance is predicated on the following clarifications, additions or modifications to the order," including a substitute warranty clause limiting Seller's liability. Buyer made no written objection to the terms in Seller's letter but by telephone requested a change in the payment terms, which Seller granted. Seller shipped, and Buyer installed the conveyor system.

When the conveyor system did not operate as desired, Buyer sued Seller for breach of warranty. Seller defended by reference to the substitute warranty clause.

Did the parties enter a contract? If so, under what part of § 2–207? Is the substitute warranty clause part of the contract?

3-30. Buyer was in need of window gaskets to install in a building Buyer was constructing. Buyer solicited price quotations from several companies, including Seller. Seller sent a price quotation form that included the following statements:

> Any order placed in response to this quotation shall be deemed an express acceptance of each and every term and condition of sale contained herein and on the reverse side hereof.

> This proposal is for immediate acceptance only and is subject to change at any time before orders are accepted by us. This proposal and our acceptance of your orders, signed by a representative of our Company, together with your order, constitutes the entire contract between us. Modifications, changes, additions, cancellations or suspensions will not be binding upon us unless accepted by a representative of our Company in writing upon terms which will indemnify us against all loss. The terms and conditions contained in this quotation shall prevail over any inconsistent terms contained in buyer's purchase order.

Following receipt of the quotation, Buyer sent a purchase order to Seller, containing the following declaration:

> THIS PURCHASE ORDER IS EFFECTIVE AND EXPRESSLY CONDITIONAL ON SUPPLIER'S ASSENT TO ALL TERMS AND CONDITIONS IN THIS PURCHASE ORDER THAT ARE

ADDITIONAL TO OR DIFFERENT FROM THOSE STATED
IN SUPPLIER'S QUOTATION OR OTHER OFFERING DOC-
UMENTS. SUPPLIER'S ASSENT TO THIS PROVISION WILL
BE MANIFESTED BY DELIVERY OF ANY PORTION OF THE
GOODS DESIGNATED HEREIN.

The reverse side of the purchase order included a provision stating that
"Seller agrees to indemnify Buyer and agrees to binding arbitration for
the resolution of any disputes arising out of or relating to this Purchase
Order."

After receiving the purchase order, and without objecting to any of the
provisions included in it, Seller shipped the gaskets.

Serious problems of discoloration and cracking developed in the installed
windows, and Buyer was sued by and then settled with the company that
contracted with Buyer for construction of the building. Buyer commenced
arbitration proceedings against Seller for indemnification of its liability,
relying on the provision on the reverse side of its purchase order. Seller
denied those were part of the contract and filed suit in court, seeking a
declaratory judgment that the arbitration provision was not part of the
contract. Buyer moved to dismiss Seller's suit or to stay the proceedings
and compel arbitration.

The court's ruling on Buyer's motion to dismiss depends on whether the
arbitration provision is part of the contract between Buyer and Seller,
which turns on how a contract between them was created. How would
you rule? In developing your response, consider UCC §§ 2–204, 2–206,
and 2–207.

Think About It!

According to two leading commentators, "The law as to terms must be
sophisticated enough to nullify the efforts of fine-print lawyers, it must
be sufficiently reliance-oriented to protect the legitimate expectations
of the parties, and it must be fair and evenhanded." James J. White &
Robert S. Summers, *Uniform Commercial Code* § 1–2 (1972). Based on
what you have learned about how § 2–207 operates in determining
what terms are in a contract, how well does the section fulfill those
objectives?

How might offerors and offerees "game" § 2–207 by drafting their offers and purported acceptances to their advantage? Can either party ever completely "win the game"?

Test Your Knowledge

To assess your understanding of the material in this chapter, <u>click here</u> to take a quiz.

CHAPTER 4

Consideration

| How do parties demonstrate assent to a contract? | What kinds of promises will the law enforce? | What defenses to enforcement exist? | Is a writing required for enforcement? If so, what kind? | How is the content and meaning of a contract determined? | What are parties' rights and duties after breach? |

| What situations lead to excusing contract performance? | What remedies are available for breach of contract? | What contractual rights and duties do non-parties to a contract have? |

Table of Contents

§ 1. Introduction 196

§ 2. Defining Consideration 197

    § 2.1. Articulating Consideration as a Benefit-Detriment Test 198

    § 2.2. Articulating Consideration as a Bargained-for Exchange 205

        United States v. Meadors 206

        PROBLEMS: IS THERE CONSIDERATION? (4-1 TO 4-8) 221

§ 3. Common Disputes Involving Consideration 223

    § 3.1. Conditional Gifts 224

        PROBLEM: CONDITIONAL GIFTS (4-9) 229

    § 3.2. Illusory Promises 230

        PROBLEM: ILLUSORY PROMISES (4-10) 232

    § 3.3. Settlement Agreements Based on Worthless (Invalid) Claims 233

        Dyer v. National By-Products, Inc. 234

        PROBLEM: SETTLEMENT AGREEMENTS AND CONSIDERATION (4-11) 240

    § 3.4. Contract Modification and the Pre-Existing Duty Rule 241

        Angel v. Murray 242

        PROBLEMS: CONTRACT MODIFICATION AND CONSIDERATION (4-12 TO 4-14) 250

§ 3.5. Discharge of Duty and the Pre-Existing Duty Rule 251

PROBLEMS: CONTRACT DISCHARGE AND CONSIDERATION (4-15 TO
4-17).. 260

§ 4. **Stretching the Limits of Consideration Doctrine**..............................261

*Lawrence v. Ingham County Health Dept. Family Planning/Pre-Natal
Clinic* 262

§ 1. Introduction

Contracts are grounded in promises—assurances or declarations that one will do (or refrain from doing) some act. They are based on the notion that the parties created obligations to each other, so proving the existence of a contract requires a showing that the parties voluntarily took on those obligations—that they *assented* to the contract by effectively communicating their commitment. The element of manifestation of mutual assent has already been addressed in Chapters 2 and 3.

But should all promises be enforceable if assent exists? Professor Allan Farnsworth has suggested that "[n]o legal system has ever been reckless enough to make all promises enforceable. . . ."* Would it be reckless to do so? What kinds of promises should not be enforceable in court, and why? Think about the host of promises you make to friends and family, and pledges you might make to donate your time or money to a charity or cause. Should all those promises be enforceable? What rule or standard can be used to reliably distinguish enforceable from unenforceable promises?

Who's That?

E. Allan Farnsworth was one of the country's most renowned legal scholars on the subject of contract law until his death in 2005. After serving as a lawyer in the U.S. Air Force, he began his academic career in 1954 as the youngest professor at Columbia Law School, where he taught for more than 50 years. In the 1970s, after publishing several commercial law casebooks, he was chosen by the American Law Institute to be the Reporter during the drafting of the Restatement (Second) of Contracts (replacing Professor Robert Braucher, another leading contracts scholar who left the position when appointed to the Massachusetts Supreme Judicial Court). Farnsworth wrote a multi-volume treatise on contract law (also published in a single-volume version) that is one of the most frequently referenced texts on contract doctrine. The last of his many publications was *Alleviating Mistakes: Reversal and Forgiveness for Flawed Perceptions*, published in 2004.

---

*　E. Allan Farnsworth, *Contracts* 11 (4th ed. 2004).

The cases in this chapter illustrate the courts' efforts to specify which kinds of promises will be enforced, by identifying what, in addition to mutual assent, is required for contract formation. This additional requirement—the "something else" that must accompany a promise—came to be called "consideration." Historically, it arose and was developed in English courts and was further refined in early American courts. By the end of the nineteenth century, American case law on consideration represented a distillation of centuries of development.

§ 2. Defining Consideration

In a bilateral contract, each party makes one or more promises to the other party. Each promise (or set of promises) is enforceable if the recipient of a promise (the promisee) "gave consideration" for that promise (or set of promises). In the diagram below, if the promisee wants to enforce the promise(s) on the top arrow, the promisee must prove that the promisor received consideration for the promise(s):

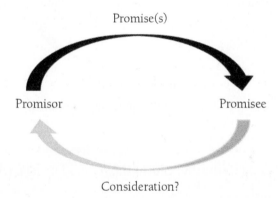

Promise(s)

Promisor   Promisee

Consideration?

Courts have articulated the test for finding consideration in two different ways, although both articulations seek the same goal and often produce the same result:

- "Benefit-detriment": The promisee must either give a benefit (usually but not always to the promisor) or suffer a detriment, in exchange for the promise(s).

- "Bargained-for exchange": The promisor (making the promise(s)) and the promisee (giving the consideration in return) must be reciprocally motivated (induced) by what the other party is giving.

The courts in older cases initially applied the benefit-detriment test. Later courts began to raise concerns about the inadequacy of the benefit-detriment test alone and eventually articulated the bargained-for exchange test. Some courts use both tests.

§ 2.1. Articulating Consideration as a Benefit-Detriment Test

Older cases articulated the test for consideration as a benefit-detriment test, under which the promisee furnished consideration by either

- providing a benefit to the promisor, or

- suffering a detriment.

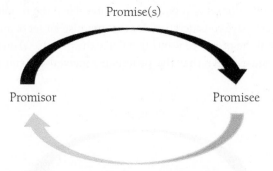

Promise(s)

Promisor   Promisee

Consideration by either
giving a benefit   OR   suffering a detriment

Reading Critically: *Clark*, *Hamer*, and *Dougherty*

The following case examples from 1889 to 1919 demonstrate the application and evolution of the benefit-detriment test. As you read them:

1. Note what each example tells you about the meaning of "benefit" and "detriment."

2. Keep in mind that where the existence of benefit or detriment was clear, there often was no need to litigate whether consideration existed, so the cases tended to highlight the outer boundaries of what benefit and detriment mean. Did any of these courts stretch the concepts of "benefit" and "detriment," perhaps to reach the most just outcome for a sympathetic party? Do you see any evidence that the courts themselves found the benefit-detriment analysis wanting or relied on something other

than the mere existence of benefit or detriment to reach the result?

Example A: *Appeal of Clark*, 19 A. 332 (Conn. 1889).

Sheldon Clark was unmarried and sick with tuberculosis, which eventually caused his death. He boarded with the family of Charles B. Clark (no relation to him) for various intervals over thirteen months, for which he paid rent. "Charles and his wife rendered services to Sheldon outside the regular contract for board—washed and mended his clothes, attended upon him when he was sick, cleaned his clothes and the bedding after a hemorrhage, took care of his cattle when he was not able to do so himself, and did the chores upon his place, etc.—matters not very great in themselves, and which seem never to have been the subject of any formal bargain between them. Sheldon appreciated their kindness and favors, and on several occasions said to Charles and to the wife of Charles that they should have their pay. In consequence of these statements by Sheldon, and in reliance upon them, Charles and his wife continued to render these services. Sheldon knew that Charles and his wife expected to be paid, and he fully intended to pay them. No price was ever fixed; it was left for Sheldon to pay such sum as in his judgment should be a full equivalent."

One day, Sheldon came to Mr. and Mrs. Clark and said that he wished them to draw a promissory note for $700, which he desired them to have for what they had done for him. Mrs. Clark said, "Why, Sheldon, that is too much; that is more than we deserve." Sheldon said, "I

What's That?

A "promissory note" is a written promise to pay a stated sum of money, usually specifying a due date or payment schedule or indicating payment will be "on demand." Free "create your own promissory note" services are available online, where you can generate samples. The form used by Sheldon Clark might have looked something like this:

PROMISSORY NOTE

For value received, _____ (the "Maker"), by this Promissory Note unconditionally promises to pay to _____ (the "Holder") the principal sum of _____, payable at or before the Maker's death. This Promissory Note shall be governed by, and construed in accordance with, the laws of the State of Connecticut. IN WITNESS WHEREOF, the Maker has duly executed this Promissory Note as of [insert date].

_____

(signed by Maker)

want you to have that if I die, but if I get well I want the note back, and I will then pay you what is right." The note was then drawn "for value received." Sheldon examined, approved, signed, and delivered it to Charles, in whose hands it remained. Just over a month later, Sheldon wrote and signed his will, without including any bequest to the Clarks; thirteen days later he died.

Analysis: The court held that the promissory note was supported by consideration and ordered Sheldon's estate to pay Charles. It defined consideration as "[a]ny benefit accruing to him who makes the promise, or any loss, trouble, or disadvantage undergone by or charge imposed upon him to whom the promise is made. . . . Any act done by the promisee at the request of the promisor, by which the former sustains any loss, trouble, or inconvenience, constitutes a sufficient consideration for a promise . . . ." The court went on to note that the value of the consideration does not matter. The benefit or "loss, trouble, or disadvantage" can constitute consideration "although the [promisor] obtains no advantage therefrom; and in respect to the extent of such loss, trouble, or inconvenience it is immaterial that it is of the most trifling description, provided it be not utterly worthless in fact and in law. . . . [C]onsideration . . . may consist either in some right, interest, profit, or benefit accruing to the one party, or some forbearance, detriment, loss, or responsibility given, suffered, or undertaken by the other. . . . If the parties, being in a situation and having the ability to do so, have exercised their own independent judgment as to the value of the subject-matter, courts of equity should not and will not interfere with such valuation."

The court reasoned that the "services rendered by Charles Clark and his wife to Sheldon Clark, and for which this note is the promise to pay, if they should be drawn out on a book in the form of an account, with times and dates, and the thing done, and prices, might not amount to $700. But to Sheldon Clark, alone in the world, unmarried, without family or near kindred to make a home for him, sick of a wasting disease, who can measure their value so well as he? He put his own estimate upon them, deliberately and without 'speck of imposition.' If he chose to pay for the services rendered a much larger sum than they were apparently worth, he had the right to do so. The note was not a gratuity or a testamentary gift. There is no standard whereby courts can limit the measure of value in such a case; and the note is not wanting, even partially, in consideration, because the value of the consideration is less than the obligation."

Example B: *Hamer v. Sidway*, 32 N.Y. St. Rep. 521, 11 N.Y.S. 182 (Sup. Gen. Term 1890), *rev'd*, 124 N.Y. 538, 27 N.E. 256 (1891).

At a family celebration, an uncle told his nephew that the uncle would pay the nephew $5000 on the nephew's 21st birthday if the nephew refrained from drinking, smoking, playing cards for money, and playing billiards until then. The nephew replied that he would endeavor to do so. Upon the nephew's 21st birthday, he wrote his uncle, asking for the $5000 because he had "lived up to the contract in every sense of the word." The uncle replied in a letter, stating that "you shall have $5000, as I promised you" and offering to hold onto the money (with interest) until the nephew was mature enough to handle such a large sum responsibly. The uncle later passed away before transferring the money. The nephew assigned his claim to the $5000 to another person, and the plaintiff eventually acquired the right to recover the payment. She sought to do so by suing the executor of the uncle's estate.

Analysis: The trial court made findings of fact that the uncle "agreed to and with" the nephew to pay $5000 in return for the nephew's abstinence, and that the nephew fully performed his part of the agreement. The trial court ruled in favor of the plaintiff, upholding the contract. On appeal, the judgment was reversed by the New York Supreme Court (an intermediate appellate court, despite its name), which held that the uncle had made a gratuitous promise, for which the nephew had not furnished consideration. In the absence of consideration, no contract was formed. The court concluded that the nephew's change in position "by abstaining from expensive habits which could in no way benefit him" was not a detriment, but instead a benefit to the nephew.

On subsequent appeal, the New York Court of Appeals (the high court) reversed again, upholding the contract and the plaintiff's right to payment. The court defined consideration as either "some right, interest, profit, or benefit accruing to the one party, or some forbearance, detriment, loss, or responsibility given, suffered, or undertaken by the other. . . . It is enough that something is promised, done, forborne, or suffered by the party to whom the promise is made as consideration for the promise made to him. . . . In general a waiver of any legal right at the request of another party is a sufficient consideration for a promise. . . . 'Consideration' means not so much that one party is profiting as that the other abandons some legal right in the present, or limits his legal freedom of action in the future, as an inducement for the promise of the first."

The nephew promised to forbear (and did in fact forbear) from smoking, drinking, playing billiards, and playing cards for money until his 21st birthday, although he had a right to pursue those activities. Thus, there was consideration in the form of a detriment to him, the promisee. That promise (and its performance) was what the uncle wanted, in return for his promise to pay the money. The court suggested that this may also have constituted consideration in the form of a benefit to the promisor, but that it was not necessary to decide this, since a detriment to the promisee is enough.

Although the case opinion is not clear about whether a contract was formed when the nephew gave the return promise or when the nephew completed performance, the net result was the same—the nephew gained a contractual right to $5000 payment from his uncle as of the nephew's 21st birthday. Because the contract arose before the uncle's death but was not paid, the estate was liable for that obligation to the assignee of the nephew's claim.

Behind the Scenes

Hamer v. Sidway was based on a promise made by W.E. Story to his nephew, William E. Story. So why was the litigation between Hamer and Sidway? The claim was brought against Franklin Sidway, the executor of W.E. Story's estate. Because Story left a will, the estate was handled by the "executor"—the person named in the will to supervise distribution of the assets. If the uncle had not made a will, the court would have appointed an "administrator" to play the same role. The executor or administrator has a legal duty to contest arguable claims in order to preserve the estate's assets for the legitimate claimants and beneficiaries, so it is common to see suits of this kind brought against the executor or administrator.

How did Hamer become the plaintiff in this case? The court of appeals said that Louisa Hamer "acquired [her claim] through several mesne assignments from William E. Story, 2d," suggesting nephew Willie transferred his claim to Louisa, or to someone else who transferred the claim to her. See Chapter 11, page 910 for a diagram of the assignment in *Hamer* and an explanation of how assignments work. The trial record shows that Louisa Hamer was Willie's mother-in-law. Louisa's original complaint said that young Willie assigned the claim to her on the day of his uncle's funeral. But Willie had previously declared bankruptcy, making all his assets (including any claim on his uncle) the property of his creditors and therefore unassignable. Perhaps to avoid that result, Louisa filed an amended complaint stating that Willie assigned the claim to his wife before the bankruptcy, and his wife later assigned it to Louisa (her mother). The bankruptcy suggests that Uncle William was rightly concerned that young Willie might fritter away the $5000 after he earned it.

The trial record can be used to support the conclusion that a bargain existed between Uncle William and nephew Willie. After William made his promise, Willie negotiated to ensure he could play cards and billiards unless money were involved, and he took the promise very seriously, even refusing to take prescribed medicine with alcohol in it while away at college. On the other hand, other evidence shows that William's promise was the culmination of a long-standing intention to help his nephew, and "the insistence that Willie cut out his bad habits was simply a string he tied to a promise." With these competing stories in mind, Douglas Baird argues that the New York Court of Appeals opinion was part of a battle over how to envision contract law—as a rigid set of rules that "forced lawyers to labor to reshape [the facts of a case] into the procrustean bed of a bargained-for exchange" or as a set of sensible principles arising from "the world as it was," where the appropriate question is "Should this promise be enforceable?" and not "Does this promise fit the previously articulated rule?" Douglas G. Baird, *Reconstructing Contracts: Hamer v. Sidway*, in *Contracts Stories* (2007).

Example C: *Dougherty v. Salt*, 227 N.Y. 200, 125 N.E. 94 (1919).

During a visit, an aunt gave her eight-year-old nephew a $3000 promissory note, payable before or at her death. The circumstances leading up to that moment were described by the nephew's guardian: "When she saw Charley coming in, she said 'Isn't he a nice boy?' I answered her, yes, that he is getting along very nice, and getting along nice in school, and I showed where he had progressed in school, having good reports, and so forth, and she told me that she was going to take care of that child, that she loved him very much. I said, 'I know you do, Tillie, but your taking care of the child will be done probably like your brother and sister done, take it out in talk.' She said: 'I don't intend to take it out in talk, I would like to take care of him now.' I said, 'Well, that is up to you.' She said, 'Why can't I make out a note to him?' I said, 'You can, if you wish to.' She said, 'Would that be right?' And I said, 'I do not know, but I guess it would; I do not know why it would not.' And she said, 'Well, will you make out a note for me?' I said, 'Yes, if you wish me to,' and she said, 'Well, I wish you would.' "

> Someone produced a blank promissory note, which the aunt filled out and signed. The form note stated that it was for "value received." The aunt handed the note to her nephew and said, "You have always done for me, and I have signed this note for you. Now, do not lose it. Some day it will be valuable."
>
> The aunt passed away some time later. The nephew's guardian presented the note to the aunt's executrix for payment. The executrix refused payment, claiming lack of consideration, and this suit followed.

Analysis: The trial judge submitted to the jury the question whether there was any consideration for the promised payment, and the jury decided in the affirmative. Afterwards, the trial judge set aside the verdict in favor of the plaintiff and dismissed the complaint.

The appellate division reversed the judgment of dismissal and reinstated the verdict on the ground that the note was sufficient evidence of consideration.

The court of appeals reversed the appellate division and reinstated the dismissal. The court reasoned that the note was a voluntary and unenforceable promise of an executory gift. ("Executory" gift means a gift that was not yet carried out. A gift is not effective until it is delivered.) The aunt was not paying a debt, but rather was conferring a bounty upon the nephew. A note so given is not made for "value received," however its maker may have labeled it.

Food for Thought: Why is Consideration Required?

The trial court in *In re Barker's Estate*, 287 N.Y.S. 841 (Surrogate's Ct. 1936), *affirmed*, 249 App. Div. 336 (N.Y. 1937), *reversed and remanded*, 279 N.Y. 449 (1939), applied the result in *Dougherty* to claims against the estate of a maker of promissory notes given to two educational institutions "for value received." The court rejected the claims, reasoning as follows:

> Subscriptions or gifts to institutions of the character of the claimants in this case are worthy and commendable and make it possible for such institutions to attain their desired goal; however, there are recognized ways in which those gifts may be accomplished. If the gift is to be immediate, it must be completed and the money delivered. A promise to make a gift at some future

date is not enforceable, for the reason that the person making the promise may, by reason of altered financial circumstances, change his mind and determine either that he cannot afford to make such a gift, or that he cannot afford to make a gift or subscription of the amount which he originally intended. And as this is purely a voluntary subscription upon his part, the law protects him and permits him to change his mind. Gifts and subscriptions of this kind may be legally carried out through the provisions of a will properly executed. This is a most wholesome way, because a will does not take effect until the death of the testator; and if he meets with adverse circumstances, he is at liberty to change his will to correspond.

Does this paragraph explain the result in *Dougherty* (Example C, above) as well? (Although the high court reversed, the reversal was on evidentiary grounds, not addressing or affecting the validity of the above paragraph about gift law and policy.)

§ 2.2. Articulating Consideration as a Bargained-for Exchange

As you saw in the preceding case examples, courts applying the benefit-detriment test sometimes struggled to fit the test to the circumstances, especially where the benefit or detriment was small or where it was unclear whether the benefit or detriment was connected to the promise when it was made. A court's finding of a benefit or detriment did not seem quite enough on its own to justify enforcement, so the courts sometimes instead looked at whether the parties were reciprocally motivated to exchange their promises. Out of these concerns arose the articulation of consideration as a "bargained-for exchange." The next case chronicles that evolution.

Reading Critically: *Meadors*

1. What definitions of consideration did the court use?

2. Which of the definitions have you seen already in the preceding case examples?

3. Why did the court find, or fail to find, consideration?

United States v. Meadors

UNITED STATES OF AMERICA, Plaintiff-Appellee

v.

BETTY JO MEADORS, Defendant-Appellant

United States Court of Appeals for the Seventh Circuit
753 F.2d 590 (7th Cir. 1985)

Before CUDAHY, POSNER and COFFEY, CIRCUIT JUDGES.

CUDAHY, CIRCUIT JUDGE.

Appellant Meadors appeals an order of the district court granting the Small Business Administration (the "SBA") summary judgment in its action to collect from appellant as guarantor on a loan. The district court found that the Equal Credit Opportunity Act did not protect Meadors from liability; that she had waived certain protections by signing the guaranty; and that no independent consideration was necessary for her signature as a guarantor. On appeal she raises these defenses again, and also argues that, should she be liable, the district judge erred in calculating the interest due on the note. We reverse and remand.

I.

In January, 1977, M.J.D., Inc. ("MJD") applied to the Bargersville State Bank (the "Bank") for a loan to pay off debts and to provide for additional working capital for a lumber company MJD owned in Bargersville, Indiana. The Bank's board of directors approved the loan subject to a guaranty by the SBA. In April, 1977, the SBA approved the request for a 56% guaranty of the $281,000 loan, but required the principals Melton Meadors, Jay Judd and Harold Ducote and Ducote's wife Marie to sign a guaranty on SBA Form 148. In the January application, listed on page four as possible guarantors had been: "Melton E. Meadors—a single person, Jay A. Judd & Wife, Harold A. Ducote, Jr., & Wife." After considering the loan application and attached balance sheets, the SBA chose to have Meadors, Judd, Ducote and Ducote's wife sign the required guaranty.

On April 2, 1977, Melton Meadors and Betty, appellant here, were married. At the April 19 closing the three principals and their wives were all present. Although the SBA had provided places on its Form 148 for the signatures only of Meadors, Judd, Ducote, & Ducote's wife, and although no one from the SBA was present to request additional signatures, all six—the three principals and their wives—signed the guaranty form. Neither the SBA nor the Bank required Betty to sign any document as a prerequisite for disbursing loan proceeds. These facts are not disputed by either side.

MJD defaulted on its loan, and the Bank asked the SBA to take over the guaranteed portion of the loan. MJD turned over the collateral securing the loan to the SBA in July, 1980 and it was later sold. An action was subsequently instituted in district court to collect the deficiency from the guarantors, including Betty Meadors. Appellant raised several defenses, including lack of consideration and impairment of collateral. In November, 1983 appellee SBA filed a motion for summary judgment which was granted by the district court on February 2, 1984. It is from that grant of summary judgment that Betty Meadors appeals. . . .

There is apparently some confusion about whether Indiana law or federal law should govern in this case. In the district court appellant appealed to Indiana common law; the government has apparently relied on federal cases. Without raising the issue, the district court applied Indiana law.

Federal law governs questions involving the rights of the United States arising under nationwide federal programs. *United States v. Kimbell Foods, Inc.*, 440 U.S. 715, 726, 99 S.Ct. 1448, 1457, 59 L.Ed.2d 711 (1979). "In the absence of an applicable Act of Congress it is for the federal courts to fashion the governing rule of law according to their own standards." *Clearfield Trust Co. v. United States*, 318 U.S. 363, 367, 63 S.Ct. 573, 575, 87 L.Ed. 838 (1943). Nevertheless, federal courts may turn to state law in attempting to give content to the federal rule in question. *United States v. Kimbell Foods, Inc.*, 440 U.S. at 727, 99 S.Ct. at 1457. Thus, on certain issues, such as impairment of collateral and the right to notice, where "the state law on which private creditors base their daily commercial transactions is derived from a uniform statute [the U.C.C.]," and there is therefore no conflict with the federal interest in uniformity, appeal to state law is appropriate. *United States v. Kukowski*, 735 F.2d 1057, 1058 (8th Cir.1984). On those issues, then, we look to the Uniform Commercial Code, the Indiana statute based on it, and Indiana common law.

II.

Summary judgment is appropriate if "the pleadings, depositions, answers to interrogatories, and admis-

Take Note!

Contract law is almost invariably a matter of state law, whether under the common law, state-adopted UCC, or other state statutes, but an applicable federal statute will supersede state law. The circumstances in *Meadors* reflect one of the few instances where federal courts have authority to fashion common law principles of contract law, but, as you see, the court may nonetheless defer to state law, if that law sufficiently protects federal interests. As acknowledged by Judge Posner several years after he joined the *Meadors* opinion, the United States Supreme Court ruled six years before *Meadors* that federal courts should use the relevant state's law as the federal common law in disputes arising over loans guaranteed by the Small Business Administration, for the same reasons articulated by the court here. *See United States v. Stump Home Specialties Mfg., Inc.*, 905 F.2d 1117, 1119 (7th Cir. 1979).

sions on file, together with the affidavits, if any, show that there is no genuine issue as to any material fact and that the moving party is entitled to a judgment as a matter of law." Fed. R. Civ. Pro. 56(c). In the case before us the parties do not disagree about the facts, and our only role is to determine whether, on the facts as agreed, the district court was right as a matter of law.

[Discussion of the Equal Credit Opportunity Act and other issues omitted.]

III.

Betty Meadors argues, finally, that she received no consideration for her signature on the guaranty form. She reasons that the signature of a volunteer, who happens upon an agreement after the negotiations have been concluded and the terms set, and who signs as a guarantor although neither side has required her to sign, has not received consideration and therefore is not bound by the agreement.

Consideration has long and consistently been treated as an essential element of every contract. Yet there is little agreement about just what consideration is, and that fact makes it difficult to assess a defense of want of consideration in a novel setting. We venture that the setting in which it is raised here is very nearly unique, and the validity of the defense would seem to depend on which interpretation of the doctrine we adopt.

Every interpretation has serious faults. It used to be said that consideration was either a benefit to the promisor, or a detriment to the promisee. In other words, the one who made the promise receives consideration if he gets something, or if the one to whom he makes the promise gives something up. Either alternative will do. If I promise you a thousand dollars if you quit smoking, and you do quit, then even though there may be no benefit to me, I have received consideration: you have given something up. Similarly, I can promise you a thousand dollars if you teach my daughter to sing. If you do teach her—or if you promise to—then I have received consideration even if all the practice sessions and even the final result are of no real benefit to me.

But reflection shows that benefit-detriment is neither necessary nor sufficient for consideration. I may promise to give you a thousand dollars if you quit smoking—I may even do it in writing—and you may give up smoking, and yet my promise may be

Take Note!

The court says that either the promise to teach the daughter or the actual teaching of the daughter can count as consideration. The former situation—a promise serving as consideration—is the most common because so many contracts are formed by an exchange of promises. As you saw in Chapter 3, page 116, the promisor (the offeror, as the master of the offer) gets to decide how the offeree accepts the offer—by return performance or a return promise.

unenforceable and may be the sort of thing that everyone would agree was without consideration. For you may have given up smoking without ever having learned of my promise. So the detriment in isolation is not sufficient for consideration. On the other hand, I might agree to pay you for something that was neither a benefit to me nor a detriment to you. I might promise to pay you for bringing a benefit on yourself. The reasoning in the classic case of *Hamer v. Sidway,* 124 N.Y. 538, 27 N.E. 256 (N.Y. App.1891), suggests that the courts will find consideration in such a case. An uncle had promised his nephew $5000 on his twenty-first birthday if the nephew would refrain from drinking, smoking, swearing and playing cards until that time. The nephew evidently fulfilled his part of the deal, but the uncle's executor resisted his claim against the estate. The court found the promise enforceable. . . .

Perhaps because of such difficulties, the benefit-detriment account of consideration was replaced by a "bargain" theory: there is consideration when each promise or performance has been bargained for, when each has been offered as inducement for the other:

> [I]t is the essence of a consideration, that, by the terms of the agreement, it is given and accepted as the motive or inducement of the promise. Conversely, the promise must be made and accepted as the conventional motive or inducement for furnishing the consideration. The root of the whole matter is the relation of reciprocal conventional inducement, each for the other, between consideration and promise.

O.W. Holmes, The Common Law 293–94 (1881).[2] The bargain-exchange account fits rather neatly into an economic analysis of common law, which sees in this version of the doctrine of consideration an attempt to select out for enforcement those contracts—namely bargained-for exchanges—that promote the increase of value in society.

The state has an independent interest in the enforcement of [bargain] promises. Exchange creates surplus, because each party presumably values what he gets more highly than what he gives. A modern free-enterprise system depends heavily on private planning and on credit transactions that involve exchanges over time. The extent to which private actors will be ready to engage in exchange, and are able to make reliable plans, rests partly on the probability that bargain promises will

---

[2]   "Going back into the past, there was an indefinite number of cases which had imposed liability, in the name of consideration, where nothing like Holmes's 'reciprocal conventional inducement' was anywhere in sight." G. Gilmore, Death of Contract 63 (1974). Gilmore saw Holmes as trying to change the law, and succeeding. "There is never any point in arguing with a successful revolution. What Holmes told the young lawyers who flocked to his lectures in the spring of 1881 promptly became the truth—the indisputable truth—of the matter for his own and succeeding generations." *Id.* at 21.

be kept. Legal enforcement of such promises increases that probability. Eisenberg, *Principles of Consideration*, 67 Cornell L. Rev., 640, 643 (1982).[3] . . .

Of course, if any theory could persuade us that the cases that stand as counterexamples to it were wrongly decided, we might accept the theory in spite of the cases. But the tendency in the courts has been to favor the accumulated wisdom of the common law over the simplicity of any single-minded theory. Thus Eisenberg argues that consideration is a guise under which judges have tried to deal fairly with contract difficulties, and argues that it is time now to relegate the doctrine and its epicycles to the history books, and bring fairness out into the open in decision-making.

> In the past courts decided issues of fairness covertly, and expressed their decisions through the manipulation of rules and exceptions purportedly designed for other ends. . . . The agenda for the legal community is . . . to encourage the courts to perform such review openly.

67 Cornell L. Rev., at 640–41.

Although it is a beguiling thought to drop the mask and do justice openly, the present case seems to us to make manifest the emptiness of such an approach. Having dropped the guise of consideration, what is the fair outcome in a case in which a wife (apparently) gratuitously affixes her name to a guaranty intended for her husband? Where the rules of contract law clearly dictate one result or the other (and there is no fraud or unconscionability) then the fair outcome might be to enforce that result. But to find such rules we are driven back to the doctrine of consideration and its exceptions.[5]

Since the just solution does not leap out at us, therefore, let us begin by pressing the doctrine of consideration as far as it will go. Where there is no consideration, it has been the general rule that the contract is not enforceable. In this case, under the versions of the doctrine we are acquainted with, there has been no consideration. The government suffered no detriment: its undertaking would have been precisely the same (on the account we have before us) whether or not Mrs. Meadors had signed the guaranty. She gained no benefit, either; whatever benefit passed to her and her husband because of the loan would have passed

---

[3] This position is subject to two different sorts of criticism: (1) unilateral promises also increase surplus, Posner, *Gratuitous Promises in Economics and Law*, 6 J. of Legal Stud. 411, 412 (1977); and (2) if it is the promotion of exchanges in the market place that is sought, why extend enforcement to, for example, intrafamilial contracts or the contract between me and the fellow who sells me his car? C. Fried, Contract as Promise 36–37 (1981).

[5] It may seem that, in our effort to find a rule that gives the just result, we have given considerations of simplicity short shrift. Although we think that the best argument for a result different from the one we reach here would be based on the simplicity of a rule that automatically bound signers, the same argument could be made for any per se rule and does not seem to us to weigh heavily in the balance.

without her signature. And no bargain was involved. The SBA gave up nothing to induce Mrs. Meadors to sign; her signature induced no act or promise on the part of the SBA. Since there has been no consideration, the general rule would deny the government enforcement of the contract.

. . . .

If the promises of the principal and the surety are made simultaneously, they may be made for a single consideration; the loan of money by the creditor to the principal is a sufficient consideration for the promises of both principal and surety. Corbin on Contracts § 213.[6] That rule, on its face, suggests that because the signing was simultaneous the appellant here cannot raise the defense of lack of consideration. On a benefit-detriment theory, there is nothing more to be said about it.

We believe, however, that that outcome is wrong, and—although cases on this point are naturally rare—we are supported in our belief by the commentators and by the bargain-exchange interpretation of the doctrine of consideration. This is not the ordinary case of the guarantor signing simultaneously with the principal; this is more like the case mentioned earlier in which X promises to pay Y a thousand dollars if Y gives up smoking, and Y gives up smoking without ever learning of X's promise. Whether or not there has been benefit to one party or detriment to the other, there has been no bargain here, and the SBA made the loan apparently in ignorance of Mrs. Meadors' signature. If those are the facts, then we believe that . . . there has been no consideration at all.

. . . .

For Corbin, the lack of consideration is clear from the fact that the signature was not originally contemplated as part of the deal. Where the creditor does not even know of the signature—as we are assured by both parties is the case here—the lack of a bargain and consequent lack of consideration is even clearer:

> Even if the promisee takes some action subsequent to the promise (so that there is no problem of past consideration), and even if the promisor sought that action in exchange for his promise, . . . that action is not bargained for unless it is given by the promisee in exchange for the promise. In other words, just as the promisor's purpose must be to induce an exchange, so the promisee's purpose must be to take advantage of the proposed exchange. *In practice, the principal effect of*

---

[6] Corbin distinguishes guaranties made subsequent to the principal agreement as requiring separate consideration. There are cases holding that even in such circumstances no separate consideration is necessary, but in each such case it is clear that the guaranty had been bargained for with the main agreement, or there is some other explanation for the apparent discrepancy.

> *this requirement is to deny enforcement of the promise if the promisee takes the action sought by the promisor without knowledge of the promise. As might be supposed, examples are infrequent.*

E. Farnsworth, Contracts 64 (1982).[8] On the undisputed facts, this case is one of Farnsworth's infrequent examples.

. . . .

Indiana law does not raise any difficulties for the position we adopt. *See especially Davis v. B.C.L. Enterprises, Inc.,* 406 N.E.2d 1204, 1205 (Ind. App.1980) ("If the guaranty is made at the time of the contract to which it relates, *so as to constitute a part of the consideration of the contract,* it is sufficient.").

We hold, therefore, that summary judgment for plaintiff was not appropriate on this point. Although the parties have apparently agreed on the relevant facts, we feel that it would also be inappropriate for us to decide as a matter of law that the guaranty is unenforceable. The district court, relying on a different construction of the law, did not take evidence on the question. Construing the law as we have construed it, it must be resolved whether in fact Betty Meadors' signature was in any respect whatsoever required, anticipated, requested or relied upon (or, in fact, known of); because if it was not, it was wholly irrelevant to the transaction and does not create an enforceable obligation.

Reversed and remanded.

The *Meadors* court eventually settled on using the "bargain" (or "bargained-for exchange") theory of consideration. Under this articulation, the promisee seeking to enforce the promisor's promise must prove that each promise or performance was induced by the other. More particularly, the promisee must prove the following:

(1)   When the promisor made its promise, the promisor was motivated (induced) by the desire to receive the promisee's return promise or performance.

---

[8]   Eisenberg also suggests the rarity of such cases:

The proposition that bargains involving the performance of a pre-existing contractual duty are often gratuitous is empirically far-fetched. Perhaps a few such cases could be found, but I have never run across one. In any event, if such cases really do arise, they neither need nor justify a special rule. As Comment a [to § 573 of the Restatement Second of Contracts] points out, "[i] f the performance was not in fact bargained for and given in ex-change for the promise, the case is not within this section: in such cases there is no consideration . . . ." 67 Cornell L.Rev., at 644–45.

(2)　When the promisee gave the promisor a return promise or performance, the promisee was motivated (induced) by the promisor's promise.

The word "bargain" in this theory has a meaning different from the layperson's meaning. It does not require the parties to bargain, negotiate, or haggle. Instead, the bargain is the parties' reciprocal inducement of each other's promise or performance.

The left-hand diagram below depicts this "bargain" theory of consideration, with the pair of vertical arrows showing the reciprocal inducement between the promise and the return promise or performance. You may find it helpful to fill in a similar diagram with the particular names and promises/performances as you analyze a case or problem. Typically, the plaintiff is the promisee, seeking to enforce the defendant's promise. It is thus the defendant's promise that appears on the top arrow, and the alleged consideration (the benefit flowing back to the promisor-defendant or the detriment to the plaintiff promisee) that appears on the bottom arrow. To find consideration, look for whether the promise on the top arrow and the promise or performance on the bottom arrow were given in exchange for each other and were motivated by the other. The right-hand diagram depicts the *Meadors* case. The SBA is the plaintiff-promisee trying to enforce Betty Meadors' promise to repay the loan. What is missing is the reciprocal inducement, because Meadors was not asked to make her promise to repay in order to receive the loan money, and the SBA was not induced to give the loan money in order to receive Meadors' promise to repay.

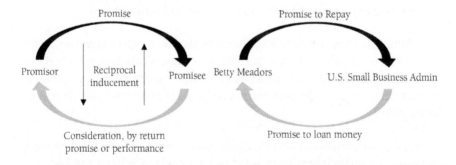

As illustrated by many of the examples you have already read, what is often—indeed, most often—sought and given as consideration for one promise is another promise. Of course, what the promisor ultimately wants is performance of what is promised, but the contract is created by exchanging one promise for another. That is worth repeating again: **A promise can and often does count as consideration for a promise**, as long as the two promises are reciprocally induced. Consider these examples:

- An insurance company enters into an agreement with a customer, in which the insurance company agrees to provide the specified insurance and the customer agrees to pay the specified premiums when due.

- A contractor enters into a building agreement with a developer, in which the contractor agrees to construct a building according to the developer's plans and the developer agrees to make periodic progress payments to the contractor.

- A landlord enters into a rental agreement with a tenant, in which the tenant agrees to pay specified monthly rent and the landlord agrees to let the apartment to the tenant for a year.

- A homeowner/seller enters into a purchase agreement, in which the buyer agrees to pay a specified price and the seller agrees to convey ownership of the house. The closing (the performance) is set for 60 days after the agreement.

Each party ultimately wants the other's performance (e.g., the insurance company wants the premium money and the customer wants insurance coverage in place; the developer wants the structure built and the contractor wants to be paid), but at the moment of contract formation what each gets is a *promise* of the desired performance. In these kinds of promise-for-promise agreements—"bilateral contracts" in the language we saw used in Chapter 3, page 117—either party can enforce the unperformed promise of the other party by proving that the promise was motivated by a return promise and therefore had consideration.

Although most contracts are formed by the exchange of promises, recall from Chapter 3, page 117, that "unilateral contracts" are formed when one party seeks (and obtains) only performance from the other party, not a promise. In those circumstances, the performance is the consideration because there is no return promise.

Note that parties can also mutually agree to void an agreement between them—to rescind their agreement—and each promise to rescind is consideration for the other promise to rescind. Each party is induced to give up its right to contract performance by the other party's agreement to do the same, thereby satisfying the bargain requirement. Each party gains a benefit from getting out of its performance obligations under the contract, and each party suffers a detriment by losing the benefit of the other party's performance.

Reading Critically: *Baehr, Meincke, Schnell,*
and Restatement Provisions

The following case examples involve the "bargained-for exchange"
articulation of consideration. As you read them, answer these questions:

1. Note what each example tells you about the meaning of "bargain"
   or "bargained-for exchange".

2. Did it make a difference that each court applied the "bargain"
   test for consideration, rather than the "benefit-detriment" test?

3. In *Meincke* (Example E, below), the appellate and supreme
   courts applied Restatement (Second) of Contracts §§ 71 and
   81, which are consistent with the common law "bargain" test
   for consideration. **Read these sections, including their comments and illustrations.** What do these sections add to your
   understanding of the "bargain" test?

4. Restatement (Second) § 79 and its comments are consistent with
   rules used by the *Clark* court (Example A) and the *Schnell* court
   (Example F). **Read this section and its comments.** The Restatement rule against any requirement of "mutuality of obligation"
   is an issue in the *Lawrence* case at the end of this chapter.

Example D: *Baehr v. Penn-O-Tex Oil Corp.*, 104 N.W.2d 661 (Minn. 1960).

Baehr leased some gasoline filling stations to Kemp, in return for Kemp's
promise to pay rent. Concurrently or nearly so, Kemp purchased Webb
Oil Co. from Penn-O-Tex Oil Corp., in return for Kemp's promise to
make periodic payments. When Kemp became unable to keep up on his
payments to Penn-O-Tex, he assigned his accounts receivable (present
and future) to Penn-O-Tex Oil Corp. and allowed Penn-O-Tex to collect
rents from the operators of the filling stations, to receive other payments
made to Webb Oil Co., to pay some of Webb's debts when Webb so
directed, and to install its own agent to run Webb's business.

Within a month, Kemp notified Baehr that he was unable to make his
rent payment to Baehr, because Penn-O-Tex had control of so much of
Kemp's cash flow. Baehr was spending the winter in his Florida residence

What's That?

An "assignment" of contract rights is a party's transfer to a third party of the right to receive contract performance from the other party to the original contract. It may be accompanied by a "delegation" of duties, making a third party responsible for performing contract obligations. Recall that an assignment of rights played a part in *Hamer v. Sidway*, Example B, page 201: The nephew promisee assigned to his wife his right to receive money from his uncle.

In this case, Baehr argued that Penn-O-Tex was responsible for the service station lease because Kemp had transferred the lease and all its obligations to Penn-O-Tex by both assigning rights (e.g., to collect money from service station customers) and delegating duties (e.g., to make lease payments to Baehr). The trial court ruled that no such transfer had taken place.

Chapter 11, § 2, further explores assignment and delegation, and features diagrams of the claimed assignments and delegation in *Hamer and Baehr*.

when he received this notice. He called Penn-O-Tex's agent, who Baehr claims told him "that Mr. Kemp's affairs were in a very mixed up form but that he would get them straightened out and mail me . . . my checks for the rent." Receiving nothing, Baehr sent a letter to Penn-O-Tex, asking what he should do to get the rent checks, and adding: "Or will I have to give it to an attorney to sue." Penn-O-Tex replied with a letter saying it was trying to help Kemp keep the business going, but denying operating or taking possession of Kemp's business and also denying any knowledge of rent due to Baehr. However, in a subsequent phone call, Baehr claimed that Penn-O-Tex said that it was interested and "would see that I got my rent, and would take care of it, and . . . would work it out with the head office. . . . [Penn-O-Tex's agent] said he would take it up with them and they would assure me my rent."

Baehr did not receive any rent payments for a few more months. After he returned to his summer residence in Minnesota, he engaged a lawyer, notified Penn-O-Tex that he was re-taking possession of the leased filling stations because of the missed rent payments, and brought suit against Penn-O-Tex for payment of rents due, seeking to enforce Penn-O-Tex's promise to pay the rent while it was receiving the payments.

Analysis: The jury found for Baehr on his breach of contract claim, but the trial court granted Penn-O-Tex's motion for judgment notwithstanding the verdict.

On appeal, the Minnesota Supreme Court stated that a promise is enforceable as a contract if it is "the product of a bargain" and therefore supported by consideration.

The court defined "bargain" in this context *not* as "an exchange of things of equivalent, or any, value" *but instead* as "a negotiation resulting in the voluntary assumption of an obligation by one party upon condition of an act or forbearance by the other." This definition ensures that "the promise enforced as a contract is not accidental, casual, or gratuitous, but has been uttered intentionally as the result of some deliberation manifested by reciprocal bargaining or negotiation." Thus, "[i]n substance, a contractual promise must be of the logical form: 'If . . . (consideration is given) . . . then I promise that . . .'." The court held that, even though Penn-O-Tex's agent had promised that the rents would be paid, that promise was not induced by, nor did it induce, any promise or action by Baehr. In particular, Baehr's forbearance from bringing suit was not requested by the Penn-O-Tex, and his failure to bring suit earlier than he did was for his own convenience, not induced by Penn-O-Tex's promise. With no inducement on either side, Penn-O-Tex's promise was unsupported by consideration and was therefore unenforceable.

Example E: *Meincke v. Northwest Bank & Trust Co.*, 2007 WL 4553476 (Iowa Ct. App.) (unpublished opinion), *vacated*, 756 N.W.2d 223 (Iowa 2008).

Janice was 82 years old, and her husband was hospitalized and in failing health. At the urgent request of her daughter and nephew, Janice loaned them $90,000 for their businesses, secured by a mortgage on property owned by their businesses (Meincke Plumbing and Scramm Enterprises). Janice's mortgage had priority over a bank's earlier mortgage on the same property (that is, she would be paid before the bank would be paid). When the daughter and nephew needed more financing for their businesses, it approached the bank, which refused to loan them additional funds

What's That?

A mortgage is a document in which the owner of real property pledges its title to the property to another as security for money owed, often as part of the purchase price for the property. If the debt is not repaid, the mortgagee (the lender) can sell the property and use the proceeds to satisfy the loan. In this case, Janice loaned money to Scramm Enterprises; Scramm pledged title to its business property to Janice so she would have something of value if Scramm did not repay. Multiple mortgages may be given on a single piece of property. If that occurs, the mortgagees' interests are satisfied in order of priority. If the property is worth less than the total of the secured debts, holders of lower-priority mortgages may not have their claims satisfied. Often—but not always—priority is controlled by the order in which the loans and security interests were established. The dispute in this case involved a change in the priority of the multiple mortgages on the Scramm property.

until Janice signed an agreement that subordinated her mortgage to the bank's mortgage (so the bank would be paid before Janice). When both businesses failed, the bank sold the mortgaged property, but the proceeds were insufficient to fully pay the bank's outstanding loans, so Janice did not receive any proceeds or further payments. Janice challenged the validity of the subordination agreement, arguing that her promise was unsupported by consideration.

Analysis: The trial court found that the agreement was supported by consideration. The court of appeals reversed that judgment. The supreme court vacated the court of appeals ruling and affirmed the trial court's ruling.

The supreme court first applied the benefit-detriment test to define consideration and noted that the test is met even if the benefit flows to a third party—it need not flow to the promisor. It agreed with the trial court that the daughter and nephew gained a benefit because their businesses were able to get more financing. Alternatively, the bank suffered a detriment by advancing more funds.

However, the court stated that the trial court also should have applied the "bargained-for exchange" test. "Consideration requires the voluntary assumption of an obligation by one party *on the condition* of an act or forbearance by the other. . . . If a detriment to a party is serving as the consideration, 'it must appear that the disadvantage was suffered *at the request* of the promisor, express or implied.' . . . These cases illustrate the requirement of reciprocal inducement or a bargained for exchange for a finding of consideration." The court also recited requirements from Restatement (Second) of Contracts §§ 71 and 72. Based on Janice's testimony, the court found that her promise to subordinate her mortgage was motivated by her wish that her daughter and nephew receive the needed loan from the bank, so the "bargain" requirement was satisfied. The facts also showed that the bank's loan was contingent on Janice subordinating her loan, so reciprocal motivation existed. Therefore, Janice's promise in the subordination agreement was supported by consideration and was enforceable by the bank.

Example F: *Schnell v. Nell*, 17 Ind. 29, 1861 WL 2779 (1861).

A woman died without owning any property in her own name because all of her property was jointly held with her husband and reverted to him at her death. Thus, her will, which promised to pay three named beneficiaries $200 each, was ineffective. After her death, her husband entered into a signed and sealed agreement with those beneficiaries, promising to pay each one $200, in equal payments spread over the next three years. The agreement recited the following consideration:

> "[W]hereas the said *Theresa Schnell* has also been a dutiful and loving wife to the said *Zach. Schnell,* and has materially aided him in the acquisition of all property, real and personal, now possessed by him;
>
> for, and in consideration of all this, and the love and respect he bears to his wife; and, furthermore, in consideration of one cent, received by him of the second parties,
>
> he, the said *Zach. Schnell,* agrees to pay the above named sums of money . . . .
>
> And the [three beneficiaries], for, and in consideration of this, agree to pay the above named sum of money [one cent], and to deliver up to said *Schnell,* and abstain from collecting any real or supposed claims upon him or his estate, arising from the said last will and testament of the said *Theresa Schnell,* deceased."

The husband subsequently refused to make any payments pursuant to the agreement, and the three beneficiaries sued the husband for non-payment under the agreement.

Analysis: The court ruled that the promises in the instrument were not supported by consideration, so the promise was simply one to make a gift. The court refuted the following forms of alleged consideration for the husband's promise to pay $600:

- *The beneficiaries' promise to pay the husband one cent*: "[I]nadequacy of consideration will not [invalidate] an agreement, [but] this doctrine does not apply to a mere exchange of sums of money, of coin, whose value is exactly fixed. . . . In this case, had the one cent mentioned been some particular one cent, a family piece, or ancient, remarkable coin, possessing an indeterminate value, extrinsic from its simple money value, a different view might be taken. . . . The consideration of one cent is, plainly, in this case, merely nominal, and intended to be so."

- *The love and affection the husband bore his deceased wife, and the fact that she had done her part, as his wife, in the acquisition of property*: "These are past considerations. Furthermore, the fact that [the husband] loved his wife, and that she had been industrious, constituted no consideration for his promise to pay [the beneficiaries] a sum of money. . . . Nor is the fact that [her husband] now venerates the memory of his deceased wife, a legal consideration for a promise to pay any third person money."

- *The beneficiaries' promise to abstain from claims against the wife's and husband's estates:* "As the will . . . of [the wife] imposed no legal obligation upon [the husband] to discharge her bequests out of his property, and as she had none of her own, his promise to discharge them was not legally binding upon him, on that ground. A moral consideration, only, will not support a promise. . . . And for the same reason, a valid consideration for his promise can not be found in the fact of a compromise of a disputed claim; for where such claim is legally groundless, a promise upon a compromise of it, or of a suit upon it, is not legally binding. . . . [T]he agreement admits the will inoperative and void. The promise was simply one to make a gift."

The *Schnell* court packed several new and important concepts into the points outlined in the three bullets above:

- As described in the first bullet point, the court noted that "inadequacy of consideration" will not invalidate an agreement, meaning that it does not matter whether the consideration is disproportionately small in value compared with the value of the promise. (In Example A, the court in *Appeal of Clark* (page 199) used similar reasoning to uphold the promise.) However, the promise in *Schnell* was unsupported by consideration because the exchange of a sum certain of money for a different and much lower amount of money ($600 for one cent) showed that the consideration was "merely nominal." So-called "nominal consideration" is invalid, not because it is too little, but because the tiny amount could not have motivated or induced the promisor to make the promise, so the "bargain" requirement is not met. In effect, this was a "sham" exchange, not really a bargained-for exchange at all.

- As described in the second bullet point, the court noted that the husband's affection for his wife and her role in helping him to acquire property are "past considerations." Past consideration is also sometimes called "antecedent consideration," which means that the alleged consideration was furnished before the promise was ever contemplated, so it could not serve as consideration by inducing or motivating the promise. Indeed, "past consideration" is an oxymoron, because something that happened in the past can never be consideration for a subsequent promise (though, as we will see in coverage of promissory restitution in Chapter 5, it may help justify enforcement of a subsequent promise under some circumstances).

- As described in the third bullet point, the court concluded that the husband's promise was not supported by consideration from the beneficiaries' promise to forgo any claims against the husband's and wife's estate, because the beneficiaries admitted in the written agreement that the wife's will was "inoperative and void." The court stated that "where such claim is legally groundless, a promise upon a compromise of it, or of a suit upon it, is not legally binding." However, as we will see later in this chapter, some courts hold that forgoing a groundless claim can be consideration in some circumstances; see *Dyer v. National By-Products, Inc.,* on page 234.

Make the Connection

In Chapter 3, page 157, you learned that an option contract is one way to make an offer irrevocable. Interestingly, courts routinely uphold option contracts for which the offeree pays seemingly nominal consideration to the offeror:

> The consideration may consist of either a promise or a performance. Often it consists of a sum of money that is small in relation to the opportunity that speculation affords the offeree and the risk that speculation imposes on the offeror. Whatever hostility may have been shown to the device of nominal consideration in general, courts have tolerated that device as a means of making an offer irrevocable and [have] upheld options for . . . as little as a dollar. Nevertheless, the prudent lawyer would do well to advise the client not to invite litigation by paying an absurdly small amount for an option.

E. Allan Farnsworth, *Contracts* § 3.23 (4th ed. 2004).

Problems: Is There Consideration?

Is there consideration for each of the promises described below? If so, what is the consideration? (Be sure to consider all the promises described in each problem.) Does it matter if you use the "benefit or detriment" or "bargain" theory? (If you get stuck or want help in thinking through some examples, reread some of the previously assigned sections, comments, and illustrations in the Restatement (Second).)

4-1.   Anna promises to mow Ben's lawn, in exchange for $25. Ben promises to pay her $25 for mowing his lawn. If Anna never mows the lawn, does that mean there was no consideration for his promise to pay?

4-2.   Anna mows Ben's lawn, as a surprise gift. Ben is delighted and promises to pay her $25 for the mowing.

4-3.   Ben says to Anna, "I'll pay you $25 if you mow my whole lawn." Anna mows the whole lawn.

4-4.   Carla promises to give her nephew Deepak a gift of her bicycle. In reliance on the promise, before Carla delivers the bike, Deepak buys a new bike light and bike rack that will fit Carla's bike. Is your answer the same if Carla delivers the bike, and, a month later, Deepak promises to pay Carla $100 for the bike?

4-5.   Ellen wants to make a binding promise to give $10,000 to her daughter Fernanda. A lawyer friend has told her that a promise of a gift is not binding, so Ellen and Fernanda sign a writing containing Ellen's promise and a false statement that Fernanda has loaned Ellen $10,000. Would your answer be different if Ellen and Fernanda instead sign a writing in which Ellen promises to pay Fernanda $10,000 for Fernanda's car that is worth $500?

4-6.   Hannah and Ivan sign a written agreement stating, "We will each buy 5 lottery tickets each week and are partners in any winnings we receive from the tickets, to be shared equally."

4-7.   Jake wishes to buy a home but, because he has an insufficient credit history, the bank is unwilling to approve a loan to him. Jake's father, Kai, promises Jake that he will co-sign the loan so Jake can make the purchase. Thereafter, Kai signs a note promising to pay the bank if the bank approves the loan and if Jake then defaults on the loan payments. Jake gets the loan and uses the loan funds to purchase the house.

4-8.   When Lee Hunter died, State Bank held a promissory note for $3700 signed by Lee and also held 50 shares of capital stock of the Hunter Company, owned by Lee, as collateral for the payment of the promissory note. The company was insolvent at the time of Lee's death (its debts exceeded its assets), and his death made the promissory note unenforceable, so there was no value to these two "assets." Lee's widow, Zennetta, asked the bank to return to her both the stock certificate and promissory note. The bank told her it would surrender both documents if she gave the bank her own promissory note in the amount of $3700. When Zennetta failed to pay the amount due under her note, the bank sued. She claimed lack of consideration. What should the result be?

Think About It!

As described by Professor Farnsworth, there are at least two ways to approach the task of framing a basis for enforcing promises. "One can begin with the assumption that promises are generally enforceable, and then create exceptions for promises considered undesirable to enforce. Or one can begin with the assumption that promises are generally unenforceable, and then create exceptions for promises thought desirable to enforce . . . . The common law courts chose this latter assumption." E. Allan Farnsworth, *Contracts* 11 (4th ed. 2004). Civil law systems usually start with the opposite assumption, that all promises are enforceable unless they fall into delineated categories. After struggling with the common law concept of "consideration," you may well wonder which choice is preferable!

§ 3. Common Disputes Involving Consideration

Although consideration is not at issue in most contract cases, when the issue does arise, one of the following is often involved:

- Conditional gifts

- Illusory promises

- Settlement agreements for worthless claims

- Contract modifications

- Discharge of duties from an existing contract

The remainder of this chapter examines each of these subjects and further refines our understanding of the doctrine of consideration.

§ 3.1. Conditional Gifts

Because the "bargain" test for consideration requires that the parties were reciprocally induced or motivated by the exchange of promise for promise (or promise for performance) we often find consideration by looking for what the promisor "asked for" and what the promisee "gave" in exchange for the promise. Recall the statement in *Baehr* that a contractual promise appears in the logical form "If . . . (consideration is given) . . . then I promise that . . . ."

However, sometimes a promisor may make a promise and ask the promisee to do something, yet not be proposing a bargain, because the promisor is promising to make a gift and is stipulating a condition that the promisee must fulfill in order to take advantage of the gift. The promise to make a conditional gift is not supported by consideration.

Reading Critically: The Tramp Hypothetical, *Tomczak*, and *Pennsy Supply*

The line between a bargained-for exchange and a conditional gift is often difficult to discern, so several examples are helpful. As you read the examples below, consider these questions:

1. What tests do the commentators and courts use to distinguish between a conditional gift and a bargained-for exchange?

2. Why is the "benefit-detriment" test ineffective in discerning between conditional gifts and bargained-for exchanges?

3. Do you agree with the result in each case?

Example G: The Tramp Hypothetical

Professor Williston, in his treatise, described a hypothetical that is often used to illustrate a conditional gift. (Keep in mind that he developed this hypothetical in an earlier era, when a "tramp" was a homeless person or a vagabond.) He noted that

> any event may be named in a promise as fixing the moment, on the happening of which a promisor (not as an exchange for the happening but as a mere coincidence in time) will perform a promise intended and understood to be gratuitous. The same

thing, therefore, stated as the condition of a promise may or may not be consideration, according as a reasonable man would or would not understand that the performance of the condition was requested as the price or exchange for the promise. If a benevolent man says to a tramp, "If you go around the corner to the clothing shop there, you may purchase an overcoat on my credit," no reasonable person would understand that the short walk was requested as the consideration for the promise, but that in the event of the tramp going to the shop the promisor would make him a gift. Yet the walk to the shop is in its nature capable of being consideration. It is a legal detriment to the tramp to take the walk, and the only reason why the walk is not consideration is because on a reasonable interpretation, it must be held that the walk was not requested as the price of the promise, but was merely a condition of a gratuitous promise.

It is often difficult to decide whether words of condition in a promise indicate a request for consideration or state a mere condition in a gratuitous promise. An aid, though not a conclusive test in determining which interpretation of the promise is more reasonable, is an inquiry whether the happening of the condition will be a benefit to the promisor. If so, it is a fair inference that the happening was requested as a consideration. On the other hand, if, as in the case of the tramp stated above, the happening of the condition will be not only of no benefit to the promisor but is obviously merely for the purpose of enabling the promisee to receive a gift, the happening of the event on which the promise is conditional, though brought about by the promisee in reliance on the promise, will not be interpreted as consideration.

1 Samuel Williston & Walter H.E. Jaeger, *A Treatise on the Law of Contracts* § 112, at 445–46 (3d ed. 1957).

Example H: *Tomczak v. Koochiching County Highway Dept.*, 1999 WL 55501 (Minn. Ct. App. Feb. 9, 1999) (unpublished opinion).

In April, residents (including Maureen and William Tomczak) were concerned that the rising water level in a nearby gravel pit was endangering houses in the neighborhood. They raised the issue at a meeting of the county board of commissioners. Even though the county did not own or operate the gravel pit, a county engineer thought that pumping water from the pit to lower the water level by two feet might solve the problem. The board authorized the highway department to furnish a pump at the county's expense. The Tomczaks offered to furnish a site for the pump and to keep it filled with fuel and oil. The engineer said the county was concerned about liability and instructed him to obtain a release from the Tomczaks. He therefore prepared and had the Tomczaks sign the following typewritten document:

> In exchange for Koochiching County furnishing a pump to dewater the abandoned gravel pit near my property, we agreed to maintain the pump by fueling and checking the oil when necessary and waived all liability to the County for any action, damages, or injury that is caused by pumping the pit.

Around-the-clock pumping began, but a single pump was not adequate, so the county added a second, larger pump. However, the pumping kept flooding adjacent and downstream properties, no matter where the county rerouted the discharge and how many hours per day it pumped. The water level in the gravel pit slowly began to drop, but then once again rose due to heavy rains.

In early June, the county stopped pumping because the heavy volume of water had washed out a catch basin and because another landowner complained that the pumping caused flooding on his property. In late June, the Tomczaks' house was flooded. The Tomczaks sued the county for breach of contract.

Analysis: The trial court dismissed the contract claim. On appeal, the Tomczaks contended that when they signed the liability release, they entered into a contract under which the county agreed to furnish a pump and the Tomczaks agreed to maintain the pump by fueling it and checking the oil. When the county withdrew the pump, they argued, the county breached the contract.

The appellate court disagreed. Noting that a "gratuitous conditional promise is unenforceable," the court quoted the Williston passage included in Example G above. It then applied Williston's test of whether there was any benefit to the promisor (the county):

> Even if we assume that the county agreed that it would provide the pump until the water level in the pit was reduced by two feet, as Maureen Tomczak stated in her deposition, there is no contract because there is no consideration. Applying the benefit-to-promisor test, we conclude that the county's promise was a gratuitous conditional

promise and that the Tomczaks' agreement to (1) operate the pump
and (2) provide the county with a liability release was a condition of
the promise. The county did no more than gratuitously promise to
provide a pump. The Tomczaks' agreement to operate the pump was
of no benefit to the county and was obviously merely for the purpose
of enabling the Tomczaks to receive some benefit from the county's
gratuitous promise.

The court concluded that the county had not entered into a contract with the
Tomczaks. It affirmed the dismissal of the contract claim.

> **Example I:** *Pennsy Supply, Inc. v. American Ash Recycling Corp.*, 895 A.2d
> 595 (Pa. Super. Ct. 2006).
>
> A school district entered into a construction contract with a general
> contractor, which subcontracted the paving portion of the contract to
> Pennsy Supply, Inc. In the construction contract, the specifications
> required the general contractor and its subcontractor to pave with certain
> base aggregates (crushed rock) or to substitute an alternate material
> known as Treated Ash Aggregate (TAA) (known as AggRite). The project
> specifications contained documents notifying contractors that a certain
> amount of free AggRite was available from American Ash, a supplier of
> AggRite, on a first-come, first-served basis. Pennsy picked up 11,000 tons
> of AggRite from American Ash and used it for the paving work.
>
> A few months after Pennsy completed the work according to specifications,
> the pavement developed extensive cracks. The school district notified the
> general contractor, which instructed Pennsy to remedy the defective work.
> Pennsy found that it would need to remove and dispose of the AggRite,
> which is classified as a hazardous waste material by the Pennsylvania
> Department of Environmental Protection. Pennsy requested American
> Ash to remove and dispose of the AggRite, but American Ash refused.
> Pennsy eventually performed the remedial work, at no cost to the school
> district. Pennsy sued American Ash, seeking $251,940 for the cost of
> its remedial work and $133,777 for its cost to dispose of the AggRite it
> removed, based on breach of contract and other claims.

Analysis: The trial court dismissed the complaint, determining that "any alleged
agreement between the parties is unenforceable for lack of consideration." Pennsy
appealed. Addressing the contract claim, the appellate court used both the "benefit-
detriment" test and the "bargain" test to define consideration and then reasoned:

It is not enough, however, that the promisee has suffered a legal detriment at the request of the promisor. The detriment incurred must be the "quid pro quo," or the "price" of the promise, and the inducement for which it was made . . . . If the promisor merely intends to make a gift to the promisee upon the performance of a condition, the promise is gratuitous and the satisfaction of the condition is not consideration for a contract.

It quoted Williston's "tramp hypothetical" (see Example G above) and Professor Murray's analysis of conditional gifts:

If the promisor made the promise for the purpose of inducing the detriment, the detriment induced the promise. *If, however, the promisor made the promise with no particular interest in the detriment that the promisee had to suffer to take advantage of the promised gift or other benefit, the detriment was incidental or conditional to the promisee's receipt of the benefit.* Even though the promisee suffered a detriment induced by the promise, the purpose of the promisor was not to have the promisee suffer the detriment because she did not seek that detriment in exchange for her promise.

John Edward Murray, Jr., *Murray on Contracts* § 60.C, at 230 (3d ed.1990) (emphasis added). It also quoted another test:

As to the distinction between consideration and a condition, it is often difficult to determine whether words of condition in a promise indicate a request for consideration or state a mere condition in a gratuitous promise. An aid, though not a conclusive test, in determining which construction of the promise is more reasonable is an inquiry into *whether the occurrence of the condition would benefit the promisor. If so, it is a fair inference that the occurrence was requested as consideration.* On the other hand, if the occurrence of the condition is no benefit to the promisor but is merely to enable the promisee to receive a gift, the occurrence of the event on which the promise is conditional, though brought about by the promisee in reliance on the promise, is not properly construed as consideration.

17A Am. Jur.2d § 104 (2004 & 2005 Supp.) (emphasis added). The court noted Pennsy's argument that

American Ash actively promotes the use of AggRite as a building material to be used in base course of paved structures, and provides the material free of charge, in an effort to have others dispose of the material and thereby avoid incurring the disposal costs itself . . . American Ash provided the AggRite to Pennsy for use on the Project, which saved American Ash thousands of dollars in disposal costs it otherwise would have incurred.

The court stated that, accepting Pennsy's allegations to be true (as it had to do to rule on the motion to dismiss), "it is a fair interpretation of the Complaint that American Ash's promise to supply AggRite free of charge induced Pennsy to assume the detriment of collecting and taking title to the material, and critically, that it was this very detriment, whether assumed by Pennsy or some other successful bidder to the paving subcontract, which induced American Ash to make the promise to provide free AggRite for the project." It reasoned that, understood as set forth in the complaint, this was not a "conditional gift to the successful bidder on the paving subcontract for which American Ash desired and expected nothing in return."

American Ash argued that consideration was lacking because Pennsy did not allege that American Ash's avoidance of disposal costs was part of any bargaining process between the parties. The court refuted that argument by noting, "The bargain theory of consideration does not actually require that the parties bargain over the terms of the agreement."

> **Take Note!**
>
> The court's point here echoes a point made earlier in this chapter: The bargain theory does not require actual bargaining or back-and-forth negotiation. Such negotiation may help demonstrate that a "bargain" exists (the parties were looking to induce each other to make certain promises), but a bargain may exist without any evidence of back-and-forth haggling.

The appellate court reversed the trial court's dismissal and remanded the case. In further proceedings, Pennsy would have to prove that the inducement alleged in its complaint did in fact occur.

Problem: Conditional Gifts

4-9. Stelmack purchased land with a building containing stores and apartments, but his rights were expressly subject to mineral rights held by Glen Alden Coal Co., due to a previous owner's conveyance of those rights. Under the deed, the coal company was "not liable for any injury or damage to the surface of the property or to the buildings on the property that might be caused by mining or removal of coal and minerals." The deed said that it was understood that the property's value and price were reduced to reflect the possibility that damage could be caused by the mining operations, without compensation to the owner of the property.

Five years later, the coal company informed Stelmack that mining was about to begin under the property, and that the mining would cause a "subsidence of the soil" (that is, sinking soil levels and likely damage to the building). The coal company and Stelmack entered into an agreement under which Stelmack would permit the coal company's employees to enter his land and prop up the building to minimize damage, and the coal company would make all repairs necessary to restore the property to its original condition.

The coal company erected ties and supports around the building, causing the building to be an eyesore and allegedly causing a loss of rents. Mining continued for five years, with the coal company making repairs to the property from time to time. Soil subsidence continued, however, and Stelmack determined that additional work would be required, at a considerable cost, to restore the land and building to its previous condition. The coal company refused to do the additional work or provide funds to Stelmack to have the work done.

Stelmack seeks to enforce the coal company's promise to restore the property to its original condition. Is that promise enforceable (that is, was there consideration for the coal company's promise)?

---

§ 3.2. Illusory Promises

As we saw in Chapter 2, § 4, some communications that look like promises are merely "illusory promises" (meaning no promise at all) because they contain no commitment. This lack of commitment may be caused by the would-be promisor retaining total discretion to decide whether to perform the particular promise or by the existence of a termination-for-convenience clause that allows the promisor to terminate the agreement for any reason at any time without any advance notice. If the would-be promise is illusory, then it cannot serve as consideration for the other party's promise, and no contract can result.

This result—that an illusory promise cannot serve as consideration—does not necessarily follow from the bargain test for consideration.

- Consider the merchant trying to enter a market who is willing to commit to fulfilling orders during the next six months if a potential customer places such orders, even though the customer does not commit to actually placing any orders. In one sense, the merchant is receiving nothing for its promise, because the customer has total discretion about whether to order anything. In another sense, however, the merchant is getting exactly what it wants—a chance to be considered by the customer, who has other more established sources of supply.

- Or consider the bicycle touring company that sends a message to past customers in November that if they place a deposit by December 31 on a trip for the following year, they can have the current year pricing, but will be free to change their minds about which trip to take, or whether to take any trip, and get back their full deposit. In one sense, the touring company is receiving nothing, because the customer is free to take back the money and never commit to a trip. In another sense, however, the touring company is getting exactly what it wants—a better chance that the customers who give a deposit will actually book a trip than if they had not.

- The same issue arises with termination-for-convenience clauses that give one party (or both parties) the right to unilaterally terminate the agreement for any reason at any time without any advance notice.

That said, even if the return "promise" appears to be nonexistent or illusory, courts generally "prefer a construction [of a so-called illusory promise] which will make the contract effective rather than one which will make it illusory or unenforceable." If the court can find an implied promise or otherwise find a commitment, then it often can find that the newly construed promise was bargained for or was a benefit or detriment.

Example J: *Questar Builders, Inc. v. CB Flooring, Inc.*, 978 A.2d 651 (Md. Ct. App. 2009).

Questar Builders hired CB Flooring to install carpeting in a new luxury midrise apartment and townhome complex for a total price of $1,120,000. The agreement's express language gave one party the right to terminate for convenience. When Questar exercised its right to terminate, CB contested that right (among other issues in a complicated dispute), claiming that Questar's right to terminate was not unrestricted.

Analysis: In considering whether the contract was enforceable despite the existence of the clause, the court explained both the challenge and the response to the enforcement issues surrounding such clauses:

Under Maryland law of contract, illusory contracts are unenforceable. . . . An unlimited right to determine how to perform, or whether to perform at all, negates the promise to perform.

This notwithstanding, courts generally "prefer a construction [of a contract] which will make the contract effective rather than one which will make it illusory or unenforceable." To that end,

> If there is a restriction, express or implied, on the promisor's ability to perform, the promise is not illusory. The tendency of the law is to avoid the finding that no contract arose due to an illusory promise when it appears that the parties intended a contract. Through the process of interpretation, in the absence of express restrictions, courts find implied promises to prevent a party's promise from being performable merely at the whim of the promisor. . . . The nature of the promise to be implied will vary with the kind of transaction and the particular context surrounding the individual transaction.

> . . . .

> Looked at woodenly, it might appear that performance is dependent upon the party's own whim, but courts are not mindless wooden sticks. Judges are cognizant of the utility of such contracts and of the understanding of reasonable parties to such contracts.

Make the Connection

In Chapter 8, we will see other instances in which courts find implied obligations, as well as additional examples of implied obligations that save a contract from unenforceability.

The court found in the agreement an implicit obligation to act reasonably (in good faith) in the exercise of discretion under the termination clause and therefore found the contract was not illusory. (It then moved on to resolve other issues).

Problem: Illusory Promises

4-10. An agreement signed by Drew, Ebony, Farley, Garret, and Hakeem provided that (1) Drew and Ebony would serve as directors of a new company, Interchange, Inc., and have the right to manage the company "for a period of ten years or until their sooner resignation"; and (2) Farley, Garret, and Hakeem would establish Interchange, Inc., install Drew and Ebony as directors, and enter a management agreement with them. After four years, Farley, Garret, and Hakeem (also directors of the company) ousted Drew and Ebony as directors and terminated the management contract. Drew and Ebony filed suit against the other three directors to compel them to continue the management contract. Defendants claim lack of consideration. What argument(s) should the plaintiffs raise, in support of consideration? Which side do you think will prevail?

§ 3.3. Settlement Agreements Based on Worthless (Invalid) Claims

Lawsuits often end not with trials and verdicts but instead with settlement agreements between the parties, in which the plaintiff promises to waive further rights to pursue its claim, in return for the other party's transfer of (or promise to transfer) specified assets (often money). Parties may enter into a settlement agreement before or after a lawsuit is filed. For example:

- A patient alleging malpractice against a doctor may agree to give up the right to file or pursue a medical malpractice suit in exchange for a sum of money paid by the doctor's insurer.

- A property owner who has sued another person for trespass may agree to voluntarily dismiss the lawsuit in return for the other person's promise to pay a specified sum.

For such settlement agreements to be binding—that is, to foreclose a subsequent claim and to enforce a promise to pay an amount to settle the asserted claim—each promise must be supported by consideration. In particular, the promise to waive the claim must constitute consideration for the promised payment or transfer.

Settlement agreements generate questions about the existence of consideration when a party forgoes a claim that is worthless (or later turns out to be worthless). Early courts held that such a settlement agreement lacked consideration. However, subsequent courts have used a more nuanced approach.

Reading Critically: *Dyer*

The *Dyer* case examined whether relinquishment of a disputed, worthless, or invalid claim can be consideration for a promise. As you read the case, answer these questions:

1. The opinion, the cases cited in the opinion, and the Restatement (Second) of Contracts § 71 all draw a distinction between the treatment of a claim that is "doubtful" or "disputed" (both terms are used), and a claim that is "invalid" or "unfounded" (again, both terms are used to describe this category of claims). What

is the difference between these two categories of claims? Give
an example of each.

2. If a party to a settlement agreement promises to forgo a claim
   with disputed validity (because of uncertainty as to the facts or
   the law), does that promise furnish consideration for a return
   promise to pay a certain sum?

3. What are the conflicting rules on whether and when forgoing
   an invalid claim can be consideration for a promise? Which rule
   did the *Schnell v. Nell* court apply above, (page 218)? Which
   rule do you think is better? Why?

4. In what respect do the rules in *Dyer* resemble the rules in *Questar
   Builders*, page 231?

Dyer v. National By-Products, Inc.

Dale Warren DYER, Plaintiff-Appellant

v.

NATIONAL BY-PRODUCTS, INC., Defendant-Appellee

Supreme Court of Iowa
380 N.W.2d 732 (Iowa 1986)

SCHULTZ, JUSTICE.

The determinative issue in this appeal is whether good faith forbearance
to litigate a claim, which proves to be invalid and unfounded, is sufficient consideration to uphold a contract of settlement. The district court determined, as a
matter of law, that consideration for the alleged settlement was lacking because
the forborne claim was not a viable cause of action. We reverse and remand.

On October 29, 1981, Dale Dyer, an employee of National By-Products, lost
his right foot in a job-related accident. Thereafter, the employer placed Dyer on a
leave of absence at full pay from the date of his injury until August 16, 1982. At
that time he returned to work as a foreman, the job he held prior to his injury. On
March 11, 1983, the employer indefinitely laid off Dyer.

Dyer then filed the present lawsuit against his employer claiming that his
discharge was a breach of an oral contract. He alleged that he in good faith believed
that he had a valid claim against his employer for his personal injury. Further, Dyer

claimed that his forbearance from litigating his claim was made in exchange for a promise from his employer that he would have lifetime employment. The employer specifically denied that it had offered a lifetime job to Dyer after his injury.

Following extensive discovery procedures, the employer filed a motion for summary judgment claiming there was no genuine factual issue and that it was entitled to judgment as a matter of law. The motion was resisted by Dyer. The district court sustained the employer's motion on the basis that: (1) no reciprocal promise to work for the employer for life was present, and (2) there was no forbearance of any viable cause of action, apparently on the ground that workers' compensation provided Dyer's sole remedy.

On appeal, Dyer claims that consideration for the alleged contract of lifetime employment was his forbearance from pursuing an action against his employer. Accordingly, he restricts his claim of error to the second reason advanced by the district court for granting summary judgment. Summary judgment is only proper when there is no genuine issue of any material fact. Iowa R. Civ. P. 237(c). Dyer generally contends that an unresolved issue of material fact remains as to whether he reasonably and in good faith forbore from asserting a claim against his employer and his co-employees in exchange for the employer's alleged promise to employ him for life. Specifically, he asserts that the trial court erred because: (1) the court did not consider the reasonableness and good faith of his belief in the validity of the claim he forbore from asserting, and (2) the court considered the legal merits of the claim itself which Dyer forbore from asserting.

The employer, on the other hand, maintains that workers' compensation benefits are Dyer's sole remedy for his injury and that his claim for damages is unfounded. It then urges that forbearance from asserting an unfounded claim cannot serve as consideration for a contract. For the purpose of this discussion, we shall assume that Dyer's tort action is clearly invalid and he had no basis for a tort suit against either his employer or his fellow employees. We recognize that the fact issue, as to whether Dyer in good faith believed that he had a cause of action based in

> **FYI**
>
> All states in the United States have adopted some form of workers' compensation system, as have many other industrialized nations. The system mandates that injured workers' claims against their employers be paid under the workers' compensation rules and processes, and it preempts the employees' rights to tort recovery for such injuries. The amounts distributed are often less than what might be recovered in a tort lawsuit, but employees are more certain to get some kind of recovery than might be true based solely on the ability to bring and win tort claims.

tort against the employer, remains unresolved. The determinative issue before the district court and now on appeal is whether the lack of consideration for the alleged promise of lifetime employment has been established as a matter of law.

Preliminarily, we observe that the law favors the adjustment and settlement of controversies without resorting to court action. *Olson v. Wilson & Co.*, 244 Iowa 895, 899, 58 N.W.2d 381, 384 (1953). Compromise is favored by law. *White v. Flood*, 258 Iowa 402, 409, 138 N.W.2d 863, 867 (1965). Compromise of a doubtful right asserted in good faith is sufficient consideration for a promise. *Id.*

The more difficult problem is whether the settlement of an unfounded claim asserted in good faith is consideration for a contract of settlement. Professor Corbin presents a view favorable to Dyer's argument when he states:

> [F]orbearance to press a claim, or a promise of such forbearance, may be a sufficient consideration even though the claim is wholly ill-founded. It may be ill-founded because the facts are not what he supposes them to be, or because the existing facts do not have the legal operation that he supposes them to have. In either case, his forbearance may be a sufficient consideration, although under certain circumstances it is not. The fact that the claim is ill-founded is not in itself enough to prevent forbearance from being a sufficient consideration for a promise.

1 *Corbin on Contracts* § 140, at 595 (1963). Further, in the same section, it is noted that:

> The most generally prevailing, and probably the most satisfactory view is that *forbearance is sufficient if there is any reasonable ground for the claimant's belief that it is just to try to enforce his claim. He must be asserting his claim "in good faith"*; but this does not mean he must believe that his suit can be won. It means that he must not be making his claim or threatening suit for purposes of vexation, or in order to realize on its "nuisance value."

Id. § 140, at 602 (emphasis added). Indeed, we find support for the Corbin view in language contained in our cases. *See White v. Flood*, 258 Iowa at 409, 138 N.W.2d at 867 ("[C]ompromise of a doubtful right asserted in good faith is sufficient consideration for a promise."); *In re Estate of Dayton*, 246 Iowa 1209, 1216, 71 N.W.2d 429, 433 (1955) ("The good faith assertion of an unfounded claim furnishes ample consideration for a settlement."); *Messer v. Washington National Insurance Co.*, 233 Iowa 1372, 1380, 11 N.W.2d 727, 731 (1943) ("[I]f the parties act in good faith, even when they know all the facts and there is promise without legal liability on which to base it, the courts hesitate to disturb the agreements of the parties. . . ."); *Lockie v. Baker*, 206 Iowa 21, 24, 218 N.W. 483, 484 (1928) (Claim settled, though perhaps not valid, must have been presented and demanded in good faith.); *First National Bank v. Browne*, 199 Iowa 981, 984, 203 N.W. 277, 278 (1925) (Settlement of a disputed or doubtful claim in good faith is sufficient consideration for a compromise, even though judicial investigation might show claim to be unfounded.).

The Restatement (Second) of Contracts section 74 (1979), supports the Corbin view and states:

Settlement of Claims

(1) Forbearance to assert or the surrender of a claim or defense which proves to be invalid is not consideration unless

(a) the claim or defense is in fact doubtful because of uncertainty as to the facts or the law, or

(b) *the forbearing or surrendering party believes that the claim or defense may be fairly determined to be valid.*

Comment b. Requirement of good faith. The policy favoring compromise of disputed claims is clearest, perhaps, where a claim is surrendered at a time when it is uncertain whether it is valid or not. Even though the invalidity later becomes clear, *the bargain is to be judged as it appeared to the parties at the time;* if the claim was then doubtful, no inquiry is necessary as to their good faith. Even though the invalidity should have been clear at the time, the settlement of an honest dispute is upheld. But a mere assertion or denial of liability does not make a claim doubtful, and *the fact that invalidity is obvious may indicate that it was known.* In such cases Subsection (1)(b) requires a showing of *good faith.*

(Emphasis added.) *See also* 15 Am.Jur.2d *Compromise and Settlement* § 16, at 787 (1976); 15A C.J.S. *Compromise and Settlement* § 11(b), at 206 (1967), quoted in *Messer v. Washington National Insurance Co.*, 233 Iowa at 1380, 11 N.W.2d at 731.

However, not all jurisdictions adhere to this view. Some courts require that the claim forborne must have some merit in fact or at law before it can provide consideration and these jurisdictions reject those claims that are obviously invalid. *See Bullard v. Curry-Cloonan*, 367 A.2d 127, 131 (D.C.App.1976) ("[A]s a general principle, the forbearance of a cause of action advanced in good faith, which is neither absurd in fact nor obviously unfounded in law, constitutes good and valuable consideration."); *Frasier v. Carter*, 92 Idaho 79, 437 P.2d 32, 34 (1968) (The forbearance of a claim which is not utterly groundless is sufficient consideration to support a contract.); *Charles v. Hill* 260 N.W.2d 571, 575 (Minn.1977) ("[A] wholly baseless or utterly unfounded claim is not consideration for a contract."); *Agristor Credit Corporation v. Unruh*, 571 P.2d 1220, 1224 (Okla.1977) (In order to constitute consideration for a contract, "claim forborne must be reasonably doubtful in law or fact."); *see generally* 15A C.J.S. *Compromise and Settlement* § 10, at 201 (There are many decisions holding that a claim which is entirely baseless does not afford consideration for a compromise.).

In fact, we find language in our own case law that supports the view which is favorable to the employer in this case. See *Vande Stouwe v. Bankers' Life Co.*, 218 Iowa 1182, 1190, 254 N.W. 790, 794 (1934) ("A claim that is entirely baseless and without foundation in law or equity will not support a compromise."); *Peterson v. Breitag*, 88 Iowa 418, 422–23, 55 N.W. 86, 88 (1893) ("It is well settled that there must at least be some appearance of a valid claim to support a settlement to avoid litigation."); *Tucker v. Ronk*, 43 Iowa 80, 82 (1876) (The settlement of an illegal and unfounded claim, upon which no proceedings have been instituted, is without consideration.); *Sullivan v. Collins*, 18 Iowa 228, 229 (1865) (A compromise of a claim is not a sufficient consideration to sustain a note, when such claim is not sustainable in law or in equity, or, at least doubtful in some respect.). Additionally, Professor Williston notes that:

> While there is a great divergence of opinion respecting the kind of forbearance which will constitute consideration, the *weight of authority holds that although forbearance from suit on a clearly invalid claim is insufficient consideration for a promise,* forbearance from suit on a claim of doubtful validity is sufficient consideration for a promise if there is a sincere belief in the validity of the claim.

1 *Williston on Contracts* § 135, at 581 (3rd ed. 1957) (emphasis added).

We believe, however, that the better reasoned approach is that expressed in the Restatement (Second) of Contracts section 74. Even the above statement from *Williston*, although it may have been the state of the law in 1957, is a questionable assessment of the current law. In fact, most of the cases cited in the cumulative supplement to *Williston* follow the "good faith and reasonable" language. 1 *Williston on Contracts* § 135B (3rd ed. 1957 & Supp.1985). Additionally, Restatement (Second) of Contracts section 74 is cited in that supplement. *Id.* As noted before, as a matter of policy the law favors compromise and such policy would be defeated if a party could second guess his settlement and litigate the validity of the compromise. The requirement that the forbearing party assert the claim in good faith sufficiently protects the policy of law that favors the settlement of controversies. Our holdings which are to the contrary to this view are overruled.

In the present case, the invalidity of Dyer's claim against the employer does not foreclose him, as a matter of law, from asserting that his forbearance was consideration for the alleged contract of settlement. However, the issue of Dyer's good faith must still be examined. In so doing, the issue of the validity of Dyer's claim should not be entirely overlooked:

> Although the courts will not inquire into the validity of a claim which was compromised in good faith, there must generally be reasonable grounds for a belief in order for the court to be convinced that the

belief was honestly entertained by the person who asserted it. Sufficient consideration requires more than the bald assertion by a claimant who has a claim, and to the extent that the validity or invalidity of a claim has a bearing upon whether there were reasonable grounds for believing in its possible validity, evidence of the validity or invalidity of a claim may be relevant to the issue of good faith.

15A Am.Jur.2d *Compromise and Settlement* § 17, at 790. We conclude that the evidence of the invalidity of the claim is relevant to show a lack of honest belief in the validity of the claim asserted or forborne.

Under the present state of the record, there remains a material [question] as to whether Dyer's forbearance to assert his claim was in good faith. Summary judgment should not have been rendered against him. Accordingly, the case is reversed and remanded for further proceedings consistent with this opinion.

Reversed and remanded.

Who's That?

As reflected in the court's opinion, opposing views on what kinds of claims may serve as consideration were presented by Samuel Williston and Arthur Corbin, two of the most influential contracts scholars of the twentieth century.

Samuel Williston[*] (1861–1963) taught at Harvard Law School from 1890 to 1938. In the photograph below, he is posing next to the manuscript for his five-volume treatise on contract law, which remains

authoritative (though now edited by others). Among other accomplishments, he drafted several uniform laws that became the basis for the Uniform Commercial Code, was one of the

---

[*] Picture appears courtesy of Historical & Special Collections, Harvard Law School Library.

original members of the American Law Institute, and was primary draftsman of the first Restatement of Contracts. Williston is known as a "formalist," emphasizing the application of general principles of law sometimes seen as divorced from normative and policy considerations.

 Arthur Corbin (1874–1967) taught at Yale Law School from 1903 until his retirement in 1943. He helped to introduce the case method of teaching at Yale and was the author of many books and articles on the subject of contracts. He published his own eight-volume treatise on contracts in 1950 (like Williston's, it is still authoritative, though now edited by others). He was an adviser to the Reporters of both the first and second Restatement of Contracts, and his scholarship was influential in the creation of the Uniform Commercial Code. Corbin is known as a "realist," concerned that the law reflect the changing social and economic context.

How are the assumptions and philosophies of these two scholars reflected in *Dyer*? You should watch for references to both Corbin and Williston in the cases you read to help you understand and evaluate the arguments made, as well as to place those arguments in historical and theoretical context.

Problem: Settlement Agreements and Consideration

4-11. Recall the facts in *Schnell v. Nell* (Example F, page 218). Assume that, instead of signing the agreement that appears in that case, Nell filed a claim against the estate of Theresa Schnell, seeking recovery of the $200 promised her in Theresa's will. Thereafter, Zacharias Schnell and Nell entered the following agreement:

> Zacharias Schnell and J.B. Nell agree as follows: Nell will withdraw her claim against the estate of Theresa Schnell and waive any further right to pursue such claim. In exchange, Zacharias Schnell agrees to pay $150 to Nell.

Schnell then refused to pay any sum to Nell. Nell filed suit to compel performance of the above agreement. Schnell claimed lack of consideration. How should the court rule?

---

§ 3.4. Contract Modification and the Pre-Existing Duty Rule

Under the traditional common law rule, the requirement that a promise have consideration to be enforceable applies not only to the formation of a contract, but also to its modification, because the modification agreement is itself a contract that must satisfy the rules on contract formation. If the duties of both parties to the contract are modified, consideration is often easy to find, because each party sought the other party's promise. Sometimes, though, the parties agree to change the responsibilities of only one party to a contract, perhaps because unanticipated circumstances have caused the performance to become unexpectedly burdensome to one of the parties. Compare the following situations:

- In a contract to build a structure, the builder may agree to add another interior wall to the original plans while the owner agrees to pay an additional amount for the work.

- A natural disaster greatly increases lumber prices and therefore the costs for a builder. In a home construction contract, the homeowner and builder agree that the increased cost to the builder will be shared in a specified ratio with the homeowner, who originally agreed to a fixed price for the construction project. The work of the builder does not change.

Under the latter circumstances, the requirement of consideration for the modification may be problematic. The duty promised under the original contract—the original structure promised by the builder, in the examples above—is already owed to the other party. It is, in legal terms, a "pre-existing duty" and therefore cannot serve as "fresh" consideration for the owner's promise to pay an additional sum.

This "pre-existing duty rule" has been roundly criticized since at least the early part of the nineteenth century in the United States and in England, where the rule originated.[*] Although the effect of the rule has been moderated by judicial

---

[*] For example, the Minnesota Supreme Court long ago described the rule as "one of the relics of antique law which should have been discarded long ago. It is evidence of the former capacity of lawyers and judges to make the requirement of consideration an overworked shibboleth rather than a logical and just standard of actionability." *Rye v. Phillips*, 282 N.W. 459, 460 (Minn. 1938). Almost 40 years earlier, the Washington Supreme Court noted that, "[f]or many years, . . . courts have been dissatisfied with this rule, and have refused to extend the doctrine, but have sought to restrict the

manipulation, common law reforms, and statutory enactments, the original rule remains the law in most jurisdictions.* The cases and statutory material in this section will introduce you to the application of the pre-existing duty rule, its exceptions, criticisms of the rule, and some of the reforms that have limited its influence.

Reading Critically: *Angel*

1. What kind of modification was made to the original contract, and why did the parties agree to it? What challenges did the pre-existing duty rule present to enforceability?

2. What justifications or rationale are or may be given for the pre-existing duty rule? What arguments are or may be made against its operation?

3. Did the court find that consideration existed, despite application of the pre-existing duty rule, or did the court create an exception to the pre-existing duty rule?

4. What mechanisms or strategies do the courts use to "get around" the pre-existing duty rule (that is, to avoid applying the rule while not changing it)?

Angel v. Murray

ALFRED L. ANGEL, Plaintiff-Appellee

v.

JOHN E. MURRAY, Jr., Director of Finance of the City of Newport, and JAMES L. MAHER, Defendants-Appellants

Supreme Court of Rhode Island
<u>322 A.2d 630 (R.I. 1974)</u>

ROBERTS, CHIEF JUSTICE.

This is a civil action brought by Alfred L. Angel and others against John E. Murray, Jr., Director of Finance of the City of Newport, the city of Newport, and

---

operation of the rule whenever it was possible. It is certainly not in accordance with ethics, and ought not to be in accord with the rules of law . . . ." *Brown v. Kern*, 57 P. 798, 799 (Wash. 1899).

* *See* E. Allan Farnsworth, *Contracts* §§ 4.21, 4.22 (4th ed. 2004).

James L. Maher, alleging that Maher had illegally been paid the sum of $20,000 by the Director of Finance and praying that the defendant Maher be ordered to repay the city such sum. The case was heard by a justice of the Superior Court, sitting without a jury, who entered a judgment ordering Maher to repay the sum of $20,000 to the city of Newport. Maher is now before this court prosecuting an appeal.

The record discloses that Maher has provided the city of Newport with a refuse-collection service under a series of five-year contracts beginning in 1946. On March 12, 1964, Maher and the city entered into another such contract for a period of five years commencing on July 1, 1964, and terminating on June 30, 1969. The contract provided, among other things, that Maher would receive $137,000 per year in return for collecting and removing all combustible and noncombustible waste materials generated within the city.

In June of 1967 Maher requested an additional $10,000 per year from the city council because there had been a substantial increase in the cost of collection due to an unexpected and unanticipated increase of 400 new dwelling units. Maher's testimony, which is uncontradicted, indicates the 1964 contract had been predicated on the fact that since 1946 there had been an average increase of 20 to 25 new dwelling units per year. After a public meeting of the city council where Maher explained in detail the reasons for his request and was questioned by members of the city council, the city council agreed to pay him an additional $10,000 for the year ending on June 30, 1968. Maher made a similar request again in June of 1968 for the same reasons, and the city council again agreed to pay an additional $10,000 for the year ending on June 30, 1969.

The trial justice found that each such $10,000 payment was made in violation of law. His decision, as we understand it, is premised on two independent grounds. First, he found that the additional payments were unlawful because they had not been recommended in writing to the city council by the city manager. Second, he found that Maher was not entitled to extra compensation because the original contract already required him to collect all refuse generated within the city and, therefore, included the 400 additional units. The trial justice further found that these 400 additional units were within the contemplation of the parties when they entered into the contract. It appears that he based this portion of the decision upon the rule that Maher had a preexisting duty to collect the refuse generated by the 400 additional units, and thus there was no consideration for the two additional payments.

[Discussion of the city council's power to modify the 1964 contract omitted.]

II.

Having found that the city council had the power to modify the 1964 contract without the written recommendation of the city manager, we are still confronted with the question of whether the additional payments were illegal because they were not supported by consideration.

A.

As previously stated, the city council made two $10,000 payments. The first was made in June of 1967 for the year beginning on July 1, 1967, and ending on June 30, 1968. Thus, by the time this action was commenced in October of 1968, the modification was completely executed. That is, the money had been paid by the city council, and Maher had collected all of the refuse. Since consideration is only a test of the enforceability of executory promises, the presence or absence of consideration for the first payment is unimportant because the city council's agreement to make the first payment was fully executed at the time of the commencement of this action. See *Salvas v. Jussaume*, 50 R.I. 75, 145 A. 97 (1929); *Young Foundation Corp. v. A. E. Ottaviano, Inc.*, 29 Misc.2d 302, 216 N.Y.S.2d 448, aff'd 15 A.D.2d 517, 222 N.Y.S.2d 685 (1961); . . . . However, since both payments were made under similar circumstances, our decision regarding the second payment (Part B, infra) is fully applicable to the first payment.

B.

It is generally held that a modification of a contract is itself a contract, which is unenforceable unless supported by consideration. See Simpson, supra, § 93. In *Rose v. Daniels*, 8 R.I. 381 (1866), this court held that an agreement by a debtor with a creditor to discharge a debt for a sum of money less than the amount due is unenforceable because it was not supported by consideration.

Rose is a perfect example of the preexisting duty rule. Under this rule an agreement modifying a contract is not supported by consideration if one of the parties to the agreement does or promises to do something that he is legally obligated to do or refrains or promises to refrain from doing something he is not legally privileged to do. See Calamari & Perillo, Contracts § 60 (1970); 1A Corbin, Contracts §§ 171–72 (1963); 1 Williston, supra, § 130; Annot., 12 A.L.R.2d 78 (1950). In *Rose* there was no consideration for the new agreement because the debtor was already legally obligated to repay the full amount of the debt.

Although the preexisting duty rule is followed by most jurisdictions, a small minority of jurisdictions, Massachusetts, for example, find that there is consideration for a promise to perform what one is already legally obligated to do because the new promise is given in place of an action for damages to secure performance. See *Swartz v. Lieberman*, 323 Mass. 109, 80 N.E.2d 5 (1948); *Munroe v. Perkins*, 26 Mass. (9 Pick.) 298 (1830). Swartz is premised on the theory that a promisor's forbearance of the power to breach his original agreement and be sued in an action for damages is consideration for a subsequent agreement by the promisee to pay extra compensation. This rule, however, has been widely criticized as an anomaly. See Calamari & Perillo, *supra*, § 61; Annot., 12 A.L.R.2d 78, 85–90 (1950).

The primary purpose of the preexisting duty rule is to prevent what has been referred to as the "hold-up game." See 1A Corbin, *supra*, § 171. A classic example of the "hold-up game" is found in *Alaska Packers' Ass'n v. Domenico*, 117 F. 99 (9th Cir. 1902). There 21 seamen entered into a written contract with Domenico to sail from San Francisco to Pyramid Harbor, Alaska. They were to work as sailors and fishermen out of Pyramid Harbor during the fishing season of 1900. The contract specified that each man would be paid $50 plus two cents for each red salmon he caught. Subsequent to their arrival at Pyramid Harbor, the men stopped work and demanded an additional $50. They threatened to return to San Francisco if Domenico did not agree to their demand. Since it was impossible for Domenico to find other men, he agreed to pay the men an additional $50. After they returned to San Francisco, Domenico refused to pay the men an additional $50. The court found that the subsequent agreement to pay the men an additional $50 was not supported by consideration because the men had a preexisting duty to work on the ship under the original contract, and thus the subsequent agreement was unenforceable.

Behind the Scenes

For a look at the history of the Alaska Packers' Association and the salmon industry, go to www.youtube.com/watch?v=qN55l8ejhdU. Recent research has suggested that the story told in *Alaska Packers' Ass'n* is more complicated, because the plaintiff seamen might well have had a legitimate claim that the defendant was breaching its responsibilities under the contract to provide adequate nets for fishing. *See* Debora L. Threedy, *A Fish Story: Alaska Packers' Association v. Domenico*, 2000 Utah L. Rev. 185. If that were so, how would that change the analysis?

Another example of the "hold-up game" is found in the area of construction contracts. Frequently, a contractor will refuse to complete work under an unprofitable contract unless he is awarded additional compensation. The courts have generally held that a subsequent agreement to award additional compensation is unenforceable if the contractor is only performing work which would have been required of him under the original contract. See, e.g., *Lingenfelder v. Wainwright Brewing Co.*, 103 Mo. 578, 15 S.W. 844 (1891), which is a leading case in this area. See also cases collected in Annot., 25 A.L.R. 1450 (1923), supplemented by Annot., 55 A.L.R. 1333 (1928), and Annot., 138 A.L.R. 136 (1942); cf. *Ford & Denning v. Shepard Co.*, 36 R.I. 497, 90 A. 805 (1914).

These examples clearly illustrate that the courts will not enforce an agreement that has been procured by coercion or duress and will hold the parties to their original contract regardless of whether it is profitable or unprofitable. However, the courts have been reluctant to apply the preexisting duty rule when a party to a contract encounters unanticipated difficulties and the other party, not influenced by coercion or duress, voluntarily agrees to pay additional compensation for work already required to be performed under the contract. For example, the courts have found that the original contract was rescinded, *Linz v. Schuck*, 106 Md. 220, 67 A. 286 (1907); abandoned, *Connelly v. Devoe*, 37 Conn. 570 (1871), or waived, *Michaud v. McGregor*, 61 Minn. 198, 63 N.W. 479 (1895).

Although the preexisting duty rule has served a useful purpose insofar as it deters parties from using coercion and duress to obtain additional compensation, it has been widely criticized as a general rule of law. With regard to the preexisting duty rule, one legal scholar has stated: "There has been a growing doubt as to the soundness of this doctrine as a matter of social policy. . . . In certain classes of cases, this doubt has influenced courts to refuse to apply the rule, or to ignore it, in their actual decisions. Like other legal rules, this rule is in process of growth and change, the process being more active here than in most instances. The result of this is that a court should no longer accept this rule as fully established. It should never use it as the major premise of a decision, at least without giving careful thought to the circumstances of the particular case, to the moral deserts of the parties, and to the social feelings and interests that are involved. It is certain that the rule, stated in general and all-inclusive terms, is no longer so well-settled that a court must apply it though the heavens fall." 1A Corbin, *supra*, § 171; see also Calamari & Perillo, *supra*, § 61.

Think About It!

The *Angel* court said that some courts avoid the pre-existing duty rule by finding that the original contract was rescinded, abandoned, or waived.

- Rescission is the unmaking or avoidance of a contract, unilaterally or by agreement.

- Abandonment is the voluntary relinquishment of a right or interest with the intent never to reclaim it.

- Waiver is the voluntary relinquishment or abandonment, express or implied, of a right or advantage, with knowledge of the right and the intent to forgo it.

How would these theories allow courts to "get around" the preexisting duty rule? Would such theories have worked in *Angel*? Why or why not?

The modern trend appears to recognize the necessity that courts should enforce agreements modifying contracts when unexpected or unanticipated difficulties arise during the course of the performance of a contract, even though there is no consideration for the modification, as long as the parties agree voluntarily.

Under the Uniform Commercial Code, § 2–209(1), which has been adopted by 49 states, "(a)n agreement modifying a contract (for the sale of goods) needs no consideration to be binding." See G.L.1956 (1969 Reenactment) § 6A–2–209(1). Although at first blush this section appears to validate modifications obtained by coercion and duress, the comments to this section indicate that a modification under this section must meet the test of good faith imposed by the Code, and a modification obtained by extortion without a legitimate commercial reason is unenforceable.

The modern trend away from a rigid application of the preexisting duty rule is reflected by § 89D(a) of the American Law Institute's Restatement

Draft § 89(D)(a) became § 89 in the Restatement (Second).

Second of the Law of Contracts, which provides: "A promise modifying a duty under a contract not fully performed on either side is binding (a) if the modification is fair and equitable in view of circumstances not anticipated by the parties when the contract was made . . . ."

We believe that § 89D(a) is the proper rule of law and find it applicable to the facts of this case. It not only prohibits modifications obtained by coercion, duress, or extortion but also fulfills society's expectation that agreements entered into voluntarily will be enforced by the courts. See generally Horwitz, The Historical Foundations of Modern Contract Law, 87 Harv. L. Rev. 917 (1974). Section 89D(a), of course, does not compel a modification of an unprofitable or unfair contract; it only enforces a modification if the parties voluntarily agree and if (1) the promise modifying the original contract was made before the contract was fully performed on either side, (2) the underlying circumstances which prompted the modification were unanticipated by the parties, and (3) the modification is fair and equitable.

The evidence, which is uncontradicted, reveals that in June of 1968 Maher requested the city council to pay him an additional $10,000 for the year beginning on July 1, 1968, and ending on June 30, 1969. This request was made at a public meeting of the city council, where Maher explained in detail his reasons for making the request. Thereafter, the city council voted to authorize the Mayor to sign an amendment to the 1964 contract which provided that Maher would receive an additional $10,000 per year for the duration of the contract. Under such circumstances we have no doubt that the city voluntarily agreed to modify the 1964 contract.

Having determined the voluntariness of this agreement, we turn our attention to the three criteria delineated above. First, the modification was made in June of 1968 at a time when the five-year contract which was made in 1964 had not been fully performed by either party. Second, although the 1964 contract provided that Maher collect all refuse generated within the city, it appears this contract was premised on Maher's past experience that the number of refuse-generating units would increase at a rate of 20 to 25 per year. Furthermore, the evidence is uncontradicted that the 1967–1968 increase of 400 units "went beyond any previous expectation." Clearly, the circumstances which prompted the city council to modify the 1964 contract were unanticipated.[4] Third, although the evidence does not indicate what proportion of the total this increase comprised, the evidence does indicate that it was a "substantial" increase. In light of this, we cannot say that the council's agreement to pay Maher the $10,000 increase was not fair and equitable in the circumstances.

The judgment appealed from is reversed, and the cause is remanded to the Superior Court for entry of judgment for the defendants.

Practice Pointer: Indemnification and Duty-to-Defend Clauses

The clause noted in the *Angel* court's footnote 4 is a "hold harmless" (indemnification) and duty-to-defend clause that shifts many risks from the city to the contractor.

---

[4] The trial justice found that sec. 2(a) of the 1964 contract precluded Maher from recovering extra compensation for the 400 additional units. Section 2(a) provided: "*The Contractor, having made his proposal after his own examinations and estimates, shall take all responsibility for, and bear, any losses resulting to him in carrying out the contract*; and shall assume the defence of, and hold the City, its agents and employees harmless from all suits and claims arising from the use of any invention, patent, or patent rights, material, labor or implement, by or from any act, omission or neglect of, the Contractor, his agents or employees, in carrying out the contract." (Emphasis added). The trial justice, quoting the italicized portion of sec. 2(a), found that this section required that any losses incurred in the performance of the contract were Maher's responsibility. In our opinion, however, the trial justice overlooked the thrust of sec. 2(a) when read in its entirety.

It is clearly a contractual provision requiring the contractor to hold the city harmless and to defend it in any litigation arising out of the performance of his obligations under the contract, whether a result of affirmative action or some omission or neglect on the part of Maher or his agents or employees. We are persuaded that the portion of sec. 2(a) specifically referred to by the court refers to losses resulting to Maher from some action or omission on the part of his own agents or employees. It cannot be disputed, however, that any losses that resulted from an increase in the cost of collecting from the increased number of units generating refuse in no way resulted from any action on the part of either Maher or his employees. Rather, whatever losses he did entail by reason of the requirement of such extra collection resulted from actions completely beyond his control and thus unanticipated.

An indemnification clause reallocates the risk of specified losses from the indemnified party (indemnitee) to the indemnifying party (indemnitor). If the indemnitee suffers the specified kind of loss, the indemnitor must reimburse the indemnitee for that loss. The clause may grant broad indemnification of, e.g., "all losses arising from the contract or its performance," or it may limit indemnification to a narrower scope, such as "any losses arising from the indemnitor's failure to provide non-infringing software." The clause may limit the extent of indemnification by specifying a maximum dollar amount or limiting recovery in some other fashion, e.g., by capping liability at an amount equal to the indemnitee's payments to date to indemnitor or indemnitee's insurance deficiency.

A duty-to-defend clause requires one party to defend against claims brought against another party if the claims are within the scope of the clause. The clause may cover a broad or narrow range of claims, covering, for instance, "only claims filed in court," "any copyright infringement claim," or perhaps "any and all claims brought against the defended party that relate to this contract." Clauses vary as to the type and timing of notice given to the defending party; whether the defended party has a say in the choice of lawyers, the litigation strategy, and any settlement agreement; the nature of the cooperation the defended party owes the defending party; and whether the defended party must share some of the costs.

Reading Critically: Contract Modification in the Restatement and the UCC

Read Restatement (Second) of Contracts §§ 73 and 89 and UCC § 2–209, including any comments and illustrations.

1. What exceptions and reforms to the pre-existing duty rule are reflected in the Restatement and UCC provisions?

2. What advantages and disadvantages do you see in the rules that differ between the codifications?

3. How would these provisions affect the outcomes in *Angel*?

> Note that UCC § 2–209 says that a "failed" modification may nonetheless operate as a "waiver," a concept mentioned by the *Angel* court on page 246. Unlike a valid modification, which is binding upon both parties' assent, a waiver results from the actions or communications of one party, and—as reflected in § 2–209(5) and also in case law—it may be retracted by that party, unless there has been material and reasonable reliance by the other party. We will encounter the concept of "waiver" often in the chapters dealing with performance, breach, and remedies.

Problems: Contract Modification and Consideration

In the following scenarios, what theory or theories offer support for the enforceability of the indicated promise?

4-12. Joseph Jockey was hired by the owner of the horse Winning Winnie to ride her in an important race. Ted is the owner of Winnie's sire (father) and dam (mother). In advance of the race, Ted promised Joseph that if he rode Winnie to victory, Ted would pay Joseph $5000, knowing that his own horses would be more valuable if Winnie takes first place. Is Ted's promise to Joseph enforceable? Should it matter that Joseph's original obligation is to Winnie's owner, not to Ted?

4-13. In August 2005, Terry Teacher entered into a contract with the University to work from September 1, 2005, to August 31, 2006, as "Program Leader, Home Economics" at a specified salary. Teacher's duties under this position included planning, developing and executing educational programs in home economics. On November 1, her supervisor requested that she undertake the additional duties of acting leader for the 4-H Youth Development Program because the previous 4-H Program Leader did not return from his leave as expected in early October. Teacher and the University executed a formal, written addendum to Teacher's contract through August 31, 2006. The addendum changed Teacher's title from "Program Leader, Home Economics" to "Program Leader, Home Economics and Acting Program Leader, 4-H/Youth Development." The addendum said the change in title would be effective November 15, confirmed that Teacher's salary would stay the same, and expressed the University's thanks for Teacher's cooperation in "accepting this new assignment." Is Teacher's promise to perform the additional duties as 4-H Program Leader enforceable?

4-14. On May 28, Husband and Wife signed a separation agreement. Husband agreed to convey all his right and interest in the couple's jointly owned property, including the house where they had lived together until the separation; to permit his wife absolute custody of their child; and to pay $100 per month in child support. The contract also provided that "the husband agrees to sign any and all papers necessary to effectuate the transfer of said property to the wife. The proceeds therefrom shall unconditionally and irrevocably go to the wife." Wife agreed to settle all her claims to alimony and support and waived any other claims she might have against Husband.

On the same night the agreement was signed, Wife received a phone call from her attorney requesting that she appear at his office the next day for a further conference. At that conference, she signed an "Addendum" to the agreement of the previous day. The Addendum specified that, "in exchange for consideration of one dollar," she agreed to give Husband $22,000 out of the proceeds when she sold the family home and that Husband would vacate the premises of that residence "as of today, May 29, and remove all his personal belongings therefrom." The Husband did so.

Several months later, Wife sold the residence but did not pay any money to Husband. Husband sued to enforce her promise to pay $22,000. Wife claims lack of consideration. Can Husband enforce her promise?

If the agreement of Husband and Wife had been solely about transfer and sale of items of personal property (so the contract would fall under UCC Article 2), would the result be different?

---

§ 3.5. Discharge of Duty and the Pre-Existing Duty Rule

A duty under a contract can be "discharged," which means that the obligor no longer has to perform the duty and the obligee loses the right to that performance. Part or all of a contract can be discharged by the parties' mutual assent, as long as the discharge is supported by fresh consideration and thereby meets the pre-existing duty rule. Here are some of the com-

For More Information

For a broader discussion of the concept and consequences of a discharge of duty, see Restatement (Second) of Contracts §§ 278–281, & Introductory Note to Ch. 12; E. Allan Farnsworth, *Contracts* §§ 4.23, 4.24 (4th ed. 2004); John Edward Murray, Jr., *Murray on Contracts* Ch. 12 (5th ed. 2011); Joseph M. Perillo, *Calamari & Perillo on Contracts* Ch. 21 (6th ed. 2009).

mon mechanisms for discharges by mutual assent, with or without a replacement agreement:

- **Agreement of mutual rescission:** The parties can rescind an agreement by making a subsequent promise-for-promise agreement to discharge the parties' remaining duties, but only if the contract is at least partly "executory" (unperformed) on both sides. Each party's promise satisfies the pre-existing duty rule and is therefore supported by consideration, because each party gains a benefit from getting out of its performance obligations and each party suffers a detriment by losing the benefit of the other party's performance. Each party is willing to so promise, because he or she is motivated to receive the other party's promise, thereby satisfying the bargain requirement. "A contract of rescission has only one purpose, i.e., to discharge the existing contract and, in performing that sole purpose, it discharges itself. Thus, [it] is formed, performed, and thereby discharged simultaneously. Like other contracts, a contract of rescission may be inferred from conduct."[*] It is a matter of interpretation whether the parties agreed to make restitution as to the performance already rendered. See Restatement (Second) § 283.

  > **What's That?**
  >
  > "Rescission" is "an avoidance of a transaction. . . . [T]he contract is being unmade . . . ." Dan B. Dobbs, *Law of Remedies* § 4.3(6) (2d ed. 1993). If the rescission is meant to return the parties to the "status quo ante" (the state of things at the time of contract formation), they must make restitution of benefits received thus far in the contract. Rescission differs from "termination" and "cancellation," in which the contract remains but the parties' performance duties end and they retain any remedies for breach under the contract. Earlier in this chapter, the *Angel* court, page 246, mentioned rescinding a contract as a way of getting around the pre-existing duty rule. Chapter 6 covers some contract-formation defenses under which the aggrieved party can choose to rescind a "voidable contract."

- **Substituted contract:** If an obligor as to some duty (contractual or not) offers the obligee a *promise* of a different performance in satisfaction of the original duty, the obligee is free to refuse or accept that promise. If the obligee accepts that promise, it immediately discharges the obligor's original duty *if* the discharge is supported by consideration. If either party breaches the substituted contract, the other party can bring a claim under that contract, but not the original one. See Restatement (Second) of Contracts § 279.

---

[*] John Edward Murray, Jr., *Murray on Contracts* § 144[C] (5th ed. 2011).

- **Novation:** If the parties to a substituted contract bring a new party into the substituted contract, it is called a "novation." "The obvious consideration for a novation is the obligee's surrender of its right against the original obligor and the third party's assumption of a duty to the obligee."* As with a substituted contract, a party aggrieved by a breach can sue under the novation, but not the original contract. See Restatement (Second) of Contracts § 280. A common type of novation gives the duties of the original obligor to the new party and relieves the original obligor of any duties.

- **Accord and satisfaction:** If the obligee is willing to take performance of a substitute promise by the obligor but is unwilling to give up its right to the obligor's promise in the original contract until the obligor performs the substitute promise, then the parties should agree to an "accord," rather than a substituted contract or novation. Under an accord, the obligee promises to accept a stated performance in satisfaction of the obligor's original duty, and the obligor promises to render the stated performance. Until the accord is performed (that is, while it is still "executory"), the obligor's original duty is suspended but not yet discharged. If and when the obligor performs, its original duty (and the obligee's corresponding right) is discharged. This performance is called "satisfaction." If the obligor does not fully and timely perform the accord, the obligee can choose whether to sue under the original contract or the accord. An accord can involve one or more new parties. In a common example of an accord, a creditor promises to accept the agreed-upon partial payments from the debtor, and the debtor promises to make those partial payments. Satisfaction occurs when the debtor makes the payments on time. See Restatement (Second) of Contracts § 281. However, as we will see below, some accords lack consideration and are therefore ineffective.

- **Substituted performance:** If an obligor (or a third party) offers the obligee a different *performance* (not a promise) from the one promised under the original contract, the obligee is free to refuse or accept that performance in substitution for the original duty under the contract. If the obligee accepts the substituted performance, it immediately discharges the obligor's original duty *if* the discharge is supported by consideration. See Restatement (Second) of Contracts § 278. However, as we will see below, some substituted performances lack consideration and are therefore ineffective.

---

* *Id.* § 146[B].

Thus, a present discharge results from an agreement of mutual rescission, a substituted performance, a substituted contract, and a novation. A future discharge can result from an accord, which is dependent on full and timely performance (the satisfaction).

This table summarizes the major differences among these kinds of discharge:

	Consideration required?	Discharges what?	Original contract/duty discharged immediately?	Involves only original contract parties?
Agreement of mutual rescission	Yes	Original contract	Depends on terms	Yes
Substituted contract	Yes	Original duty	Yes	Yes
Novation	Yes	Original duty	Yes	No, must involve third party as well
Accord & satisfaction	Yes	Original duty	No, only upon performance of accord ("satisfaction")	Third party OK but not required
Substituted performance	Yes	Original duty	Yes	Third party OK but not required

Because parties seldom label their settlement agreements as one of the five categories, courts sometimes need to interpret the settlement agreement in order to determine which method of discharge applies. As you will learn in Chapter 8, interpretation looks first and foremost to the intent of the parties. The most common dispute involves whether the discharge was deferred until performance (an accord and satisfaction) or was immediate (a substituted performance, a substituted contract, or a novation). "[A] court will be less likely to suppose that an obligee was willing to accept a mere promise in satisfaction of an original duty that was clear than in satisfaction of one that was doubtful. It will therefore be less likely to find a substituted contract and more likely to find an accord if the original duty was one to pay money, if it was undisputed, if it was liquidated, and if it was matured. A creditor owed an unquestioned debt that is already due is unlikely to assent to a substituted contract that discharges that debt in return for the debtor's promise to deliver goods in the future; the creditor is more likely to assent to an accord that will allow the creditor to enforce the debt if the goods are not forthcoming." E. Allan Farnsworth, *Farnsworth on Contracts* § 4.24, at 469–70 (1990) (citing Restatement (Second) § 279 cmt. c and § 281 cmt. e, which are nearly identical to each other).

As discussed above, if an obligee discharges the obligor's duty without the obligor or a third party furnishing fresh consideration in return, the discharge is ineffective. If the obligor offers a discharge that is really just partial performance of the original duty, the obligee's acceptance of that performance does not discharge the duty in full, only in part. For example:

Make the Connection

Note that these discharges are not governed by the rules in *Dyer,* page 234, which upheld consideration based on a claimant's good-faith promise to forgo or surrender a doubtful or invalid claim in a settlement agreement. In these discharge situations, the parties' duties are valid, undisputed, and "liquidated" (certain in amount)."

- A debtor owed a creditor $100. The debtor offered to pay $50, to fully satisfy the debt obligation, and the creditor accepted that payment. The debtor's debt was discharged only to the extent of the payment, not in full, because the debtor did not furnish fresh consideration for the discharge.

- A homeowner owed a contractor $5000 on a building contract. The homeowner offered $4000, to fully pay off the contract. The contractor took the money and told the homeowner that $1000 was still due. The contractor was correct, because the homeowner did not furnish fresh consideration for the discharge.

In both situations, the new performance (be it a substituted performance or a satisfaction) was ineffective to fully discharge the original duty to pay, because the obligor did not give any additional or different benefit to the obligee, nor did the obligor suffer any additional or different detriment, as compared with the obligor's pre-existing duty under the original contract.

But wait, you might be saying: The pre-existing duty rule says you cannot enforce the modification of a promise when no fresh consideration is given in return. But here, the pre-existing duty rule is being applied to a discharge by the obligee, even if the discharge is immediate, rather than in a promise to discharge in the future. Compare the diagram below with the diagram on page 197, where the top arrow contains a promise.

Discharge of obligor's duty

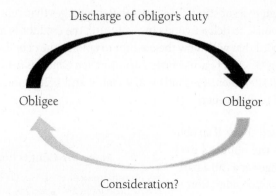

Obligee Obligor

Consideration?

Why should the pre-existing duty rule (and consideration in general) apply to the validity of something other than a promise? You're right to ask. Why should it? The answer lies in dictum from *Pin-nel's Case,* an old English case that subsequent courts followed without questioning the rationale. Subsequent courts also followed *Pinnel's Case* in allowing nominal consideration—seemingly trivial items that were not bargained for—as consideration for a discharge. These rules persist in present law, including Restatement (Second) § 273. Here is the progression of English cases and a sampling of how courts in one American state (Connecticut) accepted the English rules:

Make the Connection

Recall that, in *Schnell v. Nell,* page 218, the court disallowed nominal consider-ation for a promise.

- *Pinnel's Case,* 77 Eng. Rep. 237 (C.P. 1602): In dictum, in the English Court of Common Pleas, Lord Coke declared that "payment of a less sum on the [due] day in satisfaction of a greater [sum] cannot be any satisfac-tion for the whole." However, he noted that the needed consideration can be satisfied by the obligor providing additional or different performance, such as substitute payment by a piece of personal property ("the gift of a horse, hawk, or robe [or the like] in satisfaction is good"), payment at a time earlier than the due date, or payment in a different place (presumably a less convenient place for the debtor).

- *Cumber v. Wane,* 93 Eng. Rep. 613 (1718): The English court held that a creditor could not take 5£ in satisfaction of a 15£ debt because he received no consideration for the other 10£.

- *Sibree v. Tripp,* 153 Eng. Rep. 745, 752 (1846): The English court stated that a piece of paper or a stick of sealing wax will suffice as substitute payment.

- *Warren v. Skinner,* 20 Conn. 559 (1850): Recognizing the English rule and its exceptions, the Connecticut court stated that an agreement in satisfaction of a debt will be recognized when it "rests on a new and adequate consideration; as where the debtor pays a part of the debt . . . in a collateral article, agreed to be received in full payment." This line of rulings allowed a money debt to be paid with a piece of personal property, or even part money and part property.

- *Couldery v. Bartrum,* 19 Ch.D. 394, 399 (1880): The English court stated that a horse or a canary will suffice as substitute payment.

- *Argall v. Cook,* 43 Conn. 160 (1875): The Connecticut court held that a note endorsed by a third person may be taken in accord and satisfaction of a debt, even when the note is for a lesser amount. The court explained, "The additional security which [the creditor] received by the indorsement was a sufficient legal consideration for the discharge."

- *Foakes v. Beer,* L.R. 9 A.C. 605 (H.L. 1884): Based on Lord Coke's dictum in *Pinnel's Case,* the English House of Lords assumed that consideration was required for the discharge of a duty. It then applied the pre-existing duty rule, to bar a debtor from paying $800 to discharge a $1000 debt (translated from British pounds). The opinion discussed a ruling from 1696 (when it was accepted procedure for parties to buy time by the use of sham pleas) and noted that it was also accepted procedure for a defendant to plead that he had given the plaintiff a beaver hat. "No one for a moment supposed that a beaver hat was really given and accepted; but everyone knew that the law was that if it was really given and accepted it was a good satisfaction."[*]

Reading Critically: *Birdsall*

The following Connecticut case cited and applied all of the above cases. Answer the following questions, using the case below as well as the preceding cases:

1. Assemble the list of mostly silly items of personal property that the cases above suggested as suitable for substitute payment of a money debt. What does this list suggest about the courts'

---

[*] The courts in Minnesota and New Hampshire have "flatly rejected" the rule in *Foakes v. Beer.* See E. Allan Farnsworth, *Contracts* § 4.25 (4th ed. 2004) (also listing some states in which a discharge is valid without consideration if it is under seal or in a signed writing).

application of the rules governing consideration, as you have learned them in the preceding sections of this chapter? Did the cases above seem to be applying the benefit-detriment test or the bargain test or both?

2. In addition to the items you listed in your previous answer, how else can an obligor furnish consideration for the obligee's discharge of the obligor's duty?

3. Why did the *Birdsall* court reject the interpretation of the broker-seller arrangement (at closing) as an accord?

4. Why did the *Birdsall* court conclude that the broker-seller arrangement (at closing) was supported by consideration and therefore discharged the seller?

Example K: *Birdsall v. Saucier*, 1992 WL 37731 (Conn. Super. Ct. Feb. 24, 1992) (unpublished opinion).

[Note: To avoid confusion, this Example/Analysis uses the discharge categories from the previous pages of this section, rather than the terms used by the court in this case.] A real estate broker entered into a contract with a seller of real estate, who promised to pay the broker a cash commission of 10% of the sale price at closing, if the broker located a suitable buyer. The broker located a pair of buyers, and the seller signed a purchase agreement with them. However, prior to the closing, the seller ran into cash flow problems and asked the broker to forgo the $115,000 cash commission on the sale price of $1,150,000, and to instead accept some alternative form of payment. The broker said that he would take a third mortgage on the property, but the parties did not agree to exact terms at that time. At the closing, the broker accepted $29,500 in cash, as well as a promissory note (signed by the buyers and then assigned by the seller to the broker) entitling the broker to five years of interest payments totaling $22,500 and then a lump sum payment of $73,000. He signed a receipt saying that he had received the cash and the note and that the commission was "paid in full." The net result was that the broker would eventually receive $10,000 more than under the original contract.

Make the Connection

For coverage of assignment of rights, see Chapter 11.

The buyers made the required interest payments to the broker for three years, then ceased payments. After the broker failed in his efforts to receive further payments from the buyers, he sued the seller for $73,000 under the original broker contract. His argument was that the seller's obligation to pay was not discharged until the promissory note had been paid in full (and so was an accord and satisfaction). The seller defended by arguing that his obligation under the original broker contract had been discharged at the time of the closing (and so was a substituted performance).

Analysis: The court made a finding of fact that the broker "was satisfied with what he received." It framed the initial issue as one of interpretation: Whether the parties intended to discharge the seller's original duty to pay the broker's commission (before or at the closing) or upon the completion of performance (payment of the promissory note in full). That depended on the intent of the parties. The court noted that there is a strong presumption in favor of the later discharge date (an accord and satisfaction) if the settlement agreement gives a much smaller sum to the obligee, because an obligee who does not receive full payment under the accord ("satisfaction") can choose whether to sue on the original contract or on the accord. However, the court declined to apply that presumption because the obligee here (the broker) was to receive $10,000 more from the later arrangement, albeit over five years, and from another source (the buyers) if full payment was made. Moreover, "credible evidence [showed] that both parties intended that the original debt was to be extinguished by the assignment"; the broker signed a receipt at closing saying that his commission had been paid in full. Therefore, the better interpretation was that the parties intended a substituted performance, so that the original contract (and the seller's duty to pay the $115,000 cash commission originally due to the broker) was discharged at the closing.

The second issue was whether the discharge in the substituted performance was supported by consideration. After reviewing the English and Connecticut precedents in the examples above, the court held that the discharge in the substituted performance was valid because it was supported by fresh consideration. Compared to the original contract, the substituted performance gave the broker the right to an additional $10,000 and also gave him additional security in the form of a promissory note signed by two third parties, rather than by the seller, who was experiencing cash flow issues. Therefore, the original contract was discharged at the closing, and the broker was barred from suing the seller.

Problems: Contract Discharge and Consideration

4-15. Match the following means of discharge (A through F) with the later-listed scenarios (1 through 6):

A. an agreement of mutual rescission

B. a substituted contract

C. a novation

D. accord and satisfaction

E. a substituted performance

F. none of the above

1. On March 1, A & B make a contract under which A promises to paint B's house in Minnesota by July 1, and B promises to pay A $1,000. On April 1, A offers to paint B's summer home in Florida if B will accept his promise in satisfaction of A's duty to paint B's Minnesota home, and B accepts.

2. A & B make a contract under which A promises to paint B's house and B promises to pay A $1,000. A sells part of her painting business to C, who promises A that he will assume A's duty to B if B promises to accept it immediately and in substitution for A's duty. B so promises A.

3. A owes B $1,000. A offers B a machine in full satisfaction of her debt, and B accepts.

4. A owes B $1,000. They make a contract under which A promises to paint B's house by July 1 and B promises to accept this service in satisfaction of A's debt. A paints B's house by July 1.

5. A & B make a contract under which A promises to paint B's house and B promises to pay A $1,000. A finds, after beginning the work, that he will lose more money by finishing than by giving up at once and makes B an offer to rescind the contract. B accepts.

6. A & B make a contract under which A promises to paint B's house and B promises to pay A $1,000. After A has finished the work, B's financial condition has become impaired, and A tells B "You need never pay me the $1000 that you owe to me."

4-16. Why does a discharge under an agreement of mutual rescission or under a novation easily satisfy the pre-existing duty rule? Why do the other methods of discharge not necessarily satisfy the pre-existing duty rule?

4-17. Brook sold his farm to Pamila Corp. on January 10, 2012, for $100,000. Under the terms of sale, Pamila paid $40,000 at the time of the closing and agreed to pay 6% annual interest on the remaining $60,000 for 10 years (in $300 monthly payments on the 15th of each month) and to pay the final $60,000 on January 15, 2022. Under the terms of sale, if Pamila did not make the scheduled payments, Brook could reclaim the land and sell it to make up the deficiency in payments. Pamila made the monthly interest payments for 5 years. By then, farm prices had plummeted. On January 5, 2017, Pamila notified Brook that it probably would not be able to make the final $60,000 payment in January 2022 because of its financial difficulties caused by the market downturn. On January 10, 2017, Brook agreed to reduce the principal due to $40,000 and Pamila agreed to pay the $40,000 on January 15, 2025, and to pay 9% annual interest on the $40,000 for 8 years (in $300 monthly payments). If Pamila does not pay as specified in the 2017 arrangement, can Brook enforce the 2012 agreement or the 2017 arrangement or either? If Pamila makes full payment under the 2017 arrangement, can it enforce the discharge in that arrangement? Would your answers differ if the 2017 arrangement required Pamila to pay 10% interest for the final 3 years?

---

§ 4. Stretching the Limits of Consideration Doctrine

Admittedly, it is usually much easier to determine whether consideration exists than would appear from the cases in this chapter. The difference between gift and contract is in most instances a bright line, and in most contract disputes it is easy to identify the consideration for each party's promises. But there *are* difficult cases, as is illustrated in this chapter, and it is those difficult cases that both explore the boundaries of the doctrine and offer opportunities to practice the subtle skill of legal argumentation.

Reading Critically: *Lawrence*

The following case is a prime example of circumstances that test the limits of the doctrine of consideration and perhaps even challenge the worth of the concept as a dividing line between enforceable and unenforceable promises. Consider the arguments made by both the majority and the dissent. Who has the better position?

Lawrence v. Ingham County Health Dept. Family Planning/ Pre-Natal Clinic

ETHEL LAWRENCE, Individually and as Next Friend of JESSICA LAW-RENCE, a Minor, and DOUGLAS J. LAWRENCE, Plaintiffs-Appellants

v.

INGHAM COUNTY HEALTH DEPARTMENT FAMILY PLANNING/PRE-NATAL CLINIC, Defendant-Appellee, and A. BRECK, M.D., WILLIAM C. CARLEY, M.D., L. SANBORN, M.D., D. HOLDEN, M.D., A. CROW, M.D., EDWARD W. SPARROW HOSPITAL, ST. LAWRENCE HOSPITAL, ROBERT POSEY, M.D., and J.C. LESHOCK, M.D., Jointly and Severally, Defendants

Michigan Court of Appeals
<u>408 N.W.2d 461 (Mich. Ct. App. 1987)</u>

KELLY, PRESIDING JUDGE.

Plaintiffs appeal as of right from an order of summary disposition granted under MCR 2.116(C)(8) in favor of defendant Ingham County Health Department Family Planning/Pre-Natal Clinic. We affirm.

Plaintiffs filed this three-count complaint following the birth of their daughter, Jessica Lawrence. According to the allegations in the complaint, which are taken as true for purposes of deciding and reviewing a motion under MCR 2.116(C)(8), plaintiff Ethel Lawrence first visited defendant clinic on December 13, 1979, for a pregnancy test. She reported her last menstrual period as October 19, 1979, and tested positive for pregnancy. Plaintiff then continued routine prenatal treatment with the clinic. On August 19, 1980, she appeared at defendant St. Lawrence Hospital in labor, where she underwent an emergency Caesarean section. Jessica Lawrence suffered fetal distress and prenatal asphyxia, which plaintiffs theorized could have been prevented by applying standard procedures for postmature fetuses. Following the delivery, Jessica was resuscitated and transferred to defendant Edward W. Sparrow Hospital. She sustained permanent, serious brain damage.

Plaintiffs' original complaint alleged various acts of negligence on the part of the individual physicians, the clinic and the two hospitals. Defendant clinic was granted summary disposition as to the negligence claims on the ground of governmental immunity. See *Ross v. Consumers Power Co. (On Rehearing)*, 420 Mich. 567, 363 N.W.2d 641 (1984). Plaintiffs do not appeal from that ruling.

Plaintiffs' third amended complaint included two counts of breach of contract. In paragraphs 4 and 5 of Count II of their third amended complaint, plaintiffs allege breach of an enforceable agreement between plaintiffs Ethel and Douglas Lawrence and the clinic and clinic physicians:

> "4. That thereafter, Defendant Ingham County Health Department Family Planning/Prenatal Clinic agreed to accept Plaintiff Ethel Lutman Lawrence as a patient and Plaintiff Ethel Lutman Lawrence agreed to follow the directions of the physicians and other medical personnel at the Defendant Clinic for the benefit of her unborn child.
>
> "5. That an implied contract in law was created as a result of the Defendant Clinic's offer to provide medical services to Plaintiff Ethel Lutman Lawrence within the then-existing and applicable standard of care and Plaintiff Ethel Lutman Lawrence's acceptance of said offer by agreeing to follow the directions of the Defendant Clinic's physicians and other medical personnel for the benefit of her unborn child."

> **FYI**
>
> In *Ross v. Consumers Power Co.*, cited by the court of appeals, the Michigan Supreme Court ruled that government agencies, both state and local, are immune from tort liability when engaged in the exercise or discharge of a governmental function and are similarly immune from liability for actions of their employees carrying out such governmental functions. The court further concluded that a governmental function is any activity that is expressly or impliedly mandated or authorized by constitution, statute, or other law. The lower court in Lawrence considered the actions of the county health clinic to fall within those limits, so the clinic was immune from liability in tort for its actions and those of its doctors.

. . . .

The lower court found that plaintiffs failed to state a cause of action for breach of contract and granted summary disposition in favor of defendant clinic. Summary disposition on this ground tests the legal basis of the complaint, not whether it can be factually supported, and is proper only when the claim is so clearly unenforceable as a matter of law that no factual development can possibly justify a right to recover. *Bradford v. Michigan,* 153 Mich. App. 756, 761, 396 N.W.2d 522 (1986). The trial court concluded that plaintiffs failed to plead facts that would support a finding of adequate consideration and that plaintiffs' contract claim must therefore fail.

Plaintiffs argue that the consideration provided by plaintiff Ethel Lawrence was her agreement not to have an abortion and her agreement to follow the directions of the clinic medical staff. Plaintiffs contend that, by entering into these agreements, Ethel Lawrence refrained from doing that which she was legally privileged to do and thereby rendered valuable consideration in return for defendant clinic's promise to provide adequate prenatal care. Since plaintiffs have not alleged in their complaint that Ethel Lawrence agreed not to have an abortion in return for the promise of medical care, we will not consider this argument further.[2]

The contract described by plaintiffs involves an exchange of promises: Ethel Lawrence's promise to follow directions in exchange for the clinic's promise to provide appropriate prenatal care. In order for Ethel Lawrence's promise to rise to the level of consideration sufficient to support a contract implied in fact, however, that promise must be of some value to defendant clinic. We think this means the promise must be enforceable. Although we recognize that mutuality of obligation is not always a necessary element to every contract, we are persuaded that, in the context of this case, lack of mutuality of obligation translates into lack of consideration:

> "Inasmuch as a promise by one person is merely one of the kinds of consideration that will support a promise by another, mutuality of obligation is not an essential element in every contract. Therefore, to say the least, language which is susceptible of the interpretation that consideration and mutuality of obligation are two distinct elements lacks precision in that, while consideration is essential, mutuality of obligation is not, *unless the want of mutuality would leave one party without a valid or available consideration for his promise.*" 17 Am.Jur.2d, Contracts, § 11, pp. 347–348. (Emphasis added.)

Plaintiff Ethel Lawrence's agreement to follow the advice of the clinic's medical staff regarding prenatal health care is not a legally enforceable promise. Contrary to the position of plaintiffs below, we are not persuaded that defendant clinic has or had a cause of action for breach of contract against plaintiff for failure on her part to follow its medical advice. Plaintiff Ethel Lawrence was given advice on health care conducive to the well-being of her unborn baby. We hold that her acceptance of that advice cannot be deemed consideration for a contract. . . .

We do not evaluate the adequacy of the consideration allegedly rendered in this case since that would be a question for the factfinder rather than for us in determining the adequacy of plaintiff's pleadings. We simply conclude that

---

[2] We note, however, that our analysis would be the same on sufficient consideration even if we did address this argument. We are saved from examining the public policy implications of such an anomolous agreement by plaintiffs' complaint.

plaintiffs' claim of consideration is so clearly unenforceable as a matter of law that no factual development can possibly justify their right to recover on the theory of defendant's breach of an implied contract in fact.

Affirmed.

KNOBLOCK, J., concurred.

SAWYER, JUDGE (dissenting).

I dissent.

Defendant health clinic made a promise to Ethel Lawrence that if she would come to the clinic and promise thereafter to follow its staff's directions, it would provide her and her unborn child with appropriate prenatal care. Despite these promises, which defendants must admit as true for purposes of the summary disposition motion, the majority concludes that Ethel's promise to follow the clinic's directions had no value to the clinic and, therefore, "is not a legally enforceable promise."

It is not the office of the courts to scrutinize the adequacy of consideration. *Harwood v. Randolph Harwood, Inc.,* 124 Mich. App. 137, 142, 333 N.W.2d 609 (1983). In fact, even the majority concedes in its final paragraph that "the adequacy of the consideration . . . [is] a question for the factfinder . . . ." How, then, can the majority now say that Ethel's promise is lacking in value? As I will explain more fully below, I am unable to sign my name to an opinion which on the one hand states that it will let the factfinder worry about the adequacy of consideration and, then, on the other hand holds that plaintiff Ethel Lawrence's consideration "is so clearly unenforceable as a matter of law." . . .

Summary disposition under MCR 2.116(C)(8) tests the legal basis of the complaint, not whether it can be factually supported, and is proper only when the claim is so clearly unenforceable as a matter of law that no factual development can possibly justify a right to recover. *Bradford v. Michigan,* 153 Mich. App. 756, 761, 396 N.W.2d 522 (1986).

Regarding Count II of the complaint, plaintiffs allege that there was an implied contract which defendant health clinic breached. The trial court concluded that there could be no contract as there was no consideration on plaintiffs' behalf:

> Looking at the complaint in the light most favorable to the Plaintiff even if Plaintiff were able to sustain her proofs that she had not gotten an abortion and she had followed the directives [of the Health Department's physicians] when she was not obligated by law to do so,

the Court does not believe that under any stretch of the imagination could that be considered as adequate or any form of consideration. I think to take that as consideration would expand the definition of the contract beyond all recognition.

The majority seems to follow this view, with which I disagree.

The concept of consideration was discussed in Calamari and Perillo, Contracts (2d ed.), § 4–1, pp. 133–134:

> Since the doctrine of consideration is an historical phenomenon and therefore in some of its aspects affected by fortuitous circumstances, an encompassing definition is perhaps impossible. Nonetheless, an attempt should be made. A learned judge [Cardozo, C.J., in *Allegheny College v. Nat'l Chautauqua Co. Bank*, 246 N.Y. 369, 159 N.E. 173 (1927)] has identified the three elements which must concur before a promise is supported by consideration.
>
> (a) The promisee must suffer legal detriment; that is, do or promise to do what he is not legally obligated to do; or refrain from doing or promise to refrain from doing what he is legally privileged to do.
>
> (b) The detriment must induce the promise. In other words the promisor must have made the promise because he wished to exchange it at least in part for the detriment to be suffered by the promisee.
>
> (c) The promise must induce the detriment. This means in effect, as we have already seen, that the promisee must know of the offer and intend to accept. [Footnotes omitted.]

In this case, plaintiffs argue that the consideration given by Ethel Lawrence was her agreement not to have an abortion and her agreement to follow the directions of the attending physicians.[2] Either of these agreements, if in fact they were made, would constitute a form of consideration. Her agreement not to have an abortion constitutes an agreement to refrain from doing that which she was legally

---

[2] I recognize that, as pointed out by the majority, plaintiffs did not allege in their complaint that Ethel Lawrence agreed to refrain from undergoing an abortion as part of her agreement. However, plaintiffs did so argue in the trial court. Since plaintiffs could easily have added such an allegation to their complaint by way of amendment, and since amendments to complaints should be freely given, MCR 2.118(A)(2), *Ben P. Fyke & Sons v. Gunter Co.*, 390 Mich. 649, 213 N.W.2d 134 (1973), I believe we can properly consider that argument as part of plaintiffs' claim of consideration. However, I would reach the same result if I considered only plaintiffs' claim of consideration arising from the agreement to follow the physicians' advice.

privileged to do.[3] Her agreement to follow the advice of the physicians constitutes an agreement to do that which she was not legally obligated to do. Assuming that a factual development is made to show that Ms. Lawrence's agreements were made to induce defendant health clinic's agreement to provide services and, conversely, that defendant health clinic required Ms. Lawrence to make those agreements in order to receive the health services, then a contract would exist between the parties.

The flaw in the majority's reasoning is evident from the following statement:

Plaintiff Ethel Lawrence's agreement to follow the advice of the clinic's medical staff regarding prenatal health care is not a legally enforceable promise.

The majority, however, offers no authority for this conclusion. I am aware of no rule of law, be it statutory, regulatory or common law, which would operate to prevent a person from contractually obligating himself to following the advice of a physician. Since a person is free to do so, upon contractually binding oneself to following a physician's advice, that person exposes himself to a breach of contract action for a subsequent failure to follow the advice. The majority apparently confuses the unusualness of plaintiffs' theory in application with its viability in the abstract. That is, while I would be surprised to learn that it is common practice for patients to contractually agree to be bound by their physicians' advice, I do not believe such contracts are unenforceable as a matter of law.[4]

The same principle applies to plaintiffs' argument concerning the agreement not to have an abortion. While I am aware of no institution which demands such a promise, I can easily imagine that a private health clinic, run by a charitable or religious organization, might well offer free prenatal care as an inducement to prevent women from having an abortion.[5] While such an arrangement would undoubtedly prove difficult for a court to attempt to enforce or to provide a remedy for a breach of such an arrangement, I am unwilling to conclude at this time that such agreements are legally unenforceable.

Once the conclusion is reached that a person may legally bind himself to follow a physician's advice, or to forego an action he is legally privileged to take, it becomes a factual question whether he has made such an agreement. It is improper

---

[3] See *Roe v. Wade*, 410 U.S. 113, 93 S.Ct. 705, 35 L.Ed.2d 147 (1973).

[4] In fact, I can imagine situations in which a physician would wish to contractually bind his patient to take certain actions. For example, a physician may offer services for free or at a reduced fee in order to develop a new technique wherein the patient's obeyance is essential to the physician's perfection and evaluation of the technique. While admittedly an uncommon occurrence, it does point to the flaw in the majority's broad-sweeping principle.

[5] The question of a governmental agency demanding such a promise from a woman in exchange for services opens a Pandora's Box which, fortunately, we have not yet been called upon to open.

to resolve that factual question in the context of a motion brought pursuant to MCR 2.116(C)(8) or in an appeal from an order granted under that subrule.

The majority's and the trial court's alternative conclusion, that the consideration, if any, was inadequate is more easily disposed of. It is not ordinarily the role of the courts to question the adequacy of the consideration supporting the contract. Any consideration, no matter how economically insignificant, is sufficient to support a contract. See *Harwood, supra,* 124 Mich. App. at 142, 333 N.W.2d 609.[6]

To summarize, I would hold that a person may contractually obligate himself to follow the directions of a physician, or to forego an action he is legally privileged to perform. Where such an obligation is given in exchange for the promise of another to perform services, that obligation serves as consideration and a contract is established.

I would stress, however, the fact that this case comes to us by way of a motion for summary disposition for failure to state a claim. I express no opinion as to whether plaintiffs will be able to prove at trial, or even be able to survive a motion for summary disposition for no genuine issue of material fact, that Ms. Lawrence made her agreements in exchange for defendant health department's agreement to provide the health services. If the agreement of one did not induce the agreement of the other, then there is no contract. Similarly, we have not been called upon to consider whether defendant health department has provided consideration. Its only agreement appears to have been to provide health services. If, for example, it was under a preexisting legal duty to provide Ms. Lawrence with the health services, then its agreement to do so cannot constitute consideration. *Lowery v. Dep't of Corrections,* 146 Mich. App. 342, 359, 380 N.W.2d 99 (1985).

While I recognize that plaintiffs' claim is, at best, novel and, at worst, tenuous, I do not believe that should provide the basis for summarily dismissing the complaint. Plaintiffs' theory is novel and, I suspect, it will prove difficult for them to establish the existence of the alleged promises and that the promise of each party induced the promise of the other. That is, I am not at all convinced that defendant health department required Ethel Lawrence to make the promises she allegedly did in order to receive medical attention. However, the point which seems to elude the majority and the trial court is that plaintiffs have not yet been called upon to convince anyone, be it this Court, the trial court, or a jury, that their claim can be borne out by the facts. To date, plaintiffs have only been called upon to state a claim. In my opinion, they have done so.

---

[6]   However, the adequacy of consideration may be relevant in certain instances, such as to determine the existence of fraud. *Harwood, supra,* 124 Mich.App. at 142, 333 N.W.2d 609.

Judge Kelly once opined that "[a]s in most *trials*, somebody wins and some-body loses."[9] However, the majority today would have plaintiffs lose before they have even had their day in court. To me, that is unconscionable.

I would reverse.

Food for Thought: Contractual Liability in Doctor-Patient Relationships

In contrast to recent claims that medical malpractice claims against doctors have spun out of control, for many years it was difficult for plaintiffs to succeed in medical malpractice suits against doctors, in part because other doctors were reportedly reluctant to testify against their colleagues to establish negligence. In the face of those difficulties, some plaintiffs turned to contract law as an alternative to tort suits, often with just as little success. As articulated in *Sullivan v. O'Connor*, 296 N.E.2d 183 (Mass. 1973):

> It is not hard to see why the courts should be unenthusiastic or skeptical about the contract theory. Considering the uncertainties of medical science and the variations in the physical and psychological conditions of individual patients, doctors can seldom in good faith promise specific results. Therefore it is unlikely that physicians of even average integrity will in fact make such promises. Statements of opinion by the physician with some optimistic coloring are a different thing, and may indeed have therapeutic value. But patients may transform such statements into firm promises in their own minds, especially when they have been disappointed in the event, and testify in that sense to sympathetic juries. If actions for breach of promise can be readily maintained, doctors, so it is said, will be fright-ened into practicing "defensive medicine." On the other hand, if these actions were outlawed, leaving only the possibility of suits for malpractice, there is fear that the public might be exposed to the enticements of charlatans, and confidence in the profession might ultimately be shaken. See Miller, *The Contractual Liability of Physicians and Surgeons*, 1953 Wash. L.Q. 413, 416–423. The law has taken the middle of the road position of allowing actions based on alleged contract, but insisting on clear proof.

---

[9] *Kovacs v. Chesapeake & O. R. Co.*, 134 Mich. App. 514, 542, 351 N.W.2d 581 (1984) (emphasis added).

Reflecting concerns about protecting patients, as well as continuing reluctance to see the doctor-patient relationship as contractual in nature, courts have also consistently denied enforcement to agreements by which some doctors have sought limitations on their liability, including a patient's release of a physician from liability for negligence, a limitation of the patient to a specified damage amount, and an acceptance of binding arbitration by the patient. See Maxwell J. Mehlman, *The Patient-Physician Relationship in an Era of Scarce Resources: Is There a Duty to Treat?*, 25 Conn. L. Rev. 349 (1993).

Do you think the policies and concerns articulated here had an effect on the outcome in *Lawrence*?

Test Your Knowledge

To assess your understanding of the material in this chapter, click here to take a quiz.

CHAPTER 5

Alternatives to Consideration

How do parties demonstrate assent to a contract?

What kinds of promises will the law enforce?

What defenses to enforcement exist?

Is a writing required for enforcement? If so, what kind?

How is the content and meaning of a contract determined?

What are parties' rights and duties after breach?

What situations lead to excusing contract performance?

What remedies are available for breach of contract?

What contractual rights and duties do non-parties to a contract have?

Table of Contents

§ 1. Introduction 272

§ 2. Promissory Estoppel 274

RESTATEMENT § 90. PROMISE REASONABLY INDUCING DEFINITE AND
SUBSTANTIAL ACTION 277

RESTATEMENT (SECOND) § 90. PROMISE REASONABLY INDUCING ACTION OR
FORBEARANCE 278

Conrad v. Fields 280

Hayes v. Plantations Steel Co. 287

Maryland Nat'l Bank v. United Jewish Appeal Fed'n of Greater Wash. 292

Pavel Enterprises v. A.S. Johnson Co. 305

§ 3. Promise for Benefit Already Received ("Promissory
Restitution") 312

Mills v. Wyman 313

Drake v. Bell 318

Webb v. McGowin 322

§ 4. Liability for Restitution 329

Nursing Care Services, Inc. v. Dobos 332

Mitchell v. Moore 335

271

Bloomgarden v. Coyer 342

PROBLEMS: PROMISSORY ESTOPPEL, PROMISSORY RESTITUTION, AND RESTITUTION
(5-1 TO 5-9)..347

§ 1. Introduction

Chapter 4 explored the requirement that a promise must have "consideration" in order to be enforceable under traditional contract principles. This chapter covers two doctrines—promissory estoppel and promissory restitution—that allow promises without consideration to be enforced, and a third doctrine— non-promissory restitution—that provides compensation under contract-like circumstances even if no promise was made. These "alternatives to consideration" arose historically and rhetorically as exceptions to the requirement of consideration for contract formation, though they have since developed into separate grounds for "contract-like" liability. Because a court may choose a more limited remedy when any of these doctrines are the basis of a claim, it is almost always preferable to find a "true" contract—one with consideration as well as assent—rather than to rely on the doctrines described in this chapter. Sometimes, though, a true contract cannot plausibly be argued; one of these alternatives may be all that is available. In other circumstances, the facts may profitably be analyzed under more than one doctrine, with liability dependent on which narrative is most persuasive.

An Introduction to Contract Remedies

It is only after the existence, terms, and breach of a contract are established that the appropriate remedies for breach of contract can be determined. Accordingly, this book covers remedies for breach of contract near the end, in Chapter 10. But many cases refer to remedies as they discuss issues of formation, interpretation, and liability for breach. To help you understand those references, this note offers a brief primer on the kinds of remedies available to injured parties, including alternative ways to measure money damages to compensate for breach.

If a party is liable for injury caused by breach of a contract, a court may award an equitable remedy, such as specific performance (which orders the breaching party to perform as promised) or an injunction (which orders the party to take or refrain from taking other actions). Alternatively, the court may award damages (a dollar amount meant to compensate for the injury caused). Specific performance may seem like the most sensible relief, as it would result in the other party receiving the promised performance, but damages are generally favored over equitable relief, for reasons noted later in this chapter.

If damages are warranted, they may be calculated in several different ways:

- A court may enforce the promise made, by awarding "**expectation damages**," the amount necessary to fulfill the expectation created by the promise. These damages seek to put the promisee in the position she would have been in if the promise had been performed.

- A court may instead award "**reliance damages**," the amount necessary to compensate the promisee for expenses or costs incurred in reliance on the existence of the promise. These damages seek to put the promisee in the position she would be in today if the promise had not been made.

- If benefits have been conferred on a party (usually but not always the breaching party), a court may require that party to "disgorge" the benefit by paying the other party the value of those benefits ("**restitution damages**"). These damages seek to put the aggrieved party back in the position it was before the promise was made.

The damage remedies (expectation, reliance, and restitution) intersect with but are not identical with the theories of liability (breach of contract, promissory estoppel, and promissory and non-promissory restitution). As you will see, promissory estoppel as a theory of liability is based in reliance, but courts may (and often do) award full expectation damages rather than limiting the award to reliance damages. Similarly, a court that finds a party liable on the basis of promissory restitution may enforce the promise as made or reduce the award, perhaps to an amount reflecting restitution damages. In restitution cases, there is no promise to enforce, so the courts must necessarily choose restitution damages.

As you will see more fully in Chapter 10, courts have some flexibility, even in breach of contract actions, to award the damages that are most appropriate under the circumstances to compensate the injured party. While expectation damages are most common, courts may choose measures based on reliance or restitution, if warranted.

> Because of the overlap in terminology, it is important that you recognize and watch for the distinction between the basis of liability (contract, promissory estoppel, or restitution) and the determination of damages remedy (expectation, reliance, or restitution).

§ 2. Promissory Estoppel

Chapter 4 distinguished between consideration (where an action or forbearance is bargained for) and conditional gift (where an action is undertaken in order to receive a promised gift). In some circumstances, the action undertaken in response to a gift promise is minor (e.g., providing an email address in order to receive a coupon by return email). In other instances, the promisee may engage in more substantial action and may incur expenses to obtain the promised gift or may otherwise rely on the promise of a gift. Even though those actions would not be consideration under traditional concepts because they were not bargained for, courts are sometimes convinced that an unbargained-for gift promise should be enforced anyway.

Kirksey v. Kirksey, 8 Ala. 131 (1845) is an early case presenting just such a dilemma. The defendant in *Kirksey* (Isaac Kirksey) wrote the following letter to his sister-in-law, whose husband (defendant's brother Henry) had just died:

> Dear sister Antillico—Much to my mortification, I heard, that brother Henry was dead, and one of his children. I know that your situation is one of grief, and difficulty. You had a bad chance before, but a great deal worse now. I should like to come and see you, but cannot with convenience at present. . . . I do not know whether you have a preference on the place you live on, or not. If you had, I would advise you to obtain your preference, and sell the land and quit the country, as I understand it is very unhealthy, and I know society is very bad. If you will come down and see me, I will let you have a place to raise your family, and I have more open land than I can tend; and on the account of your situation, and that of your family, I feel like I want you and the children to do well.

Plaintiff moved with her family to the residence offered by the defendant, but after two years defendant ordered her to leave. Judge Ormond, reversing a jury verdict for plaintiff and writing for the court, stated: "The inclination of my mind, is, that the loss and inconvenience, which the plaintiff sustained in breaking up, and moving to the defendant's, a distance of sixty miles, is a sufficient consideration to support the promise, to furnish her with a house, and land to cultivate, until she could raise her family. My brothers, however, think that the promise on the part of the defendant, was a mere gratuity, and that an action will not lie for its breach." The court concluded, in other words, that defendant did not offer a place to live in exchange for the move but merely made a promise to give a gift of a place to live, conditioned on plaintiff's moving to that residence. Therefore the move was only a condition—an act necessary to receive the promised gift—and not consideration for the promise.

In contrast to his colleagues on the bench, Judge Ormond believed that the promise *should* be enforced because the move entailed loss and inconvenience to plaintiff. He would have called the loss and inconvenience "consideration," but he was overruled by the other members of the panel. The disagreement among the judges might signal a lack of consensus on the meaning of consideration at that time, with some judges favoring a narrow interpretation and others (Judge Ormond in particular) favoring a broader understanding that would include more than bargained-for acts. A modern court would agree with the *Kirksey* majority that Antillico's actions undertaken in reliance on and in order to take advantage of her brother-in-law's promise would not constitute consideration (at least on the facts as stated by the court), but, as we will see below, courts have since found alternative ways to compensate promisees in Antillico's position.

Behind the Scenes

Recent scholarship about the *Kirksey* case reveals that Isaac Kirksey may have promised Antillico a place to live partly to help his widowed sister-in-law and her children, but at least equally so that she could claim the land for him pursuant to a federal land preemption statute. He had already claimed preemption rights of his own on other land, so he could not claim the additional land for himself, but he could reach the same result if Antillico acted as his proxy. She may thus have given up her own preemption (or "preference") rights on the land where she resided in order to help her brother-in-law.

After Antillico moved, however, a new federal statute made it possible for Antillico to claim title for the land for herself if she was in physical possession of it. Probably as a result, Isaac moved his own son onto the land—once the son was old enough to take advantage of the federal statute to claim the land for himself and, indirectly, for his father—and told Antillico to leave. Procuring Antillico's help to circumvent the pre-emption statute would have been considered fraudulent and so was not discussed at trial, although the local men who served on the jury may well have understood the situation. For the details of this story, see William R. Casto and Val D. Ricks, *"Dear Sister Antillico . . .": The Story of Kirksey v. Kirksey*, 94 Georgetown L.J. 321 (2006).

Under the likely "real" facts described here, would the promise have been enforceable under traditional contract principles?

More than fifty years after *Kirksey*, in *Ricketts v. Scothorn*, 77 N.W. 365 (Neb. 1898), the Nebraska Supreme Court faced a slightly different dilemma. Katie Scothorn's grandfather, "desiring to put her in a position of independence," gave her a promissory note for $2000. According to the testimony, he asked for nothing in return, though he hoped she would give up the job she then held: " 'I have fixed out something that you have not got to work any more.' He says, 'none of my grandchildren work, and you don't have to.' " She immediately quit her job, although she returned to work as a bookkeeper a little more than a year later, with her grandfather's approval. While nothing was required of Katie Scothorn to receive the gift (unlike the situation in *Kirksey*, where Antillico had to move with her family in order to receive the gift of a place to live), she suffered some "loss and inconvenience" in reliance on the promise of $2000 when she went without employment for upwards of a year.

When Katie sued her grandfather's estate for payment of the promissory note, the executor defended by claiming that Katie had not given any consideration for her grandfather's promise. The court reviewed a number of earlier cases involving charitable donations in which courts found that an expenditure of money or assumption of liability by the charity "on the faith of the promise" constituted "a valuable and sufficient consideration," sounding much like Judge Ormond in *Kirksey*. The court did not think those actions were "consideration," and said "the true reason" for finding liability, in the earlier cases and in *Ricketts*, was the existence of an "equitable estoppel." That is, the executor, standing in the shoes of the grandfather, was "estopped" (prevented) from raising the defense of no consideration because the grandfather's actions had induced Katie to change her position, and it would be unjust to permit the estate to benefit. The *Ricketts* court relied on equitable estoppel, based on the existence of "acts, admissions, or conduct" inducing a change of position, but implicitly extended the concept to embrace what later became known as "*promissory* estoppel," preventing (estopping) a litigant from claiming no consideration when a *promise* (rather than conduct) induced reliance. "Having intentionally induced the plaintiff to alter her position for the worse on the faith of the note being paid when due, it would be grossly inequitable to permit the maker, or his executor, to resist payment on the ground that the promise was given without consideration."

In *Ricketts* and other early cases, promissory estoppel was invoked only as a response to the defense that consideration did not exist, preventing the other party from raising that defense. However, the doctrine quickly evolved to become an independent source of promissory liability, both in common law and in the Restatement of Contracts § 90, in 1932. A later version appeared in the Restatement (Second) of Contracts § 90 (the retention of the same section number reflecting the considerable importance of the provision). "Section 90 has been described as the *Restatement's* 'most notable and influential rule' [quoting E. Allan Farnsworth, *Contracts* § 2.19, at 95 (2d ed. 1990)] and as 'perhaps the most radical and expansive development of this century in the law of promissory liability.' [quoting Charles L. Knapp, *Reliance in the Revised* Restatement: *The Proliferation of Promissory Estoppel,* 81 Colum. L. Rev. 52, 53 (1981)]. The section has had a profound influence on the law of contracts because it ratifies cases enforcing a promise in the absence of bargained-for consideration. By giving its imprimatur to those cases, the *Restatement* has encouraged courts to expand contractual liability beyond the traditional doctrinal limits of consideration." Edward Yorio & Steve Thel, *The Promissory Basis of Section 90,* 101 Yale L.J. 111, 111–12 (1991).

Reading Critically: Promissory Estoppel in the Restatements

Read Restatement § 90 and Restatement (Second) § 90. While many state courts have adopted or referred favorably to the Restatement (Second) articulation of promissory estoppel in § 90, others continue to rely on the formulation in the first Restatement, so you should be familiar with both versions. The Reporter's Note accompanying Restatement (Second) § 90 says, "The principal change from former § 90 is the recognition of the possibility of partial enforcement." What other differences do you see between the two versions? How significant do you think those differences are?

Restatement § 90. Promise Reasonably Inducing Definite and Substantial Action

A promise which the promisor should reasonably expect to induce action or forbearance of a definite and substantial character on the part of the promisee and which does induce such action or forbearance is binding if injustice can be avoided only by enforcement of the promise.

Restatement (Second) § 90. Promise Reasonably Inducing Action or Forbearance

(1) A promise which the promisor should reasonably expect to induce action or forbearance on the part of the promisee or a third person and which does induce such action or forbearance is binding if injustice can be avoided only by enforcement of the promise. The remedy granted for breach may be limited as justice requires.

(2) A charitable subscription or a marriage settlement is binding under Subsection (1) without proof that the promise induced action or forbearance.

Food for Thought: Unpublished Opinions

Like *Ardente* (page 108), *Tomczak* (page 225) and *Birdsall* (page 258), the next case, *Conrad* is designated as "unpublished" by the deciding courts. An unpublished decision is publicly available (in electronic form or from the court), but generally does not appear in the hard-copy case reporters, and citation to it may be limited by state statute or rule. The Minnesota court rule, for example, says, "Unpublished opinions of the Court of Appeals . . . are not precedential" and requires counsel to give other counsel in a case at least 48 hours' notice before using an unpublished opinion in any pretrial conference, hearing, or trial. Minn. Stat. § 480A.08 subd. 3. Nebraska's Rule 2(E)(4) specifies that unpublished opinions "may be cited only when such case is related, by identity between the parties or the causes of action, to the case then before the court."

In 2000, a surprising three-quarters of the opinions of the federal courts of appeals were being issued unpublished.[*] The prevalence of such opinions led courts and commentators to consider two distinct questions. First, should (or must) courts treat their unpublished opinions as binding precedent? Second, should parties be allowed to cite unpublished opinions in their briefs? *See* Alex Kozinski & Stephen Reinhardt, *Please Don't Cite This! Why We Don't Allow Citation to Unpublished Opinions,* Cal. Lawyer, June 2000.

---

[*] *See* Administrative Office of the United States Courts, 1998 Judicial Business of the United States Courts, Table S-3 (1999)

In 2006, after some litigation and considerable discussion, the Federal Rules of Appellate Procedure were amended to bar federal courts from prohibiting or restricting parties from citing unpublished opinions issued on or after January 1, 2007. The rule does not address whether unpublished opinions are or must be treated as precedential, and the federal courts may (and some do) restrict citation to unpublished opinions issued before the designated date.

Why do you think a court would choose not to publish some of its opinions? Why might the *Conrad, Ardente, Tomczak,* and *Birdsall* courts have chosen not to publish those opinions? What are the implications of that choice? Should courts restrict citation to unpublished opinions? For an exploration of the arguments for and against citing unpublished opinions, *see* Patrick J. Schiltz, *Much Ado About Little: Explaining the Sturm und Drang over the Citation of Unpublished Opinions,* 62 Wash. & Lee L. Rev. 1429 (2005). Professor (now United States District Court Judge) Schiltz was Reporter for the Advisory Committee on the Federal Rules of Appellate Procedure during the discussion leading to adoption of the amended rule on the citation of unpublished opinions.

Whether precedential or not, unpublished opinions sometimes provide helpful explications of legal rules and interesting factual circumstances, which is why you will find several included in this textbook.

Reading Critically: *Conrad, Hayes,* and *Maryland National Bank*

Although many courts cite § 90 of the first or second Restatement with approval, some courts—even those that purport to rely on the Restatement—adopt variations of the standard. As you read the cases that follow, be alert to the details of the promissory estoppel standard adopted by each court and consider the similarities and differences between them.

In addition, consider the following questions:

1. Why wasn't the plaintiff able to establish the existence of consideration for the promise made?

2. In each case in which the promissory estoppel claim failed, which aspect of the test presented difficulty for the claimant, and why?

3. In each case in which the promissory estoppel claim succeeded, what particular facts supported the outcome? How did the court measure the damages awarded?

4. How are the various promissory estoppel standards consistent with one another? How do they differ, and do you think those differences would lead to different outcomes on the same facts? If there are differences between the court's stated standard and the Restatement's articulation, can you nonetheless fit the court's analysis into the Restatement version of the rule?

5. What policies did the courts identify that support the application of promissory estoppel? What policies did they identify that suggest limits on use of the doctrine?

Conrad v. Fields

MARJORIE CONRAD, Plaintiff-Respondent

v.

WALTER R. FIELDS, Defendant-Appellant

Court of Appeals of Minnesota
2007 WL 2106302 (Minn. Ct. App. July 24, 2007) (unpublished opinion)

PETERSON, JUDGE.

This appeal is from a judgment and an order denying posttrial motions. The judgment awarded respondent damages in the amount of the cost of her law-school tuition and books based on a determination that the elements of promissory estoppel were proved with respect to appellant's promise to pay for the tuition and books. We affirm the judgment and grant in part and deny in part respondent's motion to strike appellant's brief and appendix.

FACTS

Appellant Walter R. Fields and respondent Marjorie Conrad met and became friends when they were neighbors in an apartment complex in the early 1990's. Appellant started his own business and became a financially successful businessman. Appellant built a $1.2 million house in the Kenwood neighborhood in Minneapolis and leased a Bentley automobile for more than $50,000 a year. Appellant is a philanthropic individual who has sometimes paid education costs for others.

In the fall of 2000, appellant suggested that respondent attend law school, and he offered to pay for her education. Respondent, who had recently paid off an $11,000 medical bill and still owed about $5,000 for undergraduate student loans, did not feel capable of paying for law school on her own. Appellant promised that he would pay tuition and other expenses associated with law school as they became due. [Respondent] quit her job at Qwest, where she had been earning $45,000 per year, to attend law school. Appellant admitted at trial that before respondent enrolled in law school, he agreed to pay her tuition.

Respondent testified that she enrolled in law school in the summer of 2001 as a result of appellant's "inducement and assurance to pay for [her] education." Appellant made two tuition payments, each in the amount of $1,949.75, in August and October 2001, but he stopped payment on the check for the second payment. At some point, appellant told respondent that his assets had been frozen due to an Internal Revenue Service audit and that payment of her education expenses would be delayed until he got the matter straightened out. In May 2004, appellant and respondent exchanged e-mail messages about respondent's difficulties in managing the debts that she had incurred for law school. In response to one of respondent's messages, appellant wrote, "to be clear and in writing, when you graduate law school and pas[s] your bar exam, I will pay your tuition." Later, appellant told respondent that he would not pay her expenses, and he threatened to get a restraining order against her if she continued attempting to communicate with him.

Respondent brought suit against appellant, alleging that in reliance on appellant's promise to pay her education expenses, she gave up the opportunity to earn income through full-time employment and enrolled in law school. The case was tried to the court, which awarded respondent damages in the amount of $87,314.63 under the doctrine of promissory estoppel. The district court denied appellant's motion for a new trial or amended findings. This appeal followed.

DECISION

The district court's "[f]indings of fact, whether based on oral or documentary evidence, shall not be set aside unless clearly erroneous, and due regard shall be given to the opportunity of the trial court to judge the credibility of the witnesses." Minn. R. Civ. P. 52.01. In applying this rule, "we view the record in the light most favorable to the judgment of the district court." *Rogers v. Moore,* 603 N.W.2d 650, 656 (Minn.1999). If there is reasonable evidence to support the district court's findings of fact, this court will not disturb those findings. *Fletcher v. St. Paul Pioneer Press,* 589 N.W.2d 96, 101 (Minn.1999). While the district court's findings of fact are reviewed under the deferential "clearly erroneous" standard, this court reviews questions of law de novo. *AFSCME, Council No. 14 v. City of St. Paul,* 533 N.W.2d 623, 626 (Minn.App.1995).

"Promissory estoppel implies a contract in law where no contract exists in fact." *Deli v. Univ. of Minn.,* 578 N.W.2d 779, 781 (Minn.App.1998), *review denied* (Minn. July 16, 1998). "A promise which the promisor should reasonably expect to induce action or forbearance on the part of the promisee or a third person and which does induce such action or forbearance is binding if injustice can be avoided only by enforcement of the promise." Restatement (Second) of Contracts § 90(1) (1981).

The elements of a promissory estoppel claim are (1) a clear and definite promise, (2) the promisor intended to induce reliance by the promisee, and the promisee relied to the promisee's detriment, and (3) the promise must be enforced to prevent injustice. *Cohen v. Cowles Media Co.,* 479 N.W.2d 387, 391 (Minn.1992). Judicial determinations of injustice involve a number of considerations, "including the reasonableness of a promisee's reliance." *Faimon v. Winona State Univ.,* 540 N.W.2d, 879, 883 (Minn.App.1995), *review denied* (Minn. Feb. 9, 1996).

"Granting equitable relief is within the sound discretion of the trial court. Only a clear abuse of that discretion will result in reversal." *Nadeau v. County of Ramsey,* 277 N.W.2d 520, 524 (Minn.1979). But

> [t]he court considers the injustice factor as a matter of law, looking to the reasonableness of the promisee's reliance and weighing public policies (in favor of both enforcing bargains and preventing unjust enrichment). When the facts are taken as true, it is a question of law as to whether they rise to the level of promissory estoppel.

Greuling v. Wells Fargo Home Mortgage, Inc., 690 N.W.2d 757, 761 (Minn.App.2005) (citation omitted).

I.

Appellant argues that respondent did not plead or prove the elements of promissory estoppel. . . .

Paragraph 12 of respondent's complaint states, "That as a direct and approximate result of the negligent conduct and breach of contract conduct of [appellant], [respondent] has been damaged . . . ." But the complaint also states:

4.   That in 2000, based on the assurance and inducement of [appellant] to pay for [respondent's] legal education, [respondent] made the decision to enroll in law school at Hamline University School of Law (Hamline) in St. Paul, Minnesota which she did in 2001.

5.   That but for the inducement and assurance of [appellant] to pay for [respondent's] legal education, [respondent] would not have enrolled in law school. [Appellant] was aware of this fact.

Paragraphs four and five of the complaint are sufficient to put appellant on notice of the promissory-estoppel claim.

At a pretrial deposition, respondent testified that negligence and breach of contract were the only two causes of action that she was pleading. Because promissory estoppel is described as a contract implied at law, respondent's deposition testimony can be interpreted to include a promissory-estoppel claim.

In its legal analysis, the district court stated:

The Court finds credible [respondent's] testimony that [appellant] encouraged her to go to law school, knowing that she would not be able to pay for it on her own. He knew that she was short on money, having helped her pay for food and other necessities. He knew that she was working at Qwest and would need to quit her job to go to law school. He offered to pay for the cost of her going to law school, knowing that she had debts from her undergraduate tuition. He made a payment on her law school tuition after she enrolled. [Respondent] knew that [appellant] was a wealthy philanthropist, and that he had offered to pay for the education of strangers he had met in chance encounters. She knew that he had the wealth to pay for her law school education. She knew that [ ] he was established in society, older than she, not married, without children, an owner of a successful company, an owner of an expensive home, and a lessor of an expensive car. Moreover, [appellant] was a friend who had performed many kindnesses for her already, and she trusted him. [Appellant's] promise in fact induced [respondent] to quit her job at Qwest and enroll in law school, which she had not otherwise planned to do. . . .

. . . [T]he circumstances support a finding that it would be unjust not to enforce the promise. Upon reliance on [appellant's] promise, [respondent] quit her job. She attended law school despite a serious health condition that might otherwise have deterred her from going.

These findings are sufficient to show that respondent proved the elements of promissory estoppel.

Appellant argues that because he advised respondent shortly after she enrolled in law school that he would not be paying her law-school expenses as they came due, respondent could not have reasonably relied on his promise to pay her expenses to her detriment after he repudiated the promise. Appellant contends that the only injustice that resulted from his promise involved the original $5,000 in expenses that respondent incurred to enter law school. But appellant's statement that he would not pay the expenses as they came due did not make respondent's reliance unreasonable because appellant also told respondent that his financial problems were temporary and that he would pay her tuition when she graduated and passed the bar exam. This statement made it reasonable for respondent to continue to rely on appellant's promise that he would pay her expenses. . . .

IV.

In actions based on promissory estoppel, "[r]elief may be limited to damages measured by the promisee's reliance." *Dallum v. Farmers Union Cent. Exchange, Inc.,* 462 N.W.2d 608, 613 (Minn. App. 1990), review denied (Minn. Jan. 14, 1991). "In other words, relief may be limited to the party's out-of-pocket expenses made in reliance on the promise." *Id.*

Appellant objects to respondent seeking damages for lost income and living expenses, including housing. But the district court awarded respondent damages only for the cost of tuition and books. Appellant argues that respondent sought double recovery for the cost of tuition and the amount of her student loans. But an exhibit prepared by respondent and admitted into evidence shows that tuition totaled $86,462.21 and books cost $2,802.17. The district court awarded respondent $87,314.63 (tuition plus books minus payment made by appellant).

Make the Connection

As discussed at greater length in Chapter 10, § 2.1.6, mitigation is an important limitation on damage awards. An aggrieved party may recover only those damages caused by the breach and may not recover damages that she could have prevented by taking reasonable steps.

Appellant argues that respondent was obligated to mitigate her damages and she could have avoided all of her damages by dropping out of law school immediately after appellant refused to pay her tuition as it was incurred. But as we explained when addressing the reasonableness of respondent's reliance, appellant told respondent that his financial difficulties were temporary and that he would pay her expenses after graduation. Under these circumstances, respondent was not aware until after she graduated that she would suffer damages, and by the time she graduated, she had already paid for her tuition and books and had no opportunity to mitigate damages.

V.

Appellant argues that because respondent received a valuable law degree, she did not suffer any real detriment by relying on his promise. But receiving a law degree was the expected and intended consequence of appellant's promise, and the essence of appellant's promise was that respondent would receive the law degree without the debt associated with attending law school. Although respondent benefited from attending law school, the debt that she incurred in reliance on appellant's promise is a detriment to her. . . .

Affirmed; motion granted in part.

History of Equity

When the *Conrad* court says, "Granting equitable relief is within the sound discretion of the trial court," it is referring to the equitable roots of promissory estoppel. As is clear in *Conrad* as well as in the Restatement, promissory estoppel is premised on determining the reasonableness of the behavior of promisor and promisee and on preventing injustice. Such concerns (reasonableness, fairness, justice) are classic equitable concerns. Understanding their historical roots may help clarify the relationship between the doctrine of consideration and the alternative paths to enforcement discussed in this chapter.

In the 14th century, the English common law courts operated on a rigid system of "writs" that narrowly limited available forms of action, so that many kinds of claims—including claims based on oral promises—could not successfully be pursued there. Writs for new kinds of claims were rarely created, so many claimants had no recourse. Contract defenses based on fraud, failure of performance, and prior satisfaction of the claimed debt were often precluded in common law courts. Procedures in common law courts were also restrictive. Parties to lawsuits could not offer evidence in their cases, witnesses could not be summoned unless they owned property, and a court could not order discovery of documentary evidence.

Individuals with grievances who could not seek or obtain relief before the common law courts sometimes petitioned the King or the King's Council for redress, and such petitions were often referred to the chancellor, the King's chief councilor, who dispensed justice in individual cases. Over time, the petitions and responses became more regularized, and the Chancery Court and later other lesser equity courts emerged, handling what became known as equitable claims for relief, including some contract-related causes of action and defenses. Until the middle of the 16th century, most chancellors were religious figures, generally bishops or cardinals. Because of the religious background of the chancellor, moral conduct and good conscience played a large role in the Chancery Court's reasoning, often leading to sensible and practical results not available under the more rigid restrictions on legal relief.

Court procedures varied considerably between the chancery courts and the common law courts. Chancery courts acted "in personam" (with respect to the individual rather than to his property), so they had the ability to demand the appearance of the parties and other witnesses. Because the chancellor or, later, judges, made decisions, the chancery courts permitted parties to testify, rather than relying on the "self-informing" common law jury to decide cases based on the jurors' own knowledge. Although some chancery court process was problematic (the absence of cross-examination and juries, for example), procedural advances over the common law courts nonetheless made the chancery courts attractive to litigants. To forestall political criticism that chancery was competing with the common law courts, the judges of the Chancery Court said they were "following the law"—supplementing the common law and responding to shortcomings, not replacing it. Equitable relief was "extraordinary" and granted only if legal relief was not available.

Today, most jurisdictions have merged the courts of law and equity. However, the ghosts of the Chancery Court and its history still persist in some respects. Even though a single judge can make decisions in law and equity, an equitable claim or remedy usually is available only if the claimant has no adequate remedy at law and will suffer irreparable harm unless equitable relief is given. Equitable issues are still decided by the judge, not by a jury. Equity continues to focus on fashioning a result that is fair and morally sound. Equitable relief will be denied to a party "with unclean hands," and specific performance (an equitable remedy) may be denied if the contract has lop-sided consideration or is entered into in unfair circumstances. The standards and rules of equity generally reserve more discretion to the court than do comparable rules "at law."

As you consider the alternatives to consideration discussed in this chapter, think about the role of equitable factors in the elements of each claim.

> See John H. Langbein, Renée Lettow Lerner & Bruce P. Smith, *History of the Common Law: The Development of Anglo-American Legal Institutions* (2009); Dan B. Dobbs, *Law of Remedies: Damages—Equity—Restitution* §§ 2.2–2.4 (2d ed. 1993).

Hayes v. Plantations Steel Co.

EDWARD J. HAYES, Plaintiff-Appellee

v.

PLANTATIONS STEEL COMPANY, Defendant-Appellant

Supreme Court of Rhode Island

<u>438 A.2d 1091 (R.I. 1982)</u>

SHEA, JUSTICE.

The defendant employer, Plantations Steel Company (Plantations), appeals from a Superior Court judgment for the plaintiff employee, Edward J. Hayes (Hayes). The trial justice, sitting without a jury, found that Plantations was obligated to Hayes on the basis of an implied-in-fact contract to pay him a yearly pension of $5,000. The award covered three years in which payment had not been made. The trial justice ruled, also, that Hayes had made a sufficient showing of detrimental reliance upon Plantations's promise to pay to give rise to its obligation based on the theory of promissory estoppel. . . .

What's That?

In a contract "implied-in-fact," the required factual elements are inferred from the circumstances rather than explicitly stated by the parties.

We reverse the findings of the trial justice regarding Plantations's contractual obligation to pay Hayes a pension. . . .

Plantations is a closely held Rhode Island corporation engaged in the manufacture of steel reinforcing rods for use in concrete construction. The company was founded by Hugo R. Mainelli, Sr., and Alexander A. DiMartino. A dispute between their two families in 1976 and 1977 left the DiMartinos in full control of the corporation. Hayes was an employee of the corporation from 1947 until his retirement in 1972 at age of sixty-five. He began with Plantations as an "estimator and draftsman" and ended his career as general manager, a position of considerable responsibility. Starting in January 1973 and continuing until January 1976, Hayes received the annual sum of $5,000 from Plantations. Hayes instituted this action in December 1977, after the then company management refused to make any further payments.

Hayes testified that in January 1972 he announced his intention to retire the following July, after twenty-five years of continuous service. He decided to retire because he had worked continuously for fifty-one years. He stated, however, that he would not have retired had he not expected to receive a pension. After he stopped working for Plantations, he sought no other employment.

Approximately one week before his actual retirement Hayes spoke with Hugo R. Mainelli, Jr., who was then an officer and a stockholder of Plantations. This conversation was the first and only one concerning payments of a pension to Hayes during retirement. Mainelli said that the company "would take care" of him. There was no mention of a sum of money or a percentage of salary that Hayes would receive. There was no formal authorization for payments by Plantations's shareholders and/or board of directors. Indeed, there was never any formal provision for a pension plan for any employee other than for unionized employees, who benefit from an arrangement through their union. The plaintiff was not a union member.

Mr. Mainelli, Jr., testified that his father, Hugo R. Mainelli, Sr., had authorized the first payment "as a token of appreciation for the many years of (Hayes's) service." Furthermore, "it was implied that that check would continue on an annual basis." Mainelli also testified that it was his "personal intention" that the payments would continue for "as long as I was around."

Mainelli testified that after Hayes's retirement, [Hayes] would visit the premises each year to say hello and renew old acquaintances. During the course of his visits, Hayes would thank Mainelli for the previous check and ask how long it would continue so that he could plan an orderly retirement.

The payments were discontinued after 1976. At that time a succession of several poor business years plus the stockholders' dispute, resulting in the takeover by the DiMartino family, contributed to the decision to stop the payments.

The trial justice ruled that Plantations owed Hayes his annual sum of $5,000 for the years 1977 through 1979. The ruling implied that barring bankruptcy or the cessation of business for any other reason, Hayes had a right to expect continued annual payments.

The trial justice found that Hugo Mainelli, Jr.'s statement that Hayes would be taken care of after his retirement was a promise. Although no sum of money was mentioned in 1972, the four annual payments of $5,000 established that otherwise unspecified term of the contract. The trial justice also found that Hayes supplied consideration for the promise by voluntarily retiring, because he was under no obligation to do so. From the words and conduct of the parties and from the surrounding circumstances, the trial justice concluded that there existed an implied contract obligating the company to pay a pension to Hayes for life. The trial justice made a further finding that even if Hayes had not truly bargained for a pension by voluntarily retiring, he had nevertheless incurred the detriment of foregoing other employment in reliance upon the company's promise. He specifically held that Hayes's retirement was in response to the promise and held also that Hayes refrained from seeking other employment in further reliance thereon.

The findings of fact of a trial justice sitting without a jury are entitled to great weight when reviewed by this court. His findings will not be disturbed unless it can be shown that they are clearly wrong or that the trial justice misconceived or overlooked material evidence. Lisi v. Marra, R.I., 424 A.2d 1052 (1981); Raheb v. Lemenski, 115 R.I. 576, 350 A.2d 397 (1976). After careful review of the record, however, we conclude that the trial justice's findings and conclusions must be reversed.

Assuming for the purpose of this discussion that Plantations in legal effect made a promise to Hayes, we must ask whether Hayes did supply the required consideration that would make the promise binding? And, if Hayes did not supply consideration, was his alleged reliance sufficiently induced by the promise to estop defendant from denying its obligation to him? We answer both questions in the negative.

[The court noted that the statement of Hugo Mainelli, Jr. (that Hayes "would be taken care of"), standing alone, "was not an expression of a direct and definite promise to pay Hayes a pension." Because the parties did not enter into express contract, the court would need to determine whether the circumstances of the parties' conduct and words gave rise to a contract. Any promise by Mainelli would not be enforceable if it were not supported by consideration. The court cited cases supporting both the benefit-detriment test and the bargained-for-exchange test and noted that an alleged consideration was not valid if it was given before the promise was made, because it was "rendered in the past and apart from an alleged exchange in the present" and so was not bargained for.]

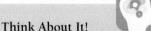

Think About It!

Recall that, at the beginning of Chapter 2, page 16, we defined a promise as an assurance or declaration that one will do or refrain from doing some act. Was Mainelli's statement a promise?

In the case before us, Plantations's promise to pay Hayes a pension is quite clearly not supported by any consideration supplied by Hayes. Hayes had announced his intent to retire well in advance of any promise, and therefore the intention to retire was arrived at without regard to any promise by Plantations. Although Hayes may have had in mind the receipt of a pension when he first informed Plantations, his expectation was not based on any statement made to him or on any conduct of the company officer relative to him in January 1972. In deciding to retire, Hayes acted on his own initiative. Hayes's long years of dedicated service also is legally insufficient because his service too was rendered without being induced by Plantations's promise.

. . . . Instead, the testimony establishes that Plantations's promise was intended "as a token of appreciation for (Hayes's) many years of service." As such it was in the nature of a gratuity paid to Hayes for as long as the company chose. . . .

. . . .

Hayes argues in the alternative that even if Plantations's promise was not the product of an exchange, its duty is grounded properly in the theory of promissory estoppel. This court adopted the theory of promissory estoppel in East Providence Credit Union v. Geremia, 103 R.I. 597, 601, 239 A.2d 725, 727 (1968) (quoting 1 Restatement Contracts § 90 at 110 (1932)) stating:

> "A promise which the promisor should reasonably expect to induce action or forbearance of a definite and substantial character on the part of the promisee and which does induce such action or forbearance is binding if injustice can be avoided only by enforcement of its promise."

In *East Providence Credit Union* this court said that the doctrine of promissory estoppel is invoked "as a substitute for a consideration, rendering a gratuitous promise enforceable as a contract." *Id.* To restate the matter differently, "the acts of reliance by the promisee to his detriment (provide) a substitute for consideration." *Id.*

. . . .

. . . . One of the essential elements of the doctrine of promissory estoppel is that the promise must induce the promisee's action or forbearance. The particular act in this regard is plaintiff's decision whether or not to retire. As we stated earlier, the record indicates that he made the decision on his own initiative. In other words, the conversation between Hayes and Mainelli which occurred a week before Hayes left his employment cannot be said to have induced his decision to leave. He had reached that decision long before.

An example taken from the Restatement provides a meaningful contrast:

"2.   A promises B to pay him an annuity during B's life. B thereupon resigns profitable employment, as A expected that he might. B receives the annuity for some years, in the meantime becoming disqualified from again obtaining good employment. A's promise is binding." (Emphasis added.) 1 Restatement Contracts § 90 at 111 (1932).

In Feinberg v. Pfeiffer Co., 322 S.W.2d 163 (Mo. App.1959), the plaintiff-employee had worked for her employer for nearly forty years. The defendant corporation's board of directors resolved, in view of her long years of service, to obligate itself to pay "retirement privileges" to her. The resolution did not require the plaintiff to retire. Instead, the decision whether and when to retire remained entirely her own. The board then informed her of its resolution. The plaintiff worked for eighteen months more before retiring. She sued the corporation when it reduced her monthly checks seven years later. The court held that a pension contract existed between the parties. Although continued employment was not a consideration to her receipt of retirement benefits, the court found sufficient reliance on the part of the plaintiff to support her claim. The court based its decision upon the above Restatement example, that is, the defendant informed the plaintiff of its plan, and the plaintiff in reliance thereon, retired. Feinberg presents factors that also appear in the case at bar. There, the plaintiff had worked many years and desired to retire; she would not have left had she not been able to rely on a pension; and once retired, she sought no other employment.

However, the important distinction between *Feinberg* and the case before us is that in *Feinberg* the employer's decision definitely shaped the thinking of the plaintiff. In this case the promise did not. It is not reasonable to infer from the facts that Hugo R. Mainelli, Jr., expected retirement to result from his conversation with Hayes. Hayes had given notice of his intention seven months previously. Here there was thus no inducement to retire which would satisfy the demands of § 90 of the Restatement. Nor can it be said that Hayes's refraining from other employment was "action or forbearance of a definite and substantial character." The underlying assumption of Hayes's initial decision to retire was that upon leaving the defendant's employ, he would no longer work. It is impossible to say that he changed his position any more so because of what Mainelli had told him in light of his own initial decision. These circumstances do not lead to a conclusion that injustice can be avoided only by enforcement of Plantations's promise. Hayes received $20,000 over the course of four years. He inquired each year about whether he could expect a check for the following year. Obviously, there was no absolute certainty on his part that the pension would continue. Furthermore, in the face of his uncertainty, the mere fact that payment for several years did occur is insufficient by itself to meet the requirements of reliance under the doctrine of promissory estoppel.

For the foregoing reasons, the defendant's appeal is sustained and the judgment of the Superior Court is reversed. The papers of the case are remanded to the Superior Court.

Maryland Nat'l Bank v. United Jewish Appeal Fed'n of Greater Wash.

MARYLAND NATIONAL BANK et al., Defendant-Appellant

v.

UNITED JEWISH APPEAL FEDERATION OF GREATER
WASHINGTON, INC., Plaintiff-Appellee

Court of Appeals of Maryland
407 A.2d 1130 (Md. Ct. App. 1979)

ORTH, JUDGE.

The issue in this case is whether a pledge to a charitable institution survives the death of the pledgor and is an enforceable obligation of his estate.

I

What's That?

In Maryland, the "Orphans' Court" is the court that handles wills and estates, often called probate or surrogate's court in other jurisdictions. The name derives from the old City of London's Court for Widows and Orphans, which Lord Baltimore brought to the colony of Maryland. In 1777, the Maryland General Assembly formally established an Orphans' Court and Register of Wills in each county and the City of Baltimore, a structure that continues to operate today.

Milton Polinger pledged $200,000 to the United Jewish Appeal Federation of Greater Washington, Inc. (UJA) for the year 1975. He died on 20 December 1976. His last will and testament was admitted to probate in the Orphans' Court for Montgomery County and letters were issued to Melvin R. Oksner and Maryland National Bank as personal representatives. At the time of Polinger's death $133,500 was unpaid on his pledge. The personal representatives disallowed the claim for the balance of the pledge. UJA filed a petition praying that the claim be allowed and moved for summary judgment. The personal representatives answered and filed a cross-motion for summary judgment. The court granted UJA's motion for summary judgment, denied the personal representatives' motion for summary judgment, allowed UJA's claim against the estate in the amount of $133,500, and assessed the costs against the personal representatives. The personal representatives noted an appeal to the Court of Special Appeals and petitioned this Court to issue a writ of certiorari to that court before decision by it. We did so.

II

The facts before the court were undisputed in material part. They showed the nature of UJA and its relationship with its beneficiaries. UJA, chartered in the District of Columbia, is a public non-profit corporation. In general, its objective is to solicit, collect and receive funds and property for the support of certain religious, charitable, philanthropic, scientific and educational organizations and institutions, and it enjoys tax exempt status federally and in Maryland, Virginia and the District of Columbia. Based on monies received and pledged, it makes allocations to tax exempt organizations. No formal commitment agreement is executed with respect to the allocations, but UJA undertakes to pay pursuant to the allocation and the beneficiary organizations "go ahead to act as though they are going to have the money and they spend it." In other words, UJA makes allocations to various beneficiary organizations based upon pledges made to it, and the beneficiary organizations incur liabilities based on the allocations. Historically 95% of the pledges are collected over a three year period, and allowance for the 5% which may be uncollected is made in determining the amount of the allocations. So, according to Meyer Brissman, Executive Vice-President Emeritus of UJA: "We always pay [the allocated amount]. I don't know of any case where we haven't paid." Pledges to "emergency funds" are not paid on the basis of an allocation by UJA. All monies actually collected on those pledges are paid to the emergency funds.

The facts before the court showed the circumstances surrounding the pledge of Polinger with which we are here concerned. It was evidenced by a card signed by Polinger under date of 9 November 1974. It recited:

In consideration of the obligation incurred based upon this pledge, I hereby promise to pay to the United Jewish Appeal the amount indicated on this card.

The amount indicated as his "1975 pledge" was $100,000 for "UJA including local national and overseas," and $100,000 for "Israel Emergency Fund."

UJA organized a "mission" to Israel in the fall of 1974. The mission was in no sense a tour. It was at the time of the missile crisis in Israel, and the members of the mission were to meet with Golda Meir, then Prime Minister, and with other government leaders to be briefed on the problems the country faced. It was to be involved with "people in the troubled settlements." Certain community leaders, including Polinger, went on the mission. Polinger had been active in the affairs of UJA and had regularly made substantial contributions to it.

"Pre-solicitation" is a process whereby it is determined who can be expected to make large pledges and specifically who will likely substantially increase their pledges of previous years. Pre-solicitation is part of a well conceived plan to obtain large contributions. It leads to a "high-pressure meeting" at which, according to Brissman,

> [t]here is no question that the technique is the interchange and people knowing everyone else in the room, and if this one is thinking of a need of being so great as to be willing to do something unusual, the others thought it was similarly important for them to demonstrate it.

The idea is that "if somebody thought it was important enough to give more than he gave before, [others would think] that they ought to give more, and they [give] more money. . . . [W]e get together and discuss reactions to what they have seen, what the needs are, and people sometimes make a speech before they decide what they are going to say about the money, and it is a free-flowing thing, and nobody knows in advance what anybody is going to say, but some of the people are talked to one by one privately to condition them to make some kind of a special response to influence the group. The whole purpose of fund raising is to get an example."

Polinger was selected to be an example on the Israel mission. He had pledged $65,000 for 1973. He had "participated willingly" in such a meeting in connection with the 1974 fund raising campaign and had pledged $150,000. He was one of those it was "felt was ready to do something unusual. . . ." He was pre-solicited by three or four individuals and went up to two hundred thousand dollars for 1975. It was agreed that his pledge would be made in a "caucus" at the King David Hotel in Jerusalem. The caucus was held and Polinger "came into the caucus," as Brissman said, "so we could announce all the gifts and influence other people of different levels." Polinger was to be a "pacesetter."

There were about thirty men at the caucus. About four of them had pledged an amount as large as $200,000 before Polinger made his announcement. Brissman thought that "there was an emotional impact that develops when a man has seen things that influence him to believe that there is something desperate and earth-shaking going on and he could do something about it beneficially, and he responds." When Polinger said he would give $200,000, he indicated that he wanted everybody to give as much as they could. He thought he was giving the greatest amount that he possibly could find himself able to so do. Of course, Polinger was only one of many people who spoke and made a pledge. Whether anyone in fact increased his pledge because of Polinger was never discussed at the meeting, and Brissman was unable to say whether anyone was influenced by Polinger's pledge.

It is just a dynamics of an involvement where after two weeks of being together night and day in a setting of that kind after a major war, meeting with individuals who lived through three or four such wars, that everybody is strung out and you are like a family, and in the process of interchange, speeches are made, and maybe somebody [who] made a gift of $5,000.00 influenced people just as much as the man who gave $200,000.00 because of what the money meant in their view of this person's ability to give.

It is just not the biggest number, but it is the concept of response to a need that these people are reacting to. And I don't know that you verbalize it in that way necessarily, but it does come out that one influences another in the interchange, because you are going around a room and everybody is talking about how they were moved by what they were into. So there is no question one influences another.

Brissman was asked "whether aside from the specific group of people who were present in Israel with Mr. Polinger, are there any other people here in the Washington area or anywhere else that you are aware of who made pledges, gifts, or increased gifts as a result of Mr. Polinger's gift?" He could not say. He could only give the procedure followed:

I solicited personally hundreds of people, some face to face, some by telephone, some by appointment with two or three people talking to an individual. And frequently I, personally, and I know of others who do likewise, start to tell people what kind of response we are getting when we get to the question of what is a standard for giving, or what you ought to consider as your share, and in the process I have used Milton Polinger as an example talking to individuals. They know who Milton is. And I would tell them what Milton had done in 1973 and in 1974 in trying to get them to respond in some way to move further ahead in their extension as far as they can, because we are talking of stretching. If you can give so much, can you give a little but more type of thing, and I frequently would use Milton as an illustration.

There is no question in my mind when I do it I know others do it, and I have seen at the time that we are talking about people reporting on the mission to others who were not there, soliciting gifts at meetings or in individual confrontations, telling what happened at the mission, and they would go down line by line everybody who made gifts, they had a list in front of them as a tool.

So it was used. There is no question about it. I cannot tell you this one increased his gift only because of that one's response, but it is part of a package. That is how you raise money.

III

We find that the law of Maryland with regard to the enforcement of pledges or subscriptions to charitable organizations is the rule thus expressed in the Restatement of Contracts § 90 (1932):

> A promise which the promisor should reasonably expect to induce action or forbearance of a definite and substantial character on the part of the promisee and which does induce such action or forbearance is binding if injustice can be avoided only by enforcement of the promise.

We reach this conclusion through opinions of this Court in four cases, *Gittings v. Mayhew*, 6 Md. 113 (1854); *Erdman v. Trustees Eutaw M. P. Ch.*, 129 Md. 595, 99 A. 793 (1917); *Sterling v. Cushwa & Sons*, 170 Md. 226, 183 A. 593 (1936); and *American University v. Collings*, 190 Md. 688, 59 A.2d 333 (1948).

Gittings concerned the building of an Atheneum. The subscription contract authorized the calling of payment of installments by the subscribers when a certain amount had been pledged. The amount was reached, installments were called for and paid, contracts to erect the building were made and the Antheneum was completed. It was in these circumstances that the Court said:

> . . . [W]here advances have been made, or expenses or liabilities incurred by others, in consequence of such subscriptions, before notice of withdrawal, this should, on general principles, be deemed sufficient to make them obligatory, provided the advances were authorized by a fair and reasonable dependence on the subscriptions. . . . (6 Md. at 131–132.)

It's Latin to Me

"Obiter dictum" is Latin for "something said in passing" and refers to a judicial comment made in an opinion that that is unnecessary to the decision in the case and therefore not precedential, though it may be considered persuasive. The reference is often shortened to simply "dictum."

This statement of the law appeared to be obiter dictum in *Gittings*, but if it were, it became the law in *Erdman*.

Erdman dealt with a suit on a promissory note whereby there was a promise to pay the Eutaw Methodist Protestant Church the sum of $500 four years after date with interest. The consideration for the note was a subscription contract made with the trustees of the church for the purpose of paying off a building debt, which had been incurred for the erection of a new church building. It had been entered on the books of the church, the trustees had subsequently borrowed $2,000 on that subscription and other subscriptions to pay off the indebtedness for the erection of the church building. The Court held that in such circumstances the subscription contract was a valid and binding one and constituted a sufficient consideration to support the note, *Id.* 129 Md. at 602, 99 A. 793, observing that "[t]he policy of the law, to sustain subscription contracts of the character of the one here in question, is clearly stated by this court, and by other appellate courts, in a number of cases," *Id.* at 600, 99 A. at 795. The only Maryland case cited was *Gittings.* The holding in *Gittings* was said to be "that as the party had authorized others by the subscription to enter into engagements for the accomplishment of the enterprise, the law requires that he should save them harmless to the extent of his subscription." *Erdman,* 129 Md. at 601, 99 A. at 795. . . . In [*Trustees v. Garvey,* 53 Ill. 401 (1870)] the court noted that "[a]s a matter of public policy, courts have been desirous of sustaining the legal obligation of subscriptions of this character, and in some cases . . . have found a sufficient consideration in the mutuality of the promises, where no

Take Note!

Note that the court used the term "consideration" broadly here, to encompass not only traditional consideration but also alternatives to consideration.

fraud or deception has been practiced." *Id.* at 403. "But," the court continued, "while we might be unwilling to go to that extent, and might hold that a subscription could be withdrawn before money had been expended or liability incurred, or work performed on the strength of the subscriptions, and in furtherance of the enterprise," the church trustees had, on the faith of the subscriptions, borrowed money, relying on the subscription as a means of payment and incurred a specific liability. *Id.* Thus, it seems that *Erdman* made law of the dictum in *Gittings,* but that law was that charitable subscriptions to be enforceable require reliance on the subscriptions by the charity which would lead to direct loss to the organization or its officers if the subscriptions were not enforced.

. . . .

In summary, the rule announced in *Gittings,* referred to in *Collings* and applied in *Erdman* and *Sterling,* is in substance the rule set out in § 90 of the Restatement of Contracts (1932). It is the settled law of this State.

IV

[Although UJA argued that the court should "view traditional contract law requirements of consideration liberally" in order to maintain a judicial policy of favoring charities, the court declined to loosen the requirements of promissory estoppel for charitable subscriptions.]

. . . [W]e are not persuaded that we should, by judicial fiat, adopt a policy of favoring charities at the expense of the law of contracts which has been long established in this state. We do not think that this law should be disregarded or modified so as to bestow a preferred status upon charitable organizations and institutions. It may be that there are cases in which judgments according to the law do not appear to subserve the purposes of justice, but this, ordinarily, the courts may not remedy. "It is safer that a private right should fail, or a wrong go unredressed, than that settled principles should be disregarded in order to meet the equity of a particular case." *Gittings* at 134. If change is to be made it should be by legislative enactment, as in the matter of the tax status of charitable organizations.

. . . .

Take Note!

Restatement (Second) of Contracts § 90(2) removes the requirement that actual reliance be shown, in cases involving charitable subscriptions. However, most courts—like the Maryland Court of Appeals here—have not been persuaded to follow that rule. When applying promissory estoppel to charitable subscriptions, courts continue to require the recipients to show actual reliance (though they sometimes seem to do so with "strained reasoning," as noted in the *Maryland National Bank opinion*).

Section 90 of the tentative draft No. 2 of the Restatement (Second) of Contracts, 1965, has not been adopted by the American Law Institute, and we are not persuaded to follow it.

"Cases throughout the country clearly reflect a conflict between the desired goal of enforcing charitable subscriptions and the realities of contract law. The result has been strained reasoning which has been the subject of considerable criticism." *Salsbury v. Northwestern Bell Telephone Company*, 221 N.W.2d 609, 611–612 (Iowa, 1974). When charitable subscriptions, even though clearly gratuitous promises, have been held either contracts or offers to contract, the "decisions are based on such a great variety of reasoning as to show the lack of any really sufficient consideration." Williston on Contracts, § 116 (3d ed. 1957) (footnotes omitted). "Very likely, conceptions of public policy have shaped, more or less subconsciously, the rulings thus made. Judges have been affected by the thought that 'defenses of [the] character [of lack of consideration are] breaches of faith towards the public, and especially towards those engaged in the same enterprise, and an unwarrantable disappointment of the reasonable expectations of those interested.' " *Allegheny College v. National Chautauqua County Bank*, 246 N.Y. 369, 159 N.E. 173, 175 (1927). Therefore, "[c]ourts have . . . purported to find consideration on various tenuous theories. . . . [The] wide variation in reasoning indicates the difficulty of enforcing a charitable subscription on grounds of consideration. Yet, the courts have generally striven to find grounds for enforcement, indicating the depth of feeling in this country that private philanthropy serves a highly important function in our society." J. Calamari & J. Perillo, The Law of Contracts, § 6–5 (1977) (footnotes omitted). Some courts have forthrightly discarded the facade of consideration and admittedly held a charitable subscription enforceable only in respect of what they conceive to be the public policy. See, for example, *Salsbury v. Northwestern Bell Telephone Company, supra; More Game Birds in America, Inc. v. Boettger*, 125 N.J.L. 97, 14 A.2d 778, 780–781 (1940).

. . . .

V

When the facts concerning the charitable subscription of Polinger are viewed in light of the Maryland law, it is manifest that his promise was not legally enforceable. There was no consideration as required by contract law. . . . The consideration recited by the pledge card was "the obligation incurred based upon this pledge. . . ." But there was no legal obligation incurred in the circumstances. Polinger's pledge was not made in consideration of the pledges of others, and there was no evidence that others in fact made pledges in consideration of Polinger's pledge. No release was given or binding agreement made by the UJA on the strength of Polinger's pledge. The pledge was not for a specific enterprise; it was to the UJA generally and to the Israel Emergency Fund. With respect to the former, no allocation by UJA to its beneficiary organization was threatened or thwarted by the failure to collect the Polinger pledge in its entirety, and, with respect to the latter, UJA practice was to pay over to the Fund only what it actually collected, not what was pledged. UJA borrowed no money on the faith and credit of the pledge. The pledge prompted no "action or forbearance of a definite and substantial character" on the part of UJA. No action was taken by UJA on the strength of the pledge that could reasonably be termed "definite and substantial" from which it should be held harmless. There was no change shown in the position of UJA made in reliance on the subscription which resulted in an economic loss, and, in fact, there was no such loss demonstrated. UJA was able to fulfill all of its allocations. Polinger's pledge was utilized as a means to obtain substantial pledges from others. But this was a technique employed to raise money. It did not supply a legal consideration to Polinger's pledge. On the facts of this case, it does not appear that injustice can be avoided only by enforcement of the promise.

. . . . UJA's function was to serve as a conduit or clearinghouse to collect gifts of money from many sources and to funnel them into various charitable organizations. It did, of course, plan for the future, in that it estimated the rate of cash flow based on the pledges it received and told its beneficiaries to expect certain amounts. In so doing, however, it expressly did not incur liabilities in reliance on specific pledges. It seems that none of the organizations to which it allocated money would have legal rights against UJA in the event of failure to pay the allocation, and, in any event, UJA, cognizant of the past history of collections, made due allowance for the fact that a certain percentage of the pledges would not be paid.

We hold that Polinger's pledge to UJA was a gratuitous promise. It had no legal consideration, and under the law of this State was unenforceable. The Orphans' Court for Montgomery County erred in allowing the claim for the unpaid balance of the subscription, and its order of 5 January 1979 is vacated with direction to enter an order disallowing the claim filed by UJA. . . .

In *Conrad, Hayes*, and *Maryland National Bank*, the courts used the doctrine of promissory estoppel to make a promise enforceable, even though it was not supported by consideration. The courts also sometimes use promissory estoppel to make an offer irrevocable. In Chapter 3, pages 156–158, we noted that an offeror's right to revoke an offer could be constrained by § 45 of the Restatement (Second), by an option contract, by a firm offer under UCC § 2–205, or by invoking promissory estoppel based on reliance by the offeree.

Almost any offer to enter a contract might induce the offeree to take some steps in reliance, perhaps to investigate whether to accept the offer or to prepare to do the work required of the offeree if she does accept. If the offeror revokes the offer before acceptance, that reliance will have been for naught. Most often, however, that kind of reliance will not be sufficient to lead a court to call the offer irrevocable, since the simple solution for the offeree is to accept the offer or negotiate an option contract. Injustice will not be the result if the offer is allowed to be withdrawn, since the offeree could protect herself.

In one specific set of circumstances, however, courts have been more willing to apply promissory estoppel to prevent revocation of an offer, at least temporarily: where contractors and their prospective subcontractors are bidding on projects. Typically, there is a project owner or its developer, who is seeking bids from general contractors, who are seeking bids from subcontractors (plumbers, electricians, paving contractors, etc.). Each general contractor uses the subcontractors' bids that it receives, to figure out its own bid to the owner. But it is very rare for a general contractor to contact a "sub" and accept the sub's bid before the general contractor submits its bid to the owner. (If a general contractor did so, it would be well advised to make its acceptance to the sub conditional on having its bid accepted by the owner.) And contractors rarely are required to list their sub on their bids to the owner, so it is often difficult to ascertain which sub's bid the contractor used in its bid. Thus, in the usual situation, no contract is formed between the general contractor and a sub unless and until the owner accepts the general contractor's bid and the general contractor accepts a sub's bid. (Remember that an acceptance must be communicated to the offeree and is usually effective upon dispatch, under the mailbox rule. See Chapter 3, § 2.6.1.)

So (you can see this problem coming) any of the subs could revoke its bid before the owner accepts the general contractor's bid and before the general contractor accepts the sub's bid. This revocation may leave the general contractor with only higher-priced bids to consider, so that the general contractor might need to seek additional bids or settle for less profit on the job.

Early courts wrestled with this problem, with differing results:

Example A: *James Baird Co. v. Gimbel Bros., Inc.*, 64 F.2d 344 (2d Cir.1933).

A general contractor was assembling a bid to construct a government building. A subcontractor sent its bid to supply linoleum to a number of bidding general contractors on December 24. The general contractor received the sub's bid on December 28. The sub realized its bid was based on an incorrect computation and notified the general contractor on December 28 that it was revoking its bid. The government awarded the general contractor the job on December 30. The general contractor formally accepted the sub's bid on January 2. When the sub refused to perform, the general contractor sued the sub for the additional cost of a substitute linoleum supplier.

Analysis: Judge Learned Hand, speaking for the court, held that the sub's initial bid was an offer to contract and, under traditional contract law, remained open only until accepted or withdrawn, despite the general contractor's reliance. Because the sub withdrew the offer before it was accepted, there was no contract. He also rejected two alternative theories of the case: unilateral contract and promissory estoppel. He held that the sub's bid was not an offer of a unilateral contract that the general contractor could accept by performing, *i.e.,* submitting the bid as part of the general bid. He also held that the theory of promissory estoppel was limited to cases involving charitable pledges. Judge Hand's opinion was widely criticized as an injustice without any relief, but it was also widely influential until *Drennan v. Star Paving*, in Example B.

Example B: *Drennan v. Star Paving*, 333 P.2d 757, 51 Cal.2d 409 (1958).

A paving subcontractor phoned the general contractor with a $7,131 bid for paving work on a school job (a common practice in some bidding settings). The bid was the lowest paving bid, so the general contractor used it in computing its bid for the school and listed the sub on its bid. The school awarded the contract to the general contractor. The next day, the general contractor stopped by the sub's office, only to be told that the sub had made a mistake in figuring its bid, which should have been $15,000. The general contractor sued the subcontractor to recover the $3,817 excess cost of using another subcontractor.

Analysis: Writing for the Supreme Court of California, Justice Roger Traynor implied a subsidiary promise, by the subcontractor, not to revoke the bid, under Restatement of Contracts § 90. The court reasoned:

> "When plaintiff [, a General Contractor,] used defendant's offer in computing his own bid, he bound himself to perform in reliance on defendant's terms. Though defendant did not bargain for the use of its bid neither did defendant make it idly, indifferent to whether it would be used or not. On the contrary it is reasonable to suppose that defendant submitted its bid to obtain the subcontract. It was bound to realize the substantial possibility that its bid would be the lowest, and that it would be included by plaintiff in his bid. It was to its own interest that the contractor be awarded the general contract; the lower the subcontract bid, the lower the general contractor's bid was likely to be and the greater its chance of acceptance and hence the greater defendant's chance of getting the paving subcontract. Defendant had reason not only to expect plaintiff to rely on its bid but to want him to. Clearly defendant had a stake in plaintiff's reliance on its bid. Given this interest and the fact that plaintiff is bound by his own bid, it is only fair that plaintiff should have at least an opportunity to accept defendant's bid after the general contract has been awarded to him."

Drennan, 51 Cal.2d at 415, 333 P.2d at 760. When the general contractor stopped by the sub's office to tell him they had been awarded the contract, he accepted the sub's bid while that bid was irrevocable, thereby forming a bilateral contract. The court granted damages to the general contractor. The *Drennan* decision has been very influential. Many states have adopted the reasoning used by Justice Traynor.

———————————

Since *Drennan* was decided in 1958, the doctrine of detrimental reliance has evolved. In 1979, the American Law Institute adopted the Restatement (Second) of Contracts, which responded to *Drennan* and sought to make detrimental reliance more applicable to construction bidding. **Restatement (Second) § 87(2)—which you should read now**—makes subcontractors' bids binding in some circumstances. Because the language of § 87(2) is not limited to construction bids, it could be applied to all offers, which could significantly change the law of offer and acceptance. However, few courts have adopted § 87(2), even in construction bid settings.

Many courts follow *Drennan* by applying § 90 to construction bidding, and some courts have considered arguments to apply § 90 more broadly to create liability for pre-contractual reliance in non-bidding cases. Extending promissory estoppel in that fashion could make an offeror potentially liable for any foreseeable expenses by an offeree considering whether to accept. However, aside from claims brought by potential franchisees induced by franchisors to incur expenses to prove themselves worthy contract partners, few such claims have succeeded. For further discussion, see E. Allan Farnsworth, *Contracts* § 3.26 & nn. 39–41 (4th ed. 2004).

As noted by the court in the next case, *Pavel Enterprises v. A.S. Johnson Co.*, 674 A.2d 521, 527–28 (Md. Ct. App. 1996), concerns linger about "the lack of symmetry of detrimental reliance in the bid process, in that subcontractors are bound to the general, but the general is not bound to the subcontractors. The result is that the general is free to bid shop,[13] bid chop,[14] and to encourage bid peddling,[15] to the detriment of the subcontractors. One commentator described the problems that these practices create:

> 'Bid shopping and peddling have long been recognized as unethical by construction trade organizations. These "unethical," but common practices have several detrimental results. First, as bid shopping becomes common within a particular trade, the subcontractors will pad their initial bids in order to make further reductions during post-award negotiations. This artificial inflation of subcontractor's offers makes the bid process less effective. Second, subcontractors who are forced into post-award negotiations with the general often must reduce their sub-bids in order to avoid losing the award. Thus, they will be faced with a Hobson's choice between doing the job at a loss or doing a less than adequate job. Third, bid shopping and peddling tend to increase the risk of loss of the time and money used in preparing a bid. This occurs because generals and subcontractors who engage in

---

[13] Bid shopping is the use of the lowest subcontractor's bid as a tool in negotiating lower bids from other subcontractors post-award.

[14] "The general contractor, having been awarded the prime contract, may pressure the subcontractor whose bid was used for a particular portion of the work in computing the overall bid on the prime contract to reduce the amount of the bid." [Michael L. Closen & Donald G. Weiland, *The Construction Industry Bidding Cases: Application of Traditional Contract, Promissory Estoppel, and Other Theories to the Relations Between General Contractors and Subcontractors*, 13 J. Marshall L. Rev. 565, 566 n.6 (1980).]

[15] An unscrupulous subcontractor can save estimating costs, and still get the job by not entering a bid or by entering an uncompetitive bid. After bid opening, this unscrupulous subcontractor, knowing the price of the low sub-bid, can then offer to perform the work for less money, precisely because the honest subcontractor has already paid for the estimate and included that cost in the original bid. This practice is called bid peddling.

these practices use, without expense, the bid estimates prepared by others. Fourth, it is often impossible for a general to obtain bids far enough in advance to have sufficient time to properly prepare his own bid because of the practice, common among many subcontractors, of holding sub-bids until the last possible moment in order to avoid pre-award bid shopping by the general. Fifth, many subcontractors refuse to submit bids for jobs on which they expect bid shopping. As a result, competition is reduced, and, consequently, construction prices are increased. Sixth, any price reductions gained through the use of post-award bid shopping by the general will be of no benefit to the awarding authority, to whom these price reductions would normally accrue as a result of open competition before the award of the prime contract. Free competition in an open market is therefore perverted because of the use of post-award bid shopping.'

[Comment, *Bid Shopping and Peddling in the Subcontract Construction Industry,* 18 UCLA L. Rev. 389, 394–96 (1970) (citations omitted)]. *See also* Note, *Once Around the Flag Pole: Construction Bidding and Contracts at Formation,* 39 N.Y.U. L. Rev. 816, 818 (1964) (bid mistake cases generally portray general contractor as victim, but market reality is that subs are usually in weaker negotiating position); Jay M. Feinman, *Promissory Estoppel and Judicial Method,* 97 Harv. L. Rev. 678, 707–08 (1984). These problems have caused at least one court to reject promissory estoppel in the contractor-subcontractor relationship. *Home Elec. Co. v. Underdown Heating & Air Conditioning Co.,* 86 N.C. App. 540, 358 S.E.2d 539 (1987). *See also* Note, *Construction Contracts—The Problem of Offer and Acceptance in the General Contractor-Subcontractor Relationship,* 37 U. Cinn. L. Rev. 798 (1980). But other courts, while aware of the limitations of promissory estoppel, have adopted it nonetheless. *See, e.g., Alaska Bussell Elec. Co. v. Vern Hickel Constr. Co.,* 688 P.2d 576 (Alaska 1984)."

The *Pavel* court engaged in the above discussion, in the process of deciding the following case:

Reading Critically: *Pavel Enterprises*

1. How is *Pavel* factually distinguishable from *Drennan*?

2. Aside from those factual differences, how did the *Pavel* court apply § 90 of the Restatement differently from the *Drennan* court? Would the *Drennan* court have reached a different result in this case? Which result seems more in keeping with § 90, and why?

3. Why does the bidding process pose these challenges to the traditional rules on acceptance and irrevocability?

Pavel Enterprises v. A.S. Johnson Co.

PAVEL ENTERPRISES, INC., Plaintiff-Appellant

v.

A.S. JOHNSON COMPANY, Defendant-Respondent

Court of Appeals of Maryland
674 A.2d 521 (Md. Ct. App. 1996)

KARWACKI, JUDGE.

In this case we are invited to adapt the "modern" contractual theory of detrimental reliance,[1] or promissory estoppel, to the relationship between general contractors and their subcontractors. Although the theory of detrimental reliance is available to general contractors, it is not applicable to the facts of this case. For that reason, and because there was no traditional bilateral contract formed, we shall affirm the trial court.

I

[The facts can be summarized as follows:

- The National Institute of Health (NIH) solicited bids for renovation of Building 30.

- Pavel Enterprise Inc. (Pavel) solicited sub-bids from various mechanical subcontractors.

- July 27, 1993: A.S. Johnson Co. (Johnson) responded to Pavel with a scope of work proposal.

- Aug. 5, 1993: Johnson verbally submitted $898,000 quote to Pavel for the HVAC components, using used Johnson's sub-bid in computing its own bid.

---

[1] We prefer to use the phrase detrimental reliance, rather than the traditional nomenclature of "promissory estoppel," because we believe it more clearly expresses the concept intended. . . . *See* Note, *The "Firm Offer" Problem in Construction Bids and the Need for Promissory Estoppel*, 10 Wm & Mary L. Rev. 212, 214 n.17 (1968) [hereinafter, *"The Firm Offer Problem"*].

- On the same day, Pavel submitted a bid of $1,585,000 to NIH.

- On the same day, NIH opened Pavel's bid.

- In mid-August, NIH disqualified the low bidder and notified Pavel that its bid would be formally accepted in September.

- Aug. 26, 1993: Pavel met with James Kick, at Johnson, to discuss the project.

- On the same day, Pavel faxed all of the mechanical subcontractors, asking them to re-submit their bids without any work on electrical controls. Earlier that day, Johnson had said that it would not object to not working on the electrical controls.

- Aug. 30, 1993: Pavel informed NIH that Johnson was to be the mechanical subcontractor.

- Sept. 1, 1993: Pavel mailed and faxed a letter to Johnson formally accepting Johnson's bid.

- Sept. 1 & 2, 1993: Johnson notified Pavel by telephone and letter that its bid contained an error, and therefore, Johnson wished to withdraw its bid. Pavel responded that it refused to allow Johnson to withdraw its bid.

- On Sept. 28, 1993: NIH formally awarded Pavel the construction contract.

- Pavel subsequently found a substitute subcontractor for $930,000.

- Pavel brought suit for damages for $32,000, the difference between the price for the substitute subcontractor and Johnson's original bid.]

The case was heard by the trial court without the aid of a jury. The trial court made several findings of fact, which we summarize:

1. PEI relied upon Johnson's sub-bid in making its bid for the entire project;

2. The fact that PEI was not the low bidder, but was awarded the project only after the apparent low bidder was disqualified, takes this case out of the ordinary;

3. Prior to NIH awarding PEI the contract on September 28, Johnson, on September 2, withdrew its bid; and

4. PEI's letter to all potential mechanical subcontractors, dated August 26, 1993, indicates that there was no definite agreement between PEI and Johnson, and that PEI was not relying upon Johnson's bid.

The trial court analyzed the case under both a traditional contract theory and under a detrimental reliance theory. PEI was unable to satisfy the trial judge that under either theory that a contractual relationship had been formed.

PEI appealed to the Court of Special Appeals, raising both traditional offer and acceptance theory, and "promissory estoppel." Before our intermediate appellate court considered the case, we issued a writ of certiorari on our own motion.

. . . .

III

. . . .

The trial court held, and we agree, that Johnson's sub-bid was an offer to contract and that it was sufficiently clear and definite. We must then determine if PEI made a timely and valid acceptance of that offer and thus created a traditional bilateral contract, or in the absence of a valid acceptance, if PEI's detrimental reliance served to bind Johnson to its sub-bid. We examine each of these alternatives, beginning with traditional contract theory.

A. Traditional Bilateral Contract

The trial judge found that there was not a traditional contract binding Johnson to PEI. A review of the record and the trial judge's findings make it clear that this was a close question. On appeal however, our job is to assure that the trial judge's findings were not clearly erroneous. Maryland Rule 8–131(c). This is an easier task.

The trial judge rejected PEI's claim of bilateral contract for two separate reasons: 1) that there was no meeting of the minds; and 2) that the offer was withdrawn prior to acceptance. Both need not be proper bases for decision; if either of these two theories is not clearly erroneous, we must affirm.

There is substantial evidence in the record to support the judge's conclusion that there was no meeting of the minds. PEI's letter of August 26, to all potential mechanical subcontractors, reproduced *supra*, indicates, as the trial judge found, that PEI and Johnson "did not have a definite, certain meeting of the minds on a certain price for a certain quantity of goods . . . ." Because this reason is itself sufficient to sustain the trial judge's finding that no contract was formed, we affirm.

Alternatively, we hold, that the evidence permitted the trial judge to find that Johnson revoked its offer prior to PEI's final acceptance. We review the relevant chronology. Johnson made its offer, in the form of a sub-bid, on August 5. On September 1, PEI accepted. Johnson withdrew its offer by letter dated September 2. On September 28, NIH awarded the contract to PEI. Thus, PEI's apparent acceptance came one day *prior* to Johnson's withdrawal.

The trial court found, however, "that before there was ever a final agreement reached with the contract awarding authorities, that Johnson made it clear to [PEI] that they were not going to continue to rely on their earlier submitted bid." Implicit in this finding is the judge's understanding of the contract. Johnson's sub-bid constituted an offer of a contingent contract. PEI accepted that offer subject to the condition precedent of PEI's receipt of the award of the contract from NIH. Prior to the occurrence of the condition precedent, Johnson was free to withdraw. *See* 2 *Williston on Contracts* § 6:14 (4th ed.). On September 2, Johnson exercised that right to revoke.[23] The trial judge's finding that withdrawal proceeded valid final acceptance is therefore logical and supported by substantial evidence in the record. It was not clearly erroneous, so we shall affirm.

B. Detrimental Reliance

PEI's alternative theory of the case is that PEI's detrimental reliance binds Johnson to its bid. . . .

. . . .

. . . [W]e now clarify that Maryland courts are to apply the test of the *Restatement (Second) of Contracts* § 90(1) (1979), which we have recast as a four-part test:

1.   a clear and definite promise;

2.   where the promisor has a reasonable expectation that the offer will induce action or forbearance on the part of the promisee;

3.   which does induce actual and reasonable action or forbearance by the promisee; and

---

[23] We have also considered the possibility that Johnson's offer was not to enter into a contingent contract. This is unlikely because there is no incentive for a general contractor to accept a non-contingent contract prior to contract award but it would bind the general to purchase the subcontractor's services even if the general did not receive the award. Moreover, PEI's September 1 letter clearly "accepted" Johnson's offer subject to the award from NIH. If John-son's bid was for a non-contingent contract, PEI's response substantially varied the offer and was therefore a counter-offer, not an acceptance. *Post v. Gillespie*, 219 Md. 378, 385–86, 149 A.2d 391, 395–96 (1959); 2 *Williston on Contracts* § 6:13 (4th ed.).

4.   causes a detriment which can only be avoided by the enforcement of the promise.

. . . .

In a construction bidding case, where the general contractor seeks to bind the subcontractor to the sub-bid offered, the general must first prove that the subcontractor's sub-bid constituted an offer to perform a job at a given price. . . . In the instant case, the trial judge found that the sub-bid was sufficiently clear and definite to constitute an offer, and his finding was not clearly erroneous.

Second, the general must prove that the subcontractor reasonably expected that the general contractor would rely upon the offer. The subcontractor's expectation that the general contractor will rely upon the sub-bid may dissipate through time.

In this case, the trial court correctly inquired into Johnson's belief that the bid remained open, and that consequently PEI was not relying on the Johnson bid. The judge found that due to the time lapse between bid opening and award, "it would be unreasonable for offers to continue." This is supported by the substantial evidence. James Kick testified that although he knew of his bid mistake, he did not bother to notify PEI because J.J. Kirlin, Inc., and not PEI, was the apparent low bidder. The trial court's finding that Johnson's reasonable expectation had dissipated in the span of a month is not clearly erroneous.

As to the third element, a general contractor must prove that he actually and reasonably relied on the subcontractor's sub-bid. We decline to provide a checklist of potential methods of proving this reliance, but we will make several observations. First, a showing by the subcontractor, that the general contractor engaged in "bid shopping," or actively encouraged "bid chopping," or "bid peddling" is strong evidence that the general did *not* rely on the sub-bid. Second, prompt notice by the general contractor to the subcontractor that the general intends to use the sub on the job, is weighty evidence that the general *did* rely on the bid.[31] Third, if a sub-bid is so low that a reasonably prudent general contractor would not rely upon it, the trier of fact may infer that the general contractor did not in fact rely upon the erroneous bid.

In this case, the trial judge did not make a specific finding that PEI failed to prove its reasonable reliance upon Johnson's sub-bid. We must assume, however, that it was his conclusion based on his statement that "the parties did not have a definite, certain meeting of the minds on a certain price for a certain quantity of

---

[31] Prompt notice and acceptance also significantly dispels the possibility of bid shopping, bid chopping, and bid peddling.

goods and wanted to renegotiate . . . ." The August 26, 1993, fax from PEI to all prospective mechanical subcontractors, is evidence supporting this conclusion. Although the finding that PEI did not rely on Johnson's bid was indisputably a close call, it was not clearly erroneous.

Finally, as to the fourth prima facie element, the trial court, and not a jury, must determine that binding the subcontractor is necessary to prevent injustice. This element is to be enforced as required by common law equity courts—the general contractor must have "clean hands." This requirement includes, as did the previous element, that the general did not engage in bid shopping, chopping or peddling, but also requires the further determination that justice compels the result. The fourth factor was not specifically mentioned by the trial judge, but we may infer that he did not find this case to merit an equitable remedy.

Because there was sufficient evidence in the record to support the trial judge's conclusion that PEI had not proven its case for detrimental reliance, we must, and hereby do, affirm the trial court's ruling.

IV

In conclusion, we emphasize that there are different ways to prove that a contractual relationship exists between a general contractor and its subcontractors. Traditional bilateral contract theory is one. Detrimental reliance can be another. However, under the evidence in this case, the trial judge was not clearly erroneous in deciding that recovery by the general contractor was not justified under either theory.

Judgment affirmed, with costs.

Practice Pointer: Bid Bonds

A project owner or the general contractor receiving offers in the form of bids can protect itself by requiring a "bid bond" from each bidding contractor, thereby guaranteeing itself compensation if a contractor withdraws. A bidding contractor obtains a bid bond by paying a fee to a bonding company and entering into a contract that requires the bonding company to pay an agreed sum to the beneficiary (the project owner or the general contractor) if the bidding contractor does not "honor the bid" (keep it available). (*See* Chapter 11 for more on such "intended third-party beneficiaries.") The agreed sum may be a percentage of the bid or the amount by which a substitute contract exceeds the withdrawn bid. Usually the party buying the bid bond tries to pass on the cost of the bid bond in its bid, but in a highly competitive bidding situation, that may not be possible. If the bonding company has to pay the beneficiary, it may or may not have the contractual right to recover its costs from the party that purchased the bond, over and above the fee already paid.

Food for Thought: Making Bids Irrevocable

So far, the courts have been unable to fashion a solution to the bid-revocability problem that evenly balances the power between the contractor and the subcontractor. Abuses and unfairness accompany each solution. Is the current state of the law as good as it gets, or can it be improved upon? Where do you think that the arc of the law on this issue will or should proceed in the coming decades? Although sophisticated parties can protect themselves in some ways, less sophisticated and less powerful parties are more likely to suffer losses under some of the current rules. Which fact situations trigger this vulnerability, and what changes in the law would ameliorate this problem?

Food for Thought: The Future of Promissory Estoppel

Promissory estoppel was initially formulated to permit enforcement of promises in a limited set of circumstances where bargain would likely be absent, primarily promises within families and promises to donate to charities. It has since been extended to apply in a wide variety of commercial contexts, though some question whether such an extension is appropriate. At the very least, invoking promissory estoppel in a commercial context requires answering the question whether it would be reasonable, under the circumstances, for a party to rely on a promise that could have been, but was not, made as part of a "bargain" (that is, made without consideration).

Promissory estoppel continues to be the focus of a substantial amount of scholarly attention, with authors addressing the nature of the doctrine (*e.g., Is it about reliance or is it about promising?*), the appropriate extent of application for the doctrine (*e.g., Should it be used to enforce a promise that otherwise would have to be in writing? Should it be used to compensate for pre-contractual reliance?*), the appropriate damage award (*Should courts limit damages to less than full contract damages?*), and the extent to which courts actually enforce promises on the basis of promissory estoppel.

While questions clearly remain regarding its present application and future scope as a rationale for enforcing promises, promissory estoppel remains one of the most important and dynamic doctrines in the field of contract enforcement.

For discussion of these and other issues related to promissory estoppel, see, e.g., Marco Jimenez, *The Many Faces of Promissory Estoppel: An Empirical Analysis Under the Restatement (Second) of Contracts*, 57 UCLA L. Rev. 669 (2010); Juliet P. Kostritsky, *The Rise and Fall of Promissory Estoppel or Is Promissory Estoppel Really as Unsuccessful as Scholars Say It Is: A New Look at the Data*, 37 Wake Forest L. Rev. 531 (2002); Robert A. Hillman, *Questioning the "New Consensus" on Promissory Estoppel: An Empirical and Theoretical Study*, 98 Colum. L. Rev. 580 (1998); Charles L. Knapp, *Rescuing Reliance: The Perils of Promissory Estoppel*, 49 Hastings L.J. 1191 (1998); Jay M. Feinman, *The Last Promissory Estoppel Article*, 61 Fordham L. Rev. 303 (1992); Edward Yorio & Steve Thel, *The Promissory Basis of Section 90*, 101 Yale L. J. 111 (1991); Daniel A. Farber & John H. Matheson, *Beyond Promissory Estoppel: Contract Law and the "Invisible Handshake,"* 52 U. Chi. L. Rev. 903 (1985).

§ 3. Promise for Benefit Already Received ("Promissory Restitution")

So far you have seen that promises may be enforced because they have consideration or because, despite the absence of consideration, the promise induced reliance by the promisee in circumstances found to justify enforcement of the promise under promissory estoppel. What if the promise was made not to induce action by the promisee, but to reward or compensate the promisee for actions already taken or expenses already incurred? By definition, benefits already conferred by the promisee cannot constitute consideration. Although courts sometimes use the expression "past consideration," that is an oxymoron; to *be* consideration, the benefit *must* be in the future. Yet courts have sometimes concluded that some promises of this kind are worthy of enforcement. The problem was finding a consistent and coherent rationale for doing so.

Reading Critically: *Mills*, *Drake*, and *Webb*

1. Why does each court enforce, or fail to enforce, the promise made?

2. On what authority does each court rely in reaching its result?

3. What role does moral obligation play in each court's analysis? Why isn't moral obligation enough to make a promise enforceable? What else is necessary to warrant enforcement?

Mills v. Wyman

DANIEL MILLS, Plaintiff-Appellant

v.

SETH WYMAN, Defendant-Appellee

Supreme Judicial Court of Massachusetts
20 Mass. 207 (1825)

This was an action of *assumpsit* brought to recover a compensation for the board, nursing, &c., of Levi Wyman, son of the defendant, from the 5th to the 20th of February, 1821. The plaintiff then lived at Hartford, in Connecticut; the defendant, at Shrewsbury, in this county. Levi Wyman, at the time when the services were rendered, was about 25 years of age, and had long ceased to be a member of his father's family. He was on his return from a voyage at sea, and being suddenly taken sick at Hartford, and being poor and in distress, was relieved by the plaintiff in the manner and to the extent above stated. On the 24th of February, after all the expenses

What's That?

"Assumpsit" is one of the old English and American forms of action or writs, used to bring suit for recovery of damages for non-performance of a promise or contract. In England, assumpsit was abolished in the 19th century along with other common law forms of action. In the United States, assumpsit became obsolete in the federal courts with adoption of the Federal Rules of Civil Procedure in 1938. Most but not all states have also ceased to use the old forms of action, replacing them with claims for breach of contract.

had been incurred, the defendant wrote a letter to the plaintiff, promising to pay him such expenses. There was no consideration for this promise, except what grew out of the relation which subsisted between Levi Wyman and the defendant, and Howe J., before whom the cause was tried in the Court of Common Pleas, thinking this not sufficient to support the action, directed a nonsuit. To this direction the plaintiff filed exceptions.

PARKER C. J.

General rules of law established for the protection and security of honest and fair-minded men, who may inconsiderately make promises without any equivalent, will sometimes screen men of a different character from engagements which they are bound in *foro conscientiæ* to perform. This is a defect inherent in all human systems of legislation. The rule that a mere verbal promise, without any consideration, cannot be enforced by action, is universal in its application, and cannot be departed from to suit particular cases in which a refusal to perform such a promise may be disgraceful.

The promise declared on in this case appears to have been made without any legal consideration. The kindness and services towards the sick son of the defendant were not bestowed at his request. The son was in no respect under the care of the defendant. He was twenty-five years old, and had long left his father's family. On his return from a foreign country, he fell sick among strangers, and the plaintiff acted the part of the good Samaritan, giving him shelter and comfort until he died. The defendant, his father, on being informed of this event, influenced by a transient feeling of gratitude, promises in writing to pay the plaintiff for the expenses he had incurred. But he has determined to break this promise, and is willing to have his case appear on record as a strong example of particular injustice sometimes necessarily resulting from the operation of general rules.

Take Note

In this case and the next, notice that a statement of facts precedes the court's opinion, and the judge in each case launches into a discourse on the legal rule without any attempt to summarize the facts. That pattern was especially common in the early years of state and federal court reports, when private individuals were the publishers of court opinions, adding their own summaries of the facts and the arguments of counsel. Although not part of the court's opinion, the reporter's statement of facts is often critical to understanding early cases, but, as we will see, it is not always correct.

The first official court reporter was named in Massachusetts in 1804. *Mills v. Wyman* was published by Octavius Pickering, the official reporter in that state from 1822 to 1839; for that reason, the original citation to the opinion was 3 Pick. 207.

For more information about the history of court reporting in the United States, see Erwin C. Surrency, *Law Reports in the United States*, 25 Am. J. Leg. History 48 (1981); Thomas Young, *A Look at American Law Reporting in the 19th Century*, 68 Law Libr. J. 294 (1975).

It is said a moral obligation is a sufficient consideration to support an express promise; and some authorities lay down the rule thus broadly; but upon examination of the cases we are satisfied that the universality of the rule cannot be supported, and that there must have been some pre-existing obligation, which has become inoperative by positive law, to form a basis for an effective promise. The cases of debts barred by the statute of limitations, of debts incurred by infants, of debts of bankrupts, are generally put for illustration of the rule. Express promises founded on such pre-existing equitable obligations may be enforced; there is a good consideration for them; they merely remove an impediment created by law to the recovery of debts honestly due, but which public policy protects the debtors from being compelled to pay. In all these cases there was originally a *quid pro quo;* and according to the principles of natural justice the party receiving ought to pay; but the legislature has said he shall not be coerced; then comes the promise to pay the debt that is barred, the promise of the man to pay the debt of the infant, of the discharged bankrupt to restore to his creditor what by the law he had lost. In all these cases there is a moral obligation founded upon an antecedent valuable consideration. These promises therefore have a sound legal basis. They are not promises to pay something for nothing; not naked pacts; but the voluntary revival or creation of obligation which before existed in natural law, but which had been dispensed with, not for the benefit of the party obliged solely, but principally for the public convenience.

If moral obligation, in its fullest sense, is a good substratum for an express promise, it is not easy to perceive why it is not equally good to support an implied promise. What a man ought to do, generally he ought to be made to do, whether he promise or refuse. But the law of society has left most of such obligations to the *interior* forum, as the tribunal of conscience has been aptly called. Is there not a moral obligation upon every son who has become affluent by means of the education and advantages bestowed upon him by his father, to relieve that father from pecuniary embarrassment, to promote his comfort and happiness, and even to share with him his riches, if thereby he will

Think About It!

Why should a gratuitous promise to pay an old unenforceable debt be itself enforceable, but not a promise to pay for other past benefits, even though the promisor wants to offer payment?

be made happy? And yet such a son may, with impunity, leave such a father in any degree of penury above that which will expose the community in which he dwells, to the danger of being obliged to preserve him from absolute want. Is not a wealthy father under strong moral obligation to advance the interest of an obedient, well disposed son, to furnish him with the means of acquiring and maintaining a becoming rank in life, to rescue him from the horrors of debt incurred by misfortune? Yet the law will uphold him in any degree of parsimony, short of that which would reduce his son to the necessity of seeking public charity.

Without doubt there are great interests of society which justify withholding the coercive arm of the law from these duties of imperfect obligation, as they are called; imperfect, not because they are less binding upon the conscience than those which are called perfect, but because the wisdom of the social law does not impose sanctions upon them.

A deliberate promise, in writing, made freely and without any mistake, one which may lead the party to whom it is made into contracts and expenses, cannot be broken without a violation of moral duty. But if there was nothing paid or promised for it, the law, perhaps wisely, leaves the execution of it to the conscience of him who makes it. It is only when the party making the promise gains something, or he to whom it is made loses something, that the law gives the promise validity. And in the case of the promise of the adult to pay the debt of the infant, of the debtor discharged by the statute of limitations or bankruptcy, the principle is preserved by looking back to the origin of the transaction, where an equivalent is to be found. An exact equivalent is not required by the law; for there being a consideration, the parties are left to estimate its value: though here the courts of equity will step in to relieve from gross inadequacy between the consideration and the promise.

These principles are deduced from the general current of decided cases upon the subject, as well as from the known maxims of the common law. The general position, that moral obligation is a sufficient consideration for an express promise, is to be limited in its application, to cases where at some time or other a good or valuable consideration has existed.

A legal obligation is always a sufficient consideration to support either an express or an implied promise; such as an infant's debt for necessaries, or a father's promise to pay for the support and education of his minor children. But when the child shall have attained to manhood, and shall have become his own agent in the world's business, the debts he incurs, whatever may be their nature, create no obligation upon the father; and it seems to follow, that his promise founded upon such a debt has no legally binding force.

Think About It!

"Necessaries" are things that are indispensable to living, for example, food, shelter, and clothing, at least at subsistence levels. Why would a father's promise to pay for his minor child's necessaries or education have "a sufficient consideration" but his promise to pay for his adult child's debts would not?

. . . .

. . . [T]here seems to be no case in which it was nakedly decided, that a promise to pay the debt of a son of full age, not living with his father, though the debt were incurred by sickness which ended in the death of the son, without a previous request by the father proved or presumed, could be enforced by action.

. . . .

For the foregoing reasons we are all of opinion that the nonsuit directed by the Court of Common Pleas was right, and that judgment be entered thereon for costs for the defendant.

Behind the Scenes

As discovered by Professor Geoffrey Watson (*see* Geoffrey Watson, *In the Tribunal of Conscience: Mills v. Wyman Reconsidered*, 71 Tul. L. Rev. 1749 (1997)), the letter written by Seth Wyman to Daniel Mills, never quoted by the court or the reporter who wrote the statement of facts, read as follows:

> Dear Sir
>
> I received a line from you relating to my Son Levi's sickness and requesting me to come up and see him, but as the going is very bad I cannot come up at the present, but I wish you to take all possible care of him and if you cannot have him at your house I wish you to remove him to some convenient place and if he cannot satisfy you for it I will.
>
> I want that you should write me again immediately how he does and greatly oblige your most obedient servant
>
> Seth Wyman Feb. 24th 1821

By the time the letter arrived, Levi was apparently leaving or had already left Mills' establishment. (Despite Justice Parker's statement that Mills cared for Levi until the latter's death, Levi survived his illness and moved to Springfield, Massachusetts.) Mills wrote back to Wyman, informing him of Levi's departure and seeking payment of a bill of $16 for lodging and $6 for the doctor's fee, but heard nothing back from Wyman and filed suit in 1824.

As also reported by Professor Watson, "while Levi outlived the Supreme Judicial Court's pronouncement of his death, he did not outgrow his habit of getting into trouble." In 1829, a legal guardian was appointed for Levi, " 'who spends and wastes his estate by excessive drinking and idleness.' "

What effect do these facts have on your evaluation of the correctness of the *Mills* opinion?

Drake v. Bell

JOSEPHINE C. DRAKE, Plaintiff

v.

EDWARD C. BELL, Defendant

Supreme Court, Kings County, New York
55 N.Y.S. 945 (Sup. Ct. 1899)

The plaintiff made a contract with a mechanic [Russell] to repair her vacant house for $210. By his own mistake he went into the vacant house of the defendant next door and repaired it instead. He discovered his mistake after the work was done. He then informed the defendant. The work was done without the defendant's knowledge. It was all of an irremovable character like plastering and painting. The defendant looked over the work, and disclaimed responsibility, but finally had the contractor reduce his bill to $194 and orally promised to pay him that sum. The work was of that value. The defendant's house which had stood vacant for lack of repair was benefited by such work to at least the value thereof, and by reason thereof was immediately let and became salable. The contractor filed a mechanic's lien against the house and the defendant as owner for the said work after the said promise, and assigned his claim against the defendant and his lien to the plaintiff. This is an action to foreclose the lien, etc.

What's That?

A "mechanic's lien" is a legal interest in property that is given to a person who has improved or repaired the property, providing security to the service provider. The right to file a mechanic's lien is granted by statute.

Take Note!

The defendant (Bell) made a promise to the contractor (Russell) to pay for the services mistakenly rendered on Bell's house. So why is Drake, Bell's neighbor (and the person who actually made a contract with Russell to repair *her* house) the plaintiff in the lawsuit? Note the second to last sentence in the case description above: contractor Russell "assigned his claim against the defendant" to Drake. That means Russell transferred to Drake any rights he had to payment. Why would he do that? A note after the case may explain his actions.

GAYNOR, J.

The defendant was under no legal obligation to pay for the work. Nor is there any question of acceptance as of a chattel, for there was

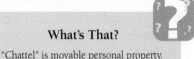

What's That?

"Chattel" is movable personal property.

nothing capable of being rejected or taken away. Did, then, his promise bind him? Lord Mansfield with his keen perception, broad mind, and aversion to alleged rules of law resting on misunderstood or inadvertent remarks of judges, instead of on foundations of reason and justice, said in Hawkes v. Saunders, Cowp. 289, that:

"Where a man is under a moral obligation, which no court of law or equity can enforce, and promises, the honesty and rectitude of the thing is a consideration."

Buller, J., said in the same case:

"If such a question were stripped of all authority it would be resolved by inquiring whether law were a rule of justice, or whether it was something that acts in direct contradiction to justice, conscience and equity."

If the rule so plainly stated by Lord Mansfield, that a moral obligation was of itself sufficient consideration for a subsequent promise, had been followed, the sole question in each case would be whether there was a moral obligation to

Who's That?

William Murray, 1st Earl of Mansfield, was Lord Chief Justice of England and Wales from 1756 to 1788, after a political career that included election to Parliament and service as Solicitor General and Attorney General. As Lord Chief Justice, Mansfield reformed court procedures and led efforts to modernize the commercial law of England. "The law relating to shipping, commercial transactions, and insurance was practically remade by Mansfield." Frederick Edwin Smith Birkenhead, *Fourteen English Judges* 186 (1926). Mansfield is perhaps best known as the author of Somerset's Case, 20 State Tr. 1 (1772), in which he condemned the practice of slavery in words that reverberated in English and later American law, though the case itself ruled more narrowly that a master could not by force remove a slave from the country. *See Oxford Dictionary of National Biography*.

support the promise. That would resolve the present case for the plaintiff. But it has not been always followed. I have examined the cases on the subject in England and here from the beginning. They are irreconcilable, and it would be no use to cite and review them.

But notwithstanding much stray remark by judges may be cited to the contrary, it seems to me that a promise to pay for antecedent value received by the promisor from the promisee binds, although there was never any obligation to pay which could be enforced. Why not? Such a case is not one of mere moral obligation resting on no consideration received, if there can be any such abstract moral obligation. The case is one of moral obligation created by a past valuable consideration derived from another. For instance, a promise after coming of age to pay a debt incurred during infancy, and which cannot be enforced, or by a woman after coming discovert to pay a like debt incurred while covert, is binding. . . . Goulding v. Davidson, 26 N. Y. 604. On the other hand, a subsequent promise by a father to pay for the care of his adult son while sick among strangers, or of a son to pay for like care of his father, is not binding. Mills v. Wyman, 3 Pick. 207 . . . . The distinction is that in the former class of cases there was past valuable consideration to the promisor, while in the latter not. The promise in the one class is not a naked pact, for it is not to pay something for nothing; while in the other class just that is the case.

. . . [O]nly a subsequent promise which revives an obligation formerly enforceable either at law or in equity, but which has grown extinct, is binding. "But a mere moral or conscientious obligation, unconnected with any prior legal or equitable claim, is not enough," is the rule reduced from the said note in a number of cases (as in Ehle v. Judson, 24 Wend. 97). And yet the same opinions say that the moral obligation "to pay a debt contracted during infancy or coverture, and the like," is sufficient to support a subsequent promise; as though in such cases the moral obligation rested on a prior legal or equitable claim, which it does not. Such is true though of a promise to pay a debt barred by the statute of limitations or by a discharge in bankruptcy, which all of the cases hold to be binding.

What's That?

The court refers to a promise by a woman to pay a debt incurred "while covert." In the 19th century and earlier, a married woman was considered under coverture, meaning she was unable to enter contracts without the consent of her husband and could not be independently liable for a debt incurred. The court here refers to a woman who, perhaps through divorce or the death of her husband, ceases to be under coverture ("discovert") and thereafter affirms a debt incurred while she was still married.

The actual decisions most worthy of attention (not feeling bound by mere general remarks of judges and their citation) make two classes. In one of them the promise is held binding because based on a former obligation enforceable at law or in equity, which obligation it revives; in the other because the promisor though never under any such obligation nevertheless received an antecedent valuable consideration. Hence the rule seems to be that a subsequent promise founded on a former enforceable obligation, or on value previously had from the promisee, is binding.

. . . .

Chancellor Kent does not confine the validity of such promises to cases of past legal obligation, but extends it to cases of the existence of a prior consideration. He says it is an unsettled point whether a moral obligation is of itself "a sufficient consideration for a promise, except in those cases in which a prior legal obligation or consideration had once existed." 2 Kent, Comm. 465.

I do not pretend that this question is free from doubt, but to use the words of Chief Justice Marshall, "I do not think that law ought to be separated from justice where it is at most doubtful" (Hoffman v. Porter, 2 Brock. 159, Fed. Cas. No. 6,577), and that has no doubt influenced me some in reaching a conclusion.

Judgment for the plaintiff.

Behind the Scenes

When *Drake v. Bell* was appealed, a few additional facts were revealed. First, during the negotiations between the carpenter (Russell) and the defendant homeowner (Bell), Bell promised that, if the plaintiff homeowner (Drake) would pay Russell the agreed sum of $194, he (Bell) would pay her that amount. Second, the appellate court noted the trial court's finding "that some of the said repairs consisted of windows and some articles which were not made part of the freehold, and could have been taken away by the said Russell, but by the defendant's said promise the said Russell was induced to leave everything there, and he did so." What effect should these facts have had on the trial court's analysis?

Webb v. McGowin

JOE WEBB, Plaintiff-Appellant

v.

N. FLOYD and JOSEPH F. McGOWIN,
as executors of the estate of J. Greeley McGowin, deceased,
Defendants-Appellees

Court of Appeals of Alabama
<u>168 So. 196 (Ala. Ct. App. 1935)</u>

BRICKEN, PRESIDING JUDGE.

This action is in assumpsit. The complaint as originally filed was amended. The demurrers to the complaint as amended were sustained, and because of this adverse ruling by the court the plaintiff took a non-suit, and the assignment of errors on this appeal are predicated upon said action or ruling of the court.

A fair statement of the case presenting the questions for decision is set out in appellant's brief, which we adopt.

"On the 3d day of August, 1925, appellant while in the employ of the W.T. Smith Lumber Company, a corporation, and acting within the scope of his employment, was engaged in clearing the upper floor of mill No. 2 of the company. While so engaged he was in the act of dropping a pine block from the upper floor of the mill to the ground below; this being the usual and ordinary way of clearing the floor, and it being the duty of the plaintiff in the course of his employment to so drop it. The block weighed about 75 pounds.

"As appellant was in the act of dropping the block to the ground below, he was on the edge of the upper floor of the mill. As he started to turn the block loose so that it would drop to the ground, he saw J. Greeley McGowin, testator of the defendants, on the ground below and directly under where the block would have fallen had appellant turned it loose. Had he turned it loose it would have struck McGowin with such force as to have caused him serious bodily harm or death. Appellant could have remained safely on the upper floor of the mill by turning the block loose and allowing it to drop, but had he done this the block would have fallen on McGowin and caused him serious injuries or death. The only safe and reasonable way to prevent this was for appellant to hold to the block and divert its direction in falling from the place where McGowin was standing and the only safe way to divert it so as to prevent its coming into contact with McGowin was for appellant to fall with it to the ground below. Appellant did this, and by holding to the block and falling with it to the ground below, he diverted the course of its fall in such way that McGowin was not injured. In thus preventing the injuries to McGowin appellant himself received serious bodily injuries, resulting in his right leg being broken, the heel of his right foot torn off and his right arm broken. He was badly crippled for life and rendered unable to do physical or mental labor.

"On September 1, 1925, in consideration of appellant having prevented him from sustaining death or serious bodily harm and in consideration of the injuries appellant had received, McGowin agreed with him to care for and maintain him for the remainder of appellant's life at the rate of $15 every two weeks from the time he sustained his injuries to and during the remainder of appellant's life; it being agreed that McGowin would pay this sum to appellant for his maintenance. Under the agreement McGowin paid or caused to be paid to appellant the sum so agreed on up until McGowin's death on January 1, 1934. After his death the payments were continued to and including January 27, 1934, at which time they were discontinued. Thereupon plaintiff brought suit to recover the unpaid installments accruing up to the time of the bringing of the suit.

"The material averments of the different counts of the original complaint and the amended complaint are predicated upon the foregoing statement of facts."

In other words, the complaint as amended averred in substance: (1) That on August 3, 1925, appellant saved J. Greeley McGowin, appellee's testator, from death or grievous bodily harm; (2) that in doing so appellant sustained bodily injury crippling him for life; (3) that in consideration of the services rendered and the injuries received by appellant, McGowin agreed to care for him the remainder of appellant's life, the amount to be paid being $15 every two weeks; (4) that McGowin complied with this agreement until he died on January 1, 1934, and the payments were kept up to January 27, 1934, after which they were discontinued.

The action was for the unpaid installments accruing after January 27, 1934, to the time of the suit.

The principal grounds of demurrer to the original and amended complaint are: (1) It states no cause of action; (2) its averments show the contract was without consideration; (3) it fails to allege that McGowin had, at or before the services were rendered, agreed to pay appellant for them; (4) the contract declared on is void under the statute of frauds.

The averments of the complaint show that appellant saved McGowin from death or grievous bodily harm. This was a material benefit to him of infinitely more value than any financial aid he could have received. Receiving this benefit, McGowin became morally bound to compensate appellant for the services rendered. Recognizing his moral obligation, he expressly agreed to pay appellant as alleged in the complaint and complied with this agreement up to the time of his death; a period of more than 8 years.

Had McGowin been accidentally poisoned and a physician, without his knowledge or request, had administered an antidote, thus saving his life, a subsequent promise by McGowin to pay the physician would have been valid. Likewise, McGowin's agreement as disclosed by the complaint to compensate appellant for saving him from death or grievous bodily injury is valid and enforceable.

Think About It!

Is the rule for which the court cites *Pittsburg Vitrified Paving* consistent with your understanding of the meaning of "consideration"? If not, how do you explain the statement?

Where the promisee cares for, improves, and preserves the property of the promisor, though done without his request, it is sufficient consideration for the promisor's subsequent agreement to pay for the service, because of the material benefit received. Pittsburg Vitrified Paving & Building Brick Co. v. Cerebus Oil Co., 79 Kan. 603, 100 P. 631; Edson v. Poppe, 24 S.D. 466, 124 N.W. 441,26 L.R.A. (N.S.) 534; Drake v. Bell, 26 Misc. 237, 55 N.Y.S. 945.

In Boothe v. Fitzpatrick, 36 Vt. 681, the court held that a promise by defendant to pay for the past keeping of a bull which had escaped from defendant's premises and been cared for by plaintiff was valid, although there was no previous request, because the subsequent promise obviated that objection; it being equivalent to a previous request. On the same principle, had the promisee saved the promisor's life or his body from grievous harm, his subsequent promise to pay for the services rendered would have been valid. Such service would have been far more material than caring for his bull. Any holding that saving a man from death or grievous bodily harm is not a material benefit sufficient to uphold a subsequent promise to pay for the service, necessarily rests on the assumption that saving life and preservation of the body from harm have only a sentimental value. The converse of this is true. Life and preservation of the body have material, pecuniary values, measurable in dollars and cents. Because of this, physicians practice their profession charging for services rendered in saving life and curing the body of its ills, and surgeons perform operations. The same is true as to the law of negligence, authorizing the assessment of damages in personal injury cases based upon the extent of the injuries, earnings, and life expectancies of those injured.

In the business of life insurance, the value of a man's life is measured in dollars and cents according to his expectancy, the soundness of his body, and his ability to pay premiums. The same is true as to health and accident insurance.

It follows that if, as alleged in the complaint, appellant saved J. Greeley McGowin from death or grievous bodily harm, and McGowin subsequently agreed to pay him for the service rendered, it became a valid and enforceable contract.

It is well settled that a moral obligation is a sufficient consideration to support a subsequent promise to pay where the promisor has received a material benefit, although there was no original duty or liability resting on the promisor. Lycoming County v. Union County, 15 Pa. 166, 53 Am.Dec. 575, 579, 580; Ferguson v. Harris, 39 S.C. 323, 17 S.E. 782, 39 Am.St.Rep. 731, 734; Muir v. Kane, 55 Wash. 131, 104 P. 153, 26 L.R.A. (N.S.) 519, 19 Ann.Cas. 1180; State ex rel. Bayer v. Funk, 105 Or. 134, 199 P. 592, 209 P. 113, 25 A.L.R. 625, 634; Hawkes v. Saunders, 1 Cowp. 290; In re Sutch's Estate, 201 Pa. 305, 50 A. 943; Edson v. Poppe, 24 S.D. 466, 124 N.W. 441, 26 L.R.A. (N.S.) 534; Park Falls State Bank v. Fordyce, 206 Wis. 628, 238 N.W. 516, 79 A.L.R. 1339; Baker v. Gregory, 28 Ala. 544, 65 Am. Dec. 366. In the case of State ex rel. Bayer v. Funk, supra, the court held that a moral obligation is a sufficient consideration to support an executory promise where the promisor has received an actual pecuniary or material benefit for which he subsequently expressly promised to pay.

The case at bar is clearly distinguishable from that class of cases where the consideration is a mere moral obligation or conscientious duty unconnected with receipt by promisor of benefits of a material or pecuniary nature. Park Falls State Bank v. Fordyce, supra. Here the promisor received a material benefit constituting a valid consideration for his promise.

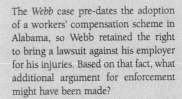

Think About It!

The *Webb* case pre-dates the adoption of a workers' compensation scheme in Alabama, so Webb retained the right to bring a lawsuit against his employer for his injuries. Based on that fact, what additional argument for enforcement might have been made?

Some authorities hold that, for a moral obligation to support a subsequent promise to pay, there must have existed a prior legal or equitable obligation, which for some reason had become unenforceable, but for which the promisor was still morally bound. This rule, however, is subject to qualification in those cases where the promisor, having received a material benefit from the promisee, is morally bound to compensate him for the services rendered and in consideration of this obligation promises to pay. In such cases the subsequent promise to pay is an affirmance or ratification of the services rendered carrying with it the presumption that a previous request for the service was made. McMorris v. Herndon, 2 Bailey (S.C.) 56, 21 Am.Dec. 515; Chadwick v. Knox, 31 N.H. 226, 64 Am.Dec. 329; Kenan v. Holloway, 16 Ala. 53, 50 Am.Dec. 162; Ross v. Pearson, 21 Ala. 473.

Under the decisions above cited, McGowin's express promise to pay appellant for the services rendered was an affirmance or ratification of what appellant had done raising the presumption that the services had been rendered at McGowin's request.

The averments of the complaint show that in saving McGowin from death or grievous bodily harm, appellant was crippled for life. This was part of the consideration of the contract declared on. McGowin was benefited. Appellant was injured. Benefit to the promisor or injury to the promisee is a sufficient legal consideration for the promisor's agreement to pay. Fisher v. Bartlett, 8 Greenl. (Me.) 122, 22 Am.Dec. 225; State ex rel. Bayer v. Funk, supra.

Under the averments of the complaint the services rendered by appellant were not gratuitous. The agreement of McGowin to pay and the acceptance of payment by appellant conclusively shows the contrary. . . .

Think About It!

What does the court mean by saying the services were "not gratuitous"? Does that conclusion seem correct on the facts? Why should it matter if the services were gratuitous?

From what has been said, we are of the opinion that the court below erred in the ruling complained of; that is to say, in sustaining the demurrer, and for this error the case is reversed and remanded.

Reversed and remanded.

SAMFORD, JUDGE (concurring).

The questions involved in this case are not free from doubt, and perhaps the strict letter of the rule, as stated by judges, though not always in accord, would bar a recovery by plaintiff, but following the principle announced by Chief Justice Marshall in Hoffman v. Porter, Fed.Cas. No. 6,577, 2 Brock. 156, 159, where he says, "I do not think that law ought to be separated from justice, where it is at most doubtful," I concur in the conclusions reached by the court.

———————

Consistent with decisions described in *Mills* and *Drake*, the first and second Restatement of Contracts each contain a provision allowing for enforcement of promises to pay antecedent debts (that is, debts incurred in the past) that would be enforceable but for the effect of the statute of limitations. Another provision allowed enforcement of a promise to perform all or part of an antecedent but voidable contract that was not voided before the new promise was made. For example, minors (individu-

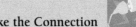

Make the Connection

The rights and liabilities of minors entering contracts are addressed in Chapter 6, page 357.

als under the age of the majority) generally can incur only "voidable" duties, so they may disavow contracts entered before they turn that age. The Restatement provisions make enforceable the promise of an adult to pay debts incurred under a voidable contract created when under the age of the majority.

Both the first and second Restatements also contain provisions making enforceable an express promise to pay all or part of an indebtedness discharged or dischargeable in bankruptcy, but federal bankruptcy law has added additional criteria that must be satisfied before such a promise will be considered binding. For example, the agreement must be made before the debt was discharged and must be filed with the court, the debtor may rescind the agreement as late as 60 days after it is so filed, and the debtor's attorney (or the court if the debtor is not represented by an attorney) must inform the debtor of the consequences of making the agreement and determine that the agreement is in the best interests of the debtor and will not cause the debtor undue hardship. *See* 11 U.S.C. § 523(c).

Think About It!

Does the existence of the protections in the bankruptcy law suggest that the "promise for material benefit received" rule has gone too far? Are similar protections warranted in circumstances other than promises to pay debts discharged in bankruptcy? Do the bankruptcy law developments support or undercut the traditional rule that consideration is required to enforce a promise?

Although by 1930 there were a significant number of cases like *Drake v. Bell* that had also found a right to recover based on "moral obligation" arising from a promise to pay for past benefits, the drafters of the first Restatement did not include any provisions reflecting those developments. Additional cases continued to accumulate, however, and the concept was added to the Restatement (Second).

Reading Critically: Restatement (Second) Provisions and Illustrations

As reflected in *Drake* and *Webb*, court decisions whether to enforce a promise made in recognition of a past benefit invoked judgments whether the past benefit created a "moral obligation" that helped support the subsequent promise. The drafters of Restatement (Second) rejected moral obligation as the justification for enforcement and sought to establish an alternative rationale by reference to the concepts underlying restitutionary recovery restoring the value of a benefit conferred. As you will see in the next section of this chapter, the courts have limited the circumstances in which restitution will be ordered solely on the basis of a benefit received, no promise having been made. Section 86 tries to articulate when adding a promise to the benefit received should be enough to warrant ordering the restitution promised. Because the Restatement analysis joins "promise" to "restitution" as the basis for relief, the doctrine described in the cases and § 86 is sometimes called "promissory restitution."

Section 86 says a promise for benefit received should be enforced "to the extent necessary to prevent injustice," a standard as difficult to apply precisely as one grounded in "moral obligation." The drafters of the Restatement provisions provided some guidance in the explanations accompanying the standard. **Read Restatement (Second) § 86 and its comments and illustrations.** Consider why each promise is or is not enforced, and whether you agree with the outcomes. What general principles can you identify to help you decide subsequent cases? You will have an opportunity to apply these principles to problems at the end of the chapter.

Food for Thought

Promissory restitution is used relatively infrequently in reported cases, perhaps because few circumstances of this kind are worth litigating and the results are relatively uncertain. The materials in this section are therefore most valuable not as a guide to important decisional rules, but instead as a study of how courts adapt legal principles to reach just results when precedent is not adequate to that task. They may also serve as a kind of cautionary tale about parties' inability to predict enforceability under some circumstances and their need to plan more effectively to reach desired results.

Some states have addressed the problem of promises after-the-fact through statutory rules rather than (or in addition to) through common law change. New York, for example, has enacted the following provision:

> A promise in writing and signed by the promisor or by his agent shall not be denied effect as a valid contractual obligation on the ground that consideration for the promise is past or executed, if the consideration is expressed in the writing and is proved to have been given or performed and would be a valid consideration but for the time when it was given or performed.

N.Y. Gen. Oblig. Law § 5–1105 (McKinney 2001). Would you recommend adoption of the New York rule in a jurisdiction still relying on the common law rule? What are the advantages and disadvantages of this statutory approach?

§ 4. Liability for Restitution

All the kinds of liability considered so far—contract, promissory estoppel, and promissory restitution—have been based on the existence of a promise. This section considers liability when there is no promise to enforce. The basis of liability here is "restitution," the claim that the defendant obtained a benefit from the plaintiff and should be required to make restitution to the plaintiff (that is, restore the benefit to its rightful owner, the plaintiff). It shares with promissory restitution the existence of a benefit conferred but is missing the other central component—a promise to compensate made after-the-fact. Unlike the other doctrines at the core of contract law, restitution as a source of liability is *not* grounded in the idea of enforcing a voluntary obligation undertaken by a party, either through making a contract or through making some other kind of promise.

Why is restitution included at all in a course focused on the enforcement of promises? While it is articulated as a separate ground for liability, restitution has historical roots in contract law, and many restitution cases arise out of failed contractual relationships. Restitution operates at the borders of contract doctrine, and understanding the nature of restitutionary liability can help define the outer limits of contract law as well. This section touches only on the aspects of the law of restitution that intersect most closely with contract theory.

Legal responsibility for restitution begins with the notion that "[a] person who is unjustly enriched at the expense of another is subject to liability in restitution." Restatement (Third) of Restitution & Unjust Enrichment § 1 (2011). "Unjust enrichment" is not precisely defined; the Reporter's comment a. refers to the "inherent flexibility of the concept" and the fact that the concept "will not, by itself, yield a reliable indication of the nature and scope of the liability imposed." To determine the limits of restitutionary liability, the critical question to be answered is: When *is* it unjust to retain a benefit conferred by another? The cases that follow—and the other 70 sections of the Restatement (Third) of Restitution—are designed to help answer that question.

Note first that restitution or unjust enrichment is *not* an appropriate ground for relief if an enforceable contract exists. Entering an enforceable contract represents a choice to define the parties' relationship according to the terms of that contract. Any adjustment to the contractual relationship arising from nonperformance should be made by bringing an action to enforce the contract, not by seeking restitution on the basis of unjust enrichment (*see* Restatement (Third) of Restitution and Unjust Enrichment § 2(z)), though restitution may be applicable as a *measure* of the compensation owed by the breaching party (see the Introduction to Contract Remedies, page 272).

But what if an agreement-in-fact of the parties turns out to be unenforceable for some reason—because, for example, one party lacks capacity, or the parties made a mutual mistake of fact about basic assumptions underlying the contract, or the contract has to be in writing to be enforceable, or the terms are too unclear for a party to enforce them? If one party or both of the parties has already performed some of the agreement's obligations, neither party can successfully claim breach of contract to be compensated for the work already performed, but restitution is available as a basis for relief to allow them each to be restored to the "status quo ante" by returning the benefits conferred on the other. There was good reason for the benefits to be conferred at the time, as part of contract performance, and probably no good reason for them to be retained when the contract failed. *See* Restatement (Third) of Restitution and Unjust Enrichment §§ 31–34. You will see the application of this rationale for restitution reappear repeatedly in this course in materials dealing with defenses against contract enforceability and excuses from contract performance (in Chapters 6 and 9). When contracts are avoided or become unenforceable for such reasons, restitution is available as a ground for liability to assist the parties in reaching a just allocation of the burdens that result.

If no contract exists, however, but an individual confers a benefit on another without being asked, when, if ever, should that individual be compensated, when no promise to pay was ever made? The rest of this section explores some answers to this question.

Take Note!

The courts use a sometimes confusing array of different terms to discuss restitution, including quasi-contract, quantum meruit, and implied-in-law contract, as well as restitution and unjust enrichment. Although they are often used interchangeably, there may be subtle differences among them, and they may be used differently (and inconsistently) by different courts.

The term "implied-in-law contract" indicates that there was no actual (in fact) agreement of the parties; instead, the law imposes a contract-like liability as a matter of law. "Quasi-contract" is similar. "Quasi" means "seemingly," "almost but not quite," or "having some resemblance." "Quasi-contract" thus carries with it the flavor of liability that is "almost but not quite" a contract; it is *not* based in agreement of the parties. As you read the cases below, ask yourself why the courts might have called this form of liability "quasi-contract" or "implied-in-law contract." What about the doctrine makes the relationship of the parties "seem" like a contract in some ways?

Quantum meruit is a Latin phrase meaning, literally, "as much as he has deserved." The term is sometimes used to describe a restitutionary measure of relief (the party gets not what was promised, since nothing was promised, but instead what he deserves based on the benefit conferred). It is also sometimes used to describe the basis for liability. Similarly, *quantum valebant* (literally, "as much as they were worth"), is used both to describe liability for goods delivered to another and to describe the measure of restitutionary relief for such delivery.

As you read the cases below, note the terminology used by each court.

Reading Critically: *Nursing Care Services,* *Mitchell,* and *Bloomgarden*

1. What kind of benefit was conferred in each set of circumstances? What motivated the plaintiff to act and thereby confer the benefit? What was the relationship of the parties when the benefit was conferred? What role, if any, do all those facts play in the court's judgment and opinion?

2. What persuades the court to conclude that restitution is or is not warranted (that is, what makes retention of the benefit just or unjust)?

3. For each case, what rules does the court articulate or follow regarding the availability of restitution? You will find statements of when restitution is appropriate as well as exceptions or limitations to recovery, and even exceptions to the exceptions.

Nursing Care Services, Inc. v. Dobos

NURSING CARE SERVICES, INC., Plaintiff-Appellant

v.

MARY DOBOS, Defendant-Appellee

District Court of Appeal of Florida
380 So. 2d 516 (Fla. Dist. Ct. App. 1980)

HURLEY, JUDGE.

Plaintiff, Nursing Care Services, Inc., appeals from that part of a final judgment which disallowed compensation for certain nursing care services. Our review of the record reveals substantial uncontradicted testimony supporting plaintiff's theory of recovery and thus we remand for entry of an amended final judgment.

Mary Dobos, the defendant, was admitted to Boca Raton Community Hospital with an abdominal aneurysm. Her condition was sufficiently serious to cause her doctor to order around-the-clock nursing care. The hospital implemented this order by calling upon the plaintiff which provides individualized nursing services.

Mrs. Dobos received nursing care which in retrospect can be divided into three periods: (1) two weeks of in-hospital care; (2) forty-eight hour post-release care; and (3) two weeks of at-home care. The second period of care (the forty-eight hour post-release care) was removed as an issue at trial when Mrs. Dobos conceded that she or her daughter authorized that period of care. The total bill for all three periods came to $3,723.90; neither the reasonableness of the fee, the competency of the nurses, nor the necessity for the services was contested at trial.

The gist of the defense was that Mrs. Dobos never signed a written contract nor orally agreed to be liable for the nursing services. Testifying about the in-hospital care, she said, "Dr. Rosen did all the work. I don't know what he done (sic), and he says, I needed a nurse." It is undisputed that Mrs. Dobos was mentally alert during her at-home recuperation period. Asked if she ever tried to fire the nurses or dispense with their care, she replied, "I didn't. I didn't know who I thought, maybe if they insist, the doctors insist so much, I thought the Medicare would take care of it, or whatever. I don't know."

After a non-jury trial, the court granted judgment for the plaintiff in the sum of $248.00, the cost of the forty-eight hour post-release care. It declined to allow compensation for the first and third periods of care, saying,

> ". . . [T]here certainly was a service rendered, but based on the total surrounding circumstances, I don't think there is sufficient communications and dealings with Mrs. Dobos to make sure that she knew that she would be responsible for those services rendered. . . ."

We concur in the trial court's determination that the plaintiff failed to prove an express contract or a contract implied in fact. It is our view, however, that the uncontradicted testimony provided by plaintiff and defendant alike, clearly established a contract implied in law which entitles the plaintiff to recover.

Contracts implied in law, or as they are more commonly called "quasi contracts", are obligations imposed by law on grounds of justice and equity. Their purpose is to prevent unjust enrichment. Unlike express contracts or contracts implied in fact, quasi contracts do not rest upon the assent of the contracting parties. See generally, 28 Fla.Jur., Restitution and Implied Contracts.

One of the most common areas in which recovery on a contract implied in law is allowed is that of work performed or services rendered. The rationale is that the defendant would be unjustly enriched at the expense of the plaintiff if she were allowed to escape payment for services rendered or work performed. There is, however, an important limitation. Ordinarily liability is imposed to pay for services rendered by another only when the person for whose benefit they were rendered requested the services or knowingly and voluntarily accepted their benefits. Yeats v. Moody, 128 Fla. 658, 175 So. 719 (1937); Strano v. Carr & Carr, Inc., 97 Fla. 150, 119 So. 864 (1929); Taylor v. Thompson, 359 So.2d 14 (Fla. 1st DCA 1978); and Tobin & Tobin Insurance Agency, Inc. v. Zeskind, 315 So.2d 518 (Fla. 3d DCA 1975).

The law's concern that needless services not be foisted upon the unsuspecting has led to the formulation of the "officious intermeddler doctrine." It holds that where a person performs labor for another without the latter's request or implied consent, however beneficial such labor may be, he cannot recover therefor. Tipper v. Great Lakes Chemical Company, 281 So.2d 10 (Fla.1973). A notable exception to this rule, however, is that of emergency aid:

A person who has supplied things or services to another, although acting without the other's knowledge or consent, is entitled to restitution therefor from the other if he acted unofficiously and with intent to charge therefore, and the things or services were necessary to prevent the other from suffering serious bodily harm or pain, and the person supplying them had no reason to know that the other would not consent to receiving them, if mentally competent, and it was impossible for the other to give consent or, because of extreme youth or mental impairment, the other's consent would have been immaterial. 66 Am.Jur.2d, Restitution and Implied Contract, § 23.

In the case at bar it is unclear whether Mrs. Dobos, during the period of in-hospital care, understood or intended that compensation be paid. Her condition was grave. She had been placed in the hospital's intensive care unit and thereafter had tubes and other medical equipment attached to her body which necessitated special attention. She was alone, unable to cope and without family assistance. It is worthy of note that at no point during the litigation was there any question as to the propriety of the professional judgment that the patient required special nursing care. To the contrary, the record demonstrates that the in-hospital nursing care was essential to Mrs. Dobos' health and safety. Given these circumstances it would be unconscionable to deny the plaintiff recovery for services which fall squarely within the emergency aid exception. Tipper v. Great Lakes Chemical Company, supra.

The third period of care is less difficult. It is unquestioned that during the at-home recuperation, Mrs. Dobos was fully aware of her circumstances and readily accepted the benefits conferred. Given such facts, we believe the rule set down in Symon v. J. Rolfe Davis, Inc., 245 So.2d 278, 279 (Fla. 4th DCA 1971) must govern:

> It is well settled that where services are rendered by one person for another which are knowingly and voluntarily accepted, the law presumes that such services are given and received in expectation of being paid for, and will imply a promise to pay what they are reasonably worth.

A patient's unannounced misconception that the cost of accepted services will be paid by an insurer or Medicare does not absolve her of responsibility to bear the cost of the services.

As a postscript we note that Mrs. Dobos' home recuperation was interrupted by her readmission to the hospital with an apparent heart attack. In this age of burgeoning malpractice actions it is not idle conjecture to ponder what her legal position might have been had the plaintiff unilaterally terminated its services at a time of vital need. To its credit, it did not and therefore it is entitled to just compensation. Accordingly, we remand the cause to the trial court with instructions to enter an amended final judgment for the plaintiff in the sum of $3,723.90 plus interest and court costs.

It is so ordered.

ANSTEAD and LETTS, JJ., concur.

Mitchell v. Moore

THOMAS MITCHELL, Plaintiff-Appellee

v.

WILLIAM MOORE, III, Defendant-Appellant

Superior Court of Pennsylvania
729 A.2d 1200 (Pa. Super. Ct. 1999)

CIRILLO, PRESIDENT JUDGE EMERITUS:

William Moore, III (Moore), appeals from the order entered in the Court of Common Pleas of Chester County denying his post-trial motions and entering judgment on a jury verdict of $130,000.00 awarded to Appellee, Thomas Mitchell (Mitchell). We affirm in part and reverse in part.

Thomas Mitchell and William Moore first met in 1980; the two men quickly developed a romantic relationship. Moore resided in Elverson, Pennsylvania and Mitchell in South Carolina. In the spring of 1981, Mitchell accepted Moore's invitation to spend his "off season"[1] at Moore's Chester County farm. By 1985, Mitchell had permanently moved to Elverson, where he resided at Moore's farm without paying rent, worked a full-time job with a company located in Lancaster, Pennsylvania, and assisted Moore in maintaining his house and farm. Among other things, Mitchell took care of the farm animals, which included aiding in the breeding of sheep and birds. In 1990, Mitchell enrolled at Penn State University for graduate studies. As a result of his academic schedule, he was unable to run the sheep and bird businesses or maintain the farm. Soon thereafter, the parties' relationship soured; Mitchell moved out of Moore's residence in June of 1994.

In 1995, Mitchell brought an action against Moore sounding in fraud, *quantum meruit*, and implied contract. Specifically, Mitchell sought compensation, in the form of restitution, for the services he rendered to Moore throughout the thirteen years the two men lived together on the farm. In his complaint, Mitchell

---

[1] Mitchell was a tobacco broker in South Carolina. He did not work during the winter months.

alleged that Moore had: promised him compensation for his services rendered to maintain and operate his farm; agreed to compensate him for his help in running an antique cooperative (co-op) that Mitchell [Moore?] had purchased; promised him future compensation and the devise of property in a will and codicil; and failed to compensate him for monetary contributions he had made towards Moore's purchase of real estate on Amelia Island, Florida.

In response to Mitchell's action, Moore filed preliminary objections seeking a demurrer. The court granted the objections in part and denied the objections in part, striking Mitchell's claim of fraud for lack of specificity, *see* Pa.R.C.P. 1019(b), but granting Mitchell leave to file an amended complaint. Mitchell filed an amended complaint, now including only counts for *quantum meruit*/unjust enrichment and implied contract. Moore filed a counterclaim seeking $139,300.00 representing reasonable rent for the 139 months Mitchell lived on his farm rent-free and as compensation for various utility and telephone bills, taxes, car payments, and other miscellaneous expenses paid by Moore on Mitchell's behalf.

After a jury trial, a verdict was rendered in favor of Mitchell on the basis of unjust enrichment and against Moore on the counterclaim. Moore filed post-trial motions seeking, among other remedies, a judgment in his favor; these motions were denied by the trial court. Moore filed a timely appeal, raising the following issues for our consideration:

(1) Whether the verdict was against the weight of the evidence in that:

    (a) appellee-plaintiff failed to produce evidence of an express contract;

    (b) appellee failed to prove an implied contract;

    (c) the nature of the relationship rebutted the presumption of a promise to pay and therefore, appellee failed to prove unjust enrichment; and

    (d) appellee failed to prove that appellant wrongfully secured or passively received benefits that would be unconscionable for him to retain?

. . .

In reviewing a denial of judgment notwithstanding the verdict, an appellate court must decide whether there was sufficient evidence to sustain the verdict; our scope of review is very narrow: all evidence and all reasonable inferences drawn therefrom must be considered in the light most favorable to the verdict winner. *Johnson v. Hyundai Motor America*, 698 A.2d 631 (Pa.Super.1997). Judgment notwithstanding the verdict can be entered only if the movant is entitled to judgment as a matter of law or if evidence is such that no two reasonable minds could disagree that the outcome should have been rendered in favor of the movant. *Jara v. Rexworks, Inc.*, 718 A.2d 788 (Pa.Super.1998) (citations omitted). We will reverse a trial court's grant or denial of a judgment notwithstanding the verdict only when we find an abuse of discretion or an error of law that controlled the outcome of the case. *Id.*, citing *Jones v. Constantino*, 429 Pa.Super. 73, 631 A.2d 1289 (1993).

Mitchell's claim for restitution for services rendered lies not upon an express contract or written agreement, but, rather, upon the equitable theory of unjust enrichment. Further, we may not make a finding of unjust enrichment, as has the trial court, where a written or express contract between parties exists. *See First Wisconsin Trust Co. v. Strausser*, 439 Pa.Super. 192, 653 A.2d 688 (1995). We, therefore, confine our review to whether the court properly found Mitchell entitled to compensation under the legal theory of unjust enrichment.

"Unjust enrichment" is essentially an equitable doctrine. *Styer v. Hugo*, 422 Pa.Super. 262, 619 A.2d 347 (1993), *aff'd*, 535 Pa. 610, 637 A.2d 276 (1994). Where unjust enrichment is found, the law implies a contract, which requires the defendant to pay to the plaintiff the value of the benefit conferred. *Schenck v. K.E. David, Ltd.*, 446 Pa.Super. 94, 666 A.2d 327 (1995). The elements necessary to prove unjust enrichment are:

> (1) benefits conferred on defendant by plaintiff; (2) appreciation of such benefits by defendant; and (3) acceptance and retention of such benefits under such circumstances that it would be inequitable for defendant to retain the benefit without payment of value. The application of the doctrine depends on the particular factual circumstances of the case at issue. **In determining if the doctrine applies, our focus is not on the intention of the parties, but rather on whether the defendant has been unjustly enriched.**[*]

Id., 666 A.2d at 328. *Accord Torchia v. Torchia*, 346 Pa.Super. 229, 499 A.2d 581, 582 (1985) ("[t]o sustain a claim of unjust enrichment, a claimant must show that the party against whom recovery is sought either 'wrongfully secured or passively received a benefit that it would be unconscionable for her to retain.' ").

In its opinion, the trial court clearly determines that a benefit was conferred upon Moore as a result of the extensive labor and services Mitchell provided him on his farm and in his home. The critical question, with regard to whether as a result of this benefit Moore was unjustly enriched, was answered in the positive by the court as follows:

---

[*] [Authors' Note: The bold font appears in the case.]

Assuming the jury established that a benefit had been conferred by Plaintiff [Mitchell] and received by Defendant [Moore], they only had to determine that Defendant's acceptance of these benefits and failure to compensate Plaintiff resulted in an unconscionable bargain. The jury was aware that Defendant [sic] moved hundreds of miles away from his job, house, friends and family to a different region of the country where he took on a new job and did work on Defendant's [Moore's] farm. It is not unreasonable to suggest that the jury believed Plaintiff [Mitchell] in that he made that life-altering change based on something besides his desire to develop his relationship with Defendant [Moore]. Given this potential scenario, it is likely that the jury could have found that the lack of compensation Plaintiff [Mitchell] received amounted to an unconscionable bargain and therefore, Defendant's [Moore's] unjust enrichment.

"It has been said, an intention to pay for work done will be assumed, except in the case of parent and child. Where, however, it is apparent that the parties, though not so related by blood, in reality bore like connection to each other, the implication does not arise." *Brown v. McCurdy*, 278 Pa. 19, 22, 122 A. 169, 170 (1923). While it has been held that the presumption of gratuitous services does not automatically arise in a daughter-in-law/mother-in-law context, where a claimant has become "part of the family" the contrary is true. *Id.*

Both parties concur that when Mitchell moved into Moore's home on a full-time basis, Moore paid many of Mitchell's bills, including car payments, VISA and Sears card charges, and phone bills. Moreover, Moore claims that Mitchell became part of his own family; Mitchell, himself, admits to having celebrated all the major holidays with Moore's immediate family and received gifts from them on special occasions.

Think About It!

On what basis does the court here decide that Mitchell's actions were gratuitous? What facts, if proved, might lead to the opposite result? Courts have suggested that relevant factors include the extent of services provided, the nature of the relationship between the provider and the recipient of the services, and whether the provider ever sought compensation or appeared to be acting out of a sense of moral obligation.

In *Brown, supra,* the law and facts centered around the issue of whether a presumption of payment, based upon an express contract to pay for services rendered by a daughter-in-law to her mother-in-law, had been successfully established based upon the evidence at trial. The court demanded strict proof of an express contract in order to overcome any presumption that the services were gratuitous. Although the instant case is not based upon either an express contract or written agreement, we find the principles espoused in *Brown* equally applicable, namely, in order to prove that the defendant in the present case had been **unjustly** enriched by plaintiff's actions and services, there must be some convincing evidence establishing that plaintiff's services were not gratuitous.

We first note that Mitchell had complete access to a large farm house where he lived rent-free and virtually unencumbered by any utility expenses. The nature and amount of benefits that plaintiff received from living at Moore's farm rebuts any presumption that the benefit conferred upon Moore was unjust. In fact, the advantages plaintiff obtained were compensation enough for all the work he offered to do on the farm; further, Mitchell derived an obvious personal benefit by living with the defendant, his partner for thirteen years, at his farm.

Having found no evidence which would imply that Moore's services were anything but gratuitous, we cannot agree with the trial court that a theory of unjust enrichment has been proved. While defendant indisputably bequeathed plaintiff his farm (found within the provisions of two wills that were later supplanted by a codicil), the gift was exactly that, an intention to reward the plaintiff through a testamentary provision. . . .

Such bequest is not equivalent to a finding that the defendant intended to compensate the plaintiff for his services and that upon failure to remit such monies the defendant became unjustly enriched. *See Meehan v. Cheltenham Township*, 410 Pa. 446, 450, 189 A.2d 593, 596 (1963) ("[t]he mere fact that one party benefits from the act of another is not of itself sufficient to justify restitution."); *see also Torchia, supra* (to sustain a claim of unjust enrichment, the claimant must show that the party against whom recovery is sought either wrongfully secured or passively received a benefit that it would be unconscionable for the party to retain).

Furthermore, the defendant testified that the plaintiff himself suggested that he move in with the defendant because he could not afford to rent an apartment on his own at the time. He, as well as the defendant, thought such potential living arrangement would give the two men more time to foster their relationship. In fact, upon learning of plaintiff's potential job opportunity in nearby Lancaster, Pennsylvania, the defendant anticipated that the two parties would be able to grow closer in a permanent "live-in" situation—another indication that there existed no expectation of payment for plaintiff's voluntary work on the defendant's farm. Moreover, plaintiff testified that he never asked the defendant for compensation for his services and that the defendant never told him he would pay him for his help around the house and the farm.

To solidify the fact that the plaintiff's actions were gratuitous services rendered during a "close, personal" relationship, the plaintiff testified at trial that after he moved in and began to help around the farm, the defendant told him he "did a great job, that he appreciated what I [plaintiff] did, and it was for—it made the house much better looking, it kept it stable, and that **we were building a future together and some day it would all be worth it for me [plaintiff].**" While Mitchell would characterize the nature of the parties' relationship as a type of business venture between partners, the evidence at trial indicates a very different aspect of their lives. As Mitchell, himself, testified, he had a "romantic or sexual aspect to his relationship with Dr. Moore." Furthermore, the parties conducted themselves around the home like parties in a loving relationship; they shared household chores, cooked dinners for each other, bestowed gifts upon one another, attended events together, and shared holidays and special occasions with Moore's family. Most potent, however, is the following language used in a letter written by Mitchell to Moore sometime in 1993, "The time I have given you breaking my back with the house and grounds were just that, **a gift to our relationship.**" Moore testified that Mitchell was "his lover and we were living together as partners, and I felt like anything I could do for him, you know, gave me pleasure." To find restitution (compensation) proper for services performed in such a relationship, we would curtail the freedom associated in forming new personal bonds based upon the important facet of mutual dependence.

After a review of the record in this case, including the pivotal testimony of both Mitchell and Moore, we cannot find that the defendant benefited unjustly from plaintiff's services. While we do not attempt to characterize the services rendered in all unmarried couple's relationships as gratuitous, we do believe that such a presumption exists and that in order to recover restitution for services rendered, the presumption must be rebutted by clear and convincing evidence. The basis of this presumption rests on the fact that services provided by plaintiff to the defendant are not of the type for which one would normally expect to be paid, nor did they confer upon the defendant a benefit that is unconscionable for him to retain without making restitution to the plaintiff. *See Feingold, supra* (Beck, J., concurring).

The circumstances of this case do not require the law to imply a contract in order to avoid an injustice. *See Feingold*, 654 A.2d at 1095 (Beck, J., concurring) ("unlike true contracts, quasi-contracts are not based on the apparent intention of the parties to undertake the performances in question, nor are they promises. They are obligations created by law for reasons of justice."), *citing Schott v. Westinghouse Elec. Corp*, 436 Pa. 279, 290–93, 259 A.2d 443, 449 (1969). Accordingly, we reverse the trial court's verdict in favor of plaintiff; the verdict should have been rendered in defendant's favor. Jara, supra. We affirm the court's denial of defendant's counterclaim on the same basis. The various benefits plaintiff received over the parties' thirteen year relationship were also gratuitous in nature; the plaintiff did not "wrongfully secure a benefit that is unconscionable for him to retain." *Torchia, supra.*

Order reversed in part and affirmed in part. Jurisdiction relinquished.

Reading Critically: Restatement of Restitution & Unjust Enrichment

The Restatement of Restitution was adopted in 1937 and remained in effect until 2011. An effort to write a second Restatement of Restitution was suspended in 1985 after two drafts were circulated, though the drafts were sometimes cited for their persuasive value. The Restatement (Third) of Restitution & Unjust Enrichment was finally adopted in 2011. While the draft of the Restatement (Second) attempted to articulate a set of precise and detailed rules, similar to those identified in the cases in this section, the provisions of Restatement (Third) largely rely on general statements of liability, with the comments and illustrations offering additional guidance. Which approach—specifying rules for decision or leaving determination to the discretion of the decision-maker—do you think is the preferable approach? Why?

For a sampling of provisions, **read Restatement (Third) of Restitution & Unjust Enrichment § 20 (protection of another's life or health), § 21 (protection of another's property), § 22 (performance of another's duty) and § 28 (unmarried cohabitants). How would the previous case, *Mitchell v. Moore*, be decided under § 28?**

Bloomgarden v. Coyer

HENRY S. BLOOMGARDEN, Plaintiff-Appellant

v.

CHARLES B. COYER et al., Defendants-Appellees

United States Court of Appeals, District of Columbia Circuit
479 F.2d 201 (D.C. Cir. 1973)

SPOTTSWOOD W. ROBINSON, III, CIRCUIT JUDGE:

Who's That?

Spottswood W. Robinson, III (1916–1998) was a Richmond, Virginia, civil rights lawyer who, as a private attorney and under the auspices of the NAACP Legal Defense and Educational Fund, litigated many significant civil rights cases, including one of the cases that led to the United States Supreme Court's 1954 decision in *Brown v. Board of Education*. He challenged discrimination in interstate transportation when he represented Irene Morgan who, more than a decade before Rosa Parks, refused to move to the "colored" seats at the back of an interstate bus, taking her case all the way to the U.S. Supreme Court. He worked on cases challenging racial restrictions in property transactions and in the use of public parks, in addition to his work challenging racial inequality in public schools. He was a faculty member at Howard University Law School from his graduation in 1939 until he joined the NAACP in 1948 and, in 1960, he returned to Howard as the law school dean. Judge Robinson "credited the law school with instilling the notion of social responsibility. 'One of the things that was drilled into my head was . . . "This legal education that you're getting is not just for you, it was for everybody. So when you leave here, you want to put it to good use." ' "*

Judge Robinson was the first African-American to serve on the United States District Court for the District of Columbia (1963–1966) and on the United States Court of Appeals for the District of Columbia

---

* *Spottswood Robinson, U.S. Appeals Judge, Dies in Virginia at 82*, Jet, (Nov. 2, 1998).

> Circuit (1966–1992). He was the author of 411 opinions on the Court of
> Appeals, "each one both a beginning and an end to the issues discussed
> . . . , a one-stop dissertation on the law in a particular area—past,
> present, and future . . . . I am told [reported Patricia Wald, who suc-
> ceeded Judge Robinson as Chief Judge of the D.C. Circuit] many law
> students found his opinions more than adequate substitute for a bar
> review cram course."*

This appeal follows appellant Bloomgarden's unsuccessful effort in the
District Court to recover a $1 million finder's fee. The fee was sought for services
leading to the inauguration of an enterprise to extensively develop certain property
on the Georgetown waterfront in Washington. . . . Bloomgarden's assertion [is that
he] brought the organizers together in this mutually beneficial venture and . . .
should be rewarded for that contribution.

   . . . .

After the close of the pleadings and some amount of discovery, Bloomgarden
moved for partial summary judgment on the issue of liability and appellees for
summary judgment on the entire case. The District Court denied Bloomgarden's
motion and granted appellees' . . . . The court held that Bloomgarden had no
enforceable claim for recompense because it appeared without dispute that at the
time he introduced the parties he did not expect to be personally compensated
for so doing. [W]e affirm.

I

Bloomgarden's suit traces its origin to a series of events commencing in the
fall of 1969 and extending into the spring of 1970. Throughout this period he was
serving as president of Socio-Dynamics Industries, Inc. (SDI), a consulting and
research firm in the field of urban and environmental affairs. Nearly half of SDI's
capital stock was owned by David Carley, president of Public Facilities Associates,
Inc. (PFA), which was engaged in the development of public and private housing
and the redevelopment of urban areas. Carley had requested Bloomgarden to
remain alert to any potentially fruitful investment opportunities for PFA in the
Washington area.

At the time, Coyer and Guy [individual real estate developers] held contracts or options on several parcels of real estate on the Georgetown waterfront.
Bloomgarden met Coyer in the summer of 1969 while arranging to lease office

---

*   Patricia M. Wald, *In Memoriam, Spottswood W. Robinson, III*, 15 Harv. Black Letter L.J. 3 (1999).

space in a building in which Coyer had an interest. At one of their meetings, Coyer revealed to Bloomgarden the details of a plan for the assembly and development of a sizeable segment of the waterfront into a multipurpose business complex. Coyer explained that he and Guy lacked the financial resources needed to carry the project through, and Bloomgarden offered to put him in touch with Carley.

Bloomgarden promptly apprised Carley of Coyer's project and set up a meeting between them and others for January 26, 1970. Ideas were then exchanged but no suggestion was made by Bloomgarden to Carley or Coyer that he expected to be paid for bringing them together. By Bloomgarden's arrangement the group attended another meeting, on February 19 in Chicago, with representatives of subsidiaries of Inland Steel Company (Inland Steel). Again the plan was discussed and again Bloomgarden gave no indication that he anticipated a fee for introducing Coyer and Guy to Carley and his Inland associates. On the contrary, during a ride to the airport on the day after the Chicago meeting, Guy inquired of Bloomgarden as to what he hoped to get out of the project, and Bloomgarden responded merely that possibly SDI, his company, might garner some work in implementing the plan. Aside from furnishing three of the principals—Coyer, Guy and Carley—with information about the others, Bloomgarden had no further role in the transaction.

An agreement in principle was reached between Coyer, Guy and the Inland Steel group in early April, 1970. This was formalized by a contract in June and a shareholders' agreement executed in August. Five corporations, among them Georgetown-Inland, were organized to handle the project. It was not until the end of March, 1970, however, that Bloomgarden asserted any monetary claim on behalf of SDI for bringing about the initial contact, and it was not until May that he asked for compensation for himself. After each of these demands was rejected, Bloomgarden, on September 14, wrote to Coyer, again claiming a fee for sparking the business opportunity culminating in the Georgetown project. That likewise failing, Bloomgarden commenced his suit on October 1.

II

. . . .

Bloomgarden . . . sought a finder's fee on a twofold basis. He said that an agreement to pay such a fee, though not express, might be implied from the circumstances in which he brought the parties together, particularly in view of an alleged custom to reward those who discover advantageous business opportunities for others. Bloomgarden also said that in the context in which he introduced the parties, they came under a legal obligation—a quasi-contract—to compensate him for his services whether or not the elements of an enforceable contract were present. . . .

In reviewing the propriety of a summary judgment, it is our responsibility to determine whether there was any issue of fact pertinent to the ruling and, if not, whether the substantive law was correctly applied. . . .

. . . . [W]e are unable to perceive any factual basis upon which it could be asserted that, at the time he introduced the parties, Bloomgarden looked forward to any finder's fee for himself, as distinguished from a fee and future business for his company. His silence on the matter at the January meeting in Washington and again at the February meeting in Chicago, followed by his statements on the day after the Chicago meeting and later in his deposition, indicated unequivocally that at most the gain he then anticipated was work and compensation for SDI, of which he was president. . . .

. . . .

III

[The court affirmed the trial court ruling against Bloomgarden's claim for an implied-in-fact contract.]

IV

We turn . . . to . . . Bloomgarden's quasi-contract theory as a basis for recovery of the finder's fee which he sought. The quasi-contract . . . is not really a contract, but a legal obligation closely akin to a duty to make restitution. . . . For the purpose of preventing unjust enrichment, however, a quasi-contract—an obligation to pay money to another—will be recognized in appropriate circumstances, even though no intention of the parties to bind themselves contractually can be discerned. . . .

. . . . [T]o make out his case, it is not enough for the plaintiff to prove merely that he has conferred an advantage upon the defendant, but he must demonstrate that retention of the benefit without compensating the one who conferred it is unjustified. What must be resolved here is whether Bloomgarden made such a showing or evinced his capability of possibly doing so at trial.

By their very nature, the equitable principles of quasi-contracts are more difficult to apply where the court must determine whether services rendered by one person to another are to go unrewarded than where it must make that determination with respect to money or property unjustly retained. . . . [I]n situations involving personal services, . . . a duty to pay will not be recognized where . . . the benefit was conferred gratuitously or officiously, or . . . the question of payment was left to the unfettered discretion of the recipient. Nor is compensation mandated where the services were rendered simply in order to gain a business advantage. And the courts have reached the same conclusion where the plaintiff did not contemplate a

Think About It!

Why would the equitable principles of quasi-contracts be more difficult to apply in the case of services rendered than in the case of money or property retained, as the court suggests?

personal fee, or the defendant could not reasonably have supposed that he did. As one court has pointed out: ". . . chagrin, disappointment, vexation, or supposed ingratitude cannot be used as a subsequent basis for a claim for compensation where none was originally intended or expected." Nor, we add, can an uncommunicated expectation of remuneration serve the plaintiff's purpose where the defendant had no cause to believe that such was the fact.

. . . . There simply was no basis on which a jury could rationally find that when he brought the parties together he entertained any thought of a finder's fee for himself, or that those with whom he dealt held the payment of such a fee in prospect. These circumstances defeat Bloomgarden's quasi-contract claim . . . . [W]e find that the District Court was fully warranted in holding that, as a matter of law, Bloomgarden was not entitled to recover on either a contract implied-in-fact or a quasi-contract, and its action in so doing is accordingly.

Affirmed.

Think About It!

The *Bloomgarden* court referred to the notion of "officiousness." Recall that in *Nursing Care Services*, on page 332, the court said the "officious intermeddler doctrine" bars recovery for services performed for another without request or consent, but then noted at least one exception to that rule, for emergency aid. Restatement (Third) of Restitution & Unjust Enrichment § 2(3) makes the point more broadly, saying there is "no liability in restitution for an unrequested benefit voluntarily conferred, unless the circumstances of the transaction justify the claimant's intervention in the absence of contract." Comment d to the section notes that those who cannot recover are variously labeled "officious," "intermeddler," or "volunteer." To say someone conferred a benefit "officiously" is thus more a conclusion than an argument: if there was no good reason to confer the benefit, the action is labeled officious interference in the affairs of others. *Nursing Care Services* established that emergency aid is not officious. What other interventions would be considered justified and therefore not officious? At least one court has suggested that an action is not officious if done "under the compulsion of a moral obligation, . . . a duty that . . . springs from the common sense of justice and fairness shared by all honorable persons" that is "perhaps best epitomized by the obligation family members commonly feel to support each other." *Estate of Cleveland*, 837 S.W.2d 68, 71 (Tenn. Ct. App. 1992). Would the actions of Mitchell in *Moore v. Mitchell* be considered officious under that standard? Perhaps not—but acts undertaken because of a sense of moral obligation might run up against the other limitation described in these cases, that restitution is not available for benefits conferred gratuitously!

Problems: Promissory Estoppel, Promissory Restitution, and Restitution

As you have seen, the standards governing promissory estoppel, promissory restitution, and restitution invite the court to make judgments about what is fair and just. In responding to the following problems, consider whether any of those doctrines could serve as the basis for relief. Sometimes your best course will be an argument in the alternative, whether it is based on alternative factual analysis or alternative bases for recovery. If your answer is that the claimant cannot recover, your analysis should refute all three bases for recovery.

5-1. Recall the case of *Hayes v. Plantations Steel Co.* (page 287). Just before Hayes retired from his job but after he had announced his intention to leave, his employer promised him the company "would take care of him" and then paid him a yearly pension of $5000 for four years before discontinuing the practice. Hayes was denied recovery as a matter of contract (no consideration) or promissory estoppel (no reliance). Could he have recovered under a theory of promissory restitution? Restitution?

5-2. Nadia Nussbaum's upstairs neighbor, Alexander, was found dead in his apartment due to natural causes. Knowing that he was Jewish (as was she) and apparently had no surviving relatives, Nadia arranged and paid $5000 for a traditional Jewish burial, which her rabbi said would be a "mitzvah." (A mitzvah refers to a Jewish religious obligation, derived from the commandments in the Torah, the first 5 books of the Bible; the word is sometimes used to refer generally to any good deed. As noted in the Jewish Virtual Library, the duty of burial, although primarily an obligation of the heirs, ultimately rests with the whole community. See www.jewishvirtuallibrary.org/jsource/judaica/ejud_0002_0004_0_03747.html.)

Shortly after the funeral was held, the neighbor's long-lost brother, Samuel, appeared. He had not seen his brother for 37 years. Samuel called on Nadia to express his gratitude for what she had done for Alexander.

Could Nadia recover the funeral expenses from Samuel under the theory of restitution? If Samuel made a promise to reimburse Nadia and then did not, could she recover under a theory of promissory restitution?

5-3.   While leasing commercial property from Leslie Landlord, Trudy Tenant hired Construction Contractor to perform renovations on the property. Under the lease, Tenant was responsible for such renovations. Tenant did not pay and Contractor will not be able to recover from her. Could Contractor recover payment from Landlord under the theory of restitution? If Landlord made a promise to reimburse Contractor and then did not, could Contractor recover under a theory of promissory restitution?

5-4.   ADS Unlimited (ADS), an advertising agency located in Minneapolis, talked with the regional manager of Staples, Inc., about the possibility of being hired on retainer by the New York-based company, which was looking to expand its national marketing. The regional manager encouraged ADS to prepare an advertising plan for submission at the quarterly Board meeting in New York "to show your stuff" and assured ADS that it will have the "inside track" to receive the advertising account. ADS submitted its plan, but the Board followed its usual practice of considering only local (to New York) agencies, so the retainer was offered to another firm. That firm made use of the work submitted by ADS as it developed its own plan, which was then used on behalf of Staples.

Could ADS recover the fair value of its plan from Staples?

5-5.   Howard Lane has filed claims against the estate of his deceased companion, Lori Masters. Howard and Lori had lived together for several years and, according to Howard, they considered their relationship to be like a marriage, "except for the vows."

Lori owned 10 acres of land, titled in her name and purchased with her own funds. During the several years preceding Lori's death, Howard used equipment from his own construction business to improve the property Lori owned, primarily by grading and landscaping, and by putting in a road. He also paid taxes, insurance, and legal bills for Lori's property, drawing from a joint checking account that contained money Howard had inherited from his family along with rental income from additional property Lori owned.

After Lori was diagnosed with terminal cancer, Howard paid Lori's medical bills, since Lori had no insurance. He provided personal care and services until Lori's death. Howard says Lori had promised Howard to give him the ten-acre parcel of land, but she died without executing a will.

Howard has filed claims against Lori's estate for the following:

a. $21,000 to compensate him for personal care given to Lori during her illness ($50 per day for taking care of Lori at home and transporting her to the hospital and other appointments);

b. 21,169 in medical bills he paid;

c. $70,000 for improvements Howard made to Lori's 10-acre parcel; and

d. An amount to cover the taxes, insurance, and legal bills for Lori's property that had been paid from the joint checking account during the three years preceding Lori's death.

Could Howard recover these amounts from Lori's estate? Consider each of the four claims separately.

5-6. Glenda owned a summer home in Minneapolis and a winter home in South Carolina. During July, high winds ripped through the South Carolina neighborhood, and a large tree fell on the house, causing considerable damage. Glenda's neighbor, Tony, who works after-hours as a handyman, did preliminary work on the house, tacking plywood over a hole in the wall and a tarp over the roof, protecting the interior from the rains that followed the winds. Tony's home was also damaged in the storms, and he hired Professional Renovators to repair both of their homes. When Glenda saw the news about the storm, she contacted Discount Builders to inspect the damage; they agreed that she would pay for two hours of their time for the inspection trip, but that amount would be deducted from the final bill if she used them to make the repairs. Discount Builders reported to Glenda that repair work was already underway and billed her $70 for the trip to the house.

a. Could Professional Renovators recover from Glenda for the work done on her home? Would it make a difference if Professional Renovators phoned Glenda after the work was completed and she said she'd "make good" on the repairs?

b. Could Tony recover from Glenda for his time working on her house? For anything he pays to Professional Renovators for the work the company did on her house? Would it make a difference if Glenda thanked Tony for everything he'd done and said, "Don't worry, I'll pay you back for everything"?

5-7. Cyclops Steel is a steel manufacturer and the owner of a dormant steel-forging facility in Aliquippa, Pennsylvania. (Forging is a manufacturing process that turns raw metal alloy into strong complex shapes for industrial use.) Ronald Crouse expressed an interest in purchasing the dormant facility, and the two parties agreed to go forward with the purchase, contingent on Crouse obtaining financing within six months.

Crouse learned that, to satisfy his investors that he had a workable business plan, he needed a commitment of future business for the facility, which he intended to operate under the name Aliquippa Forge. He discussed his needs with Cyclops, and on January 12, 2011, Cyclops issued a letter to Crouse that included the following:

> Cyclops is willing to commit to have Ronald Crouse (doing business as Aliquippa Forge) forge an average of 300,000 to 400,000 pounds of steel product per month, provided price and delivery are competitive and quality meets our requirements. Please be aware that we cannot and do not guarantee a uniform flow in quantity or type of forging work. We look forward to working with you in developing a mutually beneficial business relationship and to sending you our first lot of material in the near future.

On January 31, 2011, Crouse and Cyclops executed the agreement of sale for the facility. Aliquippa Forge started operations in February 2011, and in March 2011, Cyclops ordered 291,969 pounds of conversion work from the Forge. Cyclops made no complaints about the quality of the work performed, but made no further orders to Aliquippa. In December 2012, Aliquippa Forge ceased doing business based on financial difficulties, including an insufficient flow of business.

Does Aliquippa have any viable claims against Cyclops based on the circumstances described? If so, under what theories of recovery?

5-8. Edward Oswald is the owner of an antebellum plantation-style house, "Chateau Haut Brian," currently vacant. He entered an agreement with Charles Buchanan for the sale of the property for the price of $430,000. As part of that agreement, Oswald agreed to allow Buchanan to make alterations to the property in advance of payment and closing on the purchase of the house.

Buchanan thereafter entered a contract with Orleans Onyx for installation of marble-like onyx tile and fixtures into two of the bathrooms in the house. The interior designer working with Buchanan told him the fixtures were not compatible with the style of the house, "but he insisted, and we gave him what he wanted." The contract between Buchanan and Orleans Onyx provided for a 30% down payment of the contract price of $30,000, with the remainder due upon completion of the work. The down payment was made, but the final $20,000 check Buchanan wrote was dishonored for insufficient funds. Buchanan did not complete the purchase of the house and discharged his debt to Orleans Onyx in bankruptcy proceedings.

Oswald was unable to sell the house after Buchanan's default and moved into the house himself. Orleans Onyx seeks recovery from Buchanan for the $20,000 owed for the work done on the bathrooms. Oswald has refused, describing the bathroom décor as "too flashy and gaudy," though acknowledging that the work was well-done and the bathrooms are fully operational.

Could Orleans Onyx recover from Oswald for the work done on the Chateau? If so, how much?

5-9. General Liquors is a wholesale distributor of alcohol products. For more than 35 years, General had operated as a terminable-at-will distributor for Draco Distillers and other manufacturers. In April 2011, when two of its major suppliers withdrew their product lines from General, General faced a critical choice: It could sell the business to one of its competitors, or it could continue in business with scaled-back operations. Not sure of the best course, it entered negotiations with National Wine and Spirits to sell the business, receiving an offer of $2.5 million on July 15. At the same time, having determined that it could remain in business if it retained its remaining major supplier, it approached Draco to seek assurances about its commitment to General. After listening to General's concerns and hearing about the possible sale, Draco told General that it had no intention of taking its line to another distributor. On July 25, with the offer from National about to expire, General contacted Draco again and was again told that it was staying with General. General let the offer from National expire. The next day, Draco informed General that it was withdrawing its product line from General. Concluding that it could not continue without Draco, General approached National again, but National reduced its offer to $2 million, which General felt forced to accept.

Does General have any viable claims against Draco based on the circumstances described? If so, under what theories of recovery?

Test Your Knowledge

To assess your understanding of the material in this chapter, <u>click here</u> to take a quiz.

CHAPTER 6

Defenses to Contract Enforcement

How do parties demonstrate assent to a contract?	What kinds of promises will the law enforce?	What defenses to enforcement exist?	Is a writing required for enforcement? If so, what kind?	How is the content and meaning of a contract determined?	What are parties' rights and duties after breach?

What situations lead to excusing contract performance?	What remedies are available for breach of contract?	What contractual rights and duties do non-parties to a contract have?

Table of Contents

§ 1. Introduction 354

§ 2. Defenses Based on Lack of Capacity to Contract................................356

    § 2.1. Infancy 357

        Webster Street Partnership, Ltd. v. Sheridan 359

    § 2.2. Mental Illness or Defect..368

        Fingerhut v. Kralyn Enterprises, Inc. 369

    § 2.3. Intoxication 384

    PROBLEMS: THE INCAPACITY DEFENSES (6-1, 6-2)................................385

§ 3. Defenses Related to Defects in Mutual Assent 386

    § 3.1. Mistake..387

        PROBLEMS: DISTINGUISHING MISTAKE OF FACT, LAW, OPINION, AND
            PREDICTION (6-3 TO 6-7) 388

        § 3.1.1. Mutual Mistake...389

            Lenawee County Board of Health v. Messerly....................392

        § 3.1.2. Unilateral Mistake...399

        PROBLEMS: THE MISTAKE DEFENSE (6-8 TO 6-10)....................................402

§ 3.2. Misrepresentation...404
    PROBLEMS: THE MISREPRESENTATION DEFENSE (6-11 TO 6-14) 414

§ 3.3. Duress and Undue Influence..415
    § 3.3.1. Duress..415
        EverBank v. Marini 418
        PROBLEMS: THE DURESS DEFENSE (6-15 TO 6-17)............................430
    § 3.3.2. Undue Influence...431
        G.A.S. v. S.I.S. 433

§ 3.4. Unconscionability 440
    Williams v. Walker-Thomas Furniture Co. 442
    § 3.4.1. Codifications of the Unconscionability Defense.................450
    § 3.4.2. Substantive and Procedural Unconscionability.................452
    § 3.4.3. Unconscionability Issues in Arbitration Agreements.........459
        Disappearing Claims and the Erosion of Substantive Law 460
        Italian Colors and Freedom of Contract Under the Federal
        Arbitration Act..464
    PROBLEM: THE UNCONSCIONABILITY DEFENSE (6-18)...............................468
§ 4. **Violation of Public Policy**...471
    Tunkl v. Regents of the University of California 474
PROBLEMS: CONTRACT DEFENSES (6-19 TO 6-21) 486

§ 1. Introduction

As discussed in the earlier chapters, a contract is created if a promise is supported by consideration and the parties mutually assent to the exchange. Despite the apparent existence of a contract, however, one or both parties may have a defense to enforcement of the contract based on defects in the bargaining process, incapacity of one of the parties, or public policy constraints.

The first set of defenses, discussed in § 2, involve agreements by a party who lacked the capacity to contract by being too young or cognitively disabled to engage in the assent process. The defenses that fall into this category are:

- Infancy (a party is below the age of majority and therefore a minor)

- Mental illness or defect

- Intoxication

A second set of defenses, discussed in § 3, involve circumstances in which one or both parties' assent was fundamentally flawed, perhaps because of inaccurate or misleading information or because the assent occurred in a setting marred by exceptional pressure or unfair circumstances. Although it may appear that the parties agreed, additional facts demonstrate that one or both parties did not truly assent. These defenses are based on the same policies that underlie manifestation of mutual assent (see Chapter 3)—freedom of contract and the need for clarity and predictability in contractual terms. They also police against parties' use of unacceptable conduct during the contract formation process. The defenses that fall into this category are:

- Mistake

- Misrepresentation

- Duress

- Undue influence

- Unconscionability

The final defense, discussed in § 4, involves agreements in which the parties' mutual assent was unimpaired, but the substance of the agreement violates societal norms. In such instances, the contract may be unenforceable on the grounds of public policy.

The boundary lines among these defenses are not crisp, and overlap is possible in some fact situations, so a party challenging a contract often raises multiple defenses. For instance, a party who is misled or mistaken as to a crucial fact in a contract may raise defenses of misrepresentation and mistake. Similarly, a party whose free will has been impaired during contract formation may raise both duress and undue influence.

If a contract violates public policy, it is considered void (or void ab initio, "from its inception"), and enforcement of the agreement can be challenged by either party as well as by third parties in appropriate circumstances. Under all of the other defenses (aside from public policy and contracts with persons under guardianship due to a formal adjudication of incompetency), a contract is voidable, so the party protected by the defense has the power to affirm or avoid the agreement, which is otherwise valid and enforceable.

Make the Connection

Rescission is discussed in *Angel v. Murray* on page 242 and again in § 3.5. of Chapter 4.

In the event that the party seeks to avoid the contract, the party will seek to rescind the obligations under the contract. Rescission, thereby, being the means by which a party will avoid the contract, essentially by unmaking it.

Make the Connection

The remedy of restitution is discussed again in Chapter 10, § 2.3.

If a contract is declared void (by a court or by a party with power to avoid the agreement through rescission), it is as if the contract never existed, and the parties should generally be placed back into their "status quo ante," the situation existing before the contract was formed. A court can use the remedy of restitution to effectuate that goal, requiring each party to disgorge the benefits (or the value of the benefits) already received.

If a contract or a contract clause is determined to be unconscionable, the court has additional remedies available: It has equitable discretion to void the entire contract, to void the unconscionable clause, or to limit application of the offending clause to eliminate the unconscionability. As noted in the discussion of mistake (page 387), if the parties make a clerical ("scrivener's") error, the court may "reform" the written agreement by correcting the error.

§ 2. Defenses Based on Lack of Capacity to Contract

Contract liability is grounded in the belief that there is social and economic value to enforcing the voluntary private choices of contracting parties. Some private choices to enter contracts are not enforceable because they were not truly voluntary due to misrepresentation or some form of coercion (see later sections of this chapter). This section discusses defenses based on a party's lack of *capacity* to contract, protecting individuals whose characteristics or status are believed to make them especially vulnerable to over-reaching or unable to muster the necessary mental state to truly assent. The usual categories of incapacity on the basis of status are listed in Restatement (Second) § 12.

Defenses to contract enforcement may also be based on lack of *authority* to contract. For example, an individual may purportedly enter into a contract as an agent on behalf of a principal but not have authority to do so. A corporation or government agency may purportedly enter into a contract but it may be outside the scope of the authorized power of the contracting party ("ultra vires"), resulting in a void or voidable contract. These topics are typically covered in courses on agency, business associations, or administrative law.

§ 2.1. Infancy

The infancy defense seeks to protect all minors—children up to the age of majority[*]—from the legal consequences of entering into contracts. Subject to some limitations discussed below, the infancy defense makes all contracts formed by minors voidable at the option of the minor, giving the minor (but not the other party) the opportunity to disaffirm—that is, to rescind—the obligation.

The infancy defense is governed by common law and state statutes that vary considerably among jurisdictions, more so than other defenses. This text relies upon the Restatement (Second) provisions as a useful model for discussion because they reflect principles commonly found in state law, although the Restatement provisions are not directly adopted in most jurisdictions. The state-to-state difference in the scope of the infancy doctrine is illustrated by Examples A and B.

> **Example A:** *Douglas v. Pflueger Hawaii, Inc.*, 135 P.3d 129 (Haw. 2006).
>
> A 17-year-old employee was injured when a coworker sprayed him in the buttocks area with an air hose. The employee brought suit against the employer for a hostile and unsafe working environment, as well as sexual assault. Employer sought to enforce an arbitration agreement contained in the employee handbook, and the employee sought to disaffirm the employment contract based upon infancy.

Analysis: The court held that while Hawaii recognizes the infancy doctrine, it is not absolute and not available as a defense in the employment context due to application of Hawaii's child labor laws such that a minor employee who was injured could not avoid agreement to the arbitration clause under the infancy doctrine.

> **Example B:** *Stroupes v. Finish Line, Inc.*, 2005 WL 5610231 (E.D. Tenn. March 16, 2005).
>
> A 16-year-old employee brought suit for sexual harassment after another employee touched and kissed her and requested intimacies. Employer sought to enforce an arbitration agreement contained in the employee handbook, and the employee sought to disaffirm the employment contract based upon infancy.

---

[*]   The traditional common law age of majority was 21, but most states have lowered this age to 18, considerably reducing the number of instances in which the defense is available.

Analysis: The court held that Tennessee recognizes the infancy doctrine and that a minor employee could disaffirm an employment contract that contained an arbitration clause. The minor avoided the contract by filing the court action.

––––––––––––––

As reflected in Restatement (Second) § 14, the infancy defense as typically adopted gives the minor a defense to the enforcement of any contractual obligation if that right is exercised during the period of minority or within a reasonable time after the individual achieves the age of majority. The minor must return whatever is left of the item received from the other party (or any remaining proceeds from the sale of the item to a third party), but is not responsible for any loss or damage or depreciation to the item (with a few exceptions), nor is the minor responsible for the price of any services received. The defense is available regardless of the sophistication of the child. The minor cannot waive the defense, nor can the contracting parties agree to a contrary rule.

The policy behind the infancy defense is to protect minors from their immaturity and to prevent their exploitation by adults. The danger is especially keen in teenagers, who overestimate their ability to handle the complexities of adult life and underestimate what they do not know and what could go wrong. Making contracts voidable until the age of majority is easier and arguably more workable than deciding each teenager's capacity on a case-by-case basis in a particular setting. The sharp line also puts adult contracting parties on notice that they proceed at risk that the minor will void the proposed contract. On the other hand, the availability of the defense means that even mature teens, and those who need contracting capability, may find it difficult to find contract partners, or they may need an adult co-signer or have to pay a higher price. And merchants who do business with minors do so at their own peril, even when those merchants deal in good faith. It is such drawbacks that have led to some limitations to the infancy defense, addressed in the case below.

These competing interests and policies may be part of the reason there is so much variation in the state rules on contractual capacity for minors, as different jurisdictions have honored differing interests and policies. Another source of non-uniformity might be the "bright line" test of age, which tempts courts to carve out exceptions to accommodate the huge range of behaviors that older teenagers and young twenty-somethings exhibit.

Reading Critically: *Webster Street Partnership*

1. The opinion treats contracts for "necessaries" differently than other contracts with respect to the infancy defense. What are "necessaries," in the view of this court? Under what circumstances are contracts for necessaries enforceable or not enforceable against minors? What policies justify those rules?

2. What is the role of the minor's "emancipation" in determining liability of the minor or of his parents?

3. The minors in *Webster Street Partnership* are permitted to void their contract. What relief is then available to each party to the contract? Is that relief based on expectation, reliance, or restitutionary principles?

Webster Street Partnership, Ltd. v. Sheridan

WEBSTER STREET PARTNERSHIP, LTD., Plaintiff,
Appellant and Cross-Appellee
v.
MATTHEW SHERIDAN and PAT WILWERDING, Defendants,
Appellees and Cross-Appellants

Supreme Court of Nebraska
368 N.W.2d 439 (Neb. 1985)

KRIVOSHA, CHIEF JUSTICE.

Webster Street Partnership, Ltd. (Webster Street), appeals from an order of the district court for Douglas County, Nebraska, which modified an earlier judgment entered by the municipal court of the city of Omaha, Douglas County, Nebraska. The municipal court entered judgment in favor of Webster Street and against the appellees, Matthew Sheridan and Pat Wilwerding, in the amount of $630.94. On appeal the district court found that Webster Street was entitled to a judgment in the amount of $146.75 and that Sheridan and Wilwerding were entitled to a credit in the amount of $150. The district court therefore entered judgment in favor of Sheridan and Wilwerding and against Webster Street in the amount of $3.25. It is from this $3.25 judgment that appeal is taken to this court.

Webster Street is a partnership owning real estate in Omaha, Nebraska. On September 18, 1982, Webster Street, through one of its agents, Norman Sargent, entered into a written lease with Sheridan and Wilwerding for a second floor apartment at 3007 Webster Street. The lease provided that Sheridan and Wilwerding would pay to Webster Street by way of monthly rental the sum of $250 due on the first day of each month until August 15, 1983. The lease also required the payment of a security deposit in the amount of $150 and a payment of $20 per month for utilities during the months of December, January, February, and March. Liquidated damages in the amount of $5 per day for each day the rent was late were also provided for by the lease.

The evidence conclusively establishes that at the time the lease was executed both tenants were minors and, further, that Webster Street knew that fact. At the time the lease was entered into, Sheridan was 18 and did not become 19 until November 5, 1982.* Wilwerding was 17 at the time the lease was executed and never gained his majority during any time relevant to this case.

The tenants paid the $150 security deposit, $100 rent for the remaining portion of September 1982, and $250 rent for October 1982. They did not pay the rent for the month of November 1982, and on November 5 Sargent advised Wilwerding that unless the rent was paid immediately, both boys would be required to vacate the premises. The tenants both testified that, being unable to pay the rent, they moved from the premises on November 12. In fact, a dispute exists as to when the two tenants relinquished possession of the premises, but in view of our decision that dispute is not of any relevance.

In a letter dated January 7, 1983, Webster Street's attorney made written demand upon the tenants for damages in the amount of $630.94. On January 12, 1983, the tenants' attorney denied any liability, refused to pay any portion of the amount demanded, stated that neither tenant was of legal age at the time the lease was executed, and demanded return of $150 security deposit.

Webster Street thereafter commenced suit against the tenants and sought judgment in the amount of $630.94, which was calculated as follows:

Rent due Nov.	$250.00
Rent due Dec.	250.00
Dec. utility allowance	20.00
Garage rental	40.00

---

* [Authors' Note: By this statement, we surmise that the age of majority in this jurisdiction at the time of this case was 19 years of age.]

Clean up and repair broken window, degrease kitchen stove, shampoo carpet, etc.	46.79
Advertising	24.15
Re-rental fee	<u>150.00</u>
	780.94
Less security deposit	<u>− 150.00</u>
	$630.94

To this petition the tenants filed an answer alleging that they were minors at the time they signed the lease, that the lease was therefore voidable, and that the rental property did not constitute a necessary for which they were otherwise liable. In addition, Sheridan cross-petitioned for the return of the security deposit, and Wilwerding filed a cross-petition seeking the return of all moneys paid to Webster Street. Following trial, the municipal court of the city of Omaha found in favor of Webster Street and against both tenants in the amount of $630.94.

The tenants appealed to the district court for Douglas County. The district court found that the tenants had vacated the premises on November 12, 1982, and therefore were only liable for the 12 days in which they actually occupied the apartment and did not pay rent. The district court also permitted Webster Street to recover $46.79 for cleanup and repairs. The tenants, however, were given credit for their $150 security deposit, resulting in an order that Webster Street was indebted to the tenants in the amount of $3.25.

Webster Street then perfected an appeal to this court . . . . Webster Street's position [appears to be] that the district court erred in failing to find that Sheridan had ratified the lease within a reasonable time after obtaining majority, and was therefore responsible for the lease, and that the minors had become emancipated and were therefore liable, even though Wilwerding had not reached majority. Webster Street is simply wrong in both matters.

As a general rule, an infant does not have the capacity to bind himself absolutely by contract. See, *Smith v. Wade,* 169 Neb. 710, 100 N.W.2d 770 (1960); 43 C.J.S. *Infants* § 166 (1978). The right of the infant to avoid his contract is one conferred by law for his protection against his own improvidence and the designs of others. See *Burnand v. Irigoyen,* 30 Cal.2d 861, 186 P.2d 417 (1947). The policy of the law is to discourage adults from contracting with an infant; they cannot complain if, as a consequence of violating that rule, they are unable to enforce their contract. As stated in *Curtice Co. v. Kent,* 89 Neb. 496, 500, 131 N.W. 944, 945 (1911): "The result seems hardly just to the [adult], but persons dealing with infants do so at their peril. The law is plain as to their disability to contract, and safety lies in refusing to transact business with them."

However, the privilege of infancy will not enable an infant to escape liability in all cases and under all circumstances. For example, it is well established that an infant is liable for the value of necessaries furnished him. 42 Am.Jur.2d *Infants* § 65 (1969). See, also, *Burnand v. Irigoyen, supra; Merrick v. Stephens,* 337 S.W.2d 713 (Mo.App.1960); *Englebert v. Troxell,* 40 Neb. 195, 58 N.W. 852 (1894). An infant's liability for necessaries is based not upon his actual contract to pay for them but upon a contract implied by law, or, in other words, a quasi-contract. 42 Am.Jur.2d, *supra.*

Just what are necessaries, however, has no exact definition. The term is flexible and varies according to the facts of each individual case. In *Cobbey v. Buchanan,* 48 Neb. 391, 397, 67 N.W. 176, 178 (1896), we said: "The meaning of the term 'necessaries' cannot be defined by a general rule applicable to all cases; the question is a mixed one of law and fact, to be determined in each case from the particular facts and circumstances in such case." A number of factors must be considered before a court can conclude whether a particular product or service is a necessary. As stated in *Schoenung v. Gallet,* 206 Wis. 52, 54, 238 N.W. 852, 853 (1931):

> "The term 'necessaries,' as used in the law relating to the liability of infants therefor, is a relative term, somewhat flexible, except when applied to such things as are obviously requisite for the maintenance of existence, and depends on the social position and situation in life of the infant, as well as upon his own fortune and that of his parents. The particular infant must have an actual need for the articles furnished; not for mere ornament or pleasure. The articles must be useful and suitable, but they are not necessaries merely because useful or beneficial. Concerning the general character of the things furnished, to be necessaries the articles must supply the infant's personal needs, either those of his body or those of his mind. However, the term 'necessaries' is not confined to merely such things as are required for a bare subsistence. There is no positive rule by means of which it may be determined what are or what are not necessaries, for

Think About It!

Necessaries are often limited to food, shelter, and clothing of a reasonable kind, medical and dental services and medicines, and transportation to and from a workplace and places to shop for necessities. Why should (as the court says here) the "necessaries" be based on the needs of a reasonable person with the minor's "rank, social position, fortune, health, or other circumstances"? What policies argue for and against this flexible definition?

what may be considered necessary for one infant may not be necessaries for another infant whose state is different as to rank, social position, fortune, health, or other circumstances, the question being one to be determined from the particular facts and circumstances of each case."

. . . . This appears to be the law as it is generally followed throughout the country.

In *Ballinger v. Craig,* 95 Ohio App. 545, 121 N.E.2d 66, (1953), the defendants were husband and wife and were 19 years of age at the time they purchased a house trailer. Both were employed. However, prior to the purchase of the trailer, the defendants were living with the parents of the husband. The Court of Appeals for the State of Ohio held that under the facts presented the trailer was not a necessary. The court stated:

> "To enable an infant to contract for articles as necessaries, he must have been in actual need of them, and obliged to procure them for himself. They are not necessaries as to him, however necessary they may be in their nature, if he was already supplied with sufficient articles of the kind, or if he had a parent or guardian who was able and willing to supply them. The burden of proof is on the plaintiff to show that the infant was destitute of the articles, and had no way of procuring them except by his own contract."

. . . . *Id.* at 547, 121 N.E.2d at 67. Under Ohio law the marriage of the parties did not result in their obtaining majority.

In 42 Am.Jur.2d *Infants* § 67 at 68–69 (1969), the author notes:

> Thus, articles are not necessaries for an infant if he has a parent or guardian who is able and willing to supply them, and an infant residing with and being supported by his parent according to his station in life is not absolutely liable for things which under other circumstances would be considered necessaries.

The undisputed testimony is that both tenants were living away from home, apparently with the understanding that they could return home at any time. Sheridan testified:

> Q. During the time that you were living at 3007 Webster, did you at any time, feel free to go home or anything like that?

> A. Well, I had a feeling I could, but I just wanted to see if I could make it on my own.

> Q. Had you been driven from your home?

> A. No.

Q.   You didn't have to go?

A.   No.

Q.   You went freely?

A.   Yes.

Q.   Then, after you moved out and went to 3417 for a week or so, you were again to return home, is that correct?

A.   Yes, sir.

It would therefore appear that in the present case neither Sheridan nor Wilwerding was in need of shelter but, rather, had chosen to voluntarily leave home, with the understanding that they could return whenever they desired. One may at first blush believe that such a rule is unfair. Yet, on further consideration, the wisdom of the rule is apparent. If, indeed, landlords may not contract with minors, except at their peril, they may refuse to do so. In that event, minors who voluntarily leave home but who are free to return will be compelled to return to their parents' home—a result which is desirable. We therefore find that both the municipal court and the district court erred in finding that the apartment, under the facts in this case, was a necessary.

Having therefore concluded that the apartment was not a necessary, the question of whether Sheridan and Wilwerding were emancipated is of no significance. The effect of emancipation is only relevant with regard to necessaries. If the minors were not emancipated, then their parents would be liable for necessaries provided to the minors. As we recently noted in *Accent Service Co., Inc. v. Ebsen,* 209 Neb. 94, 96, 306 N.W.2d 575, 576 (1981):

Take Note!

Emancipation may be full or partial. Some minors are allowed by their parents to spend money earned in full-time employment but are not released from parental custody and control. For some courts, emancipation may have the effect stated in the case when the minor earns enough money to procure all necessaries without parental assistance.

"In general, even in the absence of statute, parents are under a legal as well as a moral obligation to support, maintain, and care for their children, the basis of such a duty resting not only upon the fact of the parent-child relationship, but also upon the interest of the state as parens patriae of children and of the community at large in preventing them from becoming a public burden. However, various voluntary acts of a child, such as marriage or enlistment in military service, have been held to terminate the parent's obligation of support, the issue generally being considered by the courts in terms of whether an emancipation of the child has been effectuated. In those cases involving the issue of whether a parent is obligated to support an unmarried minor child who has voluntarily left home without the consent of the parent, the courts, in actions to compel support from the parent, have uniformly held that such conduct on the part of the child terminated the support obligation. . . ."

If, on the other hand, it was determined that the minors were emancipated and the apartment was a necessary, then the minors would be liable. But where, as here, we determine that the apartment was not a necessary, then neither the parents nor the infants are liable and the question of emancipation is of no moment.

Because the rental of the apartment was not a necessary, the minors had the right to avoid the contract, either during their minority or within a reasonable time after reaching their majority. See *Smith v. Wade,* 169 Neb. 710, 100 N.W.2d 770 (1960). Disaffirmance by an infant completely puts an end to the contract's existence, both as to him and as to the adult with whom he contracted. *Curtice Co. v. Kent,* 89 Neb. 496, 131 N.W. 944 (1911). Because the parties then stand as if no contract had ever existed, the infant can recover payments made to the adult, and the adult is entitled to the return of whatever was received by the infant. *Id.*

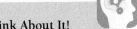

Think About It!

What amounts to a "reasonable time" for the minor to disaffirm the contract after reaching the age of majority? Compare the circumstances in *Webster Street Partnership* to *In re The Score Board, Inc.,* 238 B.R. 585 (D.N.J. 1999). In that case, Kobe Bryant attempted to disaffirm an endorsement contract that he entered when he was 17 years old, just as he began his professional basketball career. The court found Bryant had affirmed the contract when he deposited a $10,000 check from the other party 3 days after his 18th birthday and thereafter consciously performed his contractual duties by signing autographs and making personal appearances.

The record shows that Pat Wilwerding clearly disaffirmed the contract during his minority. Moreover, the record supports the view that when the agent for Webster Street ordered the minors out for failure to pay rent and they vacated the premises, Sheridan likewise disaffirmed the contract. The record indicates that Sheridan reached majority on November 5. To suggest that a lapse of 7 days was not disaffirmance within a reasonable time would be foolish. Once disaffirmed, the contract became void; therefore, no contract existed between the parties, and the minors were entitled to recover all of the moneys which they paid and to be relieved of any further obligation under the contract. The judgment of the district court for Douglas County, Nebraska, is therefore reversed and the cause remanded with directions to vacate the judgment in favor of Webster Street and to enter a judgment in favor of Matthew Sheridan and Pat Wilwerding in the amount of $500, representing September rent in the amount of $100, October rent in the amount of $250, and the security deposit in the amount of $150.

Reversed and remanded with directions.

Reading Critically: *Halbman*

1. The minor in *Halbman* was permitted to void his contract. What relief was then available to each party to the contract?

2. Based on the court's discussion, what difference does it make if a minor misrepresents his or her age? Based on the policies underlying the infancy defense, what difference should it make?

3. Toward the end of *Webster Street Partnership*, on page 365, the court says that "the adult is entitled to the return of whatever was received by the infant." What is the *Halbman* court's holding on that issue?

Example C: *Halbman v. Lemke*, 298 N.W.2d 562 (Wis. 1980).

James Halbman, a minor and an employee at L&M Standard Station, made a contract with Michael Lemke, the manager of L&M Standard, to purchase for $1250 a motor vehicle that the court determined was not a "necessity." He gave Lemke $1000 in cash and agreed to pay $25 a week until the balance was paid, at which time title to the car would be transferred to him. About five weeks later, after Halbman had paid another $100, a connecting rod on the vehicle's engine broke. Lemke denied any obligation, but offered to assist Halbman in installing a used engine, but Halbman refused. Halbman took the car to another garage for repair work, but did not pay the $637.40 repair bill and did not pick up the vehicle. Lemke endorsed the vehicle title to Halbman in an effort to avoid liability. Halbman then disaffirmed the contract. Meanwhile, as permitted under law, the repair garage removed the engine and transmission from the car to pay for the outstanding

FYI

> In this opinion, a "necessity" seems to mean the same as a "necessary" in the preceding opinion. The latter term is more common.

repair bill and towed the vehicle to Halbman's father's house where it was vandalized, making it unsalvageable. Halbman filed suit to recover the $1100 he had paid on the purchase price and Lemke counterclaimed for the unpaid contract price.

Analysis: The trial court ruled in favor of Halbman, holding that a minor who disaffirms needs only to offer return of the property as is, without restitution for any use or depreciation. The intermediate appellate court affirmed in part and reversed in part, and the case was brought to the state supreme court to consider whether Halbman must make restitution to Lemke for the damage sustained to the vehicle.

Take Note!

The seller's signing over title (that is, transferring the motor vehicle certificate of title) to the buyer might have had an impact on seller's tort liability, depending on the state's certificate-of-title law, but it did not affect the parties' contract rights.

The court noted the general rule that "a minor who disaffirms the contract is entitled to recover all consideration he has conferred incident to the transaction . . . , [but] is expected to restore as much of the consideration as, at the time of disaffirmance, remains in the minor's possession." Lemke argued that a minor should be excused only when he is seeking to avoid an obligation under contract but that different rules apply when a minor is seeking to recover the consideration paid. Halbman argued that whether a minor is using the rules of infancy as a sword or a shield should not matter unless the minor misrepresented his age to induce the contract.

The court recognized that "a minor who disaffirms a purchase and recovers his purchase price should not also be permitted to profit by retaining the property purchased . . . , but it is not to be used to bilk merchants out of property as well as proceeds of the sale." That means a minor may not both get his payment to the vendor returned and keep the property, but it does not require the minor to compensate the vendor for property he no longer retains or for damage to the property after he received it. The court explained:

> Here Lemke seeks restitution of the value of the depreciation by virtue of the damage to the vehicle prior to disaffirmance. Such a recovery would require Halbman to return more than that remaining in his possession. It seeks compensatory value for that which he cannot return. Where there is misrepresentation by a minor or willful destruction of property, the vendor may be able to recover damages in tort. But absent these factors, as in the present case, we believe that to require a disaffirming minor to make restitution for diminished value

is, in effect, to bind the minor to a part of the obligation which by law he is privileged to avoid.

. . . .

[A]bsent misrepresentation or tortious damage to the property, a minor who disaffirms a contract for the purchase of an item which is not a necessity may recover his purchase price without liability for use, depreciation, damage, or other diminution in value.

§ 2.2. Mental Illness or Defect

Although individuals suffering from mental illness or defect should be protected both from exploitation by others and from taking action that does not truly represent their voluntary choice because of their mental condition, the line dividing mental competency from incompetency is rarely a sharp one. The infancy defense can use a bright line standard based on age; no similar bright line is available for mental competency, except if the individual has already been placed under guardianship as the result of a formal ruling of incompetency. Contracts with mentally incompetent persons who have been adjudicated incompetent are generally void, but contracts with others who are (but not adjudicated to be) mentally incompetent are generally voidable at the option of the incompetent person (or someone acting on his behalf).

The policies underlying this defense tug in several, often competing, directions. Incompetent persons need protection, but so do the persons with whom they interact, especially if the incompetency is not obvious. As with minors, even incompetent individuals may have a need for contracting capability, especially if the incompetency is transitory rather than permanent, and the existence of the defense may make others wary of contracting with someone who is merely odd. The defense may be used by family and friends in an effort to control the affairs of the allegedly incompetent person, even though the incompetency is partial, transient, or not yet sufficiently advanced to meet the mental incompetency standard. Ambiguity in the definition or application of the standard of mental incompetency may invite some to use the defense to avoid choices that were merely unwise, not driven by mental illness or defect.

Issues of mental competency also arise in other areas of law, such as the competency of testators to make wills and trusts, the intent necessary to commit an intentional tort, and the ability the intent necessary or state of mind to be responsible for a criminal act. The mental competency standards in these areas of law have some similarity, but are not identical or interchangeable.

Sometimes the tests for mental competency seem arcane and even antiquated, because the law lags behind medicine's understanding of defective mental processing. Other tests may seem harsh or insensitive, mirroring society's reactions to mental illness.

Reading Critically: *Fingerhut*

1. What are the two standards the case discusses for judging mental incompetency in contract law? Which standard does plaintiff rely upon, and why?

2. What facts support plaintiff's claim of mental incapacity? What facts support defendant's position? Why does the court reject the defense?

3. In light of plaintiff's failure to establish incapacity, why does the court consider the defendant's ratification argument? Why does the court rule in favor of that argument?

4. Of what significance is plaintiff's failure to testify? Why do you suppose plaintiff and his attorney made that choice?

Fingerhut v. Kralyn Enterprises, Inc.

STANLEY FINGERHUT, Plaintiff

v.

KRALYN ENTERPRISES, INC., Defendant

Supreme Court, New York County, New York
337 N.Y.S.2d 394 (Sup. Ct. 1971)

VINCENT A. LUPIANO, J.

The plaintiff, Stanley Fingerhut, sues the defendant, Kralyn Enterprises, Inc., to rescind a contract allegedly made when he was mentally incompetent, in that he was in the manic phase of the ailment, manic-depressive psychosis.

In the summer of 1968, he was the sole general partner in a private investment company called Mt. Vernon Associates. He was then 33 years old and unmarried. He was an investment advisor, having been a customer's man for a well-known brokerage house. His yearly earnings averaged more than $50,000 over a period of five years. In 1967 he formed the investment company with 16 limited partners, which increased its capital from $3,000,000 to over $5,000,000 within a period of two years. This large increase was greatly due to plaintiff's efforts who, himself, had invested $153,000.

He was a member of a golf club and prior to the transaction involved here, toured various country clubs, because he wanted to buy one. He investigated the Bel Aire Golf & Country Club. He obtained an appraisal of Bel Aire which valued the property on February 21, 1968, at $2,728,000 exclusive of the personal property, furnishings, etc. The personal property represented an investment of $275,819.70.

On September 22, 1968 plaintiff and his attorney, Richard J. Rubin, . . . drove to Bel Aire. They informed the Krassners, majority stockholders of the club, that plaintiff desired to purchase the golf club. The Krassners then sent for their lawyer, Seymour Rabinowitz. Negotiations took place between the parties and their lawyers and the price of $3,075,000 was agreed upon. Rubin, in the presence of plaintiff, wrote the binder in longhand. The parties executed it, in the presence of their respective lawyers. Plaintiff gave a check for $25,000 to the defendant.

On September 25, 1968, the parties met at the offices of plaintiff's lawyers to discuss the making of a formal contract and after six hours of strenuous negotiating a contract was made.

On September 26, 1968 that contract was executed and plaintiff paid a further sum of $200,000. Both sums were to be held in escrow by defendant's attorney, Rabinowitz. The balance of $2,850,000, was to be paid upon the closing of title scheduled on November 15, 1968, or sooner, at the option of the purchaser who also had the right to adjourn the closing to December 15, 1968.

The property was encumbered with three mortgages aggregating $1,950,000. At least $900,000 was needed to take title, plus adjustments and inventory, depending on whether preliminary negotiations relating to the extinguishment or extensions of the existing mortgages were successful. If not successful, the buyer was obligated to cover such mortgages with cash. In this area, the binder had provided for an all cash deal. However, the buyer, in the subsequent contract, was allowed to arrange his own financing, with provision that the seller would assist the buyer in obtaining extensions of the first and second mortgages; in such case, the seller would accept a purchase-money mortgage up to $400,000. Such co-operation was afforded, apparently, on the premise that plaintiff might not have available to him sufficient funds to acquire the property free of all the mortgages at the time of closing.

At the request of plaintiff's counsel, a liquidated damages clause, providing that in the event of buyer's default, seller was entitled to retain all sums paid in escrow, was eliminated. In the contract, the escrowee was authorized to use the escrow funds in making payment of $22,894.73 for the 1968–1969 school taxes, $1,422.89 for supplies and labor to maintain the golf course, and $100,000 on account of the third mortgage, which installment was coming due in December. Such payment reduced the mortgage to $194,000. Plaintiff, having consented to such payments amounting to $124,317.62, with credit to be given the buyer at the closing, the sum of $100,682.82 was left.

> **Make the Connection**
>
> A liquidated damages clause in a contract specifies a dollar amount (or a formula for computing a dollar amount) of damages, rather than leaving damages to be determined by the court after breach. Here the liquidated damage amount was the cash previously paid into escrow, but the parties removed the clause from the final contract. Chapter 10, § 2.4, discusses limitations on the parties' right to specify liquidated and other forms of agreed damages.

The deal was never consummated.

On November 8, 1968, plaintiff, through his attorney, sent a letter to the defendant which, amongst other matters, "elected to adjourn closing of title until December 15, 1968." On November 19, 1968, plaintiff's attorneys wrote defendant's attorneys as follows:

> Yesterday, November 18, 1968, we met with Stanley Fingerhut for the purpose of discussing with him the progress, if any, of his arranging financing for the above transaction.
>
> We were apprised for the first time that Mr. Fingerhut suffers from a manic depressive psychosis, a condition for which he has received medical treatment for the past years. We were advised, and competent medical authority will substantiate, that Mr. Fingerhut prior to September 22, 1968, and until recently, was in the manic stage of his illness and wholly incompetent and totally incapable of managing his own affairs during that time.
>
> Accordingly, we submit that the binder agreement between the parties, and the contract dated September 26, 1968, were made during a period when our client wholly lacked sufficient mental competence to contract on his behalf and would not have entered into the agreement but for the existence of the mental disorder.
>
> Based upon the foregoing, our client has instructed us to give you notice, and we do so, by this letter that he elects to rescind the binder

of September 22, 1968, and the contract of September 26, 1968, and demands the return of the $225,000 given by him thereunder as a down payment. . . .

We must request that you contact us in order that we may confer on this matter.

Business Lingo

Plaintiff filed a *lis pendens* notice on the real estate at issue. "Lis pendens" means "suit pending." The lis pendens notice of pending action is usually filed in the county where the real estate is located, so that the property owner and potential buyers are put on notice of a potential claim on the property. A person who files a false lis pendens notice may have to pay attorney fees.

No agreement was reached and this action was commenced on December 16, 1968; a *lis pendens* in the sum of $124,317.62 was filed on the basis that such moneys were expended to increase defendant's equity in the property. Prior to the commencement of the action, on the date set for the closing, defendant tendered a deed and demanded payment of $2,850,000. The deed contained no recital that it was subject to any existing mortgages or encumbrances. After the plaintiff elected to rescind, the escrowee handed over the moneys to the defendant.

The complaint asks for judgment that the contract be rescinded and declared null and void, and defendant be ordered to return the down payment of $225,000, and that a lien be impressed on the property for the sum of $124,317.62.

. . . .

. . . . [D]efendant sought to amend the pleadings to conform with the proof to the extent that plaintiff, after recovery from his alleged psychotic condition, proceeded to perform acts in reliance upon and in furtherance of the September 26, 1968 contract, and thereby ratified the contract and waived any right he might have had to rescind. While not originally pleaded, defendant urges that it was impossible to plead ratification in advance of trial, since sufficient facts relating to the proposed ratification were not uncovered or divulged until the trial developed. Decision thereon was reserved.

The motion is granted in the exercise of discretion, and ratification will be considered.

It was stipulated that the defendant and its attorneys, during the crucial period involved herein, were unaware of the mental condition of the plaintiff; nor did they have any reason to believe that such condition existed; plaintiff's attorneys were also unaware of such condition, and similarly had no reason to believe such condition existed. Further, it is uncontradicted that the purchase price was fair and reasonable and there was no overreaching.

Think About It!

Why should it matter whether Kralyn Enterprises knew or had reason to know of Fingerhut's mental condition? Recall that, in the discussion of the defense of infancy, it did not matter whether the contracting party knew or had reason to know the other party was a minor. Why might the defenses differ in this respect?

The contract of a mental incompetent is voidable at the election of the incompetent (*Blinn v. Schwarz*, 177 N.Y. 252, 69 N.E. 542), and the burden of proving incompetence is upon the party alleging it.

This case, with its interesting facets, should be particularly examined in light of two recent cases: *Ortelere v. Teachers' Retirement Bd. of City of N. Y.*, 25 N.Y.2d 196, 303 N.Y.S.2d 362, 250 N.E.2d 460 (1969) and *Faber v. Sweet Style Mfg. Corp.*, 40 Misc. 2d 212, 242 N.Y.S.2d 763 (1963).

Before the advent of these cases, contractual mental capacity was measured by the so-called cognitive test (see *Aldrich v. Bailey,* 132 N.Y. 85, 30 N.E.2d 264). Similarly, in *Paine v. Aldrich,* 133 N.Y. 544, 546, 30 N.E. 725, 726, it was held that if rational judgment could be based on "[a] mental capacity at the time of the execution . . . that he could collect in his mind without prompting, all the elements of the transaction and retain them for a sufficient length of time to perceive their obvious relations to each other", such judgment would be enough to prevent avoidance of the transaction on the claim of mental incompetency.

The *Faber* case, followed by the *Ortelere* case, became landmark authorities, which legally recognized the ailment manic-depressive psychosis where the afflicted one is aware of what he is doing but cannot help himself against the compulsion which controls his actions and impairs rational judgment.

Judge Breitel, writing for the majority in *Ortelere, supra,* 25 N.Y.2d at 202, 303 N.Y.S.2d at 367, 250 N.E.2d at 464, said: "The well-established rule is that contracts of a mentally incompetent person who has not been adjudicated insane are voidable. . . . Traditionally, in this State and elsewhere, contractual mental capacity

Make the Connection

Ortelere is a well known case that is more complex than this court's references to it. For additional background on *Ortelere*, see the "Food for Thought" box following this case.

has been measured by what is largely a cognitive test [citing authorities]". In further discussion of the evolution of the law from the cognitive test based on traditional standards to a more enlightened psychiatric acceptance of the mental illness manic-depressive psychosis, Judge Breitel alluded to the standards of the past governing competency to contract which were formulated "when psychiatric knowledge was quite primitive . . . [and which] fail to account for one who by reason of mental illness is unable to control his conduct even though his cognitive ability seems unimpaired" ([25 N.Y.] at 203, 303 N.Y.S. at 368, 250 N.E.2d at 464). Thus, a motivational standard has found its place in the law by dint and force of what persuasive psychiatrists expounded.

With such progress and understanding, we have gone beyond the days when psychiatric knowledge was finding itself. And these cases, *Faber* and *Ortelere* (*supra*), representative of the problem at hand, plainly say that incompetency to contract may exist, despite the presence of cognition, when a contract is made under the compulsion of manic depressive psychosis.

In *Faber*, 40 Misc. 2d at 216, 242 N.Y.S.2d at 768, guidelines are given: "Whether under the latter test a manic will be held incompetent to enter into a particular contract will depend upon an evaluation of (1) testimony of the claimed incompetent, (2) testimony of psychiatrists, and (3) the behavior of the claimed incompetent as detailed in the testimony of others (Green, Judicial Tests of Mental Incompetency, 6 Mo. L. R. 141), including whether by usual business standards the transaction is normal or fair (Green, Proof of Mental Incompetency and the Unexpressed Major Premise, 53 Yale L.J. 271, 299–305)."

A caveat, however, in *Ortelere,* 25 N.Y.2d at 206, 303 N.Y.S.2d at 370, 250 N.E.2d at 466, is handed down by the Court of Appeals while placing its seal of approval on the motivational standard. "Of course, nothing less serious than medically classified psychosis should suffice or else few contracts would be invulnerable to some kind of psychological attack".

As this court views this problem, the evidence, for our purpose, must involve the personality of the plaintiff, the nature of the deal at stake, the circumstances and the manner in which the contract was entered into, the behavior of the plaintiff juxtaposed to the contract and in some aspects of his life going beyond the limited range of the making of the contract, the medical history and evaluations regarding plaintiff's alleged psychosis or lack thereof. Upon such considerations, the ultimate and salient determination will be made as to whether the plaintiff was a manic-depressive psychotic and, if so, was he in the manic phase of that illness when the binder and contract were executed.

Plaintiff's medical history dates back to October 14, 1964 when he was hospitalized at the Gracie Square Hospital for manic-depressive reaction, manic type. On October 21, 1964 he was transferred to Mt. Sinai Hospital, from which he was discharged on October 27, 1964. Mt. Sinai diagnosed his condition as "schizophrenic reaction with manic manifestation." On November 16, 1964 plaintiff was admitted for the second time to Gracie Square Hospital, diagnosed as "manic depressive reaction, manic," and discharged on December 2, 1964. There he received six electric shock treatments.

On September 5, 1965 plaintiff was again admitted to Gracie Square Hospital for "manic depressive reaction" and discharged on October 5, 1965.

During the period from November 14, 1964 to September 16, 1965 plaintiff was under the care of Dr. Leonard Cammer, a psychiatrist. Dr. Cammer diagnosed plaintiff's condition as manic-depressive psychosis, mixed type.

From March 31, 1966 until May, 1968 he was treated by Dr. Alexander Thomas, who made the following diagnosis: "(1) Manic depressive syndrome, (2) Psychoneurosis, character disorder. The symptoms were severe. Although he was at no time psychotic during my period of treatment of him."

. . . . In July Dr. [Richard S.] Dolins saw plaintiff 9 times; 11 times in August; 9 times in September; 3 times between October 1 and 15; 6 times in November; twice in December and, in 1969, on January 4, 7, 8 and on January 25, when he saw him for the last time. Dr. Dolins, plaintiff's witness, testified and diagnosed plaintiff's condition as manic-depressive psychosis, but qualified such finding in declaring that he did not find plaintiff psychotic until . . . about September 13, [lasting] until November 5, 1968 when he was no longer psychotic. . . .

Dr. Nathan Kline [, plaintiff's witness] . . . testified as one who has been and is still treating plaintiff from February 17, 1969. His evaluations were further based on previous reports of the doctors and the hospital records in evidence. He stated that the characteristic symptoms of manic-depressive psychosis are mood swings, which pass the bounds of normalcy, so that the individual, in one or more areas, is no longer responsible or capable of managing his life in a general fashion, particularly in areas in which he is not familiar. He further testified that the lay person might not recognize either the symptoms as being related to the illness, or that the individual was psychotic.

In his opinion, therefore, it is possible to be psychotic in certain areas and not psychotic at all in other areas, during the same time. When asked when plaintiff became psychotic, if at all in September, 1968, he responded, "I would, if you wanted to be strictly technical about it, if by psychosis you mean getting so far out of touch with reality that you are seriously injuring yourself, I would say that the time he gave a check for $25,000, which constituted this point of fact, direct evidence of his having passed over the border from normality to pathology." In answer to the question as to whether it was psychotic for this man to enter into this deal involving $3,075,000, the answer came: ". . . . For this particular man that act was psychotic. It may not have been for someone else and it may not have been for him under other circumstances."

Dr. Abrahamsen testified as defendant's expert psychiatrist. He examined plaintiff on April 6, 1971. He read plaintiff's medical history, was present in court when Dr. Dolins testified and read the stenographic record of the testimony of Dr. Kline. He states that plaintiff had some mood swings and many neurotic traits but found nothing psychotic about him. He found that plaintiff was not psychotic at all during the period from mid-September to November, 1968. He characterized plaintiff's personality makeup as a neurotic character disorder with reactive depression. He found it medically significant that plaintiff was not hospitalized in 1968, or given strong medication or shock treatment and that the frequency of treatment was not increased. He states that psychosis is a condition and that one cannot on the same day be psychotic as to some actions and not as to others. The lines are thusly drawn with respect to the crucial time involved. Plaintiff's experts say plaintiff was psychotic. Defendant's expert says plaintiff was only neurotic. In *Faber* (40 Misc. 2d 212, 216–217, *supra*) the court uttered the following:

> Moreover, in the great majority of cases psychiatrists of equal quali-fication and experience will reach diametrically opposed conclusions on the same behavioral evidence. The courts have, therefore, tended to give less weight to expert testimony than to objective behavioral evidence (Halpern, Civil Insanity: The New York Treatment of the Issue of Mental Incapacity in Non-Criminal Cases, 44 Corn. L.Q. 76; Green, *op cit.*, 53 Yale L.J., p. 306).

In September, 1968 plaintiff sought to amend the agreement of limited partnership under which Mt. Vernon Associates had been established. He retained a prestigious law firm in this connection. On October 1, 1968 plaintiff sent a memorandum to his partners in Mr. Vernon Associates asking their consent to certain transactions including:

> 1. The purchase of Stanley Fingerhut of the Bel-Aire Country Club located in Westchester County. Mr. Fingerhut does not plan to be active in the day to day management of the club but will retain professional management to do so.

On October 7, 1968 plaintiff, with his attorney, and the Krassners and their attorney, met with one Bogert, an officer of the bank which held the first mortgage on Bel Aire. They discussed the refinancing of the club mortgage on behalf of the prospective purchaser. Plaintiff gave the bank his reference and authorized the bank to check it, and it received the following report:

> The subject [Stanley Fingerhut] is an ex-broker and partner in a major brokerage house. He is the founder and manager of Mt. Vernon Associ-

ates . . . . The fund has been very successful and is now worth over $3MM . . . . He is very well versed in the operation and is one of the most respected men in the hedge fund business. His personal net worth is in seven figures.

The bank has extended loans to the fund to moderate 7 figures, secured by marketable securities. Mr. Roach and other members of Chemical's management know Fingerhut personally and have a high opinion of him and of the company. Mr. Roach expressed the opinion that Fingerhut should have no trouble paying off an $864 M mortgage over a number of years.

Bogert testified that during his conference the words and actions of plaintiff impressed him as rational.

Plaintiff sought to bolster the testimony of his medical experts by adducing bizarre conduct on his part. Within this province, Goldner, plaintiff's co-manager in Mt. Vernon Associates, testified that in about August, 1968, plaintiff began to act strangely with regard to security investments, that he gambled and lost large sums of money, contributed to the Black Panther movement, boasted about women, bought a large quantity of ducks for a party he was giving, and employed unqualified and unnecessary people for a period of a month to indulge a whim on his part. Mary Scully, plaintiff's secretary, testified about quarrels between Goldner and plaintiff concerning investment decisions and that plaintiff resorted to foul language, which had not been his custom. Other so-called "bizarre" conduct was alluded to and testified to.

Defendant, in contradiction, presented witnesses to prove plaintiff's words and actions were rational. In this framework, Donald Klopfer, the Chairman of a large publishing house and a limited partner in Mt. Vernon Associates, having invested $200,000 after meeting the plaintiff in September, 1968, testified that plaintiff's words and actions impressed him as being rational.

Martin Mayer, an author, who in September, 1968, was writing a book to be called "New Breed on Wall Street," interviewed plaintiff in connection with that book on September 20, 1968 at the office of Mt. Vernon Associates. . . . Mr. Mayer concluded that plaintiff's words and actions impressed him as rational. . . .

In similar vein, Harry G. Herman, a former Surrogate of Westchester County who has known plaintiff and his parents for many years, testified. Both plaintiff and the witness were members of the same golf club and played golf together.

Robert L. Livingston, who became a limited partner in Mt. Vernon Associates on July 1, 1968 to the extent of investing $100,000, had spoken to plaintiff on the telephone several times and had met plaintiff for lunch in the latter part of October, 1968. He, too, stated that plaintiff's words and actions were rational.

Morris Thau, an old friend of plaintiff's and his father, on the basis of that friendship and business dealings since 1964, characterized plaintiff's conduct as rational. Thau had become a limited partner in Mt. Vernon Associates when it was organized and had invested $200,000.

The situation before us here is unlike that in the *Faber* case, *supra*. Plaintiff did not go on a buying spree. He invested in a $3 million hedge fund he had started in 1967 which, in a short period of time, grew to over $5 million. Plaintiff was known as a super-salesman. Dr. Dolins agreed that he was. Plaintiff had a penchant and ability for raising money. Differently, the frenetic conduct of the incompetent, in *Faber*, as affecting that transaction, was characterized by the court as being irrational and abnormal, highlighted by "The rapidity by which the incompetent moved" in the performance of those questionable acts. Without detailing such acts, it suffices to say that the incompetent's conduct, done without the benefit of legal representation, as is found here, was so greatly abnormal that the court was convinced, with the aid of medical testimony, that he had acted under the compulsion of a psychosis. In our circumstances, the plaintiff accepted, in major and important part, the advice of his lawyers. In *Faber*, the incompetent acted against the advice given by his lawyer, and the contract was signed in the absence of any lawyer. It should be further noted, that about two weeks following the signing of the contract, the incompetent, Faber, was sent to a mental institution. There is no parallelism in the essential aspects. On the contrary, the evidence at hand moves across a wider period of time with a more calculated and studied purpose, reflected from the concerned comparison of country and golf clubs, extending to November 19, 1968, when the plaintiff elected to rescind the contract he had made with the expert advice and collaboration of his lawyers, precautionary and deliberate acts intervening.

Plaintiff, unlike the *Ortelere case*, was able and did care for himself, attended to his business, had a substantial income and net worth of about $350,000. Also, *Ortelere* deals with a sick woman who was so completely unable to manage her affairs that her husband gave up his job and devoted himself to taking care of her. Moreover, the court there observed that the defendant was, or should have been, fully aware of her condition, which gave rise to the retirement option she selected. Here, the defendant and attorneys for both parties, were unaware of any alleged psychosis, and knowledge of a condition could not be imputed to any of them.

On the whole, whatever behavior has been ascribed to the plaintiff as being irrational or bizarre does not reach sufficient level to overcome the strength and character of plaintiff's conduct, which was testified to as rational. The net result of the credible evidence in this area, conjoining with the medical evaluation of the experts and other medical evidence, convinces the court that the plaintiff was not in the manic phase of the ailment, manic-depressive psychosis, during the period the binder and the agreement were entered into. Asked by the court for a definition of "psychotic", Dr. Kline replied: "Psychotic means there is a defect in thinking, in feeling, in behaving and memory in relationship to reality in general to such a degree that the individual is incapacitated or is incapable of adequately managing his affairs".

The credible evidence does not put the plaintiff within that definition. With cognition, and without stress of psychosis, his rational judgment was not impaired during the period the binder and agreement were made. And while there were some neurotic manifestations, the condition responsible for this behavior was insufficient to render him legally incompetent to make a contract.

It follows that plaintiff has failed to sustain his burden of proving that when he executed the binder and contract he "did so solely as a result of serious mental illness, namely, psychosis". (*Ortelere, supra*, 25 N.Y.2d at 206, 303 N.Y.S.2d at 370, 250 N.E.2d at 466.)

. . . .

Therefore, plaintiff in a competent mental state, had no valid excuse in refusing to perform an enforceable contract . . . .

. . . .

Moreover, the contract may be validated on the basis that even had the binder and agreement been tainted with psychosis, the contract was later ratified by the "conscious action" of the plaintiff after November 5, 1968, when Dr. Dolins says he was free of psychosis. Dr. Dolins, plaintiff's treating and testifying doctor, declared that on November 5, 1968, plaintiff was no longer psychotic. With such a concession, the letter dated November 8, 1968, from plaintiff's lawyers to defendant's lawyer, Seymour Rabinowitz, takes on cogent and significant evidentiary meaning. Therein it was stated that "the purchaser has elected to adjourn closing of title until December 15, 1968." The letter was more than a mere request for adjournment purpose. Other matters, in recognition of the contract, were taken up. A dispute over a billing for labor was made the subject of discussion and was resolved, by authorization, to remit to Rabinowitz's client, the seller, the amount of $1,422.89, constituting "payment for material and labor as per said correspondence". Acknowledgment of that remittance was requested by letter. The letter continues:

> Your[s] of October 29 is in error concerning the furnishing of material for membership application. Mr. Fingerhut presented to seller in writing his proposed rate schedule which was unacceptable to sellers. There were several conferences between the parties concerning this schedule, the last of which was attended not only by the parties but by their respective counsel. No agreement [or] solution was arrived at and it was decided that further negotiations would continue. We will not accept any expenses incurred in the solicitation by your clients of renewal applications and preparation of any material for same . . . . You have also failed to mention whether or not your clients are notifying prospective members and existing members that a minimum food and beverage charge of $600 will be levied on the 1969 members. In light of our notice herein adjourning the closing, no comment need be made on the Thanksgiving Dinner reservations. Please be advised that we are continuing to interview prospective managers and have not as yet found someone whom we deem suitable for this position of great consequence.

The communication was written after November 5, 1968, when Dr. Dolins testified he saw plaintiff following the doctor's return from a vacation. Dr. Dolins was then satisfied that plaintiff was no longer psychotic. It was on that visit that plaintiff told the doctor he "could not raise the money" and he "was considering the adjournment of that closing from November 15 to December 15, so that he could raise the money". . . .

. . . .

On November 19, 1968, when they met again, Dr. Dolins testified, plaintiff told him he "wished he could get out of it".

The November 8 letter when read represents confirmation and indicates a purpose, on plaintiff's part, to proceed with the contract and effect the closing. For that important reason, the letter has been, in part, quoted. It bears heavily on defendant's defense that plaintiff, by acts of recognition and reliance, ratified the contract at a time he was competent to do so, if, indeed, he had not been at the time of its making.

He did not testify or raise his voice in any manner to protest that such a letter was sent without his permission or knowledge. At this point, comment on his refusal to take the stand is appropriate, since that question affects the matter being instantly considered, as well as other matters developed at the trial, which could have been the subject, or object, of his supporting or countervailing testimony. The plaintiff was in the courtroom for at least part of the trial, which extended beyond three weeks. He elected not to take the stand. He could have contradicted, corroborated or explained, if he chose, the evidence bearing upon his conduct and the motivation which prompted the making of the binder and contract. He could have even lent support to any phase which was favorable to his cause, but which had come under attack requiring bolstering.

He never reappeared at the trial. He was and is not a judicially declared incompetent. Dr. Kline testified that plaintiff is not presently psychotic and continues under his care and treatment. Yet, no opinion was sought for or advanced that because of illness, or for any cause, he was not available or unable to testify. Interestingly, at some juncture during the trial, while plaintiff was seated in the spectator part of the courtroom, the question of his age arose during the examination of a witness. Voluntarily, Mr. Fingerhut arose in and in open court, responded: "I will be 36 June 5th." That was the fullest extent of his "testimony," albeit unsworn.

> ### Think About It!
>
> Sometimes the tests for mental competency seem arcane and even antiquated, because the law lags behind medicine's understanding of defective mental processing. Other tests may seem harsh or insensitive, mirroring society's reactions to mental illness.
>
> What challenges do these tests and attitudes pose for attorneys who are seeking to be professional and compassionate about mental health issues?

Under these circumstances, the court will invoke the adverse inference rule applicable to one who is able to testify with knowledge upon certain matters in the record, but does not. Specifically, plaintiff has failed to testify concerning his participation in the making of the November 8, 1968 letter; whether he had any knowledge of it, or its purpose. In face of the evidence, it becomes an accepted fact that he did have knowledge of the letter and approved its purpose. Certainly, the testimony of Dr. Dolins, as to plaintiff's knowledge of the letter, recounted above, would in itself be corroboration of that finding.

Plaintiff cannot palliate this failure on the ground that the defendant expressed an interest to call the plaintiff on its side of the case, and did not. Firstly, plaintiff had the roles of party and witness, and the party who is naturally expected to call a witness should not be relieved of the possible unfavorable consequence of his own failure to do so [, p]articularly where the witness, such as the plaintiff, could be a hostile witness. (*Reehil v. Fraas*, 129 App. Div. 563, 566, *revd. on other grounds*, 197 N.Y. 64.) There is warrant, therefore, to apply the stamp of weakness with respect to much of the evidence that pervades the record in this particular vein (see *Perlman v. Shanck*, 192 App. Div. 179; *Milio v. Railway Motor Trucking Co.*, 257 App. Div. 640). As aptly stated in *Dowling v. Hastings* (211 N.Y. 199, 202) "where one party to an action knowing the truth of a matter in controversy and having the evidence in his possession, omits to speak, every inference warranted by the evidence will be indulged in against him."

The defendant has sustained the burden of proving ratification of the contract. The evidence clearly indicates that plaintiff, without mental disability, ratified the contract. Borrowing from *Faber*, 40 Misc. 2d at 217, 242 N.Y.S.2d at 768, there was "conscious action" on plaintiff's part which recognized the contract at a time when he was not psychotic. In adjourning the closing of title and conduct pertaining thereto, he demonstrated knowledge of the existence of the contract, with confirmation of it as a contractual obligation; and though he regretted its making, he, nevertheless, acted in furtherance of the contract.

While it may be unfortunate that the plaintiff "bit off more than he could chew", the relief he seeks must be denied.

The motion to dismiss the complaint is granted.

Think About It: *Ortelere* and the Challenges of Finding Mental Incapacity

The *Fingerhut* opinion relies on *Ortelere v. Teachers' Retirement Board of City of New York*, 25 N.Y.2d 196, 303 N.Y.S.2d 362, 250 N.E.2d 460 (1969) as establishing legal recognition of manic-depressive psychosis (now more commonly called bipolar disorder). Although *Ortelere* did recognize that mental incapacity might arise in circumstances that do not satisfy the older "cognitive" standard, the facts of the case are more challenging than acknowledged in *Fingerhut*. *Ortelere* involved "the evidently unwise and fool-hardy selection of [retirement] benefits" by a 60-year-old upon her retirement after 40 years as a public school teacher. She had suffered a "nervous breakdown," took a leave of absence, and was diagnosed as having "involutional psychosis, melancholia type." Her husband left his job to care for his wife full-time. She died a little less than two months after making her election to have maximum benefits paid during her lifetime, leaving no survivor benefits for her husband of 38 years and their two grown children. Her husband was left with meager savings and no income; as her executor, he brought suit to set aside his wife's last-minute choice to take larger benefits during the short remainder of her life with no payments to her family after her death.

Although the *Ortelere* court set aside her contractual choice based on some evidence of mental illness in her history, it is far from clear that Mrs. Ortelere was under a compulsion that was comparable to that experienced by those with bipolar disorders. The alternate view is that she was unwilling to acknowledge her physical ailments and preferred to ignore her likely impending death by choosing the benefit package she did. She might also have rationally opted to receive the larger immediate payout for the indeterminate duration of her life to help the family cash-flow when her husband quit work to take care of her. One can sympathize with the court's desire to undo Mrs. Ortelere's contractual choice, even if one questions the correctness of the court's application of the legal doctrine.

The facts of *Ortelere* and *Fingerhut* illustrate the difficulty of determining when an individual crosses the line from bad decision-making and lack of will power to compulsion based on mental illness. That is why the *Ortelere* court required "nothing less serious than medically classified psychosis" as grounds for challenging capacity, as noted by the *Fingerhut* court (page 374). But given ongoing developments in neuroscience and the changes over time in medical definitions of incompetency, relying on medical definitions does not answer all the difficult questions raised by claims of mental incompetency.

For the trial court opinion and transcript (including testimony of Mrs. Ortelere's husband, daughter, and psychiatrist) and additional background information on the case, see Richard Danzig & Geoffrey R. Watson, *The Capability Problem in Contract Law* 242–306 (2d ed. 2004).

Reading Critically

Read Restatement (Second) § 15 and Comment b.

1. What are the key differences between the alternative tests in (1)(a) (known as the "cognitive" test and drawn from criminal standards) and (1)(b) (known as the "motivational" or "affective" test)? Why do the differences make sense (if they do)?

2. Does the rule in (2) apply to both (1)(a) and (b)?

3. How does the "motivational" test in (1)(b) compare to the test applied in *Fingerhut*?

4. If you were a judge, what test would you use to decide competency for entering contracts? Why?

§ 2.3. Intoxication

The defense of intoxication raises issues of capacity similar in some respects to those raised by the defense of mental illness (inability to understand the transaction or control one's actions) but the cause of the incapacity is different, resulting from voluntary behavior (drinking) or behavior caused by a condition often akin to mental illness (alcoholism).

Reading Critically

Read Restatement (Second) § 16.

1. Compare Restatement (Second) § 16 (on the defense of intoxication) with § 15 (on the defense of mental illness or defect; see previous section). What similarities exist between these two defenses? How do they differ? What rationale would you offer for the differences?

2. Recall that the intoxication defense was discussed briefly in *Lucy v. Zehmer*, Chapter 2 (page 22). What would the result have been if § 16 had been applied to the facts of that case?

Example D: *Gonzalez v. Jurella*, 2015 WL 9943596 (D. Conn. Sept. 22, 2015).

Inmate claimed that while incarcerated he was subject to excessive force and deliberate indifference by the correctional officers. Upon release, Inmate filed a lawsuit against the State. Inmate sent an email to counsel for the State reading, "I will settle at $500. When do I get my check?" The State's attorneys confirmed the email with Inmate who replied, "Yes. I want my check as soon as possible." The State's attorneys advised Inmate that there would be paperwork to complete a settlement. Two days later, Inmate emailed the attorneys, stating, "In addition to the

$500, the defendants will also be paying the $1200 I owe to the Courts and the $400 I paid to file" the cases. The State's attorneys claimed that there was an agreement to settle all cases for $500. When the State filed a motion to enforce the email settlement agreement, Inmate claimed he was intoxicated at the time he sent his emails, being under the influence of alcohol and marijuana at the relevant time.

Analysis: Upholding the settlement agreement, the court noted there was

no indication that the defendants knew, or should have known, that the plaintiff was intoxicated, or that as a result of his intoxication he was unable to understand in a reasonable manner the nature and consequences of the transaction. The relevant emails appeared coherent. They were sent in the middle of the day, and in rapid succession. They do not contain typographical errors or other indications that Mr. Gonzalez was not in possession of his faculties. The amount of the proposed settlement was consistent with the parties' prior settlement discussions. Nothing about the interaction should have caused counsel for the defendants to suspect that Mr. Gonzalez was intoxicated. Furthermore, the fact that Mr. Gonzalez was capable of engaging in the discussion at all indicates that he was not "utterly deprived of the use of his reason" at the time.

Problems: The Incapacity Defenses

6-1. In a dispute with Husband and Wife, Sister claimed a one-half interest in property acquired by Husband and Wife from Wife's (and Sister's) Mother prior to Mother's death. In order to settle the dispute, the parties entered into mediation. Even though Husband and Wife were separated, Husband drove Wife on the date of the mediation, because he did not believe Wife was capable of driving. Husband testified that Wife became less coherent throughout the day, slurred her speech, was unable to focus or think rationally throughout the day, was crying and out of control, and ultimately left the mediation before it was over because she could not handle it. During the mediation, Sister, Husband, and Wife signed an agreement whereby Husband and Wife would sell the property and pay Sister $100,000. Husband and Wife did not follow through on the agreement, and they claimed Wife lacked capacity to execute the agreement due to her emotionally overwrought state of mind on the day of mediation. Sister sued to enforce the agreement, and Wife sought to avoid the agreement on grounds of incapacity. Should she succeed? Would Wife be required to present medical and expert evidence as to incapacity?

6-2. Mother and Father had Child out of wedlock and after contested litigation, a court entered a paternity order regarding Child. Grandfather of Child passed away. Grandfather's will established a number of trusts to benefit his children and ultimately grandchildren, with the determination of paternity being left exclusively to Executor. Child hired Attorney to investigate the matter. Attorney obtained a copy of the will and agreed to help Child be declared a beneficiary of the estate, which was very large. Attorney entered into a contingency agreement with Child for the services. The Executor ultimately advised Attorney that no monies were currently being paid to grandchildren and that Child's paternity would be evaluated at a later time, being

Ethical Issue

A contingency fee is an agreement where a lawyer agrees to accept a fixed percentage (i.e. one third) of the recovery which is ultimately paid to the client. The Model Rules of Professional Conduct § 1.5 provides "A lawyer shall not make an agreement for, charge, or collect an unreasonable fee or an unreasonable amount for expenses." It also provides guidance on what determines the reasonableness of a fee, including the amount of time involved and the amount in dispute. Do you think the contingency fee was appropriate here?

For additional information on the ethics of fees, see https://www.americanbar.org/content/dam/aba/administrative/litigation/materials/sac_2012/17-1_ethics_surrounding_attorneys_fees.authcheckdam.pdf.

not yet ripe for determination. Nevertheless, Attorney filed a complaint requesting that Child be recognized as a beneficiary of the estate and successfully obtained a court order. Upon reaching the age of majority, Child disaffirmed the contract with Attorney. If Attorney brings an action to enforce the contract, should Child succeed in his defense? If so, should Child compensate Attorney based upon an hourly rate?

---

§ 3. Defenses Related to Defects in Mutual Assent

When parties manifest assent to an agreement, both parties should be acting voluntarily and without being misled about the key aspects of the transaction. In other words, both parties have a right not to be tricked or forced into a contract ("freedom from contract") and a right to have the resulting contract be the agreement intended by them. If either party is unduly pressured to assent or is fundamentally misled as to the nature of the contract, the policies underlying the requirement of mutual assent are not met, even though the parties' assent may appear to be valid under the standards and rules discussed in Chapters 2 and 3. These policies underlie the defenses of mistake, misrepresentation, duress, undue influence, and unconscionability.

§ 3.1. Mistake

The Restatement (Second) § 151 defines a mistake as "a *belief* that is not in accord with the facts." A fact is a past or present state of things—something that actually exists or an event or circumstance that has occurred. *Facts* differ from *promises* (commitments to do or not do something in the future), *predictions* (expectations about a future occurrence or state of things), and *opinions* (personal views, attitudes, or professional appraisals about present circumstances or the future, or beliefs or judgments based on grounds insufficient to produce complete certainty).

To illustrate these distinctions, recall the case at the beginning of Chapter 2, *Lucy v. Zehmer* (page 22) (the land purchase contract negotiated in a bar). By changing the facts slightly, we can identify the kinds of mistake that could have occurred:

- *Mistake of opinion*: If Lucy had mistakenly thought that the farm was worth 50% more than the agreed-upon price

- *Mistake of prediction*: If Lucy had mistakenly thought that Zehmer's farm could produce bumper crops of soybeans, if the farm were properly run

Make the Connection

The distinctions between fact, opinion, and prediction are discussed again at the beginning of § 3.2 in this Chapter, which covers the closely related defense of misrepresentation.

- *Mistake of fact*: If Lucy (or both Lucy and Zehmer) had mistakenly believed that Zehmer's land contained valuable mineral deposits

- *Mistake of law*: If Lucy (or both Lucy and Zehmer) had mistakenly believed that Zehmer's land was eligible for agricultural subsidies for growing sunflowers

The defense of mistake applies to assertions of fact, but not to promises, predictions or opinions. Traditionally mistakes of law were denied coverage, but some recent cases have treated the existing law as part of the facts existing at the time of agreement and have allowed the defense.

If *both* parties were mistaken about a fact at the time of contract formation, the disadvantaged party can attempt to avoid the contract by using the defense of *mutual* mistake. If instead only *one* party was mistaken about a fact at contract formation, the mistaken party may be able to use the defense of *unilateral* mistake.[*]

Problems: Distinguishing Mistake of Fact, Law, Opinion, and Prediction

---

Below are statements by a party who has entered into a contract and now seeks to be excused from the contract on the basis of mistake. For each statement, indicate whether the mistake relates to fact, law, opinion, or prediction. If you think it might fit in more than one category, is there additional information that would help you decide between those possibilities?

6-3. "I bought this drought-resistant seed from the co-op because I thought it would rain only 40 inches this year, but instead it rained 92 inches."

6-4. "I bought this ring for $1,000 because the antiques store clerk told me he thought it was a diamond ring. Now I find that it's instead a cubic zirconia, which is worth only 25% of a diamond."

6-5. "I purchased an easement from Kato to cross his lakefront land because he said I could boat on that lake, but now I find that the Department of Natural Resources does not allow boating there."

6-6. "The seller and I thought that the house satisfied the building code. That's why she priced it at $250,000, and that's why I agreed to buy it for $250,000. Now I find that it met the building code of 15 years ago, but not today's building code."

6-7. "I posted this boat for sale on a website, meaning to sell it for $5,000, but I left out a zero and now a buyer has accepted my $500 offer."

---

[*] Note that these kinds of mistakes are being raised as a defense to contract formation. If instead a contract is formed but it contains ambiguous contract language, then the issue is one of contract interpretation, which is discussed in Chapter 8, page 541.

§ 3.1.1. Mutual Mistake

Example E: *Wood v. Boynton*, 25 N.W.42 (Wisc. 1885).

Wood owned and possessed a small stone, the nature and value of which she was ignorant. She sold the stone to a jewelry business for one dollar. When it turned out the stone was an uncut diamond of an alleged value of approximately $1000, Wood brought an action to recover possession of the stone.

Wood testified as follows: "The first time Boynton saw that stone he was talking about buying the topaz, or whatever it is, in September or October. I went into the store to get a little pin mended, and I had it in a small box,—the pin,—a small ear-ring; . . . this stone, and a broken sleeve-button were in the box. Mr. Boynton turned to give me a check for my pin. I thought I would ask him what the stone was, and I took it out of the box and asked him to please tell me what that was. He took it in his hand and seemed some time looking at it. I told him I had been told it was a topaz, and he said it might be. He says, 'I would buy this; would you sell it?' I told him I did not know but what I would. What would it be worth? And he said he did not know; he would give me a dollar and keep it as a specimen, and I told him I would not sell it; and it was certainly pretty to look at. He asked me where I found it, and I told him in Eagle. He asked about how far out, and I said right in the village, and I went out. Afterwards, and about the twenty-eighth of December, I needed money pretty badly, and thought every dollar would help, and I took it back to Mr. Boynton and told him I had brought back the topaz, and he says, 'Well, yes; what did I offer you for it?' and I says, 'One dollar;' and he stepped to the change drawer and gave me the dollar, and I went out." In another part of her testimony she said, "Before I sold the stone I had no knowledge whatever that it was a diamond. I told him that I had been advised that it was probably a topaz, and he said probably it was. The stone was about the size of a canary bird's egg, nearly the shape of an egg,—worn pointed at one end; it was nearly straw color,—a little darker."

Go Online!

For the diamond's history, read the Wikipedia entry on the "Eagle Diamond."

Mr. Samuel B. Boynton, the jeweler, testified that he had never dealt in or seen an uncut diamond and that "he had no idea this was a diamond, and it never entered his brain at the time."

Analysis: The court recognized that fraud or mistake about the identity of the thing sold could form the basis for rescission. Absent any proof by Wood of fraud, the court turned to consider the defense of mistake. The court observed that both parties were ignorant as to the character of the stone and its value. Mr. Boynton was a non-expert with respect to an uncut diamond and had not made a formal examination of the stone. Wood had the stone in her possession for some time, but had not determined its character. The court rejected the claim of mistake, observing that "[i]f she chose to sell it without further investigation as to its intrinsic value to a person who was guilty of no fraud or unfairness which induced her to sell it for a small sum, she cannot repudiate the sale because it is afterwards ascertained that she made a bad bargain. There is no pretense of any mistake as to the identity of the thing sold. It was produced by the plaintiff and exhibited to the vendee before the sale was made, and the thing sold was delivered to the vendee when the purchase price was paid. . . . Suppose the appellant had produced the stone, and said she had been told it was a diamond, and she believed it was, but had no knowledge herself as to its character or value, and Mr. Boynton had given her $500 for it, could he have rescinded the sale if it had turned out to be a topaz or any other stone of very small value? Could Mr. Boynton have rescinded the sale on the ground of mistake? Clearly not, nor could he rescind it on the ground that there had been a breach of warranty, because there was no warranty, nor could he rescind it on the ground of fraud, unless he could show that she falsely declared that she had been told it was a diamond, or, if she had been so told, still she knew it was not a diamond."

Moreover, the court concluded that fraud could not be based upon inadequacy of price where the value of the stone sold was open to investigation by both parties and both presumed the price was adequate. No evidence showed that Mr. Boynton had any knowledge of the real value of the stone or even that it was a diamond. While Wood's situation was "unfortunate," she had no defense that would entitle her to rescission of the sale.

Reading Critically: *Lenawee*

1. What was the parties' mistake in the sales transaction(s)? What determines whether that mistake has legal significance?

2. *Lenawee* discusses at some length, and then declines to follow, the much earlier case of *Sherwood v. Walker* (a favorite in contracts casebooks). Some jurisdictions still retain their own versions of the *Sherwood* rule, even though it is a minority rule. What is the standard articulated in *Sherwood,* and how does it

differ from the rule adopted in *Lenawee*? Which is the better rule? Why?

3. What role do the terms of the contract play in determining the result?

See It!

The *Lenawee* property transfers and lawsuits are diagrammed below:

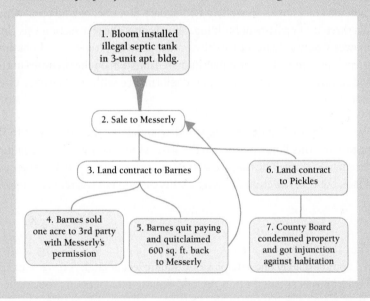

Lenawee County Board of Health v. Messerly

LENAWEE COUNTY BOARD OF HEALTH, Plaintiff

v.

WILLIAM H. MESSERLY and MARTHA B. MESSERLY, Defendants
and Cross-Plaintiffs/Appellants[*]

Supreme Court of Michigan
331 N.W.2d 203 (Mich. 1982)

RYAN, JUSTICE.

In March of 1977, Carl and Nancy Pickles, appellees, purchased from appellants, William and Martha Messerly, a 600-square-foot tract of land upon which is located a three-unit apartment building. Shortly after the transaction was closed, the Lenawee County Board of Health condemned the property and obtained a permanent injunction which prohibits human habitation on the premises until the defective sewage system is brought into conformance with the Lenawee County sanitation code.

We are required to determine whether appellees should prevail in their attempt to avoid this land contract on the basis of mutual mistake and failure of consideration. We conclude that the parties did entertain a mutual misapprehension of fact, but that the circumstances of this case do not warrant rescission.

I.

The facts of the case are not seriously in dispute. In 1971, the Messerlys acquired approximately one acre plus 600 square feet of land. A three-unit apartment building was situated upon the 600-square-foot portion. The trial court found that, prior to this transfer, the Messerlys' predecessor in title, Mr. Bloom, had installed a septic tank on the property without a permit and in violation of the applicable health code. The Messerlys used the building as an income investment property until 1973 when they sold it, upon land contract, to James Barnes who likewise used it primarily as an income-producing investment.[1]

---

[*] In this appeal, the Messerlys are the appellants and the Board of Health is no longer a party, but the Barneses (unlisted in the Supreme Court caption here) are. In the intermediate appellate court, the case title is *Board of Health v. Messerlys v. Pickles v. Barnes*. The Pickleses are both defendants (sued by the Board of Health) and cross-defendants (sued by the Messerlys). The Messerlys are defendants (sued by the Board of Health) and cross-plaintiffs (suing the Pickleses). James E. and Joan L. Barnes are also defendants (sued by the Pickleses).

[1] James Barnes was married shortly after he purchased the property. Mr. and Mrs. Barnes lived in one of the apartments on the property for three months and, after they moved, Mrs. Barnes continued to aid in the management of the property.

Mr. and Mrs. Barnes, with the permission of the Messerlys, sold approximately one acre of the property in 1976, and the remaining 600 square feet and building were offered for sale soon thereafter when Mr. and Mrs. Barnes defaulted on their land contract. Mr. and Mrs. Pickles evidenced an interest in the property, but were dissatisfied with the terms of the Barnes-Messerly land contract. Consequently, to accommodate the Pickleses' preference to enter into a land contract directly with the Messerlys, Mr. and Mrs. Barnes executed a quit-claim deed which conveyed their interest in the property back to the Messerlys. After inspecting the property, Mr. and Mrs. Pickles executed a new land contract with the Messerlys on March 21, 1977. It provided for a purchase price of $25,500. A clause was added to the end of the land contract form which provides:

> "17. Purchaser has examined this property and agrees to accept same in its present condition. There are no other or additional written or oral understandings."

Five or six days later, when the Pickleses went to introduce themselves to the tenants, they discovered raw sewage seeping out of the ground. Tests conducted by a sanitation expert indicated the inadequacy of the sewage system. The Lenawee County Board of Health subsequently condemned the property and initiated this lawsuit in the Lenawee Circuit Court against the Messerlys as land contract vendors, and the Pickleses, as vendees, to obtain a permanent injunction proscribing human habitation of the premises until the property was brought into conformance with the Lenawee County sanitation code. The injunction was granted, and the Lenawee County Board of Health was permitted to withdraw from the lawsuit by stipulation of the parties.

When no payments were made on the land contract, the Messerlys filed a cross-complaint against the Pickleses seeking foreclosure, sale of the property, and a deficiency judgment. Mr. and Mrs. Pickles then counterclaimed for rescission against the Messerlys, and filed a third-party complaint against the Barneses, which incorporated, by reference, the allegations of the counterclaim against the Messerlys. In count one, Mr. and Mrs. Pickles alleged failure of consideration. Count two charged Mr. and Mrs. Barnes with willful concealment and misrepresentation as a result of their failure to disclose the condition of the sanitation system. Additionally, Mr. and Mrs. Pickles sought to hold the Messerlys liable in equity for the Barneses' alleged misrepresentation. The Pickleses prayed that the land contract be rescinded.

After a bench trial, the court concluded that the Pickleses had no cause of action against either the Messerlys or the Barneses as there was no fraud or misrepresentation. This ruling was predicated on the trial judge's conclusion that none of the parties knew of Mr. Bloom's earlier transgression or of the resultant problem with the septic system until it was discovered by the Pickleses, and that the sanitation problem was not caused by any of the parties. The trial court held that the property was purchased "as is", after inspection and, accordingly, its "negative . . . value cannot be blamed upon an innocent seller". Foreclosure was ordered against the Pickleses, together with a judgment against them in the amount of $25,943.09.[3]

Mr. and Mrs. Pickles appealed from the adverse judgment. The Court of Appeals unanimously affirmed the trial court's ruling with respect to Mr. and Mrs. Barnes but, in a two-to-one decision, reversed the finding of no cause of action on the Pickleses' claims against the Messerlys. It concluded that the mutual mistake[5] between the Messerlys and the Pickleses went to a basic, as opposed to a collateral, element of the contract,[6] and that the parties intended to transfer income-producing rental property but, in actuality, the vendees paid $25,500 for an asset without value.[7]

We granted the Messerlys' application for leave to appeal. 411 Mich. 900 (1981).[8]

II

We must decide initially whether there was a mistaken belief entertained by one or both parties to the contract in dispute and, if so, the resultant legal significance.

A contractual mistake "is a belief that is not in accord with the facts". 1 Restatement Contracts, 2d, § 151. The erroneous belief of one or both of the parties must relate to a fact in existence at the time the contract is executed. That

---

[3]   The parties stipulated that this amount was due on the land contract, assuming that the contract was valid and enforceable.

[5]   Mr. and Mrs. Pickles did not allege mutual mistake as a ground for rescission in their pleadings. However, the trial court characterized their failure of consideration argument as mutual mistake resulting in failure of consideration. . . . Since the mutual mistake issue was dispositive in the Court of Appeals, we find its consideration necessary to a proper determination of this case.

[6]   Mr. and Mrs. Pickles did not appeal the trial court's finding that there was no fraud or misrepresentation by the Messerlys or Mr. and Mrs. Barnes. Likewise, the propriety of that ruling is not before this Court today.

[7]   The trial court found that the only way that the property could be put to residential use would be to pump and haul the sewage, a method which is economically unfeasible, as the cost of such a disposal system amounts to double the income generated by the property. There was speculation by the trial court that the adjoining land might be utilized to make the property suitable for residential use, but, in the absence of testimony directed at that point, the court refused to draw any conclusions. The trial court and the Court of Appeals both found that the property was valueless, or had a negative value.

[8]   The Court of Appeals decision to affirm the trial court's finding of no cause of action against Mr. and Mrs. Barnes has not been appealed to this Court and, accordingly, the propriety of that ruling is not before us today.

is to say, the belief which is found to be in error may not be, in substance, a prediction as to a future occurrence or non-occurrence.

The Court of Appeals concluded, after a de novo review of the record, that the parties were mistaken as to the income-producing capacity of the property in question. We agree. The vendors and the vendees each believed that the property transferred could be utilized as income-generating rental property. All of the parties subsequently learned that, in fact, the property was unsuitable for any residential use.

Make the Connection

The mistake defense applies only if the parties had an erroneous belief about facts in existence at the time of contract formation. If the erroneous belief relates not to facts at the time of formation but instead to predictions about what will or will not come to pass during the term of the contract, then the appropriate claim is not "mistake" but the "excuse" of impracticability based on the assertion that the party's performance has become impossible or extremely difficult because of the unexpected turn of events. The excuse defense is covered in Chapter 9, page 748.

Appellants assert that there was no mistake in the contractual sense because the defect in the sewage system did not arise until after the contract was executed. The appellees respond that the Messerlys are confusing the date of the inception of the defect with the date upon which the defect was discovered.

This is essentially a factual dispute which the trial court failed to resolve directly. Nevertheless, we are empowered to draw factual inferences from the facts found by the trial court. GCR 1963, 865.1(6).

An examination of the record reveals that the septic system was defective prior to the date on which the land contract was executed. The Messerlys' grantor installed a nonconforming septic system without a permit prior to the transfer of the property to the Messerlys in 1971. Moreover, virtually undisputed testimony indicates that, assuming ideal soil conditions, 2,500 square feet of property is necessary to support a sewage system adequate to serve a three-family dwelling. Likewise, 750 square feet is mandated for a one-family home. Thus, the division of the parcel and sale of one acre of the property by Mr. and Mrs. Barnes in 1976 made it impossible to remedy the already illegal septic system within the confines of the 600-square-foot parcel.[10] Appellants do not dispute these underlying facts which give rise to an inference contrary to their contentions.

---

[10] It is crucial to distinguish between the date on which a belief relating to a particular fact or set of facts becomes erroneous due to a change in the fact, and the date on which the mistaken nature of the belief is discovered. By definition, a mistake cannot be discovered until after the contract is executed. If the parties were aware, prior to the execution of a contract, that they were in error concerning a particular fact, there would be no misapprehension in signing the contract. Thus stated, it becomes obvious that the date on which a mistaken fact manifests itself is irrelevant to the determination whether or not there was a mistake.

Having determined that when these parties entered into the land contract they were laboring under a mutual mistake of fact, we now direct our attention to a determination of the legal significance of that finding.

A contract may be rescinded because of a mutual misapprehension of the parties, but this remedy is granted only in the sound discretion of the court. Appellants argue that the parties' mistake relates only to the quality or value of the real estate transferred, and that such mistakes are collateral to the agreement and do not justify rescission, citing A & M Land Development Co. v. Miller, 354 Mich. 681, 94 N.W.2d 197 (1959).

In that case, the plaintiff was the purchaser of 91 lots of real property. It sought partial rescission of the land contract when it was frustrated in its attempts to develop 42 of the lots because it could not obtain permits from the county health department to install septic tanks on these lots. This Court refused to allow rescission because the mistake, whether mutual or unilateral, related only to the value of the property.

. . .

Appellees contend, on the other hand, that in this case the parties were mistaken as to the very nature of the character of the consideration and claim that the pervasive and essential quality of this mistake renders rescission appropriate. They cite in support of that view Sherwood v. Walker, 66 Mich. 568, 33 N.W. 919 (1887), the famous "barren cow" case. In that case, the parties agreed to the sale and purchase of a cow which was thought to be barren, but which was, in reality, with calf. When the seller discovered the fertile condition of his cow, he refused to deliver her. In permitting rescission, the Court stated:

> "It seems to me, however, in the case made by this record, that the mistake or misapprehension of the parties went to the whole substance of the agreement. If the cow was a breeder, she was worth at least $750; if barren, she was worth not over $80. The parties would not have made the contract of sale except upon the understanding and belief that she was incapable of breeding, and of no use as a cow. It is true she is now the identical animal that they thought her to be when the contract was made; there is no mistake as to the identity of the creature. Yet the mistake was not of the mere quality of the animal, but went to the very nature of the thing. A barren cow is substantially a different creature than a breeding one. There is as much difference between them for all purposes of use as there is between an ox and a cow that is capable of breeding and giving milk. If the mutual mistake had simply related to the fact whether she was with calf or not for one season, then it might have been a good sale; but the mistake affected

the character of the animal for all time, and for her present and ultimate use. She was not in fact the animal, or the kind of animal, the defendants intended to sell or the plaintiff to buy. She was not a barren cow, and, if this fact had been known, there would have been no contract. The mistake affected the substance of the whole consideration, and it must be considered that there was no contract to sell or sale of the cow as she actually was. The thing sold and bought had in fact no existence. She was sold as a beef creature would be sold; she is in fact a breeding cow, and a valuable one.

"The court should have instructed the jury that if they found that the cow was sold, or contracted to be sold, upon the understanding of both parties that she was barren, and useless for the purpose of breeding, and that in fact she was not barren, but capable of breeding, then the defendants had a right to rescind, and to refuse to deliver, and the verdict should be in their favor." 66 Mich. 577–578, 33 N.W. 919.

As the parties suggest, the foregoing precedent arguably distinguishes mistakes affecting the essence of the consideration from those which go to its quality or value, affording relief on a per se basis for the former but not the latter.

However, the distinctions which may be drawn from Sherwood and A & M Land Development Co. do not provide a satisfactory analysis of the nature of a mistake sufficient to invalidate a contract. Often, a mistake relates to an underlying factual assumption which, when discovered, directly affects value, but simultaneously and materially affects the essence of the contractual consideration. It is disingenuous to label such a mistake collateral.

Appellant and appellee both mistakenly believed that the property which was the subject of their land contract would generate income as rental property. The fact that it could not be used for human habitation deprived the property of

Behind the Scenes

The dissenting opinion and some commentators doubted that Sherwood shared Walker's assessment that the cow, Rose of Aberlone, was infertile and think he bought her believing that "she would breed." 33 N.W. at 925. If the mistake lay only with the seller, then it was unilateral, not mutual (see § 3.1.2).

After winning the lawsuit, Walker sold Rose to Sherwood (again) for a higher price. Both parties were prosperous businessmen. Sherwood was an established banker who later became Michigan's first commissioner of banking, while Walker ran a liquor business that produced the widely distributed Hiram Walker's whiskey (later known as Canadian Club), which was sold in 1926 for $14 million. *See* Norman Otto Stockmeyer, *To Err is Human, to Moo, Bovine: The Rose of Aberlone Story*, 24 Cooley L. Rev. 491 (2007).

Rose of Aberlone was famously (or infamously) memorialized in an epic poem by Professor Brainerd Currie. See scholarship.law.duke.edu.

its income-earning potential and rendered it less valuable. However, this mistake, while directly and dramatically affecting the property's value, cannot accurately be characterized as collateral because it also affects the very essence of the consideration. "The thing sold and bought [income generating rental property] had in fact no existence". Sherwood v. Walker, 66 Mich. 568, 33 N.W. 919.

We find that the inexact and confusing distinction between contractual mistakes running to value and those touching the substance of the consideration serves only as an impediment to a clear and helpful analysis for the equitable resolution of cases in which mistake is alleged and proven. Accordingly, the holdings of A & M Land Development Co. and Sherwood with respect to the material or collateral nature of a mistake are limited to the facts of those cases.

Instead, we think the better-reasoned approach is a case-by-case analysis whereby rescission is indicated when the mistaken belief relates to a basic assumption of the parties upon which the contract is made, and which materially affects the agreed performances of the parties. 1 Restatement Contracts, 2d, §§ 152, 154, pp. 385–386, 402–406.

All of the parties to this contract erroneously assumed that the property transferred by the vendors to the vendees was suitable for human habitation and could be utilized to generate rental income. The fundamental nature of these assumptions is indicated by the fact that their invalidity changed the character of the property transferred, thereby frustrating, indeed precluding, Mr. and Mrs. Pickles' intended use of the real estate. Although the Pickleses are disadvantaged by enforcement of the contract, performance is advantageous to the Messerlys, as the property at issue is less valuable absent its income-earning potential. Nothing short of rescission can remedy the mistake. Thus, the parties' mistake as to a basic assumption materially affects the agreed performances of the parties.

Despite the significance of the mistake made by the parties, we reverse the Court of Appeals because we conclude that equity does not justify the remedy sought by Mr. and Mrs. Pickles.

Rescission is an equitable remedy which is granted only in the sound discretion of the court. A court need not grant rescission in every case in which the mutual mistake relates to a basic assumption and materially affects the agreed performance of the parties.

In cases of mistake by two equally innocent parties, we are required, in the exercise of our equitable powers, to determine which blameless party should assume the loss resulting from the misapprehension they shared. Normally that can only be done by drawing upon our "own notions of what is reasonable and just under all the surrounding circumstances".

Equity suggests that, in this case, the risk should be allocated to the purchasers. We are guided to that conclusion, in part, by the standards announced in § 154 of the Restatement of Contracts 2d, for determining when a party bears the risk of mistake. Section 154(a) suggests that the court should look first to whether the parties have agreed to the allocation of the risk between themselves. While there is no express assumption in the contract by either party of the risk of the property becoming uninhabitable, there was indeed some agreed allocation of the risk to the vendees by the incorporation of an "as is" clause into the contract which, we repeat, provided:

> "Purchaser has examined this property and agrees to accept same in its present condition. There are no other or additional written or oral understandings."

That is a persuasive indication that the parties considered that, as between them, such risk as related to the "present condition" of the property should lie with the purchaser. If the "as is" clause is to have any meaning at all, it must be interpreted to refer to those defects which were unknown at the time that the contract was executed. Thus, the parties themselves assigned the risk of loss to Mr. and Mrs. Pickles.

Think About It!

Do you agree that the specified contract clause allocated the risk of the mistake made by the parties to the sale? How should the case have been decided if the contract had not included the "as is" clause?

We conclude that Mr. and Mrs. Pickles are not entitled to the equitable remedy of rescission and, accordingly, reverse the decision of the Court of Appeals.

WILLIAMS, C.J., and COLEMAN, FITZGERALD, KAVANAGH and LEVIN, JJ., concur.

RILEY, J., not participating.

§ 3.1.2. Unilateral Mistake

As already noted, whether mutual or unilateral mistake applies depends on whether both or only one party was mistaken about the relevant fact. As you will see, it is more difficult to get relief for unilateral than for mutual mistake, so categorizing the mistake matters. Distinguishing between mutual and unilateral mistake is challenging.* While the problem in *Lenawee* would typically be considered a mutual mistake (both buyers and sellers were mistaken about the nature of

---

* *See* Eric Rasmussen & Ian Ayres, *Mutual and Unilateral Mistake in Contract Law*, 22 J. Legal Studies 309 (2000).

the property being sold), one could try to characterize it as a unilateral mistake by suggesting that the buyers were mistaken about the nature of the property as rental property, while the sellers were simply selling what they owned without making any assumptions about the nature of the property. That argument would not likely work in a case like *Lenawee* because the nature of the thing being sold is too important to both parties, but understanding the nature of the inquiry (who likely cared about the mistaken fact?) will help when you try to characterize a mistake as mutual or unilateral.

Despite the general difficulty with distinguishing mutual from unilateral mistake, one can at least say that bidding mistakes are clearly treated as unilateral mistakes in the caselaw. A bidding error occurs when a party makes a one-sided technical error (typographical, mathematical, or other) that results in an offer that is "incorrect" (from the perspective of the offeror), and the offeree accepts that offer. One could say that both parties were mistaken about the correctness of the bid, but the usual conclusion is that only one party made the mistake, the other party being indifferent to the particulars. In electronic commerce, such errors occur with surprising regularity not only in bids, but also in advertisements, raising unilateral mistake issues.

> **Example F:** *Wil-Fred's Inc. v. Metropolitan Sanitary District*, 372 N.E.2d 946 (Ill. App. Ct. 1978).
>
> Metropolitan Sanitary District of Greater Chicago (hereinafter Sanitary District) invited bids for rehabilitation work at one of its water reclamation plants. Wil-Fred's Inc. submitted a sealed bid of $882,600, along with a $100,000 security deposit to insure its performance. After the bids were opened and it was the low bidder, Wil-Fred's discovered that one of its subcontractors had made an error of $150,000 in its estimate to Wil-Fred's, which computation Wil-Fred's used in the preparation of its own bid. The next lowest bid by a competitor was $1,118,375. Wil-Fred's attempted to withdraw, but the Sanitary District rejected the request and stated that the contract would be awarded to Wil-Fred's. Wil-Fred's filed a complaint for preliminary injunction and rescission.

Analysis: The court found that Wil-Fred's bid represented a binding commitment in the "nature of an option to the District based upon valuable consideration: the assurance that the award would be made to the lowest bidder. . . . When the offer was accepted, a bilateral contract arose which was mutually binding on Wil-Fred's and the Sanitary District."

The court turned to the issue of whether rescission of the contract with the Sanitary District was available based upon Wil-Fred's unilateral mistake. The court articulated one rationale for affording relief based on unilateral mistake: because the mistake was "so palpable" that the other party is "put on notice" about the mistake. Basically, a party cannot snap up a deal that is "too good to be true." The court further explained that "the conditions generally required for rescission are: that the mistake relate to a material feature of the contract; that it occurred notwithstanding the exercise of reasonable care; that it is of such grave consequence that enforcement of the contract would be unconscionable; and that the other party can be placed in statu[s] quo." The court agreed with the trial court

Make the Connection

Recall that the *Pavel* case, in Chapter 5, page 305, discussed issues surrounding revocability or irrevocability of contractor bids to owners. Also recall the discussion in Chapter 3, § 2.1.2, about "Offers in the Commercial Bidding Process." The court here concludes that the District gave consideration by assuring that the award would be made to the lowest bidder. While theoretically possible, this conclusion is questionable on the facts, since the "lowest bidder wins" commitment was probably part of the governing law on municipal contracts rather than extended to bidders as part of a bargain. This case illustrates, again, the difficulties that may arise regarding subcontractors' bids to contractors. Note that, in *Wil-Fred's*, the bidder's $100,000 certified check "to insure" its performance alleviated the need for a bid bond.

that the subcontractor's "mistake related to a material feature of the rehabilitation contract and that this condition was supported by clear and positive evidence." The court also concluded that "[t]he consequences of [the subcontractor's] error were grave" because the subcontractor was not able to shoulder the loss on the project and Wil-Fred's would experience a decrease in its bonding capacity if it forfeited its $100,000 deposit. "It is evident, therefore, that either deprivation will constitute substantial hardship. The Sanitary District was not damaged seriously by the withdrawal of the bid. When the subcontractor's mistake was discovered 48 hours after the bid opening, Wil-Fred's promptly notified the District by telegram and declared its intention to withdraw. The rehabilitation contract had not been awarded at this time. Accordingly, the District suffered no change in position since it was able, with no great loss other than the windfall resulting from [the subcontractor's] error, to award the contract to the next lowest bidder . . . ."

Finally, the court concluded that Wil-Fred's exercised reasonable care in preparation of its bid and in its choice of a subcontractor that had been in business for many years and had worked on projects with Wil-Fred successfully in the past.

The court rejected the Sanitary District's argument that rescission is only available for clerical or mathematical errors, upholding rescission for the subcontractor's error which "amount[ed] to a mixed mistake of judgment and fact" arising

Make the Connection

As indicated in the note on the history of equity in Chapter 5 (page 285), an equitable remedy like an injunction is "extraordinary" relief and is available only if the claimant proves that it has no adequate remedy at law and that "irreparable injury" will result if relief is not given. The standards for awarding equitable relief are covered in more depth in Chapter 10, page 881.

partially from the Sanitary District's " misleading specifications" regarding the pipe requirements. Ultimately the court concluded that permitting rescission turned not on whether the error was one of clerical or mathematical mistake, but "in fairness to the individual bidder, that the facts surrounding the error, not the label, i.e., "mistake of fact" or "mistake of judgment," should determine whether relief is granted." Because Wil-Fred's acted in good faith and exercised reasonable care and the size of the price discrepancy was one that the Sanitary District should have noticed, equity favored Wil-Fred's. The court affirmed the trial court's order granting rescission and the return of Wil-Fred's security deposit.

Reading Critically: Mutual and Unilateral Mistake Under the Restatement (Second)

Read Restatement (Second) §§ 152, 153, 154 and 157.

1. The rules for mistake appear in § 152 (mutual mistake) and § 153 (unilateral mistake), with both making use of § 154 and § 157 to determine if the person seeking relief for mistake should bear the risk of the mistake and therefore not get relief. How do the standards for mutual and unilateral mistake in the Restatement compare to the standards used in the cases in this section?

2. If the court in *Wood* (Example E, page 389) or *Wil-Fred's, Inc.* (Example F, page 400) applied the Restatement (Second) provisions, would the decision have been the same? Why or why not?

Problems: The Mistake Defense

Could the defense of mutual or unilateral mistake apply to give relief in the following fact situations? If the result is uncertain, develop the arguments on both sides. If you would seek to discover additional facts, specify those facts.

6-8. Branch Bank was the executor of the estate of Olga Mestrovic. At the time of her death, Olga owned a residence as well as a large number of paintings and sculptures created by her husband, Sergei, a noted artist who died twenty years earlier. Olga's will provided that all works of art she owned at the time of her death should be sold and the proceeds be divided among the members of the Mestrovic family.

The Bank, in its capacity as executor of the estate, entered into a purchase agreement to sell Olga's house to Wilkin, who was familiar with Sergei's artwork and was delighted to be purchasing a house where Sergei had produced some of his art. When Wilkin was given a key to walk through the home, much of the furniture was still in place and rooms were filled with boxes of unmoved goods, making it difficult for Wilkin to thoroughly explore the residence. He mailed the Bank an inquiry about any remaining artwork, but received no reply. The purchase agreement included provisions for sale to Wilkin of specified personal property on the premises, including the stove, refrigerator, dishwasher, drapes, curtains, and sconces, but neither party made any mention of any artwork prior to or at the closing.

After the closing, Wilkin complained that the house required substantial cleaning. The Bank proposed two options: the Bank could hire a rubbish removal service to clean the property, or Wilkin could clean the premises and keep any items of personal property he wanted. Wilkin opted to clean the property himself. During the clean-up, he found eight drawings and a sculpture by Sergei. Wilkin claimed ownership, citing the agreement with the Bank—that he could keep any personal property found while cleaning up the property. The Bank argued that it had a fiduciary duty to the Mestrovics' heirs, so it had no right to enter into an agreement to transfer the artwork to Wilkin and had not done so. Should the Bank be able to rescind the "clean up and keep" agreement based on mistake?

6-9. On Sunday, Central Airlines advertised in eight metropolitan newspapers that it would be featuring special "cheapo fares" on its website during the following week. At 8 a.m. on Monday, Central Airlines posted fifteen "cheapo fares" on its website, including a Dallas-Denver fare mistakenly listed at $5, rather than $125. At 8:45 a.m., Central discovered the error and immediately corrected it. By then, 18 customers had bought Dallas-Denver tickets for $5 on Central's website, paying with credit cards. Can Central Airlines rescind the contracts with those customers based on mistake? Would your answer be different if Central's website displayed the following message just before the customer checked the "I agree" box in the purchasing process?

"If an item's price is posted incorrectly, we will, at our discretion, either contact you for instructions or cancel your order, notifying you of such cancellation."

6-10.   Joe decided to share a bottle of wine with others of a party of ten while dining at a high-end restaurant. The host of the dinner asked Joe to choose a bottle. Not knowing very much about wine, Joe asked the waitress for a recommendation. The waitress pointed to a bottle on the menu. Joe asked, "How much"? The waitress responded "thirty-seven fifty." After dinner, the waitress handed the check to the host, who was sitting opposite Joe. The dinner guests could not believe it—the total bill was $4700.61 including tax. As it turns out, the bottle of wine cost $3750.00. Joe thought the wine was $37.50. Can Joe and his party rescind the agreement to purchase the wine based on mistake? Would this be a case of unilateral mistake or of mutual mistake? If the agreement were rescinded, would Joe owe anything for the bottle of wine? How much? Would any of the following facts, if true, change your analysis?

a.   The waitress and wine steward verified the bottle requested by Joe, by bringing it to the table for inspection and tasting.

b.   The host asked about the price of the bottle after the wine was consumed, but before dinner was completed, but did not hear the answer and was not part of the conversation when Joe ordered the wine.

c.   The host learned the price of the wine after the bottle was already opened, but said nothing until the bill arrived.

———————————

§ 3.2. Misrepresentation

Recall that the purchasers in *Wood* and *Lenawee* claimed (unsuccessfully) not only that they were mistaken about the nature of what they bought, but also that they were misled about the purchase by the sellers. Such claims of misrepresentation are based on allegations that one of the parties, at the time of contract formation, made a material or fraudulent "assertion of fact" that was not in accord with the facts. An assertion of fact (a past or present fact) must be distinguished from a promise (a commitment to do or not do something in the future), a prediction (an opinion about the future), and an opinion (a guess or hypothesis).

A party can mislead another by affirmatively stating a mistruth, by taking affirmative steps to hide the truth, or by remaining silent and knowingly permitting the other party to misunderstand. Each of these may be thought of as a misrepresentation. Examples of misrepresentation through acts of concealment include a seller of real estate paneling over a leaky wall or preventing a potential buyer from viewing a room with cracks in the walls. Misrepresentation through concealment also can occur if a party makes a statement that reveals some facts but fails to disclose other related facts that would be necessary for the statement to be accurate.

While affirmatively stating a false fact is universally considered a misrepresentation, not all jurisdictions recognize concealment and nondisclosure. The following graphic suggests the relative strength of the three forms of misrepresentation, as well as the likelihood of each being recognized as actionable:

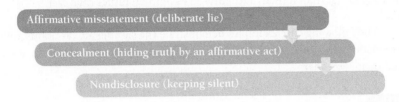

Because parties entering a contract generally must protect their own interests without depending on the other party to reveal every known relevant fact, misrepresentation through nondisclosure is rare. Some jurisdictions have found misrepresentation through nondisclosure in the following situations:

1. A relation of trust and confidence exists between the parties, entitling one of them to a disclosure of the fact in question, but the other party fails to so disclose;

2. A party makes a statement that is true at the time, but the party later acquires knowledge that makes the earlier assertion false, and that party does not disclose the subsequent knowledge; or

3. A party knows the other is acting under a mistaken impression, and it is a violation of good faith and fair dealing to remain silent.

The last thread is challenging to apply because most often parties have no responsibility to disclose their knowledge to each other.

Whether a misrepresentation is made through affirmative statement or concealment or nondisclosure of a fact, the fact itself usually must be "fraudulent" or important enough ("material") to the transaction to warrant relief, and an affirmative statement must be one on which it is reasonable for the other party to rely. In addition, an affirmative misstatement must not amount to "puffing" or "puffery"—advertising hyperbole and exaggerated statements meant to grab atten-

Make the Connection

Recall that "puffing" or "puffery" is a statement that a reasonable recipient should know is meant to promote a product and is not necessarily an accurate statement of fact. "Puffing" or "puffery" is discussed in the "What's That?" box in Chapter 3, page 93.

tion and inflate a potential buyer's estimation of a particular item being considered for purchase. Whether a statement is puffing depends on the reasonable understanding of the statement in context—is it an assertion on which it is reasonable for the recipient to rely?—and it is often devilishly hard to discern how courts and juries will rule on this issue. Puffing is more likely when the statement is general rather than specific, hedged rather than unqualified, oral rather than written, informal rather than formal, and phrased as opinion rather than fact.

The following case examples demonstrate the significant variations among jurisdictions in application of the different types of misrepresentation. As you read them, consider:

Reading Critically: *Nigro, Barrer* **and** *Kannavos*

1. What are the elements of misrepresentation applied by each court?

2. Was the representation one of fact or was it a statement of prediction, opinion, or law?

3. Was the misrepresentation an affirmative statement, an effort to conceal the truth, or a nondisclosure? If a nondisclosure, what makes it actionable as a misrepresentation? What guidelines does the court give about when a nondisclosure constitutes a misrepresentation?

4. Did the party making the misrepresentation know he was being untruthful? Did he intend to mislead? What "state of mind" was required for the claim to succeed?

5. What effect did the misrepresentation have on the decision of the other party whether to enter the contract? What effect was required for the claim to be successful?

6. Was the party who relied on the representation justified in doing so? What standard does the court use in deciding whether reliance was justified?

7. Was there any special relationship between the parties to the contract that made reliance more justifiable? Did that relationship affect any other element of the misrepresentation claim? Why should such a relationship matter in the analysis? What other kinds of relationships should receive similar treatment?

Example G: *Nigro v. Lee*, 63 A.3d 1490 (N.Y. Ct. App. 2009).

Seller from Nevada advertised a 1995 Mercedes Benz automobile on eBay as "gorgeous" and with "three minor blemishes." Buyer, a New York resident, purchased the vehicle "as is" without viewing the automobile or ordering an inspection. Upon arrival, the buyer had difficulties with the automobile. An inspection revealed that it had been in an accident; had been painted; had stained upholstery, worn-out undercoating, and rusted parts; and required a new catalytic converter and other repairs totaling more than $12,000. Buyer brought suit to rescind the contract or for damages based upon misrepresentation. The court granted summary judgment to the seller.

Analysis: The court noted that a description of goods or affirmation of facts relating to the goods will create a warranty that the goods are as promised. Ruling in favor of the seller, however, the court explained:

On the other hand, "a statement purporting to be merely the seller's opinion or commendation of the goods does not create a warranty" (UCC 2–313[2]). Here, defendants' advertisement made no promises or affirmations of fact as to the condition or quality of the electrical or sensory systems, throttle or catalytic converter. While the

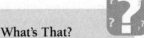

What's That?

Warranties include all contractual guarantees about the quality of the goods that the buyer is to receive. Article 2 provides for express and implied warranties. Section 2–313 governs express warranties made by a seller's affirmations about the goods, descriptions of the goods and samples or models.

advertisement did describe the car as " gorgeous," this generalized expression was merely the seller's opinion of the car and constitutes "no more than 'puffery,' which should not have been relied upon as an inducement to purchase the vehicle," particularly in light of the fact that this was a used car transaction.

Plaintiff next asserts that defendants fraudulently misrepresented that the car was gorgeous and virtually unblemished despite their knowledge that it had been used extensively, had been in an accident and was in need of significant repairs. In order to establish fraud, "a party must establish that a material misrepresentation, known to be false, has been made with the intention of inducing its reliance on the misstatement, which caused it to reasonably rely on the misrepresentation, as a result of which it sustained damages." As to the element of reliance, "if the facts represented are not matters peculiarly within the party's knowledge, and the other party has the means available to him [or her] of knowing, by the exercise of ordinary intelligence, the truth . . . of the representation, he [or she] must make use of those means, or he [or she] will not be heard to complain that he [or she] was induced to enter into the transaction by misrepresentations."

Here, all of the deficiencies that plaintiff has alleged could have been easily discovered by routine investigation. Plaintiff could have contacted defendants to inquire about the vehicle or its history (as defendants' advertisement specifically invited prospective purchasers to do), procured a vehicle history report (as recommended on eBay's Web site) or hired a mechanic in Nevada to inspect and/or examine the car before purchasing it. Instead, plaintiff made no attempt to ascertain the true condition or history of the vehicle prior to his purchase. Further, there can be no doubt that plaintiff could have ascertained the true facts with reasonable diligence, inasmuch as a mechanical examination of the vehicle and vehicle history report—steps which plaintiff took only after delivery of the vehicle—revealed exactly those conditions of which plaintiff now complains. Plaintiff's claim that he was prevented from inspecting the vehicle simply because it was located in Nevada is insufficient to defeat defendants' summary judgment motion. Thus, having "unreasonably failed to investigate the truth of the alleged misrepresentation[s]", plaintiff failed to prove that his reliance on those representations was justifiable and, therefore, his causes of action sounding in fraud were properly dismissed.

Example H: *Barrer v. Women's National Bank*, 761 F.2d 752 (D.C. Cir. 1985).

Lester Barrer brought suit against Women's National Bank (the "Bank") after the Bank rescinded a loan agreement for $17,400 that Barrer needed in order to redeem his home after a tax sale of the home by the Internal Revenue Service because of his failure to pay employment taxes. The Bank defended its rescission based upon five misrepresentations that Barrer made in his loan application: (1) that he was two months delinquent in mortgage payments (when it was really six months), (2) that Barrer did not disclose that the bank holding the mortgage on the home had begun foreclosure procedures, (3) that Barrer did not disclose an $11,000 contingent liability to the IRS for employment taxes in addition to his $38,000 assessed liability (Barrer claimed the contingent amount was included in the $38,000 assessment or that it was a corporate, not a personal, liability), (4) that Barrer did not disclose that his recently deceased wife's estate owed $5300 to IBM for which Barrer might personally be liable, and (5) that Barrer owed small amounts arising from medical bills (when it was approximately $1,500 in unsatisfied judgments pending against him).

Analysis: The court of appeals reversed and remanded the trial court's grant of summary judgment to the Bank, finding that the lower court did not use the correct legal test to determine when an innocent material misrepresentation would permit rescission of a contract. The court agreed that "misrepresentation of material facts may be the basis for the rescission of the contract, even where the misrepresentations are made innocently, without knowledge of the falsity and without fraudulent intent." However, the court found that in order for an innocent misrepresentation to be actionable, the claimant "must demonstrate that the maker made an assertion: (1) that was not in accord with the facts, (2) that was material, and (3) that was relied upon (4) justifiably by the recipient in manifesting his assent to the agreement, all factors that appear in the Restatement (Second). District of Columbia law adds a fifth condition, *i.e.,* that the recipient relied to his detriment."

The court provided further guidance on four of the conditions based upon guidance in the Restatement.

Take Note!

The court noted that a misrepresentation that induces contract formation can, in some fact situations, be a tort that results in damages, or it can be a contract defense that results in rescission of the contract. The recipient of the misrepresentation cannot "have it both ways" and therefore must elect between the tort and contract remedies.

First, with respect to defining an assertion not in accord with the facts, quoting Restatement (Second) § 159 cmt. c, the court explained that an "assertion must relate to something that is a fact at the time the assertion is made in order to be a misrepresentation. Such facts include past events as well as present circumstances but do not include future events" and "that a person's state of mind is a fact and that an assertion of one's opinion constitutes a misrepresentation if the state of mind is other than as asserted." However, according to Restatement (Second) § 161, with respect to nondisclosures, such nondisclosures are only actionable when made in a relationship of trust and confidence or "where the maker knows that disclosure: (a) is necessary to prevent a previous assertion from being a misrepresentation or from being fraudulent or material, (b) would correct a mistake of the other party as to a basic assumption on which that party is making the contract, if non-disclosure amounts to a failure to act in good faith and in accordance with reasonable standards of fair dealing, or (c) would correct a mistake of the other party as to the contents or effect of a writing."

Take Note!

This court's definition of materiality is not the only one used. Other courts have defined a misrepresentation as material if it affects the purpose of the contract, if it substantially adds to the supposed value of the contract for the other party, or if the party would not have assented to the contract without it.

Second, under Restatement (Second) § 162 cmt. c, materiality turns on whether a misrepresentation "would be likely to induce a reasonable person to manifest his assent." The court further explained, though, that this is a mixed question of law and fact based upon the expectations of a reasonable person and whether the fact that would influence that person's judgment in a transaction.

Third, as to reliance, the court applied Restatement (Second) § 167, requiring "the misrepresentation [to] be causally related to the recipient's decision to agree to the contract—that it have been an inducement to agree"; while there must be actual reliance, it does not have to be "the sole or predominant factor influencing the recipient's decision."

Fourth, as to justification of reliance, under Restatement (Second) § 169, the court observed "that reliance on an assertion of opinion often is not justified," but that in some circumstances "a statement of opinion may also be reasonably understood as carrying with it an assertion that the maker knows facts sufficient to justify him in forming it" (per § 168(2) and cmt. d).

Finally, as to the requirement of detriment, "a recipient is appropriately considered to have relied to his detriment where he receives something that is less valuable or different in some significant respect from that which he reasonably expected."

Turning to the facts of the case, the court remanded the case so that the magistrate could apply the factors above, particularly whether the Bank "actually and justifiably" relied on material misrepresentations to its detriment. The court noted the sympathy the Bank's officer expressed for Barrer's situation, the Bank's willingness to issue the loan in a short time without a credit check or inquiry into the mortgage status, and the fact that the Bank withdrew the loan only when apprised of the troubling facts by the

Think About It!

If a nondisclosure is the basis for a claim of misrepresentation, what does it mean to say that the other party "relied" on that misrepresentation? How can someone rely on silence?

purchaser of Barrer's property at the tax sale (who would lose the property if Barrer redeemed it). Moreover, the subordination agreement and security interest in the home may have adequately protected the Bank's financial position.

The court reversed the summary judgment in favor of the Bank, because of the following factual disputes: (1) whether Barrer's statement that he "thought" he was behind two months on the mortgage was a misrepresentation at all, (2) whether Barrer even knew of the foreclosure proceedings where his teenage daughter had been the one to sign for the certified letter, (3) whether the $11,000 contingent IRS liability by Barrer's business was a personal debt of Barrer's that he should have disclosed, (4) whether Barrer's disclosure about the $1500 in medical judgments was sufficient.

The court also concluded that the debt to IBM was not Barrer's as a matter of law, but rather one of his wife's estate.

Reading Critically: Fraudulent Misrepresentation Under the Restatement (Second)

Read Restatement (Second) § 162.

1. The *Barrer* court focused on whether the misrepresentation was material. Alternatively, the court could have looked at whether the misrepresentation was fraudulent. What kind of evidence would have been necessary in *Barrer* to establish that the misrepresentation was fraudulent under the Restatement (Second) definition?

2. Which kind of misrepresentation—fraudulent or material—do you suppose is proven more often? Why?

Example I: *Kannavos v. Annino*, 247 N.E.2d 708 (Mass. 1969).

The sellers, bought two properties in 1961 and 1962 with a single family home on each property. They then converted each single-family home into a multi-family apartment building, in violation of zoning ordinances and without proper building permits, and rented the apartments. The sellers later had the real estate agent advertise the properties as follows: "Income gross $9,600 yr. in lg. single house, converted to 8 lovely, completely furn. (includ. TV and china) apts. 8 baths, ideal for couple to live free with excellent income. By apt. only. Foote Realty."

In 1965, Kannavos, his wife, and Bellas (the eventual buyers) viewed the properties and obtained income and expense figures from the sellers. The court noted that Kannavos was a 38-year-old self-employed hairdresser. He "had come to the United States in 1957 from Greece where he had received the equivalent of a high school education. He learned to speak, read, and write

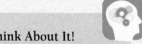

Think About It!

Why does the court note the plaintiffs' jobs, educations, English proficiencies, immigrant backgrounds, and lack of real estate experience? How are these facts relevant to this decision?

English after coming to the United States." Bellas was about thirty years old and was a produce manager in a chain grocery store. After receiving the equivalent of a high school education in Greece, he came to the United States in 1955 and learned to read and write English at night school. He had no previous experience in real estate before these events.

Sellers and the real estate agent represented to the buyers "that the property . . . consisted of . . . furnished apartments which were being rented to the public for multi-family purposes. They knew that [the buyers'] reason for buying the property was to rent the apartments to the public. . . . The [sellers] represented to [the buyers] that [the property] would be a good investment . . . as rental multi-family real estate." The sellers did not make any statements with respect to zoning or building permits, however. The buyers agreed to purchase the real estate, fixtures and personal property. At closing, the buyers were not represented by an attorney.

A short time after the closing, the city notified the buyers that the properties were in violation of the building code and zoning ordinances, along with other violations, and began abatement proceedings. The buyers brought suit to rescind the purchases. The properties are worth substantially less if operated as a single family dwelling.

Analysis: The court reasoned that "if the [sellers] had been wholly silent and had made no references whatsoever to the use of the . . . houses, they could not have been found to have made any misrepresentation . . . . [T]he parties here were dealing at arm's length, the [buyers] were in no way prevented from acquiring information, and the [sellers] stood in no fiduciary relationship to the [buyers]."

The court explained that, while there is "no duty" to speak, when a party does speak "he is bound to speak honestly and to divulge all the material facts bearing upon the point that lie within his knowledge" and that partial information can be "as misleading as active misrepresentation." In this case, the court noted that the income and expense figures furnished by the sellers helped to buttress the "express assertion" that the property was "being rented to the public for multi-family purposes" and that the buyers "could continue to operate . . . [the properties] as multi-dwelling property." In particular,

> The buildings were divided into apartments. The sales included refrigerators, stoves, and other furnishings appropriate for apartment use, as well as real estate. The [sellers] knew that the [buyers] were planning to continue to use the buildings for apartments, and yet the [sellers] still failed to disclose the zoning and building violations. We conclude that enough was done affirmatively to make the disclosure inadequate

Take Note!

As Professor Farnsworth observed, "Courts have had great difficulty in dealing with the extent to which candor, as opposed to honesty, is required." In a 1817 case, a buyer bought a large quantity of tobacco immediately after hearing that a shipping blockade had been ended by the signing of a treaty (ending the War of 1812 and the British blockade of New Orleans). The seller didn't hear about the treaty until later, when the news was made more public. When the price of tobacco subsequently increased by 30–50%, the seller sought to rescind the contract for fraud. The case eventually came before the U.S. Supreme Court, where Justice Marshall, in dictum, said that the buyer had no duty to disclose the treaty to the seller. Subsequent cases have had difficulty in defining the extent to which a party is expected to share its own separately acquired information with the other party, if the first party knows that the other party is laboring under a misapprehension material to the contract, even though the first party didn't contribute to that misapprehension. The easier cases have involved houses infested with termites, where an increasing number of courts have held that failure to disclose this fact amounts to an assertion that the house is termite-free. The gradual trend in the case law is to recognize liability for some types of non-disclosures.

and partial, and, in the circumstances, intentionally deceptive and fraudulent.

As to the character of the undisclosed information,

> the defect in the premises related to a matter of public regulation, the zoning and building ordinances. Its applicability to these premises could have been discovered by these [buyers] or by the [buyers'] counsel if, acting with prudence, they had retained counsel, which they did not. . . . Nevertheless, where there is reliance on fraudulent representations or upon statements and action treated as fraudulent, our cases have not barred plaintiffs from recovery merely because they "did not use due diligence . . . [when they] could readily have ascertained from . . . records" what the true facts were.

Ultimately, the court concluded that the sellers' representations were to the effect that the buyers would be able to continue to use the properties as multifamily housing. Because this was not true, rescission was proper.

Problems: The Misrepresentation Defense

As you saw in *Nigro, Barrer,* and *Kannavos,* liability for misrepresentation depends on (a) the nature of the misrepresentation, (b) the importance of the misrepresented fact and its effect on assent, (c) the state of mind of the person making the alleged misrepresentation, and (d) whether reliance on the misrepresentation was reasonable. Consider how those factors would affect the outcomes in the circumstances below. If you think there was a misrepresentation in fact, what was it? If the result of liability is uncertain, pinpoint the key points of contention and articulate the arguments each party would make. Also consider whether these circumstances could constitute "puffing."

6-11. Garth negotiated for two years with Hospital to donate money to Hospital, with Hospital agreeing to name a new Women's Center after Garth's mother, who died of cancer. Hospital presented Garth with mockups of Hospital buildings bearing Mother's name in neon lights and mentioned a ribbon-cutting ceremony at the opening of the building. Relying on the statements of Hospital, Garth made a $500,000 donation to Hospital. While discussions continued regarding the naming rights, Hospital informed Garth that, "without further discussion," the Hospital had earmarked the donation for another purpose. Can Garth rescind the agreement on the grounds of misrepresentation?

6-12.   Bekko negotiated with Garfield to design a new home on a lake. Garfield told Bekko that he had designed a number of homes on that lake and that there should be no problem building within 50 feet of the shoreline. The parties then entered into a written contract to have the design work completed. After Garfield completed the preliminary design, Bekko submitted it to the city for approval and was informed that the home could not be built within 75 feet of the shoreline. The lot was not large enough for the design to be set back another 25 feet, so the entire project was scrapped. Garfield sued to get payment for the work done before the project was cancelled. Can Bekko rescind the agreement based on misrepresentation?

6-13.   An elderly woman purchased a home after the sellers told her the house was in good condition and was great for an "elderly lady living alone." The sellers did not tell her that a woman and her four children had been murdered in the house ten years earlier, something well known in the neighborhood. After she purchased the house, one of her new neighbors told her about the crime and also that the sellers had asked her not to mention anything about the murders if she ran into anyone viewing the house. Can the purchaser rescind the sales contract on the grounds of misrepresentation? Would the outcome be different if the sellers did not ask the neighbors "not to tell"?

6-14.   Why would a misrepresentation/fraud defense be unsuccessful in the two cases on mutual mistake—*Wood v. Boynton* (Example E, page 389) and *Lenawee County Board of Health v. Messerly* (page 392)?

---

§ 3.3. Duress and Undue Influence

The defenses of duress and undue influence apply when a party was forced or coerced into agreeing to enter a contract so that his apparent assent was not truly voluntary. The defense of duress is based on a claim that agreement was *compelled* by threats or other forms of pressure, while the defense of undue influence is based on claims that the other party obtained assent by *coercing* agreement through abuse of a relationship of trust and dependence.

§ 3.3.1. Duress

Although the duress defense originally required physical compulsion or an unlawful threat of death or bodily harm, it has been broadened so that a variety of threats may suffice—threats of criminal prosecution, sometimes even threats of civil process, threats to withhold goods, and other threats to a person's proprietary or business interests (also known as "economic duress"). Courts have granted the duress defense in a wide range of settings. However, the duress defense fails more often than it succeeds, indicating the courts' reluctance to interfere with freedom of contract or to disturb any imbalance existing between the parties.

In the cases that follow, *Holler* and *EverBank* show the use of the classic duress defense, while *Totem Marine* discusses the use of the defense of economic duress.

Reading Critically: *Holler*, *EverBank* and *Totem Marine Tug & Barge, Inc.*

1. What are the elements of the duress defense, as articulated in *Holler, EverBank*, and *Totem Marine*? What commonalities do the definitions share? In what respects are they different?

2. What policies underlie the duress defense? What competing policies suggest caution in application of the defense?

3. What make *Holler* and *Totem Marine* appropriate cases for granting relief for duress? Can you explain the result in *Everbank*?

Example J: *Holler v. Holler*, 612 S.E.2d 469 (S.C. Ct. App. 2005).

Nataliya was from Ukraine, where she saw William's picture in a magazine and wrote to him, sending him her phone number. They talked by phone for a year, in English, and William visited Nataliya in Ukraine. On September 5, 1997, Nataliya traveled to the United States with the intention of marrying William. She had no money of her own and relied on William to pay her expenses. In October or early November, she became pregnant with William's child. Her visa was set to expire on December 4, unless she married William before then. William had told Nataliya about a premarital agreement while she was in Ukraine, but she was unable to translate the agreement in full due to her lack of English competency and did not retain legal counsel because she had no money. She finally signed the agreement on November 25. William and Nataliya were married on December 1.

When they separated in 2000, Nataliya filed an action for divorce and custody of the child. William sought to enforce the premarital agreement.

Analysis: The trial court held the premarital agreement was "invalid and unenforceable because it was signed under duress." The appellate court stated that a party claiming duress must prove "(1) coercion; (2) putting a person in such fear that he is bereft of the quality of mind essential to the making of a contract; and (3) that the contract was thereby obtained as a result of this state of mind. The fear which makes it impossible for a person to exercise his own free will is not so much to be tested by the means employed to accomplish the act, as by the state of mind produced by the means invoked. If one of the parties to an agreement is in a position to dictate its terms to such an extent as to substitute his will for the will of the other party thereto, it is not a mutual, voluntary agreement, but becomes an agreement emanating entirely from his own mind. If a party's manifestation of assent is induced by an improper threat by the other party that leaves the victim no reasonable alternative, the contract is voidable by the victim. Whether or not duress exists in a particular case is a question of fact to be determined according to the circumstances of each case, such as the age, sex, and capacity of the party influenced."

The court evaluated Nataliya's signing of the premarital agreement and concluded she "could not understand the agreement." Even assuming Nataliya was allowed the opportunity to view the premarital agreement three months in advance, "the evidence in the record indicates: (1) [she] did not understand the contents of the agreement; (2) she did not freely enter into the agreement; (3) she attempted to translate the agreement into Russian in order to better comprehend the document; (4) she became frustrated as she was unable to complete a satisfactory translation; and (5) her notes indicate there are several words for which she could not find a translation, including 'undivided,' 'equitable,' and 'pro rata.' " Moreover, William was aware of the visa deadline and Nataliya's lack of means to support herself. Therefore, she "did not enter into the agreement freely and voluntarily" and signed the agreement under duress.

EverBank v. Marini

EVERBANK, Plaintiff-Appellant

v.

GARY MARINI and CAROLINE MARINI, Defendants-Respondents

Supreme Court of Vermont
134 A.3d 189 (Vt. 2015)

EATON, J.

. . . .

. . . . In June 2005, Caroline and Gary Marini purchased a family home in the Town of Middlebury. Several years later, in early 2009, Gary began contemplating borrowing money against the Middlebury home. Caroline, however, believed that borrowing more money against their home was "financially unhealthy" for their family, and opposed the idea.

. . . . At some point thereafter, Gary told Caroline that he would mortgage the family home "whether [she] liked it or not," and regardless of whether she agreed.

Shortly thereafter, in mid-March 2009, Gary again sought to apply for an additional loan, this time through LendingTree Loans. When Caroline found out that Gary was once again attempting to secure a loan against the family home, she contacted LendingTree and informed a loan officer there that she did not want the loan, that she and Gary were in marital counseling, and that the mortgage was "a very bad thing for [them]." The LendingTree loan officer advised Caroline not to sign the mortgage documents, and stated that she would stop the process if the mortgage was not in Caroline's best interests. Notwithstanding these initial conversations, the loan officer subsequently informed Caroline that the loan application had already entered underwriting and that she was unable to stop it at that point.

. . . .

In the evening of April 5, 2009, LendingTree sent Gary an email, informing him that it had "just received confirmation from [its] notary service that [Caroline] has cancelled this transaction. Please advise. Under VT state laws, she would have needed to sign documents as well and she is refusing to at this point." Upon receipt of the email, Gary became "extremely angry." Gary brought Caroline and two of their children, ages eight and nineteen, into the kitchen and made them sit at the kitchen table while he berated Caroline, repeatedly stating that she was not a competent adult, that the children were no longer to consider her an adult, and that he was going to divorce her. Gary then removed a pair of large scissors from the knife drawer and waved them back and forth while repeating that Caroline was incompetent. Caroline was frightened for her and her children's physical safety, and told Gary that she would sign the mortgage documents if he would leave the children alone.

The following evening, a LendingTree notary came to the Marini home to witness Caroline's signature on the mortgage documentation. When the notary asked Caroline if her signature was her free act and deed, she replied, "[I]t is what it is." . . . . At some point on that same day, Gary also executed a note payable to the order of "Home Loan Center, Inc., dba LendingTree Loans, a California Corporation" in the principal amount of $311,200.00. The mortgage granted Mortgage Electronic Registration System, Inc. (MERS), as nominee for LendingTree, a security interest in the Marini's Middlebury home and was recorded with the Middlebury town clerk's office on April 15, 2009. Although Caroline signed the mortgage paperwork, she did not sign the note; however, the mortgage names both Caroline and Gary as "borrowers" with LendingTree as the "lender," and MERS acting as the nominee for LendingTree. A portion of these loan proceeds were used to refinance the existing debt on the Marinis' Middlebury home and discharge the underlying mortgage, approximately $40,000 went to paying off some of Gary's Bank of America credit card debt, and another portion stayed with Gary in cash.

Almost immediately after the Marinis signed the loan and mortgage paperwork with LendingTree in April 2009, LendingTree assigned the rights to both instruments to Bank of America, N.A., successor by merger to Countrywide Home Loans, Inc. . . . .

Thereafter, around April or May 2011, the Marinis stopped making monthly payments on the loan and defaulted. In anticipation of the impending foreclosure, MERS assigned the mortgage to Bank of America, which initiated the foreclosure action in the Addison Superior Court, Civil Division on December 3, 2012. . . . . On November 13, 2013, Bank of America moved to substitute EverBank as a party, as both the mortgage and the note had been assigned to EverBank on July 15, 2013.

. . . . When the trial court inquired with Gary whether he agreed with Caroline's recitation of the facts, he responded:

> Yes. Quite frankly, I was very surprised that the notary accepted it based on the statement of saying "it is what it is." There was clearly no desire to sign that mortgage. And, in all honesty, that was probably the basis of our subsequent divorce over this issue. You know, clearly, she was not a willing signer to this mortgage.

Upon the trial court inquiring as to whether Gary "forced her to sign" the mortgage documents, the following exchange occurred:

> [Gary]: I—yeah, I'm not a violent person, but I can't speak for how she perceived—I was very angry, you know, on what was going on at the time.

> [Judge]: So you forced her to sign it?

> [Gary]: I guess I did from that standpoint because I was very angry. I didn't physical[ly] put her hand on the paper, but I was very angry.

> . . . .

We first address EverBank's argument that the civil division erred in concluding that the mortgage was void as to Caroline as a matter of law. . . . .

. . . .

Generally speaking, improper pressure during the bargaining process, i.e., duress, operates to undermine a party's manifestation of assent and thus undermines one of the foundational cores of any agreement. See Restatement (Second) of Contracts ch. 7, topic 2, intro. note; 28 Williston on Contracts § 71:8 (4th ed. 2015) ("Duress, like . . . other invalidating causes, may completely prevent the mutual assent necessary for the formation of a contract . . . , or, as is more frequently the case, may be merely a ground for allowing the avoidance of a bargain by its victim, whose expression of mutual assent was improperly obtained."). The specific question for our resolution on appeal is when that improper pressure is of such a quality that it makes an agreement "void," which is to say there effectively never was an agreement at all, and when it makes an agreement merely "voidable," which allows a victim of duress to subsequently repudiate and thus avoid the consequences of the agreement. The distinction between a "void" contract and a "voidable" contract is not simply a theoretical exercise; indeed, it has important potential consequences because, "[f]or example, a victim of duress may be held to have ratified the contract if it is voidable, but not if it is 'void' " and "a good faith purchaser may acquire good title to property if he takes it from one who obtained voidable title by duress but not if he takes it from one who obtained 'void title' by duress." Restatement (Second) of Contracts § 174 cmt. b.

The parties agree, in essence, to this basic formulation—that duress can take two forms and that the impact on the validity of the underlying agreement varies depending on which applies. The parties also agree that duress by "physical compulsion" renders an agreement "void." The parties disagree, however, as to precisely what constitutes "physical compulsion." EverBank contends that only where one person physically compels another to give apparent consent, such as by manually forcing the victim to sign a document, is there no true expression of assent such that the purported agreement is void. Anything short of that, EverBank argues, does not prevent the victim from forming actual intent to be bound to the agreement, albeit an intent induced by improper means, although the circumstances of the agreement may create an inequity such that the agreement is later voidable by the victim. To this end, EverBank appears to concede that the civil division's alternative conclusion was correct that, even if the mortgage was not void, it was voidable by Caroline.

Caroline argues that EverBank's formulation of "physical compulsion" is underinclusive. She asserts that in addition to "actual physical compulsion," i.e., manually forcing the victim to sign, the threat of application of immediate physical force sufficient to place a person in the position of the signer in actual, reasonable, and imminent fear of death, serious personal injury, or actual imprisonment, is sufficient to render an agreement void from the start. *See United States ex rel. Trane Co. v. Bond*, 322 Md. 170, 586 A.2d 734, 740 (1991) (finding in addition to physical force, duress sufficient to render contract void consists of "the threat of application of immediate physical force sufficient to place a person in the position of the signer in actual, reasonable, and imminent fear of death, serious personal injury, or actual imprisonment."). To that end, Caroline suggests that the lethal force inherent in items such as guns, knives, scissors, baseball bats, fireplace pokers, or poison darts are all "sufficient to render the frightened victim 'a mere mechanical instrument'" and thus render a contract void for lack of mutual assent.

This Court has not yet been called upon to define the precise parameters of the defense of duress. . . . .

. . . The Restatement (Second) of Contracts, chapter 7, topic 2, addresses the concept of "duress and undue influence" and discusses at length the two forms of duress noted above—duress by physical compulsion, which renders an agreement void, *see id.* § 174, and duress by improper threat, which results in an agreement that is voidable by the victim, *see id.* §§ 175, 176. The introductory note explains the basic distinction between the two as follows:

> In one, a person physically compels conduct that appears to be a manifestation of assent by a party who has no intention of engaging in that conduct. The result of this type of duress is that the conduct is not effective to create a contract. In the other, a person makes an improper threat that induces a party who has no reasonable alternative to manifesting his assent. The result of this type of duress is that the contract that is created is voidable by the victim. This latter type of duress is in practice the more common and more important.

Id. ch. 7, topic 2, intro. note.

As to duress by physical compulsion, the Restatement provides the general formulation: "If conduct that appears to be a manifestation of assent by a party who does not intend to engage in that conduct is physically compelled by duress, the conduct is not effective as a manifestation of assent." *Id.* § 174. In other words, this section

> involves an application of [the principle that a party's conduct is not effective as a manifestation of the party's assent if the party does not intend to engage in it] to those relatively rare situations in which actual physical force has been used to compel a party to appear to assent to a contract.

Id. cmt. a (emphasis added). "The essence of this type of duress is that a party is compelled by physical force to do an act" that the party has no intention of doing; the party is therefore "a mere mechanical instrument" with the result being that "there is no contract at all, or a 'void contract' as distinguished from a voidable one." *Id.* The following illustration is provided:

> 1. A presents to B, who is physically weaker than A, a written contract prepared for B's signature and demands that B sign it. B refuses. A grasps B's hand and compels B by physical force to write his name. B's signature is not effective as a manifestation of his assent, and there is no contract.

Id. cmt. a, illus. 1.

As to duress by improper threat, the Restatement provides a two-prong test: "[i]f a party's manifestation of assent is induced by an improper threat by the other party that leaves the victim no reasonable alternative, the contract is voidable by the victim." *Id.* § 175(1). Thus, there must be both an inducement by an "improper threat" and the victim must have no "reasonable alternative" *but* to succumb. A threat is improper if "what is threatened is a crime or a tort." *Id.* § 176(1)(a); id. cmt. b ("A threat is improper if the threatened act is a crime or a tort, as in the traditional examples of threats of physical violence and of wrongful seizure or retention of goods. Where physical violence is threatened, it need not be to the recipient of the threat, nor even to a person related to him, if the threat in fact induces the recipient to manifest his assent."). Such a threat "may be expressed in words or it may be inferred from words or other conduct. Past events often import a threat." *Id.* § 175 cmt. a. Improper threats do not constitute duress, however, "if the victim has a reasonable alternative to succumbing and fails to take advantage of it." *Id.* cmt. b. This standard does not require that "the threat must arouse such fear as precludes a party from exercising free will and judgment or that it must be such as would induce assent on the part of a brave man or a man of ordinary firmness"; rather, "[t]he rule stated in this Section omits any such requirement because of its vagueness and impracticability" and "[i]t is enough if the threat actually induces assent on the part of one who has no reasonable alternative." *Id.* "The standard is a practical one under which account must be taken of the exigencies in which the victim finds himself." *Id.* The Restatement provides the following relevant illustrations:

> 1.   A is a good faith purchaser for value of a valuable painting stolen from B. When B demands the return of the painting, A threatens to poison B unless he releases all rights to the painting for $1,000. B, having no reasonable alternative, is induced by A's threat to sign the release, and A pays him $1,000. The threatened act is both a crime and a tort, and the release is voidable by B.

> 2.   A threatens B that he will kill C, an employee of B, unless B makes a contract to sell A a tract of land that B owns. B, having no reasonable alternative, is induced by A's threat to make the contract. The threatened act is both a crime and a tort, and the contract is voidable by B.

Id. § 176 cmt. b, illus. 1, 2.

In sum, under the Restatement, the fundamental distinction between the two varieties of improper conduct hinges on whether an actual manifestation of assent to enter a binding agreement existed at the time the victim signed or entered the agreement. Both varieties recognize that the manifestation of assent is flawed, but in the "voidable" context, the assent itself is compelled by circumstances that remove any reasonable alternative; in the "void" situation, there is but a shell of a manifestation of assent to enter an agreement as the victim was the conduit through which the hand of the wrongdoer acted. We generally agree with these distinctions and this approach. We have often relied upon and adopted various provisions within the Restatement (Second) of Contracts, and we do so again here. We agree that the Restatement (Second) of Contracts sets out an appropriate general framework to differentiate between the two varieties of improper conduct and their attendant impacts on and consequences for the bargaining process and, except as is discussed below with respect to physical compulsion, we adopt the legal standards of duress as set forth in §§ 174–176. Thus, in general, where one party is but a conduit through which an individual physically compels a victim to appear to manifest assent, one of the fundamental pillars of contract formation is fatally flawed and the agreement is void. On the other hand, where a party's manifestation of assent is unwillingly made but is induced by improper means without the victim having a reasonable means of avoidance, the agreement is subsequently voidable by the victim.

But this does not end our inquiry as it does not address whether the meaning of "physical compulsion" encompasses the sort of conduct Caroline argues that it should. As is clear from the above, the Restatement draws a seemingly clear line between a person manually manipulating a victim to appear to endorse an agreement and a person cajoling a victim through tortious or criminal behavior to actually endorse the same. What the Restatement does not explicitly address is the sort of immediately present lethal tortious or criminal behavior that Caroline argues effectively creates the same result as a situation involving the manual manipulation of a victim's hand. That is, according to Caroline, there is no meaningful distinction between a person with a gun to her head or a knife to her throat and a person of weaker physical ability who has her hand physically manipulated by a stronger person. To the extent that the Restatement does address this sort of potentially lethal conduct, it appears to consider it within the realm of conduct that would render an agreement voidable, but not void. *See* Restatement (Second) of Contracts § 176 cmt. b, illus. 2.

. . . .

. . . . Other commentators have noted that situations involving the immediate application of lethal force, such as the proverbial gun to the head, have no meaningful distinction from a situation where a stronger individual grabs a victim's hand and physically compels the victim to appear to manifest assent. As is explained in Williston on Contracts, in discussing the sort of improper behavior that would render a contract void under the Restatement (Second) of Contracts:

> A similar outcome should occur where the physical force or compulsion is somewhat more remote, though no less compelling, as where the victim is forced to sign a document reflecting a bargain at gunpoint; here, too, although the act appears to be that of the victim, it is no more voluntary or intentional than where the coercing party actually manipulates the victim's arm.

28 Williston on Contracts, *supra*, § 71:1. We agree with this reasoning. Thus, we conclude that in addition to "actual physical compulsion" as discussed in the Restatement, i.e., grabbing the hand of the victim and forcing the victim to appear to manifest assent, a contract may also be held void where "a threat of imminent physical violence is exerted upon the victim of such magnitude as to cause a reasonable person, in the circumstances, to fear loss of life, or serious physical injury . . . for refusal to sign the document." *Trane*, 586 A.2d at 740.5

We therefore conclude that under Vermont law improper conduct sufficient to render a contract void, as opposed to voidable, consists of the actual application of physical force that is sufficient to, and does, cause a victim to appear to assent to the execution of a document, as well as the threat of immediate application of physical force sufficient to place a person in the position of the signer in actual, reasonable, and imminent fear of death or serious personal injury. In the absence of the application of physical force, it is the immediacy of the threat of the application of the significant physical force which leaves the signer with no reasonable choice except to sign the document. We recognize, of course, that there is an overlap between what the Restatement deems to be conduct rendering an agreement voidable and conduct that we hold today renders a contract void. "Necessarily, the determination of duress is dependent upon the circumstances of each individual case," *id.*, and we have no doubt that our courts are capable of distinguishing between the varieties of improper conduct.

. . . .

Even under this expanded definition of "physical compulsion," the mortgage is not void as to Caroline as a matter of law. Nothing in the record indicates, nor does Caroline argue, that Gary overpowered Caroline and manually manipulated her hand to appear to assent. Nor does the record reveal any evidence of a threat of imminent physical violence upon Caroline such that she reasonably feared loss of life or serious physical injury at the time she signed the document, which was the day following the incident with the scissors. Although the facts present a tense situation the night prior to Caroline signing, Gary's conduct in waving the scissors and threatening to divorce Caroline if she would not sign, while obviously threatening and dangerous to some degree at the time of the conduct, was removed in time and context from Caroline's signing of the mortgage paperwork itself the next day in front of an independent person. Accordingly, the civil division erred in concluding that the undisputed material facts compelled the conclusion that the mortgage was void as a matter of law as to Caroline. We therefore reverse the trial court's decision that the mortgage was void.

Although EverBank appears to accept that the record establishes that Gary's conduct around the time Caroline signed the mortgage renders the mortgage voidable, and thus argues that the civil division erred in its ratification analysis, our review of the record leads us to a different conclusion. For summary judgment purposes, the record is insufficient to compel a conclusion as a matter of law that the mortgage was voidable by Caroline for improper threat. As noted above, to constitute improper conduct such that an agreement can be held voidable, there must be both an inducement by an "improper threat" and the victim must have no "reasonable alternative" but to succumb. In this case, even though Gary's

Think About It!

How does a court evaluate whether a "reasonable alternative" exists? Did Caroline have reasonable alternatives in lieu of signing the documents? Should her failure to seek out legal counsel or call the authorities affect the court's judgment about the existence of a reasonable choice? Was it a reasonable alternative for her to decide not to sign the documents, after Gary had threatened her with scissors?

scissor waving the night prior to Caroline signing the mortgage constitutes an improper threat as contemplated by the Restatement, see Restatement (Second) of Contracts § 176 (defining "when a threat is improper"), the record is devoid of any evidence that Caroline was without a reasonable alternative but to succumb. In this case, the improper threat occurred the night before Caroline actually signed her name to the mortgage document, and there is no indication in the record at all that the threat was so persistent that it continued through that time nor is there any indication at all that Caroline was without ability to exfiltrate herself from Gary's control. Construing the record in favor of EverBank as we must, we cannot conclude that the undisputed facts establish as a matter of law that Caroline was subjected to an improper threat for which she had no reasonable alternative but to succumb. We therefore remand the matter of whether the mortgage is voidable to the trial court.

. . . .

The civil division's decision on summary judgment in favor of Caroline Marini as to whether the mortgage is void is reversed and vacated; judgment on the matter shall issue to EverBank. Whether the mortgage is voidable and whether Caroline ratified the mortgage are remanded for further proceedings consistent with this opinion. . . .

Example K: *Totem Marine Tug & Barge, Inc. v. Alyeska Pipeline Service Co.,* 584 P.2d 15 (Alaska 1978).

Totem entered into a contract with Alyeska to transport pipeline construction materials from Houston, Texas, to southern Alaska, with one to two possible stops along the way and performance to be completed by August 15, 1975. Problems arose at the outset when Totem arrived to load the materials. Totem discovered there were three-to-four times more material to be loaded than planned and that the materials were disorganized, which increased the loading time from three days to thirty days and required Totem to remodel the barge and to hire extra cranes and stevedores. With the extra material on the

Make the Connection

In Chapter 9, § 3.3, you will learn that an aggrieved party can cancel a contract because of the other party's total breach. Cancellation differs from termination, which is a right granted by agreement. See Chapter 2, page 41. If a party puts an end to a contract without a right to terminate or cancel the contract, that party breaches the contract by repudiating it. Did the contract in this case contain any termination clause? Did Alyeska actually terminate, or cancel, or repudiate the contract?

barges, the trip was much slower than anticipated, and a second tug was required to get the material to the Panama Canal. After initial hesitations, Alyeska finally signed a contract amendment to cover the extra costs on August 21, 1975. The delays placed the vessels at the mercy of Pacific hurricane season, before the materials finally reached Long Beach, California, in September. Alyeska terminated the contract on September 14, 1975, but refused to specify a reason for the termination. Alyeska refused to pay the Totem invoices of approximately $260,000 to $300,000. Totem, facing bankruptcy, accepted a settlement offer of $97,500 from Alyeska on November 6, 1975. Totem brought suit to rescind the settlement on grounds of economic duress, to recover the balance due on the original contract and for breach of contract.

Analysis: The trial court granted Alyeska's motion for summary judgment. Reversing the grant of summary judgment and remanding for further proceedings, the appellate court recognized a claim of economic duress, sometimes called business compulsion. In particular, the court noted "the various policy considerations which are involved in cases involving economic duress,"

Make the Connection

Recall that the policy favoring finality for settlement agreements also played a major role in *Dyer*, Chapter 4, page 234, in which an injured employee signed a release of his worthless claim against the employer, apparently not knowing that his claim was precluded by the workers' compensation system.

particularly where "those claiming such coercion are attempting to avoid the consequences of a modification of an original contract or of a settlement and release agreement." While there is a "desirability of having private dispute resolutions be final," there is also "increasing recognition of the law's role in correcting inequitable or unequal exchanges between parties of disproportionate bargaining power and a greater willingness to not enforce agreements which were entered into under coercive circumstances."

After reviewing Restatement § 492(b) and historical definitions of economic duress, particularly the use of the concept of "free will," the court stated that "duress exists where: (1) one party involuntarily accepted the terms of another, (2) circumstances permitted no other alternative, and (3) such circumstances were the result of coercive acts of the other party." As to the third element, the court explained that there is no definition as to "exactly what constitutes a wrongful or coercive act, as wrongfulness depends on the particular facts in each case." The coerciveness element "may be satisfied where the alleged wrongdoer's conduct is criminal or tortious but an act or threat may also be considered wrongful if it

Make the Connection

Recall that in Chapter 4, page 245, *Angel v. Murray* discussed the public policy against contract modifications obtained by one business party "holding the other party over a barrel." This policy underlies the pre-existing duty rule and the alternative rules considered by the Angel court. The economic duress defense is an alternative solution to respond to such circumstances.

is wrongful in the moral sense." This type of conduct would include threats to breach a contract or withhold payment on a contract in bad faith. The action must not only be wrongful, leaving the victim "no choice but to agree to the other party's terms or face serious financial hardship" such that "he had no reasonable alternative to agreeing to the other party's terms, or, as it is often stated, that he had no adequate remedy if the threat were to be carried out." Of course, this would be a question of fact and available legal remedies can provide an alternative depending upon the situation in which the victim is placed. However, "[a]n available alternative or remedy may not be adequate for the delay involved in pursuing that remedy would cause immediate and irreparable loss to one's economic or business interest."

As to the case of Totem, the court concluded that:

> Totem's allegations, if proved, would support a finding that it executed a release of its contract claims against Alyeska under economic duress. Totem has alleged that Alyeska deliberately withheld payment of an acknowledged debt, knowing that Totem had no choice but to accept an inadequate sum in settlement of that debt; that Totem was faced with impending bankruptcy; that Totem was unable to meet its pressing debts other than by accepting the immediate cash payment offered by Alyeska; and that through necessity, Totem thus involuntarily accepted an inadequate settlement offer from Alyeska and executed a release of all claims under the contract. If the release was in fact executed under these circumstances,[5] we think that under the legal principles discussed above that this would constitute the type of wrongful conduct and lack of alternatives that would render the release voidable by Totem on the ground of economic duress. We would add that although Totem need not necessarily prove its allegation that Alyeska's termination of the contract was wrongful in order to sustain a claim of economic duress, the events leading to the termination would be probative as to whether Alyeska exerted any wrongful pressure on Totem and whether Alyeska wrongfully withheld payment from Totem.

---

[5]   By way of clarification, we would note that Totem would not have to prove that Alyeska admitted to owing the precise sum Totem claimed it was owed upon termination of the contract but only that Alyeska acknowledged that it owed Totem approximately that amount which Totem sought.

. . . .

Our examination of the materials presented by Totem in opposition to Alyeska's motion for summary judgment leads us to conclude that Totem has made a sufficient factual showing as to each of the elements of economic duress to withstand that motion. There is no doubt that Alyeska disputes many of the factual allegations made by Totem[7] and drawing all inferences in favor of Totem, we believe that genuine issues of material fact exist in this case such that trial is necessary. Admittedly, Totem's showing was somewhat weak in that, for example, it did not produce the testimony of Roy Bell, the attorney who represented Totem in the negotiations leading to the settlement and release. At trial,

Think About It!

How do you think the trial court will resolve the case on remand?

it will probably be necessary for Totem to produce this evidence if it is to prevail on its claim of duress. However, a party opposing a motion for summary judgment need not produce all of the evidence it may have at its disposal but need only show that issues of material fact exist. 10 C. Wright and A. Miller, Federal Practice and Procedure: Civil, § 2727 at 546 (1973). Therefore, we hold that the superior court erred in granting summary judgment for appellees and remand the case to the superior court for trial in accordance with the legal principles set forth above.

**Reading Critically: Duress Under
the Restatement (Second)**

Read Restatement (Second) § 176.

1. What kinds of threats does §176 add to what we saw in *EverBank*?

2. How and why are threats of civil suit treated differently from threats of criminal prosecution?

---

[7] For example, Alyeska has denied that it ever admitted to owing any particular sum to Totem and has disputed the truthfulness of Totem's assertions of impending bankruptcy. Other factual issues which remain unresolved include whether or not Alyeska knew of Totem's financial situation after termina-tion of the contract and whether Alyeska did in fact threaten by words or conduct to withhold payment unless Totem agreed to settle.

3. How would the Restatement section apply to the facts in *Holler* and *Totem Marine*?

Problems: The Duress Defense

6-15. Husband and Wife lived together unmarried for four years when Wife became pregnant. She went to a clinic to terminate the pregnancy, but Husband called her and asked her not to have the abortion and to marry him. She agreed. Nine or ten days before the wedding, Husband gave Wife a premarital agreement to sign, saying it was just a formality but that he would call off the wedding if she did not sign. She took the agreement to an attorney, but the attorney informed her he did not have time to fully inspect the document before the wedding.

After consulting with Husband and his counsel, Wife agreed to sign the agreement only if the life insurance benefit was increased and the alimony amount in the agreement was adjusted upwards for each year of marriage. The agreement was modified and signed. At the time, Wife had a net worth of approximately $10,000, while Husband's net worth was approximately $8.5 million.

After 18 years of marriage, Husband filed for divorce and sought enforcement of the premarital agreement, which provided Wife with $2,900 alimony per month for four years and allowed Husband to retain all the assets with which he entered the marriage and all assets they accumulated during the marriage. When he filed for divorce, Husband's net worth was $22.7 million. Wife sought to avoid the agreement on several grounds, one of which was duress. Should she succeed?

6-16. Henry, who lives in Florida, was preparing for a coming hurricane. State officials advised residents to have three day's supply of food and water on hand. All stores were completely out of basic supplies, such as foodstuffs, bottled water and fuel. Henry found a 24 pack of 16.9-ounce bottles of Spring Water on Amazon priced at $99.00 from a third-parety seller called BestSource. During normal conditions, most sellers price the same water at $9.99 delivered. If Henry purchased the water from BestSource, can he successfully claim duress to avoid the promise to pay $99.00?

6-17. Recall *Angel v. Murray* from Chapter 4 (page 242). Suppose that Maher said that his refuse collection business could not survive without being compensated for his increased costs in picking up refuse from 400 new dwelling units. The city initially resisted his request, but Maher then stirred up public sentiment in his favor by publicizing his plight. Fearful of the political consequences, the city ultimately agreed to pay the additional compensation. Could the city later rescind the modification, based on duress?

---

§ 3.3.2. Undue Influence

Undue influence is closely related but separate from the duress defense. It guards against a party's tactics that produce less than full assent by someone who is vulnerable to domination by the first party.

Reading Critically: *Ayers* and *G.A.S.*

1. How is mental incapacity relevant to the issue of undue influence?

2. What test do the courts use for the defense of undue influence? Compare that test to the standard in Restatement (Second) § 177(1).

3. How do the facts meet or not meet the test for undue influence?

4. In light of these opinions, what advice would you have given the defendants, if you had been the attorney consulted?

5. How does the defense of undue influence differ from the defense of duress? In what respects are they similar? Does each defense use the objective standard, subjective standard, or both? Recall that the objective standard uses the perspective of the reasonable person, while the subjective standard uses the actual person's perspective. *See Lucy v. Zehmer,* Chapter 2, page 22.

Example L: *Ayers v. Shaffer,* 748 S.E.2d 83 (Va. 2013).

Elsie Smith was estranged from many of her relatives during the later years of her life. Beginning April 1, 2004, Toni and Bruce Shaffer began providing assistance to Elsie, who signed a durable power of attorney

(DPOA) naming Toni as her agent and attorney-in-fact and Bruce as an alternate. Toni and Bruce made an agreement with Elsie whereby Elsie would pay them $500 per week for "needed care" and $8000 for assistance given to Elsie prior to the agreement, with the payments to be made from her estate rather than during her lifetime. Elsie's will named Toni as executrix of her estate. Toni and Bruce provided the care until October 29, 2007, when Elsie moved to an assisted living facility. In 2008, Elsie moved to a hospital and received around-the-clock care. She died on March 22, 2010.

When the estate was revealed to have fewer assets than expected, Elsie's great-grandchildren, who were beneficiaries of the estate, brought suit to challenge transactions conducted by Toni and Audrey, Elsie's sister, prior to Elsie's death, including (i) having Elsie's account at Wachovia Bank redesignated in both Elsie's and Toni's names and paying the balance of the account in the amount of $83,467.89 directly to Audrey, rather than the estate; (ii) transferring the balance of a $75,018.13 certificate of deposit (CD) into a CD in Elsie's and Toni's names; (iii) later re-designating the CD in the name of Elsie, Toni, and Bruce with a death designation in favor of Toni's son, Benjamin, with Benjamin and Audrey each receiving half of the proceeds upon Elsie's death; and (iv) redeeming CDs in the amounts of $97,206.56 and $53,766.84 and depositing the funds into an account in Elsie's and Toni's names jointly with the right of survivorship. As to the joint account, Toni was able to withdraw the account balance after Elsie's death and deposit the funds into an account in her name only. Toni, Bruce, and Audrey defended on the grounds that they did not have any undue influence over Elsie because they did not have a confidential relationship with her.

Analysis: The trial court agreed. The Supreme Court of Virginia disagreed. It noted that a court will not invalidate an agreement that is merely "rash," but it will act if the agreement is the result of undue influence proved by "clear and convincing evidence." That said, "direct proof of undue influence is often difficult to produce," but can be shown when a "great weakness of mind occurs with gross inadequacy of consideration" or when the relationship is such that a habitual influence is created so that the person cannot then accept personal benefits that are not proportional in nature. As to the existence of a confidential relationship between Elsie and Toni, the court explained:

> Unquestionably, the amended complaint pleads that Toni was in a position of trust and exercised habitual influence over Elsie, as evidenced by Elsie having entrusted the management of her property

and affairs to Toni though the DPOA, such that a confidential relationship existed between Elsie and Toni. Contrary to the [trial] court's ruling and the position urged by the defendants below and in this appeal, it was not necessary under the allegations of the amended complaint for Toni to have exercised her authority under the DPOA to accomplish the transactions that benefited her or others close to her for the presumption of undue influence to apply. Accordingly, we hold that the circuit court erred in ruling that no confidential relationship could arise between Elsie and Toni solely because Toni may not have exercised her powers under the DPOA with respect to the challenged transactions.

Moreover, because Toni, Bruce, and Audrey were all made co-owners of one or more accounts with Elsie, a confidential relationship existed as a matter of law as to those accounts. Additionally, Elsie's reliance upon Toni and Bruce for most of her daily needs prior to moving to an assisted living facility created a reasonable inference that a confidential relationship existed. Lastly, the participation of Audrey in the financial affairs, though she was less involved, gave rise to facts creating a presumption of undue influence as to those transactions that benefited Audrey. The court reversed and remanded the case for further proceedings.

G.A.S. v. S.I.S.

G.A.S., Petitioner

v.

S.I.S., Respondent

Family Court of Delaware, New Castle County

407 A.2d 253 (Del. Fam. Ct. 1978)

JAMES, JUDGE:

Action by petitioner to rescind the separation agreement he and his former wife, respondent S.I.S., executed on February 20, 1975.

Petitioner and respondent were married on January 19, 1957, and four children were born of this marriage. Petitioner's mental health problems began in 1970 when he was hospitalized at the Delaware State Hospital for eight weeks. Similar illnesses occurred in 1972 and the early part of 1974, with petitioner suffering such symptoms as acceleration of the mind followed by paranoia and loss of a sense of reality. During the two to three day onset of the illness, petitioner generally becomes violent toward himself, but not other people. After commitment, and drug therapy, petitioner slowly comes down from this state of aggressiveness, begins to communicate with others and, according to psychiatric testimony, becomes extremely dependent. After release from the hospital, petitioner usually continues to take medication for thirty to ninety days. Petitioner has been diagnosed as suffering from schizophrenia, paranoid type, and manic-depression.

On December 23, 1974, petitioner suffered a reoccurrence of this illness and was committed again to the Delaware State Hospital by police after being called by respondent. At this time, petitioner was employed by Hercules as a design engineer at a yearly salary of approximately $21,000. Although petitioner claims there had been no marital discord prior to the December 23, 1974 mental breakdown, respondent testified that she consulted an attorney in March of 1974, during petitioner's previous reoccurrence of this illness, for the purpose of securing a legal separation. However, petitioner pleaded with her to stay with him and she agreed if he promised to take his medication. In any event, respondent filed for a divorce in Superior Court alleging the mental illness of petitioner as the sole ground for the action, and petitioner was personally served with the divorce summons on January 10, 1975, while still committed to the Delaware State Hospital.

Petitioner told respondent that he did not want the divorce and he was referred, by the hospital's patient advocate, to an attorney with whom he had a very brief consultation on January 16, 1975, the details of which are the subject of some dispute. However, all parties agree that petitioner was primarily concerned with returning to the marital home and reconciling with respondent. While there may have been some discussion as to what property petitioner owned, he did not discuss with the attorney any type of proposed written separation agreement between petitioner and respondent. Although the attorney indicated he was willing to take the case, petitioner never followed up on the initial visit.

The separation agreement which is the subject of the current dispute was prepared by respondent's attorney and signed by petitioner on February 20, 1975 at her attorney's office, at her request. Petitioner never spoke with respondent's attorney about the contents of the agreement, nor did petitioner read it in the office prior to signing the document. It is clear that petitioner was not independently represented by counsel when he executed this agreement, although at the time he was still committed to the Delaware State Hospital in the night hospital program, under which he left during working hours to attend his job and returned to the hospital at night for continuing treatment. Both petitioner's testimony and the hospital records indicate that he was working with only mild success during this period. He complained of being very stiff and unable to sit or concentrate for any length of time, often returning either to the hospital or to his grandmother's house after only a few hours on the job.

Throughout February 1975, petitioner continued on extensive medication, and the hospital records reveal that on the date he signed the separation agreement he was given Akineton, Berolla C and Esidorex, medications which adversely affected petitioner's reasoning powers.

During his hospitalization from December 23, 1974 and until his discharge on February 26, 1975, petitioner was dependent upon respondent for transportation, cigarettes, money to spend and permission to leave the hospital and to return home. Furthermore, she took over his paycheck and ran the family during the course of his illness. Since petitioner did not want respondent to proceed with the divorce action, he testified that he was extremely cooperative toward her during the time when the separation agreement was executed in hopes of reconciling the marriage.

The major factual dispute centers around petitioner's knowledge and comprehension of the terms and conditions of the agreement prior to its execution, and his participation, if any, in establishing its contents.

Respondent testified that the $750 per month child support figure was established by petitioner after negotiations between them. She also indicated that during the week prior to the signing of the agreement, she and petitioner sat at the kitchen table and went over a draft of the entire separation agreement. The secretary of the respondent's attorney testified that it was office procedure that a party to the agreement would be given an original copy; however, she could not recall whether petitioner, in fact, received one.

Petitioner admits having conversations with respondent, but claims the discussions dealt only with child support, the Bethany Beach property and the Heritage Park (marital) home. Specifically, he indicated that he wished the beach property and would give the marital home to respondent; but she insisted on the beach property and, after he agreed, she also insisted on occupying the marital home with the children until the youngest reached 19. He denies setting the $750 monthly child support figure, although he does remember that respondent originally asked for $1,100 out of his $1,300 net monthly income. He further claims he did not read the separation agreement before signing it and signed it as an act of good faith and a first step toward reconciliation. In fact, he insists that he never received a copy of the agreement until August of 1977 when he requested a copy from respondent's attorney.

Petitioner did meet with respondent's attorney at his office on March 31, 1975, when settlement was made on the sale of the Marshallton property, which had been previously inherited by petitioner. The net sale proceeds were first applied to pay off the marital debts and then the balance was divided equally between petitioner and respondent.

Petitioner was released from Delaware State Hospital on February 26, 1975, six days after the agreement was signed, and subsequently lived with his grandmother. Within a few months, he was laid off by Hercules and next secured employment at Franklin Mint, as an outside contractor, through August of 1975. He then worked for Beloit Corporation in Dowington, Pennsylvania until it was sold in April of 1977, and he was transferred to Wisconsin with the successor corporation where he continued until July of 1978 when he was terminated as a result of a reoccurrence of his illness in January of 1978. This most recent illness was precipitated by his father's sickness and resulted in petitioner's commitment to Delaware Division, with subsequent transfers to Delaware State Hospital and Rockford Center until the end of February 1978, when he was discharged to live with his father in Temperanceville, Virginia. Fortunately, petitioner's last employer agreed to continue paying him his $24,000 annual salary until December of 1978.

Following his discharge from the Delaware State Hospital on February 26, 1975, petitioner began sending respondent a mortgage payment of $155, plus child support of $750 for a total of $905 each month for approximately two and a half years, until August of 1977, when he unilaterally reduced the $750 child support payment by one-fourth upon learning that his child support obligation under Delaware law ceased when a child reached 18.

The Court must answer the following questions in order to resolve the issue of the validity of the February 20, 1975 separation agreement: first, whether petitioner had the legal capacity to contract on that date; second, assuming that he did, in fact, have capacity, whether the agreement should be rescinded as a result of either constructive fraud or undue influence on the part of respondent.

Only competent persons can make a contract, and where there is no capacity to understand or agree, there can be no contract. 17 Am.Jur.2d Contracts, § 16. . . .

Although petitioner was still under commitment to Delaware State Hospital at the time of execution of the separation agreement, he had not been judicially adjudicated mentally incompetent, and therefore the agreement is not void but may be voidable. Industrial Trust Co. v. Miller, Del.Super., 170 A. 923 (1933); Poole v. Newark Trust Co., Del.Super. 8 A.2d 10 (1939).

Make the Connection

The defense of mental incapacity presented here is intermeshed with the defense of undue influence. The details of the mental incapacity defense were covered earlier in this chapter, § 2.2.

The mental incapacity sufficient to permit the [rescission] of an agreement must render the afflicted individual incapable of understanding the nature and effect of the transaction. 13 Am.Jur.2d Cancellation of Instruments, § 13; Sutcliffe v. Heatley, 232

Mass. 231, 122 N.E. 317 (1919). The Court must determine whether his mental faculties have been impaired to such an extent that he is unable to properly, intelligently and fairly protect and preserve his property rights. Monroe v. Shrives, 29 Ohio App. 109, 162 N.E. 780 (1927).

At the time of the execution of the separation agreement not only was petitioner a diagnosed paranoid schizophrenic still receiving in-patient treatment, but he was also receiving significant amounts of "anti-psychotic" medication. The only psychiatrist to testify, Dr. S, treated petitioner in February of 1978, and based his testimony upon direct knowledge of petitioner and a review of the existing medical records. Dr. S's opinion, based upon reasonable medical certainty, was that when petitioner executed the separation agreement on February 20, 1975, he would not have been fully able to understand or comprehend what he was signing nor the implications thereof. At the time of the signing, petitioner was just emerging from an acute state (psychotic decompensation) through the use of medication. Most significantly, the drugs administered to petitioner tranquilize the nervous system and permit reality orientation; however, they also adversely affect reasoning ability. Dr. S concluded that petitioner may have thought he knew what he was doing when, in fact, he did not; petitioner would neither have fully understood a complicated document nor would his value judgment have been sufficient to comprehend the effect of the transaction.

. . . .

The facts of this case do not require this Court to make the extremely difficult decision as to whether petitioner was, in fact, incapable of comprehending and acting rationally in executing the separation agreement. For even if the mental weakness of the petitioner in this case did not rise to the level of contractual incapacity, such weakness is a circumstance that operates to make the separation agreement voidable when coupled with the evidence of lack of independent counsel, undue influence and unfairness in the transaction that is present in this case. 41 Am.Jur.2d Incompetent Persons, § 95 states as follows, at 633:

> The elements of . . . undue influence and knowledge on the part of the person participating in a transaction that the other party thereto is afflicted mentally are material in many instances where the validity of a contract or deed executed on such a transaction is questioned. For example, even though the mental infirmity of a party to a contract, or the grantor in a conveyance, is not of such a degree as in itself to render the contract void or voidable, if the nature of the contract or the conveyance justifies the conclusion that the party has not exercised a deliberate judgment, but that he has been imposed upon, circumvented, or overcome by cunning, artifice, or undue influence and it appears that the other party was guilty of fraud or bad faith or imposed

upon the infirm person by taking advantage of his infirmity to secure from him a contract or conveyance that he otherwise would not have executed the contract or conveyance may be set aside.

. . . .

It is undisputed that respondent had knowledge of petitioner's mental illness. Beyond the fact of the illness, she knew both the diagnosis and the normal course of petitioner's infirmity. Indeed, she had authorized his release from Delaware State Hospital so that he could execute the agreement. Whether or not she was aware of the particular medication that petitioner had taken on the date of the execution of the agreement, the Court finds that she knew he was undergoing extensive drug therapy. However, there appears to be no fraudulent intention on the part of respondent. Nevertheless, the peculiar susceptibility of petitioner due to his mental weakness, coupled with respondent's knowledge of this infirmity, imposes upon her a higher responsibility and requires that the transaction be viewed with suspicion. 25 Am.Jur.2d Duress and Undue Influence, § 37. Such suspicion is particularly warranted where the weaker party has not been protected by the proper independent advice of competent counsel disassociated from the interest of respondent so as to be in a position to advise the petitioner impartially and confidentially as to the consequences to himself of the proposed agreement. See Post v. Hagan, 71 N.J.Eq. 234, 65 A. 1026 (1907); Hickman v. Hickman, N.J.Chanc., 121 A. 728 (1923); Giacobbi v. Anselmi, 18 N.J.Super. 600, 87 A.2d 748 (1952).

Close scrutiny of the circumstances surrounding the drafting and execution of the separation agreement, and a look at its contents, present almost textbook evidence of the elements establishing undue influence.

Undue influence is an excessive or inordinate influence considering the circumstances of the particular case. The degree of influence exerted, to be considered undue, must subjugate the free agency of the person influenced to the will of another. Conner v. Brown, 39 Del. 529, 3 A.2d 64 (1938).

> "The essentials of undue influence are a susceptible testator, opportunity to exert influence, a disposition so to do for an improper purpose, the actual exertion of such influence, and the result demonstrating its effect."

Id. at 71; 25 Am.Jur.2d Duress and Undue Influence, § 36. The facts set forth above establish petitioner's susceptibility to influence. There can be no question that there was a confidential and fiduciary relationship between the parties in view of their long marriage and the respondent's running of the family during petitioner's periodic mental breakdowns. Furthermore, petitioner's testimony revealed that when he signed the agreement, he did so in hopes of reconciling the marriage and avoiding the divorce.

In view of petitioner's mental instability and strong desire to return to the marital home, it is clear that respondent was the dominant party in the relationship at the time of the signing of the agreement.

> "Confidential relations are presumed to exist between husband and wife. . . . Confidential and fiduciary relations have the same meaning in law; and as every fiduciary relation implies a condition of superiority of one of the parties over the other, equity raises a presumption against the validity of a transaction by which the superior obtains a possible benefit at the expense of the inferior, and casts upon him the burden of showing affirmatively his compliance with all equitable requisites."

Peyton v. William C. Peyton Corp., 2 Del.Ch. 321, 7 A.2d 737, 747, 123 A.L.R. 1482 (1939).

The presumption of undue influence is present where, as here, the dominant party obtains a contract. Therefore, she has the burden of proving fairness. Swain v. Moore, Del. Ch., 71 A.2d 264 (1950). The test in such a situation is whether the separation agreement is fair and equitable, having regard for petitioner's material interests. Brown v. Mercantile Trust & Deposit Co., Md., 40 A. 256 (1898). Respondent has failed to meet this burden. The agreement goes far beyond that which would have been ordered by this Court.

The initial support agreement was for $1,000 out of the $1,300 monthly net pay of petitioner. Following the divorce, the $750 monthly child support plus $155 monthly mortgage payment bring the total charges to about 70% of petitioner's salary, and the support payments, subject to annual cost of living increases, are not deductible by petitioner nor taxable to respondent. Additionally, petitioner's support obligation extends until each child reaches 21 rather than 18.

As to the property division controlled by the agreement, respondent immediately obtained sole ownership of the parties' beach property, which had approximately the same equity as the marital home. Petitioner's right to the marital home is subject to the respondent's right to live there until the youngest child reaches 19. Furthermore, petitioner's interest in the home is subject to forfeiture if he becomes totally disabled or incapacitated, which is stipulated to mean if petitioner's income decreases to at least 50% of the salary he earned at the time of the execution of the agreement. In view of petitioner's reoccurring mental illnesses, which adversely affected his employment, it is extremely likely that respondent's attorney would have the opportunity to exercise this forfeiture option.

Petitioner has the further obligation to maintain medical and hospital insurance on respondent and the children plus responsibility for the children's extraordinary ("more than \$25 for any single visit or treatment of any specific condition") medical, dental or optical expenses.

Make the Connection

The *G.A.S.* court says that the agreement is "cancelled" when it really means "rescinded." It also orders "the parties restored as closely as possible to their status quo at the time of execution"—the remedy of restitution, which includes both restitution damages and specific restitution of items conveyed between the parties. See the FYI box on "An Introduction to Contract Remedies" at the beginning of Chapter 5, page 272.

By its terms, this agreement severely overreaches the obligation of the petitioner to either respondent to their children. Respondent in this situation clearly has received a benefit at the expense of the mentally ill petitioner. Her attorney drew up the agreement and she persuaded petitioner to accept its terms, or to sign it without in-depth knowledge of its import to him. The means of her control over him are not important, and it is irrelevant whether they consisted of importunities, overpersuasion, or moral coercion of any kind. 25 Am.Jur.2d Duress and Undue Influence, § 36.

A separation agreement procured by the undue influence of either of the parties is subject to being set aside. 41 Am.Jur.2d Husband and Wife, § 272; Rendlen v. Rendlen, Mo., 367 S.W.2d 596 (1967).

Applying the foregoing facts to the applicable law, the Court concludes that the separation agreement dated February 20, 1975 should be cancelled and declared a nullity and the parties restored as closely as possible to their status quo at the time of execution.

§ 3.4. Unconscionability

As you have seen, the defenses related to problematic behavior by one of the parties to a contract (misrepresentation, duress, and undue influence), require proof of specific elements that may be hard to establish, even where there is substantial evidence of a high degree of some kind of unfairness. The unconscionability defense gives courts the means to

Make the Connection

The unconscionability defense relates solely to the contract as it was created. It does not police against unfair conduct during the performance of the contract. As discussed in Chapter 8, § 4.2, the requirement of good faith sometimes performs that function.

police against contracts or clauses that "shock the conscience" in less defined ways. Determining exactly what shocks the conscience is not straightforward, however. In 1750, an English court said that an unconscionable contract was "such as no [person] in his senses and not under delusion would make on the one hand, and as no honest and fair [person] would accept on the other."* More than 200 years later, a New Jersey court noted the difficulty of defining unconscionability in more than abstract terms, but suggested that "there must be an inequality so strong, gross, and manifest that it must be impossible to state it to a [person] of common sense without producing an exclamation at the inequality of it."** A leading commentator has observed that unconscionability often involves "substantive unfairness . . . mixed with an absence of bargaining ability that does not fall to the level of incapacity or with an abuse of the bargaining process that does not rise to the level of misrepresentation, duress, or undue influence."***

By its nature, the unconscionability defense is raised by the contracting party with less knowledge, power, or bargaining strength in the transaction. It is an "extreme" defense, not often a winning one.

Reading Critically: *Williams*

1. How does the court define unconscionability?

2. What role does the Uniform Commercial Code provision on unconscionability play in the court's decision?

3. The contract challenged by the plaintiff is an installment sales contract. The clause at issue reads:

> The amount of each periodical installment payment to be made by [purchaser] to the Company under this present lease shall be inclusive of and not in addition to the amount of each installment payment to be made by [purchaser] under such prior leases, bills or accounts; and all payments now and hereafter made by [purchaser] shall be credited pro rata on all outstanding leases, bills and accounts due the Company by [purchaser] at the time each such payment is made.

---

* *Hume v. United States*, 132 U.S. 406 (1889) (quoting *Earl of Chesterfield v. Janssen*, 28 Eng. Rep. 82, 100 (Ch. 1750)).

** *Toker v. Westerman*, 274 A.2d 78, 80 (N.J. Dist. Ct. 1970).

*** 1 E. Allan Farnsworth, *Farnsworth on Contracts* § 4.27, at 492 (1990).

What is the meaning and effect of this clause? What effect does it have when the purchaser makes a payment? What effect does it have if she fails to pay the whole amount for a particular item? (Answer these questions before you read the opinion as well as afterwards.)

4. On remand from the decision here, what arguments would you make for and against a finding of unconscionability by the trial court? Consider both the majority and dissenting opinions in crafting your arguments. Which set of arguments do you think is stronger?

5. If the contracts are held unconscionable, on remand, what remedy should be granted?

Williams v. Walker-Thomas Furniture Co.

ORA LEE WILLIAMS, Defendant-Appellant

v.

WALKER-THOMAS FURNITURE COMPANY, Plaintiff-Appellee

WILLIAM THORNE et al., Defendants-Appellants

v.

WALKER-THOMAS FURNITURE COMPANY, Plaintiff-Appellee

United States Court of Appeals District of Columbia Circuit
350 F.2d 445 (D.C. Cir. 1965)

J. Skelly Wright, Circuit Judge:

Appellee, Walker-Thomas Furniture Company, operates a retail furniture store in the District of Columbia. During the period from 1957 to 1962 each appellant in these cases purchased a number of household items from Walker-Thomas, for which payment was to be made in installments. The terms of each purchase were contained in a printed form contract which set forth the value of the purchased item and purported to lease the item to appellant for a stipulated monthly rent payment. The contract then provided, in substance, that title would remain in Walker-Thomas until the total of all the monthly payments made equaled the stated value of the item, at which time appellants could take title. In the event of a default in the payment of any monthly installment, Walker-Thomas could repossess the item.

The contract further provided that "the amount of each periodical installment payment to be made by [purchaser] to the Company under this present lease shall be inclusive of and not in addition to the amount of each installment payment to be made by [purchaser] under such prior leases, bills or accounts; and all payments now and hereafter made by [purchaser] shall be credited pro rata on all outstanding leases, bills and accounts due the Company by [purchaser] at the time each such payment is made." The effect of this rather obscure provision was to keep a balance due on every item purchased until the balance due on all items, whenever purchased, was liquidated. As a result, the debt incurred at the time of purchase of each item was secured by the right to repossess all the items previously purchased by the same purchaser, and each new item purchased automatically became subject to a security interest arising out of the previous dealings.

What's That?

Although the contracts in *Williams* and *Thorne* were written as leases, with the seller retaining title and a right of repossession upon buyer's payment default, the law construes such a contract as a sale with an accompanying "security interest." A security interest is, loosely, a creditor's right to seize the agreed-upon collateral if the debtor defaults on a payment obligation. The "cross-collateral clause" in the contract applied each of the buyer's payments pro rata to all contracts not yet paid off, rather than "first-in, first-out" (FIFO), so that all of buyer's purchases were collateral securing all of buyer's contracts, as long as buyer had not yet paid off all of the contracts before making additional purchases.

On May 12, 1962, appellant Thorne purchased an item described as a Daveno, three tables, and two lamps, having total stated value of $391.10. Shortly thereafter, he defaulted on his monthly payments and appellee sought to replevy all the items purchased since the first transaction in 1958. Similarly, on April 17, 1962, appellant Williams bought a stereo set of stated value of $514.95.[1] She too defaulted shortly thereafter, and appellee sought to replevy all the items purchased since December, 1957. The Court of General Sessions granted judgment for appellee. The District of Columbia Court of Appeals affirmed, and we granted appellants' motion for leave to appeal to this court.

Appellants' principal contention, rejected by both the trial and the appellate courts below, is that these contracts, or at least some of them, are unconscionable and, hence, not enforceable. In its opinion in Williams v. Walker-Thomas Furniture Company, 198 A.2d 914, 916 (1964), the District of Columbia Court of Appeals explained its rejection of this contention as follows:

---

[1] At the time of this purchase her account showed a balance of $164 still owing from her prior purchases. The total of all the purchases made over the years in question came to $1,800. The total payments amounted to $1,400.

"Appellant's second argument presents a more serious question. The record reveals that prior to the last purchase appellant had reduced the balance in her account to $164. The last purchase, a stereo set, raised the balance due to $678. Significantly, at the time of this and the preceding purchases, appellee was aware of appellant's financial position. The reverse side of the stereo contract listed the name of appellant's social worker and her $218 monthly stipend from the government. Nevertheless, with full knowledge that appellant had to feed, clothe and support both herself and seven children on this amount, appellee sold her a $514 stereo set."

"We cannot condemn too strongly appellee's conduct. It raises serious questions of sharp practice and irresponsible business dealings. A review of the legislation in the District of Columbia affecting retail sales and the pertinent decisions of the highest court in this jurisdiction disclose, however, no ground upon which this court can declare the contracts in question contrary to public policy. We note that were the Maryland Retail Installment Sales Act, Art. 83 §§ 128–153, or its equivalent, in force in the District of Columbia, we could grant appellant appropriate relief. We think Congress should consider corrective legislation to protect the public from such exploitive contracts as were utilized in the case at bar."

We do not agree that the court lacked the power to refuse enforcement to contracts found to be unconscionable. In other jurisdictions, it has been held as a matter of common law that unconscionable contracts are not enforceable.[2] While no decision of this court so holding has been found, the notion that an unconscionable bargain should not be given full enforcement is by no means novel. In Scott v. United States, 79 U.S. (12 Wall.) 443, 445, 20 L.Ed. 438 (1870), the Supreme Court stated:

". . . If a contract be unreasonable and unconscionable, but not void for fraud, a court of law will give to the party who sues for its breach damages, not according to its letter, but only such as he is equitably entitled to. . . ."[3]

Since we have never adopted or rejected such a rule, the question here presented is actually one of first impression.

---

[2]   Campbell Soup Co. v. Wentz, 3 Cir., 172 F.2d 80 (1948); Indianapolis Morris Plan Corporation v. Sparks, 132 Ind.App. 145, 172 N.E.2d 899 (1961); Henningsen v. Bloomfield Motors, Inc., 32 N.J. 358, 161 A.2d 69, 84–96, 75 A.L.R.2d 1 (1960). Cf. 1 Corbin, Contracts § 128 (1963).

[3]   See Luing v. Peterson, 143 Minn. 6, 172 N.W. 692 (1919); Greer v. Tweed, N.Y.C.P., 13 Abb.Pr., N.S., 427 (1872); Schnell v. Nell, 17 Ind. 29 (1861); and see generally the discussion of the English authorities in Hume v. United States, 132 U.S. 406, 10 S.Ct. 134, 33 L.Ed. 393 (1889).

Congress has recently enacted the Uniform Commercial Code, which specifically provides that the court may refuse to enforce a contract which it finds to be unconscionable at the time it was made. 28 D.C. Code § 2–302 (Supp. IV 1965). The enactment of this section, which occurred subsequent to the contracts here in suit, does not mean that the common law of the District of Columbia was otherwise at the time of enactment, nor does it preclude the court from adopting a similar rule in the exercise

> **FYI**
>
> Because Washington, D.C., is not a state, Congress plays a special role in its governance. In 1973, the Home Rule Act gave the District of Columbia an increased measure of self-governance, including the establishment of an elected legislature (the City Council). In 1965, however, Congress was still the source of legislation for the District of Columbia. Then and now, suits in the D.C. court system, if appealed, proceed to the D.C. Circuit of the U.S. Court of Appeals.

of its powers to develop the common law for the District of Columbia. In fact, in view of the absence of prior authority on the point, we consider the congressional adoption of § 2–302 persuasive authority for following the rationale of the cases from which the section is explicitly derived. Accordingly, we hold that where the element of unconscionability is present at the time a contract is made, the contract should not be enforced.

Unconscionability has generally been recognized to include an absence of meaningful choice on the part of one of the parties together with contract terms which are unreasonably favorable to the other party. Whether a meaningful choice is present in a particular case can only be determined by consideration of all the circumstances surrounding the transaction. In many cases the meaningfulness of the choice is negated by a gross inequality of bargaining power.[7] The manner in which the contract was entered is also relevant to this consideration. Did each party to the contract, considering his obvious education or lack of it, have a reasonable opportunity to understand the terms of the contract, or were the important terms hidden in a maze of fine print and minimized by deceptive sales practices? Ordinarily, one who signs an agreement without full knowledge of its terms might be held to assume the risk that he has entered a one-sided bargain.[8]

---

[7] See Henningsen v. Bloomfield Motors, Inc., supra Note 2, 161 A.2d at 86, and authorities there cited. Inquiry into the relative bargaining power of the two parties is not an inquiry wholly divorced from the general question of unconscionability, since a one-sided bargain is itself evidence of the inequality of the bargaining parties. This fact was vaguely recognized in the common law doctrine of intrinsic fraud, that is, fraud which can be presumed from the grossly unfair nature of the terms of the contract. See the oft-quoted statement of Lord Hardwicke in Earl of Chesterfield v. Janssen, 28 Eng. Rep. 82, 100 (1751):

> ". . . [Fraud] may be apparent from the intrinsic nature and subject of the bargain itself; such as no man in his senses and not under delusion would make . . ."

[8] See Restatement, Contracts § 70 (1932); Note, 63 Harv.L.Rev. 494 (1950). See also Daley v. People's Building, Loan & Savings Ass'n, 178 Mass. 13, 59 N.E. 452, 453 (1901), in which Mr. Justice Holmes, while sitting on the Supreme Judicial Court of Massachusetts, made this observation:

Take Note!

The fact that a party does not read a contract is not enough by itself to undermine assent. Parties to contracts often do not read them. Consider the many times you have signed a contract or clicked your agreement without reading the terms. Courts usually respond by concluding that a person who objectively manifests assent to an agreement has assented to all of the terms in it, regardless of whether he or she has read the agreement. These cases are colloquially called "duty to read" cases, although there is not actually a duty to read. Rather, the assenting party is barred from using its lack of actual knowledge of a term or terms to claim no assent. If an agreement is presented in a foreign language, however, a court may not impose a "duty to read" in this fashion. Why would courts view such circumstances as different and therefore not apply the rule?

Restatement (Second) § 211(3) contains the following controversial exception to the "duty to read:" "Where the other party has reason to believe that the party manifesting . . . assent would not do so if he knew that the writing contained a particular term, the term is not part of the agreement." This provision has generated intense opposition by companies that utilize standard-form agreements, has been adopted only a few jurisdictions, and has mainly been applied to insurance contracts.

But when a party of little bargaining power, and hence little real choice, signs a commercially unreasonable contract with little or no knowledge of its terms, it is hardly likely that his consent, or even an objective manifestation of his consent, was ever given to all the terms. In such a case the usual rule that the terms of the agreement are not to be questioned[9] should be abandoned and the court should consider whether the terms of the contract are so unfair that enforcement should be withheld.

In determining reasonableness or fairness, the primary concern must be with the terms of the contract considered in light of the circumstances existing when the contract was made. The test is not simple, nor can it be mechanically applied. The terms are to be considered "in the light of the general commercial background and the commercial needs of the particular trade or case."[11] Corbin suggests the test as being whether the terms are "so extreme as to appear unconscionable according to the mores and business practices of the time and place." 1 Corbin, op. cit. supra

---

". . . Courts are less and less disposed to interfere with parties making such contracts as they choose, so long as they interfere with no one's welfare but their own. . . . It will be understood that we are speaking of parties standing in an equal position where neither has any oppressive advantage or power . . . ."

[9] This rule has never been without exception. In cases involving merely the transfer of unequal amounts of the same commodity, the courts have held the bargain unenforceable for the reason that "in such a case, it is clear, that the law cannot indulge in the presumption of equivalence between the consideration and the promise." 1 Williston, Contracts § 115 (3d ed. 1957).

[11] Comment, Uniform Commercial Code § 2–307.

Note 2.[12] We think this formulation correctly states the test to be applied in those cases where no meaningful choice was exercised upon entering the contract.

Because the trial court and the appellate court did not feel that enforcement could be refused, no findings were made on the possible unconscionability of the contracts in these cases. Since the record is not sufficient for our deciding the issue as a matter of law, the cases must be remanded to the trial court for further proceedings.

So ordered.

DANAHER, CIRCUIT JUDGE (dissenting):

The District of Columbia Court of Appeals obviously was as unhappy about the situation here presented as any of us can possibly be. Its opinion in the Williams case, quoted in the majority text, concludes: "We think Congress should consider corrective legislation to protect the public from such exploitive contracts as were utilized in the case at bar."

My view is thus summed up by an able court which made no finding that there had actually been sharp practice. Rather the appellant seems to have known precisely where she stood.

There are many aspects of public policy here involved. What is a luxury to some may seem an outright necessity to others. Is public oversight to be required of the expenditures of relief funds? A washing machine, e.g., in the hands of a relief client might become a fruitful source of income. Many relief clients may well need credit, and certain business establishments will take long chances on the sale of items, expecting their pricing policies will afford a degree of protection commensurate with the risk. Perhaps a remedy when necessary will be found within the provisions of the "Loan Shark" law, D.C. Code §§ 26–601 et seq. (1961).

I mention such matters only to emphasize the desirability of a cautious approach to any such problem, particularly since the law for so long has allowed parties such great latitude in making their own contracts. I dare say there must annually be thousands upon thousands of installment credit transactions in this jurisdiction, and one can only speculate as to the effect the decision in these cases will have.[1]

---

[12] See Henningsen v. Bloomfield Motors, Inc., supra Note 2; Mandel v. Liebman, 303 N.Y. 88, 100 N.E.2d 149 (1951). The traditional test as stated in Greer v. Tweed, supra Note 3, 13 Abb.Pr.,N.S., at 429, is "such as no man in his senses and not under delusion would make on the one hand, and as no honest or fair man would accept, on the other."

[1] However the provision ultimately may be applied or in what circumstances, D.C. Code § 28–2–301 (Supp. IV, 1965) did not become effective until January 1, 1965.

I join the District of Columbia Court of Appeals in its disposition of the issues.

Behind the Scenes

Much has been written about the facts in *Walker-Thomas Furniture*. Williams had seven children and received $218 per month from public assistance from the welfare department. Her initial purchase from Walker-Thomas Furniture was in 1957, when she bought two pairs of draperies for $12.95 after signing the form presented by the store. The form was in closely spaced 4-point type and contained the language at issue in the case. Over the next five years, she purchased a wallet, an apron set, a pot holder set, several rugs, more draperies and curtains, two beds, a mattress, a chest, sheets, a fan, a typewriter, a toy gun and holster, four chairs, a bath mat set, a washing machine, and, finally, the $514 stereophonic record player on which she did not keep up the payments. Her purchases totaled about $1500, on which she had paid about $1056. She signed the same form each time, and most of the purchases were made when a store representative came to her house. The store (pictured below) knew she was on welfare; the name of her social worker was listed on the reverse side of the form for the stereo. One study of sales practices in the District of Columbia showed that sales representatives often approached customers and suggested new

purchases just before they paid off their debts.

After Williams defaulted on her payments, the store filed an action for replevin of all of the items listed above, based on the contract's lease-to-own clause and the cross-collateral clause. The store's records showed that Williams still owed 25¢ for the first pair of draperies (out of $45.65), 3¢ on the second item (out of $13.21), $2.34 on the third item (out of $127.40), and so on. The other defendants, the Thornes, were in a similar position. They faced repossession of items purchased in eleven transactions over four years, on which they had paid $1422 and had $433.13 yet owing. After the U.S. Marshal seized all of the items under the writ, the subsequent appraisal of their worth valued them at $209.

In the picture below, the sign in the right-hand window says, "Credit . . . Buy Now, Pay Later!" Thanks to Professor Franklin Snyder at Texas A&M University School of Law for permission to reproduce this picture.

In the decade before *Williams v. Walker-Thomas Furniture*, the same furniture store had filed and success-fully executed as many as a thousand writs of replevin to enforce contracts against its customers. Other

merchants serving poor neighborhoods were using similar practices, saying that the harsh credit practices were necessary because the stores' profits were slim as a result of their customers' default rates. The attorneys representing Williams and Thorne asked for the assistance of the Federal Trade Commission in curbing the abusive credit practices, but the FTC declined to help. A year after the case, the Federal Trade Commission conducted a study at the small claims court in which the furniture store and other stores in the area filed their actions. The FTC found 2,690 court judgments, most by default. This translated into one judgment for every $2,200 in sales. The stores often sold with the "expectation and hope" that the goods would eventually be repos-sessed and resold. As one commentator put it, Walker-Thomas was "a middle-class solution to a lower-class problem." For more background, *see* Eben Colby, *What Did the Doctrine of Unconscionability Do to the Walker-Thomas Furniture Company?*, 34 Conn. L. Rev. 625 (2002). For the viewpoint of Williams's attorney from the Legal Assistance Office of The Bar Association of the District of Columbia, *see* Pierre E. Dostert, *Appellate Restatement of Unconscionability: Civil Legal Aid Work*, 54 A.B.A.J. 1183 (1968), cited in Robert H. Skilton & Orrin L. Helstad, *Protection of the Installment Buyer of Goods under the Uniform Commercial Code*, 65 Mich. L. Rev. 1465, 1476–777 (1967).

Predatory lending practices did not end with this case, at the Walker-Thomas furniture store or elsewhere. Although legislation and court action have made the cross-collateralization clause obsolete in consumer contracts, lenders have developed other aggressive models for offering credit to the poor.

For instance, banks and credit card issuers regularly engage in "fee harvesting" of their customers. National Consumer Law Center, Fee Harvesters: Low-Credit, High-Cost Cards Bleed Consumers (Nov. 2007) (available at www.consumerlaw.org).

Four years after Judge Wright wrote the opinion in *Walker-Thomas Furniture*, he wrote *The Courts Have Failed the Poor*, which appeared in The New York Times Magazine, p. 26 (March 9, 1969). "Though our most pressing social, moral and political imperative is to liberate the urban poor from their degradation," he wrote, "the courts continue to apply ancient legal doctrines which merely compound the plight of the poverty-stricken." He quoted former Attorney General Nicholas Katzenbach, who said, " '[L]aws and regulations are protections and guides, established for our benefit and for us to use,' but to the poor they are 'a hostile maze, established as harassment, at all costs to be avoided.' " Using examples from *Williams v. Walker-Thomas Furniture*, criminal law, service of process, default judgments, the holder-in-due-course rule, confession-of-judgment clauses, small claims courts, deficiency judgments, wage garnishment, landlord-tenant law, and welfare, he concluded that "[t]here is a law for the poor and a law for the rest of us." Quoting a Yale professor, he said, " 'All too often, law is used as an excuse for maintaining an unjust status quo . . . . But no form of law is ever necessary or inevitable. Law is the servant of social policy, not a determinant of it. It is our policy that must change.' The courts can and must participate in bringing about that change by changing the law, at least in the areas where judges made the offending law in the first place."

§ 3.4.1. Codifications of the Unconscionability Defense

Unconscionability had its roots in the English chancellor's office (later the chancery court), which had exclusive jurisdiction over equitable remedies such as specific performance and injunctive relief. The chancellor could withhold equitable relief for a breach of contract if the consideration was greatly disproportionate ("gross inadequacy of consideration"), if the parties' rights or obligations were too lop-sided ("lack of mutuality of obligation"), or if the contract was otherwise unfair, unjust, or unconscionable. Underlying these discretionary withholdings of relief was the belief that a court of equity ought not be a party to the enforcement of such contracts, even though courts of law were not bound by the same limitations. For perhaps as long as 500 years, these doctrines were applied *only* to requests for equitable relief, even after the merger of law and equity jurisdiction in many American courts. The first Restatement (promulgated in 1932) had no rule on unconscionability.

Whether intending to change the common law rules or not, some courts in the first half of the twentieth century began to apply unconscionability and lack of mutuality to breach-of-contract suits for damages, even though no equitable remedy was involved. Then, in the 1950s, UCC § 2–302 codified the doctrine of unconscionability for contracts for sale of goods, even when an equitable remedy was not sought. Since then, courts have extended the defense more regularly to contracts not within UCC Article 2, whether by applying § 2–302 by analogy or by simply applying the common law defense of unconscionability. The drafters of the Restatement (Second) followed suit in 1979.

The equitable roots of the doctrine continue to influence its use. A court has equitable discretion whether to grant relief based on unconscionability, making the doctrine unpredictable and incapable of precise definition.

Unconscionability is most often successfully invoked by consumers (individuals contracting for their own personal, family, or household purposes, usually with a company or corporation). It has also been raised successfully by franchisees against franchisors and by employees against employers. Unconscionability claims by businesses rarely succeed.

For More Information

Dan B. Dobbs, *Law of Remedies* §§ 2.4, 12.8 (2d ed., Practitioner's Ed. 1993); 1 E. Allan Farnsworth, *Farnsworth on Contracts* §§ 4.27, 4.28 (1990).

Reading Critically: Unconscionability Under the UCC and Restatement (Second)

Read UCC § 2–302 and Comment 1, as well as Restatement (Second) § 208 and Comments c and d.

1. Neither the UCC nor the Restatement (Second) defines unconscionability. What guidance do the UCC and Restatement comments provide as to the meaning?

2. Under these provisions, is unconscionability a question of law or fact? Does the judge decide what is unconscionable, or does the jury make the decision? Why?

3. Compare the UCC provision and the Restatement provision. How do they compare to the rule applied in Williams? Consider these codifications as you read the unconscionability cases that follow.

§ 3.4.2. Substantive and Procedural Unconscionability

As unconscionability expanded beyond its limited role in equitable remedies, courts and commentators sought to define the concept with more particularity. They began to articulate unconscionability as including aspects of both substantive and procedural unconscionability, so that they could distinguish between problems with the content of the contract and concerns about the circumstances of contract formation. As cases developed additional guidelines for determining whether unconscionability should or should not be found, jurisdictions began to diverge between stricter or more lenient standards for finding unconscionability.

Reading Critically: *Sitogum Holdings* and *American Software*

1. Which facts in each case are categorized as related to procedural unconscionability? Substantive unconscionability? Which facts in *Williams v. Walker-Thomas Furniture* fit into each category?

2. Do these cases require both procedural and substantive unconscionability to establish the defense? Does *Williams*? How do the courts use the two categories of unconscionability to decide whether to grant the defense?

3. What might explain the differences in approach and result between these two cases? Do they differ on policy or law, or do the differing outcomes result purely from differing facts?

4. Based on these cases, what specific advice would you offer a client to avoid having a contract be found unconscionable?

Example M: *Sitogum Holdings, Inc. v. Ropes*, 800 A.2d 915 (N.J. Sup. Ct. 2002).

When seller was 81 years old, her husband died. Within the next few weeks, she executed several powers of attorney (POAs) related to a piece of waterfront real estate that she owned, worth between $1,500,000 and $1,750,000. One of those POA holders, on behalf of seller, entered into a contract giving Sitogum Holdings, Inc. an option to purchase the property for $800,000, in return for a monthly $1000 fee for the option, which had to be exercised within eight months. Sitogum allegedly prepaid six months of the option fee. A few months later, seller entered into an agreement to sell the property to another buyer for $1,500,000. Upon learning of this agreement, Sitogum exercised its option to purchase the property. Seller declined to sell. Sitogum sued her, seeking specific performance (delivery of the property). Seller moved for summary judgment, claiming that the Sitogum agreement was unconscionable.

Analysis: The court began by noting that only the unconscionability issue was ripe for summary judgment. (Unresolved facts prevented any summary judgment on issues of seller's capacity and the voluntariness of the POA.) The court noted that "the doctrine of unconscionability has a place in our jurisprudence so that grossly unfair or one-sided contracts may be properly 'policed.' " Yet, even with Uniform Commercial Code § 2–302 and the Restatement's explanation of unconscionability, "the erecting of parameters has been left to the courts to consider in light of their general experience with contract disputes and upon an understanding of the particular facts of each case." In general, most courts adhere to two factors: "(1) unfairness in the formation of the contract, and (2) excessively disproportionate terms," sometimes referred to as "procedural" and "substantive" unconscionability. "The first factor—procedural unconscionability—can include a variety of inadequacies, such as age, literacy, lack of sophistication, hidden or unduly complex contract terms, bargaining tactics, and the particular setting existing during the contract formation process. . . . The second factor—substantive unconscionability—simply suggests the exchange of obligations so one-sided as to shock the court's conscience." Many courts require proof of both elements in order to find a contract unconscionable, but others have found a showing of substantive unconscionability sufficient. Even courts requiring two elements have not always required an equal effect on the transaction but, rather, a "sliding-scale" applies, so that the more the substantive unconscionability, the less the procedural unconscionability that must be shown, and vice versa.[*]

---

[*]   The "sliding scale" approach has since become the majority rule. The court explained in a footnote: "There do not appear to be any decisions where procedural unconscionability was present but not

Applying the sliding-scale, the court turned to the facts, to assess procedural and substantive unconscionability.

As to procedural unconscionability, the court observed that while Mrs. Ropes was not financially vulnerable, her husband's unexpected death made her "vulnerable to an unfair transaction." Several facts pointed to irregularities in the transaction, including her lack of involvement in the transaction, her multiple POAs, and the lack of sound advice to the seller from the multiple attorneys involved (particularly with respect to obtaining the best price). The court observed:

> So many questions arise from these events. Most notable is the curious fact that Mrs. Ropes did not sign the option contract, but only signed a power of attorney which authorized Ms. Van Noord to sign the option contract. Why would she first sign a power of attorney in favor of Ms. Van Noord on one day, in the presence of an attorney, allowing Ms. Van Noord to sign an option contract the next day, apparently outside the presence of an attorney, when, according to Ms. Van Noord, the option contract had already been seen and reviewed by Mrs. Ropes? Clearly, if Ms. Van Noord's version is accurate, the events in question must be found to be quite irregular. And, most incredibly, nearly all these events appeared to occur in the presence of attorneys apparently engaged to assist in Mrs. Ropes' efforts to sell the [waterfront] property. Accepting as true all the facts asserted by Sitogum in opposition to this motion, the court must conclude that the transactions in question, leading up to the creation of the option contract, were most unusual and made in the absence of the meaningful representation of counsel. Neither Mrs. Ropes nor those acting on her behalf obtained the type of zealous and careful advocacy required by aged persons or, for that matter, any other person in Mrs. Ropes' situation. While the present record does not yet suggest sufficient irregularity about the procedural events as to rise to the level of fraud, at best Mrs. Ropes' attorney-in-fact exhibited only some desultory interest in obtaining fair value for the property. The court is satisfied that a sufficient degree of procedural

Think About It!

What defenses other than unconscionability were or might have been raised by Mrs. Ropes? What strategic decisions may have led to her choice of defenses?

> substantive unconscionability. This should not come as any surprise. No matter how the contract came about, it would be unlikely that a party would complain—or a court would listen—if the contract was otherwise fair or reasonable. It would be much like arguing about negligent conduct which failed to result in any damage."

unconscionability is present to permit examination into the substantive fairness of the contract.

As to substantive unconscionability, the option contract for $800,000 was substantively unconscionable, because it did not approximate the true value of the property, which was worth twice as much. The POA holder who executed the option argued that Mrs. Ropes "was more concerned about disposing of the property then the price," but the court noted that execution of an option contract that tied up the property for more than eight months without a guarantee of sale did not accomplish the purpose.

Accordingly, the court granted Mrs. Rope's motion for summary judgment, against Sitogum's lawsuit to compel specific performance of the purchase agreement.

> **Example N:** *American Software, Inc. v. Ali* (54 Cal. Rptr. 2d 477 (Ct. App. 1996).
>
> Ali was an employee of American Software, Inc. While employed, she generated $30,000 in commissions on software sales, but customers paid for those sales more than 30 days after she voluntarily resigned to take a position with a competitor. A provision in her employment contract terminated her right to receive commissions on customer payments that were received more than 30 days after the end of employment. Ali sued to recover those commissions.

Analysis: Although the trial court ruled in the employee's favor, the court of appeals reversed. The court noted that a court should judge unconscionability at "the moment when [the contract] is entered into by both parties" and should not judge "whether it is unconscionable in light of subsequent events." California law requires both procedural and substantive unconscionability to invalidate a contract or contract clause. "Substantive unconscionability focuses on the actual terms of the agreement, while procedural unconscionability focuses on the manner in which the contract was negotiated and the circumstances of the parties." The court went on:

> In assessing procedural unconscionability, the evidence indicates that Ali was aware of her obligations under the contract and that she voluntarily agreed to assume them. In her business as a salesperson it is reasonable to assume she had become familiar with contracts and their importance. In fact, in Ali's testimony, she indicated that as part of her responsibilities for American Software, she helped negotiate the terms of a contract with IBM representing over a million dollars in sales.

The salient provisions of the employment contract are straightforward, and the terms used are easily comprehensible to the layman. She had the benefit of counsel.[3] Nor is this a situation in which one party to the contract is confronted by an absence of meaningful choice. The very fact that Ali had enough bargaining "clout" to successfully negotiate for more favorable terms on other provisions evidences the contrary. She admits that she was aware of the post-employment commissions clause, but did not attempt to negotiate for less onerous terms.[4] In short, this case is a far cry from those cases where fine print, complex terminology, and presentation of a contract on a take-it-or-leave-it basis constitutes the groundwork for a finding of unconscionability.

Nor do we find substantive unconscionability. Ali's arguments of substantive unconscionability rest largely on events that occurred several years after the contract was entered into—her loss of sizable commissions on sales she had solicited during her employment but where payment was delayed for various reasons so that it was not received within 30 days after her departure. However, as indicated by the very wording of California's unconscionability statute, we must analyze the circumstances as they existed "at the time [the contract] was made" to determine if gross unfairness was apparent at that time.

The court concluded that the compensation arrangement was not shocking, unfair, or oppressive and was actually commonplace in sales representative contracts, where the salesperson had ongoing responsibilities after the sale. The court concluded:

In the present case, there are no unclear or hidden terms in the employment agreement and no unusual terms that would shock the conscience, all leading to the conclusion that the contract accurately reflects the reasonable expectations of the parties. Overall, the evidence establishes that this employment contract was the result of an arm's-length negotiation between two sophisticated and experienced parties of comparable bargaining power and is fairly reflective of prevailing practices in employing commissioned sales representatives. Therefore, the contract fails to qualify as unconscionable.

---

[3] Some courts have considered the presence and advice of counsel to constitute circumstantial, if not conclusive, evidence that a contract is not unconscionable. (See e.g., *Resource Management Co. v. Weston Ranch* (Utah 1985) 706 P.2d 1028, 1045; *Bernina Distributors, Inc. v. Bernina Sewing Mach.* (10th Cir.1981) 646 F.2d 434, 440.)

[4] A company representative testified at trial that a number of individuals have successfully negotiated for modification of this provision.

Relief for Substantive Unconscionability Alone?
The Refrigerator Cases

The *Sitogum* court cited three well known cases involving a consumer purchase of a new refrigerator and/or freezer. At least two of them involved door-to-door sales (a sales setting that has since been regulated by the Federal Trade Commission, to eliminate many of its common abuses).

Example O: *Frostifresh Corp. v. Reynoso*, 274 N.Y.S.2d 757 (Dist. Ct. 1966), rev'd on damages, 281 N.Y.S.2d 964 (App. Term 1967).

The seller negotiated the sale of a refrigerator/freezer unit orally in Spanish to buyers, who didn't think they could afford it. Seller told them it would be free because they would get commissions from sales to neighbors. The signed contract in English was never translated or explained to buyers. The contract price was $1,146 for a unit that cost seller $348.

Analysis: The trial court awarded seller damages of $316 (seller's cost minus buyers' payments to date). The appellate court reversed, to allow seller to "recover its net cost for the [unit], plus a reasonable profit, in addition to trucking and service charges necessarily incurred and reasonable finance charges." Focusing primarily on the price, the trial court noted "that the sale of the appliance at the price and terms indicated in this contract is shocking to the conscience." Basically, the bargain was too hard and the court would not enforce it.

Example P: *Toker v. Westerman*, 274 A.2d 78 (N.J. Union County Ct. 1970).

Buyer purchased a refrigerator/freezer unit from an appliance dealer for $899.98, plus sales tax, group life insurance, and time price differential, for a total cost of $1,230. At trial, seller testified that the unit was a "stripped unit" worth no more than $400. Buyer had paid $656 before the suit.

Analysis: The court refused to enforce the remainder of the contract price. Finding the contract unconscionable, the court stated: "Suffice it to say that in the instant case the court finds as shocking, and therefore unconscionable, the sale of goods for approximately 2 1/2 times their reasonable retail value. This is particularly so where, as here, the sale was made by a door-to-door salesman for a dealer who therefore would have less overhead expense than a dealer maintaining a store or showroom. In addition, it appeared that defendants during the course of the payments they made to plaintiff were obliged to seek welfare assistance." As to whether excessive price alone (substantive unconscionability) could be a grounds for unconscionability, the court further commented "it would also appear that those states which have considered this question have uniformly held that the purchase price alone may be found to be unconscionable, therefore bringing the statutory provision into play."

> **Example Q:** *Toker v. Perl*, 247 A.2d 701 (N.J. Super. Ct. Law Div. 1968).
>
> Seller arranged a home visit to sell a food plan to buyers. After 2½ hours, buyers claimed not to have room for the amount of food discussed. Seller replied that a freezer was included in the food plan. Around midnight, buyers signed three forms, which seller had stacked to make only the signature lines visible on a financing application and an installment contract to purchase a freezer. The freezer price was $800, plus sales tax of $24, creditor life insurance for $17, and a credit service charge (time price differential) of $252, for a total price of $1,093, but its maximum value was $300.

Analysis: The court refused to enforce the contract because it had been procured by fraud and unconscionability. Finding the "exorbitant price of the freezer makes this contract unconscionable," the court went on to state that [t]he conscience of this court is shocked by the price imposed upon these defendants for the freezer. The testimony in court valued the freezer at no more than $300. The price charged was in excess of 2 1/2 times the maximum value. The time-price differential alone almost equalled the value of the freezer. In the light of these facts, this court is constrained to hold the price in this contract unconscionable."

Courts rarely rely solely on substantive unconscionability, but these cases remain as examples of pricing that is egregious enough to support a finding of unconscionabililty, perhaps even without the accompanying facts showing procedural unconscionability as well.

§ 3.4.3. Unconscionability Issues in Arbitration Agreements

Partly in response to the delays and expense associated with litigation, businesses have more regularly included arbitration clauses and agreements in their contracts, especially in consumer transactions. Arbitration agreements have frequently been challenged based on allegations of unconscionability and violation of public policy, because arbitration is a private means of dispute resolution that may or may not lack the procedural and evidentiary safeguards of traditional litigation, and because arbitration clauses often appear in standard-form agreements and frequently are written to prevent class action suits or claims. Indeed, the increasing use of arbitration clauses has fueled a surge in unconscionability claims. Professor Charles Knapp noted a nearly tenfold increase in unconscionability cases between 1990 and 2008 after a previous slowdown, with unconscionability decisions involving arbitration clauses "account[ing] for the lion's share of the overall increase," rising "from 1 or 2 at most through 1996, up to an average of 38 from the years 2003 through 2007, and to 115 in 2008."[*] Arbitration clauses are not the only provisions regularly scrutinized for unconscionability; choice-of-law, choice-of-forum, and class-action waiver clauses have also faced many challenges. Indeed, arbitration clauses are often coupled with class-action waiver clauses, in an effort to bar class actions in court by groups of plaintiffs with similar low-dollar-amount claims.

For a number of years, the increasing number of unconscionability claims was mirrored by increased success in challenging arbitration clauses, particularly in California but also in 21 other states. That rise in successful challenges was at least stalled by several rulings by the United States Supreme Court involving the Federal Arbitration Act (FAA), 9 U.S.C. § 1 *et seq.*, which expressly validates written arbitration clauses, "save upon such grounds as exist at law or in equity for the revocation of any contract." In *AT&T Mobility LLC v. Concepcion,* 563 U.S. 333 (2011) (*Concepcion*), Justice Scalia, writing for the majority, reversed a lower court holding that an arbitration provision was unconscionable, deciding that the FAA pre-empted a California rule of law that interfered with arbitration by allowing consumer to claim unconscionability to avoid a class action waiver. In *American Express Co. v. Italian Colors Restaurant,* 570 U.S. 228 (2013) (*Italian Colors*) the Court took up class-action waivers and, in another decision authored by Justice Scalia, held the FAA does not bar contractual waivers of class arbitration even where the cost of individual arbitration would exceed the potential recovery.

---

[*]   Charles L. Knapp, *Blowing the Whistle on Mandatory Arbitration: Unconscionability as a Signaling Device,* 46 San Diego L. Rev. 609, 621–25 (2009).

Reading Critically: The FAA's Impact
on Arbitration Clauses

The following article excerpts contain two commentators' positions on the state of recent jurisprudence and its effect on unconscionability doctrine. Consider the arguments made by both. Who has the better position?

Disappearing Claims and the Erosion of Substantive Law

J. Maria Glover, 124 Yale L.J. 3052 (2015)

The Supreme Court's recent arbitration jurisprudence represents the culmination of a three-decade-long expansion of the use of private arbitration as an alternative to court adjudication in the resolution of disputes of virtually every type of justiciable claim. As a result of this jurisprudence, cases that would otherwise proceed in the public realm—the courts—have been moved to a purely private realm, which is largely shielded from judicial and public scrutiny. . . . However, the Court's arbitration jurisprudence from the last five years—and particularly its 2013 decision in *American Express Co. v. Italian Colors Restaurant*—does far more: it undermines the substantive law itself. Indeed, the Court's most recent arbitration jurisprudence has conferred upon private entities a more fundamental power, antecedent to the authority to adjust the mechanisms of adjudication used to enforce substantive law. This power is more akin to lawmaking. A private entity, through contractual arbitration provisions, can now significantly reduce or even remove its substantive legal obligations by eliminating claiming. That private contract drafter can, in effect, wield quasilawmaking power by rendering substantive law inapplicable to a great deal of its primary conduct. Given the central role of private enforcement to the achievement of legislative directives, private entities can therefore use contractual arbitration provisions effectively to erode substantive law from the books, with the consequent erosion of both the private compensatory goals and public deterrent objectives of that law.

. . . .

I. DISAPPEARING CLAIMS: THE SUPREME COURT'S
NEW ARBITRATION REVOLUTION

The Court's early arbitration jurisprudence ushered in a sea change in dispute resolution, moving vast swaths of cases from the public realm—the courts—to a private one—arbitration. . . . The vast expansion of privatized dispute resolution that came in the wake of this jurisprudence was revolutionary, particularly insofar as it led to a significant erosion of the public realm at the behest of private arbitration contracts. This change, however, was justified by two related and critical premises: first, that freedom of contract facilitated arbitration proceedings, and second, that arbitration proceedings constituted an efficient, cost-effective means for enforcing federal substantive law. Indeed, the Court had long suggested, if not expressly held, that this freedom of contract over the locus and mechanisms of adjudication did not stretch so far as to supersede substantive law. In other words, if freedom of contract and the enforcement of substantive rights through arbitration came into tension, then freedom of contract would yield. An arbitration contract that eliminated the enforcement of substantive law would not stand.

. . . In *American Express v. Italian Colors*, the Court essentially permitted, even incentivized, private parties drafting arbitration contracts to do so in a way that allowed them to reduce or even eliminate their obligations under substantive law. In so doing, the Court has effectuated what one might call a second arbitration revolution: by handing this quasi-lawmaking power to private parties and by reducing substantive statutory rights to mere formalities—to little more than empty rights—the Court has eroded the substantive law itself.

. . . .

II. THE SUPREME COURT'S ARBITRATION REVOLUTION AND THE EROSION OF THE SUBSTANTIVE LAW

The Supreme Court's three-decade-long expansion of private arbitration has long been criticized for achieving what might be called an erosion in the public realm. However, the Supreme Court's recent arbitration jurisprudence goes well beyond the oft-lamented transfer of the enforcement and development of substantive law from a public to a private forum. In fact, this jurisprudence stretches further than achieving what some have described as the near-total disappearance of the class action device. Although the Court's jurisprudence has long been providing private entities with increased discretion to choose the means of enforcing substantive law, the decision in *Italian Colors* signaled a fundamental change. It gave these private entities a power antecedent to enforcement of substantive law—a power more akin to lawmaking itself: Corporations, through arbitration provisions in contracts, can render legal obligations virtually inapplicable to any of the primary conduct associated with those contractual arrangements. In short, corporations now have the power, through contract, effectively to negate substantive law.

. . . .

A. How the Court's Recent Arbitration Revolution Threatens Substantive Law

In the wake of the Supreme Court's recent arbitration jurisprudence, private parties have significant power to control the scope of their legal obligations, with the effect (and likely intent) of using arbitration agreements to eliminate claims against them. . . .

Indeed, the Court's decision in *Italian Colors* dramatically undercuts two related principles: one, that the reworking of substantive law should be achieved by publicly accountable bodies, and two, that public disclosure and concomitant public scrutiny should accompany attempts to effectuate changes in substantive legal obligations. Regarding the former, the wholesale freedom-of-contract view cemented in *Italian Colors* means that companies or other potential defendants interested in limiting their obligations under various consumer protection laws, employment discrimination laws, antitrust laws, and securities laws, for instance, can effectively do so without lobbying Congress or relevant state legislatures for changes to those laws. They can do so even without achieving narrower interpretations of those laws in the courts. Instead, those entities can substantially alter, if not avoid, their legal obligations under any substantive legal regime through contracts containing arbitration clauses that make it extraordinarily unlikely, if not nearly impossible, for the private enforcement apparatus established by those statutes to function. As the Court's opinion in *Italian Colors* makes clear, such provisions are enforceable, period, and the fact that they may make it wholly impracticable for a plaintiff to vindicate its substantive rights is, as Justice Kagan put it in dissent, "too darn bad."

. . . .

One striking consequence of the Court's decision in *Italian Colors* is therefore that it not only facilitates legal reform through private contracts, but also encourages the reform to take place in such a way as to avoid the public and political spotlight. . . .

Imagine what would have to occur if drafters of arbitration agreements that eliminate class actions for employment discrimination lawsuits were to pursue that reform through the democratic process. They would have to lobby Congress or promote relief in court or—less obviously, but still quite saliently—seek a change in Rule 23 of the Federal Rules of Civil Procedure. Because of the Court's recent arbitration revolution, none of that is necessary. The only paper trail that corporations leave in their efforts to reduce or eliminate their legal obligations are fine-print contracts of adhesion, which are rarely read by the average consumer or employee, let alone understood as effectively exculpatory for the drafter. The provisions themselves hardly raise a specter of suspicion regarding the corporation's underlying strategic gambit to recalibrate the extent of liability and obligation under various substantive laws. Indeed, had *Italian Colors* allowed corporations to include contractual clauses that explicitly exculpated them from liability under particular laws, at least the public's attention might have been captured. To put the point slightly differently, the Supreme Court's prohibition on blatant exculpatory clauses does little good on this score: were contract drafters to include such explicit provisions, the strategic gambit of recalibrating substantive obligations would be quite obvious, and as such, more likely to incite public backlash. As it stands now, corporations can whittle down their potential liability almost as well with contractual arbitration clauses, and very few contract signers will be the wiser.

B. Why the Supreme Court's Recent Arbitration Revolution and the Erosion of Substantive Law Are Likely Here To Stay

. . . But by and large, there has been no serious legislative push to overturn the Court's arbitration jurisprudence. Why?

Divided government is, of course, part of the answer. With the Republicans in control of the House of Representatives, the odds of congressional passage of an amendment to the FAA are slim. But part of the answer also lies in the brilliance of pursuing deregulatory reform through the interpretation of the FAA. As William Eskridge found in a landmark study, overriding the Court's statutory decisions is always a difficult business. Even "[t]he Supreme Court's most controversial statutory decisions are usually not overridden because there are strong interest group alignments on both sides of the issues, leaving the Court's decisions firmly intact." But such overrides are virtually impossible if those critical of the Court's decision lack a concentrated political constituency ready to use its clout in the political process. . . .

These political realities mean that amending the FAA is an extremely difficult political task. To begin with, arbitration is not the kind of thing that the American public gets worked up about. Its political salience is extremely low. As the Court is fond of saying, arbitration is merely a shift in forum, from the courts to private arbitrators. . . .

. . . .

In fact, the Court's FAA jurisprudence creates a political dynamic that systematically favors large corporations, the "winners" in the Court's arbitration jurisprudence, over those who enter into arbitration agreements (the "losers"). On the one hand, repeat-player large corporations and other commercial contract drafters with substantial market power have a vested interest in drafting self-deregulatory clauses and in protecting the interpretation of the FAA that enables them to do so. On the other hand, the impact of those contracts is felt by many members of the public on a wide swath of issues, which actually renders any action by the public against these decisions difficult and unlikely.

. . . .

In conclusion, with very few exceptions, the FAA has remained unchanged by Congress since its introduction in 1925, and recent efforts at legislative amendment show little promise. That fact renders the historical arc of the FAA somewhat astonishing, given that the scope of the FAA has nonetheless expanded significantly since its enactment. These dramatic and repeated changes to the FAA, however, have been rendered not by Congress, but by the Supreme Court. As a consequence, any changes to the Court's recent arbitration jurisprudence, and its far-reaching implications for the substantive law, are unlikely to emanate from anywhere except perhaps a future—and different—Court. Until such time, it is likely that this erosion of substantive law will continue unabated.

. . . .

Italian Colors *and Freedom of Contract Under the Federal Arbitration Act: Has the Supreme Court Enabled Disappearing Claims and the Erosion of Substantive Law?*

Steven W. Feldman, 2016 Mich. St. L. Rev. 109

INTRODUCTION

In her article, *Disappearing Claims and the Erosion of Substantive Law*, . . . , J. Maria Glover criticizes the U.S. Supreme Court for enabling a private arbitration takeover of civil dispute resolution. Glover contends that the Court's emerging approach distorts freedom of contract. In response, I will explore the relationship of freedom of contract and arbitration in Supreme Court and lower court decisions. My counter thesis will demonstrate that the courts, in compliance with the arbitration statutes, have faithfully implemented the various strands of freedom of contract.

. . . .

I respectfully disagree with Glover's key premises and conclusions. My counter-thesis is (1) freedom of contract in arbitration cases properly construed is not limited to devising streamlined cost-effective procedures but is broadly interpreted to allow parties the leeway to select the terms governing the arbitration; (2) the need to enforce the parties' mutual assent exists independently from arbitral efficiency and the enforcement of mutual assent takes priority over arbitral efficiency when there is a conflict; (3) "pure freedom of contract" does not exist (as claimed by Glover) because many limits from law and public policy (largely unmentioned by Glover) maintain the integrity of the arbitral process; and (4) *Italian Colors* is a legitimate evolution and not a revolution in FAA practice and procedure.

This debate is important because courts and other commentators say freedom of contract is a "fundamental" element of arbitration, and an in-depth study of case law is needed to determine the validity of this observation. While various writers have touched upon the relationship of arbitration and freedom of contract, and a number of articles discuss *Italian Colors*, no article or treatise comprehensively examines the strong connection between arbitration and the various strands of freedom of contract. Accordingly, this Article goes beyond the bounds of Glover's thesis and fills that gap in the literature.

. . . .

IV. FREEDOM OF CONTRACT IN ARBITRATION: THE PARTIES' GENERAL RIGHT TO CUSTOMIZE THE RULES OF PROCEDURE

Glover claims that, in earlier Court decisions, "arbitration served merely as an alternative mechanism for dispute proceedings and claim resolution, and thus . . . the freedom to craft arbitration contracts was simply a freedom to streamline adjudicative mechanisms." The slippery concept of "streamlined proceedings" that she advocates so strongly raises intractable problems in gauging what Glover means regarding activities constituting "procedural adaptability" and "efficient dispute resolution mechanisms." These circumstances often exist only in the eye of the beholder, and no bright line separates efficient and inefficient arbitral proceedings. Significantly, no cases support the view that freedom of contract in arbitration is restricted to achieving efficient procedures.

. . . .

As in other areas of contract doctrine, traditional autonomy aspects of freedom of contract are an important element of arbitration proceedings. The judicial position is that "parties are as free to specify idiosyncratic terms of arbitration as they are to specify any other terms in their contract." Absent a violation of law or public policy, or a contrary contract term, the proceedings can be as efficient or inefficient as the parties intend. Again, consistent with traditional notions of freedom of contract, the FAA does not forbid parties from agreeing to rules that, in hindsight, result in an unequal or even foolhardy bargain for one party or the other; such is the accountability element of freedom of contract. . . .

. . . .

VI. THE LIMITS OF FREEDOM OF CONTRACT: MAINTAINING THE INTEGRITY OF THE ARBITRAL PROCESS

In arguing that *Italian Colors* improperly approved a "reductionist" theory of freedom of contract, Glover contends parties may now prescribe "any set of procedures, no matter how onerous to the arbitration of claims." Glover repeatedly mentions that the Court has adopted a "pure" version of freedom of contract under the FAA.

The cases do not support—as a legal doctrine—that freedom of contract is enforceable in a "pure" or absolutist fashion. As explained below, the state of the law is that "freedom of contract has its limits." This last quote aligns with established Supreme Court precedent. For many years, the Supreme Court has accepted as a general proposition that "freedom of contract is a qualified, and not an absolute, right. There is no absolute freedom to do as one wills or to contract as one chooses."

The true rule is that private parties may neither override FAA proscriptions nor ignore the requirement for fundamental arbitral fairness within the limits of the FAA. The statutory rule is that arbitration agreements are on an "equal footing with all other contracts" such that the FAA will allow a claimant to challenge an agreement revocable on general grounds, such as (but not limited to) fraud, duress, and unconscionability. As part of this rule, the law accepts some key defenses . . . that can overturn an arbitration agreement.

. . . .

VII. ITALIAN COLORS: A "SUBTLE BUT DEFINITIVE" ABANDONMENT OF PRECEDENT OR A LOGICAL EVOLUTION OF ARBITRATION DOCTRINE?

What is Glover's evidence for the assertion that in *Italian Colors*, "the Supreme Court subtly, but definitively," accomplished a fundamental theoretical shift in its conception of arbitration? Her main argument is that the *Italian Colors* Court never explicitly acknowledged that the FAA allows the parties to use streamlined proceedings tailored to the type of dispute. For Glover, this omission in the Court's opinion means the Court "effectuated a subtle, but quite significant shift in lawmaking power."

In point of fact, no such omission occurred. The *Italian Colors* Court did indeed specifically mention the policy to enhance efficiency in arbitral disputes.

The Court expressly commented that imposing a class action remedy in the face of a waiver of that procedure contradicts the efficiency of arbitration:

> [Class arbitration] . . . would require—before a plaintiff can be held to contractually agreed bilateral arbitration—that a federal court determine (and the parties litigate) the legal requirements for success on the merits claim-by-claim and theory-by-theory, the evidence necessary to meet those requirements, the cost of developing that evidence, and the damages that would be recovered in the event of success. Such a preliminary litigating hurdle would undoubtedly destroy the prospect of speedy resolution that arbitration in general and bilateral arbitration in particular was meant to secure.

In her unqualified endorsement of aggregate procedures, Glover neither cites the above passage nor mentions the inefficiencies of class actions as an FAA remedy.

The *Italian Colors* decision is a logical and incremental extension of the principles in *AT&T Mobility LLC v. Concepcion*. The *Concepcion* Court held that the FAA preempts California's case-law rule permitting an unconscionability defense that allows the consumer to bypass a class-action waiver to an arbitration clause. Further, the *Concepcion* Court held that state courts may not automatically base a finding of unconscionability on the value of class arbitration to litigants with "small-dollar claims." In so ruling, *Concepcion* "makes . . . clear that freedom of contract is now the law of the land." The *Italian Colors* Court, expressly applying *Concepcion*, sensibly took the reasoning one step further. The *Italian Colors* Court held that "an arbitration agreement may not be invalidated based on individualized proof that what the plaintiffs have waived—the right to class arbitration—is so valuable that, without it, the costs of pursuing their claims are prohibitive."

Ultimately, the *Italian Colors* Court's reasoning and conclusion falls comfortably within the traditional doctrine of freedom of contract. The Court recognized the autonomy of the parties to select the contract terms and the accountability of those parties and their need to stand by their agreements. In this respect, *Italian Colors* relied on the bedrock FAA principle that "the overarching principle [is] that arbitration is a matter of contract;" therefore, "courts must 'rigorously enforce' arbitration agreements according to their terms, including terms that 'specify with whom [the parties] choose to arbitrate their disputes,' and 'the rules under which that arbitration will be conducted.' ' Here, the "with whom" reference above applied undeniably to the arbitrators required by the agreement.

While the Court accepted that freedom of contract was not absolute, *Italian Colors* deemed the respondent's public policy argument unpersuasive. The Court rejected the suggestion that plaintiffs with a small-dollar claim that could go unvindicated were entitled to a judge-made remedy beyond what Congress intended was needed to enforce the antitrust statutes. This ruling comported with consistent case law that courts should strictly cabin the public policy objection to those policies that are explicit, well-defined, and dominant. Because the *Italian Colors* Court properly enforced the parties' stated intent for a class-action waiver, as allowed by public policy, *Italian Colors* is a logical confirmation, and not the repudiation, of FAA policies and freedom of contract.

A final observation is that by emphasizing standard notions of freedom of contract principles and by noting that arbitration is a matter of contract, the *Italian Colors* Court reaffirmed what some commentators call the "contractual approach to arbitration." This approach stems from the explicit text of § 2 of the FAA, which "compels courts to enforce arbitration agreements 'save upon such grounds as exist at law or in equity for the revocation of any contract,' ' which determination expressly adopts some state contract law. Indeed, the contemporary legislative history to the first version of the FAA in 1924 further confirms this observation. Accordingly, Glover's view that "the Court's increasing embrace of pure freedom of contract in the arbitration setting is reminiscent of *Lochner*-era due process jurisprudence" is rhetoric rather than reality.

Problem: The Unconscionability Defense

6-18.   Ms. Carla Sosa signed a document entitled "Physician-Patient Arbitration Agreement" shortly before undergoing knee surgery performed by Dr. Paulos, an orthopedic surgeon. Ms. Sosa was undressed and in her surgical clothing, when one of Dr. Paulos' staff presented her with three documents, less than an hour before surgery. No one discussed the documents with Ms. Sosa, either before she was scheduled for surgery, when she signed the document, after surgery, or at any subsequent hospital visits. Above the signature line was the following notice:

> NOTICE: BY SIGNING THIS DOCUMENT, YOU ARE AGREE-ING TO NEUTRAL ARBITRATION IN THE EVENT OF ANY MALPRACTICE CLAIM YOU MAY BRING AGAINST DR. PAULOS AND WAIVING YOUR RIGHT TO A JURY TRIAL.

> IF YOU HAVE QUESTIONS ABOUT THIS FORM, PLEASE DIRECT THEM TO HOSPITAL ADMINISTRATION.

The document's fine print (1) required any medical malpractice disputes to be submitted to arbitration; (2) required any arbitrator to be a board-certified orthopedic surgeon; and (3) awarded Dr. Paulos $150 per hour spent in arbitration in addition to payment of all other expenses, costs, arbitrator fees, and attorney fees in the event that Ms. Sosa was awarded less than half of the amount she sought. The document also provided that Ms. Sosa could revoke the agreement within ten days after her discharge from the hospital.

The surgery was an apparent success, and Ms. Sosa was released the next day. She was given a two-week prescription for hydrocodone to suppress the pain. The medication substantially reduced Ms. Sosa's pain and allowed her to sleep restfully, often throughout the day.

Ms. Sosa's first visit to the hospital, a week after the surgery, was to check for pain and examine the stitching. There were no problems, and Ms. Sosa was again released. However, on the second visit, three weeks after the surgery, Ms. Sosa complained that her pain had drastically increased after she finished taking the hydrocodone. Dr. Paulos X-rayed the incision and discovered that he had dropped an orthopedic screw into Ms. Sosa's knee incision, which he failed to remove before closing the incision. The screw was causing inflammation and needed to be removed. Ms. Sosa had to undergo an additional surgery.

Ms. Sosa brought suit against Dr. Paulos for medical malpractice, claiming damages for pain, further surgery, pain medication, recovery time, and lost wages. Dr. Paulos moved to stay the proceedings and compel arbitration, referencing the "Physician-Patient Arbitration Agreement."

Is the "Physician-Patient Arbitration Agreement" unconscionable? What factors point to and against procedural unconscionability? What factors point to and against substantive unconscionability? Would any of your answers change if the agreement allowed Ms. Sosa to revoke the agreement within thirty days of discharge? What impact, if any, does the ruling in *Concepcion* have on this situation?

Food for Thought: Unfair or Deceptive Acts or Practices (UDAP)

Conduct that triggers the defense of misrepresentation, unconscionability, or economic duress may also trigger an enforcement action based on an "unfair or deceptive act or practice" (UDAP). At the federal level, the Federal Trade Commission enforces the UDAP provision in § 5 of the Federal Trade Commission Act (FTCA), 15 U.S.C. § 45. Similar provisions appear in statutes in all fifty states; they are often called "little FTC Acts" and "consumer protection acts" (CPAs).[*]

A state consumer protection act typically authorizes the state attorney general (AG) to bring claims against a deceptive business on behalf of groups of consumers, by obtaining a "cease and desist order" or other injunctive relief, a declaratory judgment, or a settlement agreement with the business, to prevent further instances of that UDAP. States' AGs interact through the National Association of Attorneys General (NAAG), to coordinate their consumer protection efforts and share evidence of UDAPs that occur in multiple states.

A prominent feature of most state CPAs is express authorization for a consumer to act as a "private attorney general" by bringing a private enforcement action against a business's unfair or deceptive conduct affecting that consumer. The FTCA has no comparable provision.[**]

Here is a sampling of enforcement actions by state AGs:

- In 2016, state and federal settlements of $15 billion were made to compensate owners of Volkswagen diesel vehicles over emissions fraud. The settlement requires repurchase or modification of vehicles, as well as prohibiting future unfair or deceptive practices on diesel vehicles. Under the agreement, affected owners would receive at least $5100 and a potential maximum of $10,000 and a choice of a buy back of the vehicle or a modification of the vehicle. The settlement also provides an environmental mitigation fund and payments to States.

- In 2015, the New York attorney general reached a settlement with the nation's three leading national credit reporting agencies, Experian Information Solutions, Inc., ("Experian"), Equifax Information Services, LLC ("Equifax"), and TransUnion LLC ("TransUnion"). The settlement sought to improve credit reporting and fairness of dispute resolution of credit histories, particularly with respect to medical debt. One primary consumer complaint covered by the settlement was debt collection by creditors that were not owed any money and other mistakes that misrepresented consumer creditworthiness. The settle-

---

[*] Jack E. Karns, *State Regulation of Deceptive Trade Practices Under "Little FTC Acts": Should Federal Standards Control?*, 94 Dick. L. Rev. 373 (1990).

[**] Howard J. Alperin & Roland F. Chase, *Consumer Law: Sales & Credit Regulation* § 133 (Westlaw, through Sept. 2012).

ment increased protections over a three-year period, with many protections applying nationwide. For instance, the settlement requires Experion, Equifax, and TransUnion to employ specially trained employees to review documentation in disputes involving "mixed files, fraud or identity theft."

- In fall 2017, the New York attorney general launched an investigation into the massive Equifax data breach, affecting the data of 140 million Americans. It issued consumer alerts, and it pushed Equifax to improve its outreach and remedies for affected consumers.

§ 4. Violation of Public Policy

Many of the defenses discussed in this chapter could be characterized as based on public policy because they are grounded in protection of party autonomy and prevention of oppression. However, when a court refuses to enforce part or all of a contract expressly on the grounds of public policy, it is focused not on protecting the promisor, as is true in those other defenses, but on avoiding enforcement of contracts seen as being against the public interest.

It is easy to determine that a contract violates public policy if the legislature has enacted a statute saying so explicitly. In most states, statutes invalidate contracts involving the following activities, based on underlying public policy:

- Buying an individual's vote

- Engaging in certain kinds of restraint of trade

- Obstructing justice

- Lending at usurious interest rates

- Buying favorable treatment from a government worker or elected representative

In these situations, the common-law defense of violation of public policy is not necessary to invalidate the contract.

In a second set of cases, no statute explicitly invalidates the contract, but a statute forbids or criminalizes the activity promised or engaged in by a party to the contract, such as

- Committing murder

- Selling alcohol to a minor

- Extorting money

- Performing services without a license

In these situations, a court will look to the purpose of the statute and the legislative history for indications of the legislature's intentions regarding the validity of the underlying contract. A court will easily conclude that a contract to commit murder will be unenforceable because the legislative purpose in forbidding the act of murder will be furthered by also denying enforceability to a contract to arrange for that act. Other cases are more complex. For instance, a statute may bar an individual from performing a particular job without a license but not declare the contract itself to be illegal or unenforceable. If the licensing statute was meant to certify critical skills or ensure moral fitness of the contracting party, there is more reason to deny enforcement than if the statute was meant as a measure to obtain revenue from the sale of licenses.[*] The more attenuated the connection between the agreement and the public policy, the more likely the contract will be enforceable.[**]

In yet a third set of cases, the legislature is silent about the legality of and public interests surrounding a particular activity, such as

- Wagering or gambling (in jurisdictions where this activity is legal)

- Committing a non-criminalized tort

- Breaching a fiduciary duty

- Restricting a person from the right to marry (depending on the facts)

In these situations, the court must discern whether the contract involving that activity should be upheld or struck down based on the court's own assessment of public policy. The court derives public policy from "community common sense and common conscience . . . applied . . . to matters of public morals, public health, public safety, public welfare, and the like."[***] These determinations are made by the judge, not a jury. Given the breadth of concerns that may be involved and the difficulty of obtaining clear guidance on public policy from sources other than legislation directly addressing the contractual concern, it is hardly surprising that courts are hesitant to establish new bases for denying enforcement. This

---

[*] *See* Joseph M. Perillo, *Calamari and Perillo on Contracts* § 22.3, at 737 (6th ed. 2009).

[**] *See* E. Allan Farnsworth, *Contracts* § 5.1 (4th ed. 2004).

[***] *Naylor, Benzon & Co. v. Krainische Industrie Gesellschaft*, 1 K.B. 331 (1881) (McCardie, J.).

final section of Chapter 6 focuses on this third set of cases—how a court decides whether public policy warrants refusing to enforce a contract in the absence of legislative mandate or clear guidance.

If an illegal contract is unenforceable or void, a court most often leaves the parties as they are, refusing to order restitution or other compensation. This deters parties from engaging in similar contracts in the future, and it avoids having the court be involved in the sometimes sordid details of the parties' transaction. As one court said, "The law will not aid a man who founds his cause of action upon his own illegal acts. The courts should leave such parties where they found them. . . . Straight shooters should always win, but when there are none, bad guys need not look to us for help."[*] Exceptions exist, however. A court may order restitution in favor of a party who would otherwise suffer a forfeiture disproportionate to the magnitude and significance of the public policy violation, for a party who was excusably ignorant of the facts or law related to a minor public policy matter, or for a party who is not equally in the wrong as the other party or who withdrew from the transaction before the improper purpose was achieved.[**] Restatement (Second) § 178 articulates many of the factors that courts consider when ruling on this defense.

Reading Critically: *Tunkl* and *Johnson*

1. In the two cases that follow, what concerns do the courts take into account in determining whether the contract violates the public interest? How do the courts balance the wide range of considerations?

2. How do the factors the court considers compare to the factors identified in Restatement (Second) § 178?

3. If you were the judge, how would you resolve each case? Should the contract be enforceable? Why or why not?

4. Is the court or the legislature the more appropriate body to make a decision about unenforceability based on public policy concerns? What effect should the answer to that question have on the court's decision?

---

[*]   *Certa v. Wittman*, 370 A.2d 573, 577 (Md. 1977).
[**]   *See* Restatement (Second) §§ 198, 199.

Tunkl v. Regents of the University of California

OLGA TUNKL, as Executrix of the Estate of Hugo Tunkl,
Deceased, Plaintiff-Appellant

v.

The REGENTS OF THE UNIVERSITY OF CALIFORNIA,
Defendant-Respondent

Supreme Court of California, In Bank
383 P.2d 441 (Cal. 1963)

Tobriner, Justice.

This case concerns the validity of a release from liability for future negligence imposed as a condition for admission to a charitable research hospital. For the reasons we hereinafter specify, we have concluded that an agreement between a hospital and an entering patient affects the public interest and that, in consequence, the exculpatory provision included within it must be invalid under Civil Code section 1668.

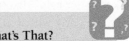

What's That?

This case was decided "in bank" (often spelled "en banc"), meaning that all the active justices on the court participated, the usual practice in most state supreme courts as well as at the United States Supreme Court. Until adoption of a constitutional amendment in 1966, the California Supreme Court heard many cases in smaller panels and only some cases were designated to be heard in bank. Courts sit "in bank" for only a limited set of cases.

Hugo Tunkl brought this action to recover damages for personal injuries alleged to have resulted from the negligence of two physicians in the employ of the University of California Los Angeles Medical Center, a hospital operated and maintained by the Regents of the University of California as a nonprofit charitable institution. Mr. Tunkl died after suit was brought, and his surviving wife, as executrix, was substituted as plaintiff.

The University of California at Los Angeles Medical Center admitted Tunkl as a patient on June 11, 1956. The Regents maintain the hospital for the primary purpose of aiding and developing a program of research and education in the field of medicine; patients are selected and admitted if the study and treatment of their condition would tend to achieve these purposes. Upon his entry to the hospital, Tunkl signed a document setting forth certain "Conditions of Admission." The crucial condition number six reads as follows: "RELEASE: The hospital is a nonprofit, charitable institution. In consideration of the hospital and allied services to be rendered and the rates charged therefor, the patient or his legal representative agrees to and hereby releases The Regents of the University of California, and the hospital from any and all liability for the negligent or wrongful acts or omissions of its employees, if the hospital has used due care in selecting its employees."

Plaintiff stipulated that the hospital had selected its employees with due care. The trial court ordered that the issue of the validity of the exculpatory clause be first submitted to the jury and that, if the jury found that the provision did not bind plaintiff, a second jury try the issue of alleged malpractice. When, on the preliminary issue, the jury returned a verdict sustaining the validity of the executed release, the court entered judgment in favor of the Regents.[1] Plaintiff appeals from the judgment.

We shall first set out the basis for our prime ruling that the exculpatory provision of the hospital's contract fell under the proscription of Civil Code section 1668; we then dispose of two answering arguments of defendant.

We begin with the dictate of the relevant Civil Code section 1668. The section states: "All contracts which have for their object, directly or indirectly, to exempt anyone from responsibility for his own fraud, or willful injury to the person or property of another, or violation of law, whether willful or negligent, are against the policy of the law."

The course of section 1668, however, has been a troubled one. Although, as we shall explain, the decisions uniformly uphold its prohibitory impact in one circumstance, the courts' interpretations of it have been diverse. Some of the cases have applied the statute strictly, invalidating any contract for exemption from liability for negligence. The court in England v. Lyon Fireproof Storage Co. (1928) 94 Cal.App.562, 271 P. 532, categorically states, "The court correctly instructed the jury that 'The defendant cannot limit its liability against its own negligence by contract, and any contract to that effect would be void.' ". . . The recent case of Mills v. Ruppert (1959) 167 Cal.App.2d 58, 62–63, 333 P.2d 818; however, apparently limits "[N]egligent . . . violation of law" exclusively to statutory law.[3] Other cases hold that the statute prohibits the exculpation of gross negligence

---

[1] Plaintiff at the time of signing the release was in great pain, under sedation, and probably unable to read. At trial plaintiff contended that the release was invalid, asserting that a release does not bind the releasor if at the time of its execution he suffered from so weak a mental condition that he was unable to comprehend the effect of his act . . . . The jury, however, found against plaintiff on this issue. Since the verdict of the jury established that plaintiff either knew or should have known the significance of the release, this appeal raises the sole question of whether the release can stand as a matter of law.

[3] To the same effect: Werner v. Knoll (1948) 89 Cal.App.2d 474, 201 P.2d 45; 15 Cal.L.Rev. 46 (1926). This interpretation was criticized in Barkett v. Brucato (1953) 122 Cal.App.2d 264, 277, 264 P.2d 978, and 1 Witkin, Summary of California Law 228 (7th ed. 1960). The latter states: "Apart from the debatable interpretation of 'violation of law' as limited strictly to violation of statutes, the explanation appears to make an unsatisfactory distinction between (1) valid exemptions from liability for injury or death resulting from types of ordinary or gross negligence not expressed in statutes, and (2) invalid exemptions where the negligence consists of violation of one of the many hundreds of statutory provisions setting forth standards of care."

only;[4] still another case states that the section forbids exemption from active as contrasted with passive negligence.[5]

In one respect, as we have said, the decisions are uniform. The cases have consistently held that the exculpatory provision may stand only if it does not involve "the public interest."[6] Interestingly enough, this theory found its first expression in a decision which did not expressly refer to section 1668. In Stephens v. Southern Pacific Co. (1895) 109 Cal. 86, 41 P. 783, 29 L.R.A. 751, a railroad company had leased land, which adjoined its depot, to a lessee who had constructed a warehouse upon it. The lessee covenanted that the railroad company would not be responsible for damage from fire "caused by any . . . means." (109 Cal. p. 87, 41 P. p. 783.) This exemption, under the court ruling applied to the lessee's damage resulting from the railroad company's carelessly burning dry grass and rubbish. Declaring the contract not "violative of sound public policy" (109 Cal. p. 89, 41 P. p. 784), the court pointed out ". . . As far as this transaction was concerned, the parties, when contracting, stood upon common ground, and dealt with each other as A. and B. might deal with each other with reference to any private business undertaking. . . ." (109 Cal. p. 88, 41 P. p. 784.) The court concluded "that the interests of the public in the contract are more sentimental than real" (109 Cal. p. 95, 41 P. p. 786; emphasis added) and that the exculpatory provision was therefore enforceable.

In applying this approach and in manifesting their reaction as to the effect of the exemptive clause upon the public interest, some later courts enforced, and others invalidated such provisions under section 1668. Thus in Nichols v. Hitchcock Motor Co. (1937) 22 Cal.App.2d 151, 159, 70 P.2d 654, 658, the court enforced an exculpatory clause on the ground that "the public neither had nor could have any interest whatsoever in the subject-matter of the contract, considered either as a whole or as to the incidental covenant in question. The agreement between the parties concerned "their private affairs" only."[7]

---

[4]   See Butt v. Bertola (1952) 110 Cal.App.2d 128, 242 P.2d 32; Ryan Mercantile Co. v. Great Northern Ry. Co. (D.Mont.1960) 186 F.Supp. 660, 667–668. . . .

[5]   Barkett v. Brucato (1953) 122 Cal.App.2d 264, 277, 264 P.2d 978.

[6]   The view that the exculpatory contract is valid only if the public interest is not involved represents the majority holding in the United States. Only New Hampshire, in definite opposition to "public interest" test, categorically refuses to enforce exculpatory provisions. The cases are collected in an extensive annotation in 175 A.L.R. 8 (1948). . . .

[7]   See also Hischemoeller v. Nat. Ice etc. Storage Co. (1956) 46 Cal.2d 318, 328, 294 P.2d 433 (contract upheld as an "ordinary business transaction between businessmen"); Mills v. Ruppert (1959) 167 Cal.App.2d 58, 62, 333 P.2d 818 (lease held not a matter of public interest); Inglis v. Garland (1936) 19 Cal.App.2d Supp. 767, 773, 64 P.2d 501 (same); cf. Northwestern Mutual Fire Ass'n v. Pacific Co. (1921) 187 Cal. 38, 41, 200 P. 934 (exculpatory clause in bailment upheld because of special business situation).

In Barkett v. Brucato (1953) 122 Cal.App.2d 264, 276, 264 P.2d 978, 987, which involved a waiver clause in a private lease, Justice Peters summarizes the previous decisions in this language: "These cases hold that the matter is simply one of interpreting a contract; that both parties are free to contract; that the relationship of landlord and tenant does not affect the public interest; that such a provision affects only the private affairs of the parties. . . ." (Emphasis added.)

On the other hand, courts struck down exculpatory clauses as contrary to public policy in the case of a contract to transmit a telegraph message (Union Constr. Co. v. Western Union Tel. Co. (1912) 163 Cal. 298, 125 P. 242) and in the instance of a contract of bailment (England v. Lyon Fireproof Storage Co. (1928) 94 Cal.App. 562, 271 P. 532). In Hiroshima v. Bank of Italy (1926) 78 Cal.App. 362, 248 P. 947, the court invalidated an exemption provision in the form used by a payee in directing a bank to stop payment on a check. The court relied in part upon the fact that "the banking public, as well as the particular individual who may be concerned in the giving of any stop notice, is interested in seeing that the bank is held accountable for the ordinary and regular performance of its duties, and also in seeing that directions in relation to the disposition of funds deposited in the bank are not heedlessly, negligently, and carelessly disobeyed, and money paid out contrary to directions given." . . .

If, then, the exculpatory clause which affects the public interest cannot stand, we must ascertain those factors or characteristics which constitute the public interest. The social forces that have led to such characterization are volatile and dynamic. No definition of the concept of public interest can be contained within the four corners of a formula. The concept, always the subject of great debate, has ranged over the whole course of the common law; rather than attempt to prescribe its nature, we can only designate the situations in which it has been applied. We can determine whether the instant contract does or does not manifest the characteristics which have been held to stamp a contract as one affected with a public interest.

In placing particular contracts within or without the category of those affected with a public interest, the courts have revealed a rough outline of that type of transaction in which exculpatory provisions will be held invalid. Thus the attempted but invalid exemption involves a transaction which exhibits some or all of the following characteristics. It concerns a business of a type generally thought suitable for public regulation.[9] The party seeking exculpation is engaged

---

[9]   "Though the standard followed does not always clearly appear, a distinction seems to be made between those contracts which modify the responsibilities normally attaching to a relationship which has been regarded in other connections as a fit subject for special regulatory treatment and those which affect a relationship not generally subjected to particularlized control." (11 So.Cal.L.Rev. 296, 297 (1938)); see also Note 175 A.L.R. 8, 38–41 (1948).

in performing a service of great importance to the public,[10] which is often a matter of practical necessity for some members of the public.[11] The party holds himself out as willing to perform this service for any member of the public who seeks it, or at least for any member coming within certain established standards.[12] As a result of the essential nature of the service, in the economic setting of the transaction, the party invoking exculpation possesses a decisive advantage of bargaining strength against any member of the public who seeks his services.[13] In exercising

---

In *Munn v. Illinois* (1877) 94 U.S. 133, the Supreme Court appropriated the common law concept of a business affected with a public interest to serve as the test of the constitutionality of state price fixing laws, a role it retained until *Nebbia v. New York* (1934) 291 U.S. 502, and *Olsen v. Nebraska* (1941) 313, U.S. 236. For discussion of the constitutional use and application of the "public interest" concept, see generally Hall, Concept of Public Business (1940); Hamilton, *Affectation with a Public Interest* 39 Yale L.J. 1089 (1930).

[10] See *New York Cent. Railroad Co. v. Lockwood* (1873) 84 U.S. 357, 378–382; *Millers Mut. Fire Ins. Assn. v. Parker* (1951) 234 N.C. 20, 65 S.E.2d 341; *Hiroshima v. Bank of Italy* (1926) 78 Cal.App. 362, 377 248 P. 947; cf. *Lombard v. Louisiana* (1963) 373 U.S. (Douglass J., concurring) (holding that restaurants cannot discriminate on racial grounds, and noting that "places of public accommodation such as retail stores, restaurants, and the like render a 'service which has become a public interest' . . . in the manner of the innkeepers and common carriers of old."); *Charles Wolff Packing Co. v. Court of Industrial Relations* (1923) 262 U.S. 522 ("public interest" as test of constitutionality of price fixing); *German Alliance Ins. Co. v. Lewis* (1914) 233 U.S. 389 (same); Hamilton, *Affectation with a Public Interest* (1930) 39 Yale L.J. 1089 (same); Arterburn, *The Origin and First Test of Public Callings*, 75 U.Pa.L.Rev. 411, 428 (1927) ("public interest" as one test of whether business has duty to serve all comers). But see *Simmons v. Columbus Venetian Stevens Buildings, Inc.* (1958) 20 Ill.App.2d 1, 25–32, 155 N.E.2d 372, 384–387 (apartment leases, in which exculpatory clauses are generally permit-ted, are in aggregate as important to society as contracts with common carriers).

[11] See *Bisso v. Inland Waterways Corp.* (1955) 349 U.S. 85, 91; *New York Cent. Railroad Co. v. Lockwood, supra*; *Fairfax Gas & Supply Co. v. Hadary* (4th Cir. 1945) 151 F.2d 939; *Millers Mut. Fire Ins. Assn. v. Parker* (1951) 234 N.C. 20, 65 S.E.2d 341; *Irish & Swartz Stores v. First Nat. Bank of Eugene* (1960) 220 Ore. 362, 375, 349 P.2d 814, 821; 15 U.Pitt.L.Rev. 493, 499–500 (1954); Note 175 A.L.R. 8, 16–17 (1948); cf. *Charles Wolff Packing Co. v. Court of Industrial Relations* (1923) 262 U.S. 522 (constitutional law); *Munn v. Illinois* (1877) 94 U.S. 133 (same); Hall, Concept of Public Business 94 (1940) (same).

[12] See Burdick, *The Origin of the Peculiar Duties of Public Service Companies* (1911), 11 Colum.L.Rev. 514, 616, 743; *Lombard v. Louisiana, supra*, n.10. There is a close historical relationship between the duty of common carriers, public warehousemen, innkeepers, etc. to give reasonable service to all persons who apply, and refusal of courts to permit such businesses to obtain exemption from liability for negligence. See generally Arterburn, *supra*. n.10. This relationship has led occasional courts and writers to assert that exculpatory contracts are invalid only if the seller has a duty of public service. 28 Brooklyn L.Rev. 357, 359 (1962); see *Ciofalo v. Vic Tanney Gyms, Inc.* (1961) 10 N.Y.2d 294, 220 N.Y.S.2d 962, 177 N.E.2d 925. A seller under a duty to serve is generally denied exemption from liability for negligence; (however, the converse is not necessarily true) 44 Cal.L.Rev. 120 (1956); cf. *Charles Wolff Packing Co. v. Court of Industrial Relations* (1923) 262 U.S. 522, 538 (absence of duty to serve public does not necessarily exclude business from class of those constitutionally subject to state price regulation under test of *Munn v. Illinois*); *German Alliance Ins. Co. v. Lewis* (1914) 233 U.S. 389, 407 (same). A number of cases have denied enforcement to exculpatory provisions although the seller had no duty to serve. See, e.g., *Bisso v. Inland Waterways Corp.* (1955) 349 U.S. 85; *Millers Mut. Fire Ins. Assn. v. Parker* (1951) 234 N.C. 20, 65 S.E.2d 341; cases on exculpatory provisions in employment contracts collected in 35 Am.Jur., Master & Servant, § 136.

[13] Prosser, Torts (2d ed. 1955) p. 306: "The courts have refused to uphold such agreements . . . where one party is at such obvious disadvantage in bar-gaining power that the effect of the contract is to put him at the mercy of the other's negligence." Note 175 A.L.R. 8, 18 (1948): "Validity is almost universally denied to contracts exempting from liability for its negligence the party which occupies a

a superior bargaining power the party confronts the public with a standardized adhesion contract of exculpation,[14] and makes no provision whereby a purchaser may pay additional reasonable fees and obtain protection against negligence.[15] Finally, as a result of the transaction, the person or property of the purchaser is placed under the control of the seller,[16] subject to the risk of carelessness by the seller or his agents.

While obviously no public policy opposes private, voluntary transactions in which one party, for a consideration, agrees to shoulder a risk which the law would otherwise have placed upon the other party, the above circumstances pose a different situation. In this situation the releasing party does not really acquiesce voluntarily in the contractual shifting of the risk, nor can we be reasonably certain that he receives an adequate consideration for the transfer. Since the service is one which each member of the public, presently or potentially, may find essential to him, he faces, despite his economic inability to do so, the prospect of a compulsory assumption of the risk of another's negligence. The public policy of this state has been, in substance, to posit the risk of negligence upon the actor; in instances in which this policy has been abandoned, it has generally been to allow or require that the risk shift to another party better or equally able to bear it, not to shift the risk to the weak bargainer.

In the light of the decisions, we think that the hospital-patient contract clearly falls within the category of agreements affecting the public interest. To meet that test, the agreement need only fulfill some of the characteristics above outlined; here, the relationship fulfills all of them. Thus the contract of exculpation

---

superior bargaining position." Accord: *Bisso v. Inland Waterways Corp.* (1955) 349 U.S. 85, 91; *Hiroshima v. Bank of Italy* (1926) 78 Cal.App. 362, 377, 248 P. 947; *Ciofalo v. Vic Tanney Gyms, Inc.* (1961) 13 App.Div.2d 702, 214 N.Y.S.2d 99; (Kleinfeld, J. dissenting); 6 Williston, Contracts (Rev. ed. 1938) § 1751C; Note, *The Significance of Comparative Bargaining Power in the Law of Exculpation* (1937) 37 Colum.L.Rev. 248; 20 Corn. L.Q. 352 (1935); 8 U.Fla.L.Rev. 109, 120–121 (1955); 15 U.Pitt.L.Rev. 493 (1954); 19 So.Cal.L.Rev. 441 (1946); *see New York Cent. Railroad Co. v. Lockwood* (1873) 17 Wall. 357, 84 U.S. 357, 378–382, 21 L.Ed. 627; *Fairfax Gas & Supply Co. v. Hadary* (4th Cir. 1945) 151 F.2d 939; *Northwestern Mut. Fire Assn. v. Pacific Co.* (1921) 187 Cal. 38, 43–44, 200 P. 934; *Inglis v. Garland* (1936) 19 Cal. App. 2d Supp. 767, 773, 64 P.2d 501; *Jackson v. First Nat. Bank of Lake Forest* (1953) 415 Ill. 453, 462–463, 114 N.E.2d 721, 726; *Simmons v. Columbus Venetian Stevens Buildings, Inc.* (1958) 20 Ill.App.2d 1, 26–32, 155 N.E.2d 372, 384–387; *Hall v. Sinclair Refining Co.* (1955) 242 N.C. 707, 89 S.E.2d 396; *Millers Mut. Fire Ins. Assn. v. Parker* (1951) 234 N.C. 20, 65 S.E.2d 341; *Irish & Swartz Stores v. First Nat. Bank of Eugene* (1960) 220 Ore. 362, 375, 349 P.2d 814, 821; 44 Cal.L.Rev. 120 (1956); 4 Mo.L.Rev. 55 (1939).

[14] See *Simmons v. Columbus Venetian Stevens Buildings, Inc.* (1958) 20 Ill.App.2d 1, 30–33, 155 N.E.2d 372, 386–387; *Irish & Swartz Stores v. First Nat. Bank of Eugene* (1960) 220 Ore. 362, 376, 349 P.2d 814, 821; Note 175 A.L.R. 8, 15–16, 112 (1948).

[15] See 6A Corbin, Contracts (1962) § 1472 at p. 595; Note 175 A.L.R. 8, 17–18 (1948).

[16] See *Franklin v. Southern Pac. Co.* (1928) 203 Cal. 680, 689–690, 265 P. 936, 59 A.L.R. 118; *Stephens v. Southern Pac. Co.* (1895) 109 Cal. 86, 90–91, 41 P. 783, 29 L.R.A. 751; *Irish & Swartz Stores v. First Nat. Bank of Eugene* (1960) 220 Ore. 362, 377, 349 P.2d 814, 822; 44 Cal.L.Rev. 120, 128 (1956); 20 Corn.L.Q. 352, 358 (1935).

involves an institution suitable for, and a subject of, public regulation. That the services of the hospital to those members of the public who are in special need of the particular skill of its staff and facilities constitute a practical and crucial necessity is hardly open to question.

The hospital, likewise, holds itself out as willing to perform its services for those members of the public who qualify for its research and training facilities. While it is true that the hospital is selective as to the patients it will accept, such selectivity does not negate its public aspect or the public interest in it. The hospital is selective only in the sense that it accepts from the public at large certain types of cases which qualify for the research and training in which it specializes. But the hospital does hold itself out to the public as an institution which performs such services for those members of the public who can qualify for them.[18]

In insisting that the patient accept the provision of waiver in the contract, the hospital certainly exercises a decisive advantage in bargaining. The would-be patient is in no position to reject the proffered agreement, to bargain with the hospital, or in lieu of agreement to find another hospital. The admission room of a hospital contains no bargaining table where, as in a private business transaction, the parties can debate the terms of their contract. As a result, we cannot but conclude that the instant agreement manifested the characteristics of the so-called adhesion contract. Finally, when the patient signed the contract, he completely placed himself in the control of the hospital; he subjected himself to the risk of its carelessness.

In brief, the patient here sought the services which the hospital offered to a selective portion of the public; the patient, as the price of admission and as a result of his inferior bargaining position, accepted a clause in a contract of adhesion waiving the hospital's negligence; the patient thereby subjected himself to control of the hospital and the possible infliction of the negligence which he had thus been compelled to waive. The hospital, under such circumstances, occupied a status different than a mere private party; its contract with the patient affected the public interest. We see no cogent current reason for according to the patron of the inn a greater protection than the patient of the hospital; we cannot hold the innkeeper's performance affords a greater public service than that of the hospital.

Think About It!

Could the plaintiffs also have raised unconscionability as a defense? Would it have been an easier or more difficult defense?

---

[18] See *Wilmington General Hospital v. Manlove* (Del.1961) 174 A.2d 135, holding that a private hospital which holds itself out as rendering emergency service cannot refuse to admit a patient in an emergency[,] and comment on the above case in 14 Stan.L.Rev. 910 (1962).

We turn to a consideration of the two arguments urged by defendant to save the exemptive clause. Defendant first contends that while the public interest may possibly invalidate the exculpatory provision as to the paying patient, it certainly cannot do so as to the charitable one. Defendant secondly argues that even if the hospital cannot obtain exemption as to its 'own' negligence it should be in a position to do so as to that of its employees. We have found neither proposition persuasive.

As to the first, we see no distinction in the hospital's duty of due care between the paying and nonpaying patient. (But see Rest., Contracts, § 575(1) (b).) The duty, emanating not merely from contract but also tort, imports no discrimination based upon economic status. (See Malloy v. Fong (1951) 37 Cal.2d 356, 366, 232 P.2d 241; Rest., Torts, §§ 323–324.) Rejecting a proposed differentiation between paying and nonpaying patients, we refused in Malloy to retain charitable immunity for charitable patients. Quoting Rutledge, J. in President & Directors of Georgetown College v. Hughes (1942) 76 U.S.App.D.C. 123, 130 F.2d 810, 827, we said: "Retention (of charitable immunity) for the nonpaying patient is the least defensible and most unfortunate of the distinction's refinements. He, least of all, is able to bear the burden. More than all others, he has no choice. . . . He should be the first to have reparation, not last and least among those who receive it." (37 Cal.2d p. 365, 232 P.2d p. 246.) To immunize the hospital from negligence as to the charitable patient because he does not pay would be as abhorrent to medical ethics as it is to legal principle.

Defendant's second attempted distinction, the differentiation between its own and vicarious liability, strikes a similar discordant note. In form defendant is a corporation. In everything it does, including the selection of its employees, it necessarily acts through agents. A legion of decisions involving contracts between common carriers and their customers, public utilities and their customers, bailees and bailors, and the like, have drawn no distinction

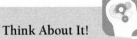

Think About It!

To what extent does tort law policy play a role in this decision?

between the corporation's 'own' liability and vicarious liability resulting from negligence of agents. We see no reason to initiate so far-reaching a distinction now. If, as defendant argues, a right of action against the negligent agent is in fact a sufficient remedy, then defendant by paying a judgment against it may be subrogated to the right of the patient against the negligent agent, and thus may exercise that remedy.

In substance defendant here asks us to modify our decision in Malloy, which removed the charitable immunity; defendant urges that otherwise the funds of the research hospital may be deflected from the real objective of the extension of medical knowledge to the payment of claims for alleged negligence. Since a research hospital necessarily entails surgery and treatment in which fixed standards of care may not yet be evolved, defendant says the hospital should in this situation be excused from such care. But the answer lies in the fact that possible plaintiffs must prove negligence; the standards of care will themselves reflect the research nature of the treatment; the hospital will not become an insurer or guarantor of the patient's recovery. To exempt the hospital completely from any standard of due care is to grant it immunity by the side-door method of a contractual clause exacted of the patient. We cannot reconcile that technique with the teaching of Malloy.

We must note, finally, that the integrated and specialized society of today, structured upon mutual dependency, cannot rigidly narrow the concept of the public interest. From the observance of simple standards of due care in the driving of a car to the performance of the high standards of hospital practice, the individual citizen must be completely dependent upon the responsibility of others. The fabric of this pattern is so closely woven that the snarling of a single thread affects the whole. We cannot lightly accept a sought immunity from careless failure to provide the hospital service upon which many must depend. Even if the hospital's doors are open only to those in a specialized category, the hospital cannot claim isolated immunity in the interdependent community of our time. It, too, is part of the social fabric, and prearranged exculpation from its negligence must partly rend the pattern and necessarily affect the public interest.

The judgment is reversed.

> **Example R:** *Johnson v. Calvert*, 851 P.2d 776 (Cal. 1993).
>
> Mark and Crispina Calvert entered into a surrogacy agreement with Anna Johnson. The parties agreed that the resulting child would be the Calverts' child and that Johnson would relinquish all claims as to the child, in return for $10,000 and a life insurance policy. Pursuant to the agreement, an embryo created from Mark's sperm and Crispina's egg was implanted into Anna. After the relationship deteriorated and after the child was born, both sides brought suit claiming parental rights to the child.

Analysis: The trial court concluded that the Calverts were the child's genetic parents and that Anna had no parental rights to the child. The Court of Appeals affirmed, as did the Supreme Court of California, which upheld the surrogacy agreement as not offending public policy or the state or federal constitution.

Applying the Uniform Parentage Act, adopted in California in 1975 prior to the advent of surrogacy contracts, the court examined the relationship of both women with the child and the contract:

> Because two women each have presented acceptable proof of maternity, we do not believe this case can be decided without enquiring into the parties' intentions as manifested in the surrogacy agreement. Mark and Crispina are a couple who desired to have a child of their own genetic stock but are physically unable to do so without the help of reproductive technology. They affirmatively intended the birth of the child, and took the steps necessary to effect in vitro fertilization. But for their acted-on intention, the child would not exist. Anna agreed to facilitate the procreation of Mark's and Crispina's child. The parties' aim was to bring Mark's and Crispina's child into the world, not for Mark and Crispina to donate a zygote to Anna. Crispina from the outset intended to be the child's mother. Although the gestative function Anna performed was necessary to bring about the child's birth, it is safe to say that Anna would not have been given the opportunity to gestate or deliver the child had she, prior to implantation of the zygote, manifested her own intent to be the child's mother. No reason appears why Anna's later change of heart should vitiate the determination that Crispina is the child's natural mother.
>
> We conclude that although the Act recognizes both genetic consanguinity and giving birth as means of establishing a mother and child relationship, when the two means do not coincide in one woman, she who intended to procreate the child—that is, she who intended to bring about the birth of a child that she intended to raise as her own—is the natural mother under California law.[10]

---

[10] Thus, under our analysis, in a true "egg donation" situation, where a woman gestates and gives birth to a child formed from the egg of another woman with the intent to raise the child as her own, the birth mother is the natural mother under California law.

The dissent would decide *parentage* based on the best interests of the child. Such an approach raises the repugnant specter of governmental interference in matters implicating our most fundamental notions of privacy, and confuses concepts of parentage and custody. Logically, the determination of parentage must precede, and should not be dictated by, eventual custody decisions. The implicit assumption of the dissent is that a recognition of the genetic intending mother as the natural mother may sometimes harm the child. This assumption overlooks California's dependency laws, which are designed to protect *all* children irrespective of the manner of birth or conception. Moreover, the best interests standard poorly serves the child in the present situation: it fosters instability during litigation and, if applied to recognize the gestator as the natural mother, results in a split of custody between the natural father and the gestator, an outcome not likely to benefit the child. Further, it may be argued that, by voluntarily contracting away any rights to the child, the gestator has, in effect, conceded the best interests of the child are not with her.

Ruling in favor of the Calverts, the court found the agreement not inconsistent with public policy. The court rejected arguments of Anna based upon state law prohibiting "payment for consent to adoption of a child "and "pre-birth waiver of her parental rights." The court distinguished adoption from surrogacy, concluding that "[t]he parties voluntarily agreed to participate in **in vitro fertilization** and related medical procedures before the child was conceived; at the time when Anna entered into the contract, therefore, she was not vulnerable to financial inducements to part with her own expected offspring." Moreover, "Anna was not the genetic mother of the child," and any payments were meant to compensate her for services, rather than for her parental rights. As such, the court concluded that it did not violate public policy involving the adoption statutes or termination of parental rights. The court also rejected arguments of involuntary servitude in light of provisions of the contract that gave Anna decision-making relative to terminating the pregnancy. Finally, the court rejected arguments regarding exportation and dehumanization of women of lower economic status, finding "no proof that surrogacy contracts exploit poor women to any greater degree than economic necessity in general exploits them by inducing them to accept lower-paid or otherwise undesirable employment."

Think About It!

Another way to view this dispute is from the perspective of a "stakeholder diagram." On a blank piece of paper, draw a circle in the middle and place the child in the circle. Then draw two spokes from the circle, to the left and right. Place Mark and Crispina on the left spoke and Anna on the right spoke. Now ask yourself who else in society might have a stake or interest in this case or its precedential value. For instance, what about the child's grandparents? What about other couples considering a similar procedure? And so on. Arrange those parties on additional spokes around the circle, so that they align with the party whose interests match theirs.

Ultimately the court upheld the contract:

> The argument that a woman cannot knowingly and intelligently agree to gestate and deliver a baby for intending parents carries overtones of the reasoning that for centuries prevented women from attaining equal economic rights and professional status under the law. To resurrect this view is both to foreclose a personal and economic choice on the part of the surrogate mother, and to deny intending parents what may be their only means of procreating a child of their own genetic stock. Certainly in the present case it cannot seriously be argued that Anna, a licensed vocational nurse who had done well in school and who had previously borne a child, lacked the intellectual wherewithal or life experience necessary to make an informed decision to enter into the surrogacy contract.

Food for Thought: Surrogacy Contracts in Flux

The law concerning surrogacy contracts is complex, changing and non-uniform. The contracts are legal in nearly all states, but some states, such as New York, have held them to be unenforceable. Some states have adopted different rules for traditional and gestational surrogacy contracts. In a gestational surrogacy, a surrogate mother more or less "rents" her womb for an implanted fertilized zygote. In a traditional surrogacy, the surrogate provides the egg herself. A gestational surrogacy agreement is more likely to be upheld than a traditional surrogacy agreement. For instance, in 2017, the District of Columbia ended a 25-year ban that had criminalized gestational surrogacy. New Mexico permits surrogacy contracts so long as the surrogate mother does not receive compensation. In 2017, several Minnesota state lawmakers introduced a Gestational Carrier Act, seeking to validate surrogacy contracts that comply with its provisions.

In Minnesota and elsewhere, a controversial issue is whether a contract can promise reasonable compensation to the gestational carrier. Compensation for surrogacy arrangements is generally disfavored and could make an otherwise enforceable contract void, although some courts regard reimbursement of medical expenses and other pregnancy-related costs as being outside the realm of compensation.

In some situations, whether or not the intended parents are married or LGBT can have an effect on the enforceability of the contract. It is also possible that state adoption laws and laws regulating foster care may narrow the interpretation of an otherwise broadly worded surrogacy statute to exclude LGBT parents. Darra L. Hofman, *"Mama's Baby, Daddy's Maybe:" A State-By-State Survey of Surrogacy Laws and Their Disparate Gender Impact*, 35 Wm. Mitchell L. Rev. 449 (2009) (including a detailed chart documenting various states' approaches to this issue).

Problems: Contract Defenses

In Problems 6-19 to 6-21, identify which defense(s) might be raised. Evaluate each defense. If more than one defense is available, determine which one has the greatest chance of succeeding and whether it will.

6-19. Aaron is a criminal defense attorney at a large firm in New York. Sarah is the vice dean of labor relations at a large university. As part of the dissolution of their marriage, Aaron and Sarah entered into settlement negotiations about division of their vehicles, miscellaneous personal property, real estate, financial accounts and instruments, and retirement accounts. They intended to divide their combined estate equally. Only Sarah was represented by counsel—an experienced divorce attorney with considerable negotiation expertise.

The final settlement document stated that the retirement accounts were to be divided equally. Aaron was to retain two vehicles; Sarah, three. Aaron was to retain the residences in New York and Paris; Sarah, the residence in Los Angeles, plus a $445,000 payment from Aaron. Both parties retained the retirement accounts held in their respective names. Aaron's investment fund of $5.4 million was used to pay Sarah a one-time payment of $2.7 million "in satisfaction for the Wife's support and marital property rights." They signed the settlement. The court approved the settlement and the divorce.

For three years Aaron continued to invest in the mutual fund. Then, the parties learned that Aaron's investment fund was part of a Ponzi scheme (check Wikipedia if you need a definition), so its assets ended up being used to pay off other investors in order to keep the scheme going. The $2.7 million paid to Sarah had actually come from an investment made by a newer victim to the scheme. By good fortune, Sarah did not need to relinquish the funds to the bankruptcy trustee, due to statutes of limitations and bankruptcy law. Aaron, however, had a balance of zero in his investment fund. If Aaron brings suit to adjust the divorce settlement, which defense(s) should he raise, and will he succeed?

6-20. Contractor wanted a $100,000 loan at 4% interest so he could build a house and sell it for a profit. Banker lied and told Contractor that he did not qualify for a bank loan, but she offered to personally loan Contractor $100,000 for six months at 10% interest per annum, with interest and principal payable upon maturity of the note. They signed a note and a mortgage with these terms. The mortgage was properly recorded and all taxes paid. The note also provided that Banker would be entitled to attorneys fees in any collection action including foreclosure on the mortgage. Contractor signed the note and mortgage without reading them. Six months later and without the money to repay the note, Contractor asked for an extension. In discussion with Contractor, Banker, feeling guilty, confessed that Contractor originally qualified for the bank loan. Banker and Contractor then agreed on the extension and they shook hands on a three-month extension.

Three months later when the loan was due, Contractor had finished the house but had not sold it. Banker threatened foreclosure. She then suggested that Contractor sell the house to Banker's mother, Mavis, for $150,000. Contractor recognized that $150,000 is the amount he spent to build the house, and he reluctantly agreed to the price. Contractor would have liked $180,000. Banker wrote down all the details of the sale listing her Mavis as purchaser, and both Banker and Contractor signed the sale agreement.

Before closing, the parties learned that the county had abandoned plans for an expressway behind the new house. Instead, the land will be dedicated as a nature preserve. The house's appraisal value rose to $250,000 ($70,000 more than what the contractor would have liked). Banker and Mavis arrived at closing with a check for $150,000, but Contractor refused to close. Which defenses would be helpful to Contractor, and why?

6-21. At age 64, Kai lost his wife after her long battle with cancer. A month later, he retired from his job. Exhausted and bereft, he sat around his house for several months. He got some grief counseling, and, at the advice of his counselor, decided to do something he had wanted to do for a long time—take painting lessons. He went to the local art center and paid $300 for a twelve-lesson beginner package in a group setting, so that he could see others progress. He enjoyed the camaraderie of the group and the praise of his young instructor. At the beginning of the tenth lesson, his instructor told him that he was "a natural" and could soon be painting well enough to exhibit and sell his paintings. She encouraged him to buy the "master painter super-package" of 24 private weekly lessons for $2400. Flattered and enheartened, he did so, signing up for the same instructor. Toward the end of the 24 private lessons, she told him that he will have enough high-quality paintings to exhibit if he signed up for another 12 private lessons for $1200. He did so, even though these lessons and his painting supplies were straining his household budget. He finished his paintings for exhibit and paid the art center an additional $1000 for exhibit space for a week. He invited his friends and family, who were appalled at his lack of talent. No paintings sold. Several of his friends eventually took him aside to tell him the harsh truth—they thought he got preyed upon because of his emotional vulnerability after his wife's death, and they urged him to get his money back. He was able to contest payment on the final $2200 in payments, which were on his credit card bill. The art center sued him for $2200. He consults you as his attorney. What kinds of evidence will you look for, in trying to determine whether he has a valid defense to the contract?

Test Your Knowledge

To assess your understanding of the material in this chapter, click here to take a quiz.

CHAPTER 7

Statute of Frauds

| How do parties demonstrate assent to a contract? | What kinds of promises will the law enforce? | What defenses to enforcement exist? | Is a writing required for enforcement? If so, what kind? | How is the content and meaning of a contract determined? | What are parties' rights and duties after breach? |

| What situations lead to excusing contract performance? | What remedies are available for breach of contract? | What contractual rights and duties do non-parties to a contract have? |

Table of Contents

§ 1. Introduction..490

§ 2. Manner and Effect of Invoking the Statute of Frauds.......................493

    PROBLEM: BURDEN OF PROOF IN THE STATUTE OF FRAUDS (7-1) 493

§ 3. Is the Contract Within the Statute of Frauds?...................................493

    § 3.1. Is the Contract Within a Category of Contracts Covered by the
    Statute of Frauds? 494

        PROBLEMS: THE ONE-YEAR PROVISION (7-2 TO 7-7) 497

    § 3.2. Does the Agreement Fall Within an Exception to the Writing
    Requirement?..500

        § 3.2.1. Exceptions for Contracts for the Sale of Goods.................500

        § 3.2.2. Part Performance Exception 501

        § 3.2.3. Equitable and Promissory Estoppel 503

§ 4. Is There a Writing That Satisfies the Statute of Frauds? 507

    § 4.1. What Kind of Writing Is Required? 507

        Howard Construction Co. v. Jeff-Cole Quarries, Inc.....................511

        PROBLEMS: WHAT KIND OF WRITING IS REQUIRED? (7-8 TO 7-12) 520

    § 4.2. Writing or Writings? 521

        Crabtree v. Elizabeth Arden Sales Corp. 525

§ 4.3. The Statute of Frauds in Electronic Commerce..............................530

Problems: Applying the Statute of Frauds (7-13 to 7-16) 532

§ 1. Introduction

Even if a contract has been formed according to traditional contract principles, it will not be enforceable in court unless the contract satisfies the relevant "statute of frauds," a set of statutes that specify which contracts must be evidenced by some kind of writing. Modern statute of frauds provisions are descended from the English Act for Prevention of Frauds and Perjuries of 1677. A state's statute of frauds is likely to be embodied in more than one legislative enactment, addressing both general contracts and contracts related to specific subject matters. The UCC includes a statute of frauds for contracts predominated by the sale of goods, and this chapter explores that provision along with general principles pertinent to application of any statute of frauds.

The English statute of frauds, as its full name implies, was enacted to counter use of perjured testimony and other fraudulent practices by requiring that certain contracts could not be enforced "unless the agreement . . . or some memorandum or note thereof, shall be in writing, and signed by the party to be charged therewith, or some other person . . . by him lawfully authorized." By requiring some form of written acknowledgement of an agreement, the statute was designed to prevent oral testimony alone from serving as sufficient evidence of the existence of a contract. It was enacted at a time when parties were not permitted to testify, jurors could use their own knowledge of the facts in rendering decisions, and judges had few tools to control decisions that might be based on sympathy or prejudice, rather than on fact. Having written evidence of the existence of a contract was seen as a way to provide some certainty that a contract existed, in order to counter such evidentiary limitations.

Today, courts and commentators have somewhat different rationales for requiring a signed writing, focusing on the functions that a writing may serve:

- **Evidentiary:** to ensure that a court that enforces a contract does so on the basis of reliable evidence. Written evidence is more reliable than oral testimony, whether because of shaky memories or the temptation to lie about past events, and having a signed writing helps to document the existence of an agreement.

- **Cautionary:** so that persons entering into contracts will recognize the significance of the contractual relationship that they are about to establish. People are usually more cautious when they need to sign a document, rather than simply conversing or shaking hands on an oral deal.

- **Channeling:** so that contractual parties can signal their intent to be bound by using a signed writing. People often think an agreement has to be in writing to be enforceable, which is not always true, but that belief underscores that a writing does serve a channeling purpose.

As you review the materials that follow, consider whether these functions help explain the ways in which the statute of frauds is interpreted and applied.

Whether the purposes of the statute of frauds are adequately and effectively served by modern use of the rule is a subject of some controversy. In a 1934 report, an English Law Revision Committee summarized the major criticisms of the statute, saying it was "a product of conditions which have long passed away," that the requirement of a writing is "out of accord with the way in which business is normally done" and "promotes more frauds than it prevents . . . ," and that the "operation [of the statute] is often lopsided and partial."[*] In 1954, Parliament repealed most of the British statute of frauds. The Convention on the International Sale of Goods (CISG) also dispenses with a writing requirement. The UCC and U.S. states retain their statutes of frauds, however, so you should understand when and how to apply the statute of frauds, as well as varying attitudes that lead some courts to support and others to limit application of the rules.

Applying the statute of frauds requires answering a series of related questions:

1. Is a writing required because the contract is within the scope of the statute of frauds? That question involves answering two sub-questions:

   a. Does the statute of frauds require this category of contract to be evidenced in a signed writing?

   b. If so, does the contract nevertheless fall within an exception to the statute of frauds, which eliminates the requirement of a writing under particular circumstances?

2. If the contract is within the scope of the statute of frauds, what kind of writing evidencing the contract is required to satisfy the statute, and does such a writing exist?

If the contract is within the scope of the statute of frauds so a writing is required, but there is no writing that meets the requirements of the statute, the consequence is that the contract is "unenforceable"—it cannot be enforced in court.

---

[*] Report of the English Law Revision Committee on the Statute of Frauds and the Doctrine of Consideration (Sixth Interim Report, Cmd. 5449, 1937), reprinted in 15 Can. B. Rev. 585, 589 (1937).

Some statutes and courts incorrectly say that the contract is "void," "invalid," or "not binding," but that is not accurate. The bar to enforcement does not prevent the parties from resolving their claims in arbitration, mediation, or settlement agreements. Nor does it bar the use of the contract for other purposes, even in court. For example, the existence of the contract may help establish a right to, or help defend against, a claim of restitution, or serve as evidence in a misrepresentation or fraud claim. Unenforceability is a significant consequence, but it falls short of making the contract void.

If the contract is *not* within the scope of the statute of frauds, or if the requirements of the statute *are* met, then the court may proceed to consider the merits of the contract claim.

In flowchart form, the statute of frauds (S/F) inquiry might look like this:

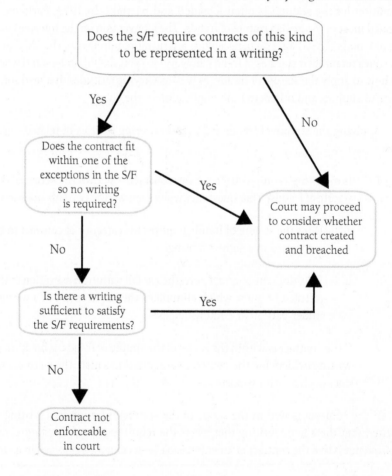

§ 2. Manner and Effect of Invoking the Statute of Frauds

If a plaintiff brings a breach-of-contract claim, the defendant—the "party against whom [contract] enforcement is sought" or the "party to be charged"—may move to dismiss the claim based on the statute of frauds, if the facts warrant such a motion. If the defendant is seeking to enforce a contract (perhaps in a counterclaim or based on a settlement agreement), then the plaintiff (who in that instance is the "party against whom enforcement is sought" or the "party to be charged") may move to dismiss the counterclaim based on the statute of frauds, to deny enforcement of that contract.

The *party raising the statute of frauds* has the burden of showing that the alleged contract is of a kind that is within the statute of frauds (that is, it is of a kind that is required to have a writing). If that is established, *the party seeking enforcement of the contract* then has the burden of (1) demonstrating that the contract fits within an exception to the statute or (2) providing a writing that meets the requirements. If she fails—that is, (1) the contract is found to be not within an exception the statute of frauds and (2) the statute's requirements are not satisfied—then the contract claim will be dismissed, and the party seeking contract enforcement will have no opportunity to present evidence about the existence and breach of the contract. On the other hand, if the party seeking enforcement succeeds in establishing that (1) no writing is required or (2) the statute of frauds is satisfied, the court proceeds to consider the merits of the breach of contract claim, where that party must still prove the existence, terms, and breach of the contract in order to win her suit.

Problem: Burden of Proof in the Statute of Frauds

7-1.   Return to the chart in § 1, and label each pair of arrows to show which party has the burden of proof for that step and whether that party must prove the answer to be Yes or No.

---

§ 3. Is the Contract Within the Statute of Frauds?

As indicated in the introduction to this chapter, the question whether a writing is required because the alleged contract is within the scope of the statute of frauds is really two related questions: (1) Is the contract within the category of contracts identified as requiring a writing; and (2) if so, does it nevertheless fit within an exception to the statute of frauds?

§ 3.1. Is the Contract Within a Category of Contracts Covered by the Statute of Frauds?

The following categories of contracts are listed in many states' general statutes of frauds, as well as in Restatement (Second) § 110(1), as requiring that there be a signed writing evidencing the contract:

- A contract containing a promise by the executor or administrator of an estate to personally pay a creditor, from her own funds (not the estate's funds), a sum owed by the decedent at the time of death;

- A suretyship contract in which the promisor guarantees personal payment of another's obligation if the primary obligor does not pay;

- A contract containing a promise made to a third party in anticipation of marriage;

- A contract for the sale of an interest in land; and

- A contract that cannot be fully performed within one year of the making of the contract.

Of these categories, the most common is that covering sale of an interest in land.

In addition, subject-matter-specific statutes sometimes contain their own statutes of frauds that vary among jurisdictions and may include:

- A contract to arbitrate contract disputes;

- A contract to extend a statute of limitations;

- An ante-nuptial (pre-nuptial) agreement;

- A contract for real-estate broker commission;

- A contract to make a testamentary distribution, to make a will, or not to revoke an existing will;

- A loan agreement above a certain dollar amount or a certain interest rate;

- A contract that cannot be performed within a lifetime; and

- A contract in which the sale of goods predominates and the contract price is $500 or more (UCC § 2–201).

A contract can be in more than one category (such as a contract for sale of goods that cannot be performed within a year). If so, the contract must meet the requirements of each category of statute of frauds (e.g., a contract for sale of goods for the price of $400 that cannot be performed within a year must be evidenced by a writing because of the one-year provision, though a writing would not be required under the UCC).

The following examples illustrate some of the particular categories covered by the statute of frauds:

Example A: Edward, the executor of Deborah's estate, personally (not on behalf of the estate) guaranteed to pay Charles 50% of the amount Deborah owed Charles on a promissory note at the time of her death, in exchange for Charles's promise not to seek payment of the additional 50% from the estate. The contract containing Edward's promise is within the statute of frauds.

Example B: Drew agreed to co-sign a loan agreement between Ethan and a bank, promising to pay the bank if Ethan defaulted. The loan agreement containing Drew's promise is within the statute of frauds because Drew promised to pay Ethan's obligation and the loan agreement is therefore a suretyship contract.

Example C: Craig caused an auto accident in which Violet was injured. Sam, Craig's uncle, signed the settlement agreement entered by Craig and Violet, promising to pay Violet if Craig does not deliver the payment agreed to in the settlement. Sam's promise is part of a suretyship agreement and so is within the statute of frauds. But if Sam promised to pay Violet in exchange for her promise not to sue Craig, Sam would be creating an obligation of his own, not acting as a surety, so an oral promise may be enforced.

Example D: Beverly promised to purchase Landacre from Stella for $100,000, and Stella agreed to sell Landacre. The contract is within the statute of frauds because it is for a sale of land. If Beverly and Stella agreed to a short-term lease of Landacre for 1 month, the contract would typically not be within the statute of frauds.

The most challenging of the categories to apply is the one-year provision, the requirement of a writing for a contract "not to be performed within one year from the making thereof." The time is to be measured from the day after the contract is entered (not the date of the contract or when performance begins).

Most courts construe the one-year provision narrowly, thereby limiting the number of contracts that need be in writing:

> Under the prevailing interpretation, the enforceability of a contract under the one-year provision does not turn on the actual course of subsequent events, nor on the expectations of the parties as to the probabilities. Contracts of uncertain duration are simply excluded; *the provision covers only those contracts whose performance cannot possibly be completed within a year.*

Restatement (Second) § 110 cmt. a (emphasis added). Using this narrow interpretation, the Supreme Court of Connecticut ruled that an oral contract for the "construction of twenty industrial buildings, a 280-room hotel and convention center, and housing for 592 graduate students and professors" was enforceable without a writing because the contract did not explicitly indicate it could not be fully performed within a year, even though the construction was expected to take well more than that amount of time.[*] Similarly, a contract to insure against a contingency that could *possibly* occur within a year (e.g., a life insurance contract payable upon death of the insured) would not be within the statute of frauds (no writing required). Nor would a contract to confer property to another upon death (of the promisor or another), because the death could occur within a year.

But not all courts agree with such a narrow interpretation, and some ask what is possible in fact, not just what is possible in theory. Thus, a court required a writing for a joint venture agreement to construct a condominium complex where there was no "reasonable possibility of performance within a year."[**] Another noted that "the possibility of performance which would take an agreement out of the statute of frauds must be such as could fairly and reasonably be said to have been within the contemplation of the parties." An "unforeseen or remote possibility" that the contract could be performed within a year "will not rescue the agreement from invalidity."[***]

---

[*]   *C.R. Klewin, Inc. v. Flagship Properties*, 600 A.2d 772, 773 (Conn. 1991).
[**] *Dean v. Myers*, 466 So. 2d 952 (Ala. 1985).
[***] *Stanley v. A. Levy & J. Zentner Co.*, 112 P.2d 1047, 1052 (Nev. 1941).

Problems: The One-Year Provision

Consider the following examples. Would the specified contracts likely (or definitely) be within the statute of frauds (so a writing would be required)?

7-2. Contract for 18 months of window-cleaning service

7-3. Contract for construction of an apartment complex, with construction expected to be completed in 18 months

7-4. Contract for performance of a single concert, to be held on a specified date 13 months after the contract was entered

7-5. Contract for 72 (or 260, or 2600) one-hour piano lessons, to be completed within 18 months

7-6. Contract for 11 months of technology service, with service to begin 2 months after the contract was entered

7-7. Contract to provide a life-time supply of Brand X car wax to the winner of a contest to submit "the best Brand X jingle"

In any of these cases, would it matter if the breach occurred the day after the contract was entered or, instead, the day before completion of contract performance? Would it matter whether the injured party filed a lawsuit immediately after breach or, instead, one day before expiration of the applicable statute of limitations?

If the parties agree to modify their contract (see Chapter 4, § 3.4), that raises the issue of whether the modification must be in a signed writing in order to be enforceable. The statute of frauds applies when the contract *as modified* is in a category of contracts that must be in writing, so the modified agreement will not be enforceable unless the statute of frauds is satisfied. Courts disagree about whether that requirement means that the *modification* must have a writing or, instead, that the *modified contract* must have a writing (a requirement that could be satisfied by the original written contract). Courts also disagree as to whether a renewal of a contract must be in writing. Some courts have viewed the renewal as a new and different agreement that requires a separate writing. Other courts have concluded that a renewal merely makes the original agreement operative for an extended period of time, so a writing that satisfies the statute of frauds for the original agreement satisfies it for the renewal as well.

Parties to a contract may create their own private statute-of-frauds requirement by including a "no oral modification" (NOM) clause specifying that all changes to the contract must be in writing. However, if the parties engage in one or more oral modifications after executing the written contract, their conduct may be found to have waived the NOM clause. Even a non-waiver clause will not prevent this result, because the parties may also be found to have waived the non-waiver clause through their later actions! A waiver may be express or implied by conduct, and the waiver may operate with respect to a particular modification or it may have continuing effect. Some (but not all) courts require that the party claiming waiver must show reasonable reliance on the waiver.

Example E: *3637 Green Road Co. v. Specialized Component Sales*, 69 N.E.3d 1083 (Ohio Ct. App. 2016).

Green Road entered into a three-year agreement to lease a warehouse and office space to Specialized Component Sales (SCS), a distributor of industrial electrical components, at a monthly rent of $1,600. The lease contained the following two provisions that appeared to require all changes to be in writing.

¶ 24: [N]o waiver of any condition or covenant shall be valid unless it be in writing signed by the Lessor.

¶ 42: This Lease contains the entire agreement between the parties, and any other agreement hereafter made shall be ineffective to change, modify or discharge it in whole or in part unless in writing and signed by the party against whom enforcement of the change, modification or discharge is sought.

The original lease was extended in writing six times, with adjustments to the rent as appropriate. At the time of the last written lease extension, the monthly rent was $1,824. After the expiration of the last written lease extension, SCS remained in possession of the premises as a month-to-month tenant. Sulzberger, a principal of SCS, testified that sometime around that time he had a conversation with Green Road's property manager, telling him that their business was doing poorly, and that SCS would have to find a cheaper place to rent unless Green Road would reduce the rent. Sulzberger also testified that Green Road agreed to reduce the monthly rent to $1,473.75. No written agreement was ever executed documenting this reduction. For the next eight years, Sulzberger paid the reduced rent, and Green Road never communicated that additional rent was owed. After SCS vacated the premises, Green Road sued for the difference between the rent paid and the rent owed under the last written lease extension.

Green Road argued that there was no enforceable oral agreement to modify the rent because (1) the lease expressly prohibited any oral modification of its terms, and (2) oral modification of the lease was barred by the statute of frauds.

Analysis: The court rejected both of Green Road's arguments. It found that there was "substantial, competent credible evidence in the record to support the conclusion that . . . Green Road waived the lease's no-oral-modification and written waiver provisions by its subsequent course of conduct acknowledging the rent reduction." Green Road offered no evidence contradicting Sulzberger's testimony about the conversations he had with the property manager. Green Road's own records demonstrated that it had treated the oral modification as effective, invoicing SCS for the reduced monthly rent and indicating a zero balance owed on the statement of account after every reduced payment. Further, there was no evidence that Green Road ever notified SCS that it was delinquent in its rent or, until the filing of its lawsuit, ever claimed that the lease's ¶¶ 24 or 42 precluded enforcement of the oral agreement to reduce the rent.

Make the Connection

Green Road also argued that there was no consideration for the oral modification of the lease. Recall that, under the pre-existing duty rule, new consideration is required for modifications (at least under the common law; see Chapter 4, § 3.4). The court rejected this argument, holding that SCS's continued leasing of the premises on a month-to-month basis constituted sufficient new consideration for the rent reduction, since it enabled the landlord to continue to earn income after the expiration of the original term lease.

Addressing the statute of frauds argument, the court acknowledged that Ohio law includes a statute of frauds for all lease agreements and that "[a] modification or reduction of the rent stated in a written lease cannot generally be proven by evidence of an oral agreement based on the statute of frauds." However, it went on to find that this modification was enforceable under an exception for partial performance, discussed below.

§ 3.2. Does the Agreement Fall Within an Exception to the Writing Requirement?

As discussed in § 1, the requirement of a signed writing is designed to provide courts with sufficient reliable evidence that a contract was formed, ensure the contracting parties make thoughtful judgments in deciding to enter contracts, and allow parties to easily signal when they intend to enter an enforceable contract. The exceptions to the statute of frauds are grounded in the judgment that, under some circumstances, those purposes are served even without a writing.

§ 3.2.1. Exceptions for Contracts for the Sale of Goods

> ### Reading Critically: UCC Article 2 Exceptions
>
> **Read UCC § 2–201(2) & (3).**
>
> 1. UCC § 2–201(2) and (3) set out four exceptions to the statute of frauds provision in § 2–201(1):
>
>   - a confirmation between merchants,
>
>   - specially manufactured goods,
>
>   - admission made by a party, and
>
>   - part performance.
>
>   For each exception, make a bullet list of the elements necessary to establish the exception. Some of the subsections contain multiple elements compressed into complex sentences; be sure to identify each separate requirement embedded in those provisions.
>
> 2. How should a party raise the statute of frauds defense so as not to risk invoking § 2–201(3)(b)?
>
> 3. Can performance by one party satisfy § 2–201(3)(c)?
>
> 4. Consider whether and how the purposes of the statute of frauds are accommodated by each exception (that is, why the exception should be recognized, given the purposes of the statute of frauds).

§ 3.2.2. Part Performance Exception

The fact that a contractual promise has already been partially performed is a basis for enforcing some but not all oral contracts.

The most frequent application of this exception is to contracts for the sale of an interest in land. In absence of a writing, the party seeking enforcement must prove at least some acts in performance of

Make the Connection

The previous section reviewed the UCC Article 2 exceptions to the UCC requirement of a writing, applicable only to contracts for the sale of goods. This section and the next one discuss exceptions that are applicable to other types of contracts. What similarities do you see between the UCC and non-UCC exceptions?

the alleged contract (1) that demonstrate the injustice of failing to enforce the alleged contract and (2) that are, in the words of Judge Cardozo, " 'unequivocally referable' to the agreement, performance which alone and without the aid of words of promise is unintelligible or at least extraordinary unless an incident of ownership."[*] The acts in performance thus serve as compelling evidence of the existence of the contract even in the absence of a signed written memorandum. Courts consider only steps taken in performance of the contract terms, such as taking possession of the land or making permanent improvements on it with the knowledge of the seller; paying all or part of the purchase price; paying taxes on the land; and extensive services performed for the seller without other compensation.

Restatement (Second) § 129 broadens the exception for part performance of land transfer contracts to allow enforcement of any contract "if it is established that the party seeking enforcement, in reasonable reliance on the contract and on the continuing assent of the party against whom enforcement is sought, has so changed his position that injustice can be avoided only by specific enforcement." However, most courts have refused to go as far as the Restatement, expressing concern that modifying the standard in this fashion would undermine the statute of frauds for land sale contracts by weakening the evidentiary purpose of the part performance requirements. These courts typically consider only acts of performance when deciding whether the party seeking enforcement has sufficiently shown the existence of the contract, though they will consider all acts of reliance to determine whether she has demonstrated a compelling need for intervention on equitable grounds.

---

[*] *Burns v. McCormick*, 135 N.E. 273 (N.Y. 1922). Similarly, Corbin said that "the performance must be one that is in some degree evidential of the contract and not readily explainable on any other ground." 2 Arthur L. Corbin, *Corbin on Contracts* § 425 (1950). For a modern statement of a similar rule, *see, e.g., Owens v. M.E. Schepp Ltd. Partnership*, 182 P.3d 664, 668 (Ariz. 2008) ("So that this exception does not swallow the rule, the acts of part performance take an alleged contract outside the statute only if they cannot be explained in the absence of the contract.").

Although not involving a contract for the sale of land, the following example illustrates how courts consider the concerns discussed above in a lease agreement.

> **Example F:** *3637 Green Road Co. v. Specialized Component Sales*, 69 N.E.3d 1083 (Ohio Ct. App. 2016).
>
> (See Example E for the facts.)

Analysis: As noted at the end of the Analysis of Example E, the court used the partial performance exception to enforce an oral modification of a rental agreement. The court explained,

> The equitable doctrine of partial performance is applied in situations where it would be inequitable to permit the statute of frauds to operate and where the acts done sufficiently establish the alleged agreement to provide a safeguard against fraud in lieu of the statutory requirements.

The court held that there was little doubt that the parties had, in fact, agreed to reduce the rent, since SCS paid, and Green Road accepted the reduced rent without objection, for perhaps as long as eight or nine years. In addition, SCS changed its position in reliance on this rent reduction "by remaining as a month-to-month tenant rather than finding a cheaper place to rent, so as to make it 'impossible or impractical' to return the parties to status quo.' "

The part performance exception has been applied to prenuptial contracts (contracts "in consideration of marriage") and to contracts to pay the debts of another. As with contracts for the transfer of interests in land, the party seeking enforcement must show part performance that is unequivocally referable to the alleged contract. *See, e.g., Hall v. Hall*, 222 Cal. App. 3d 578 (1990).

Think About It!

Why would the evidence of part performance be problematic with respect to the one-year provision, as *Coca-Cola Co.* suggests?

Courts have generally refused to apply the part performance exception to the one-year provision. Typical is the comment in *Coca-Cola Co. v. Babyback's International, Inc.*, 841 N.E.2d 557, 567 (Ind. 2006): "In contrast to real estate contracts, where evidence of part performance is relatively clear, definite, and substantial, the nature of evidentiary facts potentially asserted to show part performance of an agreement not performable within one year would be vague, subjective, imprecise, and susceptible to fraudulent application."

§ 3.2.3. Equitable and Promissory Estoppel

Recall that a party may invoke equitable estoppel based on her reasonable reliance on the acts or representations of the other party inducing such reliance (see Chapter 5, § 2). Thus, if a party to a contract represents that a writing is not needed or already was executed and the other party reasonably relies on that representation, the relying party may invoke *equitable* estoppel to prevent the party who made the representation from thereafter contradicting the representation by claiming that a writing *is* needed or was *not* executed. In effect, that party is barred from using the statute of frauds as a defense because of the other party's reasonable reliance on the representations. Similarly, if a party had *promised* to put an agreement in writing or *promised* not to insist upon a writing for enforcement, the relying party may invoke *promissory* estoppel to prevent the promisor from reneging on that promise, effectively preventing her from raising the statute of frauds as a defense.

In the absence of any such promises to execute a writing or not to insist on having one, can a party's reasonable reliance on a promise in an oral contract justify enforcement of that contract, based on promissory estoppel, even though a writing is required by the statute of frauds? Courts are divided on that question. Such a use of promissory estoppel, it is argued, undermines the very purpose of requiring a writing. Failing to enforce the statute of frauds based on the promisee's reliance rewards and thereby encourages reliance on oral promises and directly circumvents a rule designed to deter such reliance. Nonetheless, the trend favors this use of promissory estoppel, although—perhaps in recognition of those difficulties—courts often require that a promisee make an especially strong showing that the promise was made or that she suffered a substantial detriment, more than might be required to satisfy the Restatement (Second) § 90 standard.

Reading Critically: Promissory Estoppel
and the Statute of Frauds

Read Restatement (Second) § 139.

How much does the language in § 139 differ from the language of Restatement (Second) § 90? How does the language in § 139 compare to the language of Restatement (Second) § 87(2)? Does the language in § 139 make it more or less likely that a judge will apply promissory estoppel in a statute-of-frauds situation than in the situations addressed by §§ 90 (a binding promise) and 87(2) (offer binding as an option contract)?

Since the promulgation of § 139, more courts have been willing to entertain the promissory estoppel exception, but a minority of courts still hold that reliance should not be grounds for circumventing the statute of frauds, so the controversy continues. In that connection, compare the outcomes and analysis in Examples G and H below. Because application of the promissory estoppel exception is uncertain, it is wise to use other exceptions to the statute of frauds before trying to invoke promissory estoppel.

Example G: *McIntosh v. Murphy*, 469 P.2d 177 (Haw. 1970).

Murphy visited California in March to interview management personnel for his Chevrolet-Oldsmobile dealerships in Hawaii. He interviewed McIntosh two times during that visit, discussing a position as sales manager for one of the dealership. In April, McIntosh got a call from the general manager of Murphy Motors who told him that they might have a job for him to start within 30 days, if he was still interested. McIntosh told him that he was interested and available for the job. McIntosh sold some of his possessions, rented an apartment in Hawaii, and made the 2200-mile move from Los Angeles to Honolulu. He sent Murphy a telegram telling him he would be arriving in Honolulu on Sunday, April 26. On Saturday, April 25, Murphy telephoned McIntosh telling him that he could start working on Monday, April 27. McIntosh worked for Murphy for about two and a half months, until he was fired. McIntosh sued Murphy for breaching an alleged one-year oral employment contract.

At the jury trial, McIntosh argued that he had accepted the offer for a year's employment the day he began working; if the contract were for one year, he could perform it in exactly one year, so no writing was required under the statute of frauds. Murphy argued that McIntosh had accepted during the April 25 phone call, so the alleged one-year employment contract could not be performed in one year. Murphy moved for directed verdict, based on the statute of frauds.

Analysis: The trial judge refused to grant Murphy's motion, because the two extra days Murphy was relying on to subject the contract to the statute of frauds were weekend days. The jury returned a verdict for McIntosh, and Murphy appealed, arguing that the trial court erred in refusing to instruct the jury to consider whether the statute of frauds applied to the contract.

The Supreme Court upheld the jury's verdict. The court determined that it did not have to rule on whether the contract could or could not be performed within one year, because the doctrine of promissory estoppel rendered the contract enforceable even if the statute of frauds did apply. The court noted that the applicability of the statute of frauds "has been drastically limited by judicial construction over the years in order to mitigate the harshness of a mechanical application. . . . Another method of judicial circumvention of the Statute of Frauds has grown out of the exercise of the equity powers of the courts." The court cited the draft version of what became Restatement (Second) § 139 as "the proper method of giving the trial court the necessary latitude to relieve a party of the hardships of the Statute of Frauds. . . . This is to be preferred over having the trial court bend over backwards to take the contract out of the Statute of Frauds." Here, McIntosh's moving 2200 miles from Los Angeles to Hawaii was foreseeable by Murphy, since it was a job requirement. Injustice could be avoided only by enforcing the contract and paying damages, since McIntosh found himself living in Hawaii without a job. The court also stressed that some sort of contract clearly existed, as evidenced by the fact that McIntosh performed the contract for two and a half months, and was paid for that work. The exact length and nature of the contract was correctly left to the jury to determine.

The dissent objected to the majority's application of promissory estoppel to in effect overturn the legislature's decision to enact a statute of frauds:

> Here on one hand the plaintiff claimed that he had a one-year employment contract; on the other hand, the defendant claimed that the plaintiff had not been hired for one year but on a trial basis for so long as his services were satisfactory. I believe the Statute of Frauds was enacted to avoid the consequences this court is forcing upon the defendant. In my opinion, the legislature enacted the Statute of Frauds to negate claims such as has been made by the plaintiff in this case. But this court holds that because the plaintiff in reliance of the one-year employment contract (alleged to have been entered into by the plaintiff, but denied by the defendant) has changed his position, "injustice could only be avoided by enforcement of the contract." Where is the sense of justice?

> Now assuming that the defendant had agreed to hire the plaintiff under a one-year employment contract and the contract came within the Statute of Frauds, I cannot agree, as intimated by this court, that we should circumvent the Statute of Frauds by the exercise of the equity powers of courts. As to statutory law, the sole function of the judiciary is to interpret the statute and the judiciary should not usurp legislative power and enter into the legislative field. . . . Thus, if the Statute of Frauds is too harsh as intimated by this court, and it brings about undue hardship, it is for the legislature to amend or repeal the statute and not for this court to legislate.

Example H: *Stearns v. Emery-Waterhouse Co.*, 596 A.2d 72 (Me. 1991).

Stearns managed a Sears store in Massachusetts; he was 50 years old, had worked for Sears for 27 years, and was earning $99,000 a year. He was approached by Hildreth, the president of Emery-Waterhouse ("Emery"), a hardware wholesaler headquartered in Portland, Maine, which owned a number of hardware stores. Hildreth offered Stearns a job as Emery's director of retail sales. When Stearns expressed concerns about retaining his Sears job security, since it would be hard for him to find another marketing job at his age, Hildreth allegedly offered him an oral contract of employment to age 55, with a guaranteed annual salary of $85,000. Stearns accepted, resigned from Sears, and moved to Maine. Two years later, Hildreth moved him to the job of national accounts manager, at an annual salary of $68,000. Six months later, Stearns's position was eliminated and his employment was terminated. Stearns sued Emery for breach of contract.

Analysis: The trial court denied Emery's motion for summary judgment based on the statute of frauds, and held that Emery was estopped from asserting the statute of frauds because of Stearns' detrimental reliance on its promise. The jury held in favor of Stearns, and Emery appealed.

The supreme court overturned the trial court. Although the court affirmed that equitable estoppel based on *fraudulent* conduct by a promisor can avoid the application of the statute of frauds, it declined to allow promissory estoppel as an exception to the statute of frauds in employment contracts that take over a year to perform. The court reasoned:

> Although section 139 of the Restatement may promote justice in other situations, in the employment context it contravenes the policy of the Statute to prevent fraud. It is too easy for a disgruntled former employee to allege reliance on a promise, but difficult factually to distinguish such reliance from the ordinary preparations that attend any new employment. Thus, such pre-employment actions of reliance do not properly serve the evidentiary function of the writing required by the statute. An employee who establishes an employer's fraudulent conduct by clear and convincing evidence may recover damages for deceit, . . . or may avoid the statute of frauds and recover under an oral contract. The policy of the statute commands, however, that the focus remain upon the employer's conduct rather than upon the employee's reliance.

§ 4. Is There a Writing That Satisfies the Statute of Frauds?

§ 4.1. What Kind of Writing Is Required?

If a contract is within the scope of the statute of frauds (it is in a category of contracts identified as requiring the existence of a writing and it does not fall within one of the exceptions), and if the other party raises the statute of frauds issue (see § 2, above), the party seeking to enforce the contract in court must demonstrate that there is a writing that meets the requirements set out in the particular statute of frauds. Many of the state statutes require that the contract "or some note or memorandum thereof" be in writing and "subscribed" (signed) by the party to be charged. Some statutes also require the writing to "express the consideration." Restatement (Second) § 131 identifies the following typical requirements for such writings:

- the signature of the party to be charged,

- reasonable identification of the subject matter of the contract,

- language that is "sufficient to indicate that a contract with respect thereto has been made between the parties or offered by the signer to the other party", and

- language that "states with reasonable certainty the essential terms of the unperformed promises in the contract."

The requirement of a sufficient writing is generally also understood to mean:

- The writing does not have to be made as a memorandum of a contract; that is, the party need not have had the intent of writing down the contract, as long as the writing has the appropriate content. See Restatement (Second) § 133 cmt. b (the memorandum "may consist of an entry in a diary or in the minutes of a meeting . . . or . . . communication of an informal letter to a third person").

Make the Connection

Note the similarity between the statute of frauds requirement of a writing that "states with reasonable certainty the essential terms" of the contract and the requirement that, for a contract to be enforceable, its terms must be sufficiently definite for the court to determine whether there has been a breach (see Chapter 2, § 5).

- The writing does not have to be communicated to the other party to the contract. See Restatement (Second) § 133 cmt. b.

- The writing may be made "at any time before or after the formation of the contract." Restatement (Second) § 136.

- The writing need not exist at the time of trial; if the writing is lost or destroyed, "the contents of a memorandum [sufficient to satisfy the statute] may be shown by an unsigned copy or by oral evidence." Restatement (Second) § 137.

The requirement that the writing be "subscribed" or "signed" does not require a handwritten signature. Restatement (Second) § 134 defines "signature" as "any symbol made or adopted with an intention, actual or apparent, to authenticate the writing as that of the signer." The comments further explain:

The traditional form of signature is of course the name of the signer, handwritten in ink. But initials, thumbprint or an arbitrary code sign may also be used; and the signature may be written in pencil, typed, printed, made with a rubber stamp, or impressed into the paper. Signed copies may be made with carbon paper or by photographic process. . . . [T]he signature need not appear on any particular part of the writing. Although it is usual to sign at the end of a document, a printed letterhead or billhead may be adopted as a signature."

Example I: *Sterling v. Taylor,* 152 P.3d 420 (Cal 2007).

Sterling and Taylor met to discuss the sale of three apartment buildings in Santa Monica. At the meeting, Sterling drafted a handwritten memorandum entitled "Contract for Sale of Real Property." The memorandum identified the three properties for sale by street address and included a price term of "approx. 10.468xgross income[,] estimated income 1.600.000, *Price 16,750.00*." Both parties acknowledged that the notation of 16,750.00 was an error based on how Sterling wrote the price (there was reference to "superscript notation employed by plaintiff") and that the intended figure was $16,750,000. But the parties disagreed over the meaning of the price term as a whole. Taylor (the seller) claimed that the intended price was exactly $16,750,000. Sterling (the buyer) claimed that the price was to be set by a formula applying the 10.468 multiplier noted in the memorandum times the actual gross income from the buildings, which was estimated in the memorandum as $1,600,000 but was to be established precisely later. Sterling sued to enforce a sale. Taylor defended by claiming the memorandum did not satisfy the statute of frauds because it did not state the price with reasonable certainty.

Analysis: The trial court granted the defendant's motion for summary judgment on the grounds that the writing violated the statute of frauds and was too uncertain for enforcement. The intermediate appellate court disagreed and sent the case back to the trial court to consider the merits of the breach claim. The court noted:

> The terms of the writings as presented by plaintiffs suggest that the parties reached an agreement. The writings "import[ ] the essentials of a contractual obligation although [they fail] to do so in an explicit, definite or complete manner. . . ." [Later evidence] ultimately may show that the parties did not agree on material terms, but the statute of frauds does not, as a matter of law, preclude the enforcement of the alleged agreement. The writings have sufficient elements so that "by reasonable implication" they "demonstrate[ ] the existence of a contractual intent on the part of the one to be charged, and extrinsic evidence was necessary to define the limits thereof."

The Supreme Court reversed and reinstated the trial court summary judgment on behalf of the defendant. The court first noted that a memorandum of a contract for sale of real property must identify the buyer, the seller, the price, and the property, and that "[i]f a term is stated in a memorandum with sufficient certainty to be enforced, it satisfies the statute of frauds." The buyer was fully identified in the memorandum, and as for specifying the seller, it was sufficient to identify the agent for the actual seller, since a contract made in the name of an agent may be enforced against an undisclosed principal. The properties were identified by brief street address, not legal description, but "neither party displayed any confusion over their actual location. The purchase agreements Taylor prepared included full legal description, and when Sterling received those agreements he did not object that he wanted to buy buildings on 4th and 14th Streets in Manhattan rather than Santa Monica."

But the court concluded that the price was not specified with "sufficient certainty to be enforced." Two competing interpretations of the memorandum statement on price were presented to the trial court. The court concluded that the plaintiff's version of the price term

> is not reflected in the memorandum; indeed, it is inconsistent with the price term that appears in the memorandum. Under these circumstances, we conclude the evidence is insufficient to establish Sterling's price term with the reasonable certainty required by the statute of frauds.

> The statute of frauds demands written evidence that reflects the parties' mutual understanding of the essential terms of their agreement, when viewed in light of the transaction at issue and the dispute before the

court. The writing requirement is intended to permit the enforcement of agreements actually reached, but "to prevent enforcement through fraud or perjury of contracts never in fact made." The sufficiency of a memorandum to fulfill this purpose may depend on the quality of the extrinsic evidence offered to explain its terms. . . .

. . .

. . . [T]he extrinsic evidence offered by plaintiffs is at odds with the writing, which states a specific price and does not indicate that the parties contemplated any change based on actual rental income. Therefore, the evidence is insufficient to show with reasonable certainty that the parties understood and agreed to the price alleged by the plaintiffs. The price terms stated in the memorandum, considered together with the extrinsic evidence of the contemplated price, leave a degree of doubt that the statute of frauds does not tolerate.

Reading Critically: Sufficiency of a Writing Under UCC Article 2

Read UCC § 2–201 and comment 1; § 1–201(37), (43), and comment 37.

In what ways, if any, is the Restatement standard summarized above harder to satisfy than the UCC standard? In what ways, if any, is the UCC standard harder?

Reading Critically: *Howard Construction Co.*

1. The parties disagreed about whether they ever reached an agreement for the sale of a particular kind of rock. Why did the court conclude that whether the contract was made was not a "material issue of fact"?

2. What particular language in UCC § 2–201 was the focus of the court's analysis? How did the court interpret that language?

3. Many sales of goods occur not through execution of a single contract document, but through the exchange of documents sent by buyer and seller to each other, identifying the goods to be sold, along with quantity and price. In view of the court's

> analysis, what should a seller of goods put in a document it uses
> to respond to a purchase order, in order to ensure that the buyer
> will not be able to successfully raise a statute of frauds defense?
> What should a buyer of goods put in a purchase order it sends
> in response to an offer to sell, in order to ensure that the seller
> will not be able to successfully raise a statute of frauds defense?

Howard Construction Co. v. Jeff-Cole Quarries, Inc.

HOWARD CONSTRUCTION CO., Plaintiff-Appellant

v.

JEFF-COLE QUARRIES, INC., Defendant-Respondent

Missouri Court of Appeals

669 S.W.2d 221 (Mo. Ct. App. 1983)

NUGENT, JUDGE.

This case arose out of an action brought by Howard Construction Company (hereinafter "Howard Construction" or "Plaintiff") against Jeff-Cole Quarries, Inc. (hereinafter "Jeff-Cole" or "Defendant"), seeking damages on a breach of contract theory (Count I), or in the alternative, a promissory estoppel theory (Count II). The trial court granted summary judgment in favor of defendant on both Counts. Plaintiff contends on appeal that the trial court (1) erred in granting defendant's motion for summary judgment as to Count I . . . and (2) erred in finding that the statute of frauds barred Count I of plaintiff's complaint. We affirm the judgment.

Howard Construction was the successful bidder on a Missouri Highway Department project to construct a portion of Highway 54. Before Howard Construction was awarded the contract, it received from Jeff-Cole a typewritten document entitled "Proposal" [contained in an Appendix to the opinion] which referred to the Missouri Highway Project and listed descriptions, quantities and prices on types of rock needed for the project. The proposal contains six separate entries including a base type and asphaltic types of rock. It was dated November 21, 1972, and was signed by Harry Adrian, president of Jeff-Cole. The bid letting for the highway project took place in December, 1972, and Howard Construction was awarded the contract. Within a few weeks after the bid letting, the general superintendent of Howard Construction, Glenn Moore, met with Harry Adrian at defendant's office. The foregoing facts are not in dispute.

The parties do disagree, however, as to what occurred at that meeting. Plaintiff contends that Glenn Moore and Harry Adrian reached an oral agreement at the meeting and that Glenn Moore altered the typewritten prices on the proposal in his own handwriting to reflect the agreement that was reached. Plaintiff relies on Glenn Moore's deposition which reads as follows:

Q: Now, this particular document appears to have some figures written on it. Do you know anything about the various figures that are written in over the typing?

A: Yes, sir.

Q: What are those figures?

A: Those is [sic] after we got the job I went to Jeff-Cole's office and sat down with them. And those are the prices we came up with.

Q: All right, when you say you sat down with them, are you talking about Roger Adrian and Harry Adrian?

A: I'm talking about Harry Adrian.

. . . .

Q: Whose handwriting are those figures in if you know?

A: They are mine.

Q: You after discussion with Harry Adrian, changed—

A: We agreed on those prices that's [sic] written in.

Although defendant admits in its pleadings that discussions ensued between Jeff-Cole and Howard Construction, defendant denies that any agreement was ever reached in those discussions. Thus, the only disputed fact is whether the parties ever arrived at an agreement for the sale of asphaltic rock.

After the meeting between Mr. Moore and Mr. Adrian, at which the proposal was altered, Howard Construction, on January 12, 1973, mailed a purchase order to Jeff-Cole. It contained essentially the same items, quantities and prices listed on the altered proposal. The only other written document is a formal contract dated June 12, 1973, for the sale of base rock signed by agents of both parties. The subject matter of the contract, a base rock, is of the same description, quantity and price as the second entry on the altered proposal and the first entry on the purchase order.[3] The contract, however, does not refer to any of the other types of rock which the proposal and the purchase order listed.

On appeal, Howard Construction first claims that . . . the trial court's grant of summary judgment was . . . in error. Howard Construction contends that a

---

[3] The contract was for the sale of: "ITEM NO. 304–01.02 TYPE 1 AGGR. FOR BASE APPROX. 99,600 TONS FOR A PRICE PER TON OF $1.55 WATER INCLUDED." The purchase order is reproduced in the appendix to this opinion.

genuine issue exists as to a material fact because the parties dispute whether or not they ever entered into an agreement for the sale of asphaltic rock.

. . . .

. . . Defendant argues that the dispute over whether an agreement was reached does not involve material facts because even if the court accepts as true plaintiff's assertion that an oral agreement was reached, the statute of frauds bars enforcement of that agreement.

If the contract for the sale of asphaltic rock is indeed unenforceable because of the statute of frauds, then the issue whether the oral contract was made is not a material issue of fact which would preclude the entry of summary judgment for Jeff-Cole. *Hammonds v. Calhoun Distributing Co., Inc.,* 584 S.W.2d 473, 475 (Tex. Civ.App.1979).

[The court quotes the text of UCC § 2–201.] Subsection (1) sets forth the basic rules for satisfying the statute of frauds in a contract for the sale of goods for $500 or more. The Official Comment to the Uniform Commercial Code establishes "three definite and invariable requirements" as to the writing. First, the memorandum must evidence a contract for the sale of goods; second, it must be "signed," a word which includes any authentication which identifies the party to be charged; and third, the memorandum must specify a quantity.

Subsection (2) eliminates the signature requirement when both parties are merchants. If the merchant sending the confirmatory memorandum has met the requirements of the subsection and if the merchant receiving the writing does not give any notice of objection within ten days of its receipt, then the confirmatory writing need not be signed by the receiving merchant in order to satisfy the statute of frauds. Courts have, however, required that the writing be signed by the sender in order to be "sufficient against the sender." *E.g., Evans Implement Co. v. Thomas Industries, Inc.,* 117 Ga. App. 279, 160 S.E.2d 462, 463 (1968). The confirmatory memorandum must also state a quantity term and must be sufficient to indicate that a contract for sale has been made. Thus, in order for a writing to satisfy the requirements of subsection (2) it must meet the basic requirements of subsection (1) except that the confirmatory memorandum under subsection (2) need not be signed by the party to be charged; only the signature of the sender is required. *See Perdue Farms, Inc. v. Motts, Inc. of Mississippi,* 459 F. Supp. 7, 16 and nn. 15–16 (N.D.Miss.1978).

The primary requirement under both subsections (1) and (2) is that the writing evidence an agreement between the parties. Although the language of the two subsections differs in that subsection (1) requires "some writing sufficient to indicate that a contract for sale has been made" and subsection (2) requires "a writing in confirmation of the contract and sufficient against the sender," courts have found that the § 2–201(2) confirmatory memorandum must satisfy the "sufficient to indicate" requirement of § 2–201(1). *Harry Rubin & Sons, Inc. v. Consolidated Pipe Co. of America, Inc.*, 396 Pa. 506, 153 A.2d 472, 476 (1959). *See also* J. White & R. Summers, Handbook of the Law Under the Uniform Commercial Code, 62, 64 (2d ed. 1980).

The official comment to U.C.C. § 2–201 explains that "[a]ll that is required" for a writing to sufficiently indicate that a contract for sale has been made "is that the writing afford a basis for believing that the offered oral evidence rests on a real transaction." One writer has suggested that the spirit of the comments seems to be that "sufficient to indicate" is roughly equivalent to "more probably than not." J. White, *supra*, at 62. In other words, if it is more probable than not that the writing evidences a deal between the parties, then the writing should be found sufficient.

Case law on the "sufficient to indicate" requirement arises from interpretations of both § 2–201(1) and (2). Most courts have required that the writing indicate the consummation of a contract, not mere negotiations. *See, e.g., Oakley v. Little*, 49 N.C. App. 650, 272 S.E.2d 370, 372–73 (1980); *Rockland Industries, Inc. v. Frank Kasmir Associates*, 470 F. Supp. 1176, 1178–79 (N.D.Tex.1979). Thus, a writing which contained language indicating a tentative agreement has been found insufficient to indicate that a contract for sale had been made. *Arcuri v. Weiss*, 198 Pa. Super. Ct. 506, 184 A.2d 24, 26 (1962) (check inscribed with "tentative deposit on tentative purchase" held insufficient because it indicated no final commitment had been made). Writings which do not contain words indicating that a binding or completed transaction has occurred have been found insufficient. *E.g., Trilco Terminal v. Prebilt Corp.*, 167 N.J. Super. 449, 400 A.2d 1237, 1240–41 (N.J. Super. Ct. Law Div.1979) *aff'd. per curiam*, 174 N.J. Super. 24, 415 A.2d 356 (N.J.Super. Ct.App.Div.1980) (mere purchase orders which did not refer to previous agreement held insufficient). Some courts have required that the writings completely acknowledge the evidence of an agreement. *E.g., N. Dorman & Co., Inc. v. Noon Hour Food Products, Inc.*, 501 F. Supp. 294 (E.D.N.Y.1980). Even those courts giving a liberal interpretation to the requirement that the writing evidence an agreement have insisted that the terms of the writing at least must allow for the inference that an agreement had been reached between the parties. *See, e.g., Harry Rubin & Sons v. Consolidated Pipe Co. of America, Inc., supra*, 153 A.2d at 475–76; *Perdue Farms, Inc. v. Motts, Inc. of Mississippi, supra*, at 17 (where the words "confirmation of purchase" allow for inferences that writing confirmed some agreement previously made by the parties); *M.K. Metals, Inc. v. Container Recovery Corp.*, 645 F.2d 583, 591 (8th Cir.1981) (where the terms of the purchase order were so specifically and clearly geared to the desires of the party to be charged that the purchase order reflected a completed contract).

The Kansas Supreme Court, however, in *Southwest Engineering Co., Inc. v. Martin Tractor Co., Inc.*, 205 Kan. 684, 473 P.2d 18 (1970), held at 473 P.2d 26 that a mere price list afforded "a substantial basis for the belief that it rest[ed] on a real transaction." In that case, employees of the buyer and seller met and discussed the sale of a generator. The seller's employee listed the generator, various accessories, and their prices on a piece of paper on which he also handprinted his name and his company's name. The seller later refused to deliver the generator, and the buyer purchased a substitute for $27,541. The buyer sued for the difference in price, and the seller contended that the contract was unenforceable because of the statute of frauds, Kan. Stat. Ann. § 84.2–201 (1965). The Kansas Supreme Court held for the buyer and found that the writing met the statutory requirements.

The court's finding that the writing evidenced a contract has been severely criticized. See 84 Harv. L. Rev. 1737 (1971). That criticism stems from the fact that "[t]he memorandum before the court—on its face nothing more than a price list—was proof not of agreement, but, at most, only of negotiations." Id. at 1738. Finding such writing sufficient plants the seeds for allowing the statute of frauds to be satisfied by any evidence of mere negotiations.

While U.C.C. § 2–201 was indeed designed to eliminate much of the rigidity produced by prior interpretations of the statute of frauds, it retained some safeguards against fraudulent commercial practices. *Arcuri v. Weiss, supra*, 184 A.2d at 26. The requirement that the writing indicate that a contract for sale has been made is one of those safeguards. The words "as per our agreement," "in confirmation of," or "sold to buyer," would indicate that the parties had reached an agreement. Even the terms of the writing itself might be so specific and favorable to the party against whom the writing is offered that the court at least could draw the inference that an agreement had been reached. *See, e.g., M.K. Metals, Inc. v. Container Recovery Corp., supra*, at 591. Such writings would deter fraudulent assertions that a contract had been agreed upon where in fact only negotiations had taken place. The price list which the Kansas Supreme Court found sufficient to indicate that a contract had been made, however, contained no such words or terms. Thus, the decision in *Southwest Engineering* has been criticized as one that substantially weakens the protection offered by the statute of frauds, 84 *Harv. L. Rev., supra*, at 1739, and as a "case that may go too far." J. White, *supra*, at 62 n. 63.

In the case at bar, the writings are similar to the document in *Southwest Engineering*. We hold that they do not satisfy the requirements of U.C.C. § 2–201(1) or (2) because the writings, considered either separately or together, do not even allow for the inference that an agreement had been reached between the parties for the sale of asphaltic rock.

Although the typewritten proposal was signed by an agent of Jeff-Cole (prior to the handwritten alterations made thereon by plaintiff's agent) and states specific quantity terms, no words on the writing allow for the inference that any agreement was reached between the parties and therefore it does not by itself meet the primary requirement of either § 2–201(1) or (2).[6] Viewed in the light most favorable to the plaintiff, the unaltered proposal could be no more than an offer by Jeff-Cole.[7]

Make the Connection

In footnote 7, the court discussed whether the price quotation in the proposal constituted an offer or instead an invitation to deal. The court's approach was consistent with the treatment in Chapter 3, Example C, which covered when a price quotation may be understood as an offer.

[The court concludes that the hand-written notations on the Proposal added by the plaintiff's agent did not constitute an acceptance under UCC § 2–207 because the changes in pricing were "significant divergences of material terms." The formal contract between Jeff-Cole and Howard also was not an acceptance for sale of asphaltic rock because it showed an agreement only as to sale of base rock.]

Thus, the writings when taken together do not evidence a contract for the sale of asphaltic rock. At best, they evidence negotiations for the sale of asphaltic rock and a separate and completed contract for the sale of base rock.

Although Howard Construction concedes that the handwritten alterations on the proposal were made by Glenn Moore (Howard Construction's agent) *after* the proposal was signed by Jeff-Cole's agent, Howard Construction appears to argue that the proposal as altered reflects an agreement reached by the parties and thus satisfies § 2–201(1). Plaintiff argues that Glenn Moore's deposition, in which he asserted that he and Harry Adrian "agreed on those prices that's written in," tends to prove that an agreement was reached. While such evidence is indeed relevant to the issue of whether an agreement was reached between the parties (and would prevent the grant of summary judgment in favor of Jeff-Cole were it not for the bar of the statute of frauds), it is not relevant to the issue of whether the *writing*

---

[6]   The proposal could not suffice as a confirmatory memorandum under § 2–201(2) for the obvious reason that it was not delivered to Jeff-Cole.

[7]   A question remains as to whether the unaltered proposal even constituted an offer as opposed to a mere invitation to deal. Ordinarily, preliminary price quotations are not considered offers binding on the supplier. Thomas J. Sheehan Co. v. Crane Co., 418 F.2d 642, 645–46 (8th Cir. 1969). Whether the proposal was an offer, and not merely a quotation of prices, depends upon the intentions of the offerer as manifested by the facts and circumstances of each particular case. Interstate Indus. v. Barclay Indus., 540 F.2d 868, 871 (7th Cir. 1976); La Grange Metal Prod. v. Pettibone Mulliken Corp., 106 Ill. App.3d 1046, 62 Ill.Dec. 619, 624, 436 N.E.2d 645, 650 (1982). The *Sheehan* case does not control here because of the "specific terms" contained in the unaltered proposal. Moreover, Jeff-Cole refers to the unaltered proposal as an offer in its motion for summary judgment.

itself reflects an agreement. *R.S. Bennett & Co., Inc. v. Economy Mechanical Industries, Inc.*, 606 F.2d 182 (7th Cir.1979).

. . . .

Thus, the determination of whether the altered proposal satisfies the statute of frauds requirement that the writing at least allow for the inference that an agreement was reached, must be made by looking solely to the writing itself. In so doing, we find that the proposal as altered by Glenn Moore's handprinted figures does not contain any terms which indicate that an agreement had been reached. The altered proposal is similar to the typewritten proposal in that neither contains terms from which the inference can be drawn that an agreement was reached between the parties. *Compare M.K. Metals, Inc. v. Container Corp., supra.* At best, the altered proposal may allow for the inference that the parties had negotiated.[8]

Howard Construction next contends that the purchase order sent by them to Jeff-Cole is a confirmatory memorandum which meets the requirements of § 2–201(2). The requirement under § 2–201(1) that the writing evidence an agreement applies with equal force to § 2–201(2). *Perdue Farms, Inc. v. Motts, Inc. of Mississippi, supra.* The purchase order thus fails to meet the requirements of § 2–201(2) for the same reason that the proposal (in its typewritten and altered form) failed to meet the requirements of § 2–201(1). It does not indicate that an agreement had been made. The purchase order, like the proposal, is void of any terms on its face which indicate or would allow us to infer that an agreement was ever reached between the parties. *See Trilco Terminal v. Prebilt Corp., supra; Harry Rubin & Sons v. Consolidated Pipe Co. of America, Inc., supra.* Nor does the fact that the terms of the purchase order correspond to the terms of the altered proposal create any basis on which we can make such an inference, either. *Compare M.K. Metals, Inc. v. Container Recovery Corp., supra* (where the terms of the purchase order allowed for inference of agreement even though no words indicating or referring to an agreement appeared in the writing). As we stated above, the altered proposal, at best, reflects nothing more than negotiations. It does not indicate that an agreement was ever reached between the parties for the sale of asphaltic rock.

None of the writings, whether analyzed separately or in conjunction with each other allows for the inference that an agreement was reached between Jeff-Cole and Howard Construction. The primary requirement under § 2–201(1) and (2) that the writing evidence a contract has thus not been satisfied. The statute of frauds therefore bars further evidence of the alleged agreement and bars enforcement of the same as a matter of law. *Womack v. Worthington, supra; Hammonds v.*

---

[8] As was explained above, the altered proposal might also constitute a counteroffer by Howard Construction but as no acceptance was ever given by Jeff-Cole to Howard Construction for the sale of asphaltic rock, the writings evidence only negotiations.

Calhoun Distributing Co., supra. Because the alleged oral contract for the sale of asphaltic rock is unenforceable as a matter of law under the statute of frauds, we hold that the trial court's grant of summary judgment in favor of Jeff-Cole was proper.

Howard Construction's contention that the statute of frauds should not bar Count I of its complaint because the "defendant has performed in part," is without merit. U.C.C. § 2–201(3)(c) provides:

> (3)   A contract which does not satisfy the requirements of subsection (1) but which is valid in other respects is enforceable
>
> . . . .
>
> (c)   with respect to goods for which payment has been made and accepted or which have been received and accepted . . . .

The exception to the writing requirement in this subsection limits enforceability to the goods that the buyer has received and accepted or paid for. *Sedmak v. Charlie's Chevrolet, Inc.*, 622 S.W.2d 694 (Mo.App.1981).

This subsection validates a divisible contract only for as much of the goods as have been delivered and paid for. *Sedmak v. Charlie's Chevrolet, Inc., supra.* Only the base rock—the subject matter of the formal contract—was delivered and paid for. No asphaltic rock—the subject matter of the alleged oral contract—was ever delivered or paid for. The delivery of the base rock can only be deemed complete performance of the parties' separate contract for the sale of base rock. Thus, the statute of frauds still bars enforcement of Howard Construction's alleged oral contract for the sale of asphaltic rock.

. . . .

Accordingly, we affirm the judgment of the trial court.

All concur.

APPENDIX EXHIBIT 1

JEFF-COLE QUARRIES, INC.
GENERAL CONTRACTORS
HIGHWAY 54 SOUTH
JEFFERSON CITY, MISSOURI 65101

NOVEMBER 21, 1972

P R O P O S A L

RE: MISSOURI STATE HIGHWAY
PROJ. DP-F-54-3(37)
ROUTE 54, COLE COUNTY

ITEM NO.	DESCRIPTION	QUANTITY	UNIT	UNIT PRICE	TOTAL AMOUNT
301-20.00	MINERAL AGGR. BITUM. BASE	85,795.0	TONS	1.55 1.65	1.70
304-01.02	TYPE 1 AGGR. FOR BASE	99,600.0	TONS	1.55	
310-50.02	GRAVEL (A) OR STONE (B)	3,908.0	TONS	1.80 1.85	2.43
390-90.00	TEMPORARY SURFACING	150.0	TONS	1.40 1.85	2.43
403-70.00	1" MIN'L AGGR. TYPE "B" ASPH.	13,090 35,996.0	TONS	2.45	2.65
403-80.00	½" MIN'L AGGR. TYPE "C" ASPH.	13,117.0	TONS	2.45	2.65

TOTAL FOR PROJECT.....................

WE HAVE THREE (3) SITES AVAILABLE ON THE PROJECT. SITE A IS BETWEEN STA. 763+00 AND STA. 775+00, APPROX. 500 FT. OFF RT. 54. SITE B IS BETWEEN STA. 815+00 AND STA. 830+00, APPROX. 2000 FT. OFF RT. 54. SITE C IS BETWEEN STA. 940+00 AND STA. 970+00, APPROX. 500 FT. OFF RT. 54.

WE PREFER SITE _____, HOWEVER, IT WILL BE OUR OPTION TO SELECT THE SITE AFTER FINAL DETERMINATION OF THE ROCK QUALITY IS MADE. AN ASPHALT PLANT SITE WILL BE AVAILABLE AT ALL 3 LOCATIONS.

THE PRICE FOR TYPE 1 AGGR. FOR BASE ABOVE INCLUDES PUGGING. IF YOU PREFER TO USE HIGHWAY DEPARTMENT BATCH WEIGHTS IN LIEU OF OUR SCALE WEIGHTS ON THE MINERAL AGGR. BITUMINOUS BASE AND AGGR. FOR TYPES "B" & "C" ASPHALT MIX, ADD THE FOLLOWING:

MINERAL AGGR. BITUM. BASE 15% 10% 1.70
MINERAL AGGR. TYPE "B" 10% 10% 15
MINERAL AGGR. TYPE "C" 10% 10% 1.70

RESPECTFULLY SUBMITTED,

HARRY M. ADRIAN, PRESIDENT
JEFF-COLE QUARRIES, INC.

APPENDIX EXHIBIT 2

PURCHASE ORDER   № 322

Howard Construction Company
& AFFILIATED COMPANIES
1504 North Osage — Sedalia, Missouri

SHIP TO ... **Jeff**
XXXX Cole Quarries.   PROJECT: DP-J-54-3(37)
Highway 54 South   Route 54
Jefferson City, Missouri   Cole, County.

☐ BRIDGE
lease Invoice   HOWARD ☒ CONSTRUCTION COMPANY.   Job #91
☐ QUARRIES

PRICES AS PER QUOTATION DATED: **1/2/73**

QUANTITY	ITEM		UNIT PRICE	TOTAL PRICE
99,600 Tons	Type 1 Aggregate for Base (Pugged)		1.55	154,380.00
3,908 Tons	Crushed Stone (B)		1.80	7,034.40
150 Tons	Temporary Surfacing		1.80	270.00
85,795 Tons	Mineral Aggregate (Bit. Base)		1.70	145,851.50
33,000 Tons	Crushed Rock for Type B & C Asphalt		2.65	87,450.00

Rock for Mineral Aggregate (Bit. Base) and
Type B & C Asphalt will be batch weights
from job mix approved by the M.S.H.D.

Net 15 Days   TOTAL

ALL MATERIAL TO MEET THE MINIMUM REQUIREMENTS OF THE SPECIFICATIONS FOR THE PROJECT SHOWN ABOVE.

By *Jake Moore*
General Supt.   ACCEPTED BY: ....
                        Title ....

──

Problems: What Kind of Writing Is Required?

Under each standard (the Restatement and the UCC):

7-8.   True or False: The statute of frauds requires certain kinds of contracts to be entirely written.

7-9.   If the plaintiff sues, alleging breach of contract, and the defendant raises the statute of frauds defense, whose signature is necessary for enforcement of the contract?

7-10. Does a printed copy of a word-processing document constitute a "writing"?

7-11. Does the name in the "From" field of an email constitute a signature under the statute of frauds?

7-12. Does a written signed offer satisfy the statute of frauds in a suit against the offeror? In a suit against the offeree?

---

§ 4.2. Writing or Writings?

Under both the Restatement and UCC provisions, the statute of frauds is satisfied if a single writing exists that contains the required elements and is signed by the party to be charged. But what if multiple writings must be considered to find the required elements, and not all of them are signed by that party? May a court combine the documents in evaluating whether the statute of frauds is satisfied? If so, what relationship must there be between the various writings? Courts have reached differing answers to these questions.

> **Example J:** *Owen v. Hendricks*, 433 S.W.2d 164 (Tex. 1968).
>
> Owen was a real estate broker in Texas. Hendricks owned some land for which Owen had a potential buyer. Owen contacted Hendricks about arranging the sale, for which Owen would expect to receive a broker's commission from Hendricks. When Owen sued Hendricks for the commission, Hendricks asserted a provision of Texas law that requires contracts for real estate broker commissions to be in writing and signed by the person to be charged. The court explained, "To satisfy the requirements of this statute, the written memorandum must furnish within itself, or by reference to some other existing writing, the means or data by which the particular land may be identified."
>
> Owen argued that a writing sufficient to satisfy this statute of frauds could be found in two letters exchanged by the parties. The first letter, which was written and signed by Owen, read:
>
> > October 7, 1965
> > Mr. Ray Hendricks
> > Roscoe, Texas
> >
> > Dear Mr. Hendricks:
> >
> > I wrote you earlier pertaining to your 960 acres in Dallam County. Also, talked with you on the phone about the possibility of selling the place for you.
> >
> > There is a party I wish to talk with about the place, but thought that perhaps you should be contacted before going ahead. If you

will sell the place, would you advise me by return letter, stating price, terms and allotments. Did I understand that you were guaranteeing the water?

Will you do some trading on this place?

Have been thinking that I would get down to see you before now, but have been trying to get some ranch deals working.

Enclosed self-addressed, stamped envelope for your convenience.

Very truly yours,

/s/ H. B. Owen

The second letter, which was written and signed by Hendricks, read:

October 11, 1965
H. B. Owen
Box 658
Canyon, Texas

Mr. Owen:

The 960 acres in Dallam County is for sale. The price is $225.00 per acre net to me. If you sell the place, you will need to add your commission on top of this.

I can take a large down payment at this time and would require as much down as possible.

The allotment status is 100% Milo.

I will not guarantee water, but the place has good water on two sides of it and I feel that water is a certainty.

I will not do any trading.

Sincerely,

/s/ Ray Hendricks

Owen argued that these two letters should be read together, since they obviously related to the same transaction. Read together, the reference in his letter to "your 960 acres in Dallam County" satisfied the requirement that the writing contains a reference to the particular piece of property being sold, under Texas precedent holding that

> the use in the memorandum or contract of such words as 'my
> property', 'my land', or 'owned by me', is sufficient when it is
> shown by extrinsic evidence that the party to be charged and who
> has signed the contract or memorandum owns a tract and only
> one tract of land answering the description in the memorandum.

Analysis: Assuming that Hendricks owned only one parcel of land in Dallam
County, the court considered whether the two letters could be considered together
to be the writing that evidenced the agreement. The court analyzed the different
approaches taken with respect to this question by contrasting the views held by
Professors Williston and Corbin:

> It is uniformly held that an unsigned paper may be incorporated by
> reference in the paper signed by the person sought to be charged.
> The language used is not important provided the document signed
> by the defendant plainly refers to another writing. An extension of
> this doctrine may be observed in some decisions, where it is said that
> several instruments may be read together when it appears from their
> terms that they necessarily relate to the same transaction. . . .
>
> The rule that several writings may be taken together provided there is
> internal evidence showing that they relate to the same transaction was
> recognized [in a number of Texas cases]. According to the American
> Law Institute, the memorandum may consist of several writings when
> an examination of all the writings shows that the one executed by the
> defendant was signed with reference to the other writings. Restatement,
> Contracts, § 208. Professor Corbin favors a flexible approach and
> suggests that internal references may be dispensed with if, in the light
> of the surrounding circumstances, the court is convinced that no fraud
> is being perpetrated and that the several writings, taken together,
> evidence with reasonable certitude the terms of the contract. . . .
>
> As pointed out by Professor Williston, however, it is difficult to justify
> the extension of the doctrine of incorporation to permit several writings
> to be read together simply because it appears that they relate to the
> same transaction. "There is no difficulty in making out a written
> memorandum that evidently relates to the same transaction, but the
> memorandum is not signed by the party to be charged" as required by
> the statute. The only permissible extension "of the doctrine requiring
> an express reference in the signed paper is where the signed paper at
> the time of the signature can be shown from its contents to be based
> on an adoption of a then existing unsigned paper." . . .

We agree with Professor Williston. Any further extension of the doctrine of incorporation would permit the defendant to be bound, contrary to the terms of the statute, by a writing which he had not signed. An unsigned instrument which is not referred to in or adopted by the signed memorandum is as easily fabricated as false testimony. When the two letters in the present case are read together, it appears that the one written by respondent is in reply to the earlier letter written by petitioner. The two letters obviously relate to the same subject matter, but there is nothing in the letter signed by respondent that even remotely suggests the existence of another writing. Since the contents of such letter do not show that it is based on an adoption of the letter written by petitioner, we hold that the two letters cannot be taken together as constituting the signed memorandum required . . . .

Make the Connection

Recall that Professors Williston and Corbin took opposing positions whether forbearance from suing on a claim that turns out to be invalid can constitute consideration for a settlement agreement. See *Dyer v. National By-Products, Inc.*, Chapter 4, page 234. The "Who's That" box following *Dyer* characterized Williston as a "formalist" and Corbin as a "realist." Are these characterizations consistent with their positions taken on the issues in this case?

Reading Critically: *Crabtree*

1. What did the court say must be in the required writing to satisfy the statute of frauds? Which aspects were in the signed writing in the alleged contract at issue? Which were in the unsigned writing?

2. Did the court permit the signed and unsigned contract documents to be considered together to satisfy the statute of frauds? If not, why not? If so, what connection between the documents did the court require be demonstrated to allow the unsigned document to be used to satisfy the statute of frauds? Did the court permit the use of extrinsic evidence to connect the writings?

3. Did the court apply the Corbin analysis or the Williston analysis, as described in Example J above, or something else?

Crabtree v. Elizabeth Arden Sales Corp.

NATE CRABTREE, Plaintiff-Appellee

v.

ELIZABETH ARDEN SALES CORP., Defendant-Appellant

Court of Appeals of New York

110 N.E.2d 551 (N.Y. 1953)

FULD, JUDGE.

In September of 1947, Nate Crabtree entered into preliminary negotiations with Elizabeth Arden Sales Corporation, manufacturers and sellers of cosmetics, looking toward his employment as sales manager. Interviewed on September 26th, by Robert P. Johns, executive vice-president and general manager of the corporation, who had apprised him of the possible opening, Crabtree requested a three-year contract at $25,000 a year. Explaining that he would be giving up a secure well-paying job to take a position in an entirely new field of endeavor which he believed would take him some years to master he insisted upon an agreement for a definite term. And he repeated his desire for a contract for three years to Miss Elizabeth Arden, the corporation's president. When Miss Arden finally indicated that she was prepared to offer a two-year contract, based on an annual salary of $20,000 for the first six months, $25,000 for the second six months and $30,000 for the second year, plus expenses of $5,000 a year for each of those years, Crabtree replied that that offer was "interesting." Miss Arden thereupon had her personal secretary make this memorandum on a telephone order blank that happened to be at hand:

"EMPLOYMENT AGREEMENT WITH NATE CRABTREE
Date Sept. 26-1947 6: PM
At 681-5th Ave
* * *

Begin	20000.
6 months	25000.
6 months	30000.

5000.-per year
Expense money
[2 years to make good]
Arrangement with
Mr Crabtree
By Miss Arden
Present Miss Arden
Mr John
Mr Crabtree
Miss OLeary"

A few days later, Crabtree phoned Mr. Johns and telegraphed Miss Arden; he accepted the "invitation to join the Arden organization", and Miss Arden wired back her "welcome". When he reported for work, a "pay-roll change" card was made up and initialed by Mr. Johns, and then forwarded to the payroll department. Reciting that it was prepared on September 30, 1947, and was to be effective as of October 22d, it specified the names of the parties, Crabtree's "Job Classification" and, in addition, contained the notation that "This employee is to be paid as follows:

```
First six months of employment          $20,000. per annum
Next six months of employment            25,000. per annum
After one year of employment             30,000. per annum
        Approved by RPJ (initialed)
```

After six months of employment, Crabtree received the scheduled increase from $20,000 to $25,000, but the further specified increase at the end of the year was not paid. Both Mr. Johns and the comptroller of the corporation, Mr. Carstens, told Crabtree that they would attempt to straighten out the matter with Miss Arden, and, with that in mind, the comptroller prepared another "pay-roll change" card, to which his signature is appended, noting that there was to be a "Salary increase" from $25,000 to $30,000 a year, "per contractual arrangements with Miss Arden". The latter, however, refused to approve the increase and, after further fruitless discussion, plaintiff left defendant's employ and commenced this action for breach of contract.

At the ensuing trial, defendant denied the existence of any agreement to employ plaintiff for two years, and further contended that, even if one had been made, the statute of frauds barred its enforcement. The trial court found against defendant on both issues and awarded plaintiff damages of about $14,000, and the Appellate Division, two justices dissenting, affirmed. Since the contract relied upon was not to be performed within a year, the primary question for decision is whether there was a memorandum of its terms, subscribed by defendant, to satisfy the statute of frauds, Personal Property Law, § 31.

Each of the two payroll cards, the one initialed by defendant's general manager, the other signed by its comptroller, unquestionably constitutes a memorandum under the statute. That they were not prepared or signed with the intention of evidencing the contract, or that they came into existence subsequent to its execution, is of no consequence, see Marks v. Cowdin, 226 N.Y. 138, 145, 123 N.E. 139, 141; Spiegel v. Lowenstein, 162 App. Div. 443, 448–449, 147 N.Y.S. 655, 658; see, also, Restatement, Contracts, §§ 209, 210, 214; it is enough, to meet the statute's demands, that they were signed with intent to authenticate the information contained therein and that such information does evidence the terms of the contract.

See Marks v. Cowdin, supra, 226 N.Y. 138, 123 N.E. 139; Bayles v. Strong, 185 N.Y. 582, 78 N.E. 1099, affirming 104 App. Div. 153, 93 N.Y.S. 346; Spiegel v. Lowenstein, supra, 162 App. Div. 443, 448, 147 N.Y.S. 655, 658; see, also, 2 Corbin on Contracts (1951), pp. 732–733, 763–764; 2 Williston on Contracts (Rev. ed., 1936), pp. 1682–1683. Those two writings contain all of the essential terms of the contract: the parties to it, the position that plaintiff was to assume, the salary that he was to receive, except that relating to the duration of plaintiff's employment. Accordingly, we must consider whether that item, the length of the contract, may be supplied by reference to the earlier unsigned office memorandum, and, if so, whether its notation, "2 years to make good", sufficiently designates a period of employment.

The statute of frauds does not require the "memorandum . . . to be in one document. It may be pieced together out of separate writings, connected with one another either expressly or by the internal evidence of subject-matter and occasion.": Marks v. Cowdin, supra, 226 N.Y. 138, 145, 123 N.E. 139, 141, see also, 2 Williston, op cit., p. 1671; Restatement, Contracts, § 208, subd. (a).

Who's That?

Elizabeth Arden (born Florence Nightingale Graham in 1884) was a Canadian-American businesswoman who as a young immigrant to the United States started her first salon on Fifth Avenue in New York in 1910 and over the next half-century built a world-wide cosmetics empire that made her one of the wealthiest women in the world. She was instrumental in introducing cosmetics to American women at a time when their use was mostly confined to celebrities. "In 1912, she participated in a march for women's rights. The 15,000 suffragettes she marched with wore red lipstick as a sign of solidarity—lipstick that was supplied by Arden." See https://www.biography.com/people/elizabeth-arden-9187777. During World War II, she created a lipstick called Montezuma Red for women in the armed forces. In recognition of her contribution to the cosmetics industry, she was awarded the Légion d'Honneur by the French government in 1962. She died in 1966, apparently without having arranged her affairs to minimize estate taxes, resulting in the sale of many of the company's salons.

Where each of the separate writings has been subscribed by the party to be charged, little if any difficulty is encountered. See, e. g., Marks v. Cowdin, supra, 226 N.Y. 138, 144–145, 123 N.E. 139, 141. Where, however, some writings have been signed and others have not, as in the case before us, there is basic disagreement as to what constitutes a sufficient connection permitting the unsigned papers to be considered as part of the statutory memorandum. The courts of some jurisdictions insist that there be a reference, of varying degrees of specificity, in the signed writing to that unsigned, and, if there is no such reference, they refuse to permit consideration of the latter in determining whether the memorandum satisfies the statute. See, e.g., Osborn v. Phelps, 19 Conn. 63; Hewett Grain & Provision Co. v. Spear, 222 Mich. 608, 193 N.W. 291. That conclusion is based upon a construction of the statute which requires that the connection between the writings and defendant's acknowledgment of the one not subscribed appear from examination of the papers alone, without the aid of parol evidence. The other position which has gained increasing support over the years is that a sufficient connection between the papers is established simply by a reference in them to the same subject matter or transaction. See, e. g., Frost v. Alward, 176 Cal. 691, 169 P. 379; Lerned v. Wannemacher, 9 Allen, 412, 91 Mass. 412. The statute is not pressed "to the extreme of a literal and rigid logic", Marks v. Cowdin, supra, 226 N.Y. 138, 144, 123 N.E. 139, 141, and oral testimony is admitted to show the connection between the documents and to establish the acquiescence, of the party to be charged, to the contents of the one unsigned. See Beckwith v. Talbot, 95 U.S. 289, 24 L.Ed. 496; Oliver v. Hunting, 44 Ch.D. 205, 208–209; see, also, 2 Corbin, op. cit., §§ 512–518; cf. Restatement, Contracts § 208, subd. (b), par. (iii).

The view last expressed impresses us as the more sound, and, indeed although several of our cases appear to have gone the other way, see, e. g., Newbery v. Wall, 65 N.Y. 484; Wilson v. Lewiston Mill Co., 150 N.Y. 314, 44 N.E. 959 this court has on a number of occasions approved the rule, and we now definitively adopt it, permitting the signed and unsigned writings to be read together, provided that they clearly refer to the same subject matter or transaction. See, e. g., Peabody v. Speyers, 56 N.Y. 230; Raubitscheck v. Blank, 80 N.Y. 478; Peck v. Vandemark, 99 N.Y. 29, 1 N.E. 41; Coe v. Tough, 116 N.Y. 273, 22 N.E. 550; Delware Mills v. Carpenter Bros., 235 N.Y. 537, 139 N.E. 725, affirming 200 App. Div. 324, 193 N.Y.S. 201.

The language of the statute—"Every agreement . . . is void, unless . . . some note or memorandum thereof be in writing, and subscribed by the party to be charged", Personal Property Law, § 31—does not impose the requirement that the signed acknowledgment of the contract must appear from the writings alone, unaided by oral testimony. The danger of fraud and perjury, generally attendant upon the admission of parol evidence, is at a minimum in a case such as this. None of the terms of the contract are supplied by parol. All of them must be set out in the various writings presented to the court, and at least one writing, the one establishing a contractual relationship between the parties, must bear the signature of the party to be charged, while the unsigned document must on its face refer to the same transaction as that set forth in the one that was signed. Parol evidence to portray the circumstances surrounding the making of the memorandum serves only to connect the separate documents and to show that there was assent, by the party to be charged, to the contents of the one unsigned. If that testimony does not convincingly connect the papers, or does not show assent to the unsigned paper, it is within the province of the judge to conclude, as a matter of law, that the statute has not been satisfied. True, the possibility still remains that, by fraud or perjury, an agreement never in fact made may occasionally be enforced under the subject matter or transaction test. It is better to run that risk, though, than to deny enforcement to all agreements, merely because the signed document made no specific mention of the

Think About It!

The opinion says the judge may decide "as a matter of law" that the statute is not satisfied. The conclusion that the statute is not satisfied is based on a factual finding about the evidence of assent to the unsigned document, however. Why is a judge's ruling under such circumstances considered "a matter of law"?

unsigned writing. As the United States Supreme Court declared, in sanctioning the admission of parol evidence to establish the connection between the signed and unsigned writings. "There may be cases in which it would be a violation of reason and common sense to ignore a reference which derives its significance from such (parol) proof. If there is ground for any doubt in the matter, the general rule should be enforced. But where there is no ground for doubt, its enforcement would aid, instead of discouraging, fraud." Beckwith v. Talbot, supra, 95 U.S. 289, 292, 24 L. Ed. 496; see, also, Raubitschek v. Blank, supra, 80 N.Y. 478; Freeland v. Ritz, 154 Mass. 257, 259, 28 N.E. 226,12 L.R.A. 561; Gall v. Brashier, 10 Cir., 169 F.2d 704, 708–709, 12 A.L.R.2d 500; 2 Corbin, op. cit. § 512, and cases there cited.

Turning to the writings in the case before us—the unsigned office memo, the payroll change form initialed by the general manager Johns, and the paper signed by the comptroller Carstens—it is apparent, and most patently, that all three refer on their face to the same transaction. The parties, the position to be filled by plaintiff, the salary to be paid him, are all identically set forth; it is hardly possible that such detailed information could refer to another or a different agreement. Even more, the card signed by Carstens notes that it was prepared for the purpose of a "Salary increase per contractual arrangements with Miss Arden". That certainly constitutes a reference of sorts to a more comprehensive "arrangement," and parol is permissible to furnish the explanation.

The corroborative evidence of defendant's assent to the contents of the unsigned office memorandum is also convincing. Prepared by defendant's agent, Miss Arden's personal secretary, there is little likelihood that that paper was fraudulently manufactured or that defendant had not assented to its contents. Furthermore, the evidence as to the conduct of the parties at the time it was prepared persuasively demonstrates defendant's assent to its terms. Under such circumstances, the courts below were fully justified in finding that the three papers constituted the "memorandum" of their agreement within the meaning of the statute.

Nor can there be any doubt that the memorandum contains all of the essential terms of the contract. See N. E. D. Holding Co. v. McKinley, 246 N.Y. 40, 157 N.E. 923; Donald Friedman & Co. v. Newman, 255 N.Y. 340, 174 N.E. 703, 73 A.L.R. 95. Only one term, the length of the employment, is in dispute. The September 26th office memorandum contains the notation, "2 years to make good". What purpose, other than to denote the length of the contract term, such a notation could have, is hard to imagine. Without it, the employment would be at will, see Martin v. New York Life Ins. Co., 148 N.Y. 117, 121,42 N.E. 416, 417, and its inclusion may not be treated as meaningless or purposeless. Quite obviously, as the courts below decided, the phrase signifies that the parties agreed to a term, a certain and definite term, of two years, after which, if plaintiff did not "make good", he would be subject to discharge. And examination of other parts of the memorandum supports that construction. Throughout the writings, a scale of wages, increasing plaintiff's salary periodically, is set out; that type of arrangement is hardly consistent with the hypothesis that the employment was meant to be at will. The most that may be argued from defendant's standpoint is that "2 years to make good", is a cryptic and ambiguous statement. But, in such a case, parol evidence is admissible to explain its meaning. See Martocci v. Greater New York Brewery, 301 N.Y. 57, 63, 92 N.E.2d 887, 889; Marks v. Cowdin, supra, 226 N.Y. 138, 143–144, 123 N.E. 139, 140, 141; 2 Williston, op. cit., § 576; 2 Corbin, op. cit., § 527. Having in mind the relations of the parties, the course of the negotiations and plaintiff's insistence upon security of employment, the purpose of the phrase or so the trier of the facts was warranted in finding was to grant plaintiff the tenure he desired.

What's That?

If employment is "at will," either party may terminate the employment at any time, even without any justification. A promise to employ someone for a specified period of time means the employment is not at will, so the employee could not be terminated without cause.

The judgment should be affirmed, with costs.

LOUGHRAN, C. J., and LEWIS, CONWAY, DESMOND, DYE and FROESSEL, JJ., concur.

§ 4.3. The Statute of Frauds in Electronic Commerce

What happens when the parties' contract or correspondence or notes are in electronic form? Do those constitute "writings"? How are they "signed"? Those were difficult questions until 1999 and 2000, when a pair of statutes resolved such issues under many circumstances. In 1999, the ALI promulgated the Uniform Electronic Transactions Act (UETA), which was quickly adopted by 47 state legislatures. In 2000, Congress passed a similar statute at the federal level, called the Electronic Signatures in Global and National Commerce Act (E-SIGN), *codified at* 15 U.S.C. §§ 7001–7031. Both UETA and E-SIGN establish that electronic records and signatures can satisfy statutes of frauds.

Reading Critically: UETA and E-SIGN

Read the definitions of "electronic record", "electronic signature", and "record" in UETA § 2(7), (8), (13) and in E-SIGN § 106(4), (5), (9), 15 U.S.C. § 7006(4), (5), (9).

   1. How do the definitions compare?

Read UETA § 7 and E-SIGN § 101(a), 15 U.S.C. § 7001(a).

   2. Compare these provisions. Is there any substantive difference in their effect?

Note the connection between the definition of "electronic signature" in UETA and E-SIGN ("executed or adopted by a person with the intent to sign the record") and the definition of "signed" in the UCC ("executed or adopted with the present intention to adopt or accept a writing") and the Restatement ("made or adopted with an intention, actual or apparent, to authenticate the writing as that of the signer"). UETA and E-SIGN allow a party to use an electronic mechanism to sign; the electronic mechanism counts as a signature if it is used with an intent to adopt/accept/authenticate the electronic record.

The provisions of UETA and E-SIGN are parallel (and often identical), but the scope of coverage of the two statutes is different. UETA applies to transactions between parties "each of which has agreed to conduct transactions by electronic means." UETA § 5. Under UETA, parties are not required to use electronic records or electronic signatures, but if they have agreed to do so (which may be implied from "the context and surrounding circumstances, including the parties' conduct", *id.*), electronic records and signatures satisfy provisions that require writings and signatures. E-SIGN, in contrast, applies to all interstate commerce transactions, whether or not the parties have agreed to the use of electronic means of contract formation.

Because the two acts cover much of the same subject matter, Congress could have used E-SIGN to pre-empt UETA but chose not to do so.* Thus, in most states, E-SIGN and UETA both apply, providing a wider scope for the rules covering electronic contracting practices than would be provided by either statute alone.

Although E-SIGN and UETA make clear that an electronic communication *may* serve as a writing, and an electronic signature *may* count as a signature for the statute of frauds, the critical question remains whether the purported signature satisfies the requirement that the sender was manifesting her intention to authenticate the document, as required by the definition of "signed." The requirement is satisfied by a sender who adds her name or a signature block to an email or acquiesces in the software program doing so for her (despite possible concerns about the "quick and casual nature" of e-mails and the absence of the "cautionary and memorializing functions a traditional signed writing serves").** Whether information such as the automatic identifier of the sender accompanying an e-mail also serves that purpose depends on the particular factual circumstances.

While the intricacies of UETA and E-SIGN are beyond the scope of this textbook, it is worth noting that the effect of E-SIGN and UETA on the statute of frauds is to greatly expand the range of "writings" and "signatures" that satisfy the statute and greatly decrease the number of contracts that are unenforceable because of the statute of frauds.

Problems: Applying the Statute of Frauds

Problems 7-13 through 7-15 are based on the following facts:

Therese ran a business that sold restaurant equipment. On December 1, a local customer called to inquire whether Therese had 400 water glasses, catalog # 36CX, available on very short notice. The catalog price was $1.25 per glass. These glasses sold elsewhere for $1.50 each, but Therese sold some items at a discount to build a customer base. Therese replied that she would have to check her inventory. When she located the 400 glasses, she called the customer back and left a message saying she did have 400 glasses, with delivery time of 2 days. The customer called back and orally placed an order for 400 glasses.

---

* E-SIGN contains a "savings clause" that exempts UETA from federal pre-emption, as long as the state legislature enacts the uniform version of UETA (or an equivalent statute) and that statute (if adopted after E-SIGN) refers to E-SIGN. E-SIGN § 102.
** See *Singer v. Adamson*, 2003 WL 23641985, *5 (Mass. Land Ct. 2003).

7-13. Does the statute of frauds require the existence of an appropriate writing for the contract for the sale of the glasses to be enforceable?

    a. No, because the contract could be performed within a year.

    b. No, because the price of each glass was only $1.25.

    c. Yes, because the contract specified a quantity.

    d. Yes, because the value of the goods was more than $500.

    e. Yes, because the contract price was $500.

7-14. Assume that a writing is required for enforcement. When the customer called in the order, Therese's order department recorded it on a Sales Confirmation form pre-printed with the company letterhead and mailed a copy to the customer. Is the contract enforceable by the customer? By Therese?

7-15. Assume that a writing is required for enforcement. Ignore the facts in Problem 7-14 and assume that all the phone calls described in the basic facts were emails. Therese delivered the glasses to the customer on December 3, but the customer refused them, saying that no contract was formed. If Therese sues the customer for breach of contract, will the customer be successful in its motion to dismiss the lawsuit based on the statute of frauds?

    a. No, because the emails met the requirements for a signed writing.

    b. No, because the part performance exception was met.

    c. No, because the customer admitted the contract's existence when it placed the order.

    d. No, because of the promissory estoppel exception to the statute of frauds.

    e. Yes, because the emails did not contain price, an essential term.

    f. Yes, because the customer's email was an order, not a confirmation.

    g. Yes, because Therese did not object to the customer's email within ten days after receipt.

7-16. Annie ran a business that produced leather briefcases and handbags for sale at retail outlets. While touring the local art fair, she was impressed with the work displayed in one of the booths and stopped to talk with the owner, Barry. Barry worked alone and was able to produce only a small number of items each year. Annie offered to hire Barry to design a new line of bags that her company would produce in quantity; Barry would earn a royalty on each bag sold, but would have to stop selling competing products on his own. Barry was interested, but said, to make it worth his while, he wanted a two-year agreement and to be paid a guaranteed amount for each design in addition to the royalty fee. Annie said she wanted to see some new designs first, if she was going to commit to a longer term arrangement. She wrote her name and contact information on one of Barry's invoice pads and said that she would be in touch.

A week later, Annie sent Barry a letter suggesting he produce a sample design that she could review and show to her production staff. He produced a design for a small handbag and sent it to Annie with a note that said, "Here's a sample of what I can do. I hope you're satisfied and we can move forward." Annie sent back a letter saying: "Thanks for sending us a sample of your work. Everyone here is impressed. We have to see if the numbers look good on production before we can commit." Several days later, she called and said: "Everything looks great. We think we can swing $1000 for each design you submit and 5% royalty for each copy sold." Barry was pleased, and they orally agreed to work together.

Barry began work and sent six new designs to Annie at the rate of about one a month, each time with an invoice for $1000 annotated "per our agreement." In response, Annie sent back a "confirmation of receipt of your design" and a company check for $1000. The memo line on the check said "For bag design."

When Barry sent a seventh design, Annie returned it to Barry with a note saying, "Thanks for the work you've done for us over the last several months. You've done everything we asked, but in the current market we're not able to continue production of new products." Barry protested that they had a two-year agreement and asked about the royalty payments due him. Annie said that she had paid him everything he was owed and that they paid for designs they liked but had made no promises either to take further designs or to pay him any royalties on production. Barry was livid; among other things, he had stopped producing any bags of his own based on the agreement with Annie and had given up his preferred spot in several important art fairs, making it more difficult for him to market his bags once he began to produce more of them on his own.

Barry sued Annie for breach of contract, alleging a two-year agreement for design work, including payment of 5% royalty on each item sold. Annie moved to dismiss based on the statute of frauds. Will she succeed in her motion?

_____

Test Your Knowledge

To assess your understanding of the material in this chapter, <u>click here</u> to take a quiz.

CHAPTER 8

Content and Meaning of the Contract

| How do parties demonstrate assent to a contract? | What kinds of promises will the law enforce? | What defenses to enforcement exist? | Is a writing required for enforcement? If so, what kind? | How is the content and meaning of a contract determined? | What are parties' rights and duties after breach? |

| What situations lead to excusing contract performance? | What remedies are available for breach of contract? | What contractual rights and duties do non-parties to a contract have? |

Table of Contents

§ 1. Introduction 539

§ 2. Interpreting Express Contract Terms.......................................541

  § 2.1. The Types of Evidence Relevant to Interpretation.........................541

    § 2.1.1. A Case Study in Interpretation..541

      Frigaliment Importing Co. v. B.N.S. International Sales Corp.........542

    § 2.1.2. The Special Role of "Course of Performance," "Course of Dealing," and "Trade Usage" 549

  § 2.2. Canons of Construction 552

    PROBLEMS: CANONS OF CONSTRUCTION (8-1, 8-2) 552

  PROBLEMS: INTERPRETING EXPRESS TERMS (8-3 TO 8-5) 558

  § 2.3. Subjective Intent vs. Objective Meaning.......................................560

  § 2.4. Is Interpretation a Question of Fact or Law?................................561

§ 3. Using Extrinsic Evidence to Understand a Contract..........................564

  § 3.1. Determining Ambiguity..565

    C. & A. Construction Co. v. Benning Construction Co.............................566

    Pacific Gas & Electric Co. v. G.W. Thomas Drayage & Rigging Co........572

§ 3.2. The Parol Evidence Rule 579

§ 3.2.1. Applying the Parol Evidence Rule: Two Sets of
Questions 581

§ 3.2.2. The Nature of the Written Contract....................................581

UAW-GM Human Resource Center v. KSL Recreation Corp. 584

Problem: Merger or Integration Clauses (8-6) 599

§ 3.2.3. The Nature of the Evidence Introduced 601

Problems: Parol Evidence Rule (8-7 to 8-16)............................607

§ 3.3. Reviewing § 3: Using Extrinsic Evidence to Understand a
Contract 610

§ 4. **Implied Contract Terms and Provisions**...611

§ 4.1. Terms Implied from the Circumstances...613

Fisher v. Congregation B'nai Yitzhok..613

First National Bank of Lawrence v. Methodist Home for the Aged 617

Wood v. Lucy, Lady Duff-Gordon 623

§ 4.2. Duty of Good Faith...625

§ 4.2.1. The General Duty of Good Faith in Performance or
Enforcement 627

Market Street Associates Limited Partnership v. Frey 627

§ 4.2.2. Duty of Good Faith in Requirements and Output
Contracts...639

§ 4.2.3. Duty of Good Faith in Exercising Termination Rights 642

§ 5. **Express Conditions**..645

§ 5.1. General Introduction to Conditions 645

§ 5.2. Types of Conditions 647

§ 5.2.1. Conditions to Contract Formation Versus Contract
Performance...647

§ 5.2.2. Conditions Precedent, Conditions Subsequent, and
Concurrent Conditions 648

§ 5.2.3. Express Conditions and Implied Conditions.....................649

§ 5.3. Identifying and Enforcing Express Conditions..............................650

Morrison v. Bare..651

Internatio-Rotterdam, Inc. v. River Brand Rice Mills, Inc. 656

Peacock Construction Co. v. Modern Air Conditioning, Inc. 660

§ 5.4. Waiver and Excuse of Conditions...666

§ 5.4.1. Waiver of Conditions...666

§ 5.4.2. Excuse of Condition to Avoid Forfeiture............................668

J.N.A. Realty Corp. v. Cross Bay Chelsea, Inc. 671

§ 1. Introduction

Once a party suing for breach of contract has established that a contract exists, that no defense bars enforcement, and that the statute of frauds either is not applicable or is satisfied, the next step is the often surprisingly complicated process of determining what promise or promises were made in the contract so that we can evaluate whether, and to what extent, the parties performed. That process only begins with looking at the words written or spoken in creating the contract. If those words clearly and unambiguously set forth the promise, determining whether a contract was breached can be a simple matter, and the parties may well reach an informal resolution of their differences rather than litigating a claim of breach of contract. But a critical look at the words of a contract by disappointed partners in a deal that has gone sour will often expose vagueness or ambiguity in the words establishing promises that seemed perfectly clear at the time of signing. Or it may unearth aspects of the deal that were not directly addressed at all when the contract was created. Or it may reveal understandings that were shared (or believed by the disappointed party to be shared) by both parties as part of the deal but never directly expressed in the words of the contract. In addition, a court may find that "implied terms" fill a gap in the contract or are necessary to effectuate a public policy or fundamental expectation of contract performance or enforcement.

Issues of contract interpretation constitute "the largest single source of contract litigation between business firms."[*] You have already seen that issues of language interpretation are relevant to applying the rules governing mutual assent, consideration, and defenses to contract formation. Indeed, any aspect of contract involving communication between the parties may create questions of interpretation. As the examples of interpretative issues provided in this chapter illustrate (and as your legal writing classes are no doubt proving), achieving perfect clarity with words can be extremely difficult. As explained by recently retired Judge Richard Posner,

"[C]ontractual performance generally occurs over time rather than being complete at the instant the contract is signed. This is a central rather than an accidental feature of the institution of contract. Were exchange

Make the Connection

See the "Who's That?" box in § 4.2.1, for more background on Judge Posner.

simultaneous and limited to goods the quality of which was obvious on inspection, so that there was no danger of unwanted surprises, there would be little need either for contracts or for legal remedies for breach of contract. . . . So contracts regulate the future, and interpretive problems are bound to arise simply because the future is unpredictable. Stated otherwise, perfect foresight is infinitely costly,

---

[*]   Alan Schwartz & Robert E. Scott, *Contract Interpretation Redux*, 119 Yale L.J. 926, 928 (2010).

so that, as the economic literature on contract interpretation emphasizes, the costs of foreseeing and providing for every possible contingency that may affect the costs of performance to either party over the life of the contract are prohibitive."[*]

This chapter covers a wide range of tools for determining the legal effect of the words used (or not used) by parties to a contract. Some of these tools will be based on common-sense observations about the way language usually works, adopted as contract interpretation rules by common law. Others will be rules of law reflecting specific contract policies, adopted by common law or statute (such as the UCC). Courts and commentators sometimes distinguish between "interpreting" contract language (ascertaining the meaning intended by the parties) and "construing" it (using legal rules to choose a meaning and determining the legal effect of contract language). More often, the two terms are used interchangeably, and this textbook will do the same. It may be helpful, though, to think about which of those two tasks a particular legal rule is trying to accomplish.

One final note of caution. The tools of interpretation are applied by courts (and even judges) from different starting points. Some courts place a premium on the "plain language" of the contract, and on the words included within the "four corners" of a written contract, resisting consideration of any other evidence that might throw light on what the parties meant. Other courts are more skeptical of the ability of language to convey precise meaning absent relevant evidence about the context in which an agreement was reached. Contract interpretation cases require particularly careful attention to reflections of those perspectives in the common law of the jurisdiction governing the contract, as well as to the particular legal scheme (such as the UCC) applicable to the contract.

Chapter 3 addressed one issue relevant to determining what promises were made in the contract: the impact of UCC § 2–207 on ascertaining what terms are incorporated in a contract for sale of goods. This chapter addresses additional questions that often arise in establishing the content and meaning of a contract:

- Interpreting express contract terms (§ 2);

- Determining when extrinsic evidence may be used to understand and supplement a contract (§ 3);

- Supplementing express terms with implied contract terms (§ 4);

- Understanding the implied covenant of good faith (§ 4.2); and

- Distinguishing between promises and conditions as contract terms (§ 5).

---

[*] Richard A. Posner, *The Law and Economics of Contract Interpretation*, 83 Tex. L. Rev. 1581, 1582 (2005).

§ 2. Interpreting Express Contract Terms

Recall that in determining whether parties assented to a contract, courts consider the meaning a reasonable person would give to each communication and whether the recipient of the communication understood it that way. In other words, courts judge a manifestation of assent objectively (based on what a reasonable person observing the communication would have understood) rather than subjectively (based on what the "speaking" party was thinking at the time of the communication). Remember, too, that if the parties have different reasonable understandings of a critical contract term (as in the case of the two ships "Peerless," discussed in Chapter 2, page 30), they may not have created a contract. The courts treat contract interpretation in a similar fashion, determining a reasonable meaning by considering what each party claims to have meant by the contract language and whether either party knew or should have known of the meaning intended by the other party. Keep that perspective in mind as you consider each issue of interpretation in this chapter.

§ 2.1. The Types of Evidence Relevant to Interpretation

§ 2.1.1. A Case Study in Interpretation

Frigaliment v. B.N.S. International Sales is a classic case involving the meaning of the word "chicken" as used to describe the subject matter of the contract. It provides a rich introduction to how even commonly understood contract terms can be ambiguous and the arsenal of tools a party might use to persuade a court to adopt its interpretation of a contested contract term.

Reading Critically: *Frigaliment*

1. What does each party argue "chicken" means?

2. Find the opinion's discussion of each of the following types of evidence introduced by a party to support its interpretation of "chicken":

   • Language in the contract

   • Language used by the parties in negotiating the contract

   • Trade usage

- Definitions from other sources

- The logic of the overall deal between the parties

- Behavior of the parties after the contract was signed

How does each party support its interpretation by reference to that evidence?

3. Does the court decide what the contract meant by "chicken"? Note which party (buyer or seller) is the plaintiff in the litigation. Would the interpretive outcome have been different if the other contracting party had sued?

Frigaliment Importing Co. v. B.N.S. International Sales Corp.

FRIGALIMENT IMPORTING CO., Plaintiff

v.

B.N.S. INTERNATIONAL SALES CORP., Defendant

United States District Court
190 F. Supp. 116 (S.D.N.Y. 1960)

FRIENDLY, CIRCUIT JUDGE.

Who's That?

Called by fellow federal judge Jon O. Newman "quite simply the pre-eminent appellate judge of his era," Judge Henry J. Friendly clerked for Justice Louis Brandeis after graduating from Harvard Law School with the highest numeric average earned in the 20th century. In private practice, he built a reputation as an expert in railroad reorganizations and then worked for Pan American World Airways, where he became vice president and general counsel. He served on the United States Court of Appeals from his appointment by President Eisenhower in 1959 until his death in 1986. Even in semi-retirement he worked on more than 125 opinions a year and took on the additional role of presiding judge of a special court that dealt with the bankruptcy and reorganization of many of the nation's railroads. He decided *Frigaliment* while sitting by designation as a district court judge in his first year on the bench. On the Court of Appeals, Friendly "became known for crafting lucid legal opinions on a wide range of legal issues—business, criminal matters, admiralty law, jurisdiction of the courts"* and was said to have "authored the definitive opinions for the nation in each area of the law that he had occasion to consider."** His working methods reflected his erudition. As described by former Friendly clerk and now United States Court of Appeals Judge Pierre Leval: "After reading the briefs and appendices in a case, [the judge] would begin writing, as quickly as he would if he were copying a text. When he wanted a citation or quotation, he could simply pluck the exact volume he needed off the shelf. . . . Judge Friendly had all of law in his head, with an extraordinary understanding of the interrelationships between all different doctrines." See http://www.law.harvard.edu/news/2012/11/28_judge-henry-friendly-event.html (November 2012 panel discussion on his legacy held at Harvard Law School); see also David M. Dorsen, *Henry Friendly: Greatest Judge of His Era* (2012).

The issue is, what is chicken? Plaintiff says "chicken" means a young chicken, suitable for broiling and frying. Defendant says "chicken" means any bird of that genus that meets contract specifications on weight and quality, including what it calls "stewing chicken" and plaintiff pejoratively terms "fowl". Dictionaries give both meanings, as well as some others not relevant here. To support its, plaintiff sends a number of volleys over the net; defendant essays to return them and adds a few serves of its own. Assuming that both parties were acting in good faith, the case nicely illustrates Holmes' remark "that the making of a contract depends not on the agreement of two minds in one intention, but on the agreement of two sets of external signs—not on the parties' having meant the same thing but on their having said the same thing." The Path of the Law, in Collected Legal Papers, p. 178. I have concluded that plaintiff has not sustained its burden of persuasion that the contract used "chicken" in the narrower sense.

The action is for breach of the warranty that goods sold shall correspond to the description, New York Personal Property Law, McKinney's Consol. Laws, c.

---

*   Henry J. Friendly, Federal Judge in Court Of Appeals, is Dead at 82, New York Times, 3/12/86.
**   Letter from United States Court of Appeals Judge Jon O. Newman, New York Times, 3/24/86.

41, § 95. Two contracts are in suit. In the first, dated May 2, 1957, defendant, a New York sales corporation, confirmed the sale to plaintiff, a Swiss corporation, of

> "US Fresh Frozen Chicken, Grade A, Government Inspected, Eviscerated 2½–3 lbs. and 1½–2 lbs. each all chicken individually wrapped in cryovac, packed in secured fiber cartons or wooden boxes, suitable for export

> 75,000 lbs. 2½–3 lbs.............. @$33.00
> 25,000 lbs. 1½–2 lbs.............. @$36.50
> per 100 lbs. FAS New York

> scheduled May 10, 1957 pursuant to instructions from Penson & Co., New York."

The second contract, also dated May 2, 1957, was identical save that only 50,000 lbs. of the heavier "chicken" were called for, the price of the smaller birds was $37 per 100 lbs., and shipment was scheduled for May 30. The initial shipment under the first contract was short but the balance was shipped on May 17. When the initial shipment arrived in Switzerland, plaintiff found, on May 28, that the 2½–3 lbs. birds were not young chicken suitable for broiling and frying but stewing chicken or "fowl'; indeed, many of the cartons and bags plainly so indicated. Protests ensued. Nevertheless, shipment under the second contract was made on May 29, the 2½–3 lbs. birds again being stewing chicken. Defendant stopped the transportation of these at Rotterdam.

This action followed. Plaintiff says that, notwithstanding that its acceptance was in Switzerland, New York law controls under the principle of Rubin v. Irving Trust Co., 1953, 305 N.Y. 288, 305, 113 N.E.2d 424, 431; defendant does not dispute this, and relies on New York decisions. I shall follow the apparent agreement of the parties as to the applicable law.

Since the word "chicken" standing alone is ambiguous, I turn first to see whether the contract itself offers any aid to its interpretation. Plaintiff says the 1½–2 lbs. birds necessarily had to be young chicken since the older birds do not come in that size, hence the 2½–3 lbs. birds must likewise be young. This is unpersuasive—a contract for "apples" of two different sizes could be filled with different kinds of apples even though only one species came in both sizes. Defendant notes that the contract called not simply for chicken but for "US Fresh Frozen Chicken, Grade A, Government Inspected." It says the contract thereby incorporated by reference the Department of Agriculture's regulations, which favor its interpretation; I shall return to this after reviewing plaintiff's other contentions.

The first hinges on an exchange of cablegrams which preceded execution of the formal contracts. The negotiations leading up to the contracts were conducted in New York between defendant's secretary, Ernest R. Bauer, and a Mr. Stovicek, who was in New York for the Czechoslovak government at the World Trade Fair. A few days after meeting Bauer at the fair, Stovicek telephoned and inquired whether defendant would be interested in exporting poultry to Switzerland. Bauer then met with Stovicek, who showed him a cable from plaintiff dated April 26, 1957, announcing that they "are buyer" of 25,000 lbs. of chicken 2½–3 lbs. weight, Cryovac packed, grade A Government inspected, at a price up to 33¢ per pound, for shipment on May 10, to be confirmed by the following morning, and were interested in further offerings. After testing the market for price, Bauer accepted, and Stovicek sent a confirmation that evening. Plaintiff stresses that, although these and subsequent cables between plaintiff and defendant, which laid the basis for the additional quantities under the first and for all of the second contract, were predominantly in German, they used the English word "chicken"; it claims this was done because it understood "chicken" meant young chicken whereas the German word, "Huhn," included both "Brathuhn" (broilers) and "Suppenhuhn" (stewing chicken), and that defendant, whose officers were thoroughly conversant with German, should have realized this. Whatever force this argument might otherwise have is largely drained away by Bauer's testimony that he asked Stovicek what kind of chickens were wanted, received the answer "any kind of chickens," and then, in German, asked whether the cable meant "Huhn" and received an affirmative response. Plaintiff attacks this as contrary to what Bauer testified on his deposition in March, 1959, and also on the ground that Stovicek had no authority to interpret the meaning of the cable. The first contention would be persuasive if sustained by the record, since Bauer was free at the trial from the threat of contradiction by Stovicek as he was not at the time of the deposition; however, review of the deposition does not convince me of the claimed inconsistency. As to the second contention, it may well be that Stovicek lacked authority to commit plaintiff for prices or delivery dates other than those specified in the cable; but plaintiff cannot at the same time rely on its cable to Stovicek as its dictionary to the meaning of the contract and repudiate the interpretation given the dictionary by the man in whose hands it was put. See Restatement of the Law of Agency, 2d, § 145; 2 Mecham, Agency § 1781 (2d ed. 1914); Park v. Moorman Mfg. co., 1952, 121 Utah 339, 241 P.2d 914, 919, 40 A.L.R.2d 273; Henderson v. Jimmerson, Tex. Civ.App.1950, 234 S.W.2d 710, 717–718. Plaintiff's reliance on the fact that the contract forms contain the words "through the intermediary of:", with the blank not filled, as negating agency, is wholly unpersuasive; the purpose of this clause was to permit filling in the name of an intermediary to whom a commission would be payable, not to blot out what had been the fact.

Plaintiff's next contention is that there was a definite trade usage that "chicken" meant "young chicken." Defendant showed that it was only beginning in the poultry trade in 1957, thereby bringing itself within the principle that "when one of the parties is not a member of the trade or other circle, his acceptance of the standard must be made to appear" by proving either that he had actual knowledge of the usage or that the usage is "so generally known in the community that his actual individual knowledge of it may be inferred." 9 Wigmore, Evidence (3d ed. § 1940) 2464. Here there was no proof of actual knowledge of the alleged usage; indeed, it is quite plain that defendant's belief was to the contrary. In order to meet the alternative requirement, the law of New York demands a showing that "the usage is of so long continuance, so well established, so notorious, so universal and so reasonable in itself, as that the presumption is violent that the parties contracted with reference to it, and made it a part of their agreement." *Walls v. Bailey,* 1872, 49 N.Y. 464, 472–473.

Plaintiff endeavored to establish such a usage by the testimony of three witnesses and certain other evidence. Strasser, resident buyer in New York for a large chain of Swiss cooperatives, testified that "on chicken I would definitely understand a broiler." However, the force of this testimony was considerably weakened by the fact that in his own transactions the witness, a careful businessman, protected himself by using "broiler" when that was what he wanted and "fowl" when he wished older birds. Indeed, there are some indications, dating back to a remark of Lord Mansfield, Edie v. East India Co., 2 Burr. 1216, 1222 (1761), that no credit should be given "witnesses to usage, who could not adduce instances in verification." 7 Wigmore, Evidence (3d ed. 1940), § 1954; see McDonald v. Acker, Merrall & Condit Co., 2d Dept.1920, 192 App.Div. 123, 126, 182 N.Y.S. 607. While Wigmore thinks this goes too far, a witness' consistent failure to rely on the alleged usage deprives his opinion testimony of much of its effect. Niesielowski, an officer of one of the companies that had furnished the stewing chicken to defendant, testified that "chicken" meant "the male species of the poultry industry. That could be a broiler, a fryer or a roaster", but not a stewing chicken; however, he also testified that upon receiving defendant's inquiry for "chickens", he asked whether the desire was for "fowl or frying chickens" and, in fact, supplied fowl, although taking the precaution of asking defendant, a day or two after plaintiff's acceptance of the contracts in suit, to change its confirmation of its order from "chickens," as defendant had originally prepared it, to "stewing chickens." Dates, an employee of Urner-Barry Company, which publishes a daily market report on the poultry trade, gave it as his view that the trade meaning of "chicken" was "broilers and fryers." In addition to this opinion testimony, plaintiff relied on the fact that the Urner-Barry service, the Journal of Commerce, and Weinberg Bros. & Co. of Chicago, a large supplier of poultry, published quotations in a manner which, in one way or another, distinguish between "chicken," comprising broilers, fryers and certain other categories, and "fowl," which, Bauer acknowledged, included stewing chickens. This material would be impressive if there were nothing to the contrary. However, there was, as will now be seen.

Defendant's witness Weininger, who operates a chicken eviscerating plant in New Jersey, testified "Chicken is everything except a goose, a duck, and a turkey. Everything is a chicken, but then you have to say, you have to specify which category you want or that you are talking about." Its witness Fox said that in the trade "chicken" would encompass all the various classifications. Sadina, who conducts a food inspection service, testified that he would consider any bird coming within the classes of "chicken" in the Department of Agriculture's regulations to be a chicken. The specifications approved by the General Services Administration include fowl as well as broilers and fryers under the classification "chickens." Statistics of the Institute of American Poultry Industries use the phrases "Young chickens" and "Mature chickens," under the general heading "Total chickens." and the Department of Agriculture's daily and weekly price reports avoid use of the word "chicken" without specification.

Defendant advances several other points which it claims affirmatively support its construction. Primary among these is the regulation of the Department of Agriculture, 7 C.F.R. § 70.300–70.370, entitled, "Grading and Inspection of Poultry and Edible Products Thereof." and in particular 70.301 which recited:

Go Online!

For an amusing display of the many kinds of chicken, see Julia Child presenting "the chicken sisters" on YouTube, https://www.youtube.com/watch?v=d2kYAF6qw6I and R.B. Craswell's musical rendition of the case at www.youtube.com/watch?v=ELwt-KXz8GA.

"*Chickens*. The following are the various classes of chickens:

(a)   Broiler or fryer . . .

(b)   Roaster . . .

(c)   Capon . . .

(d)   Stag . . .

(e)   Hen or stewing chicken or fowl . . .

(f)   Cock or old rooster . . ."

Defendant argues, as previously noted, that the contract incorporated these regulations by reference. Plaintiff answers that the contract provision related simply to grade and Government inspection and did not incorporate the Government definition of "chicken," and also that the definition in the Regulations is ignored in the trade. However, the latter contention was contradicted by Weininger and Sadina; and there is force in defendant's argument that the contract made the regulations a dictionary, particularly since the reference to Government grading was already in plaintiff's initial cable to Stovicek.

Defendant makes a further argument based on the impossibility of its obtaining broilers and fryers at the 33¢ price offered by plaintiff for the 2½–3 lbs. birds. There is no substantial dispute that, in late April, 1957, the price for 2½–3 lbs. broilers was between 35 and 37¢ per pound, and that when defendant entered into the contracts, it was well aware of this and intended to fill them by supplying fowl in these weights. It claims that plaintiff must likewise have known the market since plaintiff had reserved shipping space on April 23, three days before plaintiff's cable to Stovicek, or, at least, that Stovicek was chargeable with such knowledge. It is scarcely an answer to say, as plaintiff does in its brief, that the 33¢ price offered by the 2½–3 lbs. "chickens" was closer to the prevailing 35¢ price for broilers than to the 30¢ at which defendant procured fowl. Plaintiff must have expected defendant to make some profit—certainly it could not have expected defendant deliberately to incur a loss.

Finally, defendant relies on conduct by the plaintiff after the first shipment had been received. On May 28 plaintiff sent two cables complaining that the larger birds in the first shipment constituted "fowl." Defendant answered with a cable refusing to recognize plaintiff's objection and announcing "We have today ready for shipment 50,000 lbs. chicken 2½–3 lbs. 25,000 lbs. broilers 1½–2 lbs.," these being the goods procured for shipment under the second contract, and asked immediate answer "whether we are to ship this merchandise to you and whether you will accept the merchandise." After several other cable exchanges, plaintiff replied on May 29 "Confirm again that merchandise is to be shipped since resold by us if not enough pursuant to contract chickens are shipped the missing quantity is to be shipped within ten days stop we resold to our customers pursuant to your contract chickens grade A you have to deliver us said merchandise we again state that we shall make you fully responsible for all resulting costs."[2] Defendant argues that if plaintiff was sincere in thinking it was entitled to young chickens, plaintiff would not have allowed the shipment under the second contract to go forward, since the distinction between broilers and chickens drawn in defendant's cablegram must have made it clear that the larger birds would not be broilers. However, plaintiff answers that the cables show plaintiff was insisting on delivery of young chickens and that defendant shipped old ones at its peril. Defendant's point would be highly relevant on another disputed issue—whether if liability were established, the measure of damages should be the difference in market value of broilers and stewing chicken in New York or the larger difference in Europe, but I cannot give it weight on the issue of interpretation. Defendant points out also that plaintiff proceeded to deliver some of the larger birds in Europe, describing

---

[2] These cables were in German; "chicken", "broilers" and, on some occasions, "fowl," were in English.

them as "poulets"; defendant argues that it was only when plaintiff's customers complained about this that plaintiff developed the idea that "chicken" meant "young chicken." There is little force in this in view of plaintiff's immediate and consistent protests.

When all the evidence is reviewed, it is clear that defendant believed it could comply with the contracts by delivering stewing chicken in the 2½–3 lbs. size. Defendant's subjective intent would not be significant if this did not coincide with an objective meaning of "chicken." Here it did coincide with one of the dictionary meanings, with the definition in the Department of Agriculture Regulations to which the contract made at least oblique reference, with at least some usage in the trade, with the realities of the market, and with what plaintiff's spokesman had said. Plaintiff asserts it to be equally plain that plaintiff's own subjective intent was to obtain broilers and fryers; the only evidence against this is the material as to market prices and this may not have been sufficiently brought home. In any event it is unnecessary to determine that issue. For plaintiff has the burden of showing that "chicken" was used in the narrower rather than in the broader sense, and this it has not sustained.

This opinion constitutes the Court's findings of fact and conclusions of law. Judgment shall be entered dismissing the complaint with costs.

§ 2.1.2. The Special Role of "Course of Performance," "Course of Dealing," and "Trade Usage"

Two years after *Frigaliment* was decided, in 1962, New York adopted Article 2 of the Uniform Commercial Code, including provisions dealing with two of the types of evidence considered by Judge Friendly: "trade usage" and the conduct of the parties after the contract was signed (referred to in the UCC as "course of performance"). The UCC also identified a related type of evidence called "course of dealing." These three categories of evidence deserve special consideration because such evidence of "commercial context" has played an important role in both sale-of-goods contracts, to which the UCC specifically applies, and common law contracts, where similar concepts have been adopted, as evidenced in the Restatement (Second) §§ 202(4) & (5) and 203(b).

Reading Critically: The UCC on Contract Interpretation

Read UCC § 1–303 and its Comments.

1. What are the similarities and differences among "course of dealing," "course of performance," and "usage of trade"?

2. Section 1–303(e) sets out specific rules for resolving conflicts between different sources of meaning of contract terms. What are those rules, and why do they make sense?

The case described in the following example is considered a classic illustration of the expansive way the UCC may interpret the contract by applying the commercial context, even when that evidence seems to contradict the express contract language. Although the case itself is decided only on application of Article 2 rules, its impact may extend to interpretation questions under the common law as well.

Example A: *Nanakuli Paving and Rock Co. v. Shell Oil Co.*, 664 F.2d 772 (9th Cir. 1981).

Nanakuli Paving and Rock Co. was an asphaltic paving contractor in Hawaii. It bought all of its asphalt from Shell Oil Company, under a contract entered into in 1969 that expressly required Nanakuli to pay "Shell's Posted Price at time of delivery" of the asphalt. In 1974, the cost of asphalt increased dramatically due to a world-wide oil shortage, and Shell raised the price for its asphalt from $44 to $76. Nanakuli sued Shell for breach of contract and presented evidence that it was standard trade usage in the asphaltic paving business in Hawaii for sellers to "price protect" (that is, not to impose increases in price for shipments of asphalt that a buyer under a contract had already committed to use in bids already submitted or contracts already awarded). In addition to evidence of "trade usage," Nanakuli presented evidence of "course of performance" showing that Shell had price-protected Nanakuli twice before under the same contract. (The reason for this practice was "found in one reality of the Oahu asphaltic paving market: the largest paving contracts were let by government agencies and none of the three levels of government—local, state, or federal—allowed escalation clauses for paving materials. If a paver bid at one price and another went into effect before the award was made, the paving company would lose a great deal of money, since it could not pass on increases to any government agency or to most general contractors.") In 1973, Shell underwent a major corporate reorganization, leaving no one "who was knowledgeable about the peculiarities of the Hawaiian market or about Shell's long-time relations with Nanakuli or its 1969 agreement, beyond the printed contract." Shell then discontinued its price protection practice in Hawaii.

Analysis: The jury found for Nanakuli, but the district court set aside the verdict and granted Shell's motion for judgement n.o.v., deciding that the agreement had not included price protection. The court of appeals reinstated the jury verdict. It reasoned that the UCC requires a court to "look beyond the printed pages of the contract to usages and the entire commercial context of the agreement in order to reach the 'true understanding' of the parties." In the court's view, evidence of trade usage and course of performance are always relevant to interpreting the words of a contract, even when they would initially seem to contradict the express language of the contract. The price protection practice established by trade usage did not completely contradict the express price language, since increases in the posted price were effective with respect to new orders of asphalt for new projects. The practice "formed an exception to, rather than a total negation of, the express price term."

Thus, the commercial context of a contract—trade usage, course of dealing, and course of performance—is relevant to determining the meaning of an agreement, but courts disagree on how far that practice should extend. Frigaliment is an example of a typical use of commercial context evidence. *Nanakuli* is an example of the expansive use of commercial context to overcome explicit contract language, because the court used evidence of commercial context to interpret contract language that appeared to mean one thing so that it was understood very differently. Similarly, the court in *Columbia Nitrogen v. Royster*, 451 F.2d 3 (4th Cir. 1971), relied on evidence of usage of trade to conclude that the seemingly firm commitment in a long-term contract to purchase phosphate was subject to cancellation based on market price changes. Some commentators have celebrated these cases as appropriately recognizing the importance of interpreting even seemingly clear words of a contract in context, while other commentators have reviled them as undermining certainty by allowing parties to challenge and even reword clear contract language. In *Framing Contract Law: An Economic Perspective* (2006), Professor Victor Goldberg called *Nanakuli* and *Columbia Nitrogen* the "Terrible Twosome." Although he endorsed interpreting a contract in context, Goldberg believed that, by "rewrit[ing] contracts that were plain on their face," the

Think About It!

In your view, did the *Nanakuli* court go too far? One way for a contracting party to avoid what happened to Shell is to include in its contracts a statement that trade usage cannot be used to interpret the contract. Would that be a wise choice?

Nanakuli court opened the door to an anything-goes approach. "The danger of a *Nanakuli-Columbia Nitrogen* interpretive strategy is that parties will be frustrated in trying to devise the terms of their agreement, and they will have little confidence in their ability to predict the outcomes if their disputes do end up in litigation." *Id.* at 162. On the other hand, Professor Douglas Newell saw *Nanakuli* as affording "an opportunity to examine major changes from the classical contract law of Williston to the realism of Llewellyn incorporated into the Uniform Commercial Code." Douglas K. Newell, *Will Kindness Kill Contract?*, 24 Hofstra L. Rev. 455, 458 (1995).

§ 2.2. Canons of Construction

As demonstrated in *Frigaliment* and *Nanakuli*, a variety of sources may be relevant in interpreting contract language, but the text of the contract is always the place to start. Courts have articulated a variety of rules ("canons") of construction to assist in interpretation. Many of these rules are "semantic canons": rules based on assumptions about ordinary language usage, leading to presumptions about what the parties likely intended particular language to mean in the absence of contrary evidence regarding the parties' actual intent. Some are "substantive canons": rules that construe contract meaning in light of public policy concerns. Some canons combine public policy concerns with semantic assumptions about the likely intent of the parties.

Problems: Canons of Construction

8-1.   Below is a list of the most widely used canons, including the Latin phrases by which some of them are known. As you read them, try to identify which are semantic canons, which are policy-based, and which have elements of both.

> 1.   If a provision has two reasonable meanings, the court should prefer the meaning less favorable to the party drafting the contract language, unless the parties have equal bargaining power or the contract is otherwise the product of negotiation rather than imposed by one party on the other (in Latin, "omnia praesumuntur contra proferentem").

2. If a contractual provision is susceptible of two reasonable constructions, only one of which comports with law, the court should choose the interpretation that will make the provision legal.

3. An interpretation is preferred that gives force to every term and provision of the contract (there should be no surplusage) and that does not create an irreconcilable conflict between provisions.

4. A writing is interpreted as a whole, and all writings that are part of the same transaction are interpreted together.

5. Words derive meaning from the words with which they are associated in an agreement (in Latin, "noscitur a sociis").

6. General terms derive meaning from the specific terms that precede them (in Latin, "ejusdem generis").

7. When some things are specified in detail in a contract, other things of the same character are excluded by implication (in Latin, "expressio unius est exclusio alterius").

8. A modifying phrase at the end of a list is understood as referring only to the last item in the list, unless there is reason to understand the phrase as applying to the rest of the items in the list (the "last antecedent rule"; in Latin, "reddondo singular singuilis").

9. Specific terms and exact terms are given greater weight than general language.

10. Separately negotiated or added terms are given greater weight than standardized terms or other terms not separately negotiated. As a result, terms handwritten on a form are given greater weight than standard terms.

11. When the same word is used in different parts of the contract, it will be presumed to be used in the same sense throughout the contract.

12. Technical terms and words of art are given their technical meaning when used in a transaction within that technical field.

8-2. Below are examples from cases that applied the canons of construction. Identify which canon or canons of construction were applied in each example.

Example B: *Moraine Prods., Inc. v. Parke*, Davis & Co., 203 N.W.2d 917 (Mich. Ct. App. 1972).

Whether Mylanta is a "compound combination" within the meaning and intentions of the contracting parties in a patent license agreement is interpreted according to the meaning attributed by experts in the field.

Example C: *Mealey v. Kanealy*, 286 N.W. 500 (Iowa 1939).

An agreement for sale of real estate provided that the broker would be paid a commission "upon the signing of this agreement" by both buyer and seller. In the last paragraph, the seller added: "The commission being due and payable upon the transfer of the property." The property was never transferred because the buyer was unable to go forward with the sale. The court ruled that the commission was not owed, because the former statement must be read with the final clause, which shows the commission was owed not upon signing but upon transfer.

Example D: *Harding v. Cargo of 4,698 Tons of New Rivers Steam Coal*, 147 F. 971 (D. Me. 1906).

A printed term in a charter contract said "vessel to have turn in loading." Handwritten below that was the phrase "vessel to be loaded promptly." One party argued that the second phrase took precedence over the first, so that the vessel did not have to wait its turn for loading when it arrived. The court concluded that, read together, the terms meant the vessel would wait its turn, but when it reached the front of the line it would be loaded expeditiously.

Example E: *Hills Materials Co. v. Rice*, 982 F.2d 514 (Fed. Cir. 1992).

A specific clause shifting the cost of conforming to regulations enacted after the bid was submitted took precedence over a more general clause requiring that the contractor's work conform with all relevant regulations.

Example F: *Holter v. Nat'l Union Fire Ins. Co.*, 459 P.2d 61 (Wash. Ct. App. 1969).

An insurance contract identified the "insured" as the named company and "any executive officer, director or stockholder thereof while acting within the scope of his duties . . . ." The court interpreted an exclusion of coverage for injury to or destruction of property "in the care, custody or control of the insured" to exclude coverage for damage to a piece of equipment operated by a company employee. Employees were not mentioned in the definition, and the average person would consider the word "insured" to mean the same thing throughout the document.

Example G: *Popkin v. Sec. Mut. Ins. Co.*, 367 N.Y.S.2d 492 (App. Div. 1975).

In an insurance contract, "flood" meant inundation from natural water sources, not damage from a broken water main, because the contract referred to loss from "flood, surface water, waves, tidal water or tidal wave, overflow of streams or other bodies of water or spray from any of the foregoing, all whether driven by wind or not."

Example H: *Central Drug Store v. Adams*, 201 S.W.2d 682 (Tenn. 1947).

A lease contract that prohibited the lessee from subletting the property "for use as a pool parlor, beer parlor, or other business which would be undesirable and objectionable to the tenants in other parts of the building" did not prevent lessee from subletting for use as a restaurant, even though a tenant who already operated a restaurant in the same property objected. The court reasoned, "Under the language 'or other businesses which would be undesirable and objectionable to tenants', the words 'or other businesses' must in all reason embrace a business that is of a similar type to that of 'pool parlors or beer parlors', or 'such as from its nature or extent or the manner of conducting it would amount to a nuisance.'"

Example I: *Roylex, Inc. v. Avco Cmty. Developers, Inc.*, 559 S.W.2d 833 (Tex. Civ. App. 1977).

Invoice from contractor contained a smaller typewritten amount and a larger handwritten number. Although normally the handwritten amount would control, testimony showed they were written to record a disputed amount claimed, not to record the amount agreed to.

Example J: *S.M.R. Enters., Inc. v. S. Haircutters, Inc.,* 662 S.W.2d 944 (Tenn. Ct. App. 1983).

A franchise contract mentioned approval of two specific locations but did not mention a third location, so the logical implication was that the third site was not approved.

Example K: *Ford Motor Credit Co. v. McDaniel,* 613 S.W.2d 513 (Tex. App. 1981).

An ambiguous installment contract clause was interpreted to mean the company could not collect unearned interest, because the alternative construction would violate usury laws.

Example L: *Newport Associates Phase I Developers Ltd. v. Travelers Cas. and Sur. Co.,* 2013 WL 10090299 (N.J. Sup. Ct. 2015).

An insurance contract extended coverage to all companies "controlled by" the holding company that bought the insurance. Two subsidiaries argued that the interpretation of "controlled by" that would have excluded them from coverage should be rejected, since the insurance company had drafted the language. The court rejected that argument, because the insured company and its subsidiaries "are sophisticated commercial entities that procured insurance through regional and national brokers" who negotiated with the insurance company.

Example M: *JRG Capital Investors I v. Doppelt,* 2012 WL 2529256 (S.D. Tex. 2012).

A guaranty agreement contains the following phrase: "All amounts due, debts, liabilities and payment obligations described in clauses (i) and (ii), above, are referred to herein as 'Indebtedness.'" The court concluded that "described in clauses (i) and (ii)" applies only to the "payment obligations," not to "amounts due, debts, liabilities."

Another canon of construction is that punctuation, grammar, and the choice of words such as "and" vs. "or" and "may" vs. "shall" vs. "must", matter. In the 2006 dispute discussed below, a million Canadian dollars revolved around the placement of a single comma in a 14-page contract.

> **Example N:** *Rogers Communications Inc. v. Bell Aliant Regional Communications Income Fund,* 2007 CarswellNat 7307(CRTC 2007), *as reported in* Catherine McLean, *Rogers' comma victory found in translation*, The Globe and Mail, Aug. 21, 2007.
>
> Rogers Communications of Toronto, Canada's largest cable television provider, entered into a contract with the telephone company Bell Aliant, for the use of Bell's telephone poles. The contract stated: "Subject to the termination provisions of this Agreement, this Agreement shall be effective from the date it is made and shall continue in force for a period of five (5) years from the date it is made, and thereafter for successive five (5) year terms, unless and until terminated by one year prior notice in writing by either party." During the first five-year term of the contract, Bell informed Rogers that it was terminating the contract one year early. Rogers argued that the termination provision did not apply to the initial five-year term of the contract.

Analysis: The Canadian Radio-television and Telecommunications Commission (CRTC), the regulatory body with jurisdiction to review this dispute, initially ruled that the second comma in the disputed phrase meant that the termination clause applied to both the initial terms and renewal terms. The regulator concluded that "[t]he meaning of the clause was clear and unambiguous." Rogers appealed this ruling, challenging the rule of grammar applied by the Commission, and introducing the official French version of the agreement, which did not contain the ambiguity about the term of the contract introduced by the placement of the comma in the English version. On appeal, the Commission agreed that the French version removed the ambiguity, but concluded that it did not have jurisdiction to resolve this contractual dispute, thus it did "not consider it necessary to reach any conclusions with respect to Rogers' arguments on the history of negotiations, contractual rules of interpretation, or punctuation rules."

Problems: Interpreting Express Terms

In each of the following problems, answer the interpretation question using only the contract document and any applicable canons of construction. You may also use dictionary definitions, but consider whether and how those might be relevant to understanding the contract terms. Not all of the contract language will be relevant to the question you are asked to address, but you should read carefully through all the contract text in order to create the best arguments you can muster for the competing interpretations.

8-3.   Guardian Casualty provides its customers with homeowners insurance that protects against "accidental direct physical loss." The policy contains a clause excluding coverage for "loss resulting directly or indirectly from: . . . discharge, release, escape, seepage, migration or dispersal of pollutants." The policy defines "pollutants" as "any solid, liquid, gaseous or thermal irritant or contaminant, including smoke, vapor, soot, fumes, acids, alkalis, chemicals, liquids, gases and waste. Waste includes materials to be recycled, reconditioned or reclaimed."

Customers of Guardian have filed claims, seeking recovery for losses resulting from (1) inadequate ventilation of exhaled carbon dioxide; (2) lead-based paint chips, flakes, and dust; and (3) the presence of bats and bat guano between the structure's siding and walls, making the building uninhabitable. Guardian has denied all of the claims, asserting that they are all covered by the pollutant exclusions clause.

For each claim, identify the arguments that Guardian and its customers would make, for and against coverage. How would you interpret the contract on the contested point if you were the judge?

8-4.   In November 1998, the attorneys general of 46 states entered a settlement agreement with major manufacturers of cigarettes, including R.J. Reynolds, as part of litigation over medical expenses from tobacco-related diseases. The settlement agreement barred Reynolds and the other manufacturers from "using or causing to be used . . . any Cartoon in the advertising, promoting, packaging or labeling of tobacco products." The agreement defined "Cartoon" as

> Any drawing or other depiction of an object, person, animal, creature or other similar caricature that satisfies any of the following criteria:
>
> (1)   The use of comically exaggerated features;

(2) The attribution of human characteristics to animals, plants or the similar use of anthropormorphic technique; or

(3) The attribution of unnatural or extra-human abilities, such as imperviousness to pain or injury, X-ray vision, tunneling at very high speeds or transformation

While operating under the settlement agreement, Reynolds placed an advertisement in Rolling Stone magazine, promoting independent rock music and record labels in connection with its Camel cigarette brand. The advertisement included a page depicting an "odd pastoral scene." The images are each realistic photographs, but they are arranged in a surreal fashion. A woman drives a floating tractor that has enormous film reels for wheels and a telephoto camera lens protruding from the engine. A rooster rides on top, with a bird on his back. A radio with a propeller is flying through the air above an eagle carrying a picture frame through which a human hand protrudes. Old-style radios, televisions, and speakers are perched on stems as if growing out of the ground. Above the images is the Camel logo and the heading "The Farm Free Range Music, Committed to Supporting and Promoting Independent Record Labels." You can view the Rolling Stone advertisement at: https://www.ok.gov/okswat/documents/ Microsoft%20PowerPoint%20-%20Farm%20PDF.pdf and other sites.

The attorneys general of several states claimed that Reynolds violated the settlement agreement by promoting its cigarettes using cartoons. Reynolds claimed that the advertisement did not contain cartoons as that term is used in the settlement agreement.

Articulate the arguments that you think would support each side's interpretation of the contract. How would you rule if you were the judge?

8-5. On Jan. 1, 2000, Rappaport (Lessor) entered into a lease giving Interbroad, LLC (Lessee) the right to use the rooftop of a building to display a billboard. The lease ran until April 11, 2094. The lease gave Rappaport the following termination rights:

> In the event that Lessor's building is damaged by fire or other casualty and Lessor elects not to restore such building, or Lessor elects to demolish the building, Lessor may terminate the Lease upon not less than 60 days notice to Lessee upon paying Lessee ten (10) times the net operating income earned by Lessee from the Advertising Structures or the Premises for the immediately preceding twelve (12) month period.

In 2015, the building subject to the lease was purchased by BL Partners, Inc., which assumed the rights and obligations of Rappaport and so became the Lessor under the original lease. BL Partners sent Interbroad a letter stating that it had taken over the lease, had elected to demolish the building, and was terminating the lease effective 60 days from that date. The building had not been damaged by fire or any other casualty. BL Partners asked Interbroad to provide its net operating income earned by the billboard for the preceding twelve months, in order to calculate the amount owed in connection with the termination. Interbroad refused, arguing that BL Partners had no right to terminate the lease. BL Partners sought a declaratory judgment that it had the right to terminate the lease.

Articulate the arguments that you think would support each side's interpretation of the contract. How would you rule if you were the judge?

---

§ 2.3. Subjective Intent vs. Objective Meaning

As we saw in Chapter 2, the general approach to contract interpretation is objective, seeking to determine what a reasonable person in the position of the recipient of a communication would understand, rather than what the speaker subjectively meant by the communication. But there is a touch of subjectivity involved as well: a court would be unlikely to use an objectively reasonable interpretation if it were demonstrated that the proponent of that interpretation did not believe it herself. Similarly, if the recipient of a communication understood it the same way in which the sender subjectively intended it, a court would likely enforce the shared subjective understanding of the parties, no matter how objectively unreasonable that meaning might be.

The semantic canons of construction generally reflect the same combination of objective and subjective perspectives. A canon may point in the direction of a particular interpretation, but that canon will not be followed if the court is convinced a different meaning was intended, considering the parties' words and conduct, as well as the surrounding context. Substantive canons may operate differently, however, because they implement policy considerations that may be independent of the parties' intent.

Courts may shift back and forth between the objective and subjective views as they state the legal standard and consider the evidence, so you should be alert to the way the court combines the two standards. In *Frigaliment*, on page 542, for example, Judge Friendly quoted Justice Holmes as saying, "[T]he making of a contract depends not on the agreement of two minds in one intention, but on the agreement of two sets of external signs—not on the parties' having meant the same thing but on their having said the same thing." Taken literally, this purely objective approach would mean that parties could be bound by a contractual promise that neither of them actually intended, if a court determined that their words objectively communicated such a promise. But Judge Friendly did not stop with the purely objective approach. He went on to consider what each party apparently subjectively meant by "chicken," and ultimately concluded that the buyer's meaning was not shared by the seller (no subjective agreement) and the buyer did not meet his burden of proof that his narrow meaning of the word chicken should prevail (so the buyer did not prove the contract had adopted his subjective understanding).

As applied to the interpretation of contract terms, then, the subjective view of interpretation means that "[w]here the parties have attached the same meaning to a promise or agreement or a term thereof, it is interpreted in accordance with that meaning." Restatement (Second) § 201(1). Where the subjective meanings do not agree, the subjective meaning of one party will be used if that is the objectively reasonable interpretation. See Restatement (Second) § 201(2). If there is no way to choose between the two subjective meanings—if both are plausible and neither party knew or had reason to know of the meaning attached by the other—there may be no agreement at all, especially if the term at issue is critically important to the contract. Recall the discussion of the case of the two ships named "Peerless," in Chapter 2, page 30.

§ 2.4. Is Interpretation a Question of Fact or Law?

A fundamental question affecting contract interpretation is whether such interpretation is a question of law for the judge to decide or a question of fact for the jury (or judge sitting as finder of fact) to decide. The characterization as law or fact also affects the scope of an appellate court's review of a trial court's decisions; findings of fact are reviewable only if clearly erroneous, while questions of law are subject to *de novo* review. Finally, if a matter of interpretation is a question of law, it might be considered *stare decisis* in subsequent cases; if it is a question of fact, it will have no such effect.

Both the issue of what the parties meant by their words (subjective intent) and what a reasonable person would think the words mean (objective intent) seem like questions of fact. To the extent that decisions about meaning turn on evaluation of credibility or require "a choice among reasonable inferences to be drawn from extrinsic evidence," they are indeed questions of fact. See Restatement (Second) § 212(2). But if meaning is to be derived from the words themselves, especially in a written contract document, courts have often treated it as a question of law to be decided by the judge, as reflected in Restatement (Second) § 212 comment d:

[G]eneral usage as to the meaning of words in the English language is commonly a proper subject for judicial notice without the aid of evidence extrinsic to the writing. Historically, moreover, partly perhaps because of the fact that jurors were often illiterate, questions of interpretation of written documents have been treated as questions of law in the sense that they are decided by the trial judge rather than the jury. Likewise, since an appellate court is commonly in as good a position to decide such questions as the trial judge, they have been treated as questions of law for purposes of appellate review.

Moreover, a question of fact as to interpretation will be taken from the jury if the judge determines that there is only one reasonable outcome of the factual inquiry.

It is sometimes hard to tell where a court has placed the boundary line between questions of law and fact in matters of interpretation, but you should keep the issue in mind as you read cases dealing with interpretation. Consider the following case, which deals with the meaning of a written contract, the use of extrinsic evidence, and the application of both a semantic and a substantive canon.

Example O: *Klapp v. United Insurance Group Agency, Inc.*, 663 N.W.2d 447 (Mich. 2003).

Craig Klapp worked for United Insurance Group Agency from 1990 to 1997. After his employment with United Insurance was terminated, Klapp claimed that the company failed to pay him commissions due when his former clients renewed their insurance policies. Klapp interpreted the contract to require such payments after an individual served as an insurance agent for seven years. United Insurance denied Klapp was owed commissions, interpreting the contract to require that an agent have worked for at least ten years and have reached the age of sixty-five in order to be eligible to receive renewal commissions.

The different interpretations were based on conflicting understandings of language that appeared in the Agent's Agreement and in the Agent's Manual, which was incorporated by reference in the Agreement. Section 5(B) of the Agent's Agreement listed the percentage of renewal commissions that vest, beginning at 2 years of service with the company, and specified that such commissions are payable "in the event of a termination of this Agreement for reasons of death, disability, and retirement." The percentages ranged from 10% at 2 years of service to 100% at 7 years to 150% at 12 years. Section 5(A) of the Agent's Agreement provided for payment of 100% of renewal commissions "[u]pon the death, disability, or retirement" of an agent with fewer than 8 years of service. A provision

> in the Agent's Manual specified that vesting for retirement occurs only when the agent reaches age 65 or after 10 years of service, whichever comes later.

Analysis: The trial court found that the language of the contract was ambiguous and sent it to the jury to interpret. The jury was also permitted to consider extrinsic evidence (evidence outside the written contract itself) favoring Klapp's interpretation: language from an older version of the Agent's Agreement and deposition testimony from United Insurance executives showing that its past practice had been to pay former agents in accordance with Klapp's interpretation. The jury found in favor of Klapp. The court of appeals reversed, interpreting the written contract to unambiguously favor the interpretation pressed by United Insurance.

The supreme court reversed the court of appeals, rejected the finding that the contract was unambiguous, and concluded that there was an irreconcilable conflict between the language in the Agent's Agreement and the Agent's Manual on the payment of commissions.

The court's opinion began with a vivid illustration of the complexity of determining whether a particular question of interpretation is a question of law or fact, as well as the challenge of construing complex contractual language. With respect to the scope of its review, the court noted that both "whether contract language is ambiguous" and "the proper interpretation of a contract" are "question[s] of law that we review de novo." The court also noted: "It is well settled that the meaning of an ambiguous contract is a question of fact that must be decided by the jury. . . . 'Where a contract is to be construed by its terms alone, it is the duty of the court to interpret it; but where its meaning is obscure and its construction depends upon other and extrinsic facts in connection with what is written, the question of interpretation should be submitted to the jury, under proper instructions.' "

The court of appeals had compared Section 5(B) of the Agreement with the Agent's Manual and concluded there was no ambiguity. The Agent's Manual clearly said renewal commissions would not vest for retirees until they reached age 65 and had worked for at least 10 years, but that did not conflict with Section 5(B) because the vesting schedule for years 2 through 10 was meant to apply to agents who died or became disabled. The supreme court rejected that understanding, pointing to Section 5(A) of the Agreement, which explicitly granted 100% vesting to agents who died or became disabled. That created an irreconcilable conflict between Section 5(B), which said there was vesting for retirement after year 2, and the Agent's Manual, which said there was no vesting for retirement until there was 10 years of service. It also created a problem of "surplusage" (recall the third canon on page 553). "If the contract is read, as the Court of Appeals read it, to require an agent to be at least sixty-five years old and to have served as an agent for defendant for at least ten years to be considered retired, years two through nine of the vesting scheduled are rendered meaningless. Because there is no way to read the provisions of this contract in reasonable harmony, the language of the contract is ambiguous."

In addition to disagreeing about the meaning of the words in the contract, the judges also disagreed about how to apply the substantive canon of *contra preferentum* to the issue of interpretation. The majority reasoned that once the contract's language was determined to be ambiguous, the jury should look at the extrinsic evidence (the older version of the contract and deposition testimony, in this instance) to understand it. If the extrinsic evidence convinces the jury that a particular meaning is the one intended, the inquiry ends. But if ambiguity remains after the extrinsic evidence is considered, then the fact-finder may apply the canon of *contra preferentum* (construe the contract against the drafter of the contract in appropriate circumstances) as a tie-breaker. In contrast, the concurring judge believed that the canon of *contra preferentum* should be applied *before* considering extrinsic evidence "when the contract is drafted entirely by one party without bilateral negotiation." If the language on its face was found to be ambiguous, the contract would be construed against the drafter, and extrinsic evidence should not have been considered to resolve the ambiguity.

The justifications offered for these different positions reveal the judges' different perspectives on the role of judicial interpretation of contracts. The majority reasoned that the point of contract interpretation is to understand the intent of the parties, and extrinsic evidence is the most appropriate way to understand that intent, if such evidence is available. Construing against the drafter is not finding intent. Rather, it is substituting for intent when intent cannot be adequately determined. Understood that way, the canon should be applied only when all else fails. The concurring judge thought the canon was designed, among other things, to provide "strong incentive for a party drafting a contract to use clear and unambiguous language." He also argued that the canon helps ensure that cases are decided more easily, by barring lengthy consideration of oral testimony, and it helps protect stability of contracts by allowing parties to rely "on a written contract with the understanding that any ambiguity should be construed against the drafter." Both opinions were supported by extensive case law, and both have merit, depending on the perspective one has on the role of judicial interpretation.

§ 3. Using Extrinsic Evidence to Understand a Contract

We have seen that contract interpretation begins with the words themselves. In *Frigaliment*, Judge Friendly began his analysis by "turn[ing] first to see whether the contract itself offers any aid to its interpretation." But when that first step failed to clarify the meaning of "chicken," he considered the broader context, including the speech and conduct of the parties before and after entering the contract, as well as the surrounding commercial and other circumstances. The evidence of that context is often called *extrinsic* evidence because it is outside the express terms of the agreement.

One might think that the judge or jury would consider all relevant extrinsic evidence when construing the contract terms, but that is not always the case. You have already seen one example of a limitation on the use of extrinsic evidence. In *Klapp*, described in Example O, the majority and dissent disagreed about whether extrinsic evidence of intent should be considered to clarify ambiguous contract language if the ambiguity could be resolved by reference to the substantive canon of *contra proferentem*, and both opinions cited authority for their competing arguments. In the materials that follow, you will see other examples of rules that operate to limit the admissibility of extrinsic evidence to determine contract meaning, and other instances of disagreement among the courts on the appropriateness and applicability of those rules.

§ 3.1. Determining Ambiguity

In *Frigaliment,* Judge Friendly declared that the critical word "chicken" was ambiguous and proceeded to consider additional evidence, including the parties' negotiations prior to entering the contract, to resolve the meaning of that word in the contract. But what if the critical word is not obviously ambiguous? Should a seemingly clear contract term be interpreted according to its "plain meaning" without reference to the prior negotiations? Must a judge make a finding that a term is ambiguous before the fact-finder (judge or jury) is allowed to consider all relevant evidence, including prior negotiations, to determine contract meaning? If so, what evidence should the judge consider in deciding whether the term is ambiguous? In particular, should the judge consider the parties' prior negotiations, even if the contract term, understood in the context of the surrounding circumstances, appears clear? The following two cases reflect a philosophical split regarding the answer to that question.

Reading Critically: *C. & A. Construction*
and *Pacific Gas & Electric Co.*

1. According to each opinion (the majority and dissent in *C. & A. Construction Co.* and the decision in *Pacific Gas & Electric Co.*),

what kinds of evidence should be considered to determine whether contract language is ambiguous? What rationales are offered for the different approaches? Which do you think is the best rule? Why?

2. According to the opinions, is the decision whether extrinsic evidence should be considered a question of law or a question of fact? Is the determination of the meaning of the contract a question of law or of fact?

3. Do you think there was ambiguity in the contract terms being construed? If so, was it patent or latent ambiguity? On what evidence do you base your conclusions?

C. & A. Construction Co. v. Benning Construction Co.

C. & A. CONSTRUCTION CO., Defendant-Appellant

v.

BENNING CONSTRUCTION CO., Plaintiff-Appellee

Supreme Court of Arkansas
509 S.W.2d 302 (Ark. 1974)

HOLT, JUSTICE.

The appellant and appellee are subcontractors who entered into an agreement involving the installation of sewer lines. Paragraph 7 of the agreement between these parties provided:

It is further agreed that the 2nd subcontractor will receive $20,000 for supervision which will be added to the actual cost figure.

[Appellee sued for underpayment of the amount owed. The trial court, sitting as a jury, after hearing parol evidence, awarded appellee an amount that included, in addition to actual costs and $20,000 for supervision, an amount of $18,600 for the salary and living expenses of appellee's president and sole stockholder during the time he was personally engaged in the supervision of the construction.] Appellant contends that the extra award of $18,600 is double recovery in that it is contrary to the terms of the contract which designates a specific sum of $20,000 for supervision.

When contracting parties express their intention in a written instrument in clear and unambiguous language, it is our duty to construe the written agreement according to the plain meaning of the language employed. Miller v. Dyer, 243 Ark. 981, 423 S.W.2d 275 (1968). However, where the meaning of a written contract is ambiguous, parol evidence is admissible to explain the writing. Brown and Hackney v. Daubs, 139 Ark. 53, 213 S.W. 4 (1919). Ambiguities are both patent and latent. When, on its face, the reader can tell that something must be added to the written contract to determine the parties' intent, the ambiguity is patent; a latent ambiguity arises from undisclosed facts or uncertainties of the written instrument. Dorr v. School District No. 26 &c, 40 Ark. 237 (1882) . . . . However, the initial determination of the existence of an ambiguity rests with the court and if ambiguity exists, then parol evidence is admissible and the meaning of the term becomes a question for the factfinder. . . . Easton v. Washington County Insurance Co., 391 Pa. 28, 137 A.2d 332 (1957), cited in 4 Williston on Contracts, § 627 (3d Ed. 1961). . . .

In the case at bar, we cannot strain the plain, obvious, and unambiguous language of the contract. Appellee agreed to a definite amount for supervision. Had appellee's president and sole owner of the corporation desired that the sum of $20,000 represent a guaranteed profit, as he and his witnesses so understood from their verbal agreement during negotiations, the wording of the contract should have so indicated. Had appellee's president and owner intended, as he now contends was their verbal understanding, that his salary should be in addition to the $20,000 for supervision, the written contract could easily have so reflected. The lower court's award for salary ($15,500) is contrary to the plain and unambiguous terms of their written agreement and the judgment should be adjusted accordingly.

. . . .

. . .[I]n the case at bar, even though the verbal evidence and tentative drafts attending the negotiations be true, it cannot alter the terms of the clearly unambiguous written agreement as to his compensation for supervisory services. The contracting parties were knowledgeable and certainly capable of reducing their negotiations to unambiguous written terms. In such situations, we cannot interfere.

The court found that appellee was entitled to $3,100 for its owner's expenses during the time he actually was "on the job." The contract clearly provides for recovery of actual costs. In the circumstances, the court was justified in this award.

We deem it unnecessary to discuss appellant's other contentions.

The judgment is modified to exclude the salary allowance.

Affirmed as modified.

Fogleman and Brown, JJ., dissent.

FOGLEMAN, JUSTICE.

The majority opinion is apparently based upon the premise that the existence of ambiguity must be determined by the court upon the basis of an examination of the contract. This is the case in determining whether there is a patent ambiguity. It is not in the case of a latent ambiguity. By definition, a latent ambiguity is one which does not appear upon the face of the instrument and cannot be detected by examination of the document. It arises from facts not disclosed in the instrument. Dorr v. School District No. 26, 40 Ark. 237. . . .

The term "latent ambiguity" is defined to mean an ambiguity which arises not upon the words of the instrument, as looked at in themselves, but upon those 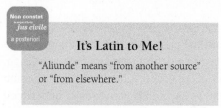 words when applied to the object or subject which they describe. It is one which does not appear on the face of the language used or the instrument being considered, or when the words apply equally to two or more different subjects or things, as where the language employed is clear and intelligible and suggests but a single meaning, but some extrinsic fact or evidence *aliunde*, creates a necessity for interpretation or a choice among two or more possible meanings.

It's Latin to Me!

"Aliunde" means "from another source" or "from elsewhere."

. . . .

In order for the court to determine whether a latent ambiguity exists, it is obviously necessary that it consider evidence of extraneous and collateral facts as to extrinsic circumstances. Logan v. Wiley, 357 Pa. 547, 55 A.2d 366 (1947). It is a well settled rule that extrinsic evidence is admissible to show that a latent ambiguity exists. Hall v. Equitable Life Assurance Society, 295 Mich. 404, 295 N.W. 204 . . . .

It is generally held that the question whether an ambiguity exists is one of law for the court. Steele v. McCargo, 260 F.2d 753 (8th Cir. 1958) . . . . In determining whether an ambiguity exists, a contract must be read in the light of what the parties intended as gathered from the language thereof in view of all surrounding circumstances. Arkansas Amusement Corp. v. Kempner, 57 F.2d 466 (8th Cir. 1932). . . . The words of a contract, which are not ambiguous in the abstract, may, when considered in relation to the circumstances surrounding the making of it, create an ambiguity requiring interpretation. . . . In making the determination, courts may acquaint themselves with the persons and circumstances that are the subjects of the statements in the written agreement and place themselves in the position of the parties who made the contract, so as to view the circumstances as they did. Wood v. Kelsey, 90 Ark. 272, 119 S.W. 258.

There is another facet of the problem of admissibility of parol testimony to explain a contract very closely related to the question whether a latent ambiguity exists. Our cases clearly recognize that parol evidence is admissible to explain the meaning of the terms or words used when they have a technical meaning or, by custom and usage, are used in a sense other than in an ordinary meaning of the words. . . . Wilkes v. Stacy, 113 Ark. 556, 169 S.W. 796. In the case last cited, we quoted from Lawson on Contracts, Second Edition, § 390, p. 450, as follows:

> The customs of particular classes of men soon give to particular words different meanings from those which they may have among other classes, or in the community generally. Mercantile contracts are commonly framed in a language peculiar to merchants, and hardly understood outside their world. Agreements which are entered into every day in the year between members of different trades and professions are expressed in technical and uncommon terms. The intentions of the parties, though perfectly well known to themselves, would be defeated were the language employed to be strictly construed according to its ordinary meaning in the world at large. Hence, while words in a contract relating to the ordinary transactions of life [are] to be construed according to their plain, ordinary, and popular meaning, yet if, in reference to the subject-matter of the contract, particular words and expressions have, by usage, acquired a meaning different from their plain, ordinary, and popular meaning, the parties using those words in such a contract must be taken to have used them in their peculiar sense. And so words, technical or ambiguous on their face, or foreign or peculiar to the sciences or the arts, or to particular trades, professions, occupations, or localities, may be explained, where they are employed in written instruments, by parol evidence of usage.

Obviously the trial court found that an ambiguity existed. The pertinent contract terms hang upon the meaning of the words "supervision" and "actual cost." The real issue is whether the salary and expenses of Benning while he was acting as superintendent of the Crossett job are a part of the "actual costs" as distinguished from the allowance of $20,000 for "supervision." Benning testified that the charge in question covered only the time he spent on the North Crossett job, and that appellee employed no superintendent on the job, although there were four working foremen. It is significant that appellant thought that evidence of the original negotiations was admissible, because its attorney introduced evidence thereof by cross-examination of Benning over appellee's attorney's objection that it should be considered for impeachment only.

There was evidence that the following circumstances existed at the time that contract being construed was entered into:

Sutton Construction Company had failed. A representative of appellant had prepared a contract relating to unfinished sewer jobs at Hope and McGehee. Benning agreed with the two persons then representing appellant that he would not charge any of his time to these two jobs, but that it would be charged for the North Crossett job, which apparently had not been commenced by Sutton. Benning told the interested parties how much salary he was drawing ($300 per week) and that he was drawing $50 per week as expenses, which he said was to be charged to the Hope and McGehee jobs. According to Benning, it was agreed that he was to get a guaranteed profit of $20,000 on the North Crossett job and one-third of any profit, and his salary to be charged to the job was not included in the $20,000 figure. The first estimate made by appellee included two $20,000 items, one for profit and the other for supervision. On most construction jobs the size of the North Crossett job there is a construction superintendent. The original contract required that a construction superintendent or foreman who had full authority to act for the contractor be employed at the site.

Carrie New testified that he was familiar with the custom in the construction business as to whether the managing executive of a company is entitled to charge his salary to the job in addition to a fixed fee for supervision. He stated that the practice is that when the contract is let on a cost-plus fixed fee basis, the fee is over and above all job costs, which include office overhead, executives' salaries, general contractor's labor, material and all subcontract costs. Normally, he said, a corporation would have an office staff and executive officers, and the duties of the latter may vary in that they double as superintendents, estimators, expeditors and purchasers. In a small organization, he said that one man may act as all these. He was present when the final draft of the contract was made and did not understand that the $20,000 figure therein was to be for Benning's salary and expenses, but did understand that was a fee to be paid over and above any profit or whether any profit was realized or not. John W. Cole, Jr., appellee's attorney at the drafting, was not familiar with usage in the construction field, but had the same understanding as New as to the $20,000. He recalled that there was discussion directed at the amount of Benning's personal salary and stated that it was agreed that the $20,000 payment would not be a substitute for it. A portion of the stated contract form of the American Institute of Architects for use when cost of work plus a fixed fee forms the basis of payment was introduced as an exhibit. It contained a clause under the heading of "Costs to be Reimbursed" providing for payment of salaries of the contractor's employees stationed at the field office in whatever capacity employed.

The contract in question was not abstracted but the paragraph in question is stated thus:

> It is further agreed that 2nd Subcontractor will receive $20,000.00 for supervision which will be added to actual cost figure. . . .

It must be noted that the payment of this $20,000 was to be made to appellee, a corporation, and not to Benning. Appellant's attorney emphasizes the fact that this language constituted a change of the same paragraph in the next preceding draft in that it was therein provided that "the 2nd Subcontractor will, nevertheless, receive the sum of $20,000 for his supervisory services."

I do not see how we can say the court erred in holding that the contract was ambiguous in view of the surrounding circumstances and collateral facts. If it was ambiguous, then we only have to determine whether there is any substantial evidence to support the judgment, since the judge also sat as the jury, and the question was for the jury. Ft. Smith Appliance & Service Co. v. Smith, 218 Ark. 411, 236 S.W.2d 583 . . . .

Once it was shown that there was a latent ambiguity or that the words used by the parties were commonly accorded a meaning different from their ordinary meaning, oral evidence was admissible to explain them. . . . Ellege v. Henderson, 142 Ark. 421, 218 S.W. 831. Evidence of the way in which a particular term is understood commercially, or in a particular trade or business is admissible, as is evidence of custom and usage, including local popular and general use. . . . Davis v. Martin Stave Co., 113 Ark. 325, 168 S.W. 553. Testimony of the parties as to the meaning of the terms is also admissible. Ellege v. Henderson, supra. Parol evidence is also competent to explain the situation and relation of the parties and the surrounding circumstances at the time of the execution of the contract. Clear Creek Oil & Gas Co. v. Bushmaier, 165 Ark. 303, 264 S.W. 830.

In addition to the evidence set out above, there was other substantial evidence in appellee's favor. Benning testified he spent 95% of his time on the North Crossett sewer job. Carrie New said that Benning acted as construction superintendent on the North Crossett job and that he knew of no other person employed in that capacity.

It is true that there is also evidence from which a contrary result might have been reached, but this does not affect the substantiality of the evidence to support the conclusion reached by the court sitting as a jury. I would affirm the judgment.

I am authorized to state that Mr. Justice BROWN joins in this dissent.

Pacific Gas & Electric Co. v. G.W. Thomas Drayage & Rigging Co.

PACIFIC GAS & ELECTRIC CO., Plaintiff-Respondent

v.

G. W. THOMAS DRAYAGE & RIGGING CO., Defendant-Appellant

Supreme Court of California, In Bank

442 P.2d 641 (Cal. 1968)

TRAYNOR, CHIEF JUSTICE.

Who's That?

Justice Roger Traynor served on the California Supreme Court from 1940–1970, the last six as chief justice. Upon his death in 1983, the *New York Times* noted that he "was often called one of the greatest judicial talents never to sit on the United States Supreme Court."[*] Born in 1900 in a small mining community in Utah, his humble beginnings reportedly led to "a lifelong disdain for display and pomposity, a beautiful simplicity and directness, an empathy with common people of heterogeneous race and background, and an abiding humanity."[**]

After earning a law degree and a Ph.D. in political science at the University of California at Berkeley, he joined the Berkeley faculty, first in the political science department and the next year at the law school. He became a leading scholar on state and federal tax, serving as a consultant to both the U.S. Treasury Department and the California State Board of Equalization.

In his 30 years on the California Supreme Court, Traynor published some 900 opinions and more than two dozen law review articles. He is widely viewed as enormously influential in a broad variety of

---

[*] Les Ledbetter, "Roger J. Traynor, California Justice," *New York Times*, 17 May 1983.

[**] California Associate Supreme Court Justice Mathew Tobriner, *Chief Justice Roger Traynor*, 83 Harv. L. Rev. 1769 (1970).

subject areas, from torts (leading the move to strict product liability and away from charitable and sovereign immunity) to conflicts (proposing analysis of the interests and public policies of the states affected rather than using the law of the site of the tort or contract) to criminal law (opening the door to discovery by defendants in criminal cases) to civil procedure (rejecting the mutuality requirement for collateral estoppel).

United States Court of Appeals Judge Henry Friendly (author of the *Frigaliment* opinion) said Traynor "illuminated and modernized every field of law that he touched, and, in the course of his long judicial service, he touched almost all."[*] Donald Barrett, senior attorney at the California Supreme Court, said Traynor "was always able to detect cant, hypocrisy, or pettifogging. He had an innate sense that told him when a seemingly irrefragable legal argument was leading to an impossible result, and was therefore necessarily flawed; a conclusion he often telegraphed with the terse observation, 'ain't law wonderful.'"[**]

Defendant appeals from a judgment for plaintiff in an action for damages for injury to property under an indemnity clause of a contract.

In 1960 defendant entered into a contract with plaintiff to furnish the labor and equipment necessary to remove and replace the upper metal cover of plaintiff's steam turbine. Defendant agreed to perform the work "at [its] own risk and expense" and to "indemnify" plaintiff "against all loss, damage, expense and liability resulting from . . . injury to property, arising out of or in any way connected with the performance of this contract." Defendant also agreed to procure not less than $50,000 insurance to cover liability for injury to property. Plaintiff was to be an additional named insured, but the policy was to contain a cross-liability clause extending the coverage to plaintiff's property.

During the work the cover fell and injured the exposed rotor of the turbine. Plaintiff brought this action to recover $25,144.51, the amount it subsequently spent on repairs. During the trial it dismissed a count based on negligence and thereafter secured judgment on the theory that the indemnity provision covered injury to all property regardless of ownership.

Defendant offered to prove by admissions of plaintiff's agents, by defendant's conduct under similar contracts entered into with plaintiff, and by other proof

---

[*]   *Henry Friendly, Ablest Judge of His Generation*, 71 Calif. L. Rev. 1039 (1983).

[**]   Donald Barrett, *Master of Judicial Wisdom*, 71 Cal. L. Rev. 1060 (1983). In addition to the sources noted above, see Stewart Macaulay, *Justice Traynor and the Law of Contracts*, 13 Stan. L. Rev. 812 (1961) and John Poulos, *The Judicial Philosophy of Roger Traynor*, 46 Hastings L. J. 1643 (1995).

that in the indemnity clause the parties meant to cover injury to property of third parties only and not to plaintiff's property. Although the trial court observed that the language used was "the classic language for a third party indemnity provision" and that "one could very easily conclude that . . . its whole intendment is to indemnify third parties," it nevertheless held that the "plain language" of the agreement also required defendant to indemnify plaintiff for injuries to plaintiff's property. Having determined that the contract had a plain meaning, the court refused to admit any extrinsic evidence that would contradict its interpretation.

When a court interprets a contract on this basis, it determines the meaning of the instrument in accordance with the ". . . extrinsic evidence of the judge's own linguistic education and experience." (3 Corbin on Contracts (1960 ed.) (1964 Supp. § 579, p. 225, fn. 56).) The exclusion of testimony that might contradict the linguistic background of the judge reflects a judicial belief in the possibility of perfect verbal expression. (9 Wigmore on Evidence (3d ed. 1940) § 2461, p. 187.) This belief is a remnant of a primitive faith in the inherent potency[2] and inherent meaning of words.[3]

The test of admissibility of extrinsic evidence to explain the meaning of a written instrument is not whether it appears to the court to be plain and unambiguous on its face, but whether the offered evidence is relevant to prove a meaning to which the language of the instrument is reasonably susceptible. (*Continental Baking Co. v. Katz* (1968) 68 A.C. 527, 536–537, 67 Cal.Rptr. 761, 439 P.2d 889; *Parsons v. Bristol Development Co.* (1965) 62 Cal.2d 861, 865, 44 Cal.Rptr. 767, 402 P.2d 839; Hulse v. Juillard Fancy Foods Co. (1964) 61 Cal.2d 571, 573, 39 Cal. Rptr. 529, 394 P.2d 65; [additional citations omitted].

A rule that would limit the determination of the meaning of a written instrument to its four-corners merely because it seems to the court to be clear and unambiguous, would either deny the relevance of the intention of the parties or presuppose a degree of verbal precision and stability our language has not attained.

Some courts have expressed the opinion that contractual obligations are created by the mere use of certain words, whether or not there was any intention

---

[2]   E.g., "The elaborate system of taboo and verbal prohibitions in primitive groups; the ancient Egyptian myth of Khern, the apotheosis of the word, and of Thoth, the Scribe of Truth, the Giver of Words and Script, the Master of Incantations; the avoidance of the name of God in Brahmanism, Judaism and Islam; totemistic and protective names in mediaeval Turkish and Finno-Ugrian languages; the misplaced verbal scruples of the 'Precieuses'; the Swedish peasant custom of curing sick cattle smitten by witchcraft, by making them swallow a page torn out of the psalter and put in dough. . . ." from Ullman, The Principles of Semantics (1963 ed.) 43. (See also Ogden and Richards, The Meaning of Meaning (rev. ed. 1956) pp. 24–47.)

[3]   "Rerum enim vocabula immutabilia sunt, homines mutabilia," (Words are unchangeable, men changeable) from Dig. XXXIII, 10, 7, § 2, de sup. leg. as quoted in 9 Wigmore on Evidence, op. cit. supra, § 2461, p. 187.

to incur such obligations.[4] Under this view, contractual obligations flow, not from the intention of the parties but from the fact that they used certain magic words. Evidence of the parties' intention therefore becomes irrelevant.

In this state, however, the intention of the parties as expressed in the contract is the source of contractual rights and duties. A court must ascertain and give effect to this intention by determining what the parties meant by the words they used. Accordingly, the exclusion of relevant, extrinsic evidence to explain the meaning of a written instrument could be justified only if it were feasible to determine the meaning the parties gave to the words from the instrument alone.

If words had absolute and constant referents, it might be possible to discover contractual intention in the words themselves and in the manner in which they were arranged. Words, however, do not have absolute and constant referents. "A word is a symbol of thought but has no arbitrary and fixed meaning like a symbol of algebra or chemistry . . . ." (Pearson v. State Social Welfare Board (1960) 54 Cal.2d 184, 195, 5 Cal.Rptr. 553, 559, 353 P.2d 33, 39.) The meaning of particular words or groups of words varies with the "verbal context and surrounding circumstances and purposes in view of the linguistic education and experience of their users and their hearers or readers (not excluding judges). . . . A word has no meaning apart from these factors; much less does it have an objective meaning, one true meaning." (Corbin, The Interpretation of Words and the Parol Evidence Rule (1965) 50 Cornell L.Q. 161, 187.) Accordingly, the meaning of a writing "can only be found by interpretation in the light of all the circumstances that reveal the sense in which the writer used the words. The exclusion of parol evidence regarding such circumstances merely because the words do not appear ambiguous to the reader can easily lead to the attribution to a written instrument of a meaning that was never intended." (Universal Sales Corp. v. Cal. Press Mfg. Co., supra, 20 Cal.2d 751, 776, 128 P.2d 665, 679 (concurring opinion); see also, e.g., Garden State Plaza Corp. v. S. S. Kresge Co. (1963) 78 N.J.Super. 485, 189 A.2d 448, 454; Hurst v. W. J. Lake & Co. (1932) 141 Or. 306, 310, 16 P.2d 627, 629, 89 A.L.R. 1222; 3 Corbin on Contracts (1960 ed.) § 579, pp. 412–431; Ogden and Richards, The Meaning of Meaning, op. cit. 15; Ullmann, The Principles of Semantics, supra, 61; McBaine, The Rule Against Disturbing Plain Meaning of Writings (1943) 31 Cal.L.Rev. 145.)

Although extrinsic evidence is not admissible to add to, detract from, or vary the terms of a written contract, these terms must first be determined before it can be decided whether or not extrinsic evidence is being offered for a prohibited purpose. The fact that the terms of an instrument appear clear to a judge does not

---

[4]   "A contract has, strictly speaking, nothing to do with the personal, or individual, intent of the parties. A contract is an obligation attached by the mere force of law to certain acts of the parties, usually words, which ordinarily accompany and represent a known intent." Hotchkiss v. National City Bank of New York (S.D.N.Y. 1911) 200 F. 287, 293. . . .

Take Note!

The statement made here—"extrinsic evidence is not admissible to add to, detract from, or vary the terms of a written contract"—is a version of the "parol evidence rule," which will be considered in the section that follows. As you will see, the question whether extrinsic evidence is admissible to establish ambiguity—the question dealt with in this section—is separate from, but intimately related to, the application of the parol evidence rule to decide whether extrinsic evidence is admissible to change or add to terms of a written contract.

preclude the possibility that the parties chose the language of the instrument to express different terms. That possibility is not limited to contracts whose terms have acquired a particular meaning by trade usage,[6] but exists whenever the parties' understanding of the words used may have differed from the judge's understanding.

Accordingly, rational interpretation requires at least a preliminary consideration of all credible evidence offered to prove the intention of the parties.[7] (Civ.Code, § 1647; Code Civ. Proc. § 1860; see also 9 Wigmore on Evidence, op. cit. supra, § 2470, fn. 11, p. 227.) Such evidence includes testimony as to the "circumstances surrounding the making of the agreement . . . including the object, nature and subject matter of the writing . . ." so that the court can "place itself in the same situation in which the parties found themselves at the time of contracting." (Universal Sales Corp. v. Cal. Press Mfg. Co., supra, 20 Cal.2d 751, 761, 128 P.2d 665, 671; Lemm v. Stillwater Land & Cattle Co., supra, 217 Cal. 474, 480–481, 19 P.2d 785.) If the court decides, after considering this evidence, that the language of a contract, in the light of all the circumstances, is "fairly susceptible of either one of the two interpretations contended for . . . ," extrinsic evidence relevant to prove either of such meanings is admissible.[8]

---

[6] Extrinsic evidence of trade usage or custom has been admitted to show that the term "United Kingdom" in a motion picture distribution contract included Ireland (Ermolieff v. R.K.O. Radio Pictures (1942) 19 Cal.2d 543, 549–552, 122 P.2d 3); that the word "ton" in a lease meant a long ton or 2,240 pounds and not the statutory ton of 2,000 pounds (Higgins v. Cal. Petroleum, etc., Co. (1898) 120 Cal. 629, 630–632, 52 P. 1080); that the word "stubble" in a lease included not only stumps left in the ground but everything "left on the ground after the harvest time" (Callahan v. Stanley (1881) 57 Cal. 476, 477–479); that the term "north" in a contract dividing mining claims indicated a boundary line running along the "magnetic and not the true meridian" (Jenny Lind Co. v. Bower & Co. (1858) 11 Cal. 194, 197–199) and that a form contract for purchase and sale was actually an agency contract (Body-Steffner Co. v. Flotill Products (1944) 63 Cal.App.2d 555, 558–562, 147 P.2d 84). See also Code Civ.Proc. § 1861; Annot., 89 A.L.R. 1228; Note (1942) 30 Cal.L.Rev. 679.)

[7] When objection is made to any particular item of evidence offered to prove the intention of the parties, the trial court may not yet be in a position to determine whether in the light of all of the offered evidence, the item objected to will turn out to be admissible as tending to prove a meaning of which the language of the instrument is reasonably susceptible or inadmissible as tending to prove a meaning of which the language is not reasonably susceptible. In such case the court may admit the evidence conditionally by either reserving its ruling on the objection or by admitting the evidence subject to a motion to strike. (See Evid.Code, § 403.)

[8] Extrinsic evidence has often been admitted in such cases on the stated ground that the contract was ambiguous (e.g., Universal Sales Corp. v. Cal. Press Mfg. Co., supra, 20 Cal.2d 751, 761, 128 P.2d

In the present case the court erroneously refused to consider extrinsic evidence offered to show that the indemnity clause in the contract was not intended to cover injuries to plaintiff's property. Although that evidence was not necessary to show that the indemnity clause was reasonably susceptible of the meaning contended for by defendant, it was nevertheless relevant and admissible on that issue. Moreover, since that clause was reasonably susceptible of that meaning, the offered evidence was also admissible to prove that the clause had that meaning, and did not cover injuries to plaintiff's property.[9] Accordingly, the judgment must be reversed.

---

665). This statement of the rule is harmless if it is kept in mind that the ambiguity may be exposed by extrinsic evidence that reveals more than one possible meaning.

[9] The court's exclusion of extrinsic evidence in this case would be error even under a rule that excluded such evidence when the instrument appeared to the court to be clear and unambiguous on its face. The controversy centers on the meaning of the word "indemnify" and the phrase "all loss, damage, expense and liability." The trial court's recognition of the language as typical of a third party indemnity clause and the double sense in which the word "indemnify" is used in statutes and defined in dictionaries demonstrate the existence of an ambiguity. (Compare Civ.Code, § 2772, "Indemnity is a contract by which one engages to save another from a legal consequence of the conduct of one of the parties, or of some other person," with Civ.Code, § 2527, "Insurance is a contract whereby by one undertakes to indemnify another against loss, damage, or liability, arising from an unknown or contingent event." Black's Law Dictionary (4th ed. 1951) defines "indemnity" as "A collateral contract or assurance, by which one person engages to secure another against an anticipated loss or to prevent him from being damnified by the legal consequences of an act or forbearance on the part of one of the parties or of some third person." Stroud's Judicial Dictionary (2d ed. 1903) defines it as a "Contract . . . to indemnify against a liability. . . ." One of the definitions given to "indemnify" by Webster's Third New Internat. Dict. (1961 ed.) is "to exempt from incurred penalties or liabilities.")

Plaintiff's assertion that the use of the word "all" to modify "loss, damage, expense and liability" dictates an all inclusive interpretation is not persuasive. If the word "indemnify" encompasses only third-party claims, the word "all" simply refers to all such claims. The use of the words "loss," "damage," and "expense" in addition to the word "liability" is likewise inconclusive. These words do not imply an agreement to reimburse for injury to an indemnitee's property since they are commonly inserted in third-party indemnity clauses, to enable an indemnitee who settles a claim to recover from his indemnitor without proving his liability. (Carpenter Paper Co. v. Kellogg (1952) 114 Cal. App.2d 640, 651, 251 P.2d 40.Civ.Code, § 2778, provides: "1. Upon an indemnity against liability . . . the person indemnified is entitled to recover upon becoming liable; 2. Upon an indemnity against claims, or demands, or damages, or costs . . . the person indemnified is not entitled to recover without payment thereof; . . . .")

The provision that defendant perform the work "at his own risk and expense" and the provisions relating to insurance are equally inconclusive. By agreeing to work at its own risk defendant may have released plaintiff from liability for any injuries to defendant's property arising out of the contract's performance, but this provision did not necessarily make defendant an insurer against injuries to plaintiff's property. Defendant's agreement to procure liability insurance to cover damages to plaintiff's property does not indicate whether the insurance was to cover all injuries or only injuries caused by defendant's negligence.

Food for Thought

Pacific Gas & Electric Co. has been criticized by some judges and commentators as undercutting the finality of written contracts in unacceptable ways, a criticism that might also be made of the dissenting opinion in *C. & A. Construction Co.* See, for example, the comment by Judge Kozinski in *Trident Center v. Connecticut General Life Insurance Co.*, 847 F.2d 564 (9th Cir. 1988):

> Under *Pacific Gas*, it matters not how clearly a contract is written, nor how completely it is integrated, nor how carefully it is negotiated, nor how squarely it addresses the issue before the court: the contract cannot be rendered impervious to attack by parol evidence. If one side is willing to claim that the parties intended one thing but the agreement provides for another, the court must consider extrinsic evidence of possible ambiguity. If that evidence raises the specter of ambiguity where there was none before, the contract language is displaced and the intention of the parties must be divined from self-serving testimony offered by partisan witnesses whose recollection is hazy from passage of time and colored by their conflicting interests. . . . *Pacific Gas* casts a long shadow of uncertainty over all transactions negotiated and executed under the law of California. As this case illustrates, even when the transaction is very sizeable, even if it involves only sophisticated parties, even if it was negotiated with the aid of counsel, even if it results in contract language that is devoid of ambiguity, costly and protracted litigation cannot be avoided if one party has a strong enough motive for challenging the contract. While this rule creates much business for lawyers and an occasional windfall to some clients, it leads only to frustration and delay for most litigants and clogs already overburdened courts.

Id. at 569. California Supreme Court Justice Mosk expressed similar concerns in his dissent in *Delta Dynamics, Inc. v. Arioto*, 446 P.2d 785, 789 (Cal. 1968), noting that "I had misgivings at the time, [but] I must confess to joining the majority [in *Pacific Gas* and in *Masterson v. Sine*, 436 P.2d 561 (Cal. 1968)]. Now, however, that the majority deem negotiations leading to execution of contracts admissible, the trend has become so unmistakably ominous that I must urge a halt."

> Others have continued to offer support for context-based interpretation as articulated in *Pacific Gas*:
>
>> We recognize that *Pacific Gas* has its critics. . . . We too would recoil if *Pacific Gas* meant that mere complexity required a finding of ambiguity or that courts must listen to wholly unpersuasive extrinsic evidence to create ambiguity where words are clear beyond dispute. . . . [T]he court must first decide what the agreement says and, as a preliminary matter, must decide if it reasonably could be interpreted in different ways, given the language and the factual context surrounding the making of the agreement. Admittedly, the process is not without risk, but we believe the game is worth the candle. After all, the purpose is to produce the contract result the parties intended, not that which the judge intends. Some words are clear beyond dispute. Some may mean one thing to the judge but could have meant something else to the parties. It is the latter meaning that is important.
>
> *Taylor v. State Farm Mutual Automobile Insurance Co.*, 854 P.2d 1134, 1141 (Ariz. 1993).
>
> In your view, which interpretation methodology is preferable?

§ 3.2. The Parol Evidence Rule

As we have seen, courts disagree about whether to allow parties to introduce evidence from their pre-contract negotiations to show ambiguity in the contract terms, or whether they must instead establish ambiguity only from the words of the contract and the general circumstances surrounding its adoption. This section addresses a different but related question: in the absence of ambiguity (however established), may either party use evidence of prior negotiations to *add to or alter* the terms of a written agreement? The answer appears in the "parol evidence rule," which, when applicable, (1) bars use of such evidence to alter a term that the parties considered final in the written contract and (2) bars use of such evidence to add a term to a contract the parties considered fully expressed in the written contract. The rule is deceptively simple to state, but notoriously hard to apply.

Take Note!

"Parol" means "oral," but the parol evidence rule controls the use of both oral and written evidence of the results of prior negotiations.

The policies underlying the parol evidence rule are sensible ideas. The rule presumes that written evidence is better than conflicting oral evidence on the same term. It presumes that a subsequent written agreement is better evidence than a conflicting earlier agreement on the same topic. It presumes that when parties produce a written contract document,* they usually intend it to take priority over what they said or did leading up to the adoption of the written contract. It affirms that certainty and stability of contracts is promoted if parties can depend upon written terms. And it presumes that, if the parties expressly say that their written agreement supersedes all of their previous agreements and dealings, all evidence from those prior dealings should be excluded, even to add additional terms consistent with those in the written document. At the same time, the rule acknowledges that words must always be understood in their commercial context and that courts may need additional evidence to explain ambiguous or incomplete terms.

The parol evidence rule is a rule of substantive (not procedural or evidentiary) law because it is at base a rule about which terms become part of a contract. Although it operates by controlling what evidence is admissible, the decision on admissibility is not based on evidentiary considerations of credibility or trustworthiness. Rather, the underlying question is whether the written expression of a contract should take precedence over terms discussed or agreed upon before the written expression was adopted.

The rule is generally considered a rule of law, to be applied by the court, not the jury; that is, the judge must apply the rule and decide that the evidence is admissible to prove a term of the contract before the evidence can be presented to the fact-finder.** Some factual questions may need to be answered in order to apply the rule (e.g., whether the parties intended their written contract to be a "final expression" that would supersede earlier agreements). Some courts submit such factual questions to a jury for decision, while other jurisdictions allow the jury to see only the evidence that has "run the gauntlet" of the parol evidence rule.

The parol evidence rule is challenging to understand and apply because the lines that the rule draws are often indistinct, and judges disagree about how to apply them. "'Few things,' wrote Professor Thayer, 'are darker than . . . [the parol evidence rule] or fuller of subtle difficulties'; and this condition of the law all

---

* Recall from Chapter 7 (page 531) that UETA and ESIGN ensure that references to writing and to written documents encompass both physical writings and electronic records. References in this chapter to written contracts should be understood to have that broader meaning.

** The fact-finder could be the judge, not a jury, if the parties waive their rights to a jury trial (or if no jury trial is available on the matter, as with equitable claims). In that case, the judge rules first whether the extrinsic evidence can be considered to find the content of the contract; if the answer is "no", then the judge decides the content of the contract without reference to the excluded evidence. For ease of reference, this chapter uses "the jury" to mean the fact-finder.

members of the profession will concede. . . . [T]he so-called parol evidence rule is attended with confusion and obscurity which make it the most discouraging subject in the whole field of evidence."* Moreover, some courts are skeptical of the parol evidence rule, much as they are of the statute of frauds, because it operates to keep evidence—often credible evidence—from the jury and may prevent the fact-finder from considering apparently legitimate disputes about the substance of the agreement reached. As with the statute of frauds, courts therefore differ in how they apply the rule as a result of the variations in their commitment to the rule itself.

With some exceptions, the common law and UCC versions of the parol evidence rule are similar, though they use different terminology. The materials below draw on both sources.

§ 3.2.1. Applying the Parol Evidence Rule: Two Sets of Questions

Application of the parol evidence rule requires careful analysis of two factors: (1) the nature of the written contract and (2) the nature of the evidence that a party offers (where does it come from, and what is the evidence intended to prove?). Those factors are critical because only some written contract documents are intended by the parties to preclude consideration of evidence from outside the document, and because only some kinds of evidence are problematic under the policies underlying the parol evidence rule. These two factors trigger two distinct sets of questions:

1. **Questions about the written contract:** Using the terminology of the parol evidence rule, is the writing a "final expression" of the terms it contains (is it "integrated")? Is the writing a "complete and exclusive statement" of the contract terms (is it "completely integrated")? Or is the writing neither of these (in which case the parol evidence rule does not apply)?

2. **Questions about the evidence:** Is the evidence offered *to add to* the written contract terms? To *change* the written terms? Or is it offered for some other reason (in which case the parol evidence rule does not apply)?

§ 3.2.2. The Nature of the Written Contract

The parol evidence rule is designed to implement the parties' intent as to the effect of a written memorialization of the contract terms. To do so, the rule first

---

*   9 John Henry Wigmore, *Evidence* § 2400, at 3 (Chadbourn rev. ed. 1981).

categorizes the kind of document the writing represents, based on the parties' intent. As articulated in UCC § 2–202, the rule asks:

- First, did the parties intend the document to be a "final expression of the parties' agreement" (superseding any *conflicting* terms they may have agreed to before creating the document).

- Second, did the parties *also* intend the document to be a "complete and exclusive statement of the terms of the agreement" (superseding *all* terms they may have agreed to before creating the document, whether conflicting or not).

The common law asks the same questions, but what the UCC calls a "final expression" is instead called an "integrated agreement" (or "partially integrated agreement") and what the UCC calls a "complete and exclusive statement" is instead called a "completely integrated agreement." The following chart summarizes these categories and their meaning:

Intent of parties	UCC terminology	Common law terminology
Written terms supersede conflicting terms previously agreed to	"Final expression of the parties' agreement"	Integrated agreement; partially integrated agreement
Written terms supersede *all* terms previously agreed to, whether conflicting or additional	"Complete and exclusive statement of the terms of the agreement"	Completely integrated agreement

Determining whether a contract is a final expression (or integrated or partially integrated agreement) or a complete and exclusive statement (or completely integrated agreement) will matter in determining the significance of the second factor in any parol evidence analysis—that is, understanding the fate (admissible or not) of the type of evidence sought to be introduced. In particular, a final expression of the parties' agreement is intended to be final *as to terms that are part of that final expression*, so it supersedes all previous agreements (written or oral) and contemporaneous oral agreements; therefore, such extrinsic evidence may not be used to *contradict* or *change* the terms written into the contract document but may be used to *add* express terms. A complete and exclusive statement of the parties' agreement is intended to comprise *all* terms to which the parties agreed, so it completely supersedes all previous agreements (written or oral) and contemporaneous oral agreements and therefore use of such extrinsic evidence is barred both to *add* express terms and to *contradict* or *vary* the terms in the written contract document.

As explained in the next section, however, no matter what kind of integrated agreement the parties might have, evidence of a prior agreement may be admissible if it is offered for reasons that fall outside the scope of the parol evidence rule.

FYI

Why the difference in treatment between oral agreements (barred if they occurred before or at the same time as the writing) and written agreements (barred only if they occurred before the writing)? Two or more writings adopted at the same time would generally be considered part of the same written memorialization of the contract terms and so would together constitute the written contract that would be protected by the parol evidence rule.

How, and based on what evidence, does a court determine whether a writing is integrated, and if integrated, whether it is a partial or a complete integration? Whether a writing is partially or fully integrated (whether it is a "final statement" or a "complete and exclusive statement") depends on the intent of the parties: Did they intend the contract document to be final as to the terms contained in it, incorporating their final agreed-upon understanding of those terms? Did they intend it to incorporate the whole agreement between them? All evidence relevant to that inquiry may be considered, e.g., the complexity and length of the negotiation process and the resulting agreement, whether the parties are themselves experienced in the particular kind of transaction or are represented by counsel in the drafting process, whether the contract document appears to be thorough and complete, what the parties said to each other about finality or completeness. Determining the kind of contract document at issue, and the factual basis for that determination, is a critical first step in applying the parol evidence rule, though courts often simply conclude summarily that the written contract is integrated or completely integrated without much analysis.

In addition to other relevant evidence, the written contract may contain a particular kind of provision, known as a "merger clause" or an "integration clause," declaring the writing to be the final, or final and exclusive, agreement. The existence of such a clause is important evidence of the intent of the parties but is not always conclusive as to integration of the writing, as the following case illustrates.

Reading Critically: *UAW-GM Human Resource Center*

1. What evidence is the UAW seeking to introduce? What term does that party seek to prove?

2. What is the language in the merger clause?

3. What evidence does majority opinion say should be considered in deciding whether the contract document is integrated, and what are the reasons for its conclusion?

4. What evidence does the dissent say should be considered in deciding whether the contract document is integrated, and what are the reasons for its conclusion?

UAW-GM Human Resource Center v. KSL Recreation Corp.

UAW-GM HUMAN RESOURCE CENTER, Plaintiff-Appellee

v.

KSL RECREATION CORP. and KSL HOTEL CORP., Defendants-Appellants

Court of Appeals of Michigan

579 N.W.2d 411 (Mich. Ct. App. 1998)

MARKMAN, PRESIDING JUDGE.

Defendants appeal as of right a trial court order granting summary disposition to plaintiff on its claims of breach of contract, conversion, and fraud. Defendants also appeal as of right the trial court's denial of their motion for summary disposition. We reverse and remand for determination of damages pursuant to the liquidated damages formula set forth in the contract.

What's That?

An "appeal as of right" is an appeal that a higher court is required to consider if a party chooses to file. In contrast, some appeals in both state and federal courts will be considered only if the higher court grants permission or leave to appeal. The categories of cases that result in appeals as of right or by leave are specified by statute or by court rule.

Facts

In December 1993, plaintiff entered into a contract with Carol Management Corporation (CMC) for the use of its property, Doral Resort and Country Club, for a convention scheduled in October 1994. The "letter of agreement" included a merger clause that stated that such agreement constituted "a merger of all proposals, negotiations and representations with reference to the subject matter and provisions." The letter of agreement did not contain any provision requiring that Doral Resort employees be union-represented. However, plaintiff contends in its appellate brief that it signed the letter of agreement in reliance on an "independent, collateral promise to provide [plaintiff] with a union-represented hotel." Plaintiff provided the affidavits of Herschel Nix, plaintiff's agent, and Barbara Roush, CMC's agent, who negotiated the contract. In his affidavit, Nix states that during the contract negotiation he and Roush discussed plaintiff's requirement that the hotel employees be union-represented and that Roush agreed to this requirement. In her affidavit, Roush states that "prior to and at the time" the contract at issue was negotiated she "was well aware" of plaintiff's requirement that the hotel employees be union-represented and that "that there is no doubt that I agreed on behalf of the Doral Resort to provide a union hotel." The letter of agreement also included a liquidated damages clause in the event plaintiff canceled the reservation "for any reason other than the following: Acts of God, Government Regulation, Disaster, Civil Disorders or other emergencies making it illegal to hold the meeting/convention."

Later in December 1993, the hotel was sold to defendants, who subsequently replaced the resort's union employees with a nonunionized work force. In June 1994, when plaintiff learned that the hotel no longer had union employees, it canceled the contract and demanded a refund of its down payment. Defendants refused to refund the down payment, retaining it as a portion of the liquidated damages allegedly owed to them pursuant to the contract. Plaintiff filed suit for return

Make the Connection

A liquidated damages clause is a contract term that specifies, by amount or formula, the damages that will be owed for a contract breach, rather than leaving determination of damages to a court enforcing the contract. The parties are free to agree to such a term, but courts do not always enforce them. The limitations on liquidated damages clauses are discussed in Chapter 10, § 2.4.

of the down payment and asserted claims of breach of contract, conversion of the deposit, and fraud. Defendants filed a counterclaim and moved for summary disposition and enforcement of the liquidated damages clause. Plaintiff filed a cross-motion for summary disposition. The trial court granted plaintiff's motion for summary disposition regarding the breach of contract count on the basis of its determination that there was a separate agreement requiring that the hotel employees be union-represented. . . .

This Court reviews decisions on motions for summary disposition de novo to determine if the moving party was entitled to judgment as a matter of law. *Stehlik v. Johnson* (On Rehearing), 206 Mich.App. 83, 85, 520 N.W.2d 633 (1994). . . .

Merger Clause

Defendants claim that the trial court erred in granting plaintiff's motion for summary disposition and in denying defendants' motion for summary disposition. Regarding the breach of contract count, they specifically contend that parol evidence of a separate agreement providing that the hotel would have union employees at the time of the convention was inadmissible because the letter of agreement included an express merger clause.

We begin by reiterating the basic rules regarding contract interpretation. "The primary goal in the construction or interpretation of any contract is to honor the intent of the parties." *Rasheed v. Chrysler Corp.*, 445 Mich. 109, 127, n. 28, 517 N.W.2d 19 (1994).

> We must look for the intent of the parties in the words used in the instrument. This court does not have the right to make a different contract for the parties or to look to extrinsic testimony to determine their intent when the words used by them are clear and unambiguous and have a definite meaning." [*Sheldon-Seatz, Inc. v. Coles*, 319 Mich. 401, 406–407, 29 N.W.2d 832 (1947), *quoting Michigan Chandelier Co. v. Morse*, 297 Mich. 41, 49, 297 N.W. 64 (1941).]

In *Port Huron Ed. Ass'n v. Port Huron Area School Dist.*, 452 Mich. 309, 323, 550 N.W.2d 228 (1996), the Court stated:

> The initial question whether contract language is ambiguous is a question of law. If the contract language is clear and unambiguous, its meaning is a question of law. Where the contract language is unclear or susceptible to multiple meanings, interpretation becomes a question of fact.

A contract is ambiguous if "its words may reasonably be understood in different ways." *Raska v. Farm Bureau Ins. Co.*, 412 Mich. 355, 362, 314 N.W.2d 440 (1982). Courts are not to create ambiguity where none exists. *Smith v. Physicians Health Plan, Inc.*, 444 Mich. 743, 759, 514 N.W.2d 150 (1994). "Contractual language is construed according to its plain and ordinary meaning, and technical or constrained constructions are to be avoided." *Dillon v. DeNooyer Chevrolet Geo*, 217 Mich.App. 163, 166, 550 N.W.2d 846 (1996). If the meaning of an agreement is ambiguous or unclear, the trier of fact is to determine the intent of the parties. *Chrysler Corp. v. Brencal Contractors, Inc.*, 146 Mich.App. 766, 775, 381 N.W.2d 814 (1985).

The parol evidence rule may be summarized as follows: "[p]arol evidence of contract negotiations, or of prior or contemporaneous agreements that contradict or vary the written contract, is not admissible to vary the terms of a contract which is clear and unambiguous." *Schmude Oil Co. v. Omar Operating Co.*, 184 Mich.App. 574, 580, 458 N.W.2d 659 (1990). This rule recognizes that in "[b]ack of nearly every written instrument lies a parol agreement, merged therein." *Lee State Bank v. McElheny*, 227 Mich. 322, 327, 198 N.W. 928 (1924). "The practical justification for the rule lies in the stability that it gives to written contracts; for otherwise either party might avoid his obligation by testifying that a contemporaneous oral agreement released him from the duties that he had simultaneously assumed in writing." 4 Williston, Contracts, § 631. In other words, the parol evidence rule addresses the fact that "disappointed parties will have a great incentive to describe circumstances in ways that escape the explicit terms of their contracts." Fried, *Contract as Promise* (Cambridge: Harvard University Press, 1981) at 60.

However, parol evidence of prior or contemporaneous agreements or negotiations is admissible on the threshold question whether a written contract is an integrated instrument that is a complete expression of the parties' agreement. *In re Skotzke Estate*, 216 Mich.App. 247, 251–252, 548 N.W.2d 695 (1996); *NAG Enterprises, Inc. v. All State Industries, Inc.*, 407 Mich. 407, 410–411, 285 N.W.2d 770 (1979). The *NAG* Court noted four exceptions to the parol evidence rule, stating that extrinsic evidence is admissible to show (1) that the writing was a sham, not intended to create legal relations, (2) that the contract has no efficacy or effect because of fraud, illegality, or mistake, (3) that the parties did not integrate their agreement or assent to it as the final embodiment of their understanding, or (4) that the agreement was only partially integrated because essential elements were not reduced to writing. *NAG, supra* at 410–411, 285 N.W.2d 770. See also 4 Williston, Contracts, § 631. Importantly, neither *NAG* nor *Skotzke* involved a contract with an explicit integration clause.

The first issue before us is whether parol evidence is admissible with regard to the threshold question of integration even when the written agreement includes an explicit merger or integration clause. In other words, the issue is whether *NAG* applies to allow parol evidence regarding this threshold issue when a contract includes an explicit merger clause. . . .

. . . [B]oth Corbin and Williston indicate that an explicit integration clause is conclusive and that parol evidence is not admissible to determine whether a contract is integrated when a written contract contains such a clause. In the context of an explicit integration clause, Corbin recognizes exceptions to the barring of parol evidence only for fraud (or other grounds sufficient to set aside a contract) and for the rare situation when the written document is obviously incomplete "on its face" and, therefore, parol evidence is necessary "for the filling of gaps." *Id.* The conclusion that parol evidence is not admissible to show that a written agreement is not integrated when the agreement itself includes an integration clause is consistent with the general contract principles of honoring parties' agreements as expressed in their written contracts and not creating ambiguities where none exist.[4] See *Rasheed, supra* at 127, n. 28, 517 N.W.2d 19; *Sheldon-Seatz, supra* at 406–407, 29 N.W.2d 832; Smith, supra at 759, 514 N.W.2d 150. This conclusion accords respect to the rules that the parties themselves have set forth to resolve controversies arising under the contract. The parties are bound by the contract because they have chosen to be so bound.

Further, and most fundamentally, if parol evidence were admissible with regard to the threshold issue whether the written agreement was integrated despite the existence of an integration clause, there would be little distinction between contracts that include an integration clause and those that do not. When the parties choose to include an integration clause, they clearly indicate that the written agreement is integrated; accordingly, there is no longer any "threshold issue" whether the agreement is integrated and, correspondingly, no need to resort to parol evidence to resolve this issue.[5] Thus *NAG,* which allows resort to parol evidence to resolve this "threshold issue," does not control when a contract includes a valid merger clause. . . .

This rule is especially compelling in cases such as the present one, where defendants, successor corporations, assumed performance of another corporation's obligations under a letter of agreement. Because defendants were not parties to the negotiations resulting in the letter of agreement, they would obviously be

---

[4] This is the only rule that treats the parties to the contract as consenting adults who are able to establish their own rules for the resolution of future controversies between themselves. The dissenting opinion fails to respect the parties' clearly expressed intent to be bound only by the terms of the letter of agreement. While the dissenting opinion attempts to minimize the import of the merger clause, the merger clause is an explicit term of the parties' contract and therefore an expression of their intent to which this Court is obligated to give meaning.

[5] The increased use of explicit integration clauses appears to be a response to the growing number of exceptions that have arisen in modern contract law to the traditional rule that courts will not look beyond the language of the contract itself in order to interpret the contract. Plaintiff now proposes to embark upon the same course by creating exceptions even to contracts that contain explicit integration clauses. We do not agree with plaintiff's contention during oral argument that there is no effective means by which parties to a contract can preclude courts from looking beyond the four corners of a contract in interpreting such contract. Were we to accept plaintiff's contention, as the dissenting opinion does, the likely response by members of the bar would be increasingly explicit merger clauses designed to compel the judiciary to respect the parties' decision to be bound only by the terms of the written agreement. Such "super-merger" clauses should not be necessary, but clear merger provisions of the sort contained in the instant contract are apparently insufficient to convince some that the parties mean what they say when they agree to a contract that includes an integration clause. Would it have made any difference if the parties had included language in the contract to the effect that the merger clause here "means what it says" or that the clause was "consciously" included in the agreement or that "it is not intended to be mere boilerplate"? What can parties to a contract do to ensure that they are held *only* to the terms explicitly agreed to in a written agreement?

unaware of any oral representations made by CMC's agent to plaintiff's agent in the course of those negotiations. Defendants assumed CMC's obligations under the letter of agreement, which included an explicit merger clause. Defendants could not reasonably have been expected to discuss with every party to every contract with CMC whether any parol agreements existed that would place further burdens upon defendants in the context of a contract with an explicit merger clause. Under these circumstances, it would be fundamentally unfair to hold defendants to oral representations allegedly made by CMC's agent. Of the participants involved in this controversy, defendants are clearly the least blameworthy and the least able to protect themselves. Unlike plaintiff, which could have addressed its concerns by including appropriate language in the contract, and unlike CMC, which allegedly agreed to carry out obligations not included within the contract, defendants did nothing more than rely upon the express language of the instant contract, to wit, that the letter of agreement represented the full understanding between plaintiff and CMC. We believe that defendants acted reasonably in their reliance and that the contract should be interpreted in accordance with its express provisions.

Fraud

. . . Parol evidence is generally admissible to demonstrate fraud. . . . [W]hen a contract contains a valid merger clause, the only fraud that could vitiate the contract is fraud that would invalidate the merger clause itself, i.e., fraud relating to the merger clause or fraud that invalidates the entire contract including the merger clause. 3 Corbin, Contracts, § 578.

. . . In its fraud count, plaintiff contends that Roush's representations that the hotel would have union employees and her failure to inform plaintiff of the impending sale of the hotel constituted fraud. . . . Here, the merger clause made it unreasonable for plaintiff's agent to rely on any representations not included in the letter of agreement. Any injury suffered by plaintiff appears to have resulted from its agent's failure to include a requirement that hotel employees be union-represented in the integrated letter of agreement rather than from reliance on any misrepresentations by Roush. Thus, the allegations in plaintiff's fraud count are not the type of fraud claims that could invalidate a contract with a valid merger clause.[9]

---

[9] Although not necessary to our analysis, we additionally note that plaintiff's allegations fail to meet the elements of fraud . . . . Here, plaintiff offered no documentary evidence to indicate that, at the time she allegedly represented that the hotel employees would be union-represented, Roush knew that defendants intended to eliminate the union work force, Roush knew that the possible sale of the hotel to defendants would be significant to the contract negotiations or that she had a duty to disclose the fact that negotiations for the sale of the hotel were under way. According to defendants' answer to the complaint, they purchased the hotel on or about December 30, 1993; thus, they purchased the hotel after the letter of agreement at issue was signed. Plaintiff's belated claim for innocent misrepresentation would have similarly failed because plaintiff failed to demonstrate that Roush had any duty to disclose the impending sale that would make a failure to disclose this information a representation that was false in fact.

Plaintiff made no allegations of fraud that would invalidate the contract or the merger clause itself. Nix, plaintiff's agent, had over seven years' experience in negotiating contracts for such conventions as demonstrated by his own affidavit. There is no allegation that he was defrauded regarding the integration clause or defrauded into believing that the written contract included a provision requiring the hotel to use union-represented employees when it did not. In his affidavit, he states that in a 1991 letter of agreement with the same hotel, provisions were made for the hotel to provide bus transportation with union drivers. This evidence demonstrates that the plaintiff's agent knew how to include agreements regarding the union status of employees in a written contract, had done so in the past when negotiating with CMC, and yet apparently decided not to include any such agreement here. In light of the obvious importance of this issue to plaintiff, it is difficult to understand why an agreement regarding the union status of employees was not included in the same way in the instant agreement. Instead, the letter of agreement contained no such provision and included a clear integration clause.[11] The written agreement is detailed and complete on its face, see 3 Corbin, Contracts, § 578,[12] and its words are unambiguous, see Raska, supra at 362, 314 N.W.2d 440; Smith, supra at 759, 514 N.W.2d 150. There is no indication that the integration clause itself is void for any reason. Accordingly, as a matter of law, parol evidence was not admissible here to contradict the explicit integration clause.[13]

---

[11] Although not necessary to our analysis, we note that the letter of agreement expressly set forth reasons justifying cancellation, i.e., "Acts of God, Government Regulation, Disaster, Civil Disorders or other emergencies making it illegal to hold the meeting/convention." These reasons did not include failure to maintain a union-represented staff. This cancellation clause would have been the logical place to provide for termination of the contract if the hotel employees did not continue to be union-represented.

[12] This exception applies when a contract with a merger clause fails to specify obvious elements of the deal struck. [Authors' Note: The exception the court refers to is "where an agreement is obviously incomplete 'on its face' and, therefore, parol evidence is necessary for the 'filling of gaps .'" 3 Corbin, Contracts § 578.] For example, under the letter of agreement at issue, if the hotel were to provide rooms without furniture or running water, this Court could fill the gaps in the letter of agreement by recognizing that such minimal amenities are essential to what constitutes a hotel room. But union-represented hotel employees are not essential to providing a hotel room. Rather, it is a particular desire of plaintiff, not common to all hotel patrons, that it use only hotels with union-represented employees. Unlike a failure to specify obvious elements of a contract, a party's failure to specify particular requests it may have will not make a contract with a merger clause "obviously incomplete on its face" such that parol evidence may be used "for the filling of gaps." . . .

[13] Here, the merger clause, which was not void for fraud and not part of a contract that was incomplete on its face, dispositively answers the question whether the letter of agreement was integrated. Accordingly, here, there is no longer a threshold question whether the letter of agreement is integrated. The dissenting opinion cites Corbin, §§ 582 and 583 for the proposition that parol evidence is admissible to make the threshold determination whether a contract is completely integrated. However, Corbin, § 578 clearly states that a merger clause that is neither void itself nor part of a contract that is "obviously incomplete on its face" is conclusive. It is unclear whether there is anything that consenting parties can do in Michigan, pursuant to the theory of the dissenting opinion, to ensure that their future contract disputes will be resolved exclusively through resort to the language of their agreements.

Therefore, we hold that the trial court erred in granting plaintiff's motion for summary disposition and equally erred in denying defendants' motion for summary disposition.[14]

. . . .

Reversed and remanded for proceedings consistent with this opinion. We do not retain jurisdiction.

HOLBROOK, JR., J., (dissenting).

I respectfully dissent.

The event that precipitated this legal dispute was Carol Management's sale of the resort to defendants, without informing plaintiff during contract negotiations that the resort was for sale or that a sale was pending, and defendants' subsequent firing of the resort's union staff, less than one month after the contract with plaintiff was negotiated and signed. The contract—drafted by Carol Management—included a standardized integration or merger clause, but was silent regarding plaintiff's acknowledged requirement that the resort employ a union-represented staff. Attempts to pigeonhole these unusual facts into established black-letter rules of contract law lead to harsh and unintended results. Hard cases do, indeed, make bad law.[1]

The contract's merger clause—"a merger of all proposals, negotiations and representations with reference to the subject matter and provisions"—appears plain and unambiguous. While it is often stated that courts may not create an ambiguity in a contract where none exists, and that parol evidence is generally not

---

[14] To construe the integration clause as precluding summary disposition for plaintiff, but not also as requiring summary disposition for defendants, is to accept the premise that the integration clause does not mean what it says. Contrary to plaintiff's contention during oral argument, we believe that the parties to a contract can agree to an integration clause that will effectively preclude courts from looking outside the contract to interpret the contract. The raison d'etre of an integration clause is to prohibit consideration of parol evidence by nullifying agreements not included in the written agreement. See 3 Corbin, Contracts, § 578. To consider parol evidence in interpreting a written contract that includes an integration clause is to accord the integration clause no meaning. An integration clause is not merely an additional "factor" to be weighed in light of the affidavits and other extrinsic evidence to determine the parties' understandings, nor is it merely one more piece of evidence to be used to determine whether there is a "genuine issue of material fact" to be evaluated at trial. Rather, an integration clause, if construed as precluding summary disposition for plaintiff, does so because it establishes an internal rule of construction for the contract explicitly agreed to by the parties to the contract. Specifically, an integration clause is an internal rule of construction that any previous or contemporaneous agreements are nullified. The parties' choice to include such an internal rule of construction precludes consideration of any prior or contemporaneous agreements and compels summary disposition here for defendants.

[1] Paraphrasing Justice Holmes' statement, "Great cases, like hard cases, make bad law." *Northern Securities Co. v. United States*, 193 U.S. 197, 400–401, 24 S.Ct. 436, 468, 48 L.Ed. 679 (1904).

admissible to vary or contradict the terms of a written contract, Professor Corbin acknowledges that strict adherence to these rules can be problematic:

> The fact that the [parol evidence] rule has been stated in such a definite and dogmatic form as a rule of admissibility is unfortunate. It has an air of authority and certainty that has grown with much repetition. Without doubt, it has deterred counsel from making an adequate analysis and research and from offering parol testimony that was admissible for many purposes. Without doubt, also it has caused a court to refuse to hear testimony that ought to have been heard. The mystery of the written word is still such that a paper document may close the door to a showing that it was never assented to as a complete integration.

> No injustice is done by exclusion of the testimony if the written integration is in fact what the court assumes or decides that it is. . . .

> The trouble is that the court's assumption or decision as to the completeness and accuracy of the integration may be quite erroneous. *The writing cannot prove its own completeness and accuracy. Even though it contains an express statement to that effect, the assent of the parties thereto must still be proved. Proof of its completeness and accuracy, discharging all antecedent agreements, must be made in large part by the oral testimony of parties and other witnesses.* The very testimony that the "parol evidence rule" is supposed to exclude is frequently, if not always, necessary before the court can determine that the parties have agreed upon the writing as a complete and accurate statement of terms. The evidence that the rule seems to exclude must sometimes be heard and weighed before it can be excluded by the rule. This is one reason why the working of this rule has been so inconsistent and unsatisfactory. This is why so many exceptions and limitations to the supposed rule of evidence have been recognized by various courts.

> There is ample judicial authority showing that, in determining the issue of completeness of the integration in writing, evidence extrinsic to the writing itself is admissible. *The oral admissions of the plaintiff that the agreement included matters not contained in the writing may be proved to show that it was not assented to as a complete integration, however complete it may look on its face.* On this issue, parol testimony is certainly admissible to show the circumstances under which the agreement was made and the purposes for which the instrument was executed. [3 Corbin, Contracts, § 582, pp. 447–451 (emphasis added).]

And, in § 583 of his treatise, Professor Corbin continues:

> No written document can prove its own execution or that it was ever assented to as a complete integration, supplanting and discharging

> what preceded it. . . . There are plenty of decisions that additional terms
> and provisions can be proved by parol evidence, thereby showing that
> the written document in court is not a complete integration. This is
> true, even though it is clear that the additional terms form a part of one
> contractual transaction along with the writing. [3 Corbin on Contracts,
> § 583, pp. 465–467.]

Accord Stimac v. Wissman, 342 Mich. 20, 26–27, 69 N.W.2d 151 (1955) (extrinsic
evidence was admissible regarding a collateral independent promise so as to give
full effect to the intent of the contracting parties); Restatement Contracts, 2d, § 216,
comment e, p. 140 (observing that a merger "clause does not control the question
of whether the writing was assented to as an integrated agreement").

The fact that plaintiff's representative read and signed the contract does not
obviate the applicability of the principles outlined in Corbin, §§ 582 and 583.
Indeed, Professor Corbin illustrates the principles of the section by analyzing the
case of Int'l Milling Co. v. Hachmeister, Inc., 380 Pa. 407, 110 A.2d 186 (1955), in
which the parties entered into a contract for the sale and purchase of flour. During
negotiations, buyer insisted that each shipment of flour meet certain established
specifications and that such a provision be included in the contract. Seller refused
to put the provision in the contract, but agreed to write a confirmation letter to
buyer tying in the required specifications. Buyer placed a written order, indicating
that the flour must meet the required specifications. Seller sent to buyer a printed
contract form, which contained none of the specifications, but did contain an
express integration clause. Seller also sent a separate letter assuring delivery in
accordance with the required specifications. Buyer signed the written contract
form. When a subsequent shipment of flour failed to meet the specifications, buyer
rejected it and canceled all other orders. The Pennsylvania Supreme Court held
that extrinsic evidence of the parties' negotiations and antecedent agreements was
admissible with regard to the issue whether buyer had assented to the printed
contract form as a complete and accurate integration of the contract, *notwithstanding
its express provision to the contrary.* Corbin, *supra* at 458.[2] Professor Corbin notes
that the court's decision was fully supported by § 582, and explained at p. 459:

> It appears that in the instant case the buyer's evidence was very strong,
> so strong that it would be a travesty on justice to keep it from the jury.
> This is not because the express provision of integration was concealed
> from the buyer; he was familiar with the printed contract form and
> knew that the provision was in it and the specifications were not. The
> court rightly refuses to deprive him of the opportunity to prove that

---

[2]   The presence of an integration clause cannot invest a writing with any greater sanctity than the
writing merits where, as here, it assuredly does not fully express the essential elements of the parties'
undertakings." *Hachmeister, supra* at 417, 110 A.2d 186.

its statement was untrue. . . . Bear in mind, however, that throughout the chapter the author has warned against the acceptance of flimsy and implausible assertions by parties to what has turned out to be a losing contract.

Section 582 of Corbin, allowing admission of extrinsic evidence with regard to the threshold question whether in fact the parties mutually assented to the written document as a completely integrated contract, does not contradict, but rather dovetails with, § 578, on which the lead opinion relies. Indeed, in § 578, p. 402, Professor Corbin hinges a finding of conclusiveness of an express integration clause on whether the written document was *"mutually assented to."* Further, in language excerpted out of the lead opinion's quotation of § 578, Professor Corbin observes:

> The fact that a written document contains one of these express provisions does not prove that the document itself was ever assented to or ever became operative as a contract. Neither does it exclude evidence that the document was not in fact assented to and therefore never became operative.
>
> . . . .
>
> . . . [P]aper and ink possess no magic power to cause statements of fact to be true when they are actually untrue. Written admissions are evidential; *but they are not conclusive.* [*Id.* at 405, 407 (emphasis added).]

Thus, examination of the written document alone is insufficient to determine its completeness; extrinsic evidence that is neither flimsy nor implausible is admissible to establish whether the writing was in fact intended by the parties as a completely integrated contract. See *Brady v. Central Excavators, Inc.,* 316 Mich. 594, 25 N.W.2d 630 (1947); *In re Frost,* 130 Mich. App. 556, 562, n. 1, 344 N.W.2d 331 (1983) (parol evidence admissible where it was clear from the face of the writing that the writing did not contain the complete agreement as assented to by the parties); *Franklin v. White,* 493 N.E.2d 161, 166 (Ind., 1986) ("An integration clause is only some evidence of the parties' intentions. The trial court should consider an integration clause along with all other relevant evidence on the question of integration."); *Sutton v. Stacey's Fuel Mart, Inc.,* 431 A.2d 1319, 1322, n. 3 (Me., 1981) (citing Restatement Contracts, 2d for the proposition that a "merger clause does not control the question of whether a writing was intended to be a completely integrated agreement"); Restatement Contracts, 2d, § 209, comment b, p. 115 ("Written contracts . . . may include an explicit declaration that there are no other agreements between the parties, but such a declaration may not be conclusive.").

"The cardinal rule in the interpretation of contracts is to ascertain the intention of the parties. To this rule all others are subordinate." *McIntosh v. Groomes,* 227 Mich. 215, 218, 198 N.W. 954 (1924). It is undisputed in this case that plaintiff's decision to hold its convention at the resort was predicated on the understanding of the representatives for both defendants' predecessor and plaintiff that the resort employed a unionized staff. Had plaintiff been made aware that the resort was for sale or that a sale was pending, I believe it is reasonable to assume that plaintiff's representative would have insisted that such a clause be incorporated into the agreement. Courts should not require that contracting parties include provisions in their agreement contemplating every conceivable, but highly improbable, manner of breach. In my opinion, the circumstances surrounding execution of the contract, as well as the material change in circumstance that occurred when the resort was sold and the union staff fired, establishes as a matter of law that plaintiff did not assent to a completely integrated agreement. Corbin's warning against the admission of "flimsy and implausible" evidence is not implicated here.

Accordingly, I would affirm the trial court's order granting summary disposition in favor of plaintiff pursuant to MCR 2.116(C)(10).

———————————

The majority in UAW gave full effect to the "plain language" of the merger clause to bar any consideration of the alleged oral understanding between the parties to the contract. The dissent was skeptical that the presence of the standard merger clause language in the contract was conclusive proof that the parties had intended to exclude that oral understanding from their contract because of the circumstances surrounding the signing of the contract and the subsequent change in ownership of one of the parties. The following examples illustrate other factors that may be relevant in challenging whether a merger clause effectively establishes that a contract is completely integrated.

Example P: *Sierra Diesel Injection Service v. Burroughs Corp.*, 656 F. Supp. 426 (D. Nev. 1987).

James Cathey, the President of Sierra Diesel, contacted Burroughs for advice on how best to upgrade its bookkeeping machine. Burroughs recommended that Sierra replace its bookkeeping machine with a computer. Cathey and his daughter-In-law (who was apparently in charge of Sierra's accounting and bookkeeping) negotiated the purchase of a computer with Burroughs, relying heavily on the Burroughs salesperson's representations as to what computer equipment and software should be purchased and what it was expected to accomplish. Before signing the contracts that Burroughs prepared, Cathey read only the portions dealing with the equipment to be purchased, the price, the parties involved, and the delivery dates. The contracts were minimal, merely identifying the items be purchased by names, numbers, and brief descriptions; the court noted that a "reasonable person in Mr. Cathey's position would not have had any way of knowing from the contracts themselves what he was purchasing or what the equipment would do." The contracts included the following integration clause:

> This Agreement constitutes the entire agreement, understanding and representations, express or implied, between the Customer and Burroughs with respect to the equipment and/or related services to be furnished and this Agreement supersedes all prior communications between the parties including all oral and written proposals.

When Cathey attempted to sue for breach of some of Burroughs' representations about the equipment, Burroughs argued that the integration clause precluded consideration of the oral representations.

Analysis: The court held that the contracts were not integrated. It reasoned as follows:

> Mr. Cathey was an experienced businessman with some knowledge of warranties, but was not particularly versed in contract law or computer science. He scanned and in part read the agreements, as noted above, but he did not understand that the integration clause meant that the representations of defendant's salespersons as to what the computer could accomplish might be nullified. On the other hand, what the computer would accomplish was an essential part of the agreement of the parties. The equipment and software were useless to plaintiff unless they would accomplish the specific needed tasks in question. They were just so much useless metal, plastic and paper if they would not do the job required for plaintiff's business. A reasonable buyer would have insisted that these representations as to what the computer would do be included in the agreement if he believed they would otherwise not be binding on the seller.

> Provided he understood the possible legal effect of the integration clause in question, a reasonable businessman in Mr. Cathey's position would have insisted that the prior written and oral representations which had been made regarding the computer be included in the written agreement. The preponderance of the evidence is that Mr. Cathey did not understand that the integration clause would relieve defendant of the representations it had made as to what the computer would do.

From the standpoint of defendant, on the other hand, it wanted to sell the equipment and this necessitated making the representations which were made. Yet, defendant apparently may have believed or hoped that the integration clause would protect it from responsibility or liability for the representations of its salespersons, so long as they were not included in the agreement. Plaintiff, however, was relying upon defendant's expertise as to what the purchase of these items would accomplish. From the standpoint of plaintiff, there could be no agreement at all for the sale of the computer absent the accompanying representations.

Integration requires a mutual intent by both of the contracting parties that the written agreement contain all of the agreements of the parties and the further mutual intent that the written agreement is intended to be the sole agreement, barring reliance upon any other prior or contemporaneous representations or agreements. The preponderance of the evidence is that there was no such mutual intent of the parties in this case that the agreement be integrated.

Example Q: *Middletown Concrete Products v. Black Clawson Co.*, 802 F. Supp. 1135 (D. Del. 1992).

Middletown Concrete Products (MCP), a precast concrete manufacturing plant, entered into a series of contracts with Hydrotile Machinery to purchase a machinery system to manufacture concrete pipe (the "System"). During the negotiations, the parties had heated discussions over whether Hydrotile would guarantee specific production rates for the System. Hydrotile was reluctant to do so, because actual production levels depended on too many factors. At some point in the negotiations, Hydrotile presented MCP with a letter listing a production rate (the "Acceptable Performance Letter"), and told MCP that it would guarantee that production rate; MCP maintains that it informed Hydrotile representatives that It was relying on that guarantee in making its decision to purchase the System.

MCP signed a series of three separate contracts for the System. Each contract contained the following language near the top of the first page:

> We [Hydrotile] hereby offer for a limited period of 30 days following the date hereof the items described below and/or in the specifications, if any consisting of [ ] pages attached hereto. This offer is subject to the terms and conditions contained on this and

the other side hereof and in said specifications, if any, and to no others whatsoever.

On the reverse side of each contract was the following limitation of warranties:

> THE FOREGOING WARRANTY [that the equipment will be free from defects in material and workmanship under normal use and service for a period of 90 days from delivery] IS EXCLUSIVE AND IS IN LIEU OF ALL OTHER WARRANTIES (WHETHER WRITTEN, ORAL OR IMPLIED) INCLUDING THE WARRANTY OF MERCHANTABILITY IN OTHER RESPECTS THAN EXPRESSLY SET FORTH ABOVE AND WARRANTY OF FITNESS FOR A PARTICULAR PURPOSE.

Also on the reverse side of each writing was the following clause:

> There are no rights, warranties or conditions, express or implied, statutory or otherwise, other than those herein contained. This agreement between Buyer and Seller can be modified or rescinded only by a writing signed by both parties. No waiver of any provision of this agreement shall be binding unless in writing signed by an authorized representative of the party against whom the waiver is asserted and unless expressly made generally applicable shall only apply to the specific case for which the waiver is given.

When MCP sued Hydrotile after the System failed to meet the specified production rates, Hydrotile asserted that the parol evidence rule barred consideration of the Acceptable Performance Letter.

Analysis: The court agreed with Hydrotile that the parol evidence rule barred consideration of the Acceptable Performance Letter. MCP had argued that the individual contracts were not completely integrated because its representatives only signed the individual contracts based on Hydrotile's assurances that the Acceptable Performance Letter would be part of the contract between the parties. The court rejected that argument, emphasizing that MCP's principals were "sophisticated businessmen who negotiated with defendants for several months"; that "the relative bargaining strengths of the parties were commensurate"; and that the entire set of documents were reviewed by MCP's counsel. The court also stressed the clear language of the merger clause and the warranty limitation in the contracts signed by MCP representatives.

However, the court also rejected Hydrotile's argument that the presence of a merger clause in each of the three writings should, as a matter of law, mean that the three writings together were the complete and exclusive agreement between the parties. The fact that each of the three separate contract documents contained language stating that it contained the entire agreement between the parties "belies the conclusion that any one of the writings alone is the entire agreement between the parties." However, the court concluded that each writing was "final as to the terms each writing contains"—in other words, each writing was partially integrated. Since the Acceptable Performance Letter contradicted the partially integrated agreements, which excluded all warranties not contained in the writings, the parol evidence rule prohibited evidence of the Acceptable Performance Letter.

Problem: Merger or Integration Clauses

8-6. As reflected in the case and examples above, the existence of a "merger" or "integration" clause is an important factor to be considered in determining whether a contract is partially or completely integrated. The mere existence of a merger clause is not sufficient by itself to determine the outcome, but a well drafted clause can influence the court's conclusion.

Consider the language of each of the following clauses standing alone. Which ones appear to create "final agreements" or "complete and exclusive agreements"? Which are ambiguous? What changes would you make to improve the drafting of any of the clauses?

a. This Agreement supersedes all prior agreements and representations, written or oral, concerning the subject matter herein.

b. This writing is the final embodiment of the parties' contractual rights and obligations.

c. These documents contain the exclusive statement of the parties' contract terms.

d. This Contract represents the complete agreement of the parties and supersedes all prior agreements and representations.

e. This agreement contains the parties' entire agreement with respect to the specifications of the goods.

Food for Thought

The *UAW* case, and the examples that follow it, all involve contracts that contain an integration or merger clause—that is, an express indication that the writing is integrated. What if a contract does not contain any such clause, as was the case in the *Skotzke* and *NAG* cases cited on page 587 of the *UAW* opinion? In that event, the court is free to use any general tool of interpretation and any type of evidence offered, to determine whether the parties actually intended the written document to be the final expression of their agreement. In other words, the court interprets the language of the contract using all of the tools that you learned about in § 2 of this chapter, and subject to the same diverging views about the effect of the "plain meaning" of contract language that were displayed by the courts in *C&A Construction* and *Pacific Gas & Electric*, discussed in § 3.1 of this chapter.

Two commentators have postulated that "American courts . . . divide over the appropriate test for determining whether or not parties intended to integrate part or all of their agreement into an exclusive, legally enforceable writing." Alan Schwartz & Robert E. Scott, *Contract Interpretation Redux*, 119 Yale L. J. 926, 959 (2010). They name these divergent approaches as "formalist" and "antiformalist":

> Formalist courts, such as common law courts in New York, use a hard parol evidence rule. Derived from the traditional rule at common law, a hard parol evidence rule gives presumptively conclusive effect to merger clauses, and, in the absence of such a clause, determines whether the written agreement is fully integrated by applying the four corners presumption. This presumption holds that the contract is fully integrated if it appears final and complete on its face. A hard parol evidence rule thus maximizes party discretion over the content of the legally enforceable contract: it functions as a procedural default rule that shrinks the evidentiary base on which the court finds the terms of the contract, but the rule permits parties to expand that base as they see fit. When parties fully integrate the agreement and use a merger clause, an interpretation dispute over contract terms may be resolved on summary judgment.
>
> Antiformalist jurisdictions, such as California, favor a soft parol evidence rule. The test for integration in these states admits extrinsic evidence of meaning, even if the writing has an unam-

biguous merger clause or would appear final and complete on its face under the four corners presumption. Antiformalist courts believe that a merger clause raises a rebuttable presumption of integration that may be overridden by extrinsic evidence that the parties lacked the intent to integrate. When a merger clause is absent, soft rule courts reject the four corners presumption in favor of admitting any extrinsic evidence that may aid in determining the parties' intent to integrate their writing. A court that uses a soft parol evidence rule is likely to deny a motion for summary judgment, thus increasing the expected litigation costs of both parties. Moreover, a soft parol evidence rule functions, in effect if not formally, as an open gate: any extrinsic evidence that a party sees as advantageous ex post will likely be considered. Thus, contrary to the stated purposes of the rule, the soft version withdraws from parties the ability to determine the evidentiary base that the court will later see.

Id. at 959–961. Do you favor the New York or the California approach to interpretation? Does your answer reflect your philosophy of contracts, or your assessment of the practical consequences of each position on this issue?

§ 3.2.3. The Nature of the Evidence Introduced

As you have seen, the types of evidence excluded by the parol evidence rule are determined by whether a written contract is integrated (a final expression) and, if it is, whether it is completely integrated (a complete and exclusive statement). For a partially integrated agreement (a final expression), the parol evidence rule excludes evidence of *prior agreements and contemporaneous oral agreements that contradict or change terms in the written agreement*, but allows evidence that adds to the terms to the written agreement. For a completely integrated agreement (a complete and exclusive statement), the parol evidence rule excludes evidence of *any prior agreements and contemporary oral agreements that contradict, change, or add to terms in the written agreement.*

Other kinds of evidence—anything *not* from a *prior or contemporaneous* oral agreement offered to contradict, change, or add to terms in the written agreement—are not addressed by the parol evidence rule. The rule is designed to implement the parties' commitment to the finality of their integrated written agreement by preventing them from undercutting that finality after that written agreement was entered into. So the rule blocks either party from later attempting to incorporate into the contract any written agreements made before, or any oral agreements made before or at the same time as, the writing was adopted. These limitations are sometimes identified as "exceptions" to the parol evidence rule, but they are better understood as instances outside the scope of the rule ("exemptions"). Thus, the parol evidence rule does not bar use of evidence to establish:

The meaning of an ambiguous term: Relevant evidence of all kinds (including prior agreements, course of performance, course of dealing, and usage of trade) is always admissible to explain ambiguity or clarify terms that cannot be interpreted without the assistance of that evidence. As we saw in § 3.1, courts differ on whether they will consider prior negotiations or agreements to *find* ambiguity, but once ambiguity is established, all courts will consider any relevant evidence (including evidence from prior or contemporaneous agreements) to resolve the ambiguity. See Restatement (Second) § 214, Illustrations 1–4.

A course of performance, course of dealing, or usage of trade: Under the UCC, evidence of course of performance, course of dealing, and usage of trade is admissible to establish the existence of contract terms as well as to interpret contract language, even if the agreement is "complete and exclusive," because it is presumed—unless carefully negated by the parties' agreement—that course of dealing and usage of trade provide the commercial context for the agreement and course of performance reflects the parties' intentions. The contract thus cannot be understood without that evidence. Terms that become part of a contract through proof of course of dealing or usage of trade are considered part of the original agreement, not "added" to the agreement from prior negotiations. See Example A above.

> **Practice Pointer:**
> **Is Course of Performance Evidence Always Admissible?**
>
> As reflected in the text, course of performance enjoys a favored position with respect to the parol evidence rule because of the number of ways in which it can escape the effect of the rule. Evidence of course of performance is admissible:
>
> - To interpret the express terms of the agreement if there is ambiguity;
> - To supplement or explain the writing, unless the parties carefully negate that possibility in the agreement; or
> - To show modification of the agreement.
>
> A skillful use of one or more of these arguments should prevent the parol evidence rule from blocking admission of evidence of course of performance.

Subsequent modifications of contract: The parol evidence rule has no effect on admissibility of the negotiations or agreements that occurred *after* the writing was executed. Nor does it affect evidence of course of performance because that always arises *after* contract formation. The function of the parol evidence rule is to ensure that the written final expression prevails over much of the evidence leading up to the moment of contract formation, not to set the contract in stone so that the parties cannot change it in the future. See Example R below.

Existence and contents of a collateral agreement: Evidence of an agreement on a separate (or "collateral") topic is allowed, because the parties did not intend it to be part of the integrated contract. What the court will consider to be a separate or collateral agreement is not always clear. See Example S below.

Problems with contract formation: Evidence is admissible if offered to show fraud, duress, undue influence, mistake, illegality, lack of consideration, or other circumstances that would invalidate the formation of a contract. The parol evidence rule does not apply to such evidence because a writing that is considered the "final expression of the parties' agreement" does not take on its privileged status until the court is convinced that there was, in fact, an agreement. Similarly, evidence to show that the contract was created only if a particular condition was satisfied is admissible, because it relates to the issue of whether a contract was formed, not to determination of the terms of the contract. See Restatement (Second) § 214, Illustrations 5 & 6.

Grounds for granting particular remedies: Evidence offered to show circumstances that support the availability of particular remedies is not subject to the parol evidence rule because that evidence is not being used to vary or add to the terms of the contract but instead to show whether the criteria for a particular remedy are satisfied. See Restatement (Second) § 214, Illustration 7.

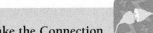

Make the Connection

A condition may affect whether a contract exists at all, as described in the text here and in Chapter 2 (page 42), or it may be a term of the contract, affecting whether particular acts of contract performance will be required or excused (addressed in § 5 of this chapter). For example, the parties may agree that a buyer will commit to a house purchase only if he is able to get financing at or below a particular interest rate (no contract formed unless the condition is satisfied) or they may commit to a house purchase but the buyer will be excused from performing if he cannot get such financing (contract formed but a contract term creates a condition that may excuse performance). The parol evidence rule does not prevent introduction of evidence of a condition affecting contract formation, but it may prevent introduction of extrinsic evidence that performance was understood as being conditional on particular events or actions.

Consider the following additional examples of the application of particular "exemptions":

> **Example R:** *Muther-Ballenger v. Griffin Electronic Consultants*, 897 S.E.2d 247 (N.C. App. 1990).
>
> Muther-Ballenger, a medical partnership, bought from Griffin Electronic a used Pfizer CT scanner, for scanning the spinal region of the human body. In the course of negotiating the purchase agreement, Griffin made a number of representations about the quality of the scans that would be produced from that scanner, including that it would produce acceptable spinal scans for the diagnostic purposes of Muther-Ballenger's practice. At the time of the sale, Muther-Ballenger signed a set of documents that included the following language:
>
> > ALL THE TERMS AND CONDITIONS OF THIS AGREEMENT INCLUDING THOSE SET OUT IN THE ATTACHED ADDENDUM AND THOSE SPECIFICALLY INCORPORATED HEREIN BY REFERENCE CONSTITUTE THE ENTIRE AGREEMENT BETWEEN THE PARTIES. THERE ARE NO WARRANTIES, EXPRESSED OR IMPLIED, OF MERCHANTABILITY, FITNESS FOR A PARTICULAR PURPOSE, OR OTHERWISE, EXCEPT AS SET FORTH IN THIS AGREEMENT.
>
> None of the written documents signed by the parties contained any mention of the representations made by Griffin before the purchase. Upon installation, the scanner failed to produce diagnostically acceptable spinal scans. Muther-Ballenger requested Griffin to service the scanner as provided in their agreements. During their attempts to resolve these issues, Griffin made a number of specific representations to Muther-Ballenger, stating that the scanner would produce spinal scans for diagnostic purposes and that the problems with the scanner would be resolved. Muther-Ballenger eventually rejected the scanner and sued for breach of warranty. Griffin argued that the parol evidence rule barred consideration of Griffin's oral representations about the quality of the scans.

Analysis: The court held that the parol evidence rule did not bar admission of evidence of Griffin's statements after the signing of the sales document, since that would be evidence of oral modifications made *subsequent* to the written contract.

Example S: *Harold S. Lee v. Joseph E. Seagram & Sons*, 552 F.2d 447 (2d Cir. 1977).

Harold Lee, his two sons, brother, and nephew jointly owned Capitol City Liquor Company, a wholesale liquor distributor In Washington D.C. Lee approached Jack Yogman, Executive Vice President of Joseph Seagram & Sons, about possibly selling Capital City to Seagram. Lee had worked for Seagram for 36 years before acquiring his interest in Capital City and had known Yogman for many years. In their conversations about the sale, Lee conditioned his offer on Seagram's agreement to relocate Lee and his two sons in a new distributorship in a different city. The sale of Capital City to Seagram was negotiated by Yogman's assistant. The written purchase agreement did not contain the promise to relocate Lee and his sons. When Seagram failed to provide the Lees another distributorship, Lee sued for breach of contract. The jury found In favor of the Lees. Seagram appealed, arguing that Lee's proof of the alleged oral agreement was barred by the parol evidence rule.

Analysis: The court held that the alleged oral agreement was "collateral" to the written sale agreement and, therefore, not barred by the parol evidence rule. Seagram argued that the oral agreement was "part and parcel" of the subject matter of the sales contract and would have affected the consideration for the sale; if it were intended to be part of the agreement, it should have been mentioned in the written agreement. Lee countered that the oral agreement was a "collateral" or separate side agreement; the integrative effect of the written sales agreement applied only to the terms of that sale, none of which were contradicted by the oral agreement. The court reasoned that "the overarching question is whether, in the context of the particular setting, the oral agreement was one which the parties would ordinarily be expected to embody in the writing." In this case, the court identified several reasons why this oral agreement would not be expected to be included in the sales contract. First, the sales contract was between Seagram and the five co-owners of Capitol City; it was reasonable to expect that a separate agreement between Seagram and only three of those parties would not be included in the sales contract. Second, given the "close relationship of confidence and friendship over many years between two old men . . . [i]t would not be surprising that a handshake for the benefit of Harold's sons would have been thought sufficient." Third, the sales agreement did not contain an integration clause. Finally, the oral agreement did not contradict the terms of the sales agreement.

The following chart summarizes the operation and scope of the parol evidence rule, including the evidentiary questions that are outside the scope of the rule:

	If document is not integrated	If document is a final expression (integrated)	If document is a complete and exclusive statement (completely integrated)
Evidence of prior agreement	May be used to establish contract terms	May be used to add terms but not to change terms in the written contract	May not be used to add or to change terms in the written contract
Evidence to interpret ambiguous contract term	Admissible; outside scope of parol evidence rule		
Evidence to show course of performance, usage of trade, or course of dealing	Admissible; outside scope of parol evidence rule		
Evidence from separate (collateral) agreement	Admissible; outside scope of parol evidence rule		
Evidence to show formation problems (e.g., duress)	Admissible; outside scope of parol evidence rule		
Evidence to show grounds for granting a particular remedy	Admissible; outside scope of parol evidence rule		
Evidence to show modification	Admissible; outside scope of parol evidence rule		

The chart graphically illustrates the many purposes for which evidence may be admitted, even though the same evidence would be barred by the parol evidence rule if offered for a forbidden purpose. If the evidence is admitted, though, it may be used only for the allowed purpose, (e.g., to challenge that agreement was reached between the parties) not for the forbidden purpose. (e.g., to show the agreement meant something different than was written), However, once evidence has been admitted, it may be hard for the court to limit its effect on the fact-finder.

Problems: Parol Evidence Rule

8-7. If a written agreement is final, complete, and exclusive, which item or items does it bar?

   a. a collateral agreement

   b. evidence to interpret a contract term

   c. evidence of fraud or mistake

   d. course of performance, course of dealing, usage of trade

   e. a subsequent agreement

   f. none of the above

   g. all of the above

8-8. Evidence of a course of performance can be used, in spite of the parol evidence rule, for all of the following purposes except one. Which is that one?

   a. To interpret a term.

   b. To show a defect in the contract formation process.

   c. To show an agreement subsequent to the final writing.

   d. To supplement the agreement.

   e. To show modification.

8-9. Which statement is not accurate with respect to a "collateral agreement"?

   a. It is outside the application of the parol evidence rule.

   b. It is collateral in form, does not contradict the main agreement, and is the kind of agreement that the parties wouldn't ordinarily put in their writing.

c. It would certainly have been put in the writing, had the parties agreed to it.

d. It is unaffected by a merger clause.

8-10. Evidence of course of dealing

a. is excluded by a merger clause.

b. is controlled by a conflicting usage of trade.

c. is not admissible when the agreement is completely integrated.

d. is admissible to establish the meaning of an ambiguous term.

8-11. True or False: If evidence is offered to prove terms from an oral agreement not later memorialized in writing, the parol evidence rule will bar that evidence.

8-12. Penny's Painting Service gets a call from Bob, who wants most of the interior of his new house painted and who has heard that Penny is a very careful painter. Penny walks through the house, orally discussing the job with Bob. The next day, she gives him a bid on a pre-printed form that includes her business's name, address, phone number, fax number, and email, as well as blanks to be filled in for customer's name and phone number, address of painting job, which rooms are to be painted, which such as plaster repair. She has filled in the blanks with the pertinent information and has bid the job at $3100, including $600 in paint and $2500 in services. Bob likes the bid amount and the care with which Penny prepared it, so he accepts the bid by signing and dating the bid form on the customer's signature line at the bottom of the form, then sending it back to Penny. Would you characterize the agreement as partially integrated, completely integrated, or not integrated? Why?

8-13. Same facts as in previous question. Later that month, when Penny is in the middle of the job, Penny and Bob disagree over whether, during her pre-bid walk-through, she orally agreed to paint the closet interiors in each room. Penny says that she doesn't remember any such thing, but Bob is sure that Penny had orally agreed to that task. If their dispute ends up in small claims court, Bob's best two arguments in favor of introducing evidence of this oral conversation are that the oral conversation

a. is a collateral agreement.

b. interprets the written terms that list the rooms to be painted.

    c. is a prior agreement.

    d. is a contemporaneous oral agreement.

    e. shows fraud on Penny's part.

    f. is a consistent additional term that supplements the agreement.

8-14. Adam purchases an old painting from Betty pursuant to a written purchase agreement that lists the parties, the painting, the price, and the delivery date. After Adam discovers that the painting is a valuable original by a well-known local artist, worth more than twice the purchase price, Betty sues to get the painting back. She wants to testify that in a conversation before Adam bought the painting, they agreed that he would have it appraised after the purchase and if the value was more than 50% higher than the contract price, Betty would have the option of buying back the painting at 175% of the purchase price. Betty tried to exercise that option, but Adam refused, denying that such promises had been made. If Betty seeks to introduce evidence of the alleged oral agreement, will it be admissible?

8-15. Suppose that the written agreement in *Lee v. Seagram & Sons, Inc.* (Example S) expressly promised that Seagram would find a replacement liquor distributorship for the seller's sons in a "suitable city." If the seller tried to introduce evidence about conversations the parties had regarding which cities might be appropriate, would that evidence be allowed by a court?

    a. The evidence will not be allowed in a context jurisdiction (represented by the dissenting opinion in *UAW*), but it will be allowed in a four-corners jurisdiction (represented by the majority opinion in *UAW*).

    b. The evidence will be allowed because it is a collateral agreement.

    c. The evidence will be allowed in either a context jurisdiction or a four-corners jurisdiction.

    d. The evidence will not be allowed in a four-corners jurisdiction, but it will be allowed in a context jurisdiction.

8-16. Ted has been admiring Terra's three-year-old mountain bike for a year, since he saw it on several bicycle trips sponsored by a local bicycling club. Terra is now ready to buy a new bike and wants to sell her old one to provide cash for the new purchase. While drinking Gatorade after a bike trip, Terra and Ted orally agree that Terra will sell her bike to Ted for $350, and that Ted can pick up the bike two weekends from now, in return for cash. They write out the following agreement on a notepad:

March 27, 2009

> Terra will sell Ted her Bianca gray-blue mountain bike for $350 cash, to be picked up and paid for by Ted on April 10, 2009, at Terra's house. The sale includes the water bottle holster on the bike and the water bottle that fits it, the Kryptonite lock/cable/bracket attached to the bike, and the spiffy bell on the handlebar. It doesn't include Terra's helmet. We're done bargaining about this bike, so this really is our final agreement.

Both Ted and Terra sign the agreement. When Ted shows up at Terra's house on April 10th, he's disappointed to find that Terra is not including the lightweight Blackberry bike pump that's always been clipped onto the bike with a spring-loaded clamp. He claims that during their off-and-on negotiations over the bike, they had a conversation in which Terra said that the pump would be included. Terra disagrees. If they went to small claims court over the dispute, would the court admit Ted's evidence of this conversation?

---

§ 3.3. Reviewing § 3: Using Extrinsic Evidence to Understand a Contract

Section 3 in this chapter has considered the following question: When is it permissible to consider evidence *extrinsic* to the express contract terms to interpret or supplement a contract? As you have seen, the question arises in three contexts, and each has generated varying approaches in different courts.

First, a court will always consider extrinsic evidence to determine the meaning of ambiguous text. But can or should a court consider extrinsic evidence when the language of a contract is not clearly ambiguous? In § 3.1, the majority opinion in *C&A Construction* articulated the strict "plain meaning" approach (if there is no ambiguity, do not look at extrinsic evidence), while the dissenting opinion, and Judge Traynor's opinion in *Pacific Gas & Electric*, displayed a more liberal approach (extrinsic evidence may be considered even in the absence of patent ambiguity and may convince the fact-finder that ambiguity exists and the meaning is different than first appeared).

Second, whether a contract document is meant by the parties to be "integrated" or "completely integrated" has a critical impact on whether the parties can supplement the agreement due to the application of the parol evidence rule. Can or should a court consider extrinsic evidence to determine whether an agreement is integrated or completely integrated? In § 3.2.2, the majority and dissenting opinions in *UAW* display different perspectives on this question.

Third, once a court has determined whether a contract is integrated or completely integrated, the parol evidence rule applies to discern which extrinsic evidence can be admitted. In § 3.2.3, we saw that the answer depends on the nature of the evidence offered and whether it is being offered to add to or vary the written terms or for some other purpose.

§ 4. Implied Contract Terms and Provisions

In addition to interpreting express terms and adding terms through extrinsic evidence, a court may need to imply additional terms not supplied expressly by the parties, if those terms are necessary to effectuate the purposes of the contract. These terms can be missing from the parties' agreement for a variety of reasons:

- The parties did not foresee the circumstances that later arose.

- The parties foresaw the circumstances, but they chose not to deal with it at contract formation.

- An agreement that contains every possible term would be far too long— and transaction costs far too high.[*]

Assuming the agreement is sufficiently definite and complete to be enforceable, a court will try to select terms to fill the gaps.

Sometimes a court will be able to select a term that effectuates the parties' intent and expectations at contract formation, based on the broader purposes of the contract and the context in which it was created. It may be unclear whether such terms should be considered "implied in fact" (agreed to by the parties implicitly rather than explicitly) or "implied in law" (selected by the court to fill in the gap, consistent with but not representing the parties' choice). Course of performance, course of dealing, or usage of trade may also be a source of implied terms, representing the presumed intent of the parties.

Sometimes a court will fill a gap by using default provisions (off-the-rack solutions that are binding only if the parties did not agree to the contrary) or by reference to relevant public policies (such as preventing unjust enrichment, forfeiture, and overreaching) that form a backdrop to the articulated terms. Default

---

[*] Recall that, if too many terms are omitted, the resulting agreement may not be enforceable. See Chapter 2, § 5.

provisions ("gap-fillers") are drawn from case law or statutes. They usually identify terms that reasonable parties would likely have agreed upon if they were acting fairly and sensibly. Examples of gap-fillers include:

- A real estate lease is month-by-month (rather than yearly or a fixed term) if no lease term is specified.

- In the absence of any provision on assignment of contract rights, most rights are assignable by the obligee unless the rights are personal to the obligee. (*See* Chapter 11, § 2, for more on assignability.)

For sale-of-goods contracts:

- If nothing is said as to price, the contract price is a reasonable price (usually fair market value) at the time of delivery. UCC § 2–305.

- Goods will be delivered in a single lot (not multiple lots) if no selection is made in the contract. UCC § 2–307.

- If no place of delivery is specified, goods will be delivered to the seller's place of business, or, if none exists, to seller's residence. But if the parties know at the time of contract formation that the goods are elsewhere, the place of delivery is where the goods are. UCC § 2–308.

- The time for delivery, shipment, or other contractual actions is "a reasonable time" if no time is specified. UCC § 2–309.

- The goods are covered by Article 2's implied warranties, unless the seller disclaims the warranties effectively. UCC §§ 2–314, 2–315.

Gap-fillers allow parties to expressly agree on the important dickered terms and leave others to be filled in as default terms. Thus, they decrease transaction costs in contract negotiation and drafting. They also decrease the number of disputes about the topics governed by those gap-fillers. However, using default terms does not preclude disputes over the meaning of the contract, especially because a number of the gap-fillers depend upon determining what is "reasonable" under all the facts and circumstances.

Contracting parties are also bound by mandatory rules of law that specify fundamental expectations regarding contract performance or enforcement. These rules are added as "implied" contract terms, whether or not the parties agreed to them. Mandatory rules might come from statutes, regulations, or court decisions. Examples include statutes of limitations, statutes of frauds, the parol evidence rule, regulations on unfair and deceptive trade and business practices, rulings on the (in)validity of certain clauses, and regulations governing the businesses of one or both of the parties (e.g., insurance or banking).

The subsections that follow address implied-in-fact terms and the meaning of particular default and mandatory provisions.

§ 4.1. Terms Implied from the Circumstances

Reading Critically: *Fisher*, *First National Bank of Lawrence*, and *Wood*

1. What terms do the courts supply in enforcing the contracts? Why were the terms left out by the parties? What arguments might be made against the conclusion that those terms were implied?

2. Do the courts supply terms based on the intent of the parties? If not, how do the courts determine the terms?

3. In each case, are the added terms implied "in fact" or implied "in law"?

4. What similarities/differences do you see in the approaches of the courts?

Fisher v. Congregation B'nai Yitzhok

HERMAN FISHER, Plaintiff-Appellee

v.

CONGREGATION B'NAI YITZHOK, Defendant-Appellant

Pennsylvania Superior Court
110 A.2d 881 (Pa. Super. 1955)

HIRT, JUDGE.

Plaintiff is an ordained rabbi of the orthodox Hebrew faith. He however does not officiate except on occasion as a professional rabbi-cantor in the liturgical service of a synagogue. The defendant is an incorporated Hebrew congregation with a synagogue in Philadelphia. Plaintiff, in response to defendant's advertisement in a Yiddish newspaper, appeared in Philadelphia for an audition before a committee representing the congregation. As a result, a written contract was entered into on June 26, 1950, under the terms of which plaintiff agreed to officiate as cantor at the synagogue of the defendant congregation "for the High Holiday Season of 1950", at six specified services during the month of September 1950. As full compensation for the above services the defendant agreed to pay plaintiff the sum of $1,200.

The purpose upon which the defendant congregation was incorporated is thus stated in its charter: "The worship of Almighty God according to the faith, discipline, forms and rites of the orthodox Jewish religion." And up to the time of the execution of the contract the defendant congregation conducted its religious services in accordance with the practices of the orthodox Hebrew faith. On behalf of the plaintiff there is evidence that under the law of the Torah and other binding authority of the Jewish law, men and women may not sit together at services in the synagogue. In the orthodox synagogue, where the practice is observed, the women sit apart from the men in a gallery, or they are separated from the men by means of a partition between the two groups.

The contract in this case is entirely silent as to the character of the defendant as an orthodox Hebrew congregation and the practices observed by it as to the seating at the services in the synagogue. At a general meeting of the congregation on July 12, 1950, on the eve of moving into a new synagogue, the practice of separate seating by the defendant formerly observed was modified and for the future the first four rows of seats during religious services were set aside exclusively for the men, and the next four rows for the women, and the remainder for mixed seating of both men and women.

When plaintiff was informed of the action of the defendant congregation in deviating from the traditional practice as to separate seating, he through his attorney notified the defendant that he, a rabbi of the orthodox faith, would be unable to officiate as cantor because "this would be a violation of his beliefs." Plaintiff persisted in the stand taken that he would not under any circumstances serve as cantor for defendant as long as men and women were not seated separately. And when defendant failed to rescind its action permitting men and women to sit together during services, plaintiff refused to officiate. It then was too late for him to secure other employment as cantor during the 1950 Holiday season except for one service which paid him $100, and he brought suit for the balance of the contract price.

. . . . Judge Smith did specifically find that defendant, at the time the contract was entered into, "Was conducting its services according to the Orthodox Hebrew Faith." Judge Smith accepted the testimony of three rabbis learned in Hebrew law, who appeared for plaintiff, to the effect: "That Orthodox Judaism required a definite and physical separation of the sexes in the synagogue." And he also considered it established by the testimony that an orthodox rabbi-cantor "could not conscientiously officiate in a 'trefah' synagogue, that is, one that violates Jewish law"; and it was specifically found that the old building which the congregation left, "had separation in accordance with Jewish orthodoxy." The ultimate finding was for the plaintiff in the sum of $1,100 plus interest. And the court entered judgment for the plaintiff on the finding. In this appeal it is contended that the defendant is entitled to judgment as a matter of law.

The finding for the plaintiff in this trial without a jury has the force and effect of a verdict of a jury and in support of the judgment entered by the lower court, the plaintiff is entitled to the benefit of the most favorable inferences from the evidence. Jann v. Linton's Lunch, 150 Pa.Super. 653, 29 A.2d 219. Findings of fact by a trial judge, sitting without a jury, which are supported by competent substantial evidence are conclusive on appeal. Scott-Smith Cadillac Co., Inc., v. Rajeski, 166 Pa.Super. 116, 70 A.2d 454.

Although the contract is silent as to the nature of the defendant congregation, there is no ambiguity in the writing on that score and certainly nothing was omitted from its terms by fraud, accident or mistake. The terms of the contract therefore could not be varied under the parol evidence rule. Bardwell v. Willis Co., 375 Pa. 503, 100 A.2d 102; Mathers v. Roxy Auto Co., 375 Pa. 640, 101 A.2d 680. Another principle controls the interpretation of this contract.

There is sufficient competent evidence in support of the finding that this defendant was an orthodox congregation, which observed the rule of the ancient Hebrew law as to separate seating during the services of the High Holiday Season; and also to the effect that the rule had been observed immemorially and invariably by the defendant in these services, without exception. As bearing on plaintiff's bona fide belief that such was the fact, at the time he contracted with the defendant, plaintiff was permitted to introduce in evidence the declarations of Rabbi Ebert, the rabbi of the defendant congregation, made to him prior to signing of the contract, in which the rabbi said: "There always was a separation between men and women" and "there is going to be strict separation between men and women", referring to the seating in the new synagogue. Rabbi Lipschitz, who was present, testified that Rabbi Ebert, in response to plaintiff's question "Will services be conducted as in the old Congregation" replied "Sure. There is no question about that" referring to the prior practice of separate seating. The relationship of rabbi to the congregation which he serves does not create the legal relationship of principal and agent. Cf. Reifsnyder v. Dougherty, 301 Pa. 328, 152 A. 98. And Rabbi Ebert in the absence of special authority to speak for the congregation could not legally bind the defendant by his declarations to the plaintiff prior to the execution of the contract. Davidsville First Nat. Bank v. St. John's Church, 296 Pa. 467, 472, 146 A. 102. But while the declarations of Rabbi Ebert, above referred to would have been inadmissible hearsay as proof of the truth of what was said, yet his declarations were properly admissible as bearing upon plaintiff's state of mind and his intent in entering into the contract. 1 Henry Pa. Evid., 4th Ed., §§ 22, 469. "Statements tending to show intent are admissible in evidence although self-serving. Ickes v. Ickes, 237 Pa. 582, 591, 85 A. 885", 44 L.R.A.,N.S., 1118. Smith v. Smith, 364 Pa. 1, 9, 70 A.2d 630, 635.

In determining the right of recovery in this case the question is to be determined under the rules of our civil law, and the ancient provision of the Hebrew law relating to separate seating is read into the contract only because implicit in the writing as to the basis—according to the evidence—upon which the parties dealt. Cf. Canovaro v. Brothers of Order of H. of St. Aug., 326 Pa. 76, 86, 191 A. 140. In our law the provision became a part of the written contract under a principle analogous to the rule applicable to the construction of contracts in the light of custom or immemorial and invariable usage. It has been said that: "When a custom or usage is once established, in absence of express provision to the contrary it is considered a part of a contract and binding on the parties though not mentioned therein, the presumption being that they knew of and contracted with reference to it". 1 Henry, Pa.Evid., 4th Ed., § 203. Cf. Restatement, Contracts, § 248(2) and § 249. In this case there was more than a presumption. From the findings of the trial judge supported by the evidence it is clear that the parties contracted on the common understanding that the defendant was an orthodox synagogue which observed the mandate of the Jewish law as to separate seating. That intention was implicit in this contract though not referred to in the writing, and therefore must be read into it. It was on this ground that the court entered judgment for plaintiff in this case.

Judgment affirmed.

First National Bank of Lawrence v. Methodist Home for the Aged

FIRST NATIONAL BANK OF LAWRENCE, KANSAS, Plaintiff-Respondent

v.

METHODIST HOME FOR THE AGED, Defendant-Appellant

Kansas Supreme Court

309 P.2d 389 (Kan. 1957)

PARKER, CHIEF JUSTICE.

Plaintiff is a banking corporation with its place of business at Lawrence, Kansas, and the duly appointed administrator, with the will annexed, of the will of Bertha C. Ellsworth, deceased. Defendant is the Methodist Home For the Aged, a corporation, with its principal place of business at Topeka, Kansas, where it operates a home for the aged.

The events leading up to the institution of this litigation are not in controversy and should be stated at the outset in order to insure a proper understanding of the appellate issues involved.

On September 13, 1953, Bertha C. Ellsworth, who desired to be admitted to the defendant's home and was then single and more than seventy-one years of age, made a written application for admission to such home. Thereafter, having been advised her application had been approved, she was admitted to the home on May 10, 1954, and on the same date entered into the written agreement with defendant which is actually the subject of this litigation. Pertinent portions of such agreement, which we pause to note had been prepared by defendant on one of its standard forms, used for admission of members, read:

> "This Agreement, made and entered into this 10th day of May, 1954, by and between The Methodist Home for the Aged, a Corporation, of Topeka, Kansas, Party of the First Part and Bertha C. Ellsworth, of Lawrence, Kansas, Party of the Second Part, Witnesseth:

> "Party of the Second Part having this day given Party of the First Part, *without reservation*, the sum of $10,779.60 to be used and disposed of in the furtherance of its benevolence and charitable work as it may deem best, Party of the First Part *admits Party of the Second Part into its Home as a member thereof during the period of her natural life, and agrees to furnish*:

> . . . .

"Fifth: *It is clearly understood that Party of the Second Part has been received in accordance with the new regulations on a probation period of two months in which time she has the opportunity of finding out whether she desires to remain in the Home; and also find out whether the Home is able to satisfy the requirements. If it should be found advisable to discontinue her stay in the Home, then her gift, with the exception of $80.00 per month shall be refunded.*

"*The rules and regulations and bylaws of the Home as they now are and as they from time to time may be adopted and promulgated by the Board of Directors of said Party of the First Part are hereby referred to and made a part hereof and the Party of the Second Part hereby agrees to be bound by same.* It is especially understood and agreed that in case of serious mental illness requiring hospital care and attention, that the First Party shall have the right to make proper arrangements for the treatment and care of the Second Party in a lawful manner in a proper State Institution, provided that if Second Party is discharged as completely cured to admit Second Party into the Home without further financial requirements." (Emphasis supplied.)

The parties concede that defendant's bylaw, article 12, was in full force and effect on the date of the execution of the agreement and therefore, according to the terms of that agreement, is a part of the contract. It reads:

"*Probationary membership means a short trial period while the member becomes adjusted to the life of the Home. The probationary membership shall not continue for a longer period than two consecutive months. If for any reason the trial member does not desire to remain in the Home he or she shall have the privilege of leaving. On the other hand, if the Home for any reason does not desire to continue the membership then the member shall be notified in writing and leave the Home within a week after such notice is given.* Only members who do not have the money or securities to pay for their life Membership shall be granted the privilege of paying by the month." (Emphasis supplied.)

After execution of the May 10, 1954, agreement Bertha C. Ellsworth remained in the home until she died on June 10, 1954. At that time neither she nor the home had made an election as to whether she was to leave the home or remain therein after the expiration of the probationary period specified by its terms. However, it is conceded that during the interim, and on June 4, 1954, the plaintiff bank in its capacity as trustee had paid the defendant the sum of $10,799.60 by a check, which defendant had cashed, specifying that such check was "In Payment of Life Membership for Bertha C. Ellsworth in the Methodist Home for the Aged, as specified in Agreement dated May 10, 1954", and that defendant had acknowledged payment of that sum by a receipt of like import.

Upon the death of Bertha Ellsworth plaintiff was appointed by the probate court of Douglas County, Kansas, as Administrator CTA of such decedent. Thereafter it made written demand on defendant for performance under the agreement, including pertinent by-laws, and demanded that defendant refund the estate of its decedent the amount paid pursuant thereto, less any amounts due the Home under its terms, particularly the fifth clause thereof. When this demand was refused plaintiff procured authority from the probate court to institute the instant action to recover such amount as an asset of the estate of Bertha C. Ellsworth, deceased.

Following action as above indicated plaintiff commenced this lawsuit by filing a petition which . . . recites in a general way that . . . the defendant had never attained a life membership in the home by reason of her death prior to the expiration of the probationary membership period prescribed by the contract, hence the contract should be construed as contemplating her estate was entitled to a return of the money paid by her to defendant for such a membership. When a demurrer to this pleading, based on the ground it failed to state a cause of action, was overruled by the trial court defendant filed an answer alleging in substance that under the same facts, conditions and circumstances the contract between it and the decedent is to be construed as warranting its retention of the sum paid by such decedent for the life membership even though, prior to her death, such decedent neither indicated that she did not desire to remain in the Home nor that she desired the privilege of leaving it. It should perhaps be added that such answer contains an allegation that on May 10, 1954, decedent was permitted to enter the home without having paid her life membership; admits subsequent payment of such membership in the manner heretofore indicated; and makes decedent's application for admission to the home a part of such pleading.

. . . [T]he trial court, after holding that the salient question in the case was purely a question of law involving the interpretation of the contract, rendered judgment decreeing that plaintiff was entitled to recover the amount paid by Bertha C. Ellsworth to the Home, less $235 paid by the Home for her funeral expenses and less the sum of $80 provided for in the contract in the event she had elected not to remain in the Home. Thereupon defendant perfected this appeal wherein under proper specification of errors it charges the trial court erred in overruling the demurrer to the petition; in rendering judgment for plaintiff and against defendant, wholly contrary to the law and the terms of the agreement; and in overruling its motion for a new trial.

In a preliminary way it can be said a careful examination of the record leads to the inescapable conclusion the trial court was eminently correct in holding that the all decisive question involved in this case is purely a question of law involving the interpretation of the contract entered into between the appellant and Bertha C. Ellsworth, deceased. Indeed the parties make no serious contention to the contrary. For that reason, and others to be presently disclosed, we turn directly to appellant's claim the trial court's judgment was contrary to the terms of the agreement and to the law, mindful as we do so that where—as here—the terms of a contract are ambiguous, obscure or susceptible of more than one meaning there are certain well defined rules to which courts must adhere in construing its provisions. Four of such rules, which we believe have special application here, can be stated as follows:

1.   That doubtful language in a contract is construed most strongly against the party preparing the instrument or employing the words concerning which doubt arises. [citations omitted]

2.   That where a contract is susceptible of more than one construction its terms and provisions must, if possible, be construed in such manner as to give effect to the intention of the parties at the time of its execution. Braly v. Commercial Casualty Ins. Co., 170 Kan. 531, 227 P.2d 571.

3.   That in determining intention of the parties where ambiguity exists in a contract the test is not what the party preparing the instrument intended its doubtful or ambiguous words to mean but what a reasonable person, in the position of the other party to the agreement, would have understood them to mean under the existing conditions and circumstances. Braly v. Commercial Casualty Ins. Co., supra.

4.   That the intent and purpose of a contract is not to be determined by considering one isolated sentence or provision thereof but by considering and construing the instrument in its entirety. [citations omitted]

Stated, substantially in its own language, the principal contention advanced by appellant as grounds for reversal of the judgment is that the membership agreement between it and the involved decedent was fully executed inasmuch as decedent had been admitted to the Home as a life member on May 10, 1954, and thereafter caused her life membership to be paid; hence, since nothing further needed to be done by the parties to make the portion of the agreement relating to life membership binding, provisions of the contract with respect thereto had become fully executed and title to the fee paid for such membership had vested in appellant.

If we could limit our construction of the contract to its first two paragraphs, as heretofore quoted, we might well conclude that appellant's views respecting the status of the agreement and the gift therein mentioned could be upheld. However, as has been previously demonstrated, our obligation is not to consider isolated provisions of the contract but to consider and construe such instrument in its entirety. When succeeding paragraphs of the agreement, and the incorporated by-laws, particularly portions thereof which we have heretofore italicized for purposes of emphasis, are reviewed in the light of the rule to which we have just referred, as well as others heretofore mentioned, we have little difficulty in concurring in the views expressed by the trial court in rendering its judgment that the contract had never become executed and that title to the gift paid by the decedent for a life membership had not vested in the Home. In fact, and without repeating the emphasized portions of the agreement on which we base our conclusion, we go further and hold that, under the clear import and meaning of such emphasized provisions, Bertha C. Ellsworth, because of her untimely death during the probationary and/or trial period expressly required by their terms, never attained a life membership status in the Home. Indeed to hold otherwise would not only do violence to the language of the contract but read into it something that is not there.

One question remains in this lawsuit. Who, the Home or the decedent's estate, is entitled to the life membership fee paid by decedent to appellant? In this connection it is interesting to note that the money was paid by decedent by a check and receipted for by appellant in writing, each of which instruments contain a recital "In Payment of Life Membership for Bertha C. Ellsworth in the Methodist Home for the Aged, as specified in Agreement dated May 10, 1954." So, since it cannot be denied the contract contains no express provisions relating to where the money was to go if Bertha Ellsworth died during the probationary and/or trial period prescribed by its terms, it appears we are faced with the obligation of determining what was intended by the parties at the time of the execution of the agreement in the event of such a contingency.

Strange as it may seem, the question thus presented has been before the Courts on but few occasions. However, it has been decided under similar circumstances. An interesting discussion on the subject appears in 10 A.L.R.2d., Annotation, pp. 874, 875, § 12. It reads:

> "Many entrance contracts provide for a probationary period during which the applicant for admission to the charitable home as well as the home itself can dissolve the agreement without cause. In case the applicant is refused permanent admission at the end of the trial period or withdraws during the period of his own volition, all payments made, less a fixed weekly charge for the time he stayed at the home, are refunded to him and his property rights are restored.

> "An interesting situation arises if the applicant dies during the probationary period without having been either accepted or rejected as a permanent inmate. The legal question then is whether or not the

charitable home may retain the applicant's property on the ground that the agreement had not been dissolved by either party.

"In a majority of cases this question has been answered in the negative and it has been held that the home may not claim or retain the applicant's property, on the ground that the death of the applicant has made it impossible to determine whether he would have become a permanent inmate at the end of the probationary period."

In connection with the foregoing quotation the author cites Evangelical Lutheran St. S. Cong. v. Bishop, 213 Ill. App. 137; Christenson v. Board of Charities, 253 Ill. App. 380; Kirkpatrick Home for Childless Women v. Kenyon, 119 Misc. 349, 196 N.Y.S. 250; Sup., 196 N.Y.S. 475; 206 App. Div. 728, 199 N.Y.S. 851, as supporting the conclusion reached by him in the concluding paragraph of his discussion and one case only, Dodge v. New Hampshire Centennial Home for the Aged, 95 N.H. 472, 67 A.2d 10, 10 A.L.R.2d 858, as holding to the contrary. We may add our somewhat extended research of the books, including our own reports, discloses no other cases which can be regarded as decisive of the question presented under similar facts, conditions and circumstances.

Again reviewing the contract in the light of the heretofore stated rules, and mindful that appellant, not the decedent, prepared the involved contract, we are impelled to the view that a reasonable person, in the position of the decedent at the time of the execution of the contract, would have understood the provisions of that instrument to mean that unless and until she attained the status of a life member in the appellant's home she, or her estate would be entitled to a return of the money paid by her for that right, less amounts specified in the agreement. Moreover we are convinced, that having prepared the contract, appellant's failure to make express provision therein for retaining the money paid by Bertha C. Ellsworth as a life membership fee, in the event of her death during the period of her probationary and/or trial membership status, precludes any construction of that agreement which would warrant its retention of such money upon the happening of that contingency.

After careful consideration of the decisions last above cited we have concluded those having the effect of holding, under similar circumstances, that the appellant cannot claim or retain Bertha Ellsworth's lifetime payment for the reason her death made it impossible for her to determine whether she was to become a permanent inmate of the Home at the end of the probation period, are more sound in principle and better reasoned than the one case holding to the contrary. Therefore, based on the conclusions heretofore announced and on what is said and held in such decisions, we hold that the trial court did not err in rendering the judgment from which the Home has appealed. . . .

The judgment is affirmed.

Wood v. Lucy, Lady Duff-Gordon

WOOD, Plaintiff-Appellant

v.

LUCY, LADY DUFF-GORDON, Defendant-Respondent

Court of Appeals of New York
118 N.E. 214 (N.Y. 1917)

CARDOZO, J.

The defendant styles herself "a creator of fashions." Her favor helps a sale. Manufacturers of dresses, millinery, and like articles are glad to pay for a certificate of her approval. The things which she designs, fabrics, parasols, and what not, have a new value in the public mind when issued in her name. She employed the plaintiff to help her to turn this vogue into money. He was to have the exclusive right, subject always to her approval, to place her indorsements on the designs of others. He was also to have the exclusive right to place her own designs on sale, or to license others to market them. In return she was to have one-half of "all profits and revenues" derived from any contracts he might make. The exclusive right was to last at least one year from April 1, 1915, and thereafter from year to year unless terminated by notice of 90 days. The plaintiff says that he kept the contract on his part, and that the defendant broke it. She placed her indorsement on fabrics, dresses, and millinery without his knowledge, and withheld the profits. He sues her for the damages, and the case comes here on demurrer.

The agreement of employment is signed by both parties. It has a wealth of recitals. The defendant insists, however, that it lacks the elements of a contract. She says that the plaintiff does not bind himself to anything. It is true that he does not promise in so many words that he will use reasonable efforts to place the defendant's indorsements and market her designs. We think, however, that such a promise is fairly to be implied. The law has outgrown its primitive stage of formalism when the precise word was the sovereign talisman, and every slip was fatal. It takes a broader view today. A promise may be lacking, and yet the whole writing may be "instinct with an obligation," imper-

> **Go Online!**
>
> You can find much information online about Lucy, Lady Duff Gordon, including pictures of some of the dresses she designed and the story of her other claim to fame (or infamy) as a passenger on the Titanic.

fectly expressed (Scott, J., in McCall Co. v. Wright, 133 App. Div. 62, 117 N. Y. Supp. 775; Moran v. Standard Oil Co., 211 N. Y. 187, 198, 105 N. E. 217). If that is so, there is a contract.

The implication of a promise here finds support in many circumstances. The defendant gave an exclusive privilege. She was to have no right for at least a year to place her own indorsements or market her own designs except through the agency of the plaintiff. The acceptance of the exclusive agency was an assumption of its duties. Phoenix Hermetic Co. v. Filtrine Mfg. Co., 164 App. Div. 424, 150 N. Y. Supp. 193; W. G. Taylor Co. v. Bannerman, 120 Wis. 189, 97 N. W. 918; Mueller v. Mineral Spring Co., 88 Mich. 390, 50 N. W. 319. We are not to suppose that one party was to be placed at the mercy of the other. Hearn v. Stevens & Bro., 111 App. Div. 101, 106, 97 N. Y. Supp. 566; Russell v. Allerton, 108 N. Y. 288, 15 N. E. 391. Many other terms of the agreement point the same way. We are told at the outset by way of recital that:

> "The said Otis F. Wood possesses a business organization adapted to
> the placing of such indorsements as the said Lucy, Lady Duff-Gordon,
> has approved."

The implication is that the plaintiff's business organization will be used for the purpose for which it is adapted. But the terms of the defendant's compensation are even more significant. Her sole compensation for the grant of an exclusive agency is to be one-half of all the profits resulting from the plaintiff's efforts. Unless he gave his efforts, she could never get anything. Without an implied promise, the transaction cannot have such business "efficacy, as both parties must have intended that at all events it should have." . . . But the contract does not stop there. The plaintiff goes on to promise that he will account monthly for all moneys received by him, and that he will take out all such patents and copyrights and trade-marks as may in his judgment be necessary to protect the rights and articles affected by the agreement. It is true, of course, as the Appellate Division has said, that if he was under no duty to try to market designs or to place certificates of indorsement, his promise to account for profits or take out copyrights would be valueless. But in determining the intention of the parties the promise has a value. It helps to enforce the conclusion that the plaintiff had some duties. His promise to pay the defendant one-half of the profits and revenues resulting from the exclusive agency and to render accounts monthly was a promise to use reasonable efforts to bring profits and revenues into existence. For this conclusion, the authorities are ample. [citations omitted]

The judgment of the Appellate Division should be reversed, and the order of the Special Term affirmed, with costs in the Appellate Division and in this court.

CUDDEBACK, MCLAUGHLIN, and ANDREWS, JJ., concur. HISCOCK, C. J., and CHASE and CRANE, JJ., dissent.

§ 4.2. Duty of Good Faith

Parties may, in their contracts, explicitly create an obligation to perform in good faith,* but even in the absence of such a clause, it is generally agreed that every contract carries with it an implied covenant of good faith that may not be disclaimed. The Restatement (Second) § 205 and the UCC § 1–304 use almost identical language to state that parties to every contract are subject to a duty of good faith and fair dealing in the performance and enforcement of the contract.

Saying there is a covenant of good faith and fair dealing is only the starting point. What constitutes acting in good or bad faith? In an influential article in 1968, Professor Robert Summers suggested that good faith "is best understood as an 'excluder,' " a phrase with no general meaning of its own "but which serves to exclude many heterogeneous forms of bad faith" that may be found in the cases.** If a court finds a seller acted in bad faith because he concealed a defect in delivered goods, one can conclude that good faith includes fully disclosing material facts. If a court finds a contractor acted in bad faith because she abused her bargaining power to coerce an increase in contract price, one can conclude that good faith includes refraining from abusing bargaining power. Summers suggested that case law reveals a wide variety of forms of bad faith, including "evading the spirit of the transaction, lack of diligence, willfully rendering only substantial performance, and abusing the power to specify terms or to determine compliance[,] . . . interfering with or failing to cooperate in the other party's performance, pretending to dispute or arbitrarily disputing, adopting overreaching or 'weaseling' interpretations or constructions of contract language, taking advantage of the other party's weaknesses to get a favorable readjustment or settlement of a dispute, abusing the right to adequate assurances of performance, refusing for ulterior reasons to accept the other party's slightly defective performance, willfully failing to mitigate the other party's damages, and abusing a privilege to terminate contractual relations."***

The Restatement (Second) offers a series of examples of the sorts of behavior that courts have found to constitute good or bad faith:

Good faith performance or enforcement of a contract emphasizes faithfulness to an agreed common purpose and consistency with the

---

* The duty of good faith arises as part of the commitment each party makes to the other in the contract, so it generally applies to contract performance, enforcement, and modification, but not to contract formation.

** Robert S. Summers, *"Good Faith" in General Contract Law and the Sales Provisions of the Uniform Commercial Code*, 54 Va. L. Rev. 195, 196 (1968).

*** *Id.* at 216–17.

justified expectations of the other party; it excludes a variety of types of conduct characterized as involving "bad faith" because they violate community standards of decency, fairness or reasonableness. . . . (§ 205, Cmt. a)

Subterfuges and evasions violate the obligation of good faith in performance even though the actor believes his conduct to be justified. But the obligation goes further: bad faith may be overt or may consist of inaction, and fair dealing may require more than honesty. A complete catalogue of types of bad faith is impossible, but the following types are among those which have been recognized in judicial decisions: evasion of the spirit of the bargain, lack of diligence and slacking off, willful rendering of imperfect performance, abuse of a power to specify terms, and interference with or failure to cooperate in the other party's performance. (§ 205, Cmt. d)

The obligation of good faith and fair dealing extends to the assertion, settlement and litigation of contract claims and defenses. . . . The obligation is violated by dishonest conduct such as conjuring up a pretended dispute, asserting an interpretation contrary to one's own understanding, or falsification of facts. It also extends to dealing which is candid but unfair, such as taking advantage of the necessitous circumstances of the other party to extort a modification of a contract for the sale of goods without legitimate commercial reason. Other types of violation have been recognized in judicial decisions: harassing demands for assurances of performance, rejection of performance for unstated reasons, willful failure to mitigate damages, and abuse of a power to determine compliance or to terminate the contract. . . . (§ 205, Cmt. e)

As suggested by even this brief overview, good faith is notoriously hard to define specifically, and therefore, to apply successfully. Some courts refuse to recognize a separate obligation of good faith, believing that a claim of bad faith performance must be grounded in violation of express or implied contract terms. Even courts that do recognize it are understandably reluctant to find a breach of so undefined an obligation. As a result, breach of the implied obligation of good faith should be invoked as a last resort, only after identifying breaches of express terms of the contract and other implied terms. Any claim of bad faith must identify as precisely as possible the actions deemed troubling and why those actions should be considered to violate the other party's reasonable expectations regarding how the contract will be performed.

The following case offers a thorough and nuanced explanation of the existence, nature, and limits of the general obligation of good faith. This case is followed by some examples illustrating the nature of the obligation of good faith in two particular circumstances in which it often arises: specifying the quantity of goods in output and requirements contracts and exercising rights under termination clauses.

§ 4.2.1. The General Duty of Good Faith in Performance or Enforcement

Reading Critically: *Market Street Associates*

1. How does the court identify or define the meaning of "good faith" both generally and in the specific context of this contract?

2. What evidence is relevant to establishing the existence of good or bad faith? What story will the plaintiffs and defendants each tell to the court on remand to establish that Market Street Associates acted in good or bad faith?

3. In his opinion for the court, Judge Posner says, "We could of course do without the term 'good faith,' and maybe even without the doctrine." Is he suggesting there are no obligations of good faith?

Market Street Associates Limited Partnership v. Frey

MARKET STREET ASSOCIATES LIMITED PARTNERSHIP
and WILLIAM ORENSTEIN, Plaintiffs-Appellants

v.

DALE FREY, et al., Defendants-Appellees

United States Court of Appeals, Seventh Circuit
941 F.2d 588 (7th Cir. 1991)

POSNER, CIRCUIT JUDGE.

Who's That?

Judge Richard Posner is the author of the *Market Street Associates* case (as well as *Morin Building Products Co.* and *Northern Indiana Public*

Service Co.) and is now retired from the bench. He is a leading proponent of the law and economics school of legal theory (see the note in Chapter 10, page 872) and one of the country's most prominent, prolific, and most often-cited legal thinkers and scholars. After clerking for Justice William Brennan, he served as Attorney-Advisor at the Federal Trade Commission, worked in the office of the U.S. Solicitor General, and served as general counsel of the President's Task Force on Communications Policy before becoming a member of the faculty at Stanford Law School and, later, at the University of Chicago Law School. In 1981, he was appointed to the Seventh Circuit Court of Appeals, serving as Chief Judge from 1993 to 2000. When he announced his retirement in September 2017, the New York Times called him a man "whose restless intellect, withering candor and superhuman output made him among the most provocative figures in American law in the last half-century."[*] He remains a senior lecturer at Chicago, co-authors a blog with Nobel-prize winning economist Gary Becker (see www.becker-posner-blog.com/), and has written more than 40 books on an extraordinary range of topics, including law and economics, law and literature, how judges think, moral philosophy, intellectual property, political theory, and legal history. Demonstrating the breadth of his expertise, he has taught administrative law, antitrust, economic analysis of law, history of legal thought, conflict of laws, regulated industries, law and literature, the legislative process, family law, primitive law, torts, civil procedure, evidence, health law and economics, law and science, and jurisprudence. He was the founding editor of the *Journal of Legal Studies* and the *American Law and Economics Review.* Generations of law students may sympathize with his advocacy of "Bluebook abolitionism," criticizing the citation system as "a monstrous growth, remote from the functional need for legal citation forms that serves obscure needs of the legal culture and its student subculture." In his review of the then newly published 19th edition of the Bluebook, he noted that he had "dipped into it, much as one might dip one's toes in a pail of freezing water. I am put in mind of Mr. Kurtz's dying words in Heart of Darkness—"The horror! The horror!" . . . ."[**]

---

[*] Adam Liptak, "An Exit Interview with Richard Posner, Judicial Provocateur," New York Times (Sept. 11, 2017).

[**] Richard Posner, *The Bluebook Blues*, 120 Yale L.J. 850 (2011).

Market Street Associates Limited Partnership and its general partner appeal from a judgment for the defendants, General Electric Pension Trust and its trustees, entered upon cross-motions for summary judgment in a diversity suit that pivots on the doctrine of "good faith" performance of a contract. Cf. Robert Summers, "'Good Faith' in General Contract Law and the Sales Provisions of the Uniform Commercial Code," 54 Va. L. Rev. 195, 232–43 (1968). Wisconsin law applies common law rather than Uniform Commercial Code, because the contract is for land rather than for goods, UCC § 2–102; Wis. Stat. § 402.102, and because it is a lease rather than a sale and Wisconsin has not adopted UCC art. 2A, which governs leases. . . .

In 1968, J.C. Penney Company, the retail chain, entered into a sale and leaseback arrangement with General Electric Pension Trust in order to finance Penney's growth. Under the arrangement Penney sold properties to the pension trust which the trust then leased back to Penney for a term of 25 years. Paragraph 34 of the lease entitles the lessee to "request Lessor [the pension trust] to finance the costs and expenses of construction of additional Improvements upon the Premises," provided the amount of the costs and expenses is at least $250,000. Upon receiving the request, the pension trust "agrees to give reasonable consideration to providing the financing of such additional Improvements and Lessor and Lessee shall negotiate in good faith concerning the construction of such Improvements and the financing by Lessor of such costs and expenses." Paragraph 34 goes on to provide that, should the negotiations fail, the lessee shall be entitled to repurchase the property at a price roughly equal to the price at which Penney sold it to the pension trust in the first place, plus 6 percent a year for each year since the original purchase. So if the average annual appreciation in the property exceeded 6 percent, a breakdown in negotiations over the financing of improvements would entitle Penney to buy back the property for less than its market value (assuming it had sold the property to the pension trust in the first place at its then market value).

What's That?

In a "sale and leaseback," a financing company (like G.E. Pension Trust here) buys the property (realty or personalty), then leases it back to the seller. The seller retains possession and use of the property, but exchanges its capital interest in the property for a lump sum payment of cash and is able to claim the lease payments as business operating expenses. The buyer obtains title to the property purchased, a guaranteed income stream from the lease payments, and the right to the tax benefits from the property's depreciation. The buyer also benefits from a lower-than-market-value purchase price, and the lease payments may be enough to finance any loan the buyer obtained to finance the purchase.

One of these leases was for a shopping center in Milwaukee. In 1987 Penney assigned this lease to Market Street Associates, which the following year received an inquiry from a drugstore chain that wanted to open a store in the shopping center, provided (as is customary) that Market Street Associates built the store for it. Whether Market Street Associates was pessimistic about obtaining financing from the pension trust, still the lessor of the shopping center, or for other reasons, it initially sought financing for the project from other sources. But they were unwilling to lend the necessary funds without a mortgage on the shopping center, which Market Street Associates could not give because it was not the owner but only the lessee. It decided therefore to try to buy the property back from the pension trust. Market Street Associates' general partner, Orenstein, tried to call David Erb of the pension trust, who was responsible for the property in question. Erb did not return his calls, so Orenstein wrote him, expressing an interest in buying the property and asking him to "review your file on this matter and call me so that we can discuss it further." At first, Erb did not reply. Eventually Orenstein did reach Erb, who promised to review the file and get back to him. A few days later an associate of Erb called Orenstein and indicated an interest in selling the property for $3 million, which Orenstein considered much too high.

That was in June of 1988. On July 28, Market Street Associates wrote a letter to the pension trust formally requesting funding for $2 million in improvements to the shopping center. The letter made no reference to paragraph 34 of the lease; indeed, it did not mention the lease. The letter asked Erb to call Orenstein to discuss the matter. Erb, in what was becoming a habit of unresponsiveness, did not call. On August 16, Orenstein sent a second letter—certified mail, return receipt requested—again requesting financing and this time referring to the lease, though not expressly to paragraph 34. The heart of the letter is the following two sentences: "The purpose of this letter is to ask again that you advise us immediately if you are willing to provide the financing pursuant to the lease. If you are willing, we propose to enter into negotiation to amend the ground lease appropriately." The very next day, Market Street Associates received from Erb a letter, dated August 10, turning down the original request for financing on the ground that it did not "meet our current investment criteria": the pension trust was not interested in making loans for less than $7 million. On August 22, Orenstein replied to Erb by letter, noting that his letter of August 10 and Erb's letter of August 16 had evidently crossed in the mails, expressing disappointment at the turn-down, and stating that Market Street Associates would seek financing elsewhere. That was the last contact between the parties until September 27, when Orenstein sent Erb a letter stating that Market Street Associates was exercising the option granted it by paragraph 34 to purchase the property upon the terms specified in that paragraph in the event that negotiations over financing broke down.

The pension trust refused to sell, and this suit to compel specific performance followed. Apparently the price computed by the formula in paragraph 34 is only $1 million. The market value must be higher, or Market Street Associates wouldn't be trying to coerce conveyance at the paragraph 34 price; whether it is as high as $3 million, however, the record does not reveal.

The district judge granted summary judgment for the pension trust on two grounds that he believed to be separate although closely related. The first was that, by failing in its correspondence with the pension trust to mention paragraph 34 of the lease, Market Street Associates had prevented the negotiations over financing that are a condition precedent to the lessee's exercise of the purchase option from taking place. Second, this same failure violated the duty of good faith, which the common law of Wisconsin, as of other states, reads into every contract. *In re Estate of Chayka,* 47 Wis.2d 102, 107, 176 N.W.2d 561, 564 (1970); *Super Valu Stores, Inc. v. D-Mart Food Stores, Inc.,* 146 Wis.2d 568, 577, 431 N.W.2d 721, 726 (App.1988); *Ford Motor Co. v. Lyons,* 137 Wis.2d 397, 442, 405 N.W.2d 354, 372 (App.1987); *Sunds Defibrator AB v. Beloit Corp.,* 930 F.2d 564, 566 (7th Cir.1991); *Restatement (Second) of Contracts* § 205 (1981); 2 E. Allan Farnsworth, *Farnsworth on Contracts* § 7.17a (1990). In support of both grounds the judge emphasized a statement by Orenstein in his deposition that it had occurred to him that Erb mightn't know about paragraph 34, though this was unlikely (Orenstein testified) because Erb or someone else at the pension trust would probably check the file and discover the paragraph and realize that if the trust refused to negotiate over the request for financing, Market Street Associates, as Penney's assignee, would be entitled to walk off with the property for (perhaps) a song. The judge inferred that Market Street Associates didn't want financing from the pension trust—that it just wanted an opportunity to buy the property at a bargain price and hoped that the pension trust wouldn't realize the implications of turning down the request for financing. Market Street Associates should, the judge opined, have advised the pension trust that it was requesting financing pursuant to paragraph 34, so that the trust would understand the penalty for refusing to negotiate.

We begin our analysis by setting to one side two extreme contentions by the parties. The pension trust argues that the option to purchase created by paragraph 34 cannot be exercised until negotiations over financing break down; there were no negotiations; therefore they did not break down; therefore Market Street Associates had no right to exercise the option. This argument misreads the contract. Although the option to purchase is indeed contingent, paragraph 34 requires the pension trust, upon demand by the lessee for the financing of improvements worth at least $250,000, "to give reasonable consideration to providing the financing." The lessor who fails to give reasonable consideration and thereby prevents the negotiations from taking place is breaking the contract; and a contracting party cannot be allowed to use his own breach to gain an advantage by impairing the rights that the contract confers on the other party. *Variance, Inc. v. Losinske,* 71 Wis.2d 31, 40, 237 N.W.2d 22, 26 (1976); *Ethyl Corp. v. United Steelworkers of America,* 768 F.2d 180, 185 (7th Cir.1985); *Spanos v. Skouras Theatres Corp.,* 364 F.2d 161, 169 (2d Cir.1966) (en banc) (Friendly, J.); 3A *Corbin on Contracts* § 767, at p. 540 (1960). Often, it is true, if one party breaks the contract, the other can walk away from it without liability[—]can in other words exercise self-help. *First National Bank v. Continental Illinois National Bank,* 933 F.2d 466, 469 (7th Cir.1991). But he is not required to follow that course. He can stand on his contract rights.

But what exactly are those rights in this case? The contract entitles the lessee to reasonable consideration of its request for financing, and only if negotiations over the request fail is the lessee entitled to purchase the property at the price computed in accordance with paragraph 34. It might seem therefore that the proper legal remedy for a lessor's breach that consists of failure to give the lessee's request for financing reasonable consideration would not be an order that the lessor sell the property to the lessee at the paragraph 34 price, but an order that the lessor bargain with the lessee in good faith. But we do not understand the pension trust to be arguing that Market Street Associates is seeking the wrong remedy. We understand it to be arguing that Market Street Associates has no possible remedy. That is an untenable position.

Market Street Associates argues, with equal unreason as it seems to us, that it could not have broken the contract because paragraph 34 contains no express requirement that in requesting financing the lessee mention the lease or paragraph 34 or otherwise alert the lessor to the consequences of his failing to give reasonable consideration to granting the request. There is indeed no such requirement (all that the contract requires is a demand). But no one says there is. The pension trust's argument, which the district judge bought, is that either as a matter of simple contract interpretation or under the compulsion of the doctrine of good faith, a provision requiring Market Street Associates to remind the pension trust of paragraph 34 should be read into the lease.

It seems to us that these are one ground rather than two. A court has to have a reason to interpolate a clause into a contract. The only reason that has been suggested here is that it is necessary to prevent Market Street Associates from reaping a reward for what the pension trust believes to have been Market Street's bad faith. So we must consider the meaning of the contract duty of "good faith." The Wisconsin cases are cryptic as to its meaning though emphatic about its existence, so we must cast our net wider. We do so mindful of Learned Hand's warning, that "such words as 'fraud,' 'good faith,' 'whim,' 'caprice,' 'arbitrary action,' and 'legal fraud' . . . obscure the issue." *Thompson-Starrett Co. v. La Belle Iron Works,* 17 F.2d 536, 541 (2d Cir.1927). Indeed they do. Summers, *supra,* at 207–20; 2 *Farnsworth on Contracts,* supra, § 7.17a, at pp. 328–32. The particular confusion

to which the vaguely moralistic overtones of "good faith" give rise is the
belief that every contract establishes a
fiduciary relationship. A fiduciary is
required to treat his principal as if the
principal were he, and therefore he
may not take advantage of the principal's incapacity, ignorance, inexperi-
ence, or even naïveté. *Olympia Hotels
Corp. v. Johnson Wax Development Corp.,*
908 F.2d 1363, 1373–74 (7th
Cir.1990); *United States v. Dial,* 757
F.2d 163, 168 (7th Cir.1985); *Faulter-
sack v. Clintonville Sales Corp.,* 253 Wis.
432, 435–37, 34 N.W.2d 682, 683–84
(1948); *Schweiger v. Loewi & Co.,* 65
Wis.2d 56, 64–65, 221 N.W.2d 882,
888 (1974); *Meinhard v. Salmon,* 249

What's That?

A "fiduciary" is a person required to act
solely for the benefit of another person,
not for his own benefit, usually on the
basis of a special relationship of trust
and confidence. For example, the executor of an estate is a fiduciary with
respect to the estate of the person who
wrote the will; a guardian is a fiduciary
with respect to her ward. A fiduciary
duty is the highest standard of care in
law or equity. It requires undivided loyalty as well as reasonable care for the
other person's assets. Although a contract may give rise to fiduciary obligations, contracting parties are not typically fiduciaries for one another, as the
court opinion notes.

N.Y. 458, 463–64, 164 N.E. 545, 546 (1928) (Cardozo, C.J.). If Market Street
Associates were the fiduciary of General Electric Pension Trust, then (we may
assume) it could not take advantage of Mr. Erb's apparent ignorance of paragraph
34, however exasperating Erb's failure to return Orenstein's phone calls was and
however negligent Erb or his associates were in failing to read the lease before
turning down Orenstein's request for financing.

But it is unlikely that Wisconsin wishes, in the name of good faith, to
make every contract signatory his brother's keeper, especially when the brother
is the immense and sophisticated General Electric Pension Trust, whose lofty
indifference to small (= < $7 million) transactions is the signifier of its grandeur.
In fact the law contemplates that people frequently will take advantage of the
ignorance of those with whom they contract, without thereby incurring liability.
Restatement, supra, § 161, comment d. The duty of honesty, of good faith even
expansively conceived, is not a duty of candor. You can make a binding contract
to purchase something you know your seller undervalues. *Laidlaw v. Organ,* 15
U.S. (2 Wheat.) 178, 181 n.2, 4 L.Ed. 214 (1817); *Teamsters Local 282 Pension Trust
Fund v. Angelos,* 762 F.2d 522, 528 (7th Cir.1985); *United States v. Dial, supra,* 757
F.2d at 168; 1 *Farnsworth on Contracts, supra,* § 4.11, at pp. 406–10; Anthony T.
Kronman, "Mistake, Disclosure, Information, and the Law of Contracts," 7 *J. Legal
Stud.* 1 (1978). That of course is a question about formation, not performance,
and the particular duty of good faith under examination here relates to the latter
rather than to the former. But even after you have signed a contract, you are not
obliged to become an altruist toward the other party and relax the terms if he
gets into trouble in performing his side of the bargain. *Kham & Nate's Shoes No. 2,*

Inc. v. First Bank, 908 F.2d 1351, 1357 (7th Cir.1990). Otherwise mere difficulty of performance would excuse a contracting party—which it does not. *Northern Indiana Public Service Co. v. Carbon County Coal Co.,* 799 F.2d 265, 276–78 (7th Cir.1986); *Jennie-O Foods, Inc. v. United States,* 217 Ct.Cl. 314, 580 F.2d 400, 409 (1978) (per curiam); 2 *Farnsworth on Contracts, supra,* § 7.17a, at p. 330.

But it is one thing to say that you can exploit your superior knowledge of the market—for, if you cannot, you will not be able to recoup the investment you made in obtaining that knowledge—or that you are not required to spend money bailing out a contract partner who has gotten into trouble. It is another thing to say that you can take deliberate advantage of an oversight by your contract partner concerning his rights under the contract. Such taking advantage is not the exploitation of superior knowledge or the avoidance of unbargained-for expense; it is sharp dealing. Like theft, it has no social product, and also like theft it induces costly defensive expenditures, in the form of overelaborate disclaimers or investigations into the trustworthiness of a prospective contract partner, just as the prospect of theft induces expenditures on locks. See generally Steven J. Burton, "Breach of Contract and the Common Law Duty to Perform in Good Faith," 94 Harv. L. Rev. 369, 393 (1980).

The form of sharp dealing that we are discussing might or might not be actionable as fraud or deceit. That is a question of tort law and there the rule is that if the information is readily available to both parties the failure of one to disclose it to the other, even if done in the knowledge that the other party is acting on mistaken premises, is not actionable. *Kamuchey v. Trzesniewski,* 8 Wis.2d 94, 98 N.W.2d 403 (1959); *Southard v. Occidental Life Ins. Co.,* 36 Wis.2d 708, 154 N.W.2d 326 (1967); *Lenzi v. Morkin,* 103 Ill.2d 290, 82 Ill. Dec. 644, 469 N.E.2d 178 (1984); *Guyer v. Cities Service Oil Co.,* 440 F.Supp. 630 (E.D.Wis.1977); W. Page Keeton et al., *Prosser and Keeton on the Law of Torts* § 106, at p. 737 (5th ed. 1984). All of these cases, however, with the debatable exception of *Guyer,* involve failure to disclose something in the negotiations leading up to the signing of the contract, rather than failure to disclose after the contract has been signed. (*Guyer* involved failure to disclose during the negotiations leading up to a renewal of the contract.) The distinction is important, as we explained in *Maksym v. Loesch,* 937 F.2d 1237, 1242 (7th Cir.1991). Before the contract is signed, the parties confront each other with a natural wariness. Neither expects the other to be particularly forthcoming, and therefore there is no deception when one is not. Afterwards the situation is different. The parties are now in a cooperative relationship the costs of which will be considerably reduced by a measure of trust. So each lowers his guard a bit, and now silence is more apt to be deceptive. Cf. *AMPAT/Midwest, Inc. v. Illinois Tool Works Inc.,* 896 F.2d 1035, 1040–41 (7th Cir.1990).

Moreover, this is a contract case rather than a tort case, and conduct that might not rise to the level of fraud may nonetheless violate the duty of good faith in dealing with one's contractual partners and thereby give rise to a remedy under contract law. Burton, *supra*, at 372 n. 17. This duty is, as it were, halfway between a fiduciary duty (the duty of *utmost* good faith) and the duty merely to refrain from active fraud. Despite its moralistic overtones it is no more the injection of moral principles into contract law than the fiduciary concept itself is. *Tymshare, Inc. v. Covell*, 727 F.2d 1145, 1152 (D.C.Cir.1984); Summers, *supra*, at 204–07, 265–66. It would be quixotic as well as presumptuous for judges to undertake through contract law to raise the ethical standards of the nation's business people. The concept of the duty of good faith like the concept of fiduciary duty is a stab at approximating the terms the parties would have negotiated had they foreseen the circumstances that have given rise to their dispute. The parties want to minimize the costs of performance. To the extent that a doctrine of good faith designed to do this by reducing defensive expenditures is a reasonable measure to this end, interpolating it into the contract advances the parties' joint goal.

It is true that an essential function of contracts is to allocate risk, and would be defeated if courts treated the materializing of a bargained-over, allocated risk as a misfortune the burden of which is required to be shared between the parties (as it might be within a family, for example) rather than borne entirely by the party to whom the risk had been allocated by mutual agreement. But contracts do not just allocate risk. They also (or some of them) set in motion a cooperative enterprise, which may to some extent place one party at the other's mercy. "The parties to a contract are embarked on a cooperative venture, and a minimum of cooperativeness in the event unforeseen problems arise at the performance stage is required even if not an explicit duty of the contract." *AMPAT/Midwest, Inc. v. Illinois Tool Works, Inc., supra*, 896 F.2d at 1041. The office of the doctrine of good faith is to forbid the kinds of opportunistic behavior that a mutually dependent, cooperative relationship might enable in the absence of rule. "'Good faith' is a compact reference to an implied undertaking not to take opportunistic advantage in a way that could not have been contemplated at the time of drafting, and which therefore was not resolved explicitly by the parties." *Kham & Nate's Shoes No. 2, Inc. v. First Bank, supra*, 908 F.2d at 1357. The contractual duty of good faith is thus not some newfangled bit of welfare-state paternalism or . . . the sediment of an altruistic strain in contract law, and we are therefore not surprised to find the essentials of the modern doctrine well established in nineteenth-century cases, a few examples being *Bush v. Marshall*, 47 U.S. (6 How.) 284, 291, 12 L. Ed. 440 (1848); *Chicago, Rock Island & Pac. R.R. v. Howard*, 74 U.S. (7 Wall.) 392, 413, 19 L. Ed. 117 (1868); *Marsh v. Masterson*, 101 N.Y. 401, 410–11, 5 N.E. 59, 63 (1886), and *Uhrig v. Williamsburg City Fire Ins. Co.*, 101 N.Y. 362, 4 N.E. 745 (1886).

. . . .

We could of course do without the term "good faith," and maybe even without the doctrine. We could, as just suggested, speak instead of implied conditions necessitated by the unpredictability of the future at the time the contract was made. Farnsworth, "Good Faith Performance and Commercial Reasonableness under the Uniform Commercial Code," 30 U. Chi. L. Rev. 666, 670 (1963). Suppose a party has promised work to the promisee's "satisfaction." As Learned Hand explained, "he may refuse to look at the work, or to exercise any real judgment on it, in which case he has prevented performance and excused the condition." *Thompson-Starrett Co. v. La Belle Iron Works, supra,* 17 F.2d at 541. See also *Morin Building Products Co. v. Baystone Construction, Inc.,* 717 F.2d 413, 415 (7th Cir.1983). That is, it was an implicit condition that the promisee examine the work to the extent necessary to determine whether it was satisfactory; otherwise the performing party would have been placing himself at the complete mercy of the promisee. The parties didn't write this condition into the contract either because they thought such behavior unlikely or failed to foresee it altogether. In just the same way—to switch to another familiar example of the operation of the duty of good faith—parties to a requirements contract surely do not intend that if the price of the product covered by the contract rises, the buyer shall be free to increase his "requirements" so that he can take advantage of the rise in the market price over the contract price to resell the product on the open market at a guaranteed profit. *Empire Gas Corp. v. American Bakeries Co.,* 840 F.2d 1333 (7th Cir.1988). If they fail to insert an express condition to this effect, the court will read it in, confident that the parties would have inserted the condition if they had known what the future held. Of similar character is the implied condition that an exclusive dealer will use his best efforts to promote the supplier's goods, since otherwise the exclusive feature of the dealership contract would place the supplier at the dealer's mercy. *Wood v. Duff-Gordon,* 222 N.Y. 88, 118 N.E. 214 (1917) (Cardozo, J.).

What's That?

In a "requirements contract," the seller promises to meet the buyer's needs (or requirements) in terms of quantity. The contract does not otherwise contain a quantity term. Requirements contracts are covered in greater detail in § 4.2.2 of this chapter.

But whether we say that a contract shall be deemed to contain such implied conditions as are necessary to make sense of the contract, or that a contract obligates the parties to cooperate in its performance in "good faith" to the extent necessary to carry out the purposes of the contract, comes to much the same thing. They are different ways of formulating the overriding purpose of contract law, which is to give the parties what they would have stipulated for expressly if at the time of making the contract they had had complete knowledge of the future and the costs of negotiating and adding provisions to the contract had been zero.

The two formulations would have different meanings only if "good faith" were thought limited to "honesty in fact," an interpretation perhaps permitted but certainly not compelled by the Uniform Commercial Code, see Summers, *supra*, at 207–20—and anyway this is not a case governed by the UCC. We need not pursue this issue. The dispositive question in the present case is simply whether Market Street Associates tried to trick the pension trust and succeeded in doing so. If it did, this would be the type of opportunistic behavior in an ongoing contractual relationship that would violate the duty of good faith performance however the duty is formulated. There is much common sense in Judge Reynolds' conclusion that Market Street Associates did just that. The situation as he saw it was as follows. Market Street Associates didn't want financing from the pension trust (initially it had looked elsewhere, remember), and when it learned it couldn't get the financing without owning the property, it decided to try to buy the property. But the pension trust set a stiff price, so Orenstein decided to trick the pension trust into selling at the bargain price fixed in paragraph 34 by requesting financing and hoping that the pension trust would turn the request down without noticing the paragraph. His preliminary dealings with the pension trust made this hope a realistic one by revealing a sluggish and hidebound bureaucracy unlikely to have retained in its brontosaurus's memory, or to be able at short notice to retrieve, the details of a small lease made twenty years earlier. So by requesting financing without mentioning the lease Market Street Associates might well precipitate a refusal before the pension trust woke up to paragraph 34. It is true that Orenstein's second letter requested financing "pursuant to the lease." But when the next day he received a reply to his first letter indicating that the pension trust was indeed oblivious to paragraph 34, his response was to send a lulling letter designed to convince the pension trust that the matter was closed and could be forgotten. The stage was set for his thunderbolt: the notification the next month that Market Street Associates was taking up the option in paragraph 34. Only then did the pension trust look up the lease and discover that it had been had.

The only problem with this recital is that it construes the facts as favorably to the pension trust as the record will permit, and that of course is not the right standard for summary judgment. The facts must be construed as favorably to the nonmoving party, to Market Street Associates, as the record permits (that Market Street Associates filed its own motion for summary judgment is irrelevant, as we have seen). When that is done, a different picture emerges. On Market Street Associates' construal of the record, $3 million was a grossly excessive price for the property, and while $1 million might be a bargain it would not confer so great a windfall as to warrant an inference that if the pension trust had known about paragraph 34 it never would have turned down Market Street Associates' request for financing cold. And in fact the pension trust may have known about paragraph 34, and either it didn't care or it believed that unless the request mentioned that paragraph the pension trust would incur no liability by turning it down. Market

Street Associates may have assumed and have been entitled to assume that in reviewing a request for financing from one of its lessees the pension trust would take the time to read the lease to see whether it bore on the request. Market Street Associates did not desire financing from the pension trust initially—that is undeniable—yet when it discovered that it could not get financing elsewhere unless it had the title to the property it may have realized that it would have to negotiate with the pension trust over financing before it could hope to buy the property at the price specified in the lease.

On this interpretation of the facts there was no bad faith on the part of Market Street Associates. It acted honestly, reasonably, without ulterior motive, in the face of circumstances as they actually and reasonably appeared to it. The fault was the pension trust's incredible inattention, which misled Market Street Associates into believing that the pension trust had no interest in financing the improvements regardless of the purchase option. We do not usually excuse contracting parties from failing to read and understand the contents of their contract; and in the end what this case comes down to—or so at least it can be strongly argued—is that an immensely sophisticated enterprise simply failed to read the contract. On the other hand, such enterprises make mistakes just like the rest of us, and deliberately to take advantage of your contracting partner's mistake during the performance stage (for we are not talking about taking advantage of superior knowledge at the formation stage) is a breach of good faith. To be able to correct your contract partner's mistake at zero cost to yourself, and decide not to do so, is a species of opportunistic behavior that the parties would have expressly forbidden in the contract had they foreseen it. The immensely long term of the lease amplified the possibility of errors but did not license either party to take advantage of them.

The district judge jumped the gun in choosing between these alternative characterizations. The essential issue bearing on Market Street Associates' good faith was Orenstein's state of mind, a type of inquiry that ordinarily cannot be concluded on summary judgment, and could not be here. If Orenstein believed that Erb knew or would surely find out about paragraph 34, it was not dishonest or opportunistic to fail to flag that paragraph, or even to fail to mention the lease, in his correspondence and (rare) conversations with Erb, especially given the uninterest in dealing with Market Street Associates that Erb fairly radiated. To decide what Orenstein believed, a trial is necessary. As for the pension trust's intimation that a bench trial (for remember that this is an equity case, since the only relief sought by the plaintiff is specific performance) will add no illumination beyond what the summary judgment proceeding has done, this overlooks the fact that at trial the judge will for the first time have a chance to see the witnesses whose depositions he has read, to hear their testimony elaborated, and to assess their believability.

The judgment is reversed and the case is remanded for further proceedings consistent with this opinion.

§ 4.2.2. Duty of Good Faith in Requirements and Output Contracts

Most contracts for sale of goods contain express terms selecting the quantity of goods to be bought and sold. There is a breach of contract if the buyer refuses to take or pay for the full quantity in the contract or if the seller refuses to deliver that amount. In contrast, a requirements or an output contract measures the quantity of goods by the needs of the buyer ("requirements") or by the production of the seller ("output"), thereby allowing the parties to enter into a contract without knowing the precise quantity of goods, but agreeing to let the quantity be controlled by business operations and needs.

Older cases questioned whether the flexible quantity in requirements and output contracts made those contracts unenforceable because of indefiniteness or because they lacked a quantity term to satisfy any applicable statutes of frauds. Later cases resolved those issues in favor of enforceability (there is a quantity term, even if the quantity is defined by the buyer's needs or the seller's output, and using buyer's needs or seller's output is *not* too indefinite).

However, requirements and output contracts generate a new issue: whether the buyer or seller breached by demanding "too much" or supplying "too little" of the contracted-for goods. UCC § 2–306 uses "good faith" to furnish bounds on the quantity range in the contract.

Reading Critically: UCC 2–306

Read UCC § 2–306(1) and Official Comments 1 to 3.

1. What terms are implied in a sales contract in which the quantity of goods sold is defined as the seller's output or the buyer's requirements?

2. What terms are implied in any such contract that includes an estimate of the seller's output or the buyer's requirements?

3. What guidance do the Official Comments provide to a seller considering ceasing production of goods subject to an output contract, or a buyer considering expanding sales of goods subject to a requirements contract?

The following two examples illustrate the application of the concept of good faith in these sorts of contracts:

Example T: *Feld v. Henry S. Levy & Sons, Inc.,* 335 N.E.2d 320 (N.Y. 1975).

Feld entered into a contract with Levy to buy all the bread crumbs produced by Levy in its factory for one year. The contract was to be automatically renewed at the end of the first year for successive one-year terms, unless either party cancelled by giving not less than six months notice to the other by certified mail. During the first 11 months of the contract, Levy sold over 250 tons of bread crumbs to Feld. Then, however, Levy stopped production of bread crumbs, claiming that the operation of the bread-crumb producing oven was "very uneconomical." Levy told Feld that it would resume bread crumb production if Feld agreed to pay 7 cents per pound, rather than the 6 cents per pound specified in the contract. The toasting oven was dismantled, and Levy started selling the raw materials used in making crumbs to other buyers.

When Feld sued for breach of contract, Levy argued that the contract did not require Levy to produce any bread crumbs, but only to sell those that it did produce to Feld; since none were produced after the oven was dismantled, Levy had no obligation to sell any breadcrumbs to Feld.

Analysis: The court rejected Levy's argument, distinguishing this case from a situation where a seller might have a good-faith reason for ceasing production. The court noted that Levy stopped producing breadcrumbs only after Feld refused to pay the increased price. The court explained:

> The parties by their contract gave the right of cancellation to either by providing for a six months' notice to the other. The apparent purpose of such a stipulation was to provide an opportunity to either the seller or buyer to conclude their dealings in the event that the transactions were not as profitable or advantageous as desired or expected, or for any other reason. Correspondingly, such a notice would also furnish the receiver of it a chance to secure another outlet or source of supply, as the case might be. Short of such a cancellation, defendant was expected to continue to perform in good faith and could cease production of the bread crumbs, a single facet of its operation, only in good faith. Obviously, a bankruptcy or genuine imperiling of the very existence if its entire business caused by the production of the crumbs would warrant cessation of production of that item; the yield of less profit from its sale than expected would not. Since bread crumbs were but

a part of defendant's enterprise and since there was a contractual right of cancellation, good faith required continued production until cancellation, even if there be no profit. In circumstances such as these and without more, defendant would be justified, in good faith, in ceasing production of the single item prior to cancellation only if its losses from continuance would be more than trivial, which, overall, is a question of fact.

> **Example U:** *Orange & Rockland Utilities, Inc. v. Amerada Hess Corp.*, 397 N.Y.S.2d 814 (App. Div. 1977).
>
> Amerada Hess Corp, an oil company, entered into a contract to supply a utility company with all of the utility company's needs for fuel oil at a fixed price for five years. When the price of fuel oil greatly increased, the utility burned more of the fixed-price oil to "suddenly and dramatically propel itself into the position of a large seller of power to other utilities," rather than just selling power to its own customers. The utility's increased demands vastly exceeded the estimates stated in the contract, including in one case by 65%. When Amerada refused to supply the full increased amount of oil claimed to be required by the utility company, the utility obtained the extra oil from other suppliers and later sued Amerada for damages for the excess cost of that oil.

Analysis: The court ruled that, to the extent the utility company was using the oil to generate excess power to resell to other utilities, its "requirements" were not incurred in good faith. The court also ruled that any demand for more than double the stated estimates would be considered unreasonably disproportionate and, thus, barred by UCC § 2–306. The court did not "adopt the factor of more than double the contract estimates as any sort of an inflexible yardstick." Rather, it considered a number of factors "calculated to limit a party's risk In accordance with the reasonable expectations of the parties":

> (1) the amount by which the requirements exceed the contract estimate; (2) whether the seller had any reasonable basis on which to forecast or anticipate the requested Increase . . . ; (3) the amount, If any, by which the market price of the goods In question exceeded the contract price; (4) whether such an Increase In market price was Itself fortuitous; and (5) the reason for the increase in requirements.

§ 4.2.3. Duty of Good Faith in Exercising Termination Rights

Agreements may contain express clauses that permit one or both parties to the contract to terminate it, either for particular reasons ("termination for cause") or for any reason ("termination for convenience"). If a contract contains no specified end for performance obligations and no provision for termination by the parties, a court may supply an implied term identifying when the contract may be terminated. The following examples consider what restrictions on exercise of such terms are imposed by the implied covenant of good faith and fair dealing

Example V: *Bak-A-Lum Corp. v. Alcoa Building Products, Inc.,* 351 A.2d 349 (N.J. 1976).

Make the Connection

Recall the Chapter 2 discussion of the possibility that a very broad "termination for convenience" clause may make a contract promise illusory (page 35). However, if termination for convenience may be invoked only in good faith, the contract promise may have enough substance to no longer be illusory.

Sometime in 1962 or 1963, Bak-A-Lum (BAL) entered into a verbal agreement with Alcoa under which BAL would be the exclusive distributor in northern New Jersey for Alcoa's aluminum siding and related products. This exclusive relationship lasted until 1970, when Alcoa appointed four additional distributors for the same territory. In the spring of 1969, BAL had untaken a major expansion of its warehouse facilities in view of the expected enlargement of its business with ALCOA, including entering into a five-year lease for the new warehouse space. Alcoa knew of BAL's expansion efforts, but concealed from BAL its intention to add the new distributors, "in order to avoid any risk of cooling [BAL's] interest in selling Alcoa products during the several months before the new distributors were named and made ready to go." Indeed, Alcoa's salesman encouraged BAL to place a very heavy order of Alcoa merchandise just before the announcement of the termination of the exclusivity of BAL's distributorship. BAL sued for breach of the exclusive distributorship agreement.

Analysis: The trial court held that the oral agreement between the two parties included an implied requirement of reasonable notice before termination. The court determined that seven months would be a reasonable time for notice in this case, based on "the amount of time the notified party needs to make adjustments and to plan and arrange for business activities to replace those which are to be eliminated." It assessed damages to BAL based on Alcoa's violation of this implied contract term.

The supreme court concurred that there was an implied requirement of reasonable notice and it relied upon the implied covenant of good faith and fair dealing to find that BAL was entitled to twenty months rather than seven months notice. The supreme court explained:

> It may be true that defendant ordinarily would be under no strictly legal obligation to inform plaintiff that it was about to terminate its exclusive distributorship although it knew that in all probability plaintiff was enlarging its plant upon an assumption of the continuation of the business arrangement for the indefinite future. However, we have been at pains recently to point out that "[i]n every contract there is an implied covenant that 'neither party shall do anything which will have the effect of destroying or injuring the right of the other party to receive the fruits of the contract; in other words, in every contract there exists an implied covenant of good faith and fair dealing.'" . . . [W]e distinguish[ ] between an absence of literal violation of a contract and the breach of the implied covenant of good faith therein which could give rise to the sanction of damages. . . .

So, too, here. While the contractual relation of manufacturer and exclusive territorial distributor continued between the parties an obligation of reciprocal good-faith dealing similarly persisted between them. In such circumstances defendant's selfish withholding from plaintiff of its intention seriously to impair its distributorship although knowing plaintiff was embarking on an investment substantially predicated upon its continuation constituted a breach of the implied covenant of dealing in good faith of which we have spoken. As such it must be given substantial weight in determining the reasonableness of a period of notice of termination of the distributorship.

Example W: *Questar Builders, Inc. v. CB Flooring*, 978 A.2d 651 (Md. Ct. App. 2009).

Questar and CB Flooring entered a contract for CB Flooring to install carpeting in a luxury midrise apartment and townhome complex being built by Questar, for a price of $1,120,000. Subsequently, Questar's interior designer changed the quality of carpet to be used in the project, causing CB Flooring to submit a change order requesting an upward adjustment to the contract price by $103,371. In the meantime, Questar had contacted a competitor of CB Flooring, Creative Touch Interiors

(CTI), which proposed to complete the project (with the upgraded carpet style) for $1,119,000. Questar terminated the agreement with CB Flooring and entered into a contract with CTI for $1,120,000.

Questar claimed that the termination was for cause, based on CB Flooring's refusal to perform the original contract and CB Flooring's breach of the duty of good faith in using the interior designer's changes to seek an increase in the contract price. Even absent any breach by CB Flooring, Questar asserted the right to terminate the contract under Paragraph 14 of the contract, which provided:

> **Termination for Convenience:** If this Subcontract Agreement is terminated for convenience, Subcontractor shall be entitled, as its sole compensation, to be paid that portion of the total price provided in this Subcontract Agreement that is equal to the reasonable value of the authorized materials, equipment and incidentals furnished and delivered to the job site prior to the termination plus the reasonable value of properly authorized materials fabricated and properly stored ("Stored Materials") by Subcontractor prior to the termination, and of properly authorized special inventory items specifically purchased ("Special Inventory") by the Subcontractor for this project prior to the termination. The Subcontractor shall only be paid for Stored Materials and Special Inventory after the Subcontractor has delivered, at its expense, such Stored Materials and Special Inventory to a location specified by the Contractor and the Contractor has inspected and acknowledged in writing the acceptance of the Stored Materials and Special Inventory.

Analysis: The trial court held that Questar did not have adequate cause to terminate the contract and that Questar could not rely on the termination-for-convenience clause because it had acted in bad faith. Questar appealed, asking for a ruling whether a termination for convenience clause was enforceable under state law and whether the trial court had erred in applying the particular termination-for-convenience clause.

The court of appeals reviewed the history of the development of termination-for-convenience clauses and the evolution of the concept that, to avoid creating illusory contracts, such clauses must be exercised "subject to an implied obligation to exercise the right to terminate in good faith and in accordance with fair dealing." Finding that the trial court had not adequately determined that issue, the court of appeals remanded to the trial court, offering what it described as "guidance on how the implied obligation of good faith and fair dealing may apply in this case."

The court noted, "Where, as here, personal taste does not provide the basis for the exercise of discretion, an objective standard of what constitutes good faith and fair dealing applies." The court further reasoned that:

> On remand, the trial judge must be persuaded that Questar breached the Subcontract by exercising its right to terminate for convenience in bad faith, or, stated otherwise, by not exercising its discretion to terminate in accordance with the implied obligation of good faith and fair dealing. As the party with the discretion to terminate for convenience, Questar was entitled to decide whether continuing with the contract would subject it to an unnecessary risk. It is not the court's role to make that decision for Questar; the court's role is to determine only whether Questar's determination was consistent with the reasonable expectations of CB Flooring, in light of the terms of the Subcontract.

> CB Flooring may prevail if the trial court is convinced that Questar's asserted basis for the termination—a deterioration in its business relationship with CB Flooring—was not commercially reasonable under the circumstances, and therefore inconsistent with CB Flooring's reasonable expectations. Additionally, if the trial judge were to conclude that Questar sought to recapture a better bargain with CTI or that Questar did not make reasonable efforts to ensure that continuing its contractual relationship with CB Flooring remained convenient, CB Flooring may prevail. If the court resolves that Questar invoked its right to terminate for convenience in order to evade its obligation to perform . . . , as such an exercise would have been inconsistent with the subcontractor's reasonable expectations as well, CB Flooring may prevail.

§ 5. Express Conditions

§ 5.1. General Introduction to Conditions

Up to this point, the main focus of our attention has been on the promises that create legally enforceable contractual duties. In this section (and in the next chapter), our focus shifts to contractual provisions known as "conditions," because they in some way condition, or qualify, a party's obligation to perform a contractual promise. The Restatement (Second) § 224 defines a condition as "an event, not certain to occur, which must occur, unless its nonoccurrence is excused, before performance under a contract becomes due." Consider the following examples of common contractual conditions:

Example X: A construction company's duty to perform (to begin building) is subject to the approval of a zoning exception at an upcoming meeting of the metropolitan planning commission.

Example Y: Under a securities purchase agreement, the parties' obligations to sell the securities and to pay the purchase price are contingent on an expert's determination that the purchase will generate favorable tax consequences for both parties.

Example Z: A homebuyer's duty to close on a purchase is conditional on the buyer being able to obtain a 30-year mortgage at not more than 6% interest with no points.

Example AA: An insurance company has a duty to pay the insured for a covered occurrence, provided that the insured files a claim within 60 days after the insured event.

Example BB: A law student agrees to buy another law student's used study aid for $20, payable in cash at 9:00 the next morning in exchange for the book. The buyer's duty to deliver the payment is conditional on the seller showing up the next morning with the study aid. The seller's duty to deliver the study aid is conditional on the buyer's delivery of the purchase price.

As seen in these examples, a condition can be articulated in a variety of ways, but however articulated, it establishes that performance A is due if, but only if, B occurs. B may be an event (e.g., the expert determining that the purchase will have a favorable tax outcome in Example Y) and it may also be an event tied to a promise (e.g., the law student's promise to deliver a book in Example BB). A promise by definition is a commitment to do (or refrain from doing) something, so failure to fulfill that promise is a breach. A stand alone condition that is not also tied to a promise operates differently: if the condition is not fulfilled, performance of the connected obligation is excused but there is no breach. For example, if the planning commission does not approve the zoning exception in Example X, the construction company does not have to perform and there is no breach. A condition that is also tied to a promise has characteristics of both: failure to perform is a breach, and the connected performance is not required. In Example BB, if the seller does not deliver the book, the seller has breached her promise to deliver the book, and the buyer does not have to pay $20.

The following chart summarizes the basic differences between promises and conditions:

	PROMISE	CONDITION
WHAT IS IT?	**A manifestation of intention to act** or refrain from acting in a specified way, so made as to justify a promisee in understanding that a commitment has been made. (Restatement (2nd) of Contracts § 2(1)	**An event,** not certain to occur, which must occur . . . before performance under a contract becomes due (Restatement (2nd) of Contracts § 224)
WHAT IS THE LEGAL CON-SEQUENCE OF HAVING ONE IN A CONTRACT?	Creates a legal duty in the promisor and a right in the promisee	Creates no right or duty; rather, it limits or modifies the legal duty created by a promise
WHAT IS THE CONSEQUENCE IF: The promise is not performed, or The condition does not occur?	The contract is breached (*unless the breach is excused, see Chapter 9*)	The legal duty that was conditioned is discharged

§ 5.2. Types of Conditions

§ 5.2.1. Conditions to Contract Formation Versus Contract Performance

Examples X to BB above all involve conditions to contract *performance*. In each example, a binding contract exists (the parties have committed themselves to the agreement), but the condition included in the contract means that some (or all) contractual duties may not be owed because the specified triggering circumstance may not occur.

Alternatively, a party may propose or the parties may agree to a condition on contract *formation*. For example, the parties in Example Y might agree that they will become obligated—that the agreement will come into existence—only if the expert's report shows favorable tax consequences. If a condition for contract formation is not satisfied, the parties have no enforceable contract at all.

One consequence of the choice between establishing a condition to formation and a condition to performance is the application of the parol evidence rule. Recall that proving the existence of a condition to contract formation is not subject to the parol evidence rule, but the content and meaning of a clause in the contract that creates a condition to contract performance would be subject to parol evidence rule.

§ 5.2.2. Conditions Precedent, Conditions Subsequent, and Concurrent Conditions

A condition to contract performance may be a "condition precedent" or a "condition subsequent" depending upon whether it *triggers* a duty (that is, the duty does not exist unless the condition occurs) or instead *terminates* a duty (that is, the duty exists but is extinguished if the condition does not occur). If parties agree to exchange performances at the exact same time, the conditions to performance are called "concurrent conditions."

The Restatement has rejected these particular words as descriptors, even though the concepts themselves survive. A condition precedent is instead a "condition," and a condition subsequent is instead an "event that terminates a duty."[*]

The conditions in Examples X, Y, and Z are all conditions precedent because the duties are not owed unless the condition occurs (e.g., the construction company has no duty to build until the required approval is made). The condition in Example AA is an example of a condition subsequent: the insurance company has a duty to pay upon the happening of a contingency (e.g., a death), but the duty to pay is terminated if the insured individual does not file a claim within a specified number of days after the loss-causing event. Example BB (the two law students exchanging money for a book) illustrates a transaction that involves concurrent conditions; if either the cash or the book is not delivered, the other party's duty is not owed.

---

[*] Restatement (Second) §§ 224 and 230.

The major consequence of these distinctions among conditions is evidentiary: the plaintiff has the duty of establishing the existence of a condition precedent to the defendant's contract duty while the defendant has the duty of establishing the existence of a condition subsequent that would extinguish its duty of performance.

§ 5.2.3. Express Conditions and Implied Conditions

Probably the most legally significant distinction among conditions is the distinction between express and implied conditions. Express conditions are explicitly specified in the contract, making clear that one party is protected from the need to perform if the condition does not occur. Examples X through AA are likely to be expressly stated in the contract in this fashion, using language of the kind indicated (A is "subject to" B, A is "contingent on" B, B will be done, "provided that" A happens).

Some conditions may go unsaid, however. This is often the case when promises are made by both parties, and those promises are (implicitly) connected by a condition. For example, the two law students in Example BB would state their promises to each other (one will deliver the study aid, the other will deliver payment) but the connection between the two promises—that performance of one is dependent on concurrent performance of the other—may be understood but not be stated in the contract terms. Not all such conditions are concurrent, of course. If a homeowner calls a plumber to fix a leaking pipe, the plumber promises to fix the pipe, and the homeowner promises to pay a stated hourly rate for the work done, it may be understood that the homeowner's duty to pay is conditional on the plumber's completion of the promised repair. Implied conditions reflect judgments about the implied order of performance (whether duties by one party must be performed before the other party is required to perform) and will be treated in Chapter 9, when other issues related to performance or contract promises are addressed.

Distinguishing between express and implied conditions is legally significant because express conditions are subject to a rule of strict compliance. In other words, courts will demand literal compliance with the condition as expressed in the contract, regardless of whether the nonoccurrence of the condition is important or insignificant. As one court explained, "The reasoning behind this rule is that when the parties expressly condition their performance upon the occurrence or non-occurrence of an event, rather than simply including the event as one of the general terms of the contract, the parties' bargained-for expectation of strict compliance should be given effect."* As you will learn in Chapter 9, a very different rule applies to implied conditions.

---

* Renovest Co. v. Hodges Development Corp., 600 A.2d 448 (N.H. 1991).

§ 5.3. Identifying and Enforcing Express Conditions

In some cases, the judge must use the tools of interpretation to determine whether a contractual provision is a condition, a promise, both, or neither.

Reading Critically: *Morrison,*
Internatio-Rotterdam, and *Peacock*

As you read each of the next three cases, consider these questions:

1. What are the promises made by each party to the contract? What is one party arguing is a condition to one of those promises?

2. Does the court decide that the contested provision is

    *   A condition,

    *   A promise,

    *   Both a condition and promise, or

    *   Neither a condition nor a promise?

    How does the court reach that conclusion? What tools of contract interpretation are invoked?

3. What impact does the court's conclusion about the contested provision have on each party's duty to perform the promises in the contract?

Morrison v. Bare

JACK W. MORRISON, Jr., Plaintiff-Appellant

v.

JONAS BARE, et al., Defendants-Appellees

Court of Appeals of Ohio

2007 WL 4415307 (Ohio Ct. App. Dec. 19, 2007)

DICKINSON, JUDGE.

INTRODUCTION

Jack W. Morrison Jr. is in the business of buying houses, refurbishing them, and renting them to college students. Tom Campensa, a real estate agent, showed Mr. Morrison a house owned by Jonas Bare. Mr. Morrison noticed a sticker on the furnace that indicated it had a cracked heat exchanger. After checking with Mr. Bare, Mr. Campensa told Mr. Morrison that the furnace had been repaired in 2004. Mr. Morrison executed a contract to purchase the house, but included a "special condition" in the contract that Mr. Bare would provide him a copy of the 2004 furnace repair bill within 14 days. Mr. Bare supplied a copy of a 2004 bill for repairs, but those repairs did not include replacing the heat exchanger. Instead of closing on the house, Mr. Morrison sued Mr. Bare for specific performance and breach of contract and sued Mr. Bare, Mr. Campensa, and Mr. Campensa's real estate agency for fraud. The trial court granted summary judgment to all three defendants, and Mr. Morrison appealed. His sole assignment of error is that the trial court incorrectly granted the defendants summary judgment. This court affirms the trial court's judgment because: (1) Mr. Morrison neither performed his part of the contract nor showed his "readiness and ability" to do so; (2) the requirement that Mr. Bare provide a bill showing that the heat exchanger was repaired was a condition for Mr. Morrison's performance, not a promise; and (3) Mr. Morrison did not justifiably rely upon Mr. Campensa's statement that the heat exchanger had been repaired.

BACKGROUND

Mr. Morrison noticed a for-sale sign on the house at issue in this case and told Mr. Campensa he would like to look at it. Mr. Campensa walked through the house with Mr. Morrison and Mr. Morrison's father. The house was in disrepair, and the utilities were disconnected. During the walkthrough, Mr. Morrison noticed a sticker on the furnace that indicated it had a cracked heat exchanger. When he was deposed, he said the sticker had caused him concern because he knew that a cracked heat exchanger meant the furnace would have to be replaced. He further testified that he questioned Mr. Campensa about the heat exchanger and

Mr. Campensa said that he would check with the seller, Mr. Bare, to see whether it had been fixed.

At some point after the walkthrough, Mr. Campensa talked to Mr. Bare about the furnace. Mr. Campensa testified that he told Mr. Bare that the furnace had a sticker on it indicating that it had a cracked heat exchanger and that Mr. Bare told him the furnace had been repaired. Mr. Bare testified that he did not recall whether Mr. Campensa had specifically mentioned the cracked heat exchanger, but that he had told Mr. Campensa the furnace had been repaired. Either way, Mr. Morrison and Mr. Campensa agree that Mr. Campensa told Mr. Morrison that the heat exchanger had been repaired.

Mr. Morrison did a second walkthrough of the house, this time with an inspector. He testified that his purpose for having the inspector look at the house with him was to try to estimate the cost of needed repairs and to "generally just look [ ] around the property." The utilities were still off at the time of his second walkthrough. During the second walkthrough, Mr. Morrison concluded that the kitchen floor would have to be replaced. He and his inspector also noted some problems with windows and drywall. They looked at the sticker on the furnace, but did not attempt to independently determine whether the heat exchanger had been repaired.

Following his second walkthrough, Mr. Morrison made a written offer to purchase the house for $40,000, using a form real estate purchase agreement. The form included a provision permitting Mr. Morrison to have the house inspected and, if not satisfied, to notify Mr. Bare within fourteen days of the date of the agreement. If any unsatisfactory conditions could not be resolved, Mr. Morrison could void the agreement or accept the property in its "as is" condition. The form further provided that, if Mr. Morrison did not have the home inspected or did not notify Mr. Bare of any unsatisfactory conditions, he would take the property in its "as is" condition.

Under the heading "Special Conditions," Mr. Morrison wrote: "Seller to supply buyer with copy of furnace repair bill from 2004 within 14 days." Mr. Campensa acknowledged at his deposition that the purpose of the "special condition" was to allow Mr. Morrison to satisfy himself that the heat exchanger had been repaired. At the same time he signed the written offer, Mr. Morrison also signed a property disclosure form in which he acknowledged that he was purchasing the property "as is."

Four days after he made his written offer, Mr. Morrison signed an amendment to that offer, removing his right to inspect the property. The amendment further provided that Mr. Morrison recognized that neither Mr. Bare nor Mr. Campensa was warranting the property in any manner:

> In exercising or waiving their right to inspect, the Buyer(s) are not relying upon any representation about the property made by the Seller(s), Broker(s), Agent(s), other than those representations specified in the purchase agreement. The Buyer(s) understand that the Seller(s), Broker(s), Agent(s), and/or inspector(s) do not warrant or guarantee the condition of the property in any manner whatsoever.

Three days later, Mr. Bare signed both the form purchase agreement and the amendment, thereby accepting Mr. Morrison's offer to purchase the house.

Prior to the date set for closing, Mr. Campensa obtained a copy of the 2004 furnace repair bill. That bill indicated that repairs totaling $234 had been made to the furnace, but that the heat exchanger had not been repaired. In fact, it included a quote to replace the furnace for $1600 and a notation that, if a new furnace was installed within 30 days, the $234 for repairs would be deducted from the cost of the new furnace.

Mr. Campensa telephoned Mr. Morrison and told him that the heat exchanger had not been repaired. At that point, Mr. Morrison told Mr. Campensa that he would close on the house only if Mr. Bare either replaced the furnace or reduced the purchase price in an amount equal to what it would cost to replace the furnace. Mr. Bare was unwilling to do either.

Mr. Campensa sent Mr. Morrison a copy of the bill, along with a proposed addendum to the purchase agreement. The proposed addendum provided that Mr. Morrison agreed to accept the property with the furnace "in its as is condition and assume all responsibility for its repair and/or replacement." Mr. Morrison refused to execute the proposed addendum.

Prior to the date set for closing, Mr. Morrison filed his complaint in this case. Mr. Bare subsequently sold the house to another purchaser, who refurbished it and rented it to college students. . . .

MR. MORRISON'S CONTRACT CLAIMS

. . . .

By his second cause of action, Mr. Morrison sought damages for breach of contract. Mr. Bare has argued that the "special condition" was satisfied when he provided Mr. Morrison a copy of the 2004 bill for repairs to the furnace, even though, instead of showing that the heat exchanger had been repaired, it showed that it had not been repaired.

There can be no doubt that, in order to satisfy the "special condition" that Mr. Morrison included in his offer, the repair bill had to show that the heat exchanger had been repaired. Mr. Campensa, who was Mr. Bare's agent, acknowledged that the purpose of the "special condition" was to allow Mr. Morrison to satisfy himself that the heat exchanger had been fixed:

Q.   All right. On line 103 it says, "Seller to supply buyer with copy of furnace repair bill from 2004 within 14 days," correct?

A.   Correct.

Q.   Why was that provision put in the contract?

A.   Because there was the potential that that was cracked in there was a cracked thing and Jack wanted to know if it was fixed or not.

Q.   Okay. Because you believed it had been repaired based on your conversation with Jonas Bare, correct?

A.   Yes.

Q.   And you had told Jack that it had been repaired, did you not?

A.   Yes.

Q.   So Jack wanted to make sure as part of this deal that that furnace had already been repaired, correct?

A.   Correct.

Mr. Bare's argument that he satisfied the condition by supplying a bill showing that the heat exchanger had not been repaired is, at best, disingenuous. Both parties knew at the time they entered the contract that the bill Mr. Bare needed to supply to satisfy the "special condition" was a bill showing that the heat exchanger had been repaired.

That, however, does not mean that Mr. Bare breached the purchase agreement by not delivering a bill that showed the heat exchanger had been repaired and by not replacing the furnace or lowering the purchase price. To begin with, the contract does not include a promise by Mr. Bare that, if the heat exchanger was not repaired in 2004, he would replace the furnace or reduce the purchase price. Further, the "special condition" that Mr. Morrison included in the contract was just that, a condition, not a promise:

[P]romise and condition are very clearly different in character. One who makes a promise thereby expresses an intention that some future performance will be rendered and gives assurance of its rendition to the promisee. Whether the promise is express or implied, there must be either words or conduct by the promisor by the interpretation of which the court can discover promissory intention; a condition is a fact or an event and is not an expression of intention or an assurance. A promise in a contract creates a legal duty in the promisor and a right in the promisee; the fact or event constituting a condition creates no right or duty and is merely a limiting or modifying factor.

8 Catherine M.A. McCauliff, *Corbin on Contracts*, Section 30.12 (rev. ed.1999).

Mr. Campensa told Mr. Morrison that the heat exchanger had been repaired. Mr. Morrison made his offer to purchase the house contingent upon receiving proof that it had been:

In contract law, "condition" is an event, other than the mere lapse of time, that is not certain to occur but must occur to *activate* an existing contractual duty, unless the condition is excused. The fact or event properly called a condition occurs during the *performance* stage of a contract, i.e., after the contract is formed and prior to its discharge.

John Edward Murray Jr., *Murray on Contracts*, Section 99B (4th ed.2001) (emphasis in original); Restatement (Second) of Contracts, Section 224 (1981). While the failure to perform a promise is a breach of contract, the failure to satisfy a condition is not:

A promise is always made by the act or acts of one of the parties, such acts being words or other conduct expressing intention. A fact can be made to operate as a condition only by the agreement of both parties or by the construction of the law. The purpose of a promise is to create a duty in the promisor. The purpose of constituting some fact as a condition is always the postponement or discharge of an instant duty (or other specified legal relation). The non-fulfillment of a promise is called a breach of contract, and creates in the other party a secondary right to damages. It is the failure to perform a legal duty. The non-occurrence of a condition will prevent the existence of a duty in the other party; but it may not create any remedial rights and duties at all, and it will not unless someone has promised that it shall occur.

Corbin on Contracts, at Section 30.12.

The fact that, to satisfy the "special condition," Mr. Bare would have had to do something (supply the bill showing that the heat exchanger had been repaired) did not mean that it was a promise rather than a condition. A condition can be an act to be done by one of the parties to the contract:

Virtually any act or event may constitute a condition. The event may be an act to be performed or forborne by one of the parties to the contract, an act to be performed or forborne by a third party, or some fact or event over which neither party, or any other party, has any control.

Murray on Contracts, at Section 99C. In this case, Mr. Bare had partial control over the condition. Even if he had a bill showing that the heat exchanger had been repaired in 2004, he could have chosen not to deliver it to Mr. Morrison, in which case the condition would not have been satisfied. It also, however, was partially out of his control. Since the heat exchanger had not been repaired in 2004, he was unable to satisfy the condition. The material part of the condition was that Mr. Morrison had to be satisfied that the heat exchanger had been repaired. . . .

. . .

In this case, Mr. Morrison's duty to pay the purchase price did not come due because Mr. Bare could not produce a 2004 bill showing that the heat exchanger had been repaired. . . .

By informing Mr. Campensa that he was unwilling to close on the house unless Mr. Bare replaced the furnace or reduced the purchase price, Mr. Morrison chose to treat his duty to pay the original purchase price as discharged and the contract as terminated. His proposal to go forward under different conditions was, in effect, an offer to enter into a new contract; a new contract that Mr. Bare was free to reject, which he did.

Upon the failure of the "special condition" that he included in the real estate purchase agreement, Mr. Morrison treated the agreement as terminated, as he was entitled to do. The failure of the "special condition" was not a breach of contract. . . .

Judgment affirmed.

Internatio-Rotterdam, Inc. v. River Brand Rice Mills, Inc.

INTERNATIO-ROTTERDAM, INC., Plaintiff-Appellant

v.

RIVER BRAND RICE MILLS, INC., Defendant-Appellee

United States Court of Appeals Second Circuit
259 F.2d 137 (2d Cir. 1958)

HINCKS, CIRCUIT JUDGE.

The defendant-appellee, a processor [and seller] of rice, in July 1952 entered into an agreement with the plaintiff-appellant, an exporter [and buyer of rice], for the sale of 95,600 pockets of rice. The terms of the agreement, evidenced by a purchase memorandum, indicated that the price per pocket was to be "$8.25 F.A.S. Lake Charles and/or Houston, Texas"; that shipment was to be "December, 1952, with two weeks call from buyer"; and that payment was to be by "irrevocable letter of credit to be opened immediately payable against" dock receipts and other specified documents.

In the fall, the appellant, which had already committed itself to supplying this rice to a Japanese buyer, was unexpectedly confronted with United States export restrictions upon its December shipments and was attempting to get an export license from the government. December is a peak month in the rice and cotton seasons in Louisiana and Texas, and the appellee became concerned about shipping instructions under the contract, since congested conditions prevailed at both the mills and the docks. The appellee seasonably elected to deliver 50,000 pockets at Lake Charles and on December 10 it received from the appellant instructions for the Lake Charles shipments. Thereupon it promptly began shipments to Lake Charles which continued until December 23, the last car at Lake Charles being unloaded on December 31.

December 17 was the last date in December which would allow appellee the two week period provided in the contract for delivery of the rice to the ports and ships designated. Prior thereto, the appellant had been having difficulty obtaining either a ship or a dock in this busy season in Houston. On December 17, the appellee had still received no shipping instructions for the 45,600 pockets destined for Houston. On the morning of the 18th, the appellee rescinded the contract for the Houston shipments, although continuing to make the Lake Charles deliveries. It is clear that one of the reasons for the prompt cancellation of the contract was the rise in market price of rice from $8.25 per pocket, the contract price, to $9.75. The appellant brought this suit for refusal to deliver the Houston quota.

Business Lingo

"F.A.S" stands for "Free Along Side" and "F.A.S. Lake Charles and/or Houston" means the seller is required to deliver the goods to a named port (in Lake Charles or Houston, Texas) alongside a vessel designated by the buyer. "Alongside" means that the goods are within reach of the ship's lifting tackle. "Dock receipts" are documents issued by an ocean carrier to acknowledge receipt of freight. The contract required Internatio-Rotterdam to obtain financing that guaranteed payment to River Brand once it presented the dock receipts evidencing its delivery of the goods.

FYI

It appears that under the contract provisions, the seller had the option of specifying the port for delivery (Lake Charles or Houston) but the buyer had to issue the call for the goods to be delivered and had to identify the ship alongside which the goods would be delivered.

. . . .

The area of contest is also considerably reduced by the appellant's candid concession that the appellee's duty to ship, by virtue of the two-week notice provision, did not arise until two weeks after complete shipping instructions had been given by the appellant. Thus on brief the appellant says: "we concede (as we have done from the beginning) that on a fair interpretation of the contract appellant had a duty to instruct appellee by December 17, 1952 as to the place to which it desired appellee to ship . . . and that, being late with its instructions in this respect, appellant could not have demanded delivery (at either port) until sometime after December 31, 1952." This position was taken, of course, with a view to the contract provision for shipment "December, 1952": a two-week period ending December 31 would begin to run on December 17. But although appellant concedes that the two weeks' notice to which appellee was entitled could not be shortened by the failure to give shipping instructions on or before December 17, it stoutly insists that upon receipt of shipping instructions subsequent to December 17 the appellee thereupon became obligated to deliver within two weeks thereafter. We do not agree.

It is plain that a giving of the notice by the appellant was a condition precedent to the appellee's duty to ship. Corbin on Contracts, Vol. 3, § 640. Id. § 724. Obviously, the appellee could not deliver free alongside ship, as the contract required, until the appellant identified its ship and its location. Jacksboro Stone Co. v. Fairbanks Co., 48 Tex. Civ. App. 639, 107 S.W. 567; Fortson Grocery Co. v. Pritchard Rice Milling Co., Tex. Civ. App., 220 S.W. 1116. Thus the giving of shipping instructions was what Professor Corbin would classify as a "promissory condition": the appellant promised to give the notice and the appellee's duty to ship was conditioned on the receipt of the notice. Op. cit. § 633, p. 523, § 634, footnote 38. The crucial question is whether that condition was performed. And that depends on whether the appellee's duty of shipment was conditioned on notice on or before December 17, so that the appellee would have two weeks wholly within December within which to perform, or whether, as we understand the appellant to contend, the appellant could perform the condition by giving the notice later in December, in which case the appellee would be under a duty to ship within two weeks thereafter. The answer depends upon the proper interpretation of the contract: if the contract properly interpreted made shipment in December of the essence then the failure to give the notice on or before December 17 was nonperformance by the appellant of a condition upon which the appellee's duty to ship in December depended.

In the setting of this case, we hold that the provision for December delivery went to the essence of the contract. In support of the plainly stated provision of the contract there was evidence that the appellee's mills and the facilities appurtenant thereto were working at full capacity in December when the rice market was at peak activity and that appellee had numerous other contracts in January as well as in December to fill. It is reasonable to infer that in July, when the contract was made, each party wanted the protection of the specified delivery period; the appellee so that it could schedule its production without undue congestion of its storage facilities and the appellant so that it could surely meet commitments which it in turn should make to its customers. There was also evidence that prices on the rice market were fluctuating. In view of this factor it is not reasonable to infer that when the contract was made in July for December delivery, the parties intended that the appellant should have an option exercisable subsequent to December 17 to postpone delivery until January. United Irr. Co. v. Carson Petroleum Co., Tex. Civ. App., 283 S.W. 692; Steiner v. United States, D.C., 36 F. Supp. 496. That in effect would have given the appellant an option to postpone its breach of the contract, if one should then be in prospect, to a time when, so far as could have been foreseen when the contract was made, the price of rice might be falling. A postponement in such circumstances would inure to the disadvantage of the appellee who was given no reciprocal option. Further indication that December delivery was of the essence is found in the letter of credit which was provided for in the contract and established by the appellant. Under this letter, the bank was authorized to pay appellee only for deliveries "during December, 1952." It thus appears that the appellant's interpretation of the contract, under which the appellee would be obligated, upon receipt of shipping instructions subsequent to December 17, to deliver in January, would deprive the appellee of the security for payment of the purchase price for which it had contracted.

Since, as we hold, December delivery was of the essence, notice of shipping instructions on or before December 17 was not merely a "duty" of the appellant—as it concedes: it was a condition precedent to the performance which might be required of the appellee. The nonoccurrence of that condition entitled the appellee . . . to treat its contractual obligations as discharged. Corbin on Contracts, §§ 640, 724 and 1252; Williston on Sales, §§ 452, 457; Restatement, Contracts, § 262; National Commodity Corp. v. American Fruit Growers, 6 Terry 169, 45 Del. 169, 70 A.2d 28; Alpena Portland Cement Co. v. Backus, 8 Cir., 156 F. 944; Jungmann & Co. v. Atterbury Bros., Inc., 249 N.Y. 119, 163 N.E. 123; Arnolt Corp. v. Stansen Corp., 7 Cir., 189 F.2d 5. On December 18th the appellant unequivocally exercised its right to rescind. Having done so, its obligations as to the Houston deliveries under the contract were at an end. And of course its obligations would not revive thereafter when the appellant finally succeeded in obtaining an export permit, a ship and a dock and then gave shipping instructions; when it expressed willingness to accept deliveries in January; or when it accomplished a "liberalization" of the outstanding letter of credit whereby payments might be made against simple forwarder's receipts instead of dock receipts.

. . . .

Affirmed.

Peacock Construction Co. v. Modern Air Conditioning, Inc.

PEACOCK CONSTRUCTION CO., Defendant-Petitioner

v.

MODERN AIR CONDITIONING, INC. and OVERLY
MANUFACTURING CO., Plaintiffs-Respondents

Supreme Court of Florida
353 So. 2d 840 (Fla. 1977)

Boyd, Acting Chief Justice.

We issued an order allowing certiorari in these two causes because the decisions in them of the District Court of Appeal, Second District, conflict with the decision in Edward J. Gerrits, Inc. v. Astor Electric Service, Inc., 328 So. 2d 522 (Fla. 3d DCA 1976). The two causes have been consolidated for all appellate purposes in this Court because they involve the same issue. That issue is whether the plaintiffs, Modern Air Conditioning and Overly Manufacturing, were entitled to summary judgments against Peacock Construction Company in actions for breaches of identical contractual provisions.

Peacock Construction was the builder of a condominium project. Modern Air Conditioning subcontracted with Peacock to do the heating and air conditioning work and Overly Manufacturing subcontracted with Peacock to do the "rooftop swimming pool" work. Both written subcontracts provided that Peacock would make final payment to the subcontractors,

> "within 30 days after the completion of the work included in this sub-contract, written acceptance by the Architect and full payment therefor by the Owner."

Modern Air Conditioning and Overly Manufacturing completed the work specified in their contracts and requested final payment. When Peacock refused to make the final payments the two subcontractors separately brought actions in the Lee County Circuit Court for breach of contract. In both actions it was established that no deficiencies had been found in the completed work. But Peacock established that it had not received from the owner full payment for the subcontractors' work. And it defended on the basis that such payment was a condition which, by express term of the final payment provision, had to be fulfilled before it was obligated to perform under the contract. On motions by the plaintiffs, the trial judges granted summary judgments in their favor. The orders of judgment implicitly interpreted the contract not to require payment by the owner as a condition precedent to Peacock's duty to perform.

The Second District Court of Appeal affirmed the lower court's judgment in the appeal brought by [Peacock]. In so doing it adopted the view of the majority of jurisdictions in this country that provisions of the kind disputed here do not set conditions precedent but rather constitute absolute promises to pay, fixing payment by the owner as a reasonable time for when payment to the subcontractor is to be made. When the judgment in the *Overly Manufacturing* case reached the Second District Court, *Modern Air Conditioning* had been decided and the judgment, therefore, was affirmed on the authority of the latter decision. These two decisions plainly conflict with *Gerrits*, supra.

In *Gerrits*, the Court had summarily ordered judgment for the plaintiff/subcontractor against the defendant/general contractor on a contractual provision for payment to the subcontractor which read,

> "The money to be paid in current funds and at such times as the General Contractor receives it from the Owner."

Id. at 523.

In its review of the judgment, the Third District Court of Appeal referred to the fundamental rule of interpretation of contracts that it be done in accordance with the intention of the parties. Since the defendant had introduced below the issue of intention, a material issue, and since the issue was one that could be resolved through a factual determination by the jury, the Third District reversed the summary judgment and remanded for trial.

Peacock urges us to adopt *Gerrits* as the controlling law in this State. It concedes that the Second District's decisions are backed by the weight of authority. But it argues that they are incorrect because the issue of intention is a factual one which should be resolved after the parties have had an opportunity to present evidence on it. Peacock urges, therefore, that the causes be remanded for trial. If there is produced no evidence that the parties intended there be condition precedents, only then, says Peacock, should the judge, by way of a directed verdict for the subcontractors, be allowed to take the issue of intention from the jury.

The contractual provisions in dispute here are susceptible to two interpretations. They may be interpreted as setting a condition precedent or as fixing a reasonable time for payment. The provision disputed in *Gerrits* is susceptible to the same two interpretations. The questions presented by the conflict between these decisions, then, are whether ambiguous contractual provisions of the kind disputed here may be interpreted only by the factfinder, usually the jury, or if they should be interpreted as a matter of law by the court, and if so what interpretation they should be given.

Although it must be admitted that the meaning of language is a factual question, the general rule is that interpretation of a document is a question of law rather than of fact. 4 Williston on Contracts, 3rd Ed., § 616. If an issue of contract interpretation concerns the intention of parties, that intention may be determined from the written contract, as a matter of law, when the nature of the transaction lends itself to judicial interpretation. A number of courts, with whom we agree,

Think About It!

What policies support the competing rules being considered by the court? If you were the judge, which rule would you favor and why?

have recognized that contracts between small subcontractors and general contractors on large construction projects are such transactions. Cf. Thos. J. Dyer Co. v. Bishop International Engineering Co., 6 Cir., 303 F.2d 655 (1962). The reason is that the relationship between the parties is a common one and usually their intent will not differ from transaction to transaction, although it may be differently expressed.

That intent in most cases is that payment by the owner to the general contractor is not a condition precedent to the general contractor's duty to pay the subcontractors. This is because small subcontractors, who must have payment for their work in order to remain in business, will not ordinarily assume the risk of the owner's failure to pay the general contractor. And this is the reason for the majority view in this country, which we now join.

Our decision to require judicial interpretation of ambiguous provisions for final payment in subcontracts in favor of subcontractors should not be regarded as anti-general contractor. It is simply a recognition that this is the fairest way to deal with the problem. There is nothing in this opinion, however, to prevent parties to these contracts from shifting the risk of payment failure by the owner to the subcontractor. But in order to make such a shift the contract must unam-

Think About It!

How could the contractual language here have been clearer? What would you advise future subcontractor clients, in light of this ruling?

biguously express that intention. And the burden of clear expression is on the general contractor.

The decisions of the Second District Court of Appeal to affirm the summary judgments were correct. We adopt, therefore, these two decisions as the controlling law in Florida and we overrule *Gerrits*, to the extent it is inconsistent with this opinion.

The orders allowing certiorari in these two causes are discharged. It is so ordered.

Conditions of Satisfaction

One way an express condition may be used in a contract is to make one party's contractual duty conditional on the other party's (or a third party's) "satisfaction" with the other party's performance. For example, a contract for a commissioned painting might make the recipient's duty to pay dependent on his satisfaction with the painting the artist produces. Or an owner's duty to pay for construction work may be conditioned on the satisfaction of an architect or engineer. Because express conditions are subject to the rule of strict construction, we know that a conditioned event must occur precisely as articulated in the condition. But what does it mean to fulfill such a "condition of satisfaction"? Does it require showing that a reasonable person would be satisfied with the performance (an objective test) or that the designated person was in fact satisfied (a subjective test)?

The answer is, it depends. As with other contract terms, the question is what the parties meant by including a satisfaction clause. The parties may specify explicitly that satisfaction is to a subjective or objective standard (e.g., "the painting to be done to the subject's personal satisfaction" or "the structure to be completed to the satisfaction of the architect, whose approval will not be unreasonably withheld"). If they do not, the court considers the nature of the contract and its context, to determine what standard was understood. As one court explained:

> Where the satisfaction clause requires satisfaction as to such matters as commercial value or quality, operative fitness, or mechanical utility, dissatisfaction cannot be claimed unreasonably. In these contracts, an objective standard is applied to the satisfaction clause and the test is whether the performance would satisfy a reasonable person. . . .

> If, on the other hand, the satisfaction clause relates to matters involving fancy, personal taste, or judgment, then a subjective standard is applied, and the test is whether the party is actually satisfied. . . . Although application of a subjective standard to

a satisfaction clause would seem to give the obligor virtually unlimited latitude to avoid his duty of performance, such is not the case. In these situations, courts impose the limitation that the obligor act in good faith. . . . Thus, under the subjective standard, the promisor can avoid the contract as long as he is genuinely, albeit unreasonably, dissatisfied. Which standard applies in a given transaction is a matter of the actual or constructive intent of the parties, which, in turn, is a function of the express language of the contract, or the subject matter of the contract.[*]

The court also noted that even in a commercial context, where an objective standard might be expected, a subjective standard might be used if application of an objective standard would be impracticable. For example, in *Mattei v. Hopper*, 330 P.2d 625 (Cal. 1958), the purchaser of real estate intended for use as a shopping center was to tender payment if leases were obtained that were satisfactory to the purchaser. Although the commercial context would typically call for application of an objective standard, the court determined a subjective standard would apply because "the factors involved in determining whether a lease is satisfactory to the lessor are too numerous and varied to permit the application of a reasonable man standard . . . . This multiplicity of factors which must be considered in evaluating a lease shows that this case more appropriately falls within the . . . line of authorities dealing with 'satisfaction' clauses . . . involving fancy, taste, or judgment."

As noted, the court will first look to the express language of the contract to understand the satisfaction clause. If the intent is not clear, the court will then rely on other tools of contract interpretation. A few additional examples will provide a sense of how the courts make judgments on this issue:

In *Ard Dr. Pepper Bottling Co. v. Dr. Pepper Co.*, 202 F.2d 372 (5th Cir. 1953), Dr. Pepper Bottling Company granted Ard an exclusive license to bottle Dr. Pepper soda in a particular territory. The contract provided that Ard was to

at all times loyally and faithfully promote the sale of and secure thorough distribution of Dr. Pepper throughout every part of said territory and to all dealers therein, and to develop an increase in volume of sales of Dr. Pepper satisfactory to the

---

[*] Hutton v. Monograms Plus, Inc., 604 N.E.2d 200 (Ohio Ct. App. 1992).

Grantor. And in this connection, the Grantee agrees, represents and guarantees that the said territory included in this license . . . will be fully covered, solicited and worked by the Grantee in a systematic and business-like manner now, and at all times hereafter while this license agreement remains in effect. The determination and judgment of Dr. Pepper Company as to whether or not this clause is being complied with when made in good faith, shall be sole, exclusive and final, and such determination by the Dr. Pepper Company that this clause is not being complied with shall in addition to any other grounds herein mentioned, be grounds for forfeiture of this license at the option of Grantor.

Although the commercial context of this transaction might suggest that an objective standard should apply, the court determined that the language in the contract clearly expressed the intent that Dr. Pepper's satisfaction should be judged subjectively, limited only by the obligation of good faith. "Dr. Pepper was the party to be satisfied, not some imaginary reasonable person. It was not unreasonable for Dr. Pepper to reserve to its own business judgment the question of whether the agreement had been properly and faithfully performed. . . . If Ard would make out his case by proof of performance, such proof must extend to such perfect performance as would negative Dr. Pepper's good faith. The proof in this case fails by a wide margin to meet that exacting standard."

In *Hutton v. Monograms Plus, Inc.*, 604 N.E.2d 200 (Ohio Ct. App. 1992), David Hutton signed an agreement to purchase a monogramming franchise from MPI. A clause of the contract said that Hutton could cancel his franchise agreement with MPI and receive a refund of his $25,000 franchise fee if he was "unable . . . to obtain financing suitable to him" within ninety days of signing the agreement. One of the primary costs for Hutton was for leasing monogramming equipment. MPI offered terms for lease of the equipment, but Hutton rejected them because they were substantially less advantageous to him than the terms offered in a circular from MPI. He submitted a financing application to another company, but it was rejected due to Hutton's inadequate financial position. Hutton also submitted a loan application to a bank, which rejected the application because of insufficient collateral. Hutton subsequently requested a refund of the franchise fee from MPI. MPI refused, and Hutton sued. The appellate court concluded that the satisfaction clause appeared in a commercial contract and therefore would be understood as establishing an objective standard for satisfaction. "There was nothing unique about this commercial contract that would implicate a subjective assessment of Hutton's satisfaction. Indeed, this contract presents a classic example of an arm's-length business transaction in which reasonable business concerns, relevant to the financing of equipment, dictated the terms of the contract." The court remanded for a factual inquiry into whether Hutton was "unable" to obtain financing objectively suitable for him.

§ 5.4. Waiver and Excuse of Conditions

As we have seen, the requirement of strict satisfaction of express conditions can result in harsh consequences because it often means that contract performance of one or both parties is no longer due. As illustrated in cases already considered in this section, courts may use interpretative tools to avoid such outcomes. For example, in *Peacock*, page 660, the court interpreted the contract language to find that the contract clause created a due date, not an express condition. As explained above, courts may also interpret the meaning of a condition to find that it is satisfied, as by understanding a condition of satisfaction to impose an objective rather than a subjective standard, thus reducing the risk of non-compliance.

Courts have two additional tools at their disposal to alleviate the harshness of the requirement of strict compliance with express conditions:

- **Waiver:** finding that the person for whose protection the condition was placed in the contract has waived compliance with that condition, and

- **Excuse:** excusing the occurrence of the condition for equitable reasons, for example, to avoid disproportionate forfeiture, or because the condition was not satisfied because of interference by the party that would be benefited if the condition were enforced.

§ 5.4.1. Waiver of Conditions

Recall *Morrison v. Bare*, page 651. Morrison, noting a sticker on the furnace indicating that it had a cracked heat exchanger, wrote into the contract an express condition to his purchase of the house—that the seller deliver a furnace repair bill within 24 days showing the heat exchanger had already been fixed. Morrison added the condition so he could make sure the house he was buying had a fully operational furnace. The seller did not (and could not) satisfy the condition because he discovered that the heat exchanger had, in fact, not been repaired. Morrison asked the seller to lower the sale price, but the seller refused and sold the house to someone else. When Morrison sued for breach, the court held that "Mr. Morrison chose to treat his duty to pay the original purchase price as discharged and the contract as terminated." That is, the delivery of the repair bill was a condition on Morrison's duty to purchase, and when Morrison began to negotiate for a reduced price, he indicated he was not planning on paying the contract price and was therefore invoking the condition. In a part of the opinion not included earlier, the court observed, "Once it became clear that it was impossible for Mr. Bare to produce such a bill, Mr. Morrison could have excused the condition and closed on the property." In other words, Morrison could have waived satisfaction of the condition—"let it go" by informing Bare that he would not require compliance—had he wanted to proceed with the purchase at the negotiated price, but he chose not to.

Note that only the party protected by a condition—Morrison, in the example case—has the right to waive it. A party cannot waive a condition designed to protect the other party to the contract (so the seller could not have waived the requirement of producing the receipt). Nor can a party unilaterally waive a condition intended to protect both parties. That limitation is sensible; waiver is voluntarily relinquishing a right—saying "I don't have to perform, but I choose to do so anyway"—so the party who has the right to enforce the condition is the one who has a right to waive it.

A waiver must be communicated to be effective. As one court has noted, "A finding of waiver must be 'based upon an intention expressed in explicit language to forego a right, or upon conduct under the circumstances justifying an inference of a relinquishment of it.' . . . A waiver may be express or implied."* In effect, the "waiver" is a promise to perform despite the non-occurrence of the condition (see Restatement (Second) § 84), and that promise must be communicated as are other contractual promises. Morrison's waiver might have been conveyed expressly if he told the seller he intended to purchase even though bill showing repair hadn't been delivered, or implicitly if he reconfirmed a closing date for the sale after the deadline for delivery of the bill. Note that a waiver may be partial, so Morrison might have waived the due date for delivery of the bill ("It's fine to take an extra week to get me that bill") without waiving the entirety of the condition.

Because it is a one-sided action (not, for instance, a modification to the contract terms made with consideration), a waiver that excuses a condition may

---

* *Renovest Co. v. Hodges Development Corp.*, 600 A.2d 448 (N.H. 1991).

be retracted, unless retraction would be unjust because of reliance on the waiver by the other party. See Restatement (Second) § 84(2). Moreover, the concept of waiver will not apply if waiving the condition will amount to a material change in the obligations of the parties. So, for example, "[a] vendor that has made an offer coupled with an option contract to sell land on condition that the purchaser pay $100,000 cannot waive this condition. . . . An insurance company that has promised to pay the owner of a house $100,000 on condition that the house is destroyed by fire cannot waive that condition."* Examples of waivable conditions are those that "merely relate to the time or manner of the return performance or provide for the giving of notice or the supplying of proofs," such as conditions of notice and proof of loss or time of suit in insurance policies. Restatement (Second) § 84, cmt. d.

§ 5.4.2. Excuse of Condition to Avoid Forfeiture

Courts may exercise their equitable powers to alleviate the harshness of the strict compliance requirement for express conditions in situations where they decide that justice demands leniency. The most common situation is when the party who did not satisfy the condition would suffer "disproportionate forfeiture." The Restatement drafters explain that "forfeiture" means "the denial of compensation that results when [a party] loses his right to the agreed exchange after he has relied substantially, as by preparation or performance on the expectation of that exchange." To determine whether a forfeiture is "disproportionate"

> a court must weigh the extent of the forfeiture by [one party] against the importance to the [other party] of the risk from which he sought to be protected and the degree to which that protection will be lost if the non-occurrence of the condition is excused to the extent required to prevent forfeiture.

Restatement (Second) of Contracts § 229, Comment b. The following example and case illustrate the application of this concept.

Example CC: *Burger King Corp. v. Family Dining, Inc.*, 426 F. Supp. 485 (E.D. Pa. 1977).

Family Dining entered into a contract with Burger King under which Family Dining was to be granted the exclusive right to open and operate Burger King restaurants in Bucks and Montgomery Counties in Pennsylvania (the "exclusive territory"), provided Family Dining maintained

---

* Farnsworth, *Contracts* 527 (4th ed. 2004).

a specified schedule of opening one new restaurant a year for the next ten years. The pertinent contract language read:

> For a period of one year, beginning on the date hereof, [Burger King] will not operate or license others for the operation of any BURGER KING restaurant within the [exclusive territory] as long as [Family Dining] operates each BURGER KING restaurant pursuant to BURGER KING restaurant licenses . . . and faithfully performs each of the covenants contained.

> This agreement shall remain in effect and [Family Dining] shall retain the exclusive territory for a period of ninety (90) years from the date hereof, provided that at the end of one, two, three, four, five six, seven, eight, nine and ten years from the date hereof, and continuously thereafter during the next eighty years, Licensee has the . . . requisite number of BURGER KING restaurants in operation or under active construction. . . . .

> If at the end of either one, two, three, four, five, six, seven, eight, nine or ten years from the date hereof, or anytime thereafter during the next eighty (80) years, there are less than the respective requisite number of BURGER KING operations or under active construction in the "exclusive territory" pursuant to licenses by Company this agreement shall terminate and be of no further force and effect."

Family Dining opened the first three restaurants right on schedule. Family Dining encountered some delays in opening the fourth and sixth restaurants according to the schedule, but Burger King granted Family Dining extensions for those two openings. The fifth, seventh, and eight restaurants were opened on schedule. When Family Dining encountered delays in opening the last two restaurants, however, Burger King was not as accommodating. (The court suggested that this change in attitude was in part due to the change in management at Burger King, and in part due to Burger King's realization that the exclusive territory could support substantially more than the ten restaurants contemplated in the agreement.) After the deadline for opening all ten restaurants had passed, Burger King began warning Family Dining that it was in default under their contract. Family Dining proceeded to open the last two restaurants, despite Burger King's insistence that their agreement was terminated. Burger King sued to enjoin Family Dining from using the Burger King trademarks at these restaurants and asked the court for a declaratory judgment that the contract between the two parties was no longer in effect.

Analysis: The court declined to declare the agreement terminated, dismissing Burger King's suit. Burger King argued that Family Dining had breached its promise to open the restaurants according to the schedule prescribed in the contract, and that therefore, under the clear language of the contract, the contract was terminated, freeing Burger King to permit others to open restaurants in the exclusive territory. The court rejected this argument, holding that meeting the schedule for opening restaurants was not a *promise* by Family Dining, but instead a *condition subsequent*, "which operates to divest Family Dining of exclusivity." The court explained:

> Whether words constitute a condition or a promise is a matter of the intention of the parties to be ascertained from a reasonable construction of the language used, considered in light of the surrounding circumstances. . . . It seems clear that the true purpose of the [agreement] was to create a long-term promise of exclusivity to act as an inducement to Family Dining to develop [the exclusive territory] within a certain time frame. A careful reading of the agreement indicates that it raises no duties, as such, in Family Dining. . . . Failure to comply with the development rate operates to defeat liability on Burger King's promise of exclusivity.

Having found that the schedule was an express condition rather than a promise, the court proceeded to consider whether the condition had been waived by Burger King or was excused due to the "disproportionate forfeiture" by Family Dining. The court determined that Burger King had waived strict compliance with the schedule due to its pattern of granting extensions and failure to object to the delays until very late in the first ten years of the contract. Further, the court found that "if the right of exclusivity were to be distinguished by termination it would constitute a forfeiture. . . . [I]f Family Dining were forced to forfeit the right of exclusivity it would lose something of incalculable value based on its investment of time and money developing the area, the significant risks assumed and the fact that there remains some 76 years of exclusivity under the [agreement]. Such a loss would be without any commensurate breach on its part since the injury caused to Burger King by the delay is relatively modest and within definable limits. Thus, a termination of the [agreement] would result in an extreme forfeiture to Family Dining."

Reading Critically: *J.N.A Realty Corp.*

1. What is the condition identified in the contract? Why is it understood to be a condition rather than a promise?

2. What will happen if the condition is strictly enforced? Why is that consequence considered a forfeiture rather than simply the loss of an expectation under the contract?

3. According to the court, when should a condition be excused based on forfeiture? On remand, should the lower court enforce the condition or excuse it? Why?

4. Why would the dissenting judge deny relief, enforcing the strict requirements of the condition? Do you agree with the majority or with the dissent?

J.N.A. Realty Corp. v. Cross Bay Chelsea, Inc.

J.N.A. REALTY CORP., Petitioner-Appellee
CROSS BAY CHELSEA, INC. et al., Appellants-Respondents

Court of Appeals of New York
366 N.E.2d 1313 (N.Y. 1977)

WACHTLER, JUDGE.

J.N.A. Realty Corp., the owner of a building in Howard Beach, commenced this proceeding to recover possession of the premises claiming that the lease has expired. The lease grants the tenant, Cross Bay Chelsea, Inc., an option to renew and although the notice was sent, through negligence or inadvertence, it was not sent within the time prescribed in the lease. The landlord seeks to enforce the letter of the agreement. The tenant asks for equity to relieve it from a forfeiture.

The Civil Court, after a trial, held that the tenant was entitled to equitable relief. The Appellate Term affirmed, without opinion, but the Appellate Division, after granting leave, reversed and granted the petition. The tenant has appealed to this court.

Two primary questions are raised on the appeal. First, will the tenant suffer a forfeiture if the landlord is permitted to enforce the letter of the agreement.

Secondly, if there will be a forfeiture, may a court of equity grant the tenant relief when the forfeiture would result from the tenant's own neglect or inadvertence.

At the trial it was shown that J.N.A. Realty Corp. (hereafter JNA) originally leased the premises to Victor Palermo and Sylvester Vascellero for a 10-year term commencing on January 1, 1964. Paragraph 58 of the lease, which was attached as part of 12-page rider, granted the tenants an option to renew for a 10-year term provided "that Tenant shall notify the landlord in writing by registered or certified mail six (6) months prior to the last day of the term of the lease that tenant desires such renewal." The tenants opened a restaurant on the premises. In February, 1964 they formed the Foro Romano Corp. (Foro) and assigned the lease to the corporation.

By December of 1967 the restaurant was operating at a loss and Foro decided to close it down and offer it for sale or lease. In March, 1968 Foro entered into a contract with Cross Bay Chelsea, Inc. (hereafter Chelsea), to sell the restaurant and assign the lease. As a condition of the sale Foro was required to obtain a modification of the option to renew so that Chelsea would have the right to renew the lease for an additional term of 24 years.

The closing took place in June of 1968. First JNA modified the option and consented to the assignment. The modification, which consists of a separate document to be attached to the lease, states: "the Tenant shall have a right to renew this lease for a further period of Twenty-Four (24) years, instead of Ten (10) years, from the expiration of the original term of said lease . . . All other provisions of Paragraph # 58 in said lease, . . . shall remain in full force and effect, except as hereinabove modified." Foro then assigned the lease and sold its interest in the restaurant to Chelsea for $155,000. The bill of sale states that "the value of the fixtures and chattels included in this sale is the sum of $40,000 and that the remainder of the purchase price is the value of the leasehold and possession of the restaurant premises." At that point five and one-half years remained on the original term of the lease.

In the summer of 1968 Chelsea reopened the restaurant. JNA's president, Nicholas Arena, admitted on the stand that throughout the tenancy it regularly informed Chelsea in writing of its obligations under the lease, such as the need to pay taxes and insurance by certain dates. For instance on June 13, 1973 JNA sent a letter to Chelsea informing them that certain taxes were due to be paid. When that letter was sent the option to renew was due to expire in approximately two weeks but JNA made no mention of this. A similar letter was sent to Chelsea in September, 1973.

Arena also admitted that throughout the term of the tenancy he was "most assuredly" aware of the time limitation on the option. In fact there is some indication in the record that JNA had previously used this device in an attempt to evict another tenant. Nevertheless it was not until November 12, 1973 that JNA took any action to inform the tenant that the option had lapsed. Then it sent a letter noting that the date had passed and, the letter states, "not having heard from you as prescribed by paragraph # 58 in our lease we must assume you will vacate the premises" at the expiration of the original term, January 1, 1974. By letter dated November 16, 1973 Chelsea, through its attorney, sent written notice of intention to renew the option which, of course, JNA refused to honor.

At the trial Chelsea's principals claimed that they were not aware of the time limitation because they had never received a copy of paragraph 58 of the rider. They had received a copy of the modification but they had assumed that it gave them an absolute right to retain the tenancy for 24 years after the expiration of the original term. However, at the trial and later at the Appellate Division, it was found that Chelsea had knowledge of, or at least was "chargeable with notice" of, the time limitation in the rider and thus was negligent in failing to renew within the time prescribed.

Chelsea's principals also testified that they had spent an additional $15,000 on improvements, at least part of which had been expended after the option had expired. Toward the end of the trial JNA's attorney asked the court whether it would "take evidence from" Arena that he had negotiated with another tenant after the option to renew had lapsed. However, the court held that this testimony would be immaterial.

It is a settled principle of law that a notice exercising an option is ineffective if it is not given within the time specified (see, e.g., Restatement, Contracts 2d (Tent. Draft No. 1, 1964), § 64, subd. (b); 1A Corbin, Contracts (1963), § 264; 1 Williston, Contracts (3d ed. 1957), § 87; Sy Jack Realty Co. v. Pergament Syosset Corp., 27 N.Y.2d 449, 318 N.Y.S.2d 720, 267 N.E.2d 462). "At law, of course, time is always of the essence of the contract" (De Funiak, Modern Equity, § 80, p. 223). Thus the tenant had no legal right to exercise the option when it did, but to say that is simply to pose the issue; it does not resolve it. Of course the tenant would not be asking for equitable relief if it could establish its rights at law.

The major obstacle to obtaining equitable relief in these cases is that default on an option usually does not result in a forfeiture. The reason is that the option itself does not create any interest in the property, and no rights accrue until the condition precedent has been met by giving notice within the time specified. Thus equity will not intervene because the loss of the option does not ordinarily result in the forfeiture of any vested rights (see, e.g., *Fidelity & Columbia Trust Co. v. Levin,*

128 Misc. 838, 221 N.Y.S. 269, *aff'd,* 221 App.Div. 786, 223 N.Y.S.2d 866, *aff'd,* 248 N.Y. 551, 162 N.E. 521; *Doepfner v. Bowers,* 55 Misc. 561, 106 N.Y.S. 932; cf. *People's Bank of City of N. Y. v. Mitchell,* 73 N.Y. 406; but see *Noyes v. Anderson,* 124 N.Y. 175, 179–180, 26 N.E. 316, 317, where it is indicated that the "rule may not be without exception"). The general rule is customarily stated as follows: "There is a wide distinction between a condition precedent, where no title has vested and none is to vest until the condition is performed, and a condition subsequent, operating by way of a defeasance. In the former case equity can give no relief. The failure to perform is an inevitable bar. No right can ever vest. The result is very different where the condition is subsequent. There equity will interpose and relieve against the forfeiture". (*Davis v. Gray,* 16 Wall. (83 U.S.) 203, 229–230, 21 L.Ed. 447.) It has been suggested that even when the option has been paid for, nothing is forfeited when it expires, because the amount paid "is the exact agreed equivalent" of the power to exercise the right for the time allotted (*see* 1 Corbin, *Contracts,* § 35, p. 147).

But when a tenant in possession under an existing lease has neglected to exercise an option to renew, he might suffer a forfeiture if he has made valuable improvements on the property. This of course generally distinguishes the lease option, to renew or purchase, from the stock option or the option to buy goods. This was a distinction which some of the older cases failed to recognize (*see, e.g., Fidelity & Columbia Trust Co. v. Levin, supra; Doepfner v. Bowers, supra;* cf. *People's Bank of City of N. Y. v. Mitchell,* supra). More recently it has been noted that "although the tenant has no legal interest in the renewal period until the required notice is given, yet an equitable interest is recognized and protected against forfeiture in some cases where the tenant has in good faith made improvements of a substantial character, intending to renew the lease, if the landlord is not harmed by the delay in the giving of the notice and the lessee would sustain substantial loss in case the lease were not renewed" (2 Pomeroy, Equity Jurisprudence (5th ed.), § 453b, p. 296).

The leading case on this point is *Fountain Co. v. Stein,* 97 Conn. 619, 118 A. 47, 27 A.L.R. 976 and the rule has been accepted by noted commentators (see, e.g., 1 Corbin, op. cit., § 35, p. 146; 1 Williston, Contracts (3d ed.), § 76, p. 249, n. 4; 2 Pomeroy, op. cit., § 453b, p. 296). It has also been accepted and applied by this court. In *Jones v. Gianferante,* 305 N.Y. 135, 138, 111 N.E.2d 419, 420, citing the Fountain case we held that the tenant was entitled to "the benefit of the rule or practice in equity which relieves against such forfeitures of valuable lease terms when default in notice has not prejudiced the landlord, and has resulted from an honest mistake, or similar excusable fault." The rule was extended in *Sy Jack Realty Co. v. Pergament Syosset Corp.,* 27 N.Y.2d 449, 453, 318 N.Y.S.2d 720, 722, 267 N.E.2d 462, 464, *supra,* to preserve the tenant's interest in a "long-standing location for a retail business" because this is "an important part of the good will of that enterprise, [and thus] the tenant stands to lose a substantial and valuable asset."

In neither of those cases were we asked to consider whether the tenant would be entitled to equitable relief from the consequences of his own neglect or "mere forgetfulness" as the court had held in the Fountain case, supra. In Gianferante the default was due to an ambiguous lease, and in Sy Jack the notice was mailed but never delivered (but see *Roy's of North Syracuse v. P & C Food Markets*, 51 A.D.2d 641, 377 N.Y.S.2d 1019, mot. for lv. to app. den. 38 N.Y.2d 711, 384 N.Y.S.2d 1026, 348 N.E.2d 927; and the dissenting opn. in *Sy Jack, supra*, 27 N.Y.2d p. 456, n. 1, 318 N.Y.S.2d p. 725, 267 N.E.2d p. 466, where it is noted that the three cases cited in Williston the principle one being the Fountain case "obviously warranted equitable relief. For not only in those cases was there 'excusable fault', but also in each one the tenant had made substantial improvements"). But the principle involved is well established in this State. A tenant or mortgagor should not be denied equitable relief from the consequences of his own neglect or inadvertence if a forfeiture would result (*Giles v. Austin*, 62 N.Y. 486; *Noyes v. Anderson*, 124 N.Y. 175, 26 N.E. 316; *Roy's of North Syracuse v. P & C Food Markets, supra*; see, also, 2 Pomeroy, Equity Jurisprudence (5th ed.), § 452, p. 287). The rule applies even though the tenant or mortgagor, by his inadvertence, has neglected to perform an affirmative duty and thus breached a covenant in the agreement (Giles v. Austin, supra; Noyes v. Anderson, supra).

On occasion the court has cautioned that equitable relief would be denied where there has been a willful or gross neglect (*Noyes v. Anderson, supra*, 124 N.Y. p. 179, 26 N.E. p. 317), but it has been reluctant to employ the sanction when a forfeiture would result. In *Giles v. Austin, supra*, p. 491, for instance, the landlord sought to recover possession of the premises after the tenant had neglected to pay the taxes as required by a covenant in the lease. We held that although the tenant had not paid the taxes since the inception of the lease in 1859, and had only paid them after suit was commenced in 1868, the tenant's default was not "so willful, or his neglect so inexcusable, that a court of equity should have denied him any relief."

There are several cases in which this court has denied a tenant or mortgagor equitable relief because of his own neglect to perform within the time fixed in the lease or mortgage, but only when it has found that there was "no penalty, no forfeiture" (*Graf v. Hope Bldg. Corp.*, 254 N.Y. 1, 4, 171 N.E. 884, 885; *Fidelity & Columbia Trust Co. v. Levin*, 128 Misc. 838, 221

Make the Connection

Note Judge Cardozo's position in the cited case of *Graf v. Hope Bldg. Corp.* and compare his opinion in *Jacob & Youngs v. Kent* (page 692), in which he also contrasts the venial (that is, minor and easy to forgive) failure to follow contract terms with the grave hardship to be suffered if the contract were to be enforced as written.

N.Y.S. 269, *aff'd*, 221 App. Div. 786, 223 N.Y.S.2d 866, *aff'd*, 248 N.Y. 551, 162 N.E. 521, supra; *People's Bank of City of N. Y. v. Mitchell*, 73 N.Y. 406, *supra*). Cardozo took a different view. He felt that even though there may be no penalty or forfeiture "in a strict or proper sense" equity should "relieve against it if default has been due to mere venial inattention and if relief can be granted without damage to the lender". Even in those cases he would apply the general equitable principle that "the gravity of the fault must be compared with the gravity of the hardship" (*Graf v. Hope Bldg. Corp., supra*, 254 N.Y. pp. 9–10, 13, 171 N.E. p. 888 (Cardozo, Ch. J., dissenting); see, also, 2 Pomeroy, Equity Jurisprudence (5th ed.), § 439, p. 220).

Here, as noted, the tenant has made a considerable investment in improvements on the premises $40,000 at the time of purchase, and an additional $15,000 during the tenancy. In addition, if the location is lost, the restaurant would undoubtedly lose a considerable amount of its customer good will. The tenant was at fault, but not in a culpable sense. It was, as Cardozo says, "mere venial inattention." There would be a forfeiture and the gravity of the loss is certainly out of all proportion to the gravity of the fault. Thus, under the circumstances of this case, the tenant would be entitled to equitable relief if there is no prejudice to the landlord.

However, it is not clear from the record whether JNA would be prejudiced if the tenant is relieved of its default. Because of the trial court's ruling, JNA was unable to submit proof that it might be prejudiced if the terms of the agreement were not enforced literally. Its proof of other negotiations was considered immaterial. It may be that after the tenant's default the landlord, relying on the agreement, in good faith, made other commitments for the premises. But if JNA did not rely on the letter of the agreement then, it should not be permitted to rely on it now to exact a substantial forfeiture for the tenant's unwitting default. This, however, must be resolved at a new trial.

Finally we would note, as the dissenters do, that it is possible to imagine a situation in which a tenant holding an option to renew might intentionally delay beyond the time prescribed in order to exploit a fluctuating market. However, as the dissenters also note, there is no evidence to suggest that that is what occurred here. On the contrary there has been an affirmed finding of fact that the tenant's late notice was due to negligence. Of course a tenant who has intentionally delayed should not be relieved of a forfeiture simply because this tenant, who was merely inadvertent, may be granted equitable relief. But, on the other hand, we do not believe that this tenant, or any tenant, guilty only of negligence should be denied equitable relief because some other tenant, in some other case, may be found to have acted in bad faith. By its nature equitable relief must always depend on the facts of the particular case and not on hypotheticals.

Accordingly, the order of the Appellate Division should be reversed and a new trial granted.

Breitel, Chief Judge (dissenting).

Relieving the tenant of its negligent failure to exercise its option to renew a lease within the prescribed time upsets established precedent, introduces instability in business transactions, and disregards commercial realities. I therefore dissent.

This case involves an option to renew a lease, not a mortgage foreclosure or an acceleration clause in a lease or mortgage. The categories and applicable precedents are not to be confused.

. . . .

At issue is the availability of equitable relief to remedy a commercial tenant's failure, by the appointed date, to exercise its option to renew a lease when the only explanation is sheer negligence.

The order of the Appellate Division should be affirmed, and the landlord awarded possession. Mere negligence does not justify departing from the rule that notice of intention to exercise an option to renew must be given within the prescribed period. Equitable relief is never justified by the fact alone, always present, that the tenant will suffer some sort of economic detriment.

The record is unusually deficient in many respects. From it, however, may be culled what follows.

. . . .

. . . [In February 1968,] Peter and John Morfogen, principals of the present tenant Cross Bay Chelsea, responded to an advertisement in the New York Times and indicated their interest in purchasing the leasehold and the closed-down business.

The precise details of the initial conversations between the parties cannot be extracted from the record because they are included only in bits and pieces. Apparently, however, the prospective buyer, who at the time of trial was operating four other restaurants in Manhattan, Queens, and Nassau County, was ready to agree only if a 30-year lease could be arranged. To that effect, a meeting of the principals of landlord J.N.A., Foro, and Chelsea was held on March 16, 1968, and a "modification and extension of lease" agreement executed. While the modification agreement provided that the tenant have the "right to renew this lease for a further period of Twenty-Four (24) years, instead of Ten (10) years", it also continued in full force and effect "[a]ll other provisions of Paragraph # 58", which contained the requirement of six months' notice of election of the option to renew. The modified lease provided that a portion of the taxes and insurance premiums, and all of the interior repairs, be borne by the tenant. The starting rent reserved in the option was $1,000 per month.

J.N.A.'s principals attended this critical meeting without counsel, although the Chelsea principals, who now claim ignorance of the conditions to exercising the 24-year renewal option, were accompanied by their lawyer and an accountant. The transaction eventually involved a gross price of $155,000, much of it deferred, for the restaurant, fixtures, and the assignment of the leasehold. Of the $155,000, $40,000 was allocated to the chattels and fixtures, and the balance to the leasehold. Chelsea's lawyer also attended the June 8 closing of the transfer of the modified lease and the sale of the restaurant, following the March 16 lease modification meeting. Between the closing of the lease modification agreement in March, 1968 and the final closing in June, 1968, Chelsea arranged for a liquor license. Also before the June, 1968 closing, Chelsea had invested $15,000 in undescribed improvements in the premises. In short order the restaurant was reopened and was quite successful, or else this litigation would never have ensued.

On July 1, 1973, the date the renewal option was to be exercised, no notice or advice of any kind was sent or given to the landlord. It was not until November 16, 1973, some four and a-half months later, that Chelsea, in response to a letter from J.N.A., sent to the landlord a purported notice to exercise the option. J.N.A. refused to recognize the notice, and on March 4, 1974, instituted this holdover proceeding. The record is silent about the intervening period except to indicate that there were negotiations.

To excuse its failure to send a renewal notice by the July 1 deadline and to support a claim to equitable relief, Chelsea asserts that it never received a copy of the 12-page rider attached to the original lease. In addition to the 1968 modification agreement's reference to the 1963 rider, the entire lease, including that rider, was filed in April, 1968 with the Division of Alcoholic Beverage Control on Chelsea's preclosing application for a liquor license. While Chelsea contends that the 1963 rider found in the agency's file must have been taken from an earlier application submission, the trial court resolved this issue of fact in favor of the landlord. The Appellate Division expressly found that Chelsea had knowledge, or at least should be chargeable with notice, of the provisions of paragraph 58 of the 1963 rider requiring six months' notice to renew.

Chelsea contends that J.N.A.'s representative was on the premises in the summer of 1973, after law day had passed, and failed to comment when he saw that additional improvements were still being made. There is no evidence of what these improvements were, how extensive they were, their value, or whether they were fixed or movable fixtures or equipment. J.N.A. never conceded that the visits had occurred or that such post law day improvements had been made.

What's That?

"Law day" is archaic terminology for the day appointed for a debtor to discharge a mortgage or else forfeit the property to the lender. The words are used here to refer to the day on which notice to renew the lease was due to be given.

Had an honest mistake or similar "excusable fault", as opposed to what is undoubtedly mere carelessness, occasioned the tenant's tardiness, absent prejudice to the landlord, equitable relief would be available (e.g., *Sy Jack Realty Co. v. Pergament Syosset Corp.*, 27 N.Y.2d 449, 453, 318 N.Y.S.2d 720, 722, 267 N.E.2d 462, 464; *Jones v. Gianferante*, 305 N.Y. 135, 138, 111 N.E.2d 419). At issue, instead, is the availability of equitable relief where the only excuse for the commercial tenant's dilatory failure to exercise its option to renew is sheer carelessness.

Enough has been said to uncover a common situation. Experienced and even hardened businessmen at cross-purposes over the renewal of a valuable lease term seek on the one hand to stand by the written agreement, and on the other, to loosen the applicable rules to receive ad hoc adjustment of equities and relief from economic detriment. The landlord wants a higher return. The tenant wants to keep the old bargain. Which of the profit-seeking parties in this particular case should prevail as a matter of morals is not within the province of the courts. The well-settled doctrine is that with respect to options, whether they be lease renewal options, options to purchase real or personal property, or stock options, time is of the essence. The exceptions, namely, estoppel, fraud, mistake, accident, or overreaching, are few. Commercial stability and certainty are paramount, and always the dangers of unsolvable issues of fact and speculative manipulation (as with stock options) are to be avoided.

The landlord should be awarded possession of the premises in accordance with the undisputed language and manifested intention of the written lease, its 12-page rider, and modification. It does not suffice that the tenant may suffer an economic detriment in losing the renewal period. Nor does it suffice that the delay in giving notice may have caused the landlord no "prejudice", other than loss of the opportunity to relet the property or renegotiate the terms of a lease on a fresh basis. Once an option to renew a lease has been conditioned upon the tenant's giving timely notice, the commercial lessee should not be heard to complain that through carelessness a valued asset has been lost, anymore than one would allow the landlord to complain of the economic detriment to him in agreeing to an improvident option to renew.

The court unanimously accepts the general rule at law: an option to renew a commercial lease must be exercised within the appointed time period (*e.g., Sy Jack Realty Co. v. Pergament Syosset Corp.*, 27 N.Y.2d 449, 452, 318 N.Y.S.2d 720, 721, 267 N.E.2d 462, 463, *supra*, and authorities cited; *see Restatement, Contracts 2d* (*Tent. Draft Nos. 1–7, 1973*), § 64, *Comment f; 34 N.Y. Jur., Landlord and Tenant,* §§ 418–419; 51C C.J.S. *Landlord & Tenant* § 59). Underlying the bar to equitable relief is the theory that until the condition precedent is fulfilled, that is, until the required timely notice is given, there is no "forfeiture" for which equity will extend protection (*Fidelity & Columbia Trust Co. v. Levin*, 128 Misc. 838, 844–845, 221 N.Y.S. 269, 275–276, *aff'd*, 221 App. Div. 786, 223 N.Y.S.2d 866, *aff'd*, 248 N.Y. 551, 162 N.E. 521; 2 Pomeroy, Equity Jurisprudence (5th ed.), § 453b, p. 296). While the rule has been bolstered by traditional concepts of estates in land, its basis has current commercial and economic validity.

In this State, as in others, relief has been afforded tenants threatened with loss of an expected renewal period (see, generally, Effect of Lessee's Failure or Delay in Giving Notice Within Specified Time, of Intention to Renew Lease, Ann., 44 A.L.R.2d 1359, esp. 1362–1369). But in New York, as elsewhere, the circumstances conditioning such relief have been carefully limited. It is only where the tenant can show, not mere negligence, but an excuse such as fraud, mistake, or accident, that is, one or more of the categories common and integral to invocation of equity, that courts have, despite the literal agreement and intention of the parties, stepped in to prevent a loss (see, e.g., *Jones v. Gianferante*, 305 N.Y. 135, 138–139, 111 N.E.2d 419, 420, *supra*; 1 McAdam, *Landlord and Tenant* (5th ed.), § 156, pp. 721–722).

Even in the case of excusable default by the tenant the court looks to the investment the tenant has made to bolster his right to equitable relief. But the fact of tenant investment alone is not enough to justify intervention. Thus, in the leading cases excusing the tenant's late notice, mention is perforce made of investments and improvements (e.g., *Sy Jack Realty Co. v. Pergament Syosset Corp.*, 27 N.Y.2d 449, 453, 318 N.Y.S.2d 720, 722, 267 N.E.2d 462, 464, *supra; Jones v. Gianferante*, 305 N.Y. 135, 138, 111 N.E.2d 419, *supra*). But the loss or "forfeiture" of these investments was not alone the trigger to granting relief. Indispensable is the existence of some mistake or excusable default. Thus, in *Jones v. Gianferante, supra*, p. 138, 111 N.E.2d p. 419, an ambiguous term in the lease excused the tenant's failure. And in *Sy Jack v. Pergament, supra*, 27 N.Y.2d p. 453, 318 N.Y.S.2d p. 722, 267 N.E.2d p. 464, it was reliance on the post office to deliver the notice, mailed three days before law day, that was forgiven. In no case of accepted or acceptable authority, however, were improvements alone enough to help the negligent tenant.

The majority facilely disposes of the tenant's delinquency in exercising its option by relying on cases in which a party, notwithstanding its negligence, was relieved from a forfeiture (*e.g., Giles v. Austin*, 62 N.Y. 486, 493–494, *a conditional limitation in a lease; Noyes v. Anderson,* 124 N.Y. 175, 182–183, 26 N.E. 316, 318, mortgagor's failure to pay an assessment). But indiscriminate application of principles evolved to deal with mortgage foreclosures or a lessor's right to re-enter upon a tenant's failure to pay taxes and assessments when due does not withstand analysis. Since ever so long, enforcement of a mortgage has rested in equity (see *Jamaica Sav. Bank v. M. S. Investing Co.,* 274 N.Y. 215, 219, 8 N.E.2d 493, 494; 38 N.Y. Jur., Mortgages and Deeds of Trust, § 317). It is also significant that as to foreclosure, time is not of the essence (see 10 N.Y. Jur., Contracts, s 270). Even where acceleration clauses are involved and a strong argument can be made for allowing relief, time has been of the essence and negligence has not been excused (see *Graf v. Hope Bldg. Corp.,* 254 N.Y. 1, 4, 7, 171 N.E. 884, 885, 886 (dissenting opn. per Cardozo, Ch. J.)). It is equally inappropriate to analogize to a lessee's failure to comply with a lease requirement that taxes and assessments be paid as they become due (see *Giles v. Austin, supra,* 62 N.Y. pp. 493–494). For the loss of an existing lease term subject to a condition subsequent distinguishes that situation from the loss of a possible option period subject to a condition precedent. An option is a right to purchase or acquire an interest in personal or real property in the future, and, if precise, it carries an invulnerable requirement to comply with all conditions, including that of time which is therefore of the essence in law and equity.

There are cases, not binding on this court, which express the principles discussed. For reasons that are not persuasive they would distinguish, however, between mere neglect or forgetfulness and gross or willful negligence, whatever that might be (see *Fountain Co. v. Stein,* 97 Conn. 619, 626–627, 118 A. 47; *Xanthakey v. Hayes,* 107 Conn. 459, 469, 140 A. 808; *see, generally,* 1 Williston, *Contracts* (3d ed.), § 76, p. 249, n. 4). This is not a distinction generally accepted and is hardly a pragmatic one to apply in an area where the opportunities for distortion and manipulation are so great. The instability and uncertainty would be dangerous and would allow for ad hoc dispensations in particular cases without reliable rule so essential to commercial enterprise.

To begin with, under the guise of sheer inadvertence, a tenant could gamble with a fluctuating market, at the expense of his landlord, by delaying his decision beyond the time fixed in the agreement. The market having resolved in favor of exercising the option, the landlord, even though the day appointed in the agreement has passed, could be held to the return set out in the option, although if the market had resolved otherwise, the tenant could not be held to the renewal period.

None of this is to say that the tenant in this case was guilty of any manipulation. Hardly so. But what the court is concerned with is a rule for this case which perforce must cover other cases of like kind, where there will be no assurance that the "forgetfulness" is no more than that. The worst of the matter is that the kind of paltry record made in this case is hardly one on which a new rule with potential for mischief should be based. When the option, especially one requiring notice well in advance of the expiration of the lease, permits of economic manipulation, in commercial fairness the parties, especially if represented by counsel, should be held to their bargain, if plainly expressed.

Considering investments in the premises or the renewal term a "forfeiture" as alone warranting equitable relief would undermine if not dissolve the general rule upon which there is agreement. For, it is difficult to imagine a dilatory commercial tenant, particularly one in litigation over a renewal, who would not or could not point, scrupulously or unscrupulously, to some threatened investment in the premises, be it a physical improvement or the fact of good will. As a practical matter, it is not unreasonable to expect the commercial tenant, as compared with his residential counterpart, to protect his business interests with meticulousness, a meticulousness to which he would hold his landlord. All he, or his lawyer, need do is red-flag the date on which he has to act.

Having established no excuse, other than its own carelessness, Chelsea's claim is unfounded. Even if Chelsea honestly thought it enjoyed a 30-year lease, it does not change the result. Nor is it helpful to argue that Chelsea, always represented by a lawyer, was unable to procure a copy of the entire lease agreement. Indeed, it borders on the utterly incredible that experienced, sophisticated businessmen and their lawyers would not have assembled and scrutinized every relevant document affecting a long-term lease covering, with a renewal, a 30-year period.

That adherence to well-settled principles, like a Statute of Limitations or a Statute of Frauds works a hardship on some does not, alone, permit a court to depart from sound doctrine and principles. Even if precedent did not control the same doctrines and principles discussed should be applied.

Accordingly, I dissent and vote that the order of the Appellate Division should be affirmed, and the landlord awarded possession of the premises.

Test Your Knowledge

To assess your understanding of the material in this chapter, click here to take a quiz.

CHAPTER 9

Performance, Breach, and Excuse

| How do parties demonstrate assent to a contract? | What kinds of promises will the law enforce? | What defenses to enforcement exist? | Is a writing required for enforcement? If so, what kind? | How is the content and meaning of a contract determined? | What are parties' rights and duties after breach? |

| What situations lead to excusing contract performance? | What remedies are available for breach of contract? | What contractual rights and duties do non-parties to a contract have? |

Table of Contents

§ 1. Introduction..684

§ 2. Implied Conditions and Order of Performance....................................685

    PROBLEMS: IMPLIED CONDITIONS (9-1, 9-2)...688

§ 3. Performance and Breach Under the Common Law 690

    § 3.1. Implied Conditions and the Doctrine of Substantial
    Performance...690

        Jacob & Youngs v. Kent...692

        PROBLEM: IMPLIED VERSUS EXPRESS CONDITIONS (9-3) 700

    § 3.2. Substantial Performance or Material Breach?..............................701

        PROBLEMS: SUBSTANTIAL PERFORMANCE OR MATERIAL BREACH? (9-4,
        9-5)..705

    § 3.3. Partial or Total Breach? 706

        Sackett v. Spindler..711

        PROBLEMS: PARTIAL OR TOTAL BREACH? (9-6, 9-7)..................................717

§ 4. Repudiation...724

    § 4.1. Defining Repudiation (Renunciation) 725

§ 4.2. Anticipatory Repudiation...728

    Hochster v. De la Tour 729

§ 4.3. Reasonable Insecurity About Future Performance 733

    PROBLEM: RIGHT TO ADEQUATE ASSURANCE (9-8) 736

    Hornell Brewing Co. v. Spry 737

§ 5. **Performance and Breach Under UCC Article 2** 745

    PROBLEM: PERFORMANCE UNDER UCC ARTICLE 2 (9-9).............................747

§ 6. **Excuse from Performance: Impossibility, Impracticability, and Frustration of Purpose** 748

§ 6.1. Impossibility 748

    Taylor v. Caldwell 749

§ 6.2. Impossibility Broadens into Impracticability 754

§ 6.3. Frustration of Purpose...762

    Krell v. Henry...762

    Adbar, L.C. v. New Beginnings C-Star 770

§ 6.4. When *Do* Courts Grant Excuse? 776

    PROBLEMS: IMPOSSIBILITY, IMPRACTICABILITY, AND FRUSTRATION OF PURPOSE (9-10, 9-11) 779

§ 1. Introduction

Once a contract is formed, the performance stage of the contract begins. Performance may involve, for example, providing services, delivering goods, conveying real estate, performing construction work, assigning contract rights, or paying the price for performance by the other party. In all but the simplest of contracts, performance will likely involve multiple acts by the parties, at different times over the course of the contract.

With performance comes the possibility of breach—performance that does not match the contract's terms (express and implied). In contracts involving multiple acts by the parties over extended time periods, there are many moments when breach may occur. Breaches come in many varieties:

- Repudiation (a party renounces the contract and refuses to perform)

- Nonperformance

- Late performance

- Incomplete or faulty performance (failing to finish performance, or performing defectively)

- Wrongfully rejecting the other party's performance

- Failure to perform in good faith

Once a breach occurs, attention turns to determining the consequences. This chapter focuses on the initial question for the aggrieved party: At what point is she entitled to respond to the other party's breach by terminating her own performance or by suspending her performance and demanding the breaching party cure the breach? The picture becomes more complicated if both parties breach (or are accused of breach), as may occur in complex transactions involving multiple acts of performance on both sides. Either or both parties may have the right to suspend or terminate performance. Finally, if certain unexpected circumstances arise during contract performance, a party's duty to perform may be excused, under the doctrine of impossibility, impracticability, or frustration of purpose.

Chapter 10 focuses on the second question for the aggrieved party: What remedies are available for breach? Whether or not the parties continue to perform under the contract after a breach, the aggrieved party will ultimately be entitled to money damages to compensate for injury caused by the breach and, in special circumstances, may be entitled to an equitable remedy such as specific performance (an order to perform contract obligations).

The concepts covered in this chapter—suspension or termination of performance after breach and excuse of performance after changed circumstances—are among the most important tools for transactional lawyers advising clients during the performance of contracts that are veering into breach. Skillful use of these tools may help your clients avoid a breach of contract lawsuit or put your client in the best possible position if a lawsuit ultimately is filed.

§ 2. Implied Conditions and Order of Performance

Chapter 8 introduced the concept of conditions related to contractual promises. The focus in Chapter 8 was on express conditions, explicitly identified events (conditions) on which a contractual duty depends. You encountered the rule of strict compliance for express conditions: The condition must be satisfied completely before the consequence of the condition comes to pass. Chapter 8 also introduced the idea of implied conditions, implicit conditional connections between promises in a contract. These implied conditions are crucial to understanding the relationship among the promises made in a contract, which in turn are crucial to determining who has the obligation of performing when. As you will see, implied conditions operate quite differently than do express conditions.

In the early common law of England, all contractual promises were considered independent of each other and not connected to any events external to the contract unless the parties attached an express condition to a promise. No conditions were implied. In the classic case of *Nichols v. Raynbred,*[*] Nichols promised to sell Raynbred a cow, for which Raynbred agreed to pay Nichols 50 shillings. Nichols failed to deliver the cow, but the court held that Raynbred was still obligated to keep his promise to pay Nichols 50 shillings. Nichols could presumably go into court and sue Raynbred for breaching his promise to deliver the cow, but the two promises were independent of each other.

Slowly, though, the common law evolved rules recognizing that some promises were connected to each other, even if the parties did not expressly state this in their contract. One party's non-performance sometimes was understood to mean that the other party would not have to perform its promise, or could at least delay performance while waiting for the other party's performance to occur. The path to this recognition was the courts' identification of "constructive conditions of exchange," which connected contract promises together through conditional relationships implied from the agreement, thereby determining the order of the parties' performances. These implied conditions (sometimes referred to as "constructive conditions") operate to reverse the result of *Nichols*.

Connecting promises together through implied conditions means that there is an implicit order for the parties' performances, identifying which promise has to be performed by one party before a connected performance by the other party is required, or which promises have to be performed at the same time. For example, in a contract for plumbing services for a homeowner, unless the agreement indicates otherwise, the plumber is probably required to perform before the homeowner must pay, so performing the plumbing services is an implied condition of the customer's promise to pay. In a real estate sales contract, performance of the two parties (delivery of title and delivery of payment) is ordinarily expected to occur at essentially the same time, typically at a "closing" during which both parties sign the documents that constitute performing their obligations. In such cases, the tender of performance under each promise is an implied condition of the other promise.

Note that implied conditions of the sort described above are both promises to perform and conditions connected to another performance. Not all implied conditions are also promises, however. Courts may find that a performance is implicitly dependent on the occurrence or nonoccurrence of an event rather than on the performance of the other party's promise. For instance, a landlord's promise to repair rental premises may be implicitly conditional on the tenant giving notice of needed repairs.

---

[*] 80 Eng. Rep. 238 (K.B. 1615).

Courts may and often do imply conditions based on interpretation of contract language, extrinsic evidence, usage of trade, course of dealing, public policy considerations, or what reasonable persons would have intended in the circumstances. These implied conditions "play an essential role in assuring the parties to a bilateral contract that they will actually receive the performance that they have been promised. In the centuries since [the next case], courts have sensibly imposed such conditions whenever possible."[*]

> **Example A:** *Kingston v. Preston*, 99 Eng. Rep. 437 (K.B. 1773).
>
> Preston, a "silk-mercer" (silk merchant) and Kingston came to an agreement whereby Kingston would learn Preston's business and eventually buy it from him. Preston promised to hire Kingston, for a rate of £200 per year, to work in Preston's business for 15 months, and Kingston agreed to serve. Preston promised to sell to Kingston and Preston's nephew the silk-mercer business and "his stock and trade, at a fair valuation" at the end of this 15 months. Preston promised to allow Kingston to conduct the business in Preston's house after the buyers executed 14-year deeds of partnership with Preston. Kingston promised to accept the business and stock in trade; to give Preston "good and sufficient security . . . to be approved of by" Preston; and to guarantee Preston a monthly payment of £250 in lieu of Preston receiving a share of the business's income each month after the sale, payments to continue "until the value of the stock should be reduced to £4000."
>
> At the end of the 15 months, Preston refused to sell the business to Kingston. When Kingston sued for breach of contract, Preston claimed that Kingston had not offered or furnished sufficient security for the future monthly payments of £250. Kingston countered that the parties' promises were mutual and independent; even if he had breached one of his own promises, he could still recover from Preston for Preston's breach.
>
> Preston countered that the promises were impliedly dependent, so that Kingston had to give Preston adequate security before Preston had any duty to sell the business to Kingston. Otherwise Preston would have to give up a valuable business and stock in trade, based only on Kingston's promise, when Kingston's worth was admittedly zero.

Analysis: The court ruled for Preston, holding that performance of Kingston's promise to provide sufficient security was "clearly a condition precedent" to

---

[*]   E. Allan Farnsworth, *Contracts* § 8.9, at 538 (4th ed. 2004).

Preston's duty to sell the business. Lord Chief Justice Mansfield, writing for the court, distinguished among three types of relationships between promises:[*]

1. "Mutual and independent promises," in which either party may recover damages from the other for the injury incurred by the breach of the other's promise; breach of one party's promise is not an excuse for the other party's failure to perform.

> **Make the Connection**
>
> Despite its age, *Kingston* remains a foundational opinion for the American law of conditions, reflecting the influence of the judge who authored the opinion. See Mansfield's biography in Chapter 5, page 319.

2. "Sequential dependent promises" in which "the performance of one depends on the *prior* performance of another"; until the prior promise is performed, the other party does not owe a duty to perform his promise.

3. "Simultaneous dependent promises," to be performed at the same time. "[I]f one party [is] ready, and offer[s], to perform his part, and the other neglect[s], or refuse[s], to perform his part, [the first party, upon] fulfill[ing] his engagement, . . . may maintain an action for the default of the other. . . . "

The court explained that the determination of whether promises are dependent or independent is "to be collected from the evident sense and meaning of the parties." The order of their performance "must depend on the order of time in which the intent of the transaction requires their performance."

In this case, the court held that the "essence" of the agreement was that Preston did not trust the personal security of Kingston, and that he agreed to sell his business and stock only if Preston could provide good security for the future payments.

Problems: Implied Conditions

9-1. To ensure your understanding of the three *Kingston* categories, fill in the chart below, by identifying the relationships between the promises or performances of the parties, for each category defined in *Kingston*. The first row is filled in for you, reminding you of the characteristics

---

[*] Mansfield identified the three types of relationships noted in the text, though he used slightly different terminology. We have modified the archaic language in the opinion to bring clarity to the distinctions Mansfield made.

associated with conditions that involve performance but no promise (e.g., the seller in *Morrison v. Bare,* Chapter 8, page 651, who was to deliver a receipt proving the furnace was repaired in order to trigger Morrison's obligation to buy, but who did not make an enforceable promise to deliver the receipt).

	Effect of one party's performance on the other's duty to perform	Whether *nonperformance* by A or B is a breach	Effect of either party's *nonperformance* on the other's duty to perform
A's action is a condition of B's duty to perform, but not a promise	Party A's performance triggers B's duty to perform	A's failure to perform is not a breach; if A fails to perform, B's failure to perform is not a breach	A's nonperformance means B does not have to perform
Mutual and independent promises by A and B			
Sequential dependent promises (A, then B)			
Simultaneous dependent promises (A at the same time as B)			

9-2. For the following descriptions of contractual arrangements, identify the promises made and the *Kingston* category to which each pair of promises belongs (that is, what is the relationship between the promises?). If the example contains more than one pair of promises, identify the relationship between each pair. Does the example contain a condition that is *not* a promise?

   a. A hardware store enters into a contract with a local distributor to purchase 16 wheelbarrows, to be delivered within 7 days, with the payment to be made when the goods are delivered.

b. A promises to make a loan to B, in return for B's signed promissory note, which says that B will repay the loan in 8 years with 5% interest compounded annually.

c A business contracts with a technology firm for the firm to install and test a system on the business's premises and teach the business's staff to use the new system. In the contract, the business promises to pay the technology firm's monthly invoices within 30 days; the technology firm promises to provide training on avoiding sexual harassment to its employees who will be sent to work on-site at the business's office.

d. A contracts with B, an amusement park, to design and install all the plumbing and mechanical parts for a water park feature. A agrees to defend any lawsuits brought against B arising out of its work and to pay any damages recovered in such an action, provided B notifies A of such suits within two weeks of the filing of such lawsuits. The contract does not expressly give B any obligation to give A notice of the filing of such law suits.

e. A contracts to make alterations in B's home for $5,000. $500 is to be paid on the signing of the contract, $1,500 when work is started, $2,000 on the completion of rough carpentry and rough plumbing, and $1,000 on the completion of the job.*

---

§ 3. Performance and Breach Under the Common Law

When one party to a contract breaches its performance obligations, a critical question for the aggrieved party is whether or when she is permitted to suspend performance or to cancel the contract in response. The answer to this question differs between the common law and Article 2. This section addresses the common law rules; § 5 covers the rules in UCC Article 2. In either situation, and regardless of whether the aggrieved party is permitted to suspend performance or cancel, she can obtain a remedy for the breach, covered in Chapter 10.

§ 3.1. Implied Conditions and the Doctrine of Substantial Performance

You have seen that promises in a contract may be connected by means of an implied condition. Performance of one promise (perhaps by performing a service

---

* Restatement (Second) § 234 illus. 11.

or by delivering a deed and the property it represents) must be completed in order to trigger the other party's duty to perform (perhaps to pay). If the implied conditional relationship had to be treated the same way in which express conditions are treated, then the first promise would have to be performed perfectly or the conditioned performance (payment) would not be due.

But often, the first performance is flawed, even if the flaws are minor. For instance, at the end of the contractor's performance in a construction contract, the architect and perhaps the owner will walk through the building to determine whether the general contractor is entitled to the final payment. The building will not be flawless. Some corners will not be perfect 90° angles, the plaster skim coat will have some blemishes, a few closets might be minus the requisite coat-hooks, and there no doubt will be other defects as well. The owner or architect will make a "punch list" of the remaining defects, and most of them will be remedied by the contractor, but some likely will not (perhaps the imperfect corners). If flawless construction (perfect performance) is a condition precedent that must be satisfied before the owner has a duty to pay, then the contractor will not receive payment.[*]

Is that the fairest result? What is the general expectation about the operation of such implied conditions, where the next performance in the chain is conditioned on earlier performance of some act or acts by the other party? Is precise and exact performance of the condition required, as with express conditions? If not, what should the rule be, in order to be fair to both parties (the contractor, who has done considerable though not perfect work, and the homeowner, who received reasonably good but not perfect performance)? In the next case, Judge Cardozo used two of the categories set out in *Kingston v. Preston,* page 687, to fashion a solution to this dilemma.

Reading Critically: *Jacob & Youngs*

1. Under the construction contract, Jacob & Youngs promised to build and Kent promised to pay. One would likely start with the assumption that Kent's promise to pay is conditional on the contractor's performance (just as the plumbing customer's

---

[*] In a complex contract such as a major construction project, it is likely that the parties will not have written it as an all-or-nothing arrangement, with all construction work done before any payment is due. Instead, the contract may have established a sequence of progress payments along the way, so that there are a series of connected promises—the builder to complete various stages of work and the owner to make periodic payments, with the final payment due upon completion of the whole project. The principles discussed in this section apply to each set of connected promises (performance of part of the construction project and the related progress payment), as well as to the final step in the sequence.

promise to pay is presumed to be conditional on the plumber's performance), so the promises would fall into the second of the *Kingston* categories (sequential dependent promises). However, the court ruled that these dependent promises at some point shift to a different *Kingston* category.

   a. What is that different category?

   b. Why does the category change? What policies support this ruling?

   c. What effect did this change have on the parties' rights and obligations?

2. After noting the shift from one *Kingston* category to another, the court suggested a variety of factors (as many as 8) that may be used to decide when the dependent condition between the parties' promises shifts into this new category. Identify as many of those factors as you can; you will have to look in several places in the court's discussion. Why is each factor relevant? How did these factors apply to the facts in this case?

3. What was the fundamental disagreement between the majority and the dissent? Did the dissenting judge disagree with the court's categorization of the relationship between the promises or with some other aspect of the ruling? What result would the dissent have supported? What policy supported the dissent's reasoning?

Jacob & Youngs v. Kent

JACOB & YOUNGS, Plaintiff

v.

George KENT, Defendant

Court of Appeals of New York
129 N.E. 889 (N.Y. 1921)

CARDOZO, J.

The plaintiff built a country residence for the defendant at a cost of upwards of $77,000, and now sues to recover a balance of $3,483.46, remaining unpaid.

The work of construction ceased in June, 1914, and the defendant then began to occupy the dwelling. There was no complaint of defective performance until March, 1915. One of the specifications for the plumbing work provides that—

> "All wrought-iron pipe must be well galvanized, lap welded pipe of the grade known as 'standard pipe' of Reading manufacture."

The defendant learned in March, 1915, that some of the pipe, instead of being made in Reading, was the product of other factories. The plaintiff was accordingly directed by the architect to do the work anew. The plumbing was then encased within the walls except in a few places where it had to be exposed. Obedience to the order meant more than the substitution of other pipe. It meant the demolition at great expense of substantial parts of the completed structure. The plaintiff left the work untouched, and asked for a certificate that the final payment was due. Refusal of the certificate was followed by this suit.

The evidence sustains a finding that the omission of the prescribed brand of pipe was neither fraudulent nor willful. It was the result of the oversight and inattention of the plaintiff's subcontractor. Reading pipe is distinguished from Cohoes pipe and other brands only by the name of the manufacturer stamped upon it at intervals of between six and seven feet. Even the defendant's architect, though he inspected the pipe upon arrival, failed to notice the discrepancy. The plaintiff tried to show that the brands installed, though made by other manufacturers, were the same in quality, in appearance, in market value, and in cost as the brand stated in the contract—that they were, indeed, the same thing, though manufactured in another place. The evidence was excluded, and a verdict directed for the defendant. The Appellate Division reversed, and granted a new trial.

We think the evidence, if admitted, would have supplied some basis for the inference that the defect was insignificant in its relation to the project. The courts never say that one who makes a contract fills the measure of his duty by less than full performance. They do say, however, that an omission, both trivial and innocent, will sometimes be atoned for by allowance of the resulting damage, and will

Take Note!

The "certificate" mentioned here is the architect's certification to the owner that the contractor has complied with the building plans. A contract of this type typically requires the architect's certification before the owner has a duty to make the final payment of the contract price. Note that the court did not suggest that the issuance of this certificate was an *express* condition to payment, even though it might have been argued that the language of the contract should be interpreted that way. Instead, the court used this case to articulate the doctrine of substantial performance of *implied* conditions. Why might the court have rejected the idea that an express condition was involved?

not always be the breach of a condition to be followed by a forfeiture. Spence v. Ham, 163 N.Y. 220, 57 N.E. 412, 51 L. R. A. 238 . . . . The distinction is akin to that between dependent and independent promises, or between promises and conditions. Anson on Contracts (Corbin's Ed.) § 367; 2 Williston on Contracts, § 842. Some promises are so plainly independent that they can never by fair construction be conditions of one another. Rosenthal Paper Co. v. Nat. Folding Box & Paper Co., 226 N.Y. 313, 123 N.E. 766 . . . . Others are so plainly dependent that they must always be conditions. Others, though dependent and thus conditions when there is departure in point of substance, will be viewed as independent and collateral when the departure is insignificant. 2 Williston on Contracts, §§ 841, 842; Eastern Forge Co. v. Corbin, 182 Mass. 590, 592, 66 N.E. 419 . . . . Considerations partly of justice and partly of presumable intention are to tell us whether this or that promise shall be placed in one class or in another. The simple and the uniform will call for different remedies from the multifarious and the intricate. The margin of departure within the range of normal expectation upon a sale of common chattels will vary from the margin to be expected upon a contract for the construction of a mansion or a "skyscraper." There will be harshness sometimes and oppression in the implication of a condition when the thing upon which labor has been expended is incapable of surrender because united to the land, and equity and reason in the implication of a like condition when the subject-matter, if defective, is in shape to be returned. From the conclusion that promises may not be treated as dependent to the extent of their uttermost minutiae without a sacrifice of justice, the progress is a short one to the conclusion that they may not be so treated without a perversion of intention. Intention not otherwise revealed may be presumed to hold in contemplation the reasonable and probable. If something else is in view, it must not be left to implication. There will be no assumption of a purpose to visit venial [trivial or small] faults with oppressive retribution.

Those who think more of symmetry and logic in the development of legal rules than of practical adaptation to the attainment of a just result will be troubled by a classification where the lines of division are so wavering and blurred. Something, doubtless, may be said on the score of consistency and certainty in favor of a stricter standard. The courts have balanced such considerations against those of equity and fairness, and found the latter to be the weightier. The decisions in this state commit us to the liberal view, which is making its way, nowadays, in jurisdictions slow to welcome it. Dakin & Co. v. Lee, 1916, 1 K. B. 566, 579. Where the line is to be drawn between the important and the trivial cannot be settled by a formula. "In the nature of the case precise boundaries are impossible." 2 Williston on Contracts, § 841. The same omission may take on one aspect or another according to its setting. Substitution of equivalents may not have the same significance in fields of art on the one side and in those of mere utility on the other. Nowhere will change be tolerated, however, if it is so dominant or pervasive as in any real or substantial measure to frustrate the purpose of the contract. Crouch v. Gutmann, 134 N.Y. 45, 51, 31 N.E. 271, 30 Am. St. Rep. 608. There is no general license to install whatever, in the builder's judgment, may be regarded as "just as good." Easthampton L. & C. Co., Ltd., v. Worthington, 186 N.Y. 407, 412, 79 N.E. 323. The question is one of degree, to be answered, if there is doubt, by the triers of the facts (Crouch v. Gutmann; Woodward v. Fuller, supra), and, if the inferences are certain, by the judges of the law (Easthampton L. & C. Co., Ltd., v. Worthington, supra). We must weigh the purpose to be served, the desire to be gratified, the excuse for deviation from the letter, the cruelty of enforced adherence. Then only can we tell whether literal fulfillment is to be implied by law as a condition. This is not to say that the parties are not free by apt and certain words to effectuate a purpose that performance of every term shall be a condition of recovery. That question is not here. This is merely to say that the law will be slow to impute the purpose, in the silence of the parties, where the significance of the default is grievously out of proportion to the oppression of the forfeiture. The willful transgressor must accept the penalty of his transgression. Schultze v. Goodstein, 180 N.Y. 248, 251, 73 N.E. 21 . . . . For him there is no occasion to mitigate the rigor of implied conditions. The transgressor whose default is unintentional and trivial may hope for mercy if he will offer atonement for his wrong. Spence v. Ham, supra.

Think About It!

If you had a client who wanted to be absolutely sure Reading pipe was used in constructing his home, how would you structure the contract between the contractor and your client in view of the majority opinion?

[Damages analysis from this case discussed in Chapter 10, page 802.]

The order should be affirmed, and judgment absolute directed in favor of the plaintiff upon the stipulation, with costs in all courts.

McLaughlin, J.

I dissent. The plaintiff did not perform its contract. Its failure to do so was either intentional or due to gross neglect which, under the uncontradicted facts, amounted to the same thing, nor did it make any proof of the cost of compliance, where compliance was possible.

Under its contract it obligated itself to use in the plumbing only pipe (between 2,000 and 2,500 feet) made by the Reading Manufacturing Company. The first pipe delivered was about 1,000 feet and the plaintiff's superintendent then called the attention of the foreman of the subcontractor, who was doing the plumbing, to the fact that the specifications annexed to the contract required all pipe used in the plumbing to be of the Reading Manufacturing Company. They then examined it for the purpose of ascertaining whether this delivery was of that manufacture and found it was. Thereafter, as pipe was required in the progress of the work, the foreman of the subcontractor would leave word at its shop that he wanted a specified number of feet of pipe, without in any way indicating of what manufacture. Pipe would thereafter be delivered and installed in the building, without any examination whatever. Indeed, no examination, so far as appears, was made by the plaintiff, the subcontractor, defendant's architect, or any one else, of any of the pipe except the first delivery, until after the building had been completed. Plaintiff's architect then refused to give the certificate of completion, upon which the final payment depended, because all of the pipe used in the plumbing was not of the kind called for by the contract. After such refusal, the subcontractor removed the covering or insulation from about 900 feet of pipe which was exposed in the basement, cellar, and attic, and all but 70 feet was found to have been manufactured, not by the Reading Company, but by other manufacturers, some by the Cohoes Rolling Mill Company, some by the National Steel Works, some by the South Chester Tubing Company, and some which bore no manufacturer's mark at all. The balance of the pipe had been so installed in the building that an inspection of it could not be had without demolishing, in part at least, the building itself.

I am of the opinion the trial court was right in directing a verdict for the defendant. The plaintiff agreed that all the pipe used should be of the Reading Manufacturing Company. Only about two-fifths of it, so far as appears, was of that kind. If more were used, then the burden of proving that fact was upon the plaintiff, which it could easily have done, since it knew where the pipe was obtained. The question of substantial performance of a contract of the character of the one under consideration depends in no small degree upon the good faith of the contractor. If the plaintiff had intended to, and had, complied with the terms of the contract except as to minor omissions, due to inadvertence, then he might be allowed to recover the contract price, less the amount necessary to fully compensate the defendant for damages caused by such omissions. Woodward v. Fuller, 80 N. Y. 312 . . . . But that is not this case. It installed between 2,000 and 2,500 feet of pipe, of which only 1,000 feet at most complied with the contract. No explanation was given why pipe called for by the contract was not used, nor that any effort made to show what it would cost to remove the pipe of other manufacturers and install that of the Reading Manufacturing Company. The defendant had a right to contract for what he wanted. He had a right before making payment to get what the contract called for. It is no answer to this suggestion to say that the pipe put in was just as good as that made by the Reading Manufacturing Company, or that the difference in value between such pipe and the pipe made by the Reading Manufacturing Company would be either "nominal or nothing." Defendant contracted for pipe made by the Reading Manufacturing Company. What his reason was for requiring this kind of pipe is of no importance. He wanted that and was entitled to it. It may have been a mere whim on his part, but even so, he had a right to this kind of pipe, regardless of whether some other kind, according to the opinion of the contractor or experts, would have been "just as good, better, or done just as well." He agreed to pay only upon condition that the pipe installed were made by that company and he ought not to be compelled to pay unless that condition be performed. Schultze v. Goodstein, 180 N.Y. 248, 73 N.E. 21 . . . . The rule, therefore, of substantial performance . . . has no application. Crouch v. Gutmann, 134 N.Y. 45, 31 N.E. 271, 30 Am. St. Rep. 608 . . . . What was said by this court in Smith v. Brady, supra, is quite applicable here:

> "I suppose it will be conceded that every one has a right to build his house, his cottage or his store after such a model and in such style as shall best accord with his notions of utility or be most agreeable to his fancy. The specifications of the contract become the law between the parties until voluntarily changed. If the owner prefers a plain and simple Doric column, and has so provided in the agreement, the contractor has no right to put in its place the more costly and elegant Corinthian. If the owner, having regard to strength and durability, has contracted for walls of specified materials to be laid in a particular manner, or for a given number of joists and beams, the builder has no right to substitute his own judgment or that of others. Having departed from the agreement, if performance has not been waived by the other party, the law will not allow him to allege that he has made as good a building as the one he engaged to erect. He can demand payment only upon and according to the terms of his contract, and if the conditions on which payment is due have not been performed, then the right to demand it does not exist. To hold a different doctrine would be simply to make another contract, and would be giving to parties an encouragement to violate their engagements, which the just policy of the law does not permit." (17 N.Y. 186, 72 Am. Dec. 422).

I am of the opinion the trial court did not err in ruling on the admission of evidence or in directing a verdict for the defendant.

For the foregoing reasons I think the judgment of the Appellate Division should be reversed and the judgment of the Trial Term affirmed.

Make the Connection

The dissent would not have required Kent to pay the contract price; it reasoned that the condition precedent to his duty to pay was not satisfied. The majority holds Kent liable for the contract price and holds Jacob & Youngs liable for damages caused by its failure to perform completely under the contract. The remainder of the majority opinion, specifying damages, is discussed in Chapter 10, Example G.

Hiscock, C. J., and Hogan and Crane, JJ., concur with Cardozo, J.

Pound and Andrews, JJ., concur with McLaughlin, J.

Order affirmed, etc.

Behind the Scenes

In the early 1900s, George Edward Kent was a lawyer in New York City. He and his wife, Lillias, arranged to have a country home built on Long Island (near the summer White House of Theodore Roosevelt). The lot's location on the Jericho Turnpike made it a convenient commute from the city. The town of Jericho was inhabited by fewer than 600 people, chiefly Quaker farmers. The cost of construction of the house was about $80,000 (at today's value, $1.95 million according to the consumer price index, or $37 million using the relative share of the GDP).[*]

Landscaped gardens were added to the house a few years later, designed by Olmsted Brothers & Company, the successor company to Frederick Law Olmstead (who was a collaborator on the plan for Central Park, and later designed the U.S. Capitol Grounds, the park systems in Milwaukee and Rochester, New York, and, and the World's Columbian Exposition in Chicago). The Kent residence was later demolished.[**]

When the Kent home was built, wrought iron pipe was enjoying a surge in sales in New York City, where it was being used in construction of skyscrapers and upscale homes, apparently because of its claimed superiority to steel pipe. (Reading Pipe was used in the Chrysler Building and other famous buildings.) However, at trial, Kent was unable to prove that Reading's wrought iron pipe was superior to the competing wrought iron pipe that was substituted in Kent's house. It was common in that day for construction contracts to specify one of the four competing brands for wrought iron pipe as a standard, to avoid substitution of inferior steel pipe or other pretenders, so some

---

[*]   *See*   http://lawprofessors.typepad.com/contractsprof_blog/2005/12/today_in_histor_10.html (including two pictures in Jericho). For excerpts from the parties' contract, see Richard Danzig & Geoffrey R. Watson, *The Capability Problem in Contract Law* 96 (2d ed. 2004). Danzig and Watson were unable to uncover any business or family connections between Kent and the Reading Pipe Company. *Id.* at 109–10.

[**]   Further information about the house appears at http://www.philadelphiabuildings.org/pab/app/pj_display.cfm/126806, a website about Philadelphia architects and buildings.

have speculated that the clause was meant to require wrought iron pipe, but not a particular brand.[*]

The parties' correspondence and the pleadings show that, as their interactions became more contentious, the parties agreed to several contract modifications concerning time extensions and cost increases on the project. No particular dispute seemed to predominate. The Kent family moved into the house in June 1914; the contractor completed its work five months later, in November 1914, except for "minor details." Kent's architect discovered the non-Reading pipe in March 1915 and demanded its replacement, to no avail. (Commentators speculate that the architect probably was negligent in not discovering it before it was installed or covered over.) In January 1916, the architect used the non-conforming unreplaced pipe as the basis for exercising the owners' contractual right to terminate the contract with Jacob & Youngs, who waited until November 1916 to demand the architect's certificate and then filed suit in December.[**]

Even decades later, Reading Pipe's advertisements continued to focus on the claimed superiority of the company's wrought iron pipe, over steel and cheaper products:

> Unfailing supplies of clear, sparkling water, unclogged heating lines, and freedom from repairs at low cost are made possible by metal tested for 83 years.

> For 83 years, Reading has been assuring clean water, unclogged pipe lines, and freedom from repairs for many, many years, by making pipe of genuine puddled wrought iron.

> In modest home, in mansion, in factories and buildings, large and small, on locomotives, railroad cars and ships, under water, under ground, on the surface, between walls and floors, this pipe has been given all the terrible tests of service in every conceivable way for over four generations.

> Only seven years ago, every inch of Reading Genuine Puddled Wrought Iron Pipe was marked with an indestructible indented spiral so that you can be sure of getting the pipe that has passed the tests of time.

---

[*]   See Richard Danzig & Geoffrey R. Watson, *The Capability Problem in Contract Law* 110–12 (2d ed. 2004).

[**]   *Id.* at 114–15.

It had to be marked because many people had become careless in using the word "iron". For many years "iron" had popularly meant puddled wrought iron as Reading made it then and still makes it. Quickly-rusting materials were developed that look like "iron", and often are sold as an "iron". But, of course, they failed to give the service which only genuine puddled wrought iron gives.

That's why, if you want permanence, freedom from repairs, and unfailing flow of water air, gas, oil, or other liquids, look for the honest spiral, mark of the pipe that has been tested for four generations.

Fortune Magazine, vol. 111, no. 2, p. 134 (Feb. 1931).

Problem: Implied Versus Express Conditions

9-3.   This problem explores how the substantial performance doctrine for implied conditions differs from the strict compliance rule governing express conditions. As suggested in the "Take Note" box on page 693, the architect's certificate could have been viewed as an *express* condition to Kent's obligation to pay. How would that have changed Kent's options in reacting to the breach by Jacob & Youngs? Answer the following questions exploring how this alternative analysis would change the outcome in the case.

	Holding: The promise to use Reading Pipe was an implied condition to Kent's obligation to make final payment (*following Cardozo's ruling*)	Alternative holding: The architect's certification that Reading Pipe was used was an express condition to Kent's obligation to make the final payment (*hypothetical variation of Cardozo's ruling*)
1. Does Kent have the right to damages caused by the breach?		

2. What standard is used to judge J&Y's performance to decide if Kent has the right to withhold the final payment?		
3. Is Kent's duty to make the final payment excused because of the failure to use Reading Pipe?	According to the majority: According to the dissent:	

§ 3.2. Substantial Performance or Material Breach?

As reflected in *Jacob & Youngs*, the level of performance required to satisfy a condition differs between an implied condition and an express condition. If party A achieves the level of performance necessary to satisfy the implied condition, even though the performance might be defective in some respect, that satisfaction of the implied condition triggers party B's duty to perform the connected promise(s). Party A is then said to have rendered "substantial performance." *Substantial* performance does not mean *full* performance; if party A breaches in some respect while substantially performing, party B must perform the connected promise(s), but is owed damages for any breach by party A.

If party A does *not* achieve substantial performance, then party A has not satisfied the implied condition and therefore has committed a "material breach," so party B's duty to perform the connected promise(s) does not arise. In a construction contract, that would mean that party A (the builder) cannot enforce the contract, to make party B (the owner) pay. As you will see, party A—who has done work benefiting party B, even while materially breaching—is not left without recourse. Chapter 10 examines the availability of restitution for party A if party B has no duty to pay under the contract.

Section 237 of the Restatement expresses the doctrine of substantial performance in slightly different language, saying that party B's duty to pay is conditional on the absence of "uncured material failure" of performance by party A. In other words, to demand performance by party B, party A must not have committed a material breach—which is the same thing as saying party A must have substantially performed. The concept of substantial performance focuses on how much the performing party has done, and whether it is enough to satisfy the condition. The concept of material breach focuses on how much the performing party has failed to do, and whether it is enough to *not* satisfy the condition. These two articulations are "flip-sides of the same coin," and you will see courts using one (or both) of these different ways of saying the same thing. Note that sometimes courts use the term "immaterial" to mean that the breach was not material. It is important to understand that, in this context, the term "immaterial" does not follow the standard dictionary definition of the word (unimportant or trivial). Instead, it simply means "non-material"—large enough to matter (and have to be paid for in money damages) but not large enough to be a material breach (which means there was substantial performance).

As explained by Justice Cardozo in *Jacob & Youngs*, and as demonstrated in the next two examples, the line between substantial performance and material breach is a fuzzy one. It is decided by an aggregate rule—a standard that depends on the weighing of a number of factors arising from the particular circumstances in the case. Not all the factors need be present, and the articulations of the rule do not name every factor that may be taken into account. The outcome depends on an analysis of the strength or weakness of each factor that is present, making outcomes hard to compare from case to case. This level of uncertainty enhances the chance of litigation on this critical issue.

> **Example B:** *Khiterer v. Bell*, 2005 WL 192354 (N.Y. City Civ. Ct. Jan. 28, 2005) (unreported opinion).
>
> Inna Khiterer visited dentist Dr. Mina Bell for root canal therapy on two teeth, as well as the fabrication and fitting of crowns for those two teeth and a replacement crown for a third tooth. The following summer, Khiterer visited another dentist, whose x-rays revealed that the crowns Bell had placed in her mouth were made totally of porcelain, rather than porcelain on gold, which Khiterer claimed she had expressly requested. Bell said that their contract contemplated porcelain crowns. Khiterer sued Bell, seeking return of the full amount of her payment.

Analysis: The court found that the contract did call for crowns of porcelain on gold and that Bell had thus breached the contract by providing porcelain crowns. However, the court determined that because Bell had substantially performed, Khiterer could sue for damages, but was not entitled to return of the full contract price. (The damages portion of this opinion is discussed in Chapter 10, Example H, page 803.)

The court quoted extensively from *Jacob & Youngs* (which was governing law for this New York civil court). The following factors were relevant to its decision:

1.   There was no indication that Bell intentionally substituted all porcelain for porcelain on gold.

2.   All-porcelain crowns were clearly suitable for the intended purpose; indeed, Bell testified that porcelain crowns are therapeutically superior to porcelain on gold crowns, and Khiterer did not contradict this.

3.   Porcelain crowns cost the same as porcelain-on-gold crowns, while the cement binding porcelain crowns is more expensive than the cement binding gold crowns. In fact, Khiterer testified that Bell charged her was significantly less than the fee she had been quoted by other dentists.

4.   There was no evidence of physical harm to Khiterer from the all-porcelain crowns.

5.   Ms. Khiterer was satisfied with the all-porcelain crowns from an aesthetic perspective.

Example C: *Roberts Contracting Co. v. Valentine-Wooten Road Public Facility Board*, 320 S.W.3d 1 (Ark. Ct. App. 2009).

Roberts Contracting Co. (Roberts) entered into a contract to build a sewer system for the Valentine-Wooten Road Public Facility Board (VWB), to be completed by April 12, 2005, for $2,088,166. The project was plagued with complications, including wet weather and a contract dispute with the project engineer responsible for periodic on-site inspections, which resulted in suspension of the inspections. In addition, VWB failed to obtain required easements from two of the landowners along the sewer route until very late in the project. Roberts obtained an extension from VWB until October 20, 2005, by which time Roberts had installed and tested the sewer lines, installed five pump stations and the force-mail pipes, and related equipment. However, VWB was not able to settle the two easement disputes until January and May of 2006. On May 1, 2006, Roberts walked off the job, and VWB refused to make the final payment of approximately $162,000. At that time, although Roberts had completed 90% of its work, the sewer system was not operational.

Roberts sued for breach of contract, alleging it had substantially performed its obligations under the contract. VWB denied that Roberts had substantially performed, because Roberts had not yet

*   installed a working SCADA system (an electronic monitoring system) for each pump station;

*   adequately tested its work;

- completed the sewer system so that it could be accepted by the City of Jacksonville; and

- after completing the system, submitted "as-built" drawings of the completed system.

The trial court found that Roberts had not substantially performed the contract, because it had failed to perform the four contractual requirements listed above, and Roberts appealed.

Analysis: Although the appellate court ultimately upheld the trial court's ruling that Roberts had not substantially performed, it rejected many of the trial court's rulings on substantial performance of the specific duties under the contract.

First, echoing Justice Cardozo in *Jacob & Youngs,* the court noted that "[s]ubstantial performance cannot be determined by a mathematical rule relating to the percentage of the cost of completion. . . . There is no precise formula to use . . . ." The court cited case law adopting the language of Restatement (Second) § 241 and identified the following considerations as significant in determining whether performance is substantial:

(1) the extent to which the injured party will be deprived of the benefit that he reasonably expected;

(2) the extent to which the injured party can be adequately compensated for the part of that benefit of which he will be deprived;

(3) the extent to which the party failing to perform or to offer to perform will suffer forfeiture;

(4) the likelihood that the party failing to perform or offer to perform will cure his failure, taking account of all the circumstances, including any reasonable assurances; and

(5) the extent to which the behavior of the party failing to perform or to offer to perform comports with standards of good faith and fair dealing.

Then the court turned to the trial court's findings on the specific breaches alleged by VWB. Both courts agreed that Roberts' failure to deliver the as-built drawings did not render performance less than substantial, since all Roberts was required to do was deliver drawings to be prepared by the engineers. The trial court had found that Roberts' failure to test its work rendered its performance less than substantial, but the appellate court disagreed. The testing of the pumping stations could not be completed until the electricity was provided to the stations, and the failure to provide electricity was at least partly the responsibility of VWB. The appellate court also rejected the trial court's finding that Roberts' failure to install the SCADA-system rendered the performance less than substantial, because the SCADA system was not essential to the sewer system's operation. The pump stations could be monitored manually.

Nevertheless, the appellate court affirmed the trial court's finding that Roberts had failed to substantially perform, turning to the enumerated factors to be considered in such a determination. The most significant factor, in this case, was factor (1) above: "When Roberts walked off the job, VWR did not yet have the benefit it expected, a working sewer system. . . . A working sewer system was the essence of this contract." Factor (4) was also significant, because Roberts "walked out rather than continuing to push to resolve this important issue. There was no likelihood of Roberts curing, another factor that weighted against a finding of substantial performance." Next, the court pointed to factor (3), noting that, because Roberts had already been paid for almost all of its work along the way, the scope of its potential forfeiture was small. The court noted that factor (2) might also be an issue, since the passage of time on the project might make it difficult for VWR to establish a damage award with the required certainty. (The requirement of certainty in establishing damages will be addressed in Chapter 10.)

Problems: Substantial Performance or Material Breach?

9-4. Homeowners hired Rothco (a company selling and installing windows, doors, and millwork) to replace all fifteen windows and two external doors in their home with more energy-efficient ones. One of the doors was in a bedroom and led out to a second-story balcony. Rothco assured them that they would not have drafts or frost with their new doors and windows and that they would save considerably on energy costs. The entire job cost $12,000. As required by contract, they paid half up front, with the remaining half due upon completion. Although most of the replacements fit well, Homeowners had numerous problems with the bedroom patio door, including cold drafts, moisture and frost, and the entry of bugs. They refused to pay the invoice for the remaining $6000 until Rothco fixed the problems. Representatives from Rothco and the door manufacturer examined the patio door, said that there was no defect in the door or its installation, and recommended Homeowners buy and attach weather-stripping to the door to address the problems. Homeowners continued to refuse to pay the Rothco bill. Rothco sued Homeowners for the unpaid price. Did Rothco materially breach (that is, did Rothco fail to substantially perform)?

9-5.   The multi-factor aggregate test for determining substantial performance is merely a default rule, so contractual parties can "contract out" of this test. What terms might a construction contractor favor? What terms might an owner/payor favor? How might parties draft terms to make the contract rights and duties more certain than the default rule does?

———————

§ 3.3. Partial or Total Breach?

Reading Critically: Partial or Total Breach

Read this portion of the text—through the diagram—twice. It contains several crucial concepts packed into a small space. Be sure you understand the text well enough to answer the following questions.

1. What distinguishes "partial breach" from "total breach"?

2. What remedies does the aggrieved party have after a breach? After a partial breach? After a total breach?

3. Does the breaching party have a right to cure after a breach? After a partial breach? After a total breach?

4. Does the diagram following the text make sense to you? If not, try to create your own diagram or flow chart to illustrate the relationship between breach, partial breach, and total breach.

Upon *any breach*, the aggrieved party acquires the right to a remedy for the breach. This makes sense, because all breaches give rise to a remedy for the injury caused by the breach, if the requirements for the remedy are met. (Chapter 10 addresses remedies.) If the breach is immaterial, the collection of a remedy is the extent of the aggrieved party's rights.

Upon a *material breach* (a lack of substantial performance), the aggrieved party acquires the right to withhold ("suspend") its own performance until the breaching party "cures" its defective performance and renders at least substantial performance. For example, if a building contractor has materially breached, the owner can withhold payment until the contractor renders substantial performance (so that only immaterial breach remains, if any). After cure, the parties resume performances, but retain any rights to remedies for past breaches. (Note that an aggrieved party with a right to suspend its performance does not have to exercise that right; it may, for various reasons, decide to continue performing.)

Cure can be by furnishing the missing performance, re-performing the flawed performance, or repairing a defective item, depending on the contract and the nature of the breach. The breaching party has only a "reasonable time" to cure, and in some circumstances, that reasonable time can be very short. Some breaches cannot be cured, usually because the time or opportunity to perform has passed.

If the breaching party has a right to cure, then a material breach is considered only to be a "*partial breach*." As noted earlier, the aggrieved party has both a right to a remedy for the breach and a right to suspend/withhold its performance until the breaching party's cure results in at least substantial performance.

If the breaching party has no right to cure, then the material breach is a "*total breach*." The aggrieved party retains both the right to a remedy for the breach and the right to suspend/withhold its performance. The aggrieved party also acquires an important new right—the right to declare that the contract performances are at an end—that is, neither party has any further duties to perform under the contract. This action by the aggrieved party is called "cancellation," and it is effective when the aggrieved party so notifies the breaching party. Then the aggrieved party can walk away from the present contract and, if desired, enter into a substitute contract to complete the desired performance. Thus, an aggrieved party can initially choose to suspend its performance and then choose to cancel the contract. Or it can choose to cancel the contract right away, without suspending its performance. Or it can choose to not exercise any of those rights, for various practical reasons, but an aggrieved party who waits to long to exercise its rights may eventually waive some of those rights and may even "waive the breach."

> **Take Note!**
>
> "Cancelling" a contract differs from "terminating" a contract. Cancellation is the aggrieved party's right to put an end to any further performance by either party under the contract because of a total breach by the other party. Recall that termination (page 34) is a right granted in the parties' agreement, allowing one or both parties to declare contract performance to be at an end for a particular reason (termination for cause) or for no reason (termination for convenience).
>
> Courts are not consistent in their use of these terms, however, so you should always consider which concept is at issue, not simply which word a court uses. Whether a party terminates or cancels, it retains the right to remedies for any preceding breaches.

The key pivot point between partial and total breach is whether the breaching party has a "right to cure." If breach is not total, the breaching party should have the chance to "get it right." But when does breaching party lose its "right to cure"?

Like the line between an immaterial and material breach, this is a fuzzy line that is difficult to define. The material breach becomes a total breach if the breach is serious enough—for example, because the defects in performance are large, the need to find replacement performance is pressing, and the likelihood the breaching party will cure is remote. The courts have had difficulty articulating and defining exactly what constitutes total breach. In *San Carlos Irrigation & Drainage Dist. v. United States,*[*] the court said a total breach "may be by repudiation or by such a material failure of performance when due as to 'go to the essence' and frustrate substantially the purpose for which the contract was agreed to by the injured party." Restatement (Second) § 242 uses an aggregate test that considers

(1)　the aggregate-test factors used in determining a material breach (from Restatement (Second) § 241; see page 704),

(2)　"the extent to which . . . delay may prevent or hinder [the aggrieved party] from making reasonable substitute arrangements" (judged from the perspective of a reasonable person in the aggrieved party's position), and

(3)　"the extent to which the agreement provides for performance without delay" (not just a stated deadline, but also circumstances show that the deadline is important).

If this aggregate test is met, then the breaching party loses its right to cure, and the aggrieved party gains the right to cancel.

Of course, any aggregate test generates more uncertainty than does a rule that does not use an aggregate test. This uncertainty leads to additional disputes and litigation between the parties. If the parties' dispute is in the "gray area" of the aggregate test, neither party should feel secure in its determinations and arguments about how the aggregate test applies. That insecurity should drive the parties to settle the dispute and move on, if they are accurately assessing the risk of their own erroneous judgment.

The aggrieved party is in an especially tricky position. It must judge correctly whether the breach is material (and therefore at least partial), so that she may at least suspend performance. The aggrieved party must also judge correctly whether the breach is total, so that she may cancel the contract. If the aggrieved party is wrong and withholds its own performance temporarily when there is no material breach or cancels the contract when there is no total breach, the originally aggrieved party may itself be breaching and may end up being in material or even

---

[*]　23 Cl. Ct. 276, 280 (1991).

total breach when the other party is not. Case law is replete with these kinds of mistaken judgments.

The following diagram shows how the different remedies apply to breaches depending on whether the breach constitutes an immaterial breach (substantial performance) or a material breach, and whether a material breach is a partial breach or a total breach:

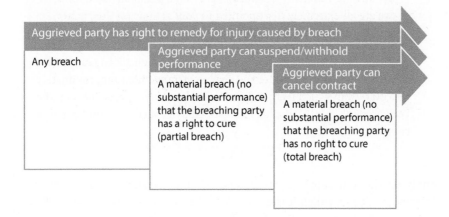

Example D: *Stanley Gudyka Sales Co. v. Lacy Forest Products*, 915 F.2d 273 (7th Cir. 1990).

Gudyka and Lacy were both in the business of marketing lumber and wood products. The parties entered a contract for Gudyka to market the products, with the two companies sharing the resulting commissions equally. Customers would pay Lacy, and Lacy would send Gudyka its share of the commissions. A "special exception" was carved out for one customer, P&E Woodworking. P&E paid Gudyka directly, and Gudyka would then pay Lacy its share of the commissions. Between December 1982 and June 1983, Gudyka received payments from P&E but did not remit the half owed to Lacy, despite questions from Lacy about the payments due. On June 14, Lacy notified Gudyka it was terminating their contract. After noting Lacy's several attempts to obtain an "update on the commissions due," and after noting that it had waited for two weeks following the latest request for information, Lacy wrote:

> We now have evidence that $5,839.82 was paid to Stanley Gudyka
> Sales Co. since December of 1982. These were direct commissions
> paid by P&E Woodworking to your company as a result of sales
> to the Andersen Corp. By our previous agreement and approval,
> . . . Gudyka : . . owes Lacy Forest Products $2,919.91.

> The partners of Lacy . . . feel very strongly that you really had no
> intention of reimbursing [us] for [our] share of this commission per
> our original agreement. If you had, you would have been issuing
> checks to Lacy . . . right along as you received the commission
> checks . . . . From a purely technical standpoint, this puts you in
> clear violation of our sales agreement and gives the partners . . . just
> cause to terminate this agreement. From a personal standpoint,
> we are all extremely disappointed in your actions on this matter,
> and our unanimous decision to terminate is final.
>
> After issuing the termination letter, Lacy sent a check to Gudyka for
> amounts due Gudyka under the sharing arrangement (approximately
> $46,000) from which Lacy had deducted the commissions due it on the
> P&E account ($2,919.91 plus interest). Gudyka sued Lacy for breach of
> contract.

Analysis: The court, applying an Illinois version of the substantial performance doctrine (the court called it the "doctrine of conditions"), held that Gudyka's failure to pay Lacy the portion of the P&E commissions owed was not grounds for termination. The court found that the termination was out of proportion to the breach, especially because Lacy owed far more in commissions to Gudyka than Gudyka had failed to pay from the P&E sales. Lacy argued that its loss of trust in Gudyka was reason for the termination, but the trial court found the testimony about loss of trust was not credible. The court concluded that Gudyka had at most committed a partial material breach, so Lacy was obligated to give Gudyka notice and an opportunity to cure its breach. By terminating rather than offering Gudyka a chance to cure, Lacy committed a material breach and owed damages to Lacy for the unjustified termination.

Reading Critically: *Sackett*

The *Sackett* opinion is divided into three parts, which appear in Chapters 9 and 10. The two parts of the case included in Chapter 10 address the issues of computing direct damages (Example E, page 799) and mitigation of damages (Example O, page 836).

1. The facts in *Sackett* present typical questions about when failure to perform constitutes material or total breach and therefore when the aggrieved party is entitled to suspend performance or cancel. (As is also somewhat typical, the court's terminology

is not entirely consistent with the Restatement terminology, so be cautious as you consider the application of the categories of breach to the facts.)

   a. At what point did Sackett's actions constitute material breach?

   b. At what point did they constitute total breach?

   c. Could any of Sackett's actions be characterized as attempts to cure his breaches?

2. What rights did Spindler have at each stage of the transaction? When was he entitled to cancel the transaction?

Sackett v. Spindler

SHELDON SACKETT, Plaintiff, Cross-Defendant and Appellant

v.

PAUL R. SPINDLER, Defendant, Cross-Complainant and Respondent

California Court of Appeal
56 Cal. Rptr. 435 (Ct. App. 1967)

MOLINARI, PRESIDING JUSTICE.

Plaintiff and cross-defendant, Sheldon Sackett, appeals from the judgment of the trial court determining that he take nothing on his complaint for money had and received and further awarding defendant and cross-complainant, Paul Spindler, $34,575.74 plus interest on his cross-complaint against Sackett for breach of contract. . . .

The Record

As of July 8, 1961 Spindler was the owner of a majority of the shares of S & S Newspapers, a corporation which, since April 1, 1959, had owned and operated a newspaper in Santa Clara known as the Santa Clara Journal. In addition, Spindler, as president of S & S Newspapers, served as publisher, editor, and general manager of the Journal. On July 8, 1961,[1] Spindler entered into a written agreement with Sackett whereby the latter agreed to purchase 6,316 shares of stock in S & S

---

[1] Unless otherwise indicated, all dates refer to the year 1961.

Newspapers, this number representing the total number of shares outstanding. The contract provided for a total purchase price of $85,000 payable as follows: $6,000 on or before July 10, $20,000 on or before July 14, and $59,000 on or before August 15. In addition the agreement obligated Sackett to pay interest at the rate of 6 percent on any unpaid balance. And finally, the contract provided for delivery of the full amount of stock to Sackett free of encumbrances when he made his final payment under the contract.

Sackett paid the initial $6,000 installment on time and made an additional $19,800 payment on July 21. On August 10 Sackett gave Spindler a check for the $59,200 balance due under the contract; however, due to the fact that the account on which this check was drawn contained insufficient funds to cover the check, the check was never paid. Meanwhile, however, Spindler had acquired the stock owned by the minority shareholders of S & S Newspapers, had endorsed the stock certificates, and had given all but 454 shares to Sackett's attorneys to hold in escrow until Sackett had paid Spindler the $59,200 balance due under the contract. However, on September 1, after the $59,200 check had not cleared, Spindler reclaimed the stock certificates held by Sackett's attorney.

Thereafter, on September 12 Spindler received a telegram from Sackett to the effect that the latter "had secured payments our transaction and was ready, willing and eager to transfer them" and that Sackett's new attorney would contact Spindler's attorney. In response to this telegram Spindler, by return telegram, gave Sackett the name of Spindler's attorney. Subsequently, Sackett's attorney contacted Spindler's attorney and arranged a meeting to discuss Sackett's performance of the contract. At this meeting, which was held on September 19 at the office of Sackett's attorney, in response to Sackett's representation that he would be able to pay Spindler the balance due under the contract by September 22, Spindler served Sackett with a notice to the effect that unless the latter paid the $59,200 balance due under the contract plus interest by that date, Spindler would not consider completing the sale and would assess damages for Sackett's breach of the agreement. Also discussed at this meeting was the newspaper's urgent need for working capital. Pursuant to this discussion Sackett on the same date paid Spindler $3,944.26 as an advance for working capital. However, Sackett failed to make any further payments or to communicate with Spindler by September 22, and on that date the latter, by letter addressed to Sackett, again extended the time for Sackett's performance until September 29. Again Sackett failed to tender the amount owing under the contract or to contact Spindler by that date, the next communication between the parties occurring on October 4 in the form of a telegram by which Sackett advised Spindler that Sackett's assets were now free as a result of the fact that his wife's petition to impress a receivership on his assets had been dismissed by the trial court in which divorce proceedings between Sackett and his wife were pending; that he was "ready, eager and willing to proceed to . . . consummate all details of our previously settled sale and purchase"; and that the decision of the trial court dismissing his wife's petition for receivership "will clear way shortly for full financing any unpaid balance." Accordingly, Sackett, in this telegram, urged Spindler to have his attorney contact Sackett's attorney "regarding any unfinished details." In response to this telegram Spindler's attorney, on October 5, wrote a letter to Sackett's attorney stating that as a result of Sackett's delay in performing the contract and his unwillingness to consummate the agreement, "there will be no sale and purchase of the stock . . . ." Following this letter Sackett's attorney, on October 6, telephoned Spindler's attorney and offered to pay the balance due under the contract over a period of time through a "liquidating trust." This proposal was rejected by Spindler's attorney, who, however, informed Sackett's attorney at that time that Spindler was still willing to consummate the sale of the stock provided Sackett would pay the balance in cash or its equivalent. No tender or offer of cash or its equivalent was made and Sackett thereafter failed to communicate with Spindler until shortly before the commencement of this action.

Beginning during the period scheduled for Sackett's performance of the contract Spindler found it increasingly difficult to operate the paper at a profit, particularly due to the lack of adequate working capital. In an attempt to remedy this situation Spindler obtained a loan of approximately $4,000 by mortgaging various items of personal property owned by him. In addition, in November, Spindler sold half of his stock in S & S Newspapers for $10,000. Thereafter, in December, in an effort to minimize the cost of operating the newspaper, Spindler converted the paper from a daily to a weekly. Finally, in July 1962 Spindler repurchased for $10,000 the stock which he had sold the previous November and sold the full 6,316 shares for $22,000, which sale netted Spindler $20,680 after payment of brokerage commission.

Breach of Contract

Sackett contends that the evidence reveals no "actionable breach" on his part. The basis of his argument is that despite his failure to tender over half of the purchase price for the stock of S & S Newspapers, his duty to consummate the contract was discharged by Spindler's conduct in two respects, namely, Spindler's "rescission" of the purchase agreement as a result of his reclamation of the stock certificates from Sackett's attorney on September 1 and Spindler's "repudiation" of the contract on October 5.

To begin with, the undisputed evidence shows that of the $85,000

Think About It!

The court writes of "Spindler's 'rescission' of the purchase agreement" and "Spindler's 'repudiation' of the contract on October 5." How would you more accurately describe Spindler's actions?

due from Sackett to Spindler under the purchase agreement the total amount which the former paid to the latter up to the time of trial was $29,744.26. Moreover, the purchase agreement reveals that Sackett's promise to pay Spindler $85,000 was an unconditional one once the respective dates on which the payments were due had arrived. Accordingly, since the trial court found that it was not impossible for Sackett to perform the subject contract either by virtue of his illness and hospitalization or his pending divorce litigation, it is clear that his failure to tender the balance due under the contract constituted a breach of the agreement, a breach being defined as an unjustified or unexcused failure to perform all or any part of what is promised in a contract. (Rest., Contracts, §§ 312, 314, pp. 462, 465.) The question remains, therefore, as to whether Sackett's duty to consummate the contract or to respond to Spindler in damages for the former's failure to perform the subject contract was in any way discharged by Spindler's conduct.

. . . . [W]ith regard to Sackett's claim that Spindler "repudiated" the contract on October 5, it is clear that the letter which Spindler's attorney wrote to Sackett's attorney on that date informing the latter that as a result of the "many delays" on the part of Sackett "there will be no sale and purchase of the [newspaper] stock" constituted notification to Sackett that Spindler considered his own duty of performance under the contract discharged as a result of Sackett's breach of the contract and that Spindler was thereby terminating the contract and substituting his legal remedies for his contractual rights. Such action was justifiable on Spindler's part if, but only if, Sackett's breach could properly be classified as a total, rather than a partial, breach of the contract. (Rest., Contracts, § 313, p. 464; 4 Corbin on Contracts, § 946, p. 809.) If, on the other hand, Sackett's breach at that time was not total so that Spindler was not entitled to consider himself discharged under the contract, then Spindler's action would constitute an unlawful repudiation of the contract, which would in turn be a total breach of the contract sufficient to discharge Sackett from any further duty to perform the contract. (6 Corbin on Contracts, § 1253, pp. 7, 13–16.)

Whether a breach of contract is total or partial depends upon its materiality. (Rest., Contracts, § 317.) In determining the materiality of a failure to fully perform a promise the following factors are to be considered:

(1) The extent to which the injured party will obtain the substantial benefit which he could have reasonably anticipated;

(2) the extent to which the injured party may be adequately compensated in damages for lack of complete performance;

(3) the extent to which the party failing to perform has already partly performed or made preparations for performance;

(4)   the greater or less hardship on the party failing to
perform in terminating the
contract;

(5)   the wilful, negligent, or
innocent behavior of the
party failing to perform;
and

> **Think About It!**
>
> This is the predecessor section to Re-
> statement (Second) § 241, discussed in
> Example C on page 703. What are the
> major differences?

(6)   the greater or less uncertainty that the party failing to perform will
perform the remainder of the contract.

(Rest., Contracts, § 275.) In the instant case, although Sackett had paid part of
the purchase price for the newspaper stock and although his delay in paying the
balance due under the contract could probably be compensated for in damages,
we are of the opinion that Spindler was justified in terminating the contract on
October 5 on the basis that despite Sackett's "offers" to perform and his assurances
to Spindler that he would perform, it was extremely uncertain as to whether in
fact Sackett intended to complete the contract. In addition, in light of Spindlers'
numerous requests of Sackett for the balance due under the contract, the latter's
failure to perform could certainly not be characterized as innocent; rather it could
be but ascribed to gross negligence or wilful conduct on his part.

The facts in the instant case are similar to those in Coughlin v. Blair, 41
Cal.2d 587, 262 P.2d 305. There the plaintiffs purchased a lot from the defendants,
who, in the deposit receipt evidencing the sale, agreed to install utilities and to
pave the road to the subject lot within one year from the date of the agreement. On
May 30, 1949, the date that performance was due under the contract, the utilities
had not been installed nor had the road been paved. During the following year
the plaintiffs wrote several letters to the defendants demanding performance. The
defendants, however, did not perform their obligations nor did they repudiate the
contract. Ultimately, on May 24, 1950, the work still not having been done, the
plaintiffs brought an action for general damages based on the difference in value of
the property with and without the performance promised in the contract and for
special damages. In affirming the judgment of the trial court insofar as it awarded
the plaintiffs general damages, the Supreme Court considered whether, in view of
the defendants' assertion that they intended to perform their obligations under the
contract in the future, the trial court's award of damages to the plaintiffs allowed
them a double recovery, that is, both the improvements and damages for failure
to secure the improvements. In this context the Supreme Court pointed out that
if the defendants' breach was total, the plaintiffs could recover all their damages,
past and prospective, in one action and that a judgment for the plaintiffs in such

an action would absolve the defendants from any duty to perform the contract. The Supreme Court then proceeded to consider whether the plaintiffs were entitled to treat the defendants' breach as total as of the date of the commencement of the action and concluded that "Although defendants had not expressly repudiated the contract, their conduct clearly justified plaintiffs' belief that performance was either unlikely or would be forthcoming only when it suited defendants' convenience." Under these circumstances it was held that the plaintiffs were not required to endure that uncertainty or to await the defendants' convenience but were justified in treating the defendants' nonperformance as a total breach of the contract. (Pp. 599–600, 262 P.2d p. 312; see also Gold Mining & Water Co. v. Swinerton, 23 Cal.2d 19, 29–30, 142 P.2d 22; Walker v. Harbor Business Blocks Co., 181 Cal. 773, 780–781, 186 P. 356.)

Similarly, in the instant case although Sackett at no time repudiated the contract and although he frequently expressed willingness to perform, the evidence was such as to warrant the inference that he did not intend to perform the subject contract. Certainly, the state of the record was such as to justify the conclusion either that it was unlikely that Sackett would tender the balance due or that he would do so at his own convenience. Spindler was not required to endure the uncertainty or to await Sackett's convenience and was therefore justified in treating the latter's nonperformance as a total breach of the contract. Accordingly, we conclude that the letter which Spindler's attorney wrote to Sackett's attorney on October 5 did not constitute an unlawful repudiation of the contract on Spindler's part, was therefore not a breach of the contract by him, and thus did not discharge Sackett's duty to perform the contract or, alternatively, to respond to Spindler in damages.

In any event, even if Spindler was not justified in treating Sackett's breach as total as of October 5, the latter's contention that his duty to perform was discharged by Spindler's repudiation of the contract as of that date is untenable. Since Spindler was not obligated to perform his promise at that time due to Sackett's failure to tender the balance due under the contract, Spindler's repudiation was, at best, anticipatory in nature. Its effect was nullified by Sackett's disregard of it and his treating the contract as still in force as evidenced by his attempt, through his attorney, to arrange an alternative method of financing the balance due under the agreement. (See Cook v. Nordstrand, 83 Cal.App.2d 188, 195, 188 P.2d 282; Rest., Contracts, § 319, p. 481.) Moreover, Spindler's repudiation was itself retracted by his attorney who, on Spindler's behalf, told Sackett's attorney in the same conversation at which the latter suggested an alternative method of financing that Spindler was still willing to consummate the sale provided Sackett would pay the balance due in cash or its equivalent. Such a retraction constitutes a nullification of the original effectiveness of the repudiation. (Rest., Contracts, § 319, p. 481.)

. . . .

The judgment is modified by deleting therefrom the award of interest from September 29, 1961 to the date of the entry of judgment. As so modified, the judgment is affirmed. Respondent Spindler to recover costs.

Sims and Bray, JJ., concur

From the text and cases in the previous sections, you have seen the difficulty of determining whether a breach is material or total and, therefore, the difficulty for the aggrieved party determining whether she has the right to suspend performance or cancel the contract. The picture becomes even more complex if the contract has a series of linked performances so the aggrieved party must decide *which* performance may be suspended. Even if there is a total breach and the aggrieved party has the right to terminate, she may wish to keep the contract operating and therefore encourage continued performance by the breaching party, rather than declare total breach.

Problems: Partial or Total Breach?

9-6. This problem illustrates the challenges of advising clients involved in such situations. The problem is based on a case involving a construction contract with progress payments due at various performance milestones, thereby creating a typical series of linked performances.[*] In the cascading sequence of alleged breaches, each of the parties thought that it could justifiably suspend its performance, but (at least) one party was incorrect and therefore materially breached the contract. This kind of legal miscalculation is a surprisingly common cause of breach. The facts are complicated further by the aggrieved party's willingness or desire to try to keep the construction project going, despite a material and perhaps total breach by the other party. As you work through this problem, consider carefully the questions posed to you as the hypothetical lawyer for each of the parties. How would you have counselled your client at the time the client had to react, without the benefit of the hindsight of the court's decision?

K & G Construction Co. (Contractor), the owner and general contractor of a housing development project, engaged Harris and Brooks (Subcon-

---

[*] See K & G Construction Co. v. Harris, 164 A.2d 451 (Md. Ct. App. 1960).

tractor) as subcontractor to do excavating and earth moving work on the project. Their contract included the following terms:

Section 3. The Subcontractor agrees to complete the several portions and the whole of the work herein sublet by the time or times following:

(a)   Without delay, as called for by the Contractor.

(b)   It is expressly agreed that time is of the essence of this contract, and that the Contractor will have the right to terminate this contract and employ a substitute to perform the work in the event of delay on the part of Subcontractor, and Subcontractor agrees to indemnify the Contractor for any loss sustained thereby, provided, however, that nothing in this paragraph shall be construed to deprive Contractor of any rights or remedies it would otherwise have as to damage for delay.

Practice Pointer

A clause saying "time is of the essence" represents an attempt by one or both parties to indicate the importance of performance due dates. Such a clause may make it more likely that the performance deadline will be understood to be an express condition or that a failure to meet the deadline will be considered a material or total breach. But such declarations should not be taken at face value (as courts sometimes do). A "time-is-of-the-essence" clause should be read in context to determine the parties' manifested understanding of contract responsibilities.

Section 4.

. . . .

(b)   Progress payments will be made each month during the performance of the work. Subcontractor will submit to Contractor, by the 25th of each month, a requisition for work performed during the preceding month. Contractor will pay these requisitions, less a retainer equal to ten per cent (10%), by the 10th of the months in which such requisitions are received.[*]

———————————————
[*] This section is not a model for clarity.

(c)   No payments will be made under this contract until the insurance requirements of Sec. 9 hereof have been complied with.

Section 5. The Contractor agrees—

(1)   That no claim for services rendered or materials furnished by the Contractor to the Subcontractor shall be valid unless written notice thereof is given by the Contractor to the Subcontractor during the first ten days of the calendar month following that in which the claim originated.

. . . .

Section 8. . . . All work shall be performed in a workmanlike manner, and in accordance with the best practices.

Section 9. Subcontractor agrees to carry, during the progress of the work, . . . liability insurance against . . . property damage, in such amounts and with such companies as may be satisfactory to Contractor and shall provide Contractor with certificates showing the same to be in force.

Subcontractor commenced work under the contract. On July 25, Subcontractor submitted a requisition for work done prior to that date, payable by the Contractor under the terms of the contract on or before August 10.

On August 9, Subcontractor's bulldozer operator drove his machine too close to Contractor's house while grading the yard, causing the immediate collapse of a wall and other damage to the house. Subcontractor reported this incident to its liability insurance carrier. The Subcontractor and its insurance carrier refused to repair damage or compensate Contractor for damage to the house, claiming that there was no liability on the part of the Subcontractor.

Contractor failed to give Subcontractor any written notice of a claim against the Subcontractor for this damage pursuant to Section 5 of the contract. However, Contractor refused to pay the Subcontractor's requisition due on August 10.

FREEZE! TRY TO ANSWER THESE TWO QUESTIONS BEFORE READING ANY FURTHER!

Question 1: If you were Contractor's attorney, how would you analyze Contractor's right to refuse to make this payment at this stage in

their dispute? Would you have advised Contractor not to make the payment?

Question 2: If you were Subcontractor's attorney, how would you analyze Contractor's action?

Subcontractor continued to work on the project until September 12, when Subcontractor notified Contractor by registered letter that it was discontinuing its work, but was willing to return to the job upon payment. Contractor requested Subcontractor to continue its work, but refused to pay Subcontractor anything more.

FREEZE! TRY TO ANSWER THIS QUESTION BEFORE READING ANY FURTHER!

Question 3: If you were Subcontractor's attorney, how would you analyze Subcontractor's right to discontinue its work at this point in the dispute? Would you have advised Subcontractor to discontinue its work? What significance would you attribute to the fact that Contractor allowed Subcontractor to continue work from August 10 to September 12?

Contractor eventually hired another excavating contractor to complete the remaining work.

FREEZE! TRY TO ANSWER THIS QUESTION BEFORE READING ANY FURTHER!

Question 4: If you were Contractor's attorney, how would you analyze Contractor's right to hire a substitute excavating contractor?

At trial, the parties stipulated to the following figures:

- Subcontractor had completed work under the contract for which it had not been paid $1,484.50.

- If the Subcontractor had completed the remaining work, Subcontractor would have made a profit of $1,340 for this work.

- It cost the Contractor $450 above the contract price to hire the replacement excavating contractor.

- Damage to the house caused by the bulldozer incident amounted to $3,400.

Contractor sued Subcontractor on two counts: (1) for the bulldozer damage to Contractor's house due to alleged negligence of the bulldozer operator, and (2) for the $450 costs above the contract price for hiring the substitute excavating subcontractor. Subcontractor filed a counter-claim for the value of $1,484.50 for which it had not received payment and for loss of $1,340 in anticipated profits.

A jury held for Contractor on the first claim in the amount of $3,400. Subcontractor paid that judgment. The second count and counterclaim were submitted to the trial judge rather than jury. The judge found for the Subcontractor in the amount of $2,824.50. Contractor appealed.

Question 5: If you were the appellate court judge, how would you rule?

9-7.   Pursuant to an Agreement for Sale for a condominium unit, Buyer deposited $118,643 into an escrow account to hold for later payment to the seller. The condominium was part of a planned development project converting an old warehouse into living space, and reconstruction work had not yet begun at the time the contract was signed. The Agreement stated that "the Premises shall include the standard features and other items described in Exhibit B." Exhibit B included a "Summary of Features," which listed, among other things, "high ceilings and expansive room arrangements." Exhibit B also included "Outline Specifications" for the condominiums, which stated:

> Ceilings will be painted drywall at approximately 9'-6" height in perimeter bedroom and living areas. Interior areas such as bathrooms, kitchens and closets will generally have slightly lower ceilings of approximately 9'-0". Some drywall soffits or ceiling height variation may result in these areas to conceal ductwork, sprinkler piping, electrical conduit and wiring, structural beams, drain piping, terrace insulation and to address other conditions as required by the construction documents and field conditions.

When built, the ceilings in the bedrooms and living areas of the condominium unit were approximately 8'-9". The contractor refused to correct the mistakes. Buyer sought to cancel the purchase agreement and demanded the return of the $118,643 deposit, claiming that the shorter ceilings were a total breach of the agreement. Is Buyer correct?

Practice Pointer: Divisible Contracts

Contracts that are "divisible" are understood as being divided into two or more parts, each of which can stand on its own as a free-standing contract. If a court finds a contract to be divisible, the court will judge the performance of each separate part of the contract independently, so, for each divisible part of the contract, the court decides whether the performing party accomplished substantial performance or materially or totally breached. Dividing the contract in this fashion means that the performing party can more easily prove substantial performance of some parts of the contract, because the court compares the performance against the promises in only the divisible part. That may disadvantage the paying party, who would have to pay for part of the contract without receiving the other part(s) of the performance, so the test for divisibility looks at whether that kind of harm would occur. Dividing the contract also means that either party can more easily prove a total breach of some parts of the contract, because the court judges whether there has been a total breach of the divisible part of the contract, not the whole.

The courts' tests for divisibility often include the following factors:

- Did the parties intend that the agreement be divisible;

- Is the contract, "by its terms, nature, and purpose, . . . susceptible of division and apportionment"* (E.g., is it possible to determine the price of each separate performance?); and

- Would the division harms the value of performance reasonably expected by each party? (E.g., can the injured party make full use of the incomplete performance? Has the injured party received the full value for its payments to date?)

Divisibility may play a role in analyzing many other issues of contract law, in addition to substantial performance and total/partial breach.** A contract may be divisible for one purpose, but not for another. For instance, a contract may be divisible for statute of frauds purposes, allowing part of the contract to be enforced, rather than barring enforcement of the whole contract. But the same contract may

---

*   *In re American Home Mortgage, Inc.*, 379 Bankr. Rep. 503, 521 (D.Del. 2008).
**   For an astute discussion of the range of issues affected by divisibility, follow the index entries for divisibility in the three-volume treatise, E. Allan Farnsworth, *Farnsworth on Contracts* (3d ed. 2004).

not be divisible for purposes of substantial performance, because it would allow a payee to achieve substantial performance of a portion of the contract too easily, while the rest of the contract was materially breached.

Consider the following cases, in which the court determined the contract was divisible with respect to the issue of substantial performance:

- *Gill v. Johnstown Lumber Co.*, 25 A. 120 (Pa. 1892): Plaintiff laborer agreed to drive four million feet of logs from various upstream points to the defendant's boom downstream. The promised compensation was $1 per 1000 feet of oak logs and 75¢ per 1000 feet of other logs. In addition, the laborer agreed to drive cross-ties downstream to another location, for another price per cross-tie. A flood carried away many of the logs, but plaintiff sued for partial payment. The court found that the contract was divisible so that plaintiff could recover compensation for each log and tie delivered to the promised location. However, the court refused to apportion the contract so as to allow compensation for logs and ties that plaintiff had driven part-way along the route. The court also refused compensation for logs transported or swept away by the flood.

- *Lowy v. United Pacific Insurance Co.*, 429 P.2d 577 (Cal. 1967): A real estate development company hired a contractor to do excavation and grading work, as well as street improvement work. The contract specified separate prices for each kind of work. The contractor completed 98% of the excavation and grading work, but ceased performance before doing the street improvement work. The court found that the contract was divisible for purposes of determining substantial performance. It allowed the contractor to recover the contract price for the excavation and grading work (minus the cost of finishing the remaining 2%), based on his substantial performance of that portion of the contract.

More often, though, the courts have rejected arguments claiming divisibility for purposes of determining substantial performance:

- *Menorah Chapels at Millburn v. Needle*, 899 A.2d 316 (N.J. Super. A.D. 2006): The son-in-law of the deceased contracted with a funeral home for services consistent with orthodox Jewish rituals, including the requirement that the body be attended by watchers ("shomers") who maintain their vigil in shifts. The funeral home's price list gave a separate price for this service. The funeral home failed to provide watchers for half of the time, and the son-in-law refused to pay. The funeral home sued for the contract price minus the price of the missing watchers. The court refused to find the contract to be divisible (in spite of the price list), because the contract's purpose was for a complete orthodox funeral. The court remanded the case on the issue of whether the breach was material and, if so, what the funeral home's recovery would be in quantum meruit.

- *Pittsburgh-Des Moines Steel Co. v. Brookhaven Manor Water Co.*, 532 F.2d 572 (7th Cir. 1976): The contract required the steel company to supply pieces of a water tank and to assemble it on site into a fixed water tank on a concrete base. Thus, the contract included goods (the water tank parts and the components of the concrete) as well as services (mixing and pouring the concrete into molds, and assembling the parts of the water tank). The court regarded the contract as non-divisible, applying UCC Article 2 to the entire contract because the goods predominated over the services.

- *K & G Construction Co. v. Harris*, 164 A.2d 451 (Md. Ct. App. 1960) (see Problem 9-6, page 717): The court said that "where a total price for work is fixed by a contract, the work is *not rendered divisible* by progress payments."

§ 4. Repudiation

The previous section dealt with breaches through defective performance or from failure to perform when performance was due. What happens if a party renounces or repudiates the contract, indicating before performance is due that she will not perform the contract or will not perform it further? If a party repudiates in response to a total breach, the repudiation of future performance is not a breach; it is a justified cancellation of the contract. But if done without such justification, repudiation is itself a breach of contract. This section deals with a variety of issues that arise with respect to repudiation: what counts as repudiation, whether a repudiation can be retracted, the consequences of a repudiation, and what a party may do to protect itself if the conduct of the other party is problematic but may not yet have created a repudiation.

As is true with respect to analysis of breach (material/immaterial, partial/total), beware of accepting the labels the parties place on their actions. Parties may claim material breach when it does not exist; may claim to be terminating or cancelling a contract for cause when they are in fact breaching, and may claim the other party has repudiated when she has not. In each instance, you must evaluate the parties' actions based on the standards governing repudiation and breach, rather than accepting the parties' self-characterizations.

§ 4.1. Defining Repudiation (Renunciation)

As with other communications between parties, courts judge whether a party's words and conduct constitutes a repudiation by using the objective standard. As you might expect, establishing exactly what constitutes a repudiation often presents challenges.

> **Example E:** *McCloskey & Co. v. Minweld Steel Co.*, 220 F.2d 101 (3d Cir. 1955).
>
> McCloskey was the general contractor for a hospital construction project. McCloskey entered into a contract with Minweld Steel for Minweld to furnish and erect the structural steel and long-span steel joists for two buildings in the project. The three separate contracts documenting their agreement all contained the following Article V:
>
>> Should the Sub-Contractor. . . at any time refuse or neglect to supply a sufficiency . . . of materials of the proper quality, . . . in and about the performance of the work required to be done pursuant to the provisions of this agreement . . . , or fail, in the performance of any of the agreements herein contained, the Contractor shall be at liberty, without prejudice to any other right or remedy, on two days' written notice to the Sub-Contractor, either to provide any such . . . materials and to deduct the cost thereof from any payments then or thereafter due the Sub-Contractor, or to terminate the employment of the Sub-Contractor for the said work and to enter upon the premises . . . .
>
> There were no specific dates in the contract for Minweld's performance. The contract provided that Minweld would receive contract drawings and specifications for the buildings from McCloskey and would then "immediately" submit to the project architects its schedule for completion. Article VI also generally provided:

> All labor, materials and equipment required under this contract are to be furnished at such times as may be directed by the Contractor, and in such a manner so as to at no time delay the final completion of the building.
>
> It being mutually understood and agreed that prompt delivery and installation of all materials required to be furnished under this contract is to be the essence of this Agreement.

Minweld received contract drawings and specifications for both buildings in May 1950. On June 13, 1950, Minweld submitted a schedule estimating that delivery of the steel would begin by September 1 and erection would be completed approximately November 15. On July 20 McCloskey wrote Minweld threatening to terminate the contracts unless Minweld gave unqualified assurances that it had made definite arrangements to acquire the steel, and would process and deliver it within 30 days. In fact, Minweld was experiencing difficulty obtaining the required steel due to a national steel shortage connected with the outbreak of the Korean War in June 1950.

Minweld sent McCloskey the following letter:

> Dear Sir:
>
> This will acknowledge receipt of your letter of July 20th, 1950, which was received by us today.
>
> Upon receipt of the architect's specifications, we completed the engineering and erection plans on the said specifications. Immediately after those details were available, we attempted to place orders for the steel with the Bethlehem Steel Company. Our order was held in the offices of the Bethlehem Steel Company for two weeks before we were notified that it could not be supplied. Since that time, we have tried the U.S. Steel Corporation and Carnegie-Illinois, both companies informing us that they were under contract for approximately one year and could not fulfill the order.
>
> The recent directive by the President of the United States, with which we assume you are familiar, has further tightened up the steel market so that at the present writing we cannot give you any positive promise as to our ability to obtain the steel or delivery dates.

In view of the directive from Washington and the tightening up of the entire steel industry, we solicit your help and that of the General State Authority in aiding us to obtain the steel for these contracts.

We are as anxious as you are that there be no delay in the final completion of the buildings or in the performance of our contract, but we have nowhere else to turn at the present time for the supply of steel necessary under said contracts, unless through your aid and assistance, and that of the General State Authority, a supplier can be induced to give us the materials needed.

The U.S. Steel Corporation informs us that you have discussed this matter with them and are presently aware of our present difficulties.

If steel is to be supplied to these hospital buildings by governmental directive, we feel that the steel should be supplied to us for completion under our contract.

Very truly yours,

Minweld Steel Company, Inc. J. A. Roberts Sales Manager

Upon receiving this letter, on July 26, 1950, McCloskey cancelled the contracts, claiming that Minweld's letter constituted an admission of their inability to perform the contract. McCloskey immediately acquired the required steel itself and hired new subcontractors to do the work. McCloskey then sued Minweld for anticipatory breach of the three contracts.

Analysis: Both the trial court and the court of appeals held that McCloskey had failed to make a prima facie case. The court of appeals said that to find "a renunciation amounting to a breach of contract, there must be an absolute and unequivocal refusal to perform or a distinct and positive statement of an inability to do so." Minweld's letter did not satisfy that standard, the court reasoned:

It is true as [McCloskey] urges that Minweld knew and was concerned about the tightening up of the steel market. And as is evident from the letter it, being a fabricator and not a producer, realized that without the help of the general contractor on this hospital project particularly by it enlisting the assistance of the General State Authority [the Pennsylvania state agency that owned the hospital being built], Minweld was in a bad way for the needed steel. However, the letter conveys no idea of contract repudiation by Minweld. That company admittedly was in a desperate situation. Perhaps if it had moved earlier to seek the steel its effort might have been successful. But that is mere speculation for there is no showing that the mentioned producers had they been solicited sooner would have been willing to provide the material.

Minweld from its written statement did, we think, realistically face the problem confronting it. As a result it asked its general contractor for the aid which the latter, by the nature of the construction, should have been willing to give. Despite the circumstances there is no indication in the letter that Minweld had definitely abandoned all hope of otherwise receiving the steel and so finishing its undertaking. One of the mentioned producers might have relented. Some other supplier might have turned up. It was McCloskey & Co. who eliminated whatever chance there was. That concern instead of aiding Minweld by urging its plea for the hospital construction materials to the State Authority [that] represented the Commonwealth of Pennsylvania took the position that the subcontractor had repudiated its agreement and then moved quickly to have the work completed. Shortly thereafter, and without the slightest trouble as far as appears, McCloskey & Co. procured the steel from Bethlehem and brought in new subcontractors to do the work contemplated by the agreement with Minweld.

§ 4.2. Anticipatory Repudiation

If a repudiation occurs before the date on which contract performance is due, it is called an "anticipatory repudiation." In some sense the breach does not occur until the time for performance arrives, but the act of repudiation undermines the contract and creates questions about the consequences. May the repudiating party may change his mind and retract the repudiation? What may the other party may do in response to a repudiation—wait for the time of performance or consider the contract canceled and move on? From what point in time should damages be measured—at the time of repudiation or later, when performance would have been due? The following English case helped answer many of those questions, thereby establishing principles that provide a degree of security for an aggrieved party in the face of the uncertainty caused by anticipatory repudiation.

Reading Critically: *Hochster*

1. How are the parties' promises connected to one another, using the *Kingston* categories (page 688)?

2. The court considered the verbal renunciation of a contract, as in *Hochster*, along with other situations in which a contracting party *acts* inconsistently with an intention to perform the contract. In none of those situations, the court suggested, is there a present breach of performance obligations because contract performance remains *possible*. What obligation did the court find *was* breached in all the cases? When did that breach occur—upon renunciation, when performance was to begin, or at some other time?

3. After a renunciation by one party to the contract, are the parties' contract duties necessarily ended? May the aggrieved party continue to insist on performance?

Hochster v. De la Tour

HOCHSTER, Plaintiff

v.

DE LA TOUR, Defendant

Court of Queen's Bench
118 Eng. Rep. 922 (Q.B. 1853)

. . . [P]laintiff was a courier, who, in April, 1852, was engaged by defendant to accompany him on a tour, to commence on 1st June 1852, on the terms mentioned in the declaration. On the 11th May 1852, defendant wrote to plaintiff that he had changed his mind, and declined [plaintiff's] services. He refused to make [plaintiff] any compensation. The action was commenced on 22d May. The plaintiff, between the commencement of the action and the 1st June, obtained an engagement with Lord Ashburton, on equally good terms, but not commencing till 4th July. The defendant's counsel objected that there could be no breach of the contract before the 1st of June. The learned Judge was of a contrary opinion, but reserved leave to enter a nonsuit on this objection. The other questions were left to the jury, who found for plaintiff.

. . . .

[On appeal,] LORD CAMPBELL C.J. now delivered the judgment of the Court.

On this motion in arrest of judgment, the question arises, Whether, if there be an agreement between A. and B., whereby B. engages to employ A. on and from a future day for a given period of time, to travel with him into a foreign country as a courier, and to start with him in that capacity on that day, A. being to receive a monthly salary during the continuance of such service, B. may, before the day, refuse to perform the agreement and break and renounce it, so as to entitle A. before the day to commence an action against B. to recover damages for breach of the agreement; A. having been ready and willing to perform it, till it was broken and renounced by B.

The defendant's counsel very powerfully contended that, if the plaintiff was not contented to dissolve the contract, and to abandon all remedy upon it, he was bound to remain ready and willing to perform it till the day when the actual employment as courier in the service of the defendant was to begin; and that there could be no breach of the agreement, before that day, to give a right of action.

But it cannot be laid down as a universal rule that, where by agreement an act is to be done on a future day, no action can be brought for a breach of the agreement till the day for doing the act has arrived. If a man promises to marry a woman on a future day, and before that day marries another woman, he is instantly liable to an action for breach of promise of marriage; *Short v. Stone* (8 Q. B. 358). If a man contracts to execute a lease on and from a future day for a certain term, and, before that day, executes a lease to another for the same term, he may be immediately sued for breaking the contract; *Ford v. Tiley* (6 B. & C. 325). So, if a man contracts to sell and deliver specific goods on a future day, and before the day he sells and delivers them to another, he is immediately liable to an action at the suit of the person with whom he first contracted to sell and deliver them; *Bowdell v. Parsons* (10 East, 359).

One reason alleged in support of such an action is, that the defendant has, before the day, rendered it impossible for him to perform the contract at the day: but this does not necessarily follow; for, prior to the day fixed for doing the act, the first wife may have died, a surrender of the lease executed might be obtained, and the defendant might have repurchased the goods so as to be in a situation to sell and deliver them to the plaintiff. Another reason may be, that, where there is a contract to do an act on a future day, there is a relation constituted between the parties in the meantime by the contract, and that they impliedly promise that in the meantime neither will do anything to the prejudice of the other inconsistent with that relation. As an example, a man and woman engaged to marry are affianced to one another during the period between the time of the engagement and the celebration of the marriage. In this very case, of traveller and courier, from the day of the hiring till the day when the employment was to begin, they were engaged to each other; and it seems to be a breach of an implied contract if either of them renounces the engagement. This reasoning seems in accordance with the unanimous decision of the Exchequer Chamber in *Elderton v. Emmens* (6 C.B. 160), which we have followed in subsequent cases in this Court.

The declaration in the present case, in alleging a breach, states a great deal more than a passing intention on the part of the defendant which he may repent of, and could only be proved by evidence that he had utterly renounced the contract, or done some act which rendered it impossible for him to perform it. If the plaintiff has no remedy for breach of the contract unless he treats the contract as in force, and acts upon it down to the 1st June 1852, it follows that, till then, he must enter into no employment which will interfere with his promise "to start with the defendant on such travels on the day and year," and that he must then be properly equipped in all respects as a courier for a three months' tour on the continent of Europe.

But it is surely much more rational, and more for the benefit of both parties, that, after the renunciation of the agreement by the defendant, the plaintiff should be at liberty to consider himself absolved from any future performance of it, retaining his right to sue for any damage he has suffered from the breach of it. Thus, instead of remaining idle and laying out money in preparations which must be useless, he is at liberty to seek service under another employer, which would go in mitigation of the damages to which he would otherwise be entitled for a breach of the contract.

It seems strange that the defendant, after renouncing the contract, and absolutely declaring that he will never act under it, should be permitted to object that faith is given to his assertion, and that an opportunity is not left to him of changing his mind. If the plaintiff is barred of any remedy by entering into an engagement inconsistent with starting as a courier with the defendant on the 1st June, he is prejudiced by putting faith in the defendant's assertion . . . .

Suppose that the defendant, at the time of his renunciation, had embarked on a voyage for Australia, so as to render it physically impossible for him to employ the plaintiff as a courier on the continent of Europe in the months of June, July and August 1852: according to decided cases, the action might have been brought before the 1st June; but the renunciation may have been founded on other facts, to be given in evidence, which would equally have rendered the defendant's performance of the contract impossible. The man who wrongfully renounces a contract into which he has deliberately entered cannot justly complain if he is immediately sued for a compensation in damages by the man whom he has injured: and it seems reasonable to allow an option to the injured party, either to sue immediately, or to wait till the time when the act was to be done, still holding it as prospectively binding for the exercise of this option, which may be advantageous to the innocent party, and cannot be prejudicial to the wrongdoer.

An argument against the action before the 1st of June is urged from the difficulty of calculating the damages: but this argument is equally strong against an action before the 1st of September, when the three months would expire. In either case, the jury in assessing the damages would be justified in looking to all that had happened, or was likely to happen, to increase or mitigate the loss of the plaintiff down to the day of trial. . . .

If it should be held that, upon a contract to do an act on a future day, a renunciation of the contract by one party dispenses with a condition to be performed in the meantime by the other, there seems no reason for requiring that other to wait till the day arrives before seeking his remedy by action: and the only ground on which the condition can be dispensed with seems to be, that the renunciation may be treated as a breach of the contract.

Upon the whole, we think that the declaration in this case is sufficient. It gives us great satisfaction to reflect that, the question being on the record, our opinion may be reviewed in a Court of Error. In the meantime we must give judgment for the plaintiff. . . .

Reading Critically: Anticipatory Repudiation Under the UCC

Read UCC §§ 2–610 & 2–611.

1. Under UCC § 2–610, what may an aggrieved party do after a repudiation? Does the UCC rule differ from the common law rule articulated in *Hochster*?

2. Under UCC § 2–611, in what circumstances may the repudiating party retract the repudiation? If retraction is permitted, what is the effect on the aggrieved party's rights and obligations? Is the rule in § 2–611 consistent with the reasoning in *Hochster*? At what point would the employer in *Hochster* have been unable to retract his repudiation?

§ 4.3. Reasonable Insecurity About Future Performance

Under *Hochster*, once an anticipatory repudiation occurs, the aggrieved party may consider the contract breached, may sue, and may enter into a substitute contract. If, however, one party merely has doubts about the other party's intention or ability to perform, but no repudiation has occurred, traditional common law offered the "insecure" party no recourse. Although the party causing the sense of insecurity could be seen as breaching its implied promise not to impair the other party's expectation of receiving due performance, courts refused to extend the *Hochster* rule, continuing to require a showing of repudiation—an unequivocal refusal to perform or a statement of an inability to perform. Insecure parties were left to flounder, facing a risky choice between continuing under a contract that might not be performed or making substitute arrangements and being held liable themselves for breaching the contract.

This gap in the law remained unaddressed until the early 1900s, when the courts slowly constructed a rule to protect insecure parties. The first step was allowing parties to protect themselves through contract clauses giving them the power to act upon something less than a repudiation:

> **Example F:** *Corn Products Refining Co. v. Fasola*, 109 A. 505 (N.J. 1920).
>
> Corn Products Refining contracted to furnish Fasola with 500 cases of No. 5 Mazola over a number of deliveries, on credit. In return, Fasola would repay the credit line within 30 days, or within 10 days for a 2% discount. Three days before the first delivery, Corn Products Refining learned from another source that Fasola's credit and ability to pay had diminished. Before shipment, Corn Products Refining informed Fasola that she would need to repay the line within 10 days. Fasola failed to pay within the 10-day requirement, even though she had paid within 10 days in previous transactions. Corn Products Refining refused to make further deliveries, relying on the following contract clause: "If at any time before shipment the financial responsibility of the buyer becomes impaired or unsatisfactory to the seller, cash payment or satisfactory security may be required by the seller before shipment." Fasola claimed that Corn Products Refining had breached the contract and refused to pay the due amount.

Analysis: The lower court directed a verdict for Corn Products Refining for the amount due. The appellate court affirmed, basing its judgment on the quoted contract provision allowing the vendor to seek assurance. The court reasoned that "if for any reason not pretend or unreal, [the vendor] becomes dissatisfied with the financial responsibility of his debtor, he may invoke his contract and refuse to ship until secured according to the terms of the agreement."

———————————

The next step was recognition of an implied term giving parties the right to demand assurance in certain circumstances:

> **Example G:** *James B. Berry's Sons Co. v. Monark Gasoline & Oil Co.*, 32 F.2d 74 (8th Cir. 1929).
>
> Berry's entered into a contract to sell Monark 75 tank cars of gas, at a rate of two cars per day. The price was 10 1/2 cents per gallon, with a 1% discount for payment within 10 days. The contract provided that "in the event that the credit or the financial responsibility of the purchaser becomes impaired or unsatisfactory to the seller, the seller reserves the right to demand cash or satisfactory security before making shipments. Upon the failure of the buyer to provide cash or satisfactory security to fully satisfy the seller's demands, the seller reserves the right to . . . to cancel the sale . . . thereby terminating all obligation on the part of the seller for delivery of the goods."
>
> Berry's alleged that, before the delivery was to begin, Monark informed Berry's that it would not be able to pay for the gas and attempted to get out of the contract. Berry's was willing to let Monark out of the contract if Berry's could get out of its contract to purchase the gas from the refiner, but the refiner refused that concession. Berry's alleged that it had also heard from other sources that Monark's credit was impaired. Berry's requested that Monark pay for future shipments in cash, which Monark refused to do. Berry's sued Monark for breaching the contract. Monark responded that its credit was in fact not impaired, that Berry's concern with Monark's credit was arbitrary, and that Berry's demand for cash payment was a breach of their contract.

Analysis: The court rejected Monark's argument, affirming Berry's contractual right to demand assurance based on the contract clause cited above. The court also stated:

> [I]f the clause in controversy had not been in this contract, the plaintiff would have had the right to demand cash or security and to refuse to deliver the goods on credit, even if the contract provided for credit, if the plaintiff had "become aware . . . that buyer was unable to pay debts as they became due in the ordinary course of business."

The final step was to recognize the right to demand assurance based only on an implied term:

Example H: *Jay Dreher Corp. v. Delco Appliance Corp.*, 93 F.2d 275 (2d Cir. 1937).

Delco Appliance Corp. entered into a contract with Jay Dreher under which Dreher would be the exclusive dealer of Delco appliances in a defined territory. Their contract originally contained a clause allowing either party to cancel or terminate the agreement at any time, with or without notice, but that clause was subsequently eliminated from the contract. When Delco violated the exclusive dealing clause on a number of occasions, Dreher suspended his performance under the contract, and sued Delco for breach of contract. Delco attempted to justify its actions by referring to another contract clause giving it the power to refuse to fill any particular order, arguing that this clause "gives it power to refuse to fill the order in any given case; that what it is free to do in detail, it is free to do in gross; and that the breach of its promise to employ no other dealer could result in no loss."

Analysis: The court affirmed Dreher's right to suspend his performance based on his insecurity about Delco's performance, despite the absence of any specific clause giving him the right to do so. The court rejected Delco's justification, ruling that the right to refuse to fill a particular order was intended to protect Delco in cases of legitimate lack of supply, rather than being "a privilege to repudiate." Though the particular refusals to fill orders by Delco might not constitute a breach of the contract, Delco's breach of the exclusive dealing clause was justified based on an implied term that gave Dreher the right to reasonable security about Delco's performance.

Jay Dreher Corp. served as a model for the right to demand adequate assurance under UCC § 2–609, when it was drafted in the 1950's (see UCC § 2–609 Cmt. 3). The drafters of the Restatement followed a similar model with Restatement (Second) § 251 in 1979. Some jurisdictions have adopted § 251, and some have applied UCC § 2–609 by analogy either generally or to particular types of contracts. However, other jurisdictions have not extended these rules beyond contracts for sale of goods. The case below illustrates the complications that may arise in navigating contract performance and how UCC § 2–609 may assist in governing their resolution.

Reading Critically: Demands for Adequate Assurance Under the UCC and Restatement (Second)

Read UCC § 609 and Comment 3, as well as Restatement (Second) § 251.

1. Under the UCC provision:

   a. Under what circumstances does a party have a right to demand adequate assurance of due performance?

   b. What happens if a party does not have a right to demand adequate assurance from the other party but does so anyway?

   c. What requirements exist regarding the form or content of the demand for adequate assurance?

   d. What makes a statement an adequate assurance of due performance?

   e. What happens if the insecure party does not receive adequate assurance?

2. How does the UCC provision compare to the Restatement provision?

Problem: Right to Adequate Assurance

9-8.   If UCC § 2–609 or Restatement (Second) § 251 had been available to the parties in *McCloskey & Co. v. Minweld Steel Co.*, Example E on page 725, would either party have been able to use the section to demand adequate assurances of future performance? How might that have affected the parties' dispute?

Reading Critically: *Hornell Brewing Co.*

1. What created the reasonable grounds for insecurity for plaintiff?

2. Why did plaintiff not need to make a written demand for adequate assurance?

3. Did defendants respond with an adequate assurance of due performance? Why or why not?

Hornell Brewing Co. v. Spry

HORNELL BREWING CO., Plaintiff

v.

STEPHEN A. SPRY and ARIZONA TEA PRODUCTS LTD., Defendants

Supreme Court, New York County, New York
664 N.Y.S.2d 698 (Sup. Ct. 1997)

LOUISE GRUNER GANS, JUSTICE.

Plaintiff Hornell Brewing Co., Inc. ("Hornell"), a supplier and marketer of alcoholic and non-alcoholic beverages, including the popular iced tea drink "Arizona," commenced this action for a declaratory judgment that any rights of defendants Stephen A. Spry and Arizona Tea Products Ltd. to distribute Hornell's beverages in Canada have been duly terminated, that defendants have no further rights with respect to these products, including no right to market and distribute them, and that any such rights previously transferred to defendants have reverted to Hornell.

In late 1992, Spry approached Don Vultaggio, Hornell's Chairman of the Board, about becoming a distributor of Hornell's Arizona beverages. Vultaggio had heard about Spry as an extremely wealthy and successful beer distributor who had recently sold his business. In January 1993, Spry presented Vultaggio with an ambitious plan for distributing Arizona beverages in Canada. Based on the plan and on Spry's reputation, but without further investigation, Hornell in early 1993 granted Spry the exclusive right to purchase Arizona products for distribution in Canada, and Spry formed a Canadian corporation, Arizona Iced Tea Ltd., for that express purpose.

Initially, the arrangement was purely oral. In response to Spry's request for a letter he needed to secure financing, Hornell provided a letter in July 1993 confirming their exclusive distributorship arrangement, but without spelling out the details of the arrangement. Although Hornell usually had detailed written distributorship agreements and the parties discussed and exchanged drafts of such an agreement, none was ever executed. In the meantime, Spry, with Hornell's approval, proceeded to set himself up as Hornell's distributor in Canada. During 1993 and until May 1994, the Hornell line of beverages, including the Arizona beverages, was sold to defendants on 10-day credit terms. In May 1994, after an increasingly problematic course of business dealings, Hornell *de facto* terminated its relationship with defendants and permanently ceased selling its products to them.

The problem dominating the parties' relationship between July 1993 and early May 1994 was defendants' failure to remit timely payment for shipments of beverages received from plaintiff. Between November and December 1993, and February 1994, defendants' unpaid invoices grew from $20,000 to over $100,000, and their $31,000 check to Hornell was returned for insufficient funds. Moreover, defendants' 1993 sales in Canada were far below Spry's initial projections.

In March and April 1994, a series of meetings, telephone calls, and letter communications took place between plaintiff and defendants regarding Spry's constant arrearages and the need for him to obtain a line and/or letter of credit that would place their business relationship on a more secure footing. These contacts included a March 27, 1994 letter to Spry from Vanguard Financial Group, Inc. confirming "the approval of a $1,500,000 revolving credit facility" to Arizona Tea Products Ltd., which never materialized into an actual line of credit; Spry sent Hornell a copy of this letter in late March or early April 1994.

All these exchanges demonstrate that during this period plaintiff had two distinct goals: to collect the monies owed by Spry, and to stabilize their future business relationship based on proven, reliable credit assurances. These exchanges also establish that during March and April, 1994, Spry repeatedly broke his promises to pay by a specified deadline, causing Hornell to question whether Vanguard's $1.5 million revolving line of credit was genuine.

On April 15, 1994, during a meeting with Vultaggio, Spry arranged for Vultaggio to speak on the telephone with Richard Worthy of Metro Factors, Inc. The testimony as to the content of that brief telephone conversation is conflicting. Although Worthy testified that he identified himself and the name of his company, Metro Factors, Inc., Vultaggio testified that he believed Worthy was from an "unusual lending institution" or bank which was going to provide Spry with a line of credit, and that nothing was expressly said to make him aware that Worthy represented a factoring company. Worthy also testified that Vultaggio told him that once Spry cleared up the arrears, Hornell would provide Spry with a "$300,000 line of credit, so long as payments were made on a net 14 day basis." According to Vultaggio, he told Worthy that once he was paid in full, he was willing to resume shipments to Spry "so long as Steve fulfills his requirements with us."

Hornell's April 18, 1994 letter to Spry confirmed certain details of the April 15 conversations, including that payment of the arrears would be made by April 19, 1994. However, Hornell received no payment on that date.

What's That?

"Factoring" involves a business selling its accounts receivable to a third party (called a "factor") at a discount (less than the stated amount due in the accounts receivable). Traditionally, factoring is not a loan because the factor purchases the accounts receivable by paying the business a price. Although factoring is a perfectly legitimate way to finance a business, typically a company that could qualify for a $1.5 million revolving line of credit from Vanguard would not need to resort to the more expensive and intrusive financing mechanism of factoring. Can you tell whether Worthy represented a factoring company, as defined here?

Instead, on April 25, Hornell received from Spry a proposed letter for Hornell to address to a company named "Metro" at a post office box in Dallas, Texas. Worthy originally sent Spry a draft of this letter with "Metro Factors, Inc." named as the addressee, but in the copy Vultaggio received the words "Factors, Inc." were apparently obliterated. Hornell copied the draft letter on its own letterhead and sent it to Metro over Vultaggio's signature. In relevant part, the letter stated as follows:

> Gentlemen:
>
> Please be advised that Arizona Tea Products, Ltd. (ATP), of which Steve Spry is president, is presently indebted to us in the total amount of $79,316.24 as of the beginning of business Monday, April 25, 1994. We sell to them on "Net 14 days" terms. Such total amount is due according to the following schedule:
>
> . . . .
>
> Upon receipt of $79,316.24. (which shall be applied to the oldest balances first) by 5:00 P.M. (EST) Tuesday, May 2, 1994 by wire transfer(s) to the account described below, we shall recommence selling product to ATP on the following terms:
>
> 1) All invoices from us are due and payable by the 14th day following the release of the related product.
>
> 2) We shall allow the outstanding balance owed to us by ATP to go up to $300,000 so long as ATP remains "current" in its payment obligations to us. Wiring instructions are as follows: . . . .

Hornell received no payment on May 2, 1994. It did receive a wire transfer from Metro of the full amount on May 9, 1994. Upon immediate confirmation of that payment, Spry ordered 30 trailer loads of "product" from Hornell, at a total purchase price of $390,000 to $450,000. In the interim between April 25, 1994 and May 9, 1994, Hornell learned from several sources, including its regional sales manager Baumkel, that Spry's warehouse was empty, that he had no managerial, sales or office staff, that he had no trucks, and that in effect his operation was a sham.

On May 10, 1994, Hornell wrote to Spry, acknowledging receipt of payment and confirming that they would extend up to $300,000 of credit to him, net 14 days cash "based on your prior representation that you have secured a $1,500,000 US line of credit." The letter also stated,

> Your current balance with us reflects a 0 balance due. As you know, however, we experienced considerable difficulty and time wasted over a five week time period as we tried to collect some $130,000 which was 90–120 days past due.

> Accordingly, before we release any more product, we are asking you to provide us with a letter confirming the existence of your line of credit as well as a personal guarantee that is backed up with a personal financial statement that can be verified. Another option would be for you to provide us with an irrevocable letter of credit in the amount of $300,000.

Spry did not respond to this letter. Spry never even sent Hornell a copy of his agreement with Metro Factors, Inc., which Spry had signed on March 24, 1994 and which was fully executed on March 30, 1994. On May 26, 1994, Vultaggio met with Spry to discuss termination of their business relationship. Vultaggio presented Spry with a letter of agreement as to the termination, which Spry took with him but did not sign. After some months of futile negotiations by counsel this action by Hornell ensued.

At the outset, the court determines that an enforceable contract existed between plaintiff and defendants based on the uncontroverted facts of their conduct. Under Article 2 of the Uniform Commercial Code, parties can form a contract through their conduct rather than merely through the exchange of communications constituting an offer and acceptance. . . . Section 2–204(1) states: "A contract for sale of goods may be made in any manner sufficient to show agreement, including conduct by both parties which recognizes the existence of such a contract." Sections 2–206(1) and 2–207(3) expressly allow for the formation of a contract partly or wholly on the basis of such conduct. . . .

Here, the conduct of plaintiff and defendants which recognized the existence of a contract is sufficient to establish a contract for sale under [UCC] sections 2–204(1) and 2–207(3). Both parties' undisputed actions over a period of many months clearly manifested mutual recognition that a binding obligation was undertaken. Following plaintiff's agreement to grant defendant an exclusive distributorship for Canada, defendant Spry took certain steps to enable him to commence his distribution operation in Canada. These steps included hiring counsel in Canada to form Arizona Tea Products, Ltd., the vehicle through which defendant acted in Canada, obtaining regulatory approval for the labeling of Arizona Iced Tea in conformity with Canadian law, and obtaining importation approvals necessary to import Arizona Iced Tea into Canada. Defendants subsequently placed orders for the purchase of plaintiff's products, plaintiff shipped its products to defendants during 1993 and early 1994, and defendants remitted payments, albeit not timely nor in full. Under the [UCC], these uncontroverted business dealings constitute "conduct . . . sufficient to establish a contract for sale," even in the absence of a specific writing by the parties. UCC § 2–207(3) . . . .

Notwithstanding the parties' conflicting contentions concerning the duration and termination of defendants' distributorship, plaintiff has demonstrated a basis for lawfully terminating its contract with defendants in accordance with [UCC] section 2–609. Section 2–609(1) authorizes one party upon "reasonable grounds for insecurity" to "demand adequate assurance of due performance and until he receives such assurance . . . if commercially reasonable suspend any performance for which he has not already received the agreed return." The Official Comment to section 2–609 explains that this

> section rests on the recognition of the fact that the essential purpose of a contract between commercial men is actual performance and they do not bargain merely for a promise, or for a promise plus the right to win a lawsuit and that a continuing sense of reliance and security that the promised performance will be forthcoming when due, is an important feature of the bargain. If either the willingness or the ability of a party to perform declines materially between the time of contracting and the time for performance, the other party is threatened with the loss of a substantial part of what he has bargained for. A seller needs protection not merely against having to deliver on credit to a shaky buyer, but also against having to procure and manufacture the goods, perhaps turning down other customers. Once he has been given reason to believe that the buyer's performance has become uncertain, it is an undue hardship to force him to continue his own performance.

McKinney's Consolidated Laws of NY, Book 62½, UCC § 2–609 Official Comment 1, at 488.

Whether a seller, as the plaintiff in this case, has reasonable grounds for insecurity is an issue of fact that depends upon various factors, including the buyer's exact words or actions, the course of dealing or performance between the parties, and the nature of the sales contract and the industry. White & Summers, *Uniform Commercial Code, supra* § 6–2 at 286; *see also* Phibro Energy, Inc. v. Empresa De Polimeros De Sines Sarl, 720 F. Supp. 312, 322 (S.D.N.Y.1989); S & S Inc. v. Meyer, 478 N.W.2d 857, 863 (Iowa App.1991); AMF, Inc. v. McDonald's Corp., 536 F.2d 1167, 1170 (7th Cir.1976). Subdivision (2) defines both "reasonableness" and "adequacy" by commercial rather than legal standards, and the Official Comment notes the application of the good faith standard. White & Summers, *id.*, at 287; McKinney's Consolidated Laws of NY, Book 62½, UCC § 2–609 Official Comment at 488, 489; Turntables, Inc. v. Gestetner, 52 A.D.2d 776, 382 N.Y.S.2d 798 (1st Dep't 1976).

Once the seller correctly determines that it has reasonable grounds for insecurity, it must properly request assurances from the buyer. Although the Code requires that the request be made in writing, UCC § 2–609(1), courts have not strictly adhered to this formality as long as an unequivocal demand is made. White & Summers, *Uniform Commercial Code, supra* § 6–2 at 288; *see, e.g.,* ARB, Inc. v. E-Systems, Inc., 663 F.2d 189 (D.C.Cir.1980); Toppert v. Bunge Corp., 60 Ill. App.3d 607, 18 Ill. Dec. 171, 377 N.E.2d 324 (1978); AMF, Inc. v. McDonald's Corp., supra. After demanding assurance, the seller must determine the proper "adequate assurance." What constitutes "adequate" assurance of due performance is subject to the same test of commercial reasonableness and factual conditions. McKinney's Consolidated Laws of NY, Book 62½, UCC § 2–609 Official Comment at 489.

Applying these principles to the case at bar, the overwhelming weight of the evidence establishes that at the latest by the beginning of 1994, plaintiff had reasonable grounds to be insecure about defendants' ability to perform in the future. Defendants were substantially in arrears almost from the outset of their relationship with plaintiff, had no financing in place, bounced checks, and had failed to sell even a small fraction of the product defendant Spry originally projected.

Reasonable grounds for insecurity can arise from the sole fact that a buyer has fallen behind in his account with the seller, even where the items involved have to do with separate and legally distinct contracts, because this "impairs the seller's expectation of due performance." McKinney's Consolidated Laws of NY, Book 62½, UCC § 2–609 Official Comment 2, at 488; *see also* Waldorf Steel Fabricators, Inc. v. Consolidated Systems, Inc., 1996 WL 480902 (S.D.N.Y.) (n.o.r.); Turntables, Inc. v. Gestetner, supra.; American Bronze Corp. v. Streamway Products, 8 Ohio App.3d 223, 456 N.E.2d 1295 (1982).

Here, defendants do not dispute their poor payment history, plaintiff's right to demand adequate assurances from them and that plaintiff made such demands. Rather, defendants claim that they satisfied those demands by the April 15, 1994 telephone conversation between Vultaggio and Richard Worthy of Metro Factors, Inc., followed by Vultaggio's April 18, 1994 letter to Metro, and Metro's payment of $79,316.24 to Hornell, and that thereafter plaintiff had no right to demand further assurance.

The court disagrees with both plaintiff and defendants in their insistence that only one demand for adequate assurance was made in this case to which there was and could be only a single response. Even accepting defendants' argument that payment by Metro was the sole condition Vultaggio required when he spoke and wrote to Metro, and that such condition was met by Metro's actual payment, the court is persuaded that on May 9, 1994, Hornell had further reasonable grounds for insecurity and a new basis for seeking further adequate assurances.

Defendants cite White & Summers, *Uniform Commercial Code*, § 6–2 at 289, for the proposition that "[i]f a party demands and receives specific assurances, then absent a further change of circumstances, the assurances demanded and received are adequate, and the party who has demanded the assurances is bound to proceed." Repeated demands for adequate assurances are within the contemplation of section 2–609. *See* McKinney's Consolidated Laws of NY, Book 62½, UCC § 2–609 Official Comment at 490.

Here, there was a further change of circumstances. Vultaggio's reported conversation with Worthy on April 15 and his April 25 letter to Metro both anticipate that once payment of defendants' arrears was made, Hornell would release *up to* $300,000 worth of product on the further condition that defendants met the 14 day payment terms. The arrangement, by its terms, clearly contemplated an opportunity for Hornell to test out defendants' ability to make payment within 14-day periods.

By placing a single order worth $390,000 to $450,000 immediately after receipt of Metro's payment, Spry not only demanded a shipment of product which exceeded the proposed limit, but placed Hornell in a position where it would have *no* opportunity learn whether Spry would meet the 14-day payment terms, before Spry again became indebted to Hornell for a very large sum of money.

At this point, neither Spry nor Worthy had fully informed Hornell what assurance of payment Metro would be able to provide. Leaving aside the question whether the factoring arrangement with Metro constituted adequate assurance, Hornell never received any documentation to substantiate Spry's purported agreement with Metro. Although Spry's agreement with Metro was fully executed by the end of March, Spry never gave Hornell a copy of it, not even in response to Hornell's May 10, 1994 demand. The March 27, 1994 letter from Vanguard coincided with the date Spry signed the Metro agreement, but contained only a vague reference to a $1.5 million "revolving credit facility," without mentioning Metro Factors, Inc. Moreover, based on the Vanguard letter, Hornell had expected that payment would be forthcoming, but Spry once again offered only excuses and empty promises.

These circumstances, coupled with information received in early May (on which it reasonably relied) that Spry had misled Hornell about the scope of his operation, created new and more acute grounds for Hornell's insecurity and entitled Hornell to seek further adequate assurance from defendants in the form of a documented line of credit or other guarantee. . . . Defendants' failure to respond constituted a repudiation of the distributorship agreement, which entitled plaintiff to suspend performance and terminate the agreement. UCC § 2–609(4); Turntables, Inc. v. Gestetner, supra.; Creusot-Loire Int'l v. Coppus Engineering Corp., supra; AMF, Inc. v. McDonald's Corp., supra; ARB, Inc. v. E-Systems, Inc., supra; Toppert v. Bunge Corp., supra; *Waldorf Steel Fabricators, Inc. v. Consolidated Systems, Inc., supra.*

Even if Hornell had seen Spry's agreement with Metro, in the circumstances of this case, the agreement did not provide the adequate assurance to which plaintiff was entitled in relation to defendants' $390,000–$450,000 order. Spry admitted that much of the order was to be retained as inventory for the summer, for which there would be no receivables to factor within 14 days. Although the question of whether every aspect of Hornell's May 10 demand for credit documentation was reasonable is a close one, given the entire history of the relationship between the parties, the court determines that the demand was commercially reasonable. . . .

The court notes in conclusion that its evaluation of the evidence in this case was significantly influenced by Mr. Spry's regrettable lack of credibility. *See* Spanier v. New York City Transit Authority, 222 A.D.2d 219, 634 N.Y.S.2d 122 (1st Dep't 1995). The court agrees with plaintiff, that to an extent far greater than was known to Hornell in May 1994, Mr. Spry was not truthful, failed to pay countless other creditors almost as a matter of course, and otherwise engaged in improper and deceptive business practices.

For the foregoing reasons, it is hereby

ORDERED and ADJUDGED that plaintiff Hornell Brewing Co., Inc. have a declaratory judgment that defendants Stephen A. Spry and Arizona Tea Products, Ltd. were duly terminated and have no continuing rights with respect to plaintiff Hornell Brewing Co.'s beverage products in Canada or elsewhere.

. . . .

§ 5. Performance and Breach Under UCC Article 2

As seen in Section 3, under the common law only substantial performance, not complete performance, is required in order to trigger the other party's impliedly conditional duty to perform (unless the parties have agreed otherwise). For sales of goods under UCC Article 2, however, the rule is different, as seen in the following summary of the UCC provisions involved.

Consider § 2–601, which states what is generally known as the "perfect tender" rule. It declares that, if the goods or tender fail "in any respect" to conform to the contract, the buyer may "reject" the goods. Although this appears to mean that the buyer's responsibility to take (and pay for) the goods is dependent on the seller tendering goods in perfect conformity to the contract by the seller, in reality the perfect tender rule has some limitations:

- Section 2–601 says the rule does not apply to installment contracts or to contracts in which the parties agree the buyer will not have such a right to reject.

- A buyer is not permitted to seize on a technical defect in order to reject (which would be operating in bad faith).

- If the contract involves a so-called "shipment contract," which means the seller's tender responsibilities involve only delivering the goods to a carrier, only certain seller's breaches in transporting the goods give buyer the right to reject.

> **What's That?**
>
> Under UCC § 2-503, the "tender" of goods means seller's performance of its delivery responsibilities under the contract, which might require transporting the goods to a particular destination, or delivering them to a transport company, or making them available at a reasonable time and place for the buyer to pick up the goods.
>
> An "installment contract" is one in which the goods must or may be delivered in separate lots to be separately accepted. Under § 2-612, installment contracts are governed by a "substantial impairment" standard, similar to a substantial performance requirement for non-sale-of-goods contracts.

- Most importantly, if the buyer rejects the goods, the seller often has a right (but not a duty) to cure the non-conformity by repairing defective goods or replacing them with conforming goods.

If a buyer rejects a tender of goods that conformed to the contract specifications, the buyer breaches the contract by making a wrongful rejection.

The U.C.C. is very specific about what a buyer has to do in order to effectively reject goods, including timely notification and, in certain circumstances, some continuing duty to exercise reasonable care of the goods and take certain actions to help the seller resell the goods to another buyer. See UCC §§ 2–602, 2–603 & 2–604.

If the buyer rejects the goods, the seller may, under § 2–508, have a right (not a duty) to "cure" the defect by repair or replacement. The right is "absolute" if the time for performance (delivery of the goods) has not yet arrived. If the time for delivery *has* passed, the seller has a right to cure if he had reasonable grounds for believing the goods would be acceptable to the buyer (e.g., the seller did not know and had no reason to know about the defects or the seller delivered goods that did not technically fit the contract terms but were functionally equivalent).

If the buyer keeps the goods (perhaps because the buyer does not find the defect or can use the defective goods, or because the seller gives assurances of cure but then does not cure), the buyer "accepts" the goods, as defined in § 2–606. Even if the buyer has a right to reject goods for any nonconformity, the buyer may instead (and often does) accept the goods (or some portion of the delivery) and seek damages for any defect.

A buyer who accepts the goods can revoke that acceptance under UCC § 2–608, but this second chance to return the goods is much more limited than rejection of the goods, which allows return for "any defect." Revocation requires (1) a defect that substantially impairs the goods' value to the buyer; (2) no substantial change in the goods' condition, other than the defect; (3) acceptance occurred either (a) without discovering the defect because of seller's assurances or the difficulty of discovery, or (b) assuming that the seller would cure the defect but it has not; and (4) buyer notifies the seller within a reasonable time of actual or constructive discovery.

The following diagram illustrates the interconnection of the various aspects of performance under Article 2, if the seller tenders goods that do not conform to the contract:

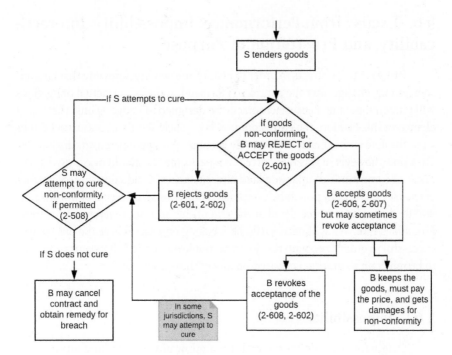

A seller may breach by repudiating the contract or otherwise failing to deliver. Under such circumstances, the buyer has no goods to reject but has other remedies available (damages or specific performance).

On the other side of the transaction, a buyer may breach by wrongfully rejecting or unjustifiably revoking acceptance, by failing to pay all or some of the contract price, by paying late, or by repudiating the contract in advance of delivery of the goods. The remedies for these breaches are introduced in Chapter 10.

Problem: Performance Under UCC Article 2

9-9.   In *Khiterer v. Bell* (Example B, page 702), as you may recall, a dentist inserted porcelain crowns rather than the porcelain-on-gold crowns that were promised in the contract, but the court found substantial performance and therefore no liability. If instead the goods had been found to predominate over the dentist's services, what would the reasoning and result have been under Article 2?

---

§ 6. Excuse from Performance: Impossibility, Impracticability, and Frustration of Purpose

Parties enter contracts in order to plan future activity, knowing that circumstances may change after the contract is formed but their contractual obligations will remain the same. Because contracts are designed to hedge against the risk of change in this fashion, the early common law concluded that contractual duties were absolute and not excusable merely because of unanticipated circumstances. Over time, however, it was recognized that performance should be excused as the result of some kinds of unanticipated circumstances. Gradually, three doctrines of excuse emerged: impossibility, impracticability, and frustration of purpose. As will be discussed in more detail at the end of this section, relief on any of these grounds is rare. We will necessarily be focusing on cases where the excuse was successful in order to explain the doctrine, but keep in mind that courts continue to be reluctant to grant relief based on any of these doctrines.

§ 6.1. Impossibility

Originally, the common law did not allow any excuse for contract non-performance, even when a later event made performance impossible, unless the contract contained an express clause granting excuse in particular circumstances or a general "force majeure" clause expressly allocating that risk between the parties. If the promise had no express qualifications, then liability was absolute.[*]

The first challenge to that understanding came in 1536, when an English court allowed the excuse of impossibility based on a supervening government action that prohibited contract performance, thereby making performance legally (though not in fact) impossible. In 1597, another court allowed excuse based on the promisor's supervening death or disability if the contract required performance by only the promisor, not someone else in his or her stead. Then, in 1628, a court excused a bailee from its bailment duty to return a horse to the owner at the end of the bailment when the horse had

What's That?

The horse case involved a "bailment" under which a "bailee" (here, defendant) took temporary possession of goods. A bailee's duties are to take reasonable care of the goods and to return them to the owner/bailor at the end of the bailment period, unless the parties' contract says otherwise.

———————————

[*] *See Paradine v. Jane*, 82 Eng. Rep. 897 (K.B. 1647).

died through no fault of the bailee.* English law remained in that posture for two centuries, recognizing a severely limited set of excuses, until the King's Bench decided *Taylor v. Caldwell* in 1863, pulling the precedents into a more cohesive (and expandable) framework.

Reading Critically: *Taylor v. Caldwell*

1. Under what circumstances does the court conclude a party may be excused from performance?

2. What limitations on excuse does the courts articulate?

3. What rationale does the court offer for finding excuse?

4. Is just one party excused, or are both parties?

Taylor v. Caldwell

TAYLOR and another [Plaintiffs]
v.
CALDWELL and another [Defendants]

Court of King's Bench
122 Eng. Rep. 309 (K.B. 1863)

BLACKBURN J:

In this case the plaintiffs and the defendants, on 27 May 1861, entered into a contract by which the defendants agreed to let the plaintiffs have the use of the Surrey Gardens and music hall on four days then to come, namely, June 17, July 16, August 5 and August 17, for the purpose of giving a series of four concerts and day and night fetes at the gardens and hall on those days, and the plaintiffs agreed to take the gardens and hall on those days, and pay 100 pounds for each day.

The parties inaccurately call this a "letting," and the money to be paid a "rent;" but the whole agreement is such as to show that the defendants were to retain the possession of the hall and gardens, so that there was to be no demise of them, and that the contract was merely to give the plaintiffs the use of them on

---

* *See Abbot of Westminster v. Clerke*, 73 Eng. Rep. 59, 63 (K.B. 1536); *Hyde v. Dean of Windsor*, 78 Eng. Rep. 798 (Q.B. 1597); *Williams v. Lloyd W. Jones*, 82 Eng. Rep. 95 (K.B. 1628).

those days. Nothing, however, in our opinion depends on this. The agreement then [sets out what each was to supply for the concerts and the entertainments.]*

See It!

Here is the music hall in Royal Surrey Gardens about three years before fire destroyed it:

For more information and pictures about the music hall, go to http://en.wikipedia.org/wiki/Royal_Surrey_Gardens.

The effect of this is to show that the existence of the music hall in the Surrey Gardens in a fit state for a concert was essential for the fulfillment of the contract; such entertainments as the parties contemplated in their agreement could not be given without it. After the making of the agreement, and before the first day on which a concert was to be given, the hall was destroyed by fire. This destruction, we must take it on the evidence, was without fault on either party, and was so complete that in consequence the concerts could not be given as intended; and the question we have to decide is whether, under these circumstances, the loss which the plaintiffs have sustained is to fall upon the defendants. The parties, when framing their agreement, evidently had not present to their minds the possibility of such a disaster, and they made no express stipulation with reference to it, so that the answer to the question must depend on the general rules of law applicable to such a contract.

There seems no doubt that, where there is a positive contract to do a thing not in itself unlawful, the contractor must perform it or pay damages for not doing it, although, in consequence of unforeseen accident, the performance of his contract has become unexpectedly burdensome, or even impossible. The law is so laid down in 1 Roll. Abr. 450, Condition (G), and in the note (2) to *Walton v. Waterhouse* (2 Wms. Saund. 421 a. 6th ed.), and is recognised as the general rule by

---

* [Authors' Note: The reporter's materials preceding the judge's opinion contain the contract language describing the elaborate events to occur during these "fêtes." The contract provided for an "organized military and quadrille band, the united bands to consist of from thirty-five to forty members; al fresco entertainments of various descriptions; . . . , fireworks and full illuminations; a ballet or divertissement, if permitted; a wizard and Grecian statues; tight rope performances; rifle galleries; air gun shooting; Chinese and Parisian games; boats on the lake, and (weather permitting) aquatic sports . . . ." *Taylor v. Caldwell*, 122 Eng. Rep. 309, 311 (K.B. 1863).]

all the Judges in the much discussed case of *Hall v. Wright* (E. B. & E. 746). But this rule is only applicable when the contract is positive and absolute and not subject to any condition either express or implied: and there are authorities which, as we think, establish the principle that where, from the nature of the contract, it appears that the parties must from the beginning have known that it could not be fulfilled unless, when the time for the fulfillment of the contract arrived, some particular specified thing continued to exist, so that when entering into the contract they must have contemplated such continued existence as the foundation of what was to be done, there, in the absence of any expressed or implied warranty that the thing shall exist, the contract is not to be construed as a positive contract, but as subject to an implied condition that the parties shall be excused in case, before breach, performance becomes impossible from the perishing of the thing without default of the contractor.

. . . [T]his implication tends to further the great object of making the legal construction such as to fulfill the intention of those who enter into the contract, for, in the course of affairs, men, in making such contracts, in general, would, if it were brought to their minds, say that there should be such a condition.

. . . .

There is a class of contracts in which a person binds himself to do something which requires to be performed by him in person, and such promises—for example, promises to marry, or promises to serve for a certain time—are never in practice qualified by an express exception of the death of the party, and, therefore, in such cases, the contract is in terms broken if the promisor dies before fulfillment; yet it was very early determined that, if the performance is personal, the executors are not liable . . . . "Thus, if an author undertakes to compose a work and dies before completing it, his executors are discharged from the contract, for the undertaking is merely personal in its nature, and by the intervention of the contractor's death has become impossible to be performed." . . . "Where a contract depends upon personal skill, and the act of God renders it impossible, as, for instance, in the case of a painter employed to paint a picture, who is struck blind, it may be that the performance might be excused."

. . . .

These are instances where the implied condition is of the life of a human being, but there are others in which the same implication is made as to the continued existence of a thing. For example, where a contract of sale is made amounting to a bargain and sale, transferring presently the property in specific chattels, which are to be delivered by the vendor at a future day. There, if the chattels, without the fault of the vendor, perished in the interval, the vendor is excused from performing his contract to deliver, which has thus become impossible.

. . . .

. . . [I]n Williams v. Lloyd . . . the plaintiff had delivered a horse to the defendant who promised to re-deliver it on request. Breach, that they requested to redeliver the horse, he refused. Plea, that the horse was sick and died, and the plaintiff made the request after its death; and, on demurrer it was held a good plea, as the bailee was discharged from his promise by the death of the horse without default or negligence on the part of the defendant. "Let it be admitted," say the Court, "that he promised to deliver it on request, if the horse die before, that has become impossible by the act of God, so the party shall be discharged as much as if an obligation were made conditioned to deliver a horse on request, and he died before it." . . .

It may, I think, be safely asserted to be now English law that in all contracts of loan of chattels or bailment, if the performance of the promise of the borrower or bailee to return the thing lent or borrowed becomes impossible because it has perished, this impossibility, if not arising from the fault of the bailee, or from some risk which he has taken upon himself, excuses the borrower or bailee from the performance of his promise to redeliver the chattel.

. . . . The principle seems to us to be that in contracts in which the performance depends on the continued existence of a given person or thing, a condition is implied that the impossibility of performance arising from the perishing of the person or thing shall excuse the performance.

In none of these cases is the promise in words other than positive, nor is there any express stipulation that the destruction of the person or thing shall excuse the performance; that excuse is by law implied, because from the nature of the contract it is apparent that the parties contracted on the basis of the continued existence of the particular person or chattel. In the present case, looking at the whole contract, we find that the parties contracted on the basis of the continued existence of the music hall at the time when the concerts were to be given, that being essential to their performance.

We think, therefore, that, the music hall having ceased to exist without fault of either party, both parties are excused, the plaintiffs from taking the gardens and paying the money, the defendants from performing their promise to give the use of the hall and gardens, and other things. Consequently the rule must be made absolute to enter the verdict for the defendants.

DISPOSITION: Rule absolute.

To explore the limits of the impossibility doctrine, compare the results in the following two examples illustrating a common situation in which impossibility is asserted: contracts to sell growing crops affected by crop failure. What explains the difference in outcome of these two cases?

Example I: *Unke v. Thorpe*, 59 N.W. 2d 419 (S.D. 1953).

Unke, the operator of a seed and feed mill, called Christopherson, another seed and feed mill operator, to ask where he might obtain alfalfa seeds. Christopherson told him about two farmers, Thorpe and Waters, who might have alfalfa seed to sell. Unke and Christopherson visited the farmers' ranch, inspected the seed, and watched the threshing operation. The parties agreed on a price for the alfalfa and signed a contract for seed that would be cleaned at Christopherson's mill within the next 30 days, with Unke paying for the cleaning. In dispute, though, was the amount of seed to be delivered. Although the contract said that the farmers would deliver "600 to 800" bushels of seed, their ranch in fact yielded only 301 bushels of seed for Unke. Thorpe and Waters claimed that they told Unke that did not know the exact amount of seed they would produce, but had only agreed to sell their entire annual crop. Unke claimed that the farmers had agreed to sell him 600 to 800 bushels of seed, regardless of where it was grown, and sued them for breaching their contract.

Analysis: The court rejected Unke's interpretation of the contract, ruling that "the only interpretation which the undisputed surrounding circumstances and the words of the contract warrant is that the parties contracted for the delivery of 600 to 800 bushels of a specific crop of alfalfa, viz, the crop the defendants were threshing." Since it was impossible for them to produce more than 301 bushels from that specific year's crop, the farmers were excused from delivering any more than those 301 bushels.

Example J: *Conagra v. Bartlett Partnership*, 540 N.W. 2d 333 (Neb. 1995).

In June 1992, ConAgra entered into four contracts to buy 300,000 bushels of corn from Bartlett, to be delivered in four shipments the following December through March. In August, Bartlett's corn crop was severely damaged by a hailstorm, leaving only about 180,000 bushels for delivery to ConAgra. ConAgra sued Bartlett for breach of contract.

Bartlett asserted, among other things, a claim of impossibility under UCC § 2–615.

Analysis: The court rejected Bartlett's impossibility claim. It ruled that "[t]he contracts did not identify the corn in any way other than by kind and amount. Nor did the contracts make any reference to corn grown or to be grown by the partnership on any identified acreage. The only limitation the contracts placed on the source of the corn was that it be grown in the continental United States." Thus, it would not have been impossible for Bartlett to have purchased the corn elsewhere and delivered it to ConAgra.

§ 6.2. Impossibility Broadens into Impracticability

The classic situations in which the common law recognizes impossibility are recognized as well in the following Restatement (Second) sections:

- § 262: Death or incapacity of person necessary for performance

- § 263: Destruction, deterioration, or failure to come into existence of thing necessary for performance

- § 264: Prevention by governmental regulation or order

Restatement (Second) § 261 and UCC § 2–615 both go beyond impossibility to allow excuse if a party's performance is made "impracticable" because an event occurs that was not expected by the parties when they entered the contract. The non-occurrence of the event must have been "a basic assumption on which the contract was made" and must not have been the fault of the party claiming excuse. The excuse does not apply if the contract language or other circumstances show that the parties allocated the risk of the event's occurrence.

How much does impracticability "broaden" impossibility? The drafters of the UCC and the Restatement (Second) attempted to circumscribe the doctrine through the cumbersome phrase requiring "the occurrence of an event the non-occurrence of which was a basic assumption on which the contract was made." The event that offers the excuse must be something that both parties reasonably assumed (usually implicitly) would *not* occur during the life of a contract. If the parties expressly allocated the risk of this event occurring in their contract, or talked about the possibility but did not mention it in the contract, then the parties clearly did contemplate the occurrence of that event and excuse will not be available. If the event is something that parties should reasonably have expected during the life of such a contract, the excuse will not be available, either. Both the Restatement and the UCC make clear that ordinary shifts in markets and financial conditions of the parties to a contract should always be expected, and the excuse of impracticability will not be available to address those occurrences. Indeed, most contracts are entered into in order to guard against such typical risks. "Increased cost alone does not excuse performance unless the rise in cost is due to some unforeseen contingency which alters the essential nature of the performance. Neither is a rise or a collapse in the market itself a justification, for that is exactly the type of business risk which business contracts made at fixed prices are intended to cover." UCC § 2–615, Cmt. 4. Comment d to Restatement (Second) § 261 explains:

> Performance may be impracticable because extreme and unreasonable difficulty, expense, injury, or loss to one of the parties will be involved. A severe shortage of raw materials or of supplies due to war, embargo, local crop failure, unforeseen shutdown of major sources of supply, or the like, which either causes a marked increase in cost or prevents performance altogether may bring the case within the rule stated in this Section. Performance may also be impracticable because it will involve a risk of injury to person or to property, of one of the parties or of others, that is disproportionate to the ends to be attained by performance. However, 'impracticability' means more than 'impracticality.' A mere change in the degree of difficulty or expense due to such causes as increased wages, prices of raw materials, or costs of construction, unless well beyond the normal range, does not amount to impracticability since it is this fort of risk that a fixed-price contract is intended to cover. Furthermore, a party is expected to use reasonable efforts to surmount obstacles to performance . . . , and a performance is impracticable only if it is so in spite of such efforts.

The following examples illustrate the application of the impracticability excuse. As you read them, recall the caution with which we began: courts rarely award relief based on impracticability. That may be especially true as disruptions from "unexpected circumstances" (flood, fire, hurricane, war) become more prevalent, as they seem to have in recent years.

Example K: *Transatlantic Financing Corp. v. United States*, 363 F.2d 312 (D.C. Cir. 1966).

The Suez Canal is an artificial waterway built in 1859–1869 that cuts through the Sinai Peninsula to connect the Mediterranean Sea with the Red Sea, allowing for shorter and quicker shipments of goods between Europe and Asia. Without the canal, ships would have to sail around the southern-most point of the African continent, the Cape of Good Hope.

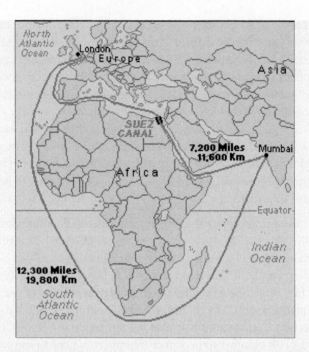

On July 26, 1956, the Government of Egypt nationalized the Suez Canal Company and took over operation of the Canal. On October 2, 1956, during the international crisis that resulted from the seizure, the United States entered into a shipping contract (a "voyage charter") with Transatlantic, to transport wheat from a Gulf of Mexico port in the United States to Iran. The contract indicated the final destination of the voyage but not the route. At the time of the contract, the "usual and customary route" for this kind of shipment was through the Suez Canal rather than around the Cape of Good Hope, which would be 30% longer. The court described the ensuing events and their impact on the contract:

> On October 27, 1956, the SS Christos sailed from Galveston for Bandar Shapur, Iran, on a course [that] would have taken her through Gibraltar and the Suez Canal. On October 29, 1956, Israel invaded Egypt. On October 31, 1956, Great Britain and France invaded the Suez Canal Zone. On November 2, 1956, the Egyptian Government obstructed the Suez Canal with sunken vessels and closed it to traffic.

Transatlantic changed the course of the SS Christos for the Cape of Good Hope, reaching Bandar Shapur on December 30, 1956. Transatlantic then filed suit against the U.S. for the additional costs of the longer route. Transatlantic argued that, under admiralty principles and practices, travel through the Suez Canal was the "usual and customary" route on which the contract was based; the closure of the Suez Canal rendered this performance commercially impracticable. When Transatlantic nevertheless completed delivery with the longer route, it rendered an additional service to the U.S. for which it should be compensated in quantum meruit (receiving the value of services rendered).

Analysis: The court reasoned that because the contract did not specify a route, the parties appeared to expect performance by the usual and customary route through the Suez Canal, and that the closure of the canal made this expected method of performance impossible. The court explained that determination of the carrier's claim required "a process which involves at least three reasonably definable steps. First, a contingency—something unexpected—must have occurred. Second, the risk of the unexpected occurrence must not have been allocated either by agreement or by custom. Finally, occurrence of the contingency must have rendered performance commercially impracticable." Recognizing that the carrier could argue the closure of the Suez Canal was such a contingency, the court went onto explain that "this unexpected development raises rather than resolves the impossibility issue, which turns additionally on whether the risk of the contingency's occurrence had been allocated and, if not, whether performance by alternative routes was rendered impracticable."

The court found nothing in the contract that expressly allocated the risk of the unavailability of the Suez route to the U.S., and nothing in custom, trade usage, or the surrounding circumstances suggesting an implied condition that the Suez route be available to Transatlantic. Indeed, the circumstances surrounding the contract suggest that this risk might have been allocated to Transatlantic, because it could be assumed that both parties were aware of the turbulent political situation in Egypt at the time. However, the court refrained from finding such an allocation, reasoning:

Foreseeability or even recognition of a risk does not necessarily prove its allocation. . . . Parties to a contract are not always able to provide for all the possibilities of which they are aware, sometimes because they cannot agree, often simply because they are too busy. Moreover, that some abnormal risk was contemplated is probative but does not necessarily establish an allocation of the risk of the contingency which actually occurs. In this case, for example, nationalization by Egypt of the Canal Corporation and formation of the Suez Users Group did not necessarily indicate that the Canal would be blocked even if a confrontation resulted. The surrounding circumstances do indicate, however, a willingness by Transatlantic to assume abnormal risks, and this fact should legitimately cause us to judge the impracticability of performance by an alternative route in stricter terms than we would were the contingency unforeseen.

The court concluded that the closure of the canal did not render the contract performance "commercially impracticable." There was nothing about the goods, the ship, or the crew that made the longer journey around the Cape of Good Hope particularly complicated. Transatlantic could easily have purchased insurance to cover the possibility of having to make the longer voyage; indeed, it was more reasonable to expect a carrier like Transatlantic to purchase such insurance than it would be to expect a shipper (here, the U.S.) to do so. The only real inconvenience to Transatlantic was the added cost of the longer route, allegedly $43,972.00 more than the contract price of $305,842.92. The court explained, "While it may be an overstatement to say that increased cost and difficulty of performance never constitute impracticability, to justify relief there must be more of a variation between expected cost and the cost of performing by an available alternative than is present in this case, where the promisor can legitimately be presumed to have accepted some degree of abnormal risk, and where impracticability is urged on the basis of added expense alone."

Example L: *Northern Indiana Public Service Co. v. Carbon County Coal Co.,* 799 F.2d 265 (7th Cir. 1986).

In 1978 Northern Indiana Public Service Company (NIPSCO) and Carbon County Coal Company signed a contract whereby Carbon County agreed to sell and NIPSCO to buy approximately 1.5 million tons of coal every year for 20 years. The original price was $24 a ton, subject to increases under the terms of an "escalation" provision. By 1985, the operation of this escalation clause had driven the price up to $44 a ton.

NIPSCO sought permission of its regulator, the Indiana Public Service Commission, to raise its rates to reflect the increased cost of coal. Some

NIPSCO customers opposed the increase, arguing that NIPSCO could reduce the cost of power by buying electrical power from neighboring utilities, rather than producing power itself with increasingly higher-priced coal from Carbon County. The Commission granted the requested increase, but also directed NIPSCO to buy more electrical power from neighboring utilities to lower the costs to customers. NIPSCO was able to find cheaper electrical power from neighboring utilities and stopped accepting coal deliveries from Carbon County.

NIPSCO brought suit seeking a declaration that it was excused from its obligation to continue purchasing coal from Carbon County because of (among other things) impracticability. Carbon County counterclaimed for breach of contract and sought a preliminary injunction requiring NIPSCO to continue to take delivery of the coal. The preliminary injunction was granted. A six-week trial resulted in a jury verdict for Carbon County for $181 million. Because NIPSCO was Carbon County's only customer, Carbon County asked the judge to grant specific performance of NIPSCO's contractual obligation to continue buying coal, in lieu of damages. But the trial judge refused specific performance, and the mine was shut down. NIPSCO appealed the damage award, and Carbon County appealed the denial of specific performance.

Analysis: First, the court rejected NIPSCO's argument that its actions were justified by the contract's *force majeure* clause, which permitted it to stop taking delivery of coal "for any cause beyond [its] reasonable control . . . including but not limited to . . . orders or acts of civil . . . authority . . . which wholly or partly prevent . . . the utilizing . . . of the coal." NIPSCO argued that the Commission's order prevented it from using the Carbon County coal. The court disagreed, explaining: "All that [the Commission's] orders do is tell NIPSCO it will not be allowed to pass on fuel costs to its ratepayers in the form of higher rates if it can buy electricity cheaper than it can generate electricity internally using Carbon County's coal. Such an order does not 'prevent,' whether wholly or in part, NIPSCO from using the coal; it just prevents NIPSCO from shifting the burden of its improvidence or bad luck in having incorrectly forecasted its fuel needs to the backs of the hapless ratepayers."

Furthermore, by agreeing to the price escalation clause in the contract, NIPSCO expressly assumed the risk of falling coal prices. The court explained: "[NIPSCO] committed itself to paying a price at or above a fixed minimum and to taking a fixed quantity at that price. It was willing to make this commitment to secure an assured supply of low-sulphur coal, but the risk it took was that the market price of coal or substitute fuels would fall. . . . The normal risk of a fixed-price contract is that the market price will change. If it rises, the buyer gains at the expense of the seller (except insofar as escalator provisions give the seller some protection); if it falls, as here, the seller gains at the expense of the buyer. The whole purpose of a fixed-price contract is to allocate risk in this way."

Because NIPSCO expressly assumed this risk of falling coal prices, the excuse of impracticability was not available to it.

Practice Pointer: Force Majeure Clauses

Although the *NIPSCO* court in Example L held that the coal contract's *force majeure* clause did not apply to the particular events that occurred, such clauses are common methods of expressly allocating risks of the type that are often the subject of impracticability claims. Force majeure clauses specify how particular risks are allocated between the parties and may also help define how the impracticability excuse will be applied. Here are two examples of force majeure clauses:

> This contract is subject to force majeure, and is contingent on strikes, accidents, acts of God, weather conditions, inability to secure labor, fire regulations or restrictions imposed by any government or governmental agency, or other delays beyond the control of the parties. If performance within the contract time is prevented by any cause of force majeure, then this contract shall be void without penalty to either party for any such portion not delivered.*

> Lesser shall not be required to perform any covenant or obligation in this Lease, or be liable in damages to Lessee, so long as the performance or nonperformance of the covenant or obligation is delayed, caused or prevented by an act of God or force majeure. . . . An "act of God" or "force majeure" is defined for purposes of this Lease as strikes, lockouts, sit-downs, material or labor restrictions by any governmental authority, unusual transportation delays, riots, floods, washouts, explosions, earthquakes, fire, storms, weather (including wet grounds or inclement weather which prevents construction), acts of the public enemy, wars, insurrections and any other cause not reasonably within the control of Lessor and which by the exercise

---

*   5 *Williston on Contracts 4th Forms* § 77F:3 (4th ed. 2012).

of due diligence Lessor is unable, wholly or in part, to prevent or overcome.[*]

A well drafted force majeure clause may serve one or more of the following functions:

- Specifying and clarifying aspects of the excuse doctrine:

    ○ which events the parties assume will not occur and why those non-occurrences are basic assumptions on which the contract is made,

    ○ a party's principal purpose (relevant for frustration of purpose),

    ○ which risks are allocated to one of the parties, and

    ○ how much difficulty of performance is necessary to find impracticability.

- Adding events that can serve as excuses (for instance, strikes, economic downturns, technology failures, etc.).

- "Contracting out" of the default rules on excuse.

Unfortunately many force majeure clauses are dropped into contracts without much thought, often as boilerplate. These clauses often purport to excuse both parties for nonperformance due to acts of God, war, earthquake, hurricane, pestilence, and other events beyond the control of the parties, but often only one party (the party delivering goods or services) is excused because the listed events will not impede the other party (the one paying for the goods or services) from performing its more limited obligation. It is important for parties to consider carefully the risks and burdens being shouldered before agreeing to any broadly worded force majeure clause.

For an analysis of force majeure clauses, a drafting checklist, and a template clause, see P.J.M. Declercq, *Modern Analysis of the Legal Effect of Force Majeure Clauses in Situations of Commercial Impracticability*, 15 J.L. & Comm. 213 (1995).

---

[*]   4A *Florida Jur. Forms Legal & Bus.* § 16A:320 (2012).

§ 6.3. Frustration of Purpose

Just as the impossibility excuse was broadened into impracticability, some courts expanded the excuse doctrine to make it available not only to the party whose performance was rendered impossible (or impracticable), but also to the party contractually obligated to pay for performance, if that party lost all or most of the performance's value due to some unexpected event. The resulting excuse of "frustration of purpose" excuses the duty to pay, under circumstances analogous to impracticability. The classic case on frustration of purpose follows.

Reading Critically: *Krell v. Henry*

1. Although the court suggests that *Krell* is an application of *Taylor v. Caldwell* (page 749), do the unanticipated circumstances here make performance impossible? What *is* the effect of the unanticipated circumstances? Whose performance is affected, and in what way?

2. According to the court, what is required to establish excuse, based on frustration of purpose? How does it differ from impossibility?

Krell v. Henry

PAUL KRELL, Plaintiff-Appellant

v.

C. S. HENRY, Defendant-Respondent

Court of King's Bench
2 K.B. 740 (1903)

The plaintiff, Paul Krell, sued the defendant, C. S. Henry, for 50£., being the balance of a sum of 75£., for which the defendant had agreed to hire a flat at 56A, Pall Mall on the days of June 26 and 27, for the purpose of viewing the processions to be held in connection with the coronation of His Majesty. The defendant denied his liability . . . .

The facts, which were not disputed, were as follows. The plaintiff on leaving the country in March, 1902, left instructions with his solicitor to let his suite of chambers at 56A, Pall Mall on such terms and for such period (not exceeding six months) as he thought proper. On June 17, 1902, the defendant noticed an announcement in the windows of the plaintiff's flat to the effect that windows to view the coronation processions were to be let. The defendant interviewed the housekeeper on the subject, when it was pointed out to him what a good view of the processions could be obtained from the premises, and he eventually agreed with the house-keeper to take the suite for the two days in question for a sum of 75£.

On June 20 the defendant wrote the following letter to the plaintiff's solicitor:—

I am in receipt of yours of the 18th instant, inclosing form of agreement for the suite of chambers on the third floor at 56A, Pall Mall, which I have agreed to take for the two days, the 26th and 27th instant, for the sum of 75£. For reasons given you I cannot enter into the agreement, but as arranged over the telephone I inclose herewith cheque for 25£. as deposit, and will thank you to confirm to me that I shall have the entire use of these rooms during the days (not the nights) of the 26th and 27th instant. You may rely that every care will be taken of the premises and their contents. On the 24th inst. I will pay the balance, viz., 50£., to complete the 75£. agreed upon.

Behind the Scenes

After having been the heir apparent for the longest period in English history, King Edward VII came to the throne at age 60 after the death of his mother, Queen Victoria. Two days before the coronation, Edward was diagnosed with appendicitis (a disease that was often fatal in that era), and he underwent life-saving surgery involving new surgical and anesthetic techniques.

The public announcement delaying the coronation and processions was made early on June 24. Under the contract in this case, defendant Henry had all day on June 24 to pay the balance due on the room, and he learned of the delay soon enough to withhold that payment. The king made a very quick recovery, and the coronation took place later that summer, on August 9. For more information about the king for whom the Edwardian era was named, see http://en.wikipedia.org/wiki/Edward_VII_of_the_United_Kingdom#Accession.

On the same day the defendant received the following reply from the plaintiff's solicitor:—

I am in receipt of your letter of to-day's date inclosing cheque for 25£. deposit on your agreeing to take Mr. Krell's chambers on the third floor at 56A, Pall Mall for the two days, the 26th and 27th June, and

I confirm the agreement that you are to have the entire use of these rooms during the days (but not the nights), the balance, 50£., to be paid to me on Tuesday next the 24th instant.

The processions not having taken place on the days originally appointed, namely, June 26 and 27, the defendant declined to pay the balance of 50£. alleged to be due from him under the contract in writing of June 20 constituted by the above two letters. Hence the present action.

Darling J., on August 11, 1902, held, upon the authority of Taylor v. Caldwell . . . , that there was an implied condition in the contract that the procession should take place, and gave judgment for the defendant on the claim . . . .

The plaintiff appealed.

. . . .

The real question in this case is the extent of the application in English law of the principle of the Roman law which has been adopted and acted on in many English decisions, and notably in the case of Taylor v. Caldwell. That case at least makes it clear that "where, from the nature of the contract, it appears that the parties must from the beginning have known that it could not be fulfilled unless, when the time for the fulfillment of the contract arrived, some particular specified thing continued to exist, so that when entering into the contract they must have contemplated such continued existence as the foundation of what was to be done; there, in the absence of any express or implied warranty that the thing shall exist, the contract is not to be considered a positive contract, but as subject to an implied condition that the parties shall be excused in case, before breach, performance becomes impossible from the perishing of the thing without default of the contractor."

. . . . English law applies the principle not only to cases where the performance of the contract becomes impossible by the cessation of existence of the thing which is the subject-matter of the contract, but also to cases where the event which renders the contract incapable of performance is the cessation or non-existence of an express condition or state of things, going to the root of the contract, and essential to its performance. It is said, on the one side, that the specified thing, state of things, or condition the continued existence of which is necessary for the fulfillment of the contract, so that the parties entering into the contract must have contemplated the continued existence of that thing, condition, or state of things as the foundation of what was to be done under the contract, is limited to things which are either the subject-matter of the contract or a condition or state of things, present or anticipated, which is expressly mentioned in the contract. But, on the other side, it is said that the condition or state of things need not be expressly specified, but that it is sufficient if that condition or state of things clearly appears by extrinsic evidence to have been assumed by the parties to be the foundation or basis of the contract, and the event which causes the impossibility . . . cannot reasonably be supposed to have been in the contemplation of the contracting parties when the contract was made. . . .

I do not think that the principle . . . is limited to cases in which the event causing the impossibility of performance is the destruction or non-existence of some thing which is the subject-matter of the contract or of some condition or state of things expressly specified as a condition of it. I think that you first have to ascertain, not necessarily from the terms of the contract, but, if required, from necessary inferences, drawn from surrounding circumstances recognised by both contracting parties, what is the substance of the contract, and then to ask the question whether that substantial contract needs for its foundation the assumption of the existence of a particular state of things. If it does, this will limit the opera-tion of the general words, and in such case, if the contract becomes impossible of performance by reason of the non-existence of the state of things assumed by both contracting parties as the foundation of the contract, there will be no breach of the contract thus limited.

Now what are the facts of the present case? . . . . In my judgment the use of the rooms was let and taken for the purpose of seeing the Royal procession. It was not a demise of the rooms, or even an agreement to let and take the rooms. It is a licence to use rooms for a particular purpose and none other. And in my judgment the taking place of those processions on the days proclaimed along the proclaimed route, which passed 56A, Pall Mall, was regarded by both contracting parties as the foundation of the contract; and I think that it cannot reasonably be supposed to have been in the contemplation of the contracting parties, when the contract was made, that the coronation would not be held on the proclaimed days, or the processions not take place on those days along the proclaimed route; and I think that the words imposing on the defendant the obligation to accept and pay for the use of the rooms for the named days, although general and unconditional, were not used with reference to the possibility of the particular contingency which afterwards occurred.

It was suggested in the course of the argument that if the occurrence, on the proclaimed days, of the coronation and the procession in this case were the foundation of the contract, and if the general words are thereby limited or quali-fied, so that in the event of the non-occurrence of the coronation and procession along the proclaimed route they would discharge both parties from further per-formance of the contract, it would follow that if a cabman was engaged to take some one to Epsom on Derby Day at a suitable enhanced price for such a journey, say 10£., both parties to the contract would be discharged in the contingency of the race at Epsom for some reason becoming impossible; but I do not think this follows, for I do not think that in the cab case the happening of the race would be the foundation of the contract. No doubt the purpose of the engager would be to go to see the Derby, and the price would be proportionately high; but the cab had no special qualifications for the purpose which led to the selection of the cab for this particular occasion. Any other cab would have done as well. Moreover, I think that, under the cab contract, the hirer, even if the race went off, could have said, "Drive me to Epsom; I will pay you the agreed sum; you have nothing to do with the purpose for which I hired the cab," and that if the cabman refused he would have been guilty of a breach of contract, there being nothing to qualify his promise to drive the hirer to Epsom on a particular day. Whereas in the case of the coronation, there is not merely the purpose of the hirer to see the coronation procession, but it is the coronation procession and the relative position of the rooms which is the basis of the contract as much for the lessor as the hirer; and I think that if the King, before the coronation day and after the contract, had died, the hirer could not have insisted on having the rooms on the days named. It could not in the cab case be reasonably said that seeing the Derby race was the foundation of the contract, as it was of the licence in this case. Whereas in the present case, where the rooms were offered and taken, by reason of their peculiar suitability from the position of the rooms for a view of the coronation procession, surely the view of the coronation procession was the foundation of the contract, which is a very different thing from the purpose of the man who engaged the cab—namely, to see the race—being held to be the foundation of the contract.

Think About It!

Do you think the court correctly distinguishes the case of hiring a cab to see the Derby? Would a party booking a hotel and flight for a vacation trip be allowed to cancel on the basis of frustration of purpose if the weather was bad at the beach destination? If a hurricane or tsunami did substantial damage to the destination location, but the hotel remained in operation?

Each case must be judged by its own circumstances. In each case one must ask oneself, first, what, having regard to all the circumstances, was the foundation of the contract? Secondly, was the performance of the contract prevented? Thirdly, was the event which prevented the performance of the contract of such a character that it cannot reasonably be said to have been in the contemplation of the parties at the date of the contract? If all these questions are answered in the affirmative (as I think they should be in this case), I think both parties are discharged from further performance of the contract. I think that the coronation procession was the foundation of this contract, and that the non-happening of it prevented the performance of the contract; and, secondly, I think that the non-happening of the procession . . . was an event "of such a character that it cannot reasonably be supposed to have been in the contemplation of the contracting parties when the contract was made, and that they are not to be held bound by general words which, though large enough to include, were not used with reference to the possibility of the particular contingency which afterwards happened." The test seems to be whether the event which causes the impossibility was or might have been anticipated and guarded against. It seems difficult to say, in a case where both parties anticipate the happening of an event, which anticipation is the foundation of the contract, that either party must be taken to have anticipated, and ought to have guarded against, the event which prevented the performance of the contract.

. . . .

It is not essential to the application of the principle of Taylor v. Caldwell that the direct subject of the contract should perish or fail to be in existence at the date of performance of the contract. It is sufficient if a state of things or condition expressed in the contract and essential to its performance perishes or fails to be in existence at that time. In the present case the condition which fails and prevents the achievement of that which was, in the contemplation of both parties, the foundation of the contract, is not expressly men-

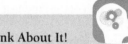

Think About It!

When the court states the rule from *Taylor*, what subtle wording change broadens the scope of the rule? How does that broader version of the *Taylor* rule assist the court in formulating its new articulation of excuse?

tioned either as a condition of the contract or the purpose of it; but I think for the reasons which I have given that the principle of Taylor v. Caldwell ought to be applied. This disposes of the plaintiff's claim for 50£. unpaid balance of the price agreed to be paid for the use of the rooms.

. . . .

See It

The distant building in the center, facing the viewer, contains the flat overlooking Pall Mall, where King Edward VII's coronation was scheduled to take place. The flat's ideal location on Pall Mall was one of Krell's primary advertising points for letting the flat and Henry's primary reason for renting the flat. Thanks to Jessica Zaiken for her permission to reproduce this photograph.

Restatement (Second) § 265 describes the excuse of frustration of purpose in terms that almost exactly parallel to the impracticability excuse of § 261:

> Where, after a contract is made, a party's principal purpose is substantially frustrated without his fault by the occurrence of an event the non-occurrence of which was a basic assumption on which the contract was made, his remaining duties to render performance are discharged, unless the language or the circumstances indicate the contrary.

As with impracticability, the excuse of frustration of purpose requires the occurrence of an event not anticipated by the parties, the non-occurrence of the event must be a basic assumption on which the contract was made, and the circumstances and language must not show the risk was allocated to the party seeking excuse. What, then, is the difference between impracticability and frustration of purpose? One commentator answered as follows:

> A person who is to supply lands, goods or services, but cannot perform, will attempt to use the impracticability defense. A buyer or any party who is obliged to pay will ordinarily attempt to use the defense of frustration. For example, if A agreed to supply B with a number of barges to carry a finished product from B's plant and A was unable to supply the barges, A would attempt to use the defense of impracticability. If B had no product to ship, B would attempt to use the frustration doctrine. Impracticability does not apply to B's promise because it is still perfectly possible for B to pay, but B is getting nothing for the money.[*]

The following example illustrates a more recent successful assertion of the excuse of frustration of purpose.

Example M: *Viking Supply v. National Cart Co.*, 310 F.3d 1092 (8th Cir. 2002).

National Cart, a manufacturer of shopping cart corrals used for the storage of shopping carts, entered into an agreement with Viking whereby Viking would sell National's cart corrals to Target as distributor, and

---

[*] Joseph M. Perillo, Calamari and Perillo on Contracts § 13.12 (6th ed. 2009).

> National Cart would refrain from selling its cart corrals to Target directly. After three years, Target informed National Cart that it would no longer purchase National Cart products through Viking, in part because of dissatisfaction with Viking's service and pricing, and in part because Target had instituted a policy of dealing only directly with manufacturers whenever possible. National Cart then terminated its distributorship relationship with Viking. Viking sued National Cart for breaching its agreement with Viking by offering to sell directly to Target before terminating the agreement with Viking.

Analysis: The district court rejected Viking's breach of contract claim, finding that the primary purpose of the contract "(to have Viking act as the distributor of National Cart's corrals to Target . . .) was frustrated by Target's refusal to buy National Cart corrals, thus excusing National Cart's performance." Viking appealed this ruling, arguing that the primary purpose of the contract was instead "to ensure that National Cart would continue to supply corrals to Target . . . without competition from other suppliers." The court of appeals cited Restatement (Second) § 265 in upholding the district court's ruling and wrote:

> It is elementary that unless Target was willing to buy corrals from Viking, the distributorship contract would make little sense, if any. Whether the purpose was, as the district court found, to have Viking act as the distributor of National Cart corrals to Target . . . or whether the purpose was, as Viking asserts, to ensure that National Cart would continue to supply corrals to Target . . . without competition from other suppliers, Target's willingness to buy National Cart corrals from Viking was clearly the basis of the contract. National Cart's essential purpose in selling corrals to Target through Viking, with or without competition, was frustrated by the occurrence of an event. This event was Target's unwillingness to do business with Viking. This event completely frustrated the basic assumption upon which the contract was made and without which the contract would make no sense.

The court also rejected Viking's arguments that National Cart contributed to the frustration of the contract by failing to notify Viking of Target's concerns about Viking's performance, by failing to notify Target of the existence of their distributorship agreement, and by trying to sell to Target directly. The court held that National Cart had no obligation to notify Viking of Target's concerns, that Target clearly knew about the distributorship agreement, and that there was no evidence that National Cart tried to sell directly to Target until after Viking had been notified of the termination of the contract.

As compared with excuse based on impracticability, courts are even more reluctant to grant excuse based on frustration of purpose. Some jurisdictions do not recognize it at all. Although the UCC does not explicitly recognize the doctrine (indeed, UCC § 2–615 makes this excuse available only to the seller of goods), UCC § 1–103(b) expressly incorporates common law doctrines not displaced by the UCC.

If a jurisdiction recognizes the excuse of frustration of purpose, it is subject to the same sorts of limits as impracticability, as the following case illustrates.

Adbar, L.C. v. New Beginnings C-Star

ADBAR, L.C., Plaintiff-Appellant
v.
NEW BEGINNINGS C-STAR, Defendant-Respondent

Missouri Court of Appeals
103 S.W.3d 799 (Mo. Ct. App. 2003)

GLENN A. NORTON, JUDGE.

Adbar, L.C. appeals the judgment in favor of New Beginnings C-Star on Adbar's claim for breach of lease. We reverse in part . . . .

I. BACKGROUND

New Beginnings provides rehabilitation services for alcohol and drug abuse to both adults and adolescents. In the fall of 1999, New Beginnings was searching for a new location and entered into negotiations with Adbar for lease of a building in the City of St. Louis. New Beginnings received a preliminary indication from the City's zoning administrator that its use of the property constituted a permitted use under the zoning regulations. New Beginnings and Adbar subsequently entered into a three-year lease. The total rent due for the three-year term was $273,000.

After the lease was executed, the City denied New Beginnings' application for an occupancy permit on the grounds that the operation constituted a nuisance use under the zoning regulations. At trial, Alderman Freeman Bosley, Sr. testified that due to his opposition to New Beginnings moving into his Ward, he had called the zoning administrator and asked him to reverse his preliminary indication that New Beginnings' operation constituted a permitted use.

New Beginnings appealed the denial of the occupancy permit to the board of adjustment. Alderman Bosley and other neighborhood residents testified in opposition to New Beginnings at the board's hearing. The board affirmed the denial of the permit. New Beginnings then sought a writ, which was granted by the circuit court, and New Beginnings was issued an occupancy permit. Alderman Bosley contacted the judge who issued the writ and asked him to reverse his decision. The judge declined. A few weeks later, at the City counselor's request, the City revoked New Beginnings' occupancy permit. New Beginnings filed a motion for contempt with the circuit court. The motion was granted, and the City re-issued the occupancy permit.

After the permit was reissued, New Beginnings began preparing to move in, including having some construction done on the building. At this same time, Alderman Bosley contacted then State Representative Paula Carter, chairwoman of the appropriations committee responsible for New Beginnings' state funding. Alderman Bosley asked Representative Carter to "pull the funding" for New Beginnings. Alderman Bosley did not get a commitment from Representative Carter, but told her that "if you don't get their funding, you are going to have trouble running" for re-election.

New Beginnings alleges that it was then contacted by Michael Couty, director of the Missouri Division of Alcohol and Drug Abuse, who threatened to rescind all state contracts with New Beginnings if it moved into the new location. New Beginnings convened a meeting of its board of directors to conduct a conference call with Director Couty. New Beginnings alleges that during that conference call Director Couty repeated his threat to rescind funding if it moved into the new location. At the end of the meeting, New Beginnings' board decided not to occupy the building they had leased from Adbar. At trial Director Couty denied making any such threats to New Beginnings.

Adbar filed a petition for breach of the lease. New Beginnings asserted a defense of legal impossibility. On the first day of the trial, New Beginnings was granted leave to amend its answer to add the defense of commercial frustration. Following a bench trial, the trial court ruled that New Beginnings was excused from its performance under the lease because of commercial frustration. This appeal follows.

II. DISCUSSION

On review of this court-tried case, we will sustain the judgment of the trial court unless there is no substantial evidence to support it, it is against the weight of the evidence, it erroneously declares the law, or it erroneously applies the law. *Murphy v. Carron,* 536 S.W.2d 30, 32 (Mo. banc 1976). We accept the evidence and inferences favorable to the prevailing party and disregard all contrary evidence. *Kassebaum v. Kassebaum,* 42 S.W.3d 685, 692 (Mo.App. E.D.2001). We will defer to the factual findings of the trial judge, who is in a superior position to assess credibility; however, we independently evaluate the court's conclusions of law. *Id.*

A. Commercial Frustration

In its first point on appeal, Adbar asserts that the trial court erroneously applied the law when it excused New Beginnings' performance under the lease due to the doctrine of commercial frustration. We agree.

The doctrine of commercial frustration grew out of demands of the commercial world to excuse performance under contracts in cases of extreme hardship. *Kassebaum,* 42 S.W.3d at 699. Under the doctrine of commercial frustration, if the occurrence of an event, not foreseen by the parties and not caused by or under the control of either party, destroys or nearly destroys the value of the performance or the object or purpose of the contract, then the parties are excused from further performance. *Id.* If, on the other hand, the event was reasonably foreseeable, then the parties should have provided for its occurrence in the contract. *Werner v. Ashcraft Bloomquist, Inc.,* 10 S.W.3d 575, 577 (Mo.App. E.D.2000). The absence of a provision in the contract providing for such an occurrence indicates an assumption of the risk by the promisor. *Id.* In determining foreseeability, courts consider the terms of the contract and the circumstances surrounding the formation of the contract. *Id.* at 577–578. The doctrine of commercial frustration should be limited in its application so as to preserve the certainty of contracts. *Id.* at 578.

New Beginnings alleged that the troubles it faced obtaining its occupancy permit, along with the actions of Alderman Bosley and Director Couty, combined to rise to commercially frustrate the lease agreement with Adbar. Ultimately, New Beginnings' funding was never rescinded. In this case the intervening event was merely the *possibility* that the funding may be rescinded. For an organization that receives funding from the State, the possibility that their funding may be reduced or even completely rescinded is foreseeable. Furthermore, while the zeal with which Alderman Bosley attempted to keep New Beginnings out of his ward may have been surprising to the parties, it is certainly foreseeable that a drug and alcohol abuse treatment facility might encounter neighborhood resistance when attempting to move into a new location. At trial, the CEO of New Beginnings admitted that both the elimination of New Beginnings' funding and opposition from neighborhood groups were foreseeable.

This court has addressed similar intervening events before. In *Conlon Group, Inc. v. City of St. Louis,* this Court found that structural defects in a 100 year-old building were foreseeable and, despite increased development costs, the agreement with the City's redevelopment authority remained intact. 980 S.W.2d 37, 40–41 (Mo.App. E.D.1998). In *Shop 'N Save Warehouse Foods, Inc. v. Soffer,* this Court found that a lessor could foresee that its supermarket tenant might bring an action to enforce a radius restriction in the lease to keep him from leasing property to another supermarket chain. 918 S.W.2d 851, 863 (Mo.App. E.D.1996). The Court noted that, while neither party wanted the eventual result, the doctrine of commercial frustration did not provide a means to avoid a bad result. *Id.* The possibility that New Beginnings' funding may be threatened was foreseeable. Yet, New Beginnings did not provide for that possibility in the lease. Therefore, New Beginnings assumed the risk that their funding may be threatened and that it might frustrate the purpose of the lease.

In addition to this event being foreseeable, neither the value of the performance nor the purpose of the lease was destroyed. The purpose of the lease was to allow New Beginnings to operate a rehabilitation center at the location of the property. New Beginnings' funding was never rescinded or even restricted. Alderman Bosley's continued interference with New Beginnings efforts to provide rehabilitation treatment to addicts of drugs and alcohol certainly made, and would have continued to make, business difficult for New Beginnings. However, neither the value of the performance nor the object or purpose of the lease was destroyed or nearly destroyed.

Therefore, the doctrine of commercial frustration does not excuse New Beginnings performance under the lease. . . .

. . . .

III. CONCLUSION

The judgment that New Beginnings is excused from the lease under the defense of commercial frustration is reversed and the cause is remanded for a new trial in accordance with this opinion. The judgment in all other respects is affirmed.

WILLIAM H. CRANDALL, P.J., and SHERRI B. SULLIVAN, J., concurring.

Think About It!

The case law on excuse tends to cluster around unexpected events. *Transatlantic Financing Corp. v. U.S.* (Example K, page 755) was one of many cases involving excuse that were brought after the Suez Canal was closed in 1956.

More recently, the terrorist attacks on the World Trade Center in New York City, on September 11, 2001, gave rise to a number of such cases:

- *U.S. Bancorp Equipment Finance, Inc. v. Ameriquest Holdings LLC*, 55 UCC Rep. Serv. 2d 423 (D. Minn. 2004) (immense losses to airline industry following Sept. 11 attacks and consequent extreme devaluation of purchased airplane did not excuse buyer from paying the contract price to purchase the plane).

- *Sub-Zero Freezer Co. v. Cunard Line Ltd.*, 2002 WL 32357103 (D. Wisc. Mar. 12, 2002) (plaintiff was not excused or entitled to a refund of its prepayment of the contract price for seven-night cruise for its employees on defendant's vessel in early October 2001; the cruise could still occur in the immediate aftermath of Sept. 11 attacks even though it might not be "the safe and relaxing cruise" plaintiff alleged that defendant had agreed to provide).

- *Bush v. Protravel International, Inc.*, 746 N.Y.S.2d 790 (Civil Ct. 2002) (defendant's summary judgment motion denied; plaintiff was permitted to proceed to trial to demonstrate excuse on basis of impossibility for her failure to cancel her safari reservation before the cancellation deadline of Sept. 15, 2001, in view of extreme circumstances in New York in the days following the Sept. 11 attack on the World Trade Center).

Was the absence of such attacks, disruptions, or losses a basic assumption on which the contracts were premised? Were any of these risks implicitly allocated in the contract? What kinds of facts might indicate an implicit allocation of risk?

The disruptions from natural disasters such as the hurricanes, fires, and floods of 2017 may give rise to claims of excuse in contracts affected by those disruptions, directly or indirectly. Professor Myanna Dellinger analyzed approximately 100 contract law cases addressing weather-related events after Hurricane Katrina 2005, examining how the courts applied excuse. She observed that climate change is responsible for problems such as "rising seas, increased storm intensity and frequency, extreme and prolonged droughts and wildfires in some regions, as well as extreme cold spells and snowfall in others."[*] These sorts of phenomenon have traditionally been considered "acts of God" under

---

[*] Mynna Dellinger, *Rethinking Contractual Impracticability*, 67 Hast. L.J. 1551 (2016).

force majeure clauses, or events "the non-occurrence of which [were] a basic assumption on which the contract was made" under excuse. However, Professor Dellinger cautions, "[T]he judiciary should more closely scrutinize arguments that parties did not actually foresee or could not reasonably have foreseen the problematic weather event. Exculpating a party from contractual liability based on the argument that the party assumed a certain supervening event would *not* become reality is troublesome from both a legal and a public policy point of view. At bottom, impracticability arguments [based on] weather problems are becoming increasingly implausible. Parties should thus exercise more caution in this respect than in even recent decades. The law is likely to change."

Do you agree with Professor Dellinger's predictions? Are catastrophic weather events sufficiently unforeseeable to the contracting parties to merit excuse? Is the absence of such events a basic assumption on which contracts can be premised? How might parties to a contract implicitly or explicitly allocate the risks of such events?

Make the Connection: The Relationship Between Mistake and Excuse

Thus far, you have encountered excuses based on unexpected circumstances that arose *after* contract formation; these excuses are known as "supervening" impossibility, impracticability, and frustration. But excuse can also be based on unexpected circumstances that existed at contract formation but were unknown to the parties until later. These excuses are known as "existing" impossibility, impracticability, and frustration.* Interestingly, these "existing" excuses overlap to some extent with the defense of mistake (covered in Chapter 6), which is based on the unexpected facts in existence at the time of contract formation. Mistake makes the contract voidable (subject to rescission), while excuse relieves one or both parties of performance duties or a breach.

Consider the case of *McCaull-Webster Elevator Co. v. Steele Bros.*, 180 N.W. 782 (S.D. 1921), presenting facts similar to Examples J and K.

---

* Restatement (Second) § 266 covers "existing impracticability or frustration." Restatement (Second) §§ 261 and 265 cover "supervening" impracticability and frustration.

(Recall that in those cases the defendants asserted the defense of impossibility.) Steele entered into a contract to sell to McCaull "5000 bushels of good sound, dry and merchantable corn to grade 3Y, 'said grain now being in my possession.' " Both parties intended as the subject of the contract corn that was growing in Steele's fields at the time of the contract, and both parties firmly believed the corn was grade 3Y. In fact, the corn did not meet the standards for grade 3Y. When Steele did not deliver the corn, McCaull sued for breach of contract. Steele asserted the defense of mistake. The court held for Steele, based on mistake, rather than impossibility, because

> both parties were so confident that the corn, then in the minds of the parties, would fulfill the conditions as to grade, that they made no provision whatsoever as to what should be done if this corn would not test No. 3. They contracted in the full belief that defendants had in their possession 5,000 bushels of yellow corn that would, at the time for delivery, grade No. 3. No corn that would, by mere lapse of time, become No. 3 corn, was in possession of defendants. Both parties assumed, as the very basis of the contract, that corn that would fulfill this contract did exist in the possession of defendants. Being mistaken as to this essential fact, there was no binding contract.

In situations where it is unclear which defense or excuse is most appropriate, it may be strategically wise for a defendant to raise both mistake and excuse, in the alternative.

§ 6.4. When *Do* Courts Grant Excuse?

Adbar (page 770), *Transatlantic* (Example K, page 755), and *NIPSCO* (Example L, page 758) are typical in denying relief based on impracticability or impossibility. *Taylor*, *Krell*, and *Unke* (Example I, page 753), illustrate the occasional but rare ruling in favor of relief.

Analyzing why certain cases have been successful may help parties draft contracts and litigate disputes when the unexpected happens. One cluster of successful cases involved health and safety concerns:

- *Northern Corp. v. Chugach Elec. Assn.*, 518 P.2d 76 (Alaska 1974) (duty to supply rock across lake discharged when unsafe ice conditions made it dangerous to haul rock across lake and this was the means of delivery "contemplated" by the parties).

- *Lakeman v. Pollard*, 43 Me. 463 (1857) (mill employee "was under no obligation to imperil his life by remaining at work in the vicinity of a [cholera] epidemic . . . nor does it make any difference that the men who remained there at work after [he] left were healthy, and continued to be so").

- *Hanford v. Connecticut Fair Assn.*, 103 A. 838 (Conn. 1918) (party excused from putting on baby show by apprehension of danger to babies from epidemic of infantile paralysis).

- *The Kronprinzessin Cecilie*, 244 U.S. 12 (1917) (owner of German steamship excused from completing voyage from US to England by apprehension on eve of WWI that she would be seized as prize).

An unusual pair of successful cases involved huge increases in the cost of performance, even though usually a large cost increase alone will not be grounds for excuse:

- *Florida Power & Light Co. v. Westinghouse Elec. Corp.*, 826 F.2d 239 (4th Cir. 1987) (difference in cost of disposing of spent fuel is "percentages in the hundreds range" and use of alternative method would not only "wipe out the expected profit but [result] in a loss some four or five times the expected profit").

- *Mineral Park Land Co. v. Howard*, 156 P. 458 (Cal. 1916) (excavator could take no further earth and gravel by "ordinary means" and "any greater amount could have been taken only at a prohibitive cost, that is, at an expense of ten or twelve times as much as the usual cost per yard").

In yet another pair of successful cases, the subject matter or purpose of the contract ceased to exist:

- *Alabama Football, Inc. v. Wright*, 452 F. Supp. 182 (N.D. Tex. 1977) (the unexpected and unplanned-for financial failure of the World Football League and Alabama Football rendered it impossible for Alabama Football to provide a team position for Wright, excusing both parties from their remaining duties under the contract).

- *Aluminum Company of America v. Essex Group, Inc.*, 499 F. Supp. 53 (W.D. Pa. 1980) (ALCOA's unexpected and huge increase in production costs excused its non-performance in conversion of alumina to molten aluminum, because performance became impracticable and because ALCOA's purpose ("an expected profit") was frustrated by the resulting extraordinary losses.

Aluminum Company of America is an oddity in the application of the excuse doctrine and has remained a controversial case among legal scholars. Some even view the court's reasoning as a misuse of the mistake doctrine because it allowed relief for mistake related to future occurrences. *See, e.g.,* E. Allan Farnsworth, *Farnsworth on Contracts* § 9.7 n.14 (3d ed. 2004).

Frustration of purpose has been an even more difficult excuse to obtain. Not all jurisdictions recognize the doctrine. In the jurisdictions that do, courts have required the party's "principal purpose" (viewed broadly) be frustrated nearly completely. If the subject of the contract can be used in some other way, albeit not as profitably or even at a loss, the excuse is often denied. Probably the most commonly discussed case is *Lloyd v. Murphy*, 153 P.2d 47 (Cal. 1944), in which a car dealer sought to be released from his payment obligations under a five-year commercial lease created shortly before the United States entered World War II. The lease limited use of the property to selling new cars and operating a gas station and forbade subletting except with lessor's permission. The government subsequently severely restricted sales of new cars, and the lessee vacated the property, even though lessor offered to waive the use restrictions, lower the rent, and allow subletting. The court noted that "the applicability of the doctrine of frustration depends on the total or nearly total destruction of the purpose for which, in the contemplation of both parties, the transaction was entered into," *id.* at 50, and found no such destruction where the leased property was on a main traffic route in Los Angeles (Wilshire Blvd. in Beverly Hills), making it usable for other purposes. Moreover, the court found that the lessee had assumed the risk of the wartime restrictions on new car sales, because the regulations were widely foreseen:

> At the time the lease in the present case was executed the National Defense Act, . . . authorizing the President to allocate materials and mobilize industry for national defense, had been law for more than a year. The automotive industry was in the process of conversion to supply the needs of our growing mechanized army and to meet lend-lease commitments. Iceland and Greenland had been occupied by the army. Automobile sales were soaring because the public anticipated that production would soon be restricted. These facts were commonly known and it cannot be said that the risk of war and its consequences necessitating restriction of the production and sale of automobiles was so remote a contingency that its risk could not be foreseen by defendant, an experienced automobile dealer. Indeed, the conditions prevailing at the time the lease was executed, and the absence of any provision in the lease contracting against the effect of war, gives rise to the inference that the risk was assumed.

Id. at 51.

Reading Critically: Temporary or Partial Excuse

Read Restatement (Second) §§ 269 and 270.

1. If the impracticability of performance or frustration of purpose is only temporary, what happens to an affected party's duty to perform? Under what circumstances would a temporary excuse discharge a duty or prevent it from arising?

2. If only part of the performance of a duty is impracticable, does the party have a duty to render the remaining (not impracticable) part of her performance?

Problems: Impossibility, Impracticability, and Frustration of Purpose

9-10. Ben is a freelance delivery driver who contracts with Callie, a horticulturist, to ship a load of tropical plants from Florida to the upper peninsula of Michigan, in January. The trailer is well insulated but poorly heated, so Ben must make the trip as quickly as possible. The written contract states that Ben "shall make the absolute minimum of stops en route to the delivery site." However, as Ben reaches southern Michigan, he encounters a severe blizzard, which reduces visibility to less than 100 feet. Snow begins to accumulate faster than plows can remove it from the highway, and crosswinds gust at 20 to 30 miles per hour.

Ben typically drives routes in the South, but he has encountered blizzards before. He debates whether or not he is capable of completing his route without stopping and waiting for the blizzard to pass. If Ben stops, the plants are likely to freeze and die. Ben finally decides that the trip may be possible, but the safety risk that he would incur by continuing is too great. Ben stops, and as expected, all of the plants die.

If Callie brings a claim for breach of contract, can Ben successfully raise a claim of impracticability? Consider arguments for both sides.

9-11. In 1979, the Vikings professional football team signed a lease with the Commission that administered the Metrodome, a domed sports stadium, to play in the Metrodome through the 2011–12 football season. Included in the lease was the following clause:

In the event of total or partial destruction rendering the Stadium not suitable for playing home games or of a valid governmental order prohibiting use of the Stadium for home games, this Agreement will be suspended immediately as to playing home games until the governmental order ceases to prohibit use for home games or the Stadium is repaired.

The Commission shall notify the Team within ninety days from the date the Stadium is no longer suitable for playing home games, whether the Commission will rebuild or repair the Stadium. If the Commission decides to rebuild or repair the Stadium, this Agreement will continue to be suspended until the Stadium is suitable for playing home games; and the Commission shall notify the Team of the Commission's best estimate of when the Stadium will be suitable for playing home games again.

For each football season, or part of football season, while this Agreement is suspended, the term of this Agreement as provided in section 3 shall be extended by one football season.

Decades later, as the Vikings lobbied to get a new stadium built and considered whether to move to a different city, the Metrodome roof tore and collapsed. The Commission argued that, under the above clause, the Vikings were bound to an additional year's lease on the stadium, even though only two of ten games had been affected by the torn roof. The Commission replaced the original roof with a stronger, more expensive roof (with some unknown amount of reimbursement from its insurance), even though the stadium might be used for only another 2–3 years, depending on the shifting politics of state funding and the worst economy since the Great Depression of the 1930s.

Now fast forward and put yourself in the shoes of counsel for the Vikings and the Commission, as they negotiated a 30-year lease for a new stadium, to be built on the Metrodome site in 2013–15. Assume that the previous lease language is the starting point for their negotiations. Construct arguments *for each side* as to how to edit or redraft the above clause. Be sure you look for counter-arguments to your arguments from the other side. Limit your efforts to the scope of the 1979 clause.

———————————————

Test Your Knowledge

To assess your understanding of the material in this chapter, click here to take a quiz.

CHAPTER 10

Remedies

How do parties demonstrate assent to a contract?

What kinds of promises will the law enforce?

What defenses to enforcement exist?

Is a writing required for enforcement? If so, what kind?

How is the content and meaning of a contract determined?

What are parties' rights and duties after breach?

What situations lead to excusing contract performance?

What remedies are available for breach of contract?

What contractual rights and duties do non-parties to a contract have?

Table of Contents

§ 1. Overview...782

    PROBLEM: COMPARING REMEDIAL PRINCIPLES (10-1)......................784

§ 2. Remedies at Law (Damages)...786

    PROBLEMS: COMPARING TYPES OF DAMAGES (10-2, 10-3)....................787

    § 2.1. Expectation Damages..790

        § 2.1.1. Categories of Expectation Damages 790

        § 2.1.2. Thinking Sensibly About Expectation Damages 792

        PROBLEMS: DETERMINING EXPECTATION DAMAGES (10-4 TO 10-9) 793

        § 2.1.3. Measuring Typical Direct Damages.........................795

        § 2.1.4. Special Problems in Measuring Direct Damages 800

            § 2.1.4.1. Damages Resulting from Anticipatory Repudiation..800

            § 2.1.4.2. Owner's Cost to Complete Versus Diminution in Value 802

            Lyon v. Belosky Construction, Inc. 804

            PROBLEM: DAMAGES FOR DEFECTIVE PERFORMANCE (10-10).....806

            Peevyhouse v. Garland Coal & Mining Co. 808

            § 2.1.4.3. Damages for "Lost Profits" and "Lost Volume"........815

§ 2.1.5. Indirect Expectation Damages 818

    § 2.1.5.1. Incidental Damages 819

        Problem: Incidental Damages (10-11) 819

    § 2.1.5.2. Consequential Damages...820

§ 2.1.6. Mitigation of Damages (Avoidable Damages) 833

    Parker v. Twentieth Century-Fox Film Corp. 837

    Problem: Mitigation of Damages (10-12) 846

§ 2.2. Reliance Damages..847

§ 2.3. Restitution Damages 851

    § 2.3.1. Damages for the Party Who Materially Breaches 854

    Eker Brothers, Inc. v. Rehders...856

    § 2.3.2. Damages for the Party Who Is Prevented from

    Performing 860

    Problem: Restitution Damages (10-13)....................................862

§ 2.4. Agreed and Liquidated Damages 862

    Wassenaar v. Panos..863

    Problems: Liquidated Damages (10-14, 10-15).......................871

§ 2.5. Punitive Damages..875

    Romero v. Mervyn's..875

§ 3. Equitable Remedies: The "Extraordinary Remedies" 881

§ 3.1. Specific Performance...882

    Ammerman v. City Stores Co. 884

    Laclede Gas Co. v. Amoco Oil Co...888

    Problem: Specific Performance (10-16)....................................894

§ 3.2. Prohibitory Injunction...894

    American Broadcasting Companies v. Wolf................................895

§ 3.3. Specific Restitution...905

§ 4. Putting the Concepts Together 906

§ 1. Overview

After a breach, the aggrieved party is entitled to seek remedies against the breaching party. These remedies may be "at law" (money damages) or "in equity" (court orders to perform, or to act or refrain from acting in specific ways). Historically, courts have preferred to award damages rather than to order equitable (often called "extraordinary") relief. As discussed in Chapter 5 (page 285), parties had access to the old English courts of chancery only if they could not be made whole by an award of damages from a court of law (King's Bench or Queen's Bench). Most U.S. courts now combine the courts of law and equity, while retaining the limitations that equitable relief is unavailable unless the aggrieved party

- has "no adequate remedy at law" and

- would suffer "irreparable harm" if the equitable remedy were not granted.

Courts' preference for damage awards is also grounded in their hesitation to become involved in administering or supervising a remedy, which is often necessary with equitable forms of relief.

The goal of contract remedies is to give the aggrieved party the benefit of the broken contract promises. It is prospective in nature, often described as putting the aggrieved party in the position it would have been in if the contract had been fully performed. Although defining what that means may be difficult, and the goal may not always be attained, it helps to keep that goal in mind and to compare it to the remedial principles that underlie two other bodies of law that sometimes apply when contracts are broken. The differing remedial principles are represented by the chart below:

	Remedial Principle
Contract	One who unjustifiably fails to perform a promise must pay to put the promisee in the position of full performance
Tort	One who unjustifiably harms another's person or property must provide compensation for the harm caused
Unjust Enrichment	One who is unjustifiably enriched at another's expense must disgorge the enrichment

The principles underlying these three areas of law appear at first glance to be quite different. Contract remedies look to the future to fulfill the broken promises. Tort remedies look to the past, to compensate for past injury. Unjust enrichment remedies focus on the breacher (making her disgorge benefits received), rather than on compensating the non-breacher. In fact, however, the content of the remedies are overlapping, as represented by the diagram below ("Δ" denotes the defendant, and "π" denotes the plaintiff).

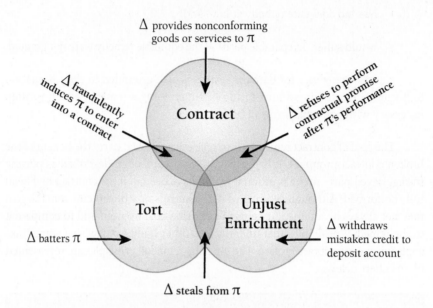

Δ provides nonconforming goods or services to π

Δ fraudulently induces π to enter into a contract

Δ refuses to perform contractual promise after π's performance

Contract

Tort

Unjust Enrichment

Δ batters π

Δ withdraws mistaken credit to deposit account

Δ steals from π

Problem: Comparing Remedial Principles

10-1. Determine where each of the examples fit in the above diagram:

a. Sam promises to watch Matilda's dog while she is on vacation for $50 per day. Sam does not watch the dog, and Matilda hires Jasmine to watch the dog for $75 per day.

b. Carol assists an elderly neighbor, Ethel, by running errands, housekeeping and cooking. Carol spends her own money for groceries, cleaning supplies and gas. Ethel later promises to reimburse Carol and pay her a reasonable hourly rate.

c. Employer wrongfully discharges Employee. Employer and Employee enter into a settlement agreement whereby both agree not to make disparaging statements about the other. Employer later makes untrue negative statements about Employee that prevent Employee from obtaining employment.

d. Manufacturer contracts to produce a table saw for Lumberman. The table saw turns out to be defective due to Manufacturer's poor design of the saw.

e. Salmon and Meinhard sign a joint venture contract to manage the Bristol Hotel for 20 years, each agreeing to not engage in competing businesses. Toward the end of the 20 years, but during the contract term, Salmon enters into a contract to purchase real property surrounding the Bristol Hotel for a competing business.

As you see in the responses to Problem 10-1, the same set of facts may give rise to a cause of action in more than one of these three areas of law, and the remedial principles driving the computation of damages may overlap as well. Keep that in mind as you consider the range of contract remedies available, and which are appropriate in a given case.

To help you navigate the complex web of remedies discussed, the flowchart below shows the organization of the chapter. A second chart providing a guide to the meaning of each remedy identified in the flowchart appears at the end of the chapter. You may find it useful to refer to that compilation periodically as you work your way through the chapter.

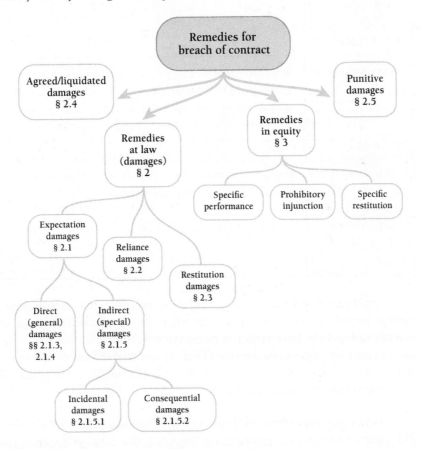

This chapter begins with the damages at law for breach of contract (the preferred set of contract remedies), followed by equitable remedies.

§ 2. Remedies at Law (Damages)

Although you may expect that contract damages are computed from a collection of formulas, determining appropriate damages is more dependent on understanding the purposes and policies underlying damage awards and their limitations than it is on any mathematical construct.

Policy	Corollary/competing policy
Award damages for injury actually caused by the breach.	Do not award damages for injuries that the aggrieved party could have avoided/prevented/mitigated (because that means they were not caused by the breaching party).
Avoid over-compensation, windfalls, and double recovery.	Avoid under-compensation, forfeitures, and penalties.
Avoid speculative damages.	Avoid letting the breaching party profit from the uncertainty caused by the breach, even if the measure of damages is somewhat uncertain, and resolve uncertainties in favor of the aggrieved party to ensure adequate compensation.
Award consequential damages for injury foreseeable to breaching party at time of contract formation.	Avoid burdening the breaching party with damages the risk of which was not reasonably contemplated when deciding whether to enter into the agreement.

Sometimes a court can satisfy all of these policies when determining a damage award. Other times—particularly when the contract performances are complicated and the interrelationships complex—courts must balance policy goals to craft the appropriate damage award. As you read the cases on damages in this chapter, note when the courts invoke (or could invoke) these policies in supporting their damage determinations.

As you may recall from the introduction to remedies in Chapter 5, page 272, contract law seeks to protect three "interests" (expectation, reliance, and restitution), each of which is reflected in a particular kind of damages:

- "Expectation damages" are designed to put the aggrieved party into the position that it would have been in if it had received the full performance promised (and had fully performed its own part of the bargain). Expectation damages make the plaintiff whole by paying the amount necessary to approximate the value of full performance.

- "Reliance damages" are designed to put the aggrieved party back in the position that it would have been in *today* if the parties had not entered the contract. Reliance damages compensate the out-of-pocket expenses incurred by the aggrieved party in reliance on the existence of the contract, as well as opportunities the aggrieved party let pass in reliance on the contract ("lost opportunity costs").

- "Restitution damages" are designed to avoid unjust enrichment of a party by forcing that party to restore ("disgorge") to the other party any as-yet-unpaid-for benefits it retained.

As already noted, the overarching goal of contract remedies is to put the aggrieved party in the position it would have been in if the contract had been performed, so expectation damages are the preferred form of damages, on the theory that full compensation should mean giving the aggrieved party the "benefit of the bargain" by enforcing the contract. But if expectation damages are inadequate or too speculative, or do not otherwise fulfill the policies noted in the chart above, courts will consider awarding reliance or restitution damages. Most often, expectation damages are the highest in amount, reliance next, and restitution the least, but sometimes there is little or no difference in the amount awarded under the various measures. The critical inquiry is to ask which measure best fulfills the policies underlying contract damage awards.

Problems: Comparing Types of Damages

10-2. Buyer purchases a toaster from Seller, paying $100 for it. The toaster does not work. Complete the chart below identifying Buyer's measure of damages under expectation, reliance and restitution.

| Expectation | The amount needed to put Buyer in the position it would have been in had the contract been fully performed. | |

Reliance	The amount needed to put Buyer in the position it would have been in had the contract not been made.	
Restitution	The amount needed to restore to the buyer the benefit conferred on Seller.	

10-3. Publisher agrees to print the manuscript of Professor, promising to pay a $2000 advance to Professor and pay royalties. Professor delivers the manuscript and Publisher pays the $2000 advance. Professor spends $500 on travel to Publisher's offices to work with Publisher on the manuscript. Publisher never publishes the book and never pays Professor any royalties. Publisher retains the manuscript. Professor sues Publisher. Complete the chart below identifying the potentially compensable items by categories of expectation, reliance, and restitution.

Expectation	The amount needed to put Professor in the position Professor would have been in had the contract been fully performed.	
Reliance	The amount needed to put Professor in the position Professor would have been in had the contract not been made.	
Restitution	The amount needed to restore to Professor the benefit conferred on Publisher.	

You will recall from Chapter 5, page 278, that in claims based on promissory estoppel, Restatement (Second) § 90 invites courts to limit the remedy for breach of promise "as justice requires." That standard suggests that in such cases courts might award reliance or restitution damages instead of expectation. In fact, many courts operating under Restatement (Second) § 90 nevertheless elect to award expectation damages, concluding that the recipient of such promises are entitled to the benefit of what was promised, even though there is often no "bargain" to be enforced. Courts operating under the first Restatement provision also typically award expectation damages, when that is possible. Some courts, though, will award an alternative measure of damages in these cases, as seen in Example A.

Example A: *Bouton v. Byers*, 321 P.3d 780 (Kan. Ct. App. 2014).

Daughter brought an action against Father on grounds of promissory estoppel arising from Father's alleged promise to leave her valuable land on his death if she quit her job as a law professor and worked on his cattle ranch. Daughter quit her job as a law professor and worked at the ranch, making much less than she did as a law professor, but Father fired her later and sold the ranch. Daughter returned to the law school and taught in a part-time position only. Daughter requested the court to award her an amount that she would have earned if she had continued working at the law school as a full-time professor.

Analysis: The court denied Father's motion for summary judgment on Daughter's promissory estoppel claim. With respect to remedy, the court noted that specific performance would be a legal impossibility as Father had sold the ranch. Kansas courts, "recognize[ ] a right to an alternative equitable remedy . . . tailored to the circumstances of the promise and the particular conduct on her part it reasonably induced—the abandonment of her teaching position." The court rejected Father's argument that she should only recover the value of services rendered to the ranch, and instead concluded that Daughter might recover an amount to place her "in the financial position she would have occupied had she not relied on the promise to her detriment." Daughter would, if she prevailed, recover her reliance damages.

If liability is based on a cause of action of restitution (recall the cases in Chapter 5, § 4), the courts will award restitution damages.

§ 2.1. Expectation Damages

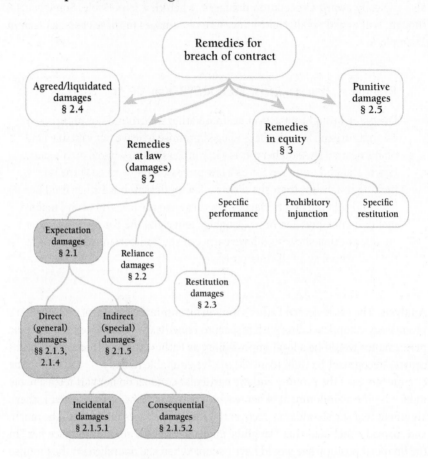

§ 2.1.1. Categories of Expectation Damages

Expectation damages include "direct" (also known as "general") damages and "indirect" (also known as "specific") damages:

- Direct damages are the amounts awarded for injury to or loss of the value of the performance promised in the contract. They measure the difference between the value of full performance and the value of performance actually received. For example, direct damages would compensate for the value of services not performed, purchased real estate or rental property not conveyed, payments not made, or a defect in the goods or services.

- Indirect damages are the amounts awarded for other secondary losses resulting from the breach. They include "incidental damages" and "consequential damages."

○ Incidental damages are extra costs incurred by the aggrieved party in dealing with the breach or mitigating losses from the breach, for example, by handling a defective delivery or arranging for purchase of substitute goods. Incidental damages can include costs incurred in storing or reshipping or reselling defective or repudiated goods, paying a broker to find a substitute buyer, boarding up and paying extra insurance on a building left unfinished by a vendor, or spending employee time negotiating a replacement contract with a new party.

○ Consequential damages are other losses arising as a consequence of the breach. They may include such items as lost profits, lost customers, lost business volume, and downstream breaches caused by the original breach. They are often the largest dollar-amount of the damages sought by an injured party.

Example B demonstrates how various damage amounts are characterized and, therefore, under which set of damages rules they are evaluated:

Example B: A professional freelance photographer purchases a digital camera for $1500 and spends $5000 to travel to Thailand to take pictures for a magazine spread on which she would earn $8000 profit. The camera malfunctions on the trip (unbeknownst to her until she returns), and all of the pictures are lost. Even the photo files on the back-up flash drive are corrupted and cannot be recovered. Repairs to the camera will cost $600, plus $20 in shipping the insured camera back to the manufacturer.

Analysis: How can the photographer's damages be characterized?

• Direct damages: The cost of repairing ($600) or replacing ($1500) the defective camera (she was promised a working camera, so the direct damages are the cost of making sure she gets one)

• Incidental damages: The cost of investigating the options for repairing or repurchasing (unknown cost), and the cost of driving to the repair shop (de minimis cost) or shipping the camera to the manufacturer ($20)

• Consequential damages: The lost profit on the magazine spread ($8000) and the reputational injury (perhaps speculative); or the cost of returning to Thailand to re-take the pictures ($5,000)

Placing damage awards in their particular categories does not mean they are all recoverable. As you will see in the material that follows, direct and incidental damages (if proved with sufficient certainty) are generally recoverable, but there are additional limits placed on the award of consequential damages. Moreover, the contract terms may limit recovery (e.g., the seller of the camera may have barred or limited consequential damages, to limit its exposure to what is likely to be the most expensive injury that might be caused by a breach).

§ 2.1.2. Thinking Sensibly About Expectation Damages

The goal of expectation damages is to put the aggrieved party in the position it would have been in if both parties had fully performed. That means ensuring the aggrieved party receives the value of the performance promised, reduced by the costs and expenses the aggrieved party would have "spent" in performing its own promises. Courts awarding expectation damages seek to "make whole" the aggrieved party, without giving a windfall or awarding speculative damages. Professor Farnsworth suggested a helpful formulation for categorizing and computing expectation damages,[*] used with slight modifications and additional explanations in the chart below:

Traditional Formula	Explanation
+ Direct Loss	Difference in value between what was promised and what was received ("direct" or "general" damages)
+ Extra loss	Additional costs and losses caused by the breach and mitigating the breach ("indirect" or "special" damages: incidental and consequential damages)
– Cost avoided	Expenses that the aggrieved party did not incur because performance stopped early
– Loss avoided	Losses that the aggrieved party would have suffered but was able to prevent/avoid because of its own mitigation efforts or other circumstances

This formulation is helpful as you begin to think about identifying and categorizing damages for breach of contract. You must compensate the aggrieved party's lost expectation from the other party's failure to perform and other losses

---

[*] E. Allan Farnsworth, *Contracts* § 12.9 (4th ed. 2004).

that may have been caused by the breach. However, you should not compensate for any costs and losses that were or could have been avoided.

However, the identification and computation of damages cannot be accomplished with a simple formula. Remember to balance the policies described in the chart on page 786. And think clearly and methodically about the circumstances following a breach, comparing the economic circumstances of the aggrieved party after breach with the economic circumstances it would have been in if the contract had been performed, and attempting to categorize and quantify each injury.

Problems: Determining Expectation Damages

In the following problems,* identify the damages that should be awarded to compensate the aggrieved party fully for the injury caused, attempting to put that party in the position it would have been in if the contract had been fully performed. Use Farnsworth's general formula above if you find it helpful, but do not feel constrained by it. If you can find an alternative way of computing damages that accommodates the policies described above, feel free to break away from the traditional formula and use your own common sense to fashion a measure. Some of the issues you are likely to identify in these problems are explored in later in this Chapter.

10-4. What damages should the aggrieved Employee recover?

- Employer and Employee enter into two-year contract for $50,000/year

- *Employer wrongfully discharges Employee after six months*

- Employee unsuccessfully looks for work for three months

- Employee hires employment agency for $1000

- After three more months (six months total out of work), Employee finds new job at $45,000/year

10-5. Should the result in Problem 10-4 change if the Employee stopped looking for work? If she had declined to take the $45,000 job, should she be able to collect her whole salary as damages? If the only job she could find was temporary work at a fast food restaurant for minimum wage and she refused, should she collect her whole lost salary as damages?

---

* These problems are based, with some variation, on examples used by Farnsworth to illustrate his formula for computing expectation damages. *See id.*

10-6. What damages should the aggrieved Employer recover?

- Employer and Employee enter into two-year contract for $50,000/year

- *Employee wrongfully quits after six months*

- For three months, the position remains vacant while Employer advertises the position.

- Having had no success in finding a suitable new hire, Employer pays employment agency $2000 to conduct search

- Employer pays $30,000 for temporary worker for three months

- After three more months (six months total after Employee quit), Employer hires permanent employee at $55,000/year

10-7. What damages should the aggrieved Builder recover?

- Builder and Owner contract for new house to be built for $200,000

- Total cost of construction estimated to be $180,000

- Value of house if completed: $225,000

- *Owner breaches by repudiating contract when construction half-completed*

- Owner has paid Builder $70,000

- Builder has spent $95,000 on labor and materials

- Builder resells materials for $10,000

10-8. What damages should the aggrieved Owner recover?

- Builder and Owner contract for new house to be built for $200,000

- Total cost of construction estimated to be $180,000

- Value of house if completed: $225,000

- *Builder breaches by walking off job when construction half-completed*

- Value of house as partially constructed: $50,000

- Owner has paid Builder $70,000

- Builder has spent $95,000 on labor and materials

- Builder resells materials for $10,000

- Owner hires another contractor to finish the job for $150,000 (what if it was $300,000?)

10-9. Consider again Problem 10-8 but assume that the Owner had so far paid the Builder nothing. Should the breaching Builder be entitled to damages? How might they be measured?

Think About It!

In the preceding problems, Problem 10-8 posits a value for the house as completed and for the structure as partially built. How would each of those values be measured? What kinds of evidence might a party submit to establish them?

§ 2.1.3. Measuring Typical Direct Damages

Two typical examples of breach occur when the buyer of goods or services refuses to take delivery of them or the seller fails to deliver the goods or services promised. In each case, the non-breaching party is likely to enter a substitute contract at a different (and often less advantageous) price than the original contract, and that difference is the measure of the direct damage to the non-breaching party. The example below involves a contract for sale of goods, so it is governed by UCC Article 2, which also employs an expectation approach to remedies functioning much the same as common law damages.

Example C: Breach by a buyer/recipient of goods or services.

Buyer contracts to buy a computer from Seller for $1500, but breaches by refusing to take delivery of the goods.

1. If Seller resells the computer for $1200 in a replacement contract (*lower* than the original breached contract price), then Seller's direct damages are typically measured by the difference between those two contract prices, here $300, as long as the resale is made reasonably (e.g., at a reasonable price under the circumstances, in a reasonable setting, and within a reasonable time after the breach). See UCC § 2–706. Seller may be able to recover indirect damages, if any (e.g., Seller's additional cost to find a new buyer). See UCC § 2–710.

2. If Seller resells the computer for $1600, then the replacement contract price is *higher* than the original (breached) contract price, and Seller has no direct damages and appears to be better off for the breach. See UCC § 2–706. Seller may be able to recover indirect damages, if any (e.g., Seller's additional cost to find a new buyer). See UCC § 2–710.

3. If Seller does not enter into a replacement contract, the market price for the promised goods or services (where a market exists) can fulfill the same function as the replacement contract price. The direct damages measure will be how much the market price is below the contract price. If the market price is used to measure damages, you would need to know when and where the market should be measured. For goods, UCC § 2–708(1) specifies using the market price at the time and place at which the seller was to tender the goods to the buyer under the contract, which amounts to a kind of hypothetical resale at the time and place the seller would have delivered the goods. The common law has similar rules.* Seller may be able to recover indirect damages, if any (e.g., Seller's additional cost to investigate the market price). See UCC § 2–710.

Again, the same principles apply if the sale is under the common law rather than the UCC, e.g., for a sale of real estate or of services.

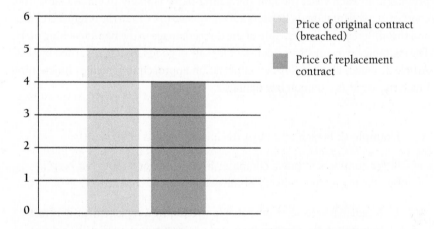

Price of original contract (breached)

Price of replacement contract

---

*   E. Allan Farnsworth, *Contracts* § 12.12 (4th ed. 2004).

Example D: Breach by a seller/supplier of goods or services.

Buyer contracts to buy a computer from Seller for $1500, but Seller breaches and fails to make delivery of the computer.

1. Buyer purchases another computer for $1600 (often called a "cover" purchase). The replacement contract price is *higher* than the original (breached) contract price, so Buyer's direct damages are typically measured by the difference between those two contract prices, here $100, so as long as the cover is made reasonably (e.g., at a reasonable price under the circumstances, within a reasonable time after the default, for comparable goods or services). See UCC § 2–712. Buyer may be able to recover indirect damages, if any (e.g., the cost of shopping around for the replacement computer and driving to the store). See UCC § 2–715 (incidental and consequential damages).

2. Buyer "covers" by purchasing another computer for $1200. The price of the replacement contract is *lower* than the price of the original (breached) contract, so the Buyer seems to be better off and appears to have no direct damages. See UCC § 2–712. Buyer may be able to recover indirect damages, if any (e.g., the cost of shopping around for the replacement computer and driving to the store). See UCC § 2–715 (incidental and consequential damages).

3. Buyer does not purchase another computer. If Buyer does not obtain cover, the market price for the promised goods or services (if a market exists) can fulfill the same function as the replacement contract price. The direct damages measure is the amount by which the market price exceeds the contract price. If the market price is used to determine damages, you need to know when and where the market should be measured. For goods, UCC § 2–713(1) specifies using the market price at the time when the buyer learned of the breach. If the seller has repudiated or failed to perform, the market price is at the place where the seller was supposed to have tendered the goods (often to a carrier, for delivery). (If the seller has tendered defective goods or otherwise breached, the market price is at the place where the goods arrive. These choices of time and place may be seen as a kind of hypothetical "cover" purchase at the place the buyer might have made such a purchase.) The common law has similar rules.[*] Buyer may be able to recover indirect damages, if any (e.g., the cost of researching the market price). See UCC § 2–715 (incidental and consequential damages).

---

[*]   E. Allan Farnsworth, *Contracts* § 12.12 (4th ed. 2004).

The same principles apply if the purchase is under the common law rather than the UCC, e.g., for a purchase of real estate or of services. In those instances, more questions may arise about whether the cover purchase is comparable to the original contract, since real estate and services may not be as interchangeable as goods would be.

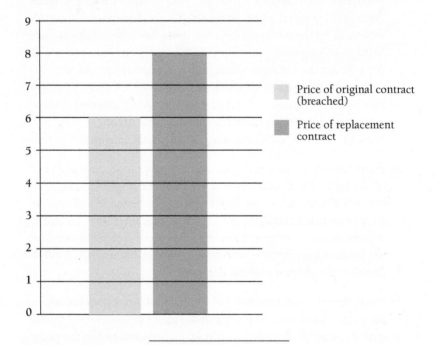

Price of original contract (breached)

Price of replacement contract

Think About It!

In Examples C and D, the market price of the goods or services that are the subject of the breach come into play. How would do we measure market price? What kinds of evidence might a party submit to establish them?

Reading Critically: *Sackett*

The first part of this case, establishing the buyer's total breach, appears in Chapter 9, page 711. The third part, on mitigation of damages appears later in this chapter, on page 836.

1. What alternative measures of damages does the court suggest? Which alternative does it adopt, and why?

2. The court says that the usual measure of damages is the difference between market price and contract price. Other courts use the difference between contract price and resale (or cover) price as the default. In some jurisdictions, the aggrieved party has a choice between the two. Which do you think is the better rule?

Example E: *Sackett v. Spindler,* 56 Cal. Rptr. 435 (Ct. App. 1967).

The parties entered into an $85,000 purchase agreement for a majority of the shares of S & S Newspapers. The buyer (plaintiff) made the first payment for $6000 on time, the second payment for $20,000 a week late and $200 short, and the third payment of $59,000 with a check that bounced. Despite several offers to cure, the buyer never paid the remaining balance. The seller eventually canceled the contract and sought another buyer. He finally sold the stock nearly a year later for a net payment of $20,680. The parties sued each other for breach. The court found that buyer/plaintiff had committed a total material breach, after which seller/defendant was entitled to cancel the contract and was therefore not in breach for doing so. On appeal, the buyer challenged the calculation of damages on two grounds: (1) that the court erred in measuring damages based upon the price of stock on the date sold, as opposed to the date of breach; and (2) that the court erred in failing to take into account additional liabilities incurred by the newspaper prior to the sale.

Analysis: Affirming, the court stressed that "the general rule . . . [is] that where the title to goods has not passed to the buyer and the seller has the property in his possession or under his control, the measure of damages upon the buyer's refusal to accept and pay for goods for which there is an available market is, in the absence of special circumstances, the difference between the contract price and the market or current price or value at the time and the place where the goods ought to have been delivered and accepted, or, if no time is fixed for acceptance, then at the time of the refusal to accept." The ordinary measure does not apply, though, "when there is no market available at the time and place of performance," but, rather, damages based upon "the value of the goods as best as can be ascertained . . . ." Testimony at trial indicated that it would have been difficult to resell the stock after the failure of the agreement with Sackett and that Spindler was fortunate to make the later sale at all. Accordingly, the unavailability of the market price at

Think About It!

How did the court calculate damages? Why did it reject the argument to use the market price of the newspaper? If the seller had breached by failing to turn over the stock, would the same measure of damages be appropriate for the buyer, with or without adjustments?

At the end of the opinion, when the court awards Spindler "costs," it is not referring to the costs included in general or specific damages, but rather to court costs such as fees to file the lawsuit, charges for serving subpoenas to compel the appearance of witnesses at trial, and the cost of ordering trial transcripts and of making copies of trial exhibits.

the time of breach supported the use of the amount obtained upon resale to calculate damages.

Taking up the issue of liabilities of the newspaper, the court concluded that the contract was one for the sale of the stock of S & S Newspapers for a fixed price, rather than one for sale of the business itself. The liabilities of the newspaper would undoubtedly impact the amount a buyer was willing to pay for the stock and therefore be reflected in the contract price for the stock at the time of sale. Accordingly, separate inclusion of this amount in damages would not be proper. The court affirmed the judgment and awarded Spindler costs.

§ 2.1.4. Special Problems in Measuring Direct Damages

Expectation damages can sometimes be measured in more than one way, and choosing among the alternatives requires you to balance and select among competing policies. Some situations present special challenges in measuring direct damages. The cases in this section demonstrate how courts have made choices among alternative measures in cases involving the following special challenges: deciding when to measure damages after anticipatory repudiation, measuring loss from incomplete or defective performance of a construction contract, and measuring lost profits.

§ 2.1.4.1. Damages Resulting from Anticipatory Repudiation

Recall from Chapter 9, page 725, that a repudiation (also called a renunciation) is "an absolute and unequivocal refusal to perform or a distinct and positive statement of an inability to do so."[*] An *anticipatory* repudiation is a repudiation that occurs *before* the date on which performance is due. Under the UCC, as noted earlier, if a repudiation occurs *at the time or after* performance is due and market price is used to determine damages, UCC § 2–713 uses the market price when the aggrieved party "learned of the breach"—when she could have acted to replace the performance lost through breach. But when should the market be measured if

---

[*] *McCloskey & Co. v. Minweld Steel Co.*, 220 F.2d 101, 104 (3d Cir. 1955).

the repudiation occurs before the time for performance? The time for performance has not yet arrived, and the aggrieved party may, but is not required to, cancel the contract immediately. So, what is the appropriate time to measure the market when using a hypothetical resale or cover contract at the market price to set damages?

Courts and commentators have identified three possible moments in time based on interpretation of the phrase "learned of the breach." If one party to a sale anticipatorily repudiates, the other party might be said to learn of the breach:

(1)   When he learns of the repudiation,

(2)   A commercially reasonable time after he learns of the repudiation, or

(3)   When performance is due under the contract.

A majority of courts (in both common law* and UCC cases) have chosen the middle solution—a commercially reasonable time after the aggrieved party learns of the other's repudiation. That time period gives the aggrieved party a chance to size up the market, locate alternative suppliers or buyers, and decide whether to merely seek market damages or to resell or obtain substitute goods ("cover") and seek cover damages. It also encourages the aggrieved party to mitigate before the contract date for performance arrives; recall that this was a strong consideration for the court in *Hochster*, page 729 (the courier case where the buyer anticipatorily repudiated). For a thorough discussion of the rationale for choosing among the three solutions for timing the measure of damages, see *Cosden Oil & Chemical Co. v. Karl O. Helm Aktiengesellschaft*, 736 F.2d 1054 (5th Cir. 1984).

> **Example F:** Buyer contracts to buy a computer from Seller for $1500, but Seller anticipatorily breaches and then fails to make delivery of the computer on the contract performance date. Buyer purchases a replacement computer ten days after learning of the breach at a cost of $1750. At the time performance is due, the market price for the computer is $1600.

Analysis: Buyer's damage is $250. As reflected in the majority approach, Buyer's direct market damages for Seller's anticipatory repudiation are measured by this formula:

Market price at a commercially reasonable time after Buyer learned of the repudiation ($1750) minus contract price ($1500)

---

*   *See* E. Allan Farnsworth, *Contracts* § 12.12, at 782–83 (4th ed. 2004).

Even though the market price dropped, so that Buyer could, in fact, have purchased a replacement at $1600 rather than $1750, the majority rule would measure the market at a commercially reasonable time after the Buyer learned of the breach, not at the time for performance. Buyer can also recover indirect damages, such as consequential and incidental damages, if any (see page 818).

§ 2.1.4.2. Owner's Cost to Complete Versus Diminution in Value

While it is clear that an aggrieved party is entitled to direct damages to give it the value of full performance, it is sometimes less clear how to measure what it would take to do so. Is the non-breaching party entitled to the amount necessary to purchase from someone else the performance that was promised in the original contract (the "cost to complete")? Or should the non-breaching party be compensated, instead, by awarding the amount representing the difference between the value that would have accrued to the aggrieved party with full performance and the value resulting from the defective performance (the "diminution in value")? The issue comes up regularly (though not exclusively) in construction contracts, where the choice is between using the cost to hire another contractor to complete the work and using the difference in the value of the property with full versus defective performance. As the next several cases demonstrate, courts have developed standards to regulate the choice between these two measures of damage, but application of the standards raises questions that go to the heart of the policies underlying award of damages.

Reading Critically: *Jacob & Youngs, Khiterer*, and *Lyon*

1. Can you reconcile the standards and outcomes in all the cases?

2. Why do you think each court chooses the damages measure that it selects?

3. Do you agree with each court's choice of damages? Why or why not? Are there circumstances under which you think the breach that occurred in each contract should be compensated by the alternative measure?

Example G: *Jacob & Youngs v. Kent*, 129 N.E. 889 (N.Y. 1921).

The facts and decision with respect to whether there was substantial performance appear in Chapter 9 on page 692 and are summarized here: The construction contractor deviated from the contract specification that Reading pipe be used, using another pipe in most of the building, but the owner and his architect did not discover the substitution until the house was nearly completed and was already occupied by owner. The owner refused to make the final payment, and contractor sued for it under the contract.

Analysis: The district court held for the defendant, concluding that the plaintiff had breached the contract. The appellate division reversed and granted a new trial. The court of appeals held that the contractor had substantially performed the contract and therefore had earned the contract price.

The court then turned to the question of measuring the damages owed by the contractor for its failure to use Reading pipe as promised; the district court and appellate division had not addressed this issue. "In the circumstances of this case, we think the measure of the allowance is not the cost of replacement, which would be great, but the difference in value, which would be either nominal or nothing. . . . It is true that in most cases the cost of replacement is the measure. The owner is entitled to the money which will permit him to complete, unless the cost of completion is grossly and unfairly out of proportion to the good to be attained. When that is true, the measure is the difference in value. . . . The rule that gives a remedy in cases of substantial performance with compensation for defects of trivial or inappreciable importance has been developed by the courts as an instrument of justice. The measure of the allowance must be shaped to the same end."

Example H: *Khiterer v. Bell*, 2005 WL 192354 (N.Y. City Civ. Ct. Jan. 28, 2005) (unreported opinion).

The facts and decision with respect to whether there was substantial performance appear in Chapter 9, Example B, on page 702 and are summarized here: Patient sued dentist for damages because her dental treatment, for which she had already paid, called for a porcelain-on-gold crown, rather than the porcelain crown that she discovered a half year later. The dentist's uncontradicted testimony showed that the porcelain crown was "therapeutically superior" and that the cost was the same, except that more expensive cement was required for the porcelain crown.

Analysis: The court held that the dental contract was predominantly for services and thus was not governed by UCC Article 2. It found that the contract had called for porcelain-on-gold crowns, but that the substitution was not intentional. The court held that the dentist's breach was not substantial and turned to the issue of damages: "Where substantial performance has been rendered, the remedy is the cost of completion or correction, unless that cost 'is grossly and unfairly out of proportion to the good to be attained. When that is true, the measure is the difference in value'" (quoting *Jacob & Youngs v. Kent*). "The 'difference in value rule' is applied to avoid 'economic waste.' " Accordingly, the court awarded Khiterer nominal damages of $10.00.

Lyon v. Belosky Construction, Inc.

Mary C. LYON et al., Plaintiffs-Respondents

v.

BELOSKY CONSTRUCTION, INC., et al., Defendants-Appellants

Supreme Court, Appellate Division, New York
669 N.Y.S.2d 400 (App. Div. 1998)

CARDONA, P. J.

Appeal from a judgment of the Supreme Court (Ellison, J.), entered November 11, 1996 in Chemung County, upon a decision of the court in favor of plaintiffs.

In October 1993, plaintiff Mary C. Lyon and her sister, plaintiff Martha Clute, entered into a contract with defendant Belosky Construction, Inc. for the construction of a custom home in the City of Elmira, Chemung County, at a base cost of $247,000 with approximately $42,000 in additional features. Lyon, who is a resident of South Carolina, retained an architectural firm in South Carolina to prepare the design drawings. Upon Belosky's advice, plaintiffs retained defendant Kirk Vieselmeyer, a professional engineer, to, *inter alia*, prepare construction documents and conduct periodic inspections to insure that the home was constructed in conformity with the drawings.

Construction commenced in November 1993. In April 1994, plaintiffs became aware of a problem with a dormer over the main entrance of the home. The dormer was removed and rebuilt. Plaintiffs, however, found the rebuilt dormer unsatisfactory and directed Belosky to remove it. The home was subsequently completed with the exception of the interior and exterior of the main entrance. After moving into the home, plaintiffs learned that the roof had been centered over the library rather than the living room as represented in the drawings resulting in a change in the roof proportions and enlargement of the overhang over the main entrance. In addition, the entrance pillars could not be used in the manner depicted in the drawings.

Plaintiffs subsequently commenced this action against defendants for breach of contract. In their respective answers, defendants raised, *inter alia*, the affirmative defense of economic waste claiming that damages, if any, should be based upon the diminution in value of the structure rather than the value of replacement. Following a nonjury trial, Supreme Court found that defendants had breached their respective contracts and plaintiffs were entitled to damages in an amount necessary to replace the roof so as to bring it in conformity with the drawings. Supreme Court awarded plaintiffs judgment in the sum of $73,182.66, the agreed-upon cost of replacement including costs and interest. Defendants appeal.

We affirm. As a general rule, the proper measure of damages in cases involving the breach of a construction contract is "the difference between the amount due on the contract and the amount necessary to properly complete the job or to replace the defective construction, whichever is appropriate" (*Sherman v. Hanu*, 195 A.D.2d 810 . . . . Where, however, "the contractor's breach was unintentional and constituted substantial performance in good faith" (*Roudis v. Hubbard*, 176 A.D.2d 388, 389), and remedying the defective performance would result in unreasonable economic waste (*see, City School Dist. v. McLane Constr. Co.*, 85 A.D.2d 749, 750, *lv denied* 56 NY2d 504), damages should be based upon "the difference between the value of the property as constructed and the value if performance had been properly completed" (*American Std. v. Schectman*, 80 A.D.2d 318, 321, *lv denied* 54 NY2d 604 . . . .)

It is undisputed that the defect in the main entrance, including the overhead dormer, was due to the misalignment of the roof which was constructed under the supervision and control of Belosky and purportedly overseen by Vieselmeyer. Belosky hired a framer to frame the roof but testified that he did not personally inspect the roof to insure that it and the dormer complied with the drawings. In fact, Belosky admitted that he had little experience reading drawings and relied upon the framer to whom he had subcontracted the work to make sure the home was constructed properly. Vieselmeyer, who was specifically hired to inspect the construction to make sure that it complied with the drawings, did not discover the problem with the roof until after he took certain field measurements at the request of plaintiffs' architect. By this time, however, the dormer had already been rebuilt and removed, and the entire roof had been shingled. Inasmuch as plaintiffs' expert testified that the misalignment of the roof should have been discovered when problems with the dormer became apparent, the evidence supports Supreme Court's finding that defendants, at the very least, acted negligently in failing to detect the problem.

In addition, there is evidence that, under the circumstances presented here, the defect was substantial.* Plaintiffs contracted to build a custom home at significant expense which, in fact, exceeded the fair market value of the home as completed per the drawings. Because they were away from the work site during most of the construction, plaintiffs retained and relied upon various professionals to assist them in successfully completing the project. It is clear from the record that the aesthetic appearance of the home, both inside and out, was of utmost importance to plaintiffs. Our review of the photographs of the home as constructed compared with the design drawings convinces us that plaintiffs did not get the benefit of their bargain and that requiring defendants to remedy the problem would not, under these particular circumstances, result in unreasonable economic waste. Accordingly, we find that Supreme Court applied the appropriate measure of damages (*see City School Dist. v. McLane Constr. Co.*, 85 A.D.2d 749, 750–751, *supra; cf., Jacob & Youngs v. Kent*, 230 N.Y. 239). Lastly, inasmuch as the evidence establishes that Vieselmeyer's breach of contract was a proximate cause of the damages sustained by plaintiffs, Supreme Court properly awarded judgment against him notwithstanding the relatively small fee he charged for services rendered to plaintiffs.

MERCURE, WHITE, SPAIN and CARPINELLO, JJ., concur.

Ordered that the judgment is affirmed, with costs.

Problem: Damages for Defective Performance

10-10. Contractor agreed to build a house for Owners based on a stock floor plan and specifications on standard printed forms. When Contractor completed construction, Owners did a final walk-through inspection during which they documented that Contractor had furnished kitchen cabinets with a much darker finish than specified (so that the countertops and woodwork in the room did not match). The Contractor also had failed to furnish gutters and downspouts, clothes closet poles, an entrance seat, and the outside sidewalks, each of which was promised in the contract. The plaster on the ceiling was cracked in the living room and kitchen. The patio floor and patio wall were defectively constructed and needed to be repaired by mud-jacking and reconstruction.

In addition, Owners noted (and the stock floor plan showed) that Contractor misplaced a wall between the living room and the kitchen by more

---

* [Authors' Note: As in *Khiterer*, the *Lyons* court found a "substantial" defect even though the court apparently believed there was substantial performance; it did not question the contractor's entitlement to the contract price, offset by the damages for its breach.]

than a foot. The record at trial was not clear why and when this wall was misplaced, but there was no evidence that, during construction, Owners had requested or demanded the repositioning of the wall called for by the specifications. Expert real estate witnesses for both parties, testifying as to the value of the house, agreed that the misplacement of the wall (resulting in a smaller living room) had no effect on the market price. A home remodeling expert witness testified that tearing down and rebuilding the wall in its proper place would cause some additional damage to other parts of the house and would require replastering and redecorating the walls and ceilings of at least two rooms. The cost of tearing down this wall and rebuilding it would be approximately $40,000.

Contractor sued Owners for breach of contract, because Owners refused to pay the contract price of $200,000. Owners claimed that Contractor had not substantially performed and therefore was not entitled to any payment. The court held that Contractor had substantially performed the contract, so it had earned the contract price, but that Owners were entitled to reduce payment by the amount of their damages. How should the court compute Owners' damages? If dollar amounts are not specified for certain injuries, identify the items for which recovery should be awarded and how the amount of recovery might be proven or ascertained.

Reading Critically: *Peevyhouse*

1. The previous cases might all be characterized as contracts for services that were performed badly, with a consequent need to measure the value of the performance defects. Is the contract in *Peevyhouse* the same kind of contract? If not, does or should the difference matter in determining the appropriate measure of damages?

2. Do you agree with the majority opinion or with the dissent? Why?

3. How could a landowner protect itself against this ruling in negotiating future coal mining leases?

Peevyhouse v. Garland Coal & Mining Co.

WILLIE PEEVYHOUSE and LUCILLE PEEVYHOUSE, Plaintiffs-Appellants

v.

GARLAND COAL & MINING COMPANY, Defendant-Respondent

Supreme Court of Oklahoma
382 P.2d 109 (Okla. 1962), *modified* (1963)

JACKSON, JUSTICE.

In the trial court, plaintiffs Willie and Lucille Peevyhouse sued the defendant, Garland Coal and Mining Company, for damages for breach of contract. Judgment was for plaintiffs in an amount considerably less than was sued for. Plaintiffs appeal and defendant cross-appeals.

[The parties' arguments all revolve around] the basic question of whether the trial court properly instructed the jury on the measure of damages.

. . . [P]laintiffs owned a farm containing coal deposits, and in November, 1954, leased the premises to defendant for a period of five years for coal mining purposes. A "stripmining" operation was contemplated in which the coal would be taken from pits on the surface of the ground, instead of from underground mine shafts. In addition to the usual covenants found in a coal mining lease, defendant specifically agreed to perform certain restorative and remedial work at the end of the lease period. It is unnecessary to set out the details of the work to be done, other than to say that it would involve the moving of many thousands of cubic yards of dirt, at a cost estimated by expert witnesses at about $29,000.00. However, plaintiffs sued for only $25,000.00.

. . . .

At the conclusion of the trial, the court instructed the jury that it must return a verdict for plaintiffs, and left the amount of damages for jury determination. On the measure of damages, the court instructed the jury that it might consider the cost of performance of the work defendant agreed to do, "together with all of the evidence offered on behalf of either party".

Think About It!

Why should the plaintiffs have objected to the jury instruction language? Why didn't they?

It thus appears that the jury was at liberty to consider the "diminution in value" of plaintiffs' farm as well as the cost of "repair work" in determining the amount of damages.

It returned a verdict for plaintiffs for $5000.00—only a fraction of the "cost of performance", *but more than the total value of the farm even after the remedial work is done.*

On appeal, . . . [p]laintiffs contend that the true measure of damages . . . is what it will cost plaintiffs to obtain performance of the work that was not done because of defendant's default. Defendant argues that the measure of damages is the cost of performance "limited, however, to the total difference in the market value before and after the work was performed".

. . . [T]his precise question has not . . . been presented to this court. . . . In the case before us, it is argued by defendant with some force that the performance of the remedial work defendant agreed to do will add at the most only a few hundred dollars to the value of plaintiffs' farm, and that the damages should be limited to that amount because that is all plaintiffs have lost.

. . . .

. . . It is highly unlikely that the ordinary property owner would agree to pay $29,000 (or its equivalent) for the construction of "improvements" upon his property that would increase its value only about ($300) three hundred dollars. The result is that we are called upon to apply principles of law theoretically based upon reason and reality to a situation which is basically unreasonable and unrealistic.

. . . .

Even in the case of contracts that are unquestionably building and construction contracts, the authorities are not in agreement as to the factors to be considered in determining whether the cost of performance rule or the value rule should be applied. The . . . Restatement of the Law, Contracts, [§] 346(1)(a)(i) and (ii) [states] that the cost of performance is the proper measure of damages "if this is possible and does not involve *unreasonable economic waste*"; and that the diminution in value caused by the breach is the proper measure "if construction and completion in accordance with the contract would involve *unreasonable economic waste*". (Emphasis supplied.) In a . . . comment . . . , the Restatement makes it clear that the "economic waste" referred to consists of the destruction of a substantially completed building or other structure. Of course no such destruction is involved in the case now before us.

On the other hand, in McCormick, Damages, Section 168, it is said with regard to building and construction contracts that "in cases where the defect is one that can be repaired or cured without *undue expense*" the cost of performance is the proper measure of damages, but where "the defect in material or construction is one that cannot be remedied without *an expenditure for reconstruction disproportion-*

ate to the end to be attained" (emphasis supplied) the value rule should be followed. The same idea was expressed in Jacob & Youngs, Inc. v. Kent, 230 N.Y. 239, 129 N.E. 889, 23 A.L.R. 1429, as follows:

> "The owner is entitled to the money which will permit him to complete, unless the cost of completion is grossly and unfairly out of proportion to the good to be attained. When that is true, the measure is the difference in value."

It thus appears that the prime consideration in the Restatement was "economic waste"; and that the prime consideration in McCormick, Damages, and in Jacob & Youngs, Inc. v. Kent, supra, was the relationship between the expense involved and the "end to be attained"—in other words, the "relative economic benefit".

In view of the unrealistic fact situation in the instant case . . . , we are of the opinion that the "relative economic benefit" is a proper consideration here. . . .

We therefore hold that where, in a coal mining lease, lessee agrees to perform certain remedial work on the premises concerned at the end of the lease period, and thereafter the contract is fully performed by both parties except that the remedial work is not done, the measure of damages in an action by lessor against lessee for damages for breach of contract is ordinarily the reasonable cost of performance of the work; however, where the contract provision breached was merely incidental to the main purpose in view, and where the economic benefit which would result to lessor by full performance of the work is grossly disproportionate to the cost of performance, the damages which lessor may recover are limited to the diminution in value resulting to the premises because of the non-performance.

Food for Thought

Why might the court state its holding in such narrow, fact-specific terms? Is the holding really limited in that fashion?

. . . .

Under the most liberal view of the evidence herein, the diminution in value resulting to the premises because of non-performance of the remedial work was $300.00. After a careful search of the record, we have found no evidence of a higher figure, and plaintiffs do not argue in their briefs that a greater diminution in value was sustained. It thus appears that the judgment was clearly excessive, and that the amount for which judgment should have been rendered is definitely and satisfactorily shown by the record.

. . . .

We are of the opinion that the judgment of the trial court for plaintiffs should be, and it is hereby, modified and reduced to the sum of $300.00, and as so modified it is affirmed.

WELCH, DAVISON, HALLEY, and JOHNSON, JJ., concur.

WILLIAMS, C. J., BLACKBIRD, V. C. J., and IRWIN and BERRY, JJ., dissent.

IRWIN, JUSTICE (dissenting).

By the specific provisions in the coal mining lease under consideration, the defendant agreed as follows:

> "7b. Lessee agrees to make fills in the pits dug on said premises on the property line in such manner that fences can be placed thereon and access had to opposite sides of the pits.

> "7c. Lessee agrees to smooth off the top of the spoil banks on the above premises.

> "7d. Lessee agrees to leave the creek crossing the above premises in such a condition that it will not interfere with the crossings to be made in pits as set out in 7b.

> . . . .

> "7f. Lessee further agrees to leave no shale or dirt on the high wall of said pits. . . ."

Following the expiration of the lease, plaintiffs made demand upon defendant that it carry out the provisions of the contract and to perform those covenants contained therein.

Defendant admits that it failed to perform its obligations that it agreed and contracted to perform under the lease contract and there is nothing in the record which indicates that defendant could not perform its obligations. Therefore, in my opinion defendant's breach of the contract was wilful and not in good faith.

Although the contract speaks for itself, there were several negotiations between the plaintiffs and defendant before the contract was executed. Defendant admitted . . . that plaintiffs insisted that the above provisions be included in the contract and that they would not agree to the coal mining lease unless the above provisions were included.

In consideration for the lease contract, plaintiffs were to receive a certain amount as royalty for the coal produced and marketed and in addition thereto their land was to be restored as provided in the contract.

Defendant received as consideration for the contract, its proportionate share of the coal produced and marketed and in addition thereto, the *right to use* plaintiffs' land in the furtherance of its mining operations.

The cost for performing the contract in question could have been reasonably approximated when the contract was negotiated and executed and there are no conditions now existing which could not have been reasonably anticipated by the parties. Therefore, defendant had knowledge, when it prevailed upon the plaintiffs to execute the lease, that the cost of performance might be disproportionate to the value or benefits received by plaintiff for the performance.

Defendant has received its benefits under the contract and now urges, in substance, that plaintiffs' measure of damages for its failure to perform should be the economic value of performance to the plaintiffs and not the cost of performance.

If a peculiar set of facts should exist where the above rule should be applied as the proper measure of damages (and in my judgment those facts do not exist in the instant case), before such rule should be applied, consideration should be given to the benefits received or contracted for by the party who asserts the application of the rule.

Food for Thought

If the Peevyhouses had instead sought relief under real property law, rather than contract law, they could have argued that they had given the mining company a "profit a prendre," a non-possessory interest in land that "consists of a right of access to land for the limited purpose of removing some naturally occurring substance from the land," such as fossil fuels, minerals, timber, sand, gravel, and confined standing water. Most commentators believe that such rights should be governed by the same rules as easements. Upon unlawful use of an easement, the owners can obtain damages or (if damages are inadequate) injunctive relief. 8 *Thompson on Real Property, Second Thomas Edition* §§ 60.03(a)(7), 60.06(a), 65.01, 65.03(b), 65.04(a) (David A. Thomas, ed., 2005) (citing Restatement of Property (Servitudes) § 1.2 (2000)). Does this affect your analysis of the case?

Defendant did not have the right to mine plaintiffs' coal or to use plaintiffs' property for its mining operations without the consent of plaintiffs. Defendant had knowledge of the benefits that it would receive under the contract and the approximate cost of performing the contract. With this knowledge, it must be presumed that defendant thought that it would be to its economic advantage to enter into the contract with plaintiffs and that it would reap benefits from the contract, or it would have not entered into the contract.

Therefore, if the value of the performance of a contract should be considered in determining the measure of damages for breach of a contract, the value of the benefits received under the contract by a party who breaches a contract should also be considered. . . .

. . . .

. . . [T]he proper measure of damages should be the cost of performance. Any other measure of damage would be holding for naught the express provisions of the contract; would be taking from the plaintiffs the benefits of the contract and placing those benefits in defendant which has failed to perform its obligations; would be granting benefits to defendant without a resulting obligation; and would be completely rescinding the solemn obligation of the contract for the benefit of the defendant to the detriment of the plaintiffs by making an entirely new contract for the parties.

I therefore respectfully dissent to the opinion promulgated by a majority of my associates.

. . . .

Food for Thought

Cases like *Peevyhouse*, *Jacob & Youngs*, and *Lyon* illustrate the importance of the advocate framing the narrative of the case in a compelling story line that demonstrates the nature of the breach and its effect on the aggrieved party. Is *Jacob & Youngs* about an owner who tried to capitalize on an ultimately unimportant choice in the contract, a careless contractor who did not check the pipe order or delivery, a contractor who chose a cheaper pipe, or an architect who did not inspect the premises carefully enough when the pipe was first installed? Is *Lyon* about two owners whose dream house was drastically altered by a careless or even negligent contractor, or is it about a perfectly good house that was rejected by two finicky owners? What alternative narratives can be constructed for *Peevyhouse*? Are some of these narratives more compelling than others? Why? The political climate may also be part of the narrative. Consider the political culture created in a region where strip mining is profitable and common. How do those pressures affect the decisions of landowners and the resulting contracts? For a similar situation, consider the present-day controversy surrounding the natural gas industry's use of fracking methods. *See generally* https://www.forbes.com/sites/judystone/2017/02/23/fracking-is-dangerous-to-your-health-heres-why/#50f2b4b75945 In light of *Peevyhouse*, what advice would you give to a landowner who has been approached by a representative of a natural gas extraction company to negotiate extraction rights on that property?

In a portion of the opinion not included here, the *Peevyhouse* court cited *Groves v. John Wunder Co.*, 286 N.W. 235 (1939) as "the only case which has come to our attention in which the cost of performance rule has been followed under circumstances where the cost of performance greatly exceeded the diminution in value resulting from the breach of contract." Groves had a sand-and-gravel extraction business on a piece of then-suburban property in Minneapolis that was zoned as heavy industrial property but so far had limited value because of lack of development in the neighborhood. Groves entered a contract in which Wunder purchased the right to remove sand and gravel from the Groves property in exchange for $105,000 and a promise to leave the property "at a uniform grade" at the level of the adjoining roadway. The court noted that Wunder "incidentally got rid of Groves as a competitor." After Wunder extracted only "the richest and best of the gravel" and then left the property with ground "broken, rugged, and uneven," Groves sued for breach of contract. The trial court awarded Groves a little over $15,000, slightly more than the value of the property if restored to grade ($12,160). The appellate court ordered a new trial on damages, concluding that the cost to complete (perhaps upwards of $60,000) would be the appropriate measure. *Groves* has sometimes been seen as an aberration, but can you see how awarding the cost to complete might be justified under the particular facts of the case? Does it matter that the property was projected to become more valuable after further development in the area? Does it matter that the promise to grade the property was part of a larger transaction between two competitors involving extraction of material from the land? Could *Groves* have served effectively as a model for the *Peevyhouse* court?

For additional background on the *Peevyhouse* case, *see* Judith L. Maute, *Peevyhouse v. Garland Coal & Mining Co. Revisited: The Ballad of Willie and Lucille*, 89 Nw. U. L. Rev. 1341 (1995); Douglas Baird, Robert Gertner, & Randal Picker, *Game Theory and the Law* 150–53, 224–32 (1994) (concluding that an award of specific performance would have been a mistake); Judith Maute, *The Unearthed Facts of Peevyhouse v. Garland Coal & Mining Co*, in *Contracts Stories* 265 (Douglas G. Baird ed. 2007). The video by Judith Maute, *The Ballad of Willie and Lucille: Disappointed Expectations of Contract Law and the Legal System*, contains interviews with Willie Peevyhouse, footage of the farm, and interviews with leading law professors discussing the outcome of the case, its rationale, and its shortcomings. You can see a Google Earth picture of the Peevyhouse Farm here. Despite much criticism of the *Peevyhouse* outcome, the judgment was affirmed in Oklahoma in 1994. *See Schneberger v. Apache Corp.*, 890 P.2d 847 (Okla. 1994).

§ 2.1.4.3. Damages for "Lost Profits" and "Lost Volume"

The following two examples consider when it is appropriate for a seller to receive lost profits from a sale (rather than the difference between contract and resale price) as direct damages for a buyer's repudiation. They also discuss how to measure a seller's lost profits.

Reading Critically: *Neri*

When a buyer breaches a purchase contract by repudiating the sale, the seller can usually be compensated fully by being awarded the amount by which the contract price exceeds the resale or market price. Under what circumstances did *Neri* say that was not sufficient, so that a seller was entitled, instead, to receive the profit lost when the original sale did not go through?

Example I: *Neri v. Retail Marine Corp.*, 334 N.Y.S.2d 165 (1972).

The buyers agreed to purchase from the seller a new boat of a specified model for $12,587.40, against which they made a deposit of $40, with delivery expected in four to six weeks. They shortly increased the deposit to $4,250 in return for the seller's agreement to arrange for immediate delivery based on a "firm sale." Six days later, the buyers sent seller a letter rescinding the sale due to one of the buyer's hospitalization and surgery that would make it "impossible for [the buyers] to make any payments." At that point, the seller had already received delivery of the boat, so it declined to refund the deposit. The seller ultimately resold the boat four months later to another buyer at the same price.

> **Think About It!**
>
> Although the buyer's letter "rescinds" the contract and says it is "impossible" for him to pay, the buyer is not claiming the legal defense of impossibility. What is the accurate legal term for buyer's action?

Buyers sued seller for return of the deposit. Seller counterclaimed for (1) its lost profit on the first sale, because it would have sold two boats and earned two profits instead of one, but for the breach by the buyers; and (2) its incidental damages for the boat's storage, upkeep, finance charges, and insurance until the boat remained unsold.

Analysis: The trial court ordered that the seller refund the buyers' deposit, minus a set-off for seller's damages. However, the trial "found untenable" the seller's counterclaim for lost profits because seller had eventually sold the boat to another buyer. It also held that seller had not proved any incidental damages. The appellate division court affirmed.

The court of appeals modified the judgment, though, holding that buyers were entitled to recover their $4,250 deposit, minus a set-off of $2579 for seller's lost profit and $674 for seller's incidental damages. For the lost-profit damages, the court applied UCC § 2–708 and concluded that "the [market-contract price differential] measure of damages is inadequate to put the seller in as good a position as performance would have done." The court therefore awarded the seller its "profit (including reasonable overhead) . . . together with any incidental damages . . . , due allowance for costs reasonably incurred and due credit for payments or proceeds of resale."

Make the Connection

For more detail on incidental damages, see page 819.

Reading Critically: *Vitex Mfg. Corp.*

The question raised in *Vitex* is whether fixed costs ("overhead" in this opinion) may be included along with variable costs (the materials and labor actually expended on the job) in determining the service-provider's lost profit and therefore its direct damages. Many cases address this issue, most of them agreeing with the outcome in *Vitex*.

1. How did the court calculate plaintiff's damages in this services contract? What rationale and policies supported the court's result?

2. What calculation did the losing party advocate? Why did the court reject it?

> **Example J:** *Vitex Manufacturing Corp. v. Caribtex Corp.*, 377 F.2d 795 (3d Cir. 1967).
>
> Vitex was located in the Virgin Islands and was in the business of treating cloth that could then be imported duty-free into the United States because of the value added in the Virgin Islands. Vitex stopped operating its plant in the Virgin Islands at a point in time when it had capacity but no customers. Vitex reopened the plant after contracting with Caribtex for processing of Italian wool to be supplied by Caribtex, but Caribtex never sent the wool.

Analysis: The trial court found that Vitex's "gross profits" (revenue) under the contract would have been $31,250 and that Vitex would have incurred costs of $10,136 for labor and materials, so Vitex's damages for loss of profit were $21,114.

On appeal, Caribtex objected to the trial court's calculation of lost profits, arguing that the calculation of lost profits should reflect *all* expenses to be paid from the contract proceeds, including a portion of general operating costs. Caribtex claimed that Vitex's damages should have been reduced by a ratable proportion of its overhead expenses, such as executive and clerical salaries and other administrative expenses incurred in operating the plant. The court reasoned, "Overhead would have remained the same whether or not Vitex and Caribtex entered their contract and whether or not Vitex actually processed Caribtex's goods. Since the overhead remained constant, in no way attributable-to or affected-by the Caribtex contract, it would be improper to consider it as a cost of Vitex's performance to be deducted from the gross proceeds of the Caribtex contract." Even though accounting principles might consider overhead a cost to be allocated to each contract, to ensure prices would be set at sufficient levels to recoup all expenses, including overhead, "it does not follow that this allocated share of fixed overhead should be considered a cost factor in the computation of lost profits on individual transactions." Alternatively, the court reasoned that overhead expenses could be awarded to Vitex as a "loss incurred,"

FYI

Students are sometimes puzzled that Vitex continued to owe executive and clerical salaries, pay property taxes, and incur general administration expenses, even when its manufacturing plant was closed or inoperative. But closing down a manufacturing plant does not mean the business itself is shut down. The business may continue to employ people who look for additional work for the business, maintain and secure the manufacturing plant, and continue to run the financial infrastructure of the business (e.g., paying taxes and other ongoing expenses of the business). Or the employees may be paid to keep them ready for additional work that is expected to follow, while the company saves some operating expenses by ceasing day-to-day operations.

since the overhead would be spread over a smaller number of transactions so that each other transaction must bear a larger share of the fixed overhead cost. Caribtex should have reasonably foreseen that its breach would not only cause a loss of "clear" profit, but also "a loss in that the profitability of other transactions [would] be reduced. Therefore, this loss is within the contemplation of 'losses caused and gains prevented,' and overhead should be considered to be a compensable item of damage." Finally, the court noted that UCC § 2–708(2) includes "reasonable overhead" in the measure of lost profits available when market or resale damages are not sufficiently compensable. While not directly applicable to a services contract like this one, the UCC "is persuasive because it embodies the foremost modern legal thought concerning commercial transactions." Therefore, the court of appeals affirmed.

§ 2.1.5. Indirect Expectation Damages

We turn now to a consideration of indirect (special) damages, which are composed of incidental and consequential damages:

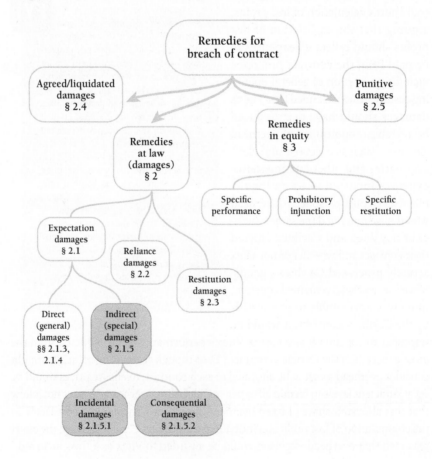

§ 2.1.5.1. Incidental Damages

As discussed on page 791, incidental damages are extra costs incurred by the aggrieved party in dealing with the breach or trying to prevent (mitigate) further losses. They may include the costs of storing or reshipping or reselling defective or repudiated goods, boarding up and paying extra insurance on a building left unfinished by a vendor, handling a defective delivery, arranging the purchase of substitute goods, paying a broker to find a substitute buyer, or spending employee time negotiating a replacement contract with a new party.

An example of incidental damages appears in *Neri v. Retail Marine Corp.*, Example I on page 815, where the court awarded the seller incidental damages of $674 for storage, upkeep, finance charges, and insurance for the boat during the time the seller held the boat for resale. UCC § 2–710 provides for recovery of incidental damages by sellers, and UCC § 2–715 does the same for buyers.

Although attorneys' fees fit conceptually into the category of incidental damages, under U.S. law they are not recoverable unless (1) the parties agree to them, (2) they are granted by statute, or (3) the lawsuit is frivolous or in bad faith.

Problem: Incidental Damages

10-11. Big Company, Inc. and Papers R Us, Inc. signed a written agreement in which Big Company agreed to buy 5000 reams of photocopy paper from Papers R Us at a stated price, deliverable as called for by the buyer. Half-way through the year, Big Company demanded that Papers R Us reduce the price for the remaining deliveries because the market price has decreased. Papers R Us refused to do so, and Big Company did not take or pay for any more deliveries. Assume that Big Company was in breach. Papers R Us sued Big Company for breach of contract.

Which **two** of the following items are clearly recoverable incidental damages under the UCC, and which additional item is arguably recoverable as incidental damages?

a. Paper R Us's costs to store the paper after Big Company refused to order according to the contract, until Papers R Us could find another buyer for it

b. Paper R Us's taxes paid on all of its paper held in inventory

c. The cost of hiring an attorney to figure out how to induce Big Company to honor the contract

d. Paper R Us's loss of profit on the Big Company contract

e. Paper R Us's costs to hire a broker to find another buyer for the paper that Big Company was supposed to take.

f. Paper R Us's interest paid on a loan to cover the missing cash flow that was supposed to result from the Big Company contract.

---

§ 2.1.5.2. Consequential Damages

As noted on page 791, consequential damages are the "downstream" *losses* caused by the breach. They are often where the "real money" is in the dispute, because these ripple effects of the breach can cause lost profits, lost customers, and lost business volume. They also include may include the aggrieved party's losses from "downstream breaches" in its contracts with third parties because those contracts depend on the now-breached performance. For contracts for sales of goods, UCC § 2–715(2) describes consequential damages resulting from seller's breach as including "(a) any loss resulting from general or particular requirements and needs of which the seller at the time of contracting had reason to know and which could not reasonably be prevented by cover or otherwise; and (b) injury to person or property proximately resulting" from the breach. The UCC definition was written to be consistent with the common law definition of consequential damages.

The aggrieved party can recover consequential damages that meet the following requirements:

- Certainty: The damages are not speculative and can be proved with reasonable certainty (a requirement for all damages).

- Causation: The breach caused the damages (a requirement for all expectation damages)

- Foreseeability: The damages "may reasonably be supposed to have been in the contemplation of both parties, at the time they made the contract, as the probable result of the breach of it" (a requirement limited to consequential damages)

- Mitigation: The aggrieved party cannot recover damages that it could have prevented by taking reasonable steps (see § 2.1.6, page 833) (a requirement for all expectation damages).

The next case, *Hadley v. Baxendale*, formulated the standard for foreseeability, in 1854. Prior to *Hadley*, courts had given juries unfettered discretion to set the amount of damages for breach of contract. In the mid-nineteenth century, judicial policy had begun to favor the growth of industry. In *Hadley*, on this appeal from a jury trial that had awarded the plaintiff full damages, Baron Alderson introduced a new rule—the rule later (and now) accepted as authoritative in limiting juries' freedom to award consequential damages.[*]

Reading Critically: *Hadley*, *Redgrave*, and *Kenford* (I) and (II)

1. What limitation(s) did the court identify for the award of consequential damages in each case?

2. What justification was or might be offered for the limitation(s)? Are there competing policies that should be taken into account?

3. Did each court apply the limitation(s) appropriately to the facts of the case?

Example K: *Hadley v. Baxendale*, 156 Eng. Rep. 145 (Ct. Exch. 1854).

Plaintiff was a grain-milling business in Gloucester; its power source was a steam engine. On May 11th, the crank shaft in the steam engine broke and stopped the mill's operation. In order to have a new crank shaft made, the mill had to send the broken shaft to the steam engine's manufacturer in Greenwich, to serve as a pattern (no standardized parts were available, so each part had to be individually made). The mill discovered the break on May 12. On May 13, the mill "sent one of their servants to the office of . . . [a carrier] . . ., for the purpose of having the shaft carried to Greenwich. *The [mill's] servant told the [carrier's] clerk that the mill was stopped, and that the shaft must be sent immediately.*"

Take Note!

Just what the mill communicated to the carrier is not clear. The version of the facts presented here was written by the reporter, not the judge. So the facts that we have italicized here do not match the facts articulated in the opinion by Baron Alderson. Whatever the mill actually communicated to the carrier, the ruling in the case is based on the facts stated in Baron Alderson's opinion.

---

[*]   Richard Danzig, Hadley v. Baxendale: *A Study in the Industrialization of the Law*, in *Contracts Stories* 1 (Douglas G. Baird ed. 2007).

The mill's servant asked when the crank shaft needed to be delivered for transport to Greenwich. The carrier's clerk replied that an item delivered to the carrier by noon on any day "would be delivered at Greenwich on the following day." On May 14, the mill delivered the broken crank shaft to the carrier before noon, arranged for it to be conveyed to Greenwich, and paid the required price of transport. *The mill told the carrier's clerk "that a special entry, if required, should be made to hasten its delivery."* The delivery of the shaft at Greenwich was delayed by some neglect [by the carrier]; and the consequence was, that the [mill] did not receive the new shaft for several days after they would otherwise have done, and the working of their mill was thereby delayed, and they thereby lost the profits they would otherwise have received. The mill brought suit against the carrier for those lost profits.

Analysis: In the trial court, "the Learned judge left the case generally to the jury," who awarded damages to the mill. On appeal, Baron Alderson wrote the opinion for the court, remanding the case for a new trial and instructing the trial court on the proper standard to apply, when instructing the jury. The court set up a test for when consequential damages should be awarded:

Where two parties have made a contract which one of them has broken, the damages which the other party ought to receive in respect of such breach of contract should be such as may fairly and reasonably be considered either arising naturally, i.e., according to the usual course of things, from such breach of contract itself, or such as may reasonably be supposed to have been in the contemplation of both parties, at the time they made the contract, as the probable result of the breach of it. Now, if the special circumstances under which the contract was actually made were communicated by the plaintiffs to the defendants, and thus known to both parties, the damages resulting from the breach of such a contract, which they would reasonably contemplate, would be the amount of injury which would ordinarily follow from a breach of contract under these special circumstances so known and communicated. But, on the other hand, if these special circumstances were wholly unknown to the party breaking the contract, he, at the most, could only be supposed to have had in his contemplation the amount of injury which would arise generally, and in the great multitude of cases not affected by any special circumstances, from such a breach of contract. For, had the special circumstances been known, the parties might have specially provided for the breach of contract by special terms as to the damages in that case; and of this advantage it would be very unjust to deprive them.

Then the court moved to apply that test to the present case:

> *[W]e find that the only circumstances here communicated by the plaintiffs to the defendants at the time of the contract was made, were, that the article to be carried was the broken shaft of a mill, and that the plaintiffs were the millers of the mill.* [Italics added.]

But how do these circumstances show reasonably that the profits of the mill must be stopped by an unreasonable delay in the delivery of the broken shaft by the carrier to the third person? Suppose the plaintiffs had another shaft in their possession put up or putting up at the time, and that they only wished to send back the broken shaft to the engineer who made it; it is clear that this would be quite consistent with the above

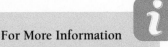

For More Information

The italicized language here contains the court's factual finding that differed from the reporter's facts recounted earlier. For more information on this controversy, see Richard Danzig & Geoffrey R. Watson, *Hadley & Another v. Baxendale & Another,* in *The Capability Problem in Contract Law* 48, at 61–64, 66–67 (2d ed. 2004); Joseph M. Perillo, *Calamari and Perillo on Contracts* 493 n.4 (6th ed. 2009).

circumstances, and yet the unreasonable delay in the delivery would have no effect upon the intermediate profits of the mill. Or, again, suppose that, at the time of the delivery to the carrier, the machinery of the mill had been in other respects defective, then, also, the same results would follow. Here it is true that the shaft was actually sent back to serve as a model for the new one, and that the want of a new one was the only cause of the stoppage of the mill, and that the loss of profits really arose from not sending down the new shaft in proper time, and that this arose from the delay in delivering the broken one to serve as a model. But it is obvious that, in the great multitude of cases of millers sending off broken shafts to third persons by a carrier under ordinary circumstances, such consequences would not, in all probability, have occurred; and these special circumstances were here never communicated by the plaintiffs to the defendants. It follows therefore, that the loss of profits here cannot reasonably be considered such a consequence of the breach of contract as could have been fairly and reasonably contemplated by both the parties when they made this contract. For such loss would neither have flowed naturally from the breach of this contract in the great multitude of such cases occurring under ordinary circumstances, nor were the special circumstances, which, perhaps, would have made it a reasonable and natural consequence of such breach of contract, communicated to or known by the defendants. The Judge ought, therefore, to have told the jury that upon the facts then before them they ought not to take the loss of profits into consideration at all in estimating the damages. There must therefore be a new trial in this case.

. . . .

See It

This print shows the type of steam engine commonly used in flour mills in England in the mid-1800s. The crankshaft is the lengthwise shaft in the right half of the picture. It transmits the power of the steam pistons to the rest of the  machine. A treatise described this kind of crankshaft as follows: "Let the crank of an engine be 2 1/2 feet radius, and the piston will make a stroke of 5 feet long; let the connecting rod be 15 feet long, and the great lever 15 feet long, or 7 1/2 feet radius." John Farey, *A Treatise on the Steam Engine: Historical, Practical and Descriptive* 415 (1827). From this description, we surmise that the crankshaft in *Hadley* was fairly heavy and long.

 To the left is a photo of Joseph and Jonah Hadley's City Flour Mills in June 2005. "This photograph shows the Mill after renovation was completed. The upper floors are now residential, and the ground floor will be occupied by a restaurant-pub. The view is looking from the Docks toward Gloucester Cathedral (seen in the background). Grain, much of it from the Ukraine and Canada, was carried by wagon from the barges to the Mill. It is believed that the steam engine was on the ground floor of the central building. The

building to the left, of typical Gloucestershire stone, was the Mill's office. The one on the right is a warehouse."*

Example L: *Redgrave v. Boston Symphony Orchestra, Inc.*, 855 F.2d 888 (1st Cir. 1988).

In March 1982, the Boston Symphony Orchestra (BSO) engaged Vanessa Redgrave to narrate Stravinsky's "Oedipus Rex" in a series of concerts in Boston and New York. Following the announcement of the engagement, the BSO received calls from its subscribers and from community members protesting the engagement because of Redgrave's political support for the Palestine Liberation Organization and because of her views on the State of Israel. Around April 1, the BSO "cancelled" (actually, repudiated) its contract with Redgrave and its perfor-

Who's That?

A member of a prestigious acting family, Vanessa Redgrave is an acclaimed actress on stage, screen, and television. She was hailed by playwrights Arthur Miller and Tennessee Williams as "the greatest living actress of our times." Her films include *Isadora* (1966), *Camelot* (1967), *Mary, Queen of Scots* (1971), and *Julia* (1978), for which she won an Academy Award. For more information, see http://en.wikipedia.org/wiki/Vanessa_redgrave.

mances of "Oedipus Rex." Redgrave sued the BSO for breach of contract, claiming direct and consequential damages.

Analysis: The jury found that the BSO had breached its contract with Redgrave. It awarded her the BSO performance fee of $27,500, as well as $100,000 in consequential damages for "loss of future professional opportunities" caused by the BSO's breach of contract. In response to special interrogatories, the jury found that the BSO's cancellation of the "Oedipus Rex" concerts caused consequential harm to Redgrave's professional career and that this harm was a foreseeable consequence within the contemplation of the parties at the time they entered the contract. BSO moved for judgment notwithstanding the verdict, and the district

---

* Formerly at http://lawprofessors.typepad.com/contractsprof_blog/2005/06/hadleys_mill.html (last viewed spring 2013). The photograph is courtesy Michael Thorpe, Gloucester City Council, which has granted permission for its use in all educational or nonprofit contexts.

court held that Redgrave's evidence of her consequential damages was sufficient, but that Redgrave could not recover these damages because of First Amendment limitations. Redgrave appealed from these rulings, and the BSO cross-appealed, arguing that the evidence of consequential damages was insufficient.

The court of appeals ruled that the district court erred in reversing the jury's award of consequential damages, but that Redgrave has presented sufficient evidence to prove only $12,000 in consequential damages, minus certain expenses.

Redgrave's consequential damages claim was based on the proposition that a significant number of movie and theater offers that she would ordinarily have received in the years 1982 and following were in fact not offered to her as a result of the BSO's cancellation in April 1982. The BSO characterized this claim as one for damage to Redgrave's reputation, and argued that Massachusetts law does not permit plaintiffs in breach of contract actions to recover consequential damages for harm to reputation, because those damages are speculative, remote, and not within the contemplation of the parties at contract formation. The court agreed that Massachusetts contract law does not allow consequential damages for harm to a claimant's reputation, but it found that Redgrave's claim was "significantly different . . . from a general claim of damage to reputation."

Redgrave's claim was about "a number of specific movie and theater performances that would have been offered to her in the usual course of events were not offered to here as a result of the BSO's cancellation." Such a claim could, in the court's view, meet the standard of *Hadley v. Baxendale* and result in recoverable consequential damages if Redgrave could prove that

> other employers refused to hire Redgrave after termination of the BSO contract because of that termination (that loss of the other employment 'followed as a natural consequence' from the termination of the contract), that this loss of other employment would reasonably have been foreseen by the parties at the time of contracting and at the time of termination, and that damages are rationally calculable . . . .

Redgrave's argument was that she had "earned more than $200,000 on the average since her company's fiscal year 1976, and she testified that she had a constant stream of offers from which she could choose films that had secure financial backing. After the BSO's cancellation in April 1982," she argued, her career underwent a "startling turnabout." She did not work at all for the fourteen months following the cancellation, and the only offers she received during that time were for films with insufficient financial backing. The court noted,

> Redgrave accepted three firm film offers in the fourteen months following the BSO cancellation. If these three films had been produced, Redgrave would have earned $850,000 during that period. The first

offer, for a film entitled *Annie's Coming Out*, was for a role in which Redgrave had expressed interest in February 1982, two months prior to the BSO cancellation. The offer for the role was made in July 1982, a short time after the BSO's cancellation, and was finalized in August 1982. . . . Redgrave's fee for the film was to be $250,000.

From July 1982 until approximately the end of October 1982, Redgrave believed that she would be filming *Annie's Coming Out* sometime during the fall. Because of that commitment, Redgrave turned down other firm offers that had secure financial backing. . . . In late October or early November 1982, Redgrave was informed that *Annie's Coming Out* would not be produced because of financial difficulties. No evidence was presented that the film's financial failure was related to the BSO cancellation.

In February 1983, Redgrave accepted an offer to appear in the film *No Alternatives*, for a fee of $350,000. Until June or July of 1983, Redgrave assumed that she would be filming *No Alternatives*. During that period, Redgrave turned down other offers . . . . In June or July of 1983, Redgrave was informed that *No Alternatives* would not be filmed because of financial difficulties. Redgrave received $25,000 as a forfeiture on the contract.

In June 1983, Redgrave accepted an offer to appear in a film entitled *Track 39*, for a fee of $250,000. This film fell through in late July 1983. There was no allegation that the financial failures of either *No Alternatives* or *Track 39* were directly related to the BSO cancellation.

Although there is no doubt that Redgrave did not have a successful financial year following the BSO cancellation, we cannot say that she presented sufficient evidence to prove that her financial difficulties were caused by the BSO cancellation. . . . If *Annie's Coming Out* had been produced, Redgrave would have earned $250,000 in the year following the BSO cancellation—an amount equal to Redgrave's average earnings before April 1982. . . .

The court engaged in similar analysis of Redgrave's claim that "the type of film offers she received in the year following the BSO cancellation were radically different from the film offers received before the cancellation." It found that Redgrave failed to carry her burden of presenting evidence sufficient to allow a jury reasonably to infer that the drop was proximately caused by the BSO cancellation and not by other, independent factors, including Redgrave's political views.

A similar fate befell Redgrave's claim that, as a result of the BSO cancellation, she no longer received offers to appear on Broadway. Although she testified about missed Broadway opportunities, she did not present sufficient proof that those missed opportunities were caused by the BSO cancellation, with the exception of one production. Redgrave testified that Theodore Mann had considered offering her a role in *Heartbreak House* at Circle in the Square, but decided not to extend the offer because of the ramifications of the BSO cancellation. Mann testified that

> the Boston Symphony Orchestra had cancelled, terminated Ms. Redgrave's contract. This had a—this is the premier or one of the premier arts organizations in America who, like ourselves, seeks support from foundations, corporations, individuals; have subscribers; sell individual tickets. I was afraid . . . and those in my organization were afraid that this termination would have a negative effect on us if we hired her. And so we had conferences about this. We were also concerned about if there would be any physical disturbances to the performance . . . . And it was finally decided . . . that we would not hire [Redgrave] because of all the events that had happened, the cancellation by the Boston Symphony and the effects that we felt it would have on us by hiring her.

The court reasoned that "Mann's testimony regarding the production of *Heartbreak House* is the one piece of evidence from which reasonable factfinders could draw conflicting inferences and upon which a reasonably ascertainable damage award could be granted. We therefore defer to the inferences drawn by the jury from that testimony and grant Redgrave damages on that basis." The court held that "Redgrave presented sufficient evidence to prove consequential damages of $12,000, the fee arrangement contemplated by Mann for Redgrave's appearance in *Heartbreak House*, minus expenses she personally would have incurred had she appeared in the play."

Example M: *Kenford Co. v. County of Erie*, 489 N.Y.S.2d 939 (App. Div. 1985), *modified*, 493 N.E.2d 234, 502 N.Y.S.2d 131 (1986).

The County of Erie contracted with Kenford Co. and Dome Stadium, Inc. ("DSI") for development and management of a proposed sports stadium. In particular, DSI would have the right to manage the stadium for twenty years under a management agreement or lease. After bids were sought, the project was $20 million over budget and, ultimately, the county abandoned the project. Kenford and DSI brought suit for breach of contract, seeking specific performance or, alternatively, $90 million in damages. Plaintiffs were granted summary judgment on the issue of liability, followed by a trial on the issue of damages only. During the lengthy trial, Kenford and DSI attempted to prove $495 million in "lost profits on a baseball franchise, a theme park, three hotels, an office park, a golf course, and a specialty retail center" they would have developed on the land surrounding the proposed stadium, lost profit on the management contract, loss of value on the land they owned adjacent to the stadium site, and out-of-pocket expenses.

Analysis by the trial court: "The trial court dismissed Kenford's claims of lost profits on the peripheral land development and the baseball franchise as being too speculative, but the court submitted the other items of damage to the jury, which awarded DSI lost profits of $25.6 million on the management contract. The jury also awarded Kenford $18 million for its lost appreciation in land value and it granted Kenford over $6 million in out-of-pocket expenses." The county appealed.

Analysis by the appellate division court: The court noted that damages must be "the natural and probable result of the breach," not "a collateral enterprise upon which [the plaintiff] might have embarked, had defendant not breached." Consequential damages must meet the foreseeability standard in *Hadley* and "must be reasonably certain," rather than speculative, possible, imaginary, or contingent. With this framework, the court approved the trial court's refusal to submit to the jury Kenford's claims regarding land development and the baseball franchise. "Although it was known that Kenford would try to buy a

Behind the Scenes

In *Kenford Co. v. County of Erie*, the court considered the claims of disappointed investors in a domed stadium project near Buffalo, New York, that never got built. One of the project developers was Roy Hofheinz, who had been the moving force behind the construction and management of the Houston Astrodome (in the photo), built in the early 1960s and the only existing stadium of that kind at the time of the case. The Astrodome was the first enclosed stadium for baseball and football and the first stadium with luxury boxes. It introduced a then-innovative four-story-high scoreboard, as well as Astroturf, the first artificial turf for ball fields.

In the late 1960s, Hofheinz joined Edward Cottrell (the president and sole shareholder of Kenford Company) to form Dome Stadium, Inc. (DSI) to lease or manage a proposed domed stadium near Buffalo, New York. When Erie County finally accepted the offer from DSI and Kenford Co. in 1969, the contract terms dictated that Kenford Co. would donate 178 acres of land for the project and that the county would negotiate a 40-year lease with DSI for the operation of the stadium. When the county terminated the contract in 1971, it prevented the project from moving forward and set the stage for this case. For more information, see Mike Acosta, *Rain or Shine: How Houston Developed Space City Baseball*, Sports (vol. 6, no. 3); www.historicamerica.net/baseballhouston.html.

baseball franchise and would try to develop the land surrounding the stadium, it was by no means certain that Kenford would have been successful in doing so or that these enterprises would have thrived." The court observed that "[n]ot all business ventures prove to be profitmaking," so "it is completely speculative to say that the franchise would have been a profitable one."

As to Kenford's loss of appreciation on the adjacent land, the evidence showed that the dome stadium would have increased the value of surrounding land fourfold. The court noted that, "[u]nlike Kenford's specific development plans, which were remote and uncertain at the time of contracting, the purchase of the land was a completed fact of which the county had full notice." As such, Kenford was entitled to recover the loss. Nevertheless, the court reversed the award of damages due to "improper appraisal evidence" because it was based on development dates for the project that the court held were speculative, concluding that "[a]ny further appreciation to the land resulting from theme parks and the like makes the evidence of value too speculative to permit recovery." The court ordered a new trial and directed that "the proper measure of damages will be the value of the land as raw acreage following construction of the Dome less the value of the land when purchased. . . . The objective . . . is simply to ascertain fair market value, i.e., what a willing buyer would pay a willing seller for the property, viewing the property exactly as it was in the early 1970s, except assuming that it was located on the periphery of a domed stadium."

Regarding Kenford's lost profits on the management contract, the court first held that there was no "per se" rule precluding recovery of lost profits for new businesses, even though they are very difficult to prove. They are recoverable if plaintiff can prove "[1] that the lost profits are the direct and proximate result of the breach; [2] that profits were contemplated by the parties; and [3] that there is a rational basis on which to calculate the lost profits." The court found the first two criteria were satisfied because "[t]he County's failure to build the stadium was clearly the proximate cause of any loss of profits stemming from the management contract and it is unquestionable that profits by DSI from the management contract were contemplated by the parties." The court found the requirement of "rational basis upon which lost profits may be calculated" was not met, because "[t]he expert had to estimate, first, how many, if any, events would be held at the stadium; how many people would attend each event; and how much each person would spend on parking and concessions," as well as estimating expense Items. The projections were mere conjecture and therefore were "insufficient as a matter of law to support an award of lost profits."

Regarding Kenford's reliance and mitigation damages, the court affirmed damages for the out-of-pocket expenses of $6,160,030.46 in mitigation after the breach, but reversed as to expenses incurred prior to the breach. It held that "proof should not include any sums expended for land acquisition expenses (i.e., brokerage commissions, recording fees, etc.) or for interest paid on the mortgages, since these sums would have been paid even without the breach and since plaintiff will be compensated for these sums by being awarded loss of appreciation of land value." However, "expenses incurred as preparatory to the aborted management agreement, for which no lost profits are recoverable, may be awarded."

Three justices dissented, being of the opinion that all damages were speculative and not recoverable, such that no new trial was needed. Justice Hancock took issue with the application of *Hadley v. Baxendale*'s foreseeability test arguing:

> The record supports the conclusion, applying the general *Hadley v. Baxendale* rule, that it was not reasonably foreseeable that plaintiffs would ultimately fail and would look to the county as their sole source of available financing. There is no evidence that plaintiffs discussed the point with the county and, indeed, no claim that this special circumstance was ever brought to the county's attention. And plaintiffs' persistent and prolonged attempts to find other sources of private and public financing after the county decided not to proceed must be taken as proof that *they* certainly did not believe that the county was the only possibility.

The dissenters concluded that "it would be unjust to compensate plaintiffs with an award of damages which would put them in the same position they would have been in if the Dome had been built." An award "put them in a far better position and to do it at vast expense to defendant."

Think About It!

Is the dissent's point about foreseeability consistent with your understanding of *Hadley*? Why should it matter whether it was foreseeable that Kenford and DSI would be unsuccessful in obtaining other financing?

Analysis by the court of appeals: The court confirmed that loss of future profits as damages are allowed in New York and that the party claiming them must demonstrate "with certainty that such damages have been caused by the breach" and the alleged loss "must be capable of proof with reasonable certainty." The court went on:

> These rules must be applied to the proof presented by DSI in this case. We note the procedure for computing damages selected by DSI was in accord with contemporary economic theory and was presented through the testimony of recognized experts. Such a procedure has been accepted in this State and many other jurisdictions (*see, De Long v. County of Erie*, 60 N.Y.2d 296, 469 N.Y.S.2d 611, 457 N.E.2d 177). DSI's economic analysis employed historical data, obtained from the operation of other domed stadiums and related facilities throughout

the country, which was then applied to the results of a comprehensive study of the marketing prospects for the proposed facility in the Buffalo area. The quantity of proof is massive and, unquestionably, represents business and industry's most advanced and sophisticated method for predicting the probable results of contemplated projects. Indeed, it is difficult to conclude what additional relevant proof could have been submitted by DSI in support of its attempt to establish, with reasonable certainty, loss of prospective profits. Nevertheless, DSI's proof is insufficient to meet the required standard.

The court stated two reasons for its conclusion. First, the court said DSI had not shown that "liability for loss of profits over a 20-year period was in the contemplation of the parties at the time of the execution of the basic contract or at the time of its breach . . . ." Second, while DSI submitted ample expert testimony, the evidence was still projections based on too many unknown factors. "DSI assumed that the facility was completed, available for use and successfully operated by it for 20 years, providing professional sporting events and other forms of entertainment, as well as hosting meetings, conventions and related commercial gatherings. . . . Quite simply, the multitude of assumptions required to establish projections of profitability over the life of this contract require speculation and conjecture, making it beyond the capability of even the most sophisticated procedures to satisfy the legal requirements of proof with reasonable certainty."

The court concluded that "[t]he economic facts of life, the whim of the general public and the fickle nature of popular support for professional athletic endeavors must be given great weight in attempting to ascertain damages 20 years in the future."

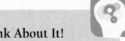

Think About It!

Which court do you agree with more— the appellate division or the court of appeals?

Food for Thought

Note that a buyer's lost profits are indirect damages (consequential damages) because a buyer's direct damages pertain to bargained-for exchange—the purchased item (real estate, services, goods, or intangibles). Any profit that the buyer could have made on that item is compensated with indirect damages. On the other hand, a seller's lost profits are direct damages, because a seller's bargained-for exchange in a contract is usually the price, and the profits are part of that price. Recall *Neri* (Example I on page 815) and *Vitex* (Example J on page 817).

> Although common law cases allow consequential damages for sellers if the damages can be proved (see *Redgrave*, Example L on page 825, and *Kenford*, Example M on page 828), UCC Article 2 does not. Why would seller's consequential damages be excluded? To answer this question, consider what kind of consequential damages a seller might suffer if a buyer fails to take the goods or pay for them.

§ 2.1.6. Mitigation of Damages (Avoidable Damages)

As noted on page 786, one of the policies underlying damages is avoiding the award of damages that the aggrieved party could reasonably have prevented or avoided, either by stopping performance or by taking affirmative steps to avoid further loss. The aggrieved party thus cannot exact revenge on the breaching party by "running up the ante," piling up damages that would punish the breaching party through actions not necessary to protect the interests of the non-breaching party. Such damages are considered to have been caused in some sense by the aggrieved party's failure to take reasonable steps to avoid further injury, rather than by the breaching party. Promoting acts in mitigation also encourages the aggrieved party to engage in productive economic behavior, rather than sit idle and rely upon being compensated for the lost expectancy or continue performing a clearly broken contract and compel the other party to pay for that performance. This is sometimes said to represent the aggrieved party's "duty to mitigate damages," though it is not a duty such that the failure to perform it makes the aggrieved party affirmatively liable.

UCC § 2–715 concurs with this approach, limiting consequential damages for buyers to those "which could not be reasonably prevented by cover or otherwise."

Declaring that the aggrieved party must take reasonable steps to avoid or mitigate damages is easier than defining just what actions are required to satisfy that responsibility. Most straightforward is the requirement that, after one party repudiates the contract, the other party should cease performing unless there is a reasonable chance that the additional work will decrease rather than increase damages.

> **Example N:** *Rockingham County v. Luten Bridge Co.*, 35 F.2d 301 (4th Cir. 1929).
>
> The County Board withdrew approval of a bridge-building project and then repudiated its contract with Luten, the builder. Despite the repudia-

tion, the company built the bridge—"in the midst of the forest" because the county had also decided not to build the road to which the bridge would connect—and then Luten sought recovery of the contract price.

Analysis: The court refused to award the company damages for any work done after receiving notice of the cancellation. The court explained:

> [W]e do not think that, after the county had given notice, while the contract was still executory, that it did not desire the bridge built and would not pay for it, plaintiff could proceed to build it and recover the contract price. It is true that the county had no right to rescind the contract, and the notice given plaintiff amounted to a breach on its part; but, after plaintiff had received notice of the breach, it was its duty to do nothing to increase the damages flowing therefrom. . . . The measure of plaintiff's damage, upon its appearing that notice was duly given not to build the bridge, is an amount sufficient to compensate plaintiff for labor and materials expended and expense incurred in the part performance of the contract, prior to its repudiation, plus the profit which would have been realized if it had been carried out in accordance with its terms.

Behind the Scenes

There was more to *Rockingham County* than a foolish contractor continuing work in the face of a clear repudiation:

> A closer look at the case reveals that the underlying dispute was more about the legitimacy of local government. The dispute emerged when angry taxpayers charged the county commissioners with pursuing a corrupt agenda on behalf of the industrialist who sponsored their political campaigns. But the conflict also revealed traditional tensions between the county's farmers and its mercantile mill owners and constituted a microcosm of the larger political conflict—endemic throughout North Carolina and the South—over investing in public improvements to promote industrialization.

> . . . [T]o [Judge] Parker, the Luten Bridge case [addressed] important issues of county government law and implicated policies that were critical to a changing North Carolina. In this

> respect, sensible rules that govern North Carolina's counties went hand-in-hand with sensible rules for contract law. Unless a county was able to commit to a contractual relationship like any individual, a county would be severely hindered from addressing the needs of an industrializing society.
>
> But perhaps the most striking lesson is the simplest—that *Rockingham County v. Luten Bridge Co.* was intended to do far more than simply reaffirm the duty to mitigate. To the contrary, the case was not so much about permitting counties to get out of contracts, but rather, about enabling counties to enter into contracts.
>
> Barak Richman, Jordi Weinstock, & Jason Mehta, *A Bridge, a Tax Revolt, and the Struggle to Industrialize: The Story and Legacy of Rockingham County v. Luten Bridge Co.*, 84 N.C. L. Rev. 1841 (2006).

The so-called "duty" to stop working is qualified. Under some circumstances, the aggrieved party may reasonably conclude that continuing to perform will reduce, not increase, damages. For instance, a seller making marketable goods for a buyer who repudiates may decide that it should complete the manufacture because it is likely the completed goods can be resold, mitigating much of the injury. Or it may decide that it should stop manufacture because the goods are unlikely to sell at a reasonable price. As long as the seller makes a reasonable judgment at the time of breach, the seller can collect the actual damages, even if the future turns out differently than expected. See UCC § 2–704.

The second, and often more difficult, mitigation question is determining what affirmative steps a party should take to avoid further losses. The following cases examine that question.

Reading Critically: *Sackett* and *Parker*

This is the third part of *Sackett*; the first and second parts appeared on pages 711 and 799.

1. According to each court, what responsibility does an aggrieved party have to mitigate damages? Are the rules articulated by the two courts consistent?

2. Did the dissenting judge in *Parker* disagree with the *Parker* majority as to the standard to be used, or as to its application to the facts of the case?

3. How does the particular type of contract (e.g., an employment contract or a sale of business) affect the application of the mitigation principles?

Example O: *Sackett v. Spindler*, 56 Cal. Rptr. 435 (Ct. App. 1967).

The contract was for sale of ownership shares in a newspaper. The buyer breached. The shares were later sold at a substantially lower price than the contract price.

Analysis: The court noted the aggrieved party had "to do everything reasonably possible to minimize his own loss and thus reduce the damages for which the other party has become liable." As to Spindler's actions:

> it is clear that the record contains ample evidence tending to show that Spindler acted reasonably in minimizing damages. Firstly, in order to improve the financial condition of the newspaper he made several efforts to raise working capital for the business. This he did by personally borrowing money for additional capital and by selling one-half of his stock. In addition, he cut costs by changing the newspaper from a daily to a weekly paper. Sackett argues that after Spindler had determined that Sackett had breached the contract, Spindler did not list the newspaper for sale with a broker nor did he take any other steps to sell the newspaper. However, according to Snyder's testimony, such action on the part of Spindler would have been futile since it would be almost impossible for him to sell the newspaper after the publicized sale to Sackett had fallen through. In addition, since the record reveals that the financial condition of the newspaper immediately after Sackett's breach was worse than its financial condition approximately one year later, it is apparent that Spindler's damages would have been greater if he had been able to sell the stock at an earlier date. Finally, Sackett contends that Spindler was required to accept Sackett's so-called "offer" of October 4 in order to minimize damages. However, Sackett's telegram of October 4 contained no tender of performance, but only an expression of willingness to proceed to consummate the sale as soon

as the release of his assets from threatened receivership in his divorce action would permit "full financing" of the unpaid balance.

Parker v. Twentieth Century-Fox Film Corp.

SHIRLEY MACLAINE PARKER, Plaintiff-Respondent

v.

TWENTIETH CENTURY-FOX FILM CORP., Defendant-Appellant

Supreme Court of California, In Bank

474 P.2d 689 (Cal. 1970)

BURKE, JUSTICE.

Defendant Twentieth Century-Fox Film Corporation appeals from a summary judgment granting to plaintiff the recovery of agreed compensation under a written contract for her services as an actress in a motion picture. As will appear, we have concluded that the trial court correctly ruled in plaintiff's favor and that the judgment should be affirmed.

Plaintiff is well known as an actress, and in the contract between plaintiff and defendant is sometimes referred to as the "Artist." Under the contract, dated August 6, 1965, plaintiff was to play the female lead in defendant's contemplated production of a motion picture entitled "Bloomer Girl." The

Who's That?

The older sister of actor Warren Beatty, Shirley MacLaine is a Hollywood film actress whose career spans from the 1950s to the present day. Discovered while performing on Broadway as an understudy replacement in *The Pajama Game*, she was signed by Paramount pictures and made her film debut in Alfred Hitchcock's *The Trouble with Harry* in 1955. She has been nominated for 5 Academy Awards for Best Actress, winning for her role in *Terms of Endearment* (1983). Her major films include *The Apartment* (1960), *Irma La Douce* (1963), *Sweet Charity* (1968), *Guarding Tess* (1994), and *Rumor Has It* (2005). She appeared in two seasons of *Downton Abbey* as Martha Levinson, mother to Cora, Countess of Grantham. In 1978, Women in Film awarded MacLaine its Crystal Award, given "to honor outstanding women who, through their endurance and the excellence of their work, have helped to expand the role of women within the entertainment industry." In 2012, she won the American Film Institute Life Achievement Award and, in 2013, received the Kennedy Center Honors for lifetime contributions to American culture through the performing arts.

contract provided that defendant would pay plaintiff a minimum "guaranteed compensation" of "53,571.42 per week for 14 weeks commencing May 23, 1966, for a total of $750,000." Prior to May 1966 defendant decided not to produce the picture and by a letter dated April 4, 1966, it notified plaintiff of that decision and that it would not "comply with our obligations to you under" the written contract.

By the same letter and with the professed purpose "to avoid any damage to you," defendant instead offered to employ plaintiff as the leading actress in another film tentatively entitled "Big Country, Big Man" (hereinafter, "Big Country"). The compensation offered was identical, as were 31 of the 34 numbered provisions or articles of the original contract.[1] Unlike "Bloomer Girl," however, which was to have been a musical production, "Big Country" was a dramatic "western type" movie. "Bloomer Girl" was to have been filmed in California; "Big Country" was to be produced in Australia. Also, certain terms in the proffered contract varied from those of the original.[2] Plaintiff was given one week within which to accept; she did not and the offer lapsed. Plaintiff then commenced this action seeking recovery of the agreed guaranteed compensation.

The complaint sets forth two causes of action. The first is for money due under the contract; the second, based upon the same allegations as the first, is for damages resulting from defendant's breach of contract. Defendant in its answer admits the existence and validity of the contract, that plaintiff complied with all the conditions, covenants and promises and stood ready to complete the performance, and that defendant breached and "anticipatorily repudiated" the contract. It denies,

---

[1]   Among the identical provisions was the following found in the last paragraph of Article 2 of the original contract: "We [defendant] shall not be obligated to utilize your [plaintiff's] services in or in connection with the Photoplay hereunder, our sole obligation, subject to the terms and conditions of this Agreement, being to pay you the guaranteed compensation herein provided for."

[2]   Article 29 of the original contract specified that plaintiff approved the director already chosen for "Bloomer Girl" and that in case he failed to act as director plaintiff was to have approval rights of any substitute director. Article 31 provided that plaintiff was to have the right of approval of the "Bloomer Girl" dance director, and Article 32 gave her the right of approval of the screenplay.

Defendant's letter of April 4 to plaintiff, which contained both defendant's notice of breach of the "Bloomer Girl" contract and offer of the lead in "Big Country," eliminated or impaired each of those rights. It read in part as follows: "The terms and conditions of our offer of employment are identical to those set forth in the 'BLOOMER GIRL' Agreement, Articles 1 through 34 and Exhibit A to the Agreement, except as follows:

1.   Article 31 of said Agreement will not be included in any contract of employment regarding 'BIG COUNTRY, BIG MAN' as it is not a musical and it thus will not need a dance director.

2.   In the 'BLOOMER GIRL' agreement, in Articles 29 and 32, you were given certain director and screenplay approvals and you had preapproved certain matters. Since there simply is insufficient time to negotiate with you regarding your choice of director and regarding the screenplay and since you already expressed an interest in performing the role in 'BIG COUNTRY, BIG MAN,' we must exclude from our offer of employment in 'BIG COUNTRY, BIG MAN' any approval rights as are contained in said Articles 29 and 32; however, we shall consult with you respecting the director to be selected to direct the photoplay and will further consult with you with respect to the screenplay and any revisions or changes therein, provided, however, that if we fail to agree . . . the decision of . . . [defendant] with respect to the selection of a director and to revisions and changes in the said screenplay shall be binding upon the parties to said agreement."

however, that any money is due to plaintiff either under the contract or as a result of its breach, and pleads as an affirmative defense to both causes of action plaintiff's allegedly deliberate failure to mitigate damages, asserting that she unreasonably refused to accept its offer of the leading role in "Big Country."

Plaintiff moved for summary judgment . . . , the motion was granted, and summary judgment for $750,000 plus interest was entered in plaintiff's favor. This appeal by defendant followed.

The familiar rules are that the matter to be determined by the trial court on a motion for summary judgment is whether facts have been presented which give rise to a triable factual issue. The court may not pass upon the issue itself. Summary judgment is proper only if the affidavits or declarations in support of the moving party would be sufficient to sustain a judgment in his favor and his opponent does not by affidavit show facts sufficient to present a triable issue of fact. . . .

The general rule is that the measure of recovery by a wrongfully discharged employee is the amount of salary agreed upon for the period of service, less the amount which the employer affirmatively proves the employee has earned or with reasonable effort might have earned from other employment. . . . However, before projected earnings from other employment opportunities not sought or accepted by the discharged employee can be applied in mitigation, the employer must show that the other employment was comparable, or substantially similar, to that of which the employee has been deprived; the employee's rejection of or failure to seek other available employment of a different or inferior kind may not be resorted to in order to mitigate damages. (Gonzales v. Internat. Assn. of Machinists (1963) 213 Cal.App.2d 817, 822–824, 29 Cal.Rptr. 190 . . . .

In the present case defendant has raised no issue of *reasonableness of efforts* by plaintiff to obtain other employment; the sole issue is whether plaintiff's refusal of defendant's substitute offer of "Big Country" may be used in mitigation. Nor, if the "Big Country" offer was of employment different or inferior when compared with the original "Bloomer Girl" employment, is there an issue as to whether or not plaintiff acted reasonably in refusing the substitute offer. Despite defendant's arguments to the contrary, no case cited or which our research has discovered holds or suggests that reasonableness is an element of a wrongfully discharged employee's option to reject, or fail to seek, different or inferior employment lest the possible earnings therefrom be charged against him in mitigation of damages.[5]

---

[5] Instead, in each case the reasonableness referred to was that of the *efforts* of the employee to obtain other employment that was not different or inferior; his right to reject the latter was declared as an unqualified rule of law. Thus, Gonzales v. Internat. Assn. of Machinists, *supra*, 213 Cal.App.2d 817, 823–824, 29 Cal.Rptr. 190, 194, holds that the trial court correctly instructed the jury that plaintiff

Applying the foregoing rules to the record in the present case, with all intendments in favor of the party opposing the summary judgment motion—here, defendant—it is clear that the trial court correctly ruled that plaintiff's failure to accept defendant's tendered substitute employment could not be applied in mitigation of damages because the offer of the "Big Country" lead was of employment both different and inferior, and that no factual dispute was presented on that issue. The mere circumstance that "Bloomer Girl" was to be a musical review calling upon plaintiff's talents as a dancer as well as an actress, and was to be produced in the City of Los Angeles, whereas "Big Country" was a straight dramatic role in a "Western Type" story taking place in an opal mine in Australia, demonstrates the difference in kind between the two employments; the female lead as a dramatic actress in a western style motion picture can by no stretch of imagination be considered the equivalent of or substantially similar to the lead in a song-and-dance production.

Additionally, the substitute "Big Country" offer proposed to eliminate or impair the director and screenplay approvals accorded to plaintiff under the original "Bloomer Girl" contract (see fn. 2, Ante), and thus constituted an offer of inferior employment. No expertise or judicial notice is required in order to hold that the deprivation or infringement of an employee's rights held under an original employment contract converts the available "other employment" relied upon by the employer to mitigate damages, into inferior employment which the employee need not seek or accept. (See Gonzales v. Internat. Asst. of Machinists, *supra*, 213 Cal.App.2d 817, 823–824, 29 Cal.Rptr. 190 . . . .)

Statements found in affidavits submitted by defendant in opposition to plaintiff's summary judgment motion, to the effect that the "Big Country" offer was not of employment different from or inferior to that under the "Bloomer Girl" contract, merely repeat the allegations of defendant's answer to the complaint in this action, constitute only conclusionary assertions with respect to undisputed facts, and do not give rise to a triable factual issue so as to defeat the motion for summary judgment. . . .

---

union member, a machinist, was required to make "such *efforts* as the average [member of his union] desiring employment would make at that particular time and place" (italics added); but, further, that the court *properly rejected* defendant's *offer of proof of the availability of other kinds of employment* at the same or higher pay than plaintiff usually received and all outside the jurisdiction of his union, as plaintiff could not be required to accept different employment or a nonunion job.

In Harris v. Nat. Union, etc., Cooks and Stewards, *supra*, 116 Cal.App.2d 759, 761, 254 P.2d 673, 676, the issues were stated to be, inter alia, whether comparable employment was open to each plaintiff employee, and if so whether each plaintiff made a *reasonable effort* to secure such employment. It was held that the trial court *properly sustained an objection to an offer to prove a custom of accepting a job in a lower rank* when work in the higher rank was not available, as "The duty of mitigation of damages . . . does not require the plaintiff 'to seek or to accept other employment of a different or inferior kind.' . . . Damages may be mitigated 'by a showing that the employee, by the exercise of reasonable diligence and effort, could have procured comparable employment. . . .'."

In view of the determination that defendant failed to present any facts showing the existence of a factual issue with respect to its sole defense—plaintiff's rejection of its substitute employment offer in mitigation of damages—we need not consider plaintiff's further contention that for various reasons, ... plaintiff was excused from attempting to mitigate damages.

The judgment is affirmed.

SULLIVAN, ACTING CHIEF JUSTICE (dissenting).

The basic question in this case is whether or not plaintiff acted reasonably in rejecting defendant's offer of alternate employment. The answer depends upon whether that offer (starring in "Big Country, Big Man") was an offer of work that was substantially similar to her former employment (starring in "Bloomer Girl") or of work that was of a different or inferior kind. To my mind this is a factual issue which the trial court should not have determined on a motion for summary judgment. The majority have not only repeated this error but have compounded it by applying the rules governing mitigation of damages in the employer-employee context in a misleading fashion. Accordingly, I respectfully dissent.

The familiar rule requiring a plaintiff in a tort or contract action to mitigate damages embodies notions of fairness and socially responsible behavior which are fundamental to our jurisprudence. Most broadly stated, it precludes the recovery of damages which, through the exercise of due diligence, could have been avoided. Thus, in essence, it is a rule requiring reasonable conduct in commercial affairs. This general principle governs the obligations of an employee after his employer has wrongfully repudiated or terminated the employment contract. Rather than permitting the employee simply to remain idle during the balance of the contract period, the law requires him to make a reasonable effort to secure other employment.[1] He is not obliged, however, to seek or accept any and all types of work which may be available. Only work which is in the same field and which is of the same quality need be accepted.[2]

---

[1] The issue is generally discussed in terms of a duty on the part of the employee to minimize loss. The practice is long-established and there is little reason to change despite Judge Cardozo's observation of its subtle inaccuracy. "The servant is free to accept employment or reject it according to his uncensored pleasure. What is meant by the supposed duty is merely this: That if he unreasonably reject, he will not be heard to say that the loss of wages from then on shall be deemed the jural consequence of the earlier discharge. He has broken the chain of causation, and loss resulting to him thereafter is suffered through his own act." (McClelland v. Climax Hosiery Mills (1930) 252 N.Y. 347, 359, 169 N.E. 605, 609, concurring opinion.)

[2] This qualification of the rule seems to reflect the simple and humane attitude that it is too severe to demand of a person that he attempt to find and perform work for which he has no training or experience. Many of the older cases hold that one need not accept work in an inferior rank or position nor work which is more menial or arduous. This suggests that the rule may have had its origin in the bourgeois fear of resubmergence in lower economic classes.

Over the years the courts have employed various phrases to define the type of employment which the employee, upon his wrongful discharge, is under an obligation to accept. Thus in California alone it has been held that he must accept employment which is "substantially similar"; "comparable employment"; employment "in the same general line of the first employment"; "equivalent to his prior position"; "employment in a similar capacity"; employment which is "not . . . of a different or inferior kind. . . ." [cites omitted throughout paragraph].

For reasons which are unexplained, the majority cite several of these cases yet select from among the various judicial formulations which contain one particular phrase, "Not of a different or inferior kind," with which to analyze this case. I have discovered no historical or theoretical reason to adopt this phrase, which is simply a negative restatement of the affirmative standards set out in the above cases, as the exclusive standard. Indeed, its emergence is an example of the dubious phenomenon of the law responding not to rational judicial choice or changing social conditions, but to unrecognized changes in the language of opinions or legal treatises. However, the phrase is a serviceable one and my concern is not with its use as the standard but rather with what I consider its distortion.

The relevant language excuses acceptance only of employment which is of a *different kind*. (Gonzales v. Internat. Assn. of Machinists, *supra*, 213 Cal.App.2d 817, 822, 29 Cal.Rptr. 190 . . .). It has never been the law that the mere existence of *differences between two jobs in the same field* is sufficient, as a matter of law, to excuse an employee wrongfully discharged from one from accepting the other in order to mitigate damages. Such an approach would effectively eliminate any obligation of an employee to attempt to minimize damage arising from a wrongful discharge. The only alternative job offer an employee would be required to accept would be an offer of his former job by his former employer.

Although the majority appear to hold that there was a difference "in kind" between the employment offered plaintiff in "Bloomer Girl" and that offered in "Big Country", an examination of the opinion makes crystal clear that the majority merely point out differences between the two *films* (an obvious circumstance) and then apodically assert that these constitute a difference in the *kind of employment*. The entire rationale of the majority boils down to this: that the *"mere circumstances"* that "Bloomer Girl" was to be a musical review while "Big Country" was a straight drama "demonstrates the difference in kind"

What's That?

The dissent may have meant that the majority "apodictically" (rather than "apodically") asserted that the differences between the two jobs meant there was a difference "in kind" between the two. "Apodictic" means "demonstrably or indisputably true"; the dissent believes the majority declared a truth about the difference between the jobs without demonstrating it.

since a female lead in a western is not "the equivalent of or substantially similar to" a lead in a musical. This is merely attempting to prove the proposition by repeating it. It shows that the vehicles for the display of the star's talents are different but it does not prove that her employment as a star in such vehicles is of necessity different *in kind* and either inferior or superior.

I believe that the approach taken by the majority (a superficial listing of differences with no attempt to assess their significance) may subvert a valuable legal doctrine.[5] The inquiry in cases such as this should not be whether differences between the two jobs exist (there will always be differences) but whether the differences which are present are substantial enough to constitute differences in the *kind* of employment or, alternatively, whether they render the substitute work employment of an *inferior kind*.

It seems to me that *this* inquiry involves, in the instant case at least, factual determinations which are improper on a motion for summary judgment. Resolving whether or not one job is substantially similar to another or whether, on the other hand, it is of a different or inferior kind, will often (as here) require a critical appraisal of the similarities and differences between them in light of the importance of these differences to the employee. This necessitates a weighing of the evidence, and it is precisely this undertaking which is forbidden on summary judgment. (Garlock v. Cole (1962) 199 Cal.App.2d 11, 14, 18 Cal.Rptr. 393.)

This is not to say that summary judgment would never be available in an action by an employee in which the employer raises the defense of failure to mitigate damages. No case has come to my attention, however, in which summary judgment has been granted on the issue of whether an employee was obliged to accept available alternate employment. Nevertheless, there may well be cases in which the substitute employment is so manifestly of a dissimilar or inferior sort, the declarations of the plaintiff so complete and those of the defendant so conclusionary and inadequate that no factual issues exist for which a trial is required. This, however, is not such a case.

It is not intuitively obvious, to me at least, that the leading female role in a dramatic motion picture is a radically different endeavor from the leading female role in a musical comedy film. Nor is it plain to me that the rather qualified rights of director and screenplay approval contained in the first contract are highly significant matters either in the entertainment industry in general or to this

---

[5] The values of the doctrine of mitigation of damages in this context are that it minimizes the unnecessary personal and social (e.g., nonproductive use of labor, litigation) costs of contractual failure. If a wrongfully discharged employee can, through his own action and without suffering financial or psychological loss in the process, reduce the damages accruing from the breach of contract, the most sensible policy is to require him to do so. I fear the majority opinion will encourage precisely opposite conduct.

plaintiff in particular. Certainly, none of the declarations introduced by plaintiff in support of her motion shed any light on these issues.

Nor do they attempt to explain why she declined the offer of starring in "Big Country, Big Man." Nevertheless, the trial court granted the motion, declaring that these approval rights were "critical" and that their elimination altered "the essential nature of the employment."

. . . .

I believe that the judgment should be reversed so that the issue of whether or not the offer of the lead role in "Big Country, Big Man" was of employment comparable to that of the lead role in "Bloomer Girl" may be determined at trial.

. . . .

Behind the Scenes: The Hollywood Studio System and "Bloomer Girl"

The Hollywood studio system functioned differently in the past than it does today. In the early years of Hollywood, the studios exerted tight contractual control over actors, who spent their entire careers working for one studio, which made decisions about an actor's physical appearance, scrutinized the actor's behavior "off the lot," and dictated which roles and movies the actor appeared in. A noncompliant actor would be placed on suspension without pay. Some studio doctors furnished drugs to actors, to help them work longer hours and sleep "on command." Judy Garland later recalled that MGM "had us working day and nights on end . . . . They'd give us pep pills to keep us on our feet long after we were exhausted, then they'd knock us cold with sleeping pills, then after four hours they'd give us the pep pills again."

Some actors rebelled against this system, initially unsuccessfully. James Cagney and Myrna Loy brought unsuccessful suits in the 1930s. Bette Davis famously became involved in a lawsuit with Warner Bros. when she walked out on her studio contract in protest for better roles. The first successful suit by a Hollywood star against a studio was mounted by Olivia de Haviland, famous for playing Melanie in *Gone with the Wind*. Her case, *De Haviland v. Warner Bros. Pictures, Inc.*, 67 Cal. App. 2d 225 (1944), limited the length of studio contracts to seven years and held that time under suspension counted as part of this time. For a fascinating account of the "De Haviland Law," see http://en.wikipedia. org/wiki/De_Havilland_Law.

During the 1950s, Hollywood stars continued to separate themselves from studios through litigation and by creating their own production companies, following the examples of Lucille Ball and husband Desi Arnaz in 1950 (Desilu Productions) and Marilyn Monroe in 1955. Many historians consider *Parker v. Twentieth Century Fox Film Corp.*, to be the official end of the Hollywood studio system. After this case, movie actors were free to pick their own roles, negotiate their own contract terms, and work for a variety of studios.

In this case, Parker entered in a contract to make a movie of a Broadway musical that had already succeeded on Broadway and that featured compelling characters and plot. "Bloomer Girl" debuted in 1944 as a Broadway musical, with lyricist E.Y. Harburg and composer Harold Arlen (who had composed "Somewhere Over the Rainbow" in 1938). In the story, "Horatio Applegate . . . [is] an upstate New York manu-facturer of hoop skirts who has married off five of his daughters to his regional salesmen. He is, as the show begins, playing Cupid with the sixth, Evelina . . . , and his new employee, Jeff Calhoun . . . , a slave owner from Kentucky. Evelina, however, is devoted to her aunt, Dolly Bloomer, a stubborn women's activist and abolitionist. . . . The battles of the sexes and North and South are played out in the courtship of Evelina and Jeff until finally love and liberalism win."* The character of Dolly, who gave the movie its name, is based on Amelia Jenks Bloomer, a suffrage pioneer and temperance advocate. Because of her promotion of changing dress standards for women to free them from activity-restricting clothing, her name became associated with the development of "bloomers," loose trousers gathered at the ankles and topped by a short dress or skirt. "Bloomer Girl" ran for 654 performances and was recorded in a cast album. In the mid-1950s, "Bloomer Girl" was resur-rected in an abridged version on TV.** The 1965 film of "Bloomer Girl" that was scrapped in this case was to have starred Shirley MacLaine (Parker) and Katharine Hepburn.

"Big Country, Big Man," which was also never made, was based on the novel "Call Me When the Cross Turns Over," a reference to a com-

---

* http://theater.nytimes.com/mem/theater/treview.html?html_title=&tols_title=BLOOMER%20 GIRL%20(PLAY)&pdate=20010324&byline=By%20BRUCE%20WEBER&id=1077011429344.

** www.answers.com/topic/bloomer-girl; http://en.wikipedia.org/wiki/Bloomer_Girl; http://www. ibdb.com/production.php?id=1583.

ment often made by sheep shearers in the Australian outback as they went to sleep (the "Cross" is the Southern Cross in the night sky). The scriptwriter of "Big Country" was Bill Strutton, who "worked on some of the best-remembered 1960s television shows including Ivanhoe, The Saint, The Avengers, and Doctor Who."[*]

Do these facts affect your analysis of the *Parker* case? If so, how?

Problem: Mitigation of Damages

10-12. Hawa, a property owner, agreed to pay $12,000 to Moore, a contractor, for installation of a recycled concrete base for a parking lot that Hawa would then cover with gravel or concrete. Hawa agreed to pay Moore $5000 down, $5000 when the work was 50% done, and the remaining $2000 when the work was 75% complete. Hawa paid $5000, and Moore began the work, delivering supplies to the job site. Hawa complained about the quality of the delivered materials and said that he would not make the second payment because he was not happy with wire in the rocks and needed his bank to inspect the work. Moore assured Hawa that he would remove the wire, and he spread about 2/3 of the materials. A dispute arose regarding payment of the next $5000, and the bank did not visit the site, so Moore walked off the job. Hawa filed a breach of contract claim in small claims court. Moore filed a counterclaim. Two months later, Moore paid $1500 to have material designated for Hawa's job transported from the supplier to his own facility.

At trial, Moore claimed the following damages:

a. $5000 cost of rock,

b. $3795 cost of the initial hauling of materials and equipment,

c. $1500 cost of the hauling of the rock after commencement of the small-claims-court action, and

d. $200 cost of front gate work requested by Hawa that was not covered in the contract.

Presuming Hawa repudiated the contract, what amount should the small claims court award Moore?

———————————

[*] http://en.wikipedia.org/wiki/Bill_Strutton.

§ 2.2. Reliance Damages

As discussed on page 787, reliance damages are designed to put the aggrieved party into the position that it would have been in *today* if the parties had not entered the contract. Reliance damages compensate for out-of-pocket expenses incurred by the aggrieved party in reliance on the existence of the contract, as well as lost opportunity costs, if provable. While forward-looking expectation damages are the preferred remedy for enforcing contractual promises, reliance damages may be appropriate if there are no identifiable expectation damages, if expectation damages are too speculative in amount, or if for other reasons expectation damages are not appropriate. Reliance damages also may be awarded when a promise is enforced under Restatement (Second) § 90; recall that the remedy for promissory estoppel "may be limited as justice requires," although few courts have chosen that route.

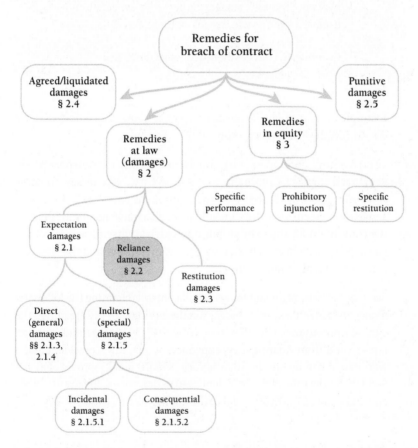

Recall the policies governing damages, as listed in the chart on page 786. Reliance damages are available only for *reasonable* expenses incurred *in reliance* on the existence of the promise, and the aggrieved party may not recover for expenses that could have been avoided through reasonable actions to mitigate or avoid losses. In a promissory estoppel case, such as Example A on page 789, the reliance must be the kind that "the promisor should reasonably expect" to have been induced by the promise. Because the promisor would not expect a promisee to spend more than it would have made on the contract, the promisee cannot recover more in reliance damages than it could have gotten in expectation damages. However, that limit may be more theoretical than actual in most cases, because reliance damages are used most often when expectation damages are not provable with sufficient certainty.

Reading Critically: *Security Stove* and *Goodman*

1. Why were reliance damages rather than expectation damages considered appropriate in each of these cases?

2. How did each court compute reliance damages?

Example P: *Security Stove & Manufacturing Co. v. American Railway Express Co.*, 51 S.W.2d 572 (Mo. Ct. App. 1932).

Security Stove contracted with American Railway to transport newly developed furnace equipment to Atlantic City, New Jersey, to show at a convention, with arrival of the equipment expected prior to the convention. Security Stove's president made arrangements to travel to the convention for the exhibit, but upon arrival, discovered one of the packages had not been delivered by American Railway, and that package contained the most important part.

Security Stove brought suit for breach of contract, claiming the following damages: "$147.00 express charges (on the exhibit); $45.12 freight on the exhibit from Atlantic City to Kansas City; $101.39 railroad and pullman fares to and from Atlantic City, expended by plaintiff's president and a workman taken by him to Atlantic City; $48.00 hotel room for the two; $150.00 for the time of the president; $40.00 for wages of plaintiff's other employee and $270.00 for rental of the booth, making a total of $801.51."

Analysis: The jury awarded Security Stove the requested damages, plus interest, and American Railway appealed.

Affirming the award of Security Stove's expenses as damages, the court rejected American Railway's argument that only lost profits were recoverable by Security Stove. The court noted that Security Stove advised American Railway of the need for prompt shipment of the equipment. With respect to recovery, the court noted:

> Ordinarily the measure of damages where the carrier fails to deliver a shipment at destination within a reasonable time is the difference between the market value of the goods at the time of the delivery and the time when they should have been delivered. But where the carrier has notice of peculiar circumstances under which the shipment is made, which will result in an unusual loss by the shipper in case of

Think About It!

This case, like *Hadley*, involves a contract directly with a carrier. Carriers are often third parties in contracts between buyers and sellers, hired to transport the goods. Why would the ordinary measure of damages for the carrier's failure to timely deliver goods be as the court describes it here? Does that measure make sense in a contract like the one in this case?

> delay in delivery, the carrier is responsible for the real damage sustained from such delay if the notice given is of such character, and goes to such extent, in informing the carrier of the shipper's situation, that the carrier will be presumed to have contracted with reference thereto. . . .

> The case at bar was to recover damages for loss of profits by reason of the failure of the defendant to transport the shipment within a reasonable time, so that it would arrive in Atlantic City for the exhibit. There were no profits contemplated. The furnace was to be shown and shipped back to Kansas City. There was no money loss, except the expenses, that was of such a nature as any court would allow as being sufficiently definite or lacking in pure speculation. Therefore, unless plaintiff is permitted to recover the expenses that it went to, which were a total loss to it by reason of its inability to exhibit the furnace and equipment, it will be deprived of any substantial compensation for its loss. The law does not contemplate any such injustice. It ought to allow plaintiff, as damages, the loss in the way of expenses that it sustained, and which it would not have been put to if it had not been for its reliance upon the defendant to perform its contract. There is no contention that the exhibit would have been entirely valueless and whatever it might have accomplished defendant knew of the circumstances and ought to respond for whatever damages plaintiff suffered. In cases of this kind the method of estimating the damages should be adopted which is the most definite and certain and which best achieves the fun-

Think About It!

If the exhibit had been shipped "in order to realize a profit on sales . . . and plaintiff failed to show loss of profits with sufficient definiteness," what would or should the result have been?

damental purpose of compensation. . . . Miller v. Robertson, 266 U. S. 243, 257, 45 S.Ct. 73, 78, 69 L. Ed. 265. Had the exhibit been shipped in order to realize a profit on sales and such profits could have been realized, or to be entered in competition for a prize, and plaintiff failed to show loss of profits with sufficient definiteness, or that he would have won the prize, defendant's cases might be in point. But as before stated, no such situation exists here.

While Security Stove contracted for some of the expenses prior to the shipping, American Railway contracted for the shipping in full knowledge of the exhibition at the convention. As such, the "damage, therefore, was suffered in contemplation of defendant performing its contract, which it failed to do, and would not have been sustained except for the reliance by plaintiff upon defendant to perform it."

Example Q: *Goodman v. Dicker,* 169 F.2d 684 (D.C. Cir. 1948).

The local distributors for Emerson Radio and Phonograph Corp. (in the District of Columbia) encouraged Dicker (and other plaintiffs) to apply for a "dealer franchise" to sell Emerson's products. The distributors "by their representations and conduct induced the plaintiffs to incurred expenses in preparation to do business under the franchise, including employment of sales personnel and solicitation of orders for radios. Among other things, [the distributors] represented that the application had been accepted, that the franchise would be granted, and that [the plaintiffs] would receive an initial delivery of thirty to forty radios." When plaintiffs were denied a franchise and did not receive any product, they sued the distributors.

Analysis: The court ruled in favor of the plaintiffs, even though there was not a contract. It awarded $1500, covering cash expenditures of $1150 and lost profits of $350 on the sale of thirty radios. The court rejected defendants' argument that the plaintiffs should collect no damages because the franchise would have been terminable at will and the plaintiffs were not guaranteed a supply of radios. "We think the contentions miss the real point of this case. . . . We are dealing with a promise by [defendants] that a franchise would be granted and radios supplied, on the faith of which [plaintiffs] with the knowledge and encouragement of [defendants] incurred expenses in making preparations to do business. . . . Justice and fair dealing require that one who acts to his detriment on the faith of conduct of the kind revealed here should be protected by estopping the party who has brought about the situation from alleging anything in opposition to the natural consequences of his own course of conduct." The court decided that:

> the trial court was correct in holding defendants liable for moneys which [plaintiffs] expended in preparation to do business under the promised dealer franchise. These items aggregated $1150. We think, though, that the court erred in adding the item of $350 for loss of profits on radios promised under an initial order. The true measure of damage is the loss sustained by expenditures made in reliance upon the assurance of a dealer franchise.

Make the Connection

Even though the plaintiffs in *Goodman* failed to prove a contract, the court ruled that the defendants were estopped from denying the contract, because promissory estoppel barred the defendants from raising the argument that no contract was formed. In *Ricketts v. Scothorn* (Chapter 5, page 276), the court used promissory estoppel in a similar fashion—to bar the defendant from raising the defense of lack of consideration. In some jurisdictions, promissory estoppel may bar the defendant from raising the defense of the statute of frauds (Chapter 7, page 503). Thus, promissory estoppel can be either a cause of action or a defense for a plaintiff.

Equitable estoppel, on the other hand, can be used only as a defense, not a cause of action. Equitable estoppel is based on a factual misrepresentation by the defendant, on which the plaintiff relies in a way that is foreseeable and reasonable. A plaintiff's cause of action for a factual misrepresentation is in tort, not contract.

As reflected in these materials, promissory estoppel can be "both a sword and a shield," while equitable estoppel can be "only a shield."

§ 2.3. Restitution Damages

Restitution is relief that seeks to return the parties to their pre-contract positions—the "status quo ante"—by requiring each party to restore to the other party any benefits conferred by that other party that it would be unjust to retain. Restitutionary relief comes in two forms—damages (paying the value of benefits conferred) and "specific restitution" (an order in equity to restore a particular object to the rightful person). Damages are preferred, as are all remedies at law. This section addresses restitution damages.

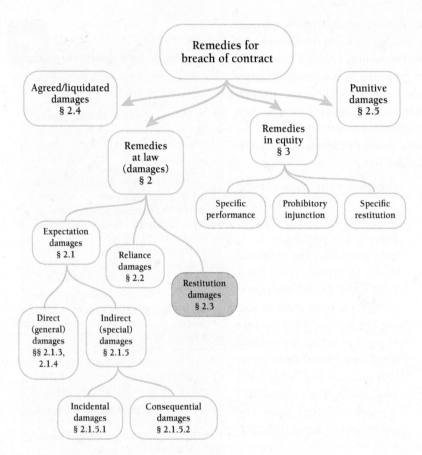

The most challenging aspect of restitution damages often is determining the value of a non-monetary benefit conferred on a party, because multiple measures may be possible. For example, if a construction contractor or other service provider has breached after doing some work and furnishing some supplies for the other party, the following measures may be considered:

- Net enrichment: How much the aggrieved party's wealth has been increased, as measured by

  - the appraised value of the construction or other material retained by the aggrieved party,
  - the amount by which the value of the aggrieved party's property has been increased, or
  - the value of the retained services and supplies to the aggrieved party.

- Cost of the services or supplies provided: What it would cost the aggrieved party to purchase the retained services or supplies on the open market ("quantum meruit" or "quantum valebant").

- Pro rata portion of the contract price.

The choice of measure may depend on what can be proved with sufficient certainty. It may also vary depending on the circumstances of the claim. For example, we have seen restitution used as a remedy when

- Restitution is the cause of action (see Chapter 5, page 329, discussing liability when benefits are conferred but no promise was made);[*]

- An agreement is voided because of mistake, misrepresentation, or other defense (see Chapter 6, page 356);

- Excuse is granted, and the parties need to be returned to their status quo ante (Chapter 9, § 6.4, page 776); and

- A repudiating buyer is entitled to refund of its deposit or other benefit conferred, while remaining liable for damages for the breach (see *Neri v. Retail Marine Corp.*, Example I (page 815).

Faced with multiple measures, a court will likely favor an aggrieved party over a breaching party, but will be more neutral if restitution follows excuse or is being awarded to prevent unjust enrichment when benefits were conferred without a promise but under circumstances where it would be unjust enrichment not to compensate for those benefits.

Example R: *Pauma Band of Luiseno Mission Indians of the Pauma & Yuima Reservation v. California*, 813 F.3d 1155 (9th Cir. 2015).

The Indian tribes entered into an agreement with the State of California for gaming on tribal lands. The Indian tribes later agreed to a modification to the agreement, requiring them to pay substantially higher rates for gaming licenses after the State misrepresented that no more gaming licenses were available at lower rates. The Indian tribes sought rescission of the modification and restitution of the overpayments made under the modified agreement.

Analysis: The trial court granted rescission and ordered the state to refund $36.2 million of overpayments, calling it "specific performance."

---

[*] The concept of restitution plays a role in promissory restitution as well, but the remedy for promissory restitution is enforcement of the promise made, perhaps limited "as justice requires."

On appeal, the Ninth Circuit affirmed the trial court grant of rescission and affirmed the monetary award, but rejected the description of the remedy as specific performance. As a result of the rescission, the State owed money as restitution, not in performance of any contract provision. The amount recoverable by the Indian tribes was the difference between the higher payments under the rescinded modification and the payments that would have been payable under the original agreement. "Under general contract principles, '[w]hen calculating restitution, we must offset the Plaintiffs' award by the value of any benefits that Plaintiffs received from the [D]efendant under the contract, so that only the actual, or net, loss is compensated.' . . . The State is not entitled to a setoff here because [the Indian tribes] would have made the same profits [under the earlier contract] if the State had not miscalculated the number of available licenses."

—————————————

The cases in the remainder of this section address two additional uses of restitution damages and suggest how restitution damages may be used and measured. As you read them, consider how the policies listed on page 786 apply to help fashion the relief in these cases.

§ 2.3.1. Damages for the Party Who Materially Breaches

As we saw in Chapter 9, a party who substantially performs is entitled to enforce the contract and therefore obtain the contract price, albeit reduced by the damages for the uncompleted performance. But what happens when that same party (the payee) has not achieved substantial performance and therefore is in material breach? Because the payee has not satisfied the condition precedent to payment, the payee is not entitled to recover any portion of the contract price. Under older common law rulings, that was the end of the inquiry, and the payee was left without further recourse, because it was in material breach. However, later courts began to use restitution to craft a more just solution:

> **Example S:** *Britton v. Turner*, 26 Am. Dec. 713, 1834 WL 1176 (N.H. 1834).
>
> A laborer contracted to perform services for an employer for a year, in return for $120, to be paid at the end of the year. (Such employment contracts were common in the 19th century for seamen and farmworkers, who employers feared would leave their jobs to look for higher wages at busy times—or perhaps abandon ship in Tahiti. Employers often provided room and board during the term of the employment, while

the employee was not receiving any payments.)* The laborer worked for nine and a half months, then left voluntarily. The employer refused to pay the laborer, based on the common law reasoning that his promise to pay $120 was conditional on the laborer doing the promised work. If the condition to the promise (one year of service) was not satisfied, then no payment was due under the contract.

Analysis: The court agreed that the employer owed no contract liability, but expressed concern that the employer was unjustly enriched by receiving the labor without having to pay for it. The closer the laborer came to satisfying the condition, the more the employer was unjustly enriched. The court turned to quasi-contract and used quantum meruit to compensate the laborer. The laborer's recovery was the *value* received and pocketed by the employer (not necessarily the same as, but no more than, the contract price), minus any damages to the employer caused by the laborer's non-completion. If the employer could and did reject and return any of the value (for instance, any goods produced by the laborer), then that amount would also be subtracted from the recovery. This result was a default rule that applied only if the parties had not agreed otherwise.

Reading Critically: *Eker Brothers, Inc.*

1. Why did the general contractor argue that the subcontractor was not entitled to recover for work done?

2. What rule did the trial court adopt with respect to recovery of damages by a breaching party? Did the Court of Appeals agree or disagree? Should parties that intentionally breach ever get recovery?

3. What rationale did the court offer for adopting the Restatement rule? Articulate the measure of restitutionary recovery under Restatement (Second) § 374.

---

* For more background information on the case, *see* Robert W. Gordon, *Britton v. Turner: A Signpost on the Crooked Road to "Freedom" in the Employment Contract*, in *Contract Stories* 186 (Douglas G. Baird ed. 2007).

Eker Brothers, Inc. v. Rehders

EKER BROTHERS, INC., Plaintiff-Appellant

v.

JOHN G. REHDERS, Defendants-Appellees

Court of Appeals of New Mexico
150 N.M. 542 (Ct. App. 2011)

BUSTAMANTE, JUDGE.

Eker Brothers, Inc. (Subcontractor) sued John G. Rehders, General Contractor, Inc. (General) seeking payment for work Subcontractor had performed. The district court found that Subcontractor was owed $74,964.05 and that General had incurred $42,448.20 in damages, but that Subcontractor's "claims [were] barred by its willful, material[,] and anticipatory breach of the parties' contract." The court awarded General $42,448.29.1 We conclude that the district court erred by not offsetting General's damages against the benefit General received from Subcontractor's unpaid work, and reverse.

I. BACKGROUND

. . . .

The district court concluded that the value of the work performed by Subcontractor between August 1 and September 7 and invoiced on September 14 was $74,964.05. To arrive at this number, the court began with the $122,099.45 from Subcontractor's September 14 invoice. The court then subtracted (1) $28,900 for grading work that had not actually been performed; (2) $7656 for curbs that were of poor quality; (3) $3,036.90 to cover General's cost to remove the defective curbs; (4) $5,512.50 for General's cost to re-stake an area that had been impacted by Subcontractor's departure; and (5) $2030 to cover half of the cost of fixing footings that had been damaged due to rain.

The district court next turned to General's damages. It found that General had "incurred [an extra] $50,194.45 in additional expenses due to [Subcontractor's] failure to complete the concrete work." It also found that General had mitigated its damages by completing the site work for $7,746.25 less than it would have paid Subcontractor. Subtracting the savings from the additional costs, the district court concluded that General's damages were $42,448.20. The district court did not offset the amount owed to Subcontractor against the damages, but instead entered judgment against Subcontractor for the full amount of the damages.

II. DISCUSSION

Subcontractor contends that the district court's decision that his claims were "barred by its willful, material[,] and anticipatory breach" was error as a matter of law, and that "[d]espite its breach, [it] was entitled to restitution for the value of the benefits its performance conferred." Subcontractor argues that New Mexico follows Restatement (Second) of Contracts § 374 (1981), which allows a breaching party to obtain restitution for benefits conferred in excess of damages. As we understand it, General's response is that the $74,964.05 of unpaid work performed by Subcontractor did not constitute a benefit to General and therefore should not be offset against General's damages. General also argues that its damages exceeded any benefit. Subcontractor has also made a substantial evidence argument, which we do not address because we agree with Subcontractor's legal argument.

A. The Nature of Restitution

Both parties have framed the issue of whether restitution must be awarded here as if it were equitable in nature, deriving from unjust enrichment. The district court denied Subcontractor's request for equitable relief in the form of restitution for unjust enrichment. That does not, however, end our analysis. To the extent that the requested restitution refers to an offset of compensatory damages by the amount of any benefit conferred, it is a legal issue which we review de novo. As an initial matter, we must determine whether the damages question at issue here is legal or equitable in order to select the appropriate standard of review.

Traditionally, restitution is thought of as an equitable remedy. However, in the context of offsetting compensatory damages, at least one court has found that restitution is a legal remedy. A popular treatise notes that "[t]he remedy of restitution, . . . [cannot] properly be described as either 'legal' or 'equitable' in any narrowly restricted signification of those terms." 12 Arthur Linton Corbin, Corbin on Contracts § 1103, at 10 (interim ed.2002). . . . As Corbin observes, modern restitution is a mixture whose rules "are the rules of equity wherever they differ from those of the common law." See Corbin on Contracts, supra, § 1103, at 5 (emphasis added).

Nevertheless, equity may still intervene, as it apparently did here. The district court ruled that Subcontractor was barred from recovering, effectively working a forfeiture on Subcontractor for the value of its work from August 1 to September 7. Our Supreme Court has observed that "a forfeiture declaration is essentially an equitable remedy." Cortez v. Cortez, 2009–NMSC–008, ¶ 25, 145 N.M. 642, 203 P.3d 857 (alteration omitted) (internal quotation marks omitted). "The question of whether, on a particular set of facts, the district court is permitted to exercise its equitable powers is a question of law, while the issue of how the district court uses its equitable powers to provide an appropriate remedy is reviewed only for abuse of discretion." United Props. Ltd. v. Walgreen Props., Inc., 2003–NMCA–140, ¶ 7, 134 N.M. 725, 82 P.3d 535.

. . . .

C. Restitution Under Restatement Section 374

Subcontractor contends that the award should be determined according to Section 374(1), which states:

> [I]f a party justifiably refuses to perform on the ground that his remaining duties of performance have been discharged by the other party's breach, the party in breach is entitled to restitution for any benefit that he has conferred by way of part performance or reliance in excess of the loss that he has caused by his own breach.

. . . .

At common law, a breaching party could not obtain restitution for benefits conferred. The common law rule reflected a belief that breach was "morally unworthy conduct," and that a breaching party should not benefit from his own wrong, see Lancellotti v. Thomas, 341 Pa.Super. 1, 491 A.2d 117, 118–19 (1985) (internal quotation marks omitted). In contrast to the common law rule, the Restatement rule reflects a policy against awarding a windfall to the non-breaching party. See id. at 119–20. The court in Lancellotti rejected the view that breach is morally wrong, see id. at 122 ("Rules of contract law are not rules of punishment; the contract breaker is not an outlaw." (internal quotation marks omitted)), and joined the many other jurisdictions that had already adopted Restatement Section 374. See id. at 120–21.

Under the Restatement, a breaching party can recover for the value of benefits conferred in excess of damages. The contract price is frequently used as evidence of the value of the benefit conferred. See generally Corbin on Contracts, supra, § 1124 & n.17, at 104. . . .

We believe that the Restatement approach is consistent with New Mexico law. We have expressed an unwillingness to award windfall damages in contract actions. . . . The same policy animates Section 374, which provides for restitution of benefits conferred pursuant to an explicit contract in order to prevent a windfall from being awarded. Accordingly, we now explicitly adopt the approach set forth in Section 374.

D. Application to This Case

Having determined that Section 374 governs the calculation of damages in this case, we must now apply it. The district court found that Subcontractor's invoice for work from August 1 to September 7 should have been in the amount of $74,964.05. The district court also found that General was damaged in the amount of $42,448.29 by Subcontractor's breach. Neither party argues that these findings are not supported by substantial evidence. The district court's finding regarding the amount owed for Subcontractor's work is essentially a finding of the contract price of the work performed. As we have discussed, this is a valid method for proving the amount of the benefit conferred. The correct amount of damages is easily concluded using the district court's findings. The amount of the benefit conferred is $74,964.05. The amount of the damages to General is $42,448.29. Applying Section 374, since the benefit is greater than the damages, Subcontractor is owed the difference of $32,515.76.

. . . .

E. Equity and Forfeiture

There remains one way that the district court's ruling can be reconciled with Section 374. The court concluded that Subcontractor's "claims [were] barred by its willful, material[,] and anticipatory breach of the parties' contract." It is conceivable that it is on this ground that the court based its decision not to offset General's damages by the amount of the benefit Subcontractor had conferred.

The decision to bar Subcontractor's claim causes a forfeiture. See Black's Law Dictionary 722 (9th ed.2009) (defining forfeiture as "[s]omething (esp. money or property) lost or confiscated"). Forfeitures are equitable remedies. See Cortez, 2009–NMSC–008, ¶ 25, 145 N.M. 642, 203 P.3d 857. However, even at equity, they are disfavored. . . .

None of the conditions prerequisite to the exercise of equity are present here. There has been no allegation or finding of fraud, hardship, oppression, mistake, or unconscionability. The district court did not make findings that would indicate Subcontractor's behavior in breaching was egregious or otherwise blameworthy, and in fact rejected proposed findings of fact to that effect. Furthermore, the district court found that a contract existed, but there is no finding that there was clear and unequivocal language requiring a forfeiture here. Absent any justification for the forfeiture, the district court erred as a matter of law in resorting to equity to deny Subcontractor restitution for the benefit it had conferred on General.

III. CONCLUSION

For the foregoing reasons, we reverse and remand for further proceedings consistent with this opinion.

§ 2.3.2. Damages for the Party Who Is Prevented from Performing

Example T: *Blanton v. Friedberg*, 819 F.2d 489 (4th Cir. 1987).

Friedberg agreed with Blanton and Landmark Enterprises, Inc. to develop a property referred to as Liberty Hall Tract and later a property referred to as Patriots Plaza. Blanton invested time and money from 1979–81 working to develop and enhance the Liberty Hall Tract, including sales of timber from the land, but was not paid the promised 5% commission. Blanton also secured leases for Patriots Plaza and referred tenants to Friedberg. Blanton received a partial payment for his services, but was terminated in 1981 by Friedberg for "unsatisfactory performance." Blanton and Landmark brought suit alleging breach of contract and *quantum meruit* claims.

Analysis: The jury returned a verdict in favor of Blanton and Landmark, awarding Blanton $20,895 and Landmark $21,000 on their breach of contract action. It also awarded Blanton $394,525 and Landmark $2,160 on the action in *quantum meruit*.

The Fourth Circuit affirmed as to the contract damages and reversed as to the *quantum meruit* damages. Friedberg claimed that Blanton and Landmark did not produce sufficient evidence of their services or the reasonable value of those services, and the court agreed. The court explained:

> In order to prove his claim against Friedberg, Blanton offered into evidence records purporting to show 1,800 hours of time which he and others who worked for him expended in attempting to develop Liberty Hall. Blanton claimed that he was entitled to an agreed-upon consulting fee of $40.00 per hour for these services, amounting to a total of $72,000.
>
> As for his services in connection with the Mt. Pleasant property, Blanton claimed $91,195.50. He arrived at this figure by subtracting a credit of $64,000 for consulting fees, which he claimed to have received, from $155,195.50, the latter figure representing 5% of the total development costs of $3,103,910. In addition, Blanton claimed entitlement to $267,525.48 for his services in connection with the Kroger lease.

Blanton points out that, pursuant to his agreement with Friedberg, he was to have been paid 5% of the gross rent for the entire 20-year lease term and that his expert testimony indicated that this type of lease commission was generally paid up front or, at least, within the first year. Blanton submits that he obtained the lease with Kroger and that Kroger occupied the shopping center based upon his efforts. Therefore, according to Blanton, the full leasing commission was due even though the lease had not been signed prior to the termination of his services. Moreover, Blanton claimed payment at the rate of 75% of projected gross rents for contacting several other tenants, arranging for leases, and laying the groundwork for tenant occupancy.

Finally, Blanton relies upon the testimony of two expert witnesses, . . . as confirmation of the reasonable value of his services. [One witness] testified that a reasonable fee for the Mt. Pleasant property development, "may be anywhere from 3 to 5 per cent of the cost," the customary fee charged in the industry, and in line with what Blanton and Landmark were to have been paid under their alleged agreement. Concerning the salary issue, [he] also testified on cross-examination that he knew of "situations where a monthly or a periodic . . . fee would be paid to a developer for his ongoing expertise and activity, and then upon completion some additional fee" would be paid. [The other witness] testified that . . . a reasonable leasing commission would be 6% of gross rents and a reasonable development fee would be between 5% and 10% of the project cost or gross rents.

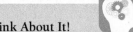

Think About It!

Did this court "cap" restitution damages so that they did not exceed the expectation measure? Courts are split on this issue, and this court followed the majority rule. Why might the courts be split on this issue? (This case doesn't discuss the split.)

Did this court subtract plaintiffs' anticipated losses from the restitution damages?

The court explained that "a mere approximation of *quantum meruit* damages was insufficient" and that Blanton and Landmark's "anticipated consulting and leasing fees, based upon percentages of development costs and gross rents, cannot provide the sole or exclusive basis for proving their *quantum meruit* damages." The court noted that Blanton and Landmark did not complete the projects, and using the customary fee for a completed project "does not control the measure of recovery for such services as they actually performed." Rather, to recover, the plaintiffs must "demonstrate[ ] *with accuracy and precision* the number of hours devoted *actually* to rendering services to Friedberg," as well as how compensation received was inadequate.

Problem: Restitution Damages

10-13. In *Roberts Contracting Co. v. Valentine-Wooten Road Public Facility Board*, 320 S.W.3d 1 (Ark. Ct. App. 2009) the court ruled that the contractor who voluntarily walked off the sewer job had not substantially performed the contract. The court awarded restitutionary damages based on the pricing in the contract, because the opposing party did not present any valuation evidence. If supporting evidence were available, what measure of recovery would best have met the goals of restitution, and why?

---

§ 2.4. Agreed and Liquidated Damages

In an agreement, the parties may agree to categories of damages not generally allowed in contract actions (e.g., attorneys fees). In addition, given the uncertainties in measuring damages, parties may agree that particular damages will be owed upon a breach or a specific kind of breach. In this "liquidated damages" provision, they can agree on the dollar amount of (or formula for computing) damages for a breach or particular type of breach. To prevent unconscionability and results contrary to public policy, the law places some limits on agreed and liquidated damages, reviewed in the case below and reflected in Restatement and UCC provisions.

Reading Critically: *Wassenaar*

1. What was the content of the liquidated damage provision in the contract?

2. What rule did the court establish for when a liquidated damage clause will, and will not, be enforceable? What is the nomenclature for an unenforceable clause?

3. What policies supported the court's rulings on burden of proof and mitigation? How did those rulings affect the court's ultimate holding?

4. Compare the court's rule to the rules appearing in UCC § 2–718(1) and in Restatement (Second) § 356(1). Under which rule(s) is a liquidated damages clause more likely to be upheld?

Wassenaar v. Panos

DONALD WASSENAAR, Plaintiff-Respondent-Petitioner

v.

THEANNE PANOS, d/b/a The Towne Hotel, Defendant-Appellant

Supreme Court of Wisconsin
331 N.W.2d 357 (Wis. 1983)

ABRAHAMSON, JUSTICE.

. . . .

The dispute centers on the stipulated damages clause of a written employment contract by which the employee-plaintiff, Donald Wassenaar, was hired as general manager of the employer-defendant, Towne Hotel. The employment contract is brief. It sets forth the employee's duties, his beginning salary, and his periodic pay increases. The contract further provides for a three-year term of employment beginning on January 1, 1977, renewable at the employee's option, and stipulates damages in case the employer terminates the employee's employment before the expiration of the contract. The stipulated damages clause in issue here reads as follows:

Who's That?

Justice Shirley S. Abrahamson was appointed to the Wisconsin Supreme Court in 1976—the first woman to serve on Wisconsin's highest court and, until 1993, the only woman member. She served as chief justice 1996–2015 and continues to serve on the court. She was president of the National Conference of Chief Justices and chair of the board of the National Center for State Courts. www.wicourts.gov/courts/supreme/justices/abrahamson.htm.

> IT IS FURTHER UNDERSTOOD, that should this contract be terminated by the Towne Hotel prior to its expiration date, the Towne Hotel will be responsible for fulfilling the entire financial obligation as set forth within this agreement for the full period of three (3) years.[1]

The employer terminated Wassenaar's employment as of March 31, 1978, 21 months prior to the contract's expiration date. Wassenaar was unemployed from April 1, 1978, until June 14, 1978, when he obtained employment in a Milwaukee area hotel where he remained employed at least until the time of trial in May, 1981.

---

[1] The clause can be interpreted to provide that the employee will receive the entire salary for three years regardless of when the employment was terminated. We reject this interpretation of the clause, as did the employee and the circuit court.

The employee sued for damages. The employer answered the complaint and as an affirmative defense asserted that the employee had failed to mitigate damages. In a pretrial motion to strike the employer's affirmative defense that the employee had failed to mitigate damages, the employee argued that mitigation was irrelevant because the contract contained a valid stipulated damages clause. The circuit court struck the employer's affirmative defense, ruling that the employee had no duty to mitigate damages, apparently inferentially ruling that the stipulated damages clause was valid.

After a trial on the remaining issues and in response to special verdict questions, the jury found that the person negotiating the contract on behalf of the employer was authorized as the employer's agent to enter into the employment contract and that the employer terminated the employment without just cause. The circuit court, over the employee's objection, submitted to the jury the question of what sum of money would compensate the employee for his losses resulting from the breach of the employment agreement. The jury answered $24,640, which is the sum the employee had calculated as his damages on the basis of the stipulated damages clause of the contract, that is, his salary for 21 months, the unexpired term of the contract.

On review, the court of appeals characterized the question of whether a stipulated damages clause should be held void as a penalty because it fixes unreasonably large damages as a question of law to be determined independently by the reviewing court. It then scrutinized the stipulated damages clause and decided that the clause was void as a penalty. The court of appeals reached that conclusion, reasoning that the amount of damages for breach of an employment contract could easily be measured and proved at trial and that the contractual formula fixing damages at full salary without considering how long the employee would need to find a new job or the probable earnings from substitute employment was unreasonable on its face. In its analysis, the court of appeals did not consider any facts other than the actual contract language and the black-letter law relating to the measure of damages for breach of employment contracts.

. . . . [T]he validity of a stipulated damages clause is a question of law for the trial judge rather than a mixed question of fact and law for the jury. The validity of a stipulated damages clause is a matter of public policy, and as in other contract cases the question of contractual validity as a matter of public policy is an issue the trial judge initially decides. . . .

. . . . The reviewing court will uphold the factual determinations underlying its legal conclusion unless they are contrary to the great weight and clear preponderance of the evidence. . . . Whether the facts fulfill the legal standard, here reasonableness, is a determination of law, . . . and ordinarily the appellate court need not defer to the trial court's determination of a question of law. . . . Nevertheless, because the trial court's legal conclusion, that is, whether the clause is reasonable, is so intertwined with the factual findings supporting that conclusion, the appellate court should give weight to the trial court's decision, although the trial court's decision is not controlling. *See* Wright, *The Doubtful Omniscence of Appellate Courts*, 41 Minn. L. Rev. 751, 778–82 (1956); Morris, *Law and Fact*, 55 Harv.L.Rev. 1303, 1304 (1942).

. . . .

Because the employer sought to set aside the bargained-for contractual provision stipulating damages, it had the burden of proving facts which would justify the trial court's concluding that the clause should not be enforced. *Northwestern Motor Car, Inc. v. Pope*, 51 Wis.2d 292, 295, 187 N.W.2d 200 (1971). Placing the burden of proof on the challenger is consistent with giving the nonbreaching party the advantage inherent in stipulated damages clauses of eliminating the need to prove damages, and with the general principle that the law assumes that bargains are enforceable and that the party asking the court to intervene to invalidate a bargain should demonstrate the justice of his or her position. As we discuss below, we conclude that the employer failed to carry its burden, and we affirm the circuit court's conclusion that the stipulated damages clause is valid.

We turn now to the test that the trial court (and the appellate court) should apply in deciding whether a stipulated damages clause is valid. The overall single test of validity is whether the clause is reasonable under the totality of circumstances.[7] *See* sec. 356(1), Restatement (Second) of Contracts (1979),[8] and sec. 402.718(1), Stats.1979–80.[9]

---

[7] . . . *Dick v. Heisler*, 184 Wis. 77, 82, 198 N.W. 734 (1924); *Fields Foundation, Ltd. v. Christensen*, 103 Wis.2d 465, 475, 309 N.W.2d 125 (Ct.App.1981).

. . . .

See also Clarkson, Miller, and Muris, *Liquidated Damages v. Penalties: Sense or Nonsense?*, 1978 Wis.L.Rev. 351, 356; Goetz and Scott, *Liquidated Damages, Penalties and the Just Compensation Principle: Some Notes on an Enforcement Model and a Theory of Efficient Breach*, 77 Colum.L.Rev. 554 (1977); Macneil, *Power of Contract and Agreed Remedies*, 47 Cornell L.Q. 495, 503 (1962) . . . .

[8] Sec. 356(1), Restatement (Second) of Contracts (1979), sets forth the test as follows:

"Damages for breach by either party may be liquidated in the agreement but only at an amount that is reasonable in the light of the anticipated or actual loss caused by the breach and the difficulties of proof of loss. A term fixing unreasonably large liquidated damages is unenforceable on grounds of public policy as a penalty."

[9] Sec. 402.718(1), Stats. 1979–80, which is U.C.C. sec. 2–718(1), provides that liquidated damages may be agreed upon, "but only at an amount which is reasonable in the light of the anticipated or actual harm caused by the breach, the difficulties of proof of loss, and the inconvenience or nonfeasibility of otherwise obtaining an adequate remedy. A term fixing unreasonably large liquidated damages is void as a penalty." . . .

The reasonableness test is a compromise the courts have struck between two competing viewpoints toward stipulated damages clauses, one favoring enforcement of stipulated damages clauses and the other disfavoring such clauses.

Enforcement of stipulated damages clauses is urged because the clauses serve several purposes. The clauses allow the parties to control their exposure to risk by setting the payment for breach in advance. They avoid the uncertainty, delay, and expense of using the judicial process to determine actual damages. They allow the parties to fashion a remedy consistent with economic efficiency in a competitive market, and they enable the parties to correct what the parties perceive to be inadequate judicial remedies by agreeing upon a formula which may include damage elements too uncertain or remote to be recovered under rules of damages applied by the courts. In addition to these policies specifically relating to stipulated damages clauses, considerations of judicial economy and freedom of contract favor enforcement of stipulated damages clauses.

A competing set of policies disfavors stipulated damages clauses, and thus courts have not been willing to enforce stipulated damages clauses blindly without carefully scrutinizing them. Public law, not private law, ordinarily defines the remedies of the parties. Stipulated damages are an exception to this rule. Stipulated damages allow private parties to perform the judicial function of providing the remedy in breach of contract cases, namely, compensation of the nonbreaching party, and courts must ensure that the private remedy does not stray too far from the legal principle of allowing compensatory damages. Stipulated damages substantially in excess of injury may justify an inference of unfairness in bargaining or an objectionable *in terrorem* agreement to deter a party from breaching the contract, to secure performance, and to punish the breaching party if the deterrent is ineffective. . . . .

The reasonableness test strikes a balance between the two competing sets of policies by ensuring that the court respects the parties' bargain but prevents abuse. . . .

Over time, the cases and commentators have established several factors to help determine whether a particular clause is reasonable: (1) Did the parties intend to provide for damages or for a penalty?[11] (2) Is the injury caused by the breach one that is difficult or incapable of accurate estimation at the time of contract?[12] and (3) Are the stipulated damages a reasonable forecast of the harm caused by the breach?[13]

---

[11] . . . *McConnell v. L.C.L. Transit Co.*, 42 Wis.2d 429, 438, 167 N.W.2d 226 (1969).

[12] . . . *Sheffield-King Milling Co. v. Jacobs*, 170 Wis. 389, 399, 175 N.W. 796 (1920). . . .

[13] *Davis v. La Crosse Hospital Association*, 121 Wis. 579, 589, 99 N.W. 351 (1904); *United Leasing & Financial Services, Inc. v. R.F. Optical*, 103 Wis.2d 488, 492, 309 N.W.2d 23 (Ct.App.1981). . . .

Recent discussions of the test of reasonableness have generally discarded the first factor, subjective intent of the parties, because subjective intent has little bearing on whether the clause is objectively reasonable.[14] The label the parties apply to the clause, which might indicate their intent, has some evidentiary value, but it is not conclusive. *Seeman v. Biemann*, 108 Wis. 365, 374, 84 N.W. 490 (1900).

The second factor, sometimes referred to as the "difficulty of ascertainment" test, is generally viewed as helpful in assessing the reasonableness of the clause. The greater the difficulty of estimating or proving damages, the more likely the stipulated damages will appear reasonable. *Sheffield-King Milling Co. v. Jacobs*, 170 Wis. 389, 402–403, 175 N.W. 796 (1920). If damages are readily ascertainable, a significant deviation between the stipulated amount and the ascertainable amount will appear unreasonable. *City of Madison v. American Sanitary Engineering Co.*, 118 Wis. 480, 503–504, 95 N.W. 1097 (1903). The "difficulty of ascertainment" test has several facets, depending on whether the stipulated damages clause is viewed from the perspective of the time of contracting or the time of breach (or trial). These facets include the difficulty of producing proof of damages at trial; the difficulty of determining what damages the breach caused; the difficulty of ascertaining what damages the parties contemplated when they contracted; the absence of a standardized measure of damages for the breach; and the difficulty of forecasting, when the contract is made, all the possible damages which may be caused or occasioned by the various possible breaches.

The third factor concerns whether the stipulated damages provision is a reasonable forecast of compensatory damages. Courts test the reasonableness of the parties' forecast, as they test the "difficulty of ascertainment" by looking at the stipulated damages clause from the perspective of both the time of contracting and the time of the breach (or trial).

The second and third factors are intertwined, and both use a combined prospective-retrospective approach. Although courts have frequently said that the reasonableness of the stipulated damages clause must be judged as of the time of contract formation (the prospective approach) and that the amount or existence of actual loss at the time of breach or trial is irrelevant, except as evidence helpful in determining what was reasonable at the time of contracting (the retrospective approach), the cases demonstrate that the facts available at trial significantly affect the courts' determination of the reasonableness of the stipulated damages clause. If the damages provided for in the contract are grossly disproportionate to the actual harm sustained, the courts usually conclude that the parties' original expectations

---

[14] 5 Williston, *Contracts*, sec. 778, p. 687, 693 (Jaeger 3d ed. 1961); 5 Corbin, *Contracts*, sec. 1058, p. 337 (1964); Calamari and Perillo, *Law of Contracts*, sec. 14–31, p. 565 (2d ed. 1977); Restatement (Second) of Contracts, sec. 356(1), comment *c* (1979).

were unreasonable.[16] Our prior decisions indicate that this court has employed the prospective-retrospective approach in determining the reasonableness of the stipulated damages clauses and has looked at the harm anticipated at the time of contract formation and the actual harm at the time of breach (or trial). *See, e.g., Fields Foundation, Ltd. v. Christensen*, 103 Wis.2d 465, 475–76, 309 N.W.2d 125 (Ct.App.1981); *Seeman v. Biemann*, 108 Wis. 365, 374–75, 84 N.W. 490 (1900).

As the above discussion demonstrates, the various factors and approaches to determine reasonableness are not separate tests, each of which must be satisfied for a stipulated damages clause to stand. Reasonableness of the stipulated damages clause cannot be determined by a mechanical application of the three factors cited above. 3 Hawkland, *Uniform Commercial Code Series*, sec. 2–718:01, p. 426 (1982). Courts may give different interpretations to or importance to the various factors in particular cases. . . .

. . . .

With the reasonableness test and the policies underlying the test in mind, we now consider the circuit court's conclusion that the stipulated damages clause is reasonable. The employer argues that the stipulated damages clause is void as a penalty because the harm to the employee was capable of estimation at the formation of the contract and was relatively easy to prove at trial. The employer further contends that calculating damages based on the entire wage for the unexpired term of the employment contract does not reasonably forecast the loss caused by the breach because such a calculation gives the employee a windfall recovery. The employer's arguments are not without merit. . . .

When the parties to an employment contract estimate the harm which might result from the employer's breach, they do not know when a breach might occur, whether the employee will find a comparable job, and if he or she does, where the job will be or what hardship the employee will suffer. Nevertheless, the standard measure of damages provides, as the court of appeals noted in its opinion, a simple formula which is generally fairly easy to apply. According to black-letter law, when an employee is wrongfully discharged, damages are the salary the employee would have received during the unexpired term of the contract plus the expenses of securing other employment reduced by the income which he or she has earned,

---

[16] 5 Corbin, *Contracts*, sec. 1063, pp. 362–64 (1964), states:

"The probable injury that the parties had reason to foresee is a fact that largely determines the question whether they made a genuine pre-estimate of that injury; but the justice and equity of enforcement depend also upon the amount of injury that has actually occurred. It is to be observed that hindsight is frequently better than foresight, and that, in passing judgment upon the honesty and genuineness of the pre-estimate made by the parties, the court cannot help but be influenced by its knowledge of subsequent events." . . .

will earn, or could with reasonable diligence earn, during the unexpired term. These damages are usually easily ascertainable at the time of trial.

The standard calculation of damages after breach, however, may not reflect the actual harm suffered because of the breach. In addition to the damages reflected in the black-letter formulation, an employee may suffer consequential damages, including permanent injury to professional reputation, loss of career development opportunities, and emotional stress. When calculating damages for wrongful discharge courts strictly apply the rules of foreseeability, mitigation, and certainty and rarely award consequential damages. Damages for injury to the employee's reputation, for example, are generally considered too remote and not in the parties' contemplation.[19] Thus, actual harm suffered and damages that would be awarded in a legal action for breach of contract may not be the same. Nevertheless, in providing for stipulated damages, the parties to the contract could anticipate the types of damages not usually awarded by law. The usual arguments against allowing recovery for consequential damages—that they are not foreseeable and that no dollar value can be set by a court—fail when the parties foresee the possibility of such harm and agree on an estimated amount.

We do not know in the case at bar how the parties calculated the stipulated amount, but we do know that both the employee and employer were concerned about job security. The employee desired a steady, long-term job and the employer wanted the employee, who was experienced in managing the Towne Hotel, to remain on the job. The parties did not suggest that the stipulated damages clause resulted from unequal bargaining power. The contract drafted by the employer provided for a fixed term of employment with a provision for stipulated damages in the amount of unpaid wages if the employer breached. Under these circumstances it is not unreasonable to assume that the parties might have anticipated elements of consequential damages and drafted the stipulated damages clause to include salary lost while out of work, expenses of finding a new job, lower salary on the new job, and consequential damages.

In examining the instant stipulated damages clause and the record, we conclude that the parties' estimate at the time of contract formation of anticipated

---

[19]   *Smith v. Beloit Corp.*, 40 Wis.2d 550, 559, 162 N.W.2d 585 (1968) . . . .

Apparently some jurisdictions do allow recovery of consequential damages for breach of certain employment contracts. *See* cases in Annot., *Recovery by Writer, Artist, or Entertainer for Loss of Publicity or Reputation Resulting from Breach of Contract*, 96 ALR 3d 437 (1979).

Dean McCormick, in his 1935 treatise on damages, foreshadowed the inadequacy of the measure of damages for wrongful discharge: "[T]he courts might expand their measure of compensation for breach of the employment *contract* by recognizing that deprivation of a job, if more than a casual one, not only affects usually a man's reputation and prestige, but ordinarily may so shake his sense of security as to inspire, even in men of firmness, deep fear and distress. . . ." McCormick, *Damages,* sec. 163, p. 639.

damages was reasonable when consequential damages are taken into account. Consequential damages may be difficult to ascertain at the time of contracting or breach and are difficult to prove at trial. The contract formula of full salary for the period after breach seems to be a simple and fair way of calculating all damages.

The employer argues that even if the stipulated amount is a reasonable forecast at the time of contract formation of anticipated loss, the amount is unreasonable from the perspective of the time of trial because the employee suffered no loss whatsoever, or if he suffered any loss it is disproportionate to (that is, significantly less than) the stipulated damages.

. . . .

In this case . . . there is evidence in the record that the employee did suffer harm in being unemployed for approximately two and a half months after his discharge. At the end of this time, the employee obtained employment at another hotel, but there is no evidence that the jobs he held were comparable in terms of salary, opportunity for advancement, etc., to the job he held as manager of the Towne Hotel. There is no evidence that the employee's total compensation from the new job was equal to or exceeded the salary under the breached contract, and the record does not reveal whether the employee suffered consequential damages. All we know is that the employee appears to have suffered some harm. . . .

Since the record in this case can be read to show that the employee suffered some harm, the question remains whether the stipulated damages are so much greater than the loss suffered by the employee that the stipulated damages constitute a penalty.

. . . . The employer argues that allowing the employee to recover the stipulated damages in this case gives the employee a windfall because he receives both the agreed upon salary and the ability to sell his services to another employer during the unexpired term of the contract: the employee will receive 21 months salary from the defendant employer and 18 months salary from the new employer. Ordinarily the circuit court would, in this type of stipulated damages case, use evidence of the employee's actual or potential earnings in assessing the overall reasonableness of the clause, since subsequent earnings would be relevant to the issue of the employee's actual loss resulting from the breach. In this case, as we discuss further below, there is no evidence in the record showing the employee's subsequent earnings, so there is no evidence supporting the employer's position that the employee would get a windfall from enforcement of the stipulated damages clause.

. . . .

At trial the employer attempted to put in evidence regarding the employee's salary at his new job. The circuit court refused to admit this evidence indicating that it had already ruled on the mitigation issue.

. . . . At trial the employer took the erroneous position that the burden was on the employee to prove the reasonableness of the stipulated damages clause, not on the employer to prove the unreasonableness of the clause. . . .

. . . .

While evidence of the employee's earnings after the employer's breach may be relevant in meeting the employer's burden of proving that the stipulated damages clause is unreasonable, once the court determines that the clause is reasonable, proof of the employee's actual loss (including what he earned or might have earned on another job) is no longer relevant. *See* 5 Corbin, *Contracts* sec. 1062, p. 355 (1964). . . . [O]nce a stipulated damages clause is found reasonable, the liquidated damages should not be reduced at trial by an amount the employee did earn or could have earned. *See Tollefson v. Green Bay Packers, Inc.*, 256 Wis. 318, 41 N.W.2d 201 (1950). Recalculating liquidated damages to credit the breaching party with the amount the employee earned or could have earned is antithetical to the policies favoring liquidated damages clauses. Our holding comports with the rule in other jurisdictions . . . .

For the reasons set forth, we conclude that the judgment of the circuit court should be affirmed. The decision of the court of appeals is reversed; the judgment of the circuit court is affirmed.

CECI, J., not participating.

Problems: Liquidated Damages

10-14. In October, Lisa contracted with Brett Mathews Photography for wedding photography the following May for a price of $4895, putting down a $1000 deposit. The contract specified that Stephen would do the photography, but that Lisa would accept a different photographer if he was "unable to perform." The Brett Mathews standard contract provided:

> REFUND & PAYMENTS: Due to the nature of this business requiring advance booking, no refunds will be given for cancellations less than twelve (12) months prior to the date of photography, including postponements. If this contract is cancelled within six (6) months of performance of the job or for any reason by you, with or without your control, the entire

balance remaining on the contract shall become immediately due and payable by you. The notification of cancellation shall be made in writing by certified mail with return receipt.

Brett Mathews fired Stephen in April. Lisa cancelled the contract and hired a different photographer. Brett Mathews brought suit for the contract balance and Lisa counterclaimed for return of her deposit. Assume that Lisa is in breach. Should Brett Mathews be able to enforce the Refund & Payments clause and prevail as to the full contract price of $4895? What arguments would Lisa make? Should Lisa be able to recover her deposit?

10-15. Sisters of Charity Health System, Inc. ("Employer") contracted with Douglass Farrago ("Doctor") for employment as a physician. At the time of contracting, Doctor was new to the area and did not have an existing patient base. The contract provided for $100,000 as reasonable liquidated damages if Doctor left Employer and sought to practice medicine within a 25-mile radius. Six years later, Doctor left Employer and went to work at a nearby medical center. Hundreds of Doctor's patients requested a transfer of their medical records to the nearby medical center where Doctor now worked. Should the court enforce the $100,000 liquidated damages provision? Why or why not? Would it matter if Employer can prove that it takes two to three years for a replacement physician to generate the income at the level of an established doctor?

Food for Thought: The Theory of Efficient Breach

Either party to a contract may have an incentive to breach if that party will reap a benefit from the breach, even after paying damages to the aggrieved party. Adherents of the "law and economics" movement support breach under such circumstances, arguing that this allows societal resources to be utilized in their most productive manner and therefore is socially desirable in the sense that it results in a gain in efficiency by moving the assets that are exchanged to higher valued uses. To assist in maximizing economic efficiency, the law should be structured to encourage such "efficient breaches" while deterring inefficient breaches. Although courts only occasionally explicitly acknowledge "efficiency" as a goal in determining damages, to some extent the law on contract remedies is structured to encourage efficient breaches. For example, courts prefer to award damages, rather than specific performance, so the party contemplating a breach can roughly quantify the cost of the breach (what it will owe in damages) and weigh it against the potential gain from the breach. In addition, willfulness of a breach does not affect damage calculations, so a party may purposely breach without increasing damage exposure, except in the rare circumstances that give rise to liability for punitive damages (page 875).

Judge Posner is a leading proponent of efficient breach. In *Lake River Corp. v. Carborundum Co.*, 769 F.2d 1284, 1288–89 (7th Cir. 1985), he included consideration of the efficient breach theory in a long disquisition about whether penalties (excessive agreed remedies) should never be enforceable:

> The hardest issue in the case is whether the formula in the minimum-guarantee clause imposes a penalty for breach of contract or is merely an effort to liquidate damages. Deep as the hostility to penalty clauses runs in the common law, . . . we still might be inclined to question, if we thought ourselves free to do so, whether a modern court should refuse to enforce a penalty clause where the signator is a substantial corporation, well able to avoid improvident commitments. Penalty clauses provide an earnest of performance. The clause here enhanced Carborundum's credibility in promising to ship the minimum amount guaranteed by showing that it was willing to pay the full contract price even if it failed to ship anything. On the other side it can be pointed out that by raising the cost of a breach of contract to the contract breaker, a penalty clause increases the risk to his other creditors; increases (what is the same thing and more, because bankruptcy imposes "deadweight" social costs) the risk of bankruptcy; and could amplify the business cycle by increasing the number of bankruptcies in bad times, which is when contracts are most likely to be broken. But since little effort is made to prevent businessmen from assuming risks, these reasons are no better than makeweights.
>
> A better argument is that a penalty clause may discourage efficient as well as inefficient breaches of contract. Suppose a breach would cost the promisee $12,000 in actual damages but would yield the promisor $20,000 in additional profits. Then there would be a net social gain from breach. After being fully compensated for his loss the promisee would be no worse off than if the contract had been performed, while the promisor would be better off by $8,000. But now suppose the contract

contains a penalty clause under which the promisor if he breaks his promise must pay the promisee $25,000. The promisor will be discouraged from breaking the contract, since $25,000, the penalty, is greater than $20,000, the profits of the breach; and a transaction that would have increased value will be forgone.

On this view, since compensatory damages should be sufficient to deter inefficient breaches (that is, breaches that cost the victim more than the gain to the contract breaker), penal damages could have no effect other than to deter some efficient breaches. But this overlooks the earlier point that the willingness to agree to a penalty clause is a way of making the promisor and his promise credible and may therefore be essential to inducing some value-maximizing contracts to be made. It also overlooks the more important point that the parties (always assuming they are fully competent) will, in deciding whether to include a penalty clause in their contract, weigh the gains against the costs—costs that include the possibility of discouraging an efficient breach somewhere down the road—and will include the clause only if the benefits exceed those costs as well as all other costs.

On this view the refusal to enforce penalty clauses is (at best) paternalistic—and it seems odd that courts should display parental solicitude for large corporations. But however this may be, we must be on guard to avoid importing our own ideas of sound public policy into an area where our proper judicial role is more than usually deferential. The responsibility for making innovations in the common law of Illinois rests with the courts of Illinois, and not with the federal courts in Illinois. And like every other state, Illinois, untroubled by academic skepticism of the wisdom of refusing to enforce penalty clauses against sophisticated promisors, . . . continues steadfastly to insist on the distinction between penalties and liquidated damages. See, e.g., *Bauer v. Sawyer*, 8 Ill.2d 351, 359–61, 134 N.E.2d 329, 333–34 (1956) . . . . [The court then applies existing Illinois precedent.]

If you were an Illinois judge or legislator, would you be receptive to Judge Posner's arguments? What are the counter-arguments to Posner's position and to the efficient breach theory in general?

§ 2.5. Punitive Damages

Courts rarely award punitive damages in a contract case. Breaking a contract is not considered "bad" behavior, and even a willful breach should simply result in compensation for the injury to the non-breaching party, not in punishment for the contract breacher. In a few special kinds of cases, however, courts have discretion to award punitive damages against a defendant, to deter that defendant and others from engaging in similar conduct in the future. The majority rule, reflected in Restatement (Second) § 355, is that punitive damages may be awarded when the breach of contract is also an independent tort for which punitive damages are recoverable.

The case below provides examples of cases in which punitive damages are allowed under various common law rules.

Reading Critically: *Romero*

1. What is the court's rule regarding when punitive damages may be awarded?

2. What policies are furthered by awarding punitive damages?

3. What guidelines did the court furnish as to the amount?

Romero v. Mervyn's

Lucy ROMERO, Plaintiff-Appellee

v.

MERVYN'S and Dennis Wolf, Defendants-Appellants

Supreme Court of New Mexico
784 P.2d 992 (N.M. 1989)

RANSOM, JUSTICE.

This is an appeal by defendant Mervyn's from a verdict in favor of plaintiff Lucy Romero for $2,041 in compensatory and $25,000 in punitive damages on a breach of contract claim. . . . We affirm.

On November 23, 1984, Romero and two of her adult daughters were shopping in Mervyn's Department Store in Albuquerque. It was the day after Thanksgiving and the store was crowded with Christmas shoppers. As Romero and her daughters were descending on an escalator, another customer either intentionally or accidentally pushed her. She fell to her hands and knees, hitting her jaw as she fell. One of her daughters testified that a commotion ensued. When Romero reached the bottom of the escalator, a salesperson at a temporary station helped her to her feet and out of the path of other shoppers. Either this employee or a security guard watching from a two-way mirror summoned the store manager to the scene.

Dennis Wolf, the acting store manager, came in response to this call. His usual job as operations manager of the store entailed responsibility for directing and training employees. It was also his duty to investigate and gather information on incidents involving customer injuries on the premises. Wolf testified that he could tell Romero was in pain and asked her whether she needed a wheelchair or ambulance. Romero replied that she did not. Wolf also testified that Romero's daughters were "very upset, a little bit hysterical," and kept asking who would pay for their mother's medical expenses. Wolf himself, according to Romero's testimony, "seemed to be kind of nervous and in a hurry since the store was busy." According to testimony by Romero and her daughters, Wolf told them that Mervyn's would pay any medical expenses. Wolf testified that, pursuant to company policy, he only told Romero that Mervyn's would submit the claim to its insurer, who would make the decision whether to pay any claims arising from the incident.

Immediately following this conversation, Romero's daughters helped their mother out of the store, brought the car around, and returned to their home in Santa Fe. The following Monday, Romero still was in pain and decided she should seek medical attention. She had another of her daughters, who lived in Albuquerque, call Mervyn's and confirm with Wolf his promise that Mervyn's would pay the expenses. She also asked him if any forms needed to be completed when her mother went to the doctor. He told her to come down to the store and pick up the necessary forms. When she did so, however, Wolf told her that he was out of the forms and then, according to her testimony, told her to go ahead and have her mother go to the doctor, and Mervyn's would pay the expenses. Wolf testified the "forms" in question were insurance claim forms. Romero's daughter confirmed that Wolf told her the forms were for the insurance company but insisted that Wolf reiterated the promise that Mervyn's would pay the bill.

Thereafter, Romero consulted a physician and underwent physical therapy. The cost of her treatment came to $2,041. Mervyn's, however, refused to pay the bills. Romero filed suit in Santa Fe District Court, alleging liability under theories of negligence and contract. She did not rely on a theory of promissory estoppel. [Facts of first trial and appeal omitted] On remand, the jury found in favor of Romero on her contract claim, and awarded punitive damages. Mervyn's appeals, arguing the court erred: . . . (5) in submitting the issue of punitive damages to the jury when there was no evidence of malice on the part of Mervyn's in refusing to pay Romero's medical bills, or in refusing to grant Mervyn's motions for judgment n.o.v. or for a new trial because the award of punitive damages was based on sympathy, passion, and prejudice . . . .

. . . .

(5) *Trial court acted correctly in instructing the jury on the issue of punitive damages and in denying j.n.o.v. or new trial.* Over Mervyn's objection, the trial court submitted an instruction that the jury could find Mervyn's liable for punitive damages if it determined the acts of Mervyn's were "maliciously intentional, fraudulent, oppressive, or committed recklessly or with a wanton disregard of the Plaintiff's rights." *See* SCRA 1986, 13–1827.

. . . .

After objecting to the absence of proof of any malicious or wanton conduct, . . . Mervyn's also stated it did not believe *any* punitive damage instruction would be proper in such a situation. Thus, . . . Mervyn's objection may be construed as an argument that malicious or wanton conduct is a prerequisite to punitive damages. We feel this argument raises important questions concerning the meaning and purpose of New Mexico's punitive damage rule when applied to contract cases. In the following two sections, therefore, we discuss these issues. We conclude our discussion on punitive damages with an examination of the evidence supporting an instruction of malice.

—*Malice, wantonness and punitive damages.* Our previous cases clearly establish that, in contract cases not involving insurance, punitive damages may be recovered for breach of contract when the defendant's conduct was malicious, fraudulent, oppressive, or committed recklessly with a wanton disregard for the plaintiff's rights. *Green Tree Acceptance, Inc. v. Layton*, 108 N.M. 171, 769 P.2d 84 (1989) . . . .

Each of the terms listed, standing alone, will support an award of punitive damages. *See Green Tree Acceptance*, 108 N.M. at 174, 769 P.2d at 87. In a literal sense, therefore, it is incorrect to argue that "malice" or "wantonness" are essential terms to the exclusion of, e.g., fraud or oppression. However, in the sense that malice and wantonness, interpreted broadly, suggest an absence either of a good faith reason or of an innocent mistake, they describe the conduct targeted by our punitive damages rule.

"Malice" as used in our punitive damages instruction does not imply "actual malice" or "malice in fact" in the sense of an intent to harm. *Galindo v. Western*

States Collection Co., 82 N.M. 149, 154, 477 P.2d 325, 330 (Ct.App.1970). Instead, malice, as defined in *Loucks*, means

> the intentional doing of a wrongful act without just cause or excuse. This means that the defendant not only intended to do the act which is ascertained to be wrongful, but that he knew it was wrong when he did it.

76 N.M. at 747, 418 P.2d at 199. This definition is a broad one and undoubtedly encompasses situations that also connote "fraudulent" or "oppressive" conduct. The term "wanton," as used in our punitive damages instruction, suggests a similar quality of wrongfulness when the evidence demonstrates conduct committed without concern for the consequences, rather than intentionally, and connotes an "utter indifference to or conscious disregard for the rights of others." *See Curtiss v. Aetna Life Ins. Co.*, 90 N.M. 105, 108, 560 P.2d 169, 172 (Ct.App.), *cert. denied*, 90 N.M. 7, 558 P.2d 619 (1976).

Thus, these words broadly distinguish "wrongful" breaches of contract from those committed intentionally for legitimate business reasons or those that are the result of inadvertence. In this sense, it may be argued that "malice" or "wantonness" are prerequisites to punitive damages. Nonetheless, we remain convinced that the nuances distinguishing the terms "malice," "fraud," and "oppression" make it useful to retain these words as distinct standards to guide the jury's exercise of discretion in particular cases.

—*Purpose of punitive damages in contract cases.* Mervyn's argues, even taking the evidence in the light most favorable to Romero, "the only thing shown was that Mr. Wolf said Mervyn's would pay the bill and then refused to do so." Mervyn's argues this conduct does not demonstrate malice or wantonness and, unless we reverse the award of punitive damages, "every breach of contract, even if justified, will result in a claim for punitive damages."

. . . .

The general rule limiting recovery in contract case to compensatory damages . . . seems in part calculated to leave undisturbed the allocation of risks and benefits to which both parties have agreed. Such a policy readily is accommodated by awarding money damages, if the measure of damages is based on the justified expectations of the injured party under the contract. Moreover, in most commercial settings,

> [t]he fact that [compensatory] damages must be paid tends directly to the prevention of breaches of contract. It makes, therefore, for the security of business transactions and helps to make possible the vast

structure of credit, upon which so large a part of our modern prosperity depends.

5 A. Corbin, *Corbin on Contracts* § 1002, at 34 (1964).

Notwithstanding the general exclusion of punitive damages from contract cases, however, exceptions long have been recognized. *See, e.g., Welborn v. Dixon,* 70 S.C. 108, 49 S.E. 232 (1904) (punitive damages allowed for fraudulent breach of contract); *Stewart v. Potter,* 44 N.M. 460, 104 P.2d 736 (1940) (same). Many courts have conceptualized the conduct necessary to afford recovery of punitive damages as consisting of an independent tort. *See, e.g., Bituminous Fire & Marine Ins. Co. v. Culligan Fyrprotexion, Inc.,* 437 N.E.2d 1360 (Ind.Ct.App.1982) (breach of contract may support an award of punitive damages when elements of fraud, malice, gross negligence, or oppression mingle in the controversy); *Consolidated Am. Life Ins. Co. v. Toche,* 410 So.2d 1303 (Miss.1982) (punitive damages available when breach attended by intentional wrong, insult, abuse, or such gross negligence as to consist of an independent tort); *see generally,* 1 J. Ghiardi and J. Kircher, *Punitive Damages Law and Practice* § 5.16 (1985); Sullivan, *Punitive Damages in the Law of Contract: The Reality and the Illusion of Legal Change,* 61 Minn.L.Rev. 207, 236–40 (1977). Similarly, the text of Section 355 of the *Restatement (Second) of Contracts* recognizes an exception when "the conduct constituting the breach is also a tort for which punitive damages are recoverable."

For More Information

For a survey of jurisdictional differences as to punitive damages, as well as a wide-ranging evaluation of various policy grounds for punitive damages, see William S. Dodge, *The Case for Punitive Damages in Contracts,* 48 Duke L.J. 629 (1999).

Other jurisdictions, including California, have justified the award of punitive damages in terms of breach of the implied covenant of good faith and fair dealing, particularly in cases involving insurance contracts. *See Gruenberg v. Aetna Ins. Co.,* 9 Cal.3d 566, 510 P.2d 1032, 108 Cal.Rptr. 480 (1973). "Broadly stated, that covenant requires that neither party do anything which will deprive the other of the benefits of the agreement." *Seaman's Direct Buying Serv.,* 36 Cal.3d at 768, 686 P.2d at 1166, 206 Cal.Rptr. at 362.

We believe, regardless of whether conceptualized in terms of an independent tort, breach of the implied covenant of good faith, or, as in New Mexico, in terms of the quality of the conduct constituting the breach itself, the award of punitive damages in some cases serves important social ends. . . .

Overreaching, malicious, or wanton conduct such as targeted by our rule is inconsistent with legitimate business interests, violates community standards of decency, and tends to undermine the stability of expectations essential to contractual relationships. When this is the case, it is appropriate to allow the jury to determine whether "the public interest will be served by the deterrent effect punitive damages will have upon future conduct." *Jones v. Abriani*, 169 Ind.App. 556, 578, 350 N.E.2d 635, 649 (1976) (quoting, *Vernon Fire & Cas. Ins. Co. v. Sharp*, 264 Ind. 599, 608, 349 N.E.2d 173, 180 (1976)).

> **FYI**
>
> The court in *Boise Dodge, Inc. v. Clark*, 453 P. 2d 551, 557 (Idaho 1969), opined, "The amount of actual damages sustained by a plaintiff is one indication of the culpability of the defendant's acts, but it cannot be the sole criterion for the assessment of punitive damages. Also relevant is the prospective deterrent effect of such an award upon persons situated similarly to the defendant, the motives actuating the defendant's conduct, the degree of calculation involved in the defendant's conduct, and the extent of the defendant's disregard of the rights of others. These are legitimate concerns of the law, and the application of any fixed arithmetic ratio to all cases in which punitive damages are assessed would be arbitrary. It therefore must be recognized that the requirement of a "reasonable relation" between actual and punitive damages serves as a rough device available to . . . courts for the purpose of paring down plainly extreme awards of punitive damages."

—*Substantial evidence supported instructions on malice and wanton conduct, denial of j.n.o.v. or new trial not error.* Contrary to Mervyn's argument, we do not believe the evidence demonstrated only that Wolf made a promise which subsequently he did not keep. Consistent with the definition of malice under *Loucks*, the trial court instructed the jury that malice denoted "the intentional doing of a wrongful act without just cause or excuse. This means * * * [Mervyn's] not only intended to do the act which is ascertained to be wrongful, but that it knew it was wrong when it did it." We note that, in closing argument to the jury, Romero's attorney contended Mervyn's made the promise to pay her client's medical bills in order to get her out of the store without causing a disturbance, but had its "fingers crossed" and never intended to keep that promise.

The evidence reasonably could be viewed as indicating the promise was made because, on one of the busiest shopping days of the year, Wolf wanted to get the Romeros out of the store as quickly as reasonably possible without causing a scene. Mervyn's also presented evidence that Wolf's promise was inconsistent with the store's policy regarding customer injuries, and that Wolf subsequently took no action other than to submit the claim to Mervyn's insurer. This evidence reasonably supports the inference that Wolf entered into the contract simply to end his encounter with Romero and her daughters, without intending to follow through on the promise, and with knowledge that his employer thereafter would not perform.

We thus conclude the jury could have inferred knowledge on Wolf's part that his employer would not honor the contract with Romero, and thus that he acted with malice. This determination leads to the conclusion that the jury also could infer Wolf made the promise with a conscious disregard for whether his employer subsequently would perform, and thus that he acted recklessly with a wanton disregard for Romero's rights. We conclude substantial evidence supported the instructions on malicious or wanton conduct. Consequently, the denial of j.n.o.v. and of a new trial was well within the discretion of the trial court. *See Cienfuegos v. Pacheco*, 56 N.M. 667, 248 P.2d 664 (1952). Furthermore, the amount of the award of punitive damages is not so plainly unrelated to the injury or actual damages, such as to raise a question of sympathy, passion and prejudice as a matter of law. *See Faubion v. Tucker*, 58 N.M. 303, 270 P.2d 713 (1954).

. . . .

For the foregoing reasons, the judgment of the trial court is affirmed in its entirety.

IT IS SO ORDERED.

§ 3. Equitable Remedies: The "Extraordinary Remedies"

As discussed on page 782, equitable remedies are reserved for instances in which

- there is no adequate remedy at law (meaning that damages are inadequate) and

- plaintiff would suffer irreparable harm in the absence of equitable relief.

This rule is an historical vestige from the separate English courts of law and equity (long since merged in nearly every U.S. jurisdiction). This English jurisdictional separation of courts still plays out in American rules about when equitable remedies may be awarded.

Make the Connection

Recall the extensive discussion of the "History of Equity" in Chapter 5, page 285.

This section considers three equitable remedies: specific performances, prohibitory injunction, and specific restitution.

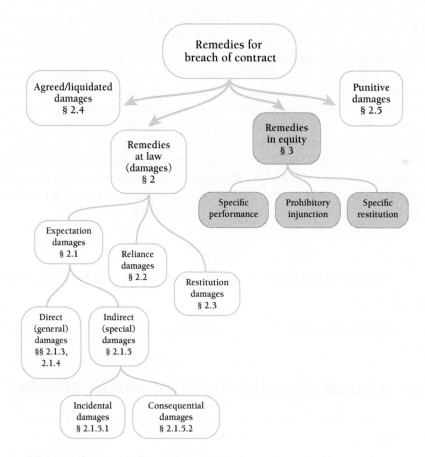

In addition, reformation due to clerical mistakes is an equitable remedy.

§ 3.1. Specific Performance

Specific performance is a remedy by which the court orders a party to perform the unfulfilled promises in the contract, rather than paying the value of those performances; the other party receives actual performance rather than damages representing the value of performance. For instance, in *Lucy v. Zehmer* (Chapter 2, page 22), the court ordered "entry of a proper decree requiring the defendants to perform the contract,"[*] and the plaintiffs received the actual land promised in the contract. Specific performance is most common as a remedy in real estate contracts, because real estate is understood to be unique in most cases; receiving money in lieu of the land is not considered adequate. Similarly, specific performance may be ordered in a contract for the purchase of rare or sentimental items, which are unique and irreplaceable. UCC § 2–716(1) expanded the class

---

[*]　84 S.E.2d at 523.

of goods for which specific performance may be ordered, allowing the remedy in "other proper circumstances," especially when the aggrieved buyer is unable to locate substitute goods ("cover") or knows that a substitute is unlikely to be available.

Grants of specific performance and other injunctive relief are within the discretion of the court, guided by a collection of factors (often in a loose aggregate test) and general policies of equity and fairness. For instance, the court may decide that the consideration supporting the promise at issue was so disproportionately small, compared to the value of the promise, that the consideration is deemed "inadequate" to support equitable enforcement. Recall from Chapter 4 that the amount of the consideration is not relevant, as long as it was bargained for. However, a court in its equitable role may consider the balance between the value of the promise and the return consideration to determine whether principles of justice and fairness support the use of an extraordinary remedy.

Reading Critically: *Ammerman* and *Laclede*

1. Why were damages inadequate for the plaintiffs in these cases?

2. What arguments did the defendants raise against the use of specific performance?

3. What factors were important to each court in deciding whether to grant specific performance? Which factors seem specific to particular fact situations, and which seem more generally applicable?

Ammerman v. City Stores Co.

H. Max AMMERMAN et al., Defendants-Appellants

v.

CITY STORES COMPANY, Plaintiff-Appellee

United States Court of Appeals, District of Columbia Circuit

394 F.2d 950 (D.C. Cir. 1968)

Before DANAHER, TAMM and ROBINSON, CIRCUIT JUDGES.

PER CURIAM:

Appellants, builders and developers of Tyson's Corner Shopping Center in Fairfax County, Virginia, challenge the District Court's decision (1) that the builders had given City Stores Company, owners of Lansburgh's Department Store, a binding option to lease one of the major buildings to be constructed at the contemplated shopping center and (2) that the option-lease agreement is sufficiently definite and certain in terms of design, type of construction, and price to be specifically enforced.

The appellants in their statement of points have here contended that the District Court erred: in ordering specific performance in that the existence and terms of the contract had not been established by clear and convincing evidence; in granting equitable relief despite the appellants' claim that the appellee had been guilty of "laches and unclean hands"; and in ordering specific performance of the contract since some substantial details will require future negotiations and yet others are said to be unclear or can not be performed.

What's That?

The defendants raise the issue of "laches." This equitable defense precludes a claimant from bringing a claim—typically an equitable claim—after waiting for an unreasonable time and prejudicing the other party. The precluded party is said to have "slept on his or her rights," or have been "estopped by laches." In that way, laches operates as a rough equivalent to a statute of limitations in equity.

At the core of the dispute is an undated letter (text, infra), from the appellants to one Jagels, then President of Lansburgh's, given at a time when the builders were attempting to obtain a ruling from the Fairfax Board of County Supervisors which would permit the rezoning of their tract of land for use as a shopping center. Prospects for a favorable outcome at a May 31, 1962, hearing, then yet in the future, were in doubt. The county planning commission and the planning staff had already recommended against the appellants' application, and another group of developers, Rouse-Reynolds, had a similar petition before the Board for a different center but in the same general area.

In early 1962, during the course of negotiations with Messrs. Gudelsky and Lerner for a lease at one of their developments in Maryland, Lansburgh's president, Jagels, had expressed an interest in the Tyson's Corner project. Thereafter Lerner requested a letter from Jagels, expressing Lansburgh's preference for appellants' site over the Rouse-Reynolds tract, which the builders could use in the Fairfax zoning hearing. Although Lansburgh's would ordinarily have been unwilling to risk offending the Rouse-Reynolds group by committing itself to the Gudelsky-Lerner project, it was eager to improve its declining economic position in the Washington area by expanding into the suburbs. Jagels provided the requested letter[4] which the appellants subsequently presented at the rezoning hearing to support their application.

Judge Gasch agreed with the appellee that the Jagels letter was given in exchange for a promise that Lansburgh's be given an opportunity to become a major tenant at Tyson's Corner on terms equal to those given other major tenants. The trial judge further found that this promise had been memorialized in the following undated letter given to Mr. Jagels on or about May 29, 1962:[6]

---

[4]　The text of the Jagels letter is reprinted in full:

May 29, 1962

Dear Mr. Gudelsky and Mr. Lerner: In view of our several discussions on the Tyson's Corner area as a place for a Regional Shopping Center, I am pleased to say that we have now completed our rather exhaustive surveys and are in a position to give you our firm position on the subject. We are convinced that the Gudelsky-Lerner tract, to which you refer as the Tyson's Triangle, is superior to any other. Being located on the Beltway, it has an unexcelled advertising value. Its location on both Route 7 and Route 123 gives it access to all local traffic. Since the Tyson's Triangle site will be developed almost exclusively to commercial uses, it also assures a live center with no dead spots. It is also readily available to automobile traffic without other competing uses within the Triangle. If you and your associates gain approval to build a Regional Shopping Center on this property, Lansburgh's would be very interested in becoming a major tenant with a full line department store. This interest is, however, restricted to this particular location only and is further conditional upon their being only one regional center in the Tyson's Corner area.

[6]　The statute of frauds for the District of Columbia reads in pertinent part:

An action may not be brought . . . to charge a person upon . . . a contract or sale of real estate (or) of any interest in or concerning it . . . unless the agreement upon which the action is brought, or a memorandum or note thereof, is in writing, which need not state the consideration and signed by the party to be charged therewith. . . .

D.C.Code § 28–3502 (1967).

The letter signed by these builders, together with appellee's full performance of the requested services, is sufficient evidence of a unilateral contract to satisfy this statute. . . . The appellee's change of position induced by the appellants' parol promise would estop the latter from setting up the statute of frauds. Brewood v. Cook, 92 U.S.App.D.C. 386, 389, 207 F.2d 439, 441 (1953). . . .

Dear Mr. Jagels:

We very much appreciate the efforts which you have expended in endeavoring to assist Mr. Gudelsky and me in our application for zoning at Tyson's Corner for a Regional Shopping Center.

You have our assurance that in the event we are successful with our application, that we will give you the opportunity to become one of our contemplated center's major tenants with rental and terms at least equal to that of any other major department store in the center.

Sincerely yours, (s) Isadore M. Gudelsky (s) Theodore N. Lerner

I.

Deeming the assistance afforded by the appellee to the appellants, particularly the May 29, 1962 letter, to be adequate consideration for a valid unilateral contract binding on the appellants, Judge Gasch considered whether the contract, so found, was an option. . . .

II.

Judge Gasch found that Lansburgh's had exercised its option and was entitled to an order compelling the builders to grant it a lease equal in terms to that of the Hecht lease. The appellants argue that the option-lease agreement is too indefinite and uncertain to be specifically enforced because substantial terms have been left to future negotiation. We approve the trial judge's recognition as a rule of law that the mere fact that a contract, definite in material respects, contains some terms which are subject to further negotiation between plaintiff and defendant will not bar a decree for specific performance, if in the court's discretion specific performance should be granted.

The rule so stated violates no precedent in this jurisdiction, but rather is in accord with such of our cases as have considered not dissimilar situations.

Treating the enforcement of construction contracts as a question novel to the District of Columbia,[17] Judge Gasch emphasized that the essential basis for

---

[17] Despite a paucity of cases in this jurisdiction, we may properly look to the decisions of other courts, recognizing that the "principles and maxims of equity as they existed in England and the colonies in 1776" are part of the law of the District of Columbia. . . . The English Chancery long ago enforced a building contract. Holt v. Holt, 2 Vern. 322, 23 Eng.Rep. 808 (Ch. 1694). There the plaintiff's father had "articled" to have a house built on part of his land but died intestate before it was constructed. The court ruled that the son, on whose inheritance the house was to be built, could compel the builder to build it and his father's administratrix to pay for it. . . . Although the Chancellor would not specifically enforce rebuilding contracts in two cases decided shortly after 1776, . . . the conflict was resolved in Mosely v. Virgin, 3 Ves.Jr. 184, 30 Eng.Rep. 959 (1796), in a rule with a remarkably modern ring: "If the transaction and agreement is in its nature defined, perhaps there would not be much difficulty to

interposition by the court is the inadequacy or impracticability of the plaintiff's legal remedy rather than the generic subject matter of the contract.

Here it is apparent that Lansburgh's could have had no adequate remedy in damages for any attempt in that respect would have been impractical because of the impossibility of an appropriate measurement. Moreover, damages could hardly compensate for the loss of the sought for opportunity to raise Lansburgh's image and economic position in the Metropolitan Washington area by its anticipated expansion into the suburbs, and for that reason alone could have been deemed inadequate.

Thus, where the contractual obligation being enforced involves more than the mere construction of a building and the building is to be built on land controlled by its owner (making it impossible for the enforcing party to have the job done by another and charged to the defaulting owner), specific enforcement becomes entirely appropriate. Nor should relief be withheld merely because it would order construction unless the difficulties of supervision by the court outweigh the importance of enforcement to the plaintiff. In this case, as the District Judge found, the construction criteria set forth in the Hecht and Woodward & Lothrop leases are sufficiently detailed to allow the court, applying the standard of equality required by the option, to enforce the lease contract with little difficulty of supervision. The District Court here has retained jurisdiction and can appoint a special master to settle such details as the parties may not agree upon or which can not be resolved through arbitration.

Affirmed.

Behind the Scenes

Lansburgh's, a large department chain like Macy's or Nieman Marcus, opened its flagship store in Washington, D.C., in 1860 and shortly thereafter supplied the black crepe for Abraham Lincoln's funeral. In the mid-twentieth century, the store's economic standing began to decline, so it sought to expand into suburban branches. In 1959, Lansburgh's opened a branch in Langley Park, Maryland, followed quickly by a branch in Arlington, Virginia. This set the context for Lansburgh's interest in expanding into Tyson's Corner International Shopping Center, in Fairfax, Virginia. However, because of the conflict discussed in *Ammerman*, the branch opening was postponed by approximately

---

decree specific performance; but if it is loose and undefined, and it is not expressed distinctly, what the building is, so that the Court could describe it as a subject for the report of the Master, the jurisdiction could not apply.". . .

seven years, until 1969. By the time the branch opened, Lansburgh's had suffered high legal fees, and its growth had slowed. The department store opened two more branches in Rockville, Maryland and Springfield, Virginia, but eventually liquidated in 1973. At that time, Lansburgh's ranked eighth in the Washington, D.C., retail market.

Although the *Ammerman* court found that there were no remedies at law adequate to compensate Lansburgh's and its owner, City Stores Co., it turned out that even an equitable remedy was inadequate to make City Stores Co. whole after a seven-year battle.

Laclede Gas Co. v. Amoco Oil Co.

LACLEDE GAS COMPANY, doing business as Midwest Missouri
Gas Company, Plaintiff-Appellant

v.

AMOCO OIL COMPANY, Defendant-Appellee

United States Court of Appeals, Eighth Circuit
522 F.2d 33 (1975)

Ross, Circuit Judge.

The Laclede Gas Company (Laclede), a Missouri corporation, brought this diversity action alleging breach of contract against the Amoco Oil Company (Amoco), a Delaware corporation. It sought relief in the form of a mandatory injunction prohibiting the continuing breach or, in the alternative, damages. The district court held a bench trial on the issues of whether there was a valid, binding contract between the parties and whether, if there was such a contract, Amoco should be enjoined from breaching it. It then ruled that the "contract is invalid due to lack of mutuality" and denied the prayer for injunctive relief. The court made no decision regarding the requested damages. Laclede Gas Co. v. Amoco Oil Co., 385 F. Supp. 1332, 1336 (E.D.Mo.1974). This appeal followed, and we reverse the district court's judgment.

On September 21, 1970, Midwest Missouri Gas Company (now Laclede), and American Oil Company (now Amoco), the predecessors of the parties to this litigation, entered into a written agreement which was designed to provide central propane gas distribution systems to various residential developments in Jefferson County, Missouri, until such time as natural gas mains were extended into these areas. The agreement contemplated that as individual developments were planned the owners or developers would apply to Laclede for central propane gas systems. If

Laclede determined that such a system was appropriate in any given development, it could request Amoco to supply the propane to that specific development. This request was made in the form of a supplemental form letter, as provided in the September 21 agreement; and if Amoco decided to supply the propane, it bound itself to do so by signing this supplemental form.

Once this supplemental form was signed the agreement placed certain duties on both Laclede and Amoco. Basically, Amoco was to "[i]nstall, own, maintain and operate . . . storage and vaporization facilities and any other facilities necessary to provide [it] with the capability of delivering to [Laclede] commercial propane gas suitable . . . for delivery by [Laclede] to its customers' facilities." Amoco's facilities were to be "adequate to provide a continuous supply of commercial propane gas at such times and in such volumes commensurate with [Laclede's] requirements for meeting the demands reasonably to be anticipated in each Development while this Agreement is in force." Amoco was deemed to be "the supplier," while Laclede was "the distributing utility."

For its part Laclede agreed to "[i]nstall, own, maintain and operate all distribution facilities" from a "point of delivery" which was defined to be "the outlet of [Amoco] header piping." Laclede also promised to pay Amoco "the Wood River Area Posted Price for propane plus four cents per gallon for all amounts of commercial propane gas delivered" to it under the agreement.

Since it was contemplated that the individual propane systems would eventually be converted to natural gas, one paragraph of the agreement provided that Laclede should give Amoco 30 days written notice of this event, after which the agreement would no longer be binding for the converted development.

Another paragraph gave Laclede the right to cancel the agreement. However, this right was expressed in the following language:

> This Agreement shall remain in effect for one (1) year following the first delivery of gas by [Amoco] to [Laclede] hereunder. Subject to termination as provided in Paragraph 11 hereof (dealing with conversions to natural gas), this Agreement shall automatically continue in effect for additional periods of one (1) year each unless [Laclede] shall, not less than 30 days prior to the expiration of the initial one (1) year period or any subsequent one (1) year period, give [Amoco] written notice of termination.

There was no provision under which Amoco could cancel the agreement.

For a time the parties operated satisfactorily under this agreement, and some 17 residential subdivisions were brought within it by supplemental letters. However, for various reasons, including conversion to natural gas, the number of developments under the agreement had shrunk to eight by the time of trial. These were all mobile home parks.

During the winter of 1972–73 Amoco experienced a shortage of propane and voluntarily placed all of its customers, including Laclede, on an 80% allocation basis, meaning that Laclede would receive only up to 80% of its previous requirements. Laclede objected to this and pushed Amoco to give it 100% of what the developments needed. Some conflict arose over this before the temporary shortage was alleviated.

Take Note

These facts suggest that Amoco provided notification that it would allocate enough propane to meet only 80% of Laclede's demand, claiming excuse under UCC § 2–615 (page 754). Upon receipt of notice, Laclede would typically have the right to terminate or modify the contract, as provided in § 2–616.

Then, on April 3, 1973, Amoco notified Laclede that its Wood River Area Posted Price of propane had been increased by three cents per gallon. Laclede objected to this increase also and demanded a full explanation. None was forth-

Think About It!

Amoco claims to have "terminated" the contract. Was it terminating, cancelling, or repudiating the contract?

coming. Instead Amoco merely sent a letter dated May 14, 1973, informing Laclede that it was "terminating" the September 21, 1970, agreement effective May 31, 1973. It claimed it had the right to do this because "the Agreement lacks 'mutuality.' "[1]

The district court felt that the entire controversy turned on whether or not Laclede's right to "arbitrarily cancel the Agreement" without Amoco having a similar right rendered the contract void "for lack of mutuality" and it resolved this question in the affirmative. We disagree with this conclusion and hold that settled principles of contract law require a reversal.

I.

A bilateral contract is not rendered invalid and unenforceable merely because one party has the right to cancellation while the other does not. There is no necessity "that for each stipulation in a contract binding the one party there must

---

[1] While Amoco sought to repudiate the agreement, it resumed supplying propane to the subdivisions on February 1, 1974, under the mandatory allocation guidelines promulgated by the Federal Energy Administration under the Federal Mandatory Allocation Program for propane. It is agreed that this is now being done under the contract.

be a corresponding stipulation binding the other." James B. Berry's Sons Co. v. Monark Gasoline & Oil Co., 32 F.2d 74, 75 (8th Cir. 1929)....

The important question in the instant case is whether Laclede's right of cancellation rendered all its other promises in the agreement illusory so that there was a complete failure of consideration. This would be the result had Laclede retained the right of immediate cancellation at any time for any reason....

Here Laclede's right to terminate was neither arbitrary nor unrestricted. It was limited by the agreement in at least three ways. First, Laclede could not cancel until one year had passed after the first delivery of propane by Amoco. Second, any cancellation could be effective only on the anniversary date of the first delivery under the agreement. Third, Laclede had to give Amoco 30 days written notice of termination. These restrictions on Laclede's power to cancel clearly bring this case within the rule [that the contract is not illusory].

. . . .

II.

Since he found that there was no binding contract, the district judge did not have to deal with the question of whether or not to grant the injunction prayed for by Laclede. He simply denied this relief because there was no contract. Laclede Gas Co. v. Amoco Oil Co., supra, 385 F.Supp. at 1336.

Generally the determination of whether or not to order specific performance of a contract lies within the sound discretion of the trial court. Landau v. St. Louis Public Service Co., 364 Mo. 1134, 273 S.W.2d 255, 259 (1954). However, this discretion is, in fact, quite limited; and it is said that when certain equitable rules have been met and the contract is fair and plain "specific performance goes as a matter of right." Miller v. Coffeen, 365 Mo. 204, 280 S.W.2d 100, 102 (1955)....

With this in mind we have carefully reviewed the very complete record on appeal and conclude that the trial court should grant the injunctive relief prayed....

Amoco contends that four of the requirements for specific performance have not been met. Its claims are: (1) [omitted]; (2) the remedy of specific performance would be difficult for the court to administer without constant and long-continued supervision; (3) the contract is indefinite and uncertain; and (4) the remedy at law available to Laclede is adequate. The first three contentions have little or no merit and do not detain us for long.

. . . .

While a court may refuse to grant specific performance where such a decree would require constant and long-continued court supervision, this is merely a discretionary rule of decision which is frequently ignored when the public interest is involved. See, e. g., Joy v. St. Louis, 138 U.S. 1, 47, 11 S.Ct. 243, 34 L.Ed. 843 (1891) . . . .

Here the public interest in providing propane to the retail customers is manifest, while any supervision required will be far from onerous. Section 370 of the Restatement of Contracts (1932) provides:

> Specific enforcement will not be decreed unless the terms of the contract are so expressed that the court can determine with reasonable certainty what is the duty of each party and the conditions under which performance is due.

We believe these criteria have been satisfied here. As discussed in part I of this opinion, as to all developments for which a supplemental agreement has been signed, Amoco is to supply all the propane which is reasonably foreseeably required, while Laclede is to purchase the required propane from Amoco and pay the contract price therefor. The parties have disagreed over what is meant by "Wood River Area Posted Price" in the agreement, but the district court can and should determine with reasonable certainty what the parties intended by this term and should mold its decree, if necessary accordingly. Likewise, the fact that the agreement does not have a definite time of duration is not fatal since the evidence established that the last subdivision should be converted to natural gas in 10 to 15 years. This sets a reasonable time limit on performance and the district court can and should mold the final decree to reflect this testimony.

It is axiomatic that specific performance will not be ordered when the party claiming breach of contract has an adequate remedy at law. Jamison Coal & Coke Co. v. Goltra, 143 F.2d 889, 894 (8th Cir.), cert. denied, 323 U.S. 769, 65 S.Ct. 122, 89 L.Ed. 615 (1944). This is especially true when the contract involves personal property as distinguished from real estate.

However, in Missouri, as elsewhere, specific performance may be ordered even though personalty is involved in the "proper circumstances." Mo.Rev.Stat. § 400.2–716(1); Restatement of Contracts, supra, § 361. And a remedy at law adequate to defeat the grant of specific performance "must be as certain, prompt, complete, and efficient to attain the ends of justice as a decree of specific performance." National Marking Mach. Co. v. Triumph Mfg. Co., 13 F.2d 6, 9 (8th Cir. 1926). Accord, Snip v. City of Lamar, 239 Mo.App. 824, 201 S.W.2d 790, 798 (1947).

One of the leading Missouri cases allowing specific performance of a contract relating to personalty because the remedy at law was inadequate is Boeving v. Vandover, 240 Mo.App. 117, 218 S.W.2d 175, 178 (1949). In that case the plaintiff sought specific performance of a contract in which the defendant had promised to sell him an automobile. At that time (near the end of and shortly after World War II) new cars were hard to come by, and the court held that specific performance was a proper remedy since a new car "could not be obtained elsewhere except at considerable expense, trouble or loss, which cannot be estimated in advance."

We are satisfied that Laclede has brought itself within this practical approach taken by the Missouri courts. As Amoco points out, Laclede has propane immediately available to it under other contracts with other suppliers. And the evidence indicates that at the present time propane is readily available on the open market. However, this analysis ignores the fact that the contract involved in this lawsuit is for a long-term supply of propane to these subdivisions. The other two contracts under which Laclede obtains the gas will remain in force only until March 31, 1977, and April 1, 1981, respectively; and there is no assurance that Laclede will be able to receive any propane under them after that time. Also it is unclear as to whether or not Laclede can use the propane obtained under these contracts to supply the Jefferson County subdivisions, since they were originally entered into to provide Laclede with propane with which to "shave" its natural gas supply during peak demand periods.[4] Additionally, there was uncontradicted expert testimony that Laclede probably could not find another supplier of propane willing to enter into a long-term contract such as the Amoco agreement, given the uncertain future of worldwide energy supplies. And, even if Laclede could obtain supplies of propane for the affected developments through its present contracts or newly negotiated ones, it would still face considerable expense and trouble which cannot be estimated in advance in making arrangements for its distribution to the subdivisions.

Specific performance is the proper remedy in this situation, and it should be granted by the district court.

CONCLUSION

For the foregoing reasons the judgment of the district court is reversed and the cause is remanded for the fashioning of appropriate injunctive relief in the form of a decree of specific performance as to those developments for which a supplemental agreement form has been signed by the parties.

---

[4] During periods of cold weather, when demand is high, Laclede does not receive enough natural gas to meet all this demand. It, therefore, adds propane to the natural gas it places in its distribution system. This practice is called "peak shaving."

Problem: Specific Performance

10-16. Osborn owned a beach house and rented the upper apartment to Kemp at the rate of $275 per month. Osborn continued to use the lower apartment from time to time. In 1985, Osborn and Kemp entered into an agreement whereby Kemp would pay Osborn $275 per month plus utilities for twenty years and thereafter could purchase the property for $50,000. Kemp paid the $275 per month plus utilities through mid-2006 and made $11,000 in improvements to the beach house, but eventually stopped making payments. In the meantime, Osborn was suffering from dementia, and her niece took over business affairs under a power of attorney. Noticing that Kemp had not paid rent, the niece brought suit to evict Kemp. Kemp counterclaimed for specific performance. Should the court order specific performance? Would it matter if the home was worth far more than Kemp paid Osborn at the end of 20 years (or at the time of the agreement)?

§ 3.2. Prohibitory Injunction

An order of specific performance is a "positive injunction," instructing one or both parties what to do to complete the contract. A court instead may issue a negative (prohibitory) injunction, forbidding a party from taking particular action in violation of the contract. A court can issue a preliminary injunction, while the case is pending or a shorter period, to preserve the status quo, so that it can make a fair ruling at the end of the case. As with other forms of equitable relief, an injunction will not be granted unless the plaintiff will suffer irreparable harm without the injunction and there is no adequate remedy at law.

Reading Critically: *American Broadcasting Companies*

1. What standard did the court establish for evaluating whether negative injunctive relief should be available during the term of the employment contract? How did that differ from the standard for granting injunctive relief after the end of the employment contract?

2. What competing policies were relevant to determining whether injunctive relief should be available?

> 3. Why was injunctive relief not granted in this case? Why did the
>   dissent disagree with that result?

American Broadcasting Companies v. Wolf

AMERICAN BROADCASTING COMPANIES, INC., Plaintiff-Appellant

v.

Warner WOLF et al., Defendants-Respondents

Court of Appeals of New York
420 N.E.2d 363, 438 N.Y.S.2d 482 (1981)

COOKE, CHIEF JUDGE. This case provides an interesting insight into the fierce competition in the television industry for popular performers and favorable ratings. It requires legal resolution of a rather novel employment imbroglio.

The issue is whether plaintiff American Broadcasting Companies, Incorporated (ABC), is entitled to equitable relief against defendant Warner Wolf, a New York City sportscaster, because of Wolf's breach of a good faith negotiation provision of a now expired broadcasting contract with ABC. In the present circumstances, it is concluded that the equitable relief sought by plaintiff—which would have the effect of forcing Wolf off the air—may not be granted.

I.

Warner Wolf, a sportscaster who has developed a rather colorful and unique on-the-air personality, had been employed by ABC since 1976. In February, 1978, ABC and Wolf entered into an employment agreement which, following exercise of renewal option, was to terminate on March 5, 1980. The contract contained a clause, known as a good-faith negotiation and first-refusal provision, that is at the crux of this litigation: "You agree, if we so elect, during the last ninety (90) days prior to the expiration of the extended term of this agreement, to enter into good faith negotiations with us for the extension of this agreement on mutually agreeable terms. You further agree that for the first forty-five (45) days of this renegotiation period, you will not negotiate for your services with any other person or company other than WABC-TV or ABC. In the event we are unable to reach an agreement for an extension by the expiration of the extended term hereof, you agree that you will not accept, in any market for a period of three (3) months following expiration of the extended term of this agreement, any offer of employment as a sportscaster, sports news reporter, commentator, program host, or analyst in broadcasting (including television, cable television, pay television and radio) without first giving us, in writing, an opportunity to employ you on substantially similar terms and you agree to enter into an agreement with us on such terms." Under this provision, Wolf was bound to negotiate in good faith with ABC for the 90-day period from December 6, 1979 through March 4, 1980. For the first 45 days, December 6 through January 19, the negotiation with ABC was to be exclusive. Following expiration of the 90-day negotiating period and the contract on March 5, 1980, Wolf was required, *before* accepting any other offer, to afford ABC a right of first refusal; he could comply with this provision either by refraining from accepting another offer or by first tendering the offer to ABC. The first-refusal period expired on June 3, 1980 and on June 4 Wolf was free to accept any job opportunity, without obligation to ABC.

Wolf first met with ABC executives in September, 1979 to discuss the terms of a renewal contract. Counterproposals were exchanged, and the parties agreed to finalize the matter by October 15. Meanwhile, unbeknownst to ABC, Wolf met with representatives of CBS in early October. Wolf related his employment requirements and also discussed the first refusal-good faith negotiation clause of his ABC contract. Wolf furnished CBS a copy of that portion of the ABC agreement. On October 12, ABC officials and Wolf met, but were unable to reach agreement on a renewal contract. A few days later, on October 16 Wolf again discussed employment possibilities with CBS.

Not until January 2, 1980 did ABC again contact Wolf. At that time, ABC expressed its willingness to meet substantially all of his demands. Wolf rejected the offer, however, citing ABC's delay in communicating with him and his desire to explore his options in light of the impending expiration of the 45-day exclusive negotiation period.

On February 1, 1980, after termination of that exclusive period, Wolf and CBS orally agreed on the terms of Wolf's employment as sportscaster for WCBS-TV, a CBS-owned affiliate in New York. During the next two days, CBS informed Wolf that it had prepared two agreements and divided his annual compensation between the two: one covered his services as an on-the-air sportscaster, and the other was an off-the-air production agreement for sports specials Wolf was to produce. The production agreement contained an exclusivity clause which barred Wolf from performing "services of any nature for" or permitting the use of his "name, likeness, voice or endorsement by, any person, firm or corporation" during the term of the agreement, unless CBS consented. The contract had an effective date of March 6, 1980.

Wolf signed the CBS production agreement on February 4, 1980. At the same time, CBS agreed in writing, in consideration of $100 received from Wolf, to hold open an offer of employment to Wolf as sportscaster until June 4, 1980, the date on which Wolf became free from ABC's right of first refusal. The next day,

February 5, Wolf submitted a letter of resignation to ABC.

Make the Connection

Notice that the agreement included the exchange of $100 for a promise "to hold open an offer of employment to Wolf as a sportscaster until June 4, 1980 . . . ." This agreement was an option contract supported by consideration, discussed in Chapter 3, page 157.

Representatives of ABC met with Wolf on February 6 and made various offers and promises that Wolf rejected. Wolf informed ABC that they had delayed negotiations with him and downgraded his worth. He stated he had no future with the company. He told the officials he had made a "gentlemen's agreement" and would leave ABC on March 5. Later in February, Wolf and ABC agreed that Wolf would continue to appear on the air during a portion of the first-refusal period, from March 6 until May 28.[1]

ABC commenced this action on May 6, 1980, by which time Wolf's move to CBS had become public knowledge. The complaint alleged that Wolf, induced by CBS breached both the good-faith negotiation and first-refusal provisions of his contract with ABC. ABC sought specific enforcement of its right of first refusal and an injunction against Wolf's employment as a sportscaster with CBS.

After a trial, Supreme Court found no breach of the contract, and went on to note that, in any event, equitable relief would be inappropriate. A divided Appellate Division, while concluding that Wolf had breached both the good-faith negotiation and first-refusal provisions, nonetheless affirmed on the ground that equitable intervention was unwarranted. There should be an affirmance.

II.

Initially, we agree with the Appellate Division that defendant Wolf breached his obligation to negotiate in good faith with ABC from December, 1979 through March [4], 1980. When Wolf signed the production agreement with CBS on February 4, 1980, he obligated himself not to render services "of any nature" to any person, firm or corporation on and after March 6, 1980. Quite simply, then, beginning on February 4 Wolf was unable to extend his contract with ABC; his contract with CBS precluded him from legally serving ABC in any capacity after March 5. Given Wolf's existing obligation to CBS, any negotiations he engaged in with ABC, without the consent of CBS, after February 4 were meaningless and could not have been in good faith.

---

[1] The agreement also provided that on or after June 4, 1980 Wolf was free to "accept an offer of employment with anyone of [his] choosing and immediately begin performing on-air services." The parties agreed that their rights and obligations under the original employment contract were in no way affected by the extension of employment.

At the same time, there is no basis in the record for the Appellate Division's conclusion that Wolf violated the first-refusal provision by entering into an oral sportscasting contract with CBS on February 4. The first-refusal provision required Wolf, for a period of 90 days after termination of the ABC agreement, either to refrain from accepting an offer of employment or to first submit the offer to ABC for its consideration. By its own terms, the right of first refusal did not apply to offers accepted by Wolf prior to the March 5 termination of the ABC employment contract. It is apparent, therefore, that Wolf could not have breached the right of first refusal by accepting an offer during the term of his employment with ABC.[2] Rather, his conduct violates only the good-faith negotiation clause of the contract. The question is whether this breach entitled ABC to injunctive relief that would bar Wolf from continued employment at CBS.[3] To resolve this issue, it is necessary to trace the principles of specific performance applicable to personal service contracts.

III.

-A-

Courts of equity historically have refused to order an individual to perform a contract for personal services (e.g., 4 Pomeroy, Equity Jurisprudence [5th ed.], § 1343, at pp. 943–944; 5A Corbin, Contracts, § 1204; see *Haight v. Badgeley*, 15 Barb. 499; Willard, Equity Jurisprudence, at pp. 276–279). Originally this rule evolved because of the inherent difficulties courts would encounter in supervising the performance of uniquely personal efforts[4] (e.g., 4 Pomeroy, Equity Jurisprudence, § 1343; 5A Corbin, Contracts, § 1204; see, also, *De Rivafinoli v. Corsetti*, 4

---

[2]   In any event, the carefully tailored written agreement between Wolf and CBS consisted only of an option prior to June 4, 1979. Acceptance of CBS's offer of employment as a sportscaster did not occur until after the expiration of the first-refusal period on June 4, 1979.

[3]   In its complaint, ABC originally sought specific enforcement of the right of first refusal. ABC now suggests that Wolf be enjoined from performing services for CBS for a two-year period. Alternatively, ABC requests this court to "turn the clock back to February 1, 1980" by: (1) setting aside Wolf's agreement with CBS and enjoining CBS from enforcing the agreement; (2) ordering Wolf to enter into good-faith negotiations with ABC for at least the period remaining under the negotiation clause when Wolf breached it; (3) ordering Wolf to honor the 90-day first-refusal period should the parties fail to reach agreement; and (4) enjoining CBS from negotiating with Wolf "for a period sufficient to render meaningful the above-described relief".

[4]   The New York Court of Chancery in *De Rivafinoli v. Corsetti* (4 Paige Chs. 264, 270) eloquently articulated the traditional rationale for refusing affirmative enforcement of personal service contracts: "I am not aware that any officer of this court has that perfect knowledge of the Italian language, or possesses that exquisite sensibility in the auricular nerve which is necessary to understand, and to enjoy with a proper zest, the peculiar beauties of the Italian opera, so fascinating to the fashionable world. There might be some difficulty, therefore, even if the defendant was compelled to sing under the direction and in the presence of a master in chancery, in ascertaining whether he performed his engagement according to its spirit and intent. It would also be very difficult for the master to determine what effect coercion might produce upon the defendant's singing, especially in the livelier airs; although the fear of imprisonment would unquestionably deepen his seriousness in the graver parts of the drama. But

Paige Ch. 264, 270). During the Civil War era, there emerged a more compelling reason for not directing the performance of personal services: the Thirteenth Amendment's prohibition of involuntary servitude. It has been strongly suggested that judicial compulsion of services would violate the express command of that amendment (*Arthur v. Oakes*, 63 F. 310, 317; Stevens, Involuntary Servitude by Injunction, 6 Corn.L.Q. 235; Calamari & Perillo, The Law of Contracts [2d ed.], § 16–5). For practical, policy and constitutional reasons, therefore, courts continue to decline to affirmatively enforce employment contracts.

Over the years, however, in certain narrowly tailored situations, the law fashioned other remedies for failure to perform an employment agreement. Thus, where an employee refuses to render services to an employer in violation of an existing contract, and the services are unique or extraordinary, an injunction may issue to prevent the employee from furnishing those services to another person for the duration of the contract (see, e.g., *Shubert Theatrical Co. v. Gallagher*, 206 App. Div. 514, 201 N.Y.S. 577). Such "negative enforcement" was initially available only when the employee had expressly stipulated not to compete with the employer for the term of the engagement (see, e.g., *Lumley v. Wagner*, 1 De G.M.&G. 604, 42 Eng.Rep. 687 . . . . Later cases permitted injunctive relief where the circumstances justified implication of a negative covenant (see, e.g., *Montague v. Flockton*, L.R. 16 Eq. 189 [1873] . . . . In these situations, an injunction is warranted because the employee either expressly or by clear implication agreed not to work elsewhere for the period of his contract. And, since the services must be unique before negative enforcement will be granted, irreparable harm will befall the employer should the employee be permitted to labor for a competitor (see 5A Corbin, Contracts, § 1206, at p. 412).

-B-

After a personal service contract terminates, the availability of equitable relief against the former employee diminishes appreciably. Since the period of service has expired, it is impossible to decree affirmative or negative specific performance. Only if the employee has expressly agreed not to compete with the employer following the term of the contract, or is threatening to disclose trade secrets or commit another tortious act, is injunctive relief generally available at the behest of the employer . . . . Even where there is an express anticompetitive covenant, however, it will be rigorously examined and specifically enforced only if it satisfies certain established requirements . . . . Indeed, a court normally will not decree specific enforcement of an employee's anticompetitive covenant unless necessary to protect the trade secrets, customer lists or good will of the employer's business, or perhaps when the employer is exposed to special harm because of the

---

one thing at least is certain; his songs will be neither comic, [n]or even semi-serious, while he remains confined in that dismal cage, the debtor's prison of New York."

unique nature of the employee's services. . . . And, an otherwise valid covenant will not be enforced if it is unreasonable in time, space or scope or would operate in a harsh or oppressive manner . . . . There is, in short, general judicial disfavor of anticompetitive covenants contained in employment contracts (e.g., *Reed, Roberts Assoc. v. Strauman, supra*, 40 N.Y.2d at p. 307, 386 N.Y.S.2d 677, 353 N.E.2d 590).

Underlying the strict approach to enforcement of these covenants is the notion that, once the term of an employment agreement has expired, the general public policy favoring robust and uninhibited competition should not give way merely because a particular employer wishes to insulate himself from competition (e.g., *Clark Paper & Mfg. Co. v. Stenacher*, 236 N.Y. 312, 319–320, 140 N.E. 708, supra; . . .). Important, too, are the "powerful considerations of public policy which militate against sanctioning the loss of a man's livelihood" (*Purchasing Assoc. v. Weitz*, 13 N.Y.2d at p. 272, 246 N.Y.S.2d 600, 196 N.E.2d 245, *supra*). At the same time, the employer is entitled to protection from unfair or illegal conduct that causes economic injury. The rules governing enforcement of anticompetitive covenants and the availability of equitable relief after termination of employment are designed to foster these interests of the employer without impairing the employee's ability to earn a living or the general competitive mold of society.

-C-

Specific enforcement of personal service contracts thus turns initially upon whether the term of employment has expired. If the employee refuses to perform during the period of employment, was furnishing unique services, has expressly or by clear implication agreed not to compete for the duration of the contract and the employer is exposed to irreparable injury, it may be appropriate to restrain the employee from competing until the agreement expires. Once the employment contract has terminated, by contrast, equitable relief is potentially available only to prevent injury from unfair competition or similar tortious behavior or to enforce an express and valid anticompetitive covenant. In the absence of such circumstances, the general policy of unfettered competition should prevail.

IV.

Applying these principles, it is apparent that ABC's request for injunctive relief must fail. There is no existing employment agreement between the parties; the original contract terminated in March, 1980. Thus, the negative enforcement that might be appropriate during the term of employment is unwarranted here. Nor is there an express anticompetitive covenant that defendant Wolf is violating, or any claim of special injury from tortious conduct such as exploitation of trade secrets. In short, ABC seeks to premise equitable relief after termination of the employment upon a simple, albeit serious, breach of a general contract negotiation clause.[7] To grant an injunction in that situation would be to unduly interfere with an individual's livelihood and to inhibit free competition where there is no corresponding injury to the employer other than the loss of a competitive edge. Indeed, if relief were granted here, any breach of an employment contract provision relating to renewal negotiations logically would serve as the basis for an open-ended restraint upon the employee's ability to earn a living should he ultimately choose not to extend his employment.[8] Our public policy, which favors the free exchange of goods and services through established market mechanisms, dictates otherwise.

Equally unavailing is ABC's request that the court create a noncompetitive covenant by implication. Although in a proper case an implied-in-fact covenant not to compete for the term of employment may be found to exist, anticompetitive covenants covering the postemployment period will not be implied. Indeed, even an express covenant will be scrutinized and enforced only in accordance with established principles.

This is not to say that ABC has not been damaged in some fashion or that Wolf should escape responsibility for the breach of his good-faith negotiation obligation. Rather, we merely conclude that ABC is not entitled to equitable relief. Because of the unique circumstances presented, however, this decision is without prejudice to ABC's right to pursue relief in the form of monetary damages, if it be so advised.

Accordingly, the order of the Appellate Division should be affirmed.

FUCHSBERG, JUDGE (dissenting).

I agree with all the members of this court, as had all the Justices at the Appellate Division, that the defendant Wolf breached his undisputed obligation to negotiate in good faith for renewal of his contract with ABC. Where we part

---

[7]   Even if Wolf had breached the first-refusal provision, it does not necessarily follow that injunctive relief would be available. Outside the personal service area, the usual equitable remedy for breach of a first-refusal clause is to order the breaching party to perform the contract with the person possessing the first-refusal right (e.g., 5A Corbin, Contracts, § 1197, at pp. 377–378). When personal services are involved, this would result in an affirmative injunction ordering the employee to perform services for plaintiff. Such relief, as discussed, cannot be granted.

[8]   Interestingly, the negative enforcement ABC seeks—an injunction barring Wolf from broadcasting for CBS—is for a two-year period. ABC's request is premised upon the fact that Wolf and CBS entered into a two-year agreement. Had the agreement been for 10 years, presumably ABC would have requested a 10-year restraint. In short, since it lacks an express anticompetitive clause to enforce, plaintiff seeks to measure its relief in a manner unrelated to the breach or the injury. This well illustrates one of the reasons why the law requires an express anticompetitive clause before it will restrain an employee from competing after termination of the employment.

company is in the majority's unwillingness to mold an equitable decree, even one more limited than the harsh one the plaintiff proposed, to right the wrong.

Central to the disposition of this case is the first-refusal provision. Its terms are worth recounting. They plainly provide that, in the 90-day period immediately succeeding the termination of his ABC contract, before Wolf could accept a position as sportscaster with another company, he first had to afford ABC the opportunity to engage him on like terms. True, he was not required to entertain offers, whether from ABC or anyone else, during that period. In that event he, of course, would be off the air for that 90 days, during which ABC could attempt to orient its listeners from Wolf to his successor. On the other hand, if Wolf wished to continue to broadcast actively during the 90 days, ABC's right of first refusal put it in a position to make sure that Wolf was not doing so for a competitor. One way or the other, however labeled, the total effect of the first refusal agreement was that of an express conditional covenant under which Wolf could be restricted from appearing on the air other than for ABC for the 90-day post-termination period.

One need not be in the broadcasting business to understand that the restriction ABC bargained for, and Wolf granted, when they entered into the original employment contract was not inconsequential. The earnings of broadcasting companies are directly related to the "ratings" they receive. This, in turn, is at least in part dependent on the popularity of personalities like Wolf. It therefore was to ABC's advantage, once Wolf came into its employ, especially since he was new to the New York market, that it enhance his popularity by featuring, advertising and otherwise promoting him. This meant that the loyalty of at least part of the station's listening audience would become identified with Wolf, thus enhancing his potential value to competitors, as witness the fact that, in place of the $250,000 he was receiving during his last year with ABC, he was able to command $400,000 to $450,000 per annum in his CBS "deal". A reasonable opportunity during which ABC could cope with such an assault on its good will had to be behind the clause in question.

Moreover, it is undisputed that, when in late February Wolf executed the contract for an extension of employment during the 90-day hiatus for which the parties had bargained, ABC had every right to expect that Wolf had not already committed himself to an exclusivity provision in a producer's contract with CBS in violation of the good-faith negotiation clause. Surely, had ABC been aware of this gross breach, had it not been duped into giving an uninformed consent, it would not have agreed to serve as a self-destructive vehicle for the further enhancement of Wolf's potential for taking his ABC-earned following with him.

In the face of these considerations, the majority rationalizes its position of powerlessness to grant equitable relief by choosing to interpret the contract as though there were no restrictive covenant, express or implied. However, as demonstrated, there is, in fact, an express three-month negative covenant which, because of Wolf's misconduct, ABC was effectively denied the opportunity to exercise. Enforcement of this covenant, by enjoining Wolf from broadcasting for a three-month period, would depart from no entrenched legal precedent. Rather, it would accord with equity's boasted flexibility (see 11 Williston, Contracts [3d ed.], § 1450, at pp. 1043–1044; 6A Corbin, Contracts, § 1394, at p. 100; see, generally, 20 N.Y.Jur. [rev.], Equity, §§ 79, 83, 84).

That said, a few words are in order regarding the majority's insistence that Wolf did not breach the first-refusal clause. It is remarkable that, to this end, it has to ignore its own crediting of the Appellate Division's express finding that, as far back as February 1, 1980, fully a month before the ABC contract was to terminate, "Wolf and CBS orally agreed on the terms of Wolf's employment as sportscaster for WCBS-TV" (majority opn.). It follows that the overt written CBS-Wolf option contract, which permitted Wolf to formally accept the CBS sportscasting offer at the end of the first-refusal period, was nothing but a charade.

Further, on this score, the majority's premise that Wolf could not have breached the first-refusal clause when he accepted the producer's agreement, exclusivity provision and all, *during* the term of his ABC contract, does not withstand analysis. So precious a reading of the arrangement with ABC frustrates the very purpose for which it had to have been made. Such a classical exaltation of form over substance is hardly to be countenanced by equity (see *Washer v. Seager*, 272 App.Div. 297, 71 N.Y.S.2d 46, affd. 297 N.Y. 918, 79 N.E.2d 745).

For all these reasons, in my view, literal as well as proverbial justice should have brought a modification of the order of the Appellate Division to include a 90-day injunction—no more and no less than the relatively short and certainly not unreasonable transitional period for which ABC and Wolf struck their bargain.

JASEN, GABRIELLI, JONES, WACHTLER and MEYER, JJ., concur with COOKE, C. J.

FUCHSBERG, J., dissents in part and votes to modify in a separate opinion.

Order affirmed, with costs.

Practice Pointer: Non-Compete Clauses

Non-compete clauses are also known as non-competition clauses and covenants not to compete. They may or may not be enforceable, at least in their entirety. On one hand, the policy of freedom of contract supports parties' agreed-upon terms. On the other hand, personal freedom and social welfare are undermined by clauses that restrict a person's ability to earn a living. A balancing of these policies dictates that an employer's non-compete clause

- must be contained within a valid contract (with consideration)

- cannot be harmful to the public:

    - For instance, in an area with a shortage of physicians, most courts would not prevent a doctor from practicing medicine, because the compelling public need for the doctor's service would outweigh the interest of the employer.

    - Non-compete clauses are rarely effective to restrict lawyers' employment by other law firms because the ethics rules governing law practice give a client the right to choose its own lawyer (and to follow her to another firm).

- must be written as narrowly as possible while protecting the legitimate business interests of the employer:

    - The employer's legitimate interests might include protecting its trade secrets and other confidential information, customer lists and customer relationships (the longer term, the better), goodwill, and unique or extraordinary skills.

    - If a non-disclosure agreement would protect trade secrets and other confidential information just as well or better, then the employer cannot use a non-compete clause for that purpose, because a non-disclosure agreement has less impact on a person's ability to earn a living.

    - Likewise, if a non-solicitation agreement would protect the employer's legitimate interests, then a non-compete clause is unlikely to be upheld.

- and therefore must be reasonable in restricting the time, place, and manner of the employee's future employment

  ○ The clause should restrict employment for as short a time period and for as small a geographical area as possible while protecting the employer's legitimate business interests.

  ○ In addition, the employee's scope of restricted activities should be drafted to cover as few activities as possible, so that the employee has the fullest possible range of ways to learn a living.

  ○ The question of reasonableness is generally for the court.

In some jurisdictions, a covenant not to compete must be ancillary to some other agreement, because a contract cannot restrain competition as its sole or primary purpose. Thus, parties often include the non-compete clause in an employment agreement or the sale of a business.

- Using the so-called "blue-pencil test," a court can "reform" (rewrite) the unreasonable aspects of a non-compete clause to prevent the clause from being invalidated. For instance, if the duration of the restraint is longer than needed to protect the employer's legitimate business interests, the court can reduce, say, a three-year period to a nine-month period, if that is the extent of a reasonable time in the circumstances. Similarly, an otherwise reasonable clause with a nationwide scope can be rewritten to encompass a narrower, more reasonable geographical area. Some courts, though, refuse to use the "blue pencil" and will strike the entire clause rather than reforming it.

§ 3.3. Specific Restitution

Specific performance is a remedy focused on granting expectation relief, because it seeks to place the non-breaching party in the position it would have been in if the contract had been fully performed voluntarily. Specific restitution is a restitutionary remedy, because it seeks to place the parties in the position they would have been in if the contract had never existed, by forcing disgorgement of unjust enrichment gained pursuant to the contract. Specific restitution is available if the court determines that restitution relief should be awarded, but restitutionary damages are not an adequate remedy. Specific restitution involves a court order that a particular item (usually something rare or of sentimental value) be restored to the plaintiff.

§ 4. Putting the Concepts Together

To help you navigate the complex web of remedies discussed in this Chapter, the flowchart we have used to show the organization of the chapter is supplemented here by a chart that identifies the meaning of each kind of remedy appearing in the flowchart. You will find both overviews useful as you review and consolidate your understanding of all the remedies available for aggrieved parties.

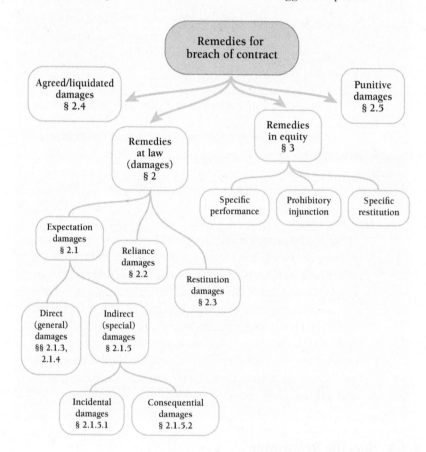

Guide to the meaning of the kinds of remedies in the flowchart:

Agreed/ Liquidated Damages	Dollar amounts of (or formula for computing) damages for a particular type of breach agreed to by the parties and included in the contract.
Conse- quential Damages	"Downstream losses" caused to the non-breaching party by the breach, including, e.g., lost profits, lost customers, lost business volume.
Direct (General) Damages	The amounts awarded for the direct loss suffered by not getting full contract performance; it measures the difference between the value of full performance and the value of performance actually received, but does not include consequential injury.
Expectation Damages	The total amount needed to put the non-breaching party in the position it would have been in had the contract been fully performed.
Incidental Damages	Extra costs incurred by the aggrieved party in dealing with the breach or in mitigating losses from the breach, for example, by handling a defective delivery or spending time or money arranging for purchase of substitute goods or negotiating a replacement contract.
Indirect (Special) Damages	Additional costs and losses caused by the breach and incurred in mitigating the breach, including incidental and consequential damages.
Prohibitory Injunction	A court order forbidding a party from taking particular action in violation of the contract.
Punitive Damages	Damages awarded to deter the breaching party and others from engaging in similar conduct in the future.
Reliance Damages	The amount needed to put the non-breaching party in the position it would have been in had the contract not been made.
Remedies in Law	The remedies of expectation, reliance and restitution damages.
Remedies in Equity	The remedies of specific performance, prohibitory injunction and specific restitution.

Restitution Damages	The amount needed to restore to the non-breaching party any benefit conferred on the breaching party in performance of contract obligations.
Specific Performance	A remedy by which the court orders a party to perform the unfulfilled promises in the contract, rather than ordering payment of the value of those performances.
Specific Restitution	A restitutionary remedy that orders the breaching party to restore to the non-breaching party a benefit gained pursuant to the contract, usually a particular rare item or one of sentimental value.

Test Your Knowledge

To assess your understanding of the material in this chapter, click here to take a quiz.

CHAPTER 11

Third-Party Rights and Duties

How do parties demonstrate assent to a contract?

What kinds of promises will the law enforce?

What defenses to enforcement exist?

Is a writing required for enforcement? If so, what kind?

How is the content and meaning of a contract determined?

What are parties' rights and duties after breach?

What situations lead to excusing contract performance?

What remedies are available for breach of contract?

What contractual rights and duties do non-parties to a contract have?

Table of Contents

§ 1. Introduction..909

§ 2. Assignment of Rights and Delegation of Duties...................................910

    § 2.1. Common Law Approach 912

    PROBLEM: DIAGRAMMING ASSIGNMENT/DELEGATION TRANSACTIONS (11-1) 920

    § 2.2. UCC and Restatement Provisions 920

    § 2.3. Beyond the Basics...923

§ 3. Third-Party Beneficiaries...925

    PROBLEM: DIAGRAMMING THIRD-PARTY BENEFICIARY TRANSACTION (11-2) 927

    § 3.1. Common Categories of Third-Party Beneficiaries 927

    § 3.2. Beyond the Basics...933

    PROBLEM: THIRD-PARTY BENEFICIARIES (11-3) 934

§ 1. Introduction

This final chapter considers the rights and duties of persons who are not in "privity" (that is, not parties) to the original contract, but who

- acquire contract rights by assignment, or

- acquire contract duties by delegation, or

- are third-party beneficiaries of contracts made by other parties.

You have seen examples of assignment, delegation, and third-party beneficiaries in cases in earlier chapters, although the focus then was on the rights of the direct parties to the contract. In complex commercial settings, however, the rights and obligations of non-parties are of significant concern. Although a complete canvassing of third-party rights and duties is beyond the scope of this book and most contracts courses, the material in this chapter introduces the issues and concepts involved.

§ 2. Assignment of Rights and Delegation of Duties

You may recall that *Hamer v. Sidway* (Chapter 4, page 201) involved a plaintiff who had acquired her claim by way of a chain of assignments from a nephew who allegedly had a right of recover money from his deceased uncle's estate. Hamer was not a party to the original contract, but had acquired her right to recover because the nephew had assigned whatever contract rights he had to his wife, who then assigned them to her mother, Louisa Hamer.

In most contracts, a third party can gain contract rights by obtaining an "assignment of rights" from a contract party, as occurred in *Hamer*. The assigning party (the nephew in *Hamer*) is the "assignor," and the receiving party (the nephew's wife) is the "assignee." The party whose payments are assigned (the uncle or his estate, in *Hamer*) is the "obligor" (the person who is obligated to perform under the original contract). The assignor is an "obligee" (the person who will receive the performance) until that right is transferred to the assignee, who becomes the obligee.

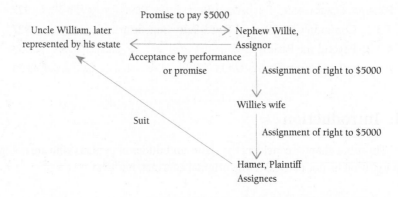

Contract performance is then owed to the assignee/obligee, not to the original obligee. A common example of assignment is in a contract for the sale of goods, services, or property, where the service provider or seller transfers ("assigns") to another person its right to payment from the purchaser, usually in exchange for a cash payment that is less than the payment due later from the purchaser.

To better understand the textual discussion and the cases, make sure that you correctly label the parties. You may find it helpful to diagram the relationships among the individuals involved in the assignments and delegations. The template below is an example of such a diagram. On it you can note the promises made by promisor and promisee, the intent of the assignor or delegator toward the third party, and the parties involved in the lawsuit seeking performance. Spend some time tracing the three sides of the triangular arrow path in this diagram:

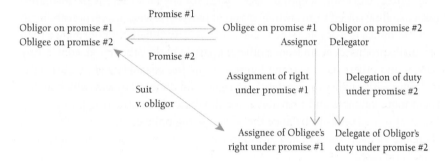

It is also possible for a party to "delegate duties" from the contract to a third party. Recall *Baehr v. Penn-O-Tex* (Chapter 4, page 215), in which Baehr claimed (unsuccessfully) that Penn-O-Tex had assumed responsibility for Kemp's duties under the service-station lease. The delegating party (allegedly Kemp) is the "delegator," and the newly responsible party (allegedly Penn-O-Tex) is the "delegatee" or "delegate." The delegate is then the "primary obligor," and the original "obligor" is then the "secondary obligor." The obligee remains the same.

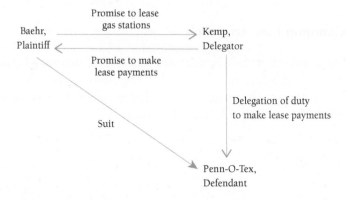

In drafting practice, many attorneys use the term "assignment" or "assignability" generically to refer to transfer of both rights and duties (assignment and delegation) under the contract. Indeed, the *Baehr* court in phrased the issue as whether Kemp had "assigned" his lease to Penn-O-Tex. However, because assignment and delegation are subject to different rules and policies, it is better to use "assignment" narrowly, to refer only to the assignment of rights, and to use "delegation" for the transfer of performance duties. This book uses the more precise terminology.

Competing policy concerns underlie common law and statutory responses to assignment and delegation. On the one hand, the original contract parties have an interest in the stability of their contract rights and duties (the *freedom to have contractual dealings with a particular chosen party*). If a right to receive performance is assigned, the obligor may be faced with somewhat different performance responsibilities owed to an entirely different party. Likewise, if a responsibility to perform duties is delegated, the obligee may receive different performance than originally promised, again from a different party. On the other hand, contracting parties and others have a strong interest in the *free alienability of contract rights and duties*—the ability to transfer those rights and duties to others, which makes them more valuable and provides more flexibility to contracting parties. The law in this area seeks to balance those competing policies, and the policies are therefore valuable tools to help attorneys and judges make the tough judgment calls in this area.

In the materials that follow, you will see that small additional burdens for obligors and obligees are tolerated to accommodate the policy of free alienability, but if substantial burdens to the other party are likely, the right to assign or delegate will be restricted because of the competing policy of stability for contract rights and duties. You will also see that delegation of duties is more restricted than assignment of rights, because assignment typically produces more economic value while creating fewer additional burdens to the other party.

§ 2.1. Common Law Approach

In the nineteenth century, British common law furnished many of the rules and principles for the developing law in the United States. The following case example shows the British struggle to define which contracts are delegable and which are not. The resulting rule is still a mainstay of U.S. law.

Example A: *British Waggon Co. v. Lea & Co.*, 5 Q.B.D. 149 (1880) (Court of Queen's Bench).

In a written lease in February 1874, Parkgate Waggon Co. leased 50 railway wagons to Lea & Co., coal merchants, for seven years, in return for yearly rent of £600, payable in equal quarterly payments. In June, the companies entered into a second lease for 50 additional wagons, for yearly rent of £625, also payable quarterly. Both leases contained the following clause:

> The owners, their executors, or administrators, will at all times during the said term, except as herein provided, keep the said waggons in good and substantial repair and working order, and, on receiving notice from the tenant of any want of repairs, and the number or numbers of the waggons requiring to be repaired, and the place or places where it or they then is or are, will, with all reasonable despatch, cause the same to be repaired and put into good working order.

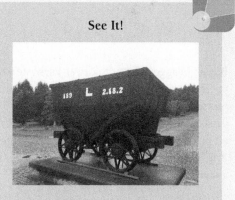

See It!

This railway wagon from the 1800s may be similar to the "waggons" in this case. Photo taken by Prof. Kunz, 2017, outside the Beamish Museum, United Kingdom.

In October 1874, Parkgate decided to voluntarily "wind up" its company. The chancery court ordered that this liquidation process should be supervised by the court. In April 1878, Parkgate entered into a written agreement with British Waggon Company, in which Parkgate assigned to British Waggon the right to all payments under the leases with Lea & Co. In return, British Waggon promised "to observe and perform such of the stipulations, conditions, provisions, and agreements contained in the said contracts as, according to the terms thereof were stipulated to be observed and performed by the Parkgate Company."

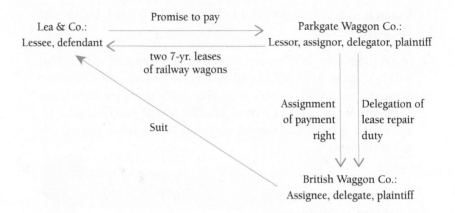

British Waggon then took over Parkgate's repair stations and staff. Lea & Co. objected to having to accept performance by British Waggon and refused to make further rent payments. It allowed performance by British Waggon only after the parties entered into an agreement preserving all parties' right to raise the issues presented in this case. Parkgate and British Waggon sued Lea & Co. to recover rent payments due after the assignment agreement.

Analysis: Lea & Co. argued that its leases with Parkgate were "at an end," because Parkgate had incapacitated itself from performing the leases by (1) going into voluntary liquidation, (2) assigning the two leases, and (3) giving up the repair stations to British Waggon, with which Lea had no privity of contract. Lea argued that Parkgate had no right to substitute a third party to perform Parkgate's duties under the leases, nor was Lea bound to accept the performance of the substituted party.

The court expressly found that British Waggon has "ever since been ready and willing to execute, and have, with all due diligence, executed all necessary repairs" to the leased wagons.

The court noted that Parkgate was not yet dissolved and had been "kept alive, the liquidator having power to carry on the business, 'so far as may be necessary for the beneficial winding-up of the company,' which the continued [leasing of the wagons] and the receipt of the rent payable in respect of them, would, we presume, be." The court refused to engage in dictum on the future position of the parties if Parkgate were dissolved.

Lea cited *Robson v. Drummond,* in which a carriage owner entered into a five-year agreement for a particular coachmaker, to keep the carriage in repair and to repaint the carriage once a year, in exchange for annual advance payments. When the coachmaker retired after the third year and assigned the contract to his partner, the carriage owner refused to accept the partner's performance and refused to make further payments.

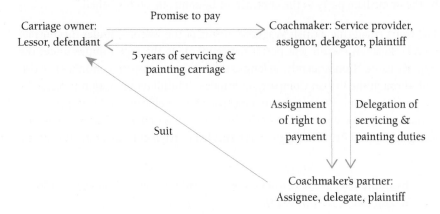

The *Robson* court reasoned that the carriage owner had entered into a long-term contract and had assented to make payments in advance because of his personal confidence in that particular coachmaker. The carriage owner was entitled to the personal services, judgment, and taste of the original coachmaker and therefore had a right to object to performance by another person. "[W]here a person contracts with another to do work or perform service, and it can be inferred that the person employed has been selected with reference to his individual skill, competency, or other personal qualification, the inability or unwillingness of the party so employed to execute the work or perform the service . . . entitles the [other party] to treat the contract as at an end, notwithstanding that the person tendered to take the place of the contracting party may be equally well qualified to do the service. Personal performance is in such a case of the essence of the contract, which, consequently, cannot in its absence be enforced against an unwilling party."

The court in *British Waggon Co v. Lea & Co.* concluded that the contract between Lea & Co. and Parkgate was not a "personal service contract" like the one in *Robson,* because the facts did not indicate that Lea & Co. had chosen Parkgate and its wagons because of any particular skill, judgment, or taste by Parkgate or its workers. "All that [Lea & Co.] cared for . . . was that the [wagons] should be kept in repair; it was indifferent to them by whom the repairs should be done. Thus if, without going into liquidation, or assigning these contracts, [Parkgate] had entered into a contract with any competent party to do the repairs, and so had procured them to be done, we cannot think that this would have been a departure from the terms of the contract to keep the [wagons] in repair." In dictum, the court voiced skepticism of the actual ruling in *Robson,* saying that "it is difficult to see how[,] in repairing a carriage when necessary, or painting it once a year, preference would be given to one coachmaker over another. Much work is contracted for, which it is known can only be executed by means of subcontracts; much is contracted for as to which it is indifferent to the party for whom it is to be done, whether it is done by the immediate party to the contract, or by someone on his behalf."

The court ruled that British Waggon's repair of the wagons, under its contract with Parkgate, was sufficient performance to satisfy the repair duties under the original leases. "Consequently, so long as the Parkgate Company continues to exist, and, through the British Company, continues to fulfill its obligation to keep the [wagons] in repair," Parkgate has not incapacitated itself from performing its lease duties and has not absolved Lea & Co. from its duties under the leases. Therefore, Parkgate Co. and British Waggon were entitled to payment due under the leases.

Example B: *Crane Ice Cream Co. v. Terminal Freezing & Heating Co.*, 128 A. 280 (Md. Ct. App. 1925).

Terminal Freezing & Heating Co. ("Terminal") was a corporation that manufactured and sold ice to businesses within Maryland. In 1917, it entered into a three-year contract to deliver ice to an ice cream plant in Baltimore, owned by W.C. Frederick, an individual. The contract required Terminal to sell and deliver to Frederick the quantities of ice he needed each week for his plant's ice cream manufacturing, up to 250 tons per week, on his plant's loading platform. In return, Frederick agreed (a) to pay Terminal on every Tuesday during the continuation of the contract, for all ice purchased by Frederick during the week ending at midnight upon the next preceding Saturday; and (b) to refrain from buying or accepting ice from any other source than Terminal, except in excess of the weekly maximum of 250 tons. Terminal gained the right (c) to "annul" the contract upon any violation of the agreement by Frederick; and (d) to sustain no liability for any breach of contract growing out of causes beyond its control. The contract was terminable at the will of either party upon 60 days' written notice. It did not contain any terms about either party's right to assign the contract. In 1918, the parties modified the contract to increase the price per ton from $2.75 to $3.25. Before the contract expired, the parties renewed it for another three years, until 1923.

Think About It!

What kind of supply contract did the appellee have with Frederick? What difference did this fact ultimately make in the court's decision?

In 1921, Frederick executed an assignment of the contract to Crane Ice Cream Co. without the consent or knowledge of Terminal, in return for consideration. It was a part of the transaction between Frederick and Crane, whereby Crane purchased the plant, equipment, rights, and credits, choses in action, "good will, trade, custom, patronage, rights, contracts," and other assets of Frederick's ice cream business in Baltimore.

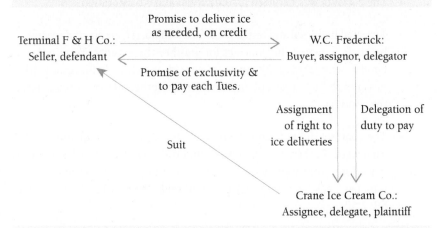

Crane took full possession and continued the business formerly carried on by Frederick, as well as continuing its existing and much-larger ice cream business in Philadelphia, Baltimore, and elsewhere in Maryland. It had ample resources and credit to meet any of its obligations, including the terms of the contract with Terminal, and it was prepared to pay cash for all ice deliverable under the contract.

When Terminal learned of the assignment and the absorption of Frederick's business by Crane, it notified Frederick that the contract was at an end and declined to deliver any ice to Crane. Crane then sued Terminal to recover damages for the alleged breach.

Analysis: The court found that Frederick attempted to assign the following rights: "(a) to take no ice, if [he] used none in his business, but, if he did (b) to require [Terminal] to deliver, on [Frederick's] loading platform . . . , all the ice he might need in his business to the extent of 250 tons a week, and (c) to buy any ice he might need in excess of the weekly 250 tons from any other person." The court found that Frederick attempted to delegate the following duties: "(a) to pay to [Terminal] on every Tuesday during the continuance of the contract the stipulated price for all ice purchased and weighed by [Frederick] during the week ending at midnight upon the next preceding Saturday, and (b) not directly or indirectly, during the existence of this agreement, to buy or accept any ice from any other person, firm, or corporation than [Terminal], except such amounts as might be in excess of the weekly limit of 250 tons."

To determine whether the attempted assignment or delegation must fail because the rights or duties were too personal to the original contract parties, the court noted the following facts:

- The contract was between an individual and a corporation.

- Terminal had tried and tested Frederick's character, credit, and resources before it renewed the contract for another three years. Terminal was familiar with (a) his ability to pay as agreed, as well as (b) his trustworthiness not to buy or accept any ice from any other source as required in the contract.

- The contract did not require Frederick to buy a specific quantity of ice each week. Rather, Terminal was comfortable with Frederick's quantity variations from week to week, which could range between 0 to 250 tons per week, so the weekly payment might be nothing or as much as $812.50.

- Each week, Terminal delivered ice to Frederick on credit, with payment due eight days after the beginning of each week's delivery. Terminal granted this credit without getting any security for its payment except in the integrity and solvency of Frederick. The performances, therefore, were not concurrent, but the performance of the non-assigning party to the contract was to precede the payments by the assignor.

- Frederick's weekly payments were based on the weight of the delivered ice on Frederick's loading platform.

The court concluded that Terminal was induced to enter into the original contract and its renewal because it relied "upon its knowledge of an average quantity of ice consumed, and probably to be needed, in the usual course of Frederick's business, at all times throughout the year, and its confidence in the stability of his enterprise, in his competency in commercial affairs, in his probity, personal judgment, and in his continuing financial responsibility. The contract itself emphasized the personal equation by specifying that the ice was to be bought for 'use in his business as an ice cream manufacturer,' and was to be paid for according to its weight 'on the loading platform of the said W. C. Frederick.' "

The court noted that, after Frederick transferred his business to Crane, the business was transformed from being a small free-standing ice cream manufacturer in Baltimore to being one of a group of plants serving Baltimore, Philadelphia, and other parts of Maryland. It was "the business of a stranger, whose skill, competency, and requirements of ice were altogether different from those of Frederick." Terminal had no guarantees that Crane would not (1) concentrate its manufacturing in Philadelphia and have no use for ice at Frederick's former plant, or (2) redirect its ice cream manufacturing to Frederick's former plant if the price of ice was higher in Philadelphia, or (3) order 250 tons per week each week on a continuing basis. These changes in quantity would not have occurred under Terminal's contract with Frederick.

The court applied turned to policy considerations, saying that "the law accords to every man freedom of choice in the party with whom he deals and the terms of his dealing. He cannot be forced to do a thing which he did not agree to do because it is like and no more burdensome than something which he did contract to do." It concluded that "the rights and duties of the contract under consideration were of so personal a character that the rights of Frederick cannot be assigned nor his duties be delegated without defeating the intention of the parties to the original contract."

The court also concluded that Frederick's attempted delegation of his duties was a repudiation of the contract. Although a contract party may usually assign its rights, except where a personal relation is involved, it cannot completely escape its contractual duties and substitute another's performance without the assent of the other party. Otherwise, obligors could free themselves of their obligations by simply delegating them. A party is entitled to know to whom it must look for the satisfaction of its rights under the contract and has a right to rely upon the character, credit, and substance of the other contractual party. Thus, a contract party can delegate a duty to third party, if the third party's performance of the duty will be substantially the same. Then the performance of the third party is the act of the promisor, who remains liable under the contract and answerable in damages for any defect in performance. The court cited *British Waggon Co. v. Lea & Co.* and *Robson v. Drummond* (both cases appear in Example A above).

The appellate court affirmed the judgment against Crane, refusing to hold Terminal to the assigned contract.

Think About It!

Would the result in *Crane Ice Cream* have been different today under the UCC? More specifically, would Terminal have been adequately protected by the good faith duties under § 2–306(1)? See Chapter 8, § 4.2. If the seller/obligor had felt insecure, would its rights have been adequately protected by the right to demand adequate assurance under 2–609? See Chapter 9, § 4.3.

Problem: Diagramming Assignment/Delegation Transactions

11-1. In each scenario below, diagram and label the persons involved. Identify whether the scenario involves an assignment of contract right(s), a delegation of contract duty(ies), both, or neither.

   a. An inventor who needs cash transfers his right to receive licensing royalties under one of his patents to his bank, in return for a loan.

   b. A partnership sells its assets and transfers its accounts receivable (unpaid customer accounts) to a corporation, in return for the corporation's cash payment and its promise to take over customer service obligations on those accounts.

   c. A parent of a college student agrees to co-sign an agreement for a car loan for the college student.

   d. An agricultural cooperative sells its used truck to an urban farm for $1400 and the farm's promise to pay the remainder of the cooperative's vehicle loan with the bank.

   e. A class-action claimant with a right to damages donates that right to his favorite charity.

   f. A piano teacher who is retiring refers her students to another piano teacher.

---

§ 2.2. UCC and Restatement Provisions

Many jurisdictions still retain their common law rules, but some jurisdictions have adopted the Restatement's approach, which tracks some of the rules in UCC § 2–210.

Reading Critically: Assignment and Delegation Under the UCC and Restatement (Second)

Read UCC § 2–210 and Restatement (Second) §§ 317, 318, and 322.

1. Read the comparisons in the table below. How, if at all, do these rules reshape the common law rules in *British Waggon* and in *Crane Ice Cream*?

	UCC § 2–210	Restatement (Second) §§ 317, 318, 322
a. Upon an assignment, what happens to the assignor's right under the contract?	Silent	317(1): It is extinguished

b. In what situations would an assignment be invalid?	2–210(2) 1st sentence: Rights are assignable
	
	• unless § 9–406 says otherwise, or
	• unless otherwise agreed (except as set out in the 2nd sentence), or
	• if the assignment
	  ° would materially change the other party's duty or
	  ° would increase materially the burden or risk imposed on the other party by K or
	  ° would impair materially his chance of obtaining return performance
		317(2): same rule as UCC, plus:
		
		• if the assignment
		  ° would materially reduce its value to him or
		  ° is barred by statute or public policy

c. Upon a delegation, what happens to the delegator's obligation under the contract? Are there any exceptions to that rule?	2–210(1): no change in duty or liability No exceptions	318(3): same as UCC rule Exception: "unless the obligee agrees otherwise"
d. In what situations would a delegation be invalid?	2–210(1) 1st sentence: Duties are delegable • unless otherwise agreed or • unless the other party [recipient of performance] has a substantial interest in having his original promisor perform or control the acts required by the contract	318(1), (2): Duties are delegable • unless contrary to public policy or • unless contrary to the terms of delegator's promise To interpret promise, see (2), which resembles 2nd UCC bullet

2. Consider each of the following clauses (commonly called "non-assignment clauses"). In light of the noted UCC and the Restatement (Second) provisions, what is the legal effect of each of these non-assignment clauses? Note any exceptions to or limitations imposed by the provisions. Analyze each clause separately from the others.

	UCC § 2–210	Restatement (Second) §§ 317, 318, 322
a. "Neither party may assign the contract."		
b. "Neither party may assign its rights under the contract."		

c. "Neither party may delegate its duties under the contract."		
d. "Neither party may assign its rights or delegate its duties under the contract. Any attempted assignment or delegation is void."		

3. If you were an attorney drafting a contract for a client, in a transaction not governed by UCC Art. 2, how would you draft what's called a "non-assignment clause" so that it has the maximum effect in limiting or barring assignments and delegations?

§ 2.3. Beyond the Basics

Assignment and delegation have a huge range of uses, especially in business transactions. Consider the following examples:

- In the sale of a business, the seller of the business can assign/delegate to the buyer the rights/duties under the lease that governs the business's location, if the landlord consents.

- A business that has accounts receivable (money due from customers) can assign those accounts (and the right to collect from those customers) to its bank, in return for a cash payment or credit from the bank, albeit at a lesser amount than the total value of the accounts receivable.

- A building contractor can delegate some of its duties to subcontractors, but the contractor remains responsible to the owner for the overall construction project.

This chapter's brief coverage of assignment and delegation just scratches the surface with respect to accompanying legal issues. Here is a sampling of other of issues that can arise:

- *After an assignment, what rights remain for the original contracting parties?* If an assignment of rights is made, the assignor no longer has the right to receive the performance owed under the original contract. By definition, that right now belongs to the assignee. The picture is complicated further if the obligor performs for the wrong person after an assignment is made or revoked. Whether the obligor remains liable after such performance depends on whether proper notice of assignment (or revocation) was received by the obligor.

- *After a delegation, what liabilities remain for the original contracting parties?* If a delegation of duties is made, the original obligor remains responsible to the obligee, unless the obligee consents to a substitution. "While an obligee can rid itself of a right merely by making an effective assignment, an obligor cannot rid itself of a duty merely by making an effective delegation. If obligors could do so, they could discharge their duties simply by finding obliging insolvents to whom performance could be delegated."[*]

- *Under what circumstances may a person making an assignment or a delegation revoke it?* If the assignment or delegation is part of a contract, supported by consideration, the assignment or delegation cannot be revoked. However, if an assignment is made as a gift (for example, if the nephew in *Hamer* had assigned his contract right to his wife as an anniversary gift), then it is governed by the rules regarding gifts, which makes it revocable until "delivered." How a gift of this kind might be delivered is complicated because an assignment is an intangible right, but it could be manifested in a deliverable instrument such as a promissory note or other written form.

- *If the obligor could have asserted a defense against paying the original obligee (the other party to the contract), can the obligor assert that defense against payment to the assignee?* For example, if services are performed unsatisfactorily but the right to receive payment for the services was assigned to a bank, can the buyer of those services defend against the bank's suit for payment by pointing to the defects in performance rendered by the assignor? The simple answer is yes; the assignee stands in the shoes of the assignor. But this picture is complicated by the existence of contract clauses that purport to waive the assertion of defenses if the right to collect is assigned (so-called "waiver-of-defense" clauses). Another complication occurs when the buyer of services has signed a promissory note (a written promise to pay), which are often "negotiable," so that the service provider can sell the note to a third party, who will not be encumbered by the defenses from the buyer of the services. The buyer must continue to

---

[*]   See Gary Monserud, *Blending the Law of Sales with the Common Law of Third Party Beneficiaries*, 39 Duq. L. Rev. 111, 114–15 (2000).

honor its payment obligation, unless a protective rule of law has evolved to cover that situation.

As you take additional courses in law school, expect to see additional settings, uses, and complexities in the law governing assignment and delegation.

§ 3. **Third-Party Beneficiaries**

In earlier chapters, you encountered several third-party beneficiaries, although you might not have recognized them as such. For instance, some construction contracts require that the general contractor purchase a performance bond for the protection of the project owner, to compensate the project owner for the contractor's deficient or incomplete construction work. The obligated party (the general contractor in the example) obtains a bond by entering into a contract with the bonding company. The benefited party (the project owner) is named as the beneficiary of the bond but is not a party to the bonding contract. The benefited party is a "third-party beneficiary" to the bonding contract. A third-party beneficiary to a contract may be expressly identified, as in this example, or may be implied from the nature of the contract. Identifying a benefited party as a third-party beneficiary is only the first step of the analysis. The second step of the analysis is ascertaining whether the third-party beneficiary is an "intended" or "incidental" beneficiary. Only intended third-party beneficiaries have a right to enforce the contract, while incidental third-party beneficiaries do not. This final section of the book examines the standards that determine whether a third-party beneficiary may enforce a contract to which it is not a party.

As with assignment and delegation, diagramming the relationships of the parties and third-party beneficiary may be helpful. The template below provides a model for that purpose:

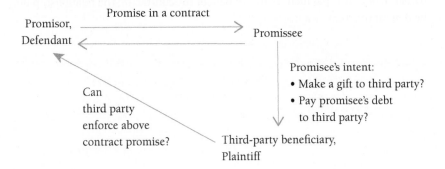

Here is how to draw the diagram:

1. Start by figuring out which contract promise the third party would like to enforce. Place that promise on the top horizontal line. Place the person who made that promise in the "promisor" position on the left side and the recipient in the "promisee" position on the right side.

2. Place the third party at the bottom of the diagram, beneath the promisee. On the vertical arrow between the two, note what the promisee intended to do for the third party (make a gift? pay promisee's debt?).

3. Now draw a diagonal arrow from the third party to promisor, and ask the crucial question: Can the third party enforce the contract promise made by the promisor? That is the focus of this portion of Chapter 10.

For instance, if a construction contract requires the general contractor to obtain a performance bond to benefit the owner of the project, the relationship may be diagrammed this way:

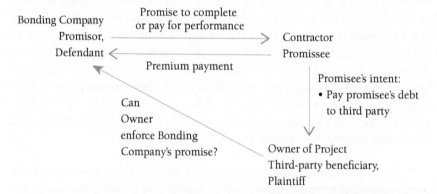

If the contract between the general contractor and the owner requires the owner to obtain a "payment bond" to benefit the contractor, the relationship may be diagrammed this way:

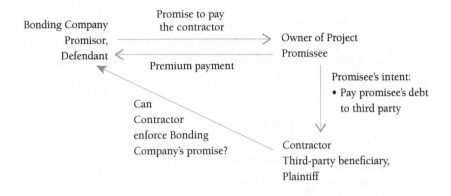

Problem: Diagramming Third-Party Beneficiary Transactions

11-2. Recall that, in *McCloskey & Co. v. Minweld Steel Co.* (Chapter 9, page 725), the contract required the subcontractor to obtain a performance bond for the benefit of the contractor. Diagram and label the third-party beneficiary relationship described in this case.

---

§ 3.1. Common Categories of Third-Party Beneficiaries

As early as 1677, the English courts recognized the right of a third-party beneficiary to enforce a contract created by other parties. English courts reaffirmed the rule a century later but repudiated it in 1861. The English common law rule remained opposed to third-party beneficiary rights. However, statutory law in the United Kingdom slowly expanded third-party beneficiary rights in the late twentieth century, culminating in a 1999 statute that conferred rights on contract beneficiaries generally.*

Meanwhile, the New York high court recognized third-party beneficiary rights in 1857 and expanded them in 1918. The cases in Examples C and D were important cases in those historical developments.

Example C: *Lawrence v. Fox*, 1859 WL 8352 (N.Y. 1859).

Fox approached Holly to get a 1-day loan of $300. In return for Holly's loan, Fox promised to repay the loan, not to Holly, but instead to Law-

---

* See E. Allen Farnsworth, *Contracts*, § 11.10 (4th ed. 2004); Gary Monserud, *Blending the Law of Sales with the Common Law of Third Party Beneficiaries*, 39 Duq. L. Rev. 111, 114–15 (2000).

rence, to whom Holly already owed $300. When Fox did not repay Lawrence, Lawrence sued Fox, claiming to be a third-party beneficiary of the loan contract between Holly and Fox. This diagram will help you sort out the parties.)

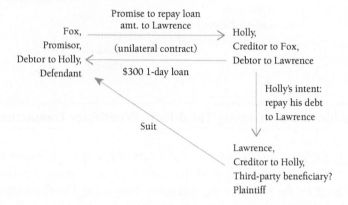

Analysis: The court began with the following New York rule (from an 1806 case and based on English precedent): "[W]here one person makes a promise to another for the benefit of a third person, that third person may maintain an action upon it," so lack of privity was not necessarily an obstacle to recovery. The court then discussed *Farley v. Cleaveland*, 4 Cow. 432 (N.Y. 1825), in which Cleaveland's promise to pay Moon's debt to Farley was made both to Moon and to Farley. The *Farley* court held that the contract was supported by consideration even though the promise benefited a third party, and Farley was able to recover on the contract as a third-party beneficiary.

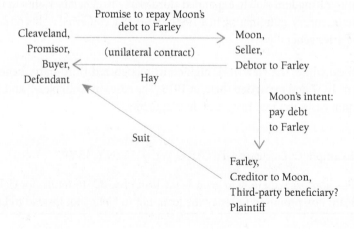

The *Lawrence* court took the *Farley* ruling a step further by holding that, even though Fox expressly made his promise *only* to Holly, to pay Holly's debt to Lawrence, the contract between Fox and Holly (like the contract between Cleaveland and Moon) was supported by consideration, and Lawrence could recover under that contract as a third-party beneficiary. In American jurisprudence, this case stands for the rule that a person to whom a debt is owed (a creditor) may recover as a third-party beneficiary for breach of another person's promise to the debtor, to pay that debt to the creditor.

> **Behind the Scenes**
>
> For an interesting "back story" on the circumstances of *Lawrence v. Fox,* see Anthony Waters, *The Property in the Promise: A Study of the Third Party Beneficiary Rule,* 98 Harv. L. Rev. 1109 (1985),

Example D: *Seaver v. Ransom,* 120 N.E. 639 (N.Y. 1918).

A judge's wife had desired to make a bequest to her niece, but that bequest was not in the will that the wife was presented with at her bedside as she was dying. Rather than risking that the wife might not execute the will before her death, the judge promised to leave the niece an equivalent bequest if the wife would execute the will right away. The wife did so, but the judge did not fulfill his promise in his own will, so the niece sued the judge's estate as a third-party beneficiary of the contract between the judge and his wife.

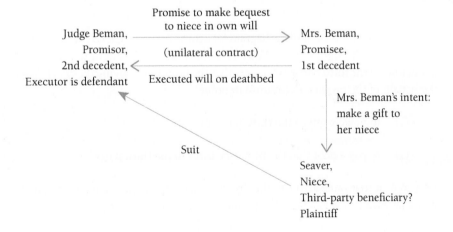

Analysis: The court noted that *Farley v. Cleaveland* and *Lawrence v. Fox* (see Example C), allowed a third-party beneficiary to recover under a contract made in order to have the promisor pay the debt obligation running from the promisee to a beneficiary. The court examined the so-called "close relationship" cases, which allowed a wife, fiancée, or child of a promisee to recover on a contract made in order to give a gift to the close family member. It also noted cases in which a municipality can protect its inhabitants by covenants for their benefit, as well as cases in which a contract party requests and obtains a return promise running directly to the beneficiary. It then synthesized these some of these cases into a broader category of cases in which the promisee intended to make a gift to a third party—the "donee beneficiaries"—regardless of whether the promisee had a close relationship or moral duty to the third party.

The court reasoned that "[i]f Mrs. Beman had left her husband the house on condition that he pay the plaintiff $6,000, and he had accepted the devise, he would have become personally liable to pay the legacy, and plaintiff could have recovered in an action at law against him, whatever the value of the house . . . because the testatrix had in substance bequeathed the promise to plaintiff, and not because close relationship or moral obligation sustained the contract. . . . The tendency of American authority is to sustain the gift in all such cases and to permit the donee beneficiary to recover on the contract. The equities are with the plaintiff, and they may be enforced in this action, whether it be regarded as an action for damages or an action for specific performance to convert the defendants into trustees for plaintiff's benefit under the agreement." The court therefore allowed the niece to recover under the contract between the judge and his wife, despite the objections of the judge's executor.

Look again at the template diagram for a third-party beneficiary relationship, on page 925. The right-hand column contains a question about the promisee's intent toward the third party. It asks whether the promisee is giving the beneficiary the benefit of the promisor's promise in order

(1)   to make a gift to the third party or

(2)   to pay a debt that the promisee owes to the third party.

Now look at that same arrow in the diagrams accompanying Examples C and D; note that each arrow is labelled with one of these two categories.

Over the centuries in which third-party beneficiary law developed (including the cases in Examples C and D above), these two fact categories presented compelling situations for which the law eventually crafted exceptions to the rule of privity of contract. By the time the first Restatement was drafted, these two fact categories had become known as "donee beneficiaries" and "creditor beneficiaries." These two categories largely persisted into the Restatement (Second), albeit under the umbrella term "intended beneficiaries" and with differing wording. Both Restatements label a beneficiary who is not entitled to recover under the contract as an "incidental beneficiary." They also contain additional provisions creating a duty from the promisor to the third-party beneficiary and allowing either the promisee or the third-party beneficiary to enforce the promisor's promise.

Prototype case:	*Seaver v. Ransom* (Example D)	*Lawrence v. Fox* (Example C)
Category in first Restatement §§ 133, 135, 136:	"Donee beneficiary"	"Creditor beneficiary"
If it appears from the terms of the promise in view of the accompanying circumstances that:	"the purpose of the promisee in obtaining the promise of all or part of the performance thereof is • to make a gift to the beneficiary *or* • to confer upon him a right against the promisor to some performance neither due nor supposed or asserted to be due from the promisee to the beneficiary"	there is "no purpose to make a gift . . . and performance of the promise will satisfy • an actual or supposed or asserted duty of the promisee to the beneficiary, or • a right of the beneficiary against the promisee which has been barred by ○ the Statute of Limitations or ○ . . . a discharge in bankruptcy, or ○ . . . the Statute of Frauds"

Category in Restatement (Second) §§ 302, 304, 315:	"Intended beneficiary"	
Unless otherwise agreed between promisor and promisee, if recognition of a right to performance in the beneficiary is appropriate to effectuate the intention of the parties and:	"the circumstances indicate that the promisee intends to give the beneficiary the benefit of the promised performance [or]"	"the performance of the promise will satisfy an ob-ligation of the promisee to pay money to the beneficiary"

Reading Critically: Third-Party Beneficiaries Under the Restatement (Second)

Read the Restatement (Second) provisions in the table above.

1. How, if at all, do these rules reshape the common law rules in *Lawrence v. Fox* and *Seaver v. Ransom* (Examples C and D, pages 927 and 929)?

2. Would these cases have come out the same under the first Restatement? the Restatement (Second)?

Food for Thought

The Restatement (Second) provisions on third-party beneficiaries were drafted in response to criticism of the two-pronged definition of donee beneficiaries in Restatement § 133, but the Restatement (Second) categories have also continued to raise problems. Among the concerns is the fact that Restatement (Second) § 302 first says that whether a beneficiary is "intended" or not depends on "the intentions of *the parties*" but then adds a requirement, in one branch, that "the *promisee* intends" to give the beneficiary the benefit of the performance. "This double use of intent, coupled with the inherent ambiguity of the term 'intent,' has perplexed courts and stimulated commentators since the Restatement Second's adoption."* Suggestions for reconfiguring the categories to bring more coherence to the doctrine can be found in Harry G. Prince, *Perfecting the Third Party Beneficiary Standing Rule Under Section 302 of the Restatement (Second) Contracts*, 25 B.C. L. Rev. 919 (1984); Jean F. Powers, *Expanded Liability and Intent Requirement in Third Party Beneficiary Contracts*, 1993 Utah L. Rev. 67; Melvin A. Eisenberg, *Third Party Beneficiaries*, 92 Colum. L. Rev. 1358 (1992); Orma S. Paglin, *Criteria for the Recognition of Third Party Beneficiaries' Rights*, 24 New Eng. L. Rev. 63 (1989).

§ 3.2. Beyond the Basics

The current state of third-party beneficiary law in the United States is a mix of common law (often following the New York cases in Examples C and D), the first Restatement, and the Restatement (Second). Courts continue to struggle with how to articulate and apply the most appropriate rule regarding the rights of third-party beneficiaries to contracts.

It is important to remember that a third-party beneficiary "stands in the shoes of" the promisee, so if the promisor and promisee modify or rescind the contract, the beneficiary's right to recover is also modified or rescinded. However, if the beneficiary has reasonably relied upon the contract as originally agreed upon, then, at some point, the beneficiary's rights "vest" and become "irrevocably settled" so that the beneficiary's rights cannot be changed without his or her consent. Then the parties can change the contract as between them, but they cannot change how it operates on the beneficiary. Courts differ as to when these rights "vest" in the beneficiary, and some courts do not require any reliance. If the original contract reserves to the parties the power to change the beneficiary's rights, then any vesting is subject to that power.

Another application of the beneficiary "standing in the shoes of" the promisee is that the promisor can raise contractual defenses against the promisee, and hence, also against the beneficiary, unless the contract says otherwise. These defenses include defects in contract formation (lack of consideration, lack of assent, etc.); voidability on the basis of fraud, mistake, duress, etc.; failure to comply with the statute of frauds; excuse; and breach by the promisee.

---

*   Gary Monserud, *Blending the Law of Sales with the Common Law of Third Party Beneficiaries,* 39 Duq. L. Rev. 111, 124 (2000).

Problem: Third-Party Beneficiaries

11-3.   In each situation below, diagram and label the persons involved. Would you allow each third-party beneficiary to recover under the contract? On what reasoning and under which authority (case law, first Restatement, or Restatement (Second))? Would the result be the same under all of those authorities?

a.   In an insurance policy, an insurance company promised a parent to pay her three children $50,000 apiece upon her death. The parent paid premiums for forty years before passing away.

b.   A disappointed football fan sued the umpire of a particular football game that was disastrous for the fan's team, seeking to recover damages under the football league's contract with the umpire.

c.   A son promised his mother that he would furnish lifetime care to his sibling with a disability, after the mother's death, in return for the mother naming him as the recipient of her retirement funds, which she did, before she passed away. The son abandoned his sibling to a state agency. Can the sibling recover from the son?

d.   A homeowner lived across the street from the site of a proposed amusement park. If the park were built, the homeowner's property would escalate greatly in value. But the development contract ran into difficulties, and the park was cancelled. The homeowner sued the parties to the development contract. Will he succeed?

e.   A city granted a zoning variance to a metal-coating factory, to expand near a residential neighborhood, but required the factory to enter into an agreement to limit air emissions and thereby prevent harm to the neighbors within a 2-mile radius. The factory violated the agreement and harmed neighbors' health. Can the neighbors recover directly from the factory?

f.   A buyer owed a start-up business $750, but the transaction did not comply with the statute of frauds, so the business could not recover the amount from the buyer. Because the business was in danger of failing, a neighborhood business incubator fund promised the buyer that it would pay the $750 to the business, in return for the buyer's promise to pay the fund $800 over the next three years. If the buyer does not repay the incubator fund, can the business sue the buyer directly?

Test Your Knowledge

To assess your understanding of the material in this chapter, <u>click here</u> to take a quiz.

Index

Because the electronic version of this book is searchable, only a brief index is included here. In most instances, only references in authors' text (not in cases) are included. If a discussion continues over multiple pages, only the first reference is noted in the index. The tables of contents (at the beginning of the book and the beginning of each chapter) provide an additional tool for navigating through the contents.

Abrahamson, Shirley S., 863
Acceptance, *see* Mutual Assent
Accord, meaning of, 253
Agent-principal relationship, 109, 356
Aliunde, meaning of, 568
American Law Institute (ALI), 6
Appeal as of right, meaning of, 584
Arbitration clause or agreement, 270, 177, 459
Arden, Elizabeth, 527
Assent, *see* Mutual assent
Assignment and delegation, *see* Third-party rights and duties
Assignment of contract, 202, 216, 318, 612
Assumpsit, meaning of, 313
Attorney fees, as remedy, 819
Bailment, meaning of, 748
Battle of the Forms under UCC § 2–207, 169
Bid bond, 310, 401
Breach, *see* Performance and breach
Cancellation or termination of a contract, 34, 41, 231, 426, 440, 707, 890
Canons of construction, *see* Interpreting/construing express terms
Cardozo, Benjamin, 50
Chancery Court, 285, 441, 782
Chattel, meaning of, 319
Cheever, John, 57
CISG, *see* Convention on Contracts for the International Sale of Goods
Civil law, application of, 6
Closing, as moment of performance, 114
Common law, application of, 6

Conditions, generally, 645
   Concurrent conditions, 648
   Condition precedent, 42, 308, 631, 648, 658, 661, 673, 687, 691, 697, 854
   Condition subsequent, 648, 674, 681
   Contract formation, affecting, 603, 647
   Express, 645, 649
      Conditions of satisfaction, 663
      Excuse of, 666, 668
      Forfeiture, causing, 668
      Waiver of, 666
   Implied, 649, 685
      Kingston categories, 688
      Substantial performance, relationship to, 690
   Promises distinguished, 647
Consideration, 197
   Bargain, as, 205
   Benefit or detriment, as, 198
   Conditional gift distinguished, 224
   Discharge of duty, 251
      Accord and satisfaction, 253
      Mutual rescission, agreement of, 252
      Novation, 253
      Substituted contract, 252
      Substituted performance, 253
   Historical development, 197
   Illusory promises and termination clauses, 230

Modification and the pre-existing duty
    rule, 241, 428
Nominal, 219, 220
Pre-existing duty rule, 241, 251, 256,
    428
Settlement agreements, in, 433
Convention on Contracts for the Interna-
    tional Sale of Goods (CISG), generally,
    9
Contract implied in fact, meaning of, 287
Contract implied in law, meaning of, 331
Contract law, sources of, 5, 207
Corbin, Arthur, 239
Course of dealing, 180, 549, 602, 611
Course of performance, 180, 549, 602, 611
Court reports, history of, 314
Coverture, meaning of, 320
Cross-collateral clause, 443
Damages, *see* Remedies
Defenses to contract enforcement, generally,
    353
    Duress, 415
        Economic, 427
        Reasonable alternative, existence
            of, 425
    Illegality, 471
    Incapacity, 356
        Infancy, 357
            Disaffirmance, 365
            Emancipation, effect on
                defense of, 364
            Necessaries, effect on def-
                ense of, 362, 366
        Intoxication, 27, 384
        Mental illness or defect, 436, 368,
            382
    Misrepresentation, 404
        Concealment, 405
        Fraudulent, 405, 411
        Material, 405, 410
        Nondisclosure, 405, 411, 413
        Tortious, 409
    Mistake, 387
        Clerical error, 356, 401, 882
        Comparison to excuse of imprac-
            ticability, 395
        Kinds of mistake, distinctions
            among, 387
        Mutual, 388, 389
        Unilateral, 388, 399
    Public policy, violation of, 471

Surrogacy contracts, 482, 485
Unconscionability, 440
    Arbitration agreements, applied
        to, 459
    Codification, 450
    Duty-to-read, and, 136, 446
    Predatory loans, and, 448
    Procedural versus substantive,
        452
    Regulatory alternatives to assert-
        ing, 469
Undue influence, 415, 431
Void versus voidable contract, 327,
    355, 368
Delegation and assignment, *see* Third-party
    rights and duties
Demurrer, meaning of, 31
Divisible contract, *see* Performance and
    Breach
Doctor-patient relationship, contractual
    liability in, 269
Duress, *see* Defenses to contract enforce-
    ment
Duty to defend clause, 248
Duty to read, 136, 446
Efficient breach, theory of, 872
Employment at will, meaning of, 530
En banc, meaning of, 474
Equitable estoppel, 276, 503, 851
Equity, history of, 285
Essential terms, 81
Ethical Issues, 386
    Contingency fee agreements, 386
Exclusive dealings, 735
Excuse defenses, generally, 748
    Force majeure clause, 748, 760, 775
    Frustration of purpose, 762
    Historical background, 748
    Impossibility, 748, 754
    Impracticability, 754
    Mistake, compared to, 395, 775
    UCC, under, 754
Executor or administrator, role of, 202
Executory, meaning of, 204, 252, 253
Extrinsic evidence, using to understand a
    contract, 59, 510, 564, 576
    Ambiguity, determination of, 565
    Parol evidence rule, generally, 579
        Collateral agreements, treatment
            of, 603, 605
        Conditions, treatment of, 603

Course of performance, treatment of, 602

Final expression vs. complete and exclusive statement, 581

Merger or Integration clause, 583

Absence of merger or integration clause, 600

Nature of evidence excluded, 601

Partial versus complete integration, 582

Policies underlying, 580

Factoring, meaning of, 739

Farnsworth, E. Allan, 196

FAS term, 657

Federal common law of contracts, 207

Federal Trade Commission (FTC), *see* Unfair or deceptive acts or practices

Fiduciary, meaning of, 633

Firm offer, 158

Force majeure clause, *see* Excuse defenses

Foreseeability, 758, 772, 820

Forum selection clause, 137

Freedom of contract, 3, 355, 416, 461, 464, 866, 904

Friendly, Henry J., 542

Frustration of purpose, *see* Excuse defenses

Gap-fillers, *see* Implied terms and provisions

Gift promises, 204, 219, 274

Good faith, *see* Implied terms and provisions

Gratuitous promise, 224, 274, 315, 326, 338

Houston Astrodome, history of, 829

Illegality, *see* Defenses to contract enforcement

Illusory promises, *see* Promises

Implied terms and provisions, 611

Best efforts, 636

Exclusive dealings, implied obligations from, 735

Gap-fillers, 180, 612

Good faith, 36, 232, 440, 625

Requirements and output contracts, in, 369

Settlement agreements, 234, 237

Termination clause, exercise of, 36, 232, 642

Implied conditions, *see* Conditions

Reasonable efforts, 623, 645, 755, 839

Terms implied from the circumstances, 613

Impossibility or Impracticability, *see* Excuse defenses

Incapacity, *see* Defenses to contract enforcement

Indefinite or incomplete agreement, *see* Mutual assent

Indemnification clause, 186, 248

Infancy, *see* Defenses to contract enforcement

Installment contract, meaning of, 458, 745

Integration clause, *see* Extrinsic evidence

Interpreting/construing express terms, 541

Canons of construction, 552

Commercial context, 551

Contextual interpretation, 551, 578

Question of law or fact, 561

Parol evidence rule, effect on, *see* Extrinsic evidence

Intoxication, *see* Defenses to contract enforcement

Jurisprudential philosophy, impact of, 62

King Edward VII, 763

Laches, 884

Law Day, meaning of, 679

Liquidated damages, *see* Remedies

Lis pendens, meaning of, 372

MacLaine Parker, Shirley, 837

Magistrate judges, role of, 185

Mansfield, Lord, 319

Material benefit received, promise for, 324, 327

Mechanic's lien, meaning of, 318

Mental illness or defect, *see* Defenses to contract enforcement

Merger clause, *see* Extrinsic evidence

Misrepresentation, *see* Defenses to contract enforcement

Missing terms, *see* Mutual assent

Mistake, *see* Defenses to contract enforcement

Modification and the pre-existing duty rule, 241, 428

Moral obligation, 314, 319, 327, 328, 338

Mortgage, meaning of, 217

Mutual assent, manifestation of, 15, 65

Acceptance, 106

By conduct, 126, 176

By inaction or silence, 129

By performance or promise, 116, 208

Clickwrap and browsewrap,
    effect on acceptance, 140
Conditional, 110, 114
Counteroffers distinguished, 107,
    114
"Grumbling" acceptance, 107,
    114, 136
Mailbox rule, 154, 159
Manner of, 116
Method of, 116
Mirror image rule, 112, 169
Notification of acceptance, 164
Terms included in, 137, 178
Time of effectiveness, 159, 164
UCC § 2–207, under, 171, 176
Unsolicited merchandise, 133
Electronic offer and acceptance, 161,
    149
Incompleteness and indefiniteness,
    31, 38
Letters of intent, 39
Missing terms, 38, 63, 180
Misunderstandings (the two ships
    "Peerless"), 30
Objective versus subjective meaning
    Perspective in contract interpreta-
      tion, 560
    Test for assent, 17, 31, 92
Offer, 69
    Advertisements, 75, 95
    Bids as offers, 98, 401
    For unilateral or bilateral con-
      tract, 77, 89, 117, 81, 156,
      157
    Preliminary negotiations distin-
      guished, 70, 92
    Price quotations, 72, 74, 516
    Rewards, 75
    RFI, RFP, RFB, RFQ, 98
Terminating the power of acceptance,
    101, 150, 152
    Condition, non-occurrence of,
      648
    Death of offeror, 105
    Incapacity of offeror, 105
    Lapse, 68, 91, 101
    Rejection by offeree, 150
    Revocation by offeror, 152
    Limitations on, 156
      Firm offer, 158
      Irrevocable offer, 157

      Option contract, 157, 221,
        300
        Unilateral contract, 117, 156
    UCC, under, 166, 169
    Vagueness, effect of, 38
National Conference of Commissioners on
    Uniform State Laws, 8
Necessaries, meaning of, 185
No oral modification (NOM) clause, 498
Non-compete clause, 904
Obiter dictum, meaning of, 296
Officious intermeddler, 333, 346
Option contract, 154, 157, 221, 300
Orphans' Court, 292
Output contract, 639
Parol evidence rule, generally, *see* Extrinsic
    evidence
Payment bond, 41, 926
Performance and breach, generally, 690
    Cancellation upon breach, 34, 41, 252,
      426, 707, 724
    Demand for assurance of future per-
      formance, 733
    Divisible contract, 722
    Efficient breach, 872
    Excuse of, *see* Excuse defenses
    Material breach, 701
    Partial versus total breach, 706
    Repudiation, 724
      Anticipatory repudiation, 728
      Damages resulting from, *see*
        Remedies
      Defining, 725
    Substantial performance, 690, 701
    Under the UCC, 745, 747
Performance bond, 41, 925, 926
Posner, Richard, 628
Pre-existing duty rule, 241, 251
Principles of International Commercial
    Contracts, 10
Profit á prendre, meaning of, 812
Promise, 15, 31
    Condition distinguished, 647
    For benefit already received, 312
    Illusory, 33
    Restatement provisions, 328
Promissory estoppel, generally, 274
    Charitable pledge, 292, 298
    Damages for, 847
    Future of, 311

Statute of Frauds, and, *see* Statute of frauds
Promissory note, meaning of, 199
Promissory restitution, 312
Public policy, violation of, *see* Defenses to contract enforcement
Puffing, 93, 406
Quantum meruit, meaning of, 331
Quantum valebant, meaning of, 331
Quasi-contract, meaning of, 331
Redgrave, Vanessa, 825
Reliance, pre-contractual, 300
Remedies, 781
    Damages, 786
        Agreed, *see* Remedies, Damages, Liquidated
        Anticipatory repudiation, damages for, 800
        Attorney fees, 819
        Avoidable, *see* Remedies, Damages, Mitigation of
        Court costs, 800
        Expectation, 787, 790, 907
            Computing, 792
            Direct, 790, 795, 800, 907
                Cost to complete, 802
                Diminution in value, 802
                Lost profits and lost volume, 815
                Market price, measured by, 796, 797, 801
            Indirect, 790, 818, 907
                Consequential, 791, 820, 832, 907
                Incidental, 791, 816, 819, 907
        Liquidated, 371, 862, 907
        Mitigation of, 820, 833
        Overhead, 816
        Policies to be balanced in determining, 786
        Promissory estoppel, damages for, 847
        Punitive, 875, 907
        Reliance, 787, 847, 907
        Restitution, 787, 851, 907
            Party who is prevented from performing, for, 860
            Party who materially breaches, for, 854

Uncertainty of amount, 77, 786
Declaratory judgment, 57
Equitable, generally, 402, 881
Injunction, 894, 907
Reformation, 356, 401, 882, 905
Remedial principles, 783
Remedies in equity, 783, 905
Remedies in law, 783, 905
Rescission, 356
Specific performance, 882, 907
Specific restitution, 905, 907
Requirements contract, meaning of, 639
Rescission of contract, 246, 252, 356
Restatements as source of authority, 6
Restitution, liability for, 329, 356
    Promissory, 312
Robinson III, Spottswood W., 342
Sale and leaseback contract, 629
Seal, contracts under, 257
Security interest, meaning of, 443
Settlement agreements, policy favoring, 236, 427
Shipment contract, meaning of, 745
Specific performance, *see* Remedies Statute of Frauds, 489
    Applying, 493
    Burden of proof for, 493
    Classes of contracts covered by, 493
        One-year provision, 496
    Effect of invoking, 491, 493
    Exceptions to, 500
        Contracts for sale of goods, 500
        Estoppel, equitable and promissory, 503
        Part performance, 501
    Manner of invoking, 493
    Modifications, applied to, 497
    Rationales for, 490
    Reasonable certainty, 507
    Writing and signature requirements, 507
        Electronic commerce, 530
        Multiple writings, 521
Substantial performance, *see* Conditions
Suez Canal, 755
Surrogacy contracts, 482
Tender of goods, meaning of, 745
Termination clauses, 34, 230, 426, 557, 642
Termination of a contract, *see* Cancellation or termination of a contract

Third-party rights and duties, 909
    Assignment and delegation, 910
        Common law, under, 912
        UCC and Restatement, under, 920
    Third-party beneficiaries, 925
        Common law, under, 927
        Intended and incidental beneficiaries, 931
        Restatements, under, 931
Time-is-of-the-essence clause, 718
Trade usage, *see* Usage of trade
Traynor, Roger, 572
Unconscionability, *see* Defenses to contract enforcement
Undue influence, *see* Defenses to contract enforcement
Unfair or deceptive acts or practices (UDAP), 469
UNIDROIT, 10
Uniform Commercial Code (UCC), generally, 8
    Application by analogy, 451, 735
    Article 1, 8, 9
    Article 2, 9
        Scope of, 166
    Contract formation in, 166
    Modification of contracts, 241
    Overview of contents, 8
    Performance and breach, 745
    Source of authority, as, 8
Uniform Law Commission (ULC), 8
Unilateral contracts, 81, 117, 156
Unsolicited merchandise, 133
Usage of trade, 180, 546, 549, 551, 602, 611
Vagueness, *see* Mutual assent
Waiver, 246, 250, 498, 598, 666
Warranty, meaning of, 407
Williston, Samuel, 239
Workers compensation, 235, 325